HOYT SHERWIN
P9-DTR-068

HOYT SHERWIN

WILLIAM McKANE

PROVERBS

THE OLD TESTAMENT LIBRARY

General Editors

PETER ACKROYD, University of London
JAMES BARR, University of Manchester
JOHN BRIGHT, Union Theological Seminary, Richmond, Virginia
G. ERNEST WRIGHT, The Divinity School, Harvard University

HOYT SHERWIN

WILLIAM McKANE

PROVERBS

A New Approach

The Westminster Press
PHILADELPHIA

© SCM Press Ltd 1970
Standard Book No. 664–20887–8
Library of Congress Catalog Card No. 75–108185

PUBLISHED BY THE WESTMINSTER PRESS ®
PHILADELPHIA 7, PENNSYLVANIA

PRINTED IN GREAT BRITAIN

CONTENTS

PART ONE

INTERNATIONAL WISDOM

PART TWO

THE BOOK OF PROVERBS

PREFACE

It is with a sense of relief and yet inadequacy that I come to the end of this study which has taken up much of my time and thought in recent years. The thesis that Prov. 1–9, 22.17–24.22 and 31.1–9 are a different literary kind from the sentences in 10.1–22.16 and 24.23–29.27 is one which is gaining recognition and which will stand the test of further enquiry. The argument that the history of the wisdom tradition in Israel and the direction of its development are mirrored in the book of Proverbs is more difficult to conduct, involving as it does the division of the sentences into three classes. Although I have reached considered conclusions here too, I am aware that I have touched on more contentious matters. The analysis of the constituents of a 'proverb' is, so far as I am aware, an original contribution which should serve to focus attention on the special concreteness or organization of imagery which produces a 'proverb'.

Alongside these lines of argument and in some measure independent of them, there is the exegetical work which I have done on the sometimes difficult and often fascinating text of Proverbs. My friend and former teacher Eric F. F. Bishop generously handed over to me material on the Palestinian background of the book of Proverbs. Where I have used this, I have indicated the source with the abbreviation EFFB.

Since the order of exposition does not follow the verse order in 10.1–22.16 and 24.23–29.27, the verse under discussion is given in bold type and the same procedure is followed where necessary in the other parts of Proverbs. In the translation I have used italics to indicate an emended text or an uncertain translation. The related discussion will be found in the body of the commentary and the page number is given in the margin of the translation.

I am deeply grateful to my colleagues Mr P. W. Coxon and Mr J. D. Martin for the careful and skilful way in whch they have read the proofs of this work, and for having urged upon me the need for a final reconsideration of a number of points.

St Mary's College,
University of St Andrews

ABBREVIATIONS

ABL	* R. F. Harper, *Assyrian and Babylonian Letters*
AJSL	*American Journal of Semitic Languages*
ANET	* J. B. Pritchard, *Ancient Near Eastern Texts*
An.Or.	*Analecta Orientalia*
ATD	Das Alte Testament Deutsch
AV	Authorized Version
BASOR	*Bulletin of the American Schools of Oriental Research*
BDB	* Brown-Driver-Briggs, *Hebrew and English Lexicon*
BEThL	*Bibliotheca Ephemeridum Theologicarum Lovaniensium*
BJ	La Bible de Jérusalem
BL	* H. Bauer- P. Leander, *Historische Grammatik*
BWANT	*Beiträge zur Wissenschaft vom alten und neuen Testament*
BWL	* W. G. Lambert, *Babylonian Wisdom Literature*
BZAW	Beihefte zur *Zeitschrift für die alttestamentliche Wissenschaft*
CAD	*Chicago Assyrian Dictionary*
CML	* G. R. Driver, *Canaanite Myths and Legends*
E.F.F.B.	† Eric F. F. Bishop
ET	English Translation
ET	*The Expository Times*
EThL	*Ephemerides Theologicae Lovanienses*
EV	English Version
GK	* Gesenius-Kautzsch, *Hebrew Grammar*
HAT	Handbuch zum alten Testament
HTR	*Harvard Theological Review*
HUCA	*Hebrew Union College Annual*
ICC	The International Critical Commentary
JBL	*Journal of Biblical Literature*
JEA	*Journal of Egyptian Archaeology*
JJS	*Journal of Jewish Studies*
JNES	*Journal of Near Eastern Studies*
JPOS	*Journal of the Palestine Oriental Society*
JQR	*Jewish Quarterly Review*
JRAS	*Journal of the Royal Asiatic Society*
JSS	*Journal of Semitic Studies*

†See Preface, p. vii.

JTS	*Journal of Theological Studies*
K.	*Kᵉtīb*
KB	* Koehler-Baumgartner
KD	*Kerygma und Dogma*
KS	* A. Alt, *Kleine Schriften*
LXX	The Septuagint
MT	Masoretic Text
MVAG	*Mitteilungen der vorderasiatisch-ägyptischen Gesellschaft*
NEB	New English Bible
NTT	*Nieuw Theologisch Tijdschrift*
OLZ	*Orientalistische Literaturzeitung*
Or.	*Orientalia*
OTS	*Oudtestamentische Studien*
PEQ	*Palestine Exploration Quarterly*
Pesh.	Peshitta
PWM	* W. McKane, *Prophets and Wise Men*
Q.	*Qᵉrē*
RB	*Revue Biblique*
RSV	Revised Standard Version
RV	Revised Version
SBOT	Sacred Books of the Old Testament (editor, P. Haupt)
SBT	Studies in Biblical Theology
SJT	*Scottish Journal of Theology*
Targ.	Targum
TGUOS	*Transactions of the Glasgow University Oriental Society*
ThLZ	*Theologische Literaturzeitung*
ThZ	*Theologische Zeitschrift*
TT	*Theologisch Tijdschrift*
V	Vulgate
VT	*Vetus Testamentum*
VTS	*Supplements to Vetus Testamentum*
WMANT	*Wissenschaftliche Monographien zum alten und neuen Testament*
ZA	*Zeitschrift für Assyriologie*
ZAeS	*Zeitschrift für ägyptische Sprache und Altertumskunde*
ZAW	*Zeitschrift für die alttestamentliche Wissenschaft*
ZDMG	*Zeitschrift der deutschen morgenländischen Gesellschaft*
ZThK	*Zeitschrift für Theologie und Kirche*

For full details of entries marked*, see Bibliography

BIBLIOGRAPHY

P. R. Ackroyd, 'A Note on the Hebrew Roots *b'š* and *bwš*', *JTS* xliii (1942), pp. 160f.

'The Meaning of Hebrew *dōr* considered', *JSS* xiii (1968), pp. 3–10

Y. Aharoni, 'Beth-haccherem', *Archaeology and Old Testament Study* (ed. D. Winton Thomas) (1967), pp. 171–4

J. Aistleitner (O. Eissfeldt), *Wörterbuch der ugaritischen Sprache*³ (1967). Berichte über die Verhandlungen der sächsischen Akademie der Wissenschaften zu Leipzig, Phil.-hist. Klasse, Band 106, Heft 3

W. F. Albright, 'An archaic Hebrew Proverb in an Amarna Letter from Central Palestine', *BASOR* 89 (1943), pp. 29–32

'A Prince of Taanach in the Fifteenth Century B.C.', *BASOR* 94 (1944), pp. 12–27

'A new Hebrew Word for "Glaze" in Proverbs 26.23', *BASOR* 98 (1945), pp. 24f.

'Canaanite-Phoenician Sources of Hebrew Wisdom', *Wisdom in Israel and The Ancient Near East* (Rowley Festschrift), *VTS* iii (1955), pp. 1–15

A. Alt, 'Die Ursprünge des israelitischen Rechts', *Kleine Schriften zur Geschichte des Volkes Israel*³, vol. i (1963), pp. 278–332; ET (R. A. Wilson), *Essays in Old Testament History and Religion* (1966), pp. 79–132

'Die Weisheit Salomos', *op. cit.*, vol. ii (1964), pp. 90–99

R. Anthes, 'Lebensregeln und Lebensweisheit der alten Aegypter', *Der alte Orient*, 32, 2 (1933)

P. Auvray, 'Sur le sens du mot *'ayin* en Ez. i.18 et x.12', *VT* iv (1954), p. 5

D. H. Baneth, 'Bemerkungen zu den Achikarpapyri', *OLZ* 17 (1914), pp. 248–52, 295–9, 348–53

A. Barucq, *Le Livre des Proverbes* (Sources Bibliques, 1964)

J. B. Bauer, 'Encore une fois Proverbes viii.22', *VT* viii (1958), pp. 91f.

A. J. Baumgartner, *Étude critique sur l'état du texte du Livre des Proverbes d'après les principales traductions anciennes* (1890)

H. Bauer, P. Leander, *Historische Grammatik der hebräischen Sprache* (1922)

W. Baumgartner, *Israelitische und altorientalische Weisheit* (1933)

'Die literarischen Gattungen in der Weisheit des Jesus Sirach', *ZAW* 34 (1914), pp. 161–98

A. Bentzen, *Introduction to the Old Testament*⁵, vols. i–ii (1959)
G. Bertram, 'Die religiöse Umdeutung altorientalischer Lebensweisheit in der griechischen Übersetzung des AT', *ZAW* 54 (1936), pp. 153–67
J. Bewer, 'Two Suggestions on Prov. 30.31 and Zech. 9.16', *JBL* lxvii (1948), pp. 61f.
G. Bickell, 'Kritische Bearbeitung der Proverbien', *Wiener Zeitschrift für die Kunde des Morgenlandes* (1891), pp. 79–102, 191–214, 271–99
A. M. Blackman and T. E. Peat, 'Papyrus Lansing: a translation with notes', *JEA* xi (1925), pp. 284–98
P. A. H. de Boer, 'The Counsellor', *VTS* iii (1955), pp. 42–71
G. Boström, *Proverbia Studien: die Weisheit und das fremde Weib in Spr. 1–9* (Lunds Universitets Årsskrift, N.F., Avd. I, Bd. 30, Nr. 3, 1935)
F. Brown, S. R. Driver, C. A. Briggs, *A Hebrew and English Lexicon of the Old Testament* (1966)
H. Brunner, *Altägyptische Erziehung* (1957)
'Gerechtigkeit als Fundament des Thrones', *VT* viii (1958), pp. 426–8
A. de Buck, 'Het religieus karakter der oudste egyptische wijsheid', *NTT* xxi (1932), pp. 322–49
'The Instruction of Amenemmes', *Mélanges Maspero I, Orient Ancien*, second fascicule, pp. 847–52. Mémoires publiés par les membres de l'Institut Français d'Archéologie Orientale du Caire, sous la direction de M. Pierre Jougnet, tome lxvi, 1935–38
H. J. Byington, 'Hebrew Marginalia III', *JBL* lxiv (1945), pp. 339–55
M. A. Canney, 'The Hebrew *mēlîṣ*', *AJSL* xl (1923–4), pp. 135–7
H. Cazelles, 'L'enfantement de las Sagesse en Prov. viii', *Sacra Pagina* i (*BEThL* xii, 1959), pp. 511–15
G. Contenau, *Trente Tablettes Cappadociennes*, 1919
F. C. Conybeare, J. Rendell Harris, A. S. Lewis, *The Story of Ahikar*² (1913)
A. E. Cowley, *Aramaic Papyri of the Fifth Century BC* (1923)
M. B. Crook, 'The Marriageable Maiden of Prov. 31.10–31', *JNES* xiii (1954), pp. 137–40
M. Dahood, *Proverbs and Northwest Semitic Philology* (1963)
'Immortality in Proverbs 12.28', *Biblica* 41 (1960), pp. 176–81
'To pawn one's cloak', *Biblica* 42 (1961), pp. 359–66
G. Dalman, *Arbeit und Sitte in Palästina*, I.1 (1928)
*Grammatik des jüdisch-palästinischen Aramäisch*², 1905

A. Deimel, *Akkadisch-Šumerisches Glossar* (*Šumerisches Lexicon*, Teil 3, Band 2, 1937)

F. Delitzsch (tr. M. G. Easton), *A Biblical Commentary on the Proverbs of Solomon* (1875)

J. Derembourg (ed.), *Version arabe du livre des Proverbes de R. Saadia* (1894)

E. Dhorme (tr. Harold Knight), *A Commentary on the Book of Job* (1967)

J. C. Döderlein, *Scholia in libros Veteris Testamenti poeticos. Iobum, Psalmos et tres Salomonis* (1779)

H. Donner, 'Die religionsgeschichtlichen Ursprünge von Prov. Sal. 8', *ZAeS* 82 (1958), pp. 8–18

E. Drioton, 'Sur la sagesse d'Aménémopé', *Robert Festschrift* (ed. H. Cazelles), 1957, pp. 254–80

'Le Livre des Proverbes et la Sagesse d'Aménémopé', *Sacra Pagina* I (*BEThL* xii, 1959), pp. 229–41

G. R. Driver, 'Some Hebrew Words', *JTS* xxix (1928), pp. 390–6

'Some Hebrew Verbs, Nouns and Pronouns', *JTS* xxx (1929), pp. 371–8

'The Aramaic Papyri from Egypt: Notes on Obscure Passages', *JRAS* (1932), pp. 77–90

'Studies in the Vocabulary of the Old Testament I', *JTS* xxxiii (1932), pp. 38–47

'Problems in "Proverbs"', *ZAW* 50 (1932), pp. 141–8

'Studies in the Vocabulary of the Old Testament VI', *JTS* xxxiv (1933), pp. 375–85

'Studies in the Vocabulary of the Old Testament VII', *JTS* xxxv (1934), pp. 380–93

'Hebrew Notes', *ZAW* 52 (1934), pp. 51–56

'Problems in Aramaic and Hebrew Texts', *An.Or.* 12 (1935), pp. 46–70

'Notes on the Psalms', *JTS* xxxvi (1935), pp. 147–56

'Textual and Linguistic Problems of the Book of Psalms', *HTR* xxix (1936), pp. 171–95

'Suggestions and Objections', *ZAW* 55 (1937), pp. 68–72

'Ecclesiasticus: A New Fragment of the Hebrew Text', *ET* xlix (1938), pp. 37–41

'Hebrew Notes on Prophets and Proverbs', *JTS* xli (1940), pp. 162–75

'Witchcraft in the Old Testament', *JRAS* (1943), pp. 6–16

'Notes on the Psalms II, 73–150', *JTS* xliv (1943), pp. 12–23

'On a Pronoun in the Baal Epic (IVAB iii.24) and Proverbs xxxi.21', *BASOR* 105 (1947), p. 11
'Hebrew Studies', *JRAS* (1948), pp. 164–76
'L'interprétation du texte masorétique à la lumière de la lexicographie hébräique', *EThL* xxvi (1950), pp. 337–53
'Hebrew Notes', *VT* i (1951), pp. 241–50
'Problems in the Hebrew Text of Proverbs', *Biblica* 32 (1951), pp. 173–97
'Problems and Solutions', *VT* iv (1954), pp. 225–45
'Two Misunderstood Passages of the Old Testament', *JTS* vi (1955), pp. 82–87
'Proverbs xix.26', *ThZ* xi (1955), pp. 373f.
Canaanite Myths and Legends (1956)
Aramaic Documents of the Fifth Century BC (1957)
G. R. Driver and J. C. Miles, *The Babylonian Laws*, vol. ii (1955)
H. Duesberg et P. Auvray, *Le Livre des Proverbes*², La Sainte Bible traduite en français sous la direction de l'école biblique de Jérusalem (1956)
M. Dunand, 'La maison de la Sagesse', *Bulletin du Musée de Beyrouth* iv (1940), pp. 69–84
L. Dürr, 'Hebrew *nepeš* = Akkadian *napištu* = Gurgel, Kehle', *ZAW* 43 (1925), pp. 262–9
Das Erziehungswesen im alten Testament und im antiken Orient, MVAG 36, 2 (1932)
J. Dyserinck, 'Kritische Scholiën bij de vertaling van het Boek der Spreuken', *TT* (1883), pp. 577–87
A. B. Ehrlich, *Randglossen zur hebräischen Bibel*, Bd. 6 (1913)
W. Eichrodt (tr. J. A. Baker), *Theology of the Old Testament*, vols. i–ii (1961, 1967)
O. Eissfeldt, *Der Maschal im Alten Testament*, *BZAW* 24 (1913)
(tr. P. R. Ackroyd), *The Old Testament: An Introduction* (1965)
I. Eitan, 'A Contribution to Isaiah Exegesis' (Notes and Short Studies in Biblical Philology), *HUCA* xii (1937), pp. 55–88
A Contribution to Biblical Lexicography (1954)
J. A. Emerton, 'A Note on Proverbs xii.26', *ZAW* 76 (1964), pp. 191–3
'Spring and Torrent in Ps. lxxiv.15', *VTS* xv (1965), pp. 122–33
A. Erman, 'Eine ägyptische Quelle der Sprüche Salomos', Sitzungsberichte der preussischen Akademie der Wissenschaften zu Berlin, Phil. Hist. Klasse, xv (1924), pp. 86–93
(tr. A. M. Blackman), *The Literature of the Ancient Egyptians* (1927)

A. Erman and H. Grapow, *Das Wörterbuch der ägyptischen Sprache* (1955)
I. Engnell, '"Knowledge" and "Life" in the Creation Story', *VTS* iii (1955), pp. 103–19
H. G. A. von Ewald, *Die Dichter des alten Bundes*², Bd. ii (1867)
J. Fichtner, *Die altorientalische Weisheit in ihrer israelitisch-jüdischen Ausprägung: ein Studie zur Nationalisierung der Weisheit in Israel*, *BZAW* 62 (1933)
F. Field, *Origenis Hexaplorum*, vols. i–ii (1875)
J. J. Finkelstein, 'Hebrew *ḥbr* and Semitic **ḫbr*', *JBL* lxxv (1956), pp. 328–31
G. Fohrer, 'Das sogenannte apodiktisch formulierte Recht und der Dekalog', *KD* 11 (1965), pp. 49–74
W. Frankenberg, *Die Sprüche übersetzt und erklärt*, Nowack's Hand-Kommentar zum Alten Testament (1898)
H. Frankfort, *Ancient Egyptian Religion* (1961)
J. Friedrich, *Phönizisch-Punische Grammatik*, *An. Or.* 32 (1951)
A. H. Gardiner, 'New Literary Works from Ancient Egypt', *JEA* i (1914), pp. 20–36
'The Earliest Manuscripts of the Instruction of Amenemmes I', *Mélanges Maspero I, Orient Ancien*, second fascicule, pp. 479–96. Mémoires publiés par les membres de l'Institut Français d'Archéologie Orientale du Caire, sous la direction de M. Pierre Jougnet, tome lxvi, 1935–8
'The Instruction addressed to Kagemni and His Brethren', *JEA* 32 (1946), pp. 71–74
A. H. Gardiner (ed.), *Hieratic Papyri in the British Museum, Third Series* (1935)
T. H. Gaster, 'Proverbs', *VT* iv (1954), pp. 77–79
B. Gemser, 'The Instructions of Onchsheshonqy and Biblical Wisdom Literature', *VTS* vii (1960), pp. 102–28
Sprüche Salomos,² Handbuch zum Alten Testament 16 (1963)
G. Gerleman, 'The Septuagint Proverbs as a Hellenistic Document', *OTS* viii (1950), pp. 15–27
Studies in the Septuagint, III, Proverbs, Lunds Universitets Årsskrift, N.F., Avd. I, Bd. 52, Nr. 3 (1956)
E. Gerstenberger, *Wesen und Herkunft des 'apodiktischen Rechts'* (1965)
H. Gese, *Lehre und Wirklichkeit in der alten Weisheit* (1958)
'The Idea of History in the Ancient Near East and the Old Testament', *Journal for Theology and Church*, vol. 1 (1965), pp. 49–64

Gesenius-Kautzsch (tr. A. E. Cowley), *Gesenius' Hebrew Grammar*[2] (1910)

H. L. Ginsberg, 'Baal's Two Messengers', *BASOR* 95 (1944), pp. 25–30

'The North-Canaanite Myth of Anath and Aqhat', *BASOR* 98 (1945), 15–23

S. R. K. Glanville, *The Instruction of Onchsheshonqy*, Catalogue of Demotic Papyri in the British Museum, vol. ii (1955)

J. J. Glueck, 'Proverbs xxx.15a', *VT* xiv (1964), pp. 367–70

A. H. Godbey, 'The Hebrew Mašal', *AJSL* xxxix (1922/3), pp. 89–108

R. Gordis, 'Quotations in Wisdom Literature', *JQR* xxx (1939), pp. 123–47

C. H. Gordon, *Ugaritic Literature* (1949)

Ugaritic Textbook, An. Or. 38 (1965)

E. I. Gordon, *Sumerian Proverbs* (1959)

J. C. Greenfield, 'Lexicographical Notes I', *HUCA* xxix (1958), pp. 203–28

P. Grelot, 'Les Proverbes araméens d'Aḥiqar', *RB* lxviii (1961), pp. 178–94

H. Gressmann, 'Die neugefundene Lehre des Amenemope und die vorexilische Spruchdichtung Israels', *ZAW* 42 (1924), pp. 272–96

Israels Spruchweisheit im Zusammenhang der Weltliteratur (1925)

F. Ll. Griffith, 'The Millingen Papyrus (Teaching of Amenemhat)', *ZAeS* 34 (1896), pp. 35–51

'The Teaching of Amenophis, The Son of Kanakht. Papyrus B.M. 10474', *JEA* xii (1926), pp. 191–231

L. H. Grollenberg, 'A propos de Prov. viii.6 et xvii.27', *RB* lix (1952), pp. 40–43

A. Guillaume, 'A Note on the √*bl*'', *JTS* xiii (1962), pp. 320–2

'A Note on the Roots *ry*', *yr*' and *r*'' in Hebrew', *JTS* xv (1964), pp. 293–5

B. Gunn, *The Instruction of Ptah-hotep and the Instruction of Ke'gemni* (1909)

R. F. Harper, *Assyrian and Babylonian Letters*, Parts i–xiv, 1892–1914

J. G. Hava, *Arabic–English Dictionary* (1915)

J. Hempel, *Die althebräische Literatur und ihr hellenistisch-jüdisches Nachleben* (1930)

'Pathos und Humor in der israelitischen Erziehung', *Von Ugarit nach Qumran* (ed. O. Eissfeldt), *BZAW* 77 (1958), pp. 63–81

A. S. Herbert, 'The Parable (*māšāl*) in the Old Testament', *SJT* 7 (1954), pp. 180–96
F. Hitzig, *Die Sprüche Salomos übersetzt und ausgelegt* (1858)
B. Hodgson, *The Proverbs of Solomon Translated from the Hebrew* (1788)
A. M. Honeyman, 'Epigraphic Discoveries at Karatepe', *PEQ* (1949), pp. 21–39
F. Horst, 'Exilsgemeinde und Jerusalem in Ez. viii–ix. Eine literarische Untersuchung', *VT* iii (1953), 337–60
P. Humbert, *Recherches sur les sources égyptiennes de la littérature sapientiale d'Israël* (1929)
'Le substantif *tōʿēbā* et le verbe *tʿb* dans l'Ancien Testament', *ZAW* 72 (1960), pp. 217–37
W. A. Irwin, 'Where shall Wisdom be found?', *JBL* lxxx (1961), pp. 133–42
J. G. Jäger, *Observationes in Proverbiorum Salomonis Versionem Alexandrinam* (1788)
C. F. Jean-J. Hoftijzer, *Dictionnaire des inscriptions sémitiques de l'ouest* (1960–5)
A. Jirku, 'Das n.pr. Lemu'el (Prov. 31.1) und der Gott Lim', *ZAW* 66 (1954), p. 151
A. R. Johnson, *The Vitality of the Individual in the Thought of Ancient Israel*[2] (1964)
E. Jones, *Proverbs and Ecclesiastes*, Torch Bible Commentaries (1961)
A. Kaminka, 'Septuaginta und Targum zu Prov.', *HUCA* viii-ix (1931/2), pp. 169–91
A. Kamphausen in E. Kautzsch, *Die Heilige Schrift des alten Testaments*[3] (1896)
C. Kayatz, *Studien zu Proverbien 1–9: eine form- und motivgeschichtliche Untersuchung unter Einbeziehung ägyptischen Vergleichsmaterials*, *WMANT* 22 (1966)
C. F. Kent and M. Burrows, *Proverbs and Didactic Poems* (1927)
R. O. Kevin, 'The Wisdom of Amen-em-apt and its possible dependence upon the Hebrew Book of Proverbs' (*Journal of the Society for Oriental Research*, 14 (1930), pp. 115–57
J. A. Knudtzon, *Die El-Amarna Tafeln*, vols. i–ii (1908–15)
K. Koch, 'Gibt es ein Vergeltungsdogma im alten Testament?', *ZThK* 52 (1955), pp. 1–42
L. Koehler, 'Archäologisches Nr. 16–19', *ZAW* 40 (1922), pp. 15–46
L. Koehler, W. Baumgartner, *Lexicon in Veteris Testamenti Libros*[2] (1958)

L. Koehler, W. Baumgartner (W. Baumgartner, B. Hartmann, E. Y. Kutscher), *Hebräisches und Aramäisches Lexicon zum Alten Testament*³, Lieferung I (1967)

J. J. Koopmans, *Aramäische Chrestomathie*, vols. i–ii (1962)

S. N. Kramer, 'Man and his God. A Sumerian variation of the "Job" motif', *VTS* iii (1955), pp. 170–82

*History Begins at Sumer*² (1961)

H. J. Kraus, *Die Verkündigung der Weisheit*, *Spr. 8*, Bibl. Studien 2 (1956)

G. Kuhn, *Beiträge zur Erklärung des salomonischen Spruchbuches*, *BWANT* 3, 16 (1931)

P. de Lagarde, *Anmerkungen zur griechischen Übersetzung der Proverbien* (1863)

W. G. Lambert, *Babylonian Wisdom Literature* (1960)

B. Landsberger, 'Jahreszeiten im Sumerisch-Akkadischen', *JNES* viii (1949), pp. 248–97

S. Langdon, *Babylonian Wisdom* (1922)

I. Lévi, *The Hebrew Text of the Book of Ecclesiasticus*, Semitic Study Series No. iii (1904)

J. Lewy, 'On some Institutions of the Old Assyrian Empire', *HUCA* xxvii (1956), pp. 1–79

W. McKane, *Al-Ghazali's Book of Fear and Hope* (1962)

'A Note on II Kings xii.10 (Evv. xii.9)', *ZAW* 71 (1959), pp. 260–5

'Ruth and Boaz', *TGUOS* xix (1963), pp. 29–40

I and II Samuel, Torch Bible Commentaries (1963)

Prophets and Wise Men, Studies in Biblical Theology No. 44 (1965)

'The Interpretation of Isaiah vii.14–25', *VT* xvii (1967), pp. 208–19

R. Marcus, 'The Tree of Life in Proverbs', *JBL* lxii (1943), pp. 117–20

G. C. C. Maspero, *Les Enseignments d'Amenemhait Ier à son fils Sanouascrit Ier* (1914)

T. B. Mitford, 'Religious Documents from Roman Cyprus', *Journal of Hellenic Studies* lxvi (1946), pp. 24–42

S. Morenz, 'Feurige Kohlen auf dem Haupt', *ThLZ* lxxviii (1953), cols. 187–92

S. Mowinckel, *Prophecy and Tradition* (1946)

(tr. D. Ap-Thomas), *The Psalms in Israel's Worship*, i–ii (1962)

'Israelite Historiography', *Annual of the Swedish Theological Institute* ii (1963), pp. 4–26

A. Müller and E. Kautzsch, *The Book of Proverbs*, Sacred Books of the Old Testament xv, ed. P. Haupt (1901)
F. S. North, 'The Four Insatiables', *VT* xv (1965), pp. 281f.
M. Noth (tr. V. I. Gruhn) *The Old Testament World* (1966)
R. T. O'Callaghan, 'The Great Phoenician Portal Inscription from Karatepe', *Or.* 18 (1949), pp. 173–205
'Echoes of Canaanite Literature in the Psalms', *VT* iv (1954), pp. 164–76
W. O. E. Oesterley, 'The Teaching of Amenemope and the Old Testament', *ZAW* 45 (1927), pp. 9–24
The Wisdom of Egypt and the Old Testament in the Light of the newly discovered Teaching of Amenemope (1927)
Proverbs, Westminster Commentaries (1929)
A. L. Oppenheim, 'Mesopotamian Mythology I', *Or.* 16 (1947), pp. 207–38
R. H. Pfeiffer, *Introduction to the Old Testament*² (1952)
S. Pinsker, *Einleitung in das babylonisch-hebräische Punktationssystem* (1863)
J. P. M. van der Ploeg, *Spreuken*, Boeken O. T., viii, 1 (1952)
'Prov. xxv.23', *VT* iii (1953), pp. 189–92
J. B. Pritchard, *Ancient Near Eastern Texts Relating to the Old Testament*² (1955)
G. von Rad, 'Die Anrechnung des Glaubens zur Gerechtigkeit', *Gesammelte Studien zum Alten Testament* (1958), pp. 130–5; ET by E. W. T. Dicken, *The Problem of the Hexateuch and other Essays* (1966), pp. 125–30
' "Gerechtigkeit" und "Leben" in der Kultsprache der Psalmen', *op. cit.*, pp. 225–47; ET, pp. 243–66
(tr. D. M. G. Stalker), *Old Testament Theology*, vols. i–ii (1962, 1965)
(tr. J. H. Marks), *Genesis*, Old Testament Library, 1961
O. S. Rankin, *Israel's Wisdom Literature* (1936)
J. Reider, 'Etymological Studies in Biblical Hebrew', *VT* ii (1952), pp. 113–30
'Etymological Studies in Biblical Hebrew', *VT* iv (1954), pp. 276–95
H. Renard, *Le Livre des Proverbes*, La Sainte Bible Pirot-Clamer, v (1943)
E. Reuss, *La Bible* vol. vi (1878)
P. Reymond, *L'eau, sa vie et sa signification dans l'Ancien Testament*, *VTS* vi (1958)

H. N. Richardson, 'Some Notes on *lyṣ* and its Derivatives', *VT* v (1955), pp. 163–79
W. Richter, *Recht und Ethos: Versuch einer Ortung des weisheitlichen Mahnspruches*, Studien zum alten und neuen Testament (1966)
H. Ringgren, *Word and Wisdom* (1947)
Sprüche/Prediger, ATD, 16/1 (1962)
A. Robert, 'Les attaches littéraires bibliques de Prov. i-ix', *RB* xliii (1934), pp. 42–68, 172–204, 374–84; *RB* xliv (1935), pp. 344–65, 502–25
F. Rosenthal, *A Grammar of Biblical Aramaic*, Porta Linguarum Orientalium, N.S., v (1961)
W. M. W. Roth, *Numerical Sayings in the Old Testament*, *VTS* xiii (1965)
W. Rudolph, *Esra und Nehemia* (HAT 20, 1949)
G. Sauer, *Die Sprüche Agur*, BWANT V, 4 (1953)
J. de Savignac, 'La sagesse en Proverbes viii.22–31', *VT* xii (1962), pp. 211–15
J. Sawyer, 'What was a *mōšīa'*?', *VT* xv (1965), pp. 475–86
H. H. Schmid, *Wesen und Geschichte der Weisheit. Eine Untersuchung zur altorientalischen und israelitischen Weisheitsliteratur*, BZAW 101 (1966)
J. Schmidt, *Studien zur Stilistik der alttestamentlichen Spruchliteratur*, Alttestamentliche Abhandlungen, 13, 1 (1936)
H. Schneider, 'Die "Tochter" des Blutegels in Spr. 30.15', *Lex tua veritas*, Festschrift für Hubert Junker (1961), pp. 257–64
R. B. Y. Scott, 'Solomon and the Beginnings of Wisdom in Israel', *VTS* iii (1955), pp. 262–79
'Wisdom in Creation: the *'āmōn* of Proverbs viii.30', *VT* x (1960), pp. 213–23
Proverbs/Ecclesiastes, The Anchor Bible (1965)
J. L. Seeligman, 'Voraussetzungen der Midraschexegese', *VTS* i (1953), pp. 150–81
E. Sellin (W. Montgomery), *Introduction to the Old Testament* (1923)
U. Skladny, *Die ältesten Spruchsammlungen in Israel* (1962)
J. Payne Smith, *A Compendious Syriac Dictionary* (1903)
L. A. Snijders, 'The Meaning of *zār* in the Old Testament: an exegetical Study', *OTS* x (1954), pp. 1–154
W. von Soden, 'Zu *ZAW* 52, 53f.', *ZAW* 53 (1935), pp. 291f.
'Die Unterweltsvision eines assyrischen Kronprinzen', *ZA* 43 (1937), 1–13
Akkadisches Handwörterbuch (1959–)

C. Steuernagel, Kautzsch-Bertholet, *Die heilige Schrift des alten Testaments*[4] (1923)

W. B. Stevenson, 'A Mnemonic Use of Numbers in Proverbs and Ben Sira', *TGUOS* ix (1938/9), pp. 26–38

H. L. Strack, Strack und Zöckler, *Kurzgefasster Kommentar zu den heiligen Schriften alten und neuen Testaments* (1888)

D. W. Thomas, 'The Root *yd'* in Hebrew', *JTS* xxxv (1934), pp. 298–306

'The Root *šnh*=Arabic *sny* in Hebrew', *ZAW* 52 (1934), pp. 236–8

'The Root *yd'* in Hebrew II', *JTS* xxxvi (1935), pp. 409–12

'A Note on *lō' tēda'* in Proverbs v.6', *JTS* xxxvii (1936), pp. 59f.

D. W. Thomas, 'Notes on some Passages in the Book of Proverbs', *JTS* xxxviii (1937), pp. 400–3

'The Root *šnh*=Arabic *sny* in Hebrew, II', *ZAW* 55 (1937), pp. 174–6

'A Note on *lyqht* in Prov. xxx.17', *JTS* xlii (1941), pp. 154f.

'A Note on *bal yāde'ā* in Prov. ix.13', *JTS* iv (1953), pp. 23f.

'' *ēw* in Proverbs xxxi.4', *VT* xii (1962), pp. 499f.

'Textual and Philological Notes on some Passages in the Book of Proverbs', *VTS* iii (1955), pp. 280–92

'A Note on *da'at* in Proverbs xxii.12', *JTS* xiv (1963), pp. 93f.

'*beliya'al* in the Old Testament', *Biblical and Patristic Studies in memory of R. P. Casey*, ed. J. N. Birdsall and R. W. Thomson (1963), pp. 11–19

'Additional Notes on the Root *yd'* in Hebrew', *JTS* xv (1964), pp. 54–57

'The Meaning of *ḥaṭṭā't* in Proverbs x.16', *JTS* xv (1964), pp. 295f.

'Proverbs xx.26', *JJS* xv (1964), pp. 155f.

'Notes on some Passages in the Book of Proverbs', *VT* xv (1965), pp. 271–9

W. M. Thomson, *The Land and the Book* (1860)

F. Thureau-Dangin, 'Deux proverbes babyloniens', *An. Or.* 12 (1935), pp. 307–11

H. Torczyner, 'The Riddle in the Bible', *HUCA* i (1924), pp. 125–49

Mišelē Selōmō (1947)

N. H. Tur Sinai, *Sēper 'īyōb* (1957)

C. C. Torrey, 'Proverbs, chapter 30', *JBL* lxxiii (1954), pp. 93–103

R. Tournay, 'Relectures bibliques concernant la vie future et l'angélologie', *RB* lxix (1962), pp. 481–505

C. H. Toy, *A Critical and Exegetical Commentary on the book of Proverbs*, The International Critical Commentary (1899)

G. Vermes, 'The Torah is a Light', *VT* viii (1958), pp. 436–8

G. J. L. Vogel, in A. Schultens, *Proverbia Salomonis* (1769)

A. Volten, 'Der Begriff der Maat in der ägyptischen Weisheit', *Les Sagesses du Proche-Orient Ancien* (1963), pp. 73–101

J. Weil, 'Le sens de *nepeš* dans Prov. 23.7a', *ZAW* 44 (1926), pp. 62f.

A. Weiser (tr. D. M. Barton), *Introduction to the Old Testament* (1961)

R. N. Whybray, *Wisdom in Proverbs*, Studies in Biblical Theology, No. 45 (1965)

G. Widengren, *The King and the Tree of Life in Ancient Near Eastern Religion*, Uppsala Universitets Årsskrift (1951)

G. Wildeboer, in Marti, *Kurzer Hand-Commentar zum Alten Testament* (1897)

R. J. Williams, 'The alleged Semitic Original of the Wisdom of Amenemope', *JEA* 47 (1961), pp. 100–6

H. A. Wolfson, 'Notes on Proverbs 22.10 and Psalms of Solomon 17.48', *JQR* xxxvii (1946/7), p. 87

A. Wünsche, 'Die Zahlensprüche in Talmud und Midrasch', *ZDMG* 65 (1911), pp. 57–100

E. ben Yehuda, 'The Edomite Language', *JPOS* i (1920/21), pp. 113–15

W. Zimmerli, 'Zur Struktur der alttestamentlichen Weisheit', *ZAW* 51 (1933), pp. 177–204

'"Leben" und "Tod" im Buche des Propheten Ezechiel', *Gottes Offenbarung* (1963), pp. 178–91

'Ort und Grenze der Weisheit im Rahmen der alttestamentlichen Theologie', *op. cit.*, pp. 300–15

INTRODUCTION

A. PROVERBS 1–9

IN HIS IMPORTANT BOOK, Schmidt[1] argues that Proverbs 1–9 represents an advanced stage in the history of a process of formal development based on the wisdom sentence. Schmidt identifies *māšāl* with a single-verse saying of which there are three variants: (*a*) the one-limbed saying; (*b*) the two-limbed saying; (*c*) the multi-limbed saying. Since the Old Testament wisdom literature (*Spruchliteratur*) has a literary and artistic character, there are few examples in it of the single-limbed verse, but in spite of this striving after literary finesse the single-limbed verse has been preserved and is found in two forms: (*a*) as a simple sentence consisting of subject, predicate and object. This form is found, for the most part, in those sayings transmitted as popular proverbs (e.g., Gen. 22.14; I Sam. 24.13[14]; Ezek. 16.44); (*b*) in an extended form which marks a stage of transition from a single-limbed saying to a two-limbed saying, since the final clause is not a grammatical entity and only makes sense in relation to what precedes it. An effort is made to extend the scope of the saying. 'A wise man's teaching is a fountain of life' (13.14) is a good saying without the supplementary 'offering escape from the snares of death'. The two-limbed saying with *parallelismus membrorum* is a typical feature of Old Testament wisdom literature, and the expanded single-limbed saying is an indication that the most primitive form of the *māšāl* is the single-limbed verse. To this group of single-limbed sayings which show a tendency towards the two-limbed form there belong those sayings which employ the different modes of comparison.

While it may be said that the single-limbed verse is the primitive form (*Urform*) of the popular proverb, the two-limbed verse is the basic stylistic element (*Stilform*) of the literary *māšāl*. The two limbs of a verse must each be a grammatical entity and the grammatical construction of the second may be either the same as, or different from, the first. When two limbs are similarly constructed, *parallelismus membrorum* is produced. Among all the uncertainties attaching to its origins, what seems assured is that it is a characteristic of elevated speech. Two reasons may be suggested for its use in Old Testament

[1] J. Schmidt, *Studien zur Stilistik der alttestamentlichen Spruchliteratur*, Alttestamentliche Abhandlungen 13, 1 (1936), pp. 1f.

wisdom literature: (*a*) the poetic character of this literature. The author sought a certain rhythm for his sentences. When it is remembered that this literature emerged from popular wisdom and arrived gradually at the form in which it is known to us today, the influence of poetry is a reasonable postulate. Because the literature grew out of popular wisdom and was not originally poetry, something of the prosaic still attaches to its form and content. Hence *parallelismus membrorum* is not native to Old Testament wisdom literature, but derives from the influence of poetry and a form of elevated speech on that literature; (*b*) the didactic function of the *māšāl*. Instruction was made more effective and easier for the student by its use.

The multi-limbed saying is compounded of a plurality of limbs, each of which is an independent grammatical entity. It also comprises the case of two-limbed verses which have been united. The multi-limbed verse may arise through the association of single-limbed sayings of similar content or by grammatical-syntactical compounding by means of principal and subordinate clauses.

The striving of Old Testament wisdom literature to exceed the limits of a single verse and the continuous working-over of wisdom sayings produced units containing more than one verse. Two verses were joined: (*a*) by a running-together of the verses, which resulted in a parallelism of verses; (*b*) without parallelism of verses; (*c*) grammatically-syntactically, as principal and subordinate clauses. The unit with a plurality of verses is developed from the single verse in the same way as the multi-limbed verse is developed from the single-limbed verse.

The way in which the wisdom literature has developed formally is thus clear. It proceeds from the unit of one verse to the unit which contains a plurality of verses. The primitive element of form is the one-limbed, single-verse saying. Generally valid and practically applicable wisdom was acquired through experience and such teaching is best imparted by brief, simple sentences. The one-limbed, single-verse saying becomes the two-limbed and multi-limbed verse by a literary process, for it was a natural development that two or more clauses related in content should be attached to each other as a means of emphasizing the instruction which was given. When reasons or consequences were added to the instruction by attaching motive or final clauses, the multi-verse unit came into being. It was not a great step from this to the larger literary units of the wisdom literature, the strophes and the didactic poems (*Lehrgedichten*).

The Old Testament wisdom literature has popular origins and takes on literary characteristics when the collectors of individual sayings come on the scene. These collectors have altered and expanded the sayings greatly, but it is not to be supposed that the sayings themselves stem from individual authors; they have a popular or folk origin. From this circumstance light can be cast on the origins of the Old Testament wisdom literature. All that can be determined is the relative priorities of the known literary forms. It is certain that the single-verse and multi-verse sayings are temporally prior to all greater units. At the beginning stands the one-limbed, single-verse saying which has a popular character and was, in the first place, transmitted orally. It was developed into the two-limbed verse, which is the basic literary form of the wisdom sentence, and the way then led to the multi-limbed and multi-verse unit and had its form-critical consummation in the didactic poem which stemmed from one author and was a literary product from the outset.

Schmidt confidently builds on the statement in Prov. 1.1 that the book is made up of *m*e*šālīm*, and concludes from this that the basic form of all the material in the book of Proverbs is the wisdom sentence (pp. 9f.). But the book contains material (1–9; 22.17–24.22; 31.1–9) which cannot be classified as *m*e*šālīm* in Schmidt's sense, and which has not been formed into larger literary units from the basic unit of the wisdom sentence by a process of form-critical evolution. This material belongs to the Instruction genre (see below, pp. 262f.), and the most important formal distinction between Instruction and the wisdom sentence is that the imperative is proper to the first and the indicative to the second. The Instruction commands and exhorts and gives reasons why its directives should be obeyed. These reasons are contained in subordinate clauses of which the most typical is the motive (*kī*) clause, but final and consecutive clauses are also common. The Instruction is marked by direct address and its aim is to command and persuade. The wisdom sentence is an observation with an impersonal form which states a truth but neither exhorts nor persuades.

Schmidt has pointed to some of the characteristics of the Instruction, but he is never aware of the true character of this material. He observes that there are complexes in the book of Proverbs which extend over several verses, which are concerned with instruction (pp. 29f.) and which employ the imperative (p. 42). He holds, however, that they have been built up from the wisdom sentence, that it is the function of the wisdom sentence to instruct and that it can accommodate the imperative as well as the indicative. In illustrating his thesis that the wisdom sentence is the basic element of form throughout the book of Proverbs, he makes an invalid use of material from the Instruction, and his statements, although true of the Instruction, cannot be used to prove that this genre is an aggregate of wisdom sentences.

This is particularly so with his treatment of the subordinate clause, and he is wrong in asserting that the wisdom sentence evolves characteristically through a process of subordination. He gives two examples (p. 26) to show how a two-limbed wisdom sentence becomes multilimbed by subordination (23.5; 27.11), but what he is describing is the syntactical structure of the Instruction and not, as he supposes, the formal evolution of the wisdom sentence. His treatment of 23.5 is particularly capricious, since it belongs to a section (22.17–23.11) which shows direct literary dependence on the Instruction of *Amenemope* and which could not possibly have undergone on Israelite soil the process of formal evolution described by Schmidt.

The consequence of Schmidt's failure to identify the Instruction in the book of Proverbs is that he applies a formal argument which is invalid in respect of this material, because it rests on the assumption that the wisdom sentence is the basic element of form throughout, and that those parts of the book which have the most advanced groupings of wisdom sentences belong to the latest stage of formal evolution (pp. 33f.). As applied to Proverbs 1–9 in particular, this argument is thought to demonstrate that since the section represents an advanced stage in the history of a process of formal development based on the wisdom sentence, it must be regarded for such formal reasons as the latest part of the book of Proverbs.

About this there is now so impressive a unanimity that it might almost be described as an article of form-critical orthodoxy.[2] A special aspect of the argument in Zimmerli[3] is the attempt to show

[2] B. Gemser, *Sprüche Salomos*², Handbuch zum Alten Testament 16 (1963), p. 5; H. Ringgren, *Word and Wisdom* (1947), p. 9; R. B. Y. Scott, *Proverbs/Ecclesiastes*, The Anchor Bible (1965), p. 15; P. Humbert, *Recherches sur les sources egyptiennes de la littérature sapientale d'Israel* (1929), pp. 53f.; J. Hempel, *Die althebräische Literatur und ihr hellenistisch-jüdisches Nachleben* (1930), pp. 49f.; O. Eissfeldt, *The Old Testament: An Introduction* (1965), pp. 472f.; A. Bentzen, *Introduction to the Old Testament*⁵, ii (1959), p. 172; A. Weiser, *Introduction to the Old Testament* (1961), p. 296.

[3] W. Zimmerli, 'Zur Struktur der alttestamentlichen Weisheit', *ZAW* 10 (1933), pp. 185f.; 'Ort und Grenze der Weisheit im Rahmen der alttestamentlichen Theologie', *Gottes Offenbarung* (1963), p. 304.

that *ʿēṣā* is primary and *miṣwā* secondary, that the admonition (*Mahnspruch*) is developed from the sentence, that statement is formally prior to command or instruction. It is now clear, however, that the lateness of Proverbs 1–9 cannot be demonstrated by such a form-critical argument, because the Instruction is a separate genre whose syntactical structure can be described and which is not constituted by an agglomeration of wisdom sentences. This is generally conceded for 22.17–23.11. Whatever the precise character of the dependence of this passage on *Amenemope*, there is little doubt that an appropriation of formal elements of the Egyptian Instruction is involved (see below, pp. 369ff.).

The recent contention of Richter[4] that 22.17–23.11 is not formally dependent on *Amenemope* puzzles me, since I cannot find any reason to doubt that the international Instruction is the model of 22.17–24.22. I can see no virtue in the suggestion that Israelite formal elements (*Vorformen*) may have been used in 22.17–23.11. Richter (pp. 147f.) traces the imperious element in the Instruction to the 'school' and there is a measure of truth in this, since the Instruction is a scholastic form. Instead of an international genre of which the Israelite wisdom teacher made use, Richter postulates an Israelite admonition (*Mahnspruch*), and he draws into the discussion the prohibitive form of the so-called apodeictic laws (pp. 68f.).

This attempt to broaden the field of the enquiry and to reduce differing areas of literary activity to simple, common elements does not seem to me to be a sensible use of the form-critical method nor to be far removed from a *reductio ad absurdum*. A comparison of the Instruction in Proverbs with extra-Israelite examples of the genre has that degree of particularity and historical definition which is necessary for a satisfactory discussion. The formal structure of the Instruction can be described and its *Sitz im Leben* defined. The objection which I am raising against Richter is one which I also have against Gerstenberger's work,[5] which, however, is only marginally related to the present enquiry. Fohrer[6] makes a good point when he notes that a method which ends up with such generalities as 'Thou shalt' and 'Thou shalt not' is threatened with vacuity. I am not inclined to seek a common origin for the imperative of the Instruction and the

[4] W. Richter, *Recht und Ethos* (1966), pp. 36f.
[5] E. Gerstenberger, *Wesen und Herkunft des 'apodiktischen Rechts'* (1965).
[6] G. Fohrer, 'Das sogenannte apodiktisch formulierte Recht und der Dekalog', *KD* 11 (1965), pp. 49f.

prohibition of the apodeictic law, but, in any case, I am convinced that the imperative of the Instruction is one formal element among others of a clearly demarcated international genre and that this indicates the need for a narrower and more precise approach to the Instruction in the book of Proverbs than that followed by Richter and Gerstenberger.

Although much of a general character had been done to establish the connections of the book of Proverbs with foreign and especially Egyptian wisdom,[7] Whybray[8] was the first to base his treatment of 1–9 on a direct comparison between these chapters and the Egyptian Instruction (there is some awareness of this affinity in Fichtner and Humbert). While he indicated his disagreement with the form-critical argument for the lateness of 1–9, he did not undertake an analysis of the formal structure of these chapters in relation to the Egyptian Instruction. This has now been done by Kayatz,[9] and her results are in all essential respects in agreement with mine (see below, pp. 262ff.), though, as might be expected in a monograph devoted entirely to this enterprise, certain refinements are incorporated as compared with the analysis which I had completed independently of either her or Whybray. In particular, she has suggested that the prototype of the personified Wisdom (1.20–33; 8) may be found in the speeches of the gods which constitute a literary genre in Egypt (pp. 76f.).

The analysis of the Egyptian, Babylonian and Assyrian Instruction given below will show that there was an international genre with definable formal characteristics which can be described in syntactical terms, and that those sections of the book of Proverbs which are explained by Schmidt and others as agglomerations of wisdom sentences can be identified by their formal characteristics as examples of this international genre. There is the further consideration that 1–9 has the same formal structure as 22.17–23.11. That the latter is formally dependent on *Amenemope* is generally acknowledged, but if this is so, the logic of the form-critical argument in relation to 1–9

[7] H. Gressmann, *Israels Spruchweisheit im Zusammenhang der Weltliteratur* (1925); P. Humbert, *op. cit.* (see note 2 above); J. Hempel, *op. cit.* (see note 2 above); J. Fichtner, *Die altorientalische Weisheit in ihrer israelitisch-jüdischen Ausprägung*, BZAW 62 (1933); L. Dürr, *Das Erziehungswesen im alten Testament und im antiken Orient*, MVAG 36, 2 (1932); W. Baumgartner, *Israelitische und altorientalische Weisheit* (1933).

[8] R. N. Whybray, *Wisdom in Proverbs*, SBT 45 (1965).

[9] C. Kayatz, *Studien zu Proverbien 1–9; eine form- und motivgeschichtliche Untersuchung unter Einbeziehung ägyptischen Vergleichsmaterials*, WMANT 22 (1966), pp. 15–75.

collapses. The conclusion to be drawn is that the formal structure of 1–9, 22.17–24.22 and 31.1–9 is that of an international Instruction genre, and that it is not the consequence of a process of form-critical evolution involving the agglomeration of wisdom sentences. The Instruction is a separate genre from the wisdom sentence and the form-critical argument for the lateness of these sections of the book of Proverbs, involving as it does the assumption that their basic formal unit is the wisdom sentence, falls to the ground.

My own investigation will show that Proverbs 1–9 is largely made up of: (*a*) pieces which are strictly Instruction (1.8–19; 3.1–12, 21–35; 4; 5; 6.1–5, 20–35; 7.1–5, 24–27); (*b*) those in which there is a development and slackening of the formal structure of the Instruction (2; 3.13–20; 6.6–11; 7.6–23). In ch. 2 the imperative has disappeared and crisp, authoritative Instruction has given place to diffuse preaching which is organized in a series of protases and apodoses. The transition to a hymnic style can be seen in 3.13–20, where imperatives are lacking and the expression 'Happy is' is halfway between statement and exhortation. In 6.6–11 the element of command is minimal and the assumptions are different from those which obtain in the Instruction proper. The sluggard is so addressed that his incorrigibility is taken for granted and a 'son' is not addressed by his teacher in such a manner. The form of 7.6–23 (cf. 24.30–34) affords greater imaginative and descriptive scope than the didactic employment of imperatives and motive clauses in order to inculcate authoritative instruction. There is rather a reliance on descriptive power in order to win acquiescence for the point which is being made.

In 1.20–33 there is a complete absence of imperatives and the influence of prophetic modes of address can be detected, while ch. 8, which may also be subject to similar influences, does contain imperious elements (vv. 5f., 32–36) and to this extent relics of Instruction are preserved in it. I have noted above the special account of these passages given by Kayatz. Two passages in ch. 6 have no connection with Instruction: vv. 12–15 are descriptive of a malevolent person, and vv. 16–19 are, in Roth's terminology (see below, pp. 654f.), 'a graded numerical saying'. There are traces of Instruction in ch. 9 (vv. 6, 8, 9), but otherwise it exercises no formal influence on this chapter, whose keynote is invitation rather than instruction in a setting where Wisdom competes with the *'iššā zārā* for guests. Chapter 1.1–7 is a general introduction to the book of Proverbs.

It may still be true that a late date should be assigned to 1–9 because of its contents, and this has been argued consistently either along with or independent of the form-critical argument which I have been criticizing.[10] A variety of reasons have been given for placing the collection in the fifth century BC or later, among them the *'iššā zārā* theme (Sellin, Ringgren), the account of the antiquity of Wisdom in ch. 8 with its mythological background (Sellin, Gemser), the union of wisdom and the fear of Yahweh (Baumgartner, Weiser) and the word *'ēṭūn* (7.16), which is thought to be a Greek loan word *(ὀθόνη)*.[11]

I am not concerned to show that the 'Collection' was completed at an earlier date than these arguments indicate, but only that in so far as 1–9 reproduces the form of the Instruction it need not be late for that reason. My account of this section will reveal an unevenness of content in those parts which are strictly Instruction (see below, p. 303). Most inculcate earthy and hard-headed wisdom and have nothing in them that would stamp them as distinctively Israelite, certainly not as Yahwistic (1.8–19; 4; 5; 6.1–5, 20–35; 7.1–5, 24–27; also 31.1–9). In a few places, the Instruction has been brought into the fold of Yahwistic piety and retains no recognizable contact with its primary educational *Sitz* (3.1–12, 21–26, 31–35). There are one or two passages which are concerned particularly with anti-social behaviour (3.27–30; 4.14f.; also 6.12–19 which is not Instruction) and so the three classes of material which appear in the sentence literature (see below, pp. 10, 415) are also present in 1–9.

The concept of a 'Collection' may perhaps be more legitimately applied to 1–9 than to the sentence literature, but even here there is a need to be clear about the degree of usefulness which attaches to the notion. I have shown that there is some formal heterogeneity in 1–9 as well as diversity of content. The dating of the collection (even if this can be done accurately) will only show when 1–9 first existed as a literary entity, and will not touch the traditio-historical questions about the form and contents of 1–9. This is the matter which primarily interests me. It is a reasonable assumption that the Instruction was appropriated by Israel as early as the reign of Solomon, when a

[10] C. H. Toy, *Proverbs*, ICC (1899), p. xxviii; Gemser, *op. cit.* (see note 2 above), pp. 5f.; Ringgren, *op. cit.* (see note 2 above), pp. 8f.; Scott, *op. cit.* (see note 2 above), p. 15; A. Barucq, *Le Livre des Proverbes*, Sources Bibliques (1964), p. 17; E. Sellin, *Introduction to the Old Testament* (1923), p. 208; W. Baumgartner, *op. cit.* (see note 7 above), p. 27; O. Eissfeldt, *op. cit.* (see note 2 above), pp. 472f.; A. Weiser, *op. cit.* (see note 2 above), pp. 296f.

[11] Sellin, Bentzen, Weiser. KB³ derives it from Egyptian *jmdj*, 'red-coloured linen'. BDB says that the derivation is unknown.

class of officials came into existence to serve the new structure of the state, and when there was a consequent need for Instruction with the same educational function as it had in Egypt. There it was located in schools where an *élite* was trained for the service of the state; likewise, when Solomon created a civil service (perhaps on the Egyptian model) there would have been a demand for a similar type of school and for such an instrument of vocational education.[12]

The Instruction may have established itself in Israel in these circumstances and, if so, a traditio-historical account of the genre should begin there. This is a very different starting-place from that allocated to the Instruction by those who describe it formally as a stringing together of wisdom sentences. In that case the Instruction had no existence at all in an Israelite context until this most advanced stage in the formal evolution of the wisdom sentence had been reached. The effect of this fallacious formal argument is to obliterate the history of the genre in the context of the Old Testament. The extant examples in 1–9 do not have the character of career advice for officials, so that the argument for its introduction to Israel in the reign of Solomon does involve a process of extrapolation. This does not seem to me to be unreasonable. In other words, it has to be assumed that the pieces in 1–9 are representative of later stages in the history of the tradition of the Instruction and that we are not able to inspect it at its point of origin (see my remarks on *Onchsheshonqy*, below, p. 123). Even those passages which are strictly educational in tone have the character of instruction for a way of life and not for a successful career, though it should be noted that Brunner[13] and Gese[14] make this claim for the Egyptian Instruction and urge that it is not adequately described as career guidance. It may be conceded that there is some justice in this, but there is an important distinction between the Egyptian and Israelite specimens of the Instruction which should not be blurred. The former has a specialized constituency in view, an *élite* who aspire to positions of responsibility and power in the state, whereas the latter is broadly-based instruction for the community and especially for the young men of the community.[15] The history of the tradition of the Instruction is parallel to that of the

[12] Cf. Humbert, *op. cit.*, pp. 63f., 107, 180f.; W. McKane, *Prophets and Wise Men*, SBT 44 (1965), pp. 23f. (henceforth *PWM*); S. Mowinckel, 'Israelite Historiography', *ASTI* 2 (1963), p. 7.

[13] H. Brunner, *Altägyptische Erziehung* (1957), pp. 117f.

[14] H. Gese, *Lehre und Wirklichkeit in der alten Weisheit* (1958), pp. 30f.

[15] Cf. Gemser, *op. cit.*, pp. 6f.

wisdom sentence; both are eventually integrated into the fabric of Yahwistic piety and become the instruments of its propagation. We may conclude that the Instruction which is originally, in Egypt if not in Israel, a means of educating officials, becomes in Israel a method of generalized mundane instruction and thereafter a way of inculcating Yahwistic piety.

B. THE SENTENCE LITERATURE IN THE BOOK OF PROVERBS

I argue below that there is, for the most part, no context in the sentence literature and that the individual wisdom sentence is a complete entity (see below, pp. 413ff.). The logical outcome of this argument is the allocation of the sentences to different classes, since the necessity for such a system of classification follows from the random way in which wisdom sentences follow one upon another in any chapter. I am aware that the word 'random' might be challenged, since I admit that there are editorial principles of different kinds according to which sentences are grouped. I shall call attention to some of these, while maintaining that they have a secondary character and do not contradict the statement that there is, for the most part, no context in the sentence literature. There is therefore need for more fundamental criteria to be brought to bear on the classification of the material and this is what I try to do.

It will be clear that I do not place a very high value on the concept of a 'collection' as applied to the sentence literature, and I am sceptical of Skladny's[16] efforts to discover in 'collections' of wisdom sentences such a coherence of theme and consistency of artistic intention that he can describe a 'collection' as if it constituted an architectonic unity. His work is useful within certain limits and his statistics are helpful (pp. 67f.). It can be said incontrovertibly that nearly all the sentences collected in 10–15 have antithetic parallelism or, again, that those in 25–27 have a more developed literary character than is commonly found elsewhere in the book. Such similes are found in other chapters, but the consistency of their occurrence and the consequent density of the imagery in 25–27 give these chapters a character of their own, and we may speak of a 'collection' of similes. On the other hand, the marks of literary artifice in 25–27 ill accord with

[16] U. Skladny, *Die ältesten Spruchsammlungen in Israel* (1962).

Skladny's view (pp. 55f.) that this is a popular proverbial collection addressed to simple people – artisans and farmers.

All this, however, is a much more limited concept of 'collection' than that employed by Skladny, who seeks to show that his collections have a thematic coherence. A (10–15) is occupied with a righteousness – wickedness antithesis. B (16–22.16) is principally constituted by sentences on two topics, Yahweh and the king. C (25–27) is characterized by its connection with nature and its high estimate of agriculture. In D (28–29) the sentences concerning the king have in mind particularly the young man who is to become a member of the ruling class. The collection can be described as a *Regentenspiegel*.

I shall come presently to the relative chronology proposed by Skladny for his collections and comment on some of the criteria which he employs. First of all I must introduce into the discussion the results obtained from my own method of analysing the sentence literature. I shall set out the statistics for 10–22.16 and 25–29 (all of the sentences except 24.23–34). Then I shall present them in a form which makes possible a direct comparison with Skladny's collections. The system of classification I adopt is as follows:

Class A: These sentences are set in the framework of old wisdom and are concerned with the education of the individual for a successful and harmonious life.

Class B: Here the centre of concern is the community rather than the individual, and the sentences in this class have, for the most part, a negative character, in that they describe the harmful effects on the life of the community of various manifestations of anti-social behaviour.

Class C: These are identified by the presence of God-language or by other items of vocabulary expressive of a moralism which derives from Yahwistic piety.

This classification is discussed again at the appropriate place in the Commentary (see below, pp. 413f.).

My argument will be that the class C material represents a reinterpretation of the class A material and a later stage in the history of the Old Testament wisdom tradition.[17] This later stage (if the assumption is accepted) is more fully represented in 10–22.16 (33 per cent) than it is in 25–29 (23 per cent). For the class A sentences, which I have described as old wisdom, the figures are 52 per cent in the former and 57 per cent in the latter. If my assumptions are

[17] This is in general agreement with Fichtner, *op. cit.*, pp. 24f.; Sellin, *op. cit.*, p. 207; Scott, *op. cit.*, p. 17.

	Total	Class A	Class B	Class C
Ch. 10	32	9	7	16
11	31	8	9	14
12	28	12	5	11
13	25*	16	3	5
14	35	23	3	9
15	33	19	4	10
16	33	10	8	15
17	28	17	7	4
18	24	16	3	5
19	29	22	1	6
20	30	21	1	8
21	31	14	4	13
22	16	9	1	6
	375	196	56	122
		52%	15%	33%

* One sentence unclassified in ch. 13.

25	27	22	4	1
26	28	19	9	
27	27	25	1	1
28	28		8	20
29	27	12	5	10
	137	78	27	32
		57%	20%	23%

	Total	Class A	Class B	Class C
A (Skladny) Ch. 10–15	184	87	31	65
		47·5%	17%	35·5%
B 16–22.16	191	109	25	57
		57%	13%	30%
C 25–27	82	66	14	2
		80·5%	17%	2·5%
D 28–29	55	12	13	30
		22%	24%	54%

correct, there is no ground for maintaining that the contents of 10–22.16 are earlier than those of 25–29. Both collections are deposits of material in which the course of development followed by the wisdom tradition is mirrored. Both contain the earlier and the later wisdom as well as the sentences with the special social emphasis which I have allocated to class B. It may be that 10–22.16 came into existence as an editorial collection earlier than 25–29, but the traditio-historical question is a separate one and the sentences in both collections are comparable in range.

When my statistics are set against Skladny's observations (pp. 76f.) about the relative chronology of his collections, they do not support his conclusions. He maintains that his collection A is earlier than B, but B has more class A sentences and less class C sentences than A. If the argument is about the contents of the two collections, there is not a great deal to choose between the one and the other in terms of the range of material which they contain. It will be noticed that Skladny's collection C has a very high incidence of class A sentences (80·5 per cent) and only two class C sentences (2·5 per cent). It is evident that the contents are preponderantly old wisdom,[18] though this does not settle the question when the collection was edited, and I acknowledge that it has marks of literary polish.[19]

In fixing the place of 25–27 in his relative chronology, Skladny supposes that the higher incidence of Instruction in these chapters (see below, pp. 577ff. especially p. 607) is a mark of lateness, and relies on the fallacious form-critical argument which I have criticized, that the *Mahnspruch* is a secondary development from the statement (see above, pp. 4ff.). His disagreement with Gese (p. 76, n.5)[20] shows that further factors are involved in his assessment of 25–27. Gese shares his form-critical assumption about the relation of statement to command, but disagrees with his concept of a 'Collection'.[21] A collection of sentences does not have the coherence and compactness of structure which Skladny supposes it to have,[22] and so a collection in which

[18] Cf. Fichtner, *op. cit.*, pp. 56, 62, n.3; Scott, *op. cit.*, p. 17; H. H. Schmid, *Wesen und Geschichte der Weisheit*, BZAW 101 (1966), pp. 145f.

[19] Cf. Sellin, *op. cit.*, p. 209, who dates 10–22.16 earlier than 25–27, because the latter with its carefully worked out comparisons represents a higher stage in the formal development of poetry (also Gemser, *op. cit.*, p. 4; Hempel, *op. cit.*, p. 175).

[20] Cf. Gese, *op. cit.*, p. 32, n.1.

[21] Cf. Scott, *op. cit.*, p. 17; Weiser, *op. cit.*, p. 297; O. Eissfeldt, *Der Maschal im Alten Testament*, BZAW 24 (1913), p. 36.

[22] Gemser (p. 5) has a somewhat similar concept of a collection. He discovers a unity in 10–22.16 in terms of Böstrom's 'agricultural ideal'.

fragments of Instruction are mixed with sentences has neither more nor less of structure than a collection of sentences. Nowhere do my results clash more obviously with those of Skladny than in collection D, which is earlier than B and C in his relative chronology. In D, 54 per cent of the sentences are in class C and 22 per cent in class A, so that the contents, on my assumptions, are relatively later than those of his collections A, B and C. In respect of incidence of antithetic parallelism and content, 28–29 has affinities with 10–15.

These results underline the need for clarity in any discussion about the dating of the 'collections' in Proverbs and, particularly, for a distinction to be drawn between editorial collecting and the content which is collected. The ascription of 25–29 to the men of Hezekiah (i.e., to the *ḥakāmīm* engaged in literary and editorial tasks under his patronage) is generally regarded as trustworthy,[23] and the collection is dated to *c.* 700 BC. Eissfeldt, Ringgren and Scott are aware that this is a statement about when the material in 25–29 was collected and edited, and not about the date of the contents of 25–29. Eissfeldt (*Introduction*, p. 474) and Scott (pp. 17f.) also make this distinction in their discussion of 10–22.16. Eissfeldt describes *ḥesed* (15.34), *nāḥat* (17.10), *rāʿaʿ* (18.24) and *qibbēl* (19.20) as Aramaisms and holds that the collection must be post-exilic, while recognizing that this is not a verdict on the age of the individual sentences in these chapters. Scott argues that 10–22.16 reached its present form in the fifth or fourth century BC, but that much of the material is pre-exilic in origin. Gemser (pp. 4f.) does not succeed so well in distinguishing between collection and contents. When he dates 10–22.16 *c.* 150 years after the reign of Solomon, this would seem not just to be a statement about an editorial collection, but also about its contents; so also with his statement that 25–29 comes from the time of Hezekiah.

The classification of the sentence literature into classes A, B and C has an element of arbitrariness in it, though not such as to call in question the validity of the procedure. Obviously there are sentences which are difficult to classify in the terms which I have drawn, and there is doubt as to whether they belong to one class or another. On the level of description, however, there does not seem to me to be any serious difficulty here. The contentious part of the exercise is the explanation which I have given of the relation of the class A sentences to the class C sentences, since this transcends mere description. It

[23] Gemser, *op. cit.*, p. 4; Ringgren, *op. cit.*, p. 8; Gressmann, *op. cit.* (see note 7 above), p. 34; Eissfeldt, *Introduction*, p. 475; Weiser, *op. cit.*, p. 297.

brings me into conflict with arguments that 10.1–22.16 contains the oldest material in the book of Proverbs and, in particular, with Skladny's special reasons for upholding this opinion in respect of 10–15. The antithesis of *ṣaddīq-rāšāʿ* which I take as evidence of a Yahwistic reinterpretation of old wisdom and as evidence that the wisdom sentence had become an instrument for inculcating Yahwistic dogma is thought by him to point to the earliness of the collection.[24] He rejects the view that these sentences give expression to a doctrine of theodicy (*Vergeltungsdogma*) and speaks instead of a character-consequence nexus. Deed and consequence are intrinsically related, but 10–15 treat not so much the actions of righteous and wicked as their settled attitudes and the consequences which can almost be regarded as part and parcel of these attitudes (pp. 7f., 71f.).

Skladny notices that in some sentences Yahweh is mentioned explicitly as the one who brings about the consequences. He urges that this does not involve any modification of the character-consequence nexus in 10–15, but that the matter is different in collection B (16–22.16), where in association with the mention of Yahweh's action he observes a new departure in some seventy-five verses. Even then there is no dogma of recompense and retribution, nor is there any abrogation of the nexus such as Gese (pp. 37f.) maintains. Yahweh inserts himself between plan and act so as to determine the direction of human action without, however, breaching his order. The distinctive element in Gese's account is that he supposes a secondary Yahwistic reinterpretation to have operated on certain of the verses in which there is an explicit mention of Yahweh's action, and that with this reinterpretation the sentences are no longer compatible with the concept of order characteristic of the older wisdom in Israel and comparable with the Egyptian *Maat*.[25] According to Gese, these sentences (10.22; 16.1, 9, 33; 20.24; 21.1, 30, 31; 25.2) emphasize the freedom of Yahweh from any metaphysical order[26] and are evidence of a tension between Yahwism and old wisdom which ultimately

[24] Also Gemser, *op. cit.*, p. 4; Barucq, *op. cit.*, p. 17; O. S. Rankin, *Israel's Wisdom Literature* (1936), pp. 69f. H. H. Schmid (pp. 159f.) likens the *ṣaddīq-rāšāʿ* antithesis to the Egyptian concept of *Maat*. He makes a distinction between the original intention of the antithesis and how it was understood by the collector.

[25] This view is criticized by Gemser (p. 8, n.2) on the ground that Gese has too restricted a view of the Israelite doctrine of God: Yahweh as independent of the order; cf. W. Zimmerli, 'Struktur' (see note 3 above), p. 203, who speaks of a concept of order not dissimilar to the Egyptian one.

[26] Cf. W. Zimmerli, 'Ort', p. 311. The freedom of God is threatened by the concept of order in Proverbs; also H. H. Schmid, *op. cit.*, pp. 146f.

precipitates the crisis of wisdom in Job and Ecclesiastes. I have explained most of these verses (16.1, 9, 33; 20.24; 21.30, 31) in a manner which presupposes a differently motivated Yahwistic reinterpretation.

The debate over the propriety of the term theodicy in relation to these sentences – whether it is proper to speak about reward and retribution – does not seem to me to have a great deal in it.[27] The evil disposition or the evil act (the righteous disposition or the righteous act) contains the seed of its consequences and we are not to think of punishment as brought about by a forensic act of Yahweh. It will be seen from my exegesis of the class C sentences in 10–15 that, in my judgement, they have more of a forensic character than this analysis allows. But even if this concept of an immanent order is associated with these sentences, it does not reduce the impression of an unreal black and white schematism which they make on me. Schmid (pp. 161f.) has observed that there is a tendency for wisdom at a certain stage of its development to lose touch with mundane realities and to construct an ideal scheme of things. Something of this kind has happened in those sentences which are marked by a *ṣaddīq-rāšāʿ* antithesis or a similar antithesis formulated in ethical terms which belong to the same framework of piety. Here is a theory, whether it is described in Skladny's terms or mine, that for the *ṣaddīq* this is the best of all possible worlds. The extreme tidiness of the doctrine is an indication of its sterility and its disengagement from mundane realities. This is not old wisdom but the theory of a kind of Yahwistic piety which is condemned to emptiness because it has disengaged itself from the realities of life and has left all problems behind.

It should be realized that my account of the relation of the class C sentences to the class A sentences cannot adequately be refuted by entering objections of a very general character. It is not enough to assert that wisdom in the Ancient Near East had a religious character from the outset and that this must have been true of Israelite wisdom also. In the present connection, too much should not be made of the circumstance that the trend is now to minimize the empirical or even pragmatic aspects of the Egyptian Instruction and to emphasize its religious character. I have tried to do justice to this newer point of view, but the nature of Old Testament wisdom cannot be determined from such a distance and regard must be paid to the results which flow from the examination of the Old Testament material itself.

[27] Cf. Gemser (p. 7, n.13), who resists the attack on 'theodicy' and 'retribution'. See below p. 271.

I am still of the opinion, after having taken the other possibilities into account, that the class C material is best explained as a Yahwistic reinterpretation of an older, empirical, mundane wisdom represented by the class A material. In particular, there are evidences in the class C sentences of a reinterpretation of the vocabulary of old wisdom. Words which in class A are set in an educational framework have a different meaning in class C in a framework of Yahwistic piety. I reproduce here briefly some of the more telling linguistic details which support a theory of a Yahwistic reinterpretation:

1. Words which are indicative of positive educational attainment in class A are pejorative and redolent of impiety in class C.

(*a*) In 8.12b (p. 347) and 14.17b (p. 468) *m^e^zimmā* is an intellectual virtue, while in 12.2b (p. 448) it is pejorative.

(*b*) In 12.5 (p. 450) *taḥbūlōt* is a pejorative antithesis of *maḥ^a^šābōt*, but both words have an equally positive and constructive connotation in the framework of old wisdom. Thus in 11.14a (p. 429), *taḥbūlōt* is indispensable for a state of political well-being.

(*c*) There is a group of sentences where the vocabulary of old wisdom is used pejoratively or else it is suggested that the intellectual grasp and range to which the *ḥakāmīm* lay claim when they use this vocabulary of themselves is properly attributable only to Yahweh (see *PWM*, pp. 79f.). In 19.21 (pp. 534f.), *maḥ^a^šābōt* and *lēb* ('intellectual grasp') are pejorative and *ʿēṣā* ('policy') is said to belong to Yahweh alone. According to 20.24 (p. 546), man's *bīnā* is inadequate, while 21.30 (pp. 558f.) maintains that *ḥokmā*, *t^e^būnā* ('perceptiveness') and *ʿēṣā* are all insufficient.

(*d*) The same process of reinterpretation can be detected in 1–9. *bīnā* is pejorative in 3.5 and *ḥākām b^eʿ^ēnāw* has a different sense in 3.7 (p. 292; *PWM*, p. 66: cf. Isa. 5.21) from what it has in 26.5, 12, 16; 28.11. It is not the fool (26.5, 12) nor the sluggard (26.16) nor the rich man who is not *mēbīn* (28.11) who is *ḥākām b^eʿ^ēnāw*, but the sage himself. In opposing the *dābār* of Yahweh to *ʿēṣā*, Isaiah shares the point of view of Prov. 3.7, where the meaning 'wise in your own eyes' is significantly changed as compared with the other passages from Proverbs cited above. 'Be not wise in your own eyes, fear Yahweh and turn away from evil.' Being wise in one's own eyes is not now an intellectual flaw nor a defect of character, but a form of impiety, and the implication of this usage is that there is no educational process, however severe, which can make a man into a *ḥākām*. In the other passages, the *ḥākām beʿênāw* is the incorrigible person who supposes that he knows everything already or who otherwise is not amenable to educational discipline.

2. There is one interesting example where the hypothesis of reinterpretation is illustrated by a process of substitution. 13.14 and 14.27 are identical except for one item. According to 13.14 (p. 455), it is the instruction of a *ḥākām* (a wisdom teacher) which is a fountain of life; according to 14.27 (p. 474) it is the fear of Yahweh. I find it very hard to resist the conclusion that this must be explained as a case of subsequent reinterpretation associated with a new concept of *mūsār*. The discipline of piety is substituted for educational discipline and Yahweh takes the place formerly occupied by the wisdom teacher.

3. There are the differing attitudes to bribery in the sentence literature. In 17.8 (p. 502), 18.16 (p. 517), and 21.14 (p. 555), the judicious employment of the bribe as an instrument of policy is recommended, while 15.27 (p. 485) and 17.23 (p. 512) contain high-toned condemnations of bribery. If this is not evidence of reinterpretation, it is at least irreconcilable with the view that all of the material in Proverbs can be accommodated within a single theological structure or unitary ethos.

I am not therefore inclined to agree with Whybray (pp. 24f.) when he says that hardly any hints about the history of the wisdom tradition are to be gathered from the book of Proverbs, that the sentence literature lacks any specifically Israelite traits and that such as there are (allusions to Yahweh) are superficial and do not disturb the general impression that we have to do with extra-Israelite material. Whybray says that when we come to Ben Sira we meet a wise man who is a master of biblical learning and is thoroughly integrated into the Yahwistic fold,[28] but that few traces of the development which led to this conclusion are observable in the book of Proverbs. It may be conceded at once that prophetic influence can be postulated for only a few sentences (11.1; 15.8; 16.6, 11; 21.3, 27; 22.7; 28.13; 29.7) and that evidences of a cultic interest are negligible (3.9; 11.1, 20; 12.2, 22; 14.9?; 15.8, 26).[29] Nevertheless, both the Instruction and sentence literature in the book of Proverbs throw light on the history of the wisdom tradition in Israel.

[28] Cf. Fichtner, *op. cit.*, pp. 93f.; see below, p. 648.
[29] See below, pp. 448, 511f.; W. Zimmerli, 'Ort', p. 309.

I have argued (*PWM*, pp. 102f.) that in the late pre-exilic period the wise men, who stood in an international tradition of wisdom, were beginning to come to terms with Yahwism, that wisdom had begun to make its bow to distinctively Israelite biblical traditions and that the wise men were in the way of becoming biblical scholars, devoted to sacred learning. The material in class C and the Instruction in its Yahwistic dress reflect this change in the occupation of the wise men, a change whose full effects can be studied in Ben Sira. What could be more natural than that the wise men should employ their own literary forms in the service of Yahwistic piety whose exponents they had become; that the wisdom sentence, particularly with antithetic parallelism (cf. 10–15, 28–29) should be made an instrument for inculcating a doctrine of theodicy and that the Instruction, which had originated in Israel in an educational context associated with the training of officials for public life, should be integrated into a like frame of piety? The style of piety in the class C material provides the point of departure for the questionings of Job and the scepticism of Ecclesiastes.[30] However it is to be characterized (theodicy seems to me to be a fair description), it has the extreme tidiness, the sterility and the disengagement from reality that prepared the way for Job and Ecclesiastes. The book of Proverbs informs us about the history of wisdom forms (Instruction and sentence) and also about the changing content of the office of *ḥākām*. Both forms are employed to give expression to a precious piety which left no questions open, no ends untied and which secured its mathematical precision by detaching itself from the messiness and confusion of men's lives in the world and by shutting its ears to the still, sad music of humanity.

Are there other and better explanations of the relation of the class A sentences to the class C sentences than the one which I have given? There would seem to be two further possibilities, the one, in my view, more serious than the other. I begin with the one which has the lesser probability. According to this argument the sentences in the book of Proverbs are all constituent parts of a single system of wisdom.[31] Different notes are struck but the result is not irreconcilable discord; they all blend in a complicated harmony. Israelite wisdom, according to Zimmerli, is not simply instruction in reliance on God; it does not

[30] Cf. W. Zimmerli, 'Ort', p. 311.

[31] W. Zimmerli, 'Ort', pp. 302f. This was also the view of Oesterley in his commentary (p. lvi), and has been restated more recently by Gerleman (*OTS* VIII, 1950, pp. 18f.; *Lunds Universitets Årsskrift*, NF, Avd. 1, Bd. 52, Nr. 3, 1956, pp. 36f.).

repeal the definition of wisdom as shrewdness and procedural skills (*taḥbūlōt*). The fear of Yahweh is the queen of all the rules of steering. Wisdom is more than a simple, unreflective fear of Yahweh; it is the comprehensive competence which enables a man to steer the whole of his life surely. Man knows that he is empowered to observe and order phenomena and this process begins in that objective sphere which is concerned with work and reward. This activity is involved with the meaning of power and influence. But wisdom – still the same wisdom – has wider horizons and it bestows order on areas of human relationships by establishing categories of moral and immoral, true and false, right and wrong. There are one or two passages which might be thought to support such a conclusion. One could argue from these passages that the same words (*mūsār*, *bīnā*) could be used by the same men both in an educational context and in a framework of piety; that it is a partnership of intellectual competence and trust in Yahweh which constitutes a whole man.[32] I need not again rehearse the arguments which have led me to the opposite conclusion and to the rejection of the view that all of the material can be made to contribute to a unitary system of wisdom.

The more serious alternative account would say that my description of the class A and class C sentences should not be made the basis of a history of the wisdom tradition in Israel, but that it points rather to different circles simultaneously active and producing different kinds of wisdom. There are adumbrations of this point of view in Baumgartner, Rankin and Gemser. Baumgartner (pp. 28f.) observes that empirical wisdom and divine wisdom may have originated independently of each other. Gemser (p. 4) remarks that secular and theological wisdom may have co-existed, and Rankin (pp. 69f.) asserts that the religious character of Israelite wisdom is original to it and is not tacked on later in order to transform an empirical type of wisdom. Here, too, Skladny's view (pp. 7f., 71f.) that the *ṣaddīq-rāšā'* antithesis in 10–15 reflects a belief in an immanent order and that this material is conceptually related to Egyptian wisdom with its doctrine of *Maat* is a relevant consideration.

One would then have to suppose that at the outset the wisdom sentence was the instrument both of a theological and an empirical wisdom. Wisdom always had this many-sided character and it is this that the division into classes lays bare rather than a history of the wisdom tradition of the kind which I have indicated. This would touch

[32] See below, pp. 263f., 281, 498 (16.20).

on the question of what is to be made of 'the fear of Yahweh' in the context of wisdom. I have argued elsewhere (*PWM*, pp. 48f.) and in the present connection that this is a facet of the reinterpretation of old wisdom. In the framework of the Instruction it is the new *mūsār*. It could be argued consistently with the account which I am now sketching that 'the fear of Yahweh' has its *Sitz* in a theological wisdom which always co-existed with the more empirical variety.

My own position is bound up with the conviction that there are evidences in the book of Proverbs of a reinterpretation of the vocabulary of old wisdom. It might be urged that while I have described the facts correctly I have put the wrong interpretation on them; that such vocabulary was not the monopoly of empirical wisdom, but was used both in an educational framework and in a frame of Yahwistic piety. Its employment in the latter is then not indicative of a subsequent process of reinterpretation, but only of different circles of wisdom practitioners using the same vocabulary at the same time in different discourse situations. I am bound to say that I find it very difficult to accept this account, because linguistic details which I have summarized (above, pp. 17f.) point to a subsequent reinterpretation of the vocabulary of old wisdom.

I have said nothing so far about the class B sentences, though in many respects this is the most interesting part of the sentence literature in the book of Proverbs. It can be said categorically that in classes A and C interest is focused on the individual. In a sense this is true also of class B, which is occupied with the malevolent individual, but there the transition is made from individual to community and I shall have to call attention repeatedly to the strong social concern which is a feature of it. On the one hand, the misanthropic and malicious person threatens the well-being of the community; on the other, it is made clear that this is a way of death for him, since life is to be found only in healthy social experience. Although there is no God-language in this class, or perhaps because there is none, it has an appealing theological relevance and a striking modernity. This appears chiefly in the circumstance that references to 'life' move entirely within a this-worldly social context, while there are evidences of an interiorizing of the old mythology of death (Sheol) which then refers to the individual's loss of vitality – to the draining away of life – consequent upon a basic perversion which sets him at enmity with his fellows and alienates him from the social enrichment which is constitutive of 'life'.

The class B material, though it is not overtly Yahwistic and is unrelated to distinctively Israelite historical traditions, does seem to me to presuppose the Israelite community and the quality of life inherent in it, and so to preserve a particular Israelite adaptation of the wisdom sentence. One may urge, as Kayatz (pp. 102f.) has done, that in those passages in 1–9 where the personified Wisdom gives 'life' to her adherents (3.16, 18; 8.35a) we have to do with the transference of a motif attached to *Maat* in Egyptian literature. Kayatz is aware that even if this is a valid piece of motif research, it does not help with the theological interpretation of 'life' in these passages, since, with respect to what is signified by 'life', we have to reckon with the two disparate theological worlds of Egypt and the Old Testament. References to 'life' in Egypt are bound up with cults of the dead and are concerned with the everlasting life which is to be grasped at death. In so far as the book of Proverbs looks beyond death it envisages only the joyless, shadowy world of Sheol. There is no 'life' beyond death; indeed to put it this way is almost to be involved in contradiction, because 'life' is a this-worldly concept whose antithesis is death. Nor is death just physical cessation, for it, too, like life, is spoken of as a state of historical existence. Existence drained of vitality is a sentence of death or an irreversible trend towards death in its ultimate sense.

C. THE MEANING OF *MĀŠĀL*

I shall discuss in detail the absence of imagery and proverbial characteristics from the language of the Instruction genre (pp. 139f., 186ff.). The function of the Instruction is to communicate clearly and authoritatively, and it sacrifices the literary effectiveness of imaginative language in order to avoid its ambiguities and achieve a pedestrian clarity. The examination of such imagery as is found in the Egyptian Instruction (below, pp. 139ff.) and *Ahikar* (below, p. 162) shows that it is usually associated with the subordinate clauses, which give reasons why the imperatives should be obeyed, and that only rarely does the language of the imperatives themselves have an imaginative texture. The exception to all this is *Onchsheshonqy*, but it is an exception which proves the rule, because it has a popular, proverbial character and diverges both in form and content from the Instruction genre proper. The Instruction strictly defined is far removed from popular, proverbial wisdom. Its setting is the school in the shadow of the court where able young men are trained for careers in administration and government. *Onchsheshonqy* belongs to the countryside and the rural life, and even its imperatives are communicated in language which has a proverbial character (below, pp. 146f.). To a much lesser extent this also happens in *Ahikar* (below, pp. 170, 175, 180, 182).

The main conclusion to be drawn is that the Instruction has nothing to do with popular wisdom and has no contribution to make to the elucidation of *māšāl*. The contribution of *Onchsheshonqy* to my definition of 'proverb' centres on the proverbial sentences which it contains (see below, pp. 129f.) and to these I now turn. These are 'proverbs' in that they have a special kind of concreteness in virtue of which their meaning is open to the future and can be divined again and again in relation to a situation which calls forth the 'proverb' as apt comment. A 'proverb' can be generalized and the generalization does some justice to it, but it forecloses the meaning and destroys the hermeneutical openness which derives from its original concreteness (see below, pp. 123, 157, 183ff., 414ff.). I shall illustrate this with many examples from *Onchsheshonqy* and I have also taken a sample of Babylonian and Assyrian proverbs (pp. 183f.) in order to discuss the difficulty which may attend the intuiting of a 'proverb', the cryptic qualities which sometimes make its meaning uncertain and yet the clear differentiation of function between the 'proverb' and the riddle. The 'proverb' may initially present a barrier to understanding, but when it is intuited it throws a brilliant light on the situations which it fits. The function of the riddle is to mystify and baffle; it is deliberately enigmatic. Some 'proverbs' are characterized by ambivalence (see below, pp. 129f., 197f., 203); it is possible to assign a literal, pedestrian meaning to them, while they also have a proverbial potential. Other 'proverbs' have their images arranged in such a way that they stand out as literary products, consciously devised for imaginative effect (pp. 129, 195).

The presence of imagery in itself does not constitute a 'proverb', and similes and metaphors are not 'proverbs' (below, p. 138, 146), although they have a highly developed literary character (below, p. 157). In their case the interpretation or application of the imagery is indicated and its sphere of operation thereby delimited. They do not therefore have the hermeneutical openness of the 'proverb', which offers no ready-made interpretation and places no restraints on intuition. I have called attention, especially in connection with *Onchsheshonqy*, to the non-proverbial wisdom sentence (pp. 124f., 189f., 195, 197, 198, 199) which has neither special 'proverbial' concreteness nor yet the imaginative content of the simile and metaphor. These may be described as aphorisms or apophthegms, and many of the wisdom sentences in the book of Proverbs fall into this category.

I have so far avoided the complexities of *māšāl*, but something must now be said about the relation of my definition of 'proverb' to *māšāl*. It would be beyond the scope of the present work to examine all the usages of *māšāl* in the Old Testament, and I deal only with those popular proverbs which are designated *m^e^šālīm*, since they have a greater relevance for the present enquiry than the remaining occurrences of *māšāl* outside the book of Proverbs (Num. 21.27f.; 23.7, 18; 24.3, 15, 20, 21, 23; Deut. 28.37; I Kings 9.7; Isa. 14.4; Jer. 24.9; Ezek. 14.8; 17.2; 24.3; Micah 2.4; Hab. 2.6; Pss. 44.15; 49.5; 69.12; 78.2; Job 17.6 [emended]).

According to Schmidt,[33] all these usages can be elucidated in terms of a basic meaning 'to stand', and so we can speak of a single genre (*Gattung*) assuming different forms (*Formen*). The *māšāl* is *das Feststehende* and this can be paraphrased as wisdom teaching which is well established and gives valid instruction for practical affairs. Even if Schmidt's etymology of *māšāl* were acceptable, however, it does not seem reasonable to say that all of the literary pieces designated as *m^e^šālīm* can be comprehended in a single *Gattung*, and Eissfeldt[34] begins his work with the recognition that there is a diversity of *Gattungen*. The question to be asked is, then, a different one. Is it possible to find a meaning for *māšāl* which will explain why it is used of different *Gattungen*? Or, put differently: is the meaning of *māšāl* such that a relationship can be discerned between the different *Gattungen* which bear this name? The further exploration of this question, which would involve a consideration of all the usages of *māšāl*, cannot be undertaken here. It will suffice to say that the most generally canvassed explanation of *māšāl* is 'sovereign saying' or 'word of power'.[35] The linguistic assumption in this explanation is normally that *māšāl* is to be derived from *mšl* 'to rule'. In his earlier

[33] J. Schmidt, *op. cit.* (see above, note 1), pp. 1f.

[34] O. Eissfeldt, *Der Maschal*, pp. 4f.; cf. A. Bentzen, *Introduction*, i, p. 167.

[35] Gemser, *op. cit.*, p. 8 n.6; J. Hempel, *op. cit.*, p. 44; O. Eissfeldt, *Introduction*, p. 82; A. Weiser, *Introduction*, p. 40; A. Bentzen, *Introduction*, i, p. 168; A. R. Johnson, *VTS III*, p. 168.

work, Eissfeldt[36] maintained that *māšāl* should be elucidated on the assumption that the meaning of 'likeness' is basic to it. Godbey[37] with his notion of 'sympathetic magic' combines 'to rule' and 'to be like'; *māšāl* as symbolic action resembles the effects which it produces. Ringgren (pp. 7f.) does not decide between the alternatives 'comparison' and 'word of power'.

According to Schmidt, *mšl* means basically 'to stand', and according to Bentzen and others it means 'to rule'. The meaning 'to rule' is confined to Hebrew and is not attested in the other Semitic languages (Aramaic, Syriac, Arabic, Accadian, Ethiopic). Schmidt appealed to Arabic usage and argued from the fact that *mṯl* means 'to stand' in the first form of the verb and 'cause to stand' in the fourth form. Even so, when the semantic range of *mṯl* in Arabic is surveyed, the meanings which are characteristic are related to 'to be like' and not 'to stand'. Further, 'to stand' is only connected with the verb and there is no evidence that *maṯal* ever had a meaning related to 'to stand'. The attested usages of *maṯal* point clearly to 'resemblance', 'similitude', 'model', 'illustration', 'example'.

The question would almost seem to be decided for Bentzen (pp. 167f.) by *a priori* considerations concerning the power of the spoken word. A general observation to do with culture and belief in the ancient world is thought to establish a connection between *māšāl* and 'to rule'. Even if it were the case that the words of seers and poets were thought to have a magical potency, this is not a linguistic argument particularly related to *māšāl*, and it is not clear that the meaning 'to rule' in the verb has anything to do with this phenomenon. In so far as there is any evidence of a relationship between 'to rule' and 'to be like' it comes from Arabic and has a somewhat exiguous character. It may show that the idea of perfection or excellence in *mṯl* is a development from 'exemplar' or 'model', and so it may be that *al-amāṯil*, 'the leading men', are model or representative figures in the community. Hence *mumaṯṯil* is the word in modern Arabic for the diplomatic representative of a state. In so far as this contains any indications, it suggests that 'to be like' is more primary than 'to rule'. It may be a mistaken enterprise to try to establish a semantic relationship between the two meanings, though Schmidt argues that they must be connected. It is perhaps better to be content with a

[36] *Der Maschal*, pp. 6f.; also A. R. Johnson, *VTS III*, p. 161.

[37] A. H. Godbey, *AJSL* xxxix, 1922–3, p. 90; similarly A. S. Herbert, *SJT* 7, 1954, pp. 195f., perhaps originally a spoken or acted spell.

simple review of the total field of usage and to say that 'to rule' is confined to Hebrew, whereas 'to be like' is distributed throughout the Semitic languages, and that there is no evidence either in Hebrew or the other Semitic languages that *māšāl* has any connection with the meaning 'to rule'. What I propose to do now is to look at some of the popular proverbs in the Old Testament and to enquire whether they can be elucidated on the assumption that *māšāl* as applied to them has some such meaning as 'model', 'exemplar', 'paradigm'.

I Sam. 10.11f.: 'And the people said to each other: "What is this that has happened to the son of Kish? Is Saul also among the prophets?" And a man of the place said in reply: "And who is their father?".' So the saying 'Is Saul also among the prophets?' became a *māšāl*. I take it that both here and in I Sam. 19.24 we have to do with attempts to furnish a historical origin for a *māšāl* which is already current and well established. In other words, the *māšāl* itself is the primary datum and its existence encourages the aetiological enterprise which is exemplified in the two passages, both of which undertake in different ways to relate the circumstances in which the *māšāl* originated. The indications about the meaning of *māšāl* provided by I Sam. 10.11f. are not entirely clear because of the obscurity of the words 'And who is their father?'. This can be understood in at least two ways: (*a*) it means that Saul is as well-entitled to be an ecstatic prophet as any other man, since prophetic inspiration is not a hereditary possession. The verb 'answered' might be thought to support this interpretation and to imply that the man of the place was delivering a riposte to those who said: 'What is this that has happened to the son of Kish? Is Saul also among the prophets?'. To those who felt a strong incongruity in Saul's behaviour and who sensed that he was acting out of character and station the man retorted, 'Why not?'; (*b*) it means that Saul has good family connections, while the prophets are an ecstatic rabble, so that in behaving like a dervish Saul is departing from the pattern of behaviour prescribed for his social station and associating himself with the outlandish and bizarre. The question ('Who is their father?') is then not a retort to the query 'Is Saul also among the prophets?', but a comment added to it. The second interpretation would seem to me to be correct, but what emerges on either interpretation is that Saul himself is primarily the *māšāl* and is seized upon as a model of incongruous behaviour. The saying 'Is Saul also among the prophets?' is described as a *māšāl* in the sense that it is a remark on Saul's behaviour which has such representative potential that it has become a comment on incongruous behaviour in anyone, at any time and in any place.

In I Sam. 19.24 the same saying is not stated to be a *māšāl* but is introduced by the formula 'Therefore they say'. Since we know from I Sam. 10.12 that this saying is a *māšāl*, we can conclude that wherever a saying is introduced by 'Therefore they say' or a similar formula it is a popular proverb, even although it is not designated a *māšāl*. As in 10.12, the saying again is pointed towards behaviour which is out of character, but the implication in 19.24 is that Saul is not worthy of a place in Samuel's prophetic guild, and to that extent the *māšāl* is given a different aetiology. He has been rejected as king over Israel by the word which Samuel spoke for Yahweh, and it is unfitting that he should be performing ecstatic exercises among Samuel's disciples. He is not there as a true devotee and, having been made the prisoner of ecstasy, is in Samuel's and therefore Yahweh's power.

Gen. 10.9: 'Therefore it is said: "As great a hunter by Yahweh's reckoning as Nimrod".' Nimrod has become a model or paradigm of the superlative hunter, and so when you want to say that a man is an outstanding hunter you establish his resemblance to the 'model' Nimrod. We see already, therefore, two sayings very different in form and both of them popular proverbs. The first is a laconic comment in the form of a question, while the second, thanks to the simile incorporated in it, interprets itself and would be transparent even to a person who knew nothing otherwise about Nimrod.

I Sam. 24.14: 'As the *māšāl* of the ancients says: "From evil men evil issues".' In the context in which it is preserved, the *māšāl* can be taken in two ways, the first more probable than the second: (*a*) it may be intended as a comment on Saul's behaviour towards David; (*b*) it may give point to David's refusal to lay violent hands on Saul.

(*a*) The evil of Saul's actions demonstrates conclusively that he is an evil man, but, nevertheless, David will not retaliate with violence because Saul is Yahweh's Anointed. 'From evil men evil issues' would then be comparable to the dominical saying: 'Thus you will know them by their fruits' (Matt. 7.20). The generalization corresponding to it would be: 'There is a harmony between character and action.'

In whatever circumstances this is relevant comment, the *māšāl* 'From evil men evil issues' is an apt model. It is more than a statement that an evil deed condemns its doer as evil, for it embraces the converse, that a good man will never perform an evil act. Hence it may be used to indict an evil man or to dissociate a man of settled virtue from an evil act of which he is accused. Although 'From evil men evil issues' has a certain concreteness and is a model with a representative potential, it is not highly concrete, and no effort is needed to grasp the resemblance between the model and the generalization, 'There is a harmony between character and action'. The effectiveness of a *māšāl* derives from its concreteness and from the circumstance that a model of a general truth stimulates the imagination and clamours for attention, as a matter-of-fact statement would not. It may even offer some resistance in the first place to understanding, but this works to its advantage in the long run, because once the representative character of the model is grasped and the relationship of resemblance intuited, the initial effort expended adds to the impressiveness of the discovery.

(*b*) David utters this *māšāl* to give point to his refusal to retaliate with violence against Saul. Saul has sinned against Yahweh, but it is for Yahweh to bring him to judgement, and David cannot justify his action theologically by asserting that he is doing Yahweh's will and that his action cannot be judged by the ethical criteria which would normally apply. If he were to kill Saul, the deed in any circumstances would be evil and would proceed from the wickedness of his heart. There is no alchemy by which an evil act can be transmuted into a good one and, in particular, it cannot be given a theological justification so that it becomes obedience to the will of God. If the act is evil, its source cannot be traced to God; it resides in the evil character of the man who did it. Even so, the general form of the *māšāl* would still be as in (*a*): 'There is a harmony between character and action.'

The choice between (*a*) and (*b*) hinges on the translation of v. 13. If the verbs are translated as jussives, the closing words of the verse will be translated: 'but my hand will not be against you'. It is possible to translate: 'Yahweh will judge between me and you and avenge me on you and (so) my hand will not be against you' (since Yahweh is your judge). The closing words of v. 14 would be similarly translated and all this would point to (*b*). If the verbs in v. 13 are jussives and 'but my hand shall not be against you' is the correct translation in vv. 13 and 14, the choice falls on (*a*) and this is almost certainly correct.

Ezek. 16.44: 'Everyone will apply to you the *māšāl* which says: "As a mother so her daughter".' This is a *māšāl* of a similar type to the preceding one; it is concrete but not highly concrete. As a model, it is not just a particular statement that a mother has a decisive formative influence on her daughter, and the generalization corresponding to it would be something like: 'A person is what he is in virtue of his heredity and upbringing.' Hence the verses which follow deal not only with the mother of Jerusalem but with her other family connections: 'Your mother was a Hittite and your father an Amorite. Your older sister was Samaria who with her daughters lived to your north and your younger sister who lived with her daughters to your south was Sodom' (vv. 45f.). In the home where the daughter Jerusalem grew up, there was a complete lack of harmony between husband and wife and the children were starved of affection. The relationship of the mother to her husband and children determined in turn that of the sisters to theirs. 'As a mother so her daughter' is comparable to 'He (or 'she') came out of a bad nest', which is said of an individual when there is a desire to establish that misdemeanours are traceable to parentage and upbringing.

I Kings 20.11: 'Let not him that girds on his armour have the boastful air of one who is loosening his' (*sc.* after victory). This is Ahab's reply to Ben Hadad, and it means that a victory should not be celebrated before it is won. The concreteness of the model is here created by the use of imagery, and no great intuitive effort is required to make the transition from the figure of a warrior getting into his armour before a battle and congratulating himself on a victory which he has yet to win to the generalization: 'A victory should not be celebrated before it is won.'

Jer. 31.29; Ezek. 18.2: 'The fathers have eaten sour grapes and the children's teeth are set on edge.' It is possible that this was a non-theological popular proverb which has become a theological slogan in the manner illustrated by these two passages. The model or picture is that of the fathers eating sour grapes and the bitter taste being felt not by them but in the mouths of their children. The interpretation is: 'The present generation is paying the penalty for the errors or sins of previous generations.' The lack of literary distinction in the generalization as compared with the model is due to the circumstance that it is a statement from which all metaphor and imagination have been drained. As a non-theological popular proverb, the saying serves to express the conviction of every generation that those who preceded them have made a mess of things and that they have to suffer for it.

Ezek. 12.22: 'Son of man, what *māšāl* is this which you have concerning the land of Israel: "The days are drawn out and every vision come to nothing".' Yahweh tells the prophet that he will make an end of this *māšāl* and that it will no longer be used in the land of Israel. He continues: 'But say to them: "The days are near and the (subject) matter of every vision".' This *māšāl* is a theological slogan rather than a popular proverb, and it expresses a particular attitude or frame of mind induced by the activities of false prophets, by the proven unreliability of prophecy and its inability to shed any light on the course of events. The visions of the prophet are supposed to embody a revelation from Yahweh concerning his decisive shaping of future events, but life goes on with the same old patterns unaltered, the visions waste away into oblivion and Yahweh does not intervene in the manner which they had portended. The *māšāl*, because of its theological particularity, can hardly be disengaged from the context in which it is preserved, and so it lacks the universality and openness to interpretation of the popular proverb. If it could be generalized it would say: When those who say that a crisis is at hand are time and again proved wrong, people are confirmed in what they want to believe, that the world will go on in the same old way, and so they cease to pay attention to anyone who says otherwise. It is unlikely that anyone at any time has ever been tempted to employ the *māšāl*, 'The days are drawn out and every vision perishes', in order to make this observation. Nevertheless, even if it is a particular theological slogan, it is a model in the sense that it serves as a stereotype for the frame of mind of those to whom the prophet is to address his prophetic word. It is the slogan in which the popular attitude becomes articulate. So Ezekiel is commanded to tell those whose attitude to him is determined by this model that the prophetic word will destroy it (vv. 25f.).

Luke 4.23: 'No doubt you will quote to me this parable: "Doctor, cure yourself".' Jesus has acquired a reputation for healing and mighty works in other parts of the country, and the truth of these reports will be decided by his ability to do these works in his home town. This is plainly a popular proverb and Jesus suggests that it may be thought to apply to his case. Its general form would be: 'The test whether your advice and skill have proved valuable in the wider world is the success which has attended your efforts nearer home and, in particular, the extent to which your remedies are seen to have a beneficial effect on yourself.' In any situation where a man wants to put the world right before he has set his own house in order this *māšāl* is applicable. It is just possible that a clue as to the way in which some popular proverbs originate and evolve is provided by this example (see below, pp. 129f.). Such a saying as this may have originated as a retort to one who fancied himself as a medical practitioner in a community which was familiar with the quack doctor and his bogus cures. It meant simply: 'If the cure which you offer me is so good, cure yourself first with it.' The saying becomes a *māšāl* when it transcends this simple particularity and its representative potential is intuited. It can do this only because everyone knows about the quack doctor and his claims and a discourse situation is given in which the process of transference can take place. This process is bound up with the discovery that when the saying is intuited as a model its original limitations are transcended and in virtue of the representative power of the imagery it has a wide field of application.

I have tried to establish that certain Old Testament popular proverbs which are described as *m*^{e}*šālīm* or can otherwise be identified as such are 'proverbs' in the special sense which I have defined. It would be possible to argue that the name *māšāl* is a secondary attachment to these popular proverbs, and that therefore we cannot argue from the character of the popular proverb to the meaning of *māšāl*. I am, however, making the assumption which seems to me to be reasonable that the name *māšāl* is rooted in popular wisdom, that this preceded all literary usages of *māšāl* and is their *fons et origo*.[38] In working out the implications of this I limit my enquiry to the material in the book of Proverbs, all of which is described as *m*^{e}*šālīm*, and, in particular, to the wisdom sentences.

I have already remarked that the use of *māšāl* in Prov. 1.1 indicates that it had acquired so general a meaning that it could be used of the

[38] O. Eissfeldt, *Der Maschal*, pp. 26f.

contents of the book as a whole, irrespective of the different kinds of material in it.[39] If one were to try and sketch the semantic development of *māšāl* on the assumption that the popular proverb is the right point of departure, it would seem obvious that more attention should be paid to the wisdom sentence than the Instruction, because as used of the latter, the meaning of *māšāl* has lost precision and particularity.[40] Efforts have been made to explain *māšāl* by connecting it with Accadian *mišlu*, 'half', *māšāl* being a line of two stichoi.[41] This is both too wide and too narrow an explanation. It is too wide because *parallelismus membrorum* is a feature of all Hebrew poetry and is not confined to the wisdom sentence. It is too narrow and late because the wisdom sentence is a literary product and the popular proverb without *parallelismus membrorum* is already described as a *māšāl*. I have suggested that the popular proverb is a 'model' and, if so, such *mᵉšālīm* are 'proverbs' in the special sense which I have defined.[42] They have the openness to interpretation and the representative scope of the 'proverb'. There are only a few *mᵉšālīm* of this kind in the book of Proverbs (10.5; 13.4, 7, 8; 16.26; 20.4; 24.27; 26.13, 15, 27; 27.7).

If this is the most exact sense of *māšāl* which is recoverable from the Old Testament evidence, it is understandable that the term should have been widened to include the wisdom sentence, which gathers up experience into a terse memorable utterance. Such utterances are aphorisms without the openness to interpretation of the 'proverb'. The sentence literature in the book of Proverbs has this character, for the most part, and is devoid of the imaginative constituents of the popular proverb.[43] Even in 25–27, the density of imagery associated with the consistent use of the simile is clearly, on the one hand, literary artifice and, on the other, a curtailing of the openness to interpretation of the popular proverb. This is also true of the occurrences of similes and metaphors elsewhere in the book. In the wisdom sentences of a more prosaic kind there is in the parallelism and especially the antithetic parallelism, which is more exact than the other kinds, unmistakable evidence of literary composition according to

[39] See below, pp. 262f.; Ringgren, *op. cit.*, p. 7; Bentzen, *Introduction* i, p. 167.

[40] R. H. Pfeiffer, *Introduction to the Old Testament*² (1952), p. 645; A. S. Herbert, *SJT* 7 (1954), p. 194.

[41] A. Müller and E. Kautzsch, *The Book of Proverbs* (1901), pp. 32f.; cf. O. Eissfeldt, *Der Maschal*, pp. 43f.

[42] Cf. O. Eissfeldt, *Der Maschal*, pp. 50f.

[43] *Ibid.*, pp. 51f.

established stylistic conventions. Such sentences have been hammered into shape, filed and polished, and whatever their difference in content, whether they contain a this-worldly empirical wisdom or are the instruments of theological teaching, they have in common the character of self-conscious literary products.

D. THE SEPTUAGINT TEXT OF PROVERBS

In his commentary, Gemser has repeatedly called attention to the additions to MT which are a feature of LXX, and has noted the moralizing tendency of these additions. Gerleman[44] in two studies has examined deviations of LXX from MT which are non-textual in character and are not to be explained on the assumption that the Greek translator had before him a different Hebrew text from MT. These may be attributable to stylistic scruples and predilections, as when LXX creates antitheses which are not in MT (1.22; 5.16; 10.18; 11.7, 25; 13.14; 14.13; 15.10; 16.26; 17.4, 14; 19.6; 21.14; 27.9), or they may arise from a pietistic and moralizing tendency in LXX (1.4, 7, 11, 18f., 22, 28, 31, 32; 2.11; 3.9, 18, 35; 8.5; 9.7, 8; 10.22, 26; 11.15; 12.25; 13.2, 11, 16, 19, 23; 14.6, 15, 18; 15.2, 14, 28; 16.9 [MT 16.4], 33; 17.1, 8, 12, 14, 26; 19.22, 24; 20.8; 21.8, 9, 11, 16, 22, 26; 22.11; 23.3, 31; 28.14, 16, 20, 21; 29.4, 23, 25; 31.1–2, 8). Gerleman observes the tendency of LXX to reduce the metaphorical language of MT to a flatter, more pedestrian form of utterance (10.7; 12.6; 14.11, 18; 20.8), its avoidance of the frank sensuality of MT (5.19) and its spiritualizing of the materialism of MT (24.27; 27.27). He points out that the deviation of LXX from MT is sometimes to be explained by the difficulty of the latter (7.22; 23.31; 30.31), and that in these cases the Greek translator might substitute a Greek proverb for the meaningless part of the Hebrew text. Thus in 7.22 he has contributed *ὥσπερ κύων ἐπὶ δεσμούς*, and in 23.31 *περιπατήσεις γυμνότερος ὑπέρου* for the obscure *yithallēk bᵉmēšārîm* ('to be more naked than a pestle' is Greek proverb meaning to be in a state of dire poverty).

Gerleman rejects Baumgartner's thesis[45] that the schematizing of

[44] 'The Septuagint Proverbs as a Hellenistic Document', *OTS* VIII (1950), pp. 15–27; 'Studies in the Septuagint: III Proverbs', *Lunds Universitets Årsskrift*, NF, Avd. I, Bd. 52, No. 3 (1956).

[45] A. J. Baumgartner, *Étude critique sur l'état du texte du livre des Proverbes d'après les principales traductions anciennes* (1890), p. 253.

moral categories in LXX and the standardization of the ethical vocabulary of MT is to be accounted for by the habits and conventions of Jewish midrashic exegesis. He also rejects Bertram's[46] contention that it is the rigid categorizing of Jewish legal piety which is reflected in the Greek translation of Proverbs. Gerleman finds the explanation in a Stoic tendency to equate wisdom with piety and folly with impiety, and he explains the disappearance of references to diligence and laziness in MT from the text of LXX in terms of Stoic influence (10.4, 5, 26; 12.24, 27; 19.24; 20.13; 24.30f.). Diligence was not a Stoic virtue nor laziness a Stoic vice. For similar reasons, references to wealth in MT (14.23, 24; 21.20; 23.4) are recast to accord with the Stoic attitude to wealth. The meaning of 14.23 in LXX is contrary to that of MT. The latter asserts that in all hard work there is profit, but that words make only for want. LXX, on the other hand, maintains that only the poor are free from sorrows and cares, while wealth brings anxiety and trouble. In 23.4, LXX is in agreement with the Stoic conviction that a man should accept his lot and not strive to alter it. Wisdom will compensate for poverty. Gerleman supposes that *ἁρμόζουσα* in 8.30 reflects the Stoic view of nature, that all things are suitable for their several purposes, that they co-exist in a relation of complementarity and that they all contribute to the harmonious beauty of the whole.

Gerleman's approach is significantly different from earlier studies of the LXX text of Proverbs which he briefly reviews.[47] He does not make the assumption that differences between MT and LXX are necessarily or normally textually significant; that they can be used to reconstruct the 'original' Hebrew text or that they point to a Hebrew text other than MT. I set out below the conclusions which I have reached through a comparison of LXX with MT and it will be seen that they are in line with those of Gerleman. The greatest caution should be exercised in employing LXX to elucidate or emend difficult portions of MT. To use LXX in these circumstances in order to recover an 'original' Hebrew text is in fact to invent a Hebrew text which never at any time existed. One has to get away from the assumption that when LXX is different from MT the Greek translator had before him a Hebrew text different from MT.

[46] G. Bertram, *ZAW* 54 (1936), p. 159.

[47] G. J. L. Vogel in A. Schultens, *Proverbia Salomonis*, 1748. In compendium redegit et observationibus criticis auxit G. J. L. Vogel, 1769; J. G. Jäger, *Observationes in Proverbiorum Salomonis Versionem Alexandrinam*, 1788; P. de Lagarde, *Anmerkungen zur griechischen Übersetzung der Proverbien*, 1863.

One has rather to take into account the possibility that the reasons for the difference between MT and LXX are non-textual in character and to enquire what these may have been. Gerleman remarks: 'For the explanation of minor deviations in the LXX Proverbs from MT textual criticism has, indeed, very little help to afford, and any arguing which neglects the translator as a creative factor is very likely to lead astray.'

1. Retention of MT on the principle *lectio difficilior potior*

5.9: v. 9a in LXX is an exact parallel of 9b and LXX has departed from MT in both 9a (MT: *hōdekā*, 'your dignity'; LXX: *ζωήν σου*, 'your life') and 9b. *σὸν βίον* (9b) is probably, in part, an evasion of the difficulty which *šenōtekā* posed to the Greek translator.

5.11: MT: *wenāhamtā*, 'and you will cry out in anguish'; LXX: *καὶ μεταμεληθήσῃ* (*wenihamtā*), 'and you will repent'.

5.16: The *μή* of LXXB has probably no textual significance and is no more than an attempt to make sense of MT.

6.1: LXX substitutes *ἐχθρῷ* for MT *zār* (1b), because *zār* is difficult in relation to *rēʿekā* (1a).

9.13: LXX: *αἰσχύνην*, 'shame'; MT: *mā* (emended to *kelimmā* on the basis of LXX).

11.23: LXX: *ἀπολεῖται*, 'perishes'; MT: *ʿebrā*, 'rage'. The LXX rendering may aim at a more conventional expression of the opposition of righteous and wicked, and the deliberate approximation of 23b to 7b may be a factor. *ʿāberā*, 'passes away' (Driver), explains LXX as a translation of the Hebrew consonantal text.

13.1: *ὑπήκοος* registers perplexity with *mūsār* and is an attempt to make sense ('a wise son listens to his father') without grappling with the difficulties of MT.

14.33: LXX inserts the negative particle *οὐ* in order to relieve the difficulty of 33b.

16.16: LXX indicates that *mā* should be deleted and *mēḥārūṣ* retained. The text before the Greek translator was probably MT and he did not apply the principle *lectio difficilior potior* (see below, p. 489).

17.26: *οὐδὲ ὅσιον* for *ʿal yōšer* is indicative of the difficulty of *ʿal yōšer* and is an attempt to resolve it. It should not be taken as evidence of a Hebrew text with *bal yāšār* or the like.

18.19: ὡς πόλις ὀχυρὰ καὶ ὑψηλή, 'like a town fortified and elevated'. *k^e^qiryat ʿōz* (on the basis of LXX) would be easier than *miqqiryat ʿōz* (cf. 19b *kib^e^rīaḥ 'armōn*). ὀχυρὰ καὶ ὑψηλή is not an indication of a Hebrew text with *nōšāʿ*, but of the inability of the Greek translator to deal with the obscure *nipšāʿ*.

2. Acceptance of LXX where it is a shorter text than MT

3.3: 'Write them on the tablet of your heart' is absent from LXX^B^, and is perhaps a secondary expansion of the Hebrew text.

15.24: 'Upwards' (*l^e^maʿlā*) and 'downwards' (*maṭṭā*) are not represented in LXX. They are additions to the Hebrew text coming from a time when 'life' was understood as a blessed immortality and 'death' as an after-life of punishment.

21.21: *ṣ^e^dāqā* is not translated by LXX, and is to be regarded as a later, moralizing reinforcement of 'life and honour'.

3. Where LXX may point to the original Hebrew text or to a conjectural emendation of MT by the Greek translator

3.31: ζηλώσῃς indicates *tithar* (MT: *tibḥar*).

8.14: ἐμὴ φρόνησις indicates *lī bīnā*, but probably reflects the decision of the translator that the Hebrew text ought to be *lī bīnā* and not *'^a^nī bīnā* (MT), and is not evidence that *lī bīnā* was in the Hebrew text which he translated.

10.4: πενία, 'poverty', points to *rē'š* (MT: *rā'š*).

14.32: LXX: 'But he who relies on his own piety is a righteous man' (32b). τῇ ἑαυτοῦ ὁσιότητι points to *b^e^tummō* (MT: *b^e^mōtō*).

15.19: ἀνδρείων, which elsewhere translates *ḥārūṣīm* (10.4; 13.4), indicates *ḥārūṣīm*, and MT *y^e^šārīm* is a secondary moralizing of the verse.

16.22: τοῖς κεκτημένοις points to *lib^e^ʿālāw*. MT *b^e^ʿālāw* may have arisen from haplography of *l*, or the Greek translator may have conjecturally emended MT to *lib^e^ʿālāw*.

19.22: καρπὸς indicates *t^e^bū'at* (MT *ta'^a^wat*). Either the Greek translator read *t^e^bū'at* or decided that the sense required it and conjectured it.

21.6: ἐπὶ παγίδας θανάτου indicates *b*^{e}*mōq*^{e}*šē māwet* (MT *m*^{e}*baqq*^{e}*šē māwet*, metathesis of *b* and *m*).

23.7: τρίχα, 'hair', points to *śēʿār* (MT *šāʿar*).

23.18: τηρήσῃς αὐτά was probably inserted by the Greek translator to make sense of a defective Hebrew text. LXX, then, does not show that an original Hebrew text contained *tišm*^{e}*rennā*, but that the translation is based on the conjectural insertion of *tišm*^{e}*rennā* or the like.

28.23: ὁδοὺς points to *'*^{o}*rāḥōt*; *'orḥō* may have been the original Hebrew text (MT: *'aḥ*^{a}*ray*).

30.17: γῆρας points to **l*^{e}*hāqā*, **l*^{e}*hīqā*, 'old age' (MT: *y*^{e}*qāhā*, 'obedience').

4. Where the consonantal text is differently vocalized by LXX as compared with MT

6.26: τιμή indicates *baʿad*, 'price' (MT: *b*^{e}*ʿad*).

7.22: κεπφωθείς, 'simpletons', indicates *p*^{e}*tā'īm* (MT: *pit'ōm*).

12.9: δουλεύων ἑαυτῷ indicates *w*^{e}*ʿōbēd lō* (MT: *w*^{e}*ʿebed lō*).

13.10: κακός, 'wicked', is perhaps a moralizing generalization of *rēq*, 'empty-head' (MT: *raq*), and so evidence that the translator read *rq* as *rēq*.

15.14: στόμα agrees with Q. *pī* against K. *p*^{e}*nē*.

21.4: λαμπτὴρ indicates *nēr*, 'lamp' (MT: *nīr*, 'tilth').

21.6: ὁ ἐνεργῶν indicates *pōʿēl* (MT: *pōʿal*).

30.24: σοφώτερα τῶν σοφῶν perhaps indicates *mēḥ*^{a}*kāmīm* (MT: *m*^{e}*ḥukkāmīm*).

5. Where LXX confirms MT when the latter is called in question

6.23: ἔλεγχος καὶ παιδεία is an attempt to render the difficult *tōk*^{e}*ḥōt mūsār* and not evidence for *tōk*^{a}*ḥat ūmūsār*.

11.28: πεσεῖται confirms MT *yippōl* against the attractive emendation *yibbōl*.

19.22: LXX has translated *ḥasdō* (ἐλεημοσύνη) and *kāzāb* (ψευδής) thereby confirming a difficult MT in these particulars.

20.27: φῶς confirms MT *nēr*.

20.30: κακοῖς is an inaccurate rendering of MT *rāʿ* and confirms MT in this particular.

6. Where a grammatical or philological point can be made from the reading of LXX

10.31–32: *yēdeʿūn* (32) is translated by ἀποστάζει, 'distil', and so is elucidated with reference to Arabic *wadaʿa*, 'flow', Ugaritic *dʿt*, 'sweat' and Hebrew *zēʿā*, 'sweat'. *yānūb* (31), also translated by ἀποστάζει, is associated with Ugaritic *nbt*, Hebrew *nōpet*, 'honeycomb'. Hebrew *nwb* is a dialectal variant of *nwp*, 'flow' (Dahood).

11.6: LXX ἀπωλεία understood MT *hawwā* as 'destruction', not 'desire'.

14.4: φάτναι καθαραί: *bār* has been understood as 'clean'.

14.30: καρδίας ἰατρός: *marpēʾ* is derived from *rpʾ*, not *rph*.

15.4: ἴασις, 'therapy', indicates correctly that *marpēʾ* is to be derived from *rpʾ*, not *rph*.

15.7: οὐκ ἀσφαλεῖς perhaps indicates that *lōʾ kēn* has been understood as 'unstable'.

16.12: ὁ ποιῶν κακά indicates correctly that the meaning of MT (*tōʿabat melākīm ʿaśōt rěšaʿ*) is that it is abhorrent to kings when others do evil.

16.27: LXX wrongly understands *kōreh rāʿā* as ὀρύσσει ἑαυτῷ κακά, 'digs evil for himself'.

21.9: ἐν οἴκῳ κοινῷ shows that the Greek translator understood *bēt ḥābēr* as 'common house'.

22.5: τρίβολοι shows that the obscure *ṣinnīm* was understood as 'prickly plants'.

22.12: διατηροῦσιν αἴσθησιν demonstrates that *nāṣerū dāʿat* was understood as 'guard knowledge'.

24.28: μηδὲ πλατύνου, 'do not exaggerate', indicates II *pātā* (KB²: 'make spacious').

25.23: LXX (πρόσωπον δὲ ἀναιδὲς γλῶσσαν, ἐρεθίζει) takes *ūpānīm nizʿāmīm* as subject.

26.8: σφενδόνη indicates that *margēmā* (a *hapax legomenon*) is 'sling', not 'cairn'.

27.17: ὀξύνει indicates that MT *yḥd* was derived from *ḥdd* 'sharpen'.

7. Where LXX corroborates conclusions drawn from higher criticism

4.5–9: In v. 5, LXX^B, LXX^ℵac, LXX^A deviate from MT and v. 7 is absent from LXX. On form-critical grounds, vv. 6–9 can be differentiated from the preceding and following verses of the chapter and are to be regarded as a development and adaptation of the Instruction genre. 'Get wisdom, get insight' (v. 5) is the instruction of a father or a teacher, but this is taken up and elaborated in vv. 6–9 in relation to a personified Wisdom. This view that vv. 6–9 are a secondary expansion prompted by the reference to wisdom in 5a is corroborated by the instability of the text of LXX in vv. 5–9.

4.27; 9.18: Both these verses are at the end of a chapter. The effect of the addition in LXX at 4.27 is to bring God into the argument, and the long addition to 9.18 supplies a greater cautionary emphasis in relation to the *'iššā zārā* and a more explicit moral disapproval of her activities. In these places LXX shows that the Instruction genre was susceptible of expansion in the interests of piety and moralism, and this raises the question whether extended motivation of a similar kind, especially at the end of a chapter (3.32–35; 5.21–23), is not secondary expansion of an originally briefer Instruction.

9.7–12: These verses disturb the continuity of the chapter. Verses 9–10 are absent from one Hebrew manuscript, and vv. 10–12 from another. There are seven additional lines in LXX which envisage the κακός of v. 12, into which MT *laṣtā* is generalized, as a liar. This theme is developed with far-fetched comparisons. The conclusion to be drawn is that 9.7–12 has been inserted secondarily into ch. 9, disturbing the continuity between vv. 1–6 and 13–18, and that LXX is a further elaboration of this secondary theme.

8. Emendations based on LXX which are not to be accepted but which have a textual point

6.3: μὴ ἐκλυόμενος: *w^e'al titrappeh* (MT: *hitrappēs*).

7.22: κεπφωθείς, 'simpletons', points to *p^etā'īm* (MT: *pit'ōm*).

10.21: ἐπίσταται indicates *yd'w* (MT: *yir'ū*).

12.8: νωθροκάρδιος, 'sluggish in heart', points to *na'^abeh lēb* (MT: *na'^aweh lēb*).

14.8: ἐν πλάνῃ points to *m^erammeh*, 'misleads' (MT: *mirmā*).

14.16: *μίγνυται* points to *mitʿārēb* (MT: *mitʿabbēr*). The textual validity of this observation is put in question by the pious twist given to the verse in LXX. *rāʿ*, 'evil', (16a) becomes *κακός*, 'wicked man', and this is paralleled by the insertion of *ἄνομος* in 16b.

14.17: *πολλὰ ὑποφέρει* may point to *yiśśāʾ* or *yišʾanān* (MT: *yiśśānēʾ*).

14.24: *πανοῦργος* translates *ʿārūm* in 14.8 and gives some support to the emendation of *ʿošrām* (MT) to *ʿormātām*.

14.34: *ἐλασσονοῦσι* points to *ḥeser* (MT: *ḥesed*).

15.30: *θεωρῶν ὀφθαλμὸς καλά*, 'an eye which sees beautiful things', gives some support to *moreh ʿēnayim*, 'a fine sight' (MT: *meʾōr ʿēnayim*).

17.5: *ἀπολλυμένῳ* points to *leʾōbēd* (MT: *leʾēd*).

18.4: *πηγὴ ζωῆς* points to *meqōr ḥayyīm* and this is the reading of 10 Hebrew manuscripts (MT: *meqōr ḥokmā*). We should conclude that the Greek translator had before him a Hebrew text with *meqōr ḥayyīm*.

21.12: *καρδίας* points to *lbwt* (MT: *lbyt*).

22.8: *ἔργων* indicates *ʿabōdātō* (MT: *ʿebrātō*). But this observation does not lead to fruitful conclusions, even with the emendation of *šebeṭ* to *šeber* ('produce'?). 'The produce of his work will come to an end' makes poor sense.

23.31: *μεθύσκεσθε* points to *rʾh=rwh*, 'drink deeply', not to *rʾh*, 'see'.

24.12: *ὁ πλάσας πνοὴν* points to *yōṣēr napšekā*.

24.21: *καὶ μηθετέρῳ αὐτῶν ἀπειθήσῃς* indicates *ʿal šenēhem ʾal titʿabbēr* (MT: *ʿim šōnīm ʾal titʿārāb*; cf. *šenēhem*, MT 22b).

25.13: *κατὰ καῦμα* points to *behōm* (MT: *beyōm*). The free rendering of MT in LXX detracts from the textual significance of this observation.

26.23: *χείλη λεῖα* indicates *śepātayim ḥalāqīm* (MT: *śepātayim dōleqīm*).

31.11: In LXX *(ἡ τοιαύτη)*, the *ʾēšet ḥayil* and not her husband is the subject of 11b. This, however, should not be taken as evidence that the Greek translator had before him a Hebrew text with *lāh* in it. It is, rather, an exegetical adjustment – the interpretation which he has resolved to put on 11b.

9. Where the deviation of LXX from MT is connected with the difficulty of MT

6.5: *miyyād* requires emendation, but *ἐκ βρόχων*, 'from meshes (of the net)', is an attempt to deal with this difficulty rather than an indication of an original *māṣōd*, 'net'.

6.11: ἀγαθὸς δρομεύς, 'a good courier', is indicative of an inability to translate *māgēn*. This produces an inept simile and then LXX expands MT with two further inept similes one of which features 'an evil courier'.

12.13: LXX has taken MT wrongly in 13a and supplied the more conventional thought that the ἁμαρτωλός falls into snares. Hence ἐμπίπτει εἰς παγίδας should not be taken as evidence of a Hebrew text containing *nōqaš*.

12.28: μνησικάκων, 'those who harbour malice', is indicative of the difficulty caused by *n*[e]*tībā*, but it has no textual significance and does not point to *m*[e]*šūbā* or *m*[e]*šibīm*.

14.1: The difficult Hebrew in 1a (*ḥak*[e]*mōt nāšīm*) is rendered σοφαὶ γυναῖκες. This does show that if *nāšīm* is a corruption, it is an old one and was in the Hebrew text before the Greek translator.

14.7: This verse is obscure in Hebrew, especially 7b, and LXX does not grapple with the problems. It substitutes a verse which has hardly any resemblance to MT: 'Everything is contrary to a foolish man, but wise lips are discerning weapons'.

14.9: LXX could apparently make nothing of 9a (MT) and substitutes: 'The houses of the impious have need of purification'. In view of the occurrence of οἰκίαι in 9a it is doubtful whether a textual point should be made of οἰκίαι in 9b. In any case, *ūbēt y*[e]*šārīm rāṣōn* makes no sense (MT: *ūbēn y*[e]*šārīm rāṣōn*). Hence 9b, like 9a, is a free paraphrase of MT – an attempt to make sense without dealing faithfully with the Hebrew.

14.22: The awkward *h*[a]*lō'* of MT is not translated by LXX.

14.35: MT 35b is difficult and LXX bears little resemblance to it: 'By his own initiative he (the king) will remove dishonour'. In the additional line in LXX ('Anger destroys even sagacious men'), ὀργή may derive from *w*[e]*ʿebrātō* (MT 35b).

15.6: The grammatical irregularities of MT are disposed of by LXX and the obscure *neʿ*[e]*kāret* is loosely rendered by ἀπολοῦνται. Again in 15.27, LXX renders *ʿōkēr bētō* ἐξόλλυσιν ἑαυτόν, 'will destroy himself'.

16.4: LXX (16.9) more or less correctly paraphrases MT without grappling with *l*[e]*maʿ*[a]*nēhū* (μετὰ δικαιοσύνης).

19.27: υἱὸς ἀπολειπόμενος is an indication of the difficulty experienced with *ḥ*[a]*dal b*[e]*nī*. It is an effort to make the verse say what the translator thought it ought: 'A son who neglects to pay attention to a father's instruction will be practised in wicked sayings.' This involves a departure from MT (*lišgōt mēʾimrē dāʿat*) in 27b also.

21.6: The textual deduction should not be made from *μάταια διώκει* that the Greek translator read *hebel rōdēp*. Rather he had difficulty with *hebel niddāp* and he translated 6b on the analogy of 6a, where he vocalized *pʿl* as *pōʿēl* ('he who acquires wealth' is matched by 'he who pursues emptiness').

22.11: MT requires emendation, but the LXX rendering is not textually significant. It reflects the difficulty presented by the Hebrew text and the tendency of LXX to moralize and introduce a note of piety where it is absent in MT ('The Lord loves the pure in heart, all who are blameless in their ways are acceptable to him'). There is a complete lack of correspondence between MT and LXX in 11b. LXX has a moralizing reference (*ἄμωμοι*) absent from MT and has the additional *stichos*: 'A king shepherds his flock with his lips'. Although I have adopted *r^eṣōnō* for *rēʿēhū* in 11b and transposed *melek* to 11a, I recognize that there is no textual basis for these emendations.

23.34: *καὶ ὥσπερ κυβερνήτης ἐν πολλῷ κλύδωνι* (34b), 'and like a navigator in a great swell', has no resemblance to *k^ešōkēb b^erōʾš ḥibbēl*. The Greek translator has apparently replaced the difficult MT with a new line.

24.5: The Greek translator invented a new line (*κρείσσων σοφὸς ἰσχυροῦ*, 'a wise man has the better of a strong man') to replace the unintelligible 5a of MT (*geber ḥākām baʿōz*).

24.28: The rhetorical question of MT is rendered as a straightforward negative. *μηδὲ πλατύνου* should not be taken as evidence that the Greek translator read *w^eʾal t^epat* (MT: *wah^apittītā*).

25.4: *καὶ καθαρισθήσεται καθαρὸν ἅπαν*. This should be regarded as a paraphrase which removes the difficulties of MT without dealing with them, and not as a basis for emending MT on the assumption that the Greek translator read some such Hebrew text as *w^eyēṣēʾ niṣrāp kullō* or *w^eyēṣēʾ niṣrāp kālīl*.

26.7: LXX's treatment of 7b is perhaps not unconnected with the difficulty presented by the obscure *dlyw* in 7a. This is wrongly rendered as an imperative (*ἀφελοῦ*) and 7b is adjusted so that sense of a kind is had from the couplet. Instead of 'A proverb in the mouth of a fool' (MT), LXX has '(Take away) impiety from the mouth of a fool'.

27.9: It appears that the Greek translator could make nothing of MT in 9b and that he invented an antithesis to 9a ('but the soul is rent by affliction'). He misses the point of 9a, which is a figure devised to illustrate the nature and effects of friendship (9b).

27.22: LXX omits all reference to the difficult imagery of MT (mortar, pestle and powder) and is a pedestrian paraphrase: 'If you were to flog a fool in the assembly, thereby dishonouring him, you would not remove his folly.'

28.2: LXX is a free translation indicative of the difficulty which the Greek translator had with MT. It cannot, then, be a basis for a massive reconstruction of the Hebrew text. It is arguable that *rbym* was vocalized as *rībīm* and *ydʿkn* as *yidʿākūn* by the translator. On the other hand, it is likely that his Hebrew text had *'ereṣ* not *ʿārīṣ*, *śārehā* not *yēʿōrū* and *ya'ᵃrīk* (which is not translated by LXX).

28.17: LXX has not dealt faithfully with MT and has adjusted the sense so as to arrive at a forensic statement ('He who goes surety for a man on a charge of murder will be obliged to flee and will not find security'). MT is rather theological affirmation.

29.21: The Greek translator was puzzled by *mānōn*. ὀδυνηθήσεται ἐφ' ἑαυτῷ is an attempt to make sense in the face of this perplexity. LXX: 'He who is pampered from childhood will be a servant and in the end will come to grief' is an incorrect translation of MT in 21a and an evasion of the difficulty posed by *mānōn* in 21b.

10. Where the deviation of LXX from MT derives from exegetical presuppositions or from a striving after what are thought to be more fitting sentiments than those expressed by MT

7.6: παρακύπτουσα. It is the woman, not the wisdom teacher, who looks out of the window, whether or not this has the exegetical overtones attached to it by those who follow LXX (see below, pp. 334ff.).

8.5: ἔνθεσθε καρδίαν. This is not textual evidence supporting *hākīnū*, but is rather the consequence of aesthetic scruples (the avoidance of the repetition of *hābīnū*).

8.21: The addition in LXX (ἐὰν ἀναγγείλω ὑμῖν τὰ καθ' ἡμέραν γινόμενα μνημονεύσω τὰ ἐξ αἰῶνος ἀριθμῆσαι, 'If I declare to you the things of daily occurrence, I shall remember to recount the things of old') is an editorial bridge between v. 20 and v. 22.

9.6: ἀφροσύνην, 'folly', is probably a paraphrase of MT rather than a translation of *p^e^tī* (MT: *p^e^tā'īm*, 'untutored companions').

10.18: δίκαια does not indicate that the Greek translator read *yōšer* or the like (MT: *šāqer*), but is the consequence of an exegetical decision, namely, that the verse refers to the benevolent concealment of hostility.

11.7: It is the feeling for antithetic parallelism, an antithesis of piety and impiety, which produces the deviation of LXX from MT.

11.9: αἴσθησις δὲ δικαίων εὔοδος (9b) is a free paraphrase of MT and no textual point should be made of ἐν στόματι ἀσεβῶν in 9a (i.e., MT *b^e^peh* to be emended to *b^e^pī*).

11.16: LXX destroys the antithesis of the shorter MT and introduces a moral note not in MT: 'A woman who hates uprightness is a throne of dishonour.'

12.4: LXX changes the simile in 4b (MT: 'like decay in the bones'; LXX: 'like maggot in wood') and expands the application (MT: *m^e^bīšā*; LXX: οὕτως ἄνδρα ἀπόλλυσιν γυνὴ κακοποιός).

12.19: In LXX the verse is given an unambiguous forensic character as opposed to its general character in MT. The only textual point is that *'d* (19b) is apparently read as *'ēd*, 'witness' (μάρτυς; MT *'ad*).

13.13: LXX expands the verse with a particular reference to the ill in store for the crafty son and the prosperity to be enjoyed by a wise servant. The Greek translator apparently thought that 13a was concerned with filial disobedience.

14.19: LXX offers a correct exegesis of 19b rather than a translation: 'Impious men will serve the gates of the righteous', i.e., will be their domestic servants.

15.20: υἱὸς δὲ ἄφρων does not point to a different Hebrew text from MT, but registers dissatisfaction with the odd expression *k^e^sīl 'ādām*. The Greek translator replaced this with the exact antithesis of *bēn ḥākām – bēn k^e^sīl*.

15.26: 'But the words of the pure are grave' (26b) was thought by the translator to be more felicitous than, 'But gracious words are pure' (MT), although in fact it weakens the parallelism.

15.28: LXX: 'The hearts of the righteous contemplate truth' paraphrases correctly: 'A righteous man gives a considered answer' (MT), and the addition in LXX underlines the social reference of the verse:

'The way of righteous men is acceptable to the Lord, by means of them enemies become friends.'

16.26: LXX completely alters the meaning of MT and adds an additional *stichos*. The down-to-earth observation of MT that a man works so as not to starve is replaced by a contrast between the industrious (silent) man and the crooked person who busies himself with misrepresentation. The one diverts destruction from himself, the other carries it in his own mouth.

20.25: *μετανοιεῖν γίνεται* ('for after vowing comes a change of mind') is mistaken exegesis of *lᵉbaqqēr* ('to seek ways and means of fulfilling them').

21.20: LXX has interpreted so as to expunge the earthiness of MT. The allusion to wealth in MT is changed into a reference to the treasures of wisdom.

22.10: *ἐν συνεδρίῳ* (10b) should not be regarded as textually significant in view of the intrusive *ἐκ συνεδρίου* in 10a. The translator has given a precise forensic reference to the verse and has taken liberties with the Hebrew text. *λοιμός*, 'trouble-maker', is an inaccurate rendering of *lēṣ*, and *πάντας ἀτιμάζει* connects only loosely with *qālōn*. The reconstruction *wᵉyēšeb bēt dīn* (haplography of *b*) on the basis of *καθίσῃ ἐν συνεδρίῳ* is clever, but the Greek probably does not derive from a divergent Hebrew text (MT: *wᵉyišbōt dīn*).

II. Moralizing or pious paraphrase and expansion in LXX

10.6: *εὐλογία Κυρίου*, 'blessing of the Lord' (MT: *bᵉrākōt*).

10.25: LXX has a more prosaic and explicit statement of the doctrine of theodicy than MT.

10.26: LXX applies the imagery of MT to impiety, not to laziness ('so is *παρανομία* to those who practise it').

10.29: MT: 'way of Yahweh'; LXX: 'fear of the Lord' – a more exact expression of legal piety.

12.11: 'Empty pursuits' (11b, MT) is glossed with a reference to 'banquets of wine' in the additional distich of LXX.

12.26: The longer LXX takes MT wrongly in the only line where the two can be compared. LXX is constructed in accordance with the presuppositions of theodicy, i.e., weal for the righteous and woe for the sinner.

13.2: LXX moralizes: 'A good man eats from the fruit of righteousness, but the souls of impious men are destroyed prematurely.'

13.11: There might seem to be a textual point in ἐπισπουδαζομένη (i.e., it indicates *m^e^bōhāl*; MT: *mēhebel*), but LXX taken as a whole is a pious reinterpretation and expansion of LXX. Thus, 'hastily with impiety' and 'gradually with piety' and the addition, 'the righteous man pities and lends'. It is unlikely that ἐπισπουδαζομένη derives from a Hebrew text containing *m^e^bōhāl*. There is a similar pious reinterpretation in 13.12, 'good desire' and in 13.19: 'The desires of the pious give pleasure to the soul, but the deeds of the impious are far from knowledge.'

13.15: In the additional line of LXX, διανοία is defined as knowledge of the Law (cf. *śēkel* in 15a translated as σύνεσις).

13.23: LXX transforms MT, which is difficult, into a clear-cut expression of the doctrine of theodicy: 'The righteous will enjoy wealth for many years, but the unrighteous will be speedily destroyed.'

17.8: LXX substitutes παιδεία, 'instruction', for MT *haššōhad*, 'bribe', and omits all reference to a lucky stone (*'eben ḥēn*).

21.9: LXX moralizes (μετὰ ἀδικίας, 'with injustice') and omits all reference to the nagging wife who is the occasion of the sentence in MT.

21.26: In 26b, LXX takes the right sense of MT but paraphrases ('gives without sparing' becomes 'shows kindness and pity without sparing'). In 26a LXX moralizes; MT *ta'^a^wā*, 'desire', is rendered by ἐπιθυμίας κακάς, and ἀσεβής, 'impious', does not show that the translator had before him a Hebrew text containing *rāšāʿ*. The obscurity of 26a (MT) is also a factor – the translator had to make sense of it somehow.

22.3: MT is about the ability of the *ʿārūm* to take care of himself in a dangerous world as contrasted with the *p^e^tī*. πανοῦργος is recognizably a translation of *ʿārūm*, but the sentence is given a moralizing tendency and is made to turn on the ability of the πανοῦργος to learn from the punishment meted out to the πονηρός.

25.19: LXX is a moralizing paraphrase of MT which is without textual significance, and lends no support to the emendation of *rōʿā* to *rāʿā* or the deletion of *mibṭāḥ*.

26.11: LXX makes moralizing adjustments and additions to the theme of MT (the unteachability of the fool). Thus 'and becomes odious' (11a) and 'Thus the fool who by his wickedness turns back to his sin' (11b). LXX has an additional couplet in the same moralizing vein.

27.20: The moralizing addition in LXX ('He who fixes his eye is abhorrent to the Lord and the incorrigible have unruly tongues') has only the loosest connection with the point of the simile in MT.

29.13: LXX adds theological content to the statement of MT and brings the verse into line with the assumptions of a theodicy.

30.3: MT is an agnostic utterance which is converted by LXX into a pious affirmation: 'God has taught me wisdom, I have acquired knowledge of the Holy One' (or 'of holy ones', i.e., 'angelic knowledge').

PART ONE

INTERNATIONAL WISDOM

I

THE EGYPTIAN INSTRUCTION

A. *PTAHHOTEP*

B. Gunn, *The Instruction of Ptah-hotep and the Instruction of Ke-gemni* (1909); A. Erman (tr. A. M. Blackman), *The Literature of the Ancient Egyptians* (1927), pp. 54–66; *ANET*[2] (1955), pp. 412–14 (tr. John A. Wilson).

Since Ptahhotep was a vizier of a Pharaoh of the fifth dynasty, the purported date of the composition is *c.* 2450 BC. The book certainly belongs to the period of the Old Kingdom and had already been re-edited by the time of the Middle Kingdom. It was still in use as a school book as late as the eighteenth dynasty (Erman, pp. 54f.).

In his preliminary remarks to the retiring vizier, the Pharaoh says: 'Teach thou him (i.e., Ptahhotep's son who is to be groomed for his father's office) first about speaking. Then he may set an example for the children of officials. May obedience enter into him, and all heart's poise. Speak to him. There is no one born wise' (*ANET*, p. 412). 'There is no one born wise', and so wisdom has to be learned and is teachable to him who is receptive and obedient. This is traditional wisdom which is conservable, so that a bank of it, stored up from the past and containing the mature conclusions of many statesmen on the art of statesmanship and the general behaviour which befits a man of affairs, is available for the apprentice official.

Such instruction is authoritative; it demands unreserved acceptance and is not offered for critical consideration. There is one passage in the prologue where the retiring vizier seems not to confine his counsel to his son and successor, but to have a wider audience in view (cf. H. Gese, *op. cit.*, p. 30). His intention is to instruct 'the ignorant about wisdom and about the rules for good speech, as of advantage to him who will hearken and of disadvantage to him who may neglect them' (*ANET*, p. 412). R. Anthes ('Lebensregeln und Lebensweisheit der alten Aegypter', *Der alte Orient* 32, 1933, p. 11) has called in question the originality of the opening passage in which the aged vizier seeks permission of the Pharaoh to install his son as his successor. He observes that the maxims are general in character and are addressed to any young man standing on the threshold of a career as an official.

The young official must accept without qualification the authority of this corpus of instruction and must cultivate an attitude of receptivity towards it. There is a passage in the epilogue which makes much play on the word 'hear'. His whole duty is to listen, retain and obey. *Ptahhotep* is concerned with the form as well as the content of wise speaking. The apprentice must so immerse himself in the forms of elegant and incisive speech that it will become second nature to him to express himself with style and distinction. This emphasis on craftsmanship (*ANET*, p. 414) is more than a demand for speech with literary merit; it is a recognition that in high public office style of utterance is indispensable.

Hence the apprentice must also be a hearer with respect to the manner in which the great ones of the past have expressed themselves. 'Teach him first about speaking' is the advice of the Pharaoh to Ptahhotep, while in the epilogue one of the advantages claimed for 'hearing' is that 'it makes *for expressing well*, the speech of the *very* officials. It is what teaches a man to speak to the future, so that it may hear it, what produces a craftsman, who has heard what is good and who speaks to the future – and it hears it' (*ANET*, p. 414).

The son following his father in high office or the apprentice official (if we set the composition in a more general context) must first learn obedience and the right attitude of unquestioning receptivity to the treasures of political wisdom conserved from the past. The absence of this is synonymous with folly. 'As for the fool who does not hearken, he cannot do anything. He regards knowledge as ignorance and profit as loss. He does everything blameworthy, so that one finds fault with him every day' (*ANET*, p. 414). There is no virtue in originality and the innovator is a fool. So the advice given to a father is this: if you are a man of standing and your son listens to your advice and conserves your property, give him every encouragement. If he is insubordinate and unteachable, disown him (*ANET*, p. 413).

This Instruction is declared to be an educational manual for one who is to hold high public office; and even those directives which might not appear to have this direct vocational character have to be understood as addressed to an intending statesman, so that the important question is always this: what effect will a particular course of behaviour have on the career of an official? In teaching given on matters of private morality, the point of view is that unwise behaviour in relation to women (*ANET*, p. 413) or an undignified squabble over a family estate (*ANET*, p. 413) will detract from the reputation and weightiness of an official and hinder his success.

The advice, 'If you want to perpetuate friendship in any home to which you have access, beware of approaching the women, for one attains to death through touching them', has particular relevance for a statesman. Similarly with the advice, 'Do not be covetous at a division, do not be greedy except for your own share. Do not be covetous against your kinsmen, for a mild man earns greater respect than a strong one and a little covetousness turns a calm man into a contentious one.' A statesman should not become involved in a squalid quarrel over money with his relatives, for it is a fact that embittered relations with kinsmen will detract from his effectiveness in public life.

The demand for mildness does not mean that he should be weak or soft; he is entitled to his share, but he must avoid strained relationships with his relatives, for it is part of statesmanship to exercise such restraint and consideration that even tempers and civilized behaviour are preserved. If he cannot maintain a conciliatory atmosphere in a private affair, his ability to quieten passions and maintain sweet reasonableness in more complicated political contexts will be placed in question. Again, a statesman needs a stable home if he is to carry the burdens of public life and so he is advised to lay sound foundations for his household and take good care of his wife (*ANET*, p. 413).

Elsewhere the contents of *Ptahhotep* are more obviously connected with the skills and procedures required of an official and its character as a vocational manual rather than a moral code comes clearly to view. It is certainly concerned with values, but there is no moralism in it. It censures the unwise rather than the sinful; it contrasts judicious and injudicious, reasonable and unreasonable, temperate and intemperate rather than righteous and wicked, good and bad. It is arguable that this is simply a different kind of morality from moralism, one which regards the foolish and the rash action as no less sinful than the evil action and which places the highest value on reasonable behaviour.

Thus the statesman is warned against intellectual pride and professional prejudice. Wisdom may be gathered in strange places and the official should not suppose that he need not look beyond his own profession for fine speech. 'Good speech is more hidden than the emerald, but it may be found with maidservants at the grindstones' (*ANET*, p. 412). This may be a reference to the felicity and power of popular proverbial expressions. Even etiquette is important for an official and the occasion on which he dines with a superior may be an important milestone in his career. He is to take what is offered, keep his eyes on the food, avoid staring, speak when he is spoken to and laugh when his host laughs (*ANET*, p. 412). The object of all this is to put his superior in a good humour and to create a favourable impression. While this certainly has an unpleasant flavour of sycophantic servility, there is a serious point to it. It is not every day that he will dine with one who can advance his career and much may hinge on the estimate which is formed of him.

Otherwise the qualities which are required are principally concerned with intellectual discipline and integrity. A messenger in the service of a great man should be reliable, obedient and exact. He should exercise the greatest care not to worsen relations between great men either by accident or design. He should communicate his master's message with such clarity and precision as will ensure that he represents to the most delicate nuance his attitude and point of view (*ANET*, p. 413).

Then there is the art of dealing with a petitioner. It is important to listen attentively and courteously to what a petitioner has to say and not to wound his feelings unnecessarily or engender rancour by dismissing him in a brusque and officious way. Even if there is no intention of granting the crave of the petition, one should avoid injuring the self-esteem of the petitioner and a good hearing may give him as much satisfaction as the granting of his request (*ANET*, p. 413).

An official makes or breaks his reputation in the council chamber when he has the ear of his superior and he must mobilize all his resources so as to speak well and effectively when the occasion arises. He has to decide on the balance of advantage as between silence and speech, for he should speak only if he is convinced that the circumstances are propitious and that he has a weighty contribution to make. Even so it needs craftsmanship to make the point with clarity, elegance and weight. 'It is a (real) craftsman who can speak in counsel, (for) speaking is more difficult than any labour' (*ANET*, p. 414).

Then a statesman must be a good judge of a man. He should have the knack of summing up his character expeditiously and decisively, so that he may know what degree of trust can be reposed in him. An official who is uncertain about the calibre of a friend should closet himself with him, engage in discussion and unobtrusively test his mettle. If it becomes obvious that the friend is incapable of keeping a confidence or that he is in general injudicious, one should not react to this discovery in a tempestuous way nor bring matters to a head in such a manner as to sever relationships with him. He is now known for what he is, but the new situation created by this discovery can be managed and a personal relationship maintained. No one should suppose that it is his mission in life to expose another publicly and destroy his reputation (*ANET*, p. 414).

So far I have tried to describe the contents of *Ptahhotep* in a way not involving too many assumptions. I have asserted that it is an educational manual for statesmen, but I have not undertaken to define precisely the motivation of its instructions or the ethos which they presuppose. This discussion will be best advanced by avoiding words which are either too loaded and themselves beg too many questions or which have too precise a modern connotation. I shall avoid saying that this is a utilitarian ethic or that it recommends a pragmatic attitude to affairs. Nevertheless I believe that the criterion of workability or effectiveness must be employed in any attempt to describe the spirit which informs these maxims, though Frankfort has rightly objected to the term 'pragmatic', which might be taken to mean that here we have a kind of unprincipled opportunism, where the only consideration is the achievement of the best results or maximum success. (H. Frankfort, *Ancient Egyptian Religion*, 1961, pp. 62f.; also A. de Buck, *NTT*, xxi, 1932, pp. 322–49; H. Brunner, *Altägyptische Erziehung* (1957), pp. 118f.; H. Gese, *op. cit.*, pp. 7f.)

Now this is manifestly not the case, and we can say without fear of contradiction that *Ptahhotep* is not a crude recipe for success and that it is not the product of a brash society where men are in a hurry to get rich and where money is the measure of success and influence. On the contrary, it reflects the ethos of a mature civilization, in which smash-and-grab tactics, far from enhancing power and effectiveness in public life, will be seen as a revelation of a man's deficiencies and his unfitness for power: 'Wrongdoing has never brought its undertaking into port. (It may be that) it is fraud that gains riches, (but) the strength of justice is that it lasts, and a man may say: "It is the property of my father" ' (*ANET*, p. 412). I shall give closer consideration to this passage presently.

It cannot, therefore, be concluded that the intention of these instructions is simply either, 'Act in this way, for it is a means to prestige and influence', or, 'Act in this way, for it is the effective method of achieving prestige and influence'. It may be that one or two items are susceptible of a simple utilitarian explanation, although this is not altogether certain. Thus there is the advice to the man who has had a successful career as a statesman that he should be generous towards his clients, where 'clients' may refer to subordinate officials (*ANET*, p. 413, n.22), because this is a kind of insurance policy. 'One does not know what may happen, so that he may understand the morrow. If misfortunes occur among those (now) favoured, it is the clients who (still) say: "Welcome!" One does not secure satisfaction from a stranger; one has recourse to a client when there is trouble' (*ANET*, p. 413).

The advice on how to comport oneself at the table of a superior, which I have already discussed, would seem also to be simply utilitarian in its motivation, as is also the further advice: 'Bow thy back to thy superior, thy overseer from the palace. (Then) thy household will be established in its property, and thy recompense will be as it should be. Opposition to a superior is a painful thing, (for) one lives as long as he is mild' (*ANET*, p. 414).

I would suggest that the least tendentious way of describing this corpus of teaching is to say that it establishes the conditions of effective and successful statesmanship in ancient Egypt. If an official is to succeed in affairs and to become a weighty statesman, these are the conditions to which he must attend and give respect. But then we have to ask ourselves: How are these conditions determined? Why is it precisely these conditions and no others which apply? Part of the answer only, but an important part, is that these are the conditions which obtain in a society with a given structure, namely, ancient Egypt, and that it is the existing structure of this society which is presupposed by this authoritative teaching on the art of statesmanship.

We can go further and say that the practicability of authoritative instruction in the principles of statesmanship presupposes a tradition of statecraft and so a society with a high degree of stability and continuity in its institutions. Only if the society is thus stable or static (Frankfort's word) is the idea of basing statesmanship on the mature conclusions of past generations of statesmen a credible one. The framework of values in which the Instruction is set thus derives from the ethos of the Egyptian state.

The concept which is best suited to sum up this ethos is that of 'order' (*Maat*), and Anthes has observed that the aim of the Instruction is to indicate to the aspiring statesman how he must act so as to be in harmony with this order, for only by such conduct can he achieve a secure tenure of eminence and power (p. 12). This order is not merely political theory setting out the system of corporate values which should be realized in the structure of the state. Order is ultimately not a political concept but a theological doctrine (p. 13). Hence the authoritative teaching which is given to the apprentice official is related to a theological doctrine concerning the nature of Egyptian society. It is this aspect of the Instruction to which Frankfort has called attention and on which he has shed new light (pp. 30f., 59f.).

The most important theological utterance in *Ptahhotep* is not one in which the name of God or a god appears, but one in which there is a reference to this over-arching divine order. 'If thou art a leader commanding the affairs of the multitude, seek out for thyself every beneficial deed, until it may be that thine (own) affairs are without wrong. Justice is great, and its appropriateness is lasting; it has not been disturbed since the time of him who made it, (whereas) there is punishment for him who passes over its laws. It is the (right) path before him who knows nothing. Wrongdoing has never brought its undertaking into port. (It may be that) it is fraud that gains riches, (but) the strength of justice is that it lasts, and a man may say: "It is the property of my father" ' (*ANET*, p. 412).

'Justice' in Wilson's translation ('truth' in Erman, p. 57) is *Maat*, the principle of order to which I have alluded. *Maat* is a theological doctrine with cosmological and ethical-political ramifications which involves the integration of the order of nature with the order of the Egyptian state. This harmony is achieved in the person of the Pharaoh, who is a god, and kingship dates from the time of creation and belongs to the basic structure of existence. *Maat* has special relevance to the theological framework of the Instruction, because the order in which the Egyptian state participates is ultimately theological and it is this order which regulates the conditions of effective statesmanship. The Egyptian state has its centre in the god-king who is the source of *Maat* and who preserves, through the derivative powers of his officials, that immutable order of Egyptian society (Frankfort, p. 52; Erman, p. 57, n.1; cf. H. Gese, *op. cit.*, pp. 11f.; H. Brunner, *op. cit.*, pp. 118f.; A. Volten, 'Der Begriff der Maat in der ägyptischen Weisheit', *Les Sagesses du Proche-Orient Ancien*, 1963, pp. 73–101).

The Egyptian lived in a society which was perfect from the day of its creation, so that history is no more than the inevitable working-out of its original and immutable constitution. This, then, is the theological expression of the 'static' character of the Egyptian state, and it is on the basis of this doctrine that the continuing validity of a store of political wisdom accumulated from the past can be confidently asserted. 'The strength of *Maat* is that it lasts and a man may say: "It is the property of my father".' *Maat* guarantees the continuity and permanence of the structure of the Egyptian state from one generation to another.

It is also clear that *Maat* has an ethical content; it is not merely 'order' but 'just order'. The official charged with the conduct of public affairs must 'seek out every beneficial deed' (Erman: 'strive after every excellence'). This, too, is a condition of effective statesmanship. Practised delicacy of political judgement, astuteness and sagacity – these do not by themselves make a great statesman. He must also be inspired by an awareness that by his probity and integrity he participates in an immutable order of society. He must even be actuated by a spirit of benevolence and find satisfaction in holding a public trust, and in the thought that by giving to every man his due he fulfils the conditions of effective statesmanship in Egypt. 'Wrongdoing has never brought its undertaking into port' (cf. Frankfort, pp. 43–46).

If all this is so, we have now to ask: How do statesmen become attuned to this order? Are the rules of statesmanship revealed by God? Are they oracularly delivered by priests? Has statecraft the character of religious dogma? It is because the answer to all these questions is in the negative that the inner character of the Egyptian Instruction is so elusive and difficult to grasp. What Frankfort has called the 'pragmatic misinterpretation' (p. 62) is not entirely a misinterpretation. Much of the advice which is given in *Ptahhotep* would pass for diplomatic and political strategy in any age and society and is not obviously bounded by the Egyptian doctrine of order. Conserve as much goodwill as you can when there is a disagreement. Learn to deal with people without hurting them or giving them the impression that they are being managed. If you test out the character of a colleague and find him deficient, the discovery is valuable, but do not make a public exhibition of it. Reticence and even secretiveness are political virtues. Silence may sometimes advance your cause better than speech. Much depends on a sense of timing and when you speak do it clearly and weightily. All this, I say, is advice which might find a place in any manual of statesmanship anywhere.

Another way of expressing this point is to say that these maxims are not revealed by the gods. They rest on the authority of the great statesmen of the past who were guided by them in the conduct of public affairs and who found by experience that they were indispensable to effective statesmanship in Egypt and that they best served the stability and harmony of Egyptian society. With this Frankfort does not disagree. He says: 'The mature reflection of the sages, the experience accumulated through generations supplied the guidance of which men stood in need' (p. 81). It appears that the Egyptian gods left the statesmen to their own devices to work out the details of *Maat* in relation to statesmanship and required them to make proper use of their native intellectual endowment.

To advance this discussion further there are two enquiries which can be made. We can enquire more closely into the nature of this breed of officials or statesmen, and we can ask whether it is possible to give a religious expression to the idea that a statesman participates in the divine order (*Maat*) by the right use of his wits and by a receptiveness to a process of education in statesmanship.

With regard to the first of these considerations, it is necessary to examine more closely what is meant by authoritative instruction in statesmanship. One cannot become a statesman simply through learning by rote the authoritative principles laid down in the Instruction, for the manner in which these principles apply to a particular case may only be discoverable through the greatest delicacy of intellectual judgement and robustness of acumen. The hand of authority is heavy, but it is not a dead hand, and authoritative principles of statesmanship can only be applied by first-class minds. 'There is no man born wise', says the Pharaoh in commending this authoritative teaching, but it is equally true that teaching will not make him wise unless it influences his mental habits at the deepest level, so that he becomes essentially the same kind of person as the great statesman of the past.

The educational process goes much deeper than the memorizing of the principles, and whoever would model himself on those who have succeeded best in public life must assimilate the spirit of their approach to statesmanship and acquire the insight, discipline and precision which brought them their success. The Instruction is, then, for an intellectual *élite* who are to learn from the experience of statecraft acquired by statesmen of the highest calibre in the past and who, guided and enriched by this store of political sagacity, are at once to achieve eminence and prestige for themselves and to become part of the order of the Egyptian state foreordained by the gods. There is no divine revelation of the content of statecraft; no extraordinary guidance is given on matters of state. Religion leaves room for a statecraft accumulated over many generations, and a high native intelligence developed by a rigorous educational process enables a man to be attuned to (Frankfort's phrase) or to participate in the divine order for the Egyptian state.

The idea that a man in virtue of his native endowment – because of the kind of person that he is – has his appropriate place in the scheme of things finds religious expression in *Ptahhotep*, and this brings me to the second of the two enquiries on which I embarked, and to a consideration of the occurrences of 'God' in *Ptahhotep.* Wilson has remarked that 'God' in these texts 'sometimes means the king, sometimes the supreme or creator god, and sometimes the force which demands proper behaviour – a force not clearly defined, but perhaps the local god' (*ANET*, p. 413, n.10). In the phrase 'and producest a son who is pleasing to god' (*ANET*, p. 413), Wilson thinks that the reference is probably to the Pharaoh. Erman (p. 58, n.4) draws the same conclusion for the phrase 'one of good standing with the god'. Frankfort holds that the exact meaning of 'God' is 'the god with whom you have to reckon in the circumstances' (p. 67), and Anthes identifies God with a higher fate which man cannot resist and adds: 'Whether it is a god of the pantheon or a god who rules as king of the land who is thought of' (p. 13).

I am interested in these references to 'God' in so far as they are expressions in religious terms of the belief that a person has a natural or innate 'weight' of endowment. This is the gift of God and it ultimately determines his place in the order. Thus the instruction: '*If thou* standest or sittest *in the vestibule* (Gunn, 'council-chamber'), *wait quietly until thy turn cometh.* Give heed to the servant that announceth; he that is called hath a broad place. The vestibule hath its rule, and every arrangement therein is in accordance with the measuring-cord. It is God who assigneth the foremost place – *but one attaineth nothing with* the elbow' (Erman, p. 59, Gunn, pp. 47f.). In the council chamber or vestibule of the great man (where one awaits a summons to tender advice) an official should always respect protocol and not try to elbow his way into prominence. A man who is destined to attain eminence will reach the rank which he deserves. His weight and power as a counsellor will gain recognition when the time is ripe, but it is vain to try to force the pace, for it is God who assigns the foremost place.

The same thought is present in the following advice: 'If thou art a poor fellow, following a man of distinction, one of good standing with the god, know thou not his former insignificance. Thou shouldst not be puffed-up against him because of what thou didst know of him formerly. Show regard for him in conformance with what has accrued to him – property does not come of itself. . . . It is god who makes (a man's) quality and he defends him (even) while he is asleep' (*ANET*, p. 413). Erman translates: 'It is God that createth repute' (p. 58), and this is a serious religious belief even for men who are frankly ambitious and competing with each other for the highest offices of the state. Envy need not corrode ambition, for a man cannot rise above the ceiling of his innate endowment. He has a place which corresponds to his natural 'weight' as a person. The official has his appointed place in the order of the Egyptian state, and if he is surpassed by a man of lowly origins, he must conclude that this is how it has been ordained by the gods.

This belief makes a major contribution to the ethos of the Instruction and creates a pleasing impression of composure and maturity. Even in this world of strenuous competition for reputation and eminence, there is a point beyond which it is vain to strive for success, and so the official is not to torture himself with the fear of mediocrity nor to spur himself on to ever more frantic efforts to rise to the top. He need not be infected with the fever of ambition nor be afflicted with the distemper of continual frustration. He is not, after all, a competitor in a rat-race and his humanity need not be a casualty. Nor is he condemned to live in a desert of intrigue and mistrust, for there are green pastures where he can rest in tranquillity. So it is that although the Instruction is a manual in statecraft, it is set in a framework of beliefs and values which enables the statesman to preserve his integrity as a person and to live together with his superiors and inferiors in an atmosphere of mutual respect and high aspiration, free from the jaundice of envy and frustrated ambition, for a statesman has his natural place in the order.

With this tranquillity there is also confidence, and an official should not be over-anxious for the continuing stability of the régime. He should not parade himself too self-consciously as a defender of the order, nor should he suppose that it is his business to expose and denounce those whose behaviour appears not to conform to it. This can be left to the gods. So in the passage already discussed concerning the testing of a friend we read the words: 'Do not answer in a *state* of turmoil; do not *remove* thyself from him; do not trample him down. His time has never failed to come; he cannot escape from him who predetermined him' (*ANET*, p. 414).

Anthes (p. 12) has remarked that the emphasis is on wise rather than righteous behaviour, and has tended to equate the wisdom and unwisdom which are contrasted in the Instruction with cunning or shrewdness and foolishness. There is no doubt that Anthes is right in saying that there is an absence of moralism in this kind of composition. On the other hand, the intellectual attitudes which are enjoined are no less virtues because they are different in character from the demands of a more conventional morality. They belong to a structure of values and are not simply to be equated with cunning or shrewdness.

These considerations fall into their right proportions when it is remembered that the Instruction is not and does not set out to be a general ethic, but is an educational manual for statesmen. (This is contested by H. Gese, *op. cit.*, pp. 30f., and, to some extent, by H. Brunner, *op. cit.*, pp. 116f., although I do not disagree seriously with Brunner.) It does not formulate moral instruction for Everyman, but counsels the apprentice statesman in the first principles of statesmanship. It is a misconception to expect that the Instruction will be concerned with morality for its own sake. Nor have we to do with a moralism flowing from piety, where the contrast is between godly and sinful, righteous and wicked, good and bad. In such a context, unreasonable, unwise, ill-judged and intemperate behaviour may be regarded with excessive tolerance and hardly considered at all to be sinful. They are let off much more lightly than they are in the Instruction, where they are seen as major flaws in the make-up of a would-be statesman.

Further, we are not to expect that we shall find a self-effacing or self-abnegating morality which urges that it is better to be obscure and unpraised than to win reputation and exercise power; that it is a higher virtue to perform menial tasks for other men than to be at the centre of affairs and exercise great influence over their lives. Belief in the virtue of such a humility finds no place in a composition whose function is precisely to give authoritative advice to aspiring statesmen on how they can achieve maximum effectiveness and best exercise power.

I would suggest that concept of 'power' is valuable for the elucidation of the 'ethos' of the Instruction. Given the assumptions of its intellectual framework, it is evident that power cannot possibly be seen as constituting a temptation to the statesman or exercising a corrupting influence over him. Power is an unqualified good, because when he achieves the maximum power which he is capable of exercising, he is most fully participating in the order of the Egyptian state. The self-interest of the statesman and the well-being of the state are thus completely reconcilable.

But this is not naked nor arbitrary power, for the order determines in what conditions power can be effectively wielded. Power is regulated by the concept of *Maat*, and this has a positive ethical content. A statesman cannot effectively exercise power in the context of the Egyptian state unless he respects at all times the demands of equity, and endeavours scrupulously to act fairly and without respect of persons. Frankfort has observed that such graft and corruption as were found in Egyptian bureaucracy were confined to the lower ranks of officialdom (p. 45). This would tend to confirm the view that a passion for justice was an important ingredient of power and that whoever did not have this capacity for probity and fair dealing in public affairs was disqualified from holding high office by a self-regulating process of selection. Such were weighed in the balance and found wanting. They did not have a noble cast of mind, and their graft destined them for littleness and obscurity.

We might even go further and say that to rise to the highest office an Egyptian statesman must find genuine satisfaction in the work of nurturing the state; that this activity must be congenial to his nature and that he must possess a natural beneficence. He must enjoy his role as a public guardian and be mindful of the trust reposed in him. One with no such consciousness of vocation and with merely a selfish end in view would fail to fulfil one of the conditions of effective statesmanship and could not exercise power at the highest levels. If an official desires to have a successful career, he must not suppose that he can make use of the public service in order to achieve such objectives as power and comfort for himself. If these are his motives, he is unfit to hold power and is doomed to ineffectiveness and mediocrity.

Yet there is a relationship between power and wealth, in so far as it is held to be proper and fitting that wealth should accompany power. Those who have the qualities of great statesmen and who prove themselves such men of weight that they can effectively wield power are entitled to enjoy wealth. If they did not, a discordant note would be struck, and there would be something bizarre and disproportionate in the poverty of a high-ranking statesman. Nevertheless, wealth is not a measure of power, and the person who devotes most of his energies to money-grabbing is too slight ever to become influential in public affairs. In the instruction relating to the man who has risen to high office from humble beginnings we read: 'Show regard for him in conformance with what has accrued to him – property does not come of itself' (*ANET*, p. 413). The thought that property or wealth is the gift of God is present in the injunction against miserliness; the statesman who has won success and wealth should be a benefactor. 'Do not be miserly with thy wealth, which has accrued to thee as the gift of God' (*ANET*, p. 414).

Something of this thought that wealth is the gift of God perhaps relieves the impression of bald prudence in the instruction to deal generously with subordinates as an insurance against evil days, when their goodwill and helpfulness will be invaluable. 'Satisfy thy clients with what has accrued to thee, what accrues to one whom god favours' (*ANET*, p. 413). More important here, however, is the conviction that it is always wise to conserve as much goodwill as possible. This is as intrinsic to the Egyptian formula for power as the more exalted aspects of it which we have been discussing. A statesman who is to succeed has to be accomplished in the art of public relations and has to cultivate such attitudes as will minimize bitterness and alienation. If he is making enemies for himself all the time, or is seen to be the kind of person with whom it is difficult to maintain an even and harmonious relationship, he will make scant progress in his career.

The aim should always be to take the heat and acerbity out of every situation. A statesman must be able to get on with all kinds of people, and should not be prone to declaring his likes and dislikes. He has to learn to manage difficult situations and to reach his objectives without injuring feelings and trampling on sensibilities. 'Bow thy back to thy superior' (*ANET*, p. 414) is perhaps not just barefaced servility, but is also connected with the thought that a quarrelsome or cantankerous official imposes on himself a handicap above which he cannot rise. The man of power is flexible, relaxed and tolerant.

It is true that the Egyptian statesman requires to be shrewd and astute, but what I have said may perhaps serve to restore balance to his portrait. He is not so dominated by narrow, cold intellectual attitudes as to be almost sub-human. He has need of strong nerves and nice political judgement, but he is not to be likened to a chess player who never makes a wrong move. An outstanding statesman is more than a ruthlessly efficient machine. His power is proportionate to his weight as a person and weight is defined in terms of intellectual aptitudes, integrity, well-proportioned behaviour. More generally, he is humane and civilized and, if he achieves pre-eminence, success cannot be a snare to him, for the more successful he is and the more power he commands, the better is his attunement to the order which shapes Egyptian society.

B. *KAGEMNI*

B. Gunn, *op. cit.*, pp. 62–64; A. Erman, *op. cit.*, pp. 66–67: A. H. Gardiner, *JEA*, xxxii (1946), pp. 71–74.

Erman suggests that the lost beginning of this work may have related how the old king Huni (*c.* 2600 BC) commanded his vizier to write down for the benefit of his children the wisdom which he had acquired from the experience of a lifetime in public office. Since one of the children, Kagemni, became vizier, the situation which is represented is similar to that of *Ptahhotep*. Kagemni is being prepared for high office by parental instruction. Probably, as in *Ptahhotep*, this is to be taken as a literary convention rather than as a sober account of historical circumstances. Erman says of Kagemni: 'There actually was a vizier of this name, though several hundred years later, and the author of this work will have had some dim recollection of his name' (p. 66). The composition, so far as can be judged from the extant fragment, is, like *Ptahhotep*, an educational manual for apprentice officials.

Kagemni contains five directives and a concluding narrative. Of the fourth nothing remains but the heading, and two of the remaining four are concerned with table manners. The first of these is a warning against greed for food at a public meal. A keen appetite should be restrained, for this is an essential aspect of self-mastery and a man who cannot so discipline himself is exposing his limitations for all to see. 'It taketh only a brief moment to master oneself, and it is disgraceful to be greedy. . . . He is a miserable man that is greedy for his body' (Erman, p. 66). This instruction dealing with the need of moderation or even frugality in the matter of food and drink when dining in public (perhaps when dining as a guest) is supplemented by another which offers advice for the occasion when one is sitting at table with a glutton or a drunkard. 'If thou sittest with a greedy person, eat thou only when his meal is over, and if thou sittest with a drunkard, take thou only when his desire is satisfied' (Erman, p. 66).

The intention of this advice is probably: 'Let the glutton eat his fill before you eat anything and then he cannot possibly be irritated with the thought that you have taken food which he might have enjoyed; and similarly with the drunkard.' Another possible meaning is: 'Do not become involved in the degrading business of keeping pace with a glutton or a drunkard.' Gunn's translation yields quite a different sense: 'If thou sit with a glutton, eat with him, then depart (?). If thou drink with a drunkard, accept (drink) and his heart shall be satisfied. Refuse not meat when with a greedy man. Take that which he giveth thee; set it not on one side, thinking that it will be a courteous thing' (p. 63). In this case the advice is: 'Regulate your eating and drinking habits according to your company.' Or perhaps: 'The rule is moderation, but in exceptional circumstances, as when eating with a glutton or drinking with a drunkard, it is expedient to fall in with his habits.'

The instruction not to boast about one's physique or to issue challenges to contemporaries is concluded with the thought that this is to tempt fate unnecessarily. 'One knoweth not what may chance, what God doeth when he punisheth' (Erman, p. 67). The remaining piece of advice recommends circumspection, composure and economy of utterance. Gunn (p. 62) translates: 'The cautious man flourisheth, the exact one is praised; the innermost chamber openeth unto the man of silence. Wide is the seat of the man gentle of speech; but knives are prepared against one that forceth a path, that he advance not save in due season' (for the corresponding thoughts in *Ptahhotep*, see above pp. 54f., 60f.). Progress along the path of success will not be made by using the elbows, and taciturnity with a calm bearing is a mark of strength.

C. *MERIKARE*

A. H. Gardiner, *JEA* i (1914), pp. 20–36; A. Erman, *op. cit.*, pp. 75–84; *ANET*, pp. 414–18.

There is one respect in which this differs obviously from *Ptahhotep*. It is addressed by a Pharaoh to his son, and there is no doubt that the form of address is more than a literary convention. Thus, while it may be supposed that the father-son form of address in *Ptahhotep* does not preclude us from regarding it as a general educational manual for statesmen, we are bound to conclude that *Merikare* is more particular in character, that it is written against the background of a particular reign and that much of its advice has a special application to an heir-apparent. Merikare reigned in the intermediate period between the Old and Middle Kingdoms, from *c.* 2180 BC, and his father who gives him the advice was one of the kings of Herakleopolis who ruled contemporaneously and in competition with the kings of the eleventh dynasty of Thebes. Even if the historicity of the document is called in question (cf. Gardiner, pp. 35–36), the fact remains that the composition has been set in the reign of a Herakleopolite king and has been deliberately fashioned as a period piece. The circumstances of this Pharaoh's reign are recorded in some detail, and his advice to Merikare is formulated in the light of his particular historical experiences.

The idea of order which has already been discussed in connection with *Ptahhotep* is prominent in *Merikare*. One passage describes the activity of the sun-god in upholding the order: 'Well-directed are men, the cattle of the god' (Gardiner, p. 34). Every care has been taken for their welfare; the monster of chaos was destroyed by the god at the time of creation (cf. *ANET*, p. 417, n.49). Man has been made in the image of the god, who has breathed the breath of life into his nostrils. The sun-god gives light for men and sails across the sky that he may keep them under constant scrutiny. He makes his dwelling in a temple so that he may hear their weeping and cries for help, and he has furnished them with magic as a protective weapon.

All the resources of nature exist for the sake of men's needs, and rulers are appointed for their protection and good government. 'He made for them rulers (even) in the egg, a supporter to support the back of the disabled' (*ANET*, p. 417). Erman translates: 'He made for them rulers from the womb, a supporter to support the back of the weak' (p. 83).

Man's life is set in the framework of a comprehensive order – a harmonious integration of nature and society. With the phrase 'rulers in the egg' or 'rulers from the womb' should be compared: 'The (Lord of) the Two Banks is a wise man. The king and lord of courtiers cannot be a fool. He is (already) wise when he comes forth from the womb. (*The god*) has distinguished him ahead of a million lands' (*ANET*, p. 417). These are the only passages in *Merikare* which hint at the uniqueness of the Pharaoh and his transcending of human limitations. It should be noted, however, that it is the sun-god, the first king of Egypt, and not the Pharaoh who is represented as the pivot of the order in nature and society. 'Thus the whole universe was a monarchy and the king of the world had been the first king of Egypt. The function had devolved upon his son and successor, Pharaoh' (Frankfort, p. 53).

In *Merikare* it is the humanity rather than the deity of Pharaoh which comes to view. His father speaks as a fallible man and admits that he has been in error; on this Wilson remarks that confession of error was very exceptional for any Egyptian, particularly for the Pharaoh (*ANET*, p. 416, n.17; p. 417, n.44). The Pharaoh, who is normally represented as the fountainhead of order, can be the perpetrator of disorder (cf. Anthes, p. 22). Moreover, he addresses his son as a man rather than a god, and gives him advice of a like kind to that intended for would-be statesmen in *Ptahhotep*. Despite the theological doctrine that the Pharaoh was a god, he was none the less a man and had to live as a man in human society. Consequently he, too, had to have regard to the wisdom of his ancestors and so he is instructed to be a craftsman in speech and to copy his fathers. Of him who is a craftsman in speech it is said that he commands the most effective of all weapons. 'They who know his wisdom do not attack him, and no [*misfortune*] occurs where he is. Truth comes to him (fully) brewed in accordance with the sayings of the ancestors' (*ANET*, p. 415). Erman translates: 'Truth comes to him fully kneaded after the manner of that which the forefathers spake' (p. 76, cf. Frankfort, p. 82). Gardiner translates: 'Truth comes to him in pure essence like the sayings of the Ancestors' (p. 25). For Gardiner (p. 25, n.9) and Wilson the precise point of the metaphor is not the kneading and shaping of barley loaves in connection with the process of brewing (so Erman, p. 76, n.1), but the final product of the process, that is, a quintessential brew of wisdom has already been prepared. Erman takes the point rather to be: 'The task of kneading has already been done for you, for truth already worked up into shape is before you in the ancient writings.' 'Copy thy fathers and thy ancestors' (*ANET*, p. 415) then underlines this advice. It says, in effect, that the models of wisdom exist and are available for study. It is not necessary to be creative or original. 'Open, that thou mayest read and copy (their) wisdom' (*ANET*, p. 415). The Pharaoh, like his statesmen, is dependent on the wisdom of past generations – a wisdom which is the fruit of experience.

If the Pharaoh is to be effective, he must be just and beneficent, and the emphasis is laid on a positive fulfilment of the demands of the order rather than on efforts to safeguard it by defensive or repressive measures. This justice must begin at home, and the king should set his own house in order and earn the respect of those whose knowledge of him is more profound than that of the general public. Those who live with him can observe him in all his moods when the doors of the palace are shut to the outside world. 'Uprightness of heart is fitting for the lord. It is the forepart of the house that inspires respect in the back' (*ANET*, p. 415). The 'back' is the servants' quarters (*ANET*, p. 415, n.5).

Erman translates: 'It is the inside of a house that inspireth the outside with fear', and he glosses this with 'your good example in the palace influences your officials all over the country' (p. 76, n.6). According to Wilson, the instruction points to the need of a Pharaoh to win the respect of those who serve him in a personal capacity, but Erman takes the point to be that the quality of the Pharaoh's domestic administration has repercussions on the government of his entire realm.

To dispense at all times the full measure of justice which is due to his subjects, and to maintain a deep concern for their welfare, is presented as a higher conception of upholding the order than a habitual resort to punitive measures. 'Do justice whilst thou endurest upon earth. Quiet the weeper; do not oppress the widow; supplant no man in the property of his father; and impair no officials at their *posts*' (*ANET*, p. 415).

The instruction, 'Foster thy younger generation, that the residence city may love thee' (*ANET*, p. 415), would seem to be particularly directed towards securing a steady flow of recruits into the army (*ANET*, p. 415, n. 13), but its more general intention is to urge that the future lies with the younger generation and that they should be nursed for responsible office and encouraged with early promotion. 'Make thy officials great, advance thy [*soldiers*], increase the younger generation of thy [follow]ing, provided with *property*, endowed with fields and rewarded with cattle' (*ANET*, p. 415). In being just, the Pharaoh has to show boldness and initiative. Thus he is not to be influenced by a man's pedigree in assessing his fitness for promotion and responsibility. The only criterion of promotion is to be ability and aptitude for the post which has to be filled. 'Do not distinguish the son of a man (Erman, p. 78, 'the son of one of high degree'; Gardiner, p. 27, 'the son of a noble') from a poor man, (but) take to thyself a man because of the work of his hands' (*ANET*, p. 415; Gardiner, p. 27 'because of his capacity').

This enlightened attitude towards the upholding of justice will save the king from the too anxious or zealous discharge of a defensive role and from falling a prey to unreasonable suspicions or vindictiveness. 'Be on thy guard against punishing wrongfully' (*ANET*, p. 415). The king should exercise a wise restraint in the matter of punishment and should resist the temptation to justify repressive or coercive measures on the ground that they are necessary to the security of the state. He should not be obsessed with such fears, and should recognize that within very wide limits the order will take care of itself and does not tolerate too much interference. 'Be not evil: patience is good. Make thy memorial to last through the love of thee. . . . God will be praised as (thy) reward' (*ANET*, p. 415; cf. Erman, p. 76, 'Be not evil, it is good to be kindly'; Gardiner, p. 25, 'Be not evil; good is willingness of heart'). Again: 'Do not kill a single one that comes close to thee, when thou hast shown him favour: the god knows him. He who prospers on earth is one of them (cf. *ANET*, p. 418, n. 55; Gardiner, p. 35, n. 3), and they who follow the king are gods' (*ANET*, p. 418). Gardiner is puzzled by this. Wilson thinks that it is the wildest exaggeration of majesty. Either serving the Pharaoh is like being one of the gods, or the king's followers will become gods after death. Could it have something to do with the confidence in the smooth working of the order to which *Ptahhotep* gives expression? Success and eminence are a true measure of worth and a man finds the place in the order for which the gods have fitted him.

Nevertheless, vigilance in guarding the integrity of the state is the Pharaoh's duty. He should reinforce his boundaries and *frontier patrol* (*ANET*, p. 415; Gardiner, p. 26, 'thy boundaries and thy borders') and act with speed and severity in putting down seditious elements in the population. The kind of person who attracts popular support for his seditious policies – especially when he entices the young into becoming his partisans – is pointing a dagger at the vitals of the state and deserves death. The effect of his activities is to create two factions among youth, since he attracts some and repels others, and the solidarity of society is thereby damaged (*ANET*, p. 415).

While clemency is generally recommended in the administering of justice, the imposition of capital punishment is not to be shirked when the safety of the state is at stake. 'Do not slaughter: it is not of advantage to thee. (But) thou shouldst punish with beatings and with arrests; this land will be (firmly) grounded thereby – except (for) the rebel, when his plans are discovered, for the god knows the treacherous of heart and the god condemns his sins in blood' (*ANET*, p. 415). Wilson remarks that treason against the state was the one capital crime and that the Egyptians, not wishing to lay the responsibility on the Pharaoh, stated that the sentence was a divine vengeance (*ANET*, p. 415, n.6).

Anthes (pp. 17–20) has remarked that the belief in the divine order is not asserted so robustly in *Merikare* as in *Ptahhotep*. He seems to say that while the teaching of *Ptahhotep* assumes that the order operates fully and instantaneously in the here and now, that of *Merikare* supposes that the concept of order only achieves completeness in the hereafter. We might suppose from this account that we have a situation in *Merikare* somewhat similar to that which obtains in the Jewish apocalyptic literature, where everything hinges on an act of judgement in the beyond – a retrospective forensic settlement which will redress all the injustices for which there was no redress in a this-worldly context. This, however, would be misleading. The judgement at death to which *Merikare* refers is not necessitated by the breakdown of order; it is not postulated because the concept is no longer credible. On the contrary it is part of the order – its consummation. Frankfort cites the following passage from Merikare: 'Put not thy faith in length of years, for the gods regard a lifetime as but an hour. A man remains over after reaching the haven of death. His deeds are laid beside him for all treasure. Eternal is the existence yonder. A fool is he who has made light of it. But he who has reached it without wrongdoing shall continue yonder like a god, stepping forward boldly like the Lords of Eternity' (p. 118; *ANET*, p. 415).

Frankfort points out that where the judgement of the dead is discussed in serious theological terms it is part and parcel of the concept of order. 'Whether the Great God of the Old Kingdom inscriptions represents the king Re, or Osiris, is immaterial. All of these vindicated Maat. But just because the Egyptians believed justice and truth to be part of the cosmic order, there could be no question of judgement of all the dead in the sense which biblical religion gives to that conception. For the Egyptian, the righteous man was in harmony with the divine order and there the matter ended. This view, which does away with a formal judgement altogether, has great dignity' (pp. 117f.).

Frankfort's emphasis is right, but I am not certain that there is a complete absence of references to a formal judgement of the dead in the passage from *Merikare* which he has partly cited. On the words, 'The council which judges the deficient, thou knowest that they are not lenient on that day of judging the miserable, the hour of doing (their) duty' (*ANET*, p. 415), Wilson remarks: 'The reference is to a judgment after death by a tribunal of gods, at this time under the presidency of the sun-god, later with Osiris as the judge' (*ANET*, p. 415, n.10). On 'Do not trust in length of years' he says: 'The judges of the dead remember all sins no matter how long the time may be' (*ANET*, p. 415, n.11, cf. Erman, p. 77, n.9). Finally, to 'his deeds are placed beside him in heaps' he adds the explanatory gloss 'as legal exhibits' (*ANET*, p. 415, n.12; cf. Erman, p. 78, n.1). Nevertheless, I agree with Frankfort that the judgement which takes place at death does not presuppose an order which has been inoperative in a this-worldly context. Its function is rather to clear up finally the unresolved ambiguities of a man's relation to the order, and to reveal to him in a moment of truth the ultimate worth of his life measured against the demands of the order.

Yet there is an unmistakable shift in emphasis in *Merikare* as compared with *Ptahhotep*, and in so far as Anthes has called attention to this he has performed a valuable service. In both compositions, unjust measures are seen as ineffective measures. In *Merikare*, however, it may only be in the last analysis – in the light of the hereafter – that this is fully demonstrated. The reality of the order is as robustly asserted in *Merikare* as in *Ptahhotep*, but the obviousness of its workings is no longer taken for granted. If there is a loss of confidence, it is the doubt whether a man can know with certainty *now* how he is related to the order. If he infringes it, the consequences may not be immediately obvious (Gese, pp. 17f.).

This, too, is being said in *Merikare*, not of an ordinary individual but of the Pharaoh. The Pharaoh is fallible; he admits that he has acted in error and warns his son that the consequences of having acted wrongly must be suffered. If the king should go through life with the mistaken belief that he is immune from the consequences of his injustices and they do not recoil on him, he will be made to realize in the beyond that at no time did he breach the integrity of the order with impunity; that in so far as his actions were in conflict with it they resulted in his own diminishment, while the order remained whole. So Merikare is advised: 'The council which judges the deficient, thou knowest that they are not lenient on that day of judging the miserable, the hour of doing (their) duty. It is woe when the accuser is one of knowledge. Do not trust in length of years, for they regard a lifetime as (but) an hour. A man remains over after death and his deeds are placed beside him in heaps' (*ANET*, p. 415).

Thus a man cannot be deprived by arbitrary or violent action of the place in the order for which he has an intrinsic fitness. 'Do not kill a man when thou knowest his good qualities . . . (his) soul comes to the place which it knows. It does not miss the ways of yesterday. No magic can oppose it, (but) it reaches those who will give it water' (*ANET*, p. 415). The intention of this is not to establish an antithesis between the injustice of this world and the justice of the next. Both worlds belong to the same order, and in both justice is the rule. The point of view here is not so much that all injustices will be redressed at death as that there is a relationship between worth and status which nothing can abrogate. It may seem to be abrogated, but this abrogation will ultimately be seen as illusory, although perhaps only in the light of the hereafter. 'There is no river that permits itself to be concealed; that is, it breaks the [*dam*] by which it was hidden. (So) also the soul goes to the place which it knows, and deviates not from its way of yesterday' (*ANET*, p. 417).

Some of the advice given in *Merikare* is similar in character to the contents of *Ptahhotep*. The instruction, 'Advance thy great men, so that they may carry out thy laws' (*ANET*, p. 415), supplements what *Ptahhotep* has to say on the relation between power and wealth. It is necessary that men in high office should not be exposed to the corrupting influence of bribes, and they are far less vulnerable to these pressures or to subtler deviations from probity if all their material comforts are more than adequately met with the material rewards which accompany high office. 'He who is rich does not show partiality in his (own) house. He is a possessor of property who has no wants. (But) the poor man does not speak according to what is right for him. It is of no avail to say: "Would that I had!". He is partial to him who possesses rewards for him' (*ANET*, p. 415; similarly Erman, p. 76 and Gardiner, p. 26).

It would be fair to say that the horizons of the order are wider in *Merikare* than in *Ptahhotep* and that the dimension of the hereafter comes into much greater prominence. Hence the warning against covetousness in *Merikare* runs as follows: 'He who is covetous when other men possess is a fool, (because) [life] upon earth passes by, it has no length. Happy is he who [*is without*] sin in it' (*ANET*, p. 415). This is orientated differently from the corresponding warning in *Ptahhotep*. The emphasis is on the transitoriness of life and possessions, and the gaze is turned towards the beyond. The order in *Ptahhotep* is complete without reference to the hereafter, and the rigorously intellectual procedures of statesmanship make a major contribution to its functioning. The operation of the order can be seen and understood in this-worldly terms, and there is no appeal to the light of eternity for a final elucidation of its inner workings. This is not to say that in *Merikare* it is *now* inoperative, but only that men may not be aware of how it reacts when they infringe it and may remain in a state of ignorance about the degree of their positive participation in the order until the moment of truth is attained in the hereafter.

It is with this shift of emphasis that the piety of *Merikare* is to be connected. Of piety in this sense there are no traces in *Ptahhotep* except perhaps for a sentence in the closing paragraph: 'Mayest thou reach me (i.e., in the next world), with thy body sound, and with the king satisfied with all that has taken place' (*ANET*, p. 414). But in *Merikare* reverence for the god is enjoined, and the rites of religion feature prominently (*ANET*, pp. 416f.). The hereafter impinges on the present, and even now one must prepare for it. 'A single day gives for eternity, and an hour effects accomplishment for the future. The god is aware of him who works for him' (*ANET*, p. 416; Gardiner, p. 28, 'an hour makes beautiful for futurity'; Erman, p. 79, 'an hour doeth good to futurity').

The service of the god is not exhausted in building monuments, participating in rites and mysteries, furnishing sacrifices and votive inscriptions. 'More acceptable is the character of one upright of heart than the ox of the evil-doer' (*ANET*, p. 417). And it is he who lives the good life which is more that the punctilious observance of the external rites of religion – important though these are – who can confidently prepare for a blessed hereafter. 'Enrich thy house of the West; embellish thy place of the necropolis, as an upright man and as one who executes the justice on which (men's) hearts rely' (*ANET*, p. 417).

D. FORM OF *PTAHHOTEP* AND *MERIKARE*

(i) Ptahhotep

The main formal elements are easily distinguishable and show a high degree of stability. They occur again and again and are intrinsic to the formal structure. Yet they are not combined in accordance with any consistent formula and the pattern varies from one directive to another. It is evident that in this respect *Ptahhotep* does not have a tight or precise formal structure.

The main element of form is the imperative, which may be positive or negative, or a jussive or a virtual (polite) imperative ('thou shalt', 'thou shalt not'). The individual topic may contain a single imperative or a plurality of imperatives, and the latter may be organized in more than one series with motive clauses and/or consequential clauses separating one series from another. In If thou art one of those sitting (*ANET*, p. 412) there are six imperatives, in If thou art a man of intimacy (*ANET*, p. 413) seven, and in If thou art a man of standing, thou shouldst found thy household (*ANET*, p. 413) eight. For the other topics translated in *ANET* the figures are one, three, three, two, two, three, one, one, one.

In one case the imperative is elucidated by exegesis or explication. In If thou art a man of standing (p. 414) the exegesis of 'summon thy resources for good' is 'If thou art silent . . . *stick*'. It would be possible to understand this passage as motivation (see below), but 'summon thy resources for good' is a directive whose precise application is not clear and which, in the first place, needs elucidation rather than recommendation. The imperative is the principal constituent of form, because it issues the note of authority and makes a claim for receptivity and obedience. The priority of those attitudes on which prologue and epilogue dwell is therefore reflected in the form of the individual directives which communicate guidance not in statements, but in commands.

Another important formal characteristic of *Ptahhotep* is the conditional clause, and all except three of the individual directives translated in *ANET* begin with a conditional clause. In *Ptahhotep* one conditional clause preceding the imperative is normal, but there is one example of several conditional clauses. 'If thou art a man of standing . . . and producest a son . . . if he is correct . . . if he takes care of thy property . . . seek out for him every useful action' (*ANET*, p. 413). The function of the conditional clause is to define the condition or circumstances in which the imperative(s) applies. The conditional clause (or a 'when' clause) has a similar function in legal and omen formulations, and in every case it serves the ends of precise definition. It is self-evident that this is an important consideration in a legal formulation, for it is a principal concern of legal draftsmanship to define in as watertight a way as possible the circumstances in which a law applies (Ex. 21f.; G. R. Driver and J. C. Miles, *The Babylonian Laws*, vol. ii, 1955; A. Alt, *KS* i, 1953, pp. 278–332). As for the interpretation of omens, since this was regarded as an exact science, the correlations between observations and what they signified were set out by means of a conditional clause followed by a principal clause as in the so-called casuistic legal formulations (W. G. Lambert, *Babylonian Wisdom Literature*, 1960, henceforth *BWL*, p. 110).

The next element of form to which I call attention is the motive clause, whose function is to recommend the imperative(s) and demonstrate its reasonableness. In *Ptahhotep* the reasoning by which the imperatives are recommended is normally extended beyond the limits of a single clause and the clauses are asyndetic – the conjunction 'for' is not explicit. The following examples will make the position clear.

(*a*) In IF THOU ART (NOW) IMPORTANT (*ANET*, p. 414), the imperative is followed by a single asyndetic motive clause ('Thou are not behind . . . to whom the same has happened').

(*b*) In IF THOU ART A MAN OF STANDING (*ANET*, p. 413), the imperative is followed by two asyndetic motive clauses ('He is thy son . . . for thee' and 'Thou shouldst not . . . from him').

(*c*) In DO NOT BE COVETOUS (*ANET*, p. 413), there are three asyndetic motive clauses, 'Greater is . . . the strong' (for) 'he is a mean person . . . *fruits of conversation*' (for) 'it is (only) . . . into a contentious man'.

(*d*) In IF THOU ART A LEADER (*ANET*, p. 412), 'Justice is great, and its appropriateness is lasting' is an asyndetic motive clause which is further explicated by 'it has not been . . . property of my father'.

(*e*) Similarly, in IF THOU ART ONE OF THOSE SITTING (*ANET*, p. 412), 'No one . . . in the heart' is an asyndetic motive clause and 'As for the great man . . . would *complain of* it' is extended comment.

(*f*) Again, in IF THOU ART A POOR FELLOW (*ANET*, p. 413), 'property does not come of itself' is an asyndetic motive clause which is amplified by 'It is their law . . . while he is asleep'.

(*g*) In 'If thou art one to whom petition is made' (*ANET*, p. 413), 'A petitioner . . . for which he came' is an asyndetic motive clause which is further elucidated by 'He is rejoicing . . . a soothing of the heart'.

(*h*) In IF THOU DESIREST (*ANET*, p. 413), 'It does not go well . . . where that is done' is an asyndetic motive clause and what follows, although it is in part obscure, is supporting motivation. There follows another imperative ('Do not do it') supported by an asyndetic motive clause, a consequential clause (which I shall discuss below) and another asyndetic motive clause. The two motive clauses are 'it is really an abomination' and 'As for him . . . prosper with him'.

(*i*) A similar pattern is found in IF THOU ART A MAN OF STANDING THOU SHOULDST FOUND THY HOUSEHOLD (*ANET*, p. 413). The imperatives are followed by an asyndetic motive clause, 'She is a profitable field for her lord'. Then the imperatives are resumed and are supported by what is perhaps an asyndetic motive clause ('Her eye is her stormwind'). Finally comes a jussive followed by an asyndetic motive clause, 'it means keeping her long in thy house'.

(*j*) In SATISFY THY CLIENTS (*ANET*, p. 413), 'As for him . . . a *ka* of robbery' is an asyndetic motive clause and 'A proper *ka* . . . satisfied' is expanded comment. 'One does not know . . . the morrow' is another motive clause and 'If misfortunes . . . trouble' is supplementary argument.

(*k*) In IF THOU ART SEEKING OUT (*ANET*, p. 414), 'If what he may have . . . still a friend' is extended motivation connected with the preceding imperatives. The second series of imperatives are then followed by two asyndetic motive clauses, '(for) His time has never failed to come, (for) he cannot escape from him who predetermined him'.

The prominence of this formal element in *Ptahhotep* reflects the importance which is attached to demonstrating that the imperatives are reasonable. They do not have the character of naked or arbitrary commands; the authoritative aspect of the teaching is strongly emphasized, but care is taken to show that there are good reasons why the teaching can be inculcated with such assurance. In bulk the argument at least matches the imperatives, and the formal arrangement may be taken as an indication that there is an intrinsic balance between authority and reasonableness.

This would be a confirmation of a point which I have tried to make in a somewhat different way, namely, that the educational process which the Instruction serves goes much deeper than the learning of certain rules by rote. The apprentice statesman has to learn to respect the political sagacity which is the deposit of the experience of statesmen of the past, but this is not the full extent of his participation in the mental habits of these men and the intellectual climate in which they lived and worked. His intellectual kinship with them is more intense and intrinsic, and in the attaining of this educational goal the acquisition of balance and judgement is as important as respect for the authoritative principles of statesmanship.

The function of the motive clause is to show that the imperative(s) is reasonable and the function of the consequential clause (another element in the form of *Ptahhotep*) is to show that the imperative(s) is effective. Obedience to them will then facilitate the securing of the objectives which are desiderated. The following examples of consequential clauses ('and so') occur in *Ptahhotep*.

(*a*) In IF THOU ART ONE OF THOSE SITTING (*ANET*, p. 412), 'Laugh after he laughs' is followed by two consequential clauses, 'and (so) it will be very pleasing to his heart, and (so) what thou mayest do will be pleasing to the heart'. This is then followed by an asyndetic motive clause ('No one can know what is in the heart') and extended motivation.

(*b*) In IF THOU DESIREST (*ANET*, p. 413), there is the sequence: imperative, asyndetic motive clause, consequential clause. 'Do not do it – it is really an abomination – and (so) thou shalt be free from sickness of heart every day.'

(*c*) In BOW THY BACK TO THY SUPERIOR (*ANET*, p. 414), the sequence is: imperative, two consequential clauses, two asyndetic motive clauses. 'Bow thy back to thy superior, thy overseer from the palace. (And so) thy household will be established in its property, and (so) thy recompense will be as it should be, (for) opposition to a superior is a painful thing, (for) one lives as long as he is mild . . .'

(ii) MERIKARE

The number of imperatives occurring in a series varies from one to seven. DO JUSTICE WHILE THOU ENDUREST UPON EARTH (*ANET*, p. 415) contains seven and [IF] THOU [FINDEST A MAN] (*ANET*, p. 415) five. The single imperative is common in *Merikare*, and the positive preponderates over the negative. In DO JUSTICE, four of the seven imperatives are negatives, but there are only a few other cases of negatives. 'Be not evil' (*ANET*, p. 415); 'Do not kill a man' (*ANET*, p. 415); 'Do not trust in length of years' (*ANET*, p. 415); 'Do not distinguish the son of a man from a poor man' (*ANET*, p. 415); 'Do not (deal) evilly with the southern region' (*ANET*, p. 416); 'Do not say that he (the god) is weak of heart' (*ANET*, p. 417); 'Do not kill a single one that comes close to thee' (*ANET*, p. 418).

In the course of a single topic the imperative(s) may lead on to motive, final or consequential clauses and then the imperatives be subsequently resumed. Thus we find the following patterns in *Merikare*:

(*a*) [IF] THOU [FINDEST A MAN] (*ANET*, p. 415): a series of conditional clauses, five imperatives, two asyndetic motive clauses; imperative(s) (missing), two consequential clauses(?), asyndetic motive clause (I am assuming that THE CONTENTIOUS MAN IS A DISTURBANCE TO THE CITIZENS is not a new topic but an asyndetic motive clause connected with the preceding imperatives).

(*b*) ADVANCE THY GREAT MEN, SO THAT THEY MAY CARRY OUT THY LAWS (*ANET*, p. 415): imperative, final clause, asyndetic motive clause, extended motivation, three asyndetic motive clauses; imperative, final clause, two asyndetic motive clauses. The second imperative (jussive) really begins a new topic, 'Speak justice in thy (own) house'.

(*c*) DO JUSTICE WHILST THOU ENDUREST UPON EARTH (*ANET*, p. 415): seven imperatives, asyndetic motive clause, imperative, consequential clause, 'except' clause, extended motivation; imperative, extended motivation; imperative, two asyndetic motive clauses, extended motivation. I have assumed that 'The council which judges the deficient . . . is one of knowledge' is part of the argument associated with 'Do not kill a man when thou knowest his good qualities'. It may, however, be a preamble to the following imperative, in which case it is an example of motivation anticipating the imperative rather than, as is usual, coming after it.

(*d*) FOSTER THY YOUNGER GENERATION, THAT THE RESIDENCE CITY

MAY LOVE THEE (*ANET*, p. 415): imperative, final clause, imperative, two asyndetic motive clauses; three imperatives.

(*e*) MAKE MONUMENTS . . . FOR THE GOD (*ANET*, p. 416): imperative, two asyndetic motive clauses, explication of motive clauses; three imperatives, asyndetic motive clause; imperative, two asyndetic motive clauses; jussive, motive clause.

Conditional Clause

The most marked formal difference between *Ptahhotep* and *Merikare* is the paucity in the latter of the conditional clause which precedes the imperative(s). It is only in the opening paragraphs that the 'if' clause appears (Gardiner, p. 24, 2, 3, 5; *ANET*, p. 415). In [IF] THOU [FINDEST A MAN], a series of conditional clauses precede the imperatives.

Motive Clause

(*a*) Imperative(s) with one motive clause:

1. 'Do not distinguish the son of a man from a poor man . . . (for) every skilled work should be practised according to the . . . of the lord of a strong arm' (*ANET*, p. 415).

2. 'Protect thy frontier and build thy *fortresses*, (for) troops are of advantage to their lord' (*ANET*, pp. 415–16).

3. 'Make the offering-table flourish . . . (for) it is an advantage to him who does it' (*ANET*, p. 416).

4. 'Let thy statues be transported into a distant country . . . (for) only a sick man *is free* (*from*) *some hostility*, and the foe within Egypt is never calm' (*ANET*, p. 416).

5. 'Embellish thy place of the necropolis . . . (for) more acceptable is the character of one upright of heart than the ox of the evildoer' (*ANET*, p. 417).

6. 'Give the love of thee to the whole world; (for) a good character is a remembrance' (*ANET*, p. 418).

7. 'Establish thy boundaries and thy *frontier patrol*, (for) it is good to act for the future. Respect a life of attentiveness, (for) (*mere*) *credulity* will (lead) to wretchedness' (*ANET*, p. 415).

(*b*) Imperative(s) with two motive clauses:

1. 'Make thy monuments to endure . . . (for) a single day gives for eternity . . . (for) the god is aware of him who works for him' (*ANET*, p. 416).

2. 'Do not kill a single one that comes close to thee . . . (for) the god knows him, (for) he who prospers on earth is one of them, and they who follow the king are gods' (*ANET*, p. 418).

Extended Motivation

This may take the form of expansion or explication of a motive clause:

1. 'Make monuments . . . for the god, (for) that is what makes to live the name of him who does it, (for) a man should do what is of advantage to his soul' (*ANET*, p. 416). What then follows ('the monthly service . . . bread in the temple') spells out the general statement of the second motive clause.

2. 'Do not kill a man when thou knowest his good qualities' (*ANET*, p. 415) is supported by the argument 'He who reads . . . the place which it knows'. Then, 'It does not miss the ways of yesterday. No magic can oppose it, (but) it reaches those who give it water' is further comment on '(his) soul comes to the place which it knows'. 'The council which judges the deficient . . . one of knowledge' is an argument connected with the original imperative, 'Do not kill a man . . .'.

3. 'Do not trust in length of years, for they regard a lifetime as (but) an hour, (for) a man remains over after death, and his deeds are placed beside him in heaps' (*ANET*, p. 415). 'However, existence yonder is for eternity . . . like the lords of eternity' contains further reflections on the subject matter of the two motive clauses.

Final Clauses

These are more frequent in *Merikare* than in *Ptahhotep*, and the usual pattern (see above pp. 79f.) is: imperatives, final or consequential clause, motive clause.

1. 'Be a craftsman in speech, (so that) thou mayest be strong, (for) the tongue is a sword to [*a man*], and speech is more valorous than any fighting, (for) no one can circumvent the skilful of heart' (*ANET*, p. 145). 'They who know . . . sayings of the ancestors' is extended comment on the two motive clauses.

2. 'Advance thy great men, so that they may carry out thy laws, (for) he who is rich does not show partiality to his own house' (*ANET*, p. 415). The motive clause is further elucidated by, 'He is a possessor

of property . . . rewards for him'. Then follow three asyndetic motive clauses which depend on the original imperative: '(for) great is a great man when his great men are great, (for) valiant is the king possessed of courtiers, (for) august is he who is rich in his nobles'.

3. 'Mayest thou speak justice in thy (own) house, (so that) the great ones who are on earth may fear thee, (for) uprightness of heart is fitting for the lord, (for) it is the forepart of the house that inspires respect in the back' (*ANET*, p. 415).

4. 'Act for the god, (so) that he may act similarly for thee' (*ANET*, p. 417) is further elucidated by 'with oblations . . . to thy name'. Then follows a motive clause, '(for) the god is aware of him who acts for him'. 'Well-directed are men. . . . For the god knows every name' should then be regarded as extended motivation describing the beneficent régime of the sun god and supplying reasons why he should be served with offerings and votive inscriptions.

5. One example of imperative, final clause, consequential clause should be noted: '*Open* thy face, (so) that thou mayest be raised as a man, (and so) thou shalt reach me, without having an accuser' (*ANET*, p. 418).

6. 'Do not slaughter, (for) it is not of advantage to thee, (but) thou shouldst punish with beatings and with arrests, (and so) this land will be (firmly) grounded thereby, except (for) the rebel, when his plans are discovered, for the god knows the treacherous of heart, and the god condemns his sins in blood' (*ANET*, p. 415). Here we have an imperative, a motive clause, a polite imperative, a consequential clause, an 'except' clause. 'For the god . . . his sins in blood' gives reasons why the rebel is excepted from the general proscription of capital punishment, i.e., it elucidates the 'except' clause.

E. *AMENEMHET*

ANET, pp. 418f.; A. Erman, *op. cit.*, pp. 72–74; B. Gunn, *op. cit.*, pp. 65–71.

I do not intend to enter into great detail on the question of the historicity of this document, since the small use which I make of it is not affected by problems of authorship. It purports to be the advice which Amenemhet I, the first Pharaoh of the twelfth dynasty (*c.* 2000 BC) gave to his son and successor, Senusert I, whom he made his co-regent in the twentieth year of his reign. F. Ll. Griffith (*ZAeS* xxxiv, 1896, pp. 35f.) and A. H. Gardiner (*Mélanges Maspero* i, 1935–8, pp. 495f.) associate the piece with this occasion, while Maspero, De Buck and Gunn hold that what is represented rather is that Pharaoh tenders this advice after his death.

A crux is the phrase 'a message of truth' (*ANET*, p. 418) which Maspero (*Les Enseignments D'Amenemhait Ier à son fils Sanouascrit Ier*, 1914, p. xii) supposes to be a dream or revelation, to be classed with those prophetic dreams or revelations by which the gods, of whom the dead Pharaoh was one, revealed their thoughts to men (similarly De Buck, *Mélanges Maspero*, i, p. 849 and B. Gunn, *JEA* 27, 1941, pp. 2–6).

De Buck also takes into account the ascription of the work to the scribe Khety in a nineteenth-dynasty manuscript (*Hieratic Papyri in the British Museum*, Third Series, ed. A. H. Gardiner, 1935, i, pp. 43f.; ii, plates 20–21), and on this Wilson says: 'This passage must be treated as a valid or as a misapplied tradition that a scribe Khety composed the present text' (*ANET*, p. 418, n.1).

The work was popular as an exercise for schoolboys during the period of the New Kingdom (xviii-xxth dynasties, *c.* 1580–1085 BC) and it is to this that it owes its preservation. Only a small part of it has those formal characteristics which I have analysed in the compositions already studied, and in so far as the Instruction genre can be defined by these formal criteria, *Amenemhet* has not the same title as *Ptahhotep* and *Merikare* to be classed as Instruction. On the other hand, there are certain affinities between *Amenemhet* and *Merikare*. Both are decidedly occasional in character; both contain elements of historical reminiscence and reflection which relate particularly to the respective reigns of the two Pharaohs. The difference in this respect is that even the considerable block of material in *Merikare* which has this occasional character (*ANET*, pp. 416–17) is interspersed with imperatives, so that it retains something of the character of Instruction.

Thus in connection with the observations on the Southern Region the following instructions are given in *Merikare*: 'Do not (deal) evilly with the southern region.' 'Be lenient.' 'Satisfy thyself with thy (own) bread and beer.' 'Do not injure the monument of another' (*ANET*, p. 416). Out of reflections on policies pursued towards the Bedouin come the following instructions: 'Do not trouble thyself about him', i.e., do not take too seriously the annoyance caused by the Bedouin (*ANET*, p. 416). 'Dig a dyke against [half] of it and flood half of it', i.e., the east delta region. 'Guard against *encirclement by* the retainers of an enemy. . . .' 'Build structures in the Northland' (*ANET*, p. 417).

This most obscure part of *Merikare* gives an account of political conditions in Egypt during the Pharaoh's reign and comments on the various problems with which he had to deal. Partly it is a record of achievement, but it also contains an exposition of the policies pursued and even a frank admission of error (*ANET*, p. 417). The king has learned through the experience of ruling how particular situations can best be managed, and he gives his successor the benefit of his wisdom, for he may find himself exercising rule in similar political conditions.

The scope of the Instruction which is given in *Amenemhet* is extremely narrow and can be summed up in a few words: 'Trust no man.' 'Hold thyself apart from those subordinate to (thee), lest that should happen to whose terrors no attention has been given. Approach them not in thy loneliness. Fill not thy heart with a brother, nor know a friend. Create not for thyself intimates – there is no fulfilment thereby. (Even) when thou sleepest, guard thy heart thyself, because no man has adherents on the day of distress' (*ANET*, p. 418).

The remainder of the work narrates in some detail the experiences which led Amenemhet to so sombre a conclusion. The Pharaoh ought not to count on the loyalty of any subordinate. He is in a situation of utter isolation – beleaguered and in constant danger. These are the sober realities of his condition and, if he is to survive, he must cultivate a suspicious nature. Not even when he goes to sleep should he relax his vigilance. Amenemhet has experienced perfidy and betrayal and has lost his capacity for trusting other men. Loyalty has become for him a hollow word and he advises his successor that its existence should not be taken for granted. The Pharaoh lives in a jungle and fights for survival against the attacks of wild beasts. It appears that Amenemhet's taste of betrayal has left behind a permanent bitterness. For him there is no new point of equilibrium; he cannot strike a new balance between trustfulness and vigilance, credulity and suspiciousness; he is all but unhinged. He has been so disillusioned and suffers such a sense of outrage and grotesque contradiction that he would be reduced to inner confusion and speechlessness were he not to express himself in a violent indictment of all men. Only with such a grim misanthropy can he face his betrayers and salvage something of his authority and self-esteem.

There is also an absurdity, a topsy-turvy aspect, about the whole affair, and this has contributed to Amenemhet's malaise. The incredible, irrational part of the matter is that a Pharaoh, possessed of athletic prowess and personal valour, who had shown such competence and beneficence, should have been undone by a squalid intrigue in his own palace (*ANET*, pp. 418f.). It is the bizarre disproportion of this state of affairs which urges him on to such an extremity of misanthropy. 'Had women ever marshalled the battle array? Had contentious people been bred within the house? Had the water *which cuts the soil* (ever) been opened up, *so that* poor men were frustrated at their work?' (*ANET*, p. 419). The opening words of this passage may contain a specific allusion to a harem intrigue, but in any case, the general intention of all three questions is to urge that the world is out of joint and that the unthinkable has come to pass. That women should command an army, that treachery should have been cherished by those inside the palace whose loyalty was most taken for granted, that anyone would sabotage the irrigation system on which the livelihood of the peasant depended – all three propositions are equally unthinkable (cf. *ANET*, p. 419, n.11).

There is no religious element in *Amenemhet* and in this respect it contrasts with *Merikare*. Nothing is said about order; no comment is passed about a régime of justice either in a this-worldly or an otherworldly setting. Amenemhet speaks simply about the absence of loyalty and the attitude to other men which is determined by this lack. The word 'god' appears twice, in both instances referring to Senusert who is said to have 'appeared as a god', i.e., to have become Pharaoh (*ANET*, p. 418). He is also designated 'seed of a god', i.e. son of a Pharaoh (*ANET*, p. 419). The statement: 'I made for myself a house adorned with gold' (*ANET*, p. 419) probably refers to the king's palace rather than to his tomb (*ANET*, p. 419, n.16). The Pharaoh boasts of its strength and durability ('made for eternity, prepared for *everlastingness*', cf. Erman, p. 74, n.7). This phrase does not, then, as might otherwise appear, describe the tomb which he has built as a provision for a blessed hereafter in view of his expectation of immortality.

As in *Merikare*, it is the humanity of the Pharaoh which is communicated by the portrayal. He has suffered as a man and has been the victim of cruel circumstance. He is lonely and friendless and must fight for survival with every man's hand against him. But the Pharaoh of *Merikare* is a much more developed political animal and gives more robust and practical advice. He gives the impression of being able to manage men and situations and has a relish for the art of politics. It may, by contrast, be doubted whether Amenemhet's advice to Senusert is of great practical value. A king whose misanthropy is so severe as to be almost pathological no longer has the mental poise which is indispensable for a ruler. Politics cannot be practised from a position of extreme isolation in the absence of positive elements of trust, co-operation and sociability. If Amenemhet's diagnosis of Egyptian society were to be accepted, the correct conclusion to be drawn would be that the Pharaoh's task had become impossible. What this document really reflects is a profound crisis of political confidence. This may have been no more than a personal crisis for Amenemhet precipitated by his experience of treachery. For him, at any rate, order had been replaced by chaos, and Egyptian society had become a jungle.

F. *DUAUF*

ANET, pp. 432–4; A. Erman, *op. cit.*, pp. 67–72.

The purpose of this composition (cf. the fictitious letters of the New Kingdom which purport to be a correspondence between schoolboys and schoolmasters, Erman, pp. 188–98; A. M. Blackman and T. E. Peet, 'Papyrus Lansing: A Translation with Notes', *JEA* xi, 1925, pp. 284–98) is to demonstrate the favoured position of the scribe or official *vis-à-vis* all the other professions. It is preserved in documents which, for the most part, belong to the nineteenth dynasty (1320–1200 BC), but the original derived from the Middle Kingdom or earlier (2150–1750 BC; cf. *ANET*, p. 432, Erman, p. 68).

This work (and also the other compositions which have been noted) is mostly taken up with a catalogue of the various trades and professions in which much is made of the drudgery, discomfort, toil, privations, dangers and degradation to which those who follow them are exposed. A wide range of occupations is reviewed, some of them demanding mainly manual labour and others a greater degree of skill and craftsmanship, but all of these callings in commerce, crafts, agriculture, fishing, army and temple are described as vastly inferior to the privileged office of scribe (cf. A. M. Blackman and T. E. Peet, pp. 288–90).

He who is diligent at school and masters the basic skills of reading and writing is equipping himself for the best of all careers. Failure to seize such an opportunity would be the height of folly, for the schoolboy stands on the threshold of privilege and preferment, and, if he perseveres with his studies, he will one day belong to an *élite* and will possess status in an atmosphere of refinement and elegance, where he is spared the fierce and undignified toil and competitiveness of other less dignified callings. 'But if thou knowest writing, then it will go better with thee than (in) these professions which I have set before thee. . . . A day in school is of advantage to thee. The eternity of its work is (like that of) the mountains' (*ANET*, p. 434). 'Behold, there is no profession free of a boss – except for the scribe: he is the boss' (*ANET*, p. 434). On this Erman says: 'This thought is the culmination of all that the scribe has previously been saying' (p. 71, n.1). 'The Renenut of a scribe is on his shoulder on the day of his birth. He reaches the halls of the magistrates, when he *has become a man*. Behold, there is no scribe who lacks food, from the property of the House of the King – life, prosperity, health! Meskhenet is (the source of) the scribe's welfare, he being set before the magistrates' (*ANET*, p. 434). As the slave is branded with his master's name, the scribe is branded from birth with the name of the goddess of fortune (Renenut). He is destined for preferment and privilege; Meskhenet, the goddess of birth and destiny, is the source of his welfare (*ANET*, pp. 434, n.24 and 25).

Similar sentiments are expressed in the Papyrus Lansing. The apprentice scribe is enjoined to spend the whole day in writing and the night in reading and to shun everything which would distract him from these disciplines (A. M. Blackman and T. E. Peet, p. 285). He is to cultivate the friendship of the roll and the ink palette, 'for that is pleasanter than must. As for writing, to him who knoweth it more profitable is it than any other profession; it is pleasanter than bread and beer, than clothing and oil, yea it is more pleasant than a heritage (?) in Egypt, than a sepulchre in the west' (p. 286). 'Let thine heart be understanding, thy fingers skilled, thy mouth apt (in) reading' (p. 287). 'Set thine heart on being a scribe, the goodly profession of thy destiny. If thou callest to one, a thousand answer thee. . . . Thou shalt be at the head of others' (p. 290).

These compositions have affinities in form and function with *Ptahhotep*, but they are concerned with the education of the scribe at a more elementary level. There can be little doubt that the setting is the scribal school. Both *Duauf* and *Lansing* follow a literary convention similar to that of *Ptahhotep* in that they are represented in their respective introductions as particular and not general compositions. *Duauf* is said to have been composed by Khety for his son Pepy, 'as he was journeying upstream (to) the Residence City, to put him into the Writing School *among* the children of officials, *in the lower part of the* Residence City' (*ANET*, p. 432). And Lansing is introduced as a work by the king's scribe *Nebmaʿrēʿnakht* for the benefit of his apprentice *Wenemdyamūn* (pp. 285, 287).

The demand for attentiveness, application and submissiveness to authority reappears in these works. 'Young fellow, thine heart is exceeding proud and thou dost not hearken when I speak' (Lansing, p. 286). 'I spend the whole day instructing thee, but thou dost not hear. Thy mind is like a public office, what I teach thee is not in thy heart' (p. 291). On this simile Blackman and Peet observe (p. 291, n.1): 'Where all things come and go and nothing stays.' 'Behold, it is good that thou send away the multitude and hear the words of officials (only). . . . When the scribe has been seen to listen, listening becomes a heroic quality. Thou shouldst combat words *which may be* against it. Let thy legs hasten as thou goest, (or) it *cannot be attained*. Associate with him *who leads the way* to it, and make friends with a man of thy (own) generation' (*ANET*, p. 434).

The teacher in *Lansing* alludes to the youthfulness of his apprentice: 'Even if I beat thee with every kind of stick, yet thou wouldest not hearken. If only I knew another way of doing it, I would do it for thee and thou shouldst hearken and thou shouldst be a man by virtue of writing, although thou hast not yet known woman' (pp. 286f.). The apprentice who is being addressed in these pieces is in the process of learning the basic skills of reading and writing. These are his passport to privilege and eminence; if he does not master them, the door is forever closed to him. The scribes are a *corps d'élite*, but those who would gain membership of it must possess this fundamental intellectual equipment.

The advantages enjoyed by the official are painted in the brightest colours, and the apprentice who is sternly directed to pursue his studies with singleness of purpose is offered as an incentive the glittering prospects of a career of unrivalled advantages and opportunities. Perchance he will be fortified to endure the hardness and drudgery of the basic academic disciplines by the thought that great prizes may be grasped by those who endure and win the mastery. So the schoolmaster is represented as writing to his pupil: 'I place thee at school with the children of the notables, to educate thee and to have thee trained for this aggrandizing calling' (Erman, p. 189).

There are one or two directives in *Duauf* which transcend this sphere of elementary education and which touch on the principles of statesmanship in a manner comparable to *Ptahhotep*. One deals with the correct ordering of relations with a (superior) official. He should be approached in accordance with protocol and, if he is engaged when one calls at his house on an errand, the correct thing to do is to wait patiently and deferentially until he is free. On no account should an attempt be made to claim his attention while he is occupied with another person. This would be a form of gate-crashing, and thus to infringe his privacy would show a lack of good taste and a disregard for proper procedure. There is also an obscure allusion to the need for reticence and for the careful choosing of words on the occasion of sitting at table with a (superior) official (*ANET*, p. 434).

Another instruction deals with the art of effective speech and the knack of speaking as the occasion demands. There is a time when the situation demands reserve and when little should be given away, so that an opponent should be kept guessing: 'He who hides his belly (is) one who makes a shield for himself' (*ANET*, p. 434). There is a time when open hostility has to be countered with bold and resolute speech. Whatever tone may be demanded by a particular set of circumstances, utterance should on every occasion be stamped with calmness, weight and authority: 'Be dignified, (yet) be not under awe' (*ANET*, p. 434).

The need for meticulous accuracy when acting as an envoy – an aspect of professional behaviour commented on by *Ptahhotep* – is again aired in *Duauf*, and the motivation of the instruction is the same in both. The messenger should communicate the mind of his master with a stringent exactitude. This does not require initiative nor originality, but a passion for accuracy and a scrupulous care to reproduce faithfully the mind of the master. This may be a subordinate role, but it is a test of character, and the person who does it well wins the confidence of his superiors and proves his fitness for the higher reaches of statesmanship. 'If an official sends thee on an errand, say it (just) as he said it; do not take away or add to it. He who leaves (*things alone*) creates jubilation. . . . (One) trusts in every good characteristic of his. There is nothing hidden from him; there is no *separating him from* any place of his' (*ANET*, p. 434).

Finally there is a fragment which appears to recommend abstemiousness and warns against gluttony in a manner similar to the directive in *Kagemni* which I have discussed above (p. 66).

G. FORM OF *DUAUF* AND *LANSING*

These are only in small part Instructions, but the following formal patterns of the genre appear in them.

(i) DUAUF

1. IF THOU GOEST TO THE REAR OF OFFICIALS (*ANET*, p. 434): conditional clause, imperative. Conditional clause, circumstantial clause, conditional clause, circumstantial clause, imperative. Polite imperative(?). The circumstantial clauses are an interesting feature of this pattern. Thus: 'If thou enterest in, while a householder is in his house, and (if) his *activity* is for some one else before thee, as thou sittest with thy hand to thy mouth, do not ask for something beside him.'

2. IF AN OFFICIAL SENDS THEE ON AN ERRAND (*ANET*, p. 434): conditional clause, three imperatives, asyndetic motive clause, explication of motive clause. '(One) trusts . . . place of his' is a further elucidation of '(for) he who leaves (*things alone*) creates jubilation'.

3. BEHOLD, IT IS GOOD THAT THOU SEND AWAY THE MULTITUDE AND HEAR (*ANET*, p. 434): two polite imperatives, motivation(?). Polite imperative. Jussive. Two imperatives. I am assuming that 'When the scribe has been seen to listen, listening becomes a heroic quality' supports the opening injunction to 'Hear'.

4. BE DIGNIFIED, (YET) BE NOT UNDER AWE (*ANET*, p. 434): two imperatives, circumstantial phrase, parenthetical comment on circumstantial phrase, circumstantial phrase, circumstantial clause. The two circumstantial phrases, which are arranged disjunctively, so that the imperatives are related to both of them, have a function similar to the conditional clause, which normally precedes the imperative(s). The passage could be reconstructed as follows: 'If thou art speaking words of reserve – he who hides his belly (is) one who makes a shield for himself – be dignified, (yet) be not under awe; if thou art speaking words of boldness, when one sits with thee in

hostility, be dignified, (yet) be not under awe.' 'He who hides . . . makes a shield for himself' is comment recommending reticence and guarded speech.

(ii) Lansing

1. Two imperatives. 'Set not thine heart on the playing-field(?), put behind thee throwing(?) and hurling(?)' (p. 285). 'Spend thy whole day writing with thy fingers and read by night' (p. 285).

2. Imperative, motive clause, extended motivation. 'Make thyself friends of the roll and the ink-palette, for that is pleasanter than must' (p. 286). 'As for writing . . . sepulchre in the west' gives further support to the imperative.

3. Three jussives, extended motivation, asyndetic motive clause, comment on motive clause. 'Let thine heart be understanding, thy fingers skilled, thy mouth apt (in) reading' (p. 287). 'As for writing . . . in his mouth continually' is in praise of writing and so is a recommendation of the second jussive. 'Joyful is the heart . . . scribe's profession' is an argument for all three jussives and 'it grows younger every day' is further comment on this asyndetic motive clause.

4. Imperative, asyndetic motivation (conditional clause and principal clause), asyndetic motive clause, final clause, asyndetic motive clause. 'Set thine heart on being a scribe, the goodly profession of thy destiny, (for) if thou callest to one, a thousand answer thee, (for) thou goest freely upon the road, so that thou dost not become like an ox to be handed over(?), (for) thou shalt be at the head of others' (p. 290). The final clause does not depend on the imperative, but on the second asyndetic motive clause.

5. Imperative, two final clauses. 'Put writing in thy heart, (so) that thou mayest protect thyself from hard labour of any kind, and (so that thou mayest) be a magistrate of high repute' (pp. 291f.).

6. Imperative, three final clauses, motive clause, comment on motive clause. 'Be a scribe, (so) that thy body may be bright, and (so that) thy hand become soft, and (so) that thou mayest not smoke(?) like a lamp as doth one whose body is weak, for there is no bone of man in thee.' The motive clause is perhaps to be related to the third of the final clauses rather than to the imperative. 'Thou art tall and weedy . . . thy body would be in evil case' is expanded comment on the motive clause.

H. *ANI*

ANET, pp. 420f.; A. Erman, *op. cit.*, pp. 234–42.

Like other works which have already been examined, this has the form of parental instruction, but, since father and son are both scribes (Ani and Khenshotep), and since the contents have a general educational character, we are probably entitled to conclude that the parental form is a literary convention and that this is really a school-text used in the education of scribes. It belongs to the period of the New Kingdom (1580–1085 BC) and is preserved in corrupt copies which derive from a later period (the dates of the main papyri are assigned by Wilson to eleventh to eighth century BC). The names Ani and Khenshotep belong to the period of the New Kingdom (Erman, p. 235).

A supreme virtue in the official is reticence and secretiveness. To discipline the tongue is an impressive demonstration of self-control. 'Do not talk a lot. Be silent, and thou wilt be happy. Do not be garrulous' (*ANET*, p. 420). It is unwise to be too frank with a stranger and to pass remarks in his presence which are critical or derogatory and which, if repeated to those in authority, would be damaging to the prospects of an aspiring official. One should not be drawn into making injudicious comments by the leading questions of a stranger. 'If a *passing* remark issuing from thy mouth is hasty and *it is* repeated, thou wilt make enemies. A man may fall to ruin because of his tongue' (*ANET*, p. 420). To speak well, a man must make strenuous efforts and summon all the forces at his command. Speech contains possibilities of both good and evil. Injudicious and ineffective speaking can be heard from even the best equipped of men and the mark of mature wisdom is the ability to recognize that what you are about to say would be better left unsaid and to suppress it before it is audible. There is much virtue in silence and the times for speaking are to be carefully chosen. 'The belly of a man is wider than a storehouse, and it is full of every (kind of) response. Thou shouldst choose the good and say them, while the bad are shut up in thy belly. . . .' (*ANET*, p. 420).

Discretion and deference are also demanded by Ani. It is important to show proper respect and to observe protocol in dealings with superiors, 'Thou shouldst not sit when another who is older than thou is standing, or one who has been raised higher in his rank . . . Go every day according to the prescribed way, that thou mayest walk (with regard to) precedence' (*ANET*, p. 420). The scribe must exercise discretion in relation to his friends and associates. He should avoid the 'hostile man' – perhaps the man whose attitude to authority is unsound. The person who is badly orientated socially, who has a chip on his shoulder, is to be avoided.

Friends should be sought among men of integrity whose qualities have been fully tested. 'Make to thyself a friend (rather) of one that is upright and righteous, when thou seest what he hath done(?) . . .' (Erman, p. 237). Friendship with a slave should be avoided, for it may lead to great embarrassment and to a painful and damaging conflict of loyalties. Deep personal feeling for a slave may be irreconcilable with membership of the established order. 'If one pursueth him in order to seize him (the owner of the slave), and to take away him (the slave in question) that is in his house, thou are wretched and sayest: "What am I to do?" ' (Erman, p. 237). An official should make himself scarce if he happens to be one of a crowd which seems on the point of getting out of hand. He cannot afford to be involved in any conflict with authority nor to appear to have associated himself with elements of disorder. 'Enter not into a crowd, if thou findest that it standeth ready for beating . . . that thou mayest not be blamed in the Court before the magistrates after the tendering of evidence. Keep thee far from hostile people' (Erman, p. 240).

Discretion or a sense of proportion may also take the form of respect for the privacy of friends or acquaintances. The confidences of friendship must not be betrayed, but the less that is known of irregularities in the private affairs of acquaintances the better. 'Enter not the (house?) of another. . . . Gaze not on that which is not right in (his?) house: thine eye may see it, but thou keepest silent. Speak not of it to another outside, that it may not become to thee a great crime worthy of death when it is heard (?)' (Erman, p. 236). It is difficult to form a firm opinion about the precise intention of this instruction. The thought may be similar to that already noticed in *Ptahhotep*: 'Do not suppose that the order requires you to defend it by exposing or informing on those who have received you as a guest into their homes.' Perhaps, however, the thought is not so coherent nor so elevated as this. The meaning may simply be: 'Avoid all associations which might compromise you and never attempt to publish scandal about acquaintances. The fact that they are acquaintances places you in a position of danger, and you may find that the tentacles of scandal will extend so far that you yourself will be caught in them.' Similarly: 'Guard thyself against aught that injureth(?) great people, by talking of secret affairs. If anyone speaketh (of them) in thine house, make (thyself) deaf. . . .' (Erman, p. 235).

There are a number of instructions which could be classed as prudential. It is fatal to fall for the charms of a foreign woman who is far away from her husband and who throws off all restraints while she sojourns among strangers. To have an affair with such a woman is to court disaster. 'Do not *stare at* (Erman 'wink? at') her when she passes by. Do not know her carnally: a deep water, whose windings one knows not, a woman who is far away from her husband. "I am sleek," she says to thee every day. She has no witnesses when she waits to ensnare thee. It is a great crime (worthy) of death, when one hears of it. . . .' (*ANET*, p. 420). Again: 'Go not after a woman, in order that she may not steal thine heart away' (Erman, p. 240).

Also in the realm of prudence is the warning against drunkenness which is uttered. It produces incoherent speech and incapability and destroys respect and competence. 'If there (then) cometh one to seek thee in order to question thee, thou art found lying on the ground, and thou art like a little child' (Erman, pp. 236f.).

Advice is given on how to manage a superior when his mood is bad. An official who is to succeed must have the knack of pouring oil on troubled waters. A superior whose temper has deteriorated should be mollified and not controverted; silence and submissiveness are the better part. It is important not to fall foul of him at such a time, for this may prove detrimental to subsequent career prospects. On the other hand, to have blunted the sharpness of his displeasure or taken the heat out of his anger by conciliatory words is to have acquired merit for the future. 'Answer not a superior who is enraged, *get out of his way*. Say what is sweet, when he saith what is bitter to anyone, and make calm his heart. Contentious words carry rods and thy strength collapseth. . . . He turneth about and praiseth thee quickly, after his terrible hour. If thy words are soothing for the heart, the heart inclineth to receive them. Seek out silence for thyself and submit to what he doeth' (Erman, p. 240).

Then there is the emphasis on home, wife and family. The official who is to bear the burdens of public life and give the impression that he is fit to wield power must have a stable home as the secure base of his operations. So the official is given instructions on how to lay out the land around his house: 'Make thou a garden-plot. Enclose thou (a bed of) cucumbers in front of thy plough-land. . . . And fill thy hand (with) every flower which thy eye may behold. One *feels the need of* them all, and it is good fortune not to lose them' (*ANET*, p. 420).

More fundamental is the advice to establish a good personal relationship with a wife. Officiousness and interference which breed irritation are to be avoided. If a wife is efficient, her efficiency should be acknowledged and she should be left to get on with her own business. A husband who has a competent wife should cultivate the habit of silent admiration and should avoid nagging and displays of bad temper. Harmony at home is a great blessing and should not lightly be impaired or destroyed. 'Do not say to her: "Where is it? Fetch (it) for us!" when she has put (it) in the (most) useful place. Let thy eye have regard, while thou art silent, that thou mayest recognize her abilities. How happy it is when thy hand is with her! Many are here who do not know what a man should do to stop dissension in his house. . . . Every *man* who is settled in a house should hold the hasty heart firm' (*ANET*, p. 421). It is good to marry young and to produce children, especially a son and heir: 'Beget [him] for thyself while thou art (still) young. Teach him to be a man. A man whose people are many is happy; *he is* saluted (respectfully) with regard to his children' (*ANET*, p. 420).

Still in the circle of the family are the instructions which inculcate respect for parents. A man owes a special debt of gratitude to his mother, who surrounded him with her protection in his early years, cheerfully performed all the chores of motherhood, and was careful for his nurture and education. A wholesome relationship with a wife will be encouraged by preserving a fresh recollection of a mother's labour of love. In relation to his wife and the home which he builds, a man should strive not to be unworthy of a mother's sacrifices nor to bring shame and sorrow on her head (Erman, p. 239). Indeed, respect for parents is a religious duty and the ritual demands of piety should be met. 'Offer water to thy father and mother who rest in the desert valley. . . . Omit not to do it, that thy son may do the like for thee' (Erman, p. 236).

Some of the remaining instructions help to round off the portrait of the ideal scribe. Since sweet reasonableness and the ability to communicate calm and cordiality are prime virtues, the official should be on his guard against the flaw of litigiousness. 'Go not in and out in the court of justice, that thy name may not stink' (Erman, p. 236). As a member of a learned profession, he should show marks of erudition, for men will respect him if he is thoroughly versed in the authoritative literature of his profession, and he will thereby increase in stature and weight as a counsellor. When opportunities for promotion present themselves, it is ability and not heredity which counts. 'Men do all that thou sayest, if thou art skilled in the writings. Devote thyself to the writings, and put them in thine heart, and then all that thou sayest is excellent. To whatsoever office the scribe is appointed, he consulteth the writings. There is no son for the superintendent of the treasury, no heir for the superintendent of the fortress . . . the offices which have no children . . .' (Erman, p. 238).

Finally, there is an obscure directive which cannot be interpreted with certainty, but which perhaps sets out the attitude to wealth which should be cultivated by the scribe. Wealth exists to provide bread for all, and not to encourage greed and self-indulgence among the few. To ensure an adequate supply of bread for all is the most elementary function of wealth. Wealth has more significance than the wealthy man; the rich man may not be rich for long. 'The man rich in the time of last year is a vagabond this year' (*ANET*, p. 421). Let him then be given to hospitality while he has the means and not be greedy to fill his own belly (*ANET*, p. 421).

With regard to the religious quality of *Ani*, Wilson has remarked that it reflects 'the later emphases of quietude, personal piety and ritual activity' (*ANET*, p. 420). Anthes (p. 28) sees evidence of the awakening of a warm personal relationship to God which can no longer remain satisfied with the concept of order, since this sets the living God at a remove from men. The piety of *Ani* seeks a meeting-place with God *now* in the practice of prayer, and not just a rendezvous with the eternal Judge at the moment of death. Anthes is perhaps building too much on one passage: 'The dwelling of god, its abomination is clamour. Pray thou with a loving heart, all the words of which are hidden, and he will do what thou needest, he will hear what thou sayest, and he will accept thy offering' (*ANET*, p. 420). Nevertheless, the testimony of this passage is impressive. It does suggest a climate of pietism; men pray in silence in the quietness of a shrine and bring their needs before God. This would seem to be very different from the severely intellectual concept of order, and the mediation of this order would seem to have given place to an unsophisticated piety, according to which men speak directly to God and remind him of their needs.

It would be unwise, however, to build too much on this passage. In other respects there are marked similarities between the piety of *Ani* and that of *Merikare*. The awareness of the other dimension of life in the Beyond which is lively in *Merikare* is also present in *Ani*. Duty to parents does not terminate with their death. 'Offer water to thy father and thy mother who rest in the desert-valley' (Erman, p. 236). This interest in death as a momentous event does not produce an imbalance of other-worldliness in *Ani*, any more than it does in *Merikare*. The now and the then are aspects of the total significance of existence. In view of the vocational character of *Ani* and the interest which it shows in equipping the scribe for his career, one can hardly say that it has any taint of valetudinarianism, even if it does resile somewhat from the robust this-worldliness of *Ptahhotep*. The uncertainty of man's tenure of life is strongly felt and so it is wise to be prepared for the visitation of death. 'Embellish thy place which is in the desert-valley, the pit which will hide thy corpse. Set it before thee as thy business, which is of account in thy eyes, like unto the great elders *who* rest in their *store-chambers*. No blame attaches to him who does it, (but) he is happy. Prepare thou likewise, and when thy messenger comes to thee to take thee, he will find thee prepared *to come* (*to*) the place where thou hast rest, saying: "Behold, he who prepared himself before thee is coming." Do not say: "I am (too) young for thee to take," for thou knowest not thy death. When death comes, he steals away the infant which is on its mother's lap like him who has reached old age' (*ANET*, p. 420).

The statutory religious festivals are to be kept, and the god is to receive the offerings which are his due. This insistence on the importance of external religious observance was prominent in *Merikare*. In *Ani* it is said that to disregard such rites is to risk the anger of God; to fulfil them is to earn his favour. Care should even be taken to secure attestation of one's participation in the rites (*ANET*, p. 420, n.2). 'Celebrate the feast of thy god and repeat it at its season. God is angry at them who disregard him. Have witnesses attending when thou makest offering *at* the first time *of doing it*. If someone comes to *require thy examination*, have them set on papyrus thy goings-down at this time. . . . Singing, dancing, and incense are his food, and to receive prostrations is his property (right). The god will magnify the name of him who *does it*' (*ANET*, p. 420).

One passage which certainly refers to the worship of the sun-god inculcates a healthy respect for the sphere of the numinous on the occasion of fulfilling religious rites. 'Make offering to thy god, and beware of sins against him. Thou shouldst not enquire about his form (i.e., the cult image, *ANET*, p. 420, n.7; Erman, p. 239). Be not (too) free with him during his procession. Do not approach him (too closely) to carry him. Thou shouldst not *disturb the veil*; beware of *exposing what it shelters*. Let thy eye have regard to the nature of his anger, and prostrate thyself in his name' (*ANET*, p. 420). Wilson (*ANET*, p. 420, n.8) supposes that the obscure '*exposing what it shelters*' is an allusion to the fact that the images of some gods were shrouded during their public appearances.

What follows is differently interpreted by Wilson and Anthes. Wilson translates: 'He shows (his) power in a million forms. (Only) they are magnified whom he magnifies. The god of this land is the sun who is on the horizon, and (only) his images are upon earth. If incense be given as their daily food, the Lord of Appearances will be established' (*ANET*, p. 420). Wilson glosses 'and (only) his images are upon earth' with the comment: 'Some of that approach to monotheism which appeared in later Egypt. The sun is the god, appearing in a myriad of forms, including his images' (*ANET*, p. 420, n.9). Anthes comments as follows on this phrase: 'This clear formulation of thought, which was fundamentally, perhaps, already old, is clearly directed against the efforts at religious reform like those of the heretic king Akhenaton (Amenophis IV, *c.* 1375 BC), who allowed only the actual sun-disc to have the value of God and denied and suppressed the forms and images of the old cult. We recognize in the words of Ani the spirit of a time in which this attempt at reform was not only suppressed externally, but in a more healthy fashion had inwardly been overturned' (p. 28). Erman's translation, 'The god of this land is the sun which is in the horizon, (but) his images are on earth' (p. 239) is compatible with this interpretation.

With Anthes' remarks should be compared those of Frankfort: 'Akhenaten adored but one power and refused to accept a multiplicity of answers and, again, the Egyptians did not acquiesce. His monotheistic zeal offended their reverence for the phenomena and the tolerant wisdom with which they had done justice to the many-sidedness of reality. Akhenaten's doctrine was execrated and forgotten a few years after his death' (p. 25).

Finally, I take up Anthes' point that *Ani* does not belong to the higher echelons of officialdom and that the work reflects the values and aspirations of one in a much less exalted station than those statesmen for whom *Ptahhotep* was designed. Anthes says: 'While the older rules for life were put into the mouths of the highest royal officials or even the king, the authors of these later Instructions are officials of different grades. The Instruction of *Ani* takes us into the affairs of the plain middle class. The father is a temple-scribe and the mother carries alone the nursing of the child. The possession or acquisition of a house or a garden is here the mark of an elevated status in life. To these presuppositions corresponds the fact that in the whole book nothing is said about the relation of a man to his inferiors. In this respect many of the rules of *Ani* have their special emphasis, namely that a man should avoid everything that would bring him into conflict with his superior' (pp. 25f.). Anthes tends to overstate his case here, especially in the last point which he raises. Behaviour towards a superior is touched on in *Ptahhotep* and the treatment of this topic in *Ani* does not demonstrate the differing provenance of the two works. Even the most ambitious and able official must begin at least some rungs away from the top of the ladder, and the right way to manage superiors is a matter of general concern for all officials. Anthes may be right in supposing that *Ani* is addressed particularly to those of modest attainment in the scribal hierarchy, but in so far as *Ani* and *Ptahhotep* are both educational manuals for scribes (i.e., officials), they have much in common.

I. FORM OF *ANI*

1. Erman, p. 235: imperative, conditional clause, imperative. 'Guard thyself against aught that injureth (?) great people, by talking of secret affairs. If (anyone) speaketh (of them) in thine house, make (thyself?) deaf . . .'

2. TAKE TO THYSELF A WIFE (*ANET*, p. 420): imperative, circumstantial clause, final clause. Imperative, circumstantial clause. Imperative, asyndetic motive clause, explication of motive clause. '*He is* saluted (respectfully) with regard to his children' expands on 'a man whose people are many is happy'.

3. CELEBRATE THE FEAST OF THY GOD (*ANET*, p. 420): imperative, imperative, asyndetic motive clause. Imperative, circumstantial clause. Conditional clause, imperative, extended motivation. 'Singing, dancing and incense. . . . The god will magnify the name of him who *does it*' is a recommendation of the opening imperatives: 'Celebrate the feast of thy god and repeat it at its season.'

4. Be on thy guard against a woman from abroad (*ANET*, p. 420): imperative. Imperative. Imperative, asyndetic motive clause, explicatory comment on motive clause. The motive clause is virtually a metaphor. The imagery and its application are simply laid alongside each other ('a deep water whose windings one knows not, a woman who is far away from her husband').

5. Go not in and out in the court of justice (Erman, p. 236): imperative, final clause.

6. Do not talk a lot (*ANET*, p. 420): imperative. Imperative, consequential clause. Imperative.

7. The dwelling of god, its abomination is clamour (*ANET*, p. 420): preamble. Imperative, three consequential clauses. The preamble ('The dwelling of god, its abomination is clamour') argues for the imperative ('Pray thou with a loving heart, all the words of which are hidden') and so has a function similar to the motive clause which normally follows the imperative.

8. Offer water to thy father and thy mother (Erman, p. 236): imperative. Imperative, final clause.

9. Take not upon thyself(?) to drink (Erman, p. 236): imperative, extended motivation.

10. Embellish thy place (*ANET*, p. 420): imperative. Imperative, asyndetic motive clause. Imperative, consequential argumentation. Imperative, motive clause, explication of motive clause. 'When death comes, he steals away the infant which is on its mother's lap like him who has reached old age' expands on 'for thou knowest not thy death'.

11. Keep thyself far from a hostile man (Erman, p. 237): imperative, imperative. Imperative, circumstantial clause. The circumstantial clause following the imperative (cf. no. 3 above) has a function similar to the conditional clause preceding the imperative. The meaning of 'when thou seest what he hath done' is obscure, but we can perhaps paraphrase: 'If you have tested a man and found him upright and righteous, make him your friend.'

12. Make not a friend of the slave of another (Erman, p. 237): imperative, extended motivation.

13. I shall let thee know upon earth (*ANET*, p. 420): preamble. Imperative. Imperative. Imperative, final clause. Imperative, asyndetic motive clause.

14. Thou shouldst not sit (*ANET*, p. 420): polite imperative, circumstantial clause, final clause. 'If another who is older than thou

is standing, or one who has been raised higher in his rank, thou shouldst not sit' would be a fair paraphrase, with the circumstantial clause transformed into a conditional clause preceding the imperative (see no. 11 above).

15. MEN DO ALL THAT THOU SAYEST (Erman, p. 238): preamble. Imperative, imperative, consequential clause, asyndetic motive clause, explication of motive clause. 'There is no son for the superintendent of the treasury . . . the offices which have no children' develops, 'To whatever office the scribe is appointed he consulteth the writings'.

16. THOU SHOULDEST NOT EXPRESS THY (WHOLE) HEART (*ANET*, p. 420): polite imperative, consequential clause, extended motivation. Polite imperative, circumstantial clause. 'To let him discover thy speech against thee' is virtually a consequential clause, i.e., 'and so let him discover thy speech against thee'.

17. MAKE OFFERING TO THY GOD (*ANET*, p. 420): imperative, imperative. Polite imperative. Imperative. Imperative. Polite imperative. Imperative. Jussive, imperative, extended motivation.

18. DOUBLE THE FOOD WHICH THOU GIVEST TO THY MOTHER (*ANET*, p. 420): imperative, imperative, extended motivation. 'She had a heavy load . . . for three years *continuously*' is related particularly to the second imperative ('carry her as she carried thee').

19. WHEN THOU ART A YOUNG MAN (*ANET*, p. 421): three circumstantial clauses, imperative. Three jussives. The circumstantial clauses have a similar function to the conditional clause or clauses which more normally precede the imperative(s). Cf. no. 11 above.

20. THOU SHOULDST NOT EAT BREAD (*ANET*, p. 421): polite imperative, circumstantial clause, extended motivation. Imperative, extended motivation. The extended motivation following the second imperative expresses in a metaphor what was stated more prosaically after the first imperative. 'The course of the water of last year is gone, and it is in a different area this year. Great seas have become dry places, and sandbanks have become abysses.' That is, the tenure of wealth is extremely precarious, 'the man rich in the time of last year is a vagabond this year'.

21. ENTER NOT INTO A CROWD (Erman, p. 240): imperative, conditional clause, final clause(?). Imperative.

22. ACT NOT THE OFFICIAL OVER THY WIFE (Erman, p. 240, *ANET*, p. 421): imperative, conditional clause, explication of imperative. Jussive, final clause, extended motivation. 'Do not say to her: "Where

is it? Fetch (it) for us!", when she has put (it) in the (most) useful place' is explicative of 'act not the official over thy wife'.

23. THOU SHOULDST NOT PURSUE AFTER A WOMAN (*ANET*, p. 421): imperative. Imperative. According to Erman (p. 240), imperative, final clause.

24. ANSWER NOT A SUPERIOR (Erman, p. 240): imperative. Imperative. Imperative, circumstantial clause, consequential clause, extended motivation. Two imperatives.

The conditional or circumstantial clause following the imperative rather than preceding it is a special formal characteristic of *Ani*.

J. *AMENEMOPE*

ANET, pp. 421–4; F. Ll. Griffith, *JEA* xii (1926), pp. 191–231.

The following is a summary of the work:

Chapter 1 is a general introduction which enjoins receptivity and teachability.

Chapter 2 ranges over many topics and its apparent lack of unity makes it difficult to summarize but its gist is as follows: Do not rob or oppress the old and the weak. Do not use strong-arm tactics against the defenceless. Do not associate with those who intrigue and do not become their accomplice. Do not try feverishly to justify yourself when you know that you have deliberately injured a person. Give support and practical assistance to the man whose wrongdoing has brought him to a condition of destitution.

Chapter 3: Do not be provoked into impetuous speech. Refuse to be involved in a wrangle with a hot-tempered man. Do not be infected by his heat, and sleep on any rejoinder which you are tempted to make.

Chapter 4 contrasts the hot-tempered and the tranquil man. The one is a tree destined to be fuel for the fire, but the other is a tree planted in a garden which bears fruit.

Chapter 5 deals with tranquillity associated with honesty in the service of the temple. Do not be an embezzler in the temple service to satisfy your greed, for this is a theological as well as a moral flaw. The tranquil man does not strive too much to advance himself, and so he is not exposed to these temptations. He is content to place his life in the hands of Rē – to fulfil his appointed role in the order. Hold fast to the tranquil man and you will have life.

Chapter 6: Do not remove land marks or covet another's land. Cultivate your own fields and live by your own industry. Be content with what you have, for you can be prosperous only with what God gives you. Produce exacted by force and fraud is not a lasting asset. Poverty according to the will of God is better than wealth gained by oppressive self-assertion.

Chapter 7: Fate is immutable and every man has his appointed place in the order. No man is captain of his fate and it is vain that he should aspire to this role. Self-aggrandizement through exploitation is not the route to power and honour, for unjust gain evaporates and is no more. The way of life is the way of tranquillity.

Chapter 8: Cultivate a good reputation. Do not be a detractor and avoid speaking evil of others. Do not make a habit of exposing other people. If you have to judge another man, treat this as a matter of confidence and do not blab about it to all and sundry. Take every advantage of speaking well of a man. Advertise his virtues, but keep silent about his deficiencies.

Chapter 9: Do not associate with a hot-tempered man, for he is a breeding-ground of mischief, discord and bitterness. His tongue is his ruin. Do not be drawn into an argument with a superior, even if he is being deliberately provocative, for a polemical or abusive rejoinder may mean your ruin. Swallow your hot words.

Chapter 10: Do not affect affability or confidence, if this is not how you really feel. Do not be a dissembler; do not sever your heart from your tongue, for God hates lying and equivocation. There is a confidence which belongs to the man who knows that he is in the hand of God. Such a person scorns spurious posturings and is open and fearless in his relations with other people. His tranquillity makes him steadfast and immovable. He is free from the bondage of self-assertiveness.

Chapter 11 is an obscure chapter which apparently sketches the unenviable lot of a dependent and makes the point: 'Be content with your lot.'

Chapter 12: Be an honest steward and, if you are set over a man's affairs, do not betray the trust which he has set in you.

Chapter 13: As a scribe, do not use pen or tongue to do evil but to do good, for the praise and love of men are better than wealth.

Chapter 14 is obscure, but gives instructions on how to deal with a suitor. Do not show him excessive condescension, but do not repel him brutally.

Chapter 15: As a scribe use your pen to do good, for Thoth is your overseer. A scribe has his duty to his son, for his behaviour will have consequences for him.

Chapter 16: Do not falsify the balances nor diminish the measures and weights, for Thoth is the guardian of the balances.

Chapter 17: Do not employ tricks to falsify the corn measure. Do not be dishonest or oppressive in collecting harvest dues. Do not employ your legal expertise in order to engage in oppressive extortion.

Chapter 18: Be resolute, but do not talk too much nor strive too hard, for the hand of God cannot be forced. Avoid feverish fear about the morrow; do not try to do God's work for him. Do not make an exhibition of your innocence. Do not protest your righteousness. Leave the verdict on yourself to God. God has everything under control.

Chapter 19: Do not lie or equivocate when giving evidence in a law court.

Chapter 20: Do not be a perjurer. Judge fairly between man and man without respect of persons, for justice is of God. Do not falsify documents or falsify records. Do not expose yourself to God's anger over and above what Fate has in store for you. Do not misappropriate the property of others.

Chapter 21: Do not take the law into your own hands. Leave retribution to God. There is strength in silence; it inspires respect and fear. Consider the crocodile. Do not go around betraying confidences. One who blabs is not taken seriously by anybody. Silence may be more advantageous than inept speech. Do not try too hard.

Chapter 22: Let your opponent talk and treat him with respect. Do not rush in to counter him. Sleep on your riposte. Do not indulge in debating tricks. Do not be too eager to demonstrate your cleverness in 'managing the situation'.

Chapter 23: Great demands are made on the hospitality of an official, so do not indulge yourself at his expense. This is a facet of well-proportioned behaviour. Do not be a glutton and a guzzler on another man's expense account.

Chapter 24: Do not betray confidences. A secretary in the confidence of a superior must cultivate anonymity and discreetness and avoid publicity.

Chapter 25: Do not kick a man when he is down. Do not take advantage of the weak or abnormal. Your own lot is insecure and your fate unsettled until you reach the safety of the West.

Chapter 26: Do not become the drinking-companion of superiors, but be polite and helpful, for politeness and civility cost nothing and to antagonize another needlessly is dangerous.

Chapter 27: Give reverence and submission to an old person, for you are dependent on him for support and you should acknowledge your dependence as a hound does to his master.

Chapter 28: Be kind and beneficent to the widow and the stranger.

Chapter 29: Do not be officious and obstructive. You are in office to help people. If there is room in a ferry-boat, do not hinder people from coming on. Give a hand with the steering paddle. Do not charge fares for the poor.

Chapter 30: The scribe should be soaked in this teaching and adept at interpreting it for the ignorant. A distinguished career at the court lies open before the experienced scribe.

From the information supplied in i.13–ii.6, it is clear that Amenemope is not an official of the highest rank. He has not achieved the eminence of a Ptahhotep and does not exercise so decisive a political influence. He is in the administrative and not the political arm of the service, but he holds a responsible position. Griffith remarks: 'The titles attributed to the author, with the exception of i.13; ii.3, are not found in the monuments or in other papyri. They seem to be paraphrases in literary, poetical form. From them we learn that Amenophis was in charge of the land and of corn, but whether for the whole of Egypt or for a district only does not appear. He registered and leased land for the king and for "all the gods", and he raised and apportioned the corn-dues and perhaps saw to the distribution of the corn in payment of salaries or grants' (p. 226).

Amenemope thus transports us to the lower echelons of the scribal establishment as compared with *Ptahhotep*, but the end which is in view in the one as in the other is to educate the scribe for a successful career, and the closing words of *Amenemope* hint at what those who reach the pinnacle of the profession may expect:

> As to a scribe who is experienced in his office,
> He will find himself worthy (?) to be a courtier (xxvii. 16f.; Griffith, p. 224).

Thus while it is legitimate to point to what is distinctive about *Amenemope* as compared with the older examples of the Instruction, this exercise should not be carried too far. Griffith observes that no other Egyptian book of its kind makes so many concessions to the popular beliefs and local cults of the country, and that the teaching of *Amenemope* is full of religious sentiment (p. 230). Frankfort has supplied a valuable corrective to the trend of ascribing a too distinctive piety and ethos to *Amenemope* and thereby placing it in a category apart from the other examples of the Instruction (pp. 59f.; cf. Gese, p. 21). In its most fundamental features, *Amenemope* is fully in accord with these. It instructs the scribe along similar lines and it sets the office in the same theological framework. It is true that there are evidences of a personal piety which ill accords with the virtually impersonal concept of order which dominates *Ptahhotep*. Such a pietism admits the entrance of prayer:

> Thou shalt pray to the Aten when he rises,
> Saying: 'Grant me prosperity and health,'
> And he will give thee thy needs in life,
> And thou wilt be safe from fear (x.12–15; Griffith, p. 206).

Nevertheless *Amenemope* is pervaded by a demand for tranquillity set in a framework of Fate or Destiny, and in this it prescribes the same conditions for a successful career in the public service as do the other examples of the Instruction. In the last analysis, these agreements are more impressive and significant than the differences.

How is the tranquil or calm man portrayed in *Amenemope*? The gist of the portrayal is this: Do not try too hard. Do not engage in feverish self-assertiveness. Live within the limits which are fixed by Fate. Tranquillity has in it no admixture of weakness or softness, but, on the other hand, it is free from all delusions of grandeur. Whatever is extravagant or spurious in human attitudes or behaviour, even ostensible exhibitions of strength, is in reality a confession of weakness, for a man can only be effective in accordance with the order which defines the canons of effectiveness:

> God is (ever) in his success,
> Man is (ever) in his failure.
> The words which men say are one thing,
> The things which God doeth are another (xix.14–17; Griffith, p. 216).

There is thus a release from the disorganizing and destructive tensions of ambition, even for the ambitious official, for he can find repose in the paradox that the more he finds tranquillity and masters the urge to grab power by frantic self-assertiveness, the more he shows himself fit to be a man of power. There is strength in silence and weakness in garrulity or inept speech. The man who talks and talks will not be taken seriously by anyone, but the silent man inspires respect and fear (cf. H. Brunner, *op. cit.*, pp. 119–23).

Wrangling and loss of temper in debate are flaws, and the instinctive hot rejoinder should be avoided. The tranquil man will not speak if he suspects that his judgement has been impaired by the high temperature of a debate. He will sleep on his reply, turn the matter over in his mind in a cool hour and never give public expression to his mental discomposure. He will also understand that the realities of a situation can never be altered by posturing. He will not try to justify himself when he knows that he is in the wrong, nor will he suppose that lying and intrigue are suitable exercises for cleverness. He will not affect a vast confidence if this is not how he really feels, nor will he pretend affability in the presence of one whom he dislikes. The tranquil man scorns all such tricks. He is genuine and resolute, and his calmness and freedom from unbalanced egotism make him steadfast and immovable.

The tranquil man acknowledges the immutability of Fate and knows that he can be prosperous only with what God gives him. Poverty according to the will of God is better than wealth gained by oppression and dishonesty. Self-aggrandizement through exploitation is not the route to power and honour, for unjust gain evaporates and is no more. The way of life is the way of tranquillity.

The boat of the covetous is left (in) the mud,
While the bark of the tranquil sails (with the breeze). (x.10f.; Griffith, p. 206.)

There are two extremes in relation to Fate or the order which should be avoided. It is unnecessary to take up the cudgel on behalf of the order and to suppose that one's mission is to do God's work for him. The advice given in this respect is: God will look after the order, and so do not take it upon yourself to debunk reputations, expose villainy or exact retribution. At the other extreme, do not expose yourself to God's anger beyond what Fate has in store for you by sins against the order. Tranquillity has a positive, active content to which limits are set by a passive acceptance of Fate.

Verily thou knowest not the designs of God,
Thou canst not realize(?) the morrow.
Sit thee down at the hands of God;
Thy tranquillity will overthrow them (xxiii.8–11; Griffith, p. 220).

Beneficence, too, is a demand of the order and is obligatory on the official. He is not to rob or oppress the old, the weak or the abnormal, and he is not to use strong-arm methods against the defenceless. It is a scribe's duty to use his pen for good and not for evil; to divide the large debt of the poor man into three parts and to take away two of them, if it is in his power to exercise such clemency. Yet he is not to be a party to the falsification or forgery of documents to the detriment of the common weal. Even the destitute wrongdoer is not to be allowed to go under, but should be supported and sheltered, and special consideration is to be given to widows and strangers. The claim for kindliness possessed by the blind, the lame and the dwarf is noted in conjunction with a reference to Fate, so that benevolence, too, is set in a theological framework.

Verily man is clay and straw,
God is his fashioner;
He pulls down and builds up each day;
He makes a thousand dependents at his will,
[(or) He makes a thousand men into overseers(?),]
When he is in his hour of life.
How happy is he who hath reached the West,
When he is safe in the hand of God (xxiv.13–20; Griffith, p. 221).

Man does well to reckon with the precariousness and insecurity of his lot. If God has given him status and power, it is without security of tenure. He is subject to a reversal of fate; what has been built up may be broken down. Man is exposed to chance and change until the moment of death. Only when he has reached the West does he know that his life has come to an irreversible conclusion; he is safe in the hand of God and what he is at that moment he will be for ever.

That *Amenemope* still addresses itself to the education of the official is clear from the references to professional conduct which it contains. The operations which are mentioned reflect the office which was held by Amenemope (see above, p. 105), and take us into the administrative branch of officialdom, which is small beer compared with the high level of statesmanship which is reflected in *Ptahhotep*. Nevertheless, Amenemope is represented as an important official with high principles and a noble cast of mind. He recommends scrupulous honesty in the management of another's property. In the matter of collecting corn for the crown he condemns false weights and measures and supports his probity with piety. Thoth manifested as the ape is the God of the entire art of the scribe:

The Ape sitteth by the balance,
His heart being the plummet.
Where is a god so great as Thoth,
He that discovereth these things, to make them? (xviii. 1–3; Griffith, p. 214).

The corn measure is called the *waže*, i.e., the eye of Horus or Rē:

The bushel is the eye of Rē,
Its abomination is he who abstracts. (xviii. 23–xix. 1; Griffith, p. 215.)

Against falsification or forgery of documents and perjury, religious sanctions are invoked:

The beak of the Ibis is the finger of the scribe;
Beware of disturbing it.
The Ape dwelleth in the House of Khmûn,
(but) His eye travels round the Two Lands (xvii. 7–10; Griffith, p. 214).

The Ibis is a manifestation of Thoth, and Khmûn (Griffith, p. 214) is to be differentiated from Khnum, the god who shapes man on the potter's wheel or the moulder's table (Griffith, p. 229).

Secrecy and discretion are virtues in a secretary who has access to the confidences of a principal. Garrulity in an official is a weakness and a flaw, and blabbing is contemptible. An official who would prove himself fit for power and responsibility should not be gluttonous at the table of a superior. Still more important is his having a flair for good public relations; he should cultivate a good reputation and should be free from obstructiveness and officiousness. In this connection he should refrain from making barbed comments about other men. He should be generous in his estimates of others and not set himself up as a detractor or denigrator. He should know how to get the best out of men, how to avoid fraying their tempers or denting their self-esteem. The avenging Uraeus on the brow of Rē and the giant Apophis serpent, Rē's enemy, which both inspire fear, are juxtaposed to illustrate the gulf that exists between a good and a bad reputation.

Set thy goodness in the bowels of men,
That everyone salute thee;
(for) One acclaims Uraeus,
And spits on the Apophis-serpent (x.17–20; Griffith, p. 207).

The tranquil man, too, inspires fear like the crocodile, but only the wicked need tremble before him. To those who live by the rule of Rē he is the savour of life and welfare.

Part of the expertise of the well-endowed official is his sensitivity to what is the right degree of familiarity in his relations with his superiors, and his ability to regulate these relations with skill and finesse. Conviviality and excessive sociability are to be avoided. He should not become their drinking-companion, but he should not be too remote or convey the impression that he is deliberately keeping them at a distance. It goes without saying that deference, politeness and constructive co-operation are permanent elements of a good relationship. The official who has good stuff in him and who can take all this education and self-discipline to heart has excellent career prospects. If Fate has been kind to him and he is a man of weight and distinction – if he has *gravitas* – he is destined for the highest office of state:

As to a scribe who is experienced in his office,
He will find himself worthy (?) to be a courtier (xxvii. 16f.; Griffith, p. 224).

K. FORM OF *AMENEMOPE*

The special elements in the form of *Amenemope* as opposed to the other examples of the Egyptian Instruction which have been reviewed are the arrangement of the text in lines of poetry, the incidence of parallelism and the division into chapters (Griffith, p. 227). These additional features are also found in the examples of the Instruction contained in the biblical book of Proverbs (see below, pp. 262f.). Nevertheless, the basic syntactical elements of the *genre* are as faithfully reproduced by *Amenemope* as they are elsewhere, and its peculiarities do not demand a different kind of formal analysis from that undertaken in respect of the other specimens of the Instruction. Consequently the principle which I have accepted in the following analysis is that the form of *Amenemope* is basically syntactical in kind, and that if units larger than couplets are to be entertained, they should be determined by the lines of syntactical analysis.

Chapter 1: 6 couplets (Griffith: 3 quatrains)

1 3 imperatives.
2 Asyndetic motivation with antithetic parellelism.
3 Jussive, final clause.
4 Asyndetic motivation.
5 Asyndetic motivation depending generally on all preceding imperatives.
6 Same as 5.

Chapter 2: 12 couplets (Griffith: 2 quatrains, double quatrain, six-line stanza, couplet)

1 2 imperatives.
2 2 imperatives.
3 2 jussives.
4 2 imperatives.
5–8 An eight-line stanza consisting of extended motivation related to the preceding imperatives. Five lines connect with the imperatives in the first three couplets and three lines with the imperative in the fourth couplet.
9 Imperative, motive clause.
10 3 imperatives.
11 Imperative, final clause.
12 Either asyndetic motivation related to the imperatives of the fourth couplet or, more probably, a preamble to ch. 3.

Chapter 3: 6 couplets (Griffith: 3 couplets, quatrain, couplet)

1 2 imperatives.
2 2 imperatives.
3 Imperative, asyndetic motive clause.
4 Imperative.
5 Imperative, asyndetic motive clause.
6 Asyndetic motivation recommending the preceding instructions.

Chapter 4: 2 six-line stanzas (strophe and antistrophe)

Contrasted descriptions of the hot-tempered and tranquil man and, as such, reinforcing the instructions contained in ch. 3. Hence extended motivation.

Chapter 5: 8 couplets (Griffith: quatrain, double quatrain, quatrain)

1 2 imperatives, consequential clause.
2 Imperative, final clause.
3 Imperative.
4–6 } Extended motivation related to preceding imperative.
7 Preamble associated with following imperative, approximating to the motivation which normally comes after an imperative.
8 Imperative, two consequential clauses.

Chapter 6: 18 couplets (Griffith: 2 quatrains, double quatrain(?), 5 quatrains)

1 2 imperatives.
2 2 imperatives.
3–4 } Extended motivation.
5–8 } Imperative, motive clause, extended motivation.
9 Imperative, 'lest' clause.
10 Asyndetic motivation.
11 2 imperatives.
12 Imperative, asyndetic motive clause.
13 Imperative, 2 final clauses.
14 Asyndetic motivation ('better is . . . than').
15–18 } Resumptive of preceding couplet. The two final couplets have the form 'better is . . . than'.

Chapter 7: 13 couplets (Griffith: 4 quatrains, six-line stanza, quatrain)

1 Imperative, asyndetic motive clause.
2 Imperative, asyndetic motive clause.
3 Imperative, consequential(?) clause.
4 Asyndetic motivation.
5–8 } Explication of preceding couplet.

Chapter 8: 8 couplets (Griffith: quatrain, two six-line stanzas)

1–2 Imperative, final clause, motivation.

3–5 Imperative, consequential clause, consequential argumentation.

6 2 imperatives.

7 Conditional clause, imperative.

8 Imperative, circumstantial clause.

Chapter 9: 18 couplets (Griffith: couplet, 4 double quatrains, couplet)

1 2 imperatives.

2 2 imperatives.

3 2 imperatives.

4–5 2 imperatives, asyndetic motivation.

6, 7, 8, 9, 10, 11, 12, 13, 14, 15, 16, 17 Extended motivation describing the hot-tempered man and connected with the imperatives of the first couplet.

18 Imperative, 'lest' clause (resuming the instruction of the first couplet).

Chapter 10: 6 couplets (Griffith: 3 quatrains)

1 2 imperatives.

2 Imperative, circumstantial clause.

3 Imperative, asyndetic motive clause.

4 Imperative, final clause.

5–6 Imperative, motive clause, extended motivation.

Chapter 11: 11 couplets

1–2 2 imperatives, asyndetic motivation.

3, 4, 5, 6, 7, 8, 9, 10 Explication of preceding couplet, describing the unhappy lot of the 'dependent'.

11 2 polite imperatives.

Chapter 12: 5 couplets (Griffith: quatrain, 3 couplets)

1 2 imperatives.

2 Conditional clause, imperative, final clause.

3 2 imperatives.

4–5 Conditional clause, imperative, asyndetic motivation.

Chapter 13: 8 couplets (Griffith: 3 couplets, six-line stanza, 2 couplets)

1 Imperative, asyndetic motive clause.
2 2 imperatives.
3 2 imperatives.
4–6 Conditional clause, imperative. 2 imperatives, consequential clause, consequential argumentation.
7–8 Asyndetic motivation ('better is . . . than'), related generally to preceding imperatives.

Chapter 14: 5 couplets

1 2 imperatives.
2–3 Conditional clause, 3 imperatives.
4 2 imperatives, asyndetic motivation.
5 Imperative, asyndetic motive clause.

Chapter 15: 6 couplets

1–2 Imperative, final clause. Imperative, asyndetic motive clause. Imperative.
3, 4, 5, 6 Extended motivation related to preceding imperatives.

Chapter 16: 9 couplets (Griffith: 3 quatrains, six-line stanza)

1 3 imperatives.
2 2 imperatives.
3–4 Asyndetic motivation related to preceding imperatives.
5 Imperative, asyndetic motive clause.
6 Conditional clause, polite imperative.
7–9 2 imperatives, asyndetic motivation.

Chapter 17: 9 couplets (Griffith: 3 six-line stanzas)

1 Imperative, explication.
2 2 imperatives.
3 Imperative, explication.
4–6 Imperative, asyndetic motive clause, extended motivation.
7 2 imperatives, final clause.
8–9 2 imperatives, asyndetic motivation.

Chapter 18: 10 couplets (Griffith: 5 quatrains)

1–4 Imperative, asyndetic motive clause, extended motivation (inserting a line after xix.13, Griffith, p. 216).

5–6 2 imperatives, asyndetic motivation.

7–8 Extended motivation depending on the imperatives of the opening couplet.

9–10 3 imperatives, asyndetic motivation (antithetic parallelism).

Chapter 19: 6 couplets (Griffith: 2 six-line stanzas(?))

1 2 imperatives.

2 Imperative, circumstantial clause.

3 Imperative, explication.

4–6 Imperative, 'lest' clause, asyndetic consequential argumentation.

Chapter 20: 11 couplets (Griffith: quatrain, six-line stanza, 3 quatrains)

1 2 imperatives.

2 2 imperatives.

3–5 2 imperatives, asyndetic motivation.

6–7 Imperative, asyndetic motive clause, extended motivation.

8 Imperative, explication.

9 Imperative, explication.

10 2 imperatives.

11 Jussive, asyndetic motive clause.

Chapter 21: 9 couplets (Griffith: 2 quatrains, couplet, 2 quatrains)

1 Imperative, explication.

2 Imperative, explication.

3 Asyndetic motivation related to preceding imperatives.

4–5 Imperative, asyndetic consequential clause, asyndetic motivation.

6 2 imperatives.

7 2 imperatives.

8–9 Asyndetic motivation. The first couplet is associated with the immediately preceding imperatives, the second with the imperative of the fourth couplet.

Chapter 22: 7 couplets (Griffith: ten-line stanza, quatrain)

1 2 imperatives.
2 Imperative, circumstantial clause.
3 2 imperatives, asyndetic consequential clause.
4 Imperative, final clause. Imperative, consequential clause.
5 4 imperatives.
6 Asyndetic motivation related to preceding imperatives in a general way (cf. Griffith, p. 220).
7 Imperative, asyndetic consequential clause.

Chapter 23: 4 couplets

1–2 2 imperatives, asyndetic motivation.
3–4 2 imperatives, asyndetic motivation.

Chapter 24: 4 couplets

1 2 imperatives.
2 Jussive, 'lest' clause.
3 Preamble, imperative, 'lest' clause; equivalent to imperative, 'lest' clause, motive clause ('Beware lest thou neglect the heart, for it is the nose of God').
4 Asyndetic motivation related generally to the preceding imperatives.

Chapter 25: 6 couplets (Griffith: quatrain, six-line stanza, couplet)

1 3 imperatives.
2 2 imperatives, circumstantial clause.
3–6 Extended motivation.

Chapter 26: 8 couplets (Griffith: six-line stanza, 2 quatrains, couplet)

1–2 2 imperatives, couplet explicative of second imperative.
3 Imperative, asyndetic motive clause.
4 Conditional clause, imperative.
5 Imperative, circumstantial clause. Imperative.

6
7
8 Extended motivation. The first couplet appears to be specifically related to the instruction to help an old man. The second dwells on the advantages of having a civil tongue, the third on the virtue of far-sightedness. These are probably related to the advice on how to regulate social relationships with superiors.

Chapter 27: 6 couplets (Griffith: 2 six-line stanzas)

1 Imperative, motive clause.
2 Imperative, explication.
3 Asyndetic motivation referring to preceding imperatives.

4
5
6 Jussive, circumstantial clause. Jussive, circumstantial clause.
Extended motivation.

Chapter 28: 3 couplets

1 Imperative, circumstantial clause, imperative.
2 Imperative, final clause.
3 Asyndetic motivation related generally to preceding imperatives.

Chapter 29: 5 couplets

1 Imperative, circumstantial clause.
2
3 Conditional clause, polite imperative, asyndetic motivation.
4 2 imperatives.
5 2 imperatives.

L. *ONCHSHESHONQY*

S. R. K. Glanville, 'The Instructions of Onchsheshonqy', *Catalogue of Demotic Papyri in the British Museum*, vol. ii (1955); B. Gemser, *VTS* vii (1960), pp. 102–28.

Both Gemser and Glanville have indicated how *Onchsheshonqy* differs in respect of content from the other examples of the Egyptian Instruction. The criteria on which they fasten, although of a general character, are important, and provide a useful point of departure for the discussion of the text. Unlike the other texts, *Onchsheshonqy* is not located in the circles of the scribal establishment; it does not belong to the world of officials. While the others are all, more or less, occupied with the grooming of men for power and responsibility,

Onchsheshonqy reflects life in Egypt among a less exalted stratum of the community, where the stakes are not so high and where adjustment is effected within narrower horizons. Here ambition is muted and the impression of *per ardua ad astra* is not communicated. Those who are mirrored in *Onchsheshonqy* are not people of exceptional ability who aspire to become an *élite*; they are the solid people of the country-side who are strangers to the style and distinction of courtiers and officials.

The earthiness of *Onchsheshonqy* is unmistakable. It harks back to the soil and addresses itself to those who engage in the back-breaking tasks of cultivation and are resigned to the unpredictability of agri-culture. *Onchsheshonqy* prohibits the kicking at a palm tree by a donkey, lest it shake down the fruits (11.18), and the use of arable land for building purposes (14.22). It knows of the lean years when a cultivator ought to keep his schoolboy son away from the larder or storehouse (16.3). Perseverance, application and physical fitness are recipes for success, and a cultivator who is out of condition will not be up to his tasks (8.15, 10.8, 11, 14f.). A labourer ought not to be employed unless he produces more than he consumes in wages (22.19). Education is a severely practical process as defined by a farmer with an eye to equipping his son, so that he can take on the dour soil and the wanton elements and hold his own. Formal educa-tion will have to bow to the exigencies of the agricultural year and be fitted in when work is slack in the fields (17.23).

This should not be taken to mean that *Onchsheshonqy* has nothing in common with the other examples of the Instruction. If such an impression were communicated, it would only be partially true, although true in an important respect. The differences are more significant than the similarities and deserve more attention, but if resemblances are sought, they can be found without difficulty. In *Onchsheshonqy* the ability to curb the tongue is highly valued and a premium is put on timely, effective and well-disciplined utterance (7.23f.; 12.24). Even in the company of a wise man reticence may be the better policy (14.8), and at home, in relation to wife and domestic servants, secretiveness is a golden rule (13.16f.).

Onchsheshonqy, too, is concerned that a man should be good at public relations and should appear to the world as a congenial and impressive person (6.8). An important aspect of the correct ordering of relationships is the attitude which is struck towards a superior, and one should not presume to be too egalitarian or familiar (7.13; 9.13), while, at the other extreme, one should not become involved in litigation with him, unless a successful outcome is assured.

Similarly, in relation to wealth *Onchsheshonqy*'s teaching falls into a familiar pattern. Wealth is not possessed absolutely, but is administered for God, and all good fortune is from the hand of God (18.16f.; 20.6). Meanness, self-acquisitiveness and miserly hoarding are distortions associated with wealth (12.18; 15.7; 17.8), while its right use is giving to relieve need and not to receive acclaim (15.5f.; 17.7). Covetousness is a flaw, whether in the rich man who would be richer or in the poor man who covets another's affluence (6.10; 14.20).

There are some respects in which *Onchsheshonqy* recalls *Amenemope* in particular. It shows the same healthy respect for truth and integrity and roundly condemns equivocation, falsification and perjury (13.14f.; 16.13). It is impatient with the man who does not have the grace simply to say that he is in the wrong and who engages in an elaborate and perverse process of argument in an attempt to justify himself (9.10). And in the religious framework there are elements which *Onchsheshonqy* has in common with the other members of the Instruction genre. There is the paramountcy of fate (nothing happens except what God ordains) and the consequent insecurity and unpredictability of human existence (11.23; 12.5; 22.25). Fate is an irrational and inscrutable force which confronts man at the furthest limits of his existence. It blocks his way and bars his progress, and marks the point beyond which he cannot intelligently and purposefully control his own destiny; it puts every form of human boasting out of court (12.2f.). Fate is a sobering and chastening reality which cuts man down to his size and is unkind to megalomania. Arrogance in a small man is monstrous, and modesty in a great man fitting (7.19f.; 17.26).

All this is no more than a preliminary sparring with *Onchsheshonqy*; to engage more resolutely with the questions which are thrown up by this text it is necessary to give some attention to its formal structure. Glanville and Gemser have gone into this, and Gemser's analysis in particular is thorough and penetrating. He has not missed anything important, but he has not laid the emphasis in the areas which seem to me to be most significant.

The most important single fact is that there are almost as many statements in *Onchsheshonqy* as there are prohibitions or commands. The indicative occurs almost as frequently as the imperative, whether positive or negative. I have defined the Instruction in such a way that the imperative is of its essence. The imperative is a primary and indispensable element of its form. Thus almost half of *Onchsheshonqy* is not Instruction at all. It is not therefore homogeneous with respect to form as the other examples of the Instruction are. This is a straw in the wind, for the mixture of statement and command points to the popular character of *Onchsheshonqy* over against the specialized, professional character of the Instruction proper. The popular proverb has the form of a statement, and many of the statements in *Onchsheshonqy* are popular proverbs. Even its commands or prohibitions have, in some cases, something of the texture of the popular proverb; that is, they employ imagery or high concreteness of expression in a manner reminiscent of the popular proverb and not characteristic of the Instruction as encountered elsewhere.

In addition to statements and commands or prohibitions, *Onchsheshonqy* contains a group of sayings which are formulated optatively (10.11–25; 11.1–4; 25.14). These engage themselves with fundamental concerns, hopes and fears and indicate the limits within which the people whom the text had in view lived and had their being. The impression which is conveyed is that they asked for no more than the satisfaction of elemental necessities and were content that the material basis of their existence should not be threatened, and that fundamental human relationships should be undisturbed and uncorrupted (10.14f., 21f.; 25.14). There is an affecting and pleasing simplicity about this list of things desired, and it is an illuminating record of the measure of security and fulfilment which was hoped for and the mischances and calamities which were feared.

The feeling that *Onchsheshonqy* is an earthy book is here strongly reinforced. It is the order of nature, the seasons and the soil which monopolize attention and shape life for good or evil (10.17, 24). For those who stake all on the land and are naked and defenceless before the elemental insecurities, regularity is life and irregularity death. Existence is circumscribed by toil on the land and anxious preoccupation with the crops, and for aught else there is neither time nor energy. It is enough that the fields should be green and that the cow should receive her bull (10.18, 20). Even here, where the smell of the farmyard is so strong and the horizons of life so restricted, there emerges unexpectedly, among these bread-and-butter preoccupations, a wish which shakes itself free from this little world of the peasant and runs towards the furthest bounds of expectation. It is a characteristic Egyptian religious emphasis, but when it follows on wishes that the flood waters should not fail to arrive, that the fields may be green and that the cow may receive her bull, its effect on the reader is startling. 'O may life always succeed death' (10.25). This is no less the case, even if the way has been prepared by the preceding allusion to the established order of day and night. As the moon comes up after the sun has set, so may life always succeed death. It is not, however, certain that this association of ideas is intended.

In that part of *Onchsheshonqy* where the imperative is present, the formal structure is less developed than in the other specimens of the Instruction which have been reviewed. This is true despite the traces of literary refinement which may be detected here and there, such as the couplet with antithetic parallelism (8.9f.; 9.24f.; 11.21f.) or an antithetic structure within a single line (18.9, 23; 22.19, 20). In neither of these categories is the 'but' explicit. The simplicity of the structure, on the other hand, is shown by the circumstance that the directive is often communicated by a single imperative without subordinate clauses (6.17, 24; 7.5, 6, 7, 10, 12, 13, 19, 25; 11.23; 12.4, 14, 17, 21; 13.14, 17, 23, 24; 14.12, 19, 21, 22, 23; 15.14, 19; 16.3, 6, 12, 15, 16, 17, 18, 21, 23; 17.3, 4, 9, 14, 15, 16, 17, 25; 18.8; 21.17; 22.10, 11, 21; 23.22; 24.6; 25.8, 10, 11, 12, 13).

Then again, more than one subordinate clause is the exception rather than the rule and this runs contrary to what is normal in the other texts. The analysis of the directives with more than one subordinate clause is as follows:

7.9f.: imperative, conditional clause, asyndetic motive clause.
8.4–6: imperative, 2 asyndetic motive clauses.
8.7f.: imperative, 2 asyndetic motive clauses.
9.14f.: imperative, 'unless' clause. Imperative, 2 asyndetic motive clauses.
9.16f.: imperative, 2 asyndetic motive clauses.
11.19f.: imperative, 'lest' clause, asyndetic motive clause.
12.13f.: jussive, imperative, imperative.
15.21: 2 conditional clauses, imperative, asyndetic motivation.
16.13: imperative, circumstantial clause, 'lest' clause.
17.18–20: conditional clause, imperative, imperative (antithetic), asyndetic consequential clause.
19.11f.: circumstantial clause, imperative, asyndetic motive clause.
19.15–17: imperative, circumstantial clause, imperative, 2 asyndetic motive clauses.

A notable differential of *Onchsheshonqy* is the almost total absence of extended motivation. 22.21–25 is an interesting exception: 'Do not insult a nobleman, (for) when insult occurs fighting follows. When fighting occurs killing follows, and killing does not happen without God knowing, (for) nothing happens except what God ordains.' Here the extended motivation has a form akin to the 'chain syllogism' of which there is an example in the *Wisdom of Solomon*: 'The beginning of wisdom is the most sincere desire for instruction, and concern for instruction is love of her, and love of her is the keeping of her laws, and giving heed to her laws is assurance of immortality, and immortality brings one near to God' (6.17–19, *RSV*). However, the function of the chain in *Onchsheshonqy* is to construct a causal nexus; the function in the *Wisdom of Solomon* is partly this, but partly one of definition.

Onchsheshonqy is later than the other texts (it is dated by Glanville in the fifth or fourth century BC) and yet has a greater formal simplicity than they have. This combination of lateness and formal simplicity constitutes a challenge to the common form-critical procedure of equating simplicity of form with earliness and elaboration of form with lateness. Gemser has not missed the implications of *Onchsheshonqy* in this regard, as the following comments show: 'All this means a warning against constructing a straight line of development of Egyptian wisdom and proverbial literature. Its less developed products do not necessarily stand at the beginning. . . . One has to keep in mind also that in different circles and layers of society, different forms of thought and expression have been in vogue' (p. 128).

The last remark is particularly apposite, for even the part of *Onchsheshonqy* which is formally Instruction does not belong to the world of officialdom and aspiring statesmen as do the other examples of the genre (even *Amenemope*). It does not address itself to so specialized a constituency; it is popular, ordinary, humdrum. It does not give advice to a clientele of high calibre, who have expectations of eminence and power. It has to do with less distinguished individuals who have adjusted themselves to life at lower levels and whose claims to self-fulfilment are modest. The consequent difference in content has been commented on, but even more interesting are the differences of style, in forms of expression and, particularly, in the use of imagery. The instruction in *Onchsheshonqy* has something of the flavour of popular, proverbial utterance, and in this respect, too, it stands apart from the linguistic usage characteristic of the Instruction.

This enquiry will have to be pursued further, but in order to clear the ground for it some attention must first be given to the part of *Onchsheshonqy* which contains statements rather than directives, for the popular proverb is formulated as a statement, and, if the characteristics of the popular proverb are to be sought in *Onchsheshonqy*, this is where the search ought to begin. For the moment it can be said that *Onchsheshonqy* is not exclusively a medium for advancing the education of apprentice officials, and that it has the character of a more general and popular instrument of education. *Onchsheshonqy* is the only witness to this more popular function of the Instruction among the Egyptian representatives of the genre, and this should make us pause to consider whether the Instruction does not have an original association with the training of officials and only subsequently acquires a non-vocational and popular function. The lateness of *Onchsheshonqy* as compared with all the other specimens would suit this assumption.

The statements in *Onchsheshonqy* can be divided roughly into two kinds. There are those which fall into the category of plain statements and which are to be understood in a bare, literal way. These are prosaic communications and they set out to make observations in a straightforward and uncomplicated manner and in firm terms on particular topics. They are therefore specific in character and the limits of their applicability are clearly marked. Most of these statements are the fruits of observation and reflection and have the epistemological status of empirical generalizations which engage themselves with the field of human behaviour and relationships. A few give expression to sentiments of piety. Their matter-of-factness – the pedestrian character of their forms of expression – is the most important common factor, but this does not entirely exclude literary artifice and polish.

They may have the finished form of the wisdom sentence or aphorism, in which the results of disciplined and perceptive observations are gathered up and expressed with memorable finality in finely chosen words. They may employ such stylistic devices as antithetic balance or parallelism, the clustering of sayings which begin with the same word or which both begin with the same word and have a thematic coherence. Such clusters may be put down to subsequent compilation, but some, at any rate, of the clusters seem to have an intrinsic cohesiveness and a cumulative propriety to which such a view hardly does justice. But even where these statements have the character of sententious apophthegms, they are not marked by imaginative outreach. The scope of their applicability can be determined with some precision. It is possible to draw the boundary and to confine their relevance to the area which has been enclosed.

It is in this regard that they are so different from the second group. Here, in some ways, the facts are much more difficult to describe. Some of the statements in this group make some kind of sense if they are taken literally, but it is hard to resist the impression that this is a very wooden reading of them; they clamour for further interpretation. The very intensity of their concreteness or the particularity of their images confers on them a representative potential, gives them a leaning towards universality, and the sympathetic interpreter will not be satisfied with a prosaic and precise understanding of them. They are open to interpretation in the sense that limits cannot be set to the relevance and applicability of these sayings; the future lies open to them wherever their aptness is intuited. This combination of concreteness with openness to interpretation is characteristic of the popular proverb, and what we have here in *Onchsheshonqy* is proverbial in the sense which I have indicated.

Non-Proverbial Sentences

These statements are non-proverbial in relation to my definition of 'proverbial' (see above, pp. 22f.).

> 7.8: A servant who is not beaten is full of scorn.
> 7.19: The little man who behaves arrogantly is greatly detested.
> 7.20: The great man who behaves arrogantly is highly respected.

This should be regarded as a couplet with antithetic parallelism, although the 'but' is not explicit.

> 8.13: In fair weather or foul, wealth increases only by making the most of it.

There is an element of figurative language in this sentence. Instead of the more prosaic 'in favourable or adverse circumstances', the more picturesque 'in fair weather or foul' appears, but the statement is about making the best use of wealth in order to multiply it, and 'in fair weather or foul' indicates no more than that this is the right policy in every circumstance.

> 8.14: (Good) fortune will not happen to you; (good) fortune is given to him who seeks it.

In this sentence there is antithetic balance, although the 'but' has to be supplied. Otherwise it is a prosaic generalization – if you want to get on in the world, you must exert yourself.

8.17–9.4: This is what I would describe as a thematic cluster. It could be taken as an association of sentences on the catchword principle, but this is not altogether an adequate description. The sentences are diverse in subject-matter, but the opening words of each 'the blessing of' or 'the virtue of' are more than catchwords and superimpose a certain unity on the whole. The theme is how the potential of individuals or communities or things can best be realized.

8.17: The blessing of a district is the lord who executes justice.
8.18: The blessing of a temple is a priest.
8.19: The blessing of an acre is the actual working of it.
8.20: The virtue of a storehouse is in stocking it.
8.21: The virtue of a safe is cash in hand.
8.22: The blessing of a property is a prudent woman.
8.23: The blessing of a wise man is his speech.
9.2: The blessing of an army(?) is a general(?).
9.3: The blessing of a village is not taking sides.
9.4: The blessing of a craftsman is his tools.

These examples illustrate particularly well what I mean by non-proverbial wisdom sentences. They provide little incentive for further interpretation and they deal with limited, well-defined situations. I would not go so far as to say that none of them is capable of further interpretation. One thinks of the slogan of the Second World War in which servicemen are represented as addressing those who make armaments: 'Give us the tools and we will finish the job.' 'The blessing of a craftsman is his tools' could be an apt proverbial comment, wherever the ability and effectiveness of an individual is thwarted by lack of necessary equipment. Again, 'the blessing of a village is not taking sides' might be interpreted as a comment on the advisability of a balanced neutrality and a warning against striking attitudes or taking sides.

In general, however, I feel no great constraint laid on me to disengage these sentences from their particularity and to make paradigms of them. Rather, my impression is that I would not have carried through this further process of interpretation with the two sentences above, if I had not been subjecting them to an artificially close scrutiny and squeezing their proverbial possibilities. The situation is quite different where a sentence has a striking intrinsic aptness for further interpretation. It may require a certain quality of perceptiveness or insight to intuit these possibilities, but they do not have to be contrived or engineered. They may be missed by the obtuse, but they can be grasped by those who are sensitive to the capacity which a highly concrete and particular statement can have for making a comment of a most general kind.

11.11–14: A man's personality is his family.
A man's personality is his strength(?).
A man's personality (shows) in his face.
A man's personality – it is one of his members.

This is another thematic cluster. No comprehensive definition of personality is offered, but in each sentence a particular aspect of personality is noted and a cumulative description of the many-sidedness of personality is intended.

12.10: Ruin overcomes the rich man, (for) he is punished for some great crime which was before his time.

The interest in this example lies in the motive clause, since supporting argument is not characteristic of the wisdom sentence. The wisdom sentence communicates a general truth or a considered opinion ('Ruin overcomes the rich man'), but, unlike the Instruction, it neither exhorts nor commends itself by supporting argument. The motive clause, a formal element of the Instruction, has been transferred here to the wisdom sentence, and the motivation thereby introduced would seem to have a religious colouring, although the meaning is obscure. The rich man is overtaken by ruin, not because he is personally guilty of any crime, but apparently because the pursuit of riches locates him in the path of a punishment administered retrospectively for a great crime which was before his time.

12.2: A wise man is he who desires a friend(?); a fool is he who desires an enemy.
12.6: The companion of a fool is a fool; the companion of a wise man is a wise man.
12.8: The mother is the one who produces; precept only reproduces.
12.9: Every man acquires property; it is the wise man who conserves it.

All of these sentences have antithetic balance and something of the character of aphorisms, with an epigrammatic quality imparted by filing and polishing. In particular, 12.8 is elegant and urbane. The mother is productive in a unique sense and the educative process only secondarily so to the extent that it shapes, disciplines and develops the raw human product. There is no necessary connection between such finely pointed utterances and proverbial capacity as I have defined it. These are polished wisdom sentences which, nevertheless, are not proverbs.

13.19–22: The text of v. 20 is broken and the meaning of v. 21 obscure, but the group is a thematic cluster in which different traits of a woman's character are reviewed.

14.6f.: He who is stout-hearted in a misfortune shall not feel its full force.

He who steals from the property of another shall not benefit from it.

Two more sentences with an antithetical arrangement which do not make claims on the interpreter beyond the establishing of their limited literal sense.

14.9: If you do kindness to five hundred men and one of them recognizes it, part of it has not perished.

This sentence, because it entertains the thought of ingratitude in a concrete and picturesque way, has proverbial potentialities. It conjures up the picture of four hundred and ninety-nine ungrateful men and one grateful man. On the other hand, the manner of its formulation (protasis and apodosis) is more fitted to a process of argument than to a proverb, and inhibits the enhanced interpretation of which a proverb is capable. Yet the concreteness of expression does recall the proverb. Instead of saying: 'Benevolence is justified by the grateful few, even although it is wasted on the ungrateful many', the sentence says: 'If you do kindness to five hundred men and one of them recognizes it, a part of it has not perished.'

14.17: A good deed turns aside the punishment (?) of the great God.

A simple affirmation of religious belief.

15.9: The boy who has learnt his lesson meditates on the wrongs he has done.

This has proverbial possibilities and is less hampered than 14.9 by its form. As a proverb it could be reduced to something like: 'True amendment goes with a thoughtful examination of past errors.' The more circumscribed, literal meaning of the sentence is not, however, manifestly incomplete interpretation, and this is another instance where I am inclined to conclude that I have found a proverb only because my attention is artificially concentrated on the scrutinizing of every possibility.

18.13: A man who has no village – his (own) personality is his family.

This falls into the same category as the preceding saying. Its plain meaning is that a man who is not reinforced by his solidarity with a natural community is thrown back on his own resources of self-reliance. It might possibly be applied to any situation where self-reliance is particularly desiderated. Cf. 11.11, 'A man's personality is his family', which I have taken to mean something different from 18.13, namely, that the individual cannot disengage his individuality from family solidarity.

18.19f.: He who enjoys living in a house warms it to the rafters.
He who dislikes it builds one and mortgages it.

A couplet with antithetic parallelism on contrasting attitudes to a house. One man looks on it as a comfortable home, the other as a means of borrowing capital.

19.8f.: When an idiot acts by instinct, he acts wisely, (for) a man does not love what he hates.

This sentence gives evidence of literary polish – it is sententious and weighty. Instinctive behaviour is independent of any capacity for intellectual discrimination. Feelings are immediate and infallible; love and hate cannot be confused. (On the motive clause with the wisdom sentence see 12.10, above, p. 126.)

20.17: If you are burdened by a heavy tax, you sleep in its shadow.

Here there is an element of figurative language ('sleep in its shadow'), but the sentence does not at all break out of its circumscribed significance. It means: If you are burdened with a heavy tax, you are always anxious about it.

20.22–25: The waste of a house is not to live in it.
The waste of a woman is not to know her.
The waste of a donkey is carrying bricks.
The waste of a boat is carrying straw.

This group is a thematic cluster and the recurring phrase 'the waste of' defines the theme which is the failure to make the right use of resources or their wrongful use.

23.12: The precepts of God are before all men, (but) the blockhead does not see them.

A statement with a religious content and no proverbial elements. Similarly

25.5: If a woman is at peace with her husband, it is the will of God.
25.18–20: If a woman is at peace with her husband, they shall never fare badly.
If a woman whispers about her husband, [they shall never] fare well.
If a woman does not care for the property of her husband, another man is on her mind.
25.22: A bad woman shall have no husband.

This is clearly a thematic cluster in which the state of marriage is commented on from the woman's point of view and the conditions of harmony and discord defined. It is perhaps to be regarded (25.22) as advice to girls who aspire to marriage.

Proverbial Sentences

Some of the sentences in this group make sense, or almost make sense, as prosaic statements, but, in addition, they have a self-evident proverbial aptness. A few are not at all credible as prosaic statements and have demonstrably been created artistically as proverbs by the imaginative use of language.

10.4: When a crocodile surfaces, its length is measured.

This could be taken as a factual account of the correct procedure for measuring a crocodile. The operation can only be performed in given circumstances – when the crocodile is on the surface. It is also a proverb which observes that a sense of timing is all-important. 'There is a right time for every action.'

10.5: A crocodile does not die in a papyrus thicket, it dies from hunger.

This is wholly intelligible as an observation by a naturalist who has made a study of the habits of the crocodile. In addition it has proverbial potential, although I am uncertain how it should be taken. The meaning may be: 'Real dangers should be distinguished from imaginary ones', or, 'It is against the danger which brings death that care should be exercised'.

10.7: If you stumble with your foot in the house of a rich man, you will not stumble with your tongue.

This is hardly a proverb, for its significance is restricted by the reference to the house of a rich man. Yet it employs imagery in an artistic way by associating rash, ill-considered speech (stumbling with the tongue) with physical gaucheness (stumbling with the foot). It is better to appear gauche and raw in a rich man's house than to run the risks incurred by being too self-assured and articulate.

11.10: He who raises a dyke to the sky – it will fall on him.

This is not, and never was, an observation on an actual building operation and the occupational hazards associated with it. It doubtless has its ground in attentiveness to building techniques and to the difficulty of combining stability and strength with height. In no sense, however, can this be taken as practical advice on how to build a high dyke. It is interested in this operation only in so far as the images can be made to communicate the point of the proverb, and this involves taking these descriptive terms out of the realm of the practical by deliberate hyperbole. The meaning is: 'A man who tries too much and who outreaches his limitations and resources will meet disaster.'

11.15: The fisherman casts off from the shore without being able to say, 'God will dispense to every house'.

On each occasion the fisherman sets sail, he commits himself to an enterprise which is full of risk and uncertainty. There is no such thing as a guaranteed catch. But then the fisherman's situation is parabolic and his attitude to his calling can be disengaged from particularity and transferred to all classes and conditions of men. The same proverbial aptness is possessed by our phrase 'launching out into the deep'. The man who will not venture without absolute guarantees of success is condemned to stagnation.

12.15: So long as my brother did not struggle (?) to rob, I did not struggle to restrain him.

I do not interfere with another man's freedom of action, unless he directs his activities against my property. Moreover, there is a latent proverbial aptitude in the saying and I take it to mean that a law of reciprocity operates in social relationships. Action begets reaction. Aggressiveness or suspicions of aggressive intentions produce a situation of hot or cold conflict.

14.11: A thief steals by night; he is found in the day-time.

It is hard to believe that this is just a statement about the habits of thieves and the time when the police do their work. It is not nonsensical at this level of meaning, but I suspect that it is a picturesque way of saying: 'There are times when vigilance is especially demanded and it is then that one should exercise vigilance.'

14.13: A house is open to him who has something in his hand.

This might conceivably simply mean that you will be a more welcome visitor if you take a present with you, but that does not exhaust the possibilities of interpretation. I take this to be a proverbial utterance which means, 'A judicious bribe gets results'.

14.14: He who has been bitten by the bite of a snake is afraid of a coil(?) of rope.

This is an example of a sentence where the possibility of ambivalence does not have to be taken seriously. It is hardly credible that this could ever have been a matter-of-fact statement about the subsequent reactions of a man who had been bitten by a snake. Rather, the images are so organized that the collocation of snake and coil can only be an imaginative device directed towards the fashioning of a saying with wide-ranging significance. Our 'Once bitten twice shy' comes to mind, although the orientation of this Egyptian proverb is more precise. It does not just say that a man who has suffered (perhaps through over-confidence) may as a consequence become too cautious and timid. What is indicated here is that the reality of an unpleasant or frightening encounter with a particular danger in the past may make a man vulnerable to the illusion of that danger in the future. He will recoil from it when it is not there in situations where the seeming danger has only the flimsiest resemblance to the real thing.

14.15: The man who looks in front of him does not stumble and fall.

The person who looks where he is going and keeps his eyes skinned for obstacles will not trip up. This is fair sense, but it does not do justice to the proverbial aptness of the saying. A man should not worry about what is behind him; he should not brood over past mistakes or allow his attention to be distracted by them. He should give his undivided concentration to the challenges which confront him.

15.5: There is no child (?) which fails to cry(?).

On a literal level this is so laborious a truism that it may be questioned whether it would ever have been said unless there was a proverbial intention. There are some things which can be taken for granted – which are axiomatic. There are some certainties on which you can count.

18.10: He who grieves with the people of his village shall rejoice with them.

It is reasonable to understand this as an observation on human relationships in a small community where spurious or superficial affability will deceive nobody. A natural and intense feeling of solidarity expresses itself as much in times of sorrow as in those of rejoicing. Beyond this it says parabolically that a deep and genuine personal relationship which presupposes a vulnerability to compassion and even to anguish is not to be confused with a frothy affability.

18.11: The children of the fool wander in the street, but those of the wise man are by his side.

This makes sense as a precise comment on diverging parental practice. The fool lets his children run loose, while the wise man takes them with him whenever he can. It reaches out beyond such precision and particularity as a proverbial comment with some such meaning as: a fool's children are neglected and out of control; those of a wise man are under care and discipline.

18.12: He who hides behind his master shall get five hundred masters.

This sentence is hardly credible if we try to understand it in terms of a subordinate actually hiding behind his master, for the transition to five hundred masters is only intelligible on the assumption that 'hiding' is figurative. The proverb conjures up the picture of a subordinate hiding behind a master and five hundred masters who are in the offing, and such an imaginative use of language makes the point more effectively than if we were to say: 'A man who pleads his subordinate status as a reason for his never taking a stand and accepting responsibility, will be dominated by all comers.' The proverb cannot be generalized in this way without a loss of freedom and scope. To generalize or to interpret the proverb is to restrict it, to deny it its liberty, to put it in prison. The original insight, whatever precise range of application may have been intended for it, has been expressed so imaginatively that limits cannot be set to its further interpretation. No man can say in what future situations 'He who hides behind his master shall get five hundred masters' may be seized upon as an apposite comment.

19.7: There is no son of Pharaoh in the night.

When a prince is asleep in bed he looks like any other man (cf. Glanville, p. 76, n.234). It is difficult to believe that this saying originated as, say, the observation of a domestic servant in the royal palace. Rather it came into existence as a proverb based on the image of the sleeping prince and meaning not just that sleep reduces all men to equality, but that there are certain human situations in which no individual can contract out of his humanity and where the writ of a basic egalitarianism runs. Then all distinctions and inequalities created by differences of rank and degrees of privilege are dissolved and the common lot of men is a reality.

19.22: Beer matures (only) on its mash.

This makes some sense as an instruction about brewing, but as a proverb it means that a quality product will be achieved only if good materials are put into its making. More generally it means that if a plan is to mature and come to fruition, the ingredients indispensable to maturity must be put into the planning process.

19.23: Wine matures until it has been opened.

This is of the same type, and I interpret it to mean that patience must be exercised in order to get a mature product. Precipitate action is irrevocable. There is a right time to act and what is needed is patience to wait for the time and discrimination to know when the moment has arrived.

19.24: A remedy is effective only in the hands of a physician who has prescribed it.

This is intelligible as a warning against indiscriminate self-doctoring. It means further that application cannot be divorced from theory. There are some solutions which are not cut and dried, but which have to be applied with discrimination and understanding. Al-Ghazālī uses just this medical parable: 'And we make mention of the means of hope in order that they may be employed in the case of the despairing man or the one who has been overcome by fear, according to the pattern of the Book of God and the Practice of his Messenger. For both embrace hope and fear in union, since these two unite the means of healing with respect to different kinds of sick people, in order that the knowledgeable who are the heirs of the prophets may employ one or other of them according to need, just as the discriminating physician would employ them, and not the quack who supposes that everything which has therapeutic value will be salutary to every sick person, whatever may be his condition' (W. McKane, *Al-Ghazali's Book of Fear and Hope* (1962), pp. 10f.).

20.5: A weaver does not play stranger to the woof(?).

On 'woof' (?), Glanville remarks that it may be translated 'ground floor' or even 'basement' (p. 76, n.243), and recalls the scenes of weavers in the basement of a Theban house in the tomb of Thutynefer. The form of the sentence is incompatible with the supposition that it was ever intended as a prosaic communication on the art of weaving. The phrase 'play stranger' – itself a figurative expression – is decisive in this respect. Rather, the weaving process has supplied the images which constitute the proverb. The meaning is that a man should be what he is and not pretend to be what he is not.

20.9: The hissing of a snake is more significant than the braying of a donkey.

This saying has different levels of interpretation: (a) the hissing of the snake is, unlike the braying of the donkey, a sound which demands attention and vigilance; (b) there are noises which spell danger and towards which one should cultivate an attentive and watchful response, while there are others which can be consigned to the general background of noise towards which neglect is an advantage rather than a danger; (c) selective and discriminating responsiveness to stimuli produces concentration of thought and effort and wards off distraction and dissipation of energy.

20.10f.: To one who has been running sitting down is pleasant, (but) to one who has been sitting down standing up is pleasant.

This is true in terms of physical well-being. Sitting down is enjoyable after strenuous effort, while, on the other hand, a long spell of sitting down produces its own brand of discomfort and well-being is restored by stretching the legs. The saying is not, however, so limited in its significance. It means further that pleasure is constituted by contrast and change, that variety is the spice of life.

20.13: A snake which is eating has no venom.

This could be taken as a zoological observation of practical value to those who catch snakes. The saying is certainly credible on this level, whether or not it ever existed as such. The proverb means: there is a time when an adversary who is normally dangerous is harmless and it is then that he should be attacked.

20.14: A window which is wide open (or, 'a large window') gives more heat than coolness.

This is a perfectly sensible comment on what is involved in keeping a room cool in a hot climate. It does, however, have a representative potential which releases it into a wide sphere of significance. It is a lively expression of some such thought as: exaggeration defeats its own purpose.

21.14: He who is ashamed to be with his wife will not get children.

I am not inclined to suppose that this makes sense on a merely literal level, since it would be so much a truism as not to be worth saying. 'A man who will not sleep with his wife does not have children' is a picturesque way of saying: he who wills the end must also will the means.

22.5: He who shakes a stone – it will fall on his foot.

This might just possibly be understood as piece of practical advice on the foolhardiness of brute force and ignorance. The moving of a large stone which is embedded requires skill and care and not just furious tugging. It is unlikely, however, that it ever existed as anything other than a proverb and it recalls the Hebrew proverb: 'He who digs a pit falls into it, he who sets a stone rolling is caught up by it' (Prov. 26.27; cf. Eccles. 10.8). This has no sense taken prosaically, for why should a man not be able to dig a pit without falling into it or set a stone rolling without being crushed by it? The interest of such proverbial utterance is not at all with the technicalities of digging a pit or removing a large stone but with the striking communication of an idea by a contrived collocation of images. The meaning is: he who stirs up trouble will be the victim of his own mischief.

22.14: A house which is in ruins does not attract a visitor.

Possibly a piece of practical advice, say, to an inn-keeper, but also a proverb for: 'One who aspires to be a fashionable host or hostess must live in style and keep up appearances'.

22.15: A crocodile does not catch a townsman.

The empirical observation which is indirectly connected with this is that peasants who for one reason or another (irrigation works, fishing) have to venture on crocodile-infested waters face real danger. But this proverb does not at all direct itself towards peasants nor, for that matter, towards townsmen either. The crocodiles, the peasant, the townsman, are all elements of an imaginative texture. If the saying were taken literally, nothing triter could be conceived, but it is certain that it was never at any time understood in so wooden a way. On the contrary, a wealth of suggestiveness to which no pedestrian interpretation can do justice attaches to this deliberate arrangement of images. 'A danger is unreal if you are far enough away from it.'

23.8: It is more pleasant to live in your (own) small house than to live in the large house of another.

It is more pleasant to have a small place of your own than to live spaciously in another man's house. Beyond giving this piece of practical advice, the saying, in virtue of the proverbial expansion of which it is capable, can mean: a modest independence is more satisfying than grandeur which is not your own.

23.9: A small property which is intact is better than a large property which is robbed.

Possibly an observation on the economics of estate management and certainly a proverb for: 'A man should not take on more than he can do well'.

23.15: A cat which loves fruit hates him who eats it.

This makes sense as a 'scientific' observation relating to the behaviour of cats, whether or not it ever had this sense. The proverb means: a man is moved to hatred by the sight of another in the possession and enjoyment of a prize which he passionately desires and covets.

23.16: 'I agree with you', says the weakling.

This illustrates well the skilful use of concreteness for the effective expression of an idea. '"I agree with you," says the weakling', is weightier than such a flat generalization as: there is a concord which is the result of weakness. Moreover, the proverb, because of its allusiveness and creative vagueness, is open to interpretation as the generalization is not. To reduce this proverb to: there is a concord which is the result of weakness, is to define boundaries of significance which the original, in virtue of its concreteness, does not acknowledge. This is the paradox of the concreteness of the proverb.

23.19: The guests(?) are those who sit in the houses, it is the musicians who are making merry.

This apparently means that those who have been hired to make music enjoy themselves more than those for whom the music is being provided, and so enjoyment is with the practitioner and not the spectator who has a privileged seat. It is more fun to play than to watch. Stricker's translation cited by Gemser runs: 'The architects build the houses, the musicians inaugurate them.' This has meaning as a statement of customary procedure, but it also has proverbial possibilities: 'There are occasions which are not complete without the contribution of those who have no practical usefulness.'

23.20: The frogs are those who praise Hapi (i.e., the inundation); it is the mice who eat the emmer.

An observation that frogs croak when the land is inundated by the Nile, coupled with another that it is the mice who benefit from the harvest produced by the fertilizing flood. The antithesis of frogs and mice is, however, inexplicable except as a deliberate exploitation of imagery, and so the sentence must have been created as a proverb and never at any time been intended as a zoological observation. The statement that the frogs croak at the inundation and the other that the mice eat the emmer are, taken singly, intelligible at this level, but the antithetic balance of the two indicates a 'literary' rather than a 'scientific' intention. The interpretation would then be: the advantage does not accrue to those who behave as if they were about to possess it (cf. Gemser, p. 109: 'One sows, another reaps').

23.21: The oxen are those who harvest the barley and emmer; it is the asses who eat it.

Again, the intention here can hardly be to impart the information that the oxen work on the harvest and the asses eat the produce. The proverb indicated by the antithesis is: it is not the producers of wealth who enjoy its benefits.

24.7: If a donkey runs with a horse, it keeps the same pace.

Hardly a piece of information about what actually happens when a donkey has a horse as a pacemaker, but rather an arrangement of images to produce a proverb with the meaning: competition is necessary to secure maximum effort.

24.12: No drunkenness of yesterday removes today's thirst.

In some respects, this has the appearance of an informative statement, and yet the form suggests an original proverbial intention. It does not say simply, 'Excessive drinking produces a thirst the next day,' which could be taken as a correct statement of the physiological consequences of drunkenness. It rather underlines the circumstance that excessive drinking yesterday does not remove today's thirst. This is a deliberate imaginative exploitation of the connection between drunkenness and thirst, and the proverb means: to use in excess of reasonable need is always to squander.

There are a few examples of the simile and metaphor in *Onchsheshonqy*:

22.12: A fool to go with a wise man, a *bulṭi* going with its knife.

The most important distinction between this and the proverb (as I have defined it) is that the imagery is interpreted in a firm and specific way, so that the limits of its application are fixed. In this example, the interpretation and the image are simply laid side by side. The incompatibility of the fool and the wise man is illustrated by likening their association to that of a fish (*bulṭi*) and the fisherman's knife. The knife is death to the *bulṭi*, and so is the fool to the wise man.

22.13: A fool in a house is like fine clothes in a wine cellar.

If the image (fine clothes in a wine cellar) had been incorporated in a proverb, the form might have been: 'Fine clothes are not worn in a wine cellar', and this could be reduced to the generalization: it is the place and occasion which determine what is fitting. In the proverbial form no fixed interpretation is provided, whereas in the simile the image is given a quite specific interpretation. A fool is as out of place and as useless in a house as fine clothes in a wine cellar.

23.10: A slip of the tongue in the royal palace, a wrong turn of the helm at sea.

A wrong turn of the helm at sea is the image by which the crucial importance of a disciplined tongue for a royal official is illustrated. A sailor makes a navigational error, and this may turn out to be a critical lapse bringing disastrous consequences. So it is with the hasty or ill-considered or badly phrased remark of the official.

24.20: A woman is a body of stone (or 'a quarry'); the first-comer is he who exploits her (?).

A woman is a quarry and the first man who comes along can begin quarrying operations – have sexual intercourse with her. This would seem to be the meaning.

There are also three examples of the 'better . . . than' type of formulation which shares with the simile the element of comparison. Whereas the simile establishes a relationship of resemblance between the image and that to which it is compared, the 'better . . . than' sentence compares in respect of superiority and inferiority.

21.20: Better a statue of stone for a son than a fool.
21.21: Better to be without (a brother) than to have a brother who is evil.
21.22: Better death than want.

A rough division of the proverbs on which I have just commented can be made. There are those which are ambivalent and which are credible or almost credible as plain statements. There are those which are proverbs and are unintelligible on any other assumption. In the latter, concrete or picturesque language is deliberately exploited in order to give free rein to their significance, and a literal or pedestrian meaning is out of the question. The problem is to know what precisely should be concluded from the ambivalence of certain proverbs. Could it be that they originate as prosaic statements and subsequently win acceptance as proverbs when they are seen to have just that quality of particularity and concreteness which releases them into a world of new significance? Even if they do not originate as matter-of-fact statements and were never intended as other than proverbs, there is no doubt that linguistically they are much closer to the plain statement than the proverb with a contrived arrangement of images.

The Instruction in Onchsheshonqy: a comparative treatment

This completes the study of that part of *Onchsheshonqy* which consists of statements, whether non-proverbial or proverbial, and it remains now to show that some of the instructions, that is, those formulations of which the imperative is an essential element, also have a proverbial character. The best way of approaching this study is to examine the use which is made of imagery in the other examples of the Instruction. The general conclusion which can be drawn from such a study is that figurative or metaphorical language does not occupy a large place and that its use is so limited that it can be described as untypical of the Egyptian Instruction. This would be a fair comment on *Ptahhotep*, *Merikare*, *Amenemhet* and *Ani*. *Amenemope* is a partial exception, although even in respect of it this summing up would not be dangerously misleading.

The imagery in *Amenemope* is, for the most part, found in the motive clause or in extended motivation or in descriptive passages, and the characteristic figure is a type of simile. The high incidence of the simile is to be correlated with the polished literary character of *Amenemope*. It is, in my view, significant that in the specimens of the Instruction just mentioned (including *Amenemope*), it is most unusual to find imaginative language in the instruction itself, that is, in the clause which contains the imperative. The directive is addressed to a well-defined situation and it aims to do no more than to give authoritative instruction in plain words. Since what it inculcates is in the nature of professional or vocational guidance, it contents itself with crispness and clarity, without any striving after subtler literary effects. In the context of laying down the principles of a successful career in the service of the state, imaginative forms of expression are not in place. Imagery is the bearer of enhanced literary power and increases the range of significance, but it also introduces an element of uncertainty or, at any rate, openness into what is being communicated, and this makes it unsuitable for a communication with a closed area of meaning. The instructions given to apprentice officials are communications of this kind; they are vocational training and their language is not proverbial. The following are the more important uses of imagery in *Merikare*, *Amenemhet*, *Ani* and *Amenemope*. They supply some of the detail on which the above general assessment is based.

(i) *Merikare*

> Revere the god upon his way, made of costly stones and fashioned [of] metal, like a flood replaced by (another) flood. There is no river that permits itself to be concealed; that is, it breaks the [*dam*] by which it was hidden. (So) also the soul goes to the place which it knows, and deviates not from its way of yesterday (*ANET*, p. 417).

On the likening of the god to a flood replaced by another flood, Wilson (*ANET*, p. 417, n.47) remarks: 'The creator god, a sun disc of stone and metal, goes his daily way like the annual, irresistible inundation.' The daily progress of the sun across the sky is as inevitable and infallible as the annual flooding of the Nile.

The second figure also involves comparison and has the form 'even as . . . so also'. The soul will reach its appointed destination, and ultimately there is no possibility of a miscarriage of justice. There may seem now to be a lack of correspondence between worth and status, but in the light of the hereafter this discrepancy will disappear. A soul cannot be deprived of the place in the order for which it has an intrinsic fitness. This is illustrated by the image of the river which will not be contained by artificial means, but which bursts through all barriers and resumes its course.

(ii) *Amenemhet*

> Had women ever marshalled the battle array? Had contentious people been bred within the house? Had the water *which cuts the soil* (ever) been opened up, *so that* poor men were frustrated at their work? (*ANET*, p. 419).

The three questions are to be related to Amenemhet's comment on the palace conspiracy of which he had fallen foul: 'I had not prepared for it, I had not (even) thought of it, my heart had not accepted (the idea of) the slackness of servants.' The piling up of images in the three questions effectively expresses the shattering experience of disillusionment through which the king had passed. The world in which he now lives is no longer credible and he is bemused by its topsy-turvy nature. It is a world in which women might lead armies, where primary loyalties are destroyed, and where the irrigation system on which the peasant's livelihood depends is a target for sabotage. Wilson, following Gardiner, suggests that the third question implies a comparison between the beneficence of the king and the benefits conferred by the irrigation system. The king as a channel of blessing to the people is likened to the irrigation canals which bring fertility to the land (*ANET*, p. 419, n. 11).

(iii) *Ani*

> A deep water whose windings, one knows not, a woman who is far away from her husband (*ANET*, p. 420).

This is motivation connected with preceding imperatives which warn against forming any association with 'a woman from abroad'. The image and the interpretation are laid side by side (see above, pp. 138f.), and it is clear that a relationship of resemblance is implied. Thus we have a simile in intention, if not in form. A woman who is far away from her husband is as devious and unfathomable as a deep, meandering river.

> The belly of a man is wider than a storehouse, and it is full of every (kind of) response (*ANET*, p. 420).

This is part of the argument by which the instruction 'Thou shouldst not express thy (whole) heart to the stranger' is reinforced. There is a larger variety of possible responses stored in the 'belly' than there are commodities in a storehouse. A selective articulateness is part of wisdom, for the 'belly' has mixed contents, only some of which deserve to be raised to the level of utterance.

> The course of the water of last year is gone, and it is in a different area this year. Great seas have become dry places, and sandbanks have become abysses . . . (*ANET*, p. 421).

In all probability these are two motive clauses connected with the imperative, 'Be not greedy to fill thy belly'. A preceding polite imperative, 'Thou shouldst not eat bread when another is waiting', is recommended by supporting argument, part of which is contained in the motive clause, 'The man rich in the time of last year is a vagabond this year'. These words constitute an interpretation of the two imaginatively construed motive clauses at the end of the paragraph. Wealth is an opportunity for benevolence and not an occasion for greed, and the opportunity should be seized while it is there, for the rich man is not immune from change of fortune. In this respect he is like the changing watercourse or the shifting sands. As the river changes into a dry water-bed or the mountain of sand into a yawning abyss, so does wealth give place to poverty.

(iv) *Amenemope*

> Sleep a night before speaking;
> The storm, it bursts forth like flame in straw (v.13f.).

The simile is contained in a motive clause associated with the preceding imperative, and is set in the context of a warning against passionate speech and impetuous rejoinders. It is this kind of behaviour which produces angry scenes; temperatures rise and the 'storm' breaks. The erupting of passions in its suddenness, intensity and irreversibility is like the tongue of flame that leaps from straw when it catches fire.

> As to the passionate man in the temple,
> He is like a tree grown in the forest(?) (vi.1f.).

The hot-headed man is like a tree grown for its timber, whose foliage withers at the moment it falls to the woodcutter's axe, and which is destined to be used as fuel. The tranquil or serene man is like a tree planted in a garden as a permanency, and valued for its greenness, its shade and its fruitfulness.

The truly tranquil man, he setteth himself aside,
He is like a tree grown in a plot (6.7f.).

The morrow is come, to-day is gone,
The deep hath become the edge of the waves,
The crocodiles are uncovered, the hippopotami on dry land,
The fishes are gasping(?);
The jackals are sated, the wild-fowl in festival,
The nets are empty(?) (vii.1–6).

The piling up of images from the world of nature is a picturesque extension of the motive clause, 'The morrow is come, to-day is gone', which is connected with the imperative, 'Say not "to-day is as to-morrow"'. What is envisaged is probably, as Griffith suggests (p. 203), the consequences of the Nile changing its course – the jackals and the wild fowl feed on the carcases. Men are vulnerable to such sudden and catastrophic changes of circumstances.

Rejoice not thyself (because of) riches by robbery,
Nor groan over poverty;
When an archer in front pushes forward(?)
His troop leaves him (in difficulty);
The boat of the covetous is left (in) the mud,
While the bark of the tranquil sails (with the breeze) (x.6–11).

The argument, which relates particularly to the first imperative ('Rejoice not thyself because of riches by robbery'), is conducted by two distinct groups of images which, although they are not fully formed similes, intend a relationship of resemblance. The man who is in too great a hurry to get rich and who will stop at nothing to achieve his end is like the foolhardy and impetuous archer who endangers his comrades as well as himself, and who, as a consequence, is left stranded by his troop. The calm man who does not strive too hard fares well, while the covetous man of restless ambition makes no progress. The one is like a man whose boat sails before a helpful breeze, and the other like a man whose boat is stuck in the mud.

Cause him not to cast his speech to lasso thee,
And give not free rein to thine answer (Griffith, xi.17f.).

Do not make him cast his speech to lasso thee,
Nor make (too) free with thy answer (*ANET*, p. 423).

An unusual feature of this example is that the imperative itself is imaginatively constructed. I ignore the second line, because I am unable to judge whether the figure of speech is in the original or only in Griffith's translation (it does not appear in *ANET*). No similar dubeity seems to attach to the first line, and in it the superior who incites his subordinate to speak in anger and be immoderate and abusive is compared to one who is adept at casting a lasso.

Swift is speech when the heart is hurt,
More than wind before water (?) (Griffith, xii.1f.).

Swifter is speech when the heart is hurt
than wind of *the head-waters* (*ANET*, p. 423).

This belongs to the same context as the preceding example. 'Wind before water' or 'wind of the head-waters' is obscure, but the general intention of the comparison is clear. Speech which is an instinctive response to damaged self-esteem or a sense of grievance is swifter than the rushing wind.

He makes a voyage like all the world,
But he is laden with false words.
He is like a sea-going mariner who sails with a cargo of false words (xii.7f.).

Would that Khnum might bring in indeed, indeed (?),
The potter's wheel for the fiery-mouthed,
To mould and burn hearts (like vessels)
(And reform his ways!) (xii.15–17).

These similes are contained in a passage descriptive of the hot-headed man who is caught in the toils of his impetuous and undisciplined behaviour. Khnum is the god who moulds man on the potter's wheel or the moulder's table (Griffith, p. 229). He is the divine potter; vessels are shaped from clay on the potter's wheel and fired in the kiln, and these are the processes by which Khnum might reshape and 'reform' the man of undisciplined tongue.

He is like a wolf's whelp in the farmyard (xii.18).

This relates to the hot-headed man, and means that he is one who creates havoc – an agent of destruction. The idea is not quite that of 'a bull in a china shop', which is conceived in lighter vein and points rather to a blundering and destructive clumsiness.

He goes before every breeze like clouds,
He diminishes the colour of the sun (xiii.2f.).

Wherever there is a possibility of creating mischief or strife, the hot-headed man is present. In this respect he is like the clouds which go before every breeze and obscure the sun.

He bends(?) his tail like a young crocodile,
He gathers himself together, crouched(?) (xiii.4f.).

Again concerning the hot-headed man. As the crocodile bends its tail preparatory to striking, so he is poised to make his destructive intervention.

Verily the property of a dependent, it is a choking for the throat,
It is a vomiting(?) for the gullet (xiv.7f.).

Two motive clauses in connection with the imperatives 'Covet not the property of a dependent, nor hunger for his bread'. The misappropriated property of a dependant is like food which causes choking or vomiting.

Verily a crocodile which is void of proclaiming,
Inveterate is the dread of it (xxii.9f.).

A motive clause which adduces reasons why tranquillity and taciturnity should be cultivated. The silent man is as formidable and as capable of commanding respect as the silent crocodile.

Better is a man that (hides) his report within himself
Than he who tells a thing to disadvantage.
One does not run to reach perfection;
One does not throw(?) to injure himself(?) (xxii.15–18).

This constitutes motivation of the warnings communicated by the four imperatives of the preceding quatrain. To lay bare one's soul or to lavish confidences on every Tom, Dick and Harry is to invite contempt. There is strength in not speaking about oneself, and weakness in wearing one's heart on one's sleeve. The two figures in the final couplet suggest that such garrulity is associated with anxious and impatient ambition – with a lack of tranquillity. There is an initiative which is misconceived and which is a defect in character rather than a mark of fitness for power. It is a mistaken attempt to force the pace, to rush the gates of the order ('One does not run to reach perfection').

Even as a noble is great in his office,
He is like as a well aboundeth (in) drawings (of water) (xxiii.19f.).

This couplet supplies reasons why a healthy appetite for food and drink should not be indulged at the table of a man in high office. Heavy demands are made on his hospitality, and in this respect he is like a well from which large quantities of water are drawn.

A pilot who sees from afar,
He will not make his boat a wreck (xxv.14f.).

These are the last two lines of a chapter which deals in a somewhat rambling way with discreet and helpful behaviour. The final couplet appears to urge that a man should not be the slave of impulse and that his behaviour should be shaped by a consistent awareness of the direction in which he is travelling. He is to be like the pilot who sees far ahead and who makes every move with plenty of time to spare. Such a man will not permit impulse or caprice to make shipwreck of his life.

The food of a hound is (the affair) of his master,
And he barks unto him that gives it (xxvi.6f.).

Or Lange's translation, cited by Griffith:

The client is the hound of his patron,
He barks at the giver of it (i.e. bread).

The chapter urges a policy of total submission to seniors. Their curses should be borne in silence and their beatings accepted without retaliation. The recommendation has in view a condition of dependence on seniors for material support, and this is the price which has to be paid for the bread which they supply. A dog knows the hand that feeds it, and this acknowledgement determines its relationship with its master.

Two points about the foregoing imagery should be noted: (*a*) with one exception it does not occur in the Instruction (i.e., the imperative(s)), while it is often associated with the arguments which recommend the imperatives or give reasons why they should be obeyed; (*b*) since it is provided, for the most part, with a specific and well-defined interpretation, it is more akin to the simile or metaphor than to the proverb. Whereas in the proverb, as I have defined it, the significance of the concrete or imaginative sentence is left open to future interpretation, here the intention is rather to establish a precise relationship between the idea and the image, so that it is just *this* idea for which the image has particular appositeness and felicity. The master of the simile is he who finds the image which perfectly matches the idea and can be happily married to it.

In *Onchsheshonqy*, on the other hand, the instructions are proverbial in the same sense as the statements already examined are proverbial, and it is the imperatives themselves which have this proverbial potentiality.

7.21: Do not say 'young man' to one who is grown up.

It is an old trick to say 'young man' to an opponent in accents which ooze with knowledgeability and experience. It may be an indication of a bankrupt argument, or it may be an honest but infuriating paternalism. This could be taken as a precise directive to avoid the expression 'young man' in conversation or debate with a mature adult, or as a concrete and engaging way of saying: Do not be patronizing; avoid paternalism.

9.16f.: Do not say: 'It is summer', (for) there is winter to come, (for) he who does not gather wood in the summer will not be warm in the winter.

Beware of the torpor induced by blue skies and sunshine and do not abandon yourself to them, for, although the winter may seem distant and unreal, now is the time to lay in your fuel stocks. Or, disengaged from its particularity, the instruction can mean: Do not be enervated by pleasant and easy circumstances, for adversity will come back, and now is the time to prepare for it.

11.8: Do not kill a snake and leave its tail.

This would seem to me to be proverbial through and through. I find it difficult to believe that this was ever intended literally. The meaning is obscure; perhaps, 'Do not stop short of eradicating a danger', or, 'In self-defence do not be content with half-measures'.

11.9: Do not hurl a lance(?), if you are not able to control its flight.

Again, this might just be safety regulations for the throwing of lances, but I do not take this possibility seriously. Otherwise it is proverbial and means: 'Do not precipitate action, unless you are confident that you can control its development and bring it to the desired objective.'

13.12: If you find your wife with her lover, console yourself with a bride(?).

Perhaps a wordly-wise and precise instruction to a cuckold, but certainly an imaginative expression: for 'Make the best of a bad job', or even: 'Turn discomfiture to your advantage'.

13.13: Do not get a maid for your wife, if you haven't got a servant for yourself.

Let your domestic economy be all of a piece. If you cannot afford a servant for yourself and a maid for your wife, do not create privilege and a disproportionate status for her. The instruction has, moreover, a parabolic aptness and would be apposite wherever a situation demanded some such instruction as: Do not be so generous that you create for others advantages which you do not possess yourself.

15.21f.: If you are sent for a letter and find wheat, do not bring(?) [it], (for,) if you are trading in straw, when it is wanted, you do not go around offering corn.

This is a deliberate arrangement of images and a picturesque way of saying: Fulfil the commission entrusted to you, no more and no less, or: Cultivate the strictest relevance. The association of 'letter' and 'wheat' is not meaningful on a prosaic level, and the motivation confirms the proverbial intent of the concreteness of the instruction.

16.5: Do not drink water in the house of a merchant, if he charges you for it.

This makes some sense taken literally, but it is unlikely that it ever was an instruction relating to merchants who charged for water drunk in their houses. The situation is rather one which is imaginatively conceived for its wealth of allusiveness. 'Confine your wants to the fewest where living is expensive.' 'Do not pay in one place for what you can have for nothing in another.' Or a more general interpretation: 'Do not acquiesce in an arrangement financially disadvantageous to yourself.'

16.25: Do not scorn a small document, a small fire or a small gift(?).

I am in some difficulty with this example, but, if it is proverbial, I would not press the parabolic significance of 'document', 'fire' and 'gift(?)', but would make the interpretation hinge on 'small'. 'Do not adopt a high-handed attitude to even the smallest detail, for no detail is insignificant.' If the instruction is taken literally, it contains advice not to be slack in respect of the smallest legalities, to react immediately to the smallest threat of fire and to avoid taking even a small gift(?) for granted.

17.11: Do not run around in circles (simply) in order not to stand still. *Or*, Do not run too much, and do not stand still.

Whichever translation is preferred, neither instruction just means what it says. Such literalism would not be altogether ruled out in the case of the second translation, but it would be absurd for the first. The first means: 'Do not engage in purposeless activity simply to create the impression of busyness.' The second means: 'Do not try too hard to force an initiative, but do not be too passive.'

17.12f.: Do not always be purifying yourself with water only, (for) the river flows down (even) for the stones.

This is only meaningful as a contrived proverb. It means: Do not suppose that there is nothing more to purity than ritual ablutions. The point of the associated motive clause, which is also imaginatively constructed, is that the stones in a river bed are cleaned and polished by the water washing over them. If there is no more to purity than ablutions, then these stones have this purity.

18.6: If you are powerful, throw your deeds into the river; if you are weak, throw them also.

On this, Glanville (p. 75, n.22) observes that the powerful man will not need title deeds to back his claim, while the small man will find them useless. There is, however, a wealth of allusiveness attaching to 'throw your deeds into the river'. 'If you have power, the law is useless, for you are above it. If you are without power it is useless, for no redress is to be had from it.'

18.23: Take the rich man to your house, take the poor man to your boat.

Possibly clear-cut advice, but certainly more than this when its proverbial possibilities are intuited. Make the best possible impression on a wealthy and influential visitor. Receive a poor man – one of no consequence – with the barest civility and with the minimum of ceremony and hospitality. The 'boat' is analogous to the 'tradesmen's entrance'.

19.25: When you are given a loaf for stupidity,
let teaching be an abomination to you.

This is a contrived proverb with 'loaf' parabolic for 'livelihood' and 'teaching' for 'arduous occupation'. 'If you are making a livelihood without putting forth too much intellectual effort, have nothing to do with the stresses and strains of a testing profession.'

20.4: End by planting any tree, begin by planting a sycamore.

I am not inclined to suppose that this is practical advice on afforestation, although it no doubt has its basis in the knowledge that it is easy to plant a sycamore. The meaning is: Begin with the easiest operation, and gradually you will acquire the expertise for the difficult one.

22.3: Do not start a fire, if you cannot put it out.

This is hardly credible as an instruction on fire control and must have had an original proverbial intent. 'Do not set in motion a train of events which may subsequently get beyond your control' (cf. 11.9, above, p. 147).

22.19: Give one loaf to your labourer, but take two from his shoulders.

On 'shoulders', Glanville (p. 77, n.271) observes, 'from the strength of his shoulders or from the load of corn which he carries back from the harvest'. In any case, the phrase 'take two from his shoulders' demonstrates the non-literal character of this instruction and establishes its original proverbial intention. 'Make sure that a workman produces more than he costs in wages.'

23.23: Do not drink water from a well and (then) throw the pitcher back into it.

It would hardly be necessary to warn anyone not to throw a pitcher into a well after they have drawn water, but to leave it available for the next occasion. Such a literal basis is not entirely out of the question, but the proverbial sense of the instruction is more assured: 'Exercise foresight and do not be a creature of impulse.' 'Take a long-term view.'

III

THE BABYLONIAN-ASSYRIAN INSTRUCTION

The genre is not so well represented in Babylonian-Assyrian literature as in Egyptian, but there are two pieces which in respect of form and content belong to it, one Babylonian and the other Assyrian. The first is the *Counsels of Wisdom*, which Lambert assigns to the Cassite period (1500–1200 BC) and which divides itself according to topics into ten sections (*BWL*, pp. 96f.; *ANET*, pp. 426f.).

In one of the sections, a statesman of the first rank, perhaps a vizier, warns his 'son' against the temptations of high office and urges on him the strictest probity and integrity. Here the association of the Instruction with the principles of statecraft and statesmanlike behaviour, which is well-established in Egypt, reappears, and it is only in this section of the *Counsels* that the 'my son' form of address is used. Lambert (p. 96) supposes that 'my son' points to a father-son rather than a teacher-pupil relationship, and that it presupposes the hereditary character of the office of vizier. He says: 'The advice given in the section beginning "My son" can have had relevance for very few people, unlike the rest of the *Counsels*, which has a general application.'

The point that this section contains vocational instruction, while the other parts of the *Counsels* have a more general character, is well made, but we have noticed how difficult it is in the Egyptian context to assign a precise significance to 'my son'. What began as parental instruction based on the hereditary character of high political offices was carried over into the schools where apprentice statesmen were trained, and the 'my son' form of address was preserved in this scholastic setting. The authority of the teacher was an extension of the natural authority of the father.

Another important question raised by Lambert is whether the

section in the *Counsels* on the temptations of a vizier (81f.; *BWL*, pp. 102f.) can be held to establish a connection between this work and *Ahikar* – the Assyrian work which I had in mind in my opening remarks. Can the vizier of the *Counsels* be identified with Ahikar? In one respect he corresponds precisely to Ahikar – he is a bearer of the seal (82). Lambert thinks that this identification is unlikely, as the date which he tentatively assigns to the *Counsels* makes clear (1500–1200 BC). He says: 'Whether or not Ahiqar can be identified with a figure known from Late Assyrian letters, as suggested by von Soden (*ZA* 43, pp. 1–13), the well-known story is set in the reign of Esarhaddon. It is improbable that a text composed about the reign of Esarhaddon could be represented by three copies or more in the libraries of Ashurbanipal, and by at least one copy at Assur. And then there is no room for a story at the beginning of our text. However, the comparison is suggestive' (p. 96).

I have maintained elsewhere (*PWM*, p. 32) that *Ahikar* is Assyrian in origin, but I shall now summarize von Soden's arguments with which I have not previously dealt. Von Soden's observations on Ahikar and Nadin arise out of his study of a text to which he gives the title 'Die Unterweltsvision eines assyrischen Kronprinzen'. A certain *Kummâ* is identified with the crown prince Ashurbanipal, and so the text is assigned to the reign of Esarhaddon. The scribe (*ṭupsarrum*) who intrudes into the narrative is not just an ordinary scribe, but a person of some individuality and moment who followed in the post of his father. In this respect he is like Nadin, and von Soden suggests this identification. It is then conjectured that the sin of this scribe to which allusion is made was the sin of Nadin – that he defamed his foster-father. Ahikar is then equated with *Adad-sum-uṣur*, an influential counsellor of Esarhaddon, chiefly on the basis of letters in which the latter asked an office at court for his son in a manner recalling Ahikar's request on behalf of Nadin (R. F. Harper, *Assyrian and Babylonian Letters ABL* i, No. 2; vii, No. 657). From further letters (*ABL* i, No. 117 and No. 118) it is evident that Esarhaddon accedes to his request in the same way as he is said to have acceded to Ahikar's request. The letters also reveal that *Adad-sum-uṣur* fell into disfavour (*ABL* vii, No. 659), but not that this was as a consequence of his having been denounced and not that he was subsequently pardoned.

In the case of *Ahikar*, which is set in the reign of Esarhaddon (681–669 BC), the instructions are given by one Ahikar, who is a counsellor of all Assyria and a seal-bearer to the king. He is thus portrayed as the king's first minister and is described as a 'sagacious and keen-witted statesman' (*spr ḥkym wmhyr*). Hence this work, too, is set in the context of high political office and the 'my son' form of address has an original connection with the hereditary character of the office. Ahikar has no son and he asks Esarhaddon for permission to groom his nephew Nadin to succeed him as vizier. Esarhaddon agrees, and the subsequent instructions are addressed to Nadin as Ahikar's heir presumptive.

A. COUNSELS OF WISDOM

The religious tone of the *Counsels* is indicated by the fact that an entire section (135–47) urges the claims of piety and extols its benefits and perhaps even more significantly by the tendency of the motivation elsewhere towards a religious orientation (47f.; 59f.; 63f.; 129f.; 164). Šamaš and Marduk are the deities particularly mentioned and this corresponds with the situation in the prologue and epilogue of the *Code of Ḫammurabi* (G. R. Driver and J. C. Miles, *Babylonian Laws* II, 1935, pp. 7f., 94f.), where the laws are related to a concept of moral order of which Ḫammurabi is the executor and the gods, especially Marduk and Šamaš, the guarantors and upholders. The importance of Šamaš in this respect is demonstrated best in the *Šamaš Hymn* (*BWL*, pp. 121–38), while Marduk's connections with theodicy are shown by the circumstance that the author of *Ludlul Bel Nēmeqi* (*BWL*, pp. 21–62), a devotee of Marduk, writes as one who cannot reconcile his sense of blamelessness with his experience of suffering and whose belief in theodicy is subjected to great strain.

Yet the religious motivation does not prevail everywhere, and the instructions are sometimes recommended by the more practical and worldly considerations which appear in the Egyptian Instruction. Disciplined speech is recommended by the observation that it is a man's wealth (27), and the command not to marry a prostitute is laced with the following comment:

In your trouble she will not support you,
In your dispute she will be a mocker;
There is no reverence or submissiveness with her (75–77).

The vizier who is the bearer of the seal and the custodian of the treasury is urged to cultivate the strictest probity in public office, and to respect absolutely the trust which has been placed in him, on the ground that embezzlement of public funds is certain to be discovered and visited with disgrace and ruin (88–94).

In this section ((*g*) 81–. . .) the *Counsels*' affinity to the Egyptian Instruction is obvious, but in other sections also the matters entertained are those which have been taken up again and again in the Egyptian genre, as can be demonstrated section by section, following Lambert's division (*BWL*, p. 96).

(*a*): Do not associate yourself with men of bad reputation, with gossips or idlers, for you will be identified with them in the public mind and your own reputation will be tarnished (21–25).

(*b*), (*h*): These two sections deal with the well-worn topic of the unruliness of the tongue and its potentialities for good and evil. Speech which is severely rationed and judicious is a man's wealth; a tongue which is untamed may run to extravagance, insubordination, untruth, malicious slander and blasphemy (26–30; 127–34).

(*c*): Do not show a liking for involving yourself in other people's litigation, and avoid litigation on your own account like the plague. A better way is conciliation or even benevolence towards the one who has wronged you (31–. . .).

(*d*): Show respect to seniors and do not play the autocrat with the weak and depressed. Answer need with beneficence, for this is pleasing to Šamaš (. . .–65).

(*e*), (*f*): Do not make a slave girl your favourite or instal her in your bedroom, for this is to sow dragons' teeth in your household. Do not marry a prostitute, else you will establish a liaison which is full of trouble and empty of loyalty and respect (66–80).

(*i*): Worship your god every day with ceremony and piety, and you will be rewarded with favour and long life (135–47).

(*j*): Do not betray the trust which a friend places in you or fail in a promise which you have made to him. Practise candour towards him and avoid hypocrisy (148–. . .).

This kind of advice is addressed to the apprentice official in the Egyptian Instruction, and may also be vocational wisdom in the *Counsels*. Lambert supposes that these sections are addressed to a general audience and that only section (*g*) (81–. . .), which gives advice to one destined for high office, moves in the orbit of statesmanship. The 'my son' form of address, which appears only in this section, lends some support to this point of view (*BWL*, p. 96). The difficulty here, as Lambert observes, is that so little of the genre is extant in Babylonian literature as to make any judgement hazardous. In addition to the *Counsels*, Lambert mentions the *Instructions of Šuruppak* (*BWL*, pp. 92–95) and the *Counsels of a Pessimist* (*BWL*, pp. 107–9), but the quantity of material in both is small and I have not thought that there is anything to be gained by taking them into account. *Advice to a Prince* (*BWL*, pp. 110–15) does not have the form of the Instruction – the element of command is absent. The writer of this piece has imitated the style of omen literature – a style which resembles the so-called casuistic legal formulation (cf. *BWL*, p. 110).

Form of the Counsels of Wisdom

That the form of the Instruction genre is constituted essentially by the imperative emerges clearly from a study of the *Counsels*. More so than in some of the Egyptian examples, the concern to impart authoritative instruction is reflected in the ascendancy of the element of command over that of argument. The teaching on a given topic is inculcated by means of a series of imperatives, each of which is a sharp and telling thrust, filling out and reinforcing its predecessor. Two examples will suffice to illustrate this. A topic which enjoins disciplined speech and avoidance of excess and untruth is almost entirely composed of the element of command – four jussives and one imperative – and otherwise contains only two short motive clauses ('Therein is a man's wealth', and, 'A talebearer is accursed', 26–30). In the section which urges deference to seniors and kindness to the needy (57–65), there are nine imperatives interrupted twice, and on each occasion by two lines of argument (59f.: 'With this a man's god is angry, It is not pleasing to Šamaš, who will repay him with evil', and 63f.: 'In this a man's god takes pleasure, It is pleasing to Šamaš, who will repay him with favour').

The conditional clause preceding the imperative and defining the circumstances envisaged by the command appears in several places. 'When' (36) comes to the same thing as 'if', and 'Should it be a dispute of your own' is an equivalent formulation (37). In 37; 45; 78; 81f. (where two conditional clauses precede the imperatives), 'if' translates *lu*; in 150f. it translates *šumma*, the word used in the so-called casuistic legal formulations of the *Code of Ḫammurabi*.

Two other formal elements which are a commonplace of the Egyptian Instruction are represented in the *Counsels*, namely the motive and consequential clauses. The section 21–25 is made up of two imperatives (21f.), an asyndetic motive clause (23) and three consequential clauses which elaborate the consequences of neglecting the instruction imparted (24f.). A similar complex is 31–35, which is made up of two imperatives, a motive clause and two consequential clauses. In 140f., two consequential clauses follow directly upon the imperative. The asyndetic motive clause, which gives reasons why the command should be heeded, occurs frequently (23; 27; 30; 33; 79; 133; 138), and the motivation may be extended over two (47f.; 59f.; 63f.; 129f.) or more lines (38–40; 75–77; 88–...; 143–7). 73f. explicate the command in 72, and similarly 136 explicates 135.

B. *AHIKAR*

A. E. Cowley, *Aramaic Papyri of the Fifth Century BC* (1923), pp. 204f.

My remarks are confined to those 'words of Ahikar' (col. i.1: Cowley, p. 212) which are extant in Aramaic and which are assigned to the fifth or fourth century BC (*PWM*, p. 32). The statement that *Ahikar* is Instruction needs qualification, for the case of *Ahikar* is similar to that of *Onchsheshonqy*, in that only a small part of the material consists of instructions conveyed in the imperative or jussive. Even in respect of this material it is clear that the situation which is presupposed is not always that of a 'son' being groomed to succeed his father in high office, so that the expectations which are aroused by i.1, 'These are the words of one named Ahikar, a wise and keen-witted statesman, who taught his son', are not altogether fulfilled in what follows. In particular, there is the complication that Ahikar alludes to his betrayal at the hands of Nadin (139f.; p. 169) in a manner recalling Amenemhet (*ANET*, p. 418), and so it is not at all clear that such instructions as there are relate to a point in time when Nadin was being educated to fill the office of vizier. Some of the instructions are general in character and have no special application to the training of a vizier, while one or two are even inapposite to one who has expectations of such high preferment (129–31). A better case can be made out for others. That a disciplined tongue and secretiveness are political virtues is inculcated by the Egyptian Instruction, while *Ahikar* 95f. in particular seems to have in mind one who is to have the ear of a king.

The instructions of *Ahikar* do not, then, as a whole, read like the directives of Ahikar to his heir-designate. They are not so homogeneous or so consistently orientated as to give this impression, and they do not always have the 'my son' form of address. On occasions they are cast in the form of advice to a third party on how to discipline his son (81), and even as third person jussives ('let him beware of him', 163), which are almost exhortation and are too general to constitute crisp, authoritative instruction.

Besides, *Ahikar* contains much that is not Instruction and which invites comparison with *Onchsheshonqy* because of the high incidence of imagery. There is, however, by contrast with *Onchsheshonqy* little evidence in *Ahikar* of 'popular wisdom'. Such imaginative constructions as appear are, at any rate, deliberately contrived and are products of art. They are mostly of the simile type; an image or complex of images is laid out beside the idea which it sharpens and the relation, if not one of exact resemblance, is one of comparison. There is little that is 'proverbial' according to my definition, although one or two of the instructions as in *Onchsheshonqy* are communicated proverbially. A distinctive feature of *Ahikar*, which marks its kinship with Babylonian and Sumerian literature, is the fable. It preserves several examples more or less complete (118–20, 165f., 204f.) and some of these conform to the type of the contest fable (*BWL*, pp. 150–212).

There is a strong religious colouring and a moralism which flows from piety. Hence the antithesis of *ṣdq* and *rš'* (167–9, 171, cf. 126, 128), *ṭb* (157) and *lḥy* (130, 138), *hymnwt* and *kdbh* (132). The presupposition of such an ethical vocabulary is that God (126, 128, 156) or the gods (124, 160) or Šamaš (92, 93, 138, 171) will uphold the righteous man and punish the evildoer (especially 159). The righteous man should have no dealings with the wicked (163f.), nor should he take vengeance into his own hands, for this is the business of God who will not fail nor be remiss (149, 156f., 171f.). A man can achieve nothing without God or against the design of God (122–5, 151, 160).

The following examples of the different kinds of material in *Ahikar* will illustrate these general remarks:

Col. vi (Cowley, pp. 214f.; *ANET*, p. 428) is made up of diverse material. There is only one imperative (81, addressed to a third party in respect of his son, hence 'thy son' not 'my son'), although 83 is instruction formulated without an imperative, concerning the right ordering of domestic affairs. The 'my son' address occurs in 82, but this, along with 80 and 84, which all deal with the disciplining of a son, is a sentence rather than an instruction. *wytsr* is taken by Cowley (p. 234) as an *ithpeel* of *'sr*, although he translates 'the son who is trained and taught', i.e. *'sr* with the sense of *ysr* (p. 222). Since, however, he renders *ytsr* from *'sr* 'is restrained' on p. 234, his translation 'is taught' on p. 222 may assume a derivation from *ysr*. J. J. Koopmans (*Aramäische Chrestomathie*, i, 1962, p. 140) derives from *'sr*. *yit'sar* > *yittesar*, 'to be bound'. Jean-Hoftijzer (*Dictionnaire des inscriptions sémitiques de l'ouest*, p. 20, *s.v.* *'sr*) also derive from *'sr*, but contrary to what is said there, the context points as much to *ysr* (*yt'lp*) as to *'sr* (*wytśym 'rḥ'*). Moreover, the use of *ysr* is well-established in the book of Proverbs in connection with a conception of educational discipline (9.7; 19.18; 29.17, 19. Also Ben Sira 7.23) and *mūsār* 'discipline' occurs frequently in *Proverbs*. On the other hand, *ytsr* is more easily explicable as a form from *'sr* (P. Leander, *Laut- und Formenlehre des Ägyptisch-Aramäischen*, Göteborgs Högskolas Årsskrift xxxiv, 1928, p. 59, para. 37e).

Col. vi. 79 is apparently a riddle or teasing question (see below), and 92f. is, according to Roth's terminology (W. M. W. Roth, *VTS* xiii, p. 42), a graded numerical saying (see below pp. 654f.). There is one case (88f.) and perhaps a second (90f.) of the use of imagery in a similitude, and the final words of 91 are apparently the fragment of a fable ('The ass made obeisance to the she-ass from love of her, and the birds. . . .').

79: What is stronger than wine foaming in the press? (Cowley)
What is stronger than a braying ass? The load. (Ginsberg, *ANET*).

The final word is broken and Cowley and Ginsberg restore it differently (C. *bgt'*; G. *bwt'*); Ginsberg follows Baneth (*OLZ* xiv, p. 297; cf. Jean-Hoftijzer, p. 33, Cowley, pp. 233f.), and explains the line as a riddle. Cowley's explanation presupposes not quite a riddle, but perhaps a courtly contest such as that described in I Esdras 3.5: 'Let each of us state what one thing is strongest; and to him whose statement seems wisest, Darius the king will give rich gifts and great honours of victory' (RSV). The case for wine is stated thus: Gentlemen, how is wine the strongest? It leads astray the minds of those who drink it. It makes equal the mind of the king and the orphan, of the slave and the free, of the poor and the rich. It turns every thought to feasting and mirth, and forgets all sorrow and debt. It makes all hearts feel rich, forgets kings and satraps and makes every one talk in millions. When men drink they forget to be friendly with friends and brothers, and before long they draw their swords. And when they recover from the wine, they do not remember what they have done. Gentlemen, is not wine the strongest, since it forces men to do these things? (vv. 18–24). The question, 'What is stronger than wine foaming in the press?', suggests comparison with, 'Gentlemen, how is wine the strongest?'. The allusion in *Ahikar* is to the intoxicating power of new wine (wine foaming or fermenting in the press) and its absolute mastery over those who drink it.

88f.: C. The lion devours (?) the hart in the secrecy of (his) den(?), and he . . . and will shed his blood and eat his flesh: so is the contact of *men*.

G. The lion will *lie in wait* for the stag in the concealment of the . . . and he . . . and will shed its blood and eat its flesh. Even so is the meeting of *men*.

The differences in translation reflect textual uncertainties. Cowley (p. 235) takes *msmh* (pael participle) to mean 'devour'. Jean-Hoftijzer (p. 194), *s.v. smy*, suggests 'pursue' and notes that Ginsberg's meaning 'lie in wait' agrees with Joüon. *swyd* is read by Jean-Hoftijzer as *swyr* (p. 191) with the meaning 'lair' (also G. R. Driver, *An. Or.*, xii, 1935, p. 55, 'hiding-place').

The meaning of this may be that the law of the jungle also holds in human society, and that the world of man no less than the animal world is red of tooth and claw with rapine. 'So is the contact of man' is summary interpretation and makes explicit the intention to establish a comparison.

90f.: C. *From fear of* the lion the ass left *his burden* and will not carry it. He shall bear shame before his fellow *and shall* bear a burden which is not *his*, and shall be laden with a camel's load.

G. An ass which leaves [*its load*] and *does not carry it* shall take a *load* from its companion and take the burden which is not its [own with its own] and shall be made to bear a camel's load.

The text is broken at the beginning and has been conjecturally restored by Cowley (p. 235), so as to connect 'lion' with what follows. Ginsberg's translation requires the conjectural insertion of the words *ʿm zylh*. Otherwise the translations differ only in the rendering of *bwt* (Cowley, 'shame', Hebrew *bwš*; Ginsberg, following Baneth, 'burden', cf. Jean-Hoftijzer, p. 33, *s.v. bwt*).

This is probably another similitude, which, however, unlike 88f. is not furnished with an interpretation. According to the translation of Cowley the interpretation would be: The man who jettisons the burdens of duty and runs away from responsibility because of cowardice will have his back bent by more grievous burdens. Ginsberg's translation would mean: The man who will not carry his fair load of responsibility will be made to carry a double load ('camel's load' = 'what two asses can carry').

Only in the numerical saying (92f.) are the sanctions of religion invoked. Hence col. vi opens on a note of parental authority and ends by affirming what is meritorious and pleasing in the sight of Šamaš. There may be something missing after *hkmh* (Cowley, p. 236), although the three items in question are detailed satisfactorily. They are: hospitality as opposed to selfish guzzling, the acquisition of a full measure of wisdom (*kbš*, cf. Driver, *op. cit.*, p. 56), and secretiveness or the safeguarding of confidences. The rendering of Ginsberg ('one who guards wisdom') would mean one who is consistently wise and is always on his guard against any deviation from wise behaviour. Cowley translates 'one who restrains (?) wisdom', i.e., keeps his wisdom to himself or, possibly, keeps it under control and, as a contrast to *'bdh* in 94, does not let it go astray through drunkenness (cf. Jean-Hoftijzer, p. 115). As in the *Counsels of Wisdom*, Šamaš is the overseer and guarantor of morals and *mores*.

Col. vii is almost entirely Instruction, and there are two main themes, in praise of secretiveness (96–99) and correct behaviour towards a king (100–8). The formal patterns are as follows:

96f.: 'My son', imperative, motive clause, imperative (antithetic), jussive.

98: Imperative, imperative, motive clause.

99: Imperative, imperative, motive clause.

100: Imperative, jussive, asyndetic motivation.

101f.: Preliminary argument, imperative, asyndetic motive clause. Imperative. Jussive, final clause.

103–8: Preliminary argument, imperative. Imperative, motive clause, asyndetic motive clause, extended motivation (105–8).

It will be seen that the motive clause, which is a characteristic element of the form of the Instruction, is prominently represented. What I have called preliminary argument (or 'preamble') corresponds in function to the motive clause, but it anticipates the imperative(s) rather than coming after it. The reflections in 105–8 have a somewhat loose connection with the instructions conveyed by the imperatives in 100–3. The 'my son' form of address occurs only in 96, but the instructions as a whole are consistent with the assumption that they are addressed to 'my son'. This section more than any other, both in respect of form and content, suits the supposition that Ahikar is addressing Nadin, his heir-designate, and briefing him for office. The appropriateness of 100–8 in this regard is obvious, while secretiveness or taciturnity (96–99) was also, as we have seen, thought to be a statesmanlike quality.

The remnants of the section consist of an opening passage in praise of wisdom (95), a similitude connected with the theme of secretiveness (109) and the fragment of a contest (?) fable (110). The following remarks will illustrate *inter alia* the way in which imagery is employed in this section and will bear out the observation made in the general introduction that there is a paucity of popular proverbs in Ahikar, but ample evidence of the deliberate literary exploitation of imagery.

95: C. Even to gods is it precious, *to it for ever* belongs the kingdom, in *heaven* it is treasured up, for the lord of holiness has exalted *it*.

G. To gods also she is dear. *For all time* the kingdom is *hers*. In *heaven* is she established, for the lord of holy ones has exalted *her*.

Ginsberg assumes, probably rightly, that Wisdom is personified. She is spoken of in a manner which recalls Proverbs (8.22–31), Job (28), Ben Sira (Ecclus. 1.1f.; 24.3f.) and Wisdom of Solomon (7.22f.), where Wisdom is present at and presides over the creation of the world and informs the created world as a principle of order. Nothing so explicit is said of the status and functions of wisdom here, but her exalted role and power are none the less affirmed. She has been exalted by the lord of holiness (or 'holy ones', meaning angels or heavenly beings), she is established in heaven and she exercises sovereignty (*mlkwt*) in perpetuity.

98: C. For a word is (like) a bird, and when he has sent it forth a man does not *recapture it* (?).

G. For a word is a bird; once released no man *can recapture it*.

99: C. For stronger is the ambush of the mouth than the ambush of fighting.

G. For the *instruction* of a mouth is stronger than the *instruction* of war.

Ginsberg reads *'db* (*ANET*, p. 428, n.6) and Cowley (also Jean-Hoftijzer, p. 23) *'rb*.

100: C. Soft is the speech of a king, (but) it is sharper and stronger than a *two*-edged knife.

101: C. Swifter is his anger than lightning.

G. His wrath is swift as lightning.

It is doubtful whether *zʿyr* can mean 'swift' (cf. Cowley, p. 237, Jean-Hoftijzer, p. 79, *s.v. zʿr*).

103: C. *In presence* of a king, if (a thing) is commanded thee, it is a burning fire.

G. *The wrath* of a king, if thou be commanded, is a burning fire.

104: C. *Why* should wood strive with fire, flesh with a knife, a man with *a king?*

105: C. I have tasted even the bitter sloe, and the *taste* was strong, but there is nothing which is more bitter than poverty.

G. I have tasted even the bitter medlar, and *I have eaten* endives, but there is naught which is more bitter than poverty.

Cowley's reconstruction is *wṭʿm*' and Ginsberg's *w'klt*. The sense desiderated for *ḥsyn* is determined by this decision. Cowley renders 'strong' and Ginsberg 'endives', Ugaritic *ḫswn* (Cowley, p. 238, *ANET*, p. 429, n. 12, Jean-Hoftijzer, p. 93).

105f.: C. Soft is the tongue of a *king*, but it breaks the ribs of a dragon, like death which is not seen.

Ginsberg renders 'like a plague which is not seen': *mwt*, 'plague' (cf. Jean-Hoftijzer, p. 146, 'probably "plague"').

109: C. A good vessel hides a thing within itself, but *one that* is broken lets it go forth.

G. A good vessel covers a word in its heart, and a broken one lets it out.

These examples show that nearly all the imagery in this section occurs in connection with the arguments by which the pertinence and reasonableness of the imperatives are elucidated, whether these have the form of preamble, motive clause or extended motivation. The imagery is used in order to give point to the substance of the supporting arguments, and idea and images are laid side by side. Hence all the images are 'interpreted'. The basic relationship is one of comparison and this may take the form of identity (metaphor, 98), resemblance (simile, 107: 'a king is like the merciful(?)'; 108: 'like the sun' or 'like Šamaš'), comparison in respect of superiority and inferiority (100).

The injunction to secretiveness is made more memorable by the remark that a rashly spoken word is irrevocable in the circumstance that it cannot be recalled from public possession or erased from public knowledge. It is a bird which was once caged and detained in privacy, but which has flown away to freedom and can never be recaptured (98). The ambush, as a stratagem of war, is compared with 'the ambush of the tongue'. Secretiveness is not a counsel which underestimates the power of utterance or assumes that silence is always better than speech. Most men, however, err on the side of garrulity and speak ineffectively or dangerously. Speech is weighty and even devastating when it is kept for the right moment, and the wise man will lie in wait for that moment and wield the lash of his tongue to rout his adversaries (99).

The sentence (109) which compares the sound with the defective vessel, also develops the theme of taciturnity. A feature of particular interest is the effect which is secured by the ambivalence of two of the words – an ambivalence which is reflected in the differing translations of Cowley and Ginsberg. Because of this ambivalence there is a coalescence of imagery and interpretation. *mlh* can mean either 'thing' (C.) or 'word' (G.), and *lbbh* 'centre', 'midst' or 'heart' (Jean-Hoftijzer, p. 134). The vessel which retains liquid does the job for which it was made, but the vessel which leaks is useless. And the mind or heart which cannot conceal information, opinions, plans, below the level of articulation until it adjudges the time to be ripe for their disclosure or, perhaps, never to disclose them, serves its owner badly.

Where the intention is to underline the contrast between the soft, refined (*rkyk*) accents of a king and his irresistible will (his incisive and urgent authority), his speech is said to be 'sharper and stronger than a two-edged sword' (100). He will not brook interference, opposition or delay; 'his anger is swifter than lightning' (101) and his command is 'a burning fire' (103). Beneath his calm and civility there are fires of inflexible resolve and determination. He summons his servants to the urgent implementation of his demands and, if they fail, he consumes them in his anger. A king exists to be served, not to be opposed and thwarted; this is the way of futility and destruction. It is a hopelessly unequal contest, a senseless rendezvous with death. It is as if a piece of wood spoiling for a fight should advance towards the flames, or a piece of flesh should invite a contest with a knife (104). The transition to the theme of poverty (105) is perhaps to be explained by supposing that it is envisaged as the consequence of falling out of favour with a king and there may then be an allusion to Ahikar's own suffering as a result of Nadin's treachery (cf. 26f.; Tobit 1.20f.). On the other hand, this section seems to have consistently in view the situation when Nadin was heir-designate and Ahikar his instructor. In any case the bitterness and acidity of the sloe are recalled in order to point to another more unendurable bitterness, that of poverty.

The contrast between the quiet accents of a king and the terrible power which he wields (cf. 100) is resumed in 105–6. The soft tongue of a king breaks the ribs of a dragon – it conceals a power which will increase its pressure of application until even the most powerful opposition is crushed. His speech is quiet, but the embrace into which he beckons his adversaries is the embrace of death, as the ribs of a dragon might be crushed by an adversary whose demeanour belies his strength. The other simile, 'like death which is not seen', indicates the terrible, silent, invisible speed of the king's revenge. There is no defence against it, because the lethal blow has been struck before the approach of danger is cognized. The simile is enhanced if 'plague' (G.) is a legitimate translation of *mwt*. The king's revenge is like the action of a deadly plague which strikes and kills without allowing its victims even a glimpse of danger.

Only two cases of imagery in the instructions themselves call for comment. '*Count* the secrets of thy mouth' (99) in the context seems to mean: Take stock of your hidden resources of logomachy (perhaps the damaging secrets which are in your possession), and come to the help of your brother against his adversary. 'Do not put sackcloth upon thee and hide thy hands' (103) is imaginatively constructed and obscure. Cowley presupposes that *thn* is a scribal error for *tntn* and interprets: 'Do not go into mourning about it and pretend that you cannot do it' (p. 238). The fitting response to a royal imperative is not passive resignation and defeatism, but urgent and enterprising action. The following motive clause is then translated by Cowley, '*for* also the word of a king is with wrath (*ḥmr*) of heart'. Ginsberg renders quite differently: 'Let it not be kindled (*'l thnšq*) against thee and burn (*wtkwh* for *wtksh* with Baneth, cf. Cowley, p. 238) thy hands. *Cover* up the word of a king with the veil of the heart' (for *ḥmr*: 'veil', cf. Jean-Hoftijzer, p. 91). Ginsberg associates this instruction with the instant obedience required by the 'burning fire' (see above) of the king's command. The dilatory official will have his hands burned by the flame of the king's anger. 'Cover up the word of a king with the veil of the heart' is, on the other hand, another image for the ideas communicated in 109 by the contrast between the sound and leaking vessel. The confidant of a king must so discipline himself as to keep secrets and respect confidences consistently.

There are no instructions in col. viii, whose contents, for the most part, can be divided into two kinds:

(*a*) sentences in which idea and image are juxtaposed with a view to expressing the idea in a striking way. This effect may be secured by a simple co-ordination of image and idea (111, 112), where the relationship of resemblance is not fully articulated. Or the sentence may be a fully-fledged simile (125); or it may be a similitude (parable) to which a succinct interpretation is added after the manner of 88f. (116). One sentence is an example of deliberate artistic concreteness (113), and another may be a proverbial comment on a literary conceit (117);

(*b*) this is a block of fable material, a contest fable (the leopard and the goat, 117–20), and another piece which has affinities to the fable in that it attributes to sheep the attitudes and language of humans, but which may perhaps be described as a parable of master and sheep (121). It seems to have a bearing on the religious teaching – the definition of man's role under the gods and the nature of the divine order – with which the section closes (122–5, cf. 114f.).

111: C. I have lifted sand and carried salt, and there is nothing which is heavier than *debt* (G. *rage*).

Cowley conjectures *zpt'* for the missing word (cf. 130: *tzp zpt'*: 'arrange a loan', 'contract a debt'; see Jean-Hoftijzer, p. 106, *s.v. yzp*).

The intention of the imagery is obscure because of the uncertainty surrounding the last word of the line. According to Cowley's restoration the meaning is that there are burdens more grievous than the physical strain of carrying heavy weights, and such is the inexorable, unrelenting weight of debt – the gnawing anxiety which depresses the mind, the vice-like grip which does not relax until the debtor breaks under the strain. The meaning according to Ginsberg is that it is better to stagger under a heavy load which taxes the strength to the limit than to bear the weight of another man's anger. Despite this uncertainty the following sentence confirms that both Cowley and Ginsberg are on the right lines and that the intention is to compare one kind of burden (physical) with a burden of a different order.

112: C. I have lifted chaff and taken up crumbs, and there is nothing which is lighter than (to be) a sojourner.

The lack of weight in the chaff (G. 'bruised straw') and crumbs (G. 'bran') illustrates the lack of privilege and status of one who is not a first-class citizen of the community in which he resides (*twtb*, cf. Hebrew *tôšāb*). The correlation of 'weight' and status, and 'lightness' and contempt, in Hebrew *kbd* and *qll* (see below, p. 302) should not be overlooked in any assessment of the appositeness of the imagery. *qlyl* as applied to the *twtb* may be ambivalent (cf. Cowley, p. 239). If the figure of the first part of the sentence is maintained, it means that there is less weight in him than in chaff and crumbs, but the interpretation of this is that the *twtb* has no standing in the community. He is an object of contempt (cf. 141: 'Do not disclose thy secrets before thy friends and let not thy name (reputation) be held in contempt (*yql*) before them').

113: C. A sword will trouble calm waters whether they be bad (or) good.

G. War troubles calm waters between good *friends*.

The incompleteness of the line makes interpretation hazardous. Ginsberg follows Ungnad in translating *r'yn* 'friends' (also G. R. Driver, *JRAS*, 1932, p. 88). Cowley's translation is improbable and I follow Ginsberg for the most part, although I would render *ḥrb* 'sword', which, as Jean-Hoftijzer observes (pp. 95f.), is a symbol of devastation (Matt. 10.34). The sword symbolizes strife, and strife is compared to a storm at sea in respect of its effect on human relationships. As the gales whip up the calm waters into a savage fury, so strife or war creates enmity between friends when they find themselves on different sides. *dlḥ*, 'disturb' (Jean-Hoftijzer, p. 58), is cognate with Accadian *dalāḫu* and Hebrew *dālaḥ*.

114f.: C. A little man when he multiplies his words, they fly away(?) above him, for the opening of his mouth . . . gods, and if he were beloved of (the) gods they would put something good in his palate to speak.

G. If a man be small and grow great, his words *soar* above him. For the opening of his mouth is an *utterance* of gods, and if he be beloved of gods, they will put something good in his mouth to say.

These lines are obscure, and Ginsberg's translation is disallowed by Cowley who urges that *wyrbh* must govern *mlwhy* and that the intention of the phrase 'multiply words' is pejorative (p. 239; so also G. R.

Driver, *An. Or.* xii, p. 56). The two lines apparently contrast the hollow grandiloquence of the man of slight stature with the person who has been endowed by the gods with the power of weighty utterance. According to Ginsberg, the meaning is that there are no self-made men and that the rise of one from obscurity to prestige and power is always the action of the gods, who confer on him the power of weighty words – an indispensable prerequisite of preferment. Whatever precise interpretation is put on these verses, the inference can be drawn that men cannot be more than the gods have made them or achieve more than the endowment of the gods allows – the doors to places of preferment cannot be rushed; a 'little man', however he postures, cannot become great. He can only achieve status if he is beloved of the gods and elected to eminence (see above, pp. 60f.).

116: C. Many are the stars *of heaven whose* names man knows not; so man knows not men.

Cowley (p. 239) thinks that the restoration *kwkby šmy' zy* may be regarded as certain. The stars are remote from man and his knowledge of them is exiguous, but men are no less strangers to each other. The difficulty of 'naming' the stars, where 'naming' indicates a fullness of knowledge, points to the difficulty which one man has in penetrating the mystery of another's personality and thereby achieving social enrichment. It is only by an effort which in its own way is as taxing and demanding as the rigorous intellectual effort with which the study of nature is pursued, that an individual breaks out of the isolation of his individuality and penetrates the lives of other men in depth.

117: C. There *is no* lion in the sea, therefore they call the . . . lion(?).

G. There is *no* lion in the sea, therefore they call the flood a *lb'* (lion).

Cowley leaves *qp'* untranslated, observing that the verb means to float on top of water or to congeal, and suggesting the meaning 'scum'. He notes Epstein's suggestion, adopted by Ginsberg, 'they call the flood a lion', which would be a conceit. In this case ,'surf' would be a more suitable translation, and the usage would be similar to our 'white horses'. Ginsberg supposes that the principle which is enunciated is *lucus a non lucendo et canis a non canendo* (p. 429, n.18). There are those who are so offended by simplicity that they create complications which do not exist. There is an addiction to the recondite which destroys lucidity. Pedantry creates artificial difficulties and darkens counsel. The sentence would then be a genuine proverb.

118–20: G. The leopard met the goat when she was cold. The leopard answered and said to the goat, 'Come, I will cover thee with my hide'. The goat [answered] and said to the leopard, 'What need have I for it, *my lord*?. Take not my skin from me.' For he does not greet the gazelle except to suck its blood.

ṭby', 'gazelle', is probably a mistake for *'nz*', 'goat' (Cowley, p. 240; Ginsberg, p. 429, n.19). The final sentence is an explanatory comment, disclosing the motives of the leopard.

This is a contest fable in which the goat fences skilfully with the leopard, evades him with a clever feint and earns the plaudits of the reader for her canniness. The moral, if there is one, would be that it is better to be cold than to be dead.

120f.: C. The master(?) went to the *sheep* . . . I will be silent. The sheep answered and said to him, 'Take for thyself what thou wilt *take* from us. We are *thy sheep*.'

G. The bear went to the *lambs*. '*Give me one of you and I* will be content.' The lambs answered and said to him: 'Take whichever thou wilt of us. We are *thy lambs*.'

For the lacuna, Ginsberg supplies, 'Give me one of you and', following Baneth. Cowley (p. 240) queries whether *'štq* can mean 'I will be content'. Cowley reads *rb*'(?), 'master', and Ginsberg *db*', 'bear'. The following lines (122f.) incline me to the view that this is more a parable of master and sheep than a contest fable, although the sheep are made to behave and speak like human beings as in the fable. Men are as absolutely at the disposal of God and as subject to his sovereign choice as are sheep in respect of their owner. Men have no claims to make on God and there is no obligation on his part to engage in prior consultation before he disposes of them. The interpretation of the parable is contained in 122f.: 'For it is not in the power of men to lift up their feet or to put them down without the gods. For it is not in thy power to lift up thy foot or to put it down.' This is in line with the religious teaching of 114f. – a man is made or broken by the attitude of the gods.

124f.: C. If the eyes of (the) gods are over *men* a man cuts(?) wood in the dark and does not see, like a thief who breaks into(?) a house and *escapes*(?).

G. If God's eyes are on men, a man may chop wood in the dark without seeing, like a thief who demolishes a house and . . .

Cowley expresses puzzlement at this sentence (p. 240), but Ginsberg's translation makes the general sense clear, even if detailed difficulties remain. If the gods exercise a gracious vigilance over a man, he can take risks and emerge unscathed. He can, for example, cheerfully hazard his fingers chopping wood in the dark. In respect of the 'luck' which he enjoys he is like a thief who chances his arm on a highly risky and audacious piece of housebreaking and gets away with it(?).

Col. ix is almost entirely Instruction and there are seven topics:
(*a*) Do not commit aggression against the righteous (126, 128);
(*b*) Be industrious and your needs will be met (127);
(*c*) Be a discriminating borrower, but borrow when it is necessary and advantageous (129–31);
(*d*) Listen critically and sift out truth from falsehood (132–5);
(*e*) Do not despise your lot and do not be covetous or over-ambitious (136–8);
(*f*) Hold your father and mother in high regard (138–40);
(*g*) Do not give away secrets (141).

The 'my son' form of address occurs twice (127, 129), but the contents of the instructions would not lead us to suppose that they are addressed to one destined to hold high office in the state. A vizier-designate would not be advised to work hard so as to have the wherewithal to feed himself and his children (127), and certainly not to borrow corn and wheat for that purpose (129). The reminiscences in 139f. are apparently based on Ahikar's experience of betrayal at the hands of Nadin, and the section as a whole is not particularly apposite as an address to Nadin when he stands on the threshold of preferment and power. There is nothing unusual about the formal structure of the instructions, as the following outline will show:

126, 128 (interrupted by 127): 2 imperatives, 2 'lest' clauses, motivation (128).

127: 2 imperatives, consequential clause. Ginsberg reconstructs the broken text so as to supply a conditional clause before the first imperative (also in 129).

129: imperative, final clause.

130f.: imperative. Conditional clause, imperative, motivation.

132–5: imperative, 2 motive clauses, extended motivation (133–5).

136: 2 imperatives.

137: 2 imperatives.

138: jussive, motive clause. This is curse rather than Instruction, a curse invoking Šamaš.

139f.: reminiscences of Ahikar evoked by the curse in 138.

141: imperative, jussive.

The usual types of subordinate clauses are employed: the conditional clause preceding the imperative which defines the area where the instruction operates; the motive clause or extended motivation which demonstrates the reasonableness of the instruction or otherwise recommends acceptance of it; the final clause which describes the ends to be achieved by obedience; and the admonitory 'lest' clause which sketches the consequences of disobedience, a role which can be filled by the consequential clause when it follows a negatively formulated imperative and a motive clause (Do not . . . for . . . and so).

> 126, 128: C. *Bend not* thy bow and shoot not thy arrow at the righteous, lest God come to his help and turn it back upon thee. *If* thou hast *bent* thy bow and shot thy arrow at one who is more righteous than thou, it is a sin in the sight of God.
>
> 128: G. *If thou bend* thy bow and shoot thine arrow at a righteous man, from thee is the arrow, but from God the *guidance*.

Cowley (p. 241) maintains that *lṣdyq mnk* 'must go together', but Ginsberg construes differently. Cowley observes that *mn 'lhn* is difficult for 'as regards God' or 'in the sight of God', but he rejects *hdy*, because the papyrus 'is intact and blank' after *hd* (p. 241). He suggests that *hd* (or *hr*) is a slip for *hw*. Ginsberg follows Grimme (*OLZ* xiv, 1911, p. 537) in reading *hdy*' (Arabic *hudā*) 'direction', 'guidance', but this is thought improbable by Jean-Hoftijzer (p. 61, *s.v. h*'). *ḥṭ*' 'sin' is word-play on *ḥṭ* 'arrow'. Grimme and Ginsberg read *ḥṭ*' as the emphatic form of *ḥt* (Jean-Hoftijzer, p. 94, *s,v. ḥṣ*).

Two features of these lines deserve mention. The instruction is conveyed by means of imagery and does not have the prosaic exactitude which normally characterizes such directives. It is not to be taken literally as advice not to attack a righteous man with bows and arrows and, as it is not restricted to narrow semantic bounds, it lends itself to considerable freedom of interpretation. It could mean: 'Do not practise aggression against a righteous man', but it could also be open to such an interpretation as: 'Do not make an assault on the welfare and integrity of a righteous man'. There is therefore a genuine 'proverbial' element in the language of this instruction. The second point concerns the reasons which are adduced in support of this advice, which imply that the righteous man is the object of God's care and that any violation of his rights will rebound on the aggressor. There is consequently a religious doctrine involved here, according to which God will always take the side of the righteous man and uphold his cause against the evil aggressor.

127: C. . . . do thou, O my son, gather every harvest, and do every work, then thou shalt eat and be filled and give to thy children.

G. *If* thou *be hungry*, my son, *take every trouble* and do every labour, then wilt thou eat and be satisfied and give to thy children.

Cowley equates *kṣr* with *qṣr* (p. 241, cf. Jean-Hoftijzer, p. 126, *s.v.*, *kṣr*, *ksyr*). Ginsberg's translation makes the line a general injunction to diligence; Cowley's a reference to assiduousness in agricultural operations.

130f.: C. A heavy loan and from a wicked man, borrow not, and *if* thou borrow, take no rest to thy soul till *thou pay back* the loan. *A loan* is pleasant *when there is need*, but the paying of it is the filling of a *house*.

G. Take not a heavy loan from an evil man. *Moreover*, *if* thou take a loan, give no rest to thyself until *thou repay the* loan. *A loan* is sweet as . . . but its repayment is grief.

The translations differ in the second half of 131, where Cowley supplies *zy ḥsyr* and *b* (*by*, 'house', cf. Jean-Hoftijzer, p. 35, *s.v. byt*). For the phrase *mml' by* see Cowley (p. 242) and Jean-Hoftijzer (p. 151, *s.v. ml'*), who regard Cowley's interpretation as probably correct.

This is a good example of precise, firm advice communicated in plain, clear language. The one instructed is left in no doubt what he ought to do, and since the instruction has this severely practical objective, it is concerned with functional efficiency rather than literary effect. It is for this reason, as I have already suggested, that a high incidence of imagery is not to be expected in this genre. Here the advice is admirably clear and incisive. Do not borrow heavily from a wicked man and, if you borrow, make the repayment of it a first priority. A loan is sweet when there is need(?), that is, it immediately takes the sharp edge off want, but the danger is that one may be lulled into a false sense of security and well-being and forget that a debt has been contracted. The arranging of a loan is the beginning and not the end of a striving towards a more stable economic equilibrium. 'The paying of it is the filling of a house' is an obscure metaphor which may mean, as Cowley supposes, that the repaying of it is a task equivalent to the furnishing of a house.

132–5: C. *All that thou hearest thou mayest try* by thy ears, for the beauty of a man is his faithfulness, *for* his hatefulness is the lying of his lips. *At* first the throne is *set* up for the liar, but *at last* his lies *shall* find (him) out, and they shall spit in his face. A liar has his neck cut, like a maiden of the south(?) who *hides*(?) (her) face, like a man who makes a curse which came not forth from (the) gods.

G. My *son, hearken not* with thine ears to *a lying man*. For a man's charm is his truthfulness; his repulsiveness, the lies of his lips. *At first* a throne is *set* up for the liar, but in the *end they* find out his lies and spit in his face. A liar's neck is cut, like a . . . virgin that *is hidden* from sight, like a man who causes misfortune which does not proceed from God.

At the beginning of 132, Cowley reconstructs the broken text [*kl zy tšmʿ tbḥnn*]*hy* and Ginsberg, following Baneth, reads [*bry ʾyš mkdb ʾltšmʿn*]*hy* (cf. Cowley, p. 242). Ginsberg leaves *tymnh* (134) untranslated; Cowley supplies *tḥbʾ* 'hides', since he takes the *l* of *lʾnpyn* as the particle of the direct object. Ginsberg translates 'is hidden', taking *l* to mean 'in respect of'. *lḥyt* means 'evil action' rather than 'curse' (Cowley, cf. Jean-Hoftijzer, p. 137, *s.v. lḥy*).

The arguments supporting the instruction are stated picturesquely. In the beginning, lies may bring a man profit and power so that he exercises dominion over his fellows like a king on his throne, but in the long run he will be exposed for what he is, discredited and reviled. He will be such an object of contempt that men will spit in his face. The first of the two similes with which the argumentation concludes is extremely obscure. Cowley (p. 242) suggests that 'neck' may be a symbol of strength, as in the case of Hebrew *ʿrp*, and so 'a liar's neck is cut' will mean 'a liar's strength is broken'. Ginsberg suggests that the meaning of the phrase is that the liar speaks very softly, and that in respect of his soft, alluring voice he is like a virgin hidden from the eye whose voice falls pleasantly on the ears. Cowley suggests that 'like a virgin of the south who hides her face' may indicate that the liar is being likened to one who wears a mask. He is perpetually in disguise, constantly posturing, never revealing his real self to men, incapable of a genuine personal relationship.

The second simile, 'like a man who performs an evil action which does not proceed from God' means that the liar is doomed to failure. The evil action proceeding from God is the evil visited on the wrongdoer. Men can only act effectively if they are in harmony with the divine order. The ultimate theological reason why the liar will make shipwreck of his life is that he has set his face against a moral order which God will not fail to uphold. The thought that a man has his appointed place in the order and that it is dangerous for him to strive too much in case he exceeds the limits which are fixed for him and trespasses on the forbidden is the theme of 136f., especially 136, '*Despise not* that which is in thy lot, and covet not some great thing which is withheld from thee' (Ginsberg, 'denied thee'; see above pp. 60f.).

> 138–40: C. *He who* is not proud of (?) the name of his father and the name of his mother, let not the *sun* shine *upon him*, for he is an evil man. *From myself* has my curse gone forth, and with whom shall I be justified? The son of my body has spied out (?) my house, *and what* can I say to strangers? *There* was a cruel witness against me, and who then has justified me? From my own house went forth wrath, with whom shall I strive and toil?

Ginsberg reads '*My son has* been a false witness against me'. 'Let not the sun shine upon him' could be rendered 'let not Šamaš shine upon him', that is, Šamaš is invoked for the purposes of the curse. It is this curse which leads on to the reminiscences of Ahikar in 139f. The allusion would appear to be to Nadin, although *br bṭny* does not accurately describe Ahikar's relationship to his adopted son. He feels as frustrated and impotent as Amenemhet did when the incredible happened to him, and he expressed his sense of futility in a world which had gone mad (above, pp. 84f.). Ahikar's remarks are set in a forensic framework and his vocabulary is legal (*'ṣdq*, *ṣdqny*, *šhd ḥms*; and perhaps *hgšš*: 'spied out' and so 'informed against'). Ahikar has been traduced by the one closest to him who owes him most. Where then can he hope to find testimony which will establish his innocence and lead to his acquittal ('What can I say to strangers?')? He remarks despairingly: 'From my own house wrath has gone forth, with whom shall I strive and toil?' In a situation where a man's enemies are those of his own household, what is there left to strive for? What point is there in resisting or in having a will to win through? In laying information against Ahikar, to whom he owes everything, Nadin is worse than a common informer. Moreover, he is a perjurer (*šhd ḥms*) whose evidence damns Ahikar and must inevitably lead to his condemnation ('who then has acquitted me?').

Col. x has largely the character of instruction, and the topics are these:

(*a*) Do not quarrel or have a trial of strength with a superior (142–5);
(*b*) Do not forsake wisdom and do not try to be too clever (146f.);
(*c*) Do not exude too much charm, but do not be boorish (148);
(*d*) Humble yourself before God, who exalts the humble man (149f.).

The text of the following lines (151–7) is badly broken, but 151 is connected in a loose way with the instruction communicated in 149f. and 156 is a preamble to 157f. The religious sentiments in 149–51, 156–8 accord with those which have been noticed in the preceding sections. It belongs to God and not to men to defend justice and truth, to punish evil and falsehood, to bless and to curse. Man's role is to submit to God and his moral governance (cf. 122f.). As eyes are for seeing and ears for hearing, so let a mouth be for speaking the truth (157f.).

The analysis of form reveals no new features:

142: imperative.
143–5: imperative, motivation.
146: imperative. . . .
147: imperative, jussive.
148: imperative, 'lest' clause; imperative, 'lest' clause.
149: conditional clause, imperative, two relative clauses.

The relative clauses have the function of motive clauses ('who humbles the lofty man and *exalts the humble man*' instead of 'for he humbles the lofty man and *exalts the humble man*').

The theme of 142–5 (so far as this can be recovered by repairing the damaged text) is consonant with advice given to an apprentice statesman. It is unfortunate that the words which are most crucial to the establishing of the sense of the passage are those which are missing and have to be conjectured (*nṣwy* in 142, 'quarrelling'; *'l tšpṭ ky ylqḥ* in 143, 'do not contend for he will take'; *'yš rb yšpṭ* in 145, 'who contends with a great man'). It is only from the text so reconstructed (the translations of Cowley and Ginsberg rest on the same reconstruction) that the sentences are seen to be about quarrelling and litigation. The young man who would rise to the higher echelons of officialdom must eschew the bluntness or tactlessness which would produce a bad relationship between himself and his superior. He must beware of appearing before others as a too clever and self-opinionated young man; he should cultivate deference and suavity and should, to a degree, be pliant, always seeming to bend to the superior knowledge and authority of his superior. Above all, he should not suppose that he can have resort to the law in order to prove to himself and others that he is right and his superior is wrong. A superior is the wrong target for litigation, and far from serving to remove the stigma of his inferiority, such a public exhibition of his incapacity to get on with other people and his want of reasonableness and proportion will be a ruinous confirmation that he is a misfit in the public service. The danger of being too clever (or, perhaps, ambitious) and thereby forsaking wisdom is the subject of 146f. The differences in the interpretation of 147 are due to the broken text at the end of the line and to the divergent translations of *'l tstkl kbyr*. Thus:

C. Be not over crafty, *and let not thy wisdom* be extinguished.

G. Gaze not overmuch *lest* thy *vision* be dimmed.

Another suggested translation of *'l tstkl kbyr* is 'do not have too big ideas' (Jean-Hoftijzer, p. 192, *s.v. skl*), i.e., do not be overambitious.

If Ginsberg is followed, the instruction is not to be taken literally – it is not a piece of medical advice warning against possible damage to the eyes. Rather, it is an instruction clothed in imaginative language, and the image is that of a man scrutinizing an object so hard and so long that he can no longer see it. But the instruction is not concerned to issue a warning against this kind of thing; rather, it conjures up this picture and invests it with a wealth of allusiveness by making it a parable of a certain attitude of mind. The 'proverbial' character of this instruction gives it an openness and flexibility which a more orthodox, prosaic instruction could not possess. Such an instruction as this contains no cut-and-dried advice; it will not be pinned down to a limited area of 'plain meaning'. It preserves its freedom and openness, and imposes on every reader the task of interpretation. It also leaves him to decide how and when the advice which it conveys is applicable. In what situations would we do well to recall the injunction, 'Gaze not overmuch, lest thy vision be dimmed'? To try to generalize such an instruction is in a sense to imprison it, but it would be applicable wherever we wanted to say: Do not scrutinize too minutely, else you will not see the wood for the trees. Do not ponder too long, agonize too much, else you will be perplexed. Do not get bogged down in a mass of detail, else you will not be able to pick out what is salient, and will be unable to decide and act reasonably and incisively.

The phrase, 'let not thy wisdom be extinguished', in Cowley's reconstruction, is a case where the imaginative element resides in the verb, and when its significance is drawn out it is seen to imply a relationship of resemblance between the loss of wisdom and the putting out of a light or a fire. Without wisdom a man is in the cold or the dark. 'Do not let wisdom be snuffed out like a candle or doused like a fire.'

Another instruction illustrating the deliberate, artistic use of language is 148, where, unfortunately, the text is again broken, but is sufficiently complete, even without restoration, to allow the intention of the imagery to be gauged:

> G. Be not (too) sweet, lest they *swallow* thee: be not (too) bitter, *lest they spit thee out.*

In personal relationships there is a middle way between having someone eat you and having them spit you out, and this is the mean which is desiderated. Excessive sweetness, sugariness, charm will be interpreted by men as a sign of weakness and supineness. The too nice person is regarded by other men as weak and as one whom they have in their pocket. It is equally mistaken to be so boorish, thrawn, contrary, as habitually to repel and alienate people and to acquire the reputation of being jaundiced and insufferable.

> 157f.: G. Let not good *eyes* be darkened, nor *good* ears *be stopped, and let a good mouth love* the truth and speak it.

Again the interpretation is hazardous, because of the extent of the conjectural restoration, although in this particular case we can be confident that the general sense of the original text has been restored. The instruction is cast in the form of a similitude, and I take the meaning of 'good' in relation to eyes and ears to be 'sound' or 'healthy'. As the proper function of healthy eyes is to see and healthy ears to hear, so the function of a 'healthy mouth' is to love the truth (*kšyṭ*) and speak it. If *good mouth* is correctly restored, it is to be taken as a symbol of a right moral disposition – a love of the truth in thought and speech. The comparison is thus between aspects of physical and moral health, and *ṭb* in *pm ṭb*, which takes up the preceding occurrences of *ṭbn* denoting healthy eyes and ears, is indicative of moral health.

The preamble in 156 supplements these ideas. God will not permit subversion or perversion. He will not allow a man to call falsehood truth and truth falsehood. He will effectively maintain the distinction between truth and falsehood, and so preserve fitness and morality, for there are laws of moral health. The tongue is for speaking the truth as much as the eye is for seeing and the ear for hearing. 'God will subvert the mouth of the subversive and tear out *his* tongue' (cf. G. R. Driver, *An. Or.* 12, p. 56, 'gives the lie to the liar').

Col. xi, which contains only one imperative (171) and perhaps three jussives (163f., so Ginsberg), is hardly at all Instruction. It is dominated by religious reflections and by a moralism which hinges on religious dogma – belief in a theodicy. The theme of man's utter dependence on the gods is here further elaborated and developed in different ways. On the one hand nothing can be achieved by one who is at variance with the gods (160), and, on the other, retribution belongs to Šamaš alone (171). Vengeance is for the gods and not for men. It is enough that a man's behaviour is fitting and his heart good, for this arms him (Cowley) or makes him impregnable (Ginsberg) against the assaults of evil men (159). The world is arranged by the gods for the benefit of the righteous (167) and for the discomfiting and ruin of the wicked (168f.). The good man will keep a wary eye (conjecturing *yzhr*) on the bad man, for a man does not know (conjecturing *l' yd*ʿ) what is in the heart of his fellow (163). He will not be his companion or employer (*bʿl 'gr*, which Ginsberg translates 'neighbour'). Alternatively, Cowley (p. 245) suggests 'roof' for *'gr* or 'wages'. The meaning of *bʿl 'gr* in 164 is then either 'he will not be a co-tenant with him' or 'he will not employ him' (cf. Jean-Hoftijzer, p. 4, *s.v.* *'gr*$_2$ and *'gr*$_3$ 'wall', hence Ginsberg's rendering 'neighbour' for *bʿl 'gr*). One who has a social or business relationship with an evildoer may himself suffer damage in the course of the sifting process of the gods. Apart from this main theme, the section contains a broken contest fable between bramble and pomegranate (165f.), a sentence in which Ahikar appears to be reproaching Nadin for his infamous conduct (169f.), and two lines which are broken and unintelligible (161f.).

159: C. A man excellent in character and whose heart is good is like a strong *bow* which is *bent* by a *strong man.*

G. A man of becoming conduct whose heart is good is like a mighty *city* which is *situated* upon a *mountain.*

Ginsberg, following Nöldeke, reconstructs *kqryh*, 'like a city', which is in grammatical agreement with *ḥsynh*. *kqšth* (Cowley) requires *ḥsynt'*, but Cowley (p. 244) supposes that it is a mistake for *kqšt*. Cowley conjectures *bgbr*, 'by a strong man', and Ginsberg, presumably, *bgbl*, 'upon a mountain'. Cowley notes that *'yty* following the participle *mtngdh* is an unusual construction, while Ginsberg connects *'yty* with a following lacuna which he fills in conjecturally, 'There is *none that can bring him down*'.

The point of the simile, according to Cowley, is that the man whose goodness is deeply rooted and is truly inward is poised to counter and repel any attack which may be made on him. He has the resilience and the retaliatory power of the strong bow in the hands of a mighty bowman. Ginsberg's translation makes the simile hinge on the impregnability or invulnerability of the good man rather than his preparedness to take care of himself.

160: C. *If* a man stand *not* with (the) gods, how shall he be saved by(?) his own strength?

I follow Cowley in understanding 'stand with' as 'conform to', 'take the side of' (cf. Ginsberg '*dwell* with God'). The meaning is that a man cannot survive, far less prosper, if he pits his strength against the gods and determines to go it alone. He embarks on an unequal and futile contest, for he has no power to innovate on the basic order of existence. The gods will not permit him to disturb the harmony on which they have determined, and the wise man will live within these limits that his own life may be secure and harmonious (*'al*, 'by', is a difficulty noted by Cowley, p. 244).

165f.: The *bramble* sent (a message) to *the* pomegranate as follows: Bramble to pomegranate: 'What is the good of *your mass* of thorns *to the person who* touches your *fruit*?'. The *pomegranate answered* and said to the bramble: 'You are thorns in *your* entirety to whoever touches you.'

Although there are breaks in the text, it is not difficult to grasp the sense of the fable. The bramble could not have chosen worse ground on which to take issue with the pomegranate and receives the devastating rejoinder to which it laid itself open. A complaint that the thorns of the pomegranate tree are an inconvenience or hazard to those plucking its fruit might have propriety and weight if it came from the right quarter, but when it is made by a bush whose thorns are notoriously cruel to the hands and arms of those who pick its berries it is just ludicrous. The bramble, blind to its nastiness, is absurdly pretentious and a target for ridicule.

This invites comparison with the Jotham fable (Judg. 9.8–15), although *'āṭād* is perhaps rather 'thorn bush' than 'bramble' and is characterized somewhat differently. The fable is a satire on kingship, with which no self-respecting tree will associate itself. The trees prefer a useful function to an empty office (olive, fig and vine). So they ask the thorn bush, which is not endowed to make any positive contribution to the world of gods and men, to be a king. The thorn bush is flattered, but cannot suppress a twinge of misgiving that the invitation may be a leg-pull. So it replies with a mixture of grandiloquence and threat. It speaks like a cedar, as if it had the 'presence' and attributes of a royal tree ('come and take refuge in my shade', cf. Ezek. 31.1–9). Yet it makes what is no empty threat and reminds the others that it has a real destructive potential ('let fire come out of the thorn and devour the cedars of Lebanon').

The fable is political comment on the kingship which the men of Shechem have conferred on Abimelech (Judg. 9.16–21). Abimelech *qua* king and the men of Shechem are death to each other – they are mutually destructive agencies – and creative or constructive possibilities are as lacking in Abimelech as they are in the thorn bush. He will spark off a conflagration in which he himself will be engulfed, and, in this respect, the threat of Abimelech is as real as that of the thorn bush ('let fire come out from Abimelech and devour the citizens of Shechem and Beth Millo; and let fire come out from the citizens of Shechem and Beth Millo and devour Abimelech'). Kingship has no contribution to make to the well-being of human society, and the only one who will take it on is he who has nothing positive to give, but who is prepared to exercise his destructive potential.

The contrasting lots of *ṣdyq* and *ršyʿ* are described in 167–9. The world has been arranged (by the gods) for the benefit of the righteous man (all who encounter him are on his side), and the wicked are his spoil (restoring *ṣdyq hmw* in 169). The insecurity of the wicked and the ruin which hangs over them are portrayed imaginatively in 168:

C. *The house of* wicked men in the day of storm shall be destroyed(?), and in calm(?) its gates shall fall(?).

G. *A city* of wicked men shall on a gusty day be pulled apart, and in . . . its gates be brought low.

The meaning of several words is obscure and the way to an exact appraisal of the imagery is blocked. *tṯḥll* 'is profaned' and so, perhaps, 'is destroyed' (cf. Jean-Hoftijzer, p. 89, *s.v. ḥll*). For *šhynn* Cowley suggests 'tranquillity', but notes the difficulty of the form (p. 246). Cowley queries whether *yṣʿwn* may be the pael of *yṣʿ*, 'spread' and so 'cast down'. He notes that Nöldeke adduces Arabic *ṣġy* 'incline, lean' (cf. Jean-Hoftijzer, p. 246, *s.v. ṣʿy*, 'totter').

Wicked men are insecure and stand on the edge of catastrophe, just like those who are inside a jerry-built house when a gale is blowing; or, perhaps, like those who inhabit a city of flimsy and fragile buildings which will collapse like a pack of cards before the wild gusts of the wind.

171: If the wicked man takes hold of the skirts of thy garment, leave (it) in his hand. Then draw near to Šamaš; he will take his and give it to thee.

This is an example of the use of picturesque language to recommend a moral attitude or embody a moral principle. If the instruction had been conveyed prosaically, it might have read: 'Do not offer resistance to the wicked oppressor. Leave your just cause to Šamaš and he will not fail you.' There is the further possibility, however, that the taking of a garment as a pledge or surety for debt is envisaged. The righteous man who has fallen into the hands of a ruthless creditor and whose garment has been snatched off his back will not be exposed to shame or cold, for Šamaš will robe him in his garment. Even then, this would seem to be an imaginative device for communicating an instruction whose intention is general, rather than a specific piece of advice to a hapless debtor.

A similar case in which a general maxim is clothed in concrete forms of expression is found in 192, where an intelligent guess can be made as to how the text should be restored:

If thy master entrust to thee water to keep, keep it with care.
Afterwards he may leave gold with thee (cf. Cowley, p. 247).

On the level of literal interpretation, there is nothing particularly significant in the juxtaposition of water and gold. This becomes significant only because the two commodities have a paradigmatic or parabolic status within the instruction. The meaning is: first prove yourself competent in matters of routine administration, so that you may win the confidence of your master and rise to a position of exceptional trust and responsibility. The contrast is between the routine and the glamorous as well as the menial and the grand. In its own way, the keeping of water is as indispensable and vital as having charge of gold, but it is the role of the subordinate whose work is unspectacular and attracts little notice. Yet a weak link anywhere in the chain of command will disrupt the economy of a great household, and a master is always on the look-out for those who have proved themselves in positions which brought them little acclaim and are ripe for enhanced dignity and responsibility.

A similar use of language is illustrated by the fragment in 206:

C. *Between flesh* and shoe let him not put a pebble into my foot.

Cowley's translation assumes that *ynʿl* is a hanphel of *ʿll*. G. R. Driver (*JRAS*, 1932, p. 89) takes *ynʿl* as a pael of *nʿl* meaning 'cause to fester'. Grelot (*RB* lxviii, p. 193) derives *ynʿl* from *ʿll* (peal) and translates, 'may a pebble not enter my foot' (Jean-Hoftijzer, p. 180, *s.v. nʿl*; cf. P. Leander, *op.cit.*, para. 41 i).

Whichever translation is opted for, the saying has a proverbial character. A pebble between flesh and shoe is an intolerable impediment to a man who wants to be mobile. It hurts and cripples him for as long as he tries to walk with it, and it will eventually bring him to a standstill, if he is unable to remove the source of unrelenting irritation and pain. The special feature of Cowley's translation is the introduction of an adversary into the picture. The meaning then is: 'Let an opponent not insert an irritant so as best to exploit my vulnerability.' 'Let him not probe my weakness so as to sap my energy, impair my mobility, weaken my resolve, and reduce me to such a state of helplessness that my defeat is inevitable.'

Driver's translation gives the proverb a different turn of meaning: 'Let not a pebble between flesh and shoe make my foot fester.' The implication then is that if you get a pebble between flesh and shoe, you should remove it before it causes a blister or an ulcer. A stone should be removed promptly from the shoe, else it may set up an irritation which will cripple you for a long time. The interpretation of the proverb would then be: when there is a warning signal, act immediately, for delay will bring about a worsening of your situation and reduce your efficiency to act.

Of the fragments in cols. xii–xiv, only two more morsels call for comment. One is a fable (204f.) and the other a 'proverbial' instruction (208).

204f.: G. *A man* one *day said* to the wild ass: '*Let me ride upon thee* and I will maintain thee' . . . *Said the wild ass:* '*Keep* thy maintenance and thy fodder, and let me not see thy riding.'

Cowley suggests 'cushion' or 'saddle' rather than 'fodder' for *kstk* (Jean-Hoftijzer, p. 124, *s.v. kst*). On 'I will not see thy riding' he says: 'The phrase is so strange that there must be some mistake' (p. 247). It is less difficult if taken as a jussive (so Ginsberg).

This is a contest fable involving a wild ass and a man(?). The wild ass typifies freedom and utter lack of constraint, and the man(?) a capacity for organization and planning. He will put the wild ass to work, and in return can guarantee maintenance and fodder. The issue is increased security versus loss of freedom, and the ass prefers to remain as free as the wind and be exposed to chance rather than become a well-fed slave (cf. Gen. 16.12, *pere' 'ādām*, 'a wild ass of a man', referring to the freedom of the desert-dweller).

208: *Do not show* an Arab the sea nor a Sidonian the *desert*, for their work is different.

Restoring the broken text to read [*'lth*] *ḥwy* and *b*[*r'*]. The reading *pryšh*, 'different', is doubtful (Cowley, p. 248, 'not very probable'; cf. Jean-Hoftijzer, p. 237, *s.v. prš*).

The meaning is probably: 'Employ a man where his aptitude lies' (*Chacun à son métier*). The Arab is the master of caravan routes and the Sidonian knows the tracks of the sea. The one exercises his expertise on the ship of the desert and the other on the sea-going ship. This will be an apt instruction wherever a man is palpably a misfit and where his undoubted talents are squandered, because his expertise is not properly employed.

III

BABYLONIAN AND ASSYRIAN PROVERBS

What is envisaged here is not a thoroughgoing investigation of Babylonian proverbs, but a selective treatment of the available material from the point of view which will now be clear from my handling of the other 'proverbial' texts. My intention is to use these Babylonian proverbs in order to advance the examination of certain aspects of the 'proverb' in which I have been engaged. These are chiefly its representative potential and so its openness to interpretation, the function of imagery in conferring this representative capacity, and the quality of opaqueness, or even enigma, which may characterize the imagery.

It now appears that most of these proverbs are Sumerian in origin (cf. E. I. Gordon, *Sumerian Proverbs*, 1959), but I want to discuss them in their Babylonian dress for the following reasons. The ultimate objective of this study is to suggest a fresh approach to the biblical book of Proverbs, and so this material in a Semitic language (Accadian) forms a useful point of comparison. Moreover, the quantity of material in Accadian is more manageable in relation to the overall proportions of the work in which I am incorporating this section.

BWL, pp. 216f., *ll*. 42f.:

The fowler who had no fish, but [had caught] birds,
Holding his bird net jumped into the city moat.

It is not certain that this is a proverb, for the sayings in this collection do not have those characteristics on which I have seized to define a proverb. Lambert remarks on these two lines: 'A satire on those who cannot adjust themselves to the needs of a new situation' (p. 339), and this is to put a proverbial interpretation on the saying. The picture is that of a man whose occupation is catching birds and who has the necessary equipment to do this effectively, but who has no idea how to set about catching fish or what tackle is needed for the job.

There is an element of deliberate hyperbole here: this is artistic caricature rather than plain description. However clumsy or gauche a fisherman this fowler might make, it is evident that no fowler at any time tried to catch fish by jumping into a moat with his bird-net. Lambert takes the point to be a lack of flexibility or versatility and an inability to adjust oneself to a new situation and to employ the method which it demands. This interpretation fixes on certain elements of the picture, namely, that the man was an expert at catching birds and supposed that he could transfer his expertise from field to water without adjustment, and catch the fish which he needed. Another interpretation is not ruled out, namely, 'A man who is skilled in one task and well-equipped for it should not suppose that he can perform with like excellence in a totally different sphere of competence.' *Chacun à son métier* (cf. above, p. 182). Or, this might be given rather a different turn if the picture is thought to be that of a man who is not content to do the thing which he can do well, and is ambitious to do the thing which he cannot do. The general interpretation would then be: 'A man is not content to do the thing which he can do well, but is ambitious in directions where he is inept.' This interpretation would give the proverb a wide applicability and usefulness. It would be an observation on the person who is blind to his talents and also to his limitations; who neglects his gifts and cherishes illusions of fame and self-fulfilment which are incapable of realization.

BWL, pp. 228, 232, iii.13f.:

> The wise man is girded with a loin-cloth.
> The fool is clad in a scarlet cloak.

The contrasting articles of clothing indicated by the antithetic parallelism have a paradigmatic status and point to fundamental divergences between the respective bearings of wise man and fool. The wise man wears clothes only to make himself decent in public and does not suppose that they can add or take away from his essential worth; the fool wears them to call attention to himself, to make himself stand out as the object of curiosity and perhaps uncritical adulation. The fool, because he is a fool, is a showman and a hunter after publicity; there is nothing more to him than his scarlet cloak and he can only relate himself to other men on the level of spurious exhibitionism.

The wise man, because he is a wise man, cares for none of these things. The thought of employing such tricks has never occurred to him and does not constitute a temptation for him. He has no desire to appear other than he is, and he does not confront the showman with a self-conscious pride in his integrity. He hardly takes account of those who engage in such spurious pastimes. But he is available in his loin-cloth for those who value human relationships in depth, and desire to encounter a man who has kept faith with himself and is a lover of candour. The proverb, if it can be reduced to a general statement, declares that where there is real wisdom there is a shrinking from publicity, a natural and almost inevitable modesty, but where there is emptiness there is braggadocio and self-advertisement.

BWL, pp. 229, 232, iv.18–21:

Labourers without a supervisor, a field without a ploughman.
A house without an owner, a woman without a husband.

A proverb akin to 20 is quoted four times by Rib-Addi of Byblos to the Egyptian king: 'My field is like a woman without a husband because it lacks a cultivator.' Lambert observes that this is a combination of 19 and 21 (*BWL*, p. 233). Pfeiffer (*ANET*, p. 426) suggests that the original form of the proverb may have been: 'A woman without a husand is like a field without cultivation.' The Rib-Addi saying (*eqli-ia aššata ša lā muta mašil aššum bali īrišim*) is a fully articulated simile, the relationship of resemblance being indicated by *mašil* (cf. Hebrew *māšāl*, see above, pp. 22f. and below, pp. 262f., 414f.). In 18f., 20f. the image is simply set alongside the situation which it is intended to illumine in the manner which we have already noticed in *Onchsheshonqy* (p. 138) and *Ani* (p. 141). Thus the condition of labourers without a supervisor is correlated with the image of a field without a ploughman, and a home without an owner with a woman without a husband. The function of the imagery is thus indicated with the same degree of definiteness as in the simile and the metaphor. Depending on which way you look at it, you can either say that 'labourers without a supervisor' is the interpretation of 'a field without a ploughman', or that 'a field without a ploughman' enables one to grasp imaginatively the condition of labourers without a supervisor. Similarly, 'a home without an owner' is the interpretation of 'a woman without a husband' in the sense that the task which has been assigned to the imagery is to illumine this situation. That is to say, the condition of a home without an owner is analogous to that of a woman without a husband. The point of iv.18f. would then be that a field has no productive capacity if there is no ploughman to work it, and that no productive work will be got out of labourers, unless they are kept at it by a foreman. In iv.20f., the image of a woman without a husband points to the forlornness and desolation (and perhaps the vulnerability) of an ownerless and so empty house.

BWL, p. 235, *ll.* 21f.:

Would you place a lump of clay in the hand of him who throws?

This is obviously proverbial, although the interrogative form is unusual. It is not enough to take this question literally and to answer in the negative. It is not even enough to bring the question up to date and to reformulate it in such terms as: 'Would you supply missiles to a potential aggressor?' The question is capable of further disengagement from prosaic levels of interpretation, for its concreteness is not the concreteness of a pedestrian utterance. In how many situations still to take shape in the unborn future may this not be an apt and trenchant question! Would you act in a way detrimental to your own interests? Would you do what is prejudicial to your own welfare and safety? Would you add to the precariousness of your own position and contribute to its worsening and untenability?

BWL, pp. 240, 247 (*ANET*, p. 425),

ii.9f.: Eat no fat, and there will be no blood in your excrement.

11–14: Commit no crime, and fear [of (your) God] will not consume you.

15–17: Slander no one, and then grief [will not] reach your heart.

18–21: Do [no] evil, and then you will not experience lasting misfortune.

These are all formulated with an imperative followed by a consequential clause ('and so'), describing the consequences to be averted by attention to the command. These 'instructions' mean precisely what they say and no more. They are precise rules, one relating to diet and the others to behaviour. Their language consequently does not have to be investigated in depth, as the language of the 'proverb' has to be if the relation of its concreteness or imaginativeness to its representative or paradigmatic capacity is to be probed. In the biblical book of Proverbs, similarly isolated fragments of Instruction are found among material which is predominantly sentence literature (i.e., with the indicative and not the imperative), so that the observation which I make here has a bearing on my analysis of the biblical book of Proverbs (see especially below, p. 607).

BWL, pp. 240, 247, ii.22–25:

A scorpion stung a man. What did it get? [A common] informer brought about a man's death. What benefit did he receive?

A statement, then a question, followed by another statement which in turn is related to a question. The form is not that which a proverb might be expected to take, and yet the intent of this arrangement is imaginative. A feature of the proverbs of this collection is that they have no regularity of form. Sometimes, as here, they show a tendency to sprawl, and lack the laconic effectiveness of a compact proverb. But extreme brevity is also met with, as in ii.43f.: 'Intercourse brings on lactation.' In general it may be said that they are formless in comparison with the nicely balanced formulation, the *parallelismus membrorum* of the wisdom sentence in the biblical book of Proverbs.

The example under review is a kind of simile in which an observation on the habits of a scorpion is turned to the elucidation of the motives of a common informer. The effect is achieved not by a plain statement of the springs of an informer's actions, but by asking a question which the reader has to answer by connecting it with a prior question. What did the scorpion get?, and, What benefit did the informer receive? The procedure is therefore allusive – the significance of the correlation of scorpion and informer is hinted at, but not stated. The scorpion's behaviour is a matter of instinctive drives; it is compulsive and there is no more to be said about it. It stings because it cannot help stinging and the action has no end in view. What did it get? The suggestion is then that the common informer is just another amoral creature who is the slave of impulse and to whom motives cannot be ascribed, not even motives of malice and cupidity, for this would raise his behaviour to a human level. He is an informer because he cannot help being an informer, and there is no calculation in his activity. He is an unpleasant and dangerous insect. What benefit did he receive?

BWL, pp. 241, 247 (*ANET*, p. 425), ii.40–42:

Has she become pregnant without intercourse?
Has she become fat without eating?

Pfeiffer (*ANET*) translates: 'Without copulation she conceived, without eating she became plump', and cites Amos 6.12a: 'Do horses run upon rocks? Does one plough the sea with oxen?' (p. 425, n.12). If Lambert's translation is followed, the correspondence between this proverb and the Amos passage is even more striking, for both consist of two rhetorical questions which plainly demand an answer in the negative. The questions here are perhaps even better suited than those in Amos to make the point, for their effect does not lie in the conjuring up of outlandish or bizarre possibilities which are manifestly incredible – horses running on rocks or the sea being ploughed with oxen. They deal, on the contrary, with common and inescapable facts of life – sex and food – and evince a rare Rabelaisian relish and pungency. There is no moralism here; rather, the woman who is envisaged is something of a comic figure, whose protestations are to be received with a knowing and tolerant smile. The proverb is admirable just because everybody knows that a pregnant woman has had intercourse, or a fat woman has been eating too much. There are some protests or explanations or denials which are not worth entertaining, and which should be dismissed with a wink, because they contradict established laws of cause and effect. To any such lame explanation this proverb will always be a crushing rejoinder.

BWL, pp. 241, 247 (*ANET*, p. 425), ii.43f.:
Intercourse brings on lactation.

This has some connection with the preceding example in that it, too, deals with cause and effect (Pfeiffer, p. 425, n. 13), and moves in the sphere of elemental human experience, sexual intercourse and motherhood. It is not enough to say that this is an illustration of cause and effect (Pfeiffer), nor is it satisfactory to conclude that it is merely a biological observation and no more. It has the power of a proverb, and any example of cause and effect chosen at random would not necessarily be a proverb. Its proverbial status is connected with the economical and robust way in which it is expressed, and with the universality of its topic. When its representative capacity is fully exploited, it means that action is not fully responsible and realistic unless it includes acceptance of the consequences. It is possible to engage in a course of action and, at the same time, to refuse to entertain its consequences. Such an attitude is vitiated by a fundamental dishonesty or incapacity and is spurious. It is naïveté or escapism or obscurantism.

BWL, pp. 241, 247 (*ANET*, p. 425), ii.45–47:
If I put things in store, I shall be robbed. If I squander, who will give to me?

Lambert's translation is the same as that offered by Thureau-Dangin (*An. Or.* 12, 1935, pp. 310f.), except that the latter reads a little more into *lu-uš-kun*: 'If I hoard in miserly fashion'. Pfeiffer's translation is less satisfactory and does not offer a basis for the elucidation of the proverb. 'When I labour they take away (my reward): when I increase my efforts, who will give me anything?'

Thureau-Dangin supposes that the intention of the proverb is to commend a middle course between two extremes. It is the equilibrium or the mean between the extremes of miserliness and prodigality which is desiderated; one should neither be a hoarder nor yet given to squandering. I had taken the proverb rather differently, and I mention this because it illustrates the elusive properties of these proverbs and the fluidity of their interpretation. It can be taken as a statement of a dilemma between whose horns there is no way of escape. In this case the alternatives are exhaustive, and the contrast is not so much between miserly hoarding and prodigality as between providence and improvidence. The intention then is not to allow room for a middle way, but to contemplate providence and improvidence as the only two possibilities. It is an either-or situation, and whichever course a man follows he comes out badly in the end. If he saves for a rainy day, he is robbed; if he squanders his money, no one will help him in his penniless state. More generally interpreted, the proverb would then mean that there are some situations where one cannot even choose the lesser of two evils, but only one of two equal evils.

BWL, pp. 242, 248 (*ANET*, p. 425), iii.7–10:

> The strong man lives off what is paid for his strength (lit. arm),
> and the weak man off what is paid for his children.

I include this as an example of a wisdom sentence which is not a 'proverb', and so as a means of making clear the distinction which I draw between these two kinds. It is an artistically constructed sentence with antithetic balance, and contains pithy, sententious social comment, but it has no paradigmatic scope. 'What is paid for his children' probably refers to the sale of children into slavery, although the alternative translation offered by Pfeiffer ('through the wages of his child') gives a different turn to the meaning. The sentence would then mean that the strong man earns his own livelihood, while the weak man lives off the wages of his child. Oppenheim has shown that only general famine whose intensity was defined in terms of the market-price of barley – the most essential foodstuff – created the legal right for parents to sell their children. This would normally have outraged the social conscience, but it was acceptable to the community when parents resorted to it to keep themselves alive. This statement has to be qualified somewhat for Assyria, where the distress of an individual apparently entitled him to sell his children (A. L. Oppenheim, *Iraq* 17, 1955, pp. 69–89).

A general state of famine does not appear to be a relevant presupposition in our sentence, since its intention is not to contrast the different reactions of the strong and the weak man to a state of acute hunger. Indeed, the contrast between the strong man and the weak man almost loses its point in a situation where the weakness caused by hunger is the decisive factor. For this reason I am inclined to the view that the reference is not to what is paid for the sale of children into slavery but what is paid for their hire. The weak man lives off the industry of his children. Thus *ši-im i-di-šú* is paralleled by *ši-im* [*šè*]*r-ri-šú*. The first *ši-im* refers to the strong man's wages and the second to the wages earned by the weak man's children.

BWL, pp. 242, 248 (*ANET*, p. 425), iii.19–24:

> Do you strike the face of a moving ox with a *strap*? My knees are in constant motion, my feet are tireless, (yet) a half-wit pursues me with trouble.

uppu is translated 'strap' by both Lambert and Pfeiffer. Lambert discusses the difficulties of the translation at length (p. 248), and enquires how *uppu* can be both part of a lock and a strap. He suggests that in primitive locks the door-*uppu* which moved the bolt was a simple thong of leather or some other material, and that in more elaborate locks this was replaced by a handle which moved the bolt when the key was turned. Hence *uppu* is originally a thong 'from which, *via* the door lock, the meaning "handle" was obtained' (p. 249).

Neither Lambert nor Pfeiffer connect 19f. with 21–24. Pfeiffer caps 19f. neatly with 'Do not spur a free horse' (p. 425, n.16) and Lambert queries whether 21–24 may be the complaint of an overworked slave or labourer, or of a beast of burden as in 25–29. However, 19–24 is most satisfactorily elucidated if taken as a unity. It is not after the mode of a fable with an animal expressing itself like a human, but (building on Lambert's other suggestion) expresses the exasperation of a workman whose foreman is always breathing down his neck; the question of 19f. serves to make this point. The arrangement of the whole is that of a simile or similitude, in which by a process of correlation a complex of images becomes a pungent commentary on a given situation. The picture which is drawn is an incredible one, as the form of the question itself makes explicit. Do you strike, i.e., do you *ever* strike, the face of a moving ox with a strap? Of course you do not, for it would be a ludicrous, wasteful and sadistic exercise. If the animal is doing its work it should be left alone, and the man who expends energy doing damage to a willing animal is either a half-wit or a pervert. But then men are more rational in their behaviour towards animals than they are towards their fellows, and there exists the officious, bullying foreman who will not leave willing workers to get on with their job. Such a foreman hinders rather than expedites work, but it is his effect on the workers that is chiefly in view. He blunders so unbelievably in the way he handles men that he is a born maker of strikes. 'My knees are in constant motion, my feet are tireless, (yet) a half-wit pursues me with trouble.'

BWL, pp. 242, 249 (*ANET*, p. 425), iii.25–29:
I am a riding-donkey, (yet) I am yoked to an ass. I draw a chariot, and suffer the crop.

Kramer translates the Sumerian version: 'I am a thoroughbred steed, but I am hitched to a mule, and must draw a cart and carry reeds and stubble' (*History Begins at Sumer*², 1961, p. 179). Pfeiffer's translation in *ANET* is similar, 'and must draw a wagon loaded with reeds'. On the Accadian version, Lambert observes (p. 249) that the identification of *šūru* as a driver's stick is established (G. Meier, *ZA* 45, p. 212).

Following the convention of the fable, an animal bemoans its lot and complains that its worth and potentialities go without recognition, in a manner reminiscent of the badly disgruntled human being. On this piece Kramer remarks: 'Occasionally the poor man realized that he was a failure not through a fault of his own, but because he had tied up with the wrong associates.' This is not the exact shade of interpretation which the Accadian version invites. The riding-donkey has not chosen the ass as its associate; it has had no choice in the matter. This is the type of work for which, in the opinion of those who decide such things, this particular donkey is fitted. Hence it is yoked to an ass – to a common-or-garden work animal – and is condemned to mediocrity and indignity: 'I draw a chariot and suffer the crop.' It is the victim of bad managers who do not recognize a riding-donkey when they see one; who employ it wastefully and allow it to be abused by an ordinary muleteer.

The fable should therefore be interpreted as the eternal *cri de coeur* of the neglected or rejected genius, the man who is convinced within himself that he has gifts of a high order and is only prevented from exercising them by the perverseness of the society in which he lives. It is not necessary that the donkey should in fact have been a first-class riding-donkey, or that the man who labours under the grievance of unrecognized genius should in fact be a man of genius. The piquancy of the fable consists in the circumstance that it leaves entirely open whether the *cri de coeur* is valid or invalid – whether it comes from the bricklayer who would have been a great composer if the circumstances of his nurture had been kindlier, or whether it comes from the bricklayer who suffers from a grand delusion and who could never in any conceivable circumstances have been a great composer.

BWL, pp. 243, 249, iii.56–59:

Last year I ate garlic; this year my inside burns.

This is not just a cautionary tale in which some unknown individual describes the injurious effects of garlic on his stomach with the intent that others should be warned. This reading of it would not do justice to the juxtaposition of 'this year' and 'next year', for there is a strong presumption that this has some significance, namely, that it points to a delayed effect, and this delay is probably the real point of the saying. Even then, it would be possible to limit the sentence to the sphere of dietary advice, as a statement that injudicious eating will eventually catch up with you even if you get away with it for a time. But then it is capable of a further disengagement from prosaic levels of interpretation and has a wider proverbial reference. It would be an effective retort to anyone who supposed that he was immune from a retributive, causal process, who had escaped the consequences for so long that he was inclined to dismiss them with a wave of the hand as not applicable to his particular case. The eating of garlic and the delayed effect – a burning inside – is an effective parable, because nearly everyone has had indigestion and has feared something worse. The symbolism is elemental, and because it is elemental everyone can understand it; it is the kind of experience which can throw light on other levels of experience.

BWL, pp. 244, 249 (*ANET*, p. 425), iv.19–24:

When you are in the river, the water around you absolutely stinks.
When you are in a plantation, your dates are gall.

Lambert queries whether this may not be a riddle, and certainly it does not yield up its meaning easily. Pfeiffer suggests that it is a proverb which could be recited aptly against a man with persistent bad luck, or one bringing misfortune to others through the evil eye (p. 425, n.21), while Kramer refers the Sumerian version to a person who is a chronic social misfit (*op. cit.*, p. 174). The weight of interpretation should perhaps fall on 'your water' ('the water around you') and 'your dates'. This is a fatal character doomed to misery – perhaps fatal for himself rather than for others. The proverb would then be a commentary on the person who is doomed not to extract pleasure and enjoyment from situations which are made to provide them. Or, more generally, it refers to the person for whom nothing ever goes right, not even when a plain road has been prepared with no obstacles in view. There may be in it also, however, the thought of a Jonah who radiates bad luck and disaster to those in his vicinity.

BWL, pp. 244, 250 (*ANET* p. 425), iv.30–33:

Let not the furrow bear a bad shoot; let it produce no seed (rather).

I follow Lambert in construing *še-er-ú* as subject and not object (*pace* Pfeiffer, p. 425, n.22). 'Bad shoot' does not mean diseased shoot, but the shoot which has some imperfection or abnormality (W. von Soden, *Akkadisches Handwörterbuch*, p. 305, *s.v. ḫabburu*(*m*); p. 392, *s.v. išaru*(*m*)). I take seed here to have the meaning 'grain', i.e., the produce of the harvest. *ziru* can mean both the seed which produces the harvest and the harvest which results from the sowing of the seed, as the usage *ziru* 'offspring', 'descendants' shows (*CAD* xxi, p. 89, *s.v. zēru*). I am uncertain what Lambert intends by '(rather)', which he has inserted to fill out the translation. It might seem to suggest such a meaning as: 'It would be better that no seed should be sown than that the crop should have a single blemish.' On the other hand, 'rather' might indicate that the first wish is tantamount to the second, i.e., to require the furrow not to bear a bad shoot is equivalent to condemning it to barrenness. This would be in agreement with the interpretation which I am going to suggest. The meaning of the saying is that there is no such thing as a perfect crop. 'Let the furrow not bear a bad shoot' is the expression of a perfectionism which is out of touch with the realities of producing grain. The furrow which does not produce a bad shoot is a pipe-dream which is divorced from the practicalities of efficient agriculture. The important thing is to get a high-quality yield from the furrow, but a theoretical perfectionism has little bearing on this. The perfectionist would be so fussy that he would never get around to growing anything. The proverb consequently means that perfection is not obtainable in this imperfect world, and that there is a form of perfectionism which goes hand in hand with sterility, because it lays down conditions which make it impossible to participate in truly constructive or creative tasks.

BWL, pp. 244, 250 (*ANET*, p. 425), iv.34–41:

Will the early corn thrive? How can we know?
Will the late corn thrive? How can we know?

Kramer's conclusion on the basis of the Sumerian version is probably the right one, namely, that the saying is indicative of hesitation and confusion in economic matters (p. 174), except that I would not confine it to economic matters. There is a type of agonizing over problems and difficulties which can become tyrannical and incapacitate a man for resolute and decisive action. Whatever course of action he entertains (sowing early or sowing late), it appears to him so beset with difficulties and pitfalls that he cannot bring himself to embark on it. He is so obsessed with the fear of the possible miscarriage of his plans that he will never put them to the test and remains suspended in a state of pathological anxiety. The meaning of the proverb is that one has got to go on taking decisions and accepting risks, and that calculation without the release of action is not existence but neurosis.

BWL, pp. 244, 250 (*ANET*, p. 425), iv.42–45:

Should I be going to die, I would be extravagant (lit. eat).
Should I be going to survive, I would be economical (lit. store).

Thureau-Dangin suggests that the speaker is a sick man unsure whether he is to die or recover, and so torn between brief and spectacular prodigality and a prudent husbanding of his resources against the future. On this view, the proverb is directed against the miser who, on the eve of his death, continues to amass wealth which he can never enjoy (*An. Or.* xii, p. 308). Kramer (p. 174), on the other hand, thinks that the proverb should be interpreted in the same way as the preceding one. The individual who speaks is unwilling to play according to the rules and would like to lay down his own rules, and the point is that he cannot do this. He has to play according to the rules; there is no favoured treatment for him, no extraordinary knowledge in virtue of which he will be wise before the event. The interpretation does not hinge on the respective merits of extravagance and thrift nor on the uncertainty of our tenure of life. It is rather the longing for guarantees on which we should fasten, the wistful and mistaken demand that one should be assured in advance that a certain course of action is the right one. For life is not like this, and those who demand that the risk of a wrong decision should be eliminated before they act are doomed to inhibition and frustration. They will never get beyond the whirl of their feverish and unfruitful calculations.

BWL, pp. 245, 250, iv.46–50:

> They pushed me under the water and endangered my life. I caught no fish and lost my clothes.

There is little doubt that the complex of images which comprise this saying represents an artistic arrangement and that this is a deliberately contrived proverb or parable. The description conjures up indignity, danger, discomfort and loss on the debit side unbalanced by any profit or good on the credit side. It is a description of a thoroughly unsuccessful and demoralizing outing and would be an appropriate comment on the worst of bad days – a succession of rebuffs, frustrations, mishaps, alarms and excursions, and, at the end of it, not a stroke accomplished.

BWL, pp. 245, 250 (*ANET*, p. 425), iv.53–57:

> The enemy does not depart from before the gate of a city whose weapons are not powerful.

This is perhaps no more than a wisdom sentence or aphorism directed against pacifism and pacifists (so Pfeiffer, p. 425, n.25). The aphorism is not just concerned with the danger to which the inadequately armed city is exposed, but with the consequences of this weakness on the stability of the area. The near-defenceless city is a temptation which cannot be resisted and a source of instability. Stability depends on a balance of power. If it is capable of a wider interpretation its meaning would be: in human relations, softness or weakness is bad for the person who is soft and bad for those who take advantage of that softness. It is better that the encounter should take place in a context where there is respect for each other's strength.

BWL, pp. 245, 250, v.10–13:

> Like an old oven, it is hard to replace you.

The relationship of resemblance is explicitly given in this saying by *kīma*, and it is the oven's near irreplaceability which constitutes its aptness as an image and on which attention should be focused. An old oven must presumably have certain disadvantages. It lacks modern refinements and has suffered from wear and tear. To anyone coming to it as a novice it might appear to be unbearably inconvenient and sadly inefficient. It requires to be coaxed and cajoled, and only a person who has long acquaintance with its idiosyncrasies will have the knowledge and inclination to do this. But just because the old oven is not easily managed and does not give results to any Tom, Dick or Harry, the mastery of it and ability to exercise a fine control over it yields a high sense of satisfaction. It is tried and tested and yet it is always a challenge to skill, and cooking on a new oven would be an entirely new experience.

This is the kind of simile which an employer might use of an employee who has served him for so long that he is part of the business. He may be out of touch with modern techniques and unable to keep up to date; he may on occasions be crusty and even perverse, but he achieves results in his own, unalterable ways and he and his employer understand each other; their relationship is stable and discerning and they adjust to each other intuitively. No doubt he could be replaced, and will eventually have to be replaced, by a young man bursting with expertise and drive who will raise operations to a new pitch of efficiency. But then this will be the end of an order and things will never be the same again.

BWL, pp. 245, 250 (*ANET*, p. 425), v.14–17:
You went and plundered enemy territory.
The enemy came and plundered your territory.

Kramer (p. 183) observes that this is pointed against the futility of war and tit-for-tat. Pfeiffer caps it with 'Turn about is fair play', and contrasts it with iv.53–57 (p. 425, n.26). It should be noticed, however, that whereas iv.53–57 deals with the security of a city, this example is concerned with a feud between groups and with a sequence of aggression and retaliation. Whether the motive is cupidity or punishment, aggression will provoke retaliation and nothing will have been gained in the end. When the tit for tat process is over, the bitterness and hostility between the two has been so exacerbated that the process of mending and healing their relationship becomes a more protracted and complicated matter. For there is only one kind of settlement possible and that is a composition of their differences and a reconciliation which will restore a satisfactory relationship. For as long as they indulge themselves in aggressive or retaliatory measures, they have not even begun to seek such a solution; rather, they are pushing it further and further away.

BWL, pp. 246, 250, v.23f.:

For dried green-malt spreading does not come too late.

Lambert (p. 250) explains that there were two alternative methods for drying grain, the first roasting in a kiln (*na-'-pi*) and the second spreading in the sun (*meš-ṭú-ú*). The meaning of the saying is that where grain has been dried by roasting there is some advantage in following this up with spreading. The two methods are not necessarily mutually exclusive and it may be advantageous to make use of both. The proverbial element in this is probably the thought of 'making siccar', of being thorough to a fault with a view to obviating the smallest possibility of anything going wrong. Or possibly there is the idea of not putting all one's eggs in one basket, not relying too exclusively on one method or procedure. This is a type of proverb (of which *Onchsheshonqy* furnished numerous examples) which makes sense on a prosaic level as a piece of agricultural advice and which therefore has a credible ambivalence.

BWL, pp. 252f., iii.19–24:

Long life begets for you a sense of satisfaction; concealing a thing – sleepless worry; wealth – respect.

This is a wisdom sentence, marked by its elegant and compact expression, but not proverbial in the full sense. It is trenchant and sententious, but it aims at no more than aphoristic aptness. It is the fruit of an empirical vigilance which associates three different situations in respect of cause and effect. Such acute observation, succinctly summated, produces a wisdom sentence which is without the openness to interpretation characteristic of the proverb or parable.

BWL, pp. 253f., *ll.* 5–7:

When you have escaped, you are a wild bull.
When you have been caught, you fawn like a dog.

The words which contribute most to the flavour of this saying are 'escaped', 'wild bull', 'caught', 'dog'. In one kind of situation a person is a bellowing, snorting, savage bull and in another a domesticated, fawning dog. From this arrangement of images one must suppose that the possibilities of interpretation flow into such channels as the following: 'You spoil for a fight when there is no one to fight; when the fight for freedom is on, you are all conciliation and supineness.' Or: 'You have the appearance of a formidable adversary when you have plenty of room for manoeuvre and there is no pressure on you; when you are in a tight corner, you are pliant and sugary.'

BWL, pp. 253f., *ll.* 10f.:

> You lift a mountain, but you cannot hang [from(?) a reed(?)].

The text is broken and the reconstruction uncertain. If it is relied on, the meaning is: 'You have the strength to lift a mountain, but you are too heavy to be supported by a reed.' The interpretation of this would be along the following lines: 'What gives you a great advantage in one kind of situation places you at an enormous disadvantage in another.' 'Prodigious development in one narrow sector of life makes a man useless elsewhere.' 'It is better that you should be a good all-rounder than a narrow specialist.'

BWL, pp. 254f., *ll.* 3–7:

> Fire is consuming an aristocrat. The proletarian does not say: 'Where is the aristocrat?'

I am inclined to describe this as pithy social comment neatly gathered up into a wisdom sentence rather than to regard it as a proverb, although it is not incapable of such extended interpretation. Primarily it would seem to be a comment on class division and warfare. A corollary of the plebeian's solidarity with members of his own class is his supreme indifference to any danger or ill which may assail a member of the ruling class. He simply cannot muster up a grain of interest or concern. These are just the facts of life, and they illustrate the importance of class in determining the reactions and attitudes of individual men. If the saying can bear more interpretation than this, it would mean that a degree of callousness and indifference is part of the make-up of every human being. Without this defence mechanism most men would find the demands of compassion unbearable. Life would become one long, harrowing crisis. There would be no moralizing intent or evaluating element in the saying if it were thus understood. It would be a detached, factual observation.

BWL, pp. 257f., v.8–10:

> The stewards are suppressed. I am brawny arms.

Lambert caps this with, 'When the cat is away, the mice will play', but this does not quite capture the nuance of the proverb. It means rather: 'I am full of fight once I am assured that all opposition has been overcome and no fighting remains to be done' (cf. *BWL*, p. 253, *ll.* 5–7, above, p. 197). The saying would thus serve as a suitably astringent comment on any display of sham militancy.

BWL, pp. 257f. (*ANET*, p. 426), v.11–13:

A foreigner's ox eats plants; one's own ox lies in green pastures.

This wisdom sentence with antithetic balance would appear to aim at no more than making the point that different societies have different *mores* (*ANET*, p. 426, n.29). It is thus social comment picturesquely expressed.

BWL, p. 259, *ll.* 9–11:

Friendship lasts for a day, business connexions for ever.

ll. 16f.:

A resident alien in another city is a slave.

These are sayings similar in character to the preceding one. The former shrewdly observes that human associations based on an element of common interest tend to be more durable than friendships which do not have this cement. *ib-ru-tum*, 'companionship', is to be connected with Hebrew *ḥābēr*, 'companion, associate'. *ki-na-tu-tu* is rendered 'business connexions' by Lambert. Accadian *kinātu* means 'colleague' (*BWL*, p. 286 on *Ludlul* i.87) and Aramaic *kᵉnāt* is a loan word from Accadian (*KB*², *s.v. kᵉnāt*). It is used in the book of Ezra of Shimshai who was the colleague of several Persian provincial officials (Ezra 4.9, 17, 23). Pfeiffer translates *ki-na-tu-tu* 'slavery', and misses the point of the saying.

The sentence does not just observe that men are more tolerant of each other when it would hurt their purses to be intolerant. It extends to any business or professional connection which supplies men with strong reasons for maintaining their association over and above the bonds of natural friendship. Kramer (p. 181) translates the Sumerian: 'Friendship lasts a day, kinship endures for ever', and this different thought that blood is thicker than water is taken up by another proverb whose broken text is restored by Lambert to read:

Flesh is flesh, blood is blood. Alien is alien, foreigner is indeed foreigner (*BWL*, p. 271, *ll.* 16–18).

The other saying, 'A resident alien in another city is a slave', is less pedestrian and has more proverbial subtlety. The translation is not entirely assured, as Pfeiffer's rendering shows: 'A plain citizen in another city becomes its chief' (*ANET*, p. 426). The two words on which these divergent translations disagree are *u-bar-ru* and *re-e-šú*. 'Plain citizen' accords with Deimel's *Bürger* (p. 112, *s.v. ubarru, ubāru*), and one would expect *re-e-šú* to mean 'chief', although the meaning 'slave' is well-established. The issue has to be decided by the consideration that Lambert's translation yields what is more manifestly a proverb than the rendering of Pfeiffer and that 'resident alien', 'foreign resident' is a more accurate translation than 'citizen'. Lewy's remarks on *ubāru* establish this, but in turn create new difficulties for the interpretation of the proverb, since Lewy holds that the term implies neither condescension nor contempt for the strangers so described (*HUCA* xxvii, 1956, p. 59, n.250). If, however, I understand this saying correctly, the point which is being made is that some differences are merely verbal and have no corresponding *real* distinctions, and this would imply that *u-bar-ru* can be a euphemism for 'slave'. In one city the term used is *u-bar-ru*, and in another whose habits of speech are blunter the name given is *re-e-šú*; but the status and privileges of the persons so-called is the same in both places.

This would, then, be a neat way of commenting on the misuse of language which is currently fashionable in our own society, namely, the use of inflated and sometimes absurdly inflated language to describe ordinary, dull, trivial or even unpleasant things, so that words, instead of administering the cold douche of reality, create a kind of fools' paradise. The opposite tendency is to speak of terrible possibilities which would curdle the blood of any normal human being with exaggerated matter of factness and laconicism, employing a jargon, sometimes a scientific jargon which has been drained of all emotion and imagination. Military experts will predictably use this kind of language when they are discussing the weight of hydrogen bombs ('thermo-nuclear potential') which America and Russia could deliver if they went to war with each other.

BWL, p. 260, *ll.* 5–10:

> A thing which has not occurred since time immemorial: a young girl broke wind in her husband's bosom.

Jacobsen (in Gordon, p. 547) translates the Sumerian: 'A thing that never was before: the young girl was not farting in her husband's embrace.' He supposes that the saying is 'an ironical comment offered when the practice of simple and elementary decency was praised as if it were something very special' (cf. Gordon, p. 47). This proverb is obscure, but I had taken it rather differently and had supposed that the saying was made up of proverb and interpretation. 'A thing which has not occurred since time immemorial' affords us clear guidance on the meaning of the otherwise obscure proverb, 'A young girl broke wind in her husband's bosom'. This is then an economical, robust and earthy way of giving expression to feelings of incredulity. 'A young girl broke wind in her husband's bosom' would be a sinewy comment on reported behaviour which is felt to be so lacking in precedence and out of harmony with the established order as to be entirely undeserving of credence. Jacobsen's translation is a reassessment of the Sumerian (cf. Gordon, p. 452) in the light of the bilingual text published by Lambert, and so it should be noted that Lambert's reading is *iṣ-r[u-ut]*, not *[ul]iṣ-r[u-ut]* (Gordon, p. 547). Lambert (p. 260) observes: 'There does not seem room for the negative in the Akkadian'.

BWL, pp. 260, 262, *ll.* 6f.:

The unlearned is a cart; the ignorant is his road.

This recalls the saying in the Gospels, 'And if a blind man leads a blind man, both will fall into a pit' (Matt. 15.14; cf. Luke 6.39). There are two statements about the unlearned man which have to be attended to: (*a*) he is a cart or a wagon; (*b*) a companion or companions equally devoid of knowledge are his road. 'Cart' and 'road' indicate that ignorance goes hand in hand with a bustling activism. The person who is envisaged is energetic and wants to get things done; he thrives in a climate of busyness and bustle, but he has no clear idea in his own mind what it is he wants to achieve or the means which he should adopt to achieve it. So he will follow anyone who offers to show him the way without himself having any inkling of his destination. He has no critical discrimination or independence of judgement, and so he is a prey to blind guides.

BWL, pp. 270f., *ll.* 7f.:

The mother brew is bitter. How is the beer sweet?

agarinnu, translated 'mother brew' by Lambert, means 'womb', 'reservoir' (Von Soden, p. 15). This can be capped by the Scots proverb, 'Fools and bairns should not see half-done jobs'. Beer should not be tasted until the maturing process is complete which, by interpretation, means: 'A policy should not be criticized until reasonable time has been allowed to see how it works.' At an intermediate stage of its operation, a policy may seem incapable of achieving its purpose, but it is unwise to indulge in premature criticism which, however clever and effective it may appear at the time it was made, may subsequently boomerang on the person who has made it. One who is a clever or waspish critic at the beginning or middle may turn out to be absurdly wrong-headed at the end.

BWL, p. 277, *l*. 12:

He who frequently *puffs* at mountains is counted as dust.

The rendering 'puffs' for *i-te-ni-ti-ip* is uncertain, but the activity alluded to is apparently a tilting at windmills. The person who makes a habit of striking extravagant attitudes of challenge and aggression in situations where his impotence is apparent to everyone except himself will be written off as of no account. Turned round the other way, this means that to adopt a tough attitude with someone who is unassailable and invulnerable is just to be ridiculous. Bluster is a mark of weakness and not of strength, and after a time the blusterer cuts a despicable figure.

BWL, p. 278, *l*. 4:

My well does not tire (of giving water); my thirst is not excessive.

Pfeiffer's, 'We never know the worth of water till the well is dry' (*ANET*, p. 425, n.1) is not quite apt. The point here does not seem to me to be that a commodity which is in good supply is undervalued, but rather that the surest way of stimulating excessive desire for a commodity is to proclaim its scarcity or to place restrictions on its acquisition. This, then, is a proverb which could cap an argument against licensing laws on the ground that they encourage an excessive and even morbid thirst, or against rationing on the ground that it creates a black market in the commodities rationed.

BWL, p. 278, *l*.5:

The net is loosed, but the fetter is not slack.

Pfeiffer is again inept with his citation of Amos 5.19: 'As if a man fled from a lion and a bear met him; or went into a house and leaned with his hand against a wall and a serpent bit him.' This is not really a Babylonian version of 'Out of the frying pan into the fire' (*ANET*, p. 425, n.2). The saying reckons with two impediments on freedom of action. One of these is removed, but the man is still a prisoner. That he is now detained only by a fetter and not by a net and a fetter is not altogether insignificant, for there is a sense in which he is now nearer to freedom than he was. But if attention is focused on his present condition as opposed to the long-term possibilities of his becoming a free man, it is seen that nothing has changed through the removal of the net. An obstacle has been removed, while not an inch of progress is yet possible. The felicity of this proverb cannot be reproduced by a generalizing interpretation, but the nub of it is that circumstances may be ameliorated without being significantly and decisively changed. There are concessions which mean little or nothing in the total context in which they are made.

BWL, p. 279, *ll.* 7f. (*ANET*, p. 425):

> Prematurely ripe fruit is produce (bringing) grief.
> Fruit in the spring (of the year) – fruit of mourning.

The phrase which is differently translated by Lambert and Pfeiffer is *pa-an ša-at-ti*. Both translations are possible, but Landsberger has argued that *šatti* here means 'season' and not 'year' and so *pan šatti* 'premature' (*JNES* viii, 1949, pp. 257–60).

Fruit which is forced is robbed of its taste and mellowness; it is a slow and full maturing which produces mellowness. And so there are processes which cannot be rushed and where impatience for quick results can only do damage. The saying could be applied to the unnatural and injurious forcing of a young mind in the field of education or to a lack of patience, and premature, impetuous action in the sphere of diplomacy. Plans, like fruit, must be allowed to mature and there is a right time for decisive action which must not be anticipated.

BWL, p. 279, *11*.9f.:

> An irrigation ditch (running in) the direction of the wind brings a copious supply of water.

What I suggested for some of the sayings in *Onchsheshonqy* may apply here and, in that case, this may have been originally a piece of agricultural advice. It is important to neglect no detail which will contribute to the efficiency of an irrigation ditch, and the harnessing of the prevailing wind will increase the flow of water into the fields. In whatever circumstances it may have originated, there is no doubt that this saying has proverbial merit and is open to interpretation. Every effort should be made to give the optimum chance of success to any enterprise or undertaking. Nothing which can be turned to favourable account should be neglected or despised, and every factor making for efficiency should be fully exploited. Not a trick should be missed.

BWL, p. 280:

> Just like the old proverb which goes: 'The bitch in her search for food gave birth to a poor litter.'

This is in agreement with von Soden's rendering (*Orientalia* xxi, 1952, p. 76). Von Soden derives *šu-te-pu-ru* (*m*) from *epēru* ('feed, board, provide for') whose *Št* formation means 'to scramble for food' or 'to fight for food' (*Akkadisches Handwörterbuch*, p. 223, *s.v. epēru(m)*). In *CAD* vol. E (1958), p. 13, the form is read as *šuteburu* and is derived from *ebēru* 'to cross', with the meaning 'to pass backwards and forwards'. The proverb is then translated: 'The bitch, because she passed from one (dog) to the other, gave birth to lame(?) puppies.' *ḫu-up-pu-du-tim* means lameness or weakness according to *CAD* Ḫ (1956), p. 214 (cf. Lambert *BWL*, p. 280).

This proverb appears in a letter written by Šamši-Addu, king in Assyria *c.* 1700 BC, to his son Iasmaḫ-Addu, regent in Mari, and the point which the proverb apparently makes is that the son is dissipating his energies in ineffective diversions and is not coming to grips with the enemy. This does not enable us to choose between the two translations of the proverb, for either would serve equally well in this connection. Nor is it likely that this particular application exhausts the significance of the proverb, and so we are thrown back on the two possible forms of the proverb itself.

The rendering of von Soden and Lambert places the bitch in a situation which approaches a dilemma. She has to conserve her energies as best she can so that she will have something in reserve, and her puppies which are *in utero* will be born in good shape. On the other hand, she cannot nourish herself and her puppies unless she scratches around for food. It is obviously a situation in which she has to balance priorities and order her activities so as to secure the desiderated result, which is the best nourished body that conditions will allow. Consequently she should use up energy in searching for food only to the point that this contributes to her nourishment and well-being. Beyond this a law of diminishing returns operates, and she will lose more than she gains; the activity will begin to be injurious rather than advantageous. Hence the proverb means that activity is only meaningful and effective for so long as it contributes to the end which is willed, and that it should be kept constantly under review in the interests of relevance, concentration of effort and the husbanding of resources.

The other translation lays the emphasis on the promiscuity of the bitch. She is indiscriminate in respect of her mates, and the effect of her distributing her favours so freely is a sickly litter of puppies. She ought to have satisfied herself with one good dog and had regard to the importance of breeding well. The end result of her fickleness is miserable offspring. The proverb, then, points to the disappointing consequences of pursuing an end without resolution, concentrated purposefulness and dedicated single-mindedness. Action should be consistent and decisive; deviations and departures should be guarded against; whatever is irrelevant or peripheral should be pruned, and activity should be directed without wavering along the narrow line which leads to the goal. An impulsive jumping from one scheme to another will achieve poor results.

BWL, p. 281 (*ABL*, No. 403, obv. 4–7):

> The popular proverb says: 'When the potter's dog enters the kiln it will bark at the potter.'

The author of the lettter in which this appears is most probably the Assyrian king Esarhaddon, and the context indicates that it is the vulnerability of the dog's position to which the proverb alludes. The 'pseudo-Babylonians' to whom the letter is addressed have been complaining about the behaviour of trusted royal officials, and the king reminds them that, since he can harm them at will, they are not in a situation where they can afford to ventilate such criticism. The application is clear enough, but the suitability of the proverb for such an application is not so obvious. Its form does not suggest that the intention is to portray the dog snarling aggressively at its master in circumstances where docility and obedience would have accorded better with the realities of their relationship. On the other hand, the 'exegesis' of the proverb in the Syriac and especially the Arabic versions of *Ahikar* creates a picture of a vicious dog lacking in discipline and gratitude. 'O my son, you have been to me like the dog that was cold and it went into the potter's house to get warm. And when it had got warm, it began to bark at them, and they chased it out and beat it, that it might not bite them' (F. C. Conybeare, J. Rendell Harris, A. S. Lewis, *The Story of Ahikar*², p. 158; Syriac, p. 125). The meaning of the proverb, then, is that hospitality and kindness should not be abused or allowed to create in the recipients the illusion of strength. When benevolence produces impudence in the beneficiaries, they are in for a shock and a demonstration of the realities of their position.

Langdon's account (S. Langdon, *Babylonian Wisdom*, 1922, pp. 86f.) of the letter in which the proverb appears is similar to that of Lambert. The 'non-Babylonians' have slandered the king's subjects and have manoeuvred themselves into a false and dangerous position, and it is in this context that the king applies the proverb to them. A different turn of interpretation is, however, given by Langdon to the proverb.

He renders it: 'If the dog of a potter has entered into an oven, he howls to the heart of the potter.' The dog has got itself into a hot spot and it barks for help to (barks to the heart of) the only person who can get it out of its difficulties. I have no doubt that this does more justice to the form of the proverb than any other interpretation. In particular, *a-na libbi lú paḫāru ú-nam-baḫ* points more to an appealing bark than an aggressive snarl. The meaning, then, is that the dog does not suffer from any illusions. It knows who its friends are and where to direct its appeal for help, and the pseudo-Babylonians would do well to have a like appreciation of realities and to order their behaviour with this recognition of their dependence, vulnerability and fragility.

BWL, p. 281 (*ABL*, p. 403):

> The oral proverb says: 'In court the word of a sinful woman prevails over her husband's.'

This comes from the same source as the previous proverb and is used by the king to convey to the pseudo-Babylonians that they will not get the better of him, irrespective of the merits of their case. Plausibility and suave advocacy will not obscure from him the impudence of their claims, nor induce him to weaken his determination to deal firmly with them and put them in their place.

The proverb itself, apart from this special context, envisages a situation where a woman gets a favourable verdict from a court in circumstances which allow less than justice to her husband. It is not on legal grounds or because of the merits of her case that the court has found for her. Extraneous and legally irrelevant factors have obtruded themselves into the proceedings, and influenced the court in her favour. Perhaps it was the circumstance that she was a woman, and artfully communicated to the judge a delightful and affecting impression of defencelessness and bewilderment. Or, if she were beautiful, that would be a bonus and make her impact irresistible. How could the court in any circumstances decide against such a beautiful creature! In a contest between her and a very ordinary husband it would be pedantic and ungallant to pay too much attention to the law, or to enquire whether the discrepancies between her testimony and her husband's might not be accounted for most satisfactorily by the assumption that he was speaking the truth and she was not. The proverb is, then, a comment on any situation where irrelevant, irrational, perhaps powerfully emotive factors are decisive, to the exclusion of the pertinent issues which should exercise the judgement and in terms of which the decision should be made.

BWL, p. 282:

> Like a fool . . . you perform your ablutions after sacrifice; like . . . you put in a drain pipe after it has rained.

Two groups of images which picture foolish or pointless behaviour. The broken text hinders, but does not entirely frustrate interpretation. The thought is wider than that of bolting the stable door after the horse has been stolen, although it includes this. To perform ablutions before sacrifice is a proper precaution or a pious duty. It guards against possible contraventions of ritual purity which might be thought to nullify all benefits of participating in the rites, or which might even spell danger for the participant. To wash after sacrifice is a meaningless gesture which does not make any sense and effects nothing. An action which makes sense at a certain point in a series is nonsensical and even absurd when it is done out of turn.

A somewhat different nuance attaches to the picture of a man installing a drain pipe after it has rained. The contingency for which he prepares has already eventuated. What he does is not absurd or pointless, and there will be future work for the drain pipe to do, for it will rain again. Nevertheless, he has timed the installation badly and he should have had the drain pipe in position before the rain came. He lacked foresight or else he was dilatory. The general application of all this would be that in the field of action order and timing are all-important, and that neglect of these will reduce the value of action and possibly make it useless.

BWL, p. 282:

> When ants are struck, they do not take it (passively), but bite the hand that strikes them.

The proverb occurs in one of the Amarna letters, the author of which, a certain Lab'ayu, explains and justifies his behaviour to the Pharaoh (J. A. Knudtzon, *Die El-Amarna Tafeln*, ii, p. 252; W. F. Albright, *BASOR* 89, 1943, pp. 29–32). Lab'ayu represents that he has been the victim of aggression and insists that he has the right of retaliation. He has no intention of submitting meekly or remaining passive in the face of the outrage which he has suffered, and he gives notice to the Pharaoh that he will not obey any instructions to this effect. 'Further, even if thou shouldst say: "Fall beneath them, and let them smite thee", I should still repel my foe, the men who seized the town and my god, the despoilers of my father, (yea) I would repel them' (*ANET*, p. 486).

Lambert suggests that the proverb may have been coined by Lab'ayu himself and Albright describes it as 'an archaic Hebrew proverb'. It is basically a naturalist's observation – a description of how ants react to a particular stimulus – whose proverbial possibilities have been exploited. The ant is a sensible insect whose industry and resourcefulness are held up to men as an example (Prov. 6.6; 30.25), and what is implied here is that the reaction of the ants to unprovoked aggression is sensible and proper. In this respect, too, wisdom is to be learnt from the ant, and the man who allows other men to ride roughshod over him is an abject weakling whose supineness is despicable. The sentence can be used in any situation where it is desired to give notice that there is a will to retaliate, and that insult and aggression will not be taken lying down.

PART TWO

THE BOOK OF PROVERBS

IV

TRANSLATION

CHAPTER 1

pp. 262f.

1 The proverbs of Solomon, son of David, king of Israel.
2 To take note of wisdom and instruction,
to grasp perceptive sayings.
3 To receive effective instruction,
righteousness, justice and uprightness.
4 To give shrewdness to the untutored,
knowledge and resourcefulness to the young.
5 A wise man listens and appropriates more wisdom,
and a perceptive man learns the ropes.
6 To grasp a proverb and an allusion,
words of the wise and riddles.
7 The fear of Yahweh is the beginning of knowledge,
fools despise wisdom and instruction.

pp. 267f.

8 Listen, my son, to your father's instruction,
and do not forsake your mother's teaching,
9 for they are a becoming wreath for your head,
and a necklace for your throat.
10 My son, if sinners entice you,
do not consent.
11 If they say, 'Come with us,
let us lay an ambush for blood,
let us waylay the innocent at our whim;
12 let us swallow them as Sheol swallows life,
in one piece as those who go down to the Pit.
13 We shall find the rarest wealth,
we shall fill our houses with spoil.
14 Throw in your lot with us,
there is one purse for us all.'

15 My son, do not go on a raid with them,
hold back your foot from their path,
16 for their feet run to evil,
and they hurry on to shed blood.
17 For it is to no effect that the net is strewn
in the sight of any bird;
18 so they lay an ambush for their own blood,
and waylay their own lives.
19 Such *is the end* of everyone who is greedy for gain;
it takes away the lives of those who have it.

pp. 272f.

20 Wisdom cries aloud in the streets,
she raises her voice in the squares.
21 On top of the *walls* she calls out,
at the entrances of the city gates she utters her sayings.
22 'How long, untutored youths, will you love immaturity!
Scoffers are infatuated with scoffing,
and fools hate knowledge.
23 If you return when I reprove you,
I shall pour out my spirit for you,
I shall divulge my words to you.
24 Because I summoned (you) and you rejected (me),
stretched out my hand and met no response;
25 because you neglected all my advice,
and would have none of my reproof;
26 I, in turn, will laugh at your calamity,
and chuckle when terror overtakes you;
27 when terror strikes you like a disaster,
and calamity like a whirlwind,
when distress and privation alight on you.'
28 Then they will call out to me, but I will not answer,
they will seek me but not find me.
29 Because they hated knowledge,
and declined the fear of Yahweh,
30 would have none of my advice,
and despised all my reproof,
31 they will eat the fruit of their way,
and have surfeit of their plans;
32 for the untutored are killed by their indiscipline,
and fools are destroyed by their complacency.
33 But he who listens to me will dwell in safety,
and be untroubled by the fear of evil.

CHAPTER 2

pp. 282f.
1 My son, if you receive my sayings,
and store up my commandments,
2 lending your ear to wisdom,
and inclining your mind to discernment;
3 if you call out for insight,
raise your voice for discernment;
4 if you seek it as you would silver,
and dig for it as for treasure,
5 then you will discern the fear of Yahweh,
and find the knowledge of God;
6 for Yahweh gives wisdom,
from his mouth come knowledge and discernment.
7 He stores up competence for the upright,
is a shield to those whose conduct is blameless,
8 so as to guard the paths of justice,
and watch over the way of those who are loyal to him.
9 Then you will discern what is right and just
and straight, every good track;
10 for wisdom will come into your mind,
and knowledge will give pleasure to your palate.
11 Resourcefulness will keep watch over you,
discernment will guard you,
p. 284.
12 rescuing you from the evil way,
from men whose speech is twisted,
13 who forsake straight paths
to journey on ways of darkness;
14 who take pleasure in evil-doing,
who delight in perversity;
15 whose paths are tortuous,
whose tracks are labyrinthine.
pp. 284f.
16 That you may be saved from the strange woman,
from the foreigner whose speech is smooth,
17 who forsakes the *teacher* of her youth,
and has forgotten the covenant of her God;
18 for her house inclines towards death,
and her tracks towards the shades.
19 None who visit her return,
they do not regain the paths of life.
pp. 288f.
20 That you may walk in the way of good men,
and keep to the paths of righteous men,

21 for the upright will dwell in the land,
and men of integrity will be left in it;
22 but the wicked will be cut off from the land,
and the treacherous will be uprooted from it.

CHAPTER 3

pp. 290f.
1 My son, do not forget my teaching,
let your mind retain my commandments;
2 for they give you increased length of days,
and years of life with well-being.
3 Let not loyalty and constancy forsake you,
bind them on your throat,
write them on the tablet of your heart.
4 So you will find acceptance and good success,
in the eyes of God and man.
5 Trust in Yahweh with all your heart,
and do not lean on your insight.
6 In all your ways take note of him,
and he will keep you on straight paths.
7 Do not be wise in your own eyes,
fear Yahweh and relinquish evil.
8 It is a tonic for your health,
and a medicine for your frame.
9 Honour Yahweh with your wealth,
and with the first-fruits of all your produce;
10 so your granaries will be filled with plenty,
and your vats will be bursting with wine.
11 My son, do not reject Yahweh's instruction,
nor resent his reproof,
12 for Yahweh disciplines the one whom he loves,
like a father with the son in whom he takes pleasure.
pp. 294f.
13 Happy is the man who finds Wisdom,
and he who obtains Discernment,
14 for she is more profitable than silver,
and gives a higher yield than gold.
15 She is more precious than jewels,
and nothing you desire bears comparison with her.
16 Length of days are in her right hand,
in her left hand wealth and honour.

17 Her ways are pure delight,
and all her paths are peace.
18 She is a tree of life to those who grasp her,
happy are those who take hold of her.
19 By wisdom Yahweh founded the earth,
by discernment he established the heavens;
20 by his knowledge the springs well up from beneath,
and clouds drip dew.
pp. 297f.
21 My son, set a guard on competence and resourcefulness,
do not let them out of your sight,
22 that they may increase your vitality,
and adorn your neck.
23 Then you will journey in safety,
and your foot will not stumble.
24 If you are resting, no fears will trouble you,
and when you lie down, sweet sleep will come to you.
25 Do not be afraid of sudden terror,
of the moment when evil men are destroyed,
26 for Yahweh will be *your confidence*,
and will keep your foot from entanglements.
pp. 299f.
27 Do not withhold a benefit from him who has a right to it,
when it is in your power to confer it.
28 Do not say to your neighbour, 'Go away and come again,
tomorrow I shall give it to you' – and you have it to give.
29 Do not devise evil against your neighbour,
while he lives alongside you and thinks himself secure.
30 Do not pick a gratuitous quarrel with a man,
when he has done you no injury.
31 Do not envy a man given to violence,
nor *be vexed at* any of his ways,
32 for a devious man is loathed by Yahweh,
but he takes upright men into his confidence.
33 The curse of Yahweh is on the wicked man's household,
but he blesses the righteous man's dwelling.
34 Though he pours scorn on scoffers,
yet he shows favour to the humble.
35 Wise men inherit honour,
but fools exalt (their own) disgrace.

CHAPTER 4

pp. 302f.
1 Listen, (my) sons, to a father's instruction,
give heed that you may gain insight.
2 What you take from me is good,
do not forsake my teaching;
3 for I was my father's son,
an only child, my mother's darling.
4 When he taught me, he said to me,
'Let your mind grasp my words,
keep my commandments and live.
5 Get Wisdom, get Insight,
do not forget my sayings nor deviate from them.
pp. 305f.
6 Do not forsake her and she will watch over you;
love her and she will guard you.
7 Wisdom comes first, (therefore) get Wisdom,
and with all your getting get Insight.
8 Hold her in high esteem and she will get preferment for you;
she will get you honour if you embrace her.
9 She will give you a becoming wreath for your head,
she will grant you a splendid crown.'
pp. 306f.
10 My son, be attentive and receive my words,
that the years of your life may be many.
11 I shall guide you in the way of wisdom,
I shall lead you along straight tracks.
12 When you walk, your stride will not be cramped,
and when you run, you will not stumble.
13 Take hold of Instruction, do not relax your grip,
mount a guard over her, for she is your life.
14 Do not go in the path of wicked men,
and do not make for the way of evil men.
15 Put it out of your mind; do not go on to it;
turn away from it and journey on;
16 for they cannot sleep except they do evil,
their sleep is cut off except they are stumbling blocks;
17 for they eat the bread of wickedness,
and drink the wine of violence.
18 The path of the righteous is a blazing light
which gets steadily brighter until the day is full;
19 but the way of the wicked is black as pitch,
they do not know on what they stumble.

pp. 310f.

20 My son, attend to my words,
give heed to my sayings.
21 Do not let them out of your sight,
keep them deep in your mind;
22 for they are life to him who finds them,
and a complete tonic for his body.
23 Guard your mind above all else,
for the springs of life issue from it.
24 Repel perverse speech,
and repulse devious words.
25 Keep your eyes fixed ahead,
and your *glances* straight in front of you.
26 Take care where you put your feet down,
and all your routes will be established.
27 Do not deviate to right or left;
keep your feet far from evil.

CHAPTER 5

pp. 314f.

1 My son, attend to my wisdom,
give heed to my discernment,
2 that you may keep confidences,
and your lips may guard knowledge;
3 for the lips of a strange woman drip honey,
and her speech is smoother than oil;
4 but in the end she is as bitter as wormwood,
as sharp as a two-edged sword.
5 Her feet go down to death,
her steps set course for Sheol.
6 She has *no* regard for the path of life,
her tracks waver, she is never at rest.
7 Now, my sons, listen to me,
and do not deviate from my sayings.
8 Keep well clear of her,
do not come up to the door of her house;
9 lest you give your honour to others,
and your *dignity* to the cruel;
10 lest strangers feed on your strength,
and (consume) your hard-earned wealth in a foreigner's house;

11 and so you will cry out in anguish when your end
comes,
when body and flesh are consumed.
12 You will say, 'How I hated instruction
and despised reproof!
13 I did not listen to the voice of my teachers,
nor did I give heed to my instructors.
14 I was almost involved in total ruin
before assembly and congregation.'
pp. 317f.
15 Drink water from your own cistern,
the streams which flow from your own well.
16 Should your springs be dispersed outside,
channels of water in the street?
17 Let them be for yourself alone,
and not for strangers with you.
18 Let your fountain be blessed,
and take your pleasure with the wife of your youth.
19 A darling hind, a graceful doe!
Let her breasts satisfy you continually;
in her love you are to be enfolded always.
20 My son, why are you wrapped in the embrace of a
stranger?
Why do you clasp the bosom of a foreigner?
pp. 312f.
21 For a man's ways are before Yahweh's eyes,
he scrutinizes all his tracks.
22 His iniquities snare him,[1]
he is held with the cords of his sin.
23 He dies through his indiscipline,
and is wrapped in his massive folly.

CHAPTER 6

pp. 321f.
1 My son, if you have given surety to your neighbour,
and struck hands for a stranger,
2 you are snared by your own words,
trapped by your own utterances.
3 Do this then, my son, and save yourself,
for you have come into the power of your neighbour.
Go, *swallow your pride* and importune your neighbour.

[1] ʾ*et hārāšāʿ* deleted as a gloss.

4 Refuse sleep to your eyes,
and slumber to your eye-lids.
5 Save yourself like a gazelle from a *hunter*,
or a bird from a fowler.
pp. 323f. 6 Go to the ant, O sluggard,
observe her ways and be wise.
7 She has no arbitrator,
she does without officer and ruler.
8 She lays in her stocks in summer,
and stores her food at harvest.
9 How long, O sluggard, will you lie there?
When will you rise from your sleep?
10 A little sleep, a little slumber,
a little folding of the hands to lie down,
11 and poverty will come to you like a vagrant,
and want like a beggar.
pp. 325f. 12 A malicious person, a malevolent man,
goes about with twisted words.
13 Winks with his eyes, scrapes with his feet,
points with his fingers,
14 constantly devises perverse schemes,[1]
initiates strife.
15 Therefore disaster will come on him suddenly,
in a moment he will be broken beyond healing.
p. 326 16 There are six things which Yahweh hates,
seven which he loathes:
17 haughty eyes, a false tongue,
and hands which shed innocent blood;
18 a mind which devises evil plans,
feet which run swiftly to evil;
19 a perjurer, a false witness,
one who initiates strife between brothers.
pp. 326f. 20 My son, keep your father's commandments,
and do not neglect your mother's teaching.
21 Bind them on your heart always,
tie them on your neck.
22 When you journey, they will lead you,
when you lie down, they will watch over you,
when you awake, they will converse with you;
23 for commandments are a lamp and teaching a light,
and corrective instruction a way of life;

[1] Deleting *rāʿ*. Alternatively, v. 14 may be construed like v. 13, 'Perverse schemes are in his mind, he devises evil constantly, he initiates strife.'

24 to keep you from the evil woman,
from the smooth tongue of the foreigner.
25 Do not be infatuated by her beauty,
and do not let her take you captive with her glances;
26 for *a harlot's price* is a loaf of bread at the most,
but a married woman hunts a man of means.
27 Can a man put fire in his breast pocket
without his clothes being burned?
28 Or can he walk on coals
without his feet being scorched?
29 So it is with him who makes a mistress of his neighbour's wife,
no one who touches her will escape condemnation.
30 Is not a thief despised if he steals
to satisfy his appetite when he is hungry?
31 If he is found out, he will repay sevenfold;
he will surrender all the goods in his household.
32 He who commits adultery has no sense;
he acts as his own executioner.
33 Violence and disgrace he will find,
and his shame will not be erased;
34 for jealousy *inflames* a man,
he will not show mercy when he takes his revenge.
35 He will not be disposed towards damages,
nor will he acquiesce in a large bribe.

CHAPTER 7

pp. 332f. 1 My son, keep my sayings,
and store up my commandments.
2 Keep my commandments and live,
and my teaching as the pupil of your eye.
3 Bind them on your fingers,
write them on the tablet of your heart.
4 Say to Wisdom, 'You are my sister',
and call Discernment a relative;
5 to keep you from the strange woman,
from the smooth words of the foreigner.
pp. 334f. 6 For at the window of my house
I looked out through the lattice,

7 and saw among the youths,
perceived among the young men,
one devoid of sense,
8 crossing into the street beside her corner,
making his way to her house,
9 at twilight, in the evening,
at *the eye* of night and darkness.
10 A woman comes to meet him,
with the garb and wiles of a harlot;
11 wanton and feverish,
her feet do not stay in her house.
12 Now in the streets, now in the squares,
and beside every corner she skulks.
13 She grabs him and kisses him,
with a hard face she says to him,
14 'I must provide a sacrificial meal,
today I am to fulfil my vows.
15 So I have come out to meet you,
to seek you out, and I have found you.
16 I have spread my couch with covers,
with coloured Egyptian fabrics.
17 I have sprinkled my bed
with myrrh, aloes and cinnamon.
18 Come, let us take our fill of love till morning,
let us delight in each other's embraces;
19 for my husband is not at home,
he has gone on a distant journey.
20 He has taken a bag of money with him;
he will come home when the moon is full.'
21 She distracts him with her copious charm,
she routs him with her smooth words.
22 He follows her on an impulse,
he goes like an ox to the slaughter,
as a hart skips into a noose,
23 as a bird speeds towards a trap,[1]
until an arrow pierces his liver,
without his being aware that his life was at stake.
p. 341.
24 Now, (my) sons, listen to me,
and attend to my words.
25 Do not stray into her ways,
do not wander into her paths;

[1] Reversing the order of 23a and 23b.

26 for many are the slain whom she has felled,
her victims are a great company.
27 Her house is the road to Sheol,
going down to the halls of death.

CHAPTER 8

pp. 344f.
1 Does not Wisdom call out,
and Discernment raise her voice?
2 On the high ground beside the road,
and wherever paths cross, she takes up her stance.
3 Beside gates at the entrance to a town,
at its approaches her voice rings out:
4 'It is to you, O men, that I call,
and my words are for human kind.
5 O youths, discern what shrewdness is,
O fools, discern what acumen is.
6 Listen, for my speech is *straightforward*,
and my utterances plain;
7 for my mouth speaks the truth,
and my lips loathe wickedness.
8 All my sayings are honest,
nothing in them is tortuous or twisted.
9 They are all plain to the perceptive man,
and straightforward to those who are knowledgeable.
10 Choose my instruction before silver,
and knowledge before choice gold;
11 for wisdom is better than pearls,
and nothing gives pleasure like it.
pp. 346f.
12 I, Wisdom, am neighbour to shrewdness,
I find out the right procedures.
13 The fear of Yahweh is hatred of evil,
I hate pride and haughtiness, evil conduct and twisted speech.
14 I possess policy and competence,
insight and power.
15 By me kings reign,
and rulers enact what is right.
16 By me statesmen wield power,
and nobles – all entitled to rule.
17 I love those who love *me*,

and those who seek me will find me.
18 Riches and honour are with me,
solid wealth and righteousness.
19 My fruit is better than gold, even the best gold,
and my yield than choice silver.
20 I walk in the path of righteousness,
in the tracks of justice,
21 bequeathing wealth to those who love me,
and filling their treasuries.
pp. 351f.
22 Yahweh created me at the beginning of his (creative) way,
as the most primaeval of his acts in antiquity.
23 In the distant past I *was formed*,
at the beginning, before the world began to be.
24 When there were no deeps, I was brought forth,
when there were no springs, *streams* of water;
25 before the mountains were shaped,
before the hills, I was brought forth;
26 when he had not yet made earth and fields,
and the mass of the world's soil.
27 When he established the heavens, there was I,
when he fixed a disc on the surface of the deep;
28 when he strengthened the clouds above,
when he contained the springs of the deep;
29 when he assigned to the sea its limit
– and the waters do not transgress his word –
when he fixed the foundations of the earth.
30 I was beside him as his confidant,
I gave him pleasure daily,
jesting before him continually;
31 jesting about his created world,
and the pleasure I got from human beings.'
pp. 358f.
32 Now, my sons, listen to me,
happy are those who keep my ways.
33 Listen to instruction and be wise,
do not neglect it.
34 Happy is the man who listens to me,
keeping vigil at my doors daily,
setting a watch on my doorstep;
35 for whoever finds me finds life,
and obtains acceptance from Yahweh.
36 But he who sins against me does violence to his life,
all who hate me love death.

CHAPTER 9

pp. 360f.

1 Wisdom has built her house,
she has hewn her seven pillars.
2 She has sacrificed for her banquet,
she has mixed her wine,
she has spread her table.
3 She has sent out her maids to announce
on the heights of the town,
4 'Whoever is untutored let him turn in here.'
To him who lacks sense she says,
5 'Come, eat my meat,
and drink the wine which I have mixed.
6 Forsake (your) untutored companions and live;
walk in the way of insight.

pp. 368f.

7 He who instructs a scoffer gets disgrace for himself,
and he who reproves a wicked man gets his blemish.
8 Do not reprove a scoffer, lest he hate you,
reprove a wise man and he will love you.
9 Give instruction to a wise man that he may be wiser still,
inform a righteous man that he may increase his learning.
10 The fear of Yahweh is the beginning of wisdom,
and the knowledge of the Holy One is insight;
11 for by me your days are multiplied,
and the years of your life *increased*.
12 If you are wise, it is you who will benefit from it,
and, if you scoff, it is you who will have to suffer for it.'

pp. 365f.

13 A foolish woman is wanton *and seductive*,
and is never at rest.
14 She sits at the door of her house,
on her seat on the heights of the town,
15 to call to those who pass by,
who walk with purposeful step,
16 'Whoever is untutored, let him turn in here.'
To him who lacks sense she says,
17 'Stolen waters are sweet,
and bread of stealth is delicious.'
18 And he does not know that dead men are there,
her guests are in the depths of Sheol.

CHAPTER 10

Proverbs of Solomon

p. 418 1 A wise son gives pleasure to a father,
but a foolish son is his mother's sorrow.
p. 422 2 Ill-gotten gains are not profitable,
but righteousness brings deliverance from death.
p. 426 3 Yahweh will not let the righteous man go hungry,
but he will obstruct the desire of the wicked.
p. 417 4 Half-hearted effort *makes for poverty*,
but diligence makes for wealth.
pp. 414f. 5 A son who gathers crops in summer is competent,
but one who sleeps through the harvest is a disgrace.
p. 422 6 Blessings are on the head of a righteous man,
but the speech of the wicked conceals violence.
pp. 422f. 7 The remembrance of a righteous man is a source of blessing,
but the name of the wicked rots away.
p. 416 8 A man of good sense does as he is bidden,
but he who speaks nonsense is trampled upon.
p. 423 9 He whose conduct is blameless walks in safety,
but he who walks in tortuous ways is found out.
p. 418 10 He who winks his eye makes mischief,
but he who reproves to the face reconciles.
p. 418 11 The speech of a righteous man is a fountain of life,
but the speech of wicked men conceals violence.
pp. 418f. 12 Hatred awakens strife,
but love covers over all offences.
p. 416 13 Wisdom is found on the lips of a perceptive man,
but a rod is reserved for the back of one who lacks sense.
p. 416 14 Wise men store up knowledge,
but the speech of a fool is imminent catastrophe.
pp. 416f. 15 A rich man's wealth is his strong city,
but the poverty of the poor is disaster for them.
p. 425 16 The wages of a righteous man are life,
but the product of a wicked man is sin.
p. 419 17 He who regards instruction is a path to life,
but he who spurns reproof leads others astray.
pp. 419 18 He who speaks lies conceals hatred,
and he who spreads scandal is a fool.

p. 416 19 When there is a spate of words offence is always being given,
but he whose speech is restrained is a man of good sense.

p. 423 20 The tongue of a righteous man is choice silver,
but the mind of the wicked is of small value.

p. 420 21 The speech of the righteous nourishes many,
but fools die through *lack of sense.*

p. 422 22 It is Yahweh's blessing which brings wealth,
and there is no increase of vexation with it.

pp. 419f. 23 It is like sport to a fool to make mischief,
and so it is with wisdom to a man of discernment.

p. 426 24 What the wicked man fears overtakes him,
but (Yahweh) grants the desire of the righteous.

pp. 426f. 25 When the hurricane has passed, there is no trace of the wicked man,
but the righteous man is established for ever.

p. 417 26 Like vinegar to the teeth and smoke to the eyes,
so is a lazy person to those whose messenger he is.

p. 425 27 The fear of Yahweh gives an increase of days,
but the years of the wicked are cut short.

pp. 425f. 28 The righteous can expect joy,
but the hope of the wicked will perish.

p. 427 29 Yahweh is a fortress to *the man whose conduct is blameless,*
but he brings destruction to evildoers.

p. 427 30 A righteous man will never lose his footing,
but the wicked will not inhabit the land.

pp. 423f. 31 The mouth of a righteous man produces wisdom,
but a perverse tongue is cut off.

p. 424 32 A righteous man is concerned that his words win acceptance,
but the wicked care only for perverse speech.

CHAPTER 11

pp. 438f. 1 Falsified scales are loathed by Yahweh,
but a weight which is standard meets his approval.

p. 428 2 Where there is arrogance, disgrace follows,
but wisdom is with those who are modest.

p. 435 3 The integrity of upright men guides them,
but the crookedness of treacherous men destroys them.

p. 436 4 Wealth profits nothing in a day of wrath,
but righteousness gives deliverance from death.

p. 435 5 The righteousness of a blameless man gives him a level road,
but a wicked man falls through his wickedness.

p. 430 6 The righteousness of upright men saves them,
but treacherous men are trapped by desire.

pp. 439f. 7 When a wicked man dies, expectation perishes,
and hope set in riches is cut off.

pp. 436f. 8 A righteous man is rescued from distress,
and a wicked man takes his place.

p. 431 9 By his speech an impious man destroys his neighbour,
but rescue is effected by the knowledge of righteous men.

p. 432 10 When righteous men prosper, a city rejoices,
when the wicked perish, there is a shout of joy.

pp. 431f. 11 Through the blessing of upright men a city is raised up,
but by the speech of wicked men it is demolished.

p. 428 12 He who despises his neighbour has no sense,
but a man of discernment keeps silent.

p. 429 13 He who goes around carrying tales gives away confidences,
but a trustworthy man keeps a matter secret.

p. 429 14 Where there is no expertise a nation falls,
but safety lies in many advisers.

p. 429 15 He who has gone surety for a stranger *will have to suffer for it*,
but he who hates contracts will be secure.

pp. 430f. 16 A gracious woman grasps honour,
but ruthless men grasp wealth.

p. 433 17 A merciful man benefits himself,
but a cruel man does himself injury.

p. 437 18 A wicked man earns an empty reward,
but he who sows righteousness (earns) real wages.

p. 435 19 He who is steadfast in righteousness is destined for life,
but he who pursues evil suffers death for it.

p. 438 20 Men with twisted minds are loathed by Yahweh,
but those whose conduct is blameless meet his approval.

p. 437 21 There is nothing more certain than that an evil man will not be acquitted,
but the descendants of the righteous will be set free.

p. 430 22 A gold ring on a pig's snout,
a beautiful woman with no taste.

pp. 440f. 23 The desire of righteous men brings nothing but good,
but the hope of wicked men (produces) rage.

pp. 434f. 24 There is the man who disburses his wealth freely and yet is always getting richer,
there is another whose miserliness leads only to want.

pp. 437f. 25 He who creates prosperity is himself prosperous,
and he who satisfies others is himself satisfied.

p. 434 26 A community curses one who withholds grain,
but there is a blessing on the head of one who sells it.

p. 434 27 He who strives after good seeks to win approval,
but evil overtakes him who searches for it.

p. 436 28 He who relies on his wealth suffers a fall,
but the righteous flourish like a leaf.

pp. 429f. 29 He who does his household injury inherits wind,
and a fool becomes slave to a wise man.

pp. 432f. 30 The fruit of a righteous man is a tree of life,
but (the fruit) of him who takes life is *violence*.

pp. 437f. 31 If a righteous man gets his reward in the land,
much more a wicked man and a sinner are requited.

CHAPTER 12

p. 441 1 He who loves instruction loves knowledge,
but he who hates reproof is brutish.

p. 448 2 A good man wins approval from Yahweh,
but he condemns a man of devious ways.

p. 449 3 A man is not established through wickedness,
but righteous men are immovably rooted.

p. 443 4 A woman of quality is her husband's crown,
but a hussy is like decay in his bones.

p. 450 5 The plans of righteous men are equity,
but the manoeuvres of wicked men deceit.

pp. 446f. 6 The words of wicked men are a bloody ambush,
but the speech of upright men delivers them.

p. 449 7 Wicked men are overturned and are no more,
but the households of righteous men endure.

pp. 441f. 8 It is for his good sense that a man is praised,
but a muddle-headed person is a laughing-stock.

p. 444 9 A man of small means with one servant is better off
than one who makes a show of grandeur, but is short of bread.

p. 452 10 A righteous man cares for the well-being of his animals,
but the feelings of the wicked are cruel.

p. 444 11 He who tills his soil has his fill of bread,
but he whose pursuits are empty has no sense.

pp. 449f. 12 The *foundation* of evil men *is destroyed*,
but the root of the righteous abides.

p. 452 13 Offensive words are the evil man's snare,
but a righteous man comes out of distress.

pp. 448f. 14 A man eats well from the fruit of his speech,
and himself gets the recompense which his actions deserve.

p. 442 15 The way of a fool is straight in his own eyes,
but he who listens to advice is a wise man.

p. 442 16 A fool's vexation is known at once,
but a shrewd man conceals an insult.

p. 445 17 A reliable witness tells the truth,
but a false witness (speaks) lies.

p. 446 18 There is the person whose speech is like sword-thrusts,
but the speech of wise men is a therapy.

p. 445 19 Truthful speech lasts for ever,
but false speech only for a moment.

p. 447 20 Deceit is in the mind of those who devise evil,
but joy is the lot of those who plan for the common good.

p. 448 21 No ill befalls the righteous man,
but the wicked are full of trouble.

p. 448 22 Lying speech is loathed by Yahweh,
but men of integrity win his approval.

pp. 442f. 23 A shrewd man conceals knowledge,
but fools proclaim folly.

p. 444 24 Diligent men wield authority,
but slackness leads to slavery.

p. 446 25 Anxiety in a man's mind depresses *him*,
but a good word cheers *him* up.

pp. 447f. 26 A righteous man *shows his friend the way*
but the way of wicked men leads (others) astray.

pp. 444f. 27 *A languid man does not roast his prey,*
but a diligent man captures rare wealth.
pp. 450f. 28 In the path of righteousness is life,
but the *way of folly leads to* death.

CHAPTER 13

p. 453 1 A wise son *submits to his father's discipline*,
but a scoffer does not listen to reproof.
pp. 459f. 2 A man eats well from the fruit of his speech,
but treacherous men have an appetite for violence.
p. 457 3 He who is tight-lipped keeps his life,
but he who is big-mouthed brings his own downfall.
pp. 457ff. 4 A lazy man is consumed by desire and remains hungry,
but diligent men eat their fill.
p. 460 5 A righteous man hates a false word,
but a wicked man spreads the smell of scandal.
p. 461 6 Righteousness guards *the man whose conduct is blameless*,
but evil overthrows *sinners*.
p. 458 7 There is a man who affects wealth and has nothing,
and there is a man who affects poverty and has great wealth.
p. 458 8 A man's wealth is a ransom for his life,
but a poor man pays no attention to threats.
p. 461 9 The light of the righteous shines brightly,
but the lamp of the wicked goes out.
pp. 453f. 10 An empty-head produces strife by his arrogance,
but wisdom resides with those who confer.
pp. 458f. 11 Wealth gained speculatively dwindles,
but he who acquires it gradually, builds it up.
p. 459 12 Hope long drawn out is a sickness of the mind,
but realized desire is a tree of life.
pp. 454f. 13 He who despises a word *suffers ruin*,
but he who respects a ruling *is safe*.
p. 455 14 A wise man's teaching is a fountain of life,
offering escape from the snares of death.
pp. 455f. 15 Good sense makes a man acceptable,
but the way of the treacherous is *their destruction*.
p. 456 16 A shrewd man does *everything* with knowledge,
but a fool makes a display of folly.

pp. 460f. 17 A wicked messenger *devises pitfalls*,
but a trustworthy envoy is a therapy.
p. 456 18 Poverty and contempt are for him who neglects instruction,
but he who accepts reproof wins honour.
p. 459 } 19 Realized desire is sweet to the taste,
p. 460 } but the relinquishing of evil is loathed by fools.
pp. 456f. 20 He who accompanies wise men becomes wise,
but the companion of fools suffers harm.
pp. 461f. 21 Evil pursues sinners,
but righteous men are rewarded by good.
p. 462 22 A good man leaves his wealth to his posterity,
but a sinner amasses wealth for a righteous man.
pp. 462f. 23 The tilth of grandees produces an abundance of food,
but it is swept away for lack of equity.
p. 457 24 He who is sparing with his rod hates his son,
but he who loves him disciplines him from the first.
p. 462 25 The righteous man eats his fill,
but the hunger of wicked men is unsatisfied.

CHAPTER 14

p. 472 1 *Wisdom has built*[1] her house,
but Folly demolishes it with her hands.
p. 474 2 He whose conduct is upright fears Yahweh,
but he whose ways are devious despises him.
pp. 463f. 3 The speech of a fool is a rod *for his back*,
but the words of wise men keep them safe.
pp. 470f. 4 Where there are no oxen, there is a crib of grain,
but crops are increased by the strength of an ox.
p. 469 5 A reliable witness does not lie,
but a perjurer utters falsehoods.
p. 464 6 A scoffer seeks wisdom in vain,
but knowledge is easy for a perceptive man.
p. 464 7 Get out of a fool's way,
but *do not repulse* knowledgeable lips.
pp. 466f. 8 A shrewd man's wisdom *illumines* his way,
but the folly of fools is self-deceit.
pp. 475f. 9 *Fools scoff at guilt*,
but upright men discern what is acceptable.

[1] Deleting *nāšîm*.

p. 471 10 A mind knows its own bitterness,
and no stranger can share its joy.
p. 474 11 The households of wicked men are destroyed,
but the tents of upright men flourish.
pp. 467f. 12 There is a way which seems straight to a man,
but the roads leading to death are at the end of it.
p. 471 13 Even when it is merry the heart suffers pain,
and joy turns to sorrow at the last.
pp. 474f. 14 A renegade gets the satisfaction which his ways merit,
and a good man the satisfaction which *his deeds* merit.
p. 467 15 An untutored youth believes everything,
but a shrewd man picks his step.
pp. 464f. 16 A wise man knows fear and avoids harm,
but a fool is impetuous and self-assured.
p. 468 17 A short-tempered man commits folly,
but a resourceful man *holds office.*
p. 467 18 Untutored youths *are adorned with* folly,
but shrewd men wear a crown of knowledge.
p. 475 19 Evil men bow down before good men,
and the wicked at a righteous man's gates.
pp. 471f. 20 A poor man is hated even by his friend,
but a rich man's friends are numerous.
p. 473 21 He who despises his friend is a sinner,
but happy is he who is kind to the poor!
p. 473 22 Do not those who devise evil go astray?
But those who devise good (meet) loyalty and constancy.
p. 472 23 In all hard work there is profit,
but words make only for want.
pp. 465f. 24 The crown of wise men is their wealth,
but the *wreath* of fools is folly.
p. 469 25 A reliable witness saves lives,
but a perjurer is *a deceiver.*
p. 474 26 The fear of Yahweh is a (man's) stronghold,
and for his children it will be a safe place.
p. 474 27 The fear of Yahweh is a fountain of life,
offering escape from the snares of death.
pp. 469f. 28 A large population is a king's dignity,
but a lack of people is a ruler's downfall.
pp. 468f. 29 The even-tempered man has great discernment,
but the short-tempered man exalts folly.
p. 472 30 A tranquil mind promotes good health,
but jealousy (promotes) decay in the bones.

p. 473 31 He who oppresses a poor man insults his maker,
but he who is kind to a poor man honours him.
p. 475 32 A wicked man is overthrown because of his wickedness,
but a righteous man seeks safety in his *integrity*.
p. 466 33 Wisdom rests content in the mind of a perceptive man,
but within fools *it is suppressed*.
p. 475 34 Righteousness exalts a nation,
but sin is a disgrace to a people.
p. 470 35 A king's favour is reserved for an able servant,
but his rage *for* a bungler.

CHAPTER 15

p. 477 1 A conciliatory answer makes wrath subside,
but a hurtful word raises anger.
p. 478 2 The words of wise men adorn knowledge,
but the mouths of fools spout folly.
p. 484 3 Yahweh's eyes are everywhere,
watching both evil men and good.
pp. 482f. 4 Speech with healing properties is a tree of life,
but with perversion it is spiritual ruin.
p. 479 5 A fool despises his father's instruction,
but a shrewd man accepts reproof.
pp. 484f. 6 There is great wealth *in a righteous man's household*,
but *the income* of a wicked man is *interdicted*.
p. 478 7 The lips of wise men spread knowledge,
but the minds of fools are warped.
p. 486 8 The sacrifices of wicked men are loathed by Yahweh,
but the prayers of upright men meet his approval.
p. 486 9 The way of a wicked man is loathed by Yahweh,
but he loves the man who pursues righteousness.
p. 479 10 There is severe discipline for him who forsakes the path,
and he who hates reproof will die.
p. 484 11 Sheol and Abaddon are under Yahweh's scrutiny,
how much more the minds of men.
p. 480 12 A scoffer dislikes reproof,
he does not resort to wise men.
pp. 480f. 13 Inner happiness makes the face serene,
but the spirit is broken by mental suffering.

pp. 478f. 14 The mind of a perceptive man seeks knowledge,
but the speech of fools consorts with folly.

p. 481 15 The life of a poor man is a continual struggle,
but *good morale* is a never-ending banquet.

pp. 486f. 16 A little with the fear of Yahweh
is better than great wealth and turmoil with it.

p. 484 17 A dish of greens with love present
is better than a fatted calf with hostility.

p. 482 18 A hot-tempered man stirs up strife,
but an even-tempered man quiets contention.

p. 482 19 The way of a lazy man is a thorn hedge,
but the path of *diligent men* is a highway.

p. 479 20 A wise son gives his father pleasure,
but a fool despises his mother.

p. 479 21 Folly is delight to the man who lacks sense,
but the man of discernment keeps a straight course.

p. 482 22 Where there is no consultation, plans come to nothing,
but where there are many advisers, they stand the test.

pp. 477f. 23 A man gets pleasure from an (apt) rejoinder,
and what is better than a well-timed word!

pp. 479f. 24 A path of life is reserved for the discriminating man,
that he may keep his distance from Sheol.[1]

p. 485 25 Yahweh demolishes the households of proud men,
but maintains the boundaries of the widow.

p. 483 26 Evil plans are loathed by Yahweh,
but gracious words are pure.

p. 485 27 He who is greedy for gain *destroys* his household,
but he who hates a bribe lives on.

pp. 483f. 28 A righteous man gives a considered answer,
but the mouths of wicked men spout evil.

p. 486 29 Yahweh is far removed from wicked men,
but he hears the prayers of righteous men.

p. 481 30 Shining eyes cheer the mind,
and good news builds up the body.

p. 480 31 An ear which listens to reproof is life,
it lodges in the midst of wise men.

p. 480 32 He who neglects instruction rejects his life,
but he who listens to reproof is a man of sense.

p. 487 33 The fear of Yahweh is the discipline of wisdom,
and humility comes before honour.

[1] Deleting *l^{e}maʿlā* and *māṭṭā*.

CHAPTER 16

p. 496 1 Man's part is to order his thoughts,
but the reply of the tongue comes from Yahweh.

pp. 495f. 2 All of a man's conduct is pure in his own eyes,
but it is Yahweh who weighs up motives.

pp. 496f. 3 *Confide* your actions to Yahweh,
that your plans may be established.

p. 497 4 Yahweh has made everything in relation to its counterpart,
and so the wicked man for an evil day.

pp. 497f. 5 Everyone of haughty disposition is loathed by Yahweh,
there is nothing more certain than that they will not be acquitted.

p. 498 6 Iniquity is covered by loyalty and constancy,
and when Yahweh is feared, harm is avoided.

p. 491 7 When Yahweh approves a man's conduct,
he makes even his enemies at one with himself.

p. 499 8 A little with righteousness is better
than a great income without justice.

pp. 495f. 9 A man plans his way,
but Yahweh orders his step.

pp. 499f. 10 A right decision is on the lips of a king,
in giving a verdict his speech does not err.

p. 500 11 The balance and true scales are Yahweh's concern,
all the weights in the bag are his affair.

pp. 491f. 12 Evil-doing is loathed by kings,
for a throne is established by righteousness.

p. 493 13 A king approves truthful speech,
and loves *the words of upright men.*

p. 488 14 A king's anger is a herald of death,
and a wise man covers it over.

pp. 488f. 15 Life is in the light of a king's face,
and acceptance by him is like clouds that give the spring rains.

p. 489 16 What a good thing it is to acquire wisdom!
And insight is to be chosen before silver.[1]

pp. 500f. 17 The highway of the upright is the avoidance of harm,
and he who keeps his life watches his road.

[1] Deleting *mēḥārūṣ*.

p. 490 18 Pride is the precursor of a crash,
and haughtiness of a stumble.
pp. 498f. 19 It is better to be a humble man in the company of poor men,
than to divide spoil with proud men.
p. 498 20 He who is quick to take a point prospers,
but happy is he who trusts in Yahweh.
p. 489 21 A man with acumen is called 'perceptive',
and honeyed words promote learning.
p. 490 22 Good sense is a fountain of life *to those who have it*,
but the instruction of fools is folly.
pp. 489ff. 23 A man's mind informs his speech,
and *an expert speaker* promotes learning.
p. 493 24 Gracious words are a honeycomb,
sweet to the palate and a tonic for the body.
p. 490 25 There is a way which seems straight to a man,
but the roads leading to death are at the end of it.
pp. 490f. 26 A labourer's appetite toils for him,
his mouth urges him on.
pp. 493f. 27 A malicious man digs up mischief,
it is as if a blazing fire were on his lips.
p. 494 28 A perverse man initiates strife,
and a slanderer separates friends.
p. 494 29 A man given to violence deceives his friend,
and leads him along a disastrous road.
pp. 494f. 30 He who winks his eye is planning intrigue,
and he who purses his lips has completed mischief.
p. 501 31 Old age is a crown of glory,
it is found in the way of righteousness.
p. 488 32 An even-tempered man is better than a great soldier,
and a man with self-control than one who captures a city.
p. 499 33 The lot is cast into the pocket,
but the verdict is wholly from Yahweh.

CHAPTER 17

pp. 509f. 1 Better a dry crust with concord,
than a house full of sacrifices with strife.
p. 502 2 An able servant will become the master of a worthless son,

and share an inheritance with brothers.
p. 511 3 A crucible is for silver and a furnace for gold,
and Yahweh is the assayer of hearts.
p. 508 4 An evil-doer gives heed to a malicious word,
a liar has a ready ear for a destructive tongue.
p. 511 5 He who sneers at a poor man insults his maker,
he who gets pleasure from calamity is not acquitted.
p. 503 6 Grandchildren are the crown of old age,
and sons glory in their fathers.
pp. 507f. 7 Choice speech does not become a fool,
much less do lies become a nobleman.
p. 502 8 The bribe is a magic stone in the eyes of him who uses it,
he succeeds in whatever he turns to.
pp. 508f. 9 He who conceals an offence seeks love,
but he who repeats a word severs friends.
p. 504 10 A rebuke makes a deeper impression on a discerning man,
than a hundred strokes on a fool.
p. 510 11 An evil man seeks only disruption,
but a cruel messenger will be sent against him.
p. 505 12 Better that a bear which has lost its cubs should encounter a man,
than a fool with his folly.
p. 510 13 If a man repays good with evil,
evil is never absent from his household.
p. 505 14 The beginning of strife is a seepage of water;
so desist before the quarrel erupts.
pp. 511f. 15 He who acquits a wicked man and he who condemns a righteous man,
both of them are loathed by Yahweh.
pp. 504f. 16 Why then does the fool have a fee in his hand?
To buy wisdom when he has no brains?
pp. 505f. 17 A companion is always good company,
but a brother is born for adversity.
pp. 502f. 18 A man who lacks sense strikes hands,
and goes surety in his neighbour's presence.
p. 509 19 He who likes to give offence likes strife,
and he who builds a high entrance asks for a crash.
pp. 510f. 20 He whose mind is devious does not find good,
and he whose tongue is twisted falls into evil.
p. 503 21 He who produces a dolt makes sorrow for himself,
and there is no pleasure in being a fool's father.

p. 506 22 Inner happiness makes for good health,
but a broken spirit takes the sap from the bones.
p. 512 23 A wicked man takes a bribe from his breast pocket
to pervert the course of justice.
p. 504 24 A perceptive man keeps Wisdom in sight,
but the eyes of a fool are on the ends of the earth.
p. 503 25 A foolish son is a vexation to his father,
and a bitter pill to the mother who bore him.
pp. 506f. 26 To fine an innocent man is bad,
and to flog noblemen improper.
p. 507 27 He who is sparing with his words understands what knowledge is,
and he who has a cool temper is a man of discernment.
p. 507 28 If he keeps quiet, even a fool is reckoned to be a wise man,
if he is tight-lipped, he is thought to be perceptive.

CHAPTER 18

p. 519 1 The alienated man consults his own whims,
he dissents from every sound policy.
pp. 515f. 2 A fool has no pleasure in discernment,
but only in the expression of his own opinions.
p. 521 3 Where there is *wickedness*, contempt is there also,
and insult accompanies disrepute.
pp. 513f. 4 The words of a man's mouth are deep waters,
a bubbling brook, a fountain of wisdom.
p. 516 5 It is iniquitous to show partiality to a guilty man,
to deny an innocent man the verdict which is his due.
p. 515 6 A fool's lips enter upon controversy,
his speech calls out for a beating.
p. 515 7 A fool's speech is his downfall,
and his words a lethal snare.
pp. 519f. 8 A slanderer's words are like tit-bits,
they go down into the chambers of the belly.
p. 516 9 He who works in a half-hearted way,
is brother to a wrecker.
p. 521 10 The name of Yahweh is a strong tower,
the righteous man runs into it and cannot be reached.

pp. 516f. 11 A rich man's wealth is his strong city,
he envisages it as a high wall.

p. 521 12 Before a crash a man's mind is lifted up in pride,
but before honour comes humility.

p. 515 13 If a man makes a reply before he begins to listen,
it is his folly and disgrace.

p. 517 14 A man's spirit controls his illness,
but who can endure a broken spirit!

p. 516 15 A perceptive man acquires knowledge,
and wise men keep their ears pricked for knowledge.

p. 517 16 A man's bribe gives him an easy passage,
and brings him into the presence of great men.

p. 516 17 The first to speak argues his innocence convincingly,
then his opponent comes along and interrogates him.

pp. 521f. 18 The lot puts an end to controversy,
and separates powerful contestants.

p. 520 19 An aggrieved brother *is more inaccessible* than a fortified city,
and quarrels are like the bars of a palace.

p. 514 20 From the fruit of his mouth a man's stomach is filled,
he is satisfied with the produce of his lips.

pp. 514f. 21 Death and life are in the power of the tongue,
and those who cherish it eat its fruit.

p. 521 22 He who finds a wife finds good,
and obtains favour from Yahweh.

p. 518 23 A poor man speaks in wheedling tones,
but a wealthy man gives a brusque reply.

pp. 518f. 24 *There is a companion who does nothing but chatter,*
but there is a friend who sticks closer than a brother.

CHAPTER 19

p. 533 1 Better a poor man whose conduct is blameless,
than a man of twisted speech who is a fool.

p. 527 2 Energy without knowledge is not a good thing,
the man who is in a hurry goes astray.

pp. 533f. 3 Folly in a man makes for crooked conduct,
and his mind fumes against Yahweh.

p. 526 4 Wealth makes a multitude of friends,
but a poor man is alienated from his friend.

p. 529 5 A false witness is not acquitted,
and a perjurer does not escape justice.
p. 526 6 Many court the favour of a nobleman,
and everyone is the companion of the man with gifts to bestow.
pp. 526f. 7 A poor man's brothers all hate him,
much more do his companions hold themselves aloof from him.
— — — — — — — — — — — — — — —[1]
p. 528 8 A man with acumen loves his life,
and he who has regard for discernment finds what is good.
p. 529 9 A false witness is not acquitted,
and a perjurer perishes.
pp. 527f. 10 Luxury does not befit a fool,
much less does ruling over statesmen a slave.
p. 530 11 Good sense in a man makes his temper even,
and his glory is to pass over an offence.
p. 531 12 A king's anger is like the roar of a young lion,
but his favour is as dew on the grass.
p. 531 13 A foolish son is his father's ruin,
and the nagging of a wife an unrelenting drip.
p. 535 14 House and wealth are inherited from parents,
but a competent wife is from Yahweh.
p. 530 15 Laziness induces deep sleep,
and a lethargic man goes hungry.
p. 523 16 He who keeps the commandments keeps his life,
but he who despises *his ways* dies.
pp. 534f. 17 He who is kind to a poor man lends to Yahweh,
and he will repay him the debt in full.
pp. 523f. 18 Correct your son, for there is hope,
and do not bring about his death.
pp. 529f. 19 A *hot-tempered man* should pay his fine,
for if you get him out of trouble, you have to do it again and again.
p. 524 20 Listen to advice and accept instruction,
that your end may be that of a wise man.
p. 534 21 Many are the plans in a man's mind,
but it is Yahweh's policy which stands the test.
pp. 532f. 22 A man's *productivity* is his loyalty,
and a poor man is better than a false one.

[1] Verse 7c unintelligible.

p. 534 23 The fear of Yahweh makes for life,
and one passes the night replete, unvisited by evil.
pp. 530f. 24 The lazy person dips his hand into the dish,
but cannot bring it back even to his mouth.
pp. 525f. 25 Beat a scoffer and an untutored youth learns sense,
reprove a perceptive man and he himself grasps knowledge.
pp. 531f. 26 A son who maltreats his father and evicts his mother,
is a source of shame and disgrace.
p. 525 27 Cease, my son, to listen to instruction,
that you may stray from words of knowledge.
p. 529 28 A malicious witness scoffs at justice,
and the mouths of wicked men enunciate evil.
p. 526 29 Penalties are fixed for scoffers,
and strokes for the backs of fools.

CHAPTER 20

p. 541 1 Wine is a scoffer, alcohol a roisterer,
no one under its influence behaves wisely.
pp. 543f. 2 The terror inspired by a king is like the growl of a young lion,
he who trespasses on him forfeits his life.
p. 537 3 It is a man's glory to desist from strife,
but every fool explodes into controversy.
p. 542 4 A lazy man does not plough in autumn,
he expects crops at harvest and there is nothing.
pp. 536f. 5 Counsel in a man's mind is as deep waters,
and a man of discernment draws it up.
p. 545 6 Many a man proclaims his loyalty,
but who can find a faithful friend!
p. 548 7 A righteous man's conduct is blameless,
happy are his sons after him!
pp. 544f. 8 A king sits on a throne of justice,
winnowing every criminal with his eyes.
pp. 547f. 9 Who can say, 'I have purified my heart,
I am cleansed from my sin'?
p. 549 10 Variations in weights and measures,
both are loathed by Yahweh.

pp. 545f. 11 It is in what he does that a youth reveals himself,
if his action be pure and upright.
p. 547 12 An attentive ear and an observant eye,
Yahweh is the maker of them both.
pp. 541f. 13 Do not be too fond of sleep, lest you lose your inheritance,
wake up (early), eat your fill of bread.
p. 542 14 'A bad, bad bargain!', says a buyer,
but as he makes off he congratulates himself.
pp. 538f. 15 Gold there is and pearls in store,
but knowledgeable lips are a rare treasure.
pp. 542f. 16 Take his garment, for he has gone surety for a stranger;
secure yourself against him, for he is liable for foreigners.
pp. 539f. 17 Bread of falsehood tastes sweet to a man,
but afterwards his mouth is filled with gravel.
p. 537 18 Plans are fixed by counsel,
so make war by stratagems.
pp. 537f. 19 It is a talebearer who reveals a confidence,
so do not consort with a man of unguarded speech.
pp. 540f. 20 He who curses his father and mother,
his lamp is extinguished in pitch darkness.
p. 539 21 An inheritance grabbed in haste at the outset
does not lead to a happy sequel.
p. 548 22 Do not say, 'I shall get revenge for injury.'
Wait for Yahweh and he will give you your rights.
p. 549 23 Variations in weights are loathed by Yahweh,
and falsified scales are an evil.
pp. 546f. 24 A man's steps are ordered by Yahweh,
and who is the man that can discern where he is going!
p. 538 25 It is a snare for a man to make rash vows,
and after vows to seek ways and means.
pp. 544f. 26 A wise king winnows wicked men,
and brings the wheel over them.
p. 547 27 Man's spirit is Yahweh's lamp,
exploring all the chambers of the belly.
p. 546 28 Loyalty and constancy guard a king,
and by loyalty he supports his throne.
p. 541 29 The boast of young men is their strength,
and the glory of old men their gray hairs.
p. 540 30 Weals are a massage for evil,
and strokes for the chambers of the belly.

CHAPTER 21

pp. 559f. 1 A king's mind is like channels of water in Yahweh's hand,
he turns him to whatever he wills.

p. 558 2 A man's whole conduct is right in his own eyes,
but it is Yahweh who weighs up motives.

p. 560 3 The doing of what is right and just
is preferred by Yahweh to sacrifice.

pp. 558f. 4 Pride of eye and *pride of mind*,
the tilth of the wicked (*produces*) *sin*.

pp. 549f. 5 All the plans of an incisive man result in plenty,
but all who are in a hurry produce nothing but scarcity.

pp. 551f. 6 *Making* wealth with a false tongue,
is emptiness driven *among the snares of death*.

p. 560 7 The violence of wicked men nets them,
for they refuse to do what is just.

p. 562 8 The way of the crooked man is tortuous,
but the sincere man keeps a straight course.

pp. 553f. 9 It is better to live at the corner of a roof,
than to share a house with a nagging wife.

p. 556 10 A wicked man has an appetite for evil,
he does not look on his neighbour with kindness.

p. 550 11 When a scoffer is punished, an untutored youth becomes wise,
but when a wise man receives instruction, he himself appropriates knowledge.

p. 561 12 *The Righteous One* has control over the wicked man's household,
he topples evil men to their ruin.

p. 556 13 He who stops his ear to the cry of a poor man
will himself cry out and not be answered.

p. 555 14 A clandestine gift deflects rage,
and a bribe in the pocket fierce anger.

p. 560 15 Doing what is right brings joy to a righteous man,
but ruin is reserved for evil-doers.

p. 553 16 A man who strays from the way of understanding
comes to rest in the community of the dead.

p. 553 17 He who likes a good time is impecunious,
someone with a taste for wine and oil does not become rich.

p. 561 18 The wicked man is a ransom for the righteous man,
and the treacherous man for the upright.
pp. 553f. 19 It is better to live in a desert,
than to be vexed by a nagging wife.
pp. 552f. 20 Desirable *and rare* wealth are in the home of a wise man,
but a man who is a fool consumes it.
pp. 556f. 21 He who pursues righteousness and loyalty
finds life and honour.[1]
p. 551 22 A wise man scales a city of picked soldiers,
and demolishes the strength on which it relies.
p. 551 23 He who guards his mouth and tongue
keeps his life from straits.
pp. 550f. 24 He who is arrogant *to excess*, 'scoffer' is his name,
one who acts with immoderate arrogance.
p. 550 25 A lazy man's desire kills him,
for his hands refuse to act.
p. 557 26 *All the day long he is consumed with desire*,
but the righteous man gives without sparing.
p. 560 27 The sacrifices of wicked men are an abomination,
more so if they are brought with evil intent.
pp. 555f. 28 A false witness is cut short,
but *a good listener* speaks on.
p. 562 29 A wicked man hardens his face,
but an upright man reinforces his road.
p. 558 30 There is no wisdom nor discernment
nor policy to withstand Yahweh.
p. 558 31 A horse is made ready for the day of battle,
but victory belongs to Yahweh.

CHAPTER 22

p. 566 1 Reputation is preferable to great wealth,
a good presence to silver and gold.
pp. 569f. 2 Rich and poor live side by side,
it is Yahweh who makes them all.
pp. 563f. 3 A shrewd man sees trouble ahead and makes himself scarce,
but the untutored walk into it and pay the penalty.
p. 570 4 On the heels of humility *and the fear of Yahweh*
come wealth and honour and life.

[1] Deleting *ṣ^{e}dāqā*.

p. 565 5 *Traps and* snares are in the way of the twisted man,
he who preserves his life keeps his distance from them.
p. 564 6 Train up a youth in the way he ought to go,
to the end of his life he will not deviate from it.
p. 566 7 A rich man rules over poor men,
and a borrower is slave to the man who lends.
p. 570 8 He who sows iniquity reaps evil,
and the rod of his excess *smites him.*
p. 569 9 It is the kindly man who is blessed,
for he gives a share of his bread to the poor man.
pp. 566f. 10 Drive out a scoffer and strife goes out,
litigation and insult come to an end.
pp. 567f. 11 *A king* loves a man with a pure mind,
the grace of his speech (*meets*) *his approval.*
pp. 570f. 12 The eyes of Yahweh guard knowledge,
he subverts the words of the liar.
p. 569 13 A lazy man says, 'There is a lion outside,
I shall be mauled in the street.'
p. 571 14 The speech of strange women is a deep pit,
Yahweh's curse is on him who falls into it.
pp. 564f. 15 Folly is tied to the mind of a youth,
the rod of discipline severs it from him.
pp. 571f. 16 He who extorts money from a poor man succeeds only in enriching him,
but he who gives to a wealthy man produces only impoverishment.
pp. 374f. 17 Give heed and listen to *my words*,
apply your mind to my knowledge,
18 for it is a delight when you keep them within you,
when they are held together on your lips,
19 that your trust may be in Yahweh.
It is you that I inform to-day.
20 Have I not written thirty sayings for you,
containing well-informed counsel?
21 To inform you about truth and truthful words,
so that you may bring back a reliable report to him who sends you.
pp. 377f. 22 Do not rob a poor man just because he is poor,
and do not crush a needy man in court,
23 for Yahweh will fight his case,
and beat to death those who beat him.
p. 378 24 Do not take a hot-tempered man for a friend,
and do not keep company with a hothead,

25 lest you become familiar with his paths,
and alight on a lethal snare.
pp. 378f. 26 Do not make a habit of striking hands,
of going surety for debts.
27 If you have no resources to settle them,
why should your bed be taken from under you!
pp. 379f. 28 Do not remove the boundary markers which have always been there,
those which your ancestors fixed.
pp. 380f. 29 You have seen a man who is skilful at his work?
It is with kings that he will hold office;
he will not hold office with obscure men.

CHAPTER 23

pp. 381f. 1 When you sit down to eat with a ruler,
confine your attention to what is before you,
2 and put a knife in your throat,
if you have a hearty appetite.
3 Do not let your appetite be whetted by his tit-bits,
for it is deceptive food.
pp. 382f. 4 Do not wear yourself out making wealth,
be discerning enough to give it up.
5 *If you take your eyes off it for an instant*, it disappears,
for it takes to itself wings,
like an eagle it flies heavenwards.
pp. 383f. 6 Do not eat with a miser,
nor let your appetite be whetted by his tit-bits,
7 for he is like *a hair* in *the* throat.
'Eat and drink,' he says to you,
but he does not mean what he says.
8 You will vomit up what you have eaten,
and corrupt your gracious words.
p. 385 9 Do not speak into a fool's ears,
for he will despise the good sense of your words.
p. 385 10 Do not remove the boundary markers which have always been there,
nor encroach on fields belonging to orphans;
11 for their redeemer is powerful,
he will fight their case with you.

p. 385
12 Apply your mind to instruction,
and your ear to words of knowledge.
p. 386
13 Do not withhold discipline from a youth;
if you beat him with a rod, he will not die.
14 You must beat him then with a rod,
and save his life from Sheol.
pp. 386f.
15 My son, if you become a wise man,
no one will be more pleased than I.
16 I shall be overcome with joy,
when your lips speak upright words.
pp. 387f.
17 Do not let sinners excite your envy,
but let the fear of Yahweh do it at all times;
18 for if *you have regard to it*, a good end awaits you,
and your hope will not be cut off.
p. 388
19 Listen, my son, and become wise,
and get your thoughts straight about your conduct.
20 Do not keep the company of topers,
nor of those given to gluttony;
21 for the toper and glutton are disinherited,
and slumber clothes them in rags.
pp. 388f.
22 Listen to your father who begot you,
and do not despise your mother when she is old.
23 Buy truth and do not sell it,
(buy) wisdom, instruction and insight.
24 The father of a righteous man is overcome with joy,
he who begets a wise man delights in him.
25 May your father and mother be happy,
and she who bore you rejoice.
pp. 389f.
26 My son, give your mind to me,
and let your eyes approve my ways;
27 for *a strange woman* is a deep pit,
and a foreign woman a narrow well.
28 She lays an ambush like *a highwayman*,
and deceives men again and again.
pp. 393f.
29 Who has sorrow and care?
Who has quarrels and brooding?
Who has needless bruises?
Who has lustreless eyes?
30 Those who linger over wine,
who go out to savour cocktails.
31 Do not gaze at wine when it is red,
when it gleams in the cup;
it goes over (the palate) *smoothly*.

32 Its sequel is like a snake bite,
or a viper's prick.
33 Your eyes see strange things,
you think up absurdities to say.
34 You are like a man going to bed on the high seas,
like one who lies down on the top of the tackle.
35 'They beat me but I felt no pain,
they struck me but I was not aware of it.
When shall I fully wake up?
I shall go in search of another drink.'

CHAPTER 24

p. 396 1 Do not feel envious of evil men,
nor have longings to be with them;
2 for their minds meditate destruction,
and their lips speak about misery.
pp. 396f. 3 A household is built by wisdom,
and is established by discernment.
4 Its rooms are filled by knowledge,
with expensive things in the best taste.
pp. 397f. 5 *A wise man has more strength than a strong man,*
and a knowledgeable person consolidates power;
6 for expertise is needed to wage war,
and safety lies in many advisers.
p. 398 7 Wisdom is above the grasp of a fool,
he does not open his mouth in the gate.
pp. 398f. 8 He who lays plans to do evil
gets the name 'Intriguer'.
9 *A fool's* intrigue is sin,
and men loathe a scoffer.
pp. 399f. 10 If you are seen to sag on a day of adversity,
the limits of your strength are revealed.
pp. 400f. 11 Rescue prisoners condemned to death,
and do not deny help to those *about to be* executed;
12 for if you say, 'Look we know nothing about this,'
will not the one who weighs up motives get at the truth?
He who watches over you will know about it,
and he will repay every man for what he has done.
pp. 402f. 13 My son, eat honey, for it is good,

and the honeycomb is sweet to your palate;
14 so is *knowledge and* wisdom for your life.
If you find them, there will be a (happy) sequel for you,
and your hope will not be cut off.
pp. 403f. 15 Do not lay an ambush against a righteous man's dwelling,[1]
do not destroy his resting-place;
16 for a righteous man falls seven times and gets up again,
but wicked men stumble fatally.
p. 404 17 Do not gloat at the fall of your enemy,
nor chuckle when he stumbles,
18 lest Yahweh sees and disapproves,
and withdraws his anger from him.
pp. 404f. 19 Do not let evil-doers vex you,
do not be envious of wicked men;
20 for there is no sequel for the evil man,
the lamp of the wicked goes out.
pp. 405f. 21 My son, fear Yahweh and the king,
do not get involved with noblemen;
22 for disaster overtakes them suddenly,
and who knows *when their life will be cut off*!
p. 573 23 These are also attributable to the wise men:
To give a verdict which is not impartial is an evil.
p. 573 24 He who says to a guilty man, 'You are innocent,'
peoples curse him, nations fume at him;
p. 573 25 but it is well with those who exact the right penalty,
true prosperity overtakes them.
p. 575 26 He kisses the lips,
who gives an honest reply.
pp. 575f. 27 Set your outside work in order,
and cultivate your field;
afterwards set to and build your house.
pp. 573f. 28 Do not give evidence gratuitously against your neighbour.
Will you deceive with your lips?
pp. 574f. 29 Do not say, 'I shall do to him as he has done to me,
I shall repay a man according to his deed.'
pp. 576f. 30 I passed by the field of a lazy man,
and by the vineyard of one lacking in sense.
31 Thistles had sprung up all over it,
chickweed covered its surface,
its stone dyke had become a ruin.

[1] Deleting *rāšāʿ*.

32 I looked, I took note,
I observed, I learned the lesson.
33 A little sleep, a little slumber,
a little folding of the hands to lie down,
34 and poverty comes to you like a vagrant,
and want like a beggar.

CHAPTER 25

p. 577 1 These also are proverbs of Solomon
which the men of Hezekiah, king of Judah, copied.
p. 579 2 It is the glory of God to conceal a matter,
but it is the glory of kings to seek out information.
pp. 579f. 3 As the heavens are high and the earth is deep,
the mind of a king is unsearchable.
pp. 590f. 4 Take away dross from silver,
and the smith *will produce* a work of art.
p. 591 5 Take away a wicked man from a king's presence,
and his throne will be established in righteousness.
p. 580 6 Do not affect dignity in a king's presence,
nor occupy the place of great men;
7 for it is better that one should say to you, 'Come up here,'
than that he should make you give place to a nobleman.
pp. 580f. 7c–8 Do not be in a hurry to broadcast
what your eyes have seen,
for what will you do at its sequel,
when your neighbour humiliates you?
pp. 581f. 9 Fight your own case with your neighbour,
and do not reveal another's confidence,
10 lest he who overhears you puts you to shame,
and the stigma sticks to you.
p. 584 11 Apples of gold set in a silver design,
a phrase which is well-turned.
p. 585 12 A ring of gold and a trinket of fine gold,
one who gives wise reproof to a receptive ear.
pp. 585f. 13 Like the cold of snow on a day of harvest
is a reliable messenger to those who send him;
he gives new life to his masters.

p. 586 14 Clouds and wind and no rain,
a man who boasts about a non-existent gift.
pp. 584f. 15 An even temper wins over a ruler,
a soft tongue breaks down resistance.
p. 587 16 If you find honey, eat what suffices you,
lest you have surfeit of it and vomit it up.
p. 587 17 Be sparing in your visits to your neighbour's house,
lest he have surfeit of you and hate you.
pp. 583f. 18 A *club* and a sword and a sharp arrow,
a man who gives evidence against his neighbour, a false witness.
pp. 586f. 19 A *crumbling* tooth and a *palsied* foot,
a false sense of security when you are in straits.
pp. 588f. 20 Taking off one's clothes on a cold day,
vinegar on a wound;
one who sings songs with a sad heart.
pp. 591f. 21 If your enemy is hungry, give him bread to eat,
and if he is thirsty, give him water to drink;
22 for you will heap live coals on his head,
and Yahweh will give you your reward.
pp. 582f. 23 A north wind produces rain,
and gossip a look of rage.
p. 589 24 It is better to live at the corner of a roof,
than to share a house with a nagging wife.
pp. 589f. 25 Cold water on a tired throat,
good news from a distant country.
pp. 592f. 26 A fouled spring, a polluted well,
a righteous man who cannot withstand a wicked man.
pp. 587f. 27 It is bad to eat honey in excess,
so be sparing with eulogizing words.
p. 590 28 A city breached and without a wall,
a man who has no self-control.

CHAPTER 26

p. 595 1 As snow in summer and rain at harvest,
so honour is out of place for a fool.
pp. 599f. 2 As a sparrow on the wing and a swallow in flight,
so is an unmerited curse which does not alight.
pp. 595f. 3 A whip for a horse and a bridle for an ass,
and a stick for the back of a fool.

p. 596 4 Do not answer a fool when he speaks nonsense,
lest you, too, are reduced to his level.
p. 596 5 Answer a fool when he speaks nonsense,
lest he supposes himself to be a wise man.
p. 597 6 *A man who cuts off his feet, who drinks violence,*
one who sends a message by a fool.
pp. 597f. 7 Legs *hanging limp* from a lame man,
a proverb in the mouth of a fool.
p. 598 8 It is like tying a stone in a sling,
when one accords honour to a fool.
pp. 598ff. 9 A thorn bush in a drunkard's hand,
a proverb in the mouth of a fool.
p. 599 10 *An archer who wounds every passer-by,*
one who hires a fool and a *drunkard.*
p. 599 11 As a dog returns to its vomit,
a fool repeats his folly.
p. 596 12 You have seen a man wise in his own eyes?
There is more hope for the fool than for him.
p. 600 13 A sluggard says, 'There is a lion in the road,
a lion in the streets.'
pp. 600f. 14 A door turns on its hinge,
and a sluggard on his bed.
p. 600 15 A sluggard dips his hand into the dish;
he lacks the energy to raise it to his mouth.
p. 601 16 A sluggard is wiser in his own eyes
than seven masters of the right riposte.
pp. 601f. 17 A man who takes hold of the ears of a dog,
a passer-by who gets heated over a quarrel not his own.
p. 602 18 Like one who plays the fool,
shooting lethal firebrands and arrows,
19 is the man who deceives his friend
and says, 'I was only joking.'
pp. 602f. 20 For lack of sticks a fire goes out,
and where there is no slanderer, strife is quietened.
p. 603 21 Charcoal to embers, wood to fire,
a contentious man to stoke up controversy.
p. 603 22 A slanderer's words are like tit-bits,
they go down into the chambers of the belly.
pp. 603f. 23 *Like enamel* spread over earthenware,
are ardent lips and an evil intent.
p. 604 24 A misanthropist uses words as a cloak,
but within he is set on deceit.

p. 604 25 When he is charming, do not trust him,
for there are seven villainies in his mind.
pp. 604f. 26 His malevolence is concealed by deceit,
(but) his villainy will be uncovered in public.
p. 605 27 He who digs a pit falls into it,
he who sets a stone rolling is caught up by it.
pp. 605f. 28 A lying tongue *hates to see innocence established*,
and smooth speech has destructive ends.

CHAPTER 27

pp. 607f. 1 Do not boast about to-morrow,
for you do not know what a day will produce.
p. 608 2 Let a stranger praise you and not your own mouth,
a foreigner and not your own lips.
p. 609 3 The weight of a stone, the heaviness of sand,
the vexation of a fool is heavier than both.
p. 611 4 Ruthless anger and flood-waters of rage,
but who can stand before jealousy!
p. 610 5 Open reproof is better than
love which is concealed.
pp. 610f. 6 The wounds inflicted by a friend are faithful,
but the kisses of an enemy are *effusive*.
pp. 611f. 7 The person who is satiated tramples on honey,
but everything bitter is sweet to the one who is hungry.
p. 612 8 Like a bird which flies from its nest,
is a man who flies from his place.
pp. 612f. 9 Oil and incense gladden the heart,
the sweetness of friendship strengthens the spirit.
p. 614 10 Do not forsake your friend and your father's friend,
and do not go to your brother's house when you are in trouble.
A neighbour near at hand is better than a brother at a distance.
p. 616 11 My son, be wise and make me happy,
that I may have an answer for my detractor.
p. 610 12 A shrewd man who sees trouble ahead makes himself scarce,
but the untutored who walk into it pay the penalty.

p. 616 13 Take his garment, for he has gone surety for a stranger;
secure yourself against him, for he is liable for *foreigners*.

p. 619 14 He who rises early to greet his friend with a hearty voice
is to be accounted a curse to him.

p. 616 15 An unrelenting drip on a day of downpour,
is on a par with a nagging wife.

pp. 616f. 16 He who would keep her in custody would detain the wind,
oil meets his right hand.

pp. 614f. 17 Iron *is sharpened* on iron,
a man *sharpens* the wits of his friend.

p. 617 18 He who tends a fig tree eats its fruit,
he who takes care of his master gets honour.

pp. 615f. 19 As a face is reflected in water,
a man's mind is his mirror.

pp. 617f. 20 Sheol and Abaddon are insatiable,
a man's eyes are never satisfied.

pp. 608f. 21 The smelting-pot for silver, the furnace for gold,
a man with respect to his reputation.

pp. 609f. 22 If you pulverize a fool with a pestle
in a mortar among *powder*,
you will not remove his folly from him.

pp. 618f. 23 Keep a close eye on your sheep,
pay careful attention to your flocks;

24 for wealth does not last for ever,
riches are not inexhaustible.

25 When the hay is taken off and the second growth appears,
and the hill grass is gathered,

26 lambs will supply you with clothing,
and goats provide the price of a field.

27 There will be goats' milk in plenty to feed you and your household,
and there will be sustenance for your housemaids.

CHAPTER 28

p. 621 1 A wicked man *runs away* when nobody is pursuing him,
but *a righteous man* feels as secure as a lion.

pp. 630f. 2 *A country which transgresses gets one statesman after another,*
but by a perceptive man's efforts order is maintained.[1]

pp. 628f. 3 *A man in authority* who oppresses the poor,
beating rain and starvation.

p. 623 4 Those who forsake the Law applaud a wicked man,
but those who keep the Law are incensed against *him*.

p. 620 5 Evil men do not discern what is just,
but those who seek Yahweh are all-discerning.

pp. 627f. 6 Better is a poor man whose conduct is blameless
than a rich man whose *ways* are tortuous.

pp. 623f. 7 A perceptive son keeps the Law,
but a companion of profligates puts his father to shame.

p. 626 8 He who accumulates wealth by commission and interest
gathers it for the man who is kind to the poor.

p. 623 9 He who turns a deaf ear to the Law,
even his prayer is an abomination.

pp. 621f. 10 He who leads upright men astray to their hurt
himself falls *into his own pit*;
but blameless men inherit what is good.

p. 621 p. 628 11 A rich man is wise in his own eyes,
but a poor man who has discernment sees through him.

pp. 624f. 12 When righteous men rejoice, there is great splendour,
but when wicked men rise to power, citizens *make themselves scarce*.

p. 628 13 He who conceals his wrongdoings does not prosper,
but he who confesses and renounces them finds mercy.

p. 628 14 Happy is the man who constantly fears (Yahweh),
but he who hardens his heart falls into evil.

p. 629 15 A growling lion, a prowling bear,
a wicked ruler oppressing the poor.

pp. 629f. 16 An undiscriminating ruler *piles oppression upon oppression*,
but he who hates graft maintains his rule.

pp. 625f. 17 A man burdened with another's life-blood
is running away towards the Pit.
He is not to be stopped.

p. 622 18 A man of blameless conduct is safe,
but one whose *ways* are tortuous falls into *a pit*.

[1] Deleting *yōdēaʿ*.

p. 631 19 A man who works his soil has enough to eat,
but one whose pursuits are empty feeds on poverty.
p. 626 20 Many blessings accrue to the man who keeps faith,
but one in a hurry to get rich does not escape condemnation.
p. 631 21 Failure to be impartial is an evil,
a man commits injustice for a piece of bread.
pp. 626f. 22 A grasping man is impatient for wealth,
he does not know that want will overtake him.
pp. 631f. 23 He who reproves a man *about his conduct* is more highly regarded
than one who speaks smooth words.
p. 632 24 He who robs his father and mother and says, 'There is no wrong in it',
is the accomplice of a murderer.
p. 627 25 A greedy man stirs up strife,
but he who trusts in Yahweh enjoys prosperity.
pp. 620f. 26 The fool is the one who relies on his intellect,
but it is a man of wise conduct who escapes harm.
p. 627 27 He who gives to the poor is never in want,
but many curses accrue to him who shuts his eyes (to need).
pp. 624f. 28 When the wicked rise to power, citizens conceal themselves,
but when they perish, righteous men come to power.

CHAPTER 29

p. 633 1 A man whose obstinacy grows with reproof
is suddenly shattered beyond remedy.
p. 639 2 When righteous men come to power, people rejoice,
but when a wicked man rules, they groan.
pp. 633f. 3 One who loves wisdom gives pleasure to his father,
but a customer of prostitutes squanders wealth.
pp. 637f. 4 It is by justice that a king makes a country stable,
but one who levies taxes makes a ruin of it.
pp. 636f. 5 A man who speaks smooth words to his neighbour
is spreading a net about his feet.
pp. 638f. 6 There is a snare in an evil man's wrong-doing,
but a righteous man *runs on* rejoicing.

pp. 641f. 7 A righteous man is concerned that the poor get justice,
but a wicked man is devoid of insight.
p. 635 8 Arrogant men inflame a city,
but wise men cause anger to subside.
p. 636 9 When a wise man is at law with a fool,
there is no end to his ranting and sneering.
p. 637 10 Bloodthirsty men hate the man of integrity,
but upright men are careful of his life.
p. 635 11 A fool gives expression to every angry impulse,
but a wise man keeps them in check.
p. 638 12 A ruler who gives credence to a lie,
all who serve him are wicked men.
p. 640 13 A poor man and his oppressor exist side by side,
Yahweh illumines the eyes of them both.
p. 638 14 A king who gives a fair trial to the poor,
his throne is established for ever.
p. 634 15 Rod and reproof make for wisdom,
but an undisciplined youth is his mother's shame.
p. 639 16 When wicked men are on the increase, wrong-doing increases,
but righteous men look on at their downfall.
p. 634 17 Discipline your son that he may be a source of satisfaction,
and may give pleasure to you.
pp. 640f. 18 Where there is no vision people are undisciplined,
but happy is he who keeps the Law!
p. 634 19 A slave is not disciplined by words,
for he understands but is unresponsive.
pp. 635f. 20 You have seen a man of impetuous speech?
There is more hope for the fool than for him.
pp. 634f. 21 He who pampers his slave from youth
will have an insubordinate to deal with in the long run.
p. 636 22 A hot-tempered man stirs up strife,
and one quickly aroused often gives offence.
p. 633 23 A man's haughtiness brings him low,
but one of lowly disposition grasps honour.
p. 641 24 He who goes shares with a thief hates his life,
he hears the curse but gives no information.
p. 639 25 Fear of men is a snare,
but he who trusts in Yahweh is inaccessible to danger.
p. 639 26 Many court a ruler's favour,
but it is from Yahweh that one gets justice.

p. 640
27 Righteous men loathe a devious man,
but a wicked man loathes one whose conduct is upright.

CHAPTER 30

pp. 643f.
1 The words of Agur, the son of Yakeh, *of Massa*;
the utterance of the man. There is no God, there is no God
and I am exhausted;
2 for I am more a beast than a man,
and human discernment is not given to me.
3 I have not learned wisdom,
nor do I have knowledge of the Holy One.
4 Who has ascended to heaven and come down again?
Who has held the wind in his fists?
Who has wrapped the waters in a cloak?
Who has established all the ends of the earth?
What is his name and his son's name, if indeed you know (them)?
pp. 647f.
5 Every saying of God has stood the test,
he is a shield to those who take refuge in him.
6 Do not add to his words,
lest he put you right and you are seen to be a liar.
7 Two things I ask of you,
do not deny them to me as long as I live.
8 Remove falsehood and lying far from me;
do not give me poverty or wealth;
let me eat the bread that is my due;
9 lest when I am well fed I become a renegade,
and say, 'Who is Yahweh?'
Lest when I am reduced to poverty I become a thief,
and violate the name of my God.
p. 650
10 Do not denounce a slave to his master,
lest he vilify you and you are in the wrong.
pp. 650f.
11 There are those who curse their fathers,
and do not bless their mothers.
12 There are those who are pure in their own eyes,
but are not cleansed from their filth.
13 There are those with pride in their eyes,
and haughtiness in their *glance*.

14 There are those whose teeth are swords,
whose jaws are knives,
to eat up the poor from the earth,
and the needy from among men.
pp. 653f. 15a The leech has two daughters. Give. Give.
pp. 652ff. 15b–16 There are three which are never satisfied,
four which never say, 'Enough'!
Sheol, an unopened womb,
land short of water,
and fire which never says, 'Enough'!
pp. 656f. 17 The eye that mocks a father
and despises *an aged mother*;
the ravens of the canyon will tear it out,
and the vultures devour it.
pp. 657f. 18 There are three which are beyond my comprehension,
four which I do not grasp:
19 The way of an eagle in the heavens,
the way of a snake on a rock,
the way of a ship on the seas,
and the way of a man with a woman.
pp. 658f. 20 This is the way of an adultress:
she eats, wipes her mouth
and says, 'I have done no wrong.'
pp. 659f. 21 There are three which convulse a land,
four which it cannot endure:
22 that a slave should hold rule,
and that a fool should be well fed;
23 that a shrew should get a husband,
and that a maid should supplant her mistress.
pp. 660f. 24 There are four of the earth's smallest creatures
who are the wisest of the wise.
25 Ants are a weak community,
but they lay in their food stocks in summer.
26 Badgers are a weak community,
but they make their houses in the rocks.
27 Locusts have no king,
but they march in perfect formation.
28 A lizard *can be grasped* with the hand,
but they are found in kings' palaces.
pp. 662f. 29 There are three of stately step,
four of stately tread:
30 The lion, king of beasts,
there is nothing from which he retreats.

31 *A strutting cock, a he-goat,*[1]
and a king at the head of his people.

pp. 664f. 32 If you act the fool by giving yourself airs,
if you dabble in intrigue with your hand on your mouth, (watch your step);
33 for the pressing of milk produces curds,
and the pressing of the nose produces blood,
and the pressing of anger produces strife.

CHAPTER 31

pp. 407f. 1 The instruction received by Lemuel, king of Massa, from his mother.
2 *Listen*, my son, son of my womb, son of my vows.
3 Do not expend your strength on women,
your *semen* on *those who destroy kings*.
4 It is not for kings, Lemuel,
it is not for kings to drink wine,
a taste for alcohol is not for rulers;
5 lest they drink and forget the laws,
and deny justice to the poor.
6 Give alcohol to a man who is going to die,
and wine to those who are sad,
7 that they may drink and forget their poverty,
and remember their misery no more.
8 Speak out for a dumb man,
for the rights of *all victims of circumstance*.
9 Speak out to ensure that justice is done,
and that the poor and needy get their deserts.

pp. 665f. 10 Who can find a woman of parts?
Her price is higher than pearls.
11 Her husband has confidence in her,
and is not without gain.
12 She does him nothing but good
all the days of her life.
13 She acquires wool and flax,
and has pleasure in the work of her hands.
14 She is like the ships of a merchant,
bringing her bread from afar.

[1] Deleting *'ō*.

15 She rises while it is still dark
and issues *orders* to her household,
allotting her maids their tasks.
16 She considers a field and buys it,
from what her hands have produced she plants a vineyard.
17 She girdles her loins with strength,
and strengthens her arms (for work).
18 She discerns that trade is good,
she does not put out her lamp at night.
19 She occupies herself with the distaff,
and her hands hold the spindle.
20 She stretches out her hand to the poor,
and extends her help to the needy.
21 She does not fear for her household when it snows,
for all of them are clothed in scarlet.
22 She makes her own bedspreads,
fine linen and purple are in her wardrobe.
23 Her husband is well-known in the gates,
when he sits with the elders of the district.
24 She makes dresses and sells them,
she supplies sashes to merchants.
25 Strength and majesty are her clothing,
and she laughs at the uncertain future.
26 She opens her mouth to speak wisdom,
sound teaching is on her tongue.
27 She misses nothing that goes on in her household,
she does not eat the bread of idleness.
28 Her sons rise up and bless her,
her husband sings her praises.
29 'There are many women of parts,
but you have excelled them all.'
30 Charm deceives and beauty vanishes,
it is the woman who fears Yahweh that deserves praise.
31 Give her credit for her achievements,
and let her be praised in the gates for what she has done.

V

THE INSTRUCTION GENRE IN THE BOOK OF PROVERBS

A. CHAPTERS 1–9

Chapter 1

Proverbs 1.1–7 (so Ringgren) rather than 1.1–6 (Gemser) is a general introduction to chs. 1–9. Gemser suggests that besides introducing these chapters, it also serves as a superscription for the entire book, and Whybray supposes that it is an expanded form of what was originally a preface to chs. 1–9, the original preface being vv. 1–5 (R. N. Whybray, *Wisdom in Proverbs*, SBT 45, 1965, pp. 37f.). Gemser notes the practice in the Egyptian Instruction of beginning with the name and rank of the real or fancied author. The appearance is more an indication of *Gattung* than a notice about authorship (so Gemser and Ringgren). Wisdom literature was a royal genre, one which enjoyed the patronage of the court and was practised by men who were close to the king. Neither Gemser nor Ringgren preclude the possibility that Solomon may have been the author of some proverbs, but the more significant information which the appearance of Solomon's name gives is the connection of this form of literary activity with the king and those around him, just as most of the extant examples of the Egyptian Instruction derive either from the Pharaoh himself or from his officials (see above, pp. 51f.).

[1] If *mišᵉlē* in v. 1 refers to the contents of the whole book, as is probably the case, it is not altogether a satisfactory way of describing the material. It does not take sufficient account of the variety of material in the book and, in particular, it tends to obscure the fact that there are two distinct literary kinds, the Instruction and the wisdom sentence. Yet it is too high-handed to assert that v. 1 gives us erroneous information. What would appear to have happened is that *māšāl* acquired so generalized a meaning that any type of wisdom literature could be so designated (see further above, p. 31). My study of the Instruction, particularly the Egyptian Instruction, is sufficient to show that it is distinct from the wisdom sentence and is not built up from the single wisdom sentence, as is supposed by the orthodox form-critical account of Prov. 1–9 (see above pp. 1f.).

Gemser's statement, that the higher art of life which knows how best to achieve the accommodation of man and God is the concern of the book of Proverbs, will not answer all the questions which are raised by vv. 1–7. These verses do not communicate to me such harmony and inner consistency. If careful attention is paid to their vocabulary, it will be seen that the kind of wisdom which Gemser (p. 1) terms 'amoral' is represented in the book of Proverbs. Other items of vocabulary point to a differently based wisdom in which piety and its constituent morality have become dominant. In vv. 1–7, the vocabulary of old wisdom (*PWM*, pp. 15f.), with its robust intellectual content and its preoccupation with skill and aptitude, lies alongside the language of piety and morality (cf. Whybray, pp. 95f.).

This initial impression of the book of Proverbs is not misleading; it is a pointer to the constituents of the whole. I have elsewhere (*PWM*) discussed the prophetic reinterpretation of the vocabulary of old wisdom, and I would maintain that there is also evidence of a Yahwistic reinterpretation of wisdom in the book of Proverbs. Verses 1–7 give a prior indication of the range of material in the book of Proverbs, and of the nature of wisdom before and after its subjection to Yahwistic piety. The two different worlds of vv. 1–7 can best be illustrated by an examination of the vocabulary of these verses, but a word should be said first of all about the syntactical structure of this passage. Verses 2, 3, 4, 6, all begin with an infinitive construct which in each case refers back to v. 1 and introduces different specifications of the usefulness or functions of the *mešālīm*. Verse 5, which does not have this form and which diverges metrically from the other verses, is suspected as an intrusion by Gemser.

[2] 'To take note of wisdom and instruction (*mūsār*), to grasp perceptive sayings' (*'imerē bīnā*). This is the vocabulary of old wisdom and is indicative of a strenuous educational discipline which is productive of rigorous intellectual attitudes. *mūsār* is commonly correlated with Egyptian *sb'yt*, 'instruction'. It is to be associated with the demand for receptivity in the pupil (cf. v. 5) and for submission to the authority of the teacher. Those who wield this authority, as in the case of the Egyptian Instruction, are parents (v. 8) and wisdom teachers. It is not a religious authority which is claimed here. Parents have a natural claim on the obedience of their children, which they can reinforce by an appeal to a richer experience of life, and the wisdom teacher distils the sagacity of many generations for the benefit of his pupils, basing his authority on what has proved best in the past and on his own judgement.

The other words in v. 2 (*l^ehābīn, bīnā*) have been discussed in *PWM* (pp. 65f.). They describe intellectual virtues of discrimination and penetration, but they were reinterpreted by the prophets to mean religious illumination, by being made to hinge on submission to Yahweh and obedience to his demands. **[7]** If v. 2 were understood in terms of v. 7, it would undergo a similar reinterpretation. In particular, I would suggest that the fear of Yahweh (*yir'at YHWH*) is the new *mūsār* which in v. 7 is described as 'the beginning (or 'head') of knowledge'. The acquisition of knowledge and wisdom does not now depend on a severe educational discipline in which submission is made to the authority of a teacher and the pupil's attitudes formed by his assimilation of a body of traditional, empirically based wisdom. The context is now one of piety rather than of education, and the source of authority is Yahweh. Without this basic reverence for Yahweh and submission to him, there can be no acquisition of wisdom, and this is what v. 7 indicates by the words 'fools despise wisdom and instruction' where the *'^ewīl* is the person who does not have the fear of Yahweh in his heart.

Gemser agrees in part with this estimate of v. 7. He observes that it may reflect tensions which had existed between the prophetic and priestly representatives of Yahwism, on the one hand, and the international wisdom, which was the basis of the instruction given by the wisdom teachers, on the other. But this wisdom could not give effective reassurances about its compatibility with Yahwistic tradition without indicating its readiness for change, and this aspect of the matter is not emphasized by Gemser. One can say with Gemser that according to v. 7 the fear of Yahweh disposes a man towards the search for wisdom, makes him attentive to its claims and encourages him to value it properly. One has, however, then to ask what change has taken place in the concept of wisdom consequent on this new point of departure. Once wisdom is made to hinge on submission to

Yahweh and the acceptance of his authority and illumination, a reinterpretation which affects the entire vocabulary of wisdom is involved, as I have tried to show in *PWM*.

The rhythmic reasons adduced by Gemser for associating v. 7 with vv. 8–9 are outweighed by the lack of intrinsic connection between v. 7 and vv. 8–9. There is no reason to assume that v. 8 presupposes any appeal to religious authority; the motive is respect for natural parental authority and not reverence for Yahweh. That there are additional formal reasons for regarding vv. 8–19 as an entity I shall show below.

[3] 'To receive effective instruction (*mūsar haśkēl*), righteousness, justice and uprightness.' In *PWM* (pp. 65f.) I observed that vocabulary connected with Yahweh's moral demands and associated with an intense commitment to morality plays an important role in the prophetic reinterpretation of old wisdom. Words like *ṣedeq*, *mišpāṭ* and *mēšārīm* contrast strongly with the original lack of moral commitment in the vocabulary of old wisdom, and, in the context of v. 3, *mūsar haśkēl* may refer to the discipline of piety rather than to educational discipline in the old sense. Gemser and Ringgren translate 'salutary discipline', but Ringgren correctly observes that the thought of being effective in obtaining results is original to *śkl*.

[4] 'To give shrewdness to the untutored, knowledge and resourcefulness to the young' (following Targ. and Pesh. in reading *nᵉʿārīm*). There is nothing of the new *mūsār* in v. 4; the situation which it presupposes and the vocabulary which it employs both contribute to this impression. It preserves the flavour of the relationship between the wisdom teacher and the raw youths who come to be shaped by the educational process. *mᵉzimmā*, 'intrigue', 'resourcefulness', is ethically neutral and on occasions pejorative, and *ʿormā*, 'guile', 'shrewdness', is translated *Klugheit* by Gemser and Ringgren. Of both these words Zimmerli (*ZAW* 51, 1933, p. 183) says that they stand on the border of the pejorative, not far removed from knavery (*die Tücke*). The educational process was more occupied with developing mature intellectual attitudes than with morality. Its concern was to impart negotiating skills, to nurture soundness of judgement and to produce a weighty and effective individual. It did not educate men to change the existing world into something better, but to make their way successfully in the world as it was.

[5] 'A wise man listens and appropriates more (wisdom), and a perceptive man (*nābōn*) learns the ropes (*taḥbūlōt*).' We have noticed

that the demand for receptivity is prominent in the Egyptian Instruction, and it is a willingness to assimilate a body of traditional wisdom rather than any show of originality which is expected of the apprentice sage. This does not mean that the educational process is no more than the mechanical memorizing of information. Rather, it is the belief (expressed here in v. 5) that no man can be wise who has not steeped himself in that wisdom which is the deposit of the best minds of many generations. There is a strong sense of the continuity of tradition and of its organic character. The apprentice sage does not remain outside it, confronting it as an external body of knowledge, but he appropriates it in such a way that it becomes part of himself and makes him the kind of person he is, shaping his attitudes and controlling his judgements.

The effect, therefore, is not to produce men who have no independence of judgement, but rather those who exercise such independence in the spirit of the tradition in which they live and thereby ensure that it continues to grow and retains its vitality. I have translated *leqaḥ* freely in order to convey this sense of 'appropriation' and I note that Ringgren associates it with *traditio*. *taḥbūlōt* witnesses to the interest of the wisdom teacher in imparting procedural skills. There are some objectives which can only be attained by expertise in procedural techniques, by the ability to pick one's way without putting a foot wrong through a confused and tangled situation. I have connected *taḥbūlōt* with *ḥbl* 'to bind', *ḥebel* 'rope', and the more precise associations of this formation are perhaps, as is usually assumed, with navigational skill. It is then a term for a kind of nautical expertise, the ability to steer a course through the trackless sea; and it lends itself readily to becoming a metaphor for the negotiating skills which discern the beginning and the end of a problem and perform each operation in the right place at the right time. Cf. *Aqhat* II. vi. 40–41 (*CML*, p. 54), where a lacuna in *l.* 41 is made good by the insertion of *tḥblt* (following Albright). *tqny tḥblt* is then to be compared with *taḥbūlōt yiqne* in v. 5b. The vocabulary of this verse is that of old wisdom uninfluenced by any process of reinterpretation. The first half of the verse points to the old *mūsār* rather than the new, and the second half is concerned with skill and dexterity rather than morality.

[6] 'To grasp (pierce the meaning of) a proverb (*māšāl*) and an allusion (*m^e^liṣā*), words of the wise and riddles (*ḥīdōt*).' This verse describes the forms of literary art in which the wise man has a competence. Wisdom embraces form as well as content, and it matters that what is said should be said well and elegantly. The wise man is the master of compressed, polished epigrammatic utterance; he gathers his thoughts into memorable forms of expression. The function of the proverb is to illumine, and not to present a barrier to intelligibility. In this respect it is different from the *ḥīdā*, which apparently had a vogue as a courtly game and whose essence was opaqueness, mystification, enigma. Nevertheless, the meaning of a *māšāl* has to be pierced, for it may initially offer a barrier to understanding which requires an effort of intuition to surmount. When the scope and outreach of the concreteness of the proverb have been intuited, it becomes brilliantly revealing. The problems which are raised by the circumstance that *māšāl* is a more general word than 'proverb', in the sense that I have defined the latter (see above, pp. 23f.), are discussed in the introduction (see above, pp. 24f.).

The sense of *m^e^līṣā* is uncertain. Ringgren and Gemser translate 'dark saying', and *KB*[2] suggests 'allusion'. At any rate, it is so artistically contrived that the grasping of its meaning makes demands on professional skill. Canney (*AJSL* xl, 1923–4, pp. 135f.) argues that *mēlīṣ* means 'fluent speaker', 'advocate', 'ambassador' rather than 'interpreter'. *m^e^līṣā* might then be the product of an eloquent, lucid speaker. Richardson (*VT* v, 1955, pp. 163–79) derives *m^e^līṣā* from *mlṣ* on the analogy of *q^e^rīʾā*, *h^a^līkā* etc. *m^e^līṣā* is then 'a slippery saying', 'an allusion'. The suggestion is improbable. What is the connection between a 'slippery saying' and an 'allusion'?

vv. 8–19 *Flee Sin and Violence*

This is Instruction, and its formal correspondence with examples of the same genre from outside the Old Testament can easily be demonstrated. The most significant elements in its formal structure are the imperatives and the motive clauses (introduced by *kī*) which reinforce the imperatives with argument. Verse 10 contains a conditional clause preceding the imperative, and vv. 11–14 an amplified conditional clause. The function of the conditional clause in this position is to define the circumstances in which the command is applicable. The extended version of the clause in vv. 11–14 results from the *verbatim* reporting of the enticing words spoken by the tempters. The 'my son' form of address, which is a regular stylistic feature of the Instruction, occurs in vv. 8, 10, 15.

Form

Verses 8f.: 2 imperatives, motive clause.

Verse 10: conditional clause, imperative.

Verses 11–19: expanded conditional clause, 2 imperatives, extended motivation. Verses 18–19 explicate v. 17, or interpret the metaphor in v. 17. Verse 16 is identical with Isa. 59.7ab, and is absent from the manuscripts of the LXX with the exception of LXX^A. It may be a later addition (Whybray, p. 39, n.3).

[8f.] The introductory plea for attentiveness and receptivity is, as we have seen, a common feature of the genre. The child is not to rebel against the authority of his parents. The authoritative instruction of his father (*mūsār*) is a discipline to which he should submit with unquestioning obedience. Nor should he call in question the authority of his mother's teaching (*tōrā*). I have pointed out (*PWM*, p. 106) that this word is at home in the wisdom literature as well as in the cult. Here the only authority which is implied by its use is parental authority.

The home is a primary educational agency, and it is there that the foundations of civilized behaviour and general excellence are laid. The son who learns from his parents is already beginning to lose his rawness and to present a pleasing presence to the world. Parental instruction embellishes and adorns and promotes an attractiveness of manner and bearing. 'They (the *mūsār* and *tōrā* of father and mother) are a becoming wreath for your head, and a necklace(?) for your throat.'

[10] The topic is introduced by v. 10. What is envisaged is the tempting or enticing of a young man ('my son') by sinners, and he is urged to resist their subtle persuasive devices ('do not consent'). The originality of these last words is suspected on metrical grounds by BH and Gemser. Gemser suggests that the proposals of these sinners should not be understood too literally and that the references are not really to robbery with violence. The language of vv. 11–19, however, consistently gives this impression. Jones describes the passage as an exhortation against banditry, and mentions Toy's suggestion that the situation in the Persian and Greek periods, when large cities such as Jerusalem and Alexandria contained an organized criminal class, best fits the description. That the passage has so precise a historical reference is doubted by Gemser and Ringgren. Ringgren observes that there are criminals in every period of history, and Gemser notes references to the activities of highwaymen in Hos. 6.7–9 and Jer. 7.11.

[11] The intention of the 'sinners' is to waylay (*'rb*, *ṣpn*), injure and rob innocent victims against whom no sense of personal grievance is felt (*ḥinnām*), but who are sacrificed to a lust for plunder. Gemser supposes that the allusions are to the social evils and the legal corruption against which the prophets raised their voices. One can only say that it is a far-fetched description of the evils of landlordism, rapacity in trade and legal corruption. The situation against which the Instruction is directed is, in my judgement, more specific and less complicated than this, and I cannot believe that it is justifiable to introduce so much subtlety into the interpretation of these verses.

[13ff.] The young man is tempted by criminals who seek to seduce him and demoralize him by holding out the prospect of big money painlessly acquired. They represent that they are good fellows at heart and that there is honour among thieves. 'Throw in your lot with us; there is a good community spirit; we are a sociable bunch.' The figure comes from the annual redistribution of communal land in a village. It is redistributed by 'the lot and the line'. The sinners invite young men to join their community and live in their village (E.F.F.B.). They trust each other and all plunder goes into a common pool, presumably for subsequent division (fair shares for all). But wealth gained at the expense of wisdom is poisonous fruit; there is no short cut to success, for wealth is worthless unless it is a measure of the intrinsic worth of its possessor. It is right that the wise man should be prosperous, but this route by way of lawlessness, cupidity and violence leads to death.

[12] The metaphor of v. 12 derives from a piece of Canaanite mythology (cf. R. T. O'Callaghan, *VT* iv, 1954, p. 169). Mot (Death) is the god with the gaping throat and the insatiable appetite, and it is through his gullet that the living pass into the underworld of the dead. 'Verily thou must come down into the throat of Mot, son of El, into the miry gorge of the hero loved of El' (*Baal* I*. i.6–8: *CML*, pp. 102f.). This is Mot's message for Baal delivered by Gupn-and-Ugar. The use of *nepeš* for 'throat' indicates that *nepeš* in Isa. 5.14 means 'throat', and that this verse, too, is an allusion to the god Mot (cf. *CML*, p. 157, n.21): 'Therefore Sheol has widened its throat and opened its mouth beyond measure, and her (Jerusalem's) nobility and commoners go down' (into the underworld of the dead). Similar is Hab. 2.5, where it is said of the arrogant man: 'He has widened his throat (*napšō*) like Sheol and he is as insatiable as death (Death).' The phrase in Ps. 5.10, 'their throat (*gārōn*) is an open grave', has the same mythological basis, and the allusion to the god Mot is unmistakable in Jonah 2.3. The belly of the whale (v. 2) is equated with the belly of Sheol. Jonah likens his being swallowed by the fish and his lodging in its belly to a descent into the underworld through the throat of Mot.

The highwaymen in v. 12 liken themselves to Sheol, that is, to the god Mot with the gaping throat who swallows his victims whole. They encompass the destruction of their victims so swiftly and completely that it is just as if they had passed through the yawning jaws of Death. As this god never has a surfeit of 'life', so their appetite for spoil never sickens.

[17f.] *mᵉzōrā* is a crux, and the interpretation depends on how it is resolved. Winton Thomas (*VTS* iii, pp. 281f.) parses it as the pual participle of *zrh*, and with the help of Arabic *d̲r'*, 'winnow, throw, scatter', he arrives at the meaning 'strewn (with seed)'. For this he has the support of Rashi and Ibn Ezra, but the testimony of the versions, except for V, supports the meaning 'extended, spread'. This is how Gemser translates, whereas Ringgren follows Winton Thomas. G. R. Driver (*Biblica* 32, 1951, p. 173) suggests that the versions, except V, may have read the Hebrew verb as *mzr*, or else guessed the sense from the context. Driver holds that 'constrict' rather than 'extend' is the primary sense of *mzr*, and that it is cognate with *zwr* (*zrr*), 'compress'. Driver would read either *mūzārā*, hophal participle of *zwr*, or *mᵉzūrā*, qal passive participle of *mzr*, the meaning being 'drawn tight' in either case. 'To no purpose is the net drawn tight in the sight of any winged fowl', that is, it will escape before the process of closing the trap is complete.

The choice between 'drawn tight' and 'extended' or 'spread' is not so crucial, because both lean towards the same general interpretation of the figure of speech. The meaning of v. 17 then is that if a bird is watching the preparations which are being made to trap it, it will easily take evasive action. Verse 17, however, is apparently a metaphor illustrative of v. 18 and, if the meaning which I have just outlined is the correct one, it does not seem particularly apt. I take v. 18 to mean (with Winton Thomas, p. 282, n.3) that the nefarious activities of the highwaymen will recoil upon themselves. They have been careless of the lives of others; they have laid ambushes to spill blood and take lives (v. 12), but in the end it is their own blood which will be spilled and their own lives which will be lost. If this is the correct understanding of v. 18, in what way can v. 17, as explained by Driver, be an apposite metaphor? The connecting link would presumably be that it is as futile to rob with violence as it is to lay a trap for a bird which is aware of what is going on, but this is rather a tenuous link. Because Winton Thomas' translation produces a more apt metaphor in v. 17, it ought to be followed. 'For it is to no effect that the net is strewn (with seed for bait) in the sight of any winged fowl.' The bird watches the process of laying the bait, but this has no deterrent effect on it. It will go for the grain just as it would have done if it had not seen it being put down. The bird has been given every reason to exercise prudence and caution; its suspicions should have been awakened, but it is so much the slave of its appetite that it follows a compulsive desire to eat the grain. So it is with the highwaymen who cannot control their appetite for wealth and who are incapable of benefiting from the warnings which would deter reasonable and disciplined men from courses of action which must inevitably destroy them.

[19] Verse 19 is a more prosaic reiteration of v. 18. Gain which has been gotten by such insensate and insatiable pursuit of it takes away the lives of those who possess it.

There is nothing explicitly Yahwistic in the way in which the concept of retribution is handled in these verses, and there is no overt religious allusion in the entire passage. One gets the impression that there is a concept of order in the background, but it is not so clearly articulated as in the Egyptian Instruction (cf. Whybray, pp. 61f.). Von Rad has questioned the propriety of the term 'retribution' on the ground that it envisages punishment as an additional forensic act, and that this is not what is represented here and elsewhere in the Old Testament. The action itself is pregnant with consequences for good or evil. Hence the relationship between the actions of the fools and the bad end which overtakes them is inward and necessary, not superimposed as the consequence of a forensic verdict and penalty. This comes close to saying that such necessary connections between act and consequence belong to the structure of reality, and this approximates to the concept of order in the Egyptian Instruction. (G. von Rad, *Old Testament Theology*, i, 1962, pp. 384–6; cf. K. Koch, 'Gibt es ein Vergeltungsdogma im alten Testament?', *ZThK* 52, 1955, pp. 1f.; Udo Skladny, *Die ältesten Spruchsammlungen in Israel*, 1962, p. 13).

Further comparison with the Egyptian Instruction and *Ahikar* suggests the remark that there is no vocational element in the advice given in this passage (cf. Whybray, p. 52, n.1). It is not an apprentice scribe, an aspiring statesman, who stands before us, but any young man about to be exposed to the temptations of the world and in need of such advice and warning as appears here. It is advice which a father might very appropriately give to his son at the moment when he was leaving the shelter of the home to make his way in the world. The tone is not moralistic, certainly not pious, but there is an underlying morality, a scale of values and a sense of proportion. The implication of such advice as this is, perhaps, that wealth decently sought is a good thing. We can certainly conclude that wealth feverishly sought in a context of cupidity, lawlessness and violence is an evil and destructive pattern of conduct, which brings death to those who pursue it.

vv. 20–33 *Wisdom as Preacher*

[20] Albright explains *ḥokmōt* as a singular form (see below, p. 362; cf. GK § 86l); according to Gemser it is a plural of comprehensiveness. 'The all-embracing, eloquent, veracious and elevated wisdom' (Gemser). *tārōnnā* is a third person imperfect with a cohortative ending (GK§ 48d), or else the text should be read *baḥūṣōt rinnātā* (detaching the *t* from *tārōnnā* and affixing it to the preceding noun). This is done by BH and KB². If the form is derived from *rnn*, the second *n* belongs to the root and is not *nun energicum* as Dahood supposes (M. Dahood, *Proverbs and Northwest Semitic Philology*, 1963, p. 4).

[21] The second half of v. 21 appears to be too long. Gemser deletes 'in the city' and BH 'in the city her sayings'. The form *hōmīyōt* gives some difficulty. Gemser and Ringgren understand it as a formation from *hmy*, 'to roar', and translate *bᵉrō'š hōmīyōt* 'at the summit of the noisy (places)', i.e., 'in the places where there is most stir' (cf. *hᵉmī*, 'roar', which is conjectured by KB² and BH at Lam. 2.18). This agrees with the representation of v. 1 (streets and squares) and makes for good parallelism in v. 2 (2b: 'entrances of the city gates'). On the other hand, LXX supports the reading 'on the top of the walls', but Hebrew *ḥōmōt*, 'walls', does not particularly resemble *hōmīyōt* in form. There is a Phoenician plural *ḥmyt* (Jean-Hoftijzer, p. 90, *s.v. ḥmh*; J. Friedrich, *Phönizisch-Punische Grammatik*, *An. Or.* 32, 1951, p. 90, para. 204) which could be read as *ḥōmīyōt*, and this may explain the form in v. 21 (cf. Dahood, p. 5). The only emendation which would then have to be made would be *ḥ* for *h*. The verse should be translated either: 'On top of the walls she calls out, at the entrances of the city gates she utters her sayings', or: 'In the places where there is most stir she calls out, at the entrances of the city gates she utters her sayings.'

Gemser has suggested that this picture of Wisdom finding a stance in the most public places and seeking to engage the attention of men may reflect the actual practice of the wisdom teachers. They did their teaching where there was a ready-made audience, and, in particular, the gates of the city were recognized places of public assembly where all manner of business was transacted, political, legal and commercial. In view of the formal affinities of this section with prophetic modes of address (see below), the question has to be asked whether it is not also the practice of the prophet which lies at the back of this representation (so H. Ringgren, *Word and Wisdom*, 1947, p. 96; A. Robert, *RB* xliii, 1934, pp. 172f.; C. Kayatz, *Studien zu Proverbien 1–9*, WMANT 22, 1966, pp. 120f.). He was certainly a man who encountered the people in the market-place and who competed with the noise and traffic of worldly activities for their attention. He was prepared to expose himself in the public forum and to win an audience in spite of distractions, busyness and noise, by the force and intensity of his speech.

[22] There is no doubt that in v. 22 Wisdom speaks like a wisdom teacher and not like a prophet. The *petī* is the untutored, immature youth who comes to the teacher to be shaped by the educational process (see p. 265, above, on v. 4). Richardson's translation 'simpleton' is quite misleading (H. N. Richardson, *VT*, v, 1955, p. 172). 'Simpleton', according to the *Concise Oxford Dictionary*, means 'a foolish, gullible, half-witted person', and the *petī* is not that. Richardson's other suggestion that *lyṣ* means 'to talk freely' and that a *lēṣ* is a 'chatter-box' has some attractiveness, although it is dismissed by Gemser, who translates 'scorner' (also Ringgren). It is attractive, because economy of speech, as the Egyptian Instruction particularly shows, was inculcated by the wisdom teacher. Garrulity is unwisdom and is the mark of the immature and the incorrigible man (the *petī* and the *kᵉsīl*).

It is unsafe to assume that *'ad mātay* demonstrates a stylistic affinity with Jeremiah (Gemser). It is certainly a feature of the style of

Jeremiah (4.14, 21; 12.4; 13.27; 23.26; 31.22; 47.5), but it also occurs six times in the book of Psalms (6.4; 74.10; 80.5; 82.2; 90.13; 94.3). To try to argue from a single occurrence in this passage to a special relationship between it and the style of Jeremiah is a profitless enterprise. The same can be said of the other items of vocabulary cited by Gemser (*ya'an*, v. 24; *m^e^šūbā*, v. 32; *škn beṭaḥ*, v. 33).

[23] 'If you return when I reprove you' (v. 23) is either a conditional clause without a particle (GK §159b; M. Dahood, p. 6), or else *hinnē* should be transposed to stand before *tāšūbū*. G. R. Driver (*Biblica* 32, p. 174) notes that the latter has the support of Pesh. (*hinnē* a conditional particle, like Aramaic *hēn*). Wisdom likens herself to a copious gushing spring. Just as its waters gush with lavish abundance, she will cause her spirit to overflow generously on those who acknowledge her authority and incline to her instruction. The verse suggests that her teaching has negative and positive aspects, and only those who submit to her corrective discipline are poised to receive an endowment of wisdom and knowledge. Ringgren supposes that there may be here an echo of the prophetic promise of the pouring out of the spirit (Isa. 44.3), and I have discussed in *PWM* (p. 110) certain passages where wisdom is considered to be the fruit of the spirit. The intention here may be to represent Wisdom as a charismatic, spirit-filled person, who pours out on those who are receptive and submissive the spirit of wisdom. This is a disclosure or revelation ('I shall divulge my words to you'; cf. C. Kayatz, p. 127).

[24f.] Wisdom harangues her audience like a wisdom teacher or a prophet(?). On the one hand, her vocabulary is recognizably that of a wisdom teacher (*'ēṣā*, 'advice'; *tōkaḥat*, 'reproof'), while the stance, 'I stretched out my hand', is that attributed to the prophet in Isa. 65.1f. In that passage, and especially in Isa. 6.9f., the thought of an unperceptive and negligent audience is present. There is no reason, however, to suppose that the wisdom teacher did not also use his hands for rhetorical effectiveness in order to make his point, so that 'I stretched out my hand' does not necessarily point to a prophetic model. 'There is a general Semitic tendency to accompany words with gestures' (E.F.F.B.). There can be no doubt that vv. 24f. do have the form of a prophetic *Scheltrede* ('reproof', 'chiding'), and that they lead on to a *Drohrede* ('threat') in v. 26 (see, however, below).

Wisdom adduces reasons why the threat should be uttered, upbraids those against whom it is to be directed and makes certain allegations against them. *pr'* means 'to let loose', perhaps here, 'let slip through the fingers', 'neglect'. 'Because I summoned you and you rejected (me), stretched out my hand (in rhetorical appeal) and met no response; because you neglected all my advice and would have none of my reproof; I, in turn, will laugh at your calamity and will chuckle when terror overtakes you; when terror strikes you like a disaster and calamity like a whirlwind (or 'inundation'), when distress and privation alight on you' (vv. 24–27). *Qᵉrē šō'ā*, 'disaster', is to be derived from **šaw'ā*, 'evil day', Arabic *sā'a* 'to be evil'; 'inundation' is the reading of Manuscript 30 Kennicott, *ṣūpā* = Syriac *ṭūpā* (cf. G. R. Driver, *Biblica* 32, p. 174).

[26f.] Zimmerli (*ZAW* 51, 1933, p. 187, n.1; cf. C. Kayatz, pp. 120f.) calls attention to the unusual way in which the threat is formulated in vv. 26f. It is unlike the prophetic threat in which Yahweh declares that he will execute judgement. Wisdom laughs as a mere spectator at what befalls those who refuse her admonishment and reject her advice, and does not herself make any personal intervention to effect judgement. A time will come when it will be too late to turn to wisdom for instruction, and when she will be inaccessible to those who search frantically for her. The opportunity is past, for such people hate knowledge and do not choose the fear of Yahweh.

[28–30] The mention of the fear of Yahweh is important, because it supplies a framework of interpretation for the items of wisdom vocabulary which occur in this passage. To hate knowledge (*daʿat*) is equated with not having a proper respect for Yahweh – not submitting to his authority and discipline. The personified Wisdom is consequently not like the wisdom teacher who gives instruction on the basis of what he has learned from his teachers, distilled through his mature experience of life and his aptitude for sagacity. Wisdom is not such an empirical teacher, resting her case on her personal authority; she promulgates wisdom, advice and admonishment with the authority of Yahweh, and the fear of Yahweh is a new *mūsār*. This is the discipline to which she would have her audience submit, and in introducing this direct claim to divine authority for what she teaches she emerges almost as a prophet, except that she still tends to speak the language of a wisdom teacher. But this vocabulary, subordinated as it is to the demand for submission to the authority of Yahweh, is no longer set in the context of an empirical educational discipline, but in the context of religious discipline and illumination.

[31f.] The thought that actions contain consequences for good or ill is markedly present in vv. 31–32. The relation between action and consequence is that between seed and fruit; the action initiates what can be likened to an organic process of growth culminating in the effect. Or, in a change of metaphor in v. 31b, the 'reaction' is compared to that of an overloaded digestive system. Just as over-eating produces surfeit and loathing, so the pleasure which men get out of the cleverness by which they secure their advantage at the expense of their fellows will eventually turn to disgust. The *m^e^šûbā* ascribed to the *petî* in v. 32 is probably a lack of consistent application. He does not listen to his teacher nor apply himself to his studies, and consequently he does not make steady progress to maturity and wisdom. Or, if *m^e^šûbā* is thought of in relation to the fear of Yahweh, it is rather apostasy, a lack of steadfast reverence and a failure in stamina in relation to the discipline imposed by Yahweh (Dahood, p. 7, derives from *yšb* and translates *m^e^šûbā* 'idleness'). *šalwā* is the vast and imperturbable self-satisfaction of the man who has nothing to learn from anyone and who is impervious to instruction. **[33]** A receptive attitude to the instruction of Wisdom produces necessarily a condition of safety and equanimity. Those who listen submissively and attentively will live in security and will have their minds set at rest from the terror of evil.

Wisdom is a preacher in this passage, but I would hesitate to describe her as a preacher of repentance (so Gemser and Ringgren). She employs prophetic forms of address (reproof and threat) and she lays claim to the authority of Yahweh for what she speaks, but she does not speak like a prophet. Her vocabulary is that of the wisdom teacher, not that of the prophet, and there are still traces of the Instruction in this piece. Wisdom does not demand repentance; she demands attentiveness and the recognition that she is an authoritative teacher who ought to be heeded and obeyed. The curious inner inconsistency of the formal structure of the piece, to which Zimmerli has called attention, is partly to be explained by the circumstance that prophetic forms cannot easily be combined with the vocabulary and ethos of wisdom. If Wisdom were really a prophet, what we should expect in v. 26 would be such a word of Yahweh as: 'Therefore I will punish your disobedience, I will bring disaster on you.' But this would not accord with the concept of an order which maintains itself without outside intervention, and it is this thought which dominates the remainder of the passage. Hence Zimmerli's observation that vv. 26–31 constitute a very lame word of threat, since the passage from v. 26 onwards is not concerned with 'once-for-all decisive words such as obedience, repentance, judgement, but with general, universally valid considerations.' Kayatz describes the piece as a wisdom sermon into which prophetic modes of address are taken up and modified (pp. 120f.).

I would not describe vv. 20–33 as an example of the Instruction genre, although there are a few features which recall the genre, notably the emphasis on attentiveness, the vocabulary and the motive clause in v. 32. But there is not a single imperative, which is of the essence of the Instruction, and the formal structure, for the most part, follows prophetic modes of address. Whybray's opinion that this is modified Instruction and that Wisdom has been personified in order to supply the authority represented by the Egyptian concept of *Maat* (Order) is, in my view, very questionable, although I would agree with him that the personified Wisdom is an aspect of the 'nationalization' of the wisdom tradition (pp. 93f.). There is a concern to demonstrate that the acquisition of wisdom cannot begin without a right religious attitude ('fear of Yahweh'), and wisdom is a charismatic gift dispensed by a spirit-filled teacher (Wisdom). This may be no more than a picturesque way of saying that all wisdom and illumination come from Yahweh, that he is the fountain of wisdom (cf. v. 23).

Kayatz (pp. 24f.) has argued attractively that such motifs as the laugh of Wisdom, calling-on and not-hearing, seeking and not-finding, are not originally at home in the Wisdom literature and that, in particular, there is a tendency in this passage to transfer to a personified Wisdom motifs which elsewhere are associated with Yahweh, so that Wisdom is brought into the closest relationship with Yahweh and endowed with his authority. There is no indication that Wisdom is envisaged as a Person within the Godhead in a theological sense. Wisdom is located in the market-place, not in the Godhead, and the representation is probably that of a charismatic wisdom teacher and no more.

Chapter 2

Gemser's analysis of this chapter into six strophes (vv. 1–4, 5–8, 9–11, 12–15, 16–19, 20–22) under the title 'The Fivefold Blessing of Wisdom', is not one which commends itself to me. This piece is related to the Instruction ('My son', v. 1) and the best way of exploring and describing its structure is to enquire what are its formal affinities with that genre. I have hesitated to assert that this is Instruction in the full sense, although such an assertion might be legitimate. My hesitation is connected with several circumstances. First, there is the absence of the imperatives which communicate the directives crisply and authoritatively. Instead of the imperatives followed by motive clauses and final clauses (Do this . . . for . . . so that), the structure of the passage is that of protases and apodoses (If . . . if . . . then . . . then). Clauses similar in function to the motive and final clauses of the Instruction are then tacked on to the apodoses (for . . . so that).

The conditional clause is used before the imperative in the Instruction in order to define more precisely the circumstances in which the directive applies, but that is a different matter from its use in an 'if . . . then' type of construction. I have remarked already that this is the style of the Babylonian omen literature, and that it approximates to the so-called casuistic legal formulation (above, p. 155). The style is not so tightly organized here as it is in the omen and legal contexts. On the one hand, there is the tendency to pile up protases and, on the other hand, the apodoses are separated from each other by descriptive material or by motive and final clauses. The general impression is that there is a loss of compactness and precision over against the Instruction. Directives are not issued sharply, and the emphasis changes perceptibly from authoritative teaching to recommendation, exhortation and homily. One has to be careful, however, not to press the argument from diffuseness too far, since my analysis of the Egyptian Instruction has shown that a measure of diffuseness (extended motivation, epexegesis) can be associated with it. The only firm observation which can be made is that the imperative is absent from this piece.

The other reason why I hesitate to describe this as Instruction is that there is a lack of concrete, authoritative instruction on specific matters in this passage. The opening verses (vv. 1–9) are so general in their references that they might almost seem to justify the conclusion that the passage should be compared to the preamble of an Instruction (cf. *Amenemope*), rather than to its specific contents. Nevertheless, I do not believe that this would be a right conclusion and, in fact, the latter half of the chapter does deal with particular issues (the subversive man and the foreign woman).

My opinion on this chapter is that it exemplifies a process of formal development based on the Instruction. The tendency of this development is to diminish the element of authoritative instruction communicated briefly and precisely by imperatives, and so to substitute the more diffuse, rambling style of preaching for the more exact didactic procedures of the wisdom teacher. I would still hold, however, that the formal structure of the Instruction is the key to the analysis of this chapter. I would analyse it as follows: a series of protases (vv. 1–4), then an apodosis (v. 5) on which depend two pairs of motive clauses, the first introduced by *kī* and the second without an explicit 'for' (vv. 6f.). Also related to the apodosis (v. 5) are the final clauses in v. 8. The apodosis in v. 9 states a second consequence of the initial series of protases (vv. 1–4), and related to it are the motive clauses in vv. 10f. (again the first with *kī* and the second without). Also depending on v. 9 is a final clause (introduced by *l^e* with the infinitive construct), and vv. 13–15 explicate v. 12. Similarly related to the apodosis in v. 9 is the final clause in v. 16, and vv. 17–19 explicate v. 16. A final clause introduced by *l^emaʿan* (v. 20) also goes back to v. 9, and vv. 21f. consist of motivation arranged antithetically.

Since Whybray (pp. 40f.) deals drastically with the text of this chapter, I take the opportunity of discussing his approach to the Instruction genre and offering some criticisms of it. Let me first indicate the measure of my agreement with him. His recognition that most of the material in Proverbs 1–9 is Instruction and that foreign, particularly Egyptian, models are important for its elucidation is more precise than anything hitherto achieved. In this respect he and I arrived at somewhat similar positions independently. This awareness has important consequences for the criticism of Proverbs 1–9 and it is, for example, no longer possible to suppose that the resemblances in style and vocabulary between these chapters and Deuteronomy have the significance attached to them by Robert (*RB* xliii, 1934, pp. 42–68, 172–204, 374–84; xliv, 1935, pp. 344–65, 502–25; cf. Whybray, p. 37) and demonstrate the literary dependence of Proverbs 1–9 on Deuteronomy. Any criticism of Proverbs 1–9 which does not hinge on a comparison with extra-Israelite models of the Instruction is so unbalanced as to have little value. The relation between Deuteronomy and Proverbs 1–9 requires investigation, but it is not in place here. I shall remark, however, that Weinfeld has argued from the content of Deuteronomy that it is dependent on Proverbs 1–9 (*PWM*, pp. 107f.) and there are some formal features in Deuteronomy (particularly the frequency of motive clauses) which would lead me to suppose that its composition has been influenced by the form of the Instruction. On the other hand, I would not rule out the possibility of reciprocal influences, and the tendency towards a preaching or hortatory style in Proverbs 2 may owe something to Deuteronomy. Firmer conclusions must await a detailed study, but enough is now known to show that Robert's articles do not supply a sound basis for attacking this problem.

Again, I agree with Whybray that there are evidences of a Yahwistic reinterpretation in Proverbs 1–9, and that the vocabulary of wisdom is set in two different frameworks of reference, the one an educational framework of old wisdom and the other a framework of piety and moralism. Because of his uncompromising literary-critical approach, Whybray draws conclusions from this observation with which I do not agree. He supposes that where there are evidences of reinterpretation there are 'additions' to an 'original' text, and that by subtracting such passages it is possible to recover the 'original' text of the Instruction. In so far as Whybray is guided by foreign models in carrying out this critical surgery, he claims for these a formal precision which they do not possess, for they, too, can be diffuse, and diffuseness in Proverbs 1–9 cannot be taken as a proof of additions to an original text of an Instruction. I do not raise questions about the originality of the extant text, unless there are textual reasons for doing so (see below, pp. 308f.). I simply ask how Proverbs 1–9 compares with foreign models of the Instruction and whether it exemplifies new formal developments or extraneous formal influences.

The extreme consequences of Whybray's approach are seen in his handling of ch. 2, which is reduced to an original discourse consisting of vv. 1, 9, 16–19. Even then, Whybray does not get rid of all evidences of Yahwistic reinterpretation, for this can be traced in the vocabulary of v. 9 (see below). From this point of view he would have done better to retain v. 11 and reject v. 9 (*m^e^zimmā* and *t^e^būnā* belong originally to old wisdom, but the same cannot be said of *mišpāṭ*, *ṣedeq* and *mēšārīm*(?)). I am not convinced that conclusions which are founded on such a critical method can provide a basis for further advance or command a substantial measure of agreement. Whybray rejects vv. 2–8 because in them there is a change of subject-matter from that of the teacher's words to the preciousness of wisdom and wisdom as the gift of Yahweh. So also with v. 10. Verses 12–15 have been modelled on vv. 16–19 by a later hand, or are perhaps the fragment of another discourse. Verses 20–22 are the misplaced conclusion of vv. 12–15.

In ch. 2 the vocabulary of wisdom is set unmistakably in the frame of religious commitment and its derivative morality. This is best seen in the apodosis of v. 5 and the associated motive clause of v. 6. The first reads: 'Then you discern (*tābīn*) the fear of Yahweh and find the knowledge of God.' This indicates that the teacher's authority and the content of his wisdom are derived from Yahweh. Consequently his claim on the attention of his pupils (vv. 1–2) is reinforced by a note of religious authority. His commands (*miṣwōt*, v. 1) do not depend only on his professional competence as a teacher of wisdom or on his weight and integrity as an educator. Moreover, the vocabulary of wisdom which occurs in the protases (vv. 1–4) has to be interpreted in the context of a primary claim for submission to Yahweh and dependence on a knowledge which hinges on submissiveness.

Even so, it has to be admitted that the apodosis (v. 5) is somewhat inconsequential and unconvincing. The words *'āz tābīn yir'at YHWH* are something of a *tour de force* in relation to such items of vocabulary in the protases as *ḥokmā*, *tᵉbūnā*, *bīnā*, and when v. 5 is reached the reader becomes aware that the sense of the preceding verses has been given a sudden and quite violent twist. One goes along happily supposing that a wisdom teacher is using the vocabulary of old wisdom and that *ḥokmā* and *tᵉbūnā* are mental virtues of sagacity and penetration, inculcated by an educational process which addressed itself to the right shaping and maturing of intellectual attitudes. This supposition is no longer tenable once v. 5 is reached, for there it becomes clear that the vocabulary in the protases cannot be located in the frame of old wisdom with its pragmatic bent and ethical neutrality (*PWM*, pp. 65f.). One has then to speak of a reinterpretation of the vocabulary of old wisdom, but the reinterpretation in v. 5 has much more the appearance of an *ad hoc* adjustment than of a considered reinterpretation. The seam between the original sense of the vocabulary in the protases and the reinterpretation imposed by v. 5 is clearly visible.

Any doubt that may remain about the intention of v. 5 is removed once and for all by v. 6 which states: 'For Yahweh gives wisdom, from his mouth come knowledge (*da'at*) and discernment (*tᵉbūnā*).' Corresponding to this reinterpretation of *ḥokmā*, *da'at* and *tᵉbūnā* as religious illumination is the strongly marked moralism and ethical commitment of the succeeding verses, and this again is in line with the prophetic reinterpretation of the vocabulary of wisdom which I have discussed in *PWM*.

vv. 1–11 *General Advice to a Pupil*

[1–6] The pupil must have the capacity of appropriating (*tiqqaḥ*, v. 1, cf. *leqaḥ*, 1.5) his teacher's words and of retaining them in his memory ('storing them up', *tiṣpōn*). It is not originality nor argumentativeness nor critical independence in the face of instruction that is demanded of the pupil. He must indeed be attentive and keen (v. 2), like one who cries out for insight and shouts for discernment, but the authority of the teacher must not be called in question (cf. *miṣwōt*, v. 1). This is almost a personification of *bīnā* and *tebūnā*; one calls out to them in acclamation and appeal. In 1.20–33, Wisdom calls and there is a general lack of response; here the ideal pupil greets insight and discernment with a shout of acclamation. The pupil's energies are thus not divided between appropriation and criticism. He is not to have any doubts about the value of what is taught or to oppose it with a critical, questioning scrutiny. All the words that fall from his teacher's lips are pearls, and they are to be gathered up and carefully kept. The ideal pupil is he who gives his teacher his undivided attention, who places great value on his words (v. 4), whose keenness is unabated (vv. 2b–3) and who cultivates a tenacious memory, the best of all treasure-troves (cf. v. 4).

[7] In v. 7, Yahweh is said to store up *tūšīyā* for the upright (*yešārīm*) and to be a shield for those who walk in integrity (*tōm*). From this point onwards the moralism of the passage is reflected in its vocabulary, and the effect of this is to equate wisdom and unwisdom with good and evil, justice and injustice, uprightness and perversity, righteousness and unrighteousness. There is a close resemblance between this vocabulary and that associated with the prophetic reinterpretation of wisdom (*PWM*, pp. 65f.). What is happening can be well illustrated in terms of *tūšīyā*, which belongs to the vocabulary of old wisdom and has its characteristically practical bent. It means 'power, capacity, competence' (*PWM*, p. 80, n.4), but here it is made conditional on rectitude. It is not effectiveness *simpliciter*, but a competence or power which Yahweh gives to the upright. And so the corresponding thought in the second half of the line is that Yahweh is a shield for those whose way of life is flawless (*hōlekē tōm*, those whose wholeness or integrity is not impaired).

[8–10] Wisdom is bestowed by Yahweh on those who are morally qualified and is effective in upholding Yahweh's order (paths of *mišpāṭ*) and guarding the way of life (*derek*) of those who are loyal to him (*Q. ḥasîdāw*). M. Dahood (p. 8) follows Haupt in Müller and Kautzsch (*SBOT* xv, 1901, p. 52) in reading *lnṣr* as an imperfect with emphatic *l*. This eases the grammar in 8b, but v. 8 should, nevertheless, be construed as two final clauses and not as a third pair of motive clauses. This verse (v. 8), too, is controlled by presuppositions of Yahwistic faith and practice. The *ḥāsîd* is the loyal man in a community whose cement is *ḥesed*, a reciprocal loyalty, and the 'paths of justice' have been charted by Yahweh for the right ordering of common life. The function of wisdom is to conserve and guard this way of life.

In the first apodosis (v. 5), *tābîn* indicates religious insight rather than intellectual clarity, and in the second apodosis (v. 9) it refers to moral insight (Ringgren, 'sittliche Einsicht'): 'Then you will discern what is right and just and straight.' The metaphor which is sustained in this passage is that of the two ways (vv. 7, 8, 9, 12, 13, 15, 18, 19, 20), and in view of this we may say that righteousness is the state of the man who walks in Yahweh's ways. He who discerns Yahweh's order for his community and who brings his way of life – the web of his relationships – into harmony with it is *ṣaddîq*. These are plain, level roads along which good progress can be made. Every track is a good one (cf. Robert, *RB* xliii, p. 61). In this consists the coming of wisdom into the mind (*lēb*), and it is in these circumstances that knowledge will be found pleasurable to the taste (v. 10, *nepeš* 'throat', 'palate').

In view of the metaphor of the two ways of life and the occurrence of *kol ma'gal ṭôb* in v. 9, I have suggested 'plain roads' for *mēšārîm*. The grammar of v. 9 is, however, difficult ('Then you will discern what is right and just and straight, every good track') and Driver (*Biblica* 32, p. 174) supposes that 9b needs emendation to get sense out of it. LXX appears to indicate *me'aššēr* or *meyaššēr*, 'straightening every good track'. Driver retains all the consonants of MT, but rearranges them and reads *ûmešammēr kol ma'gal ṭôb*, 'and keep to every good track' (cf. BH).

[11] In the second of the motive clauses dependent on v. 9, the function of resourcefulness (*mezimmā*) and discernment (*tebûnā*) in the context of the moral discrimination described in v. 9 is defined. This charismatic ethical endowment includes these elements of a more worldly wisdom, that the good man may be saved from the consequences of naïveté. Even so this represents a significant reinterpretation of *mezimmā*, which can mean 'intrigue', 'plotting', in a pejorative sense – a very different matter from a prudential element in a charismatic morality.

vv. 12–15 *The Perverse Man*

[12] The final clause indicates what is achieved by the moral endowment described in v. 9, and its meaning is drawn out by explication in vv. 13–15. **[13–15]** Through his discernment of *ṣedeq* and *mišpāṭ* a man is kept safe from the evil way and from him who speaks perversely or subversively (*tahpūkōt*). There is the kind of person who turns Yahweh's order (*mišpāṭ*) upside down and who tries to draw others into his wrongheadedness and confusion by creating ethical chaos. He walks along paths of darkness (v. 13b), himself devoid of all ethical illumination (cf. *tābīn* in v. 9); he deserts straight roads in preference for those paths and tracks which twist and turn. This is a comparison between a man who is so devious and crafty that he loses himself and others in the maze of his cleverness, and the forthright, open man, who means what he says and whose actions are as unequivocal as his words. The good man needs *m^e^zimmā* if he is to match an opponent who regards the spreading of moral confusion and the engaging in sharp practices as a form of enjoyment (v. 14).

vv. 16–19 *The Foreign Woman*

t^e^būnā as defined by v. 9 is also a safeguard against the 'foreign woman' who woos with seductive accents (the second final clause, like the first, is introduced by *l^e^haṣṣīl^e^kā*, 'that you may be saved'). Since the Egyptian Instruction regularly warns young men of the consequences of affairs with women and even with a foreign woman (see above, p. 94), it does not seem reasonable to introduce a cultic theory in order to explain this and associated passages in Prov. 1–9 (so G. Boström, *Proverbia Studien: die Weisheit und das fremde Weib in Spr. 1–9. Lunds Universitets Årsskrift*, N.F., Avd. I, Bd. 30, Nr. 3, 1935; H. Ringgren, *Word and Wisdom*, 1947, pp. 133f.). There may be more justification for such a theory in the other passages involved (ch. 5; 6.20–25; 7; cf. 9), and each case must be judged on its merits. With respect to 2.16–19 the theory is superfluous, unless its relevance is proved for vv. 18f., which, however, in my view are susceptible of a more convincing explanation.

I would therefore suppose that the circumstances here are similar to those presupposed by the Egyptian Instruction, although there is no evidence that the setting is so specifically vocational. We cannot say that the Israelite teacher is addressing apprentice officials and warning them that many a career has been ruined through an affair with a woman. Nevertheless, the affinity of this passage with a characteristic theme of the Instruction is clear enough, and that is why it seems to me unnecessary to introduce an elaborate cultic theory in discussing it (cf. *Word and Wisdom*, pp. 134f.). The warning is uttered against the alluring, seductive charmer who woos with honeyed words (v. 16), who is unrestrained and ruthless, and to touch whom is death for the inexperienced young man.

[16] What precisely is meant by the terms *'iššā zārā* and *nokrīyā*? The fundamental question is whether *nokrīyā* means 'foreign woman' and so, in view of the parallelism, establishes the foreignness of the *'iššā zārā*. I accept Snijders' conclusion that *nokrī* does not always mean foreign in an ethnic sense, and that it can be applied to an Israelite who is an 'outsider', i.e., one who has become estranged from the natural corporate setting of his life and has severed the relationships which would normally shape and determine his behaviour (L. A. Snijders, *OTS* X, 1954, pp. 63f., 78, 89). If the *nokrīyā* of 2.16–19 is such a woman, *nokrīyā* and *'iššā zārā* are synonymous terms and denote one who is beyond the pale and who, because she is beyond the pale, is both desperate and uninhibited – desperate because she suffers ostracism and insecurity, and uninhibited because she defies religious and social sanctions and conventions and is a law to herself. As such she is particularly deadly to young men who become embroiled with her.

It is not necessary, however, to insist on the total exclusion of the idea of ethnic foreignness from *nokrīyā* in v. 16. Gemser appositely cites the passage from *Ani* about the woman who is not known in her city and who is far away from her husband (see above, p. 94). Ringgren (*Word and Wisdom*, p. 135) quotes this and another passage from *Ptahhotep*. The implication here is that the restraints and discipline to which the woman would have been subject in the context of her home and community have been removed. She is on the loose and can indulge her appetites with impunity. It may be that the non-ethnic sense of *nokrīyā* for which Snijders has argued is connected with the popular estimate which is formed of a foreign woman in any community. She is strange and nonconformist in many respects, and to the men she is fascinating, alluring and mysterious.

The women regard her with suspicion and think the worst of her, supposing that because, measured by their conventions, she is so nonconformist, she must be loose in her morals – a woman whose charms their menfolk will find irresistible. The foreign woman then becomes a type or paradigm of any woman who spurns the conventions of the society in which she lives, and is regarded generally as defiant and wanton, a *nokrīyā*.

[17] The meaning of *'allūp* in v. 17 is usually given as 'friend', 'companion' and so 'husband'. Gemser then comments on the high estimate of marriage to which the verse testifies. The adulterous wife not only renounces the conventions of society but also 'the covenant of God'. God is envisaged as a witness to the solemn contract of marriage. Boström gives this argument a different twist, and the mention of this covenant confirms him in his opinion that the *'iššā zārā* is indeed foreign. The name YHWH is used consistently in chs. 1–9, and so the phrase *b^e^rīt '^e^lōhehā* refers to a god other than YHWH. Thus we have a foreign god for a foreign woman (pp. 103f.). There is no doubt that *'allūp* can mean something like 'bosom friend' (Micah 7.5: parallel to *rēaʿ*; Jer. 11.19: *kebeś 'allūp*, 'pet lamb'; Ps. 55.14: parallel to *m^e^yuddāʿ*; Prov. 16.28; 17.9), but there are two passages in addition to Prov. 2.17 where the translation 'teacher' is apt (cf. G. R. Driver who suggests 'instruction' for *'allūp* in Prov. 2.17, according to Gemser, p. 111). Jeremiah 3.4 is a particularly significant passage, because the same collocation of *'allūp* and *n^eʿ^ūrīm* occurs there and in Prov. 2.17. In Jer. 3.4, Yahweh's faithless people address him as 'my father, the *'allūp* of my youth'. The father is, of course, the friend of his son, but he is also set in authority over him as an instructor, and this indicates their relationship more precisely. The father gives instruction and the son is under discipline. Should the translation not be, 'My father, the teacher of my youth'? The meaning 'teach' is established for *'lp* in the piel.

Jeremiah 13.21 is a difficult verse, but *limmadtā* suggests that *'allūpīm* here may also mean 'instructors' rather than 'confidants': 'What will you say when they set over you – and you taught them – teachers with authority over you?' I would therefore suggest that Prov. 2.17 does not refer to the marriage of the *'iššā zārā*, but to her early education. She is as remiss in respect of what she was taught at school (or at home, if the *'allūp* is her father, cf. Jer. 3.4), as she is forgetful of her religious obligations. She has impugned the authority of her father and the authority of God.

[18f.] Do vv. 18f. provide support for Boström's theory? According to Boström, the *'iššā zārā* is a foreigner and a devotee of the cult of the goddess of love, Ishtar. Hence her promiscuity is a cultic act, a fertility rite and a means of fulfilling her religious obligations (pp. 103f.). What the teacher utters a warning against is involvement in the fertility rites of a foreign cult, that is, against a form of idolatry which is held in particular repugnance. It is, then, not adultery which is the sin, but the participation in a strange cult and the scattering of holy Israelite semen among foreigners (p. 141). Boström brings these observations to bear on 2.18f. by remarking that the goddess of love, who is prodigal in creating life, is also prodigal in destroying it. He refers to the destructive character of Ishtar exemplified in the Gilgamesh Epic, and to the Babylonian-Assyrian 'Goddess in the Window' (cf. Prov. 7.4f.) named Kilili, who is capable of bringing destruction to her lovers (p. 136). Hence the words 'her house inclines towards death and her tracks towards the shades. None who visits her returns, they do not regain the paths of life.'

Both Snijders (p. 103) and Ringgren make important concessions to Boström's theory, although they regard the woman as Israelite and not foreign. She is the devotee of a foreign cult, and her promiscuity is a religious duty which she performs for Ishtar. Ringgren holds that *'allūp* denotes Yahweh here, as in Jer. 3.4, and that the whole of v.17 is taken up with a description of the woman's apostasy and idolatry. She has forsaken Yahweh and his covenant and become the devotee of an alien cult. He further maintains with Boström that through this exegesis the connection of the woman with death and the realm of the dead is made more intelligible. She participates in the destructive power of the goddess whom she serves (*Word and Wisdom*, pp. 133f.).

I believe that the imagery of vv. 18f. can be more precisely elucidated, and that its associations are not with Ishtar and her cult. The Ugaritic *rpūm* appear to be chthonic deities (Driver, *CML*, p. 10) and the *rᵉpā'īm* of biblical Hebrew are the inhabitants of Sheol (Hebrew *rp'* 'healed' (bound up); Arabic *rf'* 'sewed together', 'united'). Hence the dead are envisaged as a massed community leading a common life in the underworld (Driver *CML*, p. 10, n.2; cf. p. 155, n.22). I would suggest that the verse contains two Canaanite mythological allusions. The first half alludes to the god Mot, whose gaping throat is the gateway to Sheol (see on 1.12), and the second half alludes either to the gods of that underworld (the Ugaritic *rpūm*) or to the massed community of the world of the dead. The estranged woman, the outsider, lives on the borders of the land of the dead and her paths descend towards the *repā'īm*. What does this metaphor mean? It is a warning that those who become entangled with such a woman are irrevocably involved with her in her estrangement from society. They, too, will become outcasts and every door will be shut on them, every relationship severed. They will be treated like lepers, and the sentence which society passes on them will be for life. But it is not just social conventions that they flout; they step outside the framework of Yahweh's order (cf. *mišpāṭ*, v. 9), and they do this because of their lack of a charismatic *tebūnā* ('illumination', v. 9). They take a journey to the land of no return, the Babylonian name for the country of the dead.

VV. 20–22 *The Righteous will inherit the Land*

[20–22] The contents of vv. 20–22 are related to Deuteronomy in an important respect (cf. Gemser and Ringgren) – in the emphasis which is laid on possession of the land (of Canaan) and the conditional character of this possession. Von Rad (*Old Testament Theology*, i, pp. 105f.; cf. Robert *RB* xliii, p. 62) has pointed out that the *Heilsgeschichte* of the Hexateuch considers possession of the land of Canaan to be Yahweh's supreme gift of salvation and the fulfilment of the promise made to the patriarchs. In Deuteronomy, Israel's faithlessness and disobedience are seen as a threat to her continued possession of the land of Canaan. The promise can be put in jeopardy, and its continuing validity depends on Israel's response to the proclamation of the Law. Hence Israel subsequently loses her old indivisibility before Yahweh and becomes two nations (the *ṣaddīqīm* and the *rešā'īm*) instead of one. 'For the upright will dwell in the land, and men of integrity will be left in it; but the wicked will be cut off from the land, and the treacherous will be uprooted from it.' There are two ways corresponding to two classes of men. There are those who walk in the way of good men and keep the paths of the righteous (v. 20), and there are those who desert the paths of rectitude to walk in ways of darkness (v. 13). These final verses are thoroughly Yahwistic. Those who have the heightened ethical sensitivity conferred by Yahweh are *ṣaddīqīm*, *yešārīm*, *ṭōbīm*, *temīmīm*, and so they are guided along the path of life. The man who flouts the social morality of which Yahweh is the guarantor will not regain the paths of life.

Chapter 3

The material in this chapter should be divided so as to make a distinction between what is Instruction and what is not, and in this respect neither Gemser nor Ringgren is sufficiently perceptive. By reason of their formal structure, vv. 1–12 and 21–35 are unmistakably Instruction. Ringgren suggests that 'My son' in v. 11 (cf. v. 1) is a formal indication of the beginning of a new section, but the 'My son' form of address is used resumptively in the Egyptian Instruction and cannot be taken as proof of the beginning of a new piece. The subdivisions of the material in vv. 21–35 suggested by Gemser and Ringgren are not objectionable, provided too much is not read into them. An Instruction regularly contains a succession of topics, so that a change of subject-matter is not evidence of discontinuity. The grouping of directives dealing with neighbourliness (vv. 27–30) recalls the increased cohesiveness and more systematic organization which is characteristic of *Amenemope*, where an entire chapter may be devoted to the treatment of a single subject.

Whybray (p. 42) correctly observes that vv. 13–20 are different in character, although it is not clear that it is a strictly formal differentiation which he has in mind, so that the point he makes is somewhat different from mine. What I have in mind is that the imperative, which is an essential formal element of the Instruction, is lacking and that the exclamation 'Happy is' is not appropriate to the genre. Whether we think of parental or scholastic instruction, this is not the way in which it is communicated; this is not a mode of authoritative teaching. It belongs rather, as Zimmerli has remarked, to an elevated hymnic style and hence has an especially close association with the wisdom psalms. There is, however, nothing hymnic about the Instruction; it imparts plain, precise advice. Zimmerli regards 'Happy is' as halfway between statement and admonition, as having the character of summons, but lacking direct address. One can say with Zimmerli that this mode of expression has close affinities with the wisdom literature, but this does not put in question the stylistic differentiation between it and the Instruction on which I have insisted (*ZAW* 51, p. 185, n.1).

With regard to vv. 1–12, the imperative (or jussive) appears in vv. 1, 3, 5, 7, 9, 11. In v. 1 a negative imperative and a jussive are arranged antithetically and are recommended by a motive clause which explains why they should be attended to (v. 2). Then a negative jussive, followed by two imperatives, leads on to a consequential clause (vv. 3–4). Similarly vv. 5f. contain three imperatives and a consequential clause, as also vv. 7f. In vv. 9f., a single imperative is followed by two consequential clauses, and in vv. 11f. two imperatives are reinforced by a motive clause.

In vv. 21–26 the structure is somewhat similar, whereas in vv. 27–30 the Instruction appears in its crispest form, one directive following another without intervening motive or consequential clauses. The two clauses in v. 24 in the form of protasis and apodosis are supporting argument for the imperatives in v. 21. There is a tendency in vv. 21–35 (vv. 27–30 apart) towards more extended argument. Thus there are four consequential clauses in vv. 22f. followed by two motive clauses in v. 24, and in vv. 32–35 there is extended motivation antithetically arranged depending on v. 31 (see, however, below on ch. 4).

VV. 1–12 *Trust in Yahweh and submit to his Discipline*

[1f.] There is a general similarity between v. 1 and 1.8, and we might suppose that here again it is a parent or wisdom teacher who speaks, and that his instruction (*tōrā*) or directives (*miṣwōt*) are aimed at enabling the young man to find his way in the world and make a success of life. This impression is not contradicted by the motive clause in v. 2, 'for they give you increased length of days, and years of life with well-being'. Such a recommendation is wholly in character with the Egyptian Instruction, and thus far we might suppose that it is an educational discipline in the strict sense which is in view, and that the source of authority is either the seniority of the parent or the sagacity of the wisdom teacher.

[3] But as soon as v. 3 is reached, it becomes evident that the climate of this passage is really very different from that of the international Instruction. It follows its formal structure, but its contents conduct us into the heartland of Yahwistic faith and practice. It is not a manual of instruction for a career and, apart from this lack of vocational specialization, it is not even empirical sagacity or well-balanced worldliness. The son is not subject to the authority and discipline of the parent or teacher, but to Yahweh. The new discipline (*mūsār*) – respect for Yahweh and his authoritative teaching – has replaced the old wisdom of the Instruction. That this is so is clear from v. 11: 'My son, do not reject the *mūsār* of Yahweh and do not be irked with his reproof (*tōkaḥat*).' Among the biblical parallels to vv. 1–12 mentioned by Robert (*RB* xliii, pp. 67f.), only Deut. 8.5 is sufficiently close to be significant, and Robert, like Eichrodt (*Theology of the Old Testament*, i, 1961, p. 236), reverses the true direction of the relationship between this verse and Prov. 3.11f. This is a case where a stylistic trait of the Instruction has influenced Deuteronomy, and not *vice versa*. Deut. 8.5 portrays the new *mūsār* on the analogy of the old, and is probably dependent on the process of reinterpretation which the Instruction undergoes in Prov. 1–9. 'As a father disciplines his son, Yahweh, your God disciplines you' (see below, p. 294, on vv. 11f.).

In this section, the originally international Instruction has been thoroughly integrated with Yahwistic faith and practice, and so it is not surprising that the marks of reinterpretation as they are evidenced in the vocabulary bear a general similarity to those which I have discussed in *PWM* in connection with the prophetic reinterpretation of old wisdom. The commentators have observed that the phrase *ḥesed weʾemet* is used of kin solidarity as well as of covenant solidarity, but there is little doubt that it is the latter which is intended and that the phrase is as thoroughly Yahwistic as *ṣedeq ūmišpāṭ* in 2.9. These are words which have their meaning in connection with life within the covenant; they presuppose faith in Yahweh and the consequences of such faith on the structure of Yahweh's community (cf. II Sam. 2.6; Eichrodt, *Theology* i, pp. 232f.). The demand not to forsake loyalty and steadfastness is followed by phraseology redolent of law and covenant (cf. Ex. 13.9, 16; Deut. 6.8; 11.18; Jer. 31.3, cf. 17.1). 'Write them on the tablet of your heart' may be a later expansion. It makes the line unusually long and is omitted by LXX^B. For the most part, the resemblances in vocabulary between other biblical books and Proverbs 1–9 which Robert adduces are too general to serve any useful purpose, but this instance is of a different kind, and it is an unmistakable literary reminiscence (cf. *RB* xliii, p. 51). It may even represent a contrived, free conflation of passages from law and prophecy, and the application of imperatives connected with covenant and commandments ('bind', 'write') to the demand for loyalty and steadfastness. The metaphor constructed with *qšr* is a new one: *ḥesed* and *ʾemet* are envisaged as a necklace (cf. 1.9), a means of adornment and beautification. Certainly it is Jeremiah's new covenant which is in view, but this emphasis on individual responsibility and appropriation and the presupposition that law and covenant confront the individual with the necessity of decision, which in different ways are present in Deuteronomy and Jeremiah, fits in well with the personal address ('my son') of the Instruction.

[4] The motivation in v. 4, on the other hand, is not recognizably Yahwistic, and would not look strange in an international context. The reason for this is that there is some measure of agreement between the Israelite and Egyptian Instructions as to what constitutes happiness, well-being, success. Thus the description of objectives in vv. 2 and 4, a long harmonious life, favour and good success in the eyes of man and God, are not dissimilar from the goals set before the Egyptian pupil by his teacher. All this was agreeable to the robust earthiness of Yahwism, to its 'materialism' and world-affirming character. Hence *śēkel*, which belongs to the vocabulary of old wisdom (*PWM*, p. 67), does not undergo any reinterpretation, and the meaning 'competence', 'effectiveness', 'success' survives. The ability to get on well with people, the possession of an attractive personality (*ḥēn*) and the enjoyment of reputation and success are highly prized.

[5] The situation is different in v. 5, where another item of the vocabulary of wisdom (*bīnā*) is used pejoratively. *bīnā* is no longer a primary intellectual virtue (the clarity of a powerful intellect), but is a sinful *hubris* which is incompatible with trust in Yahweh. There is also a contrast between the severely intellectual use of *lēb* (cf. *ḥasar lēb*, *PWM*, p. 15) and its use here to signify total commitment to Yahweh. 'Trust in Yahweh with all your heart.' Here is a second facet of the 'nationalizing' of the Instruction. Complementary to the new *mūsār* there is a new *bīnā*. Clarity is not achieved by a severe educational discipline, but through religious illumination. [6] This is expressed in the metaphor of the way or path in v. 6. It is knowledge of Yahweh (*PWM*, p. 86) which supplies sure guidance for life, and it is he who facilitates progress along paths which lead to a destination (cf. 2.9f., above, p. 283). The Egyptian Instruction is located in the schoolroom; the Israelite Instruction is here located the congregation. Educational demands are replaced by a religious demand.

[7] This theme is resumed in v. 7 in a manner strongly reminiscent of the prophetic attack on old wisdom and its insistence that the intellectual self-determination on which the sages set such store is illusory. I have elsewhere (*PWM*, pp. 50f.) discussed similar passages in the book of Proverbs (16.9; 19.21; 20.24; 21.30f.). The point of view of this verse is the same as that of Isa. 5.21: 'Woe to those who are *ḥᵃkāmīm* in their own eyes and are *nᵉbōnīm* in their own estimation.'

It may be that *ḥākām beʿēnekā* is wisdom terminology, but its use here is distinctive as compared with its other occurrences in the book of Proverbs (26.5, 12; 26.16; 28.11; cf. *PWM*, p. 66). It is not directed against instances of unwisdom, but against the claims of those who practise *ḥokmā*. Words such as *bīnā* and *tebūnā* are descriptive of the intellectual attitudes of the sages and their reliance on rational scrutiny, and so they are bad words and inimical to the fear of Yahweh. This is the *mūsār* from which valid ethical distinctions stem so that a man may pick his way between good and evil, but the sages with their intellectual approach and pragmatic bent are indifferent to morality and even perverse, employing their cleverness to confound moral judgement.

[8] The motive clause conceives the fear of Yahweh as a beneficial therapy; it is like a medicine or a tonic which produces vigorous health and physical well-being. The general meaning of the verse is not in doubt, but the particular interpretation which I have offered assumes the meaning 'health' for *šōr* and 'medicine' (perhaps 'balsam') for *šiqqūy* (literally, 'drink'). In Ben Sira 30.16, *šr* is the equivalent of *ὑγεία* of the Greek text, and in Aramaic letters published by G. R. Driver, *šlm wšrrt śgy' hwšrt lk* means 'I send thee many greetings of peace and prosperity' (*Aramaic Documents of the Fifth Century BC*, 1957, pp. 22–24; p. 44, n.2). Aramaic *šrrt* means 'strength', 'good health', 'prosperity'. It is not therefore necessary to emend to *šērekā*<*še'ērekā*, although this or *beśārekā* is indicated by LXX and Pesh. The meaning 'navel' for *šōr* in biblical Hebrew is derivative, since Driver has shown that the semantic development 'strength'> 'cord' is regular (e.g., Accadian *qū*, Hebrew *qāw* 'cord' from the same root as Arabic *qawiya*, 'was strong'). Driver renders *ʿaṣemōtekā* as 'bodily frame', adducing Accadian *eṣimtu*, 'something knit together', which is glossed in the syllabaries by *riksu*, 'totality'. In Ben Sira 30.14, *ḥy bʿṣmw* means 'of robust constitution' (Greek offers a paraphrase, 'healthy and with a robust constitution'), and *šr ʿṣm* in v. 16 is almost synonymous, as is the Syriac *ḥay(y)e dašrīrā* cited by Driver (*Biblica* 32, p. 175): 'It is a tonic (lit. 'healing' or 'therapy') for your health, and a medicine for your frame.'

[9] The commentators remark that v.9 is the only instance of a cultic demand in the book of Proverbs, and its parallels in the Pentateuch are noted (Ex. 23.19; Num. 28.26f.; Deut. 26.1f.). That this should be an isolated case is not so surprising, since the wisdom literature is rather far removed from cultic concerns and one would not expect cultic prescriptions to be worked into it. **[10ff.]** In v. 10 the 'materialism' which I have discussed in v. 4 reappears: 'Honour Yahweh with your wealth, and with the first-fruits of all your produce; and so your granaries will be filled with a bumper crop (lit. 'plenty'), and your vats will be bursting with wine.' M. Dahood (p. 9) suggests that the Phoenician phrase *śbʿ wtrš* in the Karatepe Inscription is evidence that *śbʿ* means precisely 'grain' in Prov. 3.10 (cf. LXX *πλησμονῆς σίτῳ*). Cf. R. T. O'Callaghan, *Or.* 18 (1949), pp. 178f.; *ANET*, p. 500, n.5. A. M. Honeyman, *PEQ* (1949), pp. 25, 35, translates *śbʿ wtrš* 'sufficiency and inheritance'. Such abundant provision of good things is an essential part of the full life of those who respect Yahweh's authority and submit to his discipline (v. 11). The motive clause (v. 12) affirms, in language which recalls Yahweh's definition of his attitude towards the Davidic king (II Sam. 7.14, *ykḥ*; cf. Ps. 89.32f.), that his discipline, however severe, is always beneficent and an expression of his love. He is like a father who disciplines the son on whom he dotes. Or, if LXX *μαστιγοῖ*, 'flogs', in fact points to *weyakʾīb* and is not simply an explication of MT, the meaning is that Yahweh inflicts pain on the son on whom he dotes. Hence it is clear that it is not parental or scholastic discipline with which this piece deals. The form of address is 'My son', but the teacher claims authority for Yahweh and not for himself and the relationship between father and son is no more than a simile which sheds light on the character of Yahweh's discipline.

VV. 13–20 *In Praise of Wisdom*

This is written in praise of wisdom and the style is hymnic rather than didactic. The intention is certainly to recommend wisdom, but no one is addressed directly and no demands are formulated. Yet there is not a sharp discontinuity between this section and the preceding verses, certainly not in respect of subject-matter, while even the formal characteristics of the Instruction are not obliterated. The crucial departure is the replacement of the imperative(s) which might have been expected in v. 13 by the hymnic *ʾašerē* ('Happy is the man who finds *ḥokmā* and he who obtains *tebūnā*'). The remainder of the section contains a succession of motive clauses which give various reasons for the blessedness of the man who possesses wisdom; the whole of the argument is within the scope of the Instruction and could equally well have hinged on initial imperatives in v. 13. From the point of view of content it might seem that the prominence of the word *ḥokmā* and its personification marks a significant departure from the preceding section. This has some value as a differential, but it would be easy to exaggerate its importance. As for *t^ebûnā*, it seems to be used in v. 13 as just a convenient and colourless synonym of *ḥokmā*. It would not have been decorous to have a line containing the same word in both halves. This, at any rate, is the impression which is had from the succeeding verses, which envisage only the singular *ḥokmā*. In v. 19, *t^ebûnā* is not so colourless, for its use there recalls those passages in Deutero-Isaiah (40.12–17, 28–31) where it denotes Yahweh's architectonic insight and capacity as creator (*PWM*, pp. 81f.).

[13] The hymnic 'Blessed' suggests the appropriateness of translating the subsequent suffixes referring to *ḥokmā* as 'her' rather than 'its' and the imagery of v. 16 establishes that the intention is to personify wisdom ('Length of days are in her right hand, in her left hand wealth and honour'). Yet the substance of the motivation in vv. 14–18 is closely akin to that in vv. 2, 4, 9 and so the benefits of Wisdom are the same as those which flow from the *tōrā* and *miṣwōt* of the teacher (v. 1). In a word, these are the gifts of life in its quantitative and qualitative aspects, length of days, harmonious self-fulfilment, wealth and honour. Only it is the pursuit of Wisdom which brings wealth and so an order of priorities is established. Wisdom is to be sought first and the other things will be added.

[14] Perhaps v. 14 should be translated: 'For she is more profitable than silver, and gives a higher yield than gold.' Money can be put to work in commercial transactions so that it earns more money, but the profit yield of Wisdom is greater than that of money. **[15f.]** Verse 15 is a variation on the same theme. Wisdom is more precious than jewels and there is no delectable thing which stands comparison with her. Kayatz (*op. cit.*, p. 105) points out that there are a large number of representations of the goddess *Maat* in which she holds a symbol of life in one hand and a sceptre symbolizing wealth and dignity in the other, and urges that the portrayal of Wisdom in v. 16 is modelled on these representations of *Maat*.

All this recalls the attitude to wealth and success in the Egyptian Instruction, where the man who is in a hurry to get rich is contrasted with the truly successful man whose prosperity is a measure of his intrinsic worth (see above, pp. 60f.). There is a correspondence between a person's 'weight' (*gravitas*) and his ability to climb to the commanding heights of statesmanship, and *kābōd* might be rendered 'weight' (*kābēd* 'to be heavy'). This is what Wisdom does for a man; he becomes a weighty person in his community, a man of substance who exercises power and influence and commands respect.

[17f.] In vv. 17f., Wisdom is a reliable and beneficent guide (cf. v. 6 where Yahweh is the guide), who leads her devotees along pleasant roads and safe paths giving vitality ('tree of life') and blessedness to those who take her hand and keep hold of it. The important role of the tree of life in ancient Mesopotamian myth and ritual has been described by Widengren (G. Widengren, *The King and the Tree of Life in Ancient Near Eastern Religion*, *Uppsala Universitets Årsskrift*, 1951, p. 4), and Engnell has discussed its significance in connection with the Genesis paradise myth (*VTS* iii, pp. 103–19). The generally held opinion that the mythology is moribund in the book of Proverbs and that the expression in v. 18 is just a pretty figure of speech or metaphor is no doubt correct (see especially R. Marcus, *JBL* lxii, 1943, pp. 117–20; cf. H. Ringgren, *Word and Wisdom*, pp. 140f.). It is the vitality imparted by wisdom which is symbolized by the tree of life. This is the vitality of the tree in the temple grove which was constantly nourished by adjacent streams of the water of life (Widengren, pp. 1f., 19). Kayatz (pp. 105f.) queries whether the references to the tree of life in Proverbs may not have some ultimate relationship to the thought of taking hold of a particular tree in order to win eternal life which had currency in the mythology of the Egyptian cult of the dead (see below, p. 346).

[19f.] It is a moot point whether we should suppose that wisdom is personified in v. 19. If it is, must not knowledge in v. 20 also be a personification? One may say that these verses are transitional in relation to the role of the personified Wisdom in the creation of the world described in 8.22f., but they do not seem to represent any advance on two passages in Deutero-Isaiah (40.12–17, 28–31) which describe Yahweh's exercise of perspicacity and power in his creation of the world. Only the intellectual mastery of Yahweh as it is evidenced in the majestic sweep of his plan of creation is worthy of the name *t*ᵉ*būnā*. I would not, then, be prepared to say, as Whybray does (pp. 98f.), that the intention of vv. 19f. is to claim *ḥokmā* as an attribute of Yahweh, with whom it was associated in the creation of the world. The most significant thing about vv. 19f., in my view, is that they furnish another demonstration of the integration of wisdom with Yahwism. It is possible that the Deutero-Isaiah passages are also connected with the 'nationalization' of wisdom. The wise men became the editors and curators of the sacred writings (*PWM*, pp. 102f.). They made their bow to Yahwism, but they brought some part of their literary heritage to their new tasks. They made amends by reinterpreting the language of wisdom and stressing the derivative character of all human wisdom. Men are wise only as they participate in the wisdom of Yahweh. This means that if vv. 19f. are transitional in relation to 8.22f., the use in Deutero-Isaiah of the vocabulary of wisdom in connection with Yahweh's creative works is a factor in the development of the personified Wisdom of 8.22f. Verse 20 refers to two fertilizing agencies, rain or dew which falls from above, and the springs which well up from beneath (cf. J. A. Emerton, *VTS* xv, 1966, p. 125).

vv. 21–26 *Yahweh will guide and keep in Safety*

These verses are not bound together into a very convincing unity and, in particular, the argumentation in vv. 22–26 is related to the imperative in v. 21 by varying degrees of aptness. While v. 22 is a sufficiently convincing account of the consequences of paying attention to *tūšiyā* and *m*ᵉ*zimmā* (see on 1.4, above, p. 265; 2.7; 2.9, above, pp. 282f.), the structure of the succeeding verses is progressively looser. I have had to take this into account in coming to a decision about the title of the section, and my choice shows that I have minimized the importance of v. 21 and given pride of place to v. 26. This is quite inconsistent with a proper regard for the form of the Instruction, for the imperative in v. 21 ought to be the primary element and the subsequent argumentation (including the motive clause in v. 26) ought to be derived from it. That this is also the case here is certainly the impression created by the consequential clauses in vv. 22f. and the subsequent motive clauses in vv. 24–26, but I am unconvinced that the appearances correspond to the reality of the matter. If the connection between the imperative and the subsequent clauses were more intrinsic, I would speak of a reinterpretation of *tūšiyā* and *m*ᵉ*zimmā*, and, indeed, I believe that this is what is attempted, but it is not carried through either perceptively or felicitously. Although vv. 23–26 purport to recommend attention to *tūšiyā* and *m*ᵉ*zimmā*, what they really do is to inculcate trust in Yahweh as the ground of security.

[23–26] These are in the same mould of Yahwistic piety as 2.7f. and 3.5f., as the recurrence of the metaphor of the road is sufficient to show. The man whose confidence is Yahweh is guaranteed a sure footing. LXX: 'The Lord will be on every road that you travel' is probably a paraphrase which attempts to make sense of a difficult Hebrew text, rather than an indication that the Greek translator read *bimᵉsillōtekā* (cf. BH). M. Dahood (p. 10) translates the obscure *bᵉkisleka* 'at your side' (so V) and cites Ugaritic *ksl* (cf. G. R. Driver, *CML*, p. 145 'back'; C. H. Gordon, *Ugaritic Textbook*, 1965, p. 421, No. 1280). Along this road there are no treacherous places or traps in which his feet might be entangled (v. 26). So he can proceed safely in the knowledge that there are no hidden obstacles to foul his feet (v. 23: *tiggōp*, 'strike against an obstruction'). Such a man is a *ṣaddīq*, for this is what is implied by the reference to the *rᵉšāʿīm* in v. 25. Because he is a *ṣaddīq* and knows himself to be under the protection of Yahweh, he is confident of his immunity from the calamity which overtakes the *rᵉšāʿīm*, and is not afraid in the presence of this sudden terror (v. 25). The promise of security at rest as well as on the road is an additional feature here, but this, too, has the flavour of Yahwistic piety and recalls especially Ps. 4.9: 'In *šālōm* I shall both lie down and sleep, for it is you, O Yahweh, alone who gives me a safe dwelling' (*lābeṭaḥ tōšībēnī*). Also Ps. 139: 'You ascertain my route and my resting-place and are familiar with all my roads' (cf. Ps. 121, which is not so precise a parallel). The theme of vv. 23–36 is that the man who trusts in Yahweh and does *ṣᵉdāqā* will be guided along a safe road and will be secure at rest (LXX indicates *tēšēb* in v. 24 in place of *tiškab*) and in the embrace of sweet, untroubled sleep. Not so the wicked man, who is exposed to the sudden, fearful and devastating judgement of Yahweh.

[21f.] The literal translation of v. 21 would seem to be: 'My son, let not the keeping of competence and resourcefulness escape from your eyes'. Or it has been suggested that the order of the two halves of the line should be reversed, in which case it could be rendered: 'My son, guard competence and resourcefulness, let them not escape from your sight' (on *yālūzū* see Gemser, p. 111; Arabic *lāḏa*, 'run away'). The meaning here is 'slip away' or 'escape', i.e., 'Do not let them out of sight for a moment'. Constant attention must be given to competence and resourcefulness, and no detail bearing on them is ever to be overlooked or neglected. Such constant and rigorous attentiveness is a necessity of life, an indispensable source of vitality ('life for your *nepeš*'), but it also adds lustre to a man. Competence and resourcefulness adorn him, they make him attractive just as the brilliance of a necklace adorns the throat. Verses 21–22 are more naturally understood as a demand for nicety of judgement and incisiveness than they are in a context of Yahwistic piety (i.e., in relation to vv. 23f.), although the intention is no doubt to make these latter verses determinative of the meaning of *tûšîyā* and *m^ezimmā* in v. 21.

vv. 27–35 *Neighbourliness and Circumspection*

This section falls naturally into two parts: vv. 27–30, which contain a succession of instructions formulated negatively, and vv. 31–35, which consist of extended motivation depending on imperatives (v. 31). The first part recommends attitudes of neighbourliness, benevolence and goodwill, and there are passages in the Egyptian Instruction which urge the same behaviour in similar terms. It would be possible to interpret these verses as concrete demands which arise from *ḥesed we'ᵉmet* (see on 3.3, above, pp. 290f.), and so as presupposing the special texture of corporate life in Yahweh's community, and it might then be thought that this is another general indication of the affinity between the contents of these chapters and the book of Deuteronomy – a book with marked humanitarian sympathies (*PWM*, p. 107). There is, however, nothing in the ideas or vocabulary of vv. 27–30 which demands a Yahwistic interpretation and it fits well into the world of international wisdom. There is no evidence that these verses are set in the framework of vocational instruction in which we know that the Egyptian counterparts exist. There benevolence, helpfulness, candour and goodwill are ingredients of the make-up of a successful official, but here the context is probably not so specialized, in which case it is neighbourliness in general which is envisaged. **[27f.]** Nevertheless, the demand not to withhold a benefit which it is in one's power to confer (v. 27) would be a very salutary directive to an official, and even v. 28 (despite *rē'ᵃkā*, which suggests a more general relationship) recalls the temptation to petty tyranny and obstructiveness to which an official may succumb, so that he makes a man come a second time simply to satisfy his sense of power. The meaning of v. 28, however, may simply be: 'If you encounter a request for help, meet it instantly and cheerfully and do not seem too hesitant or grudging in your acquiescence.' 'In modern Palestinian Arabic, *bukra*, usually rendered "to-morrow", often means "the next opportunity". It is daily on the tongue of most people. The wish to put off is innate' (E.F.F.B.).

[29] Verse 29 is directed against the spiteful and malicious intrigue which takes advantage of a relationship of trust (*lābeṭaḥ*) in order to destroy a neighbour. The trustful and unsuspecting neighbour is the victim of unprovoked aggression at the hands of one who practises malevolence as an art, and shapes his evil plans with the exquisite deliberation and skill that a craftsman might be expected to lavish on an object of art (*taḥ^a^rōš*, cf. *ḥārāš*, 'craftsman'; for another explanation on the basis of *ḥrš*, 'cultivate', see below, p. 325). Such premeditated malice is not only a crime against the neighbour but is a betrayal of the relation of trust itself and trust is an indispensable condition of community.

[30] Another public menace is the person to whom strife is the breath of life, and who quarrels with anyone and everyone for no particular reason. The reference may be more exact, in which case it is the person who is incurably litigious who is the subject of v. 30 (*tārīb* is then specifically legal terminology). Such a person will engage in legal proceedings on the flimsiest of pretexts, or with no pretext at all. A case can hardly be made out for these verses as vocational wisdom, but they are nearer to the career guidance given to the apprentice official in Egypt than anything so far encountered in the book of Proverbs.

[31] Verse 31 has in mind the person who will use violence to gain his selfish ends, reckless of the consequences to others, and the temptation to feel envious of one who can do such things with apparent impunity. In v. 31b, LXX reads: 'Do not emulate (ζηλώσῃς) their ways.' This probably indicates *tiṯḥar* (BH), 'be vexed at', which is parallel to *t^e^qannē'* in Ps. 37.1 and Prov. 24.19. In Ps. 37.1, 7, 8 *tiṯḥar* is translated by παραζήλου in LXX. In Ps. 37.1 and Prov. 24.19, *t^e^qannē'* is rendered by ζήλου. 'Do not be vexed at any of his ways' furnishes better parallelism to 'Do not envy a man given to violence' than does 'Do not choose any of his ways' (MT *tibḥar*). The verse recalls the detailed description of such conduct as a way of death – a rendezvous with Sheol – in 1.11–19.

[32–35] The extended motivation is transparently Yahwistic in ideas and vocabulary, and is arranged as a succession of contrasts. The crooked man (*nālōz*), i.e., the one who is devious and given to underhand methods, is contrasted with the straight or upright man (see above on 2.13–15, p. 284). The one is an abomination to Yahweh, while the other is in the inner circle of his confidence (*sōd*). I have discussed an analogous juxtaposition of statesman and prophet in *PWM* (p. 124). It is the prophet and not the statesman who is a member of Yahweh's cabinet (*sōd*), and is in a position to make sound policy (*ʿēṣā*). Yahweh abhors the intriguer, but the candid and upright man who knows the virtue of openness and simplicity has the ear of Yahweh, is assured of unbroken guidance and will be more effective than his Machiavellian counterpart.

The phrase *tōʿabat YHWH* raises again the question of the relationship of these chapters to Deuteronomy, since it occurs only in Proverbs and Deuteronomy. Humbert has argued that its absence elsewhere indicates that it is quasi-terminological and is confined to a particular milieu. Since ten of the eleven occurrences in the book of Proverbs are in chapters 10.1–22.16, which are usually thought to contain pre-exilic material, he queries whether it may have been a usage in pre-exilic Israelite wisdom and so a borrowing of Deuteronomy from the wisdom literature (*ZAW* 72, 1960, pp. 224f.). The significance of this point is reduced when it is recalled that *tōʿabat YHWH* in Deuteronomy is everywhere connected with a demand for an exclusive devotion to the cult of Yahweh, whereas in Proverbs it is associated with moral and intellectual flaws. There is therefore no community of content in the respective usages, and this is important for any assessment of whether there is a direct literary relationship between the one and the other. Moreover, a similar formula occurs in *Amenemope* in contexts akin to some of those in Proverbs, and in these cases *tōʿabat YHWH* is explicable as an Israelite variant of the Egyptian formula with the 'international' content unaffected. In *Amenemope*, a lack of honesty and equivocation in speech are described as 'the abomination of the god' (xiii.16, *ANET*, p. 423), and documentary falsification by a scribe is similarly censured (xv.21, *ANET*, p. 423). The use of *tōʿabat YHWH* in Prov. 12.22 with reference to lying lips is a striking parallel to *Amenemope*, and there are three other occurrences which are directly comparable. In 11.20, the formula is used of persons who are wrongheaded or twisted (*ʿiqqešē lēb*), and in 15.26 of the malicious intriguer (cf. 6.16, where *tōʿabat napšō* occurs with reference to malevolence, lying and perjury). It is used of the judge who betrays his trust by acquitting the guilty and condemning the innocent (17.15), just as it is used in *Amenemope* of the scribe who is deficient in professional integrity.

My conclusion is that if a direct literary relationship is assumed between Deuteronomy and Proverbs in respect of this formula, the dependence is probably on the side of Deuteronomy, which, however, has pressed it into the service of a new cause and has put it to work in the interests of the exclusiveness of the cult of Yahweh.

Antithetic balance is a feature of the last three verses, curse and blessing, wicked and righteous, arrogant and humble, wise man and fools, repute and disrepute. The fool does not walk humbly with Yahweh nor perform *ṣᵉdāqā* (see on vv. 23–26); wisdom is piety and rectitude. Yahweh meets scorn with scorn, but he shows favour to the humble. *kābōd* is raised on the foundations of domestic stability and happiness. The blessings of wife, children and property are basic, and the *bayit* is a crucial area of personal relationships. Only if this base is secure can a man consolidate his reputation further afield in the community. 'The curse of Yahweh is on the wicked man's household, but he blesses the righteous man's dwelling.' The wise man has a weight or gravity (see above, p. 295) as a man of substance and influence, whereas the fool is a lightweight (*qālōn*: 'lightness', from *qlh*, a variant of *qll*), for whom there is an absence of esteem and a heightened (see below on *mērīm*) contempt.

There are two small textual matters, one concerning v. 34a and the other v. 35b. Driver (*Biblica* 32, p. 176) translates MT without emendation in v. 34a: 'Though he treats the arrogant arrogantly' (*lᵉ* instead of *'et*, an Aramaism). It appears unlikely, however, that *lᵉ* has a different grammatical function in v. 34a from what it has in v. 34b. The presence of *laʿᵃnīyīm*(K) in v. 34b also tells against the emendation *ʿim lēṣīm* (BH). One could accept Driver's explanation of *'im* as concessive and suppose that *lᵉ* has the sense 'with respect to' (literally: 'Though he is scornful with respect to scoffers'). There is then a difficulty with *wᵉ* of v. 34b, unless it can mean 'yet'. This is how I have translated the verse. Another possibility would be to translate *'im* 'if', and render: 'If he pours scorn on scoffers, no less does he show favour to the humble'. In v. 35b I translate *mērīm* or *mᵉrīmīm* as 'heighten', 'intensify' following Winton Thomas (*VTS* iii, pp. 282f.).

CHAPTER 4

vv. 1–5 *The Voice of Experience*

This section (and probably the whole of this chapter) is free from Yahwistic reinterpretation and, in this respect, contrasts strongly with some of the material which we have been considering. The unevenness of Proverbs 1–9 is a fact to which insufficient attention has been directed, and which has important implications. It shows that the Instruction existed in Israel as parental or scholastic *mūsār* (v. 1: *mūsar 'āb*), and not just as *mūsar YHWH* (cf. Toy, Gemser and Ringgren on ch. 4), and provides a basis for the hypothesis of Yahwistic reinterpretation which I have advanced. Israel took over the international Instruction with the concept of authority associated with it, and it is this which is expounded in vv. 1–5.

[1–5] It is not so important to determine whether these verses refer to the authority of parents or the authority of a teacher, whether the setting is the home or the school. I would not press the plural 'sons' (v. 1) in support of the latter, but the reference to 'mother' (v. 3) is a more weighty indication that it is the former. It is equally difficult to draw a distinction in the case of the Egyptian Instruction, and we must expect this, since the teacher-pupil relationship is modelled on the father-son relationship. Consequently the authority of the teacher over his pupil is defined in terms of the natural authority of the parent over his child. The reference to 'mother' is, however, damaging to a scholastic interpretation of these verses. If it is a teacher who speaks and if he is referring to what he learned from his teacher, we can equate 'father' with 'teacher', but the reference to 'mother' is so perplexing that the interpretation almost breaks down. Ringgren steers a middle course and suggests that it is a wisdom teacher who speaks, but that it is the advice which he received from his father and not from his teacher to which he alludes in v. 4. There is no doubt that the plain meaning of v. 3 is that the father transmits to his son the teaching which he received from his father and mother (cf. 1.8, above, p. 268).

The more important consideration, however, is that whether it is home or school, the same kind of authority is envisaged in either case and this is radically different from the concept of religious authority represented by *mūsar YHWH*. What is said about this instruction is not that it bears Yahweh's authority, but that it is validated by tradition and empirical testing. It is the accumulated sagacity of many generations to whose value the father or teacher can personally testify. He derives his authority from the circumstance that he is in a good succession; because he has lived inside the tradition and allowed it to shape his life, he can speak with a personal and not merely a derivative authority (cf. v. 2, 'my *tōrā*', and v. 5, 'Do not forget my sayings nor deviate from them'). The tradition is a living process, and he has made his own contribution to its ongoing life. Hence appropriation of the tradition (*leqaḥ*, v. 2; cf. 1.5, above, pp. 265f.) is not just acceptance of arbitrary external demands, but education in depth, and only one who is so thoroughly saturated in it has the authority to teach. There is no question of any appeal beyond the authority of the teacher himself, just as there is no suggestion of religious illumination. The context is educational, and *bīnā*, 'intellectual discrimination' (v. 1), will be achieved through attentiveness, receptivity and rigorous application. Hence *lēb* (v. 4) should be translated 'mind' rather than 'heart': 'Let your mind grasp my words'.

The character of the Instruction is specified formally by *miṣwā* and substantively by *tōrā*. It is instruction communicated by imperatives, and it consists of guidance; it furnishes a way of life ('and live', v. 4. The words are absent from LXX^B^. See below on v. 11). Von Rad's attempt to characterize wisdom teaching as *ʿēṣā*, with an implied antithesis between *ʿēṣā* and *miṣwā*, is consequently not entirely happy (*PWM*, p. 48). Authoritative teaching is not confined to the disclosures of Yahweh to prophet and priest. There is a special kind of authoritative teaching inside the wisdom tradition. Dahood (p. 11) cites *ṯtkḥ ttrp šmm*, 'The heavens wilted and drooped' (*Baal* I*. i.4, 20; *CML*, pp. 102f., 151, n.15) as evidence of *škḥ* 'wilt'. He suggests that as *ṯkḥ* is synonymous with *rp* in the Ugaritic text cited, so *škḥ* (v. 5) is synonymous with *rph* (4.13). 'Get wisdom, get insight; do not flag.' It is difficult to believe that *škḥ* means anything other than 'forget' in this verse.

The difference between MT and LXX in v. 5, and also the variants of the different recensions of LXX, raise important questions. 'Get wisdom, get insight' is absent from LXX^{B}, and different Hebrew texts are perhaps also indicated by $LXX^{\aleph ca}$ and LXX^{A}. In the former, 'Get wisdom, get insight' comes after 'do not forget' and in the latter after 'sayings of my mouth', with the further repetitive addition, 'do not forget my sayings nor deviate from them'. There is evidence here that the text was not stable, a further indication of which is the absence of v. 7 from LXX. This disturbance of the text has to be considered in conjunction with vv. 6–9, which are different in character from the preceding verses and are written to praise and commend a personified Wisdom (cf. 3.13–20, above, pp. 294f.; Whybray, p. 45). This is perhaps one place (cf. the end of the chapter) where there is textual evidence of the process of reinterpretation to which the Instruction was subjected.

'Get *ḥokmā*, get *bīnā*' may be part of the Instruction contained in vv. 1–5 (cf. *bīnā* in v. 1), but in view of the correspondence between 3.13f. and 4.6f., I suspect that *ḥokmā* and *bīnā* in 4.5 (cf. 4.7) have the same significance as in 3.13, i.e., *bīnā* is used simply to avoid the repetition of *ḥokmā*, so that in the subsequent verses it is simply the singular personified Wisdom which is in view (see on 3.14f., above, pp. 295f.; cf. 4.6f., the suffix 'her' and the 3rd sing. fem. verb). This is how the matter is seen in RSV, in which the order of vv. 5a and 5b is reversed. Without the preface, 'Get wisdom, get insight', vv. 6–9 lack a beginning; 'Do not forsake her' requires an antecedent reference to Wisdom and one which is not interrupted by 'Do not forget my sayings nor deviate from them'. It is to meet this difficulty that Gemser reverses the order of vv. 6 and 7.

vv. 6–9 *The Love of Wisdom and its Rewards*

[6–9] 'Get wisdom, get insight' is reinforced by the statement, 'Wisdom comes first, (therefore) get Wisdom and, with all your getting, get Insight' (v. 7). The absence of v. 7 from LXX raises the question whether v. 7 is not an expansion of 'Get Wisdom, get Insight', perhaps an attempt to improve on the original recommendation by reiteration. Verse 7a could also be translated: 'The beginning of wisdom is "Get Wisdom",' but this gives a weaker sense (cf. Ringgren). Wisdom is an unquestionable first in any order of priorities. She should determine the structure of a man's life, giving it form and proportion and establishing a scale of priorities and a right distribution of emphasis. In return for the protection which she bestows, Wisdom requires of her devotees constancy of allegiance and affection. She must be followed steadfastly and loved without fickleness (v. 6).

Is it, then, as a lover or a bride that Wisdom is to be sought? Is this the intention of the portrayal? Boström (pp. 155f.) finds here an attempt to counter the threat of the *'iššā zārā* (see on 2.16–19, above, pp. 284f.) with whom prostitution is an aspect of cultic devotion and who is a snare to young men. Similarly Ringgren (*Word and Wisdom*, p. 106), who says: 'Wisdom should be the bride of the disciple of wisdom in place of the foreign woman.' Ringgren supposes that v. 9 contains a reference to wedding customs. Wisdom, as the bride, will invest the bridegroom with his ceremonial garland and crown of glory (cf. Gemser, who notes a more general association between crowning and garlanding and times of festival). The explanation in terms of wedding customs is hardly apt in 1.9, where paternal *mūsār* and maternal *tōrā* are described as 'a becoming wreath for your head'. If the 'becoming wreath' in 1.9 is to be explained in terms of prevailing customs, we have to think of fêting in a more general festive context.

In any case, Wisdom is not portrayed consistently as a lover in vv. 6–9, not even when *salsᵉlehā* (v. 8) is taken to mean 'caress' or 'embrace' rather than 'hold high', i.e., 'hold in high esteem', for a bride does not protect her lover, she does not exalt him (*tᵉrōmᵉmekkā*), in the sense of securing his preferment, nor does she get honour for her lover (*tᵉkabbēdᵉkā*) when he embraces her. *tᵉḥabbᵉqennā* does not describe the embrace of lovers, but the embracing of an influential patron by her *protégé*. It is by thus embracing Wisdom that the pathway to advancement, esteem and reputation is opened up. There is something to be said for translating *salsᵉlehā* 'caress' (cf. LXX περιχαράκωσον, 'surround', 'embrace'?), since this yields an *a b b a* pattern for the verbs in v. 8, with *salsᵉlehā* and *tᵉḥabbᵉqennā* synonymous. Nevertheless, I would translate: 'Hold her in high esteem and she will get preferment for you; she will get you honour, if you embrace her.' Wisdom is the lofty, influential patron who condescends to her *protégé* and installs him as her favourite, expecting in return for the benefits of her patronage constant fidelity and adoration (v. 6). It is the honour and acclaim which thereby accrue to him – Wisdom's fêting of her *protégé* – which is described in v. 9. 'She will give you a becoming wreath for your head, she will grant you a splendid crown.'

VV. 10–19 *The Two Ways*

In the examples of the Instruction so far encountered in the book of Proverbs, the metaphor of the 'road' has played an important part, This is not necessarily bound up with Yahwistic reinterpretation, for, although it does feature prominently in such passages (2.8f.; 3.23f.). its presence in 1.8–19 and 4.10–19, which are not explicitly Yahwistic, suggests that it profoundly influenced the shape of the Instruction in Israel (see, however, H. Brunner, *op. cit.*, pp. 123–6, on the 'safe road' in the Egyptian Instruction). While the Egyptian Instruction has a vocational emphasis and addresses itself to apprentice officials, its Israelite counterpart is a way of life. Whether at some earlier stage the Israelite Instruction bore a closer resemblance to the Egyptian and was originally appropriated as an instrument for educating officials is a matter on which I suspend judgement for the time being. If this were so, all the examples we have been looking at are at some remove from this earliest stage, and the 'road', or 'the two roads', is a more restrained reshaping device than the heavy-handed Yahwistic reinterpretation which eventually asserted itself. Driver's discussion of *hōrētīkā* (v. 11) is of some significance in this connection (see below).

[10] The piece opens in the usual way with the teacher demanding from his pupil attentiveness and a willingness to appropriate his teaching, and describing the consequences of such disciplined assiduity – a long life (see on 3.16, pp. 295f., above). **[11f.]** Then in vv. 11f. the teacher gives additional reasons why his authority should be respected and his teaching followed, so that his imperatives may not be thought bare or arbitrary, and their beneficence may be made plain. 'I shall guide you in the way of wisdom, I shall lead you along straight tracks. When you walk, your stride will not be cramped, and when you run, you will not stumble.' **[13]** In v. 13 the opening appeal is supplemented: 'Take hold of Instruction (*mūsār*), do not relax your grip, mount a guard over her, for she is your life.' *mūsār* is elsewhere masculine, and the feminine suffix and pronoun suggest that the personified *mūsār* has been approximated to the personified *ḥokmā*. *mūsār* is not an option but a necessity of life, which is essential to survival and prosperity.

I take G. R. Driver's point (*VT* i, 1951, pp. 249f.) that there are two verbs *yrh* in Hebrew, the one cognate with Ethiopic *warawa*, 'throw', and the other with Accadian (*w*)*arū*, Ugaritic *yr*(*y*) 'go', and that *hōrētīkā* in v. 11 is to be derived from the latter. This, however, does not require the translation 'I have made you to walk', which is excessively literal and is not demanded by *hidrīk*, for it, too, indicates Yahweh's effective guidance which is the thought of the verse (cf. *hōlīk*, 'cause to go', 'guide', 'lead'). Driver has illustrated by means of a comparison of II Chron. 6.7 with I Kings 8.36 the transition from 'lead' to 'show'. 'Thou wilt lead them in the good way' (with *'ēl*). 'Thou wilt show them the good way' (direct object).

The implications of this for the meaning of *tōrā* are important and, so far as I know, they have not been drawn. The discussion of this word should be disengaged from the meaning 'throw' and attached to the meaning 'guide'. Hence, where the Instruction is presented as a way of life, it is admirably described as *tōrā*, and the word has appeared in such contexts (1.8; 3.1). If *miṣwā* is to be correlated with the imperious form of the Instruction and *mūsār* with its character as educational discipline, *tōrā* can be associated with the presentation of the Instruction as a way of life; it contains directions for the road of a mandatory kind, that is, directives.

[11f.] I am inclined to prefer 'straight tracks' to 'tracks of uprightness' in v. 11, because this accords better with v. 12, and the other rendering is too emphatically moralistic for the context. It would be possible to justify it by pointing to v. 14, where 'the path of wicked men' and 'the way of evil men' would supply the required antithesis. I am more impressed, however, by the natural and effective transition from straight or plain tracks in v. 11b, to the picture which is painted in v. 12. On a road which is well-defined and where the feet can be put down with assurance on a good surface, one can swing along with raking strides and progress is smooth and pleasurable. It is the cramped (*yēṣār*) stride necessitated by an irregular and treacherous surface which produces apprehensions and fatigue, and drains away from the wayfarer his sense of well-being. Those who pay heed to the teacher are on a road where they can walk rhythmically and even break into a run, without fear of being tripped up by unpredictable obstacles.

[14–17] There is another kind of road on which to venture is indiscipline, and neither desire nor distraction should be allowed to lure the wise man away from his dedicated progress along the way of life (see below on v. 25). He is not to make a bee-line (*tᵉ'aššēr*) for the road of evil men, and he must not even contemplate such a course. Let him dismiss it from his thoughts and as a single-minded man pursue his journey along a safe road (vv. 14f.), for there are those who have made wrong-doing and malevolence so much a part of their routine that they suffer from insomnia if a day passes free from their nefarious activities. In their addiction to evil, they are like the sleeping-pill addict who has been denied his daily dose. Wrong-doing, lawlessness and violence are their food and drink. This – an idiom which we possess – is the meaning of v. 17, and not just that they make their livelihood from crime. Not only do they live *by* these activities but they live *for* them – they nourish the very roots of their existence.

[18f.] To the discussion of vv. 18f. I bring the additions to v. 27 in LXX and also 3.32–35, in order to ventilate an issue which is nicely illustrated by the longer text of LXX at the end of ch. 4. These additions give reasons why the imperatives of v. 27 ('Do not deviate to right or left, keep your feet far from evil') should be attended to. This motivation is arranged in two lines, one with antithetic and the other with synthetic parallelism: 'For God knows the ways on the right, but the ways on the left are twisted. And he himself will make your paths straight and conduct your journeyings in peace.' Because they bring God into the argument for the first time in this chapter, and even more because their connection with the thought of v. 27 is defective, these two verses are suspect. In v. 27 (MT) it is undeviating progress along the one safe road which is enjoined as in vv. 14f., 25, and right and left are equally aberrant. In the additional motivation of LXX, the weight of the contrast falls on right and left, the one the direction of God's leading and the other the twisted, fatal road.

The purpose of these additions is probably (cf. Toy) to bring God into the argument and to make it explicit that it is he who leads men as a sure-footed guide and who smooths the track for them. The significance of the addition is that it furnishes *textual* grounds for supposing that motivation was used as an instrument of reinterpretation, and that this might conveniently be achieved at the end of a piece. Is then 3.32–35 the result of a similar process? The preceding verses (27–31) show the Instruction in its most incisive form with an almost staccato rhythm of imperatives. Then there is a striking change to diffuseness in vv. 32–35, and the first of these verses which purports to recommend the imperatives of v. 31 does not really serve this end. For v. 31 is directed against violence and lawlessness, while v. 32 contrasts straightness with crookedness, deviousness with candour, in a manner which recalls the opposition of right and left in the LXX additions to 4.27. The function of 3.32–35 could well be to stamp an unmistakable Yahwistic impress on vv. 27–31 by a process in which a rather heavy-handed explicitness takes precedence over a concern to preserve a high continuity or to display craftsmanship in devising an invisible seam. The emphasis is on Yahweh's curse and blessing, and those who are the recipients of the one or the other, righteous and wicked, arrogant and humble, wise and foolish.

The case of 4.18f. is more contentious, but again these verses are at the end of a section and represent a heavy underlining of the theme of the two ways rather than a precise continuation of the topic of vv. 14–17. The path of the righteous is a blazing light which increases in intensity until the day is full, but the way of the wicked is black as pitch and littered with obstacles which foul the feet. (In view of *we'ōraḥ* at the beginning of v. 18, the order of vv. 18 and 19 should perhaps be reversed, but I have not thought it necessary to do this.) There is no mention of Yahweh here, but the antithesis of *ṣaddīqīm* and *rešā'īm* is characteristic of Yahwistic piety (see on 2.1f., above, pp. 282f.). These verses may, therefore, owe their existence to the concern to make the message of the section loud and clear in Yahwistic terms. This opinion is reinforced by the circumstance that here again, as in 3.32–35, the argumentation at the end of the piece is more diffuse than elsewhere within it.

vv. 20–27 *The Mind is the Spring of Life*

[20–23] The heading is not intended to indicate a real change of subject as between vv. 10–19 and 20–27, which is still, in part, a description of the two ways (cf. vv. 25–27). The demand for attentiveness and retentiveness in vv. 20f. recalls 3.21, and the meaning which best suits *lēb* in v. 21 is 'mind' (so Toy) rather than 'heart', since it is concentration and tenacity of memory which are desiderated and recommended as a means to life and a therapy for the body (*bāśār*). The medical metaphor is comparable to 3.8 (see above, p. 293) and the emphasis falls (cf. 3.2, 4, 16f.) on longevity and physical and material well-being. These are important aspects of the 'wholeness' which characterizes the life of the man who keeps the words and sayings of the teacher. It is in the mind (*lēb*) that teaching is retained, revitalized and so assimilated that it belongs to a man as his inalienable possession. So the mind is a first charge on vigilance; it is the fountain-head from which issue vitalizing and fructifying springs.

[24] It is not certain that v. 24 is connected with the thought that the mind is the fountain-head of life, although it probably is. Such a thought is explicit in *Amenemope* (xiv.2f., *ANET*, p. 423): 'God hates him who falsifies words. His great abomination is the contentious of belly.' It is in the 'belly' (cf. Arabic *lubb*, Hebrew *lēb*, 'middle-part') that words are stored and it is from there that they issue. As a man speaks, so he is, and speech lacking in candour, so labyrinthine as to darken counsel, is evidence of polluted springs. Such a man is to be repulsed (cf. Gemser, who supposes that the metaphor reflects the care that was taken to guard the sources of water from pollution).

[25–27] The final verses resume the metaphor of the road with ideas which have already been utilized (see p. 308, above). Journey without deviation of feet and eyes, give your undivided attention to your road, and then all the ways in which you walk will be reliable. *ʿapʿappīm*, 'glances', gives better sense than 'eyelids'. KB² proposes it and cites Ugaritic *ʿpʿp*, which, however, Driver renders as 'eye-lid' (*Keret* I. vi.30, 34: *CML*, p. 142). I have taken *pallēs* to mean 'pay attention', 'scrutinize', associating it with Accadian *palāšu* (G. R. Driver, *JTS* xxxvi, 1935, pp. 150f.). Driver, whose discussion is centred on Ps. 58.3, accepts this meaning for all three occurrences of *pls* in Proverbs (4.27; 5.6, 21), following Haupt (p. 39), in A. Müller and E. Kautzsch (*SBOT* xv). KB² 'to level', 'to prepare', adduces Accadian *palāšu*, 'to bore through', but a reference to wakeful concentration accords better with the context.

Robert supposes (*RB* xliii, pp. 61f.) that the phrase, 'Do not deviate to right or left' (v. 27), is Deuteronomic and that the literary dependence of Proverbs on Deuteronomy is established in this particular. In the Deuteronomic passages cited (Deut. 5.32; 17.11; 28.14; Josh. 23.6) the verb is *sūr*, not *nṭh* as in Prov. 4.27, and the warnings relate to 'commandments', 'word', 'words', 'the book of the law of Moses'. This kind of general correspondence in language and idiom cannot do the work to which Robert puts it. It shows no more than that the authors of Deuteronomy and Proverbs wrote in the same language and sometimes used the same idioms. This section is compact Instruction, with the succession of imperatives broken only by the motive clause in v. 22 and the consequential clause in v. 26b.

Chapter 5

This is indubitably a specimen of the Instruction, and it does not deviate notably from the normal form. On the alternation of 'My son' (vv. 1, 20) and 'sons' (v. 7), I have nothing to add to my remarks on ch. 4 (above, pp. 303f.). The motivation of vv. 3–6 is a little out of the ordinary in that it introduces a topic which is not specifically mentioned by the preceding imperatives (v. 1), and so furnishes the first indication of what the theme of the chapter is to be. On the other hand, the two final clauses in v. 2 are more intrinsically connected with the general character of v. 1.

In vv. 7–14, the cautionary emphasis (*pēn*, vv. 9f.) is more marked than in the preceding chapters, but this is a feature of the Egyptian Instruction which has been noted (see above, pp. 111f.). After the initial imperatives (vv. 7f.), the pupils are warned of the consequences of disregarding the warning of their teacher and to bring the matter home as effectively as possible the caution is rounded off by reproducing the actual words of one who has realized his folly too late.

Verses 15–19 are a fairly compact series of imperatives and jussives without intervening argument, and v. 20 is a motive clause in the form of a question. It is possible that v. 16 should be similarly understood (so RSV, see below). The chapter concludes with motivation whose extent and content suggest that it may be secondary expansion (see below). The chapter is dominated by a single theme and it should not be supposed that the division into sections is anything more than a convenience. Certainly it should not be thought that 'My son' in v. 20 is an infallible indication of the beginning of a new 'Discourse' (Whybray, p. 48), and, if the element of reiteration is allowed for, v.7 need not be suspected on the ground that it breaks the continuity between vv. 4–6 and v. 8 (Whybray, p. 47, n.8).

The topic resembles that of ch. 2, and the point which I have made there will bear repetition. The warning against the seductive and alluring woman is a stock one in the international Instruction, and it is improbable that its appearance in the biblical book of Proverbs requires the specialized interpretation which Boström advances. Such an admonition as this has its occasion in universal conditions of human frailty, and what is envisaged here is the same vulnerability of young men to affairs with women as is touched on in the Egyptian Instruction, in the Babylonian *Counsels of Wisdom* and in *Ahikar*. It is a robust man-to-man warning against the consequences of liaisons with loose women. It is not pitched in a key of high-souled moral revulsion or pietism, but is rather a sober, earthy estimate of the disastrous results which flow from this particular manifestation of indiscipline. Ringgren's point that the *Counsels of Wisdom* has cultic prostitutes in mind does not have the weight which he supposes it to have. It would be necessary for him to show, if he were to win support for Boström's theory, that the *Counsels* have sacral prostitution in mind – sexual acts in a cultic context. It is certain, however, that the phrasing of the warnings excludes this interpretation. All that is envisaged is sexual intercourse with prostitutes, and the fact that different types of cultic prostitutes are mentioned shows no more than that many prostitutes in that particular society had learned their trade in the cult (*Word and Wisdom*, pp. 135f.).

The concept of *mūsār* which prevails in this chapter is that of the international Instruction and, apart from vv. 21–23, there are no traces of Yahwistic theological and moral categories. The reasoning which throws doubt on 3.32–35; 4.18f. and the additions to 4.27 in LXX (above, pp. 308f.) also applies to these verses. They are located at the end of a chapter and so in a place where reinterpretative expansion by means of motive clauses can be most conveniently made, and they introduce a Yahwistic note which is absent from the remainder of the chapter (contrary to Whybray, p. 48). Verses 21–23 present a concept of *mūsār* (v. 23) into which there enters a theology and moralism conspicuously absent from the remainder of the chapter. The man who dies through his indiscipline or is wrapped (*yišgeh*) (G. R. Driver, *Welt des Orients*, i, 1941, p. 410, 'is wrapped in his folly as a corpse in a winding-sheet') in the shroud of his massive folly is he who does not reckon with Yahweh's constant scrutiny of his ways, who becomes the prisoner of his iniquities and is entangled in the cords of his sin (the gloss *'et hārāšā'* confirms the tendency of this reinterpretation). Certainly the idea of the all-seeing God occurs in *Amenemope* (xvii.9–12) and in the *Šamaš Hymn* (*BWL*, pp. 121f.), but I am confident that this passage redefines *mūsār* and *'iwwelet* in Yahwistic terms.

Elsewhere in the chapter, respect for Yahweh and his infallible theodicy does not enter into the concept of *mūsār* which, together with other occurrences of the vocabulary of old wisdom (*tōkaḥat*, *tᵉbūnā* and *mᵉzimmā*), are set in a strictly educational context. There it is the authority of which the teacher is an accredited representative and a living exponent which matters. He brings to his teaching an accumulated wealth of empirical sagacity, and he expects his pupils to acknowledge the authoritative character of his teaching and to give him their undivided attention and concentration. He reiterates this claim: 'My son, attend to my wisdom, give heed to my discernment, that you may keep confidences, and your lips may guard knowledge' (v. 1). *lišmōr mᵉzimmōt*, 'that you may keep plans (secret)', is a reference to the cultivation of taciturnity on which the Egyptian Instruction places great store. The educated man keeps a tight rein on his tongue and cultivates disciplined, measured utterance. The verse could, however, be understood as a demand for an exact and retentive memory, in which case the *mᵉzimmōt* would be the shrewd and discriminating *dicta* of the teacher ('that you may have regard to what is discreet'), but the second half of the line is more resistant to this interpretation than to the other. 'And your lips may guard knowledge' would then have to mean 'that you may have something knowledgeable to say' – a store of knowledge to which you can give articulate expression when the occasion arises – but this is somewhat forced. At any rate, there is no need to emend the verse, unless the metrical reasons adduced are thought to be compelling (cf. Gemser: 'that discretion may watch over you and the knowledge of my lips guard you', pointing the contrast between the lips of the teacher and those of the *'iššā zārā*. BH: 'that discretion and knowledge may keep you, may guard you from the lips of the foreign woman').

Again the personal authority of the teacher is asserted in v. 7: 'Now, my sons, listen to me and do not deviate from my sayings'. Finally (vv. 13–14) there is the lament of the youth who is ruined through his sexual indiscipline and regrets his aversion to *mūsār* and his contemning of reproof (*tōkaḥat*). 'I did not listen to the voice of my teachers (*mōrāy*), nor did I give heed to my instructors' (*m^elamm^eday*).

VV. 1–14 *Beware of the Seductress!*

[1–5] The *zārā* (see above on ch. 2) is at first sweeter than honey, but the final taste of her is more bitter than wormwood (the leaves and buds of the plant family *Artemesia*). She speaks in accents which ooze seductive charm, and her voice, which is smoother than oil, draws her victim irresistibly towards mystery, excitement and delight. In v. 4, *'aḥ^arītā* is not 'her latter end', i.e., what eventually becomes of a prostitute, but her final effect on the man who has an affair with her. The *'iššā zārā* is like granite – beautiful, hard, shiny and unimpressionable, for in her profession survival is only possible if in her relations with men all the ingredients of a genuine human relationship are systematically excluded. Her client consequently need not expect understanding or compassion when he finds himself in deep trouble, neither has he any right to expect such consideration. He has used her ruthlessly and he will be cut to pieces by the sharp edge of her cruelty (perhaps *pīpīyōt*, a reduplicated form of *pī* should be read; so BH and KB[2]).

[6] The route followed by this woman leads to death and Sheol (for the elucidation of this metaphor see 2.18f., above, pp. 287f.); she has no regard for (reading *bal* or *lō'* with the versions for *pen*) the path of life, her tracks are unsteady, she lacks tranquillity.

This paraphrase of v. 6 assumes the correctness of Winton Thomas's derivation of *tēdaʿ* from a root cognate with Arabic *wdʿ*. The *'iššā zārā* leads a feverish, tempestuous existence; she gads about unpredictably; she lives in the way a drunken driver steers his car; she is not tranquil – in Job 20.20 *ydʿ* is glossed by *šālēw* (D. W. Thomas, *JTS* xxxvii, 1936, pp. 59f.; xxxvi, 1935, p. 411). On *pls*, 'scrutinize', see 4.26, above, p. 311.

On the other hand, if the verbs in v. 6 are construed as second person sing. masc. (so Gemser; Ringgren; Boström, p. 138) or if a mixture of third sing. fem. and second sing. masc. is supposed, the verse will have a different meaning. Thus Gemser, Ringgren and Boström: 'You do not recognize the path of life; her tracks are unstable and you do not know it.' Ringgren offers as a variant of this: 'her tracks are unstable without her being aware of it' (taking *tēdaʿ* as third fem. sing., *Word and Wisdom*, p. 105). But vv. 4f. are certainly descriptions of the woman, and this is what we anticipate in v. 6 and what we get in at least one phrase ('her tracks waver'). In view of this, it is reasonable to conclude that the other verbs in v. 6 also refer to the woman, i.e., are third fem. sing.

[7–13] Since this woman is dangerous, she is to be given a wide berth, and an important part of prudent behaviour in relation to her is not to place oneself in circumstances where exposure to her charms may have fatal consequences. 'Do not come up to the door of her house' (v. 8). If the young man disregards this advice and is caught in her web, he will be the loser in every sense and will be reduced ultimately to exhaustion and ruin (vv. 9–11). Stated in these general terms the meaning is clear enough, but a more detailed examination of these verses discloses differences of opinion and difficulties of interpretation. When it is assumed that the woman is married (Gemser, Ringgren), the reference is thought to be to damages which will have to be paid to the husband for alienating the affections of his wife and rupturing the sanctity of his marriage. Coupled with this is the thought that it is an expensive business to keep a mistress, and that there comes a day of reckoning when a man is dunned by his creditors to meet the cost of his extravagances.

These ideas, however, are not particularly prominent in vv. 9–11, although the thought of folly leading to penury can be detected in v. 10, and there may be some support for the hypothesis of an injured husband in v. 14. If the readings of Pesh. and Targ. are attended to (*hēlekā*), loss of wealth is also the subject of v. 9a, whereas LXX supplies an exact parallel to v. 9b (*ζωήν σου; σὸν βίον*). There is no reason to suppose that the versions are superior to MT, whose parallelism is made more precise if Hebrew *šnh* is associated with Arabic *saniya* and translated 'dignity' (pointed *šenātekā* from *šānā*): 'Lest thou give thine honour unto others and thy dignity unto the cruel' (D. W. Thomas, *ZAW* 55, 1937, pp. 174f.; G. R. Driver *ET* xlix, 1938, p. 38). The plural *'akzārīm* should perhaps be read (so Winton Thomas, who suggests that it is a reference to the harlot and her associates). The appearance of *nokrī* in v. 10 lends some support to the reading of Targ. in v. 9 (*lenokrīm*), but not enough to warrant its adoption. Snijders (p. 93) retains the singular *'akzārī* and translates *šenōtekā* 'thy years'. To give one's years to a merciless one probably means 'to an illness or to death'. I follow Winton Thomas and conclude that the verse does not deal with loss of wealth (so Toy) but loss of dignity.

This accords with Boström's view only in that whereas Winton Thomas thinks of this loss of dignity as a departure from 'that exalted condition of mankind which the sages visualized as the ideal', Boström supposes that it is brought about precisely by sexual intercourse with a foreign woman. The Israelite male should not scatter his semen and dissipate his virility. The situation is similar to that of Ecclus. 26.19, where the young man is admonished to keep the bloom of his ancestors intact and not to give his power to foreigners. The possibility that *'akzārī* is to be connected with the name of a special class of Ishtar prostitute (*kizritu*) should not be rejected out of hand, nor, alternatively, should the suggestion that 'the cruel one' may be Ishtar herself (see on 2.16f., above, pp. 284f.; Boström, pp. 137f.).

But if this is *precisely* what is intended, why the consistent series of masculines in vv. 9f. (*'akzārī* or *'akzārīm*, *zārīm*, *nokrī*)? It may be said that the masculine plurals refer to the harlot and her associates, but, if this is so, it is not possible to find a more exact meaning for the two verses than that an entanglement with this woman will result in a loss of dignity, a waste of energy and the squandering of hard-earned wealth. Nevertheless, it is in 'the house of a foreigner' that this is to take place, and this phrase in v. 10 does lend support to Boström's contention that the *'iššā zārā* is a foreigner (cf. *nokrīyā* in v. 20 and see 2.16f., above, pp. 284f.). Indeed, I have no quarrel with Boström's opinion that the thought of exaction by husband or lover does not enter into v. 10, the idea of which is simply that the hard-earned wealth of an Israelite passes into foreign hands. Verse 11 should then be translated: 'And so you will cry out in anguish when your end comes, when body and flesh are consumed'. *nhm* signifies 'to roar' or 'growl' (of an animal), and, since this roaring may be caused by hunger, there is the derived meaning 'to desire strongly', 'to yearn' (Arabic *nahmatu*(*n*) 'insatiable desire', 'need', 'want'; G. R. Driver, *JTS* xxxv, 1934, pp. 386f.). What is envisaged is an extremity of destitution and exhaustion which evokes an elemental, animal cry of anguish. LXX and Pesh. read: 'And you will repent (*w^e^niḥamtā*) when your end comes.'

[14] Gemser (also Ringgren) supposes that v. 14 refers to legal proceedings and public punishment, which he suggests would take the form of scourging, since the absence of any mention of stoning by the entire community is to be explained by the circumstance that it had gone out of use as a penalty for adultery (cf. Deut. 22.22f.; Lev. 20.10) by the period to which the piece belongs. Boström suggests that the penalty almost incurred may have been excommunication or confiscation of property (cf. Pss. Sol. 16.13f.), although it is not necessary to conclude from the phrasing of the verse ('I was almost involved in total ruin before assembly and congregation') that the proceedings had a strictly legal character. Hence it may simply refer to the contempt to which such a man is exposed – to loss of reputation and public denunciation (Boström, p. 140). Boström cites Ben Sira 42.11, where *'ēdā* occurs in connection with public gossip, scandal and ridicule which focuses on a man whose daughter gets out of hand (Israel Lévi, *The Hebrew Text of the Book of Ecclesiasticus*, Semitic Study Series, no. III, 1904). The verse is formulated so generally that it is impossible to say precisely what it has in mind, and so it is not clear that *qāhāl* and *'ēdā* are sufficiently specialized to afford an indication of a late date (cf. Whybray, p. 48). For those who assume that there is an injured husband in the offing, the verse can be associated with his denunciation of the adulterer in the presence of the community and the establishing of his claim for heavy damages.

VV. 15–20 *Love your Wife with all your Heart*

In my treatment of *Onchsheshonqy* (see above, pp. 146f.), I observed that where imaginative language is used to convey directives, this constitutes an exception to the rule, for the imperatives in the Instruction are usually associated with a plain, unvarnished mode of communication. Imagery creates more exalted forms of expression; its felicitous use is an important aspect of literary art and it challenges and excites the reader. The Instruction, however, does not aspire to be literature and it sacrifices imaginative outreach to pedestrian clarity. Imagery brings with it problems of interpretation, obscurity and ambiguity, and the concern of the Instruction is above all to be clear and to leave nothing to chance or doubt. The verses before us constitute another exception to this rule, and it is, in a way, a confirmation of the point which I have been making that their interpretation has given much trouble to commentators.

[15] There is nothing contentious about v. 15: 'Drink water from your own cistern, the streams which flow from your own well' means 'Have sexual intercourse only with your wife'. **[16]** In v. 16, if LXX^B is followed (*μὴ*), the translation is either: (*a*) 'lest (inserting *pen*) your springs be dispersed outside, channels of water in the streets' (Gemser), or (*b*): 'Let not (inserting *'al*) your springs be dispersed outside, channels of water in the street.' If MT is read, the translation is either: (*a*) 'Should your springs be dispersed outside, channels of water in the streets?' (Toy), or (*b*): '(and so) your springs will be dispersed outside, channels of water in the streets' (Snijders, Ringgren). 'The cistern is for collecting rain water, and the overflow from the well, which may be fed by underground springs like the one at Sychar, must be stored in a cistern and not allowed to run to waste in the streets' (E.F.F.B.).

Snijders (p. 93, also Ringgren and Jones) supposes that the imagery of v. 16 refers to the blessing of numerous progeny which will be given to the man who reserves all his virility for his wife. The overflowing of the wells represents the gift of abundant posterity. This, in my view, is improbable, for whatever guidance the passage as a whole gives on the meaning of v. 16 runs counter to this interpretation and suggests that the dissemination of the springs outside in the streets is something to be avoided (see E.F.F.B. above); this is what is indicated by the other translations. **[17]** On the other hand Snijders' understanding of v. 17, namely, that intercourse with an *'iššā zārā* is a waste of semen, since it is the fathering of children for a strange household and a consequent neglect of the building up of one's own house and posterity, is the correct one (see below).

In v. 15 the singulars *bōr* and *b^e'ēr* are symbols for the wife and it might be supposed that she remains the subject in vv. 16–17 and that these verses contemplate retaliatory promiscuity on her part. A stumbling-block to this interpretation, as Boström has pointed out (p. 140), is the plural *ma'yānōt*, for it is difficult to understand why the wife should be symbolized by singulars in v. 15 and a plural in v.

16. Gemser suggests that the basis for this metaphor is the fact that if a man does not utilize his domestic water supply, the wells will overflow and the water will go to waste. Should this indeed be the picture it would not symbolize the unfaithfulness of the wife, but simply the failure of the husband to cultivate her fertility and the wastefulness consequent on his neglect. Toy explains the transition from singular to plural by supposing that well and cistern represent sexual intercourse with one's wife in a domestic setting, whereas springs and channels of water stand for extra-marital sexual pleasures outside the domestic context. But v. 17 is hardly consonant with this symbolism, for, if springs and channels of water had this precise reference, it could not then be said: 'Let them be for yourself alone and not for strangers with you.' Boström equates the springs and channels of water with the male sperms, and this seems to be the best solution, agreeable as it is to the plural forms and to v. 17. It is the male semen which constitutes the 'springs' and 'channels of water', and this should be used exclusively to beget numerous children within the context of marriage and the home. The same thought finds expression in Ecclus. 26.19–21:

My son, keep sound the bloom of your youth,
And do not give your strength to strangers.
Seek a fertile field within the whole plain,
And sow it with your seed, trusting in your fine stock.
So your offspring will survive,
And, having confidence in their good descent, will grow great (RSV).

[18f.] Verse 18 is then a reiteration of the foregoing theme and v. 19 a description of the wife's graces, followed by a recommendation to be satisfied with her to the exclusion of all other women. 'Let your fountain be blessed' (v. 18a) has in mind the blessing of the wife who bears many children, and is superior to LXX, 'Let your fountain be for yourself alone'. The wife is a beloved hind, a graceful doe and so it is urged: 'Let her be your companion (LXX), let her breasts satisfy you continually; in her love you are to be enfolded always' (or, 'with her love you are to be intoxicated always'). The effect of the LXX addition is to produce two couplets, but I retain the tristich of MT. **[20]** On *tišgeh̲* see v. 23 (above, p. 313), where I have followed G. R. Driver's suggestion. This is particularly apt in v. 20: 'My son, why are you wrapped (in the embrace) of a stranger and clasp the bosom of a foreigner.' Nevertheless, in these three verses (19, 20, 23) 'to be intoxicated with', 'to be infatuated with' is a translation of *šgh*, which gives good sense. **[21–23]** (On vv. 21–23, see above, p. 313f.)

Chapter 6

That 6.1–19 is a later insertion cannot really be shown by the argument that in its absence there would be a thematic continuity between 5.23 and 6.20 (cf. Gemser), for the *'iššā zārā* is a recurrent subject in chs. 1–9 (2, 5, 6, 7, 9), and if it can be reintroduced after interruptions in these other places, there is not a strong case for demanding continuity between 5.23 and 6.20.

Yet in this section there is material which is formally different from anything in the earlier chapters and which, because it lacks imperatives, is certainly not Instruction. This is true of vv. 12–15, which describe a particular type of malevolence, and of vv. 16–19, an example of a graded numerical saying (W. M. W. Roth, *Numerical Sayings in the Old Testament*, *VTS* xiii, 1965, p. 86; see below, pp. 654f.).

The remove from the Instruction is less clear in vv. 6–11, which are introduced by an imperative, although here again the form is hardly consistent with either parental or scholastic instruction, for there is a significant difference between a 'My son' address, which warns against sloth, and an 'O sluggard' address, which is directed against one confirmed in habits of slothfulness. It is difficult to believe that this would be a normal presupposition in either parental or scholastic instruction. Then again, the element of command is minimal in this section. It is possible that the question addressed to the sluggard in v. 9 should be regarded as functionally akin to the imperative in v. 6, and that vv. 10f. are related to v. 9 as supporting argument in the same way as vv. 7f. are to v. 6.

The opening verses (vv. 1–5) are emphatically Instruction and are dominated by imperatives. The only new formal feature in them deserving of comment is the series of conditional clauses preceding the initial imperative and defining the circumstances in which the imperatives are to be heeded, but this is well-established in the Egyptian Instruction (see above, p. 76). There is a long addition to v. 8 in LXX and a shorter one to v. 11. Toy describes the passage on the bee (the addition to v. 8) as the creation of a Greek scribe, and Gerleman (*Lunds Universitets Årsskrift*, N.F., Avd. 1, Bd. 52, Nr. 3, 1956, pp. 30f.) argues that the passage is dependent on Aristotle. He remarks that elsewhere in the Old Testament the bee is described as a menace, while here and in Aristotle its usefulness and beneficence are praised. Moreover, Aristotle deals with the bee in his *Natural History* immediately after the ant (Prov. 6.6–8), and he uses ἐργασία and ἐργάτις in his account of it as does LXX.

The closing section (vv. 20–35) is a unity and is Instruction, with two groups of four and two imperatives respectively (20f., 25), and the rest (22f., 26–35), with the exception of v. 24, which is a final clause, extended motivation. The division of the section into two parts, proposed by Boström (see below), is unnatural and forced.

vv. 1–5 *Against going Surety*

[1] Since *ʿrb* in the sense of 'going surety for' someone usually takes the accusative, the construction with *lᵉ* is an initial difficulty in v. 1, associated with which is the question whether *zār* is intended as an exact parallel of *rēaʿ*. That some difficulty was felt in respect of this second point by LXX is suggested by the reading 'enemy' in v. 1b, for a neighbour can be an enemy, but hardly a stranger. G. R. Driver (*Biblica* 35, 1954, pp. 148f.) observes that LXX ἐχθρός is a wrong rendering of *zār*, but he argues that it proves the currency of the meaning 'enemy' for *zār*, cognate with Accadian and Arabic *zāʾiru*. This is the difficulty which Snijders meets with his theory that *zār* means 'outsider' (i.e., one who is alienated from the normal social life of the community), and not 'stranger' or 'foreigner' (pp. 82–84). On this view, *rēaʿ* and *zār* are synonymous, and the warning is against striking hands on behalf of a neighbour who is disorientated with respect to his own community and is a social misfit. One must not engage in the symbolic ceremony which indicates acceptance of financial responsibility for such an individual. Consequently, in the background of the verse there is a third party (cf. Snijders), who is the creditor of the *rēaʿ* or *zār*, and who is the person envisaged in the ceremony of striking hands (Ringgren follows Snijders).

A feature common to Boström and Snijders is that both of them approach the verse not so much for its own sake as in order to find support for their respective theories. Snijders finds in it a confirmation that *zār* does not mean foreigner, and Boström a confirmation that it does. In addition, Boström maintains that *ʿrb lᵉ* means 'giving surety to' and not 'going surety for', and that consequently the *rēaʿ* and the *zār* are different persons, the one the creditor and the other the debtor. 'My son, if you have given surety to your neighbour, and struck hands for a stranger' (i.e., in the stead of a stranger). The assumption that the neighbour is the creditor agrees well with v. 3b, 'for you have come into the power of your neighbour' (with word play on *kap*, cf. v. 1b), which refers to the process of being dunned by the neighbour as a consequence of the defaulting of the foreigner on his financial obligations (Boström, pp. 101f.). Boström's translation assumes a different force of *l^e^* in v. 1a (where it is used with a dative) as compared with v. 1b (where it means 'in place of'). This is not a decisive objection, although it is unexpected in relation to the parallelism.

Boström argues that this verse is not simply expressive of eudaimonism, or hard-headed wisdom, and that it requires a more particular elucidation. He observes that Proverbs and Ben Sira are not insensitive to the need for compassion and neighbourliness, and that more is involved here than prudence and canniness. The verse is to be connected with the antipathy of the wise men to trade and commerce and their idealization of agriculture as the proper outlet for diligence and skill, in which simplicity and dignity are joined together and where no truck is had with the devious and doubtful transactions of commerce (pp. 53f.).

This is, then, a warning not to become involved in the complicated credit arrangements of commerce and, perhaps (so Ringgren), not to get mixed up with the money-lender who, in this case, is to be identified with the *rēaʿ*. **[2]** To give an undertaking to a money-lender in respect of credit which he has made available to a foreigner is to walk into a self-constructed trap (v. 2). It is the thought of being caught in the tentacles of a money-lender, not in respect of personal borrowing, but through having gone surety for a foreigner, which lends urgency to the advice in vv. 3–5. **[3–5]** For this is like being caught in a marsh, and unless rescue is immediately effected the victim will sink deeper and deeper into the mire and eventually go under. Verse 3c reinforces the appeal for decisiveness and speed in renouncing the contract, whatever may be the precise meaning of *hitrappēs*. G. R. Driver (*JTS* xxx, 1929, pp. 374f.) derives it from Accadian *rapāsu*, 'to trample', Arabic *rafasa*, 'to kick' (cf. Hebrew *rpś*, qal, 'to stamp with the feet'). Driver suggests the semantic development 'to trample on oneself'>'to weary oneself', i.e., to be unremitting in one's efforts to dissolve the contract (cf. Gemser, Ringgren, 'without delay'). 'To trample on oneself' might mean rather 'to swallow one's pride' (so BDB); 'Go, swallow your pride and importune (lit. 'assault') your neighbour' would mean: 'Throw your self-esteem to the winds, and use all your powers of persuasiveness in order to lay siege to him and overcome his resistance to releasing you from your undertaking.' KB² (following LXX μὴ ἐκλυόμενος) emends to *wᵉ'al titrappeh*, 'do not be slack', i.e., do not be indecisive, do not leave things as they are. The suggestion that *'ēpō* is an abbreviation for *'ᵃšer 'ēlekā pāqadtī* is ingenious but improbable (Gemser/Driver, p. 111). It is possible that this was how the Greek translator *(ἃ ἐγώ σοι ἐντέλλομαι)* understood *'ēpō*.

In v. 5, the emendation of *yād* to *ṣayyād*, 'hunter', is a smaller alteration than *māṣōd*, 'net' (cf. LXX ἐκ βρόχων, 'from meshes [of the net]'). The man who has given a bond for a foreigner is to make good his escape as a gazelle would from a hunter or a bird from a fowler (LXX, Pesh., Targ., 'a bird from a snare'; some Hebrew manuscripts, 'bird from the snare of a fowler', perhaps a conflation of MT and LXX). His situation is so urgent and full of danger that his mind should be filled only with thoughts of escape, so that relaxation and sleep are out of the question (vv. 4f.).

vv. 6–11 *The Sluggard and the Ant*

[6–8] The ant is held up as a model of self-discipline and systematic industry in a manner which bears some resemblance to the procedures of the fable. In the proverb considered above (p. 207), another aspect of the ant's behaviour – the power of effective retaliation – was the point at issue. In erecting this insect into a paradigm of discipline and prudence, a blind eye is necessarily turned to its destructive effects. These were described by Thomson in a passage of great literary merit (W. M. Thomson, *The Land and the Book*, 1860, p. 509):

> Ants pilfer from the floor and the granary – they are the greatest robbers in the land. Leave a bushel of wheat in the vicinity of one of their subterranean cities and in a surprisingly short time the whole commonwealth will be summoned to plunder. A broad, black column stretches from the wheat to their hole and you are startled by the result. As if by magic, every grain seems to be accommodated with legs and walks off in a hurry along the moving column (cf. pp. 336f.).

In the fable, human behaviour is attributed to plants and animals and a situation is contrived which throws some light on human behaviour and relationships, or which constitutes a comment, perhaps satirical, on human institutions. The use of the ant as a paradigm in this passage is less artful and more heavily didactic than fable, and there is no metamorphosis of the insect. What is in view is the ant *qua* ant, whose habits are analogous to those of the disciplined, methodical and diligent man. Similarly, the bee in the longer text of LXX in v. 8 is exhibited as a model of conscientiousness and industry, which supplies a valuable and healthful product and obtains distinction through its wisdom, despite physical insignificance. Hence the bee supplies food for thought as well as honey, and men may learn from it how to overcome physical handicaps by putting their brains to work, so as to become masters of their environment and to harness their world to useful and beneficial ends.

KB² connects *'āg^erā* (v. 8) with Arabic *'ajira*. This is a puzzling equation which is not repeated in KB³. *'gr* occurs in post-biblical Hebrew with the sense which is required here, 'to store up', but its derivation needs further elucidation. It is probably not to be distinguished from *'gr* 'to rent', 'to hire', although a distinction is made by KB³. Rent is 'collected' as a recompense for a service which has been provided – use of land or property – and the grain which is stored in a granary is the reward of foresight and industry. Both are a 'yield' (cf. W. von Soden, *Akkadisches Handwörterbuch*, *s.v. agāru*; Accadian *igru(m)*; Syriac *'agrā*, 'fee', 'payment'; and *'^agōrat kesep*, 'money payment', in I Sam. 2.36).

[9–11] Drowsiness is the natural ally of sloth, and the lazy man is without the alertness and foresight by which he might anticipate difficulties ahead and make provision against them. Because he is so sleepy-headed he has no defences against the onset of poverty and privation; he eats and sleeps from day to day, and when he is not unconscious he lives in a no-man's land between sleep and waking life, his intelligence drugged by somnolence. The simile in v. 11 is transparent, despite the uncertainty which attaches to the meaning of *māgēn*. The translation of Toy, Ringgren and RSV, 'armed man', connects it with *māgēn* 'shield', while G. R. Driver derives it from Arabic *mājin* 'bold', 'insolent' (*JTS* xxxiii, 1932, p. 44; xxxiv, 1933, pp. 383f.). Albright (*VTS* iii, pp. 9f.) connects it with Ugaritic *mgn* 'to beg, intreat' (cf. G. R. Driver, *CML*, p. 160) and points either *mōgēn* or *maggān*, 'beggar' (so Gemser). *m^ehallēk* has the pejorative nuance of 'vagrant' (Driver, 'footpad'), or of the word 'tinker', which on the lips of a farmer in Scotland is often associated with a possible threat to property. Whether *māgēn* is translated 'beggar' or 'insolent man', the parallelism is in either case satisfactory, although 'beggar' has the edge in aptness. We are to think of the jolly beggar who manipulates his victims with an engaging rascality, unhindered by any vestige of compunction or scruple. The text of LXX in v. 11 is inferior to MT. The aptness of comparing need to a 'good courier' (apparently the rendering of *māgēn*) is not at all apparent, and the additional element in LXX is inept, containing as it does two similes of more than dubious felicity – harvest is like a fountain and need like an evil courier: 'If you are diligent, your harvest will come like a fountain and want will depart like an evil courier.'

vv. 12–15 *The Mischief-Maker*

[12–15] G. R. Driver has pointed out the improbability of the analysis of *bly'l* (v. 12) into the elements *b^e^lī ya'al*, 'unprofitable', 'useless', 'worthless', and has posited a form *b^e^lā'al* on the analogy of *'^a^rāpēl* or *b^e^lī'al*, from *bl'* (Arabic *balaġa*, 'slandered') with a suffixed element (cf. *karmel*), meaning 'confusion' (*ZAW* 52, 1934, pp. 52f.; cf. KB², *s.v. bly'l*). D. Winton Thomas, *Biblical and Patristic Studies* (1963), pp. 18f., reviews all the explanations of *b^e^līya'al* that have been offered. He accepts Driver's explanation of the morphology, but derives from *bl'* 'swallow' (cf. A. Guillaume, *JTS* xiii, 1962, p. 321). The *'īš b^e^līya'al* is one whose actions or words engulf a man. *b^e^līya'al* has superlative force and the phrase *'īš b^e^līya'al* is perhaps colloquial, like English 'infernal fellow'. Certainly the person described in vv. 12–15 is confused; the springs of his conduct are polluted and his speech is perverted or twisted (*'iqq^e^šūt peh*, v. 12). He is a model of malevolence, and all his energies are bent to destructive and divisive ends. All that he says and does is informed by a spirit of evil (*'āwen*, v. 12), and a deep-seated moral perversion (*tahpūkōt*). His wrong-headedness is expressed not only in diseased speech, but in a sinister sign language – he winks with his eye, draws patterns with his feet and points with his fingers. There may be a reference here to the anti-social practice of magic, and *ḥōrēš* in v. 14 (whether or not *rā'* is deleted) may mean not simply 'to engineer' or 'to devise', but 'to devise magic' (cf. *ḥ^a^kam ḥ^a^rāšīm* in Isa. 3.3). Elsewhere (Job 4.8), *ḥrš* is used with *'āwen*, which, in Mowinckel's opinion, has associations with the sphere of anti-social magic (*Psalms in Israel's Worship*, 1962, i, pp. 199f.). E. Dhorme (*A Commentary on the Book of Job*, 1967, p. cxxxi) translates *ḥrš* 'cultivate'.

The metaphor is then based on farming and not on craftsmanship (see on 3.29, above, p. 300). *midyānīm* (Q.) is legal vocabulary and may refer here (v. 14) to litigation. An aspect of his expertise as trouble-maker and agitator is his capacity to initiate the alienation and misunderstanding between man and man which comes to a head in litigation. Such a person will be overtaken suddenly by calamity and will be shattered irremediably (see on 1.19, above, p. 271).

vv. 16–19 *Anti-social Behaviour*

[16–19] The form of this is different from that of the preceding section (on *tō'ᵃbat YHWH* see the discussion on 3.32, above, pp. 300f.), but the kinds of behaviour censured in both have much in common, and the vocabulary which has been reviewed in connection with vv. 12–15 recurs in vv. 16–19 (*ḥōrēš, mᵉdānīm*). The types of behaviour under consideration have this in common, that they are all disruptive in their tendency, that they are characterized by self-assertiveness or malice or violence, and that they break the bond of confidence and loyalty between man and man. Whether it be in the abuse of inventiveness for evil ends, or in the contempt for law and the rights of others, or in lying (particularly perjury), these are men who employ their talents in order to destroy the basis of common life. What is described is a deep-seated corruption of motives which gives rise to a constant and dedicated malevolence tantamount to a total incapacity for neighbourliness. When such chronic bad will is allied to resourcefulness, thoroughness and deceit, it assumes its most dangerous shape and wreaks havoc in a community. Once again it may be specifically litigation (cf. vv. 12–15), which is envisaged as the typical outcome of the malign activities of the mischief-maker who sows the seeds of discord systematically and observes with satisfaction the widening of the gulf between man and man, the hardening of attitudes, the refusal to be reconciled, and the bitterness of legal strife which brings about a settlement of a kind, but which also may make alienation irrevocable. For the pointing *yᵉpīaḥ kᵉzābīm* (v. 19) see on 12.17 and 14.5 (below, pp. 445, 469).

vv. 20–35 *Warnings against Adultery*

[20–22] In the opening verses which form the general introduction to this section the question of literary dependence is worth raising, since vv. 21f. are most reasonably explained as a free adaptation of

Deut. 6.7 or 11.19 – the order is that of 11.19 and not 6.7. These Deuteronomic passages are set in a context of parental instruction, and it is possible that they may have had some influence on the form of v. 20, which *prima facie* is parental and not scholastic instruction. 'My son, keep your father's commandments, and do not neglect your mother's teaching.' (See, however, on 1.8, above, p. 268, and 4.3, above, p. 303). Both Gemser and Ringgren maintain that the context is scholastic. The metaphor of binding is a new one as compared with Deuteronomy. It is not a binding of the commandments as a sign upon the hand; rather, they rest on the heart like a costly locket or signet ring which hangs on a necklace. The commandments should be valued and guarded like the most highly prized personal treasure which a man possesses (cf. 3.3, above, pp. 290f.). The accompanying instructions amplify those of Deuteronomy, except that there is no reference to sitting in the house (cf. 3.24, above, p. 298). The other occasions which are simply mentioned in Deuteronomy as affording opportunity for parental instruction are each connected in Proverbs with a particular function of the commandments. It is doubtful whether a full personification of the commandments is intended here (so Gemser; cf. Toy, fem. sing. in v. 22 translated 'she' = Wisdom), although they are said to guide the person who is abroad, to guard him who sleeps and to converse with him who has awakened from sleep. If the final phrase is an addition (cf. BH), the motive was perhaps to approximate the verse more closely to the Deuteronomic passages.

[23f.] In v. 23, where the role of *miṣwā* and *tōrā* is further described with reference to the preceding verses, it looks as if figures of speech which are redolent of the piety inspired by the Law have been imported into the Instruction. In a psalm written in praise of the Law, Yahweh's words are described as a lamp (*nēr*) to the feet and a light (*'ōr*) to the path (Ps. 119.105; G. Vermes, *VT* viii, 1958, pp. 436f.). I have pointed out, however (see on 4.11–12, above, pp. 307f.), that *miṣwā* and *tōrā* belong to both Law and Wisdom, while *tōkᵉḥōt mūsār*, 'corrective discipline' (literally, 'reproofs of discipline'), is a concept of educational discipline which is native to the Instruction, so that, even if the two metaphors are borrowed from the milieu of legal piety, this verse formally (motive clause) and materially has firm associations with old wisdom. ἔλεγχος καὶ παιδεία (v. 23 LXX; similarly Pesh. and Targ.) is an attempt to render the difficult *tōkᵉḥōt mūsār*, and should not be taken as evidence that *tōkaḥat* *ūmūsār* was read (BH). I am not therefore disposed to follow Whybray (p. 49), who argues that v. 23 should be deleted, that v. 23a is a gloss on v. 20 and that *miṣwā* and *tōrā* are equated with the word of Yahweh in v. 23 as they are in Ps. 119.105, whereas they refer to the words of the wisdom teacher in v. 20. Whybray therefore supposes that v. 23 exemplifies the same dominance of Jewish legal orthodoxy as appears in Ps. 119. This is a possible interpretation; it lays great weight on the appearance of *nēr* and *'ōr*, whereas I have suggested that their significance is more limited. If this were intended to have been so thoroughgoing a piece of Yahwistic reinterpretation as Whybray submits, it is a little surprising that it was not carried through more explicitly – by introducing the name of Yahweh in a passage where it is otherwise absent. One may say that the virtues ascribed to the quasi-personified *miṣwā* or *tōrā* in vv. 20–22 are summed up in the statement of v. 23: 'For commandments are a lamp and teaching a light, and corrective discipline a way of life.'

Boström (pp. 143f.) argues that vv. 20–35 are not a unity, since the woman alluded to in vv. 20–26 is distinct from the neighbour's wife who is the subject of vv. 27–35 (cf. Whybray, p. 49, who urges on similar grounds that there is a discontinuity between these two sections). Boström identifies the *'ēšet rā'* or *nokrīyā* of v. 24 with the *'iššā zārā* or *nokrīyā* of chs. 2 and 5, whereas he maintains that the case which is dealt with in vv. 27–35 (adultery with a neighbour's wife) is quite distinct. The arguments which he adduces are these:

1. The emendation of *'ēšet rā'* (v. 24) to *'ēšet rēa'* (with LXX) which would link v. 24 with v. 29 is inadmissible, since the expression would have to be *'ēšet rē'ᵃkā*.

2. The phrase 'wife of your neighbour' does not occur in chs. 2, 5 and 7, and its absence from these contexts is inconceivable if it is a synonym of *'iššā zārā*. Again, the verb *n'p*, 'to commit adultery', does not occur in the other *'iššā zārā* passages.

3. The warning is differently grounded in 6.27–35, where the wrath of the injured husband is the most pressing danger. In the sections on the *'iššā zārā*, the thought of loss of property occurs only once (5.10b), while the danger constituted by an injured husband plays no part. The peril of the foreign woman is differently defined – her ways lead to Sheol – and this difference is connected with the circumstance that as soon as she is the topic the reference is to participation in a strange cult.

4. The passages on the foreign woman are in the second person, so that they have the form of direct address, whereas the third person appears in 6.27–35, except in v. 35b, where 'you' is equivalent to 'one'.

Boström notes that doubts have been expressed whether 6.1–19 belongs to the original collection of chs. 1–9, and he puts the same question-mark against 6.27–35. He recognizes that it is difficult to argue stringently, and is more restrained than Whybray, who urges that vv. 26–35, with the exception of v. 32, are a series of additions. Boström would perhaps not have argued the lack of unity in vv. 20–35 so rigidly, if he had not had the special concern of advancing his theory of the *'iššā zārā*. She is promiscuous in a context of cultic devotion (this is his theory), but the description of adultery in vv. 27–35 cannot be fitted into such a framework, and so it must be separated cleanly from the *'iššā zārā* passages. On balance I do not think that there is a case for maintaining the discontinuity between vv. 20–26 and vv. 27–35, and vv. 25f., with which Boström does not deal faithfully, have an important bearing on this decision.

[25f.] First of all there are one or two linguistic points to be cleared up. In v. 26 a harlot (*zōnā*) is contrasted with a married woman (*'ēšet 'īš*) in such a way as to indicate that the 'evil woman' or 'foreign woman' of vv. 24f. is envisaged as married. In v. 25 a warning is issued against her charms and coquetry by which she awakens desire in her lovers and sexually excites them. In v. 26 G. R. Driver reads *ba'ad* or *bā'ād* ('price'; so LXX τιμή) instead of *be'ad* ('in exchange for'), and explains *nepeš yeqārā* as 'costly abundance', on the basis of the meaning 'abundance' assigned to *nepeš* in Isa. 58.10 (*VT* iv, 1954, pp. 243f.; *ZAW* 52, 1934, pp. 53f.). Winton Thomas (*VTS* iii, pp. 283f.) accepts Driver's emendation in respect of *ba'ad*, but he translates *nepeš yeqārā* 'man of weight', 'person of substance' (this is adopted by Ringgren). Gemser retains the translation offered by Toy, 'dear life' and renders v. 26 without emendation: 'Since for a harlot one need only reckon up to a loaf of bread, but a man's wife hunts dear life.' Driver translates: 'Although the price of a harlot mounts up to (amounts to) a loaf of bread, while a married woman seeks costly abundance.' Gemser has pointed out that the loaf of bread is the subsistence ration allocated to the beggar, the workless, and the prisoner. Hence one would expect the antithesis to be that of meagre fare and luxurious provision, and for this reason either 'costly abundance' or 'a person of substance' is preferable to 'dear life'.

Further, the latter of these alternatives is the better, because the one metaphor is more apt and has greater intrinsic probability than the other. Hunting costly abundance is far-fetched, but the figure of this woman as a huntress skilfully stalking the man who can keep her in comfort has realism and power. It is one thing to resort to a harlot and pay her a small fee; it is quite another to set up as a mistress another man's wife who expects style and luxury as a reward.

[27–31] On the other hand, it has to be admitted that the image of the woman who hunts 'dear life' accords well with the reflections contained in vv. 27f., where the accent is on danger and ruin. To have such an affair is like using one's breast pocket as a fire-pan or walking barefoot over red-hot coals. It is to play with fire in such a way as to expose oneself inevitably to a most painful and dangerous burn (vv. 27–29). Gemser supposes that v. 30 is a statement and not a question, and the meaning then is that theft is only a crime if it is found out. The man who steals because he is hungry and does it so skilfully that he avoids detection is not an object of contempt. Nevertheless, a thief takes a calculated risk and, if he is discovered, he will have to pay a heavy penalty (the *w*^{e} of v. 31 is then adversative). The sevenfold penalty is more severe than that prescribed in the Book of the Covenant (Ex. 21.37–22.8, 'fourfold').

I am not convinced that the hunger of the thief is mentioned as a mitigating factor (BH doubts the originality of the reference to hunger and deletes *kī yirʿab*). It is, rather, his undisciplined impulsiveness on which attention is focused, and the intention is then not to justify his action because of his hunger, but to censure him for supposing that he can break into a house to 'satisfy his appetite'. Hence v. 30 may be a question (so RSV), although there is no interrogative particle.

[32] Adultery with a married woman is so lethal a business that he who perpetrates it is mentally deficient (*ḥ*^{a}*sar lēb*) and is the agent of his own destruction. The fem. sing. suffix (*yaʿ*^{a}*śennā*) is usually taken to refer to adultery ('he who does it'). Gemser takes it to refer to the woman ('To his own destruction he dishonours her'). He does not indicate how he arrives at the meaning 'to dishonour' (p. 111). L. Kopf (*VT* ix, 1959, p. 270) connects *ʿśh* with Arabic *ġašiya*, 'to cohabit with' ('as his own destroyer he cohabits with her'). Dahood (pp. 13f.) cites *grš dʿšy lnh* (*Aqhat* II.i.30: *CML*, pp. 48f.), which he translates: 'Who will drive off those who would abuse his night-guest.' Driver translates: 'drive forth those who rebel against him.'

J. Aistleitner (*Wörterbuch der ugaritischen Sprache*, 1967, p, 243, no. 2109) translates: 'Who drives off the one who disturbs his night's rest.' Dahood associates *'śh* in v. 32 with Ugaritic *'šy* and translates: 'But a destroyer of his own soul is he who violates her.' *'śh*, 'make', gives perfectly good sense. **[33–35]** However much money he may have, he will find that an outraged husband, mad with jealousy, will prefer his pound of flesh to the most handsome financial reparation, and will exact his revenge in violence and in stamping the offender with an indelible stain of disgrace. In v. 34a, 'For jealousy is the blazing anger of a man', Driver suggests *taḥēm* for *ḥᵃmat* with a view to improving the poor sense of MT ('For jealousy inflames a man', *Biblica* 32, p. 177).

On any interpretation of v. 26, it can be established that vv. 20–26, no less than vv. 27–35, have in mind an affair with a married woman. Further, it can be said that the contrast between the harlot and the mistress which is contained in v. 26 is a natural bridge to the reflections of vv. 27–35, and that it is reasonable to consider the entire section as a unity. Boström's objection to this is not that his *'iššā zārā* is unmarried, for, on his theory, she is the wife of a foreign merchant resident in Israel who travels about in the course of his business (see on 7.19, below, pp. 337f.). I agree with him in translating *nokrīyā* as 'foreign woman' as against Snijders' view that it means 'outsider', someone, not necessarily a foreigner, who is cut off from the normal channels of social intercourse. Boström's case is that the *'iššā zārā* is not spoken of as the wife of a *rēa'* ('neighbour', v. 29) in chs. 2, 5 and 7, and that it is inconceivable that she would be so described in this chapter. In so far as this is merely an argument from silence, it does not in my judgement carry very much force. The only question which has to be asked is whether it is inherently improbable that a foreigner resident in Israel would be designated a *rēa'*, and it does not seem to me inherently improbable that he would be so designated.

CHAPTER 7

Gemser's division of the chapter into six strophes is arbitrary (cf. Ringgren, who supposes that 6.20–7.27 is one piece), and does not really throw any light on its structure. This is one of the chapters on which Whybray is most severe, and his 'original discourse' consists of vv. 1–3, 5, 25–27 (pp. 49f.). The rest is rejected for a variety of reasons, v. 4 because in it Wisdom is personified; vv. 6–24 because the woman whom they describe is alleged to be other than the woman of v. 5 and because v. 25 resumes v. 5; v. 24 because it has been inserted to ease the transition from the long interpolation to the 'original discourse'.

From the point of view of form, the chapter has three significant divisions, vv. 1–5, 6–23 and 24–27. The first and the last have recognizably the form of the Instruction (cf. 'My son', v. 1, and 'sons', v. 24), and it is only the long middle section which constitutes a clear departure from the formal elements of the genre. In the opening section, the imperatives lead on to a final clause, 'to keep you from the strange woman, from the smooth words of the foreigner' (v. 5), and in the closing section to motive clauses (vv. 26f.). Into the assessment of the central part there enter some textual considerations, and my remarks assume that it is the wisdom teacher and not the woman who looks out of the window in v. 6 (see below), and that this long descriptive passage is a variation on the theme of 'instruction', 'admonition', or a development of it.

The significance of this development would seem to me to be that it affords greater imaginative and descriptive scope than is allowed by the precise didactic formulation of the Instruction. Here the teacher does not assert his authority prosaically in imperatives, nor does he argue in motive clauses that his demands are reasonable and should be obeyed. Rather, he relies on his descriptive powers and his ability to reconstruct imaginatively the woman's stratagems and seductive conversation, so that the warning is conveyed not by schematized instruction, but by introducing the young man into the ways of the world and bringing him to the woman's house, in order to show him that it is a death trap and that only a fool will satisfy his desire at such a price.

VV. 1–5 *Instruction and the Woman*

[1, 3] In these verses it is the wisdom teacher who asserts his authority and, as I have suggested above (p. 308), *miṣwā* defines the mandatory form of this instruction (it is communicated in imperatives), while *tōrā* indicates that it has the character of 'directive' or 'guidance'. The strongly conservative nature of this educational discipline is underlined by such verbs as 'keep', 'store', 'bind', 'write', in which tenacity of memory and unbroken concentration and attentiveness are desiderated. On the other hand, 'write them on the tablet of your heart' (v. 3) represents more than a demand to learn precepts by rote, and points to an inward assimilation of the tradition. Consequently, when this educational ideal of old wisdom is described as authoritative, this does not preclude an important aspect of inwardness. The tradition is not just received as so many arbitrary external demands, but is assimilated as a way of life, and it is through this assimilation that it has the character and unity of wisdom. It shapes fundamental attitudes to life, and especially intellectual attitudes, and so it makes a man what he is.

[2] In v. 2, vitality is consequential on keeping the *miṣwōt* of the wisdom teacher, a reminder which is particularly apposite in view of the connection established elsewhere between the strange woman and death (2.16f., above pp. 285f.; 5.5, above, pp. 314f.; 7.27, below, p. 341). It may be that such a reference to 'life' in Proverbs always has some distant connection with the mythological concepts of 'the tree of life' (see on 3.18, above, p. 296) or 'the fountain of life' (see on 10.11, below, p. 418), just as 'death' is related, however remotely, to the Canaanite god Mot with his gaping throat (see on 1.12, above, pp. 269f.). At any rate, it is evident that life is more than breath and that death is not just when the heart stops and the pulse ceases to beat. There is a living death, and so 'life' in the fuller sense has qualitative aspects, and it is this more abounding vitality which is said to be consequential on keeping the commandments. In saying that his *tōrā* is to be kept as 'the little man of the eye', i.e. the pupil of the eye, the wisdom teacher defines it as illumination or guidance. The pupil, because it is the light of the eye, is precious beyond reckoning, and if a man does not 'keep' it, he is consigned to a world of darkness. Likewise, the *tōrā* of the teacher is the light of the mind and without it men have no sure guidance for the conduct of their lives. This recalls the metaphor in 6.23a, 'For the *miṣwā* is a lamp and the *tōrā* a light', and the question which I raised there (above, pp. 327f.), about the dependence of this phraseology on a figure of speech characteristic of Jewish legal piety, would also to some extent be germane here. Certainly 7.3, which differs only in one word from 3.3, is phrased in a way closely resembling passages which deal with law and covenant, and may be a deliberate literary conflation of these passages (see on 3.3, above, p. 291). Gemser suggests that v. 3a may envisage the signet ring which is a valuable personal possession, or the red thread which has magical virtue. Wisdom is a more effective apotropaic than any amulet, and it is assimilated as a vital principle, not just encountered as external demand.

[4f.] It is worth asking whether there is not some connection between this emphasis on the inwardness of wisdom and the personifications of v. 4. Both Gemser and Ringgren urge that 'sister' is a form of address equivalent to 'bride' or 'wife' (also Boström, pp. 161f.), and that Wisdom is to be seen in this verse as the rival of the strange woman, countering her fatal seductiveness by emerging with the wholesome attractiveness of a bride or wife. A love for Wisdom is like love for a wife, in that it is conducive to stability, honour and welfare. The connection of this verse may, however, be with the thought of the inwardness of wisdom in v. 3, rather than with the strange woman. The relationship which has to be established with wisdom is almost personal in character, and one knows wisdom in the same way as a sister or a relative is known. A deep community with wisdom has to be experienced, and in appropriating it there is an awareness of solidarity and kinship. 'Say to Wisdom, You are my sister, and call Discernment a relative.' The description of the woman is almost identical to that of 2.16 and has features in common with 5.3, 20 and 6.24.

vv. 6–23 *The Woman and her Prey*

[6–8] Since it is with this passage that Boström leads in developing his cultic theory of the *'iššā zārā*, it is convenient to begin with a consideration of his argument. I have already indicated that I agree with Boström against Snijders that the *'iššā zārā* or *nokrīyā* means a foreign woman rather than one whose *mores* make her a social outcast from her own community and who is an 'outsider'. According to MT of v. 6, it is Wisdom personified or the wisdom teacher who looks out of the window and observes the tactics of the strange woman. Gemser has contrasted the wisdom teacher with the prophet, the one with his attention directed towards the world and its traffic, formulating his worldly wisdom by an inductive method, and the other receiving his word from beyond the world as 'revelation' or 'disclosure'. In order to make room for his theory, Boström has to assume that the original text of v. 6 is preserved in LXX (v. 6b is missing from LXX^B^), and that it is the woman, not the wisdom teacher, who looks out of the window. In this he is followed by Albright (*VTS* iii, p. 10), and both connect παρακύπτουσα with Aphrodite παρακύπτουσα, a cult attested in Cyprus and Phoenicia, in which Aphrodite or Astarte is the goddess in the window. This goddess is to be equated with the Babylonian Ishtar, named Kililu, who is designated as 'she who leans out of the window', 'she who sets herself in the window of the house', and the twin characteristics of creativeness and destructiveness (the reverse side of fertility) are reflected in her devotees who also look out of the window as part of the ritual of her cult (pp. 104f.).

In order to sustain this interpretation of v. 6 ('For at the window of her house through the lattice she gazes'), the MT of v. 7 has also to be altered to agree with LXX, and so Boström translates: 'And she sees a youth among the untutored, she perceives among the young men one who is lacking in wit' (transposing *na'ar* to v. 7a and reading third person instead of first in the verbs). To this Snijders objects (p. 98, n.72) that even when it is so emended, v. 7 depicts a woman who looks out of the window to observe and not to be observed. The latter is required by Boström's theory. His woman should stand in the window to attract attention to herself, but the woman described by the emended text looks out of the window to catch sight of young men. This is not a decisive objection, since it is arguable that she has to do this in the first place in order to judge the moment when she can display herself to most advantage. The spying-out of possible victims is a necessary reconnaissance. There are other respects in which Boström has overstated his case, for whatever virtue it may have it ought not to be supported by the claim that MT makes no sense. MT makes very good sense, and the transition from it to v. 8 is much easier than Boström allows. One cannot say that v. 8 presupposes LXX in vv. 6f., for 'her' in v. 8 can be referred naturally to the woman of v. 5 with the MT of vv. 6f. retained. It is then the observant wisdom teacher who seeks the senseless youth crossing into the street beside her corner, and walking in the direction of her house. 'Corner' perhaps refers to the harlot's 'pitch' located in convenient proximity to her house (v. 8), an interpretation which is reinforced by v. 12: 'Now in the streets, now in the squares and beside every corner she skulks.' On *'ešnabbī*, 'lattice' (v. 6), E.F.F.B. remarks: 'The lattice is familiar from old Palestinian houses with a window sill jutting out into the street and a framework of open holes through which one might look out.' The lattice affords protection from the light and heat of the sun, and contributes to privacy.

Y. Aharoni (*Archaeology and Old Testament Study*, ed. D. Winton Thomas, 1967, pp. 180f.) notes that the queen looking through the window is a narrative motif in the Old Testament (Judg. 5.28; II Sam. 6.16; II Kings 9.30), and he has supplied archaeological evidence from Beth-Hakkerem that a window with a lattice arrangement (*'ešnāb*, Judg. 5.28; Prov. 7.6), supported by a balustrade, was an architectural feature of a royal palace. This he has correlated with the 'woman in the window' motif on Phoenician ivory plaques from Samaria, Arslan Tash, Nimrud and Khorsabad, where a window of similar design is shown. Is it, then, Wisdom portrayed as a queen who looks out of the window in Prov. 7.6? If so, it would appear that a motif associated with Astarte (as queen of fertility) and her devotees has been transferred to Wisdom (see below, pp. 360f., 365f.).

[9] The action takes place at twilight in the evening of the day, a time reference which the rather obscure phrase in v. 9b may be assumed to reinforce. If so, 'at the eye (*'īšōn*, cf. v. 2b) of night and darkness' will be a picturesque synonym of v. 9a (or perhaps we should point *'ešūn* 'approach', Accadian *isinnu* 'fixed time', cf. 20.20). Boström notes that in Ethiopic Enoch 78.2, one of the four names of the moon, corresponding to its first phase, is *Asonja* ('eye of Yahweh'), and he points to Zech. 9.9, where the planets, sun and moon are designated as 'eyes of Yahweh'. He suggests that 'eye of night' is a profane or secular formulation of 'eye of Yahweh' and is to be equated with it, in which case v. 9b establishes that these proceedings took place at the time of the new moon ('the eye of night and darkness'). There is no virtue in Dahood's suggestion (pp. 14f.) that *'īšōn* is to be derived from *yšn*, since the translation 'sleep' does not suit the verse and Dahood's rendering 'quietness' can hardly be derived from *yšn*.

[10–12] In v. 10, the woman would seem to be depicted as a prostitute with the clothes and the disposition of her class. The meaning of *n^eṣūrat lēb* has been well elucidated by G. R. Driver (*VT* i, 1950, p. 250) in terms of the parallel semantic development of *ṣnʿ* and *nṣr* from 'guarded', 'reserved' to 'crafty', 'sly' (Syriac *ṣnī*, 'sly'). She has an easy and assured mastery over all the devices of seduction. She has a house, but not a home; she is a woman without roots in her family and community who can only live at fever temperature and whose wanderlust is the index of her homelessness and her alienation from authentic social experience. She is flighty, a rover and wanderer whose feet do not stay in her house (on *sōreret*, which is to be explained with reference to Accadian *sarāru*, 'to be unstable', as well as 'to be rebellious', see G. R. Driver, *ZAW* 50, 1932, pp. 141f.). It is interesting that in rejecting vv. 6–24 as an interpolation, Whybray argues that the woman described in this passage, and especially in v. 10, is not the *'iššā zārā* of v. 5. This he founds on an argument from silence, that the *'iššā zārā* is nowhere called or likened to a *zōnā* – a professional prostitute (pp. 49f.). This is no more conclusive than the attempt of Boström to show that the woman of 6.27–35 is not the *'iššā zārā*, and both illustrate the unwisdom of trying to make her conform to an exact pattern.

[13] Once the *petī* is in her clutches, she employs all her expertise on him, and she does it with an efficiency and thoroughness which is unhampered by scruple. With a practised immodesty she gets down at once to the business of seduction. **[14]** Boström's interpretation of v. 14 can be sustained only if *šillamtī* is translated as a present, 'To-day I am to fulfil my vows'. In this case we may follow him in supposing that the communion meal (*zibeḥē šelāmīm*) does not exhaust her cultic obligations, and that her vows are fulfilled in sexual intercourse. If v. 14b is translated, 'To-day I have fulfilled my vows' (Gemser, Ringgren), the meaning must be that the communion meal is the outstanding cultic obligation and that she invites the young man to share this with her. This leads naturally to the supposition (cf. Gemser) criticized by Boström that the communion meal is more or less a pretext to lure the young man to her house and that her protestations of cultic devotion are a ruse for winning a customer. This would be a more credible interpretation if in fact the invitation had been to share a communion meal and no more, but in view of the frankness of the woman in disclosing her intentions (vv. 16–20), there is weight in Boström's objections. **[15–18]** The 'therefore' of v. 15 is directed exclusively towards sexual intercourse and suggests, as Boström's translation of v. 14 allows, that it is this which constitutes the consummation of her cultic devotions. It is as a devotee that she has decked the couch for the communion meal with fine coverlets and prepared the bed for the sacred marriage (so also Ringgren), sprinkling it with myrrh, aloes and cinnamon (on *nwp*, a by-form of *npp*, 'to sprinkle', see G. R. Driver, *ZAW* 50, 1932, p. 142).

[19f.] Yet this rather rarified cultic interpretation of the passage is not entirely adequate. While she may do this out of a devotion to Aphrodite παρακύπτουσα, she knows that it has an illicit aspect and that it is an indulgence which her husband would not tolerate. By implication she is aware that it conflicts with accepted notions of domestic and social morality. Hence it has to be supposed that her natural sensuality and eroticism make this kind of religious devotion agreeable to her. This is an aspect of the matter which should not be neglected in assessing the kind of woman who emerges in these verses.

Her husband is far from home on a business trip, and Gemser suggests that enough information is given to justify the conclusion that he is a rich merchant who is engaged in extensive business transactions. He has a purse full of money, and he has a house which reflects his affluence, whose exotic furnishings have been brought from foreign parts. I am unsure how much Gemser is trying to establish. Is he calling in question the actual 'foreignness' of the woman and her husband? If so, she and her husband are both Israelites, but she creates an exotic atmosphere in her house by means of foreign furnishings and perfumes which her husband has brought home from his commercial travels. In this matter, some weight should be attached to a passage in the Instruction of *Ani* in which the young man is warned against 'a woman from abroad . . . who is far away from her husband' (above, p. 94), and it is on this analogy that I would understand the foreignness of the woman in the book of Proverbs. She is a *nokrīyā* in the full sense, as Boström says, and she has about her an air of allurement and mystery which excites the desire of young men. She is a foreigner and the wife of a foreigner, settled in a community where she is a stranger and is careless of her reputation, with a husband who is a merchant and is away from home for lengthy periods. So the situation is made for her and, if she wills it, she can be promiscuous with impunity.

Boström's equation of *'īšōn laylā* with 'new moon' (v. 9) would seem to reinforce this interpretation. If it is the new moon and her husband is not to return until the full moon, there is no danger in spending the night with her (v. 18). This is what the woman says in vv. 19–20. Her husband is not at home; he has gone on a distant journey and will not return until the day of the full moon. Gemser supposes that her husband returns when the moon is full because travel is safer and swifter at this period of the month. Boström draws v. 9 into his cultic theory by observing that the new moon has everywhere a special connection with sexual intercourse. The conjunction of the sun and moon at the new moon signified for primitive thought the coitus of sun and moon which was celebrated with sexual rites (pp. 123f.). In this he finds a confirmation that it is the ἱερὸς γάμος which the woman wishes to consummate.

This is a convenient place for me to indicate how far I am prepared to go with Boström and in what respects he has overstretched his cultic interpretation. The woman who is the wife of a merchant and whose home has an air of luxury about it is clearly not a common prostitute soliciting for a fee. She is probably, as he contends, a devotee of Aphrodite, in which case *zōnā* (v. 10) will have this specialized sense, and her clothes will also identify her in her cultic role. This does not necessarily imply, however, that it is precisely because she is a devotee that the wisdom teacher warns young men against her. So far as they are concerned she is just a special kind of prostitute, and a particularly dangerous kind, because she gives so much and asks nothing. It is here that I part company with Boström. Boström says that the wisdom teacher issues a warning against participation in a foreign cult and heathen rites. My view is that the wisdom teacher is warning young men against an affair with a married woman who is a prostitute, and that her being a devotee of Aphrodite is not the nub of the matter. Boström attributes to the wisdom teacher a Deuteronomic abhorrence of alien cultic practices, and ignores the circumstance that similar warnings are issued in the Egyptian Instruction in a context of worldly wisdom. For the wisdom teacher, the woman is as fatal to young men as any other *zōnā*, and he is not directly concerned with the special religious reasons for her promiscuity, except in so far as these make her a particularly dangerous prostitute.

The warning in the Babylonian *Counsels of Wisdom* (above, pp. 153f.) against the temple prostitute should be similarly assessed, and it does not necessarily, as Ringgren supposes (*Word and Wisdom*, pp. 135f.), lend support to Boström's interpretation of the *'iššā zārā* in Prov. 1–9. The advice is as follows:

Do not marry a prostitute whose husbands are legion,
A temple harlot who is dedicated to a god,
A courtesan whose favours are many.
In your trouble she will not support you,
In your dispute she will be a mocker;
There is no reverence or submissiveness with her.
Even if she dominate your house, get her out,
For she has directed her attention elsewhere (*ll.* 72–79, *BWL*, pp. 102f.)

Now it is probable that all three words used for prostitute (*ḫarimtu*, *ištaritu*, *kulmašitu*) refer to a cult prostitute (see W. von Soden, *Akkadisches Handwörterbuch*), but this does not mean that the point of the warning is that one should not get involved in the ritual of a fertility cult. It is clear from *ll.* 75–79 that the advice is differently weighted, and that it is the unsuitability of such a woman as a domestic partner and help-meet which is its gist. It is not so surprising that cult prostitutes are specifically mentioned, since they must have been a common type of prostitute and, moreover, the wisdom teacher may have believed that the effects of this type of prostitution on a woman were particularly demoralizing. Yet it is unlikely that he would have considered any kind of prostitute as a promising home-maker, and it is this canny, earthy concern rather than any abhorrence of cultic connections which informs his remarks. Prostitution leaves its indelible effects on a woman and she cannot be reformed so as to become a biddable, reliable and helpful wife. The old life will erupt into the new, and she will be a vamp with a relationship to her husband like that which she used to have with her clients.

[21] Winton Thomas (*VTS* iii, p. 284) has suggested that *liqḥā* (v. 21) means 'her taking ways' (her charm) rather than 'her persuasiveness'. **[22]** LXX *κεπφωθείς*, 'simpletons', would seem to indicate that *pt'm* was vocalized *pᵉtā'īm* by the Greek translator. 'He follows her as would untutored youths' makes poor sense. Nor is the singular *petī* much improvement, and in any case the point of the emendation is lost if sense cannot be had from *pᵉtā'īm*. *pit'ōm* and *pᵉtā'īm* can be referred to the same consonantal text, but not *pit'ōm* and *petī*. She distracts him (*hiṭṭattū*) with her ample resources of coquetry, and he is putty in her hands. She routs him (*taddīḥennū*; 'routs' rather than 'seduces') with her smooth words. He follows her on an impulse (*pit'ōm* 'suddenly', here 'impulsively') and the ease with which she manipulates him and the danger in which he stands are conveyed by two figures of speech. He goes, or is brought (LXX), like an ox to the slaughter (22b). The second simile is unintelligible in MT: 'Like a bangle to the discipline of a fool'. *mōsēr*, 'noose', should be read for *mūsār*, and *'ayyāl*, 'hart', for *'ᵉwīl*, with the support of the versions. There are two elucidations of the simile by G. R. Driver, the second superseding the first.

In the first, which is followed by BH, *'ks* is associated with Arabic *'akasa*, 'to tie (a camel) with a rope', and is pointed as an infinitive construct qal (*ka'ᵃkōs*), 'as a hart is tied to a cord'. The youth is likened to an animal which is caught and tied by a cord to a stake ready for killing (*ZAW* 50, 1932, p. 143). Driver's later explanation supposes that *'ks* refers to a jerky mode of walking, as in Arabic, and he points *k^e'akkēs*, 'as a hart skips into a noose' (*VT* i, 1951, p. 241). **[23]** Driver's second suggestion accords well with 'as a bird speeds towards a trap'. The sequence would be more logical if the order of 23a and 23b were reversed. The arrow kills the trapped animal or bird and so it is with the youth. He is likened to an unsuspecting animal bounding into a trap, to a bird that is in a hurry to be snared. It is an ambush from which there is no escape, for an arrow will pierce his vitals. All the while, he is sadly oblivious to the fact that his life (*nepeš*) is at stake (*b^e* of price; he pays with his life, v. 23).

vv. 24–27 *Avoid the Gate of Death*

[24] On the alternation between 'My son' (v. 1), and 'sons' (v. 24), I have already commented (see on 4.1, above, p. 303 and 4.10, above, p. 307. LXX reads 'my son' in 7.24 with singular verbs). In these closing verses the teacher renews his demands on his pupils ('sons'), and urges them to give him their unbroken attentiveness and concentration and to defer to the authority of his words. **[25–27]** The remaining verses are constructed in terms of the metaphor of the 'road' in such a way as to elucidate the destructive potential of the woman and the lethal effects of associating with her. Commenting on 2.16f. (above, pp. 285f.; cf. on 1.12, above, pp. 269f.), I have suggested that the mythology of the Canaanite god Mot exercises some influence on the construction of this figure of the woman as a way of death. To be led away by desire for her is to take the road to Sheol and to arrive at the point of no return. This is a deviation from the way of life which does not admit of subsequent correction; it is a commitment to death and there is no way back to a safe road (v. 25). This woman deals instant death to her victims, however powerful, and a great company have been 'toppled' by her in many lethal encounters (v. 26). The thought of the gaping throat of Mot is not entirely absent from v. 27 (cf. 2.18f., above, pp. 287f.), although there is an element of reinterpretation in the verse. The mythology is subject to 'transference' and the process of transfer involves some demythologizing. The ways leading to Sheol and the chambers of death converge on the woman's house and it becomes the open throat of the god who swallows up life in death. The house, like the throat of Mot, is a gate of death – the beginning of a descent into the underworld. Mythology is thus made the servant of instruction and edification, and is no longer serious mythology.

Chapter 8

Whybray supposes that there is nothing in this chapter which strictly adheres to the form of the Instruction, and he concludes that it is made up of additions to the tenth of the original ten discourses which he postulates (pp. 72f.). The element of direct, imperious address is intrinsic to the Instruction and is largely, though not entirely, absent from this chapter. It appears in vv. 1–11 and 32–36, and these verses also contain the other principal formal elements of the genre.

The representation in vv. 1–11 is similar to that in 1.20f., and the personified Wisdom is conceived as a wisdom teacher or, perhaps, in some measure as a prophet who mixes with men in the most busy and public places of the town, where they gather for social intercourse and the transaction of business. There she raises her voice loud and clear so as to address her call to them. In this, Gemser finds a contrast between Wisdom and the *'iššā zārā* who lurks at street corners when darkness falls and who speaks in secretive, seductive whispers (7.6f.). This thought that Wisdom competes against the *'iššā zārā* and offers herself to the *peta'īm* as a counter-attraction – a pure bride, not a fatal seductress – is prominent in Boström's interpretation (pp. 163f.). Wisdom, who observed the ways of the world from her window in 7.6 (if a personification of Wisdom is intended there), steps down into the arena and assumes the role of a preacher and teacher in the public forum of the town.

Her address is to men in general and to the *peta'īm*, the raw, untutored youths, in particular. Her constituency is perhaps especially young men whose powers of intellectual judgement are unformed and who need to be matured by an educational process, rather than men in general, and, if so, she takes on the role of a wisdom teacher rather than a prophet. Such *peta'īm* stand naked and defenceless before the world and are putty in the hands of knaves and tricksters. In the subsequent verses it is the teaching of a sage rather than the preaching of a prophet which is on view. This teaching is conveyed by imperatives ('hear', v. 6; 'take', v. 10) and a succession of motive clauses (vv. 6–9, 11), by means of which Wisdom gives reasons to support her claim for attention and emphasizes the incomparable value of the instruction which she imparts.

It is not until v. 32 that Wisdom resumes the direct address to her hearers, and again it is a wisdom teacher's audience which is indicated ('my sons'). In keeping with this presupposition is the demand for attentiveness ('listen', v. 32, 33a?, 'do not neglect', v. 33b) and the ordering of the supporting argument in motive clauses. There is reason in the demands which are made, for authority is in the service of wisdom and the teacher is a sage, not a despot. The wisdom which he inculcates is justified by its beneficial results.

Gemser describes the whole chapter as a recommendation of Wisdom by herself (vv. 13–31) and her teaching (vv. 1–11, 32–36), which has an affinity with passages of self-adulation in later wisdom literature of a more hymnic kind (Ecclus.; Wisdom). Consistent with his theory that Wisdom is the rival of or antidote to Astarte and her cult, Boström detects in vv. 13–21 a striking resemblance to the numerous hymns in which the goddess engages in self-adoration and praise, so that in the words of Wisdom a shimmer of the lustre of the great queen of heaven can be caught (p. 173). In this chapter there are two sharply differentiated spheres in which Wisdom establishes her reputation and rank. According to v. 12, she is the neighbour of shrewdness (see below), and exercises beneficent influence and power in a worldly context, especially in high circles of government as the confidant of kings and statesmen. It is worth noting that Wisdom begins with this assertion of her pre-eminence as a counsellor of kings and giver of success *in the world*, and then proceeds to expatiate on the status which she derives from her primaeval antiquity (vv. 22–31). It is reasonable to attach some significance to this order, since it is the reverse of what might naturally be expected. Wisdom's dwelling with God before the world and men were created would have lent perspective and sanction to her claim to dwell with shrewdness and to dominate politics and practical affairs in a this-worldly context.

The emphasis in this chapter is still on the empirical evidences of Wisdom's effectiveness, on her earthiness and her full involvement in worldly affairs. This, rather than the more rarified description of vv. 22f., which lies outside the world of ordinary human experience and assigns to Wisdom a supra-historical existence prior to the creation of the world and man, is the ground of the givenness of Wisdom. That wisdom does shape the policies of nations and the lives of men is incontestable; wisdom as expressed in the policies of statesmen or the prudent behaviour of individuals is a force in the world making both for righteousness and material prosperity. There is solid evidence to support this and it can be empirically verified. This is the point of departure, and in this respect the chapter is still firmly anchored in the ethos of old wisdom. In that case, vv. 22–31 should perhaps be regarded as a speculative superstructure which is raised on the foundations of the empirical givenness and effectiveness of wisdom, and which tries to fill out the meaning of these phenomena by tracing the history of wisdom beyond the phenomenal world to a supra-historical *locus*, thereby supplying a theological explanation for the empirical dominance of wisdom.

Kayatz argues that the apparently diverse functions of the personified Wisdom in Proverbs can be explained and unified in terms of Egyptian influence. With respect to form, ch. 8 has been modelled on speeches of Egyptian gods (pp. 86f.), while a complex of motifs associated with *Maat* (existence before the creation of the world, the divine child at play, the lover and the beloved, the giver of life and safety, the one who is effective in the rule of the king) have been transferred to Wisdom, particularly in ch. 8, but also elsewhere in chs. 1–9. Some of the examples given are interesting and deserve careful consideration; others (Wisdom as a crown, 4.9; Wisdom as jewellery and adornment, 1.9; 3.22) are obvious metaphors which could have occurred to anyone, and for which precise mythological origins do not need to be postulated. The life-and-death antithesis in Proverbs (Kayatz, pp. 102f.) is fundamentally different from that in Egypt. This, of course, does not preclude the taking over of mythological motifs related to the quest for life after death and their employment in the context of a this-worldly understanding of life and death, but the underlying mythology in Proverbs is Canaanite rather than Egyptian (see on 1.12, above, pp. 269f.). I am therefore not convinced by this attempt to unify the different functions of Wisdom in ch. 8 by an appeal to the several functions of *Maat* in Egyptian ritual and mythology.

vv. 1–11 *Wisdom as Instructress*

[1–3] Wisdom does not recoil from the rough and tumble of the market-place with its busyness and noise. She does not reserve her discourse for a learned audience or esoteric circle, claiming immunity from the cut and thrust of a less exalted and refined level of debate and disdaining to mix with the crowds. When she raises her voice it is not to deliver an academic lecture in a classroom, or a sermon in a temple to a crowd of worshippers (cf. Jer. 7), or to enlighten an *élite*, but to summon men from their occupations and distractions to take part in an open-air meeting (cf. Gemser). She has no assurance of an audience, no prior publicity, and there are no established conventions in connection with this mode of address which guarantee that she will be treated with deference and have an easy passage.

She operates where the competition is fiercest, not so much the competition of other orators as men's preoccupation with those things which they take more seriously than listening to speeches – earning their living, making bargains, getting wealth, transacting local politics, settling disputes and other less deliberate gregarious enjoyments. It is against all this that Wisdom has to compete, raising her voice and summoning an audience until she wins one by the sustained force of her eloquence. She picks a place where the human traffic is heaviest, whether on a natural pulpit at the side of the road or at a cross-roads or beside the gates which give access to the city, where there is a continual movement to and fro and where the forum on which all manner of public transactions focus is located (vv. 2–3).

[4f.] It is the young men, the wisdom teacher's constituency, to whom she particularly addresses her words, and she urges them to acquire intellectual discrimination (*hābīnū*, v. 5). The reading of LXX in v. 5b ('Set your mind in order', *hākīnū* for *hābīnū*, so BH and Gemser) has no clear superiority over MT, apart from the aesthetic objection which may be levelled against the repetition of *hābīnū* in v. 5b. With respect to sense, *hābīnū lēb* is no more difficult than *hābīnū ʿormā*. 'O untutored youths, discern what shrewdness is, O fools, discern what acumen is' (*lēb*, 'mental capacity', see *PWM*, p. 78).

[6–9] In contrast with the markedly cerebral character of v. 5, where interest focuses on worldly know-how and intellectual judgement, vv. 6–9 are more concerned with the integrity and candour of Wisdom, which are expressed in a series of antitheses and by means of a moralistic vocabulary. Wisdom's communications are characterized by a plain honesty and openness of intention, which is opposed to a calculated, shifty, ambiguity or a labyrinthine subtlety. Thus it is the straightness rather than the nobility of Wisdom's words to which v. 6a refers, and Grollenberg's change of vocalization restores the parallelism with v. 6b (*n*ᵉ*gādīm* = *n*ᵉ*kōḥīm* and parallel to *mēšārīm*, L. H. Grollenberg, *RB* lix, 1952, pp. 40f.). Kraus (H. J. Kraus, *Die Verkündigung der Weisheit*, *Spr. 8*, Bibl. Studien, Heft 2, 1956) suggests that there is the thought here of the *tōrā* of Wisdom, i.e., the guidance which she gives for the road, but the immediate reference is to her speech rather than to the plain road to which her guidance gives access. Her words are straight and 'on the level', and the man of insight or the seeker after knowledge will recognize this characteristic of forthrightness and candour (v. 9).

In v. 7, the topic is the genuineness and solidity of Wisdom's speech and her abhorrence of wickedness, and in v. 8 it is the rightness of her words and the absence of any crooked or labyrinthine (*niptāl*) tendencies. In this context the *mēbīn* (v. 9) is the person who recognizes the value of this morally right and plain speech, and who defines knowledge (*daʿat*) in terms of moral stability (*'ᵉmet*, v. 7) and rightness (*ṣedeq*, v. 8), and a rejection of malevolence and crooked ambiguity of speech. The ultimate test indicated here is perhaps a social one. Speech which is indicative of anti-social tendencies, of a desire to deceive, an incapacity for sincerity and benevolence, is not a part of knowledge. Rightness (*ṣedeq*) and knowledge (*daʿat*) are inseparable from integrity in human relationships and the consequent social enrichment.

[10f.] The intention of vv. 10f. is not to speak disparagingly of the value of coral, silver, gold and delights or pleasures. On the contrary, in order that the comparison should have point, the great value of these other commodities has to be assumed. These are indeed great prizes and they are in no way incompatible with wisdom or rightness or knowledge (cf. v. 18), provided they exist within a framework of values in which the priority of wisdom, with its derivatives, discipline and knowledge, is assumed. Otherwise wealth may be vulgarity and a man may have it without *kābōd* – without *gravitas* – in which case it will detract from, rather than add to, his status. The man of weight in the community has a material prosperity which befits his status, but the man who has gold and silver is not necessarily a man of weight.

VV. 12–21 *The Power of Wisdom in Human Affairs*

De Boer's suggestion that Wisdom is depicted in these verses as a counsellor (*yōʿēṣ*) deserves serious attention, although the effect of what he says is diminished by the additional words 'belonging to the world of God' (*VTS* iii, p. 69). There is good reason to believe that it is the role of the statesman which Wisdom claims to fill in these verses (see *PWM*, pp. 23f. on *ḥākām*, *sōpēr*, *śar*, *yōʿēṣ*), but, if this is so, it is self-evident that she is immersed in worldly affairs and tasks of government and that the situation described is the very reverse of a Wisdom withdrawn from the world and located with Yahweh as his counsellor. Whether v. 12a is translated 'I Wisdom am neighbour to shrewdness' or 'I Wisdom, my neighbour is shrewdness' (pointing *šᵉkentī*, so BH), the effect is the same. Wisdom knows her way about the world and has expertise in earthy, hard-headed procedures and negotiations.

[12, 14] A consideration of the vocabulary of vv. 12 and 14 in particular enables this point to be made more sharply. There is no doubt that Wisdom speaks in these verses like a statesman using a vocabulary descriptive of the attitudes, skills and executive incisiveness associated with good government. This is what I have described elsewhere (*PWM*, pp. 65f.) as the vocabulary of old wisdom. Such words as *ʿormā* and *mᵉzimmōt* (v. 12) are concerned with this range of intellectual skills (see on 1.4, above, p. 265 and 3.21, above, p. 298). Wisdom says: 'I discover knowledge of *mᵉzimmōt*' and, although it is difficult to translate *mᵉzimmōt*, the meaning of the phrase is not in doubt and certainly the emendation of BH ('I am found as the acquaintance of *mᵉzimmōt*,) is unnecessary. *daʿat mᵉzimmōt* means 'knowledge of procedural devices' or 'knowledge of expediencies', and Kraus is right in seeing a reference to mental agility, versatility and adroitness. Wisdom possesses the flexibility and mental keenness which contribute to the art of politics. 'I find out the right procedures.'

With regard to v. 14, I have commented in *PWM* on the collocation of *ʿēṣā* and *tūšīyā* in v. 14a matched by *bīnā* and *gᵉbūrā* in v. 14b and to be compared with *ʿēṣā* and *gᵉbūrā* in Isa. 36.5, and I have maintained that *tūšīyā* means 'power', 'capacity', 'competence' (*PWM*, pp. 67, 80f.). Wisdom therefore speaks exactly in the manner of a statesman in v. 14, and such words as *gᵉbūrā*, *tūšīyā* (and *kōaḥ*) are indicative of the power element in old wisdom. The test of *ʿēṣā* or *bīnā* is its effectiveness as policy, and those possessing such intellectual virtues are assumed to be in positions of power and responsibility and to have the energy and incisiveness which will make them successful men of action. In v. 14b the indications of the versions should be followed. This judgement is related to the interpretation of this verse which I have just offered. What Wisdom ought to say in v. 14b (as she does in v. 14a) is that she possesses statesmanlike qualities, not that she is a personification of *bīnā*. 'I possess insight and power' not 'I am insight, I possess power' (contrary to Gemser). This is not, however, to say that the versions read a different Hebrew text from

MT. The Greek translator may have had *lī bīnā* before him, but, on the other hand, *ἐμὴ φρόνησις* may reflect his decision that the Hebrew text ought to have been *lī bīnā* rather than *'ᵃnī bīnā*.

[13] I have indicated that vv. 12 and 14 belong together both with respect to thought and vocabulary. In saying this, it was not my intention to cast doubt on the originality of v. 13, although my remarks do give impetus to the raising of this question. The verse is longer than normal, and although this cannot be regarded as a decisive consideration, it has inspired the proposal that v. 13a is a gloss and that the verse consisted originally of vv. 13b and 13c (BH). Gemser is suspicious of the whole verse on the ground that it interrupts the smooth transition from v. 12 to v. 14. This argument is capable of extension, since, apart from v. 13, vv. 12–16 make up a coherent group in which Wisdom is envisaged as framing and executing policies in the highest circles of government. **[15f.]** Thus in vv. 15f. she has the ear of kings and rulers and enables them to exercise power effectively, laying down the principles of their administration and shaping a just order. Like an elder statesman, she is the power behind the throne. The textual point in v. 16b is not of great moment and whether MT ('and nobles, all entitled to rule') or LXX ('and nobles by me rule the earth') is followed the interpretation is not much affected. Dahood's translation (p. 15), 'all legitimate rulers', takes the right sense of *šōpᵉṭē ṣedeq*.

[13] When v. 13 is considered in this context it is clear that it contains a significantly different self-representation of Wisdom, especially in v. 13a. I can only repeat here the argument which I have developed elsewhere (*PWM*, pp. 48f.), that the fear of Yahweh is not an original ingredient of old wisdom as I have defined the latter, and that the intellectual attitudes indicated by such words as *ʿormā*, *ʿēṣā*, *tūšīyā* and *mᵉzimmā* are not compatible with a wisdom which is set in a pietistic and moralistic framework. This vocabulary can only be accommodated to such a framework when it is subjected to a process of reinterpretation.

From this point of view I would argue that not all of this chapter belongs to the same stage of the history of the wisdom tradition and so something of the direction of its development can be detected here. Conclusions of this kind can also be drawn from vv. 5–11, where there is a transition from the vocabulary of old wisdom in v. 5 to a passage (vv. 6–11) in which the ethical emphasis is no less marked than in vv. 13b and 13c, and there is a further trace of moralism in v. 20. I do not wish to draw any literary-historical conclusions from all this, and so I do not propose that v. 13 or any other verse should be deleted. Mowinckel has indicated that the traditio-historical approach ought, on occasions, to lead to literary-historical conclusions (*Prophecy and Tradition*, 1946, pp. 19f.), but I cannot see that in this particular case it is either helpful or possible to restore the 'original' text. One should be satisfied with asking what light the chapter throws on the history of the wisdom tradition.

When it is so interrogated, it points to a development which I have already outlined in connection with the prophetic reinterpretation of wisdom (*PWM*, pp. 65f.). One aspect of this was the shift from a position of ethical neutrality, to which the vocabulary of old wisdom bears witness, to one of unequivocal ethical commitment. A parallel development can be seen in this chapter in vv. 6–11, 13 and 20. Wisdom hates pride and arrogance, the evil way and the mouth which speaks perversely (v. 13b). Certainly pride is also a flaw in the context of old, international wisdom, but the other two dislikes of Wisdom are connected with the process of Yahwistic reinterpretation (cf. v. 13a, 'The fear of Yahweh is hatred of evil').

I have already suggested that the metaphor of the two ways is an important aspect of the Israelite appropriation and shaping of the Instruction. As the genre appears in Proverbs it does not have the character of career guidance for civil servants, but guidance for the road of life and the educational discipline prescribed is a way of life, as opposed to a way of death which is also a way of evil (cf. v. 20, Wisdom walks in a way of righteousness, in the midst of paths of justice). The reference to twisted speech in v. 13b resumes the topic of vv. 6–11, and the words *ṣᵉdāqā* and *mišpāṭ* in v. 20 are frequently on the lips of prophets and are prominent in connection with the prophetic reinterpretation of wisdom. In v. 13a, Wisdom's hatred of evil is associated with the statement that the fear of Yahweh is hatred of evil. The fear of Yahweh is the new *mūsār*, and it is a concept of discipline different from that imposed by the wisdom teacher. It is religious submission, rather than educational discipline, and it enters the Instruction at the point where the wisdom tradition bows the knee to Yahwistic piety (cf. *PWM*, pp. 102f.). If we suppose that the personified Wisdom speaks as a sage would, it has to be noted that here and here only in the chapter does she point beyond herself to Yahweh. Elsewhere it is on herself as a benefactress and on the benefits that are in her gift that she focuses attention.

[17–21] This is particularly noticeable in vv. 17–19. Wisdom returns the love of her lovers and makes herself accessible to those who seek her. Kayatz (pp. 98f.) points to 'who love her' in v. 17a (K.) and urges that this reflects the influence of an Egyptian formula in which the third person is customary. Wisdom as lover and beloved is modelled on *Maat*. As for the gifts which she bestows or bequeathes (*l*e*hanḥīl*, v. 21), these include material prosperity, which, however, as in vv. 10f., is distinguished from vulgar opulence. The fruit of Wisdom is better than gold and her produce better than silver. What she offers is wealth or property (*yēš*, v. 21) with *kābōd* and *ṣ*e*dāqā*. This is not meretricious or speculative wealth; it is located in a framework of values and is an ingredient of a way of life which bestows *gravitas* and social wholeness. Hence wealth with *kābōd* is solid wealth or wealth with a basis in a traditional evaluation of what constitutes the good life (*hōn ʿātēq*, v. 18). The paradox is that when wealth is the chief end of life it corrupts, whereas when it is subordinated to wisdom it may be enjoyed as an aspect of welfare and honour. I do not follow Ringgren or RSV in v. 18. To translate *ṣ*e*dāqā* as 'success' or 'prosperity' is to over-simplify the relation of 'rightness' to 'wealth'. What Wisdom gives essentially is a way of life which possesses ethical fitness and equity (v. 20).

I take up here the much discussed question (Gemser, Ringgren, Robert, *RB* xliii, p. 187) of the relationship of vv. 12–14 to Isa. 11.1f. I have discussed the latter passage (*PWM*, p. 110) and have argued that wisdom is there conceived as the endowment of a spirit-filled king and is described in a way which involves a radical reinterpretation of the vocabulary of old wisdom. To speak of a *rūaḥ* of *ḥokmā* and *bīnā*, a *rūaḥ* of policy (*ʿēṣā*) and power (*g*e*būrā*) is to remove this vocabulary far from the ethos of old wisdom in which Prov. 8.12–14 still abides. Hence the supposition that 8.12–14 is dependent on the Isaiah passage is incompatible with my account of the history of the wisdom tradition in Israel. Cazelles' suggestion that the figure of wisdom in vv. 12–14 develops from the liberation of the dynastic son of David into a universal and cosmic sphere is one with which I disagree (H. Cazelles, *Sacra Pagina* i, 1959, pp. 511f.). In general, discussions on the vocabulary common to the two passages have not paid sufficient attention to the precise way in which the vocabulary is employed, and to the significant differences in this regard between Prov. 8.12–14 and Isa. 11.1f.

VV. 22–31 *The Antiquity of Wisdom*

I resume the discussion of the relation of these verses to vv. 12–21. The addition in LXX (v. 21, 'If I declare to you the things of daily occurrence, I shall remember to recount the things of old') is probably, as Toy and Gemser suggest, an editorial bridge and, if so, an indication of an awareness that vv. 22f. were discontinuous with what preceded them. This literary-critical observation reinforces a conclusion which follows from a consideration of the widely diverging characteristics of the wisdom tradition represented by the two passages. In the one it is Wisdom's role in a historical community, as the adviser of kings, as politician and instructress of men in the good life which is being described. In the other, attention is riveted on the place and precedence of Wisdom in a cosmological context. Leaving aside the detailed difficulties for the moment, I would hold with von Rad (*Old Testament Theology*, i, pp. 448f.) that the intention here is to emphasize the vast intelligence of Wisdom by assigning to her an architectonic function in the ordering of the created world. This constitutes, as von Rad notes, a differently orientated, a more comprehensive and philosophical recommendation of Wisdom than the one which appears in vv. 12–21. The aim is still to magnify the authority of Wisdom, but this is now done in a cosmological dimension from different apologetic presuppositions and with a more sophisticated, reflective audience in view.

There are two passages in Deutero-Isaiah (40.12–17, 28–31, see above, on 3.19–20, pp. 296f.) where the intellectual range and capacity of Yahweh are demonstrated in connection with his grand design for the created world – this was an aspect of the prophetic reinterpretation of the vocabulary of old wisdom (*PWM*, pp. 81f.). A further step has been taken here – perhaps a long step; but, at any rate, the progress from the use of the vocabulary of wisdom to describe Yahweh's architectonic flair as creator of the world to a personification of Wisdom in a like cosmological context is perfectly intelligible and is an insight into the internal development of the Israelite wisdom tradition which should be taken into account in any discussion of 8.22f.

From these remarks it will be clear that I do not suppose vv. 12–31 to have come into being all at once as a deliberate artistic unity. The two passages (vv. 12–21 and vv. 22–31) do not have that kind of intrinsic connection which can be explained with reference to the creative design of an author. We have to reckon here not with one context but with two contexts, and the adjacency of the passages has to be explained by traditio-historical considerations. The second passage (vv. 22–31) marks a new stage in the presentation of the personified Wisdom and, as such, is intended as a reorientation, enrichment and supplementation of what has gone before (vv. 12–21). The intention is still that of powerfully recommending Wisdom to men, but new situations and a different kind of hearer or reader present the apologist with new problems, and he has to construct a portrait of Wisdom which will be conducive to his didactic objectives. 'The whole call in Prov. 8 also presupposes an intellectual need in men who can only be reached if their will to acquire knowledge is also satisfied. They are therefore told that the wisdom which calls them has a cosmic background' (G. von Rad, *Old Testament Theology*, i, p. 451).

[22f.] Gemser notes the formal resemblance of vv. 22–31 to the Egyptian and Babylonian hymns of creation (*ANET*, pp. 6f., 60f.), and Ringgren observes that the representation of creation is the usual Israelite one which derives from Canaanite models. Wisdom exists prior to this series of creative acts (*qedem mipʿālāw mēʾāz*, v. 22b. It makes little difference if *mēʾāz* is deleted; it is not indicated by LXX and Pesh.). So much is clear in a contentious passage. But was Wisdom created or begotten or acquired? What is the meaning of *qānānī* (v. 22a)? De Boer has argued for the sense 'acquired' on the ground that Wisdom exists prior to Yahweh's creative activity, but although this is a common meaning of the word, it is not apposite here, for we expect some indication of how Wisdom originated and not the bald statement that Yahweh acquired her (P. de Boer, *VTS* iii, p. 69; cf. H. Ringgren, *Word and Wisdom*, pp. 99f.). The choice between 'create' and 'beget' is more crucial, and there is support from Ugaritic for the view that *qny* means 'procreate' rather than 'create' (G. R. Driver, *CML*, pp. 144; cf. *qānītī* in Gen. 4.1), while two other words in our passage are also connected with the process of birth. In vv. 24 and 25 Wisdom says that she was brought forth with labour (*ḥōlāltī*; see, however, Gemser, who urges that *ḥll* does not indicate physical birth or sonship), and if *nᵉsakkōtī* is read in v. 23 (BH), this can perhaps be translated: 'I was hidden in the womb in antiquity', since *skk* is used of the growth of the foetus in Ps. 139.13b (*tᵉsukkēnī bᵉbeṭen ʾimmī*), where, however, the reference of *skk* is clinched as it is not in Prov. 8.23a.

Irwin has called attention to these facts (W. A. Irwin, *JBL* lxxx, 1961, pp. 133f.) and has urged that it is the birth rather than the creation of Wisdom which is portrayed in the passage. This could be brought to bear on the problems of vv. 30f. as a confirmation that it is Wisdom as a 'child of Yahweh' in a special sense who is depicted there, and further conclusions as to the intention of this portrayal of a personified Wisdom and the kind of hypostasis which it represents might then be drawn. Thus von Rad has suggested that the mythological motif of 'a child of the gods' may be the background against which this passage has to be interpreted (*Theology* i, pp. 448f.). Wisdom is begotten, not made, and is not a creature in the ordinary sense; her precedence is qualitative as well as temporal.

Irwin, however, does not work out his insight in this way, for he holds that there is no hypostasis of Wisdom – only 'a poetic figure of speech' based on Prov. 3.19–20a. Then again, as can be seen in Gemser, the denial that there is a hypostasis may be combined with the interpretation of vv. 30f. in terms of Wisdom the child at play. And in Ringgren, a protagonist of hypostasis (*Word and Wisdom*, pp. 102f.), one finds a different interpretation of vv. 30f. and a lack of conviction that the choice between 'created' and 'procreated' in vv. 22–24 is crucial ('created' in v. 22, 'installed' in v. 23, 'born' in v. 24), along with the assertion that Wisdom is portrayed as possessing royal perhaps divine rank.

On the general question of hypostasis there is to be noted finally Donner's hypothesis (H. Donner, *ZAeS* 81–82, 1957, pp. 8f.) that the mythology in which the *Maat* concept is clothed in Egypt has shaped the portrayal of Wisdom in Prov. 8. Donner notes that *Maat* is located within the Godhead and is represented as the escort of the creator god *Re*. Donner supposes that this Egyptian influence was mediated through the Jewish community at Elephantine, which was not directly influenced by *Maat* mythology, but which, nevertheless, was not immune from its intellectual environment and could not shape its speculative activity in complete isolation from it. Donner's hypothesis rests on a slender basis, and the fragment in *Ahikar* which he adduces is an exceedingly fragile link between that book and Prov. 8 (cf. Kayatz, p. 12). With some reconstruction it reads: 'Even to the gods is she (Wisdom) precious, to her for ever belongs the sovereignty, in heaven is she treasured up, for the lord of holiness has exalted her' (col. vii.95, Cowley, pp. 215, 223). Cowley's translation does not envisage a personification of Wisdom.

The other stumbling-block to the understanding of v. 22 is the phrase *rēʾšīt darkō*, especially *darkō*. Since *qedem* in v. 22b has a temporal reference, it can fairly be concluded that *rēʾšīt* is similarly temporal and does not mean 'first in importance', as Irwin contends. If the translation is to be 'first of his ways', this has to be explained as 'first of his creative modes'. Or, perhaps, *derek* should be associated with Ugaritic *drkt* 'nobility', 'dominion' (*CML*, p. 154, n.11). 'Yahweh created me (or 'procreated me') as the first manifestation of his sovereignty' (cf. J. B. Bauer, *VT* viii, 1958, pp. 91f., who argues that *drk* has this meaning in certain other biblical passages, Ps. 90.7; Hos. 10.13; Jer. 3.13; Prov. 31.3; Num. 29.17; Job 40.19; 26.14). Even if there is this link with Ugaritic usage, it is a far cry from this to Albright's confident assertion that 'v. 22 begins with four words which transparently reflect a Canaanite 'L QNN R'ŠT DRKTH, "El created me at the beginning of his dominion"' (*VTS* iii, p. 7). Albright's reasoning is as wayward here as it is in his subsequent remarks on vv. 24f. He cites the following passage from the Baal myth:

Then surely she set her face
towards El at the source (*mbk*) of the rivers,
(in) the midst of the channels of the two oceans.

(The translation is that of G. R. Driver, *Baal* II iv.20f., *CML*, pp. 96f.; cf. III. 1.5f., *CML*, pp. 108f.; III* C.4, *CML*, pp. 76f.). Albright supposes that Prov. 8.24 contains a direct allusion to the situation described in these passages and adds: 'The words THMT and MBK occur in both passages. The biblical verse reflects older Canaanite mythological imagery. El brought forth wisdom even before he had conquered the primordial dragon Tehom and established his throne. The creation of the mountains was another favourite subject in the Canaanite and Hittite mythologies.'

[24–29] It is not at all clear to me what precise exegetical application to vv. 24f. Albright has in mind for these observations. The Ugaritic passages do support the emendation of *nikbaddē* (MT) to *nibkē* (*npk* or *nbk* are variants of *mbk*, cf. *CML*, p. 157, n.20; p. 162, n.11; J. A. Emerton, *VTS* xv, p. 126, n.2), and the reference to the two oceans (*thmtm*) does point to a Canaanite variant of the Babylonian creation myth. El becomes creator in virtue of his victory over the watery chaos, just as Marduk triumphed over the primordial dragon Tiamat. But Albright produces no evidence that there is a form of the myth in Ugarit according to which 'El brought forth wisdom before he had conquered the primordial dragon Tehom'. There are two passages in which wisdom is attributed to El, but neither gives any support to Albright's statement, nor do they bear any comparison with the representation in Prov. 8. 'Thy bidding, El, is wise, thy wisdom everlasting, a life of good luck is thy bidding' (*CML*, pp. 90f.; *Baal* V v. 30–31). Also: 'Thou art great El, surely the hoar hairs of thy head are united to wisdom' (*Baal* II v. 3–4; *CML*, pp. 96f.).

Moreover, Albright has taken no account of the circumstances that v. 24 is not consistent with a pre-existent watery chaos and that this is a noteworthy feature of the passage, furnishing a contrast with P's account of creation in Gen. 1.2. The statement in the latter that darkness was on the face of the *teₕōm* prior to Yahweh's creative activity may preserve only faintly the Marduk-Tiamat myth, but it does appear, at any rate, to envisage a formless material to which the creator gave shape (cf. G. von Rad, *Genesis*, *in loc.*). According to vv. 22f., on the other hand, Wisdom existed before the *tehōmōt*, which therefore belongs to the series of Yahweh's creative acts listed in vv. 24–29. (See, however, P. Reymond, *VTS* vi, 1958, p. 175, who argues that *tehōmōt* in Prov. 8.24 does not denote the primaeval deep; cf. J. A. Emerton, *VTS* xv, p. 126, n.2.) One can certainly detect in vv. 27–29 an allusion to the threat which is posed by the *tehōm* – the watery chaos – to the created order, and to this extent the old myth is still influential. The two oceans have to be contained, and this is done by reinforcement above and below – the clouds dam the upper ocean and precautions are taken so that the springs of the nether deep will not break through the disc of the earth (reading *beʿazzezō* with the versions or *beʿazzēz* with the suffix of *beʾammeṣō* implied. So G. R. Driver, *JRAS* 1948, pp. 164f.; Dahood, p. 16).

The fixing of the *ḥūg* on the face of the *tehōm* is perhaps the manoeuvring into position of the solid vault of heaven so that it rests on the disc of the earth and describes the horizon; or it may refer to the fixing of the disc itself over the nether ocean (see the discussion of v. 27b in Toy). The 'outside places' of v. 26a are probably 'fields' (so Gemser and Ringgren), and the *rōʾš ʿaperōt tēbēl* of v. 26b, 'the mass of the earth's soil' (KB², Gemser, Ringgren), rather than 'the first of the earth's soil'.

There remains Albright's contention that v. 25 contains mythological allusions similar to those of v. 24. The fashioning (*ṭbʿ* has this meaning in Arabic; the mountains are superimposed on the earth as a design on a coin or print on a page) of the mountains is mentioned as one of a series of creative acts and has no special mythological significance. The 'mountain of God' (cf. *hr 'el*, *Baal* II ii.36, *CML*, pp. 94f.) is a mythological concept and I have discussed this paradisal mount elsewhere in connection with Ezek. 28.2f. (*PWM*, pp. 73f.). This mountain (Zaphon or Mons Casius) is where Baal resides and perhaps represents a localizing in Lebanon of an original Babylonian myth. I cannot see, however, that v. 25 is related to these or any other mythological ideas. All that is involved in the verse is an assertion by Wisdom that she existed before the mountains and hills (cf. Gemser on vv. 22, 31: Wisdom shows her patent of nobility; the messenger of God proclaims her high antiquity – she is the oldest of created beings).

[30f.] The discussion of vv. 30f. has hinged on the meaning of *'āmōn* and has ranged far and wide. There are two suggestions which need not be considered at great length. Scott's argument that the original form is *'ōmēn* meaning 'binding', 'uniting' is unconvincing. Scott translates: 'Then I was at his side a living link.' (Cf. J. de Savignac, *VT* xii, 1962, pp. 211f., who observes that if *'mn* were a participle it ought to be feminine, as *m^eśaḥeqet* is.) Scott's related suggestion that *śḥq* 'laugh', 'sport', 'jest', has here the meaning 'to be active', 'to display vitality', is also improbable (R. B. Y. Scott, *VT* x, 1960, pp. 213f.). De Savignac's proposal is too clever to carry conviction: *śḥq* means 'to play', but here 'to dance'. The connection lies in the circumstance that the movements of Wisdom's dance are analogous to the movements of pawns in a game of chess. The perfect rhythm of the dance reflects the perfection of the divine creative activity. Then there is de Boer's proposal that *'immōn*, 'mother official', should be read, and that it is the role of the queen mother as an influential counsellor on which the representation of Wisdom in v. 30a is modelled. This proposal would have had more obvious relevance if *'immōn* had appeared in the context of vv. 12–21, where Wisdom advances claims to statesmanship, but v. 30 is connected rather with Wisdom's precedence over the created world and her special relationship to Yahweh. De Boer's point is that Wisdom does for Yahweh what the queen mother does for the king. Apart from the dubiety which could be expressed about the form (a diminutive, 'little mother'. This would be appropriate for the child Wisdom, but not for a queen mother. If the form is diminutive, how does the meaning 'mother official' develop from that of 'little mother'?) there are references to the jesting and playing of Wisdom which do not naturally cohere with de Boer's interpretation. If she is represented as the dignified, senior adviser of Yahweh, how does it come about that she is so sportive, so full of jests and laughter (P. de Boer, *VTS* iii, pp. 69f.)?

If MT is read, the picture is thought to be that of the child Wisdom who is the 'darling' (*'āmōn*) or 'ward' (*'āmūn*; Aquila, τιθηνουμένη) of Yahweh, and so Gemser thinks of a time when there was no need for Wisdom to address men with imperatives as a teacher or preacher, a Golden Age when discipline and admonition were not salutary necessities, and when 'before Yahweh' and 'upon the earth' did not involve any contradiction. 'I was delights daily' can be taken to mean that Wisdom experienced pleasure without alloy or that she gave delight to Yahweh (cf. Toy; the latter is indicated by BH *ša'ᵃšū'āw*, following LXX and Pesh.). Wisdom is a child without a care, her brow unfurrowed by anxiety, the vivacious playmate of God and man, with heaven and earth as her playground. I have already indicated that this interpretation of vv. 30f. could contribute to a precise hypostasis – Wisdom as the child of Yahweh, begotten not made. Kayatz (pp. 93f.) seeks the model of all this in Egyptian texts which represent *Maat* as the beloved child of the gods, playing before them and giving them pleasure before the world was created.

The disputed form in v. 30 should be connected with Accadian *ummānu*, although I take Gemser's point that there is nothing in the passage (vv. 22–31) to support the contention that Wisdom plays an architectonic role in creation and that the translation 'master of works' or 'architect' is consequently not apt (contrary to Ringgren; also J. de Savignac, *VT* xii, pp. 211f.). The *ō* of the second syllable of *'āmōn* can stand, since Semitic *ā* appears regularly as *ō* in Hebrew, and a form *'immōn* on the analogy of *gibbōr* (not the *'immōn* of de Boer) does not require any change of the consonantal text. Alternatively, *'ommōn*, which would be nearer to *'ommān* (Song of Songs 7.2), could be read. The latter is the exact equation of Accadian *ummānu*. I am attracted by Gaster's proposal that it is the role of the court expert (Accadian *ummānu*) which is alluded to in this representation of Wisdom in vv. 30f. (*VT* iv, 1954, pp. 77f.). Oppenheim argues that this is what Mummu ('Wisdom', 'Science') does for Apsu in *Enuma Eliš* (Tablet I, *l.* 31, *ANET*, p. 61: 'O Mummu, my vizier, who brings me into a good mood'), and that this is perhaps a mythological projection of the dwarfs who acted as court confidants and jesters

(*Or.* 16, 1947, p. 212; cf. W. F. Albright, *VTS* iii, p. 8, who notes the meaning 'wizard' for *ummānu* in the Taanach tablets. See *BASOR* 94, p. 18, n.28). What v. 31 then refers to is the delightful confidences and reminiscences which Wisdom can share with Yahweh, just because she saw the world coming into existence, and because in this respect her experience is unique. To understand v. 31 thus as alluding to the topics of conversation between Yahweh and Wisdom is, in my opinion, more apt than to suppose that it describes Wisdom's use of the world as a playground, 'sporting in his created world, my delights with the sons of men'. There is some doubt, however, whether *m^e^śaḥēq b^e^* can mean 'jesting about'. Ps. 104.26, where there is a similar construction, points clearly to 'sporting in'.

vv. 32–36 *The Concluding Admonition*

[32–36] Gemser argues that a comparison with LXX, as well as considerations of syntactical connection and rhythm, show that vv. 32–34 are in a state of disorder. He would transpose v. 32b ('Happy are those who keep my ways') after v. 34a ('Happy is the man who listens to me') with LXX, delete v. 33a with LXX and insert 'my admonition' (*tōkaḥtī*) between *w^e^* and *'al* in v. 33b (cf. BH, whose rearrangement is similar, but who deletes v. 33b and transposes v. 33a after v. 32a). The effect of Gemser's rearrangement is to get rid of the long line in v. 34 and to eliminate the awkward transition from an imperative in v. 32a to *'aš^e^rē* 'blessed' in v. 32b. Instead, two new lines are formed, one with two imperatives and the other with a twofold *'aš^e^rē*. Ringgren, on the other hand, reads MT without alteration.

In these concluding verses, Wisdom addresses her audience as a wisdom teacher might his pupils, urging on them the benefits to be derived from attentiveness to her words and warning against the perils attendant on neglecting discipline. For this is the route to wisdom which is not to be found by the indisciplined or inattentive. It is a matter of life or death, of gaining or losing Yahweh's approval. Wisdom is thus a teacher authorized by Yahweh, and to submit to her is to do Yahweh's will – to fulfil ultimate religious obligations (v. 35b). As the disciples of the wisdom teacher gathered for instruction at the door of his house, Wisdom urges men to maintain a like vigil outside her residence, for to find her is to find life, whereas to miss her is to do violence to life (*nepeš*) and to hate her is to love death

(vv. 34–36). The house of the *'iššā zārā* is the mouth of death, the threshold of Sheol, so that when a man enters it he has taken the road to the underworld; this is a journey from which no traveller returns. Such are those who miss Wisdom and do violence to their 'life' (see on 7.27, above, p. 341). But the house of Wisdom is the gateway to life and those who come there amenable to discipline and hungry for wisdom (cf. v. 33a, the personified Wisdom teaches wisdom) will be established on a road ('Happy are those who keep my ways', v. 32b) along which their vitality will be progressively enhanced (on the meaning of 'life' and 'vitality' see 7.1–5, above, pp. 332f.).

Chapter 9

There are traces of the Instruction in vv. 6, 8, 9, but otherwise it exercises little formal influence on the structure of this chapter. The keynote is 'invitation' rather than 'instruction', with Wisdom competing with the *'iššā zārā* for 'guests'. Verses 7–12 disturb both the balance and continuity of the chapter and it is probable that v. 13 originally resumed v. 6. There is evidence from textual criticism which may have some bearing on the growth of vv. 7–12. Thus vv. 9f. are absent from one Hebrew MS and vv. 10–12 from another (see BH), and there are seven additional lines in LXX which envisage the κακός of v. 12 (into which *laṣtā* of MT is generalized) as a liar and compare him in a rather far-fetched way to the remiss farmer who wastes his energies on profitless pursuits.

A further indication of the fluidity of the text is the long addition in LXX after v. 18 (seven or eight lines), in which the formal elements of the Instruction are present. If the longer text of LXX[A] and LXXℵ[c.a] (cf. LXX[B]) is followed, the passage consists of two imperatives followed by two motive clauses; two imperatives followed by two final clauses. This has apparently been added in order to reinforce the warning against the *'iššā zārā* by someone who felt that a more cautionary emphasis than that supplied by the laconic observation of v. 18 was required. It was not enough to reproduce the woman's invitation and to conclude with a couplet of sententious, macabre comment. The addition reverts to the explicit directives of the Instruction, the warning against alien waters and an alien fountain recalling the metaphor of 5.15f. (see above, p. 318f.). The imagery is not entirely felicitous, although 'Drink not of an alien fountain' is more so than the rest, as a warning against illicit sexual intercourse with the *'iššā zārā.*

The addition of vv. 7–12 is perhaps intended to fulfil a function not dissimilar to the addition in LXX after v. 18, that is, to enlarge Wisdom's role as an instructress. In vv. 1–6 there is only one verse of Instruction (v. 6), which is then supplemented by vv. 7–12. It is possible, however, that the material in vv. 7–12 was not originally shaped as an address of Wisdom and that is has only become so by modification of v. 11 ('by me' for 'by it'), 'it' referring to 'the fear of Yahweh' or to *ḥokmā* in v. 10 (so Gemser, following Kuhn).

vv. 1–6 *The Invitation of Wisdom*

[1–6] I agree with Boström that the portrayal of Wisdom in vv. 1–6 is secondary in the sense that it is formed on the model of the *'iššā zārā* (pp. 156f.). In other words, although the description of Wisdom comes first, she is not really the basis of the comparison. Rather, the portrayal is a contrived antithesis of a previously existing model. The young women who are sent out to make the invitation public are probably, as Boström supposes, a somewhat pale reflection of the devotees of the goddess of love, whose activities are represented by the invitation issued by the woman in 7.10f. (see above, pp. 336f.). In the context of the fertility cult, such women have a precise function to fulfil and their invitation is related to their intention to consummate their devotion to the goddess by an act of sexual intercourse. By contrast, the young women who serve Wisdom cannot be similarly anchored to a coherent, concrete structure. There is no cult of wisdom which is served by devotees. The young women who publish the invitation of Wisdom are presumably not wisdom teachers, since these are neither youthful nor female, although they speak, for the most part, like wisdom teachers. The lack of coherence in the representation may be taken as an indication that it belongs to another setting and has only been imperfectly accommodated to Wisdom. It is only in v. 5 that their invitation to a feast rings true, and their words would pass as authentic from the lips of a devotee of Astarte.

The woman in 7.10f. invites the youth to take his fill of love until morning. She is interested in him for his virility, through which she can fulfil her service to Astarte. The young women of ch. 9 have an educational mission; they invite young men not to bed, but to school; they address themselves to the untutored youth, deficient in acumen (*ḥ^a^sar lēb*), who constitutes the raw material which the wisdom teacher shapes by an educational process. He must forsake his untutored companions and, in the face of the complexities of the world, acquire such discrimination and sagacity as will enable him to pick his steps along life's road (v. 6). The reading of LXX (*ἀφροσύνην*, BH: *p^e^tī*, 'folly', 'untutored state') is probably a paraphrase of MT: *p^e^tā'īm*, rather than a translation of an original *p^e^tī*.

The singular *tiqrā'* in v. 3a and the third person in v. 4b appear to reflect an uncertainty as to whether it is Wisdom or the attendants who speak the words of invitation. If understood distributively, *tiqrā'* is compatible with an address by each of the young women (it is explained differently by Albright, *VTS* iii, p. 9, on the analogy of a grammatical peculiarity of Ugaritic – agreement of a feminine singular verb with a plural antecedent.) If *'ām^e^rā lō* is read in 4b, it is a preface to vv. 5f. and not part of the invitation (so RSV). It is then Wisdom who speaks in vv. 5f. If *'ōm^e^rā* is read with Pesh., the address runs (carrying over 'whoever' from 4a) without interruption from vv. 4–6. 'She has sent out her maids to announce on the heights of the town: "Whoever is untutored, let him turn in here; whoever lacks sense, to him I will say."' Dahood (pp. 16f.) translates *šāl^e^ḥā* 'dismisses' (3a), and supposes that Wisdom is the subject of *tiqrā'*. But if the *athnach* is retained at *tiqrā'*, as it must be since the first *stichos* ends there, Wisdom cannot be the subject of *tiqrā'*.

Alternatively, Gemser supposes that v. 4a is not part of the invitation and that like v. 16a it is an aside by the author, supplying a commentary on the situation and indicating his own attitude. In v. 4a ('Whoever is untutored, let him turn in here'), he speaks soberly and in v. 16a ironically, with intent to warn. It is in this way that Gemser explains 'here' in 4a. The poet claims the authority of an accredited representative of Wisdom and directs the attention of the untutored youth towards himself. This is an unnatural construction to put on these words. It is more reasonable to suppose that they belong to the address both in 4a and 16a. In this case 'here' (v. 4) is another pointer to the dependence of vv. 1–6 on the model in vv. 13–18. In v. 16, where the woman sits at the door of her house and issues her invitation to the young man, 'here' is apt as it is not in v. 4, where Wisdom has prepared the feast in her house (v. 2), and has sent her maids to publicize the invitation from prominent places in the town (so Boström). Boström supposes that the address runs from v. 4 to v. 6, interrupted only by the words 'she says to him'.

This wavering between an address by Wisdom and an address by her maids is just another indication of the lack of coherence in the representation of vv. 1–6. If we subtract the apparatus of the words of invitation to a meal (v. 5) and the reference to its preparation (v. 2), all of which has been attached to Wisdom on the analogy of the cult of the goddess of love and is only imperfectly and superficially assimilated, we are left with a portrayal of Wisdom akin to that of 1.20f. and 8.1f. It is Wisdom, the teacher, who stands before us, one who avails herself of every natural rostrum (v. 3, cf. 1.21, 8.2) in order to confront men effectively with her educational demands.

As for Wisdom's house with its seven pillars (v. 1), the first question we have to ask is whether it is a domestic residence or a temple which is so represented. Gemser alludes to Dunand's article in which he discusses examples of houses of archaic design in Phoenicia, Egypt and Babylonia with seven wooden pillars on stone bases, and, although Gemser mentions the Akitu house in Babylon as a possible model, he comes down on the side of a non-cultic interpretation (Gemser, p. 111; M. Dunand, *Bulletin du Musée de Beyrouth*, iv (1940), pp. 69–84). Wisdom is envisaged as occupying a patrician residence and dispensing such hospitality as befits her station. On the other hand, Boström, Albright and Ringgren all suppose that v. 1 describes a temple rather than a house. Boström thinks of an astral myth featuring a goddess who is the queen of heaven, and supposes that the phenomenological basis of the portrayal is the system of the sun and the seven planets. The goddess has been replaced by Wisdom. This seems to me improbable; it is surprising that one of the protagonists of a cultic interpretation of the passage should see in v. 1 not the description of a cultic structure but the reflection of an astral myth. Albright (*VTS* iii, pp. 8f.) rejects the Akitu house as a possible model and substitutes a shrine with seven free-standing pillars such as that discovered by Mitford near Amathus in Cyprus (T. B. Mitford, *Journal of Hellenic Studies* lxvi, 1946, pp. 24–42). This shrine, built in the Flavian period, and dedicated by the Roman pro-consul to Aphrodite, was named 'The Holy Place of the Seven within the Stelae' (τὸ [ἱε]ρὸν τῶν ἐντὸς [τ]ῶν στηλ[ῶν ἑπ]τά). Mitford remarks: 'So few letters have been lost that no alternative restoration seems to me possible' (p. 40). He has in mind a temenos of the circular type familiar from excavations of pre-classical sites, marked out by stelae, and within this seven statues of cult figures (p. 42). Alternatively, he envisages a group of standing stones within a circle of orthostats (p.

42, n.68), and in the title of the sanctuary he detects a survival of the early religion of Cyprus. This would appear to be a temple dedicated to a goddess of love with seven 'pillars' (if the seven indeed are pillars) and is yet another pointer that Wisdom has taken the place of the goddess of love in vv. 1–6. She resides in a temple, invites her devotees to a cultic meal (v. 2, with *ʿārekā šulḥānā* Boström compares *šulḥān ʿārūk* in Ezek. 23.42, referring to alien cultic practices with which the Jerusalem temple was profaned), but presides over a cult purged of impurity and initiates her novices to insight, not folly, to life rather than death (v. 6, cf. v. 18). Ringgren, following this line of interpretation, supposes that the heights of the town in v. 3 refers to the acropolis (so also Albright) and that the temple is thought of as located on the edge of this area, so that the maids publish Wisdom's invitation to the feast from its precincts.

In the form *ḥokmōt* (see 1.20, above, p. 272), Albright discerns a 'Canaanitism' and, following Ginsberg, derives it from a postulated **ḥukmatu* (**ḥukmatu* normally appears as *ḥokmā* in Hebrew, and the form *ḥokmōt* (sing.) exemplifies a retention of the final *t*, the lengthening of the short *a* and then its change to *ō* as is usual in Hebrew). Albright cites the parallel of *Milkōt* for *Milkat* 'queen' (name of a goddess). It is just possible that *ḥokmōt* on the analogy of *Milkōt* is another indication that Wisdom is a surrogate or replacement of a goddess.

I have indicated that some of the functions of the goddess of love are ascribed to Wisdom in vv. 1–6 and that the passage consequently has a composite character, being a blend of invitation and instruction. This does not absolve the interpreter from enquiring what the passage as a whole now means, and with this in view it is important to pay some attention to the meal which is mentioned in v. 2 and v. 5. I have tended to the conclusion that this is a cultic meal in a temple rather than a banquet in Wisdom's private residence. It is likely in view of *ṭābeḥā ṭibḥāh* (v. 2) that *leḥem* (v. 5) means 'flesh' and not 'bread' (cf. Arabic *laḥm*, 'flesh'; also Ugaritic *lḥm*, *CML*, p. 158). The other possibility would be that 'bread' represents a form of understatement (cf. our 'Come and have a bite with me'). See *BDB* on Gen. 18.5; Judg. 19.5; I Sam. 28.22. Even if no more is involved than the provision of a banquet by a generous hostess, the reference to the rare luxury of meat is apt. Wisdom provides a princely feast and the wine is mixed with honey and spices (so KB²).

In 7.14, the devotee of the goddess of love refers to her *zibḥē šelāmīm*. *zbḥ* and *ṭbḥ* have two consonants in common and are obviously related in meaning. Here, then, is perhaps another respect in which Wisdom's actions run parallel to those of the *'iššā zārā* and, if so, this would suggest that *ṭbḥ* (v. 2) means not just 'slaughter' but 'sacrificial slaughter', a meaning more usually associated with *zbḥ*. This would imply that we have to reckon with a cultic meal but hardly with a cult of Wisdom, for she is a devotee (perhaps a priestess, *ṭābeḥā*, v. 2), not a goddess. This cultic meal may then be thought of as spiritual nourishment in a broad sense, so as to bring together the elements of invitation and instruction, but the concept of a sacramental meal should not be pressed. Certainly it is not a bread and wine meal, and it would seem to me to be a curious enterprise to attempt to represent it as a prototype of the Christian sacrament in any precise sense.

The difficulty of imposing a clear interpretation on vv. 1–6 stems basically from the circumstance that in these verses Wisdom is deliberately drawn as a rival to the goddess of love or her devotee (the representation seems to waver in this regard) and that she can only be imperfectly accommodated to this manner of portrayal. I do not suppose that the intention is to represent a cult of Wisdom. If the cultic interpretation is taken seriously, the cult which is hinted at can only be the Jerusalem cult, and the significance of this would be that the promise of 'life' which Wisdom makes (v. 6) has here a cultic connection. Normally this offer of life is not connected with the cult in the Wisdom literature. It is conditional, rather, on instruction, on submission to the authority of the wisdom teacher. Even where it hinges on submission to Yahweh and on obedience to his directives, it is not set in the cult in the precise way which I have in mind.

There is, however, as von Rad and Zimmerli have pointed out, an assurance of 'life' which is made in the context of the Jerusalem cult. This is a priestly declaratory formula (von Rad), and it is made in respect of the man whose 'righteousness' has been established by a priest. The procedure is related to the Entry *Tōrōt* (Ps. 15; 24.3–6) which laid down the conditions to be fulfilled by those who would participate in the worship of the Jerusalem temple. Zimmerli supposes that Ezek. 18 reflects the form of such a *tōrā*, and that v. 9 preserves the authoritative priestly ruling, 'He is righteous, he shall surely live.' The officials who regulated conditions of entry are equated by Zimmerli with 'the keepers of the threshold' (*šōmerē hassap*, see my article in *ZAW* 71, 1959, pp. 260–5). He leaves the question open whether the same officials also gave the assurance of 'life', or whether this was reserved for the high point of the festival (W. Zimmerli, *Gottes Offenbarung: Gesammelte Aufsätze zum Alten Testament*, 1963, pp. 178–91, 319f.; G. von Rad, *Old Testament Theology*, i, pp. 261f., 377f.). The Jerusalem temple is the fountain of life (Ps. 36.10) and the man who is declared righteous or counted righteous (G. von Rad, *Gesammelte Studien zum Alten Testament*, 1958, pp. 130–5) possesses 'life' (von Rad, *op. cit.*, pp. 225–47).

If these ideas have any influence on ch. 9, we have to suppose that two cults and two sacrificial meals are deliberately juxtaposed. In the alien cult, the sacrificial meal is linked to sexual intercourse and 'death'; in the cult of Yahweh, it is 'spiritual' nourishment and so linked to 'life'. 'Life', however, is not conceived as immediate, irreducible cultic experience (von Rad associates it with justification by faith or the like); it is, in the manner of the wisdom literature, conditional on instruction and insight (*bīnā*). It is the man who leaves behind intellectual rawness and immaturity who lives, and life itself is a fluid concept. It is associated with progress along a 'road' and so it has to do with keeping the right direction and having access to sure guidance. At any and every moment it may be enhanced or diminished, for no man stands still. He must journey on and, if he loses his way, he may lose his life. Hence longevity (v. 11) is a constituent part of this concept of life, for its consummation is an old age which is full of glory and to attain this one must keep on the right road to the end. 'For by me your days are multiplied, and the years of your life increased' (reading *yiwwāsᵉpū*). This is the completion of life, and then death has no terrors. The descent into Sheol is a disaster only if it overtakes a man before his life has attained its full maturity. So, even if the cultic concept of life impinges on this passage, it is, in the last analysis, the wisdom teacher's offer of life which appears, rather than the priestly ruling or benediction which assures life.

vv. 13–18 *The Invitation of the Foolish Woman*

[13–18] The designation of the unchaste woman as foolish indicates the intention to compare her directly with Wisdom. Just as features of the *'iššā zārā* or the goddess of love whom she serves have been transferred to Wisdom, so, to a lesser degree, the reverse tendency can be detected in vv. 13–18. Thus it is in keeping with the role of Wisdom to address her invitation to those who are untutored and wanting in acumen (v. 4), but it is not in character for the devotee of the goddess of love to employ such vocabulary (v. 16). Her actions and words in 7.13f. show that she is not a teacher, but a lover; that it is the young man's body, and not his mind, in which she is interested. The same is indicated by the proverbial saying in 9.17, where the woman speaks in character and gives proverbial expression to the lure of the forbidden and the delight of illicit pleasures. D. Winton Thomas (*VT* xv, 1965, p. 272) cites the Arabic proverb: 'Everything forbidden is sweet.' Here it is the ecstasy of sexual intercourse which is conjured up for the young man. Since v. 17 is a proverb, susceptible of this interpretation in the context, it should not be thought that any significant juxtaposition with vv. 2 and 5 is primarily intended. The suggestion that the woman issues an invitation to a meal whose ingredients compare badly with those of Wisdom's feast tends to obscure the proverbial character of v. 17 and its primary significance. It is marginally possible that the proverb may have been chosen so as to hint secondarily at the disparity between the two meals – bread and water as against meat and wine (cf. Gemser and Ringgren).

Another question is whether the reference to 'the heights of the town' is not a feature of the portrayal of Wisdom which has been transferred to the woman. If the woman were seated there, the words 'let him turn in here' would be as inappropriate to her as Boström thinks they are to the maids of Wisdom in vv. 3f. In other words, 'let him turn in here' presupposes that the woman is sitting at the door of the house and not on the heights of the town. This difficulty would be disposed of, if we supposed with Ringgren that the phrase 'the heights of the town' refers to the acropolis where a temple was situated. In this case, the phrase would be synonymous with 'the door of her house', and 'house' would indicate the temple of the goddess whom she serves, not her private residence. Against this is the fact that there is what might almost be described as a convention, in accordance with which Wisdom is a teacher or a preacher who encounters men in the busiest places of the town, who raises her voice at the city gate or where roads cross or where a natural pulpit enables her to command attention (1.20f.; 8.1f.; 9.3). Since there is certainly a transference from Wisdom to the woman in v. 16, it is probable that 'on the heights of the town' is another example of this.

There are some linguistic difficulties attaching to the description of the woman in v. 13. As in 7.11, *hōmīyā* is used of her – she is restless and rootless. G. R. Driver's suggestion that *p^etayyūt* should be taken with *hōmīyā* ('a foolish woman bustles about in silliness') requires a change in the Masoretic punctuation (*Biblica* 32, pp. 178f.). A weightier objection to Driver's reconstruction is that the use of *hōmīyā* in 7.11 would lead us to expect that *hōmīyā* is also a predicate here ('a foolish woman is wanton'). There is the further consideration that *hōmīyā ūm^epatte* is the same kind of phrase as *hōmīyā hī' w^esōreret* (7.11a), and that 9.13b then approximates to 7.11b (see below). I consequently read *ūm^epatte* for *p^etayyūt* and transfer the *athnach* to *ūm^epatte*.

BH follows LXX and Pesh. in reading *k^elimmā* for *mā* ('a foolish woman is wanton and deceitful and does not know shame'). The readings of LXX and Pesh. probably arise from an attempt to make sense of a difficult Hebrew text, rather than as a translation of *k^elimmā* in a Hebrew text different from MT. Driver and Gemser suppose that *yd'* means 'to be concerned' rather than 'to know'. The woman cares for nothing – she is reckless. Winton Thomas associates *yd'* with Arabic *wd'* 'to become still', 'to be at rest'. *bal yāde'ā mā* is then synonymous with *hōmīyā* (see on 5.6, above, p. 314, where *lō' tēdā'* appears to have this sense). 'The foolish woman wanders to and fro, seducing (*m^epatte*) and ever restless' (D. Winton Thomas, *JTS* iv, 1953, pp. 23f.). The analogy of 7.11b gives support to this elucidation of *bal yāde'ā mā*. In 7.11a the woman is described as 'wanton and feverish' (cf. 9.13a), and this suggests that *bal yāde'ā mā* may have a similar meaning to 'her feet do not stay in her house' (7.11b).

Boström suggests that behind the portrayal of the devotee of the goddess in 9.13f. the figure of Astarte herself may be detected, particularly in the phrase *'ēšet k^esīlūt*, where he concludes that *k^esīlūt* is a surrogate of the type *bōšet*. As Baal is replaced by *bōšet*, so Astarte is by *k^esīlūt* (p. 159).

I have already suggested that there is a mythological background to the representation of the woman's house as the gateway to Sheol (see on 1.12, above, pp. 269f., 2.18, above, pp. 285f.; 7.24–27, above, p. 341). In 9.18 her house is described as the country of the dead, as itself the deepest recess of Sheol (cf. 7.27), where that shadowy community is massed (*repā'īm*, see on 2.18) and to which her guests are annexed. The choice between Wisdom and the woman is one between life and death (see on 7.1–5, above, pp. 332f.; 7.24–27, above p. 341).

vv. 7–12 *Wisdom and Incorrigibility*

[7–12] I have indicated above that this is not a convincing nor apt continuation of Wisdom's address, and that it interrupts the original continuity of vv. 1–6 and 13–18. Both Gemser and Ringgren call attention to its pessimistic tone and suggest that it was inserted as an antidote to the buoyant optimism of vv. 1–6 by someone who had been sobered by experience, and had discovered that to teach wisdom to men who are impervious to it is to expose oneself to abuse and indignity. However this may be, vv. 7–12 certainly indicate that there are types of men who are incorrigible and that the wisdom teacher should concentrate his efforts on those who are receptive to wisdom and disposed towards it (vv. 7–9).

In addition to this limitation which is placed on the effectiveness of wisdom teaching, there is also in v. 10 a clear statement of the redefinition of wisdom in terms of Yahwistic piety. I have argued elsewhere (*PWM*, pp. 48f.) that the fear of Yahweh is not an original constituent of wisdom (Zimmerli's position is similar to that of von Rad: *Gottes Offenbarung*, pp. 306f.), and I have maintained this in relation to Prov. 1.1–7 (see above, pp. 262f.). The fear of Yahweh is the new *mūsār*, and its promulgation is associated with a shift of emphasis from education to piety, from submission to the discipline imposed by a wisdom teacher to reverence for Yahweh. Complementary to the new *mūsār* there is a new *bīnā* (cf. *PWM*, pp. 86f.), as can be seen in v. 10: 'The knowledge of the Holy One is *bīnā*.' LXX has rendered *qᵉdōšīm* by ἁγίων 'holy ones', i.e., angels (with *qᵉdōšīm* compare *'ᵉlōhīm*). 'Insight' is no longer intellectual clarity and discrimination, but religious illumination, and 'knowledge of the Holy One' is to be compared with the prophetic 'knowledge of God' or 'knowledge of Yahweh' which is defined as religious faith and commitment (*PWM*, pp. 86f.).

There are other indications in the section of this religious orientation, and the degree of pessimism expressed is not unrelated to it. Certain men resist all attempts to educate them, not only because of intellectual but also because of moral obtuseness. The person who affects intellectual superiority and who ridicules other men and their values with a show of arrogance is a common subject of criticism in the Egyptian Instruction. Here we have not only the antithesis *lēṣ* and *ḥākām*, but also the antithesis *rāšāʿ* and *ṣaddīq*. The *rāšāʿ* is as unteachable and offensive as the *lēṣ*, and conversely, the righteous man and the wise man are equally amenable to discipline and instruction. Even if it is going too far to argue, on the ground of the parallelism, that the righteous man is equated with the wise man in v. 9, at least righteousness is assumed to be an essential part of wisdom.

Finally, there is the conviction that wisdom is an inalienable possession. It is part of the man who has it; it makes him what he is and no man can take it away from him. In this sense he is responsible for his wisdom and has full disposal of it. And the same is true of the person who has intellectual pride. This is an attitude which is constitutive of him in the most inward characteristics of his selfhood. He has become this kind of man through his own obdurate pride in the most private sector of his life and it is there in his loneliness that he must endure the consequences on his personality as they work themselves out inexorably (v. 12).

B. CHAPTERS 22.17–24.22

Since the words 'These are also attributable to the wise men' (24.23) indicate the beginning of a new collection, they also mark the conclusion of the preceding composition at 24.22. Moreover, the form of this superscription suggests that it was preceded by another which introduced 22.17–24.22 as 'The words of the wise men' (cf. LXX: 'Incline your ear to the words of the wise men and hear my word'). Hence BH restores the title 'The words of the wise men' and emends v. 17a so that it reads: 'Incline your ear and hear my words' (so also Gemser and Scott).

The limits of this piece are clearly defined by its differing formal characteristics as compared with the material which precedes and follows it. Broadly speaking, it is Instruction in its formal organization, whereas before and behind it is sentence literature. The wisdom sentence has the form of a statement; it is propositional or affirmative without any elements of direct address or exhortation. The Instruction is framed in the imperative and it commands or prohibits; it is thus characterized by direct address ('my son', 23.15, 19, 26; 24.13, 21). This distinction between 22.17–24.22 and the material which surrounds it is blurred only to a small and insignificant extent by the circumstance that 22.17–24.22 itself contains a small quantity of sentence literature (24.3–10; cf. *Onchsheshonqy*, above, pp. 117f., in which there is a blend of Instruction and sentences) and that fragments of Instruction are to be found in 24.23f. (e.g., 24.27–29).

The motive clause, which we have seen to be an important formal element of the Instruction, is prominent in 22.17–24.22. To speak more strictly, the arguments with which the imperatives are supported usually overrun the limits of a clause; their character as motivation is frequently indicated by *kī* (22.18, 23; 23.5, 7, 9, 11, 21, 27; 24.2, 13, 16, 20, 22), although elsewhere they are asyndetic (22.27; 23.5a, 8, 13b, 14, 18, 24, 28; 24.12, 14?). The motivation is organized in a variety of ways. In 23.9 the motive clause in its simplest form appears, in vv. 13b–14 the supporting argument is contained in two asyndetic sentences each consisting of protasis and apodosis (cf. 22.27), while in 24.12 a possible excuse is reproduced *verbatim* in order that its invalidity may be demonstrated. In 24.16 there is an example of antithetic parallelism in a motive sentence. In the case of 23.29–35 we have a passage which precedes the imperative (v. 31), and which is preamble rather than motivation. Nevertheless, its function is approximately the same as that of the argument which follows the imperative. It is a softening-up process which creates the right conditions for ready acquiescence to the Instruction and its formal constituents are a series of staccato questions to which a firm answer is given. The imperative is consequently ringed by cautionary recital, for vv. 32–35 continue the sorry tale of vv. 29–30 with extended motivation (asyndetic). In 24.6, the motive clause is attached to a wisdom sentence, and this may represent a transference to the wisdom sentence (which normally states without justifying the statement or arguing its reasonableness) of an element of form which belongs to the Instruction.

In addition to the motive clause, there are examples of the final clause (22.19, 21), of the negative final clause (22.25; 24.18, 'lest'= 'in order that not'), of the protasis before (23.1, *kī*) and after (23.2, *'im*) the imperative, all of which are syntactical elements of the Instruction. The final clause indicates the objectives which will be attained by paying attention to the imperatives, or, in its negative form, the disasters which will be avoided. The protasis gives a precise indication of the conditions in which the imperative is operative. In 22.29 the aspect of authoritative instruction, though not of direct address ('do you see'), is lacking, and yet the intention to instruct is present. The skilful official is held up as an example to be imitated: 'If you desire to rise above the mediocre and to rank high in the service of the state, be like this man.'

I have deliberately avoided the question of the relationship between 22.17–24.22 and the *Instruction of Amenemope* in order to show that the identification of the passage as Instruction can be made without reference to *Amenemope* and is independent of whatever construction is put on the resemblances between the two pieces. Since 1924, when Erman argued for the dependence of the passage on *Amenemope* (*Sitzungsberichte d. preuss. Acad. d. Wissenschaft*, 1924, pp. 86–93), this ground has been well trodden by scholars and I have nothing new to add. The various opinions which have been expressed are well reviewed by Gemser and Ringgren. The main weight of scholarly opinion has been on the side of Erman, but it has been held that the Egyptian book is dependent on the biblical book of Proverbs (R. O. Kevin, *Journal of the Society for Oriental Research*, 14, 1930, pp. 115–57) or that both stem from a common Semitic source (W. O. E. Oesterley, *ZAW* 45, 1927, pp. 9–24; *The Wisdom of Egypt and the Old Testament in the Light of the newly discovered Teaching of Amenemope*, 1927). More recently, Drioton has argued that both works stem from an extra-canonical Hebrew source which was composed by a syncretistic Jew living in Egypt (E. Drioton, *Robert Festschrift*, 1957, pp. 254–80; *BEThL* xii, 1959, pp. 229–41). Williams has reviewed the problem, taking Drioton's opinions into account, and has endorsed the findings of Erman (R. J. Williams, *JEA* 47, 1961, pp. 100–6). Gemser and Scott follow Erman's conclusions and this is broadly the position of Ringgren who, however, leans towards Drioton to the extent that he envisages the possibility of a Canaanite original for the Egyptian book of *Amenemope*.

The resemblances with *Amenemope*, varying in degree and sometimes amounting to verbal identity, are confined to 22.17–23.11, except, perhaps, for 24.10–12. Even so, the Israelite editor exercises freedom in his choice of Egyptian material, alters its order and imagery and inserts instructions of his own or from other sources. In 23.12–24.22 there is evidence of influence from *Ahikar* (see above, pp. 156f.). Scott (pp. 20f.) suggests that the author was a scribe who was so familiar with international wisdom that he modelled his composition on *Amenemope* in so far as he had a copy of this work or remembered its contents. His copy or his memory reached as far as 23.11, and the transition to other material is marked by 'a hortatory sub-heading' in 23.12. But if 23.12 is to be regarded as 'a hortatory sub-heading', why not 23.19, 22 as well (cf. Gemser, see below)?

In the article cited, Erman proposed that MT *šilšōm* ('the day before yesterday'; Q. *šālīšīm*, 'officers', 'key-sayings'?) in v. 20 should be emended to *šᵉlōšīm*, 'thirty', thus revealing a correspondence between the thirty chapters of *Amenemope* and the structure of 22.17–24.22. The figure of thirty can be computed in different ways, and there are slight differences, for example, in the allocation of the lines by Gemser and Scott. Gemser isolates 23.19, 22 and brackets 23.23 (absent from LXX) as secondary. Scott incorporates 23.19 in the unit 23.19–21, and 23.22 in the unit 23.22, 24, 25 and isolates 23.23. Scott also isolates 24.10, which Gemser includes in the unit 24.10–12. Finally, Scott brackets 23.12 as a hortatory sub-heading (see above). Gemser observes that ch. 30 of *Amenemope* contains concluding remarks and suggests that the introduction in 22.17–21 should perhaps be taken into the reckoning in an attempt to arrive at the number thirty. This possibility should be ruled out, because the thirty sayings which are referred to in 22.20a (emended) must follow 22.20a, and so 22.17–21 cannot be the first of the thirty. I differ from both Gemser and Scott in that I am not inclined to break up the unity of 23.22–25; otherwise I follow Scott, except that I do not bracket 23.12.

The propriety of looking for thirty sayings in Proverbs has been challenged by W. Richter (*Recht und Ethos. Studien zum Alten und Neuen Testament*, xv, 1966), who distinguishes between a translator and a collector of the Egyptian material, and urges that it is a mistake to reconstruct thirty sayings out of 22.17–24.22. Even if Erman's emendation were accepted, the 'thirty' would apply only to the work of the translator, of which a third has been selected by the collector and is extant in 22.17–23.11, divided by Richter into ten sayings, exclusive of the prologue (22.17–21) which he attributes to the collector.

It is, of course, legitimate to think of each saying as a small poem based on the couplet and to speak of the predominance of quatrains (Gemser, Scott), but I would insist here as I did in relation to *Amenemope* that the syntactical analysis is still valid. In *Amenemope*, certain new elements of form appear as compared with the other examples of the Egyptian Instruction, such as the division into chapters, the arrangement of the text in lines of poetry and the incidence of parallelism. Nevertheless, the basic syntactical elements of the genre are as faithfully reproduced in *Amenemope* as they are elsewhere, and the same is true of Prov. 22.17–24.22.

The pattern, apart from the exceptions which I have noted (above, p. 369) and which do not belong to the genre, is that of imperatives with supporting argument or, in one case, the bare imperative (22.28). I have applied this type of analysis to 23.29–35 (see above, p. 370), which is longer and has a more complicated structure than any other of the sayings. The introduction (22.17–21), which is also long, consists of imperatives followed by a series of arguments arranged in motive and final clauses, a structure which I have already shown to be characteristic of the Instruction. Thus v. 18 explains the reasonableness and desirability of heeding the imperatives, while the final clauses, v. 19a and v. 21, are dependent on v. 19b and v. 20 respectively, both of which explicate the imperatives.

The sentence literature and Instruction are different genres, and a unitary form-critical approach to all the material in the book of Proverbs, based on the assumption that the single wisdom sentence is everywhere the simplest formal unit, is misconceived. The Instruction is not an agglomeration of wisdom sentences, and the lateness of Prov. 1–9 cannot be proved by an argument which hinges on the history of the form of the wisdom sentence, and which supposes that the larger unities of ch. 1–9 exemplify an advanced stage of formal evolution.

If confirmation beyond what I have supplied in 1–9 is needed, it is furnished by 22.17–23.11. With the majority of scholars I do not believe that there is any reasonable doubt that this section is dependent on the *Instruction of Amenemope*. The relationship is at least close enough to show that the formal structure of the Egyptian genre was known in Old Testament circles and could be reproduced. What puzzles me is that this is admitted in relation to Prov. 22.17–23.11 without any consequences being drawn for ch. 1–9. It is known that an Old Testament writer could appropriate the Instruction from Egypt full-grown, with its formal structure complete. Is it then conceivable that this same Instruction genre in 1–9 came into existence through a form-critical process consummated on Israelite soil, whereby individual wisdom sentences were gradually built up into the larger unities which now lie before us? The Instruction can be identified as certainly in 1–9 as it can be in 22.17–24.22, and there is no reason to doubt that there is an international model behind the one as surely as there is behind the other. The entire form-critical argument for the lateness of Prov. 1–9 falls to the ground.

I am not concerned to show that 1–9 is not late, but only that one of the most fashionable ways of arguing its lateness is unsound (see further above, pp. 1f.). I have indicated that there are marks of lateness in its contents, but there are marks of earliness as well. Much more important than fixing a date for the completion of the collection is the realization that it is a deposit of Israelite wisdom. It is a record of the history of the wisdom tradition in Israel and, more particularly, of the history of the Instruction, and it is for the light that it throws on this that it should be valued and studied earnestly. There is no single concept of wisdom in Prov. 1–9, for it has the marks of an on-going tradition which proves its vigour by its suppleness and its capacity for reappraisal and realignment. The record of this vital process is there to be read, and the old and new lie side by side. It ranges from a worldly shrewdness and know-how to a Yahwistic piety; from wisdom in the form of statecraft at the court of kings to Wisdom located with God before the creation of the world.

22.17–21 *Introductory: Listen and be instructed*

[17] The Instruction opens characteristically with a demand for attentiveness and unbroken concentration. 'Listen to my words' (on the emendation see above). 'Apply your mind to my knowledge' (v. 17). There is a readily recognizable correspondence with the opening lines of *Amenemope*:

> Give thy ears, hear what is said,
> Give thy heart to understand them (*ANET*, p. 421).

[18] In v. 18, as in *Amenemope*, the imperatives are followed by motivation which is differently organized in the one from the other. In *Amenemope* it is antithetically arranged:

> To put them in thy heart is worthwhile,
> (But) it is damaging to him who neglects them.

The argument in v. 18a appears to have closer connections with the following jussive in *Amenemope* in that it reproduces the significant word 'belly'. *Amenemope* reads: 'Let them rest in the casket of thy belly' and v. 18a, 'for it is a delight when you keep them in your belly'. The 'belly' is a reservoir of words, and there is a passage in *Amenemope* (xxii. 15, *ANET*, p. 424) which reads:

> Better is a man whose talk (remains) in his belly
> Than he who speaks it out injuriously.

This stresses the virtue of keeping words locked up in the 'belly' and not allowing them too free access to the lips. The point in v. 18a is, rather, that the teacher's words should be conserved, so that to keep them in the 'belly' is to store them up in the memory.

If MT is retained in v. 18b, one would have to translate v. 18: 'For it is a delight when you keep them within you, (when) they are held together on your lips' (cf. RSV, 'if all of them are ready on your lips'). To the power of an accurate and tenacious memory must be added the ability to reproduce the teacher's words readily and articulately. I am not convinced that the prevalent emendation (BH, Gemser, Ringgren, Scott), for which the support of *Amenemope* is claimed, really gives better sense than this. '(When) they are fixed like a tent-peg (*keyātēd* for *yaḥdāw*) on your lips' is not a very apt simile if it means 'when they are poised for shapely utterance'. All that it can say is that the words are as firmly fixed on the lips as a tent-peg is in the ground. The postulated connection with *Amenemope* is itself not certain, and it requires the assumption that the Old Testament writer has changed the figure of speech so as to make it more characteristically Israelite ('tent-peg' instead of 'mooring stake'). Moreover, the context in *Amenemope* is different. 'At a time when there is a whirlwind of words, they shall be a mooring stake for thy tongue' (*ANET*, p. 422) is directed, not towards articulateness but towards taciturnity. At a time when there is a torrent of ineffective and confused speech, the man who remembers his teacher's instruction will know the virtue of silence and will impose this discipline on himself. The teaching is the same as in the passage just cited (xxii. 15), and often occurs in the Egyptian Instruction, where the power of silence is understood and commended and where speech is held to be advantageous only where it is timely and weighty.

It is a possibility, though not in my view a serious one, that this thought is present in 22.18b and is conveyed by the tent-peg simile. The point would then be that there should be availability of utterance but that it should be kept under strict control; articulateness should be combined with calculated reserve and there should be no overspill of ill-advised or even involuntary speech. Dahood (p. 46) urges that *yaḥdāw* is meaningless, but his translation: 'Let them be fixed, seen upon your lips' (*ḥdh* dialectal for *ḥzh*) gives poor sense. How can words be seen on a man's lips? His alternative rendering based on Arabic *ḥdy*, 'settle', makes more sense: 'Let them be fixed, settled (*yēḥādū*) on your lips.'

[19] There is no doubt that v. 19 is an Israelite contribution and that it is related to the theological reorientation of the Instruction. It points beyond the wisdom teacher and focusses attention on Yahweh as the object of trust and seat of authority. In v. 19b, LXX is usually preferred to MT, although 'even thou' (MT) may emphasize the aspect of direct address: 'It is to you and to no one else that I am divulging these words to-day.' Instead of 'I am showing you your path' (LXX, BH 'your paths'), Gemser and Ringgren substitute the third person suffix, 'his paths' and 'his path' respectively. This enhances the Yahwistic emphasis of the verse. The wisdom teacher is entirely occupied with Yahweh's business; he inculcates trust and supplies guidance like a priest. It should be clear that v. 19 is not obviously consistent with the tone of vv. 17f., that it belongs to a later stage of the history of the wisdom tradition in Israel and is associated particularly with the theological reorientation of the Instruction. The wisdom teacher who speaks in vv. 17f. belongs to an international fraternity and claims a personal authority as an educator; in v. 19 instruction is subsumed under Yahwism, education, rigorously conceived, capitulates to piety and the educator is replaced by a religious teacher.

[20] The ungainly phrase in v. 20b, 'plans and knowledge', is explained by Gemser as hendiadys with *bēt essentiae* ('plans and knowledge' = 'well-informed counsel'): 'Have I not written thirty sayings for you (on the text see above, p. 372) containing well-informed counsel?' Scott emends with BH (*bām ʿēṣōt*), 'in which are pieces of advice and knowledge'. The vocabulary and the sense of v. 21b suggest that it is the international and even vocational function of the Instruction which is envisaged in vv. 20f. In the closing lines of the first chapter of *Amenemope*, success and worldly prosperity are held out as the consequences of paying attention to the words of the teacher:

> Thou wilt find it a success;
> Thou wilt find my words a treasury of life,
> And thy body will prosper upon earth (*ANET*, p. 422, iii. 18–iv. 2).

[21] In v. 21 the teacher asks for the attention of the pupil in order that he may divulge 'truthful words', i.e., words of solid worth whose reliability will never in any circumstances be suspect. Ringgren supposes that *qōšṭ*, 'truth', is an Aramaic gloss of *'imrē 'ᵉmet*. There is no important change in the sense if *'imre 'ᵉmet* is thought to be the gloss (so Scott). On *'amārîm 'ᵉmet* see GK § 131c. Dahood (p. 47) explains it as construct relationship with enclitic *m*. BH claims the support of LXX for the emendation *lᵉšō'ᵃleka* (v. 21b): 'so that you may give a reliable answer to those who enquire at you'. The meaning of LXX is rather: 'that you may give a faithful answer to those who accuse you' (*τοῖς προβαλλομένοις σοι*). Moreover, v. 21b (MT) makes perfectly good sense: 'so that you may bring back a reliable report to him who sends you'. The verse then refers to the proper conduct of negotiations on behalf of a principal, and it reverts to a theme which I have discussed in the context of the Egyptian Instruction (above, p. 54). The teacher will equip the apprentice official for the delicate task of acting as a go-between. His prime duty is to listen carefully and report accurately. It is not his business to take a diplomatic initiative, and he must avoid like the plague any suggestion of intrigue or misrepresentation. His business is to convey the mind of his principal as accurately and sensitively as he can to the other side and *vice versa*.

vv. 22f. *The First Saying*

[22f.] There is an obvious correspondence between this and the opening lines of ch. 2 of *Amenemope*:

> Guard thyself against robbing the oppressed
> And against overbearing the disabled.
> Stretch not forth thy hand against the approach of an old man,
> Nor *steal away* the speech of the *aged* (*ANET*, p. 422, iv. 4–7).

The *Amenemope* passage consists of crisp imperatives without motivation, and it forbids oppressive measures against the old and the weak. In 22.22b–23 there is a more specific reference to legal proceedings and the imperative is commended by motive clauses. Ehrlich's suggestion (cf. Gemser, p. 112), that the second *dal* in v. 22a is a variant of the more usual *delet* 'door' (cf. Ps. 141.3) and is parallel to *šaʿar* (v. 22b) as well as punning with the first *dal*, is ingenious but improbable: 'Do not rob the poor man because he is an (ever open) door.' Yet it is certainly the vulnerability of the poor to which allusion is made ('Do not rob the poor man (just) because he is poor'), and the fact that to deal thus with a poor man is a combination of injustice and cowardice. The poor man can be oppressed and robbed with impunity, which makes the injustice the more contemptible but the temptation to it the greater.

The *šaʿar* is the forum where political, legal and commercial business is transacted. That legal proceedings are in mind here is clear from the vocabulary of v. 23a (*yārīb rībām*). Litigation is not to be an instrument of oppression, resorted to in order to bring the poor man to his knees – to crush (*dk'*) his resistance. The implication of this is that the poor man does not have the resources to get justice for himself and that an unevenly matched legal contest produces injustice. So it is said that Yahweh will accept their brief and fight their case, and will rob even of their lives those who despoil the weak (*qbʿ*=Arabic *qbḍ* 'to strike a blow', 'to rob with violence', parallel to *gzl*, G. R. Driver, *ZAW* 50, 1932, p. 145).

vv. 24f. *The Second Saying*

[24f.] Chapter 9 of *Amenemope* opens with the lines:

Do not associate to thyself the heated man,
Nor visit him for conversation (*ANET*, p. 423).

The literal correspondence of this with Prov. 22.24 is striking. Gemser suggests that *'īš ḥēmōt* in v. 24b may be a translation of the Egyptian word *šem̱em̱*, 'hothead'. The polemic against impetuous behaviour and hot words is, however, one which runs through *Amenemope*, and to it corresponds the positive recommendation of the virtues of tranquillity and taciturnity. The cautionary argument in connection with the demand not to become the companion of a hothead who is subject to ungovernable spasms of anger and is a prey to unreason and excess employs the metaphor of the 'road', largely used in chs. 1–9 and fully discussed there. Such a man is incapable of self-control and measured utterance, and will involve his companions in deep trouble. Being the friend of this man is like walking along roads which are littered with man-traps, and to be caught in one of these is death. This is therefore a variation on the theme of 'the way of death' (cf. 1–9).

vv. 26f. *The Third Saying*

The theme of this saying has been discussed in 6.1–5, and there is no parallel in *Amenemope*. The striking of hands symbolizes the making of a contract, and v. 26b indicates that it is the conclusion of a particular kind of contract which is described, namely, the act of going surety for another man's debts. I have suggested (see above,

p. 370) that v. 27 is supporting argument for v. 26. It describes picturesquely and perhaps with a touch of wry humour the consequences of entering into such bonds – your house will be emptied of furniture and your bed removed while you are lying on it. One minute you are in bed and the next on the floor. If *lammā* is explained on the analogy of Syriac *lᵉmā*, 'lest' (Gemser, p. 112), v. 27a limits the application of the imperative, i.e., it is a conditional clause dependent on v. 26. The prohibition on going surety is not then intended absolutely, but applies only where there are not adequate financial resources to cope comfortably with any contingency which might arise from the bond. A man with no spare capital may be reduced to the bare boards as a consequence of a bond entered into injudiciously.

v. 28 *The Fourth Saying*

[28] The parallel to this is in *Amenemope*, ch. 6:

> Do not carry off the landmark at the boundaries of the arable land,
> Nor disturb the position of the measuring-cord etc. (*ANET*, p. 422).

The instruction in v. 28 has no formal motivation, although the words *'ōlām* and *'ᵃbōtekā* indicate that ancestral land is inalienable and inviolable (cf. Naboth's vineyard, 'I will not give to you my ancestral allotment' (*naḥᵃlā*), I Kings 21.4). The boundaries are supported by ancient tradition and may not in any circumstances be tampered with. In *Amenemope* the demand is supported with an explicitly religious argument:

> One satisfies god with the will of the Lord
> Who determines the boundaries of the arable land.

What is in view here is not so much the riding roughshod over tradition by an autocratic queen (Jezebel) or the erosion of ancient values attached to ancestral land as a consequence of economic pressures (against which the prophets protest), but more simply sharp practices to which the weak and defenceless members of the community were particularly exposed. Hence *Amenemope* warns against encroaching on the boundaries of a widow, and a similar point is made in Prov. 23.10f., in which the fields of orphans are mentioned as particularly liable to this abuse. The motive clause (v. 11) describes Yahweh as their *gō'ēl*, 'redeemer' (see my article in *TGUOS* xix, 1963, pp. 29–40). The *gō'ēl* is the one who accepts social responsibility for his nearest kinsman and who shields him in his defencelessness. Here the contest waged by Yahweh on behalf of the orphans whose land is being whittled away is described in legal terms (cf. 22.23, above, pp. 377f.). He is a powerful advocate (transferring the *athnach* to *hū'*, so BH, Gemser), who will fight their case (*yārīb 'et rībām*), and those who try to acquire land at their expense will be worsted. The verse should probably be admitted as evidence that the office of gō'ēl has legal associations. The *gō'ēl* is the one who speaks and acts for the wronged and who wins for them the justice which they would otherwise be denied because they are weak and can be wronged with impunity.

In 23.10a, BH and Gemser read *'almānā* for *'ōlām* in view of the phrase 'boundaries of a widow' in *Amenemope*. Since *g^ebūl 'ōlām* occurs in 22.28 as well as 23.10a, this alteration hardly seems justified, although it could be argued that it is the presence of *'ōlām* in 22.28 which explains the corruption in 23.10a and that *'almānā* is a good parallel to *y^etōmīm*. The correspondence between *Amenemope* and Proverbs is not sufficiently close at this point to bear the weight of an argument based on the reference to the 'boundaries of the widow' in the former, and, in general, the text of *Amenemope* is not so slavishly adhered to as to make this type of argument reliable.

v. 29 *The Fifth Saying*

[29] The closing lines of *Amenemope* ch. 30 read:

> As for the scribe who is experienced in his office,
> He will find himself worthy (to be) a courtier (*ANET*, p. 424).

The text of v. 29 has given rise to comment, and the words 'He will not hold office with obscure men' are bracketed as an addition by Ringgren and Scott (cf. BH). Gemser, following Steuernagel, suggests that the verse should be supplemented with some such stichos as: 'But he who is unskilful at his work.' The second half of the verse would then read: 'But he who is unskilful at his work cannot (even) hold his place with obscure men.' I have discussed *māhīr* at length with special reference to Ahikar, who is described as 'a sagacious and keen-witted statesman' (*PWM*, pp. 29f.). A man who has this mental nimbleness and adroitness will become a statesman of the first rank. He will not fail to make his way in the world; he will rise to the top by sheer acumen and flair for statecraft and will not bury his talents in the service of obscure and mediocre principals.

Formally this is not Instruction. It is the furnishing of a paradigm with the implied advice that this is the model to be imitated by the man who would wield power and influence. There is no doubt that here is a case where the vocational character of the Egyptian Instruction is preserved in the biblical book of Proverbs.

23.1–3 *The Sixth Saying*

[1–3] As Ringgren has noted, there is no close verbal counterpart to this in *Amenemope*, although the topic appears in *Ptahhotep* and *Kagemni*, as well as *Amenemope* ch. 23 (*ANET*, p. 424). He who would be cast in the mould of a statesman, and would commend himself to his superiors as a model of well-proportioned behaviour and self-control, can afford to neglect nothing which contributes to this impression – not even table manners. This reflects the conviction that not only must elegance and poise be evident in the smallest matters and care be exercised in the most minute details, but even that something of the essential man is revealed in how he eats, that there will be a correspondence between his habits of eating and his habits of diplomacy. In *Amenemope*, the point of the advice appears to be particularly that since great demands are made on the hospitality of one who is in public office, great care should be taken not to give the impression that you are taking advantage of his open house. Abstemiousness should even be carried to the point of pretending to eat. The words 'what is before you' or 'who is before you' (Toy) in 23.1 are ambiguous. They may be elucidated by the lines in *Amenemope*:

> Look at the cup which is before thee,
> And let it serve thy needs.

This has the force of our idiom: 'Let not your eye be larger than your stomach', i.e., do not let the sight of large quantities of food and drink excite your greed. In this case, *bīn* has the meaning 'concentrate your attention on' or 'confine your attention to'. As Gemser points out, one could with as much justification give the infinitive absolute the force of '*wohl*,' i.e., 'Mark well'. If the translation offered is 'Confine your attention to what is before you', it has rather the force of '*nur*', and the idea of limitation present in the *Amenemope* passage is matched.

Toy's suggestion that the phrase ('who is before you') refers to the superior rather than to the food is not to be rejected out of hand. The aspiring official is presented with the opportunity of observing a principal at close quarters, and he should not be distracted by food and drink so as to fail to draw the maximum advantage from this. 'Scrutinize well him who is present with you.' In v. 2a, Scott's emendation (*b^e^bilʿaka͞*) is unnecessary (cf. KB² *s.v.* **lōaʿ*), and has the effect of replacing a piquant proverbial expression with the pedestrian, 'Use a knife to eat with'. 'Put a knife in your throat' apparently means 'Curb your natural appetite', especially if you usually eat with a hearty relish (*baʿal nepeš*). Hence v. 3a: 'Do not let your appetite be whetted by his tit-bits'. This recalls the words in *Kagemni*: 'Hold the food in abhorrence even if thou desirest it' (Erman, p. 66). But in what sense is it deceptive food (v. 3b)? Not because it is offered in bad faith or without genuine hospitality, as is the case in 23.6–8, but because a public exhibition of gluttony by an ambitious official will damage his prospects and may prove to be his undoing. Here is another example of an instruction which only makes sense in a vocational context.

vv. 4f. *The Seventh Saying*

[4f.] This corresponds literally with *Amenemope*, ch. 7 (*ANET*, pp. 422f.), although it is much briefer and less complex in its thought. 'Do not wear yourself out making wealth' is close to 'Cast not thy heart in pursuit of riches', and 'It takes to itself wings, like an eagle it flies heavenwards' to 'They have made themselves wings like geese and are flown away to the heavens' (with a change of simile). There is nothing in 23.4f. corresponding to the warning in *Amenemope* against becoming rich through robbery, and the main motivation of the latter, that fate is immutable and every man has his appointed place in the divine order, so that the way of life is the way of tranquillity, is not taken up in the biblical saying. There is the appeal to intellectual discrimination (*bīnā*), rather than to a theological concept of order which allots to a man his place under the sun and sets limits to his self-assertiveness. The man who clarifies his thoughts will realize the futility of wearing himself out in the effort to get rich, because wealth is fickle and unpredictable; it is here today and gone tomorrow, and then it is as unattainable and as hopelessly distant as the eagle which has soared towards the heavens.

Verse 5a, which is obscure, might be translated: 'If you glance at it with (your) eyes, it is no longer there'. This assumes that *h^a^*, normally an interrogative particle, can be translated 'if' (LXX ἐὰν cf. Gemser) and that Q. *tāʿîp* 'cause to fly' can be rendered 'cast a glance'. I am not entirely happy with this explanation. The sense which seems to me to be desiderated in v. 5a is: 'If you take your eyes off it for an instant, it is no longer there.' Or (allowing for the interrogative force of *hᵃ*): 'You take your eyes off it for an instant, and is it there any longer?' (cf. Scott). I would suggest that this may be the idiom indicated by 'You cause your eyes to fly with respect to it.' Even if K. (*tāʿūp*) is read, this sense can be obtained (cf. Toy). This is what BH aims at with its emendation *teʿeṣeh*, 'You blink your eyes at it', but it is not clear to me that this is indicated by ἐπιστήσῃς (LXX). The meaning of LXX would appear to be: 'If you fix your eye on it, it (your eye) alights nowhere (on nothing).'

vv. 6–8 *The Eighth Saying*

[6–8] There is no real affinity of subject matter between this and *Amenemope* ch. 11 (*ANET*, p. 423), but they do coincide in respect of certain metaphorical expressions relating to sickness and vomiting. *Amenemope* warns against greedy designs on the property of a poor man, while 23.6–8 advises against accepting hospitality from a man with 'an evil eye'. Scott supposes that this is a reference to stinginess, and the phrase appears to have this meaning in 28.22 (see below, pp. 626f.). Here it may indicate, as Gemser and Ringgren suppose, a man with misanthropic or malevolent tendencies. If the phrase has an original connection with anti-social magic or spell-binding, it is unlikely that this is preserved. What may, however, be envisaged is a person who is so radically perverted that he has no capacity for sociability and is at enmity with every other man. He appears to dispense food and drink with the greatest cheerfulness and generosity, but it is a hollow hospitality which he offers, and his show of goodwill is spurious. He has no desire for concord, no genius for friendship: 'his mind is not with you' (v. 7b). It is for this reason that one should not eat food with such a man nor allow one's appetite to be whetted by his delicatessen (v. 6b, the same phrase as v. 3a). 'His mind is not with you' may mean 'He does not mean what he says', in which case the argument that *raʿ ʿāyin* means 'miser' is strengthened. He says, 'Eat and drink', but in truth he grudges you the food.

The small grammatical difficulty in v. 6a can be removed by deleting *'et* (Gemser, cf., however, Gemser p. 113) or *leḥem* (BH), or by transposing *'et* so that it follows *leḥem* with the meaning 'with' (G. R. Driver, *Biblica* 32, p. 187). More difficult problems are posed by v. 7a and particularly by *šāʿar bᵉnapšō*. In Arabic (2nd form), post-biblical Hebrew (piel) and Jewish Aramaic (pael), *šʿr* (Arabic *sʿr*) has the meaning 'fix the price of goods', but this would be the only occurrence of the verb in biblical Hebrew with the meaning 'estimate' (cf. Gen. 26.12, *šaʿar*, 'measure (of grain)'). Translations suggested by Gemser are: 'As one who makes his own plans so is he', or, 'As one who is full of calculations so is he', the second preferable to the first, because it integrates better with the general description of the misanthropic man. Scott's proposal is to translate *nepeš* 'appetite' (cf. v. 2b), and to add *lᵉkā* ('For as he estimates his appetite so will he yours'). The reference is then to the stinginess of the *raʿ ʿāyin*. Dahood (p. 47) relates *šʿr* to Ugaritic *ṯʿr* which is used of serving food in *Baal* V. i. 4 (*CML*, p. 82) *qmyṯʿn wyšlḥmnh* 'They did rise (that) they might arrange (a feast) and give him to eat' (Driver). Dahood translates v. 7, 'Like one serving his own appetite such is he!', (reading *šāʿēr*), i.e., his hospitality is not genuine.

The belief that *Amenemope* xiv. 7 (*ANET*, p. 423) can contribute to the elucidation of this verse has long been entertained (L. Dürr, *ZAW* 43, 1925, pp. 262f.). The line in *Amenemope* runs:

> As for the property of a poor man, it (is) a blocking to the throat.

Dürr suggested that like Accadian *napištu*, *nepeš* means 'throat' in v. 7a. That this is so elsewhere in biblical Hebrew I have shown in the discussion of 1.12 (above, pp. 269f.), where I have dealt with the Ugaritic evidence. The utilization of the *Amenemope* passage has been complicated by a rendering (*ein Unwetter für die Kehle*) deriving from Gressmann ('Die Neugefundene Lehre', p. 277) and adopted by Dürr (cf. J. Weil, *ZAW* 44, 1926, pp. 62f.). This translation (which is still reproduced by Ringgren) has given rise to the emendation *śaʿar* (*saʿar*), 'storm' (so BH, cf. Ringgren's translation, '*Sturm für die Kehle*'). Widengren has noted that Egyptian *snʿ* can mean 'hinder', 'block' (Erman and Grapow, *Wörterbuch*, iv, pp. 504f.), and both Griffith and Wilson (*ANET*) translate accordingly. Widengren renders Prov. 23.7a: 'For like something disgusting in the throat (emending *bᵉnapšō* to *bannepeš*), so is it' (cf. *šaʿᵃrūr*, 'horrible things', Jer. 5.30; 23.14). Gemser adopts this, except that he correctly translates *hū'* as 'he' and not 'it' (G. Widengren, *VT* iv, 1954, p. 101).

I am inclined, however, to believe with Weil that LXX furnishes the best solution to this problem, although it deviates considerably from MT in v. 7. LXX reads: 'Eating and drinking (with him) is as if one should swallow a hair. Do not introduce him to your company, nor eat bread with him.' According to LXX, eating and drinking with this man is just like swallowing a hair (τρίχα). A hair in the gullet is irritating and disgusting; it may make you actively sick, and this is the effect of accepting this man's hospitality (emending *šā'ar* to *śē'ār*). The language is, of course, metaphorical, and v. 8a does not mean that what has been eaten will actually be vomited up (the reference is also metaphorical in *Amenemope* xiv. 17), but that what appeared to be friendship will go sour and rotten, and this is what v. 8b indicates. The words of pleasant conversation spoken during the meal will be corrupted when his duplicity and insincerity emerge. They will stick in the throat like a hair. The insertion of the words 'and like something bitter in the gullet' (BH and Gemser) after v. 7a, on the model of *Amenemope* xiv. 8 ('It makes a *vomiting* to the gullet'), should not be pressed. The metrical reasons which can be adduced to support it are not compelling (cf. v. 5), and against it is the free and abridged use of *Amenemope* which is made by the biblical writer.

v. 9 *The Ninth Saying*

The point of this is really quite different from *Amenemope* ch. 21 (*ANET*, p. 424), and the resemblance is not sufficiently close to make comparison profitable. *Amenemope* is directed against the indiscriminate disclosure of one's thoughts and against the choice of a garrulous companion, whereas this verse, like 9.7f. (above, p. 368) is concerned with the incorrigibility of the fool and urges that when an effort is made to educate him he spurns good sense (*śēkel*).

vv. 10f. *The Tenth Saying* (See above, pp. 379f.)

v. 12 *The Eleventh Saying*

[12] This has to be separated from vv. 13f., because the mode of address in the one is different from what it is in the other. In v. 12 the pupil is addressed directly by the wisdom teacher, whereas in vv. 13f. it is either a father or an apprentice wisdom teacher who is being addressed. With respect to mode of address, *Ahikar* 82 is akin to v. 12 and *Ahikar* 81 to vv. 13f.; with respect to subject-matter the *Ahikar* passage is closer to vv. 13f. (A. E. Cowley, pp. 215, 222).

vv. 13f. *The Twelfth Saying*

[13f.] There is a reference to the rod in *Ahikar* 81 (cf. v. 13b), and the subject-matter of *Ahikar* 82 which alludes to the avoidance of death ('If I strike thee, my son, thou wilt not die') coincides with that of vv. 13f. The undisciplined son who is left to his own inclinations is in danger of death (vv. 13b, 14b). Winton Thomas has made the attractive suggestion that 'he will not die' is an idiomatic usage which has its counterpart in English and means 'he will come to no very great harm'. He will be none the worse for an occasional beating (*VTS* iii, p. 288). My understanding of this passage is, however, a different one. 'He will not die' means that he will be saved from 'death', which is the consequence of indiscipline. That 'death' here is to be taken seriously is confirmed by the opposition of *nepeš*, 'life', and Sheol in v. 14b. This is the antithesis of 'life' and 'death', the land of the living and the realm of the dead, which looms large in Prov. 1–9, especially in relation to the *'iššā zārā*. The theme there is the same as here: discipline leads to life and indiscipline to the land of the dead (cf. Deut. 21.18f.). The mythological elaboration whereby Sheol is portrayed as the gaping throat of the god Mot is not here in evidence (see on 1.12, above, pp. 269f.; 2.18f.; above, pp. 287f.; 4.13, above, pp. 307f.; 5.5, above, p. 314; 7.27, above, p. 341; 9.18, above, p. 367).

vv. 15f. *The Thirteenth Saying*

[15f.] This does not instruct, but it is a preliminary motivation, in so far as it is intended to incline the son or the pupil to obey the directives which are about to be issued. The assumption is that the pupil will desire that his teacher should enjoy the satisfaction which is depicted, and that this will dispose him to submit to authority. The careful construction with the reversing of the order of protasis and apodosis in v. 16 (chiasmus) has been noted, and it is perhaps not putting too fine a point on the exegesis to maintain that v. 15a refers to the teacher's intellectual satisfaction in an able pupil (both occurrences of *lēb* in v. 15 should be translated 'mind'), while v. 16 speaks rather of his emotional accord with (*kilyōt*) or the approval which his conscience gives to one whose speech is marked by plainness and integrity.

At any rate, two of the prime virtues with which the educational tradition of wisdom was occupied are here mentioned. It nurtured wisdom, which comprehended the intellectual virtues of acumen, balanced judgement and verbal restraint, and it was concerned with clarity, weightiness and elegance of speech. With *mēšārīm*, however, there is perhaps a more pronounced ethical emphasis. It not only alludes to plain speaking, but implies a contrast with deviousness of expression, with a calculated ambiguity which seeks to darken counsel. To speak *mēšārīm* means that there is no discrepancy between speech and intent and that human relationships are established on a basis of frankness and candour. The function of speech is then always to clarify and never to deceive.

vv. 17f. *The Fourteenth Saying*

[17f.] There is a small grammatical point in v. 17b which does not, however, seriously affect the interpretation, whichever way it is resolved. G. R. Driver has argued (*Biblica* 32, p. 196) that the abstract *yir'at* is here a collective term for a concrete subject, is equivalent to *yirᵉ'ē* (cf. BH) and is the antithesis of *ḥaṭṭā'īm* (cf. D. Winton Thomas, *VT* xv, 1965, p. 274, n.2). Sinners are not to be envied nor emulated (their prosperity and apparent immunity from retribution may attract and fascinate others), but those who fear Yahweh constantly deserve to be envied and imitated. There is a right and a wrong aspiration or jealousy; the one is a disease and the other a valuable spiritual exercise. If 'fear' is read in v. 17b (cf. Gemser and Ringgren), the meaning is that the only goal to be pursued is the fear of Yahweh, and that the spirit of emulation must be concentrated on this to the exclusion of all else. The strong religious emphasis of this saying is notable, and in this respect it contrasts sharply with the earthiness of the warnings against the harlot (vv. 27–28) and against wine and gluttony (vv. 20f., 29–35).

The antithetically arranged instructions of v. 17 are reinforced by supporting argument (v. 18) which sets out the rewards of piety. LXX (*τηρήσῃς αὐτά*) should be followed in v. 18a (so BH and Gemser, who insert *tišmᵉrennā*), because the stichos appears to be short of a word and *kī* almost certainly introduces motivation. The translation of *'im* as 'surely' (Ringgren; Dahood, p. 48) or *kī 'im* as 'surely' (RSV; the motivation is then asyndetic) is less satisfactory. If *tišmᵉrennā* is inserted, the correctness of the translation 'fear' in v. 17b is assumed. There is here a qualitative element in *'aḥᵃrīt*, 'good end'

(W. Zimmerli, *ZAW* 51, 1933, p. 198, n.1), but neither in it nor in the reference to the hope which will not be cut off is there any widening of the horizon beyond death (contrary to Dahood, pp. 48f.). The thought is that of a fully-rounded, mature life which attains its climax and consummation in well-being and honour, and is not foreshortened by disaster or retribution and denied fruition. The advantages of sin (cf. v. 17a), however real they may seem, are in the long run illusory, for only in the fear of Yahweh is life gathered up into a fitting and hopeful fulfilment.

vv. 19–21 *The Fifteenth Saying*

[19–21] The idea of 'right direction' is more apposite for *'šr* than Gemser's suggestion that it should be translated 'confirm' on the analogy of post-biblical Hebrew and Aramaic. The practical consequence of wisdom is this ability to think straight about the conduct of life, and here again the metaphor of the 'road' reappears, raising as it does the problem of guidance. This depends on the right use of the mind, and on the ability to translate acumen into the sphere of those practical decisions which determine the conduct and direction of life. The question has to be asked whether gluttony and drunkenness (vv. 20f.) are just fortuitous examples of unwisdom, or whether the relationship of v. 19 to vv. 20f. is of a more intrinsic kind, in the sense that these aberrations are regarded as typical manifestations of unwisdom. Some support for this can be found in Deut. 21.20, where the son who is generally described as recalcitrant and rebellious (*sōrēr ūmōre*), i.e., a paradigm of the incorrigible youth, is more specifically designated 'a toper and a glutton' (*sōbē' wᵉzōlēl*). It might be that this was thought to be a normal form for indiscipline to assume or, at least, that it was a stock category for a delinquent. The motivation (v. 21) depicts sloth (sleep) as the stablemate of debauchery and the way to destitution (rags). Those who carouse by night sleep while other men work. The ultimate consequence of this behaviour is disinheritance, for such a son will be disowned by his father.

vv. 22–25 *The Sixteenth Saying*

[22–25] It is no doubt the double mention of 'mother' in this saying which leads Ringgren (cf. Gemser) to suppose that 23.15–28 is parental rather than scholastic instruction. The reference to 'mother' here is comparable to 'mother's *tōrā*' in 1.8 and 6.20 (see above, pp. 268, 327). We have to decide here, as with the other two passages, whether the speaker is a natural father or a wisdom teacher. I have indicated that it is difficult to resolve this question, but that the mention of 'mother' points to the home rather than the school. In that case we have a *tōrā* out of the wisdom tradition which agrees with a divine *miṣwā* of the Decalogue (Ex. 20.12). The appeal for obedience to the instruction in the motive clauses (vv. 24f.) is framed in the same way as 23.15f. (see above, pp. 386f.). Wisdom has to be learned by a young man from those who are older and wiser than himself. It is a treasure accumulated from the past, appropriated fully by those of mature experience and transmitted to those youths who acknowledge the authority of their elders and are receptive of their teaching. Such wisdom results in right conduct of one's life. It is in this that parents see the confirmation that they have a son who is *ḥākām* and *ṣāddīq* and it is this which they contemplate with profound joy and satisfaction. Since *yōledet* in v. 25b is the equivalent of 'mother', *'immᵉkā* in v. 25a is superfluous and Kuhn's *mimmekā* is adopted by Gemser and BH ('you will give pleasure to your father'). The difficulty with v. 23, which is absent from LXX, is that it does not harmonize with the theme 'Honour your father and mother', and its insertion is perhaps secondary (Gemser). It emphasizes the preciousness of what is gained by submitting to an educational discipline (truth, wisdom, instruction and insight). These are of more worth than the commodities which are bought and sold in the market, and money is not commensurate with them. They are to be 'bought' whatever the cost, but they are not to be bartered for anything.

vv. 26–28 *The Seventeenth Saying*

[26] Again in v. 26, the connection between a proper disposition of the mind (*lēb*) and the right conduct of life reappears (cf. v. 19b). 'Give your mind to me' means not just 'Give me your undivided attention', but also, 'Rely absolutely on my advice', and so, 'Do not oppose your opinions to my mature judgement'. In v. 26b, K. reads 'approves' Q. and LXX, 'observe'. It is doubtful whether there is any advantage with Q., unless weight is attached to Boström's supposition that there is a pun between *tiṣṣōrnā* and *ṣārā* (v. 27b). It is adopted by Gemser, while Ringgren reads K. There is a question whether v. 26b is a final clause or a second instruction communicated by a jussive.

In the latter case, 'Let your eyes observe my ways' means simply, 'Take my life as a paradigm', whereas 'Let your eyes approve my ways' may be considered a second-stage instruction related to the demand for inner assent in v. 26a. When the teacher asserts his authority over the mind of the pupil, he has in view the practical end of shaping his way of life, and, conversely, the pupil's inner assent is matched by his approval of a pattern of conduct. The aspect of result is intensified if v. 26b is taken as a final clause. The acceptance of the intellectual authority of the teacher results in approval of a way of life, or, if Q. is followed, sharpens the pupil's powers of observation in respect of the practical consequences of what is taught.

A peculiarity of this instruction is that its precise intention and concern only become evident in the motive clauses, where it is specifically related to the avoidance of the *zōnā* (or *zārā*). It is not normally the function of the motive clause to lend to an instruction precision which it otherwise lacks. The example which the teacher holds up to the pupil thus becomes specifically the shunning of any relationship with prostitutes.

In view of the coupling of *zārā* and *nokrīyā* in 5.20 and 7.5 (cf. *zārīm* and *bēt nokrī* in 5.10), there is some point to the suggestion that *zōnā* should be emended to *zārā*. Against it is the fact that *'ēšet rāʿ*, which appears with *nokrīyā* in 6.24, may be taken as a synonym for *zōnā* (here LXX apparently translates *'ēšet rēaʿ*, since it reads ἀπὸ γυναικὸς ὑπάνδρου, 'from a married woman', as it does for *'ēšet rēʿēhū* in 6.29). If ἀλλότριος οἶκος (LXX 23.27) is an attempt to render *zārā*, the rather clumsy paraphrase may be explained by the difficulty of distinguishing in translation between *zārā* and *nokrīyā* (rendered as ἀλλότριον in 23.27b). Thus in 5.10 *zārīm* is rendered as ἀλλότριοι and *bēt nokrī* as εἰς οἴκους ἀλλοτρίων; in 5.17 *zārīm* by ἀλλότριος. In 5.20, *zārā* is translated ἀλλοτρία, while *nokrīyā* is paraphrased τῆς μὴ ἰδίας. In 7.5, *zārā* would seem to be rendered by ἀλλοτρία and *nokrīyā* by πονήρα, 'wicked', although the Greek is more fairly described as a paraphrase which lumps together *zārā* and *nokrīyā*. In 5.3, *zārā* is equated with 'prostitute', i.e., with *zōnā* (γυνή πόρνη). In contrast with this complicated picture there is the clear indication that *zōnā* is consistently translated by πόρνη (6.26; 29.3) or the like (πορνικός 'pertaining to a prostitute', 7.10). My conclusion is that ἀλλότριος οἶκος in 23.27 points to *zārā* and not *zōnā*. The significance of this for exegesis is, however, minimal, since whether or not *zōnā* is read the reference is clearly to prostitutes (thus γυνή πόρνη in 5.3 is a correct exegesis, if a bad translation of *zārā*). The foreign woman, alluring and suspected of easy morals which she has the opportunity to indulge (cf. 7.18f., above, pp. 337f.), is a particular threat to inexperienced young men. (The other problems associated with *zārā* and *nokrīyā* have been discussed above, (pp. 284f., p. 314, pp. 328f., pp. 334f., pp. 365f.) in connection with 2.16f.; 5.3f.; 6.24f.; 7.5f.; 9.13f.).

[27f.] The motive clauses (vv. 27f.) contain two metaphors and one simile, a fact worthy of note since figurative language is not a feature of the Instruction, although where it occurs it is usually associated with the supporting argumentation rather than with the directive itself (see above, pp. 139f., 317f.). Both metaphors can be well illustrated from the book of Jeremiah. The *šūḥā* is the pit which is dug to trap a wild animal (cf. KB², '*Fanggrube*'), as is clear from Jer. 18.20 ('they have dug a pit for my life') and especially Jer. 18.22, where the reference to snares concealed for the feet confirms that 'they have dug a *šūḥā* (Q.) to capture me' is also a hunting metaphor. That *bō'r* can be used for such a pit is clear from II Sam. 23.20, which records that Benaiah slew the lion in a *bō'r* (the usual form is *bōr*, and *bō'r* could be described as a mixed form combining *bōr* and *b*ᵉ*'ēr*, 'well'. These, however, must be regarded as variants of one and the same form).

The other metaphor (v. 27b) involving the *b*ᵉ*'ēr ṣārā* is elucidated by Jer. 38.6, which tells how the prophet was lowered by ropes into a disused well (*bōr*) in which there was no water and into whose muddy bottom his feet sank. The prostitute is a deep pit dug for wild animals from which there is no escape, and she is a well of narrow diameter in which one experiences intolerable confinement without even a firm foundation for the feet. Apart from outside help and ropes there is no hope of escape (cf. Jer. 38.7f.).

The only question outstanding is whether this exhausts the interpretation of these metaphors or whether there is a distant mythological allusion to the Pit (*bōr*), as there is in Prov. 1.12 and in the descriptions of the *'iššā zārā* in 1–9 (2.18f.; 5.5f.; 7.22f.; 9.18). There are other references to the *yōr*ᵉ*dē bōr* (Isa. 38.18; Ezek. 26.20; 31.14, 16; 32.18, 24, 25, 29; Pss. 28.1; 30.4; 88.5; 143.7) which show beyond all doubt that the *bōr* leads to Sheol and that its use is associated with a contrast between life and death, between the world of the living and the underworld of the dead. I have shown that the ultimate mythological concept which is involved here is that of the god Death (Mot), the god with the gaping throat and an insatiable appetite for life. The throat of Mot is the route to Sheol. In view of the associations of the earlier descriptions of the *'iššā zārā* with this mythology, there is a distinct possibility that something of this is present in 23.7. Whoever has got into the clutches of such a woman is in hell and there is no way of escape. Only, hell is not necessarily the Sheol of mythology and does not necessarily imply physical death, for there is a living death, a doomed state from which there is no reprieve and in which there is no hope (see above, p. 341). The man in the Pit is not necessarily physically dead, for surely the Psalmist did not intend to say that Yahweh had brought him up from the underworld or had raised him from physical death. In Ps. 30.4, as in Prov. 1–9, we have to reckon with a process of demythologizing or, at least, we have to demote the mythology to metaphor before we can state the intention of the passages in question. The Psalmist who says: 'O Yahweh, you have brought up my *nepeš* from Sheol, you have resuscitated me from among those who go down to the Pit', confesses that he was dead, although his pulse had not stopped and his heart was still beating, and that no one but Yahweh could have rescued him from this living death. Jeremiah's incarceration in the *bōr* is a parable of the Psalmist's state. As the prophet was doomed to perish unless his friends had pulled him out with ropes, so the Psalmist's *nepeš* is ebbing fast and the trend cannot be reversed unless Yahweh revives his *nepeš* and pulls him up from the company of the *yōr^{e}dē bōr*, of whom he is already an associate.

The simile in v. 28 likens the harlot to a highwayman who lays an ambush. It is illumined by the extended description of her technique in 7.6f. (especially 7.12, 'at every corner she lays an ambush', where *te'^{e}rōb* is used as in 23.28). The prostitute has her pitch where she skulks in the shadows as darkness falls, waiting her chance to pounce on a likely victim who is soon putty in her hands and capitulates to her allure and promises of love, not knowing that it will cost him his life. If *bōg^{e}dīm* (v. 28b) can have a singular, abstract sense ('treachery', so G. R. Driver, *Biblica* 32, p. 196), MT can stand. Gemser suggests *b^{e}gūdīm*: 'She multiplies the number of those deceived among men'. M. Dahood, *Biblica* xlii (1961), p. 363, suggests 'She collects (*te'^{e}sōp*) garments (*b^{e}gādīm*) from (*b^{e}* = 'from') men'. For the association of harlots and garments given in pledge Dahood cites 20.16 (Q. *nokrīyā*). I have followed K. *nokrīm* (below, p. 542).

vv. 29–35 *The Eighteenth Saying*

[29f.] The way in which vv. 29f. are organized as question and answer recalls the formal arrangement of the so-called 'Entry *Tōrōt*' in Pss. 15 and 24.3f. There is also an element of riddle interest in the unfolding of the questions – a challenge to discover the answer which will accommodate all the clues, constituting an invitation to a kind of jig-saw puzzle game. What manner of man is this who has sorrow and care, squabbles and worry, who suffers needless bruises and has lustreless eyes? Then the answer: these ills are the lot of the man who lingers over wine, who is a connoisseur (*ḥqr*) of mixed drinks ('cocktails'; cf. KB², *s.v. mimsāk*, 'wine with the addition of water, honey and pepper'). Dahood (p. 49) translates *mimsāk* 'mixing-bowl' (Ugaritic *mmskn*) here and in Isa. 65.11. This gives good sense in Isa. 65.11, where filling a mixing-bowl with wine furnishes good parallelism to spreading a table. 'Those who fill bowls with mixed drink' is, however, a possible sense of Isa. 65.11b. In Prov. 23.30 'to plumb (*ḥqr*) the mixing-bowl' (Dahood), i.e., to inspect its bottom, makes poor sense. Some details of exegesis in v. 29 are doubtful. Thus *'ᵃbōy*, which is usually translated 'sorrow' or 'woe' (Gemser, Ringgren), is connected by KB² with *'bh* 'to desire' and assigned the semantic development 'desire'>'uneasiness', presumably the uneasiness caused by unrequited desire (LXX θόρυβος 'din', 'groaning'). If KB²'s derivation were accepted, the meaning would be something like 'malaise', the 'malaise' of a man whose desires remain for ever suspended in unfulfilment, because his ruinous habits and chronic indiscipline prevent him from ever realizing them. They exist in a dream world, but the reality of his life is his sottishness and he suffers from the tension of this dichotomy. He is given to brooding (*śīaḥ*). He engages in drunken squabbles (*midyānīm*, Q.), and quarrels over his cups. Since v. 29c speaks of the way in which a drunk abuses his own body (cf. v. 35) there is something to be said for Byington's suggestion that *ḥaklīlūt ʿēnāyim* (v. 29d) refers to black eyes received in brawling (H. T. Byington, *JBL* lxiv, 1945, p. 351), but this inference drawn from the parallelism is shown to be false by the Accadian use of *ekēlu* (W. von Soden, *Akkadisches Handwörterbuch*, *s.v. ekēlu*; also *CAD* iv). It is used of black moods, a dark face in *Gilgameš* vii. iv.17 (*ukkulu panušu*, *ANET*, p. 87) and of dark eyes in *TTC* 27.31 (G. Contenau, *Trente Tablettes Cappadociennes*, 1919, p. 94). The reference is perhaps to lustreless eyes rather than to dark rings under the eyes.

[31] The instruction in v. 31 is ringed with a cautionary dissuasive by means of the preamble in vv. 29f. and the more normally located motive clauses in vv. 32–35. There is a fatal fascination for the eyes in red wine sparkling in the cup (*ʿēnō* is its *éclat*, Auvray, *VT* iv, 1954, p. 5; cf. *Baal* III iv.18 *yn ʿn*, 'wine of sparkle', 'sparkling wine'; *CML*, pp. 112, 113, n.2); it is smooth to the palate and lubricates the throat ('it goes over smoothly'). Since v. 31 has only three stichoi, Gemser would add 'moistening lips and teeth'. Alternatively, BH queries whether v. 31c may not be an addition from Song of Songs 7.10 (G. R. Driver, *JSS*, ix, 1964, p. 349 supposes that it is a marginal note and should be deleted). Driver asserts roundly that 'Gaze not on the wine when it is red' is absurd (*Biblica* 32, 1951, pp. 187f.). His subsequent statement that 'there is no harm in looking on wine whatever its colour may be' is irrefutable, but it does not demonstrate the absurdity of translating 'Do not gaze at wine when it is red', since the point of the warning is that if you allow yourself to be hypnotized by the rich colour of red wine, in no time at all you will be drinking it. It is the fascination of colour which is then indicated by the allusion to the redness of the wine, and not its potency ('unmixed, undiluted wine'), as Driver supposes. What Driver has shown is that 'Drink not deeply of the wine when it is red' is a possible alternative rendering, since LXX μεθύσκεσθε, 'to get drunk on', seems to point to it, and, since *r'h* is used as a variant form of *rwh* (in Isa. 53.11 along with *śbʿ* 'to be sated'; in Ps. 60.5 where it is parallel to *šqh*; in Ps. 91.16 and Job 10.15 where it is parallel to *śbʿ*). I am not, however, convinced that 'Drink not deeply of the wine when it is red' makes better sense in 23.31 than the more usual rendering, and this meaning is not clinched there by the parallelism as it is in the other passages. LXX has the appearance of a free paraphrase of MT ('Do not get drunk on wine, but associate with righteous men and take part in edifying conversations'). μεθύσκεσθε may arise from this paraphrase rather than as a rendering of *tēre*'. Driver (*JSS* ix, pp. 348f.) translates v. 31b, 'and it forms its droplets' (Arabic *ʿaynu* 'drop'), which he takes as a reference to undiluted alcohol. His explanation of v. 31b is complicated and technical, but I am unable to understand why he rejects *ʿayin* = 'gleam' and yet translates *yn ʿn* in *Baal* III iv.18 (*CML*, pp. 112, 113, n.2) as 'sparkling wine'.

[32–35] The consequences of drinking wine as they are set out with remorseless detail in vv. 32–35 and made more piquant by a resort to simile constitute a formidable dissuasive. The 'hang-over' (*'aḥarīt*) is like a snake's bite, or like the venom which a basilisk (Gemser) or cobra (Byington, p. 344) secretes (adding *rō'š* with BH). Alternatively, *prš* may be cognate with Arabic *paraṭa*, 'to wound in the liver or stomach', and mean 'prick', 'puncture'. On the morning after, the toper feels as though he has been bitten by a snake and he is the victim of distressing hallucinatory experiences (pink elephants). His brain is befuddled; it is not only that he is unable to think clearly, but that his liverishness makes him hopelessly cross-grained, wrong-headed and perverse. The similes in v. 34 describe picturesquely how badly he feels. Even when he lies on his back he feels as if he were in a ship's bunk in mid-ocean riding a swell (this rather than Ringgren's translation, 'like a ship which lies [at anchor] on the high seas', for it is a person rather than a ship who is envisaged as *šōkēb*). The second simile in v. 34 is rendered by LXX: 'Like a steersman in a great swell'. This does not help with the elucidation of MT unless one is prepared to reshape it to make it agree with LXX as BH suggests (*ūkeḥōbēl beṣa'ar gādōl*, 'and like a navigator in a great storm'). A smaller emendation is the substitution of *rōkēb* for the second *šōkēb* whose originality is doubted. If the *hapax legomenon ḥibbēl* is translated 'mast' (RSV, Gemser), the simile then becomes 'like one who rides on the top of a mast', which is possible but far-fetched. The rendering of RSV, 'like one who lies on the top of a mast', presumably envisages a condition of shipwreck, where a sailor clings to a piece of floating wreckage in peril of his life and suffering dire miseries.

Ringgren translates, 'like one who sleeps at the helm of a ship', which affords a good parallel to v. 34a, since the movement of the ship would be exaggerated at the helm. Ringgren is right in anticipating that the accent in v.34b should be on discomfort rather than danger. It is the discomfort of the drunk man even when he is lying on his back that is indicated by the simile, and for this reason *šōkēb* is superior to *rōkēb* and should be retained. But *ḥibbēl* cannot mean 'ship'; one would expect it to mean 'rigging' or 'tackle' (intensive from *ḥābāl* 'rope'), rather than 'mast' (RSV, Gemser). Cf. G. R. Driver, *Welt des Orients* i (1948), p. 236. 'Like one who lies on the top of the tackle' might still be explained as a picture of shipwreck, but I take it to refer rather to a sailor who lies on the reverse of a feather bed – who has to sleep in conditions of extreme discomfort (cf. Ps. 107.27, where sailors in a storm with their ship pitching and tossing are said to spin and totter like drunk men). Dahood (pp. 49f.) explains *ḥbl* (which he vocalizes as *ḥebel*, 'mountain') as a metathetic variant of Ugaritic *ḫlb* (Driver *CML*, p. 140, 'forest', 'jungle'; Gordon, p. 402, No. 963, 'hill'); cf. Accadian *ḫalbu*, *ḫilbu* 'wooded height' (*CML*, p. 140 n.3). The reference would then be to the rolling of the ship, one moment in the depths of the sea and next on the top of a mountain. The drunk feels as if he is sleeping in the roughest of seas.

The drunk is unconscious of the injuries which he is receiving, whether in brawls or from the police (cf. Song of Songs 5.7). Under the influence of drink he ceases to be a sensitive human being and becomes the most unfeeling of animals. Driver translates v. 35a: 'They beat me, I am unconcerned', and *ḥlh* is explained on the analogy of Ethiopic *ḥallaya*, 'to look out for', 'to be concerned' (cf. I Sam. 22.8, *weʾēn ḥōleh̲ mikkem ʿālay*, 'There is none of you that takes thought for me'; see G. R. Driver, *JTS* xxix, 1928, p. 392; I. Eitan, *HUCA* xii, 1937, p. 83). This affords a good parallel to *ydʿ*, 'to be aware', but so does *ḥlh* with the sense 'I felt no pain' (so KB[3]). It is the mark of the addict that he feels a craving for more of the stuff even before he has slept off his most recent carousal: 'When shall I fully wake up? I shall go in search of another drink.'

24.1f. *The Nineteenth Saying*

[1f.] The two instructions in v. 1 recall 23.17a. The way of evil men may appear attractive and has the power to awaken envy and desire. To identify oneself with them in longing and regret through the feeling that moral inhibitions do not pay is in itself a false step and may lead beyond desire to imitation. But this is a romantic and unreal picture of the condition of the evil man, which the first contact with reality will dispel. For this is a way of life which is dominated by destructive motives and is dedicated to the creation of misery. It is a sufficient condemnation that every ounce of intellectual energy (*lēb* 'mind') is concentrated on bringing about human ruin and unhappiness. Evil men exemplify the complete prostitution of mental powers and speech which should be devoted to building up human welfare and happiness and not destroying them.

vv. 3f. *The Twentieth Saying*

[3f.] This and the next four sayings are 'sentences' and have no element of Instruction in them. There is no reason at all why the particular sense of this saying should be abandoned and the language interpreted as merely figurative and indicative of the general idea that 'not wickedness but wisdom furnishes the right stability and fills existence with worth' (Gemser). This is not to say that Gemser's interpretation is excluded; only that, if it is allowed, one has to reckon with the kind of ambiguity to which I have referred in my treatment of *Onchsheshonqy* (above pp. 129f.). Here, however, the original intention of the sentence was to lay down the lines of domestic prosperity and there was no thought of using imagery metaphorically or proverbially. In the first place, the sentence asserts that there are certain intellectual virtues which are the foundations of domestic well-being, and it assumes that the proper consolidation of one's household is a necessary prerequisite of a more general prosperity. The acquisition of *kābōd* in the community is inseparable from the strength and harmony of the *bayit*. This includes wealth, rooms well-filled with furnishings and the money to express the ideal of gracious living tangibly through the acquisition of beautiful and expensive things. It is more important to hang on to the earthiness of this sentence than to emphasize its metaphorical possibilities. If they are pressed, it is then the intellectual foundations of the good life of which the sentence speaks and the richly furnished mind in which strength is wedded to elegance.

vv. 5f. *The Twenty-First Saying*

[5f.] It is impossible to make sense of v. 5a of MT, and there is nothing for it but to emend on the basis of LXX and read *gābar ḥākām mēʿāz*: 'A wise man has more strength than a strong man' (BH, Gemser, Ringgren). On the other hand, v. 5b (MT) is perfectly possible, although the versions indicate a more precise parallelism with v. 5a, 'and a knowledgeable man than one of great physical strength' (cf. BH). 'A knowledgeable person consolidates power' (v. 5b, MT) would mean that the intelligent deployment of power increases its effectiveness, and this is what is argued in v. 6 with special reference to waging war. There is, therefore, a good reason for retaining MT in v. 5b. The motive clause in v. 6 perhaps represents a stylistic feature of the Instruction transferred to the 'sentence'. The sentence observes and states; it confines itself to compact, matter-of-fact generalizations and does not argue the case for them in motive clauses. Here the argument of the motive clause fastens on a particular activity – the waging of war – in which the superiority of brain over brawn is demonstrated. 'For expertise is needed to wage war (on *taḥbūlōt* see 1.5, above, p. 266) and safety lies in many advisers.' Or perhaps *yōʿēṣ* is a *qōṭēl* abstract (Gemser, p. 113; G. R. Driver, *Biblica* 32, p. 196) equivalent to *ʿēṣā*. In this case *rōb yōʿēṣ* means 'consensus'. The recommendation is then to make policy by consensus and to follow the course on which there is unanimity or the broadest agreement. *lᵉkā* should not be interpreted in such a way as to make the clause metaphorical: 'By stratagems you conduct your war', i.e., the battle of life (Gemser). There is no justification here at all for the resort to metaphorical interpretation and a loss of contact with the particular reference of v. 6. *taʿᵃśeh lᵉkā* can be translated as passive (BH emends to *tēʿāśe*).

v. 7 *The Twenty-Second Saying*

[7] As in vv. 3f., wisdom expresses itself in practical competence. Such wisdom is above the grasp of the fool because he is not amenable to educational discipline and does not attain the maturity of character and nicety of judgement which lend weight to public utterance. The meaning may be that he will never attain to the status of an accredited representative of the community or municipality; he will not make a significant contribution to public debate, nor help to make policy nor settle legal disputes in the forum ('gate'). He does not have the weight (*gravitas*) of a *zāqēn* or a *yōʿēṣ*. Perhaps, however, it is not such a disqualification which is intended, but only that if he were to raise his voice in public assembly he would be completely ineffective, and that since he knows that he does not command the respect which enables a man to speak powerfully and influence public decisions, he does not speak at all. There is no difficulty in equating *rāʾmōt* with *rāmōt*, but there is the grammatical point that elsewhere *ḥokmōt* is treated as fem. sing. (1.20, 9.1; see above, p. 363). It is to deal with this that G. R. Driver suggests *rāʾmat* (*Biblica* 32, p. 188).

vv. 8f. *The Twenty-Third Saying*

[8f.] It is doubtful whether these two sentences constitute a significant unity, although there is a community of topic pin-pointed by the occurrence of *zmm* in both verses (*mᵉzimmōt* in v. 8 and *zimmā* in v. 9). I have taken them together, since this appeared to me a less objectionable compromise than any other which might be contrived to arrive at the total of thirty sayings. The activity alluded to in v. 8 recalls the subject-matter of v. 2. That *ḥšb* and *m^e^zimmā* are items of the vocabulary of old wisdom I have argued elsewhere (*PWM*, pp. 65f.) and it should be noted that the fully pejorative sense of *m^e^zimmā* is present here. This man does not commit evil impulsively or instinctively; his malevolence flows from a cold, calculating rational activity (*m^e^ḥaššēb*), and so he gets the sobriquet 'Intriguer' (*baʿal m^e^zimmōt*) and the reputation for being indefatigable in darkening counsel, creating ill-will and misunderstanding and contributing to the brokenness rather than the wholeness (*šālōm*) of the community. These thoughts are taken up again in v. 9a: 'The intrigue of folly is sin', or, 'A fool's intrigue is sin' (whether *'iwwelet* is emended to *'^e^wīl* with the versions or *'iwwelet* is taken as abstract for concrete. Cf. G. R. Driver, *Biblica* 32, p. 196). There is not much at stake exegetically here, but 'fool' furnishes a more exact parallel for *lēṣ*. Whichever is preferred, the main point which emerges is that folly is not to be equated with simple-mindedness or lack of cleverness, but with incorrigibility and ultimately with the pollution of the springs of action, which produces a fundamental perversion and a malevolent anti-social stance. The fool is capable of intense mental activity (*m^e^zimmā*), but it adds up to sin. A particular manifestation of *'iwwelet* is the supercilious affectation of superiority to which v. 9b alludes. No man earns more universal detestation or deserves it more than he who wears a perpetual sneer, who is himself incapable of deep loyalty and reverence and who supposes that it is his mission in life to promote the corrosion of the values by which individuals and society live. He is the person with the knowing wink and the clever phrase who has seen through the hollowness of everything.

v. 10 *The Twenty-Fourth Saying*

[10] The connection of this with vv. 11f. is not apparent to me, although Gemser supposes that the three verses make up a unity. If this were so, one would have to conclude – and this seems to me a strained interpretation – that the 'day of adversity' in v. 10 is to be equated with the moment of testing outlined in v. 11, where resolute and hazardous action to rescue those in danger of death is demanded (cf. Gemser: 'day of distress'='neighbour's day of distress'). In my view, v. 10 should be taken by itself, in which case it makes the quite general observation that a man does not know what reserves of stamina he possesses, until he has to live through a situation in which severe demands are made on him. The punning of *ṣārā* with *ṣar* becomes more significant if one attends to the basic meaning of *ṣrr*, 'narrowness', 'confinement'. There is in Hebrew this correlation of a physical claustrophobia with 'distress', just as 'width' (*rḥb*), space in which to live and act, room for manoeuvre, is correlated with 'well-being'. It is when a man is hemmed in and trapped by adverse circumstances that his powers of endurance are stretched and an estimate of his toughness and stamina can be made. Of course, *kōaḥ* here is not physical strength narrowly conceived, but an all-round grittiness and sinewy determination which includes physical endurance, but also embraces mental toughness and moral courage. 'If you are seen to sag (*rph*) on a day of adversity, the limits of your strength are revealed', i.e., the demands of a critical and harrowing situation show up the limitations of your resources of nerve and endurance. Gemser (cf. Ringgren) would insert *beṣorkekā* (punning with *ṣar*) for metrical reasons ('your strength is deficient when you need it'). There is no virtue in the suggestion of BH that *sār* should be substituted for *ṣar*. It would make sense only if construed with *min* or *mē'al*, as it is in the passages cited (Judg. 16.17, 19). Even then, 'If you appear to sag on a day of adversity, your strength will depart from you' is almost tautological. It could be taken to mean that if you do not brace yourself for survival, you will lose whatever strength you have; if once you sag, defeat will be inevitable. This is not a serious alternative.

vv. 11f. *The Twenty-Fifth Saying*

[11f.] It would seem that two collateral demands are made in v. 11, the first to rescue the man who is in prison awaiting death and the second to rescue the man who is on his way to execution. Driver (*ZAW* 50, 1932, p. 146) objects to the phrase 'tottering to execution' (v. 11b) because it is too strong as compared with 'taken away to death'. He suggests 'ready for execution', i.e., at the point of execution (*mṭh* = *mṭ*' 'to arrive at', 'to be ready for'). BH (also Ringgren) suggests 'are led away to execution' (*muṭṭīm*). The interpretation which I have tentatively suggested for v. 11b presupposes the '*im* of the oath with negative force. This agrees with Gemser who, however, reads *tēḥāśēk*: 'Do not hold yourself back from those who totter to execution', i.e., do not dissociate yourself from them. Driver's earlier understanding of v. 11b (*ZAW* 50, p. 146) presupposes that *'im* is negative, but more recently he has argued that *ḥśk*, like the Syriac cognate, means 'preserved', 'kept safe' and that *'im* is emphatic as in Ps. 81.9b: 'And you are to preserve those ready for execution' (*Biblica* 32, pp. 188f.). The '*liberare ne cesses*', 'keep on setting free' of V, which Driver cites in support, agrees equally well, if not better, with Gemser's 'Do not dissociate yourself from', i.e., 'Do not deny help to'.

Apart from these matters of detail, there is the larger question about the kind of meaning which can be attached to this strange and apparently extreme demand, and Gemser's remark that it contains a warning against negligence and lack of concern for neighbours threatened with danger does not deal faithfully with its exact terms. The quotation from Stricker's translation of *Onchsheshonqy* is of doubtful relevance, since Glanville's translation gives a quite different meaning to the passage. Stricker translates: 'Do not withdraw your hand from a scribe when they take him to prison; if you withdraw your hand from him, they will take him to the tomb' (B. Gemser, *VTS* vii, 1960, p. 125). By reproducing this, Gemser indicates that v. 11 is a demand not to abandon a man in deep disgrace and facing serious charges, since he needs all the support he can get if he is to survive. The question of his guilt or innocence is apparently not raised. That is for the judges to decide, but, in the meantime, his friends must stand by him and do all in their power to help him. Glanville translates: 'Do not follow after a scribe when they take him to prison; follow him when they take him to his tomb.' The instruction thus assumes a hard-headed, almost cynical form and is dominated by considerations of self-interest. It is dangerous to be loyal to an official in prison and under a cloud, but once he has been put to death he is no longer a danger to the state and no risk attaches to joining his funeral procession and paying homage as a mourner. Beyond this innocuous loyalty one should not go. If this is what it means, it does not help with v. 11.

The terms of this verse thus remain puzzling, unless we accept Ringgren's suggestion that it refers to those who are innocent and have been unjustly condemned. This is not explicitly said, but it is a less objectionable assumption than that 'death' and 'execution' are metaphors for the oppression of the poor (Gemser, Ringgren). This assumption that the victims who are to be rescued are innocent of the crimes with which they have been charged is perhaps strengthened by the religious character of the arguments by which the imperatives are reinforced (v. 12). This amounts to an appeal to a higher justice which never miscarries nor fails of execution. It will then be futile to feign ignorance or disclaim responsibility, in view of the penetrating scrutiny and comprehensive knowledge of the divine judge and the precision with which he metes out to every man his deserts.

Gressmann supposed that the phrase *tōkēn libbōt* (cf. 21.2; also *tōkēn rūḥōt* in 16.2) used of Yahweh derives from a piece of Egyptian mythology according to which the hearts of men were weighed at death by the god of wisdom Thoth and his assistant scribes. When the heart was guiltless, it was as light as a feather, and so on the other scale lay a feather as the symbol of truth (H. Gressmann, *Israels Spruchweisheit im Zusammenhang der Welt-Literatur*, 1925, pp. 43f.). Driver has urged that *tkn* means 'to examine against a norm' (*PWM*, p. 81, n.3), and the thought in v. 12 is that Yahweh knows the most hidden springs of action; that because all the truth is accessible to him, his judgements on the hidden, inward aspects of action – the labyrinth of motivation – are definitive and unerring. I take *nōṣēr napšᵉkā* to refer to Yahweh's supervision of what is going on rather than to man's dependence on Yahweh for the maintenance of his life. LXX, ὁ πλάσας πνοὴν points to *yōṣēr* instead of *nōṣēr*, 'he who formed you', but is not an improvement on MT. The element of truth which may be in Gressmann's interpretation is that the justice of Yahweh which is envisaged is ultimate rather than immediate; it is the justice which the *'aḥᵃrīt* discloses (cf. 23.18, 24.14b). This is not necessarily the same as saying that it is judgement at death, but only that in the long run the truth about a man's worth will emerge and that then he will cease to be served by whatever wrongfully or spuriously enhanced his life beyond what he deserved. Although Yahweh's name does not appear in v. 12, there is little doubt that the ideas expressed are Yahwistic, especially since the name does occur in connection with *tōkēn libbōt* in 21.2 and *tōkēn rūḥōt* in 16.2.

vv. 13f. *The Twenty-Sixth Saying*

[13f.] The advice to eat honey has independent value apart from its metaphorical application to wisdom. The health-giving properties of honey and the nourishment which it supplies to the body are analogous with the contribution of wisdom to a more comprehensive concept of health and so the medical prescription links honey with wisdom. And there is a bonus because it has medicinal value without having an evil taste; it charms the palate and wisdom, too, is a delight, just as the pleasure-giving qualities of the law of Yahweh are illustrated by a similar allusion to honey (Ps. 19.11). In v. 14, Gemser suggests the insertion of *metōqā lelibbekā we* after *dē‘ā* (emended) and *ṭōbā* after *ḥokmā* for metrical reasons: 'Thus knowledge is sweet for your mind and wisdom good for your life' (cf. BH). Winton Thomas retains *de‘e* or *de‘ē* of MT, deriving it from *d‘h*, cognate with Arabic *da‘ā*, 'sought', 'desired', 'asked': 'So seek wisdom for yourself' (*JTS* xxxviii, 1937, p. 401). Ringgren reads, 'So is knowledge and wisdom for your life', which makes good sense, with a small degree of emendation (*dē‘ā* for *de‘eh* and the insertion of *we* before *ḥokmā*). In any case, the meaning is that physical health is only one aspect of vitality, and that without wisdom there can be no wholeness of life. The considerations adduced in support of this advice are those already discussed in 23.18 (see above, p. 387), and no more need be said except to observe that, as in 24.12, the argument has a marked religious character and expresses a confidence in Yahweh's justice. In view of this unfailing apportionment of deserts, wisdom is the route to fulfilment and vindication.

vv. 15f. *The Twenty-Seventh Saying*

[15f.] If *rāšā‘* is retained, it has to be read as a vocative (Ringgren), but it is perhaps an intrusive gloss encouraged by the antithesis of *ṣaddīq* and *rāšā‘* in v. 16 (BH and Gemser). There is an element of high-flown or poetic vocabulary in v. 15. The home of the righteous man is described as his 'pasture' and his 'couching-place' – a word which describes animals at rest (Isa. 65.10; Jer. 50.6), and whose use in relation to a person indicates a cultivated picturesqueness of expression. It is consequently illegitimate to conclude that agricultural conditions of life are in view (Oesterley, Gemser), for the instruction is quite general and unspecific. It is a warning not to lay an ambush against the household of a *ṣaddīq* nor to destroy his domestic prosperity, and the reference to the *ṣaddīq* in v. 15 as well as the cast of the argument in v. 16 shows that the same pious presuppositions prevail here as in the two preceding sayings. That this is a Yahwistic theodicy, although Yahweh's name is not mentioned, appears from the opposition of *ṣaddīq* and *rāšā‘* in v. 16, and from the statement that the *saddīq* is never defeated by the assaults of evil men. He may fall down again and again ('seven times') beneath the weight of their attacks, but he will always get up again and will endure. In the long run (cf. *'aḥarīt* 23.18; 24.14) his righteousness will be vindicated, whereas evil men, because they are dedicated to evil, will stumble fatally (cf. D. Winton Thomas, *VT* xv, 1965, p. 274, who cites the Aramaic proverb: 'Seven parts for the righteous, but one for the evil-doer'). If this is indeed a concrete account of what is intended by the doctrine of the *'aḥarīt*, we see in it a tendency to depart from the classical rigour of the dogma of theodicy and to restate it so as to bring it more in line with the experiences of the *ṣaddīq* in the world. It does not then assert what is manifestly true all the time, but only what will ultimately be seen to be true, and so it becomes more difficult to contradict and less difficult to defend. Whatever exact significance is attached to the *'aḥarīt* (see on 23.18, above, p. 387), it implies suspension or delayed vindication and a loss of dynamic immediacy in the operation of a theodicy.

vv. 17f. *The Twenty-Eighth Saying*

[17f.] The most noteworthy aspect of this saying is the shape of the cautionary argumentation ('lest'), in which piety mingles with a quaint opportunism. The absence of every trace of human feeling for the enemy who is down and out is uncanny and unpleasant. The attitude which is to be adopted towards him is measured with an eery, impersonal coldness. This is not relieved by the awareness that gloating over an enemy when he is down will meet the disapproval of Yahweh, since the conclusion which is drawn from this is not that mercy should be shown to a defeated enemy, but that one should refrain from gloating over him so that Yahweh's anger may not relent and his ruin may be final.

vv. 19f. *The Twenty-Ninth Saying*

[19f.] This is a variation on the theme of 23.17, and the motivation (v. 20) introduces the thought of the *'aḥarīt*, which is similarly adduced in 23.18 (cf. 24.14). The new thought in v. 19 is that one should not be vexed or inwardly discomposed through brooding over the behaviour of evil-doers. The verb *tiṯḥar* indicates 'heat' – the heat of a feverish indignation which achieves nothing and destroys tranquillity and efficiency. 'Do not get hot under the collar because of evil-doers.' 'Do not get worked up because of evil-doers.' There is perhaps the implication that a man should not carry all the burdens of the world on his shoulders, as if God were not able to take care of his own responsibilities. Whatever is infuriating or excites envy and a sneaking desire to imitate will come right in the light of the *'aḥarīt*. The statement that the lamp of the wicked will go out (cf. Prov. 13.9; 20.20; Job 18.6; 21.17) must refer to the extinguishing of life, but *'aḥarīt* does not then necessarily imply a belief in life after death (contrary to Dahood, p. 51). It is still possible to understand it as the fully-rounded life, which achieves maturity and fulfilment contrasted with the life which is prematurely cut short and denied a fitting climax. In II Sam. 21.17, *nēr* is combined with a synonymous verb *kbh* (both *d'k* and *kbh* appear in Isa. 43.17) in a passage where the metaphor is identified particularly with the Davidic king. I have suggested (*I and II Samuel, in loc.*) that the source of this metaphor may be the *nēr tāmīd* which not only symbolized the constant presence of Yahweh in his sanctuary, but also the enduring covenant between Yahweh and the Davidic king on which the well-being of the community depended. Hence Ps. 132.17: 'I have set up a *nēr* for my Anointed.' These words occur in a psalm which praises David for his tireless efforts to bring the ark to Jerusalem and in a passage which expatiates on Yahweh's choice of the Jerusalem temple. It is in this temple that a lamp has been set up for David, with whom Yahweh has made a covenant and whom he has installed as the founder of an enduring dynasty (vv. 11–18; cf. I Kings 11.36; 15.4: 'that David, my servant, may always have a lamp before me in Jerusalem'). Hence, if the king were to die, the lamp of Israel would go out (II Sam. 21.17). This may be the primary milieu of the metaphor from which it is detached and generalized in its application to the death of the wicked.

vv. 21f. *The Thirtieth Saying*

Kopf's solution of the linguistic difficulties in these verses makes so extensive recourse to Arabic usage that it is almost tantamount to reading the Hebrew as if it were Arabic (L. Kopf, *VT* ix, 1959, pp. 280f.). In associating *šōnīm* with Arabic *saniya*, 'to be high' (*rajul sanāyā*, 'nobleman'), he has followed D. Winton Thomas (*ZAW* 52, 1934, p. 237) and G. R. Driver (*Biblica* 32, p. 189). His other suggestions do not deserve so serious consideration. He equates *pīd* with Arabic *fāʾida*, 'utility', 'advantage', and reads *mlk* as an imperative meaning 'to possess', 'to acquire' on the analogy of Arabic *mlk*. The meaning of v. 21a is then that if you fear Yahweh you will become a man of substance, while v. 22b is a rhetorical question: 'Who knows the advantage of their high rank?' means 'their high rank has no abiding worth'. The gist of the advice given is as follows: Revere the authority of Yahweh and of the king and do not dabble in the intrigues of noblemen. As an association of religion with patriotism this is readily intelligible, but there is the further fact that the Davidic king's rule derives directly from Yahweh, so that loyalty to him and respect for his person are religious duties (see above on v. 20). Noblemen who are not above intrigue, and who plot to undermine the régime because they are greedy for power, play a dangerous game for high stakes and expose themselves to the sudden onset of disaster. They are bad risks, for calamity overtakes them in mysterious circumstances which defy rational analysis, and the course of their careers is dangerously unpredictable.

Winton Thomas emends *šᵉnēhem* (v. 22b) to *šōnīm* and G. R. Driver to *haššōnīm* (assuming the displacement of *h*), 'and who knows when calamity will befall noblemen'. Instead of emending *šᵉnēhem* (v. 22), Gemser (also Scott) follows LXX in v. 21b and reads *ʿal šᵉnēhem ʾal titʿabbēr*, 'Do not rebel against (LXX 'be insubordinate to') either of them' (*titʿabbēr* presupposes that there has been a metathesis of *b* and *r*). The plural suffixes in v. 22 then refer to God and king: 'For suddenly disaster arises (from them), and who can know the calamity attributable to them both.' Gemser points out that part of the addition in LXX (v. 22de) describes the terror of the king's anger. This addition in LXX (22a–22e, eleven lines) illustrates the point which I have already made (above, pp. 308f.), that a longer text in LXX may be associated with the end of a section – a convenient place for expansion. My own view of v. 22 (contrary to Gemser's) is that the motive clauses are more apposite in relation to the intrigues of persons of high rank (v. 21b) than as a reference to the retributive power of Yahweh and king. Toy discusses the different proposals which have been made for *šōnīm* (v. 21b), one of which, 'innovators', is Barucq's translation. In v. 22b *šnyhm* was read as 'their years' by Pesh. and Targ. It is just possible that 'Who can know the destruction of their years?' means 'Who knows when their life will be cut off?'.

C. CHAPTER 31.1–9

The Instruction of Lemuel

In that this piece is addressed to a king and contains advice related to the discharge of his office, one can say that of all the specimens of the Instruction in the book of Proverbs, this is the one which is most manifestly vocational wisdom and which, in this respect, resembles most the corresponding Egyptian literature, especially *Amenemhet* and *Merikare*, in which kings are likewise tutored. A Babylonian text which Lambert entitles *Advice to a Prince* is illustrative of the same concern to equip a ruler for his tasks by providing guidance on morality, politics and protocol (*BWL*, pp. 110f.). The style of the Babylonian text is, however, the precise, impersonal one which was used to communicate omens, and it lacks the imperious, direct address of the Instruction. It neither commands nor prohibits nor exhorts, but sets out factually, by means of protasis and apodosis, the consequences of particular courses of action. In *Amenemhet* and *Merikare* the instructor is the reigning king and father of the crown prince who is addressed. It is a special feature of this passage that the king is advised by his mother (cf. 1.8, above, p. 268; 6.20, above, p. 327).

For the most part, the aspect of career wisdom which dominates the Egyptian Instruction is hardly evident in the examples of the genre in the book of Proverbs (see above, pp. 380f.), and it is therefore probably significant that this exception bears the marks of extra-Israelite provenance. There is the possibility that Massa (v. 1) is the name of a north Arabian tribe (cf. Gen. 25.14; I Chron. 1.30), and the language displays such Aramaisms as *bar*, 'son' (3 times in v. 2), and *m*[e]*lākīn*, 'kings' (v. 3). In view of the reputation which the Edomites had for wisdom (I Kings 5.10; Jer. 49.7; and Eliphaz the Temanite in Job), Gemser suggests that this may be an Edomite piece (on Edomite wisdom see *PWM*, p. 73).

Formally these verses are principally directive or command, which is the basic element of the Instruction. Imperatives or jussives prevail, and argument in subordinate clauses is found only in vv. 5 and 7. In v. 5 are two 'lest' clauses in which cautionary considerations are adduced; v. 7 contains two consequential clauses dependent on a jussive. Apart from v. 2, which is a puzzle, the structure is simple and the two identical phrases in v. 4 are to be explained on the assumption that a jussive is suppressed in each case (so G. R. Driver, *Biblica*

32, pp. 194f.), i.e., 'let it not be for kings'. The type of subordination most typical of the Instruction, namely, the motive clause, is absent.

[1] The name *l^emū'ēl* is discussed by Gemser, who suggests that it means 'belonging to El' and so is to be equated with *lā'ēl* of Num. 3.24. *l^emū* (*l^emō*) is a longer form of *l^e* (*mō* = *mā* 'what', GK §103k). The other possibility mentioned by Gemser, 'belonging to Mū'ēl', Mū'ēl to be connected with *Mauil*, which is attested as a woman's name in Minaean, is more remote. A. Jirku (*ZAW* 66, 1954, p. 151) explains the name as 'Lim is God'. He observes that names whose second part is constituted by 'Lim' appear in the Mari texts. The absence of the determinative *ilu* 'god' before such names is not an argument against taking them as the name of a god, since it is absent elsewhere in the Mari texts from names indisputably theophoric. The words of Lemuel's mother have a quite different form from the prophetic oracle with which the title *maśśā'* is normally associated. They are not Yahweh's words prefixed by some such formula as 'Thus says Yahweh'; they constitute *tōrā* or *mūsār* rather than *maśśā'* (with a change of punctuation, 'King of Massa' can be read; see above). That they are intended as *mūsār*, 'educational discipline', is indicated by the use of *yiss^erattū* to describe the advice which is given. The individual directives deal with the following topics: *a.* warning against women (v. 3) *b.* against drinking wine (vv. 4–5); *c.* wine is to be given to those who need an opiate (vv. 6–7); *d.* the legal rights of those who are weak and poor are to be safeguarded (vv. 8–9).

[2] The enigmatic v. 2 reads: 'What my son and what son of my womb and what son of my vows'. The final phrase may be in some measure elucidated by the account of the vow taken by Hannah in connection with her prayer for a son (I Sam. 1.11). It may not have been unusual for a woman to take religious vows which she fulfilled in the event of her desire for a son being realized. The longer text of LXX is easier and is followed by BH (also Gemser), which inserts *mā l^emū'ēl b^ekōrī 'ōmar 'ēlekā* after *b^erī*, 'What, my son, what Lemuel, my first born, am I to say to you? What, son of my womb? What, son of my vows?' Dahood (p. 60) renders: 'What ails my son? What ails the son of my womb? What ails the son of my vows?' This, however, does not suit what follows. It has been suggested that *mā* should be associated with the Arabic *ma*, 'listen', 'take heed'. Sense can then be had out of MT, and the thrice-repeated demand for attention conforms to the typical general introduction of the Instruction – emphasis on the need for unbroken concentration, attentiveness and receptivity

which precedes the individual and specific directives (Eliezer ben Yehuda, *JPOS* i, 1920–1, p. 114).

v. 3 *Against Women*

[3] The sense of v. 3b is unsatisfactory and some emendation of *lamḥōt* is necessary. Gemser (cf. BH) suggests a change in the vocalization, *l*ᵉ*mōḥōt m*ᵉ*lākīn* 'the destroyers of kings', a circumlocution for women. Reider associates *lamḥot* with Aramaic *m*ᵉ*ḥā'* 'destroy' and *mlkyn* with *milkā'*, 'counsel', 'advice'. He takes *lamḥōt* to be a pael participle and postulates for it the following development: *lim*ᵉ*maḥōt* > *limaḥōt* > *lamḥōt*. The meaning is 'destroyers of counsel', again a circumlocution for women. When a king is too obsessed with women, his wits are blunted and his judgement goes awry (J. Reider, *VT* iv, 1954, pp. 287f.). A bigger alteration of MT is involved in the reading *l*ᵉ*laḥ*ᵃ*nōt m*ᵉ*lākīn* 'to royal concubines' (cf. BH).

Another problem is the lack of parallelism between *ḥēlekā*, 'thy strength', and *d*ᵉ*rākekā*, 'thy ways'; *y*ᵉ*rēkekā*, 'thy thighs', is an emendation which requires only the alteration of one consonant of MT (BH and Gemser) and which would allude to the expenditure of strength in sexual intercourse. In view of the circumstance that it is a king who is addressed, the possibility that *d*ᵉ*rākekā* is to be connected with Ugaritic *drkt* 'dominion', 'nobility' (see on 8.22, above, p. 354) has to be entertained, in which case v. 3b would read: 'nor your dignity to those who destroy kings' (cf. J. B. Bauer, *VT* viii, 1958, p. 91). *y*ᵉ*rēkekā* should be adopted and *lmḥwt* vocalized as *l*ᵉ*mōḥōt*. *ḥayil*, 'strength', 'wealth', is ambivalent and v. 3a could equally well be an allusion to the enormous expense of keeping a large harem and the subsequent drain on financial resources on which there should be prior claims. A king must keep his amorous propensities in check, else he will create grotesque disproportion and distortion and will undermine the foundations of his personal authority and the principles of sound government, thereby bringing himself into contempt.

vv. 4f. *Against Wine*

vv. 6f. *Wine is to be given to Those who Need an Opiate*

[4–7] Wine is a natural ally of women and a complementary threat to a king's integrity. While it is excusable that wine should be used to induce a torpor in those who have nothing left to live for or for whom the pain of existence has become too sharp, such an addiction in a king is a flight from responsibility, a refusal to bear the burdens of power and office and a confession of cowardice and loss of nerve. When Gemser says that the warning against wine perhaps reflects nomadic conditions and associates it with the attitude of the Rechabites (II Kings 9; Jer. 35), he reads into it a puritanical rigour which is not at all intended. There is no prohibitionist fervour in this directive and no absolute veto on wine. The king is required to give wine to those who need it as an opiate, so that in sweet oblivion they may have respite from intolerable poverty or from the grind of unbearable toil. Wine is a medicine which unlike most medicines is both pleasurable and effective, but it constitutes a danger against which those in authority must be on their guard. A king whose vitality is sapped by alcohol and whose mind is never clear will be inconsistent, unpredictable and irresponsible. He will not consistently observe the constitutional limits of his rule (*m*ᵉ*ḥuqqāq*) and he will lack the moral strength to combat corruption. Here and in vv. 18f., the legal responsibility of the king is emphasized. If the machinery of justice is rusty and officialdom is obstructive, the subject is entitled to look to the king for the redress of his grievances and the obtaining of justice. In his capacity as the supreme arbiter of justice, the king must take special care of the poor and under-privileged so as to ensure that they are at no disadvantage before the law. This a drunken king will never do, since he does not have the moral stamina to withstand graft and corruption. The only textual difficulty in these verses is constituted by K. *'ō*, Q. *'ēy* in v. 4. Driver suggests that we have here an infinitive absolute written defectively (*'awwō*) or, alternatively, that *'ēw* is a noun and a permissible Aramaizing form (cf. *rēaʿ* 'purpose'): 'a desire for alcohol', or 'an appetite for alcohol'. BH (also KB³) emends to *'awwē*, piel infinitive construct. D. Winton Thomas, (*VT* xii, 1962, pp. 498f.) suggests that *'ēw* is a scribal error for *r*ᵉ*'ō* < *r*ᵉ*wō*: 'It is not for kings to drink wine, nor for rulers to imbibe strong drink' (See on 23.31, above, p. 394). *š*ᵉ*tō* (v. 4) is a mixed form which conflates *š*ᵉ*tōt* and *šātō* (G. R. Driver, *Biblica* 32, pp. 194f.).

vv. 8f. *Safeguard the Legal Rights of the Poor*

Both verses open with precisely the same words ('Open thy mouth'), and in both the king is required to assert his responsibility effectively for the maintenance of justice in his community. The legal character of the vocabulary is unmistakable. *dīn* refers to the judicial process and the just verdict which results when it is faithfully carried out, and *šᵉpoṭ ṣedeq* is just another way of demanding that justice should be done. Thus *ṣedeq* here is entirely forensic just as the hiphil *hiṣdīq* has the meaning 'to bring in a verdict of not guilty'. This responsibility weighs most heavily on the king in relation to those for whom the judicial processes are liable to miscarry because of the obstructionist or corrupt devices of those with power and influence. Where officials or judges are amenable to bribery and exposed to pressures, the scales of justice are tipped in favour of those with power and wealth, and the poor and weak may find that the processes which should lead to vindication and redress are blocked (cf. the Egyptian piece 'The Protests of the Eloquent Peasant', *ANET*, pp. 407ff.). In these circumstances, everything hangs on the vigilance and resolution of the king in asserting his legal prerogatives. In this connection I have suggested elsewhere that Nathan's story in II Sam. 12.1f. is not so much a parable as the construction of a hypothetical legal case on which David as king and supreme judge is invited to pronounce legally (*I and II Samuel, in loc.*).

Gemser urges that *'illēm* is not just to be taken literally, but refers to all who, for one reason or another, are incapable of making effective representations on their own behalf before a judge and whose case will go by default unless it is taken up by the king. This is certainly what is intended by vv. 8f. as a whole, but I take *'illēm* to be a specific reference to those with a particular physical impediment, namely, dumbness, and who, for that reason, are obviously grievously handicapped in any legal proceedings in which they may be involved. The obscure *bᵉnē ḥᵃlōp* is apparently similarly particular, as also the *ʿānī wᵉ'ebyōn* of v. 9b. The various meanings which have been attached to *bᵉnē ḥᵃlōp* are reviewed by Gemser and Driver. Gemser favours 'children of abandonment', i.e., orphans. Driver (*Biblica* 32, pp. 195f.) objects that neither this nor any of the other meanings suggested for *bᵉnē ḥᵃlōp* ('those subject to the vicissitudes of fortune', 'those likely to perish standing on the edge of a precipice') furnishes a satisfactory parallel for *'illēm*. This objection would also apply to the emendations *bᵉnē ʿālōp*, 'sons of impotence', or *bᵉnē ḥōlī*, 'sons of disease' (cf. BH), both of which indicate 'weaklings' or 'invalids'. Dahood (p. 60) supposes that *ḥᵃlōp* denotes a bodily infirmity. D. Winton Thomas (*VT* xv, 1965, p. 277) suggests a solution on the basis of Arabic *ḫalafa* 'was stupid, foolish, of defective intellect', *ḫulfatu* 'vice, stupidity, want of intellect'. He translates: 'Open thy mouth in defence of the dumb and maintain the cause of all who are without understanding.' What Driver's emendation does is not to supply a parallel for *'illēm*, but to make of v. 8 a sentence in which there is no balanced structure or parallelism. Since this balance is present in v. 9 and since the opening words of the two verses are identical, there is justification for the assumption that v. 8 and v. 9 were similarly constructed, and this consideration weighs against Driver's emendation. He connects *ḥᵃlōp* with Aramaic *ḥallēp* 'contradicted', *ḥillūp* 'what is contrary', Arabic *ḫalafa*, 'contradicted', 'dissented from', 'opposed'; *ḫilāfu*, 'controversy': 'Open your mouth for the dumb against the suit of all his adversaries' (i.e., legal opponents). This presupposes the equation of *'ēl* with *'al*, but a similar equation is assumed in Gemser's translation: 'on behalf of the legal rights of all orphans'.

The difficulty with Gemser's translation, as also with the others, is not that they offer a notably defective parallel to *'illēm*. What orphans have in common with those who are dumb is their need of the king's advocacy to get them justice in the courts. The residual difficulty is simply constituted by the linguistic obscurity of *bᵉnē ḥᵃlōp* and the consequently speculative character of all the translations offered. One of them, 'those who are the victims of circumstance', can be associated with a single usage of *ḥlp* in Nabataean, in the phrase *ḥlp mwt*, which means either 'the contingency of death' (Jean-Hoftijzer) or 'death by accident' (Cantineau). See Jean-Hoftijzer, s.v. *ḥlp*². Those who have been treated unkindly by fate or worsted by circumstances over which they had no control are then the *bᵉnē ḥᵃlōp*.

VI

SENTENCE LITERATURE IN THE BOOK OF PROVERBS

A. CHAPTERS 10–22.16

The collection 10.1–22.16, bearing the title 'Proverbs of Solomon' (omitted by LXX and Pesh.) is made up preponderantly of sentence literature. In such literature there is no context, for each sentence is an entity in itself and the collection amounts to no more than the gathering together of a large number of independent sentences, each of which is intended to be a well-considered and definitive observation on a particular topic. The atomistic character of sentence literature may be modified to some extent by a secondary grouping of sentences, whether this is based on purely mechanical considerations (word jingles, stitch-words) and is devised as a mnemonic technique to facilitate learning, or derives from editorial groupings based on the degree of common content in several sentences. Thus Gemser has suggested that the contiguity of v. 11 and v. 12 in ch. 10 is dictated by the desire to utilize the mnemonic help constituted by the jingle *y^e^kasseh – t^e^kasseh*, that vv. 14 and 15 are associated because *m^e^ḥittā* occurs in both, and that *l^e^ḥayyīm* similarly explains the contiguity of vv. 16 and 17. As editorial groupings based on affinity of content, he mentions vv. 18–21 (concerning speech) and vv. 27–30 (the blessing of the fear of Yahweh).

While it is important to pay attention to the principles which determine the association of sentences, it is none the less true that these are secondary groupings which do not significantly alter the atomistic character of sentence literature. Further, these are not necessarily the principles of grouping which are best fitted to establish a classification by which the effective study of the wisdom tradition, as it is reflected in these sentences, can be advanced. Consequently I do not propose to concern myself with the principles which are employed to group sentences in the book of Proverbs, but rather with a system of classification which is orientated towards an investigation of the history of the wisdom tradition in Israel, in so far as this can be reconstructed from the sentences.

This is an enquiry which cannot be detached entirely from a consideration of the meaning of *māšāl* (above, pp. 22f.). All the material in the book of Proverbs, both Instruction and sentence literature, is designated *m*ᵉ*šālīm* (1.1). The word has acquired a generalized meaning, and we have to look elsewhere in the Old Testament in order to get more precise indications of what a *māšāl* was thought to be. It appears that while it is understandable that a wisdom sentence should be called a *māšāl*, the Instruction has a quite separate history from the *māšāl*. Unlike the *māšāl*, it does not have popular origins; its origins are rather in the circle of the court and the establishment; in its international context it is concerned with the preparation of officials for high office in the state.

As a means of breaking the ground for this enquiry, I have developed an exact definition of 'proverb' in which the emphasis is laid on representative potential and openness to interpretation. The 'proverb', in virtue of its concreteness, sometimes in virtue of the organization of imagery, has a representative capacity which can be intuited by future interpreters. The paradox of the 'proverb' is that it acquires immortality because of its particularity; that because of its lack of explicitness, its allusiveness or even opaqueness, it does not become an antique, but awaits continually the situation to illumine which it was coined. Among the sentences of the book of Proverbs there are not many such 'proverbs', but 10.5 may be regarded as one.

[5] It is possible to take v. 5 literally, in which case it deals with a particular kind of weakness and laziness which would be regarded as a cardinal failure in an agricultural community. A son who is lazy at harvest time, and is oblivious (*nirdām*) to the urgency of the work that is in hand, will bring scandal and ridicule on his father, whereas one who is competent, and has a grasp of all the problems involved, will throw all his energies into the successful management of the harvest (on *maśkīl* see *PWM*, pp. 67f.). 'This recalls the custom of whole families going to "camp" in the vineyards outside the town to gather the grape harvest. This was an annual affair in places like Es-Salt across the Jordan, where a large variety of grapes were cultivated. The work is concentrated while it lasts' (E.F.F.B.). But v. 5 is much more than such a limited, exact statement concerning the particular duties of a son in a peasant economy. It is also a representative saying about any son who displays acumen and mettle when his father most needs him, or, contrariwise, who fails when he is put to the test and by his weakness and uselessness brings his father into contempt. A further universalizing of the 'proverb' would be its use to say that it is the testing or critical situation which constitutes the sifting process and provides a reliable indication of ability and character. The presence of figurative language in sentences does not necessarily make them 'proverbs' in this sense. There are a number of verses in ch. 10 which contain figures of speech but are not 'proverbs' (vv. 11, 15, 20, 25, 26, 29).

I adopt the following principles of classification in my treatment of the sentence literature in the book of Proverbs. (These are outlined on p. 11, above.)

Class A: These sentences are set in the framework of old wisdom and concerned with the education of the individual for a successful and harmonious life.

Class B: Here the centre of concern is the community rather than the individual, and the sentences in this class have, for the most part, a negative character, in that they describe the harmful effects on the life of the community of various manifestations of anti-social behaviour.

Class C: These are identified by the presence of God-language or by other items of vocabulary expressive of a moralism which derives from Yahwistic piety.

It is sometimes difficult to fit a sentence into this system of classification and, in particular, to decide whether it belongs to one class rather than another, but I shall endeavour to show that this is a suitable working arrangement for investigating the range of the sentence literature.

Chapter 10

Class A: vv. 1, 4, 5, 8, 13, 14, 15, 19, 26.
Class B: vv. 10, 11, 12, 17(?), 18(?), 21(?), 23.
Class C: vv. 2, 3, 6, 7, 9, 16, 20, 22, 24, 25, 27, 28, 29, 30, 31, 32.

Class A

There is a group of sentences constituted by the antithesis of wise and foolish (vv. 8, 13, 14, 19). **[8]** The *miṣwōt* of v. 8a are the directives of the wisdom teacher communicated by imperatives (i.e., Instruction, not 'recommendation' or 'advice', contrary to L. Kopf, *VT* viii, 1958, p. 197). The *ḥakam lēb* is the one amenable to educational discipline who learns wisdom through submitting to the authority of his teacher and receiving the content of his instruction. Such a person is contrasted with the *'ewīl śepātayim*, who likes the sound of his own voice too much to attend to the wisdom of a teacher, and whose garrulity is a symptom of his indiscipline and his inability to submit to authority and learn. Discipline leads to life, while indiscipline leads to extinction.

[19] The importance of speech in relation to the educational objectives of wisdom is stated positively and negatively. The wise man will keep silence unless he is assured that the time is ripe for him to speak, that he can do it effectively and that his words have been carefully weighed. A reputation for garrulity or glibness is damaging, and is the mark of the fool rather than the wise man. This conviction that it is part of wisdom to keep speech on a tight rein finds expression in v. 19. The man who talks and talks is an inveterate blunderer who lacks sensibility and who, because he never has the feel of a situation, repeatedly injures susceptibilities, raises hackles and gives offence (*lō' yeḥdal pešaʿ*). The mark of the man who can handle people and manage situations with a sure touch is disciplined speech. This, then, is the positive aspect of the evaluation of speech and the antithesis of positive and negative in relation to speech is expressed in vv. 13 and 14.

[13] In v. 13 there is a contrast between a critically perceptive man (*nābōn*) and one who is deficient in acumen (*ḥasar lēb*). When the *nābōn* speaks, the fine balance of his wisdom is evident, whereas the *ḥasar lēb* gets himself into trouble (when he speaks). **[14]** Again, wise men are those who have served their apprenticeship with a master and have wrought into the fabric of their own being the store of his wisdom. It is because they were once teachable and receptive that they now possess a maturity of wisdom in their own right and are impeccable counsellors (v. 14a). When the fool speaks, disaster is imminent for himself and those who may attend to him (v. 14b).

The earthy character of old wisdom is well illustrated by vv. 4 and 15, both of which, in different ways, assume that wealth is a good thing. **[15]** In v. 15 the rich man's wealth is described as a fortified city and the poverty of the poor man as a disaster. Wealth is an insurance against the chanciness of existence, and whoever has it is not naked and defenceless before its vicissitudes. But those who are without wealth have no margin of safety, and their vulnerability may at any time spell disaster for them. It can be seen from v. 15a that a metaphor does not have the openness to interpretation of a 'proverb' (see above, p. 414 on v. 5). By virtue of its construction the metaphor fixes exactly the interpretation of its imagery and circumscribes its field of reference. **[4]** The other sentence (v. 4) states that diligence leads to wealth, and that poverty is associated with half-hearted effort and fecklessness. In v. 4a, BH reads *ʿōśā* and *rēʾš* (LXX πενία): 'Half-hearted effort (literally 'a slack hand') makes for poverty.' Ringgren (following MT): 'Whoever works half-heartedly will be poor.'

[26] Another verse which deals with the topic of laziness is v. 26. Albright cites from Ugaritic texts lines which have the same structure as v. 26:

Like the feeling of a wild cow for her calf,
Like the feeling of a wild ewe for her lamb,
So (was) the feeling of Anath for Baal.

(*VTS* iii, p. 5; *Baal* III ii.6–8, *CML*, pp. 110f.) Another example is:

(As) the heifer lows for her calf,
(and) soldiers' sons cry for their mothers,
Surely the people of Udm moaned (*Keret* III, i.5–7, *CML*, pp. 36f.)

This is a complicated type of double simile. According to v. 26, the relationship of vinegar to the teeth or smoke to the eyes is illustrative of the relationship of a dilatory employee to his employers. 'With regard to "smoke to the eyes" we are to think of houses where the only exit for smoke (sometimes from green wood) is through smallish apertures over the door or at the top of the wall' (E.F.F.B.). What smoke, vinegar and a lazy employee all have in common in the situations which are described is that they are irritants which are unpleasant to experience and difficult to endure. We are to think of one who has been entrusted with a mission, and who lacks the drive and incisiveness to bring it to an expeditious and successful conclusion. While he procrastinates and dithers and allows matters to drift through his ineptness and idleness, those who sent him to act for them and who are at a distance from the scene experience agonies of frustration and irritation. Although the organization of this sentence is complicated, because it is a type of simile the interpretation of the imagery is fixed, and it does not have the openness of the 'proverb'.

[1] The wisdom on which these sentences discourse equips the individual for success in life. Its acquisition will earn him recognition and status, and all his efforts will be gathered up into a fitting climax. He will enjoy a full life in every sense, and so his parents covet this wisdom for him and are fearful for his future well-being, if they see the marks of incorrigibility in him. 'A wise son gives pleasure to a father, but a son who is a fool is his mother's sorrow' (v. 1).

Class B

These sentences describe various manifestations of anti-social malevolence, or else they contrast the man who contributes to the wholeness of his community with the one who seeks its injury and disintegration (vv. 10, 11, 12, 17, 18, 21, 23). **[10]** The *qōrēṣ ʿayin* is the shifty individual who is incapable of candour and who employs a language of secret signs over and above what he says, either by winking or, perhaps, by opening and shutting his fingers in front of his eyes (v. 10a). Verse 10b is a repetition of v. 8b and does not furnish a suitable parallel to v. 10a. LXX reads: 'He who reproves candidly makes peace,' and, on the basis of this, BH suggests *ūmōkīaḥ ʿal pānīm yašlīm*, 'He who reproves to the face reconciles' (also Gemser and Ringgren). This gives the antithesis 'Pain-Reconciliation'. The one kind of activity makes for social brokenness and the other for social wholeness.

[11] In view of the antithesis of *ṣaddīq* and *rāšāʿ*, v. 11 might seem to belong to class C (see below), but I have put it in class B because of its social emphasis. It is not concerned with the reward of the righteous individual and the punishment of his wicked counterpart, but with the contribution which the *ṣaddīq* makes to the well-being of the community and the damage done by the *rāšāʿ*. The metaphor 'spring of life' is used of the speech of the *ṣaddīq* in respect of its beneficent and vitalizing properties (on the mythological origins of the expression see on 3.18, above, p. 296). The phrase harks back to the water in the paradisal garden which nourishes the roots of the tree of life. The speech of a righteous man fructifies and enriches the common life, whereas when wicked men speak, there is a deep-seated malevolence behind what they say (11b=6b). This is how I understand 'conceals violence'. Dahood (pp. 8f.) argues that the piel of *ksh* means 'uncover' here and in 10.18 and 26.26. I am unconvinced that it gives better sense than 'conceal' in any of these passages. **[12]** Similarly, love and hate are antithetic social attitudes which produce opposite effects. Hate awakens strife and contention, while love covers over all offences. Hate seeks a permanent enduring expression for differences between man and man, since its objective is social fragmentation and it would be annihilated by reconciliation. Love is engaged in covering up possible causes of offence, so that they may not appear as such. This means that love suffers long and is kind. Wrongs are endured and passed over for the sake of communal peace.

[18] A different kind of concealment is alluded to in v. 18 – the concealment of hate behind lies (unless *yōšer*, LXX *δίκαια*, is read for *šāqer*, in which case the reference is again to a benevolent concealment of hatred, i.e., the throttling of barbed words where there might seem to be a justification for speaking them). The phrase *śipᵉtē yōšer* is not, however, what is needed to express this thought. It suggests plainness, candour, openness rather than charitable restraint. If MT is retained, this is one of the few verses in the chapter which does not have an antithetic structure (the others are vv. 22, 23?, 26). The syntax ('he who conceals hatred (is) lying lips') presents some difficulty, but the construction should be tolerated and is equivalent to 'He who speaks lies conceals hatred'. The fool has a kind of cleverness, but he suffers from the disease of malevolence of which his lies and dissemination of slander (*dibbā*) are expressions. He is a hater of men who devotes his life to malicious lies and the ferreting out of hurtful gossip.

[17] It is because v. 17 seems to me to be concerned with the community rather than the individual that I have located it in class B rather than class A. Nevertheless, it contains words which belong to the vocabulary of old wisdom (*mūsār*, *tōkaḥat*), and it has been understood as an educational maxim for the individual. With *'ōrēaḥ* for *'ōraḥ* and *matʿe* explained as an internal hiphil (Gemser, p. 112), the verse is translated: 'It is he who observes discipline who is on the path of (to) life, but he who spurns correction goes astray.' This is the thought of the 'Two Ways'. Educational discipline leads to life, while indiscipline leads to extinction. I take MT rather to mean: 'He who has regard to instruction (i.e., the instruction given by a teacher) is a path to life (sc. for others), but he who spurns reproof leads others astray.'

[23] The probable meaning of v. 23 is that just as intrigue or mischievous conduct is child's play to a fool, so is wisdom to a man of intellectual discrimination. We have noted that in the context of the Egyptian Instruction the successful man is not the intriguer who disrupts community and poisons sociability. The effective exercise of power is correlated with a sense of social duty and concern. This, too, is part of wisdom, and the intellectual clarity on which the Instruction places great store cannot be exhaustively defined without this reference to justice and benevolence. These are the thoughts which should be brought to the interpretation of v. 23, where *ḥokmā* is the antithesis of the anti-social *zimmā*. This introduces the idea of the clever fool, a resourceful, devious person who intrigues indefatigably, who hates his neighbour and employs his brains to disrupt and destroy human relationships. This is a perverse cleverness, but it is not wisdom nor intellectual clarity which include a right relationship to society and a benevolent intent.

[21] The problems raised by v. 21 are of the same order as those discussed in connection with v. 17. Verse 21b would seem to be located in the educational milieu of old wisdom and so to belong to class A. Fools, by reason of their lack of wits, are incapable of *mūsār* and are set for the way of death (cf. v. 17a). The vocalization of *ḥᵃsar* should be altered to *ḥeser* or *ḥōser*, and then we should expect *rōḥab lēb* (cf. *PWM*, pp. 73f.) or the like as the antithesis in v. 21a. Instead, v. 21a deals with the socially constructive role of the righteous man, and the two halves of the verse do not hang together. The *ṣaddīq* wills what is right and good for his fellows, and this is a part of wisdom (see above, p. 419, on v. 23). His words are always directed towards nourishing the common life and promoting its weal. D. Winton Thomas (*JTS* xv, 1964, pp. 54–57) notes that LXX (ἐπίσταται) and V (*erudiunt*) in v. 21a point to *ydʿw* (the reading of a few Hebrew manuscripts). 'The lips of the righteous instruct (*yōdīʿū*) many'. Winton Thomas suggests, 'The lips of the righteous bring tranquillity to many' (*ydʿ*=Arabic *wdʿ*). His alternative suggestion is that *rʿh* (*yᵉrāʿu* or *yarʿu*) means 'appease, pacify'. In that case *rʿh* is an Aramaism = Hebrew *rṣh*.

Class C

In the case of these sentences, I find it hard to resist the conclusion that the antithesis of *ṣaddīq* and *rāšāʿ* is a dogmatic classification and that it is expressive of a premise of Yahwistic piety, namely, the doctrine of theodicy. By a doctrine of theodicy I mean the assertion that God enforces a moral order in relation to individuals by rewarding the righteous man and punishing the wicked one. I shall use the word in connection with the class C sentences in this sense. If this is accepted, it has to be recognized that such sentences mark a decisive development of the wisdom tradition in Israel. There is a significant change of vocabulary as compared with those sentences which use the vocabulary of old wisdom and in which the intellectual virtues and earthy prudence associated with a concept of educational discipline are still to the fore. In such sentences, the masters of wisdom enshrine in succinct sayings definitive and memorable expressions of their considered judgements. They display the maturity and nicety of judgement which derive from their mastery of a rigorous intellectual discipline. The sentences in which the 'righteous-wicked' antithesis appears, or which are otherwise seen to be organized according to the assumptions of Yahwistic piety, are still a didactic instrument, but they are no longer the bearers of a tradition in which intellectual virtues loom large, where the educational task of providing an intellectual discipline for the young proceeds independently of dogmatic assumptions, and where the orientation of wisdom is towards the more immediate and practical issues of life.

Where the doctrine of theodicy obtrudes itself in the wisdom sentence, the limits which old wisdom set itself are exceeded, and far-reaching assumptions about the structure of human life in relation to the will of Yahweh which transcend the range of the careful empiricism of old wisdom are made. It is a much tidier world than that to which the older sages addressed their wisdom. According to this form of Yahwistic piety, it is the best possible world for the righteous and the worst possible for the wicked, and everything is to be explained by the circumstance that Yahweh has made it in this way. It is not my intention to assert that there is no affinity between these sentences and the other kind. There are affinities of content, but the dogmatic premise decisively separates the one from the other. The difference between a wisdom sentence in the strict sense and one which is the bearer of a Yahwistic dogma is an important one and must be maintained.

In vv. 2 and 22, expression is given to a thought which is the Yahwistic counterpart of an attitude which is struck in the Egyptian Instruction (above, pp. 55f.). It matters how a man acquires his wealth, and wealth by itself is not a title to dignity and influence. If it is the expression of greed, then it is vulgarity and an indication of a monstrous defect of character which disqualifies a person from earning the respect of the community and exercising a weighty influence on its affairs. Wealth is a necessary consequence of ability and character, and then it represents solid attainment and success, but this means that the significance of the acquisition of wealth must always be tested. **[2]** According to v. 2, riches acquired by wickedness are profitless, whereas righteousness gives safety from death. In the world which is ordered by Yahweh, it is *ṣ^e^dāqā* which provides a safeguard against death – a statement which contrasts with v. 15, according to which riches are a defence against the perils of existence.

The intention of v. 2a is not to deny that wealth is a blessing, but, on the other hand, the nature of the antithesis in v. 2b establishes that righteousness is a more fundamental consideration than wealth. It should not be supposed that there is any hostility to wealth in v. 2, but there is the insistence that wealth without righteousness is valueless or that wealth only has worth if it is built on the foundation of righteousness. **[22]** This interpretation is confirmed by v. 22, which describes a kind of wealth that has no degree of trouble or vexation in it and is a material expression of Yahweh's blessing. It is possible to argue that *ta'^a^šīr* is to be understood figuratively, and that it is the spiritual enrichment resulting from Yahweh's blessing which is intended by the phrase 'It is the blessing of Yahweh which enriches (a man)'. I am convinced, however, that the reference is to material wealth and not to spiritual riches, and that the sentence is saying much the same kind of thing as v. 2. Wealth without alloy of trouble derives from righteousness and Yahweh's blessing.

[6] The same thought appears in v. 6a: 'Blessings are on the head of the righteous man' (LXX, V: 'The blessings of the Lord are on the head of the righteous man'). The second half of the sentence, which reappears in v. 11b, is something of a puzzle because of its unrelatedness to v. 6a. The antithesis of blessing would be curse or punishment, but what follows is an assertion that behind the speech of wicked men there is a deep-seated aggressiveness and hostility (*ḥāmās*). This is the same thought as appears in v. 12a and v. 18. The emendation of 'mouth of the wicked' to 'face of the wicked' does little to repair the defective antithesis (cf. BH).

[7] In v. 7, a statement is made about the connection between a man's righteousness or his lack of it and the kind of reputation which he leaves behind him after death. The significance of this has to be measured against the absence of any belief in a vigorous vitality beyond death. The *zēker* or the *šēm* is in effect an indirect prolongation of a man's influence and authority beyond death. Because of the mark which he made on his community while he was alive, he has created something permanent which is incorporated into its historical memory and enriches its ongoing life. It is unnecessary to emend *yirqab* to *yūqāb* in order to have the antithesis 'blessing-curse' (BH). The sense is good with *yirqab*, for the contrast is between the beneficent persistence of the righteous man's vitality expressed in his enduring influence on the life of his community, and the process of decay which induces the memory of the wicked to rot away to nothingness. What preserves the *zēker* or *šēm* of one deceased is the value placed upon it by those yet alive and the care with which they tend it. The *šēm* of the wicked is left untended and unprized and rots away. The sentence has special interest in that it extends the normal range of the 'righteous-wicked' antithesis. This is, for the most part, confined to life here and now, where, according to the Yahwistic theodicy, the righteous are rewarded and the wicked punished, the righteous protected and the wicked exposed to disaster. In this sentence the continuing consequences of righteousness and wickedness beyond death are explored.

[9] Verse 9a repeats the assertion (cf. 2b) that true security on the road of life is afforded by integrity or sincerity (*tōm*), while v. 9b appears to say that he who is twisted in his ways (who by his perverse cleverness tries to confuse plain moral issues and obliterate the distinction between righteousness and wickedness) will be found out (sc. and punished by Yahweh). Toy (also BH) would emend *yiwwādēaʿ* to *yērōaʿ*, ('he who walks in tortuous ways suffers hurt', cf. 11.15, below, p. 429). Winton Thomas suggests 'will be made submissive' (sc. to the Law), connecting *ydʿ* with Arabic *wdʿ*. The security of those who are blameless is contrasted with the insecurity of those who will be made to submit to Yahweh's retributive discipline (D. W. Thomas, *JTS* xxxv, 1934, p. 303).

[20] In v. 20, the metaphor is 'quality silver' or 'silver purified in the fire' (cf. LXX πεπυρωμένος). It is hardly necessary to emend to *nibḥān* in order to get this meaning. Gemser notes that Syriac *bḥr* can mean 'to test metal by fire'. Here it is the high value of the speech of the righteous man which is indicated by the metaphor, and the negligible worth of the mind (*lēb*) of the wicked man. The parallelism 'lip-mind' is a little disconcerting, but the meaning is perhaps that there is little of value in the essential make-up of the *rāšāʿ* which can find expression in speech.

The opposed characteristics of the speech of righteous and wicked are further discussed in vv. 31–32. **[31]** The product or fruit (*yānūb*) of a righteous man's speech is wisdom (v. 31a). Dahood (pp. 20f.) equates Hebrew *nōpet* with Ugaritic *nbt* (cf. G. R. Driver, *CML*, pp. 58, n.2) and argues that Hebrew *nwb* means 'to flow'. The equation is correct, but it is unlikely that v. 31b refers to the cutting off of the flow of a perverse tongue (i.e., 'The mouth of a righteous man flows with wisdom, but a perverse tongue is cut off'). Dahood's argument is reinforced by his treatment of v. 32 (see below). The contrast in v. 31b deals, not with the unproductive speech of the wicked, but with the fate of those who speak with mischievous and destructive intent. Their calculated endeavours to be the devil's advocates and to confound the moral judgement of others is indicated again in v. 32b by the same word (*tahpūkōt*). **[32]** This is the moral twist which characterizes the *rešāʿīm*; it is a pathological, anti-social stance which finds its outlet in disruptive and destructive speech. Toy, BH and Gemser emend *yēdeʿūn* to *yabbīʿūn* (v. 32a): 'The lips of a *ṣaddīq* spout what meets with approval', just as water bubbles out from a spring. This emendation, as Winton Thomas points out, is not really supported by LXX ἀποστάζει and, in any case, it does not give a reading which is superior to MT. Winton Thomas (*VTS* iii, p. 285) associates *ydʿ* with Arabic *daʿā* ('sought', 'desired', 'demanded'). 'The lips of the righteous seek goodwill (i.e., his objective is a socially constructive one, namely, to create goodwill), but the mouth of the wicked (seeks) perverse utterances' (see also on 15.14, below, pp. 478f.).

This gives the sense which is required, but it is not, in my judgement, better than that achieved by translating *ydʿ* 'is concerned with' (see on 9.13b, above, p. 367; cf. Gen. 39.6 and, especially, Job 9.21, where *lō' 'ēdaʿ napšī* is synonymous with *'em'as ḥayyāy*). 'The lips of the *ṣaddīq* are concerned with approval' means that he speaks with the express intention of winning the approval of others for his words and persuading them that he is a man of goodwill and beneficent designs. While it is not entirely beyond the bounds of possibility that it is the approval of Yahweh to which v. 32a alludes (the righteous man seeks to win Yahweh's approval by what he speaks), this would seem to me not to be a serious alternative to the interpretation which I have indicated.

Another attractive proposal for v. 32 which I have not accepted is that of Dahood (pp. 20f.), who notes that LXX translates both *yānūb* (v. 31) and *yēdeʿūn* (v. 32) by ἀποστάζει, 'distil'. He equates *yēdeʿūn* with Arabic *wadaʿa*, 'flow', Ugaritic *dʿt*, 'sweat'. One would expect *yēzeʿūn* in Hebrew, and the *z* appears in *zēʿā* 'sweat'. Hebrew *dl* 'poor' (Arabic *ḏll*) shows that the Arabic *ḏ* does appear as *d* in Hebrew (cf. G. R. Driver, *JRAS*, 1948, p. 168, n.3, *zkh* (*dkh*), *nzr* (*ndr*)).

[16] In v. 16, the antithesis of 'life' is 'sin' instead of the anticipated 'death'. The explanation of this may be that if what the *rāšāʿ* produces is sin, this will inevitably draw on him punishment and death. In this verse the 'life-death' antithesis is correlated with the 'righteous-wicked' antithesis and is subsumed under the Yahwistic dogma of theodicy. The wages or reward (*peʿullā*) which a righteous man gets for his deeds is life, whereas the end-product of a wicked man's activity is sin, and so retribution and death. D. Winton Thomas (*JTS* xv, 1964, pp. 295f.) connects *ḥaṭṭā't* with Ethiopic *ḫaṭī'at*, 'penury', and renders *ḥayyīm* 'maintenance' (cf. 27.27, below, pp. 618f.). The verse is then simply a statement about income or wages and not about retribution and reward. This I regard as too restrictive; 'income' or 'product' is not to be understood so narrowly. Moreover, 'the revenue of the wicked leads to their penury' is no easier than 'the product of a wicked man is sin'. In vv. 17a and 21b, on the other hand, life and death are still correlated with discipline (*mūsār*) and indiscipline (*'iwwelet*), and so the link in these verses with the Instruction and the extensive treatment of the life-death antithesis in chs. 1–9 is closer.

'Death' may mean death in the ordinary sense, or it may be, rather, a loss of vitality which constitutes a sentence of death and which will lead inevitably to death, unless life is restored by Yahweh (see above, pp. 391f.; cf. A. R. Johnson, *The Vitality of the Individual in the Thought of Ancient Israel*,[2] 1964, pp. 104f.). The simple contrast between life and death is present in vv. 27 and 28. **[27]** Reverence for Yahweh will guarantee a long life to the righteous man, so that he will not be denied the climax of maturity and self-fulfilment, but the years of the wicked will be cut short. **[28]** The same idea is expressed by the words of v. 28: 'The righteous can expect joy (i.e., the joy of a life in which all comes to fruition and old age is crowned with attainment and honour), but the hope of the wicked will perish.' G. R. Driver objects that 'joy' makes no sense and proposes *śāmeḥā*, 'the hope of the righteous springs up' (Accadian *šamāḫu*, 'to be luxuriant'; *Biblica* 32, p. 179). The same effect is achieved by the emendation *ṣāmeḥā* (Kuhn, BH). Driver cites the English idiom, 'hope springs eternal in the human breast'. The meaning would then be that the hope of the righteous wells up irrepressibly like the water of a copious spring, or that it thrives like a healthy plant (*ṣām^{e}ḥā*). I am not entirely persuaded that it is necessary to emend and I retain MT.

Allied in content to vv. 2 and 9 are vv. 24, 25, 29 and 30, in which the belief is variously expressed that Yahweh will keep the righteous safe and visit the wicked with destructive punishment. **[24]** What the wicked man fears will overtake him, but (Yahweh) will grant the desire of the righteous. The well-founded fear (*m^{e}gōrā*) of punishment felt by the wicked is to be differentiated from the fear of Yahweh (*yir'at YHWH*) which is cardinal with a righteous man. I have suggested in my treatment of chs. 1–9 that this represents the formulation of a new discipline (*mūsār*) and the transference of the seat of authority from the wisdom teacher to Yahweh (see especially on 9.10, above p. 368). In v. 24b one has to suppose that Yahweh is the subject of *yittēn*, unless the passive is to be read with LXX (δεκτή, cf. BH *yuttān*). The antithesis is somewhat oblique, but apparently it is constituted by a contrast between a particular aspect of the negative and positive stances of wicked and righteous respectively. The wicked brood over the punishment which they fear, so that even before they are punished they present a picture of distraction and anxiety. The righteous confront life confidently, and their desires are translated into fulfilment.

[3] This antithesis of fulfilment and its denial is explicit in v. 3. Yahweh will not leave unsatisfied (literally 'hungry') the appetite (this and not 'soul' is the meaning of *nepeš*) of the righteous, but he will repulse (or 'obstruct') the desire (*hawwā* = *'awwā*) of the wicked. 'Appetite' is not to be understood narrowly; it is the inner urge towards success and fulfilment which in the case of the righteous is a dynamic tendency towards self-realization. For the wicked, such desire is predestined to lead to perpetual frustration and degenerates into neurosis. The wicked are condemned to live forever with their unfulfilled, and so sterile, desires, which cannot be transformed into practical attainment. I am unpersuaded that Driver's interpretation of the verse gives a better sense than this. He connects *r'b* with Arabic *ra'aba*, 'was fearful', and translates *nepeš* 'soul' and *hawwā* 'wind' after Arabic *hawā'u* (cf., however, Arabic *hawā* 'desire'):

Yahweh will not make the soul of the righteous to tremble,
But he will repel the windy words of the wicked.

(G. R. Driver, *JRAS*, 1943, pp. 8f.; *Biblica* 32, p. 179.)

[25] The imagery in v. 25 recalls the Gospel similitude which opposes the house built on the sand to that built on a rock (Matt. 7.24f.). The righteous man has an enduring foundation and will withstand the storms of life, but after the tempest has passed over, not a trace of the wicked will be left behind. **[29]** Yahweh is a fortress to the man whose conduct is blameless (emending *lattōm derek* to *l^e^tam derek*), but he brings destruction to evil-doers. LXX (ὀχύρωμα ὁσίου) vocalizes *ltm* as *lattām* and paraphrases 'way of Yahweh' as 'fear of Yahweh'. 'The fear of Yahweh is a pious man's fortress.' There is no doubt, however, that *derek* goes with *tam* and not Yahweh (cf. 11.20; 13.6).

[30] The righteous will always be able to put his feet down with certainty and will never stumble disastrously, but the wicked have no security of tenure and no prospect of stability and permanence in the (promised) land (on the stipulation that enjoyment of residence in the land of Canaan is conditional on righteousness, see 2.21f., above p. 288). Since this is a particular emphasis of Deuteronomy, it is an indication that a wisdom sentence with a 'righteous-wicked' antithesis can be regarded as a wisdom form with a legal content, and that it comes into existence at the point where the wise men put their forms of literary expression at the disposal of the Law (*PWM*, pp. 101f.).

In LXX, the tendency to state the dogma of theodicy in more prosaic and explicit terms can be detected. Instead of saying that a righteous man is (like) the solid foundation (of a house), LXX says: 'But the righteous elude it (the storm) and are forever safe' (v. 25b). In v. 26 LXX applies the imagery to impiety instead of laziness and departs entirely from MT: 'Thus is impiety (παρανομία) to those who practise it.' In v. 29, LXX renders 'way of Yahweh' (see above) as 'fear of Yahweh' – a more precise term of legal piety.

CHAPTER 11

The sentences in this chapter are aphorisms rather than 'proverbs'. On the whole they are marked by plainness of expression and explicitness of reference, rather than by any desire to exploit the possibilities of language. Although there are figures of speech in vv. 3, 5, 22, 28b, 29a and 30, there are no 'proverbs'. These sentences are elegantly expressed, definitive statements, but they do not employ imagery whose interpretation is left open and to whose representative potential no limits are set.

ss A: vv. 2, 12, 13, 14, 15, 16, 22, 29.
ss B: vv. 9, 10, 11, 17, 24, 25, 26, 27, 30.
Class C: vv. 1, 3, 4, 5, 6, 7, 8, 18, 19, 20, 21, 23, 28, 31.

Class A

[2] The man who behaves arrogantly and who is disproportionately self-assertive will never be able to exercise the power at which he grasps. Unbridled egotism which is disproportionate to a man's intrinsic worth and ability will have the effect of focusing attention on his deficiencies and his unfitness for the recognition for which he strives. He will not get *kābōd*, 'weight', 'honour', but instead will be exposed as a light-weight (*qālōn*, 'lightness', 'lack of esteem', *qlh* = *qll*). Modesty, a deprecation of self-advertisement and a deliberate curbing of self-assertiveness are important ingredients of wisdom, and it is the person who is capable of this measure of self-control and restraint who will acquire influence and power without striving immoderately after them. It is not the timidity or the humility of the pious man which is indicated by *ṣānūaʿ*; it is rather an intellectual reticence and reserve which are a mark of reasonableness and the ability to keep silence if the time for effective and well-considered utterance is not ripe (cf. Syriac *ṣnʿ*, 'to act with guile'; *ṣenʿā, ṣenʿ*^{e}*tā*, 'skill', 'craft', 'stratagem').

Hence there is a relationship between this brand of wisdom and the praise of taciturnity in vv. 12 and 13. This respect for the silent man who does not waste his breath, who respects confidences and has the reputation of weighing his words carefully, is characteristic of the Egyptian Instruction (above pp. 54, 109). **[12]** A special aspect of this is a studied avoidance of any campaign of denigration waged against a friend or a colleague. The supposition that a reputation can be advanced or prospects improved by bringing a friend into contempt is stupid. The denigrator exposes his own intellectual deficiences and lack of judgement – he is *ḥ*^{a}*sar lēb*. This is not just an opportunistic observation, and the silent man is not perceptive or intellectually discriminating (*'îš t*^{e}*būnā*) simply because his silence is advantageous to himself. There is also the consideration that the truly wise man will not suppose that it is his responsibility to expose the worthlessness of his friend or to inform against him. Even if the exposure were in a sense merited, to do it would be an indication of a flaw – the absence of a sense of proportion or even of benevolence in the self-appointed castigator.

[13] In v. 13 the question is rather that of respecting confidences and avoiding duplicity. There is a connection between gossip and disloyalty, and between tight lips and a sense of honour. A breach of confidence may also involve an attempt by indisciplined garrulity or malicious gossip to misrepresent or discredit the other party or parties to the confidence. Just as there is the moral flaw of duplicity and shiftiness in garrulity, so silence is more than mere secretiveness. It is the expression of loyalty and candour (*ne'eman rūaḥ*) and the refusal to compromise the integrity of the relationship which exists within the framework of the confidence.

[14] In v. 14, *taḥbūlōt* is an item of the vocabulary of old wisdom (see on 1.5, above, p. 266). It is a metaphorical expression for political expertise – the ability to steer the ship of state through troubled waters – and it is indispensable to the survival of a community in a dangerous world. Here, and also in the second half of the verse, the connections of statesmanship with old wisdom are well illustrated. Verse 14b expresses confidence in the decision which is reached in cabinet or committee, when a number of men have put their heads together, and suggests further that the wider the consensus, the better is the quality of the advice or policy likely to be. The test of the merit of the policy is its effectiveness in relation to the *t^ešū'ā* of the community (*t^ešū'ā*, perhaps 'safety' through military victory as in 24.6).

[15] The hard-headed wisdom of v. 15 reproduces exactly the ideas of 6.1. Whoever stands surety for a stranger will certainly come to grief (reading the infinitive absolute *rōa'*), whereas he who dislikes entering into binding (financial) agreements will keep out of trouble (*tq'* is the striking of hands by which the sealing of a bargain or transaction is symbolized. On the form see G. R. Driver, *Biblica* 32, p. 196). To underwrite the financial liabilities of a stranger is to court ruin, but the abstaining from such bargains is a kind of 'insurance' (*bōṭēaḥ*, 'secure'). A. Guillaume (*JTS* xv, 1964, p. 294) supposes that the contrast is between 'fear' and 'confidence'. 'He that is surety for a stranger lives in constant dread' (*rēa' yērōa'*, Arabic *ry'* or *rw'*, 'to be afraid'). **[29]** Another sentence which deals with financial competence and incompetence is v. 29. According to KB^2, the obscure *'kr* means 'to make taboo' or 'to make a social outcast of', in which case the meaning of v. 29a would be that he who makes his family social outcasts, whose behaviour results in his family being denied the normal forms of social intercourse, will find that there is nothing left for him to inherit. That *'ōkēr bētō* means this is dubious; it is supported neither by the phrase *yinḥal rūaḥ* nor by the parallelism of v. 29b. I follow Gemser's explanation of *yinḥal rūaḥ* rather than that offered by Barucq, who supposes an allusion to the Bedouin usage of pitching a tent so that the door is away from the wind (*ʿōkēr bētō* means whoever misdirects or mismanages his household – pitches it the wrong way round). The meaning of *yinḥal rūaḥ* would then be 'exposes himself to rough treatment', 'provokes a storm', i.e., is handled roughly by the other members of the family. With Gemser I take *rūaḥ* to indicate 'nothingness', 'emptiness', as elsewhere (see Gemser), and then the reference is to the dissipation of what might have been inherited. Consequently *ʿōkēr*, which is obscure, probably alludes to mismanagement or misappropriation of family resources (Gemser, Ringgren, 'he who neglects his household') which destroys its prosperity and leaves it penniless. The parallelism in v. 29b is then apt, since it deals with a lack of aptitude for affairs or a financial incompetence. The fool, because he cannot manage his business, will be so irretrievably in debt that he will lose his personal liberty and be reduced to slavery. Then he will find himself in the service of one who does have business acumen and who conducts his affairs judiciously and successfully (*ḥᵃkam lēb*).

[22] The form of v. 22 recalls that of 10.26 (see above, p. 417), and the intention of the analogy is that beauty is wasted on a woman who is lacking in good taste or intellectual discrimination (on the semantic development of *ṭaʿam* see Gemser: taste (palate) > taste (aesthetic) > discrimination). Just as a gold ring (which would be a fitting adornment for a man or woman) is wasted on a pig's snout or is grotesquely inappropriate there, so it is with physical beauty in a woman who lacks taste and discrimination. 'The nose-ring is still used as an ornament among the Bedouin' (E.F.F.B.). **[16]** In view of this disparaging of mere physical attractiveness, it is likely that something more than an attractive woman is intended by *'ēšet ḥēn* (v. 16a). This is an evaluation in depth and not just a surface description of physical beauty; it indicates the kind of impact she makes as a person on those who meet her. She has a graciousness which is neither superficial nor meretricious; she does not contrive to appear like this before the world; rather, her charm is the expression of what in fact she is. She then has personal qualities which will earn her respect and make her acceptable and influential. Verse 16b reads: 'and *ʿārīṣīm* will obtain wealth'. Gemser and Ringgren prefer the longer text of LXX: 'A gracious woman will get honour, but a woman who hates uprightness is a throne of dishonour. Lazy men lack wealth, but diligent men (*ḥārûṣîm*, LXX ἀνδρεῖοι, 'courageous men') obtain wealth.' Barucq notes the uncertainty of the versions about this longer text and comments judiciously: 'We do not see what could arouse the suspicion of a lacuna in MT, which remains very acceptable.' Barucq translates: 'And energetic men obtain wealth.' This agrees with Driver ('and vigorous men grasp wealth'), who argues on the basis of Arabic usage that *ʿrṣ* can have a good sense as well as a bad. Thus *ʿārîṣ* is 'violent man', 'oppressor', but also 'vigorous man' (*Biblica* 32, p. 180). If *ʿōšer* is intended as antithetic to *kābōd*, the sentence would be organized like most of the others in the chapter and the parallelism would be antithetic rather than synthetic. 'But energetic men grasp wealth' would indicate a contrast between the route to success and fulfilment which becomes a woman and that which is appropriate to men. A man must strive for wealth, but a gracious woman gets honour through the natural effect of her presence and personality. Or the emphasis may rather be on *ʿōšer* and *kābōd*. The woman who is gracious gets *honour*, but men have to be energetic to get *wealth*.

Class B

[9] According to KB[2] (also Ringgren), a *ḥānēp* (v. 9) is a man alienated from God and so impious. There can be little doubt that the antithesis *ḥānēp-ṣaddîq* is a variant of *rāšāʿ-ṣaddîq*. According to MT (followed by Gemser, Ringgren and Barucq), the *ḥānēp* is one whose speech has socially destructive effects; he destroys his neighbour, and so he is the opposite of the man whose speech is constructive and benevolent and expressive of his concern for the good of his neighbour. Righteous men employ their knowledge in order to effect the rescue of those who are thus threatened with destruction. In vv. 4, 6 and 8 (see class C below) the righteous are rescued (by Yahweh), and here the righteous by virtue of their social foresight and concern are able to snatch from impending destruction those who are the victims of malevolent speech. LXX reads: 'In the speech of impious men is a snare for citizens, but the perceptiveness of the righteous is a good road'; BH, following this, reads *bᵉpî ḥānēp*: 'By the speech of an impious man his companion is destroyed' (*yiššāḥēt*), or, 'In the mouth of an impious man is an evil pit' (*šaḥat rāʿā*), in which case there is no allusion to his speech but only to the dark, dangerous depths of his malice. I follow MT.

[11] Verse 11, which states that through the beneficial influence ('blessing') of upright men a city is raised (i.e., built up, elevated in status) or 'constructed' (*tērōm*, G. R. Driver, *CML*, p. 155, n.20, Ugaritic *rm* 'constructed', Hebrew **rmm*), but that by the speech of wicked men it is demolished, makes more explicit the social implications of v. 9, **[10]** whereas v. 10 confines itself to assessing the state of civic opinion in respect of the righteous and the wicked. A righteous man has the goodwill of the members of his community, and when it goes well with him there is general rejoicing. He is recognized as one who deserves his success and who will wield it for the common good. When, however, evil men go under (i.e., are submerged by misfortunes or, perhaps, it is death which is indicated), there is a shout of joy. Those who have given the town no reason to think kindly of them or respect them, and who have acted selfishly and immorally, must be prepared for a bitter and lonely demise. They have lived to themselves and they must die to themselves, conscious of a solidarity of civic opinion in which they never had a part and of which they were careless. Now the final verdict is passed – a communal shout of joy – and they can offer no riposte.

[30] In v. 30 the antithesis of 'righteous' is 'death-dealer' (literally, 'he who takes away lives'), and the intention here, as in v. 9, is apparently to contrast one kind of 'fruit' with another. Gemser's construction of the sentence should be followed – *lōqēaḥ nᵉpāšōt* is a second absolute of *pᵉrî*. If this is so, 'fruit of the righteous man' and not 'fruit of righteousness' (LXX) is what is desiderated, and it is not helpful to suggest that *ṣdyq* may be an orthographical variant of *ṣedeq* (BH, see Gemser). If, however, the structure is antithetic and the grammar is as I have indicated, no sense can be made of *ḥākām*, and *ḥāmās* has to be read (cf. LXX παρανόμων). Ringgren supposes that the sentence is synthetic and translates v. 30b: 'And the wise man wins men for himself' (cf. Barucq, 'the wise man wins souls'). But *lōqēaḥ nᵉpāšōt* cannot be so translated; the expression means to take away life – it has a destructive significance (cf. Ps. 31.14). Dahood (pp. 24f.) finds a reference here to 'eternal life', as he does in 12.28. *nᵉpāšōt* is a *pluralis excellentiae* signifying 'eternal life', and 'tree of life' has the same significance. He translates: 'The fruit of the righteous is the tree of life, and the wise man attains eternal life'. This is not a possible sense for the verse although the Ugaritic passage which he cites (*Aqhat* II. vi 34f., *CML*, pp. 54f.) illustrates the sense of 'get' for *lqḥ*. If we translate, 'The fruit of a righteous man is a tree of life, but (the fruit) of him who takes life is violence', the meaning would be that righteous men are life to a community and their opposites death to a community (on 'tree of life' see 3.18, above, p. 296). Those whose activity is directed towards destroying the lives of other men strike at the roots of the social order, and the result of such action is violence which erupts when the basis of society has been made insecure. The imagery of v. 30a is infelicitous, and 'The fruit of a righteous man is life' would be easier to follow. It would mean that he vitalizes the community. 'The fruit of a righteous man is a tree of life' constitutes a very involved metaphor, and one can only suppose that 'tree of life' is not to be taken seriously as a metaphor and is simply a circumlocution for 'life'. Then again, the sense of v. 30b is not entirely convincing, not even with an emended text, and one can understand why the Greek translator apparently gave up the struggle with the Hebrew text and wrote down something which made sense to him ('From the fruit of justice grows a tree of life, but the souls of the wicked are cut off before their time.' 'Tree of life' thus becomes a metaphor for the longevity of the righteous, cf. 10.27, above, p. 425).

The same train of thought is pursued in vv. 17, 24, 25, 26 and 27. **[17]** I take v. 17 to mean that a proper self-interest coincides with what is best for the community, so that there is no conflict between striving after the highest degree of self-realization and serving the common good. In raising his own capabilities to the highest pitch, a man makes his most effective contribution to social enrichment. The merciful man, that is, the man whose social conscience is highly developed and whose attitudes are expressive of his sense of social solidarity with his brethren, is at the same time an enlightened egotist and does well by himself. What is good for the individual is good for the whole and vice versa. Hence the ruthless egotist, who is obsessively self-assertive and acts on the assumption that every man is his enemy and that his sole objective is to do other people down, is his own worst enemy (see v. 29, above, pp. 429f.).

This general principle that there is a harmony between enlightened self-interest and the common good is restated in vv. 25 and 27, while particular instances of the working out of the general principle are mentioned in vv 24 and 26. **[25]** The man whose vitality is a source of blessing or beneficence to others will himself enjoy well-being or prosperity (literally, 'will be made fat'), and he who makes others replete will himself be replete (*yōre'* = *yūre*, GK §69w; Dahood, p. 23, postulates **wr'* 'to be fat', cf. *mr'*, *br'*). BH follows

Pesh. in v. 25b: 'But he who curses will be cursed', supplying antithetic parallelism instead of the synthetic parallelism of MT.

[27] 'He who strives after (Accadian *saḫāru*, 'to turn towards', 'to incline towards') what is good seeks (public) approval, but evil will overtake him who searches for it' (v. 27). Gemser takes *rāṣōn* to refer to God's approval, and then the meaning is that he who strives after what is good seeks (and finds) God's approval. This would make the sentence an explicit statement of the doctrine of theodicy, and it would belong to class C. My own opinion is that it expresses the same order of ideas as vv. 9–11, 25 and 30 and that v. 27a says that the person who strives after the (public) good, seeks to win the goodwill and esteem of the community. The same sense is achieved if *yᵉbaqqēš* is associated with Accadian *baqāšu* 'to be large'. 'He who eagerly seeks what is good, wins much favour' (G. R. Driver, *JSS* xii, 1967, p. 108). However, 'seek', the normal sense of *bqš* in biblical Hebrew, preserves the contrast between one who seeks public approval and one who seeks evil.

[26] The lines of the Šamaš Hymn to which Gemser alludes contrast the honest corn merchant with his dishonest counterpart (*BWL*, pp. 132f., *ll.* 110–114) and are not apposite to v. 26, whose point is a different one. Unlike v. 24, the context of v. 26 is buying and selling and not philanthropy (see, however, below). The community curses a man who will not put his grain on the market when there is no good reason for this refusal. It is possible to read into this sentence that the merchant is taking advantage of scarcity conditions and of the consequent acute public need for grain, and is holding out for the highest price without regard for the common good. His opposite sells without haggling over the price, since the well-being of the community requires that he should sell without delay whatever grain he has. He wins regard and esteem because he is motivated by a sense of social responsibility, and not by the desire for maximum economic gain. This interpretation may stretch the sense too much and the contrast may simply be between an unreasonable and wrong-headed refusal to sell, which is cantankerous or perverse rather than economically astute, and a public-spirited readiness to sell in response to the community's needs.

[24] If 'scatters' in v. 24a means 'puts money to work', 'uses it in economic ventures', the gist of the sentence is that you have to speculate in order to accumulate, and in this case, as a statement on the economic facts of life, it belongs to class A. Money which is put to work earns more money, but the man who is excessively cautious and hoards his money may end up in want. More probably v. 24 says that philanthropy is the best policy. There is the man who disburses his wealth (among those who are in need) and who becomes richer rather than poorer as a consequence. The reverse side of the paradox is that there is a type of person with a distorted sense of thrift, and that such an anti-social miserliness results in penury. This is an illustration of the thesis that an enlightened self-interest coincides with a proper social concern, while a myopic selfishness leads to a diminution of the self.

Class C

A group of sentences (vv. 3, 5, 19) are on the theme of 'The Two Ways', but this is now a metaphorical expression of a Yahwistic theodicy, and not the two ways of wisdom and folly, teachability and incorrigibility, and so not in the context of an educational discipline (cf. 10.9, above, p. 423). **[5]** It is the righteousness of sincere men which guarantees them unfailing guidance on the way of life, whereas the wicked man, who is denied passage along a safe and clear road and is like a person stumbling in the dark, will fall because of his wickedness. This is a dogmatic utterance. The *tām* is the wholly sincere or flawless man, whose piety is without defect or admixture of hypocrisy. The *tām* is therefore also the *ṣaddīq*, the one who is right with Yahweh. Security and guidance on the road of life are given where a man is designated by Yahweh as *ṣaddīq* and withheld where his condition is that of *rāšā'*. **[3]** Guidance is again the subject of v. 3, which deals with a particular aspect of the righteous-wicked antithesis. Here integrity (*tummā*) is contrasted with perversion (*selep*), and 'straight men' with 'crooked men'. Integrity guarantees safe guidance, but perversion leads to destruction.

[19] Although there is some dubiety about the meaning of *kēn* in v. 19a, *meraddēp* in v. 19b indicates that the verse deals with two opposed ways of life. He who is steadfast in righteousness (so KB² and Ringgren, reading MT) is destined for life, but he who pursues evil suffers death for it. LXX and Pesh. read 'a righteous son', and one Hebrew MS *bēn*. Gemser and Barucq read *kān* and suggest a transitive sense for it: 'strives after', 'pursues' (Gemser); 'establishes' (Barucq). Gemser points to a transitive usage of *kwn* in Job 31.15.

Another group with similar dogmatic presuppositions is constituted by vv. 4, 6, 8, 21, 28. The particular point stressed is the protection afforded to righteous men and the disaster which overtakes the wicked. **[4]** In v. 4, the antithesis between wealth and righteousness is worked out in a manner which recalls 10.2 (10.2b and 11.4b are identical). 'The day of wrath' is probably to be identified with the day of Yahweh's retribution, and the meaning of v. 4a is that wealth without righteousness does not give protection against Yahweh's judgement, so that righteousness is the only effective safeguard of 'life' and guarantee against 'death'. I take 'life' and 'death' quite simply and literally – the antithesis is between a long life and premature death (see on 10.27, above, p. 425). **[28]** A similar verdict on wealth is passed in v. 28. Whoever relies on his wealth for security will fall (see above on v. 5b, p. 435), but the righteous will flourish like a leaf (contrary to L. Kopf, *VT* ix, 1958, p. 167). The emendation of *yippōl* to *yibbōl*, 'wither', improves the parallelism, but is not supported by the versions (LXX πεσεῖται). Dahood (p. 24) suggests that **npl* is a dialectal variant of *nbl* 'wither', or that *yippōl* is to be derived from *pll* (*CML*, p. 163, n.16). The flourishing leaf is a symbol of vitality, of vigour and well-being (cf. Gemser). **[6]** The righteousness of upright men saves them (from death), but treacherous men are caught (as in a trap or snare) by desire. Dahood (p. 21) suggests that *hawwat*, 'desire', is singular absolute, i.e., the primitive Semitic form. In this verse, LXX has translated *hawwā* as 'destruction' (ἀπωλεία). 'But treacherous men are caught in their destruction' yields a sense inferior to that supplied by MT.

To indicate more exactly the degree of security enjoyed by the righteous, some comment on the repeated use of *taṣṣīl* is desiderated (10.2b; 11.4b, 6a). Their security is not a complete immunity from danger, so that no threat is ever pointed menacingly against their existence. On the contrary, the righteous man is exposed to a dangerous world and does not live behind the massive shield of Yahweh's protection with his safety and welfare never put in jeopardy. Rather, he is acquainted with perils and can even be in the jaws of death, but he will always be rescued by Yahweh if he is a righteous man. Consequently, if one says that this is the best of all possible worlds for the righteous man, one does not imply that he has a serene, untroubled and assured passage through it – a royal progress to success and fulfilment. No; it is a world in which he will have tribulation and will experience extremity and distress, but in which Yahweh will always come to his rescue. **[8]** Thus in v. 8a Barucq translates: 'A righteous man will be snatched (*neḥelāṣ*) from distress'; *ṣārā* is physical constriction and so a constriction of the possibilities of existence which is so severe that it constitutes distress. The righteous man will find himself in a situation where he is so constricted by the iron bands of circumstance that he feels as if he is being slowly asphyxiated. But Yahweh will snatch him from his prison and will replace him with an evil man.

[21] The possibility that this escape or rescue of righteous men is forensically conceived is suggested by v. 21, which states that a verdict of guilty will be brought in against the evil man (*lō' yinnāqeh*). The antithesis in v. 21b reads: 'But the descendants of the righteous will be set free.' It is just a little puzzling why the descendants of the righteous rather than the righteous themselves are mentioned here, but this extension of the doctrine of theodicy is not so interesting as the fact that *nimlāṭ* is apparently the antithesis of *lō' yinnāqeh*, and so is indicative of an escape from an unfavourable legal verdict. It is possible, therefore, that this forensic nuance is also present in *taṣṣīl* and *neḥlāṣ* and that Yahweh's rescue of the righteous is envisaged as a forensic intervention. In rescuing them from danger and distress, he effectively establishes their innocence, since otherwise they would seem to be condemned by the orthodoxy which should guarantee their position in that their tribulation might be regarded as *prima facie* evidence of their guilt, that is, of their lack of righteousness. The expression *yād lᵉyād* is derived from the practice of striking hands to symbolize the 'striking' of a bargain (cf. 6.1, 11.15, above, pp. 321, 429) and is intended to invest the statement in v. 6a with solemnity and authority.

The language of theodicy is evident in vv. 18 and 31, which make statements on the positive and negative aspects of reward. **[18]** The result of the evil man's efforts – his final product (*pᵉʿullā*) – is lacking in truth, and because it is essentially false is worthless and perishable. He who sows righteousness earns real wages (*śeker*). The righteous man's product is of abiding worth (so Gemser and Ringgren).

[31] I follow Gemser in taking v. 31 to mean that reward is an effective concept both in its positive and negative aspects. The righteous man gets his deserts and so does the sinner. However *bā'āreṣ* is to be interpreted, the suggestion that it is to be translated 'in the other world' and so points to the belief in a blessed immortality for the righteous can be ruled out (see the discussion in Barucq). Dahood (pp. 25f.) sees in the verse a reference to Sheol and to differing degrees of punishment there. This is to be rejected. Gemser supposes that LXX ('If a righteous man is hardly saved') points to *baṣṣar* or *baṣṣōr*, 'with difficulty', 'with trouble'. Barr has suggested to me privately that the Greek translator had MT before him, but construed it as if it were *ṣar* or *ṣārā*. The text of LXX is almost exactly reproduced in I Peter 4.18 (*μέν* is omitted), where the sense of the verse is consequently not correctly taken.

Driver (*Biblica* 32, p. 180) supposes that the consonants of MT are confirmed by the readings of LXX and Pesh. (*μόλις*, *lmaḥsen*), which he thinks are based on Samaritan *'rʿ*, Syriac *'lṣ* (Gemser, p. 112). Driver is saying that LXX and Pesh. read the consonants of MT; he is not saying that they read these consonants correctly. *b'rṣ* must mean 'in the land' and the reference will be to the land of Canaan. It is explicable in terms of 2.21f. (see above, p. 288) and 10.30b (see above, p. 427).

The phrase 'abomination of Yahweh', i.e., 'loathed by Yahweh', is common to vv. 1 and 20, and the moral judgements contained in both these verses are related explicitly to what Yahweh abhors and what he approves, and so to a belief that he has revealed his will on these matters. **[20]** In v. 20, as in 3.32 (see above, p. 301), it is wrong-headedness which Yahweh is said to abhor, and I have pointed out that a similar expression is used in *Amenemope* in relation to innate perverseness, and speech which is calculated to deceive and make mischief (above, p. 301). The contrast in v. 20 is between the wrong-headed man with a kink in his mind which sets him against the world and makes him unreasonable and misanthropic, and the person whose way of life is flawless, whose relationship to Yahweh and to his neighbour is utterly sincere and whose life is complete or whole (cf. vv. 3a and 5a).

[1] In v. 1, the antithesis is between falsified balances and an accurate weight – accurate in the sense that it actually weighs what it ought to weigh without the least deficiency (*šᵉlēmā*). Both prophecy and law were concerned with honesty and 'righteousness' in this particular area of commercial practice. Micah speaks of falsified weights and inequitable balances (Micah 6.11), while Amos mentions the sharp practice of selling short weight (Amos 8.5). The vocabulary of both these passages has some resemblance to v. 1 (*mō'zᵉnē mirmā, mō'zᵉnē rešaʿ*), while *'eben šᵉlēmā* has to be compared with *'eben šᵉlēmā wāṣedeq* (Deut. 25.15; cf. Lev. 19.36; Ezek. 45.10; *mō'zᵉnē ṣedeq, 'abnē ṣedeq*). Toy argues that Prov. 11.1 is directly dependent on Deut. 25.15–16, but there are not sufficient grounds for this conclusion. The Deuteronomy passage appears to give legislative expression to the demands of Micah and Amos, although it mentions only *'eben* and *'ēpā* and does not use the expressions *mō'zenē mirmā* or *mō'zenē reša'* which appear in Amos 8.5 and Micah 6.11 respectively. These are also absent from Lev. 19.36 and Ezek. 45.10, but *mō'zenē mirmā* appears in Prov. 11.1, which would therefore seem to be dependent on Amos 8.5 for this expression. The direct links between Prov. 11.1 and Deut. 25.15f. are *šelēmā* and the formula *tō'abat YHWH*. The most that one can conclude is that attitudes which are struck in Prov. 11.1 in relation to weights and balances and the language which is used is dependent on prophetic preaching and legal formulations.

One cannot entirely rule out the possibility that the phrase *tō'abat YHWH* as used by Deuteronomy represents a modification of an expression which is derived from international wisdom (see on 3.32, above, pp. 300f.). Thus in a passage in *Amenemope* which deals with the falsification of measures (xvii.8–xix.9), we read: 'Make not for thyself a bushel measure of two capacities', and such sharp practice is described as 'perversion before God' (Griffith). Again: 'The bushel is the eye of Rē; its abomination is he who abstracts', i.e., who gives short measure. Here the bushel measure is equated with the eye of Rē, so that 'its abomination' is equivalent to 'the abomination of Rē', which recalls 'the abomination of God' or 'the abomination of the god' – a phrase which occurs elsewhere in *Amenemope* (see on 3.32).

[7] Gemser is suspicious of v. 7 for various reasons. The first stichos is too long (he and Ringgren delete *'ādām*), it contains no antithesis and the repetition of *'bd* is infelicitous. Another reason adduced, whose validity is inadmissible, is that the verse accords ill with the context (see above, pp. 413f.). Both Gemser and Ringgren translate *tōḥelet 'ōnīm* 'false expectation' (cf. *'āwen*), whereas Barucq translates 'hope set in riches', which would express a thought similar to 10.2 and 11.4 (above pp. 422, 436). The antithesis whose absence is noted by Gemser is supplied by Reider's emendations. He reads *'emūnīm* for *'ōnīm* (accidental omission of *m*) and connects *'ābādā* with Arabic *'abada* 'to last', 'to be enduring':

When a wicked man dies, his hope perishes,
But the expectation of the faithful is everlasting (*VT* ii, 1952, p. 124).

But an emendation which requires a belief that there has been a scribal error and a use of *'bd* unparalleled in biblical Hebrew in the compass of one verse is not likely to gain acceptance. LXX reads:

> When the righteous man dies, hope does not perish,
> But the boast of impious men is cut off.

On the basis of τῶν ἀσεβῶν, *'ōnīm* has been emended to *'ᵉwīlīm* or *ʿawwālīm* (BH and KB²), 'and the expectation of fools perishes'. Barucq discusses the deviation of LXX from MT in v. 7a and suggests possible explanations. *rāšāʿ* was not in the Hebrew text which lay before the translator, or it was misread as *yāšār*, or the translator produced what he thought was a more edifying sentence irrespective of the Hebrew text. The rendering of *tōḥelet* by καύχημα suggests that the Greek translator had 'fame' or 'reputation' rather than life beyond death in mind, and this would bring the thought of the verse into line with 10.7. But the form of words in v. 7a (MT), 'when a wicked man dies, expectation perishes', suggests that the righteous man has hope beyond death. Wherein does this hope consist? Is it the hope of a blessed immortality? Or is it the hope of a good name or an enduring reputation as in 10.7 (above, pp. 422f.)?

[23] In v. 23, the hope of the wicked is opposed to the desire of the righteous in a manner similar to 10.3. The desire of righteous men brings nothing but good – the issue is fulfilment, not frustration (see on 10.3, above p. 426), while the hope of evil men is anger, i.e., it is, doomed to terminate in vexation and loss of temper, since Yahweh repulses the desire of wicked men. The hopes which they entertain have no consequence except an impotent frenzy by which they give vent to feelings of intolerable frustration, but through which they accomplish nothing. In v. 23b, LXX reads 'the hope of wicked men perishes', but the more difficult reading of MT should be retained (so Gemser, Ringgren and Barucq). It may have puzzled the Greek translator, who then approximated v. 23b to v. 7b, although the Greek word used in v. 7b (ὄλλυται) is not identical with the one in v. 23b (ἀπολεῖται). Driver vocalizes *ʿebrā* as *ʿābᵉrā*, which he takes as a Syriacism ('The expectation of the wicked passes away'), and this makes LXX explicable as a translation of the Hebrew consonantal text (G. R. Driver, *JTS* xli, 1940, p. 174). Even if this were adopted, the exegesis of the verse would be as I have indicated, since account has to be taken of the fact that *tiqwā* in v. 23b is a synonym of *ta'ᵃwā* in v. 23a. The antithesis is therefore not between the hope of the righteous and the hopelessness of the wicked at death, as is apparently (*'ōnīm?*) the case in v. 7, but, as I have said, between the satisfaction of fulfilled desire and the experience of being thwarted at every turn so that desires cannot be translated into achievement.

Chapter 12

Class A: vv. 1, 4, 8, 9, 11, 15, 16, 17, 19, 23, 24, 27.
Class B: vv. 6, 18, 20, 25, 26.
Class C: vv. 2, 3, 5, 7, 10, 12, 13, 14, 21, 22, 28.

Class A

There is a group (vv. 1, 8, 15, 16, 23) in which the presence of the vocabulary of old wisdom is unmistakable. Thus *mūsār* and *tōkaḥat* belong to the context of a concept of education in which the emphasis is on the authority of the teacher and the need for discipline in the pupil. The product of this discipline is wisdom, and the product of its neglect is folly. The fool is the one who is incorrigible in the sense that he will not submit to the discipline which is the only route to wisdom. **[1]** Consequently it can be said that the love of discipline is the same as the love of knowledge, and that hatred of it shows a complete lack of discrimination. 'Brutishness' is a special aspect of folly (*baʿar* has the form of a second declension noun, but it may be legitimate to translate 'brutish'), denoting the absence of the rationality which differentiates men from animals. To hate discipline is stupidity – an attitude which argues the absence of any capacity for reasonable appraisal.

[8] Verse 8 is set in the same frame of intellectual values. As I have pointed out elsewhere (*PWM*, pp. 16, 67), *śkl* is associated with 'grasp' of affairs, with competence and success, and in all these respects betrays the practical tendency of the language of old wisdom. The antithesis of v. 8 is thus constituted by lack of intellectual grasp and muddle-headedness. Intellectual clarity and incisiveness make a man master of a situation and win him acclaim, while confused thinking brings him into contempt (*lēb* is 'mind' and not 'heart', see *PWM*, pp. 15f.). LXX has νωθροκάρδιος, 'sluggish in heart' (κάρδιος is a mistranslation of *lēb*), for MT *naʿawē lēb*; hence the emendation *naʿabē lēb* 'thick-headed', 'obtuse' (Kuhn). This would be the only instance of a niphal of *ʿbh* in biblical Hebrew, but, in any case, it does not give a sense superior to that of MT. In Mishnaic Hebrew *ʿwh* means 'to act perversely', and the 7th form in Arabic means 'to be bent', so that na'awē lēb is the one whose mind is bent, who cannot think straight and who is therefore muddle-headed or wrong-headed.

[15] A variant of the antithesis of v. 1 appears in v. 15. The commodity of the wisdom teacher is 'ēṣā. This is the advice which he gives or the policy which he frames, and in it is displayed the wealth of his experience and the nicety of his intellectual discrimination. The sage applies his wide knowledge of the world and the accumulated resources of the wisdom tradition to a given problem, and the result is a finely balanced and penetrating opinion. This is 'ēṣā (see on the Ahithophel story, *PWM*, pp. 55f.). The wise man is he who has the critical sharpness to recognize good advice when he hears it and to model his action on it. The fool is so excessively self-opinionated that he is deaf to advice from any quarter and never entertains a shadow of doubt that his own courses may be wrong. He has no problems because he does not have the critical faculties to recognize them, and his unbounded confidence in himself is a symptom of his lack of intellectual discipline and rigour and even his incapacity for these virtues. He is the incorrigible fool who is incapable of beginning to learn wisdom. Do not respond to insult in the same way

[16] Another virtue of old wisdom is touched on in v. 16, which recommends self-control and inscrutability. The fool's rejoinder to an insult or an affront is a reflex action; it is immediate and is emotionally charged, a blind retaliatory swipe and not a reasonable, effective response. He reacts like an injured animal and so his opponent knows that he has been wounded. The sagacious or shrewd man, on the contrary, has mastered any tendency towards impetuosity and has learned to hide his feelings. Even when he is insulted he maintains a front of imperturbability, and does not give his adversary the satisfaction of observing the effect of his wounding words. He knows that it is better to sleep on an insult than to react emotionally and advertise how much one is hurt (BH: *yōdia'*, 'divulges his vexation', with the versions, instead of MT, 'his vexation is evident', does not alter the sense).

[23] A related topic is treated in v. 23, where the emphasis falls on tactiturnity rather than inscrutability. The shrewd man (again '*ārūm*) does not affect omniscience and is not concerned (as the fool is) that everyone should know that he knows everything. The fool who supposes that his publicizing of his fancied acumen makes a reputation for him as a wise man is in fact enabling people to see through him

quicker than would otherwise be possible. They know that only a fool is capable of such a pose. The *'ārūm* is aware that the more a man speaks the less he is able to speak effectively and to time his utterance, and so he imposes on himself an economy of speech. To appear to be always giving advice is a damning circumstance, and the shrewd man holds his tongue and bides his time, waiting for the moment and the issue on which he can speak effectively and decisively. This furnishes the right antithesis to v. 23b, and it is this rather than the thought of secretiveness – the concealing of information and so the non-disclosure of confidences – which is intended by the phrase 'a shrewd man conceals knowledge'.

[4] The value of the right kind of wife is stressed in v. 4 (cf. 11.16, 22, above, p. 430). The woman of sterling character (*'ēšet ḥayil*) is the crown of her husband – a metaphor which suggests that a wife of quality enables a man to realize his potentialities and to attain the fulness of his stature and dignity. There is a detailed description of the *'ēšet ḥayil* in 31.10–30 (see below, pp. 665f.). She has economic ability as evidenced in thrift, industry and foresight, and by her acumen she lays the foundations of domestic prosperity, thus releasing her husband for spheres of wider influence and providing for him an indispensable basis of *kābōd* ('weight', 'honour'). She also has ethical qualities; she is wise, charitable, virtuous and dependable (cf. Ruth 3.11). The opposite of an *'ēšet ḥayil* is a *m^ebīšā* – a wife who gives a man a red face, who puts him to shame before the world. While an *'ēšet ḥayil* raises him to the fulness of his powers, a *m^ebīšā* will be a drag on him all his days and an unfailing topic of gossip and ribald humour.

A man with such a wife will himself be a standing joke who will never command respect nor win influence in the community. To be saddled with such a woman is like enduring an infestation of maggots in the bones. It is an excruciating irritant and a fatal disease; it is an insidious, gnawing process of putrefaction (cf. LXX: 'But like maggot in wood, so a woman who is an evil-doer destroys a man'). The word *m^ebīšā* is quite general and a wife could earn the epithet in a variety of ways, whether through glaring incompetence or a manner which gives offence and betrays an incapacity for good personal relationships, or behaviour which is morally scandalous (cf. Gemser and Ringgren, '*schandbar*') and brings her husband into contempt.

There are four sentences (vv. 9, 11, 24, 27) which inculcate a somewhat pedestrian prudence, two of them written in praise of diligence (vv. 24, 27). **[9]** The meaning of v. 9 would appear to be that quiet, unspectacular prosperity is better (note the 'better . . . than' form) than an affectation of affluence which conceals poverty. Toy is probably right in supposing that the *niqle* is one who is low in the social scale and who enjoys little public reputation. Yet, although he stands low in public esteem, he has a solid if modest prosperity – he is able to employ a servant. Ringgren understands MT differently: 'Better is the man of slight esteem who is his own servant', in which case the contrast is between the man who is prepared to work and so to eat, and the person who prefers to have his delusions of affluence and go hungry. This would also be the effect of following LXX and Pesh. ('who does his own work'; cf. BH, which proposes: 'Better is the man of small esteem who has a product', or, 'Better is the man of slight esteem who has a plot of land'). **[11]** Both these conjectures would connect v. 9 with v. 11, which contrasts the individual who works the soil and has enough to eat with the dilettante who wastes his time and fritters away his energies on empty pursuits. Such a person is deficient in good sense (*ḥᵃsar lēb*). Gemser's emendation of *ḥᵃsar lēb* to *ḥāsēr* or *yeḥsār* is intended to strengthen the antithetic structure of the sentence. The peasant has as much bread as he needs, but the dilettante lacks (bread). Boström holds that sentences of this kind indicate that a special value was attached to the tilling of the soil which was regarded as the highest kind of work, so that it is possible to speak of an agricultural ideal in the book of Proverbs. The antithesis, according to Boström, is particularly between such elemental work and involvement in dubious mercantile and financial transactions (pp. 53f.). See on 6.1 (above, pp. 321f.) and 11.15 (above, p. 429).

[24] Diligence enables one to exercise authority and power, and so a diligent man has the mastery over others, but slack and half-hearted effort will lead to slavery (v. 24, *mas* is *corvée* or forced labour). The idea is perhaps that the person whose efforts are no more than ineffective and unconvincing gestures will get into debt and eventually lose his personal freedom (cf. 10.4, above, p. 417). **[27]** The other sentence on diligence is more obscure, principally because of the uncertain meaning of *yaḥᵃrōk*, but also because the grammar of v. 27b is uncertain. Barucq supposes that the root *ḥrk* has its Aramaic meaning of 'roast' and translates: 'Nonchalance will not roast its prey'. Barucq renders *rᵉmīyā* here and in v. 24 as an abstract noun, but the abstract form is probably being used as a collective (G. R.

Driver, *Biblica* 32, p. 196; the masculine suffix of *ṣēdō* with the feminine *r^emīyā* should be noted in this connection). Verse 27a is apparently metaphorical and the meaning is that the lazy or listless man lacks the energy and sense of urgency needed to bring an enterprise to a successful conclusion. He is the person who chases rewards after a fashion, but who never captures them and enjoys their possession. But v. 27b is a weak antithesis to such a version of v. 27a. Barucq translates v. 27b: 'But a diligent man is rare wealth' (transposing *yāqār* and *'ādām* with LXX). This has little to do with v. 27a, which would lead us to expect in v. 27b a statement that the diligent man 'grasps' wealth and so succeeds where his listless counterpart fails. This antithesis is indicated by Ringgren and RSV. Gemser emends *yaḥ^arōk* to *yadrīk* (cf. LXX ἐπιτεύξεται): 'A languid man does not catch his prey.' He translates 27b like Barucq. Whether or not *yadrīk* or the like is adopted in 27a, it should be regarded as implicit in the construction of 27b ('but a diligent man captures rare wealth').

[17] In vv. 17 and 19 the contrast is between truth and falsehood; v. 17 has legal testimony particularly in mind, while v. 19 has a more general character in MT, although in LXX it, too, has an unambiguous forensic character ('The veracious lip orders evidence well, but the witness who is too quick has an unjust tongue'). Gemser has queried whether *yāpīaḥ* in v. 17a may not be a noun and a synonym of *'ēd* (C. H. Gordon, *Ugaritic Textbook*, *An. Or.* 38, 1965, p. 176: Text 57, *l.* 9, *ypḫ kn'm*). This provides v. 17 with better balance (*y^epīaḥ 'emūnā* is antithetic to *'ēd š^eqārīm*). Moreover, *yāpīaḥ 'emūnā* = 'he who speaks the truth' is grammatically dubious. Yet the evidence for a noun *yāpīaḥ* produced by Gordon is exiguous. The contrast is between the truthful witness and the perjurer; the one by his testimony furthers the cause of justice and facilitates a right verdict, whereas the other by his deliberate falsification defeats the ends of justice.

[19] The enduring character of truth is asserted in v. 19 (*'emet*, cf. *'emūnā* in v. 17, signifies stability and permanence). When the truth is spoken it endures, but falsehood is ephemeral. Nothing is stronger than the truth, and so it will stand every test and overcome every adversary. Lies are fragile, and as soon as they are sifted lose their credibility and are exposed as worthless. The truthful man will go on from strength to strength for none of his words will fall to the ground, but the liar will speedily be detected and discredited.

Class B

[18] The wise man knows that he should always speak constructively, and that the function of speech is to cement human relationships and to be a therapy where they are damaged or broken. The person whose aim is to wound and whose words are like sword-thrusts may be a master of invective, but if he does not realize that words are a therapy for promoting social health, he is not a wise man. The sage is not primarily interested in winning debates, and he avoids speech which creates bitterness and erects barriers between himself and others. He is not the 'outsider', the alienated intellectual with the waspish tongue. Part of his wisdom is his political or social effectiveness, and this is dependent on his ability to get on with all types of people and win their confidence. His interest is to speak so as to contribute to the 'health' of the community. In order to do this, his approach to relations between man and man is as a matter of principle conciliatory. **[25]** This social concern is expressed in v. 25, whose sense is assured, although the emendations suggested by BH are needed to make the grammar normal. (BDB supposes that the third feminine singular suffix refers to *lēb*, 'depresses it', 'cheers it up'. This is how the verse is taken by Toy, Gemser and Ringgren. The grammar, however, is still abnormal, since *lēb* is masculine.) When a man is anxious, he is depressed and he needs 'a good word' to cheer him up (G. R. Driver, *JRAS*, 1948, p. 176, derives *yšḥnh* from *šwḥ* 'to sink' and vocalizes *yᵉšīḥenhū*. According to the vocalization of MT it is to be derived from *šḥh*. *šwḥ* is used of a depressed mind in Ps. 44.26; Lam. 3.20). The ability to speak effectively to a man in this condition is a manifestation of wisdom, and so wisdom comprises such a pastoral concern and discrimination. In order to speak 'a good word' to one who is depressed by anxiety, there has to be some awareness of what is involved in the condition of anxiety and a measure of identification with the anxious person. The 'good word' is not only well-chosen and judicious; it is informed by a warm humanity and a rich sympathy.

[6] The words of *rᵉšāʿīm* have destructive consequences and lead to violent courses of action. They are a 'bloody ambush' (v. 6). Here the meaning is not that the wicked are caught in the web of their own intrigues, but that they speak with the intention of laying an ambush for others (*'ᵉrob tām*, 'an ambush for the blameless man', for *'erob dām* [BH] is not an improvement and should not be adopted). The antithetic parallelism is better served if 'them' of v. 6b refers to those who are the victims of the machinations of the wicked, and not to the *y*^{e}*šārīm* themselves. The speech of upright men is salutary and effects the escape of those who would otherwise be trapped and ambushed by the words of the wicked (cf. 11.9, above, p. 431; Ringgren, p. 53 n.6). **[20]** The *ḥōr*^{e}*šē rāʿ* of v. 20 are those who lavish their craftsmanship and expertise on shaping evil plans (see on 6.14, above, pp. 325f.), and they are contrasted with those who take thought and make policies for the common good and are concerned with *šālōm* ('social wholeness'). Since *mirmā* is the antithesis of *śimḥā*, it should probably be translated 'self-deceit'. Those who devote their cleverness to evil ends are benighted, and are themselves the victims of the lie of which they are past-masters. There is then the assertion that those who act to the detriment of the community are their own worst enemies, while those who make plans for the common good enjoy a personal satisfaction and fulfilment.

[26] The sense of v. 26 is uncertain because of the obscurity of v. 26a and the consequent difficulty in applying the test of parallelism to v. 26b. Here again, however, I would suppose that 'them' (v. 26b) indicates those who are led astray by following the way of the wicked. If this is so, Barucq's translation of v. 26a supplies what is desiderated ('The righteous man shows his companion the [right] way'), but it is not clear that MT can yield this. Barucq (cf. BDB) argues that *yātēr* is hiphil of *tūr*, 'to explore', and means 'to show the way' (cf. RV, 'The righteous man is guide to his neighbour'). Gemser's proposal (following J. C. Döderlein, *Scholia in libros Veteris Testamenti poeticos, Iobum, Psalmos et tres Salomonis*, 1779, p. 148), 'searches out his pasture', to be understood metaphorically and so indicating the moral discrimination of the *ṣaddīq*, does not provide the right kind of antithesis to 26b. It assumes that 'them' of 26b refers to the wicked themselves, and then the contrast is between moral discernment and the lack of it. The same can be said of the text adopted by Toy and Ringgren, *yāsūr mērāʿā*, 'departs from evil'. J. A. Emerton (*ZAW* lxxvi, 1964, pp. 191f.) also supposes that 'them' (26b) refers to the *r*^{e}*šāʿīm*. He observes that if *ytr* is to be regarded as a hiphil of *tūr*, the pointing should be *yātīr* rather than *yātēr* (jussive). He derives *ytr* from *ntr*, hiphil 'to set free', and points as a hophal (*yuttar*). 'The righteous man is delivered from harm (*mērāʿā*), but the way of the wicked leads them astray.' Targ., which points to *yeter min* ('The righteous man is better than his companion'), is also deficient as an antithesis to v. 26b, if the latter means 'the way of wicked men leads others astray'. The longer text of LXX reads:

A righteous arbitrator is his own friend,
but the advice of impious men lacks equity (absent from LXX^B).
Evil pursues sinners,
and the way of impious men leads them astray.

Only the last line has any resemblance to MT, and then it takes v. 26b in a sense which I believe to be wrong, since there is no doubt that *αὐτούς* refers to the impious in LXX.

Class C

There is a group of sentences in which the schematism of theodicy is unmistakably present (vv. 2, 14, 21, 22). **[2]** In v. 2, the antithesis of approval (*rāṣōn*) is condemnation, and *yaršiaʿ* means precisely the passing of a verdict of guilty, and so condemnation in a forensic context. (On the possible cultic connections of these terms see G. von Rad, *Old Testament Theology* i, p. 261.) In this case *rāṣōn* is the approval reserved by Yahweh for the one whom he finds *ṣaddīq* (here described as *ṭōb*, 'a good man'). The devious person (*'īš mᵉzimmōt*) is incapable of candour; the ruse and dubious stratagem are second nature to him. The pejorative use of *mᵉzimmā* represents a reinterpretation of an item of the vocabulary of old wisdom. In the context of old wisdom there is no implied moral censure in the meaning of *mᵉzimmā*. There the important criterion is effectiveness, and the capacity for *mᵉzimmā* – for the stratagem which is well designed to attain its objective and will be successful – is an intellectual virtue (see on 8.12b, above, p. 347; *PWM*, p. 80).

[22] In v. 22, those who behave with integrity or whose action has a quality of truth are said to win Yahweh's *rāṣōn*, and they are contrasted with liars who are 'an abomination to Yahweh' (on *tōʿᵃbat YHWH* in connection with lying speech see on 3.32 (above, pp. 301f.), where the parallels in *Amenemope* are considered). *rāṣōn* and *tōʿēbā*, as expressive of approval and strong disapproval, are the emotive correlates of *ṣaddīq* and *rāšāʿ*; Yahweh's *rāṣōn* is directed towards the one and his *tōʿēbā* towards the other.

[21] In v. 21, both *'āwen* and *rāʿ* mean 'evil' in the sense of 'injury' or 'calamity'; the *ṣaddīq* is protected by Yahweh from such grievous misfortune, but the lives of evil men are full of it. **[14]** This is the schematism of reward and retribution, which is also evident in v. 14, where the structure is synthetic. In v. 14a, 'fruit' is equivalent to 'good fruit', and only creative and beneficent speech is envisaged there. The person whose speech is productive and beneficial to others will himself get satisfaction from its results (this is a blend of class B and class C). See above on vv. 18 and 25, p. 446, and cf. 10.31–32, above, pp. 423f. The thought that there is a harmony of self-interest and care for the commonweal may also be present here. In so far as he speaks therapeutically in order to heal damaged or broken relationships, he confers satisfaction and advantage on himself – he grows in personal stature and influence. It is the double-sided character of recompense which is the subject of v. 14b. A man receives the recompense which his actions merit, or, if *yāšīb* (Q.) is read, Yahweh recompenses a man according to his deserts.

There are three sentences in which the righteous man and his opposite are contrasted in respect of the stability and security which are granted to the one and denied to the other (vv. 3, 7, 12).

[3] Wickedness is a poor and insecure foundation on which to build one's life, but righteous men are well-rooted plants whose health and growth are assured (v. 3). **[7]** The wicked suffer a reversal of fortune and are overtaken by irretrievable disaster, but a righteous man's household stands firm. The *bayit* is the indispensable basis of sound prosperity on which all efforts after wider success and recognition in the community must be founded (see on 12.4, above, p. 443).

[12] Gemser's elaborate emendation of v. 12 assumes that *ḥāmad rāšāʿ* is a fragment of the addition to v. 11 in LXX ('He who indulges in banquets of wine will leave dishonour [as a legacy] to his strongholds'), and that *'ōbēd* or *weʾōbēd* has been accidentally omitted because of its resemblance to *ḥōmēd*. He reconstructs the Hebrew text as follows:

ḥōmēd bemištē yayin yaʿazōb rešaʿ bimeṣūdātō
'ōbēd meṣōd rāʿīm wešōrēš ṣaddīqīm beʾētān

He who has a craving for banquets of wine, will leave wickedness behind in his stronghold.
The fortress of evil men will perish, but the root of the righteous will endure for ever.

The emendation is too ponderous to be convincing and two more exact objections can be raised against it: (*a*) in v. 12a, LXX reads: 'The desires of impious men are evil', and this is sufficiently close to MT of v. 12a to disprove Gemser's assertion that *ḥāmad rāšāʿ* is a fragment of the Greek addition to v. 11. In other words, the Greek translator would appear to have read something like MT of v. 12a, so that if it is a fragment of the Greek addition to v. 11 one would have to suppose that this corruption was already present in the Hebrew text which was before the Greek translator, and this makes Gemser's solution improbable; (*b*) *m*ᵉ*ṣōd* ('net') is not attested elsewhere in biblical Hebrew with the meaning 'fortress'.

As it stands, v. 12a of MT gives poor sense, although it is retained by Barucq who translates: 'The impious man desires the nets of the wicked'. This is weak, and Ringgren's rendering, which presupposes a change in the vocalization of one word (*ḥāmad* to *ḥemed*), is an improvement: 'The desire of the wicked man is a hunting after evil things.' It is doubtful whether *rāʿīm* can mean 'evil things' and *m*ᵉ*ṣōd* 'the act of hunting'. BH with a larger emendation (*yiššāmēd* for *ḥāmad rāšāʿ* and *y*ᵉ*sōd* for *m*ᵉ*ṣod*) reads: 'The foundation of evil men is destroyed', and then v. 12 reproduces exactly the two metaphors of v. 3 (see above, p. 449). Finally, there is Hitzig's suggestion that *rāšāʿ* and *rāʿīm* should be transposed (*rāʿīm*=Arabic *raġāmu* 'powdery soil'), that *ḥōmer* should be read for *ḥāmad* and *m*ᵉ*ṣūdat* for *m*ᵉ*ṣōd*: 'The fortress of a wicked man is crumbling clay.' There is then an antithesis between the crumbling clay and the deep roots of the righteous in good soil. Again, however, MT has been rearranged and altered. What could have brought about the transposition of *rāšāʿ* and *rāʿīm* (cf. G. R. Driver, *JTS* vi, 1955, p. 86, n.5.)? The emendation is not likely to win acceptance and v. 12a remains a puzzle. Verse 12b, on the other hand, can be translated without altering the consonants of the Hebrew text. *ytn* should be vocalized *yītān*, Arabic *watana*, 'to remain', 'to be permanent' (see Gemser): 'But the root of the righteous abides.' This is neater than the change to *b*ᵉ*'ētān* (BH); *yittēn* (retained by Barucq) can hardly mean 'yields (fruit)'.

[5] In the setting of old wisdom, *taḥbūlōt* and *maḥ*ᵃ*šābōt* are akin in meaning, the one referring to procedural expertise (see on 1.5, above, p. 266) and the other to plans or calculations, that is, to well-reasoned policies. In 11.14a (see above, p. 429), the indispensability of *taḥbūlōt* for a state of political well-being is asserted. In 12.5 *taḥbūlōt* has become a bad word which is associated with the activities of *r*ᵉ*šāʿīm* and is opposed to *maḥš*ᵉ*bōt ṣaddīqīm*. The vocabulary of old wisdom is here drawn into a 'righteous-wicked' antithesis in such a way that a pejorative meaning is established for *taḥbūlōt* and an ethically commendable one for *maḥ*ᵃ*šābōt*. The first issues in deceit and the second in equity; the first is immoral deviousness and the second a deliberate provision for the implementation of justice.

[28] Verse 28 has the general appearance of a statement of the

'Two Ways' similar to 11.3 and 5 (see above, p. 435), where righteousness is correlated with life and its opposite with death. For this reason, as well as for the more general one that sentences with synthetic parallelism are a rarity in this chapter (only v. 14 and, as I have shown, there is an antithetic element in it), any emendation of the corrupt v. 28b which results in synthetic parallelism is suspect. This in itself weighs against Dahood's opinion (M. Dahood, *Biblica* 41, 1960, pp. 176–81; *Proverbs and Northwest Semitic Philology*, p. 28) that v. 28b should be read: 'And the treading of her path (i.e., the path of righteousness) is immortality' (*ūdᵉrōk nᵉtībā 'al māwet*). More detailed objections can be made to his proposals. The use of *'al ṭal wᵉ'al māṭār* in II Sam. 1.21 for *'al yᵉhī ṭal wᵉ'al yᵉhī māṭār*, 'let there not be dew and let there not be rain' (GK §152g) is a different matter from the use of *bl* to negate a noun illustrated by the texts which Dahood cites: *bl ṭl bl rd*, 'without dew, without showers' (*CML*, pp. 58f., *Aqhat* I i.44). Thus although Dahood can produce a sentence from an Ugaritic text with synthetic parallelism which reads, 'In your life, O father, we rejoice and in your not dying (*bl mtk*) we exult' (C. H. Gordon, *Ugaritic Textbook*, p. 192, Text 125, *ll.* 14–15), and although GK §152g concedes that *'al māwet* in Prov. 12.28b may mean 'not death', 'immortality', the balance of probability is still, in my view, against Dahood's solution.

Tournay, who makes a point similar to mine against Dahood when he says that *'al* is a different form of negation from *bl*, supposes that *nᵉtībā* is a corruption of *petī bā'* and that *'el* should be read for *'al* (*'el māwet* is attested by Hebrew manuscripts and the versions): 'But the way of folly leads to death.' Tournay explains MT on the assumption that *'al māwet* means 'immortality'. 'The change from *'el māwet* to *'al māwet* was made in the Maccabaean period after a belief in immortality had grown up' (R. Tournay, *RB* lxix, 1962, pp. 495–97). There is merit in Tournay's treatment of the verse in two respects. In the first place, his emendation *petī bā'* is closer to *nᵉtībā* than *tō'ēbā* (BH) or *mᵉšūbā* 'apostasy' (Gemser). In the second place, he is right in seeking to restore a sentence with antithetic parallelism and in arguing that 'immortality' is not an original concern of this type of opposition between life and death (cf. 10.27, above, p. 425; 11.31, above, pp. 437f.; Ringgren, p. 55, n.1).

If Tournay's emendation is adopted, *petī* undergoes the same reinterpretation as *taḥbūlōt* and *maḥᵃšābōt* in v. 5. In the educational context of old wisdom, *petī* is the antithesis of *ḥokmā*. It is the raw, uncritical condition of the untutored youth, whereas *ḥokmā* is the quality of mind possessed by the finished products of the educational discipline. In v. 28, *petī*, if the emendation were adopted, would be opposed to *ṣedāqā* and the framework of interpretation would be supplied by a doctrine of theodicy rather than by an educational theory. *petī* then becomes moral obtuseness and it is this which leads to death, whereas the path of *ṣedāqā* leads to life (cf. 11.3, 5). Barucq supposes that *μνησικάκων* (LXX) represents an attempt to translate *mešūbā* or *mešībīm* ('the way of apostasy leads to death' or 'the way of apostates leads to death'). *μνησικάκων*, however, means 'those who bear malice' or 'those who harbour grievances', and does not point either to *mešūbā* or *mešībīm*.

[10] In v. 10, *yd'* has the sense 'be concerned for' as in 10.32 (see above, p. 452). The *ṣaddīq* is a humane person who has regard for the well-being of his animals (sheep and cattle), but the *rešā'īm* are unfeeling and without compunction in this regard – they are as hard as flint.

[13] The clue to the meaning of v. 13 is probably to be found in 11.9. If this is so, the translation of LXX, according to which it is the ἁμαρτωλός (*rā'*) who is ensnared, does not take the point of the Hebrew correctly, and so *mōqēš* should not be emended to *nōqaš* on the basis of LXX (BH, Gemser, Ringgren). The point, as in 11.9a, is that there are those who speak maliciously with a view to ensnaring and destroying their fellows (Barucq translates *mōqēš rā'*, 'lethal snare'; cf. *mūsār rā'* in 15.10, below, p. 479), but the righteous man emerges from distress (on *ṣārā* see 11.8a, above, p. 436). The sentence has affinities with class B material, but it leads up to the assertion that the *ṣaddīq* will ultimately be safe, and for this reason I have allocated it to class C. The addition in LXX is apparently directed against litigiousness. The clement man (? the antithetic element in the first stichos is rather weak) is contrasted with the person who demands his pound of flesh: 'He whose looks are gentle will be pitied, but he who encounters men in (the) gates will afflict souls.'

Chapter 13

Class A: vv. 1, 3, 4, 7, 8, 10, 11, 12, 13, 14, 15, 16, 18, 19a, 20, 24.
Class B: vv. 2, 5, 17, 19b.
Class C: vv. 6, 9, 21, 22, 25.

The odd circumstance that v. 19a is in one class and v. 19b in another is to be explained by the unrelatedness of the two halves of this verse (see below). Because of the obscurity of v. 23, it is not possible to classify it with any degree of confidence.

Class A

Within this class is a large group of sentences (vv. 1, 10, 13, 14, 15, 16, 18, 20, 24) which deal with different aspects of the educational concept associated with old wisdom, as this is conveyed by certain stock items of vocabulary. **[1]** In v. 1, the antithesis of 'wise son' and 'scoffer' is significant, since it indicates that an important constituent of the stance of a wise son is teachability. It does not matter whether we understand this parentally or scholastically. In the latter case it is the attitude of a pupil to his teacher which is the subject of comment. The son must defer to his father's authority, and this unquestioned authority is also enjoyed by the wisdom teacher in school, where a kind of father-son relationship is established between teacher and pupil. What is required of the pupil is not originality or critical doubt, but the unquestioning acceptance of the dictates of the teacher and a capacity for careful listening and unbroken concentration (v. 1b). The pupil is not to match himself against the teacher as an intellectual equal, but is rather to imbibe his wisdom as an eager apprentice. But this is what the *lēṣ* will not do, for he is by nature unteachable and incorrigible, and these are the attributes of folly. Hence the *lēṣ* is a type of fool who is not amenable to the discipline imposed by the teacher, and so will never learn wisdom. It is by the acceptance of 'rebuffs' that the apprentice learns his craft and allows his intellectual attitudes to be shaped by the tradition in which the master is steeped. In v. 1a, where MT is obscure, LXX reads: 'A wise son listens to his father.' This is adopted by Barucq. BH (cf. Gemser and Ringgren) emends *'āb* to *'ōhēb*, 'a wise son loves discipline', a sense which Driver has suggested can be had from MT (*'āb* from *'wb*, an Aramaizing by-form of *'hb*; G. R. Driver, *ZAW* 50, 1932, p. 144). More recently, Driver has suggested that *m^{e}yussār* should be read, 'a wise son is one who is disciplined by his father' (*JTS* xli, 1940, p. 174). Gemser entertains the possibility that *mūsār* may be a hophal participle: 'A wise son allows himself to be disciplined by his father.' I adopt *m^{e}yussār*.

[10] The effects of *hubris* – a topic related to that of v. 1 – are stated in v. 10. Insolence or arrogance is contrasted with a willingness to confer and be guided by a consensus of informed opinion. The contrast suggests that *zādōn* indicates particularly a contempt for all other opinions, such as is characteristic of the person who takes his own omniscience for granted and will not be deterred from unwise and contentious courses by advice from any quarter. This is the conceited, supercilious ass who spoils everything which he touches, who is ham-fisted and wrong-headed and can be depended on to create strife, wound feelings and inflame passions. If *rēq* ('an empty head') is read instead of *raq* (BH and Gemser), the sense of v. 10a is improved and the above interpretation confirmed (cf. LXX κακός, which is certainly not a translation of *raq*, but which might be a generalizing or inaccurate rendering of *rēq*). Otherwise MT must mean that nothing else is produced by *zādōn* except strife (Ringgren), and not that *zādōn* and nothing but *zādōn* produces strife. BH's emendation (*ṣᵉnūʿīm* for *nōʿāṣīm*) yields good sense and would reproduce exactly 11.2b (see above, p. 428). It is, however, unnecessary, since MT is perfectly satisfactory. The point which it makes is that *ʿēṣā* emerges from the interplay of many opinions and the reaching of a consensus. The openness and flexibility which qualify a man to participate in such an exchange and to play his part in the joint enterprise are marks of wisdom. I adopt *rēq*.

[13] Gemser's opinion that 'word' and 'opinion' in v. 13 are to be explained with reference to 'this commandment' and 'the word' of Deut. 30.11–14 should not be accepted. The verse is not to be interpreted in the framework of Deuteronomy, where *miṣwā* is the demand of Yahweh and *dābār* the authoritative, revealed word. I have argued that *miṣwā* is an item of wisdom vocabulary which indicates the mandatory character of the Instruction and the authority which attaches to the utterances of the wisdom teacher, and this is how it is to be understood here. Hence *dābār* is not the word of Yahweh, but the word of the wisdom teacher, and the two words are not to be taken as 'comprehensive expressions for divine and sapiental instructions'. The antithesis is similar to that of v. 10; on the one hand, the ill-founded intellectual arrogance which dismisses with contempt the instruction of the teacher and, on the other, the respect in which his dictates are held. The parallelism constituted by the verbs is not so easily discerned. MT: *yēḥābel lō* is explained by KB² as 'will have a pledge seized from him', 'will be mortgaged', 'will be a debtor'. The meaning of v. 13a would then be that the person who contemptuously dismisses the advice of a wise man will mismanage his affairs and become burdened with debt. This is not really apposite in relation to MT *yᵉšullām* (v. 13b), 'will be rewarded'. LXX ὑγιαίνει 'is healthy' points to *yišlam*. BH and Gemser read *yeḥubbāl* and delete *lō*, whereas Barucq retains *lō* as an ethic dative. The contrast is then between ruin or shame and reward (so Gemser and Barucq). What is perhaps rather intended is a contrast between exposure to ruin and safety (so Toy), and so I would read *yeḥubbāl* (*lō*) and *yišlām*: 'He who despises a word suffers ruin, but he who respects a ruling is safe.' The addition to LXX introduces a reference to economic prosperity, but it is doubtful whether this lends any support to KB²'s understanding of *yēḥābel lō* in v. 13a ('A crafty son will have no good thing, but the affairs of a wise servant will be prosperous and his path will be directed aright').

[14] With regard to form, v. 14 appears to be a mixture of sentence and Instruction – what is accomplished by *tōrat ḥākām* is indicated in a final clause. The instruction of the wisdom teacher (on the coupling of *tōrā* and *miṣwā* see 3.1, above, p. 290) is a fountain of life (see on 3.18, above, p. 296; 10.11, above, p. 418) offering escape from the snares of death. Just as there is an ultimate mythological basis to 'water of life', so it may be with 'snares of death', that is, Death envisaged as a hunter or fowler (on the Canaanite god Mot see 1.12, above, pp. 278f.). The goals of instruction are stated positively and negatively in a manner which recalls the representation of the two ways of life and death in 1–9. To take advice is to appropriate life and to be safe from death (cf. the antithesis in v. 13).

[15] In v. 15, *'ētān*, 'perennial', 'lasting' can hardly be translated 'arduous' (Barucq), and must be regarded as a corruption. On the basis of LXX ἐν ἀπωλείᾳ, BH, Gemser and Ringgren read *'ēdām*, 'their destruction', and Kaminka *yittām*, 'will be destroyed' (A. Kaminka, *HUCA* viii–ix, 1931–32, p. 183). Driver suggests that the rare negative particle *'ī* has been omitted by haplography and that *bōgedīm* can be translated as an abstract noun, as the parallelism requires (*Biblica* 32, p. 181): 'The way of treachery passes away.' But none of these emendations produces a particularly well-pointed antithesis, and the sentence has a somewhat disjointed aspect. The ephemeral character of the way of perfidy or the destruction of perfidious men is not a precise antithesis of the attractiveness of good sense and the acceptance which it wins. This *śēkel* is the capacity for sane appraisal and sound intellectual judgement which is educed by *mūsār*, and by it a man wins approval (*yitten ḥēn*). What is intended may be that the favour enjoyed by one who has *śēkel* is assured and lasting, whereas the twisted man who lacks intellectual clarity, consistency and integrity will soon come to grief. This would then be comparable with the *'emet* (*'emūnā*)-*šeqer* antithesis in 12.17, 19. The addition to v. 15 in LXX constitutes a reinterpretation of the vocabulary of wisdom in terms of Yahwistic legal piety: 'To know the Law is (the essence) of good understanding.' διανοία (*śēkel* is translated by σύνεσις in the preceding line) is defined as knowledge of the Law (cf. *PWM*, pp. 65f.).

[16] In v. 16, the behaviour of the shrewd man is opposed to that of the fool, and the opposition is conceived in intellectual terms. The *'ārūm* with his acumen and discrimination consistently (reading *kōl* with Pesh. and V; MT: 'every shrewd man') grasps the essentials of a situation and takes the right decision ('acts with knowledge'), but, when the *kesīl* acts, he merely exposes his intellectual deficiencies: 'He spreads out folly' (for display), i.e., he shows his wares to his own disadvantage (cf. Gemser, who suggests that the figure of speech is that of a pedlar putting his wares on display). Driver supposes that the point of the sentence is rather the contrast between the reserve of the shrewd man and garrulity of the fool, in which case it would be almost an exact replica of 12.23 (see above, pp. 442f.). Driver (also I. Eitan, *A Contribution to Biblical Lexicography*, 1954, pp. 57f.) holds that *'śh* (v. 16a) is synonymous with *ksh* (12.23a), and so is cognate with Arabic *ġašiya*, 'covered'. Similarly, he would translate Gen. 6.14, 'Make thee an ark of teak(?); cover the ark with reeds' (*qānīm*), instead of, 'Make thee an ark of teak; make rooms(?) in the ark' (one has then to suppose that *'śh* is used in two different senses in two successive phrases; G. R. Driver, *VT* iv, 1954, p. 243). I have not adopted Driver's suggestion in Prov. 13.16.

[18] The emendation of *rēš* to *yōrēš* (v. 18a, cf. BH) is unnecessary and does not improve the sense, but the grammar is made easier by the insertion of *le* before *pōrēa'* (so Toy). The antithesis of 'lightness' (*qlh*) and 'heaviness' (*kbd*) should be noted. He who submits to the discipline imposed by his teacher will himself become a sage and a man of weight in the community, but he who is negligent and intellectually undisciplined will be a man of straw. 'Weight' is status, power and influence and it embraces wealth; 'lightness' is lack of esteem and slightness and it involves poverty (*rēš*).

[20] In view of the construction of v. 20b, Q. rather than K. should be followed in v. 20a. This is another way of expressing the thought of v. 18. The way to become wise is to keep the company of sages and to be always learning from them; the way to grief is to become the companion of fools. Association is contagious for good or evil. A. Guillaume (*JTS* xv, 1964, p. 294) translates: 'But he who associates with fools will be left a fool' (Hebrew **rwʿ*=Arabic *rwġ*).

[24] Verse 24 insists that corporal punishment is an element of parental discipline and an expression of parental love, and that to be soft with a child is to do him a profound disservice ('He who withholds his rod hates his son'). The meaning of *šiḥᵃrō* is uncertain. Toy proposes 'seeks him with discipline', i.e., 'chastises him' (similarly KB²). Gemser translates 'takes thought for him with discipline' (cf. LXX ἐπιμελῶς παιδεύει), and Driver (similarly Ringgren; contrary to Toy) 'treats him early with discipline', i.e., begins the process at an early age (G. R. Driver, *JTS* xli, 1940, p. 174). I follow Driver.

[3] Barucq supposes that v. 3 is ambivalent and that the antithesis is either that of abstemiousness and gluttony or that of taciturnity and garrulity; *šōmēr napšō* means either 'guards his throat' or 'keeps his life'. But *nōṣēr pīw* cannot indicate abstemiousness nor *pōśēq śᵉpātāw* gluttony. The English idiom would be better served with *pīw* and *śᵉpātāw* transposed, i.e., 'tight-lipped' and 'big-mouthed'. There is no doubt that this is what the Hebrew means, and there is no ambivalence. Indiscreet and rash speech brings ruin, but a tight rein on the tongue, so that speech is never involuntary and ill-considered but always premeditated and judicious, precludes blundering into trouble. The self-denying ordinance of silence is an aspect of self-interest and self-preservation (cf. especially 13.3b with 10.14b, above, p. 416).

[4] On the other hand, the case for ambivalence in v. 4 which is argued by Barucq is much stronger, since the translation of *nepeš* as 'throat', 'appetite' ('stomach?' according to Barucq) is directly supported by *tᵉduššān*. In translating *nepeš* 'soul', Gemser, Ringgren, RSV go to the other extreme and follow the invariable LXX rendering of *nepeš*, which is hardly ever satisfactory. At its most literal level the sentence means that the lazy man desires food and eats imaginary banquets, while the diligent man gets down to the job of providing himself with food. The one remains hungry ('nothing with respect to his appetite', accusative of nearer definition; Barucq's emendation to *lᵉnapšō* is unnecessary), while the other is replete with food. This, however, is one of the few sentences in the book of Proverbs which conforms to my definition of a 'proverb'. It can be disengaged from its literalism and would be applicable wherever laziness and industriousness are contrasted in respect of impotence and effectiveness, fecklessness and fulfilment. The ideas expressed would then resemble those of 12.27 (see above, pp. 444f.). Laziness is barren and encourages escapism; the illusory world of desire unrelated to attainment is a prison. Industriousness is an honest engagement with the real world and a relentless pursuit of tangible and attainable rewards.

Verses 7 and 8 touch on the topic of wealth and poverty, and v. 11 describes two ways of acquiring wealth. **[7]** There is the type of person who affects ostentation and has nothing; his opposite has a large fortune and behaves as if he were penniless (v. 7). This sentence, too, has proverbial potentialities in that there is more to it than the contrast between a pretence of wealth and a pretence of poverty. Both are instances of unbalanced and immoderate behaviour and so the sentence has a representative power as a comment on the loss of equilibrium. Extremism at one pole is as bad as extremism at the other (cf. Toy, who lays more emphasis on pretence in his interpretation: 'One form of pretence is as bad as another').

[8] The intention of the antithesis in v. 8 is somewhat obscure, and Gemser adopts Steuernagel's emendation (*māṣā' g*[e]*'ullā*) which simplifies the sense but is far removed from MT: 'The ransom of a man's life is his wealth, but a poor man does not find (his) redemption' (i.e., the means of redeeming his life). The sentence is rather to be understood as a statement that the poor man, unlike his rich counterpart, is not vulnerable to blackmail. This is suggested tentatively by Gemser and is indicated by Barucq's translation of *g*[e]*ʿārā* ('menace'; 'menaces' in our legal terminology). The rich man who views his wealth as a means of buying off danger and threats will always be prone to pay up if he is blackmailed, but the poor man accepts the fact that he lives in a dangerous world and that he has no shield from insecurity, so that threats leave him unmoved. There is thus a sense in which the rich man's wealth condemns him to slavery and makes a coward of him. It tantalizes him with a craven and illusory security, while the poor man who accepts his insecurity shrugs off threats and is less filled with fear.

[11] If MT were retained in v. 11a, one would have to translate, 'Wealth made out of nothing (*mēhebel*) will dwindle', and the reference would be to wealth unrelated to honest effort ('speculative gains'). If this sense can be attached to *mēhebel*, the meaning of MT is approximately the same as that which results from Driver's emendation (*Biblica* 32, p. 180; *m*[e]*hubbāl*, 'obtained fraudulently') and the antithesis of this is the wealth which is acquired gradually through consistent and purposive effort and is a confirmation of character and worth. The opposition is made more explicit in LXX, on which the emendation *m^ebōhāl* 'hastily' (BH, Gemser, Ringgren, Barucq) is based. I have discussed a similar antithesis in *Ptahhotep* (see above, p. 64), where the greedy grasping of wealth is differentiated from the wealth which is an ingredient of distinction and merit. The increase of wealth (*yarbeh*) is then an index of a life which is moving towards its fitting climax. LXX reinterprets this in terms of Yahwistic piety: 'hastily with impiety' (*ἀνομία*), 'gradually with piety' (*εὐσεβεία*). Then it adds: 'The righteous man pities and lends'.

[12] A man is sickened by frustration and vitalized by the fulfilment of his desires. Long drawn out expectation which is again and again cheated of fulfilment and which repeatedly circumvents one obstacle only to discover that another has been erected and that the objective has again receded from view results in a special kind of illness – a loss of morale, a loss of belief in the possibility of imposing one's will on a situation and of shaping events decisively. The translating of a desire into reality is an exhilarating achievement which makes the blood course through the veins and creates the feeling that it is good to be alive and that life is abundant (on the phrase 'tree of life' see 3.18, above p. 296).

[19a] The same thought is expressed in v. 19a; desire realized is pleasurable to a *nepeš*, where 'pleasurable to a *nepeš*' is a metaphor which has its basis in the sensation of tasting appetizing food (i.e., appetizing to a palate, pleasant to the taste as it goes over the throat). There attaches to realized desire an experience of pleasure analogous to the pleasure of tasting appetizing food. LXX again reinterprets pietistically in v. 12 ('good desire') and especially in v. 19: 'The desires of the pious give pleasure to the soul, but the deeds of the impious are far from knowledge.'

Class B

[2] Verse 2a is almost synonymous with 12.14a (see above, p. 448), and it is odd that Ringgren translates the one, 'The good man eats from the fruit of his mouth', and the other, 'From the fruit of his mouth a man is satisfied with good'. The correct literal translation of v. 2a, noted by Ringgren as a possibility (p. 55, n.2), is, 'From the fruit of his mouth a man eats what is good'. Gemser, who deletes *ṭōb* in 12.14a, also translates 13.2a, 'The good man eats from the fruit of his mouth'. I take the sentence to mean that a good man's speech is socially fruitful and that he himself shares in the benefits which it creates, whereas wrong-headed or perverse men have an appetite (*nepeš*, see above, p. 459 on v. 19a for the elucidation of the metaphor) for disruption and violence (Barucq, 'feast on'; see on 10.6, above, p. 422; 11.30, above, pp. 432f; 13.14, above, p. 455). I disagree with Gemser's view that v. 2b means the same as 11.27b, namely, that the wrong-headed man will be hoist with his own petard. LXX moralizes: 'A good man eats from the fruit of righteousness, but the souls of impious men are destroyed prematurely.' Gemser has some support for his understanding of v. 2b from LXX, but Ringgren and Barucq take the same line as I have done. The roles of *rāšā'* and *ṣaddīq* are similarly envisaged in vv. 5 and 19b.

[5] The *ṣaddīq* hates falsehood which poisons personal relationships and is socially destructive, but the *rāšā'* rakes up dirt (literally, 'causes a bad smell') and spreads scandal. BH reads *yābīš*, 'creates shame', for MT *yab'īš*. Ackroyd (P. R. Ackroyd, *JTS* xliii, 1942, p. 160) takes *b'š* as a by-form of *bwš* and translates: 'An evil man causes shame and brings reproach' (the translations of Gemser, Ringgren and Barucq are similar). Gemser (p. 112) cites Arabic *ba'isa*, 'to be evil', hence the hiphil of *b'š* means 'to act basely'; also Arabic *ḫafira*, 'to be shy', 'to be confused', hence the hiphil of *ḥpr* means 'to cause confusion', 'to spread shame'. This produces two strictly synonymous verbs, but I am not persuaded that it is an improvement on the other possibility that 'causes a bad odour' is idiomatic for scandalmongering – a usage which can be transported into English. I take *yab'īš w^eyaḥpīr* as a *hendiadys*, 'spreads the smell of scandal'.

[19b] Verse 19b describes the obsession of the fool with his misanthropic attitudes and policies. Such a dedication to evil and single-minded pursuit of its ends, whatever cleverness and guile goes into it, is misguided and barren. Even with guile and cunning and a mastery of intrigue, this man is a fool and to his destructive behaviour there corresponds an inner darkness and perversion. Gemser proposes that the lack of connection between the two halves of v. 19 may be explained on the hypothesis that both are answers to separate riddles: What is pleasurable to the appetite? What is an abomination? The conjecture of BH (Kuhn) is far removed from MT and by-passes the problem of the verse rather than solving it (*w^etōḥelet k^esīlīm mūsār rā'*, 'But the expectation of fools is grievous discipline').

[17] In v. 17 the contrast is between the messenger or ambassador who deliberately engages in misrepresentation and sows seeds of dissention to the injury of others (reading *yappîl*, so BH, Gemser, Ringgren, Scott, following Reuss and others) and the utterly reliable envoy whose integrity and clarity of intention are above reproach. Such a person has therapeutic virtues and contributes to the health of the community. We are perhaps to think of men entrusted by principals with negotiations on whose outcome there is a good deal socially at stake, so that they either create welfare or make misery.

Class C

This consists of a group of sentences which outline the opposite effects of righteousness and wickedness and which are therefore expressions of a doctrine of theodicy (vv. 6, 9, 21, 22, 25). **[6]** Verse 6 contrasts the secure way of righteousness with the ruinous way of evil. Righteousness will guard him whose conduct is blameless (reading *tam*, cf. LXX^A ἄκακους; the verse is absent from LXX^B. MT: 'Righteousness will guard blameless conduct'), but evil will subvert sinners (*ḥaṭṭā't* abstract for collective or emend to *ḥaṭṭā'îm*, cf. Ringgren, p. 55 n.5). The other suggestion (BH, Gemser, Barucq), that *riš'ā* is abstract for concrete collective (Gemser, p. 112) or should be emended to *r^ešā'îm* (1 Hebrew Ms., LXX^A ἀσεβεῖς) is inferior, since *riš'ā* is a more precise antithesis of *ṣ^edāqā* than *ḥaṭṭā't*, and so 'evil subverts sinners' is better than 'sin subverts evil men' (see, however, v. 21, where *ḥaṭṭā'îm* is the antithesis of *ṣaddîqîm*).

[9] In v. 9 the emendation of *yiśmaḥ* to *yizraḥ* (BH, cf. Gemser) is not required, but the meaning is 'bright' rather than 'joyful' (Barucq). Driver (*Biblica* 32, p. 180) cites Ugaritic *pnm tšmḫ*, 'his face was lit up with joy', which illustrates the semantic relationship between 'brightness' and 'joy' (*CML*, pp. 50f.; *Aqhat* II, 11.9), and Kopf derives the meaning 'shining with a full flame', from Arabic *smḫ* (L. Kopf, *VT* ix, 1959, p. 276, n.3; cf. Ringgren 'shines clear'). Gemser elucidates in a general way the symbolism of light. The burning lamp is the sign of a house which is inhabited and where there is an ongoing family life; the extinguished lamp is to be found in the deserted house, once the home of a family which is now no more. I have suggested a more precise origin for the allusion to the extinguishing of the lamp (see on 24.20, above, p. 405). The meaning of the symbolism here is that the righteous will enjoy vitality and fulfilment, but the wicked will be cut off (cf. 10.27, above, p. 425).

[21] Similarly, v. 21 states that evil will pursue sinners, while *ṭôb*, 'good fortune' or 'happiness' (Barucq), will reward the righteous – the antithesis of punishment and reward is obvious. Gemser follows LXX (τοὺς δὲ δικαίους καταλήμψεται ἀγαθά), and reads *weʾet ṣaddīqīm yaśśīgēm ṭōb*, 'but good will overtake (them) the righteous'.

[22] According to v. 22 a good man transmits the material benefits which accrue from his goodness to his posterity, but a sinner's wealth is held in store (not for his own posterity but) for a righteous man. 'A man plants olive trees for his grandchildren' (E.F.F.B.). **[25]** In v. 25 there is the contrast between the righteous man who eats his fill (*nepeš*, 'appetite'), and evil men who never have enough to eat and suffer the pangs of hunger.

[23] Verse 23, which I have not classified, apparently says that the fields (*nīr*, perhaps marginal land, newly broken in for growing crops, cf. Gemser) of poor men yield plenty, but the produce is often misappropriated (literally, 'swept away') because of inequity. In other words, it would be possible to live well by the careful cultivation of poor land were it not for the oppressive exactions which rob the peasant of the fruit of his toil. Toy's translation of v. 23b: 'but many a man perishes through injustice' supplies a weak and inconsequential antithesis to v. 23a. What is the connection between marginal land yielding an abundance of food or the like (cf. Toy) and men perishing through injustice? Boström translates v. 23b: 'But there is (a kind of wealth) which is swept away because of an absence of equity', and understands this of speculative gains in doubtful mercantile transactions – especially usury. The 'absence of equity' consists not in the confiscating of well-earned wealth, but in the manner of acquiring that wealth itself. Boström then supposes that this is one of the sentences in which the 'agricultural ideal' which he detects in the book of Proverbs finds expression. The antithesis is between the fundamentally honest and productive work of the peasant and the transient gains of the speculator (Boström, pp. 65f.; cf. 13.11, above, pp. 458f.). Toy's objection that such an 'agricultural ideal' is utopian is an argument against its validity, but not against its existence, so that it does not impinge on Boström's exegesis.

LXX transforms the sentence into a clear-cut expression of the doctrine of theodicy: 'The righteous will pass many years in wealth, but the unrighteous will be speedily destroyed.' BH's proposal to read *yešārīm* (LXX δίκαιοι) in v. 23a would introduce a note of piety into MT, as would also Gemser's suggestion (p. 112) that *rāʾšīm* should be connected with Arabic *rasā* 'to swagger', *rawsu* 'braggard', 'swaggerer', and translated 'arrogant men'. According to BH there is the antithesis of justice and injustice, and according to Gemser arrogance and inequity are the twin defects of those who are deprived of what they produce.

My own suggestion is that *rā'šîm* here, as in 28.3 (see below, pp. 628f.), should be translated 'notables', 'grandees' (literally, 'heads', 'chiefs'), and that the verse should be rendered: 'The tilth of grandees produces an abundance of food, but it is swept away for lack of equity.' The sentence would then be a statement of the doctrine of theodicy and would belong to class C. Plenty which is raised on a foundation of injustice will not be consolidated into enduring wealth. However sound its basis may seem to be, it will be overtaken by disaster and will end in want.

Chapter 14

Class A: vv. 1, 3, 4, 5, 6, 7, 8, 10, 12 (?), 13, 15, 16, 17, 18, 20, 23, 24, 25, 28, 29, 30, 33, 35.
Class B: vv. 21 (?), 22, 31.
Class C: vv. 2, 9 (?), 11, 14, 19, 26, 27, 32, 34.

The sentences have, for the most part, antithetic parallelism, the exceptions being vv. 10, 13, 19, 26 which have synthetic parallelism (see 13.14, above, p. 455, for the form of v. 27).

Class A

A group is formed by those sentences in which there features a 'fool-sage' antithesis, or the like (vv. 3, 6, 7, 16, 24, 33). [3] MT (v. 3a) is translated by Toy 'In the mouth of a fool is a sprig of pride' (similarly Barucq, 'shoot of pride', citing Isa. 11.1 in support); the meaning then is that his boastful or arrogant speech grows out of an inner *hubris* – the roots of pride are deep. This is not a particularly apt antithesis to v. 3b, which states that wise men speak in such a way as to increase rather than diminish their own security. They avoid rashness and carelessness; they take thought of the consequences of what they say and weigh their words carefully. Habits of speech which would contrast with this are indicated by emending v. 3a so that it reads: 'In the mouth of a fool is a rod for his back' (*gēwō* for *ga'awā*, so BH, Gemser, Ringgren). The fool, unlike the sage, speaks to his own disadvantage, and through his indiscretions is his own worst enemy. He brings on himself trouble and hostility which a man

Intellectual discrimination, keen critical acumen & disciplined and mature judgement

of good sense would avoid by holding his tongue or choosing his words with care.

[6] The unteachability of the arrogant man (see on 13.1, above, p. 453) is the subject of v. 6. His quest after wisdom is vain, because he does not have the capacity for intellectual humility nor for educational discipline, and so he is the despair of a wisdom teacher. Knowledge is easy for the man with intellectual discrimination (*nābōn*) whose critical acumen is keen and whose judgement is disciplined and mature. I am quite unable to agree with Toy and Gemser, who suppose that there is a religious or moralistic nuance in the contrast of *lēṣ* with *nābōn*. The *lēṣ* is here intellectually arrogant and not impious as in Ps. 1.1. Gemser's statement that 'Wisdom is a matter of reverence and the submission of the heart' does not take the point of the sentence correctly.

[7] Verse 7 is a fragment of Instruction rather than a wisdom sentence, as is indicated by the imperative in v. 7a. Since v. 7a advises avoidance of the company of a fool, the expectation is that v. 7b should recommend the companionship of those who speak knowledgeably, in which case the sentence would be saying much the same kind of thing as 13.20 (see above, pp. 456f.). But v. 7b does not yield such a contrast, and it can hardly be translated as a motive clause (as Barucq does: 'Avoid a foolish man, for you will not make the acquaintance of knowledgeable lips'). Ringgren tries to make sense of MT by translating *lēk minneged* as 'encounter' and not 'avoid': 'Encounter a foolish man and you will not make the acquaintance of knowledgeable lips.' This is a weak sentence, and 'encounter' is a mistranslation of *lēk minneged*. LXX is far removed from MT, but it does indicate the kind of antithesis which is desiderated: 'Everything is contrary to a foolish man, but wise lips are discerning weapons.' BH emends *ūbal yādaʿtā* to *ūbahēl r*^{e}*ʿōt* and Gemser to *w*^{e}*'al taddaḥ 'et*: 'But hasten to be the companion of knowledgeable lips', or, 'But do not repulse knowledgeable lips'. Dahood (p. 31) suggests that *bal* should be translated 'surely' (Ugaritic *bl*) and that *ydʿ* is dialectal for *yzʿ* as in 10.32 (see above, p. 424). 'You will surely flow with lips of knowledge' is a very odd and improbable expression. I follow Gemser.

[16] In v. 16, the cautiousness or canniness of the wise is contrasted with the rashness and vast self-assurance of the fool. That the sage is 'fearful' does not mean that he is excessively timid and irresolute, but that he does not overestimate his own capabilities and does not underrate the difficulties and dangers involved in a given course of action.

His action always depends on a careful and acute balancing of the risks and rewards, and where involvement is disadvantageous and dangerous he avoids it. The conduct of the fool is marked by a lack of self-restraint and self-criticism. His lack of moderation causes him to rush into trouble, and his inflated estimate of his powers gives him a false sense of security. An alternative sense for v. 16b is suggested by Gemser: 'But the fool is negligent (Syriac *ʿbr*, *ethpᵉel*, 'to be neglectful') and falls' (Arabic 7th form, *inbaṭaḥa*; similarly L. Kopf, *VT* viii, 1958, p. 165, n.4). The fool, unlike the sage, is unwary, and because he does not sense danger falls into it. I regard this, however, as an improbable elucidation of *bōṭēaḥ*, which is almost certainly to be rendered 'self-assured', 'over-confident'. LXX apparently read *mitʿārēb* (MT *mitʿabbēr*), which it rendered by μίγνυται, 'mixes'. This makes the sentence turn on the avoidance of bad company (cf. v. 7): 'A wise man, because he is afraid, turns aside from an evil man, but the fool, trusting in himself, mixes with an impious person.' Thus LXX understood *bōṭēaḥ* as 'self-assured'. If *mitʿārēb ūbōṭēaḥ* were read, the meaning would be that one type of fool is the man who has a greatly exaggerated and ill-founded self-confidence and who is constantly interfering in one thing or another, oblivious to the dangers which he incurs by his officiousness.

[24] MT in v. 24b is so weak ('The folly of fools is folly') that it can hardly be supposed to conserve the original. No help is offered by LXX, which apparently has substituted a moralizing generalization: 'The conduct of fools is wicked'. Nor does Reider's proposal, that there is a punning conceit in the repetition of *'iwwelet* and that the first instance should be derived from *'wl* ('to be in front', 'to lead'), have a high degree of probability. This is associated with the derivation of *ʿošrām* from a cognate of Arabic *ʿaṭara*, which should also be rejected. Reider translates: 'The crown of the wise is their cleverness, the prominence of fools is their folly' (J. Reider, *VT* ii, 1952, p. 125). Dahood (p. 31f.) translates v. 24b: 'The throne of fools is their folly, associating the first *'iwwelet* with Ugaritic *alt*, 'prop', 'support', 'throne' (?), and supposing that a deliberate pun on *'iwwelet*, 'folly', has been contrived. But the equation *alt* = *'iwwelet* is more than dubious (cf. *CML*, p. 136, n.10), and 'wreath' (see below) is a better parallel to 'crown' than 'throne'. The emendation of *ʿošrām* to *ʿormātām*, 'their shrewdness' (BH, Gemser, Ringgren), is obliquely indicated by LXX πανοῦργος, 'versatile' (used to translate *ʿārūm* in v. 8). BH (also Gemser and Ringgren) solves the problem of v. 24b by conjecturing *weliwyat* for the first *'iwwelet*, so that the translation then runs: 'The crown of sages is their shrewdness, but the wreath of fools is folly' (or 'their folly', *'iwwaltām*, so BH and Gemser). 'Wreath' is an apt antithesis of 'crown', and some such emendation is necessary, but *'ošrām*, 'their wealth', should be retained in v. 24a. The sentence means that wealth is a fitting adornment of wisdom and is an aspect of the general recognition of his worth to which a wise man is entitled. His wealth is not an extraneous factor nor an alien intrusion, but is a confirmation of his intrinsic merit as a sage and the position of commanding influence which he has attained. It is therefore associated with the climax of his career and in this sense is the crown of his efforts. The fool can only expect to be garlanded in a derisory way. His fêting will consist in the publicizing of his folly, as if he were to process ceremonially wearing a wreath of folly. The wise man can anticipate a growing recognition of his worth and the fool an increasingly more damaging exposure of his deficiencies.

[33] LXX and Pesh. appear to have solved the textual problem in v. 33b by inserting the negative particle, and are followed in this respect by Gemser. In the mind of a perceptive man Wisdom finds a congenial place to lodge, but is a stranger to the mind of fools – it (or 'she'; there is at least a quasi-personification of wisdom here) has not made their acquaintance. The substitution of *'iwwelet* for *tiwwādēa'* (Toy, BH) supplies the obvious antithesis for *ḥokmā*, but it does not at all grapple with MT. Winton Thomas (*JTS* xxxv, 1934, pp. 302f.) connects *tiwwādēa'* with Arabic *wd'* as in 10.9 (see above, p. 423). The verse can then be translated: 'Wisdom rests in the mind of a perceptive man, but within fools it is suppressed.' A man of intellectual discrimination is hospitable to Wisdom, who in turn finds him congenial. The fool is inhospitable and domineering, as his folly inevitably makes him, and Wisdom cannot thole him.

Another group is constituted by the topic of the discipline of wisdom and its bearing on conduct – wisdom as a way of life (vv. 8, 12, 15, 18). **[8]** Wisdom is a shrewdness or sagacity in virtue of which a man picks his steps along the road of life with discernment (reading *tābīn*). Opposed to this sure sense of direction and unerring precision of course is the *mirmā* which is the product of folly, and I would suggest that, as in 12.20 (see above, p. 447), this means 'self-deceit' – a state of inner darkness and confusion (cf. Gemser, who suggests a more comprehensive meaning for deceit. It means deceiving others as well as self-deceit). LXX ἐνπ λάνῃ might be thought to point to *meramme*, 'misleads', 'leads (others) astray' (D. Winton Thomas, *VTS* iii, p. 286; cf. BH *maṭʿā* = πλάνη), but it produces weaker parallelism than *mirmā*, 'self-deceit'. The contrast should be between clarity and confusion, between keeping an exact course and lacking any sense of direction (this, rather than a reference to leading others astray, is what is desiderated in v. 8b).

[15] In v. 15, the credulity of the *petī* (the untutored youth) is opposed to the nice, critical discrimination of the *ʿārūm*. The *petī* believes everything that he hears, but the *ʿārūm* picks his steps with discernment. Thus v. 15b appears to resume the metaphor of the road in the manner of v. 8a – not exactly what is expected in view of v. 15a. On the other hand, it could be supposed that to pick one's step is here metaphorical for a process of critical sifting whereby the credible is separated from the incredible, although the metaphor more naturally refers to conduct than to ratiocination. LXX 'proceeds with delibera-tion' is too general a rendering to give much help with MT. Gemser (p. 112) suggests that the consonants of MT should be vocalized *l*^{e}*'ašš*^{e}*rō* and the sentence translated: 'A *petī* believes every word, but an *ʿārūm* knows how to verify it' (*'šr* 'verify' as in Aramaic and Mishnaic Hebrew). This provides the desired antithesis, but MT should be retained. **[18]** Verse 18 also turns on the contrast between *p*^{e}*tā'īm* and *ʿ*^{a}*rūmīm*, employing imagery which resembles that of v. 24 (see above, p. 465). *nāḥ*^{a}*lū* (MT) should be vocalized *neḥ*^{e}*lū* (**ḥalā*, whence *ḥ*^{a}*lī*, 'necklace'; cf. Arabic *ḥalā*), and the sentence then reads: 'Untutored youths are adorned with folly, but shrewd men wear a crown of knowledge' (G. R. Driver, *Biblica* 32, p. 181). Verse 18a (MT), 'Untutored youths have inherited folly', gives poor sense. They do not inherit folly; rather, folly is their condition before the educational process begins to make its impact on them. The 'folly' is here the uneducated state which is characteristic of all *p*^{e}*tā'īm* and which can be changed into 'knowledge', if they are amenable to the intellectual discipline imposed by the wisdom teacher. If they are incapable of submitting to this rigorous discipline and suppose that they know everything already, such a self-opinionated stance, indicative as it is of arrogance and unteachability, will lead to death (cf. v. 12).

[12] This sentence should not be understood as an expression of pietism, but as an allusion to the two ways of life and death which are a prominent feature of chs. 1–9, where discipline is a way of life and indiscipline a way of death. Consequently it should not be thought that v. 12b touches on the subject of immortality and that *'aḥ^a^rīt* has that kind of significance. The opposite of the way of death is not immortality, but a this-worldly way of life which is assured to those who pay attention to the concrete guidance contained in the traditional teaching of wisdom. 'The ways of death' is a phrase which is probably to be traced back to the mythology which is evident in the forms of expression used in 1–9 (see on 1.12, above, pp. 269f.; 2.18f., above, pp. 287f.; 5.5, above, p. 314; 7.25–27, above, p. 341; 9.18, above, p. 367). The incorrigible man is on a road which will ultimately lead to the underworld – to the depths of Sheol. A good example of a reinterpretation of this antithesis of discipline and indiscipline in terms of Yahwistic piety is afforded by 3.7, where being wise in one's own eyes is the opposite of fearing Yahweh and relinquishing evil. Thus the authority of Yahweh has replaced that of the wisdom teacher, and being wise in one's own eyes has become a form of irreverence and impiety rather than a refusal to submit to an educational discipline.

[17] The *'īš m^e^zimmōt* is the deliberate man who can remain calm even under provocation, who shuns displays of temper and uses all his resourcefulness to take the heat out of a situation. The comparison of *'īš m^e^zimmōt* in this verse with its use in 12.2b gives an interesting insight into the reinterpretation of the vocabulary of wisdom. There *'īš m^e^zimmōt* is the one who receives Yahweh's condemnation and is the opposite of the good man (see above, p. 448). The only textual problem in v. 17 is constituted by *yiśśānē'*, 'is hated', and I would suggest that this has arisen because a pejorative sense has erroneously been attributed to *'īš m^e^zimmōt*. LXX: 'A sagacious man endures much (provocation)' furnishes a good antithesis. Hence Toy emends to *yiśśā'*, 'endures' and Kuhn (cf. BH, Gemser) to *yiš'^a^nān*, 'remains tranquil'. Winton Thomas proposes a solution which leaves the consonants of MT intact (*yišnē'* = *yišneh*, see on 5.9, above, p. 316): 'But the deliberate man is exalted', i.e., attains rank and dignity (D. W. Thomas, *VTS* iii, p. 286). The phlegmatic man is temperamentally suited to the responsibilities and strains of high office, but the man of volcanic disposition who easily erupts into ungovernable passion will act precipitately and irresponsibly at the least provocation and is a menace in a seat of power.

[29] The same kind of thinking is represented by the contrast of patience and impatience, imperturbability and testiness in v. 29. The person who will not allow himself to be ruffled or goaded into unwise courses has a great deal of insight. He has this insight or perspicacity (*tᵉbūnā*) just because he does not allow his thoughts to be clouded by passion and will not be shifted from his habit of cool appraisal. His equable temperament is an ally of his clear mind; in this he stands out in marked contrast to the person who is always reacting in temper and engendering heat and who, as a consequence, elevates (BH: *marbe*, 'multiplies') folly (cf. especially the opposition of the tranquil and the passionate man in *Amenemope* (see above, pp. 106f.)).

[5] Two sentences (vv. 5, 25) are forensic in character. A truthful witness does not tell lies, but a perjurer utters falsehoods (on *yāpīaḥ* here and in v. 25 see on 12.17, above, p. 445). **[25]** *yāpīaḥ* (a verb) is better in v. 5 and *yᵉpīaḥ* (a noun) in v. 25. 'A perjurer is a false witness' (*yᵉpīaḥ*, a noun) is weak and tautological in v. 5b. The word order of v. 5b is explicable as *chiasmus*. In 6.19 *yᵉpīaḥ kᵉzābīm* should be read and 'a perjurer, a false witness' counts as one item in the numerical saying. The truthful witness 'saves lives' in so far as his honest testimony enables the judicial processes to function effectively and obviates any miscarriage of justice. The witness who is a liar hinders the judge from arriving at the true facts of the case, and so deliberately obscures and confounds the issues. In so far as he darkens the truth and abets injustice he is 'deceit'. Ringgren (also KB[2]) suggests the pointing *mᵉrammeh*, 'misleads', i.e., leads the judge astray (see on 14.8, above, p. 466). Gemser (p. 112) suggests 'slanderer' (abstract for concrete collective, Syriac *rammī* 'slander', 'defame'). I follow Ringgren.

Two sentences (vv. 28, 35) contain 'royal wisdom'; one is occupied with the status of the king himself and the other with his attitude towards his officials. **[28]** A throne is insubstantial unless there is a kingdom to govern, and the more numerous a king's subjects, the more impressive is his royal dignity. What may be hinted at further is that a king should base his rule on a wide measure of public support, and then v. 28b would be more meaningful and not just a statement of the obvious. If a ruler has no subjects, his rule is illusory; but *mᵉḥittā* 'downfall', 'ruin' is then a strange word to use in connection with this charade. *mᵉḥittā* makes sense if the allusion is to loss of confidence in his rule and the withdrawal of popular allegiance. It is this which topples a ruler. Another possibility is that *'epes lᵉ'ōm* means 'reduction of population', in which case the sentence can be elucidated in relation to the policies of such modern states as France and the Soviet Union who are chary of birth control for political reasons – because they believe that any downward trend in their population weakens their position in the world. Verse 28b then says that erosion of population leads to the toppling of a ruler.

[35] The subject of v. 35 is the rewards and hazards of serving the king in an office of state. The *'ebed maśkīl* has a sure grasp of affairs; he always sees the point, is relevant, competent and incisive (cf. *PWM*, pp. 67f.), and it is for these reasons that he earns the king's approval and is marked out for preferment. The *mēbīš* is the bungler who botches the king's business and whose indiscretions and incapacity expose his master to scandal and criticism. The grammar of v. 35b is difficult, and *tahărōg* has been suggested for *tihye* (BH, Gemser, Ringgren). LXX reads:

> An able man is acceptable to a king,
> But by his own initiative he (i.e., the king) will remove dishonour.
> Anger destroys even a sagacious man.

The first two lines of LXX are the ones which correspond to MT (although the correspondence is defective in the second line, 'dishonour' would seem to go back to *mēbīš*), and so ἀπόλλυσιν in the third line does not really support *tahărōg*. *lᵉ* should be inserted before *mēbīš*, or *tᵉhawwe* should be read for *tihye* on the basis of Aramaic and Arabic usage, 'to bring down', 'to cause the downfall of', 'to axe' (in our idiom) (cf. Gemser, p. 112). Barr suggests (privately) that it may be the king's anger which is described as *mēbīš* (cf. the use of *pōṭēr* in 17.14; *pōṭēr mayim*, 'water which seeps'). Verse 35b would then run, 'But his anger ruins reputations'. This, however, makes *mēbīš* a defective parallel to *'ebed maśkīl*. Reference to a person, the opposite of an able servant, is required.

A larger group, less sharply defined, touches on various aspects of prudence (vv. 4, 10, 13, 20, 23, 30). **[4]** The interpretation of v. 4 is complicated by the obscurity of *bār* and the doubt whether it can mean 'clean' (so Toy). This is how it is understood by LXX (*φάτναι καθαραί*), and it has the sense 'morally pure' in Song of Songs 6.2. I regard it as unlikely that *'ēbūs bār* means 'a clean crib' or 'an empty crib' (Gemser, Barucq). Dahood (pp. 30f.) adduces Job 22.9 in support of the translation 'empty': 'The arms of the orphans are empty' (*dk'* = *dkh*, dialectal for *zkh*; cf. G. R. Driver, *JRAS*, 1948, p. 168, n.3). The suggestion is that the semantic development from 'pure' to 'empty', postulated for *bar*, is found in *zkh*. If this is how it is to be taken, the sentence is balancing the advantages of not having draught oxen against the disadvantages. It will mean a reduction of labour – the crib will not have to be cleaned out – but there will be a loss of production, since it will not be possible to grow the same weight of crops.

My own opinion is that *bār* means 'grain' (KB[2]; KB[3], 'empty'), and I am not convinced that the emendation of *'ēbūs* to *'epes* is necessary (Toy, Ringgren; cf. BH, KB[3]): 'Where there are no oxen there is no corn'. I understand the sentence to say, rather, that draught animals are an indispensable asset for a farmer and that without them his labour is unproductive. MT should be translated as it stands: 'Where there are no oxen, there is a crib of grain, but crops are increased by the strength of an ox.' The balance between the grain which oxen consume and their productive capacity has to be ascertained. They are a kind of capital equipment which has to be used economically; it is important not to have too few or too many, but to employ the number which secures the maximum production at the lowest costs. LXX finds in v. 4b a reference to the reproductive power of the bull: 'Where there are many births the strength of a bull is evident' (cf. Barucq). The supposition that the verse is an injunction to take good care of farm animals (Toy, Gemser, Barucq) is not well-founded.

[10] Verse 10 is a comment on the privacy of joy and sorrow. There is an experience of bitterness which is so inward and private that the individual must bear it in loneliness and cannot communicate it even to those who are closest to him. So it is also with joy; no one can participate except the person who immediately experiences it; it, too, in its essence, is incommunicable. **[13]** The point of v. 13 is rather that the separation of laughter and tears, of joy and sorrow, is never completely effected. There is no joy without alloy of sorrow; beneath laughter there is pain of heart and the final outcome of joy is grief (the word division of MT should be altered and *'aḥarīt haśśimḥā* read).

[20] Verse 20 observes that a poor man is a liability to his friend, who may find it difficult to beat out a smouldering resentment that the relationship makes so heavy demands on him. In spite of himself he will come to feel that the friendship is burdensome and that the poor man is a mill-stone around his neck. Consequently he will feel hatred rather than love for his friend. The terms of friendship with a rich man are altogether different. Those who surround him and enjoy his hospitality are not above suspicion of being there for what they can get. Even where there is a deeper relationship between the rich man and his friends, it is a friendship which makes no demands on them. They stand to gain, but they have no liability.

[23] The theme of v. 23 is 'deeds, not words'. Hard work results in solid gain, but verbosity is a barren occupation which produces nothing and leads to a condition of want.

[30] If *marpē'* (v. 30) is to be derived from *rph* (KB², Gemser, Ringgren), *lēb marpē'* is 'a tranquil mind' which is then contrasted with jealousy. *marpē'*, derived from *rp'*, with the sense 'therapy' as in 12.18 and 13.17, does not seem to fit the phrase *lēb marpē'*; 'mind of healing' (LXX 'doctor of the heart') can hardly be understood as 'healthy mind', which would furnish a good antithesis to jealousy. The verse apparently says that mental calmness and repose produce physical health and jealousy a feeling of extreme malaise. If this is so, the modernity of the verse is striking, since its observation has to do with psycho-somatic relationships – it states that the mind is the seat of health or illness. Calmness or repose is conducive to physical well-being and jealousy to a condition of sickness (on 'decay of the bones' see 12.4, above, p. 443).

[1] It would seem that v. 1 alludes to a personified Wisdom (Gemser, Ringgren, Barucq: 'Dame Sagesse'), and represents her in the same way as 9.1 (see above, pp. 360f.). It is therefore unlikely that the text has been correctly preserved by MT, 'The wisest of women builds her house' (LXX 'wise women'; Toy, 'The wise among women build [everyone] her house'). Dahood (p. 30) cites Ugaritic *'mq nšm* 'wisest of men' (*Aqhat* II.vi. 44, *CML*, pp. 54f.). Gemser changes the vocalization to *ḥokmōt* as in 1.20 and deletes *nāšīm*. This makes v. 1a identical with 9.1a, where I have noted Albright's suggestion that *ḥokmōt* may be singular and not plural (see above, p. 363). The antithesis in v. 1 is then tidy and credible; the constructiveness of Wisdom and perhaps also her hospitality (see on 9.1–6, above, pp. 360f.) are opposed to the destructiveness of Folly, which has no occupation other than to destroy what Wisdom has created. The unsolved puzzle is the presence of *nāšīm* in MT and the fact that it was already in the text which lay before the Greek translator (cf. Barucq). Barucq's proposal that *ḥokmōt nāšīm* means Dame Sagesse, *nāšīm* agreeing with the plural *ḥokmōt*, is a counsel of desperation. BH is no more successful, for the rightness of *bānᵉtā* is above suspicion and BH has to change this in order to accommodate his tentative emendation of *nāšīm* to *tāšīm*. I have followed Gemser.

Class B

Humanitarianism appears as a religious demand in vv. 21 and 31, which are consequently difficult to classify. Because their social concern is so manifest I have allocated them to class B rather than class C. **[21]** He who despises his neighbour is a sinner, but he who has compassion on the poor will be blessed. **[31]** To act oppressively against a poor man is to insult his Maker (the suffix refers to the poor man, not the oppressor), but in effectively expressing sympathy for him one gives honour to God (cf. Matt. 25.31f., especially v. 40: 'I tell you this: anything you did for one of my brothers here, however humble, you did for me'). **[21]** The emendation of *lᵉrēʿēhū* to *lᵉrāʿēb* in v. 21a (LXX: πένητας, 'poor') as suggested by Gemser (*rēʿēhū* a dittograph, cf. v. 20) and BH, is unnecessary.

The harmony of self-interest and humanitarian concern which is indicated by v. 21b is further expressed by v. 22. **[22]** There are those who fashion evil plans (*ḥōrᵉšē rāʿ*) with all the skill and artistry which a craftsman (*ḥārāš*) would lavish on an object of art (see on 6.14, above, p. 325). Here, then, is skill and artistry in the service of malevolence. Over against these are *ḥōrᵉšē ṭōb*, who are equally fastidious in their planning, but whose objectives are benevolent. In the one case skill is perverted and so is employed to socially destructive ends; in the other it addresses itself to the enrichment of the life of the community. The malicious planners go astray; their anti-social stance is matched by a condition of inner darkness. They have a radical taint and twist, and they are like men who have wandered far from the right road and are lost in a trackless wasteland. Those who take thought for the well-being of their fellows and whose conduct is motivated by beneficence will be repaid with loyalty and constancy. Their stance will be reciprocated and their place in the regard of their fellows assured. Or, possibly, the meaning is that those who plan what is good 'are loyalty and constancy'. Their attitudes are those of settled benevolence. They have an unwavering sense of social responsibility. The question (*hᵃlō'*) is, according to Toy (cf. Ringgren), equivalent to emphatic assertion. *hᵃlō'* is not translated by LXX.

Class C

The 'fear of Yahweh' in vv. 2, 26, 27 is a reinterpretation of the educational concept of discipline which I have discussed in vv. 8, 12, 15, and 18. Discipline consists in reverence for Yahweh and not in respect for the authority of a wisdom teacher; the transition from education to piety has been made. **[27]** This can be best demonstrated by a comparison of v. 27 with 13.14 (above, p. 455). Verse 27b and 13.14b are identical; in 13.14b it is the *tōrā* of the wisdom teacher which is a fountain of life and a safeguard against the snares of death. The reinterpretation in v. 27 has been effected by substituting *yir'at YHWH* for *tōrat ḥākām* (on 'fountain of life' and 'snares of death' see 13.14, above, p. 455). LXX, πρόσταγμα κυρίου = *tōrat YHWH* is a more precise reinterpretation than MT. For the instruction of the *ḥākām* is substituted the Law of Yahweh. Wisdom for the road of life is contained in the Law of Yahweh and not in the prudential norms of the sages. Thus piety and impiety, rather than discipline and indiscipline in relation to educational demands, constitute the two ways of life and death.

[2] Similarly v. 2 also employs the metaphor of the two ways, the straight way and the twisted way, which are correlated with piety and impiety, with reverence for Yahweh and contempt for him. No doubt there is also a moralizing nuance to straight and crooked – uprightness and candour are opposed to deviousness and shiftiness. **[26]** According to v. 26, it is in the fear of Yahweh that security is to be found, where perhaps the home of a pious man is envisaged as a stronghold, surrounded by Yahweh's protection, so that the children who live in it are also safe (translating v. 26b, 'and for his children it will be a safe place' [Gemser, cf. RSV] rather than 'and for his children he [Yahweh] will be a safe place' [Ringgren, Barucq]). The sense yielded by the latter translation is inferior.

There is a large group in which schematic opposition of reward and punishment in relation to righteous and wicked respectively is evident (vv. 11, 14, 19, 32, 34). **[11]** The household of the wicked will be destroyed, but the tent (an archaism introduced to avoid the repetition of *bayit*, but no differentiation of meaning is intended) of the upright will flourish (LXX 'will endure'). Perhaps *'ōhel* should be translated 'family' (Arabic, *'ahlu*, 'people'), i.e., those who occupy the same tent (cf. KB[3]). The *bayit* is the indispensable foundation of prosperity and status (see on 12.4, above, p. 443; on the protection afforded to the house of the pious man see 14.26, above, p. 474). **[14]** A renegade (*sūg lēb*) will receive the satisfaction which his 'ways' merit and likewise a good man for his deeds(?). MT is unintelligible in v. 14b, and *mē'ālāw* has to be emended to *mimma'alālāw*, 'deeds', or *mimma'agālāw*, 'tracks' (which would be a more precise parallel to 'ways'). Two different ways of life are portrayed, and although reward and punishment are not explicitly mentioned there is no doubt that *'îš ṭôb* is to get the one and *sûg lēb* the other.

[19] A different manifestation of the doctrine of theodicy is considered in v. 19, namely, the subordination of the wicked to the righteous in the order which is established and enforced by Yahweh. The righteous will be a ruler-class to which the wicked will be subservient. The meaning of v. 19b is probably that the wicked will be the domestic servants of the righteous. This is how it was understood by LXX: 'Impious men will serve the gates of the righteous'.

[32] The schematism of reward and punishment is unmistakably present in v. 32, although v. 32b is obscure. If it is translated, 'But the righteous man finds refuge in his (the wicked man's) death', it means that the *ṣaddîq* is protected from the disaster which overthrows the *rāšā'* (so G. Bertram, *ZAW* 54, 1936, p. 165). But *ḥsh* (see KB²) means 'seeks safety' rather than 'finds safety' and, if MT is to read, it must be translated: 'But the righteous man seeks safety (in Yahweh), even in his death' (cf. Barucq: 'But the just man has confidence even at his death'). This would have to be taken as evidence of a belief in an after-life. I do not believe that the sentence originally asserted this, and LXX (v. 32b) supplies a more apt antithesis to v. 32a: 'But he who relies on his own piety is a righteous man'. This points to *beṭummô* rather than *bemôtô* (the order of *t* and *m* accidentally reversed and *w* inserted, so BH, Gemser and Ringgren). The *rāšā'* will be destroyed because of his wickedness, but the *ṣaddîq* will seek security in his integrity, i.e., his *tôm* guarantees him safety.

[34] According to v. 34, theodicy operates in respect of nations as well as of individuals. Righteousness elevates the status of a nation, gives it a standing in the world and makes it a power for good; sin depresses its influence and brings it into disrepute. There is no difficulty in translating *ḥesed* 'disgrace', and the sense is weaker if *ḥeser*, 'want', is read, as it apparently was by the Greek translator.

[9] Verse 9 (MT) reads: 'Fools scoff at a guilt-offering, but among upright men is approval'. This is the most obscure verse in the chapter, and v. 9a is particularly suspect. There is a lack of agreement between subject and verb, and even if this is overlooked (as it is in the translations of Barucq and Ringgren), the statement that fools scoff at a guilt-offering introduces an unexpected cultic reference. If *'āšām* is to be taken seriously and not to be dismissed as an obvious corruption (G. R. Driver, *Biblica* 32, p. 181, 'The whole verse is not above suspicion'), we should have to suppose that *rāṣôn* in v. 9b is 'acceptance' in a cultic context. Driver suggests that v. 9b should be translated: 'But upright men discern (*ūbān* or *ūbānū*) what is acceptable', i.e., they do not despise the *'āšām* but avail themselves of its provisions, in order that Yahweh may regard them with *rāṣōn* (on the correlation of *rāṣōn* and *ṣᵉdāqā* see 12.2, above, p. 448). This can hardly be accepted as a satisfactory elucidation of the verse, but the only alternative is to embark on massive emendation as Gemser has done. LXX reads: 'The houses of the impious have need of purification, but the houses of the righteous are acceptable'. Gemser inserts *'ohᵒlē* (LXX οἰκίαι) as an accusative of place, emends *yalīṣ* to *yālīn* and *bēn* to *battē* (LXX οἰκίαι): 'Guilt lodges in the tents (on 'tents' see 14.11, above, p. 474) of fools, but acceptance in the houses of upright men' (cf. BH: 'Guilt is in the tents of scorners, but acceptance in the house of upright men'). There is no foundation to BH's claim that LXX supports *lēṣīm*. παρανόμων is in all probability a translation of *'ᵉwīlīm*, and there is no reason to suppose that it translates *lēṣīm*, since it is not used elsewhere in Proverbs to render *lēṣ* or *lēṣīm*. On the other hand, Gemser and BH (also Barucq) would seem to be right in taking *'āšām* as abstract and the antithesis of *rāṣōn*. This excludes the cultic reference, which seems to me to be improbable. Barucq is mistaken in his assertion that *rāṣōn* here means simply a state of contentment and not Yahweh's approval (cf. LXX δεκταί). *'āšām* is the guilt which brings Yahweh's disapproval, and is perhaps used loosely for 'disapproval', and so is the antithesis of *rāṣōn*. The verse is an unsolved problem. I translate: 'Fools scoff at guilt, but upright men discern (*ūbānū*) what is acceptable'.

Chapter 15

Class A: vv. 1, 2, 5, 7, 10, 12, 13, 14, 15, 18, 19, 20, 21, 22, 23, 24, 30, 31, 32.
Class B: vv. 4, 17(?), 26, 28.
Class C: vv. 3, 6, 8, 9, 11, 16, 25, 27, 29, 33.

The sentences have mostly an antithetic structure, but there are five cases of synthetic parallelism (vv. 12, 23, 30, 31, 33), and two with a 'better ... than' structure are contiguous for this reason (vv. 16, 17). One verse has an *a fortiori* type of formulation ('How much more', v. 11). What I have described as a mixture of sentence and Instruction (see on 13.14, above, p. 455) with a final clause as the second member of the verse appears in vv. 3, 24.

Class A

A group is formed by those sentences which deal with the use and abuse of speech (vv. 1, 2, 7, 14, 23). There is wisdom in language which cools the passions, which lowers the temperature of a debate or takes the heat out of a situation where otherwise differences would be acrimoniously expressed (see on 14.17, 29; above, pp. 468f.).

[1] It is not appeasement at any cost which is recommended, but a studied, conciliatory approach, and v. 1a should be rendered 'a conciliatory answer' rather than 'a soft answer'. It is this which 'causes heat to subside', i.e., which restores good temper and reasonable attitudes. Words which are wounding and hurtful, and which are deliberately coined and uttered to have this effect, are bound to be inflammatory, and will exacerbate whatever differences already exist. They will 'raise anger' (v. 1b) and will set in motion a slanging-match; then polemics will be paramount and speech will no longer be an instrument of understanding and conciliation. Certain characteristic convictions of old wisdom are in play here. One is the dislike of passion which is useless and dangerous and the insistence on calm, studied appraisal (see especially *Amenemope*, above, pp. 106f.). Another is the low regard for polemics, however barbed be the tongue and deadly its thrusts. In this respect the 'political' interest of old wisdom is evident. The function of speech is to provide a cement for society (cf. Gen. 11) and to resolve or lessen the conflicts between persons which inevitably arise in the social context. It should be the instrument for the calm discussion of differences, and its usefulness is in connection with negotiation and settlement, i.e., with political solutions in the broadest sense. To use it by design in order to create heat and produce alienation solves nothing, and indeed makes the possibility of solution more remote.

[23] The effect of Kuhn's emendation in v. 23 (noted by BH and Gemser) is to introduce a reference to conciliatory speech there also (*b*ᵉ*han*ʿ*īmō* for *b*ᵉ*ma*ʿᵃ*nē*), but it is unnecessary and should not be adopted. Verse 23a refers rather to the pleasure and sense of satisfaction which a man feels when he has spoken well and effectively and when he is aware that the weight and cogency of his own ʿ*ēṣā* has been generally acknowledged. The further point which is made in v. 23b is that a sense of timing is an important aspect of effective speech. This implies that there are times when there is more virtue in silence than speech, and that it is better to say nothing than to make an unimpressive or inept intervention. To know when to

intervene and then to speak incisively and elegantly was an important part of old wisdom.

In the remaining three verses of the group the speech of wise men is contrasted with that of fools. [2] When sages speak, they adorn or embellish knowledge (v. 2a, MT), i.e., they have style as well as knowledge; they are eloquent and turn their phrases nicely. When fools speak, folly overflows like water bubbling up from a copious spring. If *taṭṭīp* is read for *teṭīb* (Gemser, BH) the verb in v. 2a has a matching metaphorical element. Dahood (pp. 32f.) postulates a root **yṭp*, cognate with *nṭp*, of which *yṭb* is a dialectal variant, and argues that the meaning 'drip' can be had without emendation. The tongue of sages drips with knowledge just as honey drips from a comb. Driver suggests the vocalization *taṭṭēb* from *ṭbb* (Syriac *ṭab*(*b*), pael 'knew', aphel 'made clear, divulged'), and supposes that the rarity of the verb is the cause of the error. 'The tongue of the wise announces knowledge' (*Biblica* 32, p. 181).

[7] The interpretation of v. 7 is complicated by the obscurity of *lō' kēn*, which is variously translated ('off the straight', i.e., perverse, Gemser and Ringgren; 'unstable', Ringgren, p. 62, n.3; 'not thus', RSV, Barucq; 'untruth', Scott). LXX: 'The hearts of fools are not safe' would seem to indicate that *lō' kēn* has been understood as 'unstable'. Toy emends to *lō' yābīn* and translates 'without intelligence'. Of the translations offered, 'perverse', 'warped', is the one most likely to be correct, since a warped mind is one incapable of disseminating knowledge, so that the antithesis is apt. The coupling of *śipᵉtē* and *lēb* in v. 7 and *lēb* and *pī* (Q., LXX στόμα) in v. 14 is to be explained by the consideration that as a man speaks so he is – the quality of his speech is indicative of the quality of his mind.

[14] Hence it is the sage, and not the wrong-headed fool, who disseminates knowledge, and it is the perceptive mind which seeks knowledge (v. 14a). Verse 14b (Q.) says that the mouths of fools pasture on folly, which is taken to mean that they have an appetite for folly, strong yearnings after it (Gemser, Ringgren). A more precise synonym for *yᵉbaqqēš* (v. 14a) is supplied by Winton Thomas's emendation *yidʿeh* (to be associated with Arabic *daʿā*, 'sought', 'demanded'). This requires the substitution of *d* for *r*, two consonants of similar shape and easily confused (D. W. Thomas, *VTS* iii, p. 285). This is an improvement in so far as *pī kᵉsīlīm* can now be translated 'speech of fools', just as *śipᵉtē ḥᵃkāmīm* (v. 7) is 'speech of wise men', and so the coupling of 'mind' and 'speech' has the same significance in both verses. This then

eliminates the metaphor of fools eating folly which is indicated by 'the mouth of fools pastures on folly', and which introduces an idea foreign to v. 7. One would expect the point of v. 14 to be that just as the mind of a perceptive man searches after knowledge, so the speech of a fool seeks out folly. Might there not be the thought of companionship here? If so, v. 14b could be translated: 'The speech of fools consorts with folly' (see KB², II *rʿh*; in the passages which are cited the form is always the participial *rōʿe*, cf. Prov. 13.20; 28.7; 29.3). The wise man has an affinity for wisdom and the fool, as his speech demonstrates, finds folly a congenial companion.

Another group of sentences has discipline for its theme (vv. 5, 10, 12, 20, 21, 24, 31, 32). **[5, 20]** A foolish son despises parental discipline, whether that of father or mother (see on 1.8 and 6.20, above, pp. 268, 327). A son who is amenable to correction has good sense or gumption and gives pleasure to his father. The curious phrase *kᵉsīl 'ādām* (v. 20b) recurs in 21.20. LXX translates 'a foolish son', but this perhaps represents dissatisfaction with *kᵉsīl 'ādām* and reflection that the precise antithesis of *bēn ḥākām* is *bēn kᵉsīl*. It does not necessarily indicate that *bēn kᵉsīl* was read (cf. BH). The metaphor of the two ways of life and death runs through vv. 10, 21, 24. **[10]** If a person forsakes the (right) road, he must be prepared to submit to severe discipline in order to get back on course. Should he not be amenable to correction, so that he is incapable of learning from a teacher who would set his feet on the way of life, he will die (cf. 14.12, see above, pp. 467f.). **[21]** In v. 21, the opposite of keeping a straight course (on the way of life) is folly, and so 'folly' can be equated with treading the ways of death (cf. 14.12) and with incorrigibility. Only one who is deficient in intelligence (*ḥᵃsar lēb*) will find pleasurable satisfaction in such folly, whereas one who thinks clearly and has a penetrating mind (*'īš tᵉbūnā*) will recognize that wisdom consists in undeviating progress (along the path of life). **[24]** Thus v. 24 declares that the *maśkīl* – the man with intellectual grasp who gets at the truth and is in control of the situation – will choose the path of life and avoid Sheol. Barucq notes that 'upwards' and 'downwards' were apparently not read by the Greek translator (LXX: 'The thoughts of an intelligent man are ways of life, so that avoiding Hades he may be saved'), and should be regarded as additions coming from a time when 'life' could be interpreted as a blessed immortality and 'death' an after-life of punishment (cf. BH). These additions therefore constitute a reinterpretation of the original antithesis, 'path of life' and 'way of death'; the new antithesis is that of heaven and hell. This is evident from the consideration that if the path of life is envisaged as a this-worldly way of life conditional on submission to discipline, 'upwards' does not make any sense in relation to it. Hence the opposition of 'upwards' and 'downwards' is not apposite if the contrast is between a this-worldly pattern of conduct which ensures vitality, and Sheol – the road to the underworld, 'the ways of death' (14.12, above, pp. 467f.). This scheme can accommodate 'downwards', but not 'upwards'. The opposition of 'upwards' and 'downwards' is only intelligible on the assumption that the path of life leads to a blessed immortality rather than to a this-worldly enjoyment of vitality. Another opinion is expressed by Gemser, who argues that the deletion of *l^ema'lā* and *l^emaṭṭā* (which is to be read instead of *maṭṭā*) would spoil the punning or word-play and that these words are original.

[32] The connection between discipline and the possession of acumen (*qōne lēb*), and the neglect of discipline and death, reappears in v. 32, where *nepeš* is to be translated 'life' and not 'self', and *mō'ēs* 'reject', 'throw away' and not 'despise' (contrary to Gemser, RSV, Ringgren, Barucq). He who is remiss with respect to *mūsār* throws away his life, but he who attends to reproof possesses acumen.

[12] Verse 12 returns to the subject of the incorrigibility of the *lēṣ* (see on 13.1b, 14.6, above, pp. 453, 464), whose opposite is the man with the receptive ear (v. 31; synecdoche, see below). The one resents correction, since this implies that the teacher is wiser than himself, the other has the humility to submit to intellectual discipline. Hence one finds the company of wise men congenial, while the other finds it uncongenial and avoids it (cf. 14.33, above, p. 466). **[31]** If the translation of v. 31 which is normally adopted (Toy, Gemser, Ringgren, Barucq, RSV) is correct, there is no parallelism in the sentence: 'An ear which is attentive to salutary reproof lodges in the midst of wise men'. The translation should rather be: 'An ear which listens to reproof is life; it (synecdoche, i.e., an attentive ear=an attentive person) lodges in the midst of wise men' (cf. Scott). The parallelism is then synthetic.

A third group consists of three sentences, two of which assert the predominance of mind over circumstances (vv. 13, 15), while the third, contrariwise, describes the impact of external things on mood and morale (v. 30). **[13]** Inner happiness is reflected in the lines of the face. The glow of health as it is visible in the face and the eyes is an epiphenomenon of a healthy and happy mind, but where there is mental illness, and the suffering associated with it, a person's morale is bruised and broken (see on 14.30, above, p. 472). **[15]** Verse 15 faces up to the grimness of poverty and describes the remorseless grind of the poor man's lot. The pressure is always on him; he has no reserves to act as a buffer between him and hunger or starvation: 'The life of a poor man is a continual struggle'. But man does not live by bread alone, and there is another kind of nourishment which will sustain him and enable him to conquer the hardness of life and the cruelty of circumstances. 'Good morale (reading *ṭūb lēb*, so Gemser; BH *l*^{e}*ṭōb lēb*) is a never-ending banquet' (v. 15b). There is an inner resilience which is invulnerable to the whims of fortune, and whoever has it will not allow himself to be broken by the assaults of poverty. He will withstand them with unconquerable courage, with dignity and composure, and will not permit poverty to contaminate him. He will endure poverty without suffering degradation. LXX moralizes and introduces the antithesis of good men and evil men: 'The eyes of evil men are continually well-disposed to evil, but good men are tranquil through everything.' The first half departs entirely from MT, while the second half retains something of its point.

[30] The interpretation of v. 30 is hindered by the obscurity of the phrase *m*^{e}*'ōr ʿēnayim*. Toy, out of a regard for the parallelism ('good news' in v. 30b), took it to mean the light which shines from the eyes of a person who brings good news and so to be synonymous with good news. Gemser supposes that 'the light of the eyes' means 'shining eyes', i.e., eyes which have friendliness in them, which are full of goodwill (similarly Barucq, 'a shining look', and Scott, 'the light in [a friend's] eye'). LXX translates: 'An eye which sees beautiful things' and Winton Thomas notes that *r'h* is used in the sense of 'looking with enjoyment' at something. In Eccles. 6.9, *mar'ēh ʿēnayim* means 'the pleasure of viewing (something) with the eyes', and Winton Thomas observes that the parallel of 'good news' (something which is heard with pleasure) would be 'something which is seen with pleasure', and so he suggests the hophal participle *mōr'e*: 'a fine sight cheers the mind as good news fills out the bodily frame' (*VTS* iii, p. 285). On the one hand, mental or spiritual benefits accrue – inner happiness or contentment – and on the other, physical well-being. If *m*^{e}*'or ʿēnayim* could mean 'eyes with the light of friendliness and goodwill in them' (Gemser), MT would be satisfactory, but the obscurity of the phrase 'light of the eyes' has to be acknowledged.

[18] The contrast between the hot-tempered man and his even-tempered counterpart (see on 14.17, 29, above, pp. 468f.; 15.1, above, p. 477) reappears in v. 18. The man of heat stirs up strife, but the even-tempered man exercises a calming influence and quietens contention. In view of the vocabulary (*mādōn*, *rīb*), it is possible that there is a special reference here to litigiousness. There is the kind of person who thrives on acrimony and who seeks a pretext to transform every difference or disagreement into a bitter legal contest, and there is his opposite who will do everything in his power to minimize contention and to obviate the acerbities of litigation.

[19] Verse 19 is about the lazy man (see 6.6–9, above, pp 323f., 10.4, above, p. 417, 13.4, above, pp. 457f.), and *ḥārūṣīm* rather than *yᵉšārīm* (MT) is the desiderated antithesis (so Toy, Gemser). The suspicion that *yᵉšārīm*, 'upright', represents a secondary moralizing of the sentence is confirmed by LXX *ἀνδρείων*, which is elsewhere (10.4, 13.4) used to translate *ḥārūṣīm*. The metaphor is that of the two ways; the way of the lazy man is a thorn hedge (LXX, 'strewn with thorns'), and that of the industrious person a highway, i.e., a road built up from a good foundation, with a surface along which safe and assured progress can be made. The metaphor of MT ('the way of a lazy man is a thorn hedge') is somewhat far-fetched, and the picture of LXX is more easily envisaged, but the meaning is not in doubt. The sluggard makes little or no progress, but the industrious man presses on.

[22] In v. 22, the theme of 11.14 and 13.10 (see above, pp. 429, 453f.) is resumed. Where there is no prior consultation, plans fall apart, but where many advisers have contributed to the shaping of a policy it will stand (the test of implementation). This is an argument for committee or conference not only in the sense that the widest consensus will produce the best policy, but also from the point of view that prior consultation is a prerequisite of the success of a plan. It is necessary to explain a policy to those who are to be involved in its implementation, to listen to their criticisms and to be flexible in respect of modifications. Only thus will the plan become *their* plan and ready co-operation be assured (on the antithesis of *prr* and *qwm* see *PWM*, pp. 79, 82).

Class B

[4] In v. 4, *marpē'* is generally derived from *rph* (so KB[2]) as in 14.30 (see above, p. 472), and *marpē' lāšōn* is translated 'a conciliatory tongue' (Toy, Gemser, Ringgren, Scott, Barucq, RSV). LXX, however, renders *marpē'* by *ἴασις*, 'therapy', and I have no doubt that this is correct here, as in 12.18 and 13.17, in both of which reference is made to the therapeutic character of speech and in one of which (12.18) *marpē'* is used with *lāšōn* (see above, p. 446). Then again, 'tree of life' as it is used in 3.18 with reference to Wisdom means 'a source of vitality to others', as it does also in 11.30, and 'fountain of life' in 10.11, 13.14 and 14.27 has a similar social reference (on the mythological associations of these expressions see 3.18, above, p. 296). In view of all this, the meaning of v. 4a must be that there is a kind of speech which has a therapeutic value and which creates social health and vitality. The opposite of a *marpē' lāṣōn* is a tongue which has a twist (*selep*) in it, and the only element of incompleteness in the parallelism of v. 4b is that it describes the effect of perversion on the individual who suffers from it rather than its injurious social consequences. The second half of the sentence can be elucidated by comparing it with 11.17, 27; 12.20 (see above, pp. 433f., p. 447), and is another expression of the conviction that there is a harmony of self-interest and benevolence. The man who speaks with malevolent intent and who uses language as a socially destructive weapon is condemning himself to spiritual fragmentation and is destroying his own essential vitality – his *élan vital* – and his personality will disintegrate. He is the victim of *mirmā*, 'self-deceit' (see on 12.20, above, p. 447).

[26] According to v. 26, such 'evil plans' are an abomination to Yahweh (see below, p. 486, on vv. 8, 9), but gracious words are pure, i.e., words of goodwill spoken with benevolent intent, words which are the cement of a society. LXX: 'The words of the pure are grave (or 'decorous')' weakens the parallelism, since 'pure' in MT as a predicate is the antithesis of *tō'ēbā* and appears in place of the more normal *rāṣōn* (see on 14.9, above, pp. 475f.). Since gracious words are pure, they are such as meet with Yahweh's *rāṣōn*. Thus, although Scott's translation is too free, he does correctly indicate the connection between *ṭᵉhōrīm* and *rāṣōn*: 'But he approves the words of the virtuous.' **[28]** Another expression of the antithesis of benevolence and malevolence is found in v. 28. A righteous man gives a considered answer, but the mouths of wicked men spout (on the metaphor see v. 2b) evil. The paraphrase of LXX, 'The hearts of righteous men contemplate truth' takes the point of v. 28a correctly, and the addition in LXX underlines the social reference of the verse: 'The way of righteous men is acceptable to the Lord, by means of them even enemies become friends.' The considered answer of v. 28a is therefore the helpful answer of the person who takes trouble to give good advice and is concerned that what he recommends will be as effective as it is well-intentioned. Kuhn's emendation (*laʿanōt* to *lineʿīmōt*) is unnecessary, although it takes the right sense of v. 28a: 'A person with a fair mind ponders gracious words.'

[17] The point of v. 17 is that lavish hospitality is not necessarily indicative of goodwill, and that there is a form of civility and sociability which has style and brilliance, but which has no depth nor essential truth. Behind the urbaneness and scintillating conversation of the practised host there may be ulterior motives of malice and rancour, and, if this is so, despite all the trimmings, there is no truth in the meeting between host and guest and no experience of *κοινωνία* is possible. The table indeed is the place for fellowship, and there is a natural concord between eating and friendship; but, if this is so, a dish of greens – the simplest of dishes – with love is better than a fatted calf with hatred.

Class C

The largest group is in the service of the doctrine of theodicy (vv. 3, 6, 11, 25, 27, 29). **[3]** The eyes of Yahweh are everywhere scrutinizing good and evil men. **[11]** Sheol and Abaddon – the underworld abode of the dead – are open to Yahweh's surveillance, how much more the minds of men. So there is nothing which Yahweh misses, whether it is in the depths of Sheol or the recesses of the human mind. His knowledge is complete in scope and depth, and his rule of righteousness operates unfailingly to reward the righteous and punish the wicked (cf. Ps. 139; *The Šamaš Hymn*, *BWL*, pp. 126f.). **[6]** In v. 6, *neʿkāret* is an obscure word, and a further small difficulty in MT is that v. 6a lacks a preposition before *bēt*, while v. 6b appears to have a superfluous one before *tebūʾat* (the first is explained as haplography of *b*). LXX presents no grammatical difficulties and renders *neʿkāret* as ἀπολοῦνται: 'In the houses of righteous men there is much strength, but the fruits of impious men will be destroyed.' KB² supposes that *neʿkāret* means 'taboo' or perhaps 'interdicted'. Gemser and Ringgren translate: 'The income of an evil man is disorganized', and Barucq, retaining MT: 'In the revenues of an evil man there is trouble.' The meaning of MT would seem to be that a righteous man amasses considerable wealth, whereas the income of an evil man is thrown into disarray (Gemser, Ringgren) or interdicted, so that he can derive no benefit from it. In the additional couplet prefixed by LXX, it is 'righteousness' and not 'wealth' which is amassed. Hence there is no reference to wealth in LXX and its moralizing tendency is evident: 'In amassing righteousness is much strength, but the impious will be destroyed root and branch from the land.' The 'fruits' which are to be destroyed are the evil fruits of wickedness. The righteous man is secure and the impious man courts destruction.

[25] According to v. 25, Yahweh cares for the weak and upholds their right, but demolishes the households of proud men (cf. 14.34, above, p. 475, where there is another corporate application of the doctrine of theodicy). The boundary of the widow's piece of land is maintained by Yahweh, when otherwise she might be defenceless before the cupidity of her neighbours. This optimistic assertion contrasts with the realism of the prophetic preaching. The prophets have their eyes open and see what in fact is happening to the weak, the fatherless and the widow (cf. Amos 2.6f.; Micah 2.1f.; Isa. 1.12f.; 5.8). **[27]** The theme of v. 27 is likewise ill-gotten wealth and greed. The literal meaning of *bṣ'* is 'cut', and so *bōṣēa'* is 'one who wants a big cut' (Scott, 'profiteer'). He is in a hurry to get rich and not particular how he does it. This kind of greed is also regarded as a flaw in the Egyptian Instruction (see on 13.11, above, pp. 458f.). In view of the parallelism, one might suppose that *bōṣēa' beṣa'* is specifically one who makes money by accepting bribes, and this is how v. 27a is understood by LXX: 'He who accepts a bribe will destroy himself.' But LXX 'will destroy himself' does not give much help with *'ōkēr bētō*, which, if we followed KB² (see on v. 6b, above, pp. 484f.), would mean something like 'ostracizes his house', i.e., puts it outside the pale of normal social intercourse. One would then have to suppose that this is equivalent to a sentence of death on his house, a wasting away in the wilderness, in order to discover an apt contrast for 'live' in v. 27b. The person who hates a bribe is assured vitality and well-being, since hating a bribe is an aspect of righteousness (cf. A. R. Johnson, *The Vitality of the Individual in the Thought of Ancient Israel*², p. 98, 'will enjoy a prosperous life'). This attitude to bribery is in marked contrast to that found in 17.8; 19.6; 21.14 (see below, pp. 502, 526, 555), where it is a part of practical wisdom, and is another example of the reinterpretation of old wisdom. In this verse, as in 11.17, 29 and 15.6, we are up against the barrier to interpretation constituted by the obscurity of *'kr*. Gemser and Ringgren translate 'destroys his house', and this provides a good antithesis for 'lives'; 'troubles his house' (Barucq, Scott, RSV) is less satisfactory in this respect.

[29] The final sentence in the group asserts that Yahweh is remote from *rešāʿīm*, but accessible to the prayer of *ṣaddīqīm*. Yahweh is alienated from wicked men; his ways are not their ways and he visits them only to punish, but he listens to the prayer of the righteous and bestows his favour on them.

Two verses describe what Yahweh abhors and what he views with approval (vv. 8f.). **[8]** Verse 8 contains one of the few cultic references in the sentence literature (for the Instruction cf. 3.9, above, p. 293), and v. 9 employs the familiar metaphor of the two ways. The statement that sacrifices made by wicked men are an abomination to Yahweh, while he approves the prayer of the upright (on *rāṣōn* see 12.2, 14.9, above, pp. 448, 475) recalls similar prophetic value judgements (Isa. 1.12f.; Amos 5.21f.), so that the sentence is an instrument of prophetic teaching (see on 11.1, above, pp. 438f.). **[9]** As for v. 9, I have pointed out in connection with 12.2 (above, p. 448) that Yahweh's *rāṣōn* is for the man whom he acquits (*hiṣdīq*), i.e., the *ṣaddīq*, and his *tōʿēbā* for the one he condemns (*hiršīaʿ*), i.e., the *rāšāʿ*. He accepts and loves the man who pursues *ṣedāqā*, but he rejects and detests the conduct of a *rāšāʿ*.

[16] It is better to have a little with the fear of Yahweh than to have great wealth and turmoil with it. This is not entirely alien to the ethos of old wisdom (cf. *Amenemope* ix. 5–8), and one could invoke von Rad's concept of the fear of Yahweh as a limit or boundary which should not be transgressed (cf. *PWM*, pp. 48f.) in order to advance such an interpretation of the verse. In that case it makes the same point as the Egyptian Instruction (above, pp. 60f.), that no one should try to fill a pair of shoes which are too big for him. There is a ceiling of attainment consonant with endowment, and it is wisdom to know when the ceiling has been reached. The fear of Yahweh is a limit to self-assertion and vaulting ambition, and so it is a limit to anxiety. Wealth is then intended as an index of success and power, and small means as an index of the acceptance of a minor role. The encountering of the fear of Yahweh and the recognition of the boundary which it prescribes is not a contraction of selfhood, but the discovery of the self. It enables a man to be what he is, and it delivers him from the lash of ambition – from striving to be what he is not.

I do not, however, believe that this is really a framework of interpretation appropriate to this sentence, and I take it rather as an expression of Yahwistic piety in which small means or even poverty is assigned a positive religious value, so that there is a tendency to equate poverty and piety and, conversely, wealth and impiety (this can be seen in the ambivalence *ʿaniyīm* and *ʿanāwīm*). The wealthy man has a fevered spirit, and wealth is inimical to the fear of Yahweh (cf. the Gospels: 'It is easier for a camel to pass through the eye of a needle than for a rich man to enter the kingdom of God'; NEB, Mark 10.25 and parallels).

[33] Verse 33 illustrates a facet of the reinterpretation of old wisdom – the substitution of a new discipline, the fear of Yahweh, for the educational discipline exercised by the wisdom teacher (see on 14.27, above, p. 474). The discipline of wisdom (i.e. the discipline whose product is wisdom) is now the fear of Yahweh, and likewise a pious humility is a prerequisite of *kābōd*. The goals are still those of old wisdom, but a new regimen has been prescribed for attaining them. Neither wisdom nor status (on *kābōd* see 13.18, above, p. 456) is now achieved by intellectual discipline, but is consequent on the discipline of piety. The emendation of *mūsār* to *mūsād*, 'The fear of Yahweh is the foundation of wisdom' (Humbert, see Gemser; cf. BH), blunts the point of the sentence. Barucq notes the expanded text in certain manuscripts of LXX and remarks on the tendency to make additions to MT at the end of such chapters as might be considered the close of sections (cf. above, pp. 308f.).

Chapter 16

In this chapter there is a significant increase in the incidence of synthetic parallelism (vv. 4, 5, 6, 7, 10, 11, 13, 15, 16, 17, 18, 20?, 21, 23, 24, 27, 28, 29, 30, 31, 32) over against antithetic parallelism (vv. 1, 2, 9, 14, 22, 25, 33), as compared with the preceding chapters of sentence literature. There are two examples of the 'better . . . than' type of sentence (vv. 8, 19); v. 3 is a fragment of Instruction with an imperative and final clause, and vv. 12 and 26, with a combination of indicative and motive clause, are a mixture of sentence and Instruction (cf. 13.14; 14.27, indicative and final clause). Editorial groupings are evident in vv. 10–15 (excluding v. 11, which disturbs the sequence), all of which have something to say about a king or kings, and vv. 27–30, whose topic is anti-social behaviour.

Class A: vv. 14, 15, 16, 18, 21, 22, 23, 25, 26, 32.
Class B: vv. 7, 12, 13, 24, 27, 28, 29, 30.
Class C: vv. 1, 2, 3, 4, 5, 6, 8, 9, 10, 11, 17, 19, 20, 31, 33.

Class A

[14, 32] Two sentences are related to the awareness that heat and anger are the enemies of wisdom, and that an even temper and complete self-control are cardinal political virtues (see on 15.1, above, p. 477). In the context of high political office and diplomacy it is a golden rule to bring down the temperature and to make room for reasonable discussion. The ability to keep calm even under stress, so that judgement is not clouded by passion or panic and every impulse which would impair reasonable self-determination and make action subject to irrational constraint is repelled, is a greater attainment than military prowess and more to be desired even than the acclaim of victory (v. 32). The danger considered in v. 14 is not so much that the king acting in heat will make a bad political decision, as that an official may be the victim of his irrational anger, although he has done nothing to deserve his disfavour. The factor which has to be taken into account is that every official, however high his rank, was an *'ebed* of the king, and so his career was in the king's gift. Hence for him the king's anger is a harbinger of death (literally, 'messengers of death', i.e., those who bring disastrous news), and he has to use all his skill in a situation where his own future and, perhaps, safety is at stake in order to 'cover it' (as fire is covered and extinguished with sand). Dahood (p. 36) translates 'Death's two messengers', noting that Baal had two messengers, *gpn–w–ủgr* (*Baal* I* 1.12, *CML*, p. 102f.) and that according to H. L. Ginsberg (*BASOR* 95, 1944, p. 29, 20) there may be a reference to two messengers of Mot (Death) in *Baal* I* ii. 16f. (*CML*, pp. 104f.). Driver understands this passage as a reference to the two messengers of Baal *gpn–w–ủgr* who carry a message from Baal to Mot.

[15] That careers are made or broken by the king is also the subject of v. 15, which asserts that everything depends on finding favour with him. The king is a fountain-head of preferment; when he smiles on an official it is life for him, and when he frowns it is death. Success is life for the ambitious politician and failure death; the issue hinges on the kind of impression which he makes on the king and the relationship which he strikes up with him. Again, in another sense, approval is life (safety) and failure or disgrace is death, for the statesman plays for high stakes and lives dangerously. The king's approval fructifies the careers of those who win it; it is like the cloud which breaks to give fertilizing showers of spring rain (i.e., rain which falls in March–April before the harvest of the winter corn and the sowing of the summer fruit, in whose absence the fruit is meagre and of poor quality).

[16] In so far as it is concerned with the establishing of priorities, v. 16 recalls v. 32. It is a splendid thing to acquire wisdom (deleting *mēḥārūṣ*), and the obtaining of perceptiveness or insight (*bīnā*) is preferable to silver (*q^e^nō* for *q^e^nōt*, BL, p. 425). Verse 16a appears to be a conflation of *q^e^nō ḥokmā mā ṭōb* and *q^e^nō ḥokmā ṭōb mēḥārūṣ*. It is difficult to decide what the original may have been, but the insertion of *mēḥārūṣ* can be explained as an approximation of 16a to 16b, whereas it is not obvious why *mā* should have been incorporated secondarily. This verse, unlike 15.16 (see above, pp. 486f.) and 16.8 (see below, p. 499) is not connected with the tendency to attribute a positive religious value to poverty and to equate wealth with impiety. Rather than expressing disapproval of wealth, the verse presupposes that it is an essential ingredient of a full life, for *ḥokmā* and *bīnā* are then a greater good in relation to what is also a good, and the significance of the comparison is enhanced. Wealth without wisdom may be vulgarity or greed or ruthless individualism, and wealth must exist within a framework of values created by wisdom. On the other hand, there is no incompatibility between wisdom and wealth, for intrinsic worth should be reflected in status and material well-being.

[21] A group is constituted by three sentences which describe the intellectual virtues of the wise man (vv. 21, 22, 23). The man of acumen (*ḥ^a^kam lēb*) will be named a *nābōn* – he will acquire a reputation for intellectual clarity and perceptiveness – and honeyed words will increase comprehension (in those who are taught). If *meteq* is taken as construct of *mātēq* (so KB^2), this affords a more exact parallel to *ḥ^a^kam lēb* than *meteq* 'sweetness' (i.e., 'a man of honeyed words promotes learning'). *leqaḥ* is literally 'appropriation' (cf. Barucq, *l'acquis*). A teacher who 'increases appropriation' is one who is a master of the art of communication and whose lucidity facilitates understanding. Consequently *leqaḥ* is not persuasiveness (Gemser, Ringgren, RSV); rather it is the persuasiveness of the teacher (*meteq ś^e^pātayim*) which increases *leqaḥ* in those who are taught, *leqaḥ* being the process of understanding and appropriating the words of the teacher. *leqaḥ*, 'persuasiveness', 'coquetry', is the sense in 7.21 (above, p. 340), but it is not apt for the other occurrences in Proverbs (1.5; 4.2; 9.9; 16.21, 23). **[23]** That the wise man is one who can speak incisively and attractively is also indicated by v. 23, which states that the mind of a wise man informs his speech, making it judicious and effective (on the connection of *śkl* with effectiveness see *PWM*, pp. 67f.). The second half of the verse, 'and on his lips he increases learning', is of uncertain meaning, but it could just possibly mean 'by his speech he promotes learning', in which case it says the same as v. 21b. BH suggests *ūbaʿal śepātāw*, 'and an expert speaker promotes learning' (cf. Scott) which gives excellent sense, *baʿal śepātāw* matching *meteq śepātayim* in v. 21b. I have adopted this emendation.

[22] 'The discipline of fools is folly' (v. 22b) is just another way of saying that fools are incapable of benefiting from an educational discipline (see on 14,8, 33, above, p. 466). They are by nature unteachable and so they will never acquire *śēkel* (v. 22a), the good sense and competence which can be learned from a wisdom teacher, where there is a proper submission to his authority and the capacity for intellectual toil (see on 15.31, above, p. 480). LXX and Pesh. point to *libeʿālāw* in v. 22a, and *beʿālāw* may have arisen through haplography of *l*. Otherwise the literal translation of MT is: 'The good sense of those who possess it is a fountain of life.' On the mythological complex from which 'tree of life' and 'fountain of life' derive, see 3.18 (above, p. 296). Nothing more precise than that *śēkel* is an unfailing source of vitality to those who possess it is indicated here.

[18] A particular cause of incorrigibility is pride and intellectual arrogance (see on 13.1b, above, p. 453; 14.6, p. 464; 15.12, p. 480). Pride is the precursor of shattering (disintegration) and a haughty temper of stumbling. 'Disintegration' suggests a contrast with the man who has achieved wholeness (*šālōm*) by submitting to *mūsār* and learning wisdom; and 'stumbling' a contrast with the safe road along which the teacher directs his attentive and receptive pupils (see on 4.12, 19, above, pp. 307f.; 15.19, above, p. 482; 17, 19, below p. 500). **[25]** The road with which the self-opinionated person is well content terminates in 'the ways of death' (see on 14.12, above, p. 467, of which this is a doublet).

[26] Verse 26 states that in the absence of all other reasons for industry, the spur of hunger will drive a man on and he will work because he wants to eat (*nepeš*, 'throat' > 'appetite', hardly 'stomach', as Barucq asserts). This is about a particular type of work, the punishing toil of the manual labourer (*ʿāmēl*), which is perhaps lacking in all intrinsic interest and into which a large element of drudgery enters. Consequently the satisfaction of a purposive or creative activity is not to be had in it, and there is no sense in which, as a vehicle of self-fulfilment, the doing of it is a sufficient reward. Such work gives neither intellectual nor aesthetic satisfaction; it might conceivably be ennobled by a strong sense of vocation, but otherwise it will be done in the knowledge that the choice is between bending the back and starving.

There is a genuine 'proverbial' element in this sentence and it can signify more than what I have so far indicated. It is not just about the spur of hunger applied to a manual labourer; it has allusiveness and openness to interpretation such as enlarges its range of application. The interpretation could be that need is the most basic of all incentives, or it would be applicable in a rather different way wherever there is talk about 'the need of incentives'. If one wanted to say proverbially what the politicians say platitudinously, namely, that work for most men, even where they value it for its own sake and are absorbed in it, is a means to an end, and that they will work harder if the rewards are better, this proverb would be apt comment: 'A worker's appetite works for him, his mouth urges him on.' LXX completely alters the meaning of the sentence and makes it turn on the contrast between the industrious (silent) man and the crooked person who busies himself with misrepresentation. The one diverts destruction from himself, while the other, with his malicious speech, carries it in his own mouth. From the parallelism it would appear that his own destruction is meant, but his destructive, anti-social activities may also be indicated (LXX similarly alters v. 27, see below).

Class B

[7] All the verses in this class have to do with the social effects of righteousness and unrighteousness. The man whose conduct earns Yahweh's *rāṣōn* is at the same time one who radiates social reconciliation. He is himself approved by Yahweh and is the object of his favour because he is *ṣaddīq* (see on 15.8, 9, 26 above, pp. 486f., 483), and his righteousness enables him to incorporate his enemies in the wholeness (*šālōm*) of his own life (literally, 'he (the subject is *'īš*, not *YHWH*) makes his enemies at one with himself'). The righteous (15.9b) or the good (12.2a) or the upright (15.8b) man has a therapeutic power to mend broken relationships and to repair evidences of alienation and divisiveness in the body politic.

The correlation of *rāṣōn* and *ṣedeq* and of *tō'ēbā* and *reša'* appears in vv. 12 and 13. **[12]** The meaning of *tō'abat melākīm* (v. 12a) should be determined on the analogy of the phrase *tō'abat YHWH* and also on the analogy of *reṣōn melākīm* (v. 13a). The meaning is that it is an abomination to kings when someone else commits evil (so LXX, ὁ ποιῶν κακά, Scott, Gemser?), and not that it is an abomination (to Yahweh) when kings do evil (Toy, Ringgren, Barucq). The motive clause signifies not that the king's tenure of rule depends on the righteousness of his personal conduct, but that the throne, i.e., the regime, has stability only where there is a broad base of social justice which is not undermined by the wrongdoing of any subjects.

Brunner has argued attractively (H. Brunner, *VT* viii, 1958, pp. 420–28) that the idea of a throne being founded on righteousness derives from Egyptian mythology. It is expressed pictorially by the pedestal on which the throne of Pharaoh rests. The description of Solomon's throne in I Kings 10.18–20 shows that it is constructed on Egyptian models, both lions and steps being features of Egyptian design. Brunner urges that the mention of the six steps is particularly significant, because from it the inference can be made that the throne of Solomon, like that of Pharaoh, rested on a pedestal, and the fact that this throne was physically reproduced in Israel provides substance for the assumption that the Egyptian mythology which was 'actualized' in the construction of this throne may have been appropriated by Israel in whole or in part.

The pedestal on which the Egyptian throne rested was an ambivalent symbol. It was a representation of the primaeval hill, the first piece of firm ground from which God began his work of creation. This mythological 'place' is realized in every Egyptian temple; every royal throne rests on it, for the king in discharging his office fulfils and preserves the work of creation. But the pedestal also resembles the sign which is the hieroglyph for *Maat*, 'justice', 'truth', 'the divine order', and in this respect it indicates that the king's throne is founded on 'justice', i.e., it rests on the basis of a divinely established order and exists within its framework. Brunner supposes that the Israelites gave up the idea of the primaeval hill because it was foreign to their cast of thought, but that they clung to the thought that the throne is founded on *ṣᵉdāqā* which here represents an attempt to render the Egyptian *Maat*.

The difficulty about this argument and the reason why it is inconclusive is that the metaphor which is being explained (righteousness is the foundation of a throne) is so commonplace and obvious that it might occur to anyone at any time. It does not obviously demand the elucidation which Brunner proposes. Nevertheless, if Brunner's explanation were adopted, it would agree with the interpretation which I have offered. If the king's rule is an aspect of the divine order, it is endangered wherever men breach that order and this then is how evil is to be defined. **[13]** It also accords with v. 13, which states that lips of *ṣedeq* win the *rāṣōn* of kings (or 'of a king' with 2 Mss. and LXX), since such speech is characterized by integrity and a will to contribute creatively and benevolently to solidarity and wholeness. Sense can be made of v. 13b by changing the vocalization of MT (*dᵉbar* for *dōbēr*) or by substituting *mēšārīm* for *yᵉšārīm* (cf. BH). Whichever is read, the sense is sufficiently clear and v. 13b is simply a variation of the theme of v. 13a. I retain the consonantal text. There is no reason to suppose that v. 13 has in mind particularly the quality of advice tendered to the king by his inner circle of advisers, his cabinet of *śārīm* or *yōʿᵃṣīm* (*PWM*, pp. 15f.), as Gemser and Barucq suggest. It is rather a general statement that a community thrives on candour and that a king loves the candid man wherever he is to be found among his subjects.

[24] The metaphor 'gracious words are a honeycomb' is stated plainly in v. 24a and then is developed in v. 24b by a description of the honeycomb which makes the point of the metaphor obvious ('it is sweet to the palate [literally, 'throat'] and a tonic for the body'). Honey is pleasant to the taste and has medicinal virtue, and so it is also with gracious words (see on 15.26b, above, p. 483), which are palatable to those to whom they are addressed and have a therapeutic value for them. They are spoken with benevolent intent as a contribution to social health, and they produce a sense of well-being in those who hear them. They create social harmony and happiness. No antithesis of soul and body is intended by the juxtaposition of *nepeš* and *ʿeṣem* (contrary to Toy, Gemser) Ringgren, RSV), and Barucq has the correct sense of the verse.

By contrast, vv. 27–30 are concerned exclusively with anti-social attitudes and activities. **[27]** The *'īš bᵉlīyaʿal* (see on 6.12, above, p. 325) in v. 27a is probably to be equated with the *'īš tahpūkōt* (v. 28a), the reference in both cases being to a state of inner confusion and contrariness (*'īš bᵉlīyaʿal*, a deranged or destructive man rather than a worthless man). This 'confusion' is a deep-seated malevolence – a contamination of the springs of sociability – and it sets a man at enmity with all other men. He has no urge to use language creatively in order to make friends and enlarge brotherhood; he is obsessed with the thought of hurting his fellows. He 'digs mischief' and his words have the destructive fury of a blazing fire.

The phrase 'digs mischief' is obscure. LXX has certainly taken v. 27 wrongly in supposing it to say that the *'īš bᵉlīyaʿal* is his own worst enemy ('he digs evil for himself'), that he plays with fire and gets burned ('he stores fire on his own lips'). Toy translates 'digs (a pit of) evil', i.e., prepares pitfalls for others, which is also indicated by RSV's paraphrase 'plots evil'. The meaning may rather be that he digs up mischief, excavates it and brings it to the surface. He is then one who digs for scandal and who propagates it with words which are ablaze with misanthropy. Perhaps *kōre rāʿā* is to be correlated with Dhorme's explanation of *ḥōrēš rāʿ* (see on 6.14, above, p. 325) and the thought will then be that the destructive man 'cultivates evil', labours for a harvest of evil. His speech causes searing pain like a burn and is as destructive as fire. The emendation accepted by Gemser and Scott (*kūr* for *kōre*) produces excellent parallelism ('a furnace of evil'), but *kōre* was read by LXX and, although obscure, is not nonsensical. Dahood (p. 37) translates: 'A depraved man concocts evil', postulating **krh*, 'to cook', 'to heat', which he associates with *kūr* 'oven'. The assumption of Gemser, Scott and Dahood that the two images of v. 27a and 27b should be related is not necessarily correct. Thus vv. 27 and 28 have a common topic, **[28]** since the latter is about the pervert (*'īš tahpūkōt*) who initiates strife and the slanderer who alienates friends. The meaning of v. 28b is not that the *nirgān* alienates his own friends (contrary to Gemser, '*von sich und von einander*'), but that he makes it his deliberate policy to destroy other men's friendships by creating discord and poisoning trust (*'allūp* is collective, so LXX, 'separates friends'; also Toy, Ringgren, Barucq, RSV).

[29] The *'īš ḥāmās* is similarly misanthropic. He is aggressive and hostile and he employs deceit in order to achieve his destructive ends. 'The way which is not good' along which he entices his companion is a euphemism for the way that leads to death. His mission is to lay the hand of death on those who suppose him to be a friend. He abuses the trust and confidences of friendship in order to destroy men and this is what he lives for.

[30] In v. 30 *laḥšōb* should be taken as a 3rd masculine, singular imperfect with a prefixed *l* (Haupt, p. 52, on 19.8, in Müller and Kautzsch; Dahood, p. 37; G. Dalman, *Grammatik des jüdisch-palästinischen Aramäisch*², 1905, p. 264). G. R. Driver (*Biblica* 32, p. 196) takes *laḥšōb* as the infinitive construct form with a prefixed *l*, *l* having the sense 'is likely to'. 'He who winks his eye is likely to engage in intrigue.' Although *ʿōṣe* is a *hapax legomenon*, it should be retained

(KB2, Arabic *ġaḍā*, 'to wrinkle the eye-lids') with the sense 'wink'. The allusion is not to clandestine sign language, by means of which deceit is accomplished and evil effected, since the pursing of the lips in 30b comes after evil has been consummated. The thought is rather that there is a correspondence between mannerism and character, between appearance and purposes, and that one can read off a man's face that he is compulsively wrong-headed and malevolent, whether it is the shiftiness which indicates that he will make mischief by deliberately confounding truth and error, by calculated misrepresentation, or the nastiness of his pursed lips which are evidence that he has effectively expressed his hatred of his fellows.

Class C

[1, 2, 9] A group is comprised of three sentences (vv. 1, 2, 9) which explore in different respects the basic antithesis of man and God. I have elsewhere discussed von Rad's view that this antithesis is to be related to the awareness of the wise men that a limit has to be set to the operations of empirical wisdom and that there is a boundary at which they must make their submission to God. I have indicated that my own understanding of these verses is that they represent a Yahwistic riposte to the claims of old wisdom, and a severe circumscribing of the powers exercised by its practitioners. It is Yahweh, and not they, who has the intellectual and executive power to move the world (*PWM*, pp. 50f.). I would maintain this thesis of a Yahwistic reinterpretation, even though thoughts not dissimilar to those of vv. 1 and 9 are found in extra-Israelite wisdom. Thus v. 1b can be compared with the verse in *Ahikar*: 'If he were beloved of the gods, they would put something good in his palate to speak' (col. viii. 115, A. E. Cowley, pp. 217, 223), although I am not entirely persuaded that this is really what is being said by v. 1b (see below). Verse 9 is comparable to: 'One thing are the words which men say, another is that which the god does' (*Amenemope* xix.16f., *ANET*, p. 423), or, 'If the tongue of man (be) the rudder of a boat, the All-Lord is its pilot' (*Amenemope* xx.5f., *ANET*, p. 424), i.e., 'Man proposes, but God disposes'.

The common element in vv. 2 and 9 is their assertion that, irrespective of man's plans or value-judgements, the issue is settled by Yahweh. A man may plan his road to the last detail, but he cannot implement his planning, unless it coincides with Yahweh's plan for him. He is deluded if he supposes that he has unfettered control and can impose his will on every situation without limitation in order to make his plan a reality, for it is Yahweh who orders his step. Verse 2 touches on the discrepancy between man's estimate of his probity (cf. 14.12a) and Yahweh's considered judgement; *zak* is used of pure, unadulterated oil, and so here of an ill-founded belief in the purity of one's motives and practice which will be appraised in accordance with Yahweh's norm (*tkn* 'adjusted to standard', see *PWM*, p. 81 n.3). The meaning of v. 2b is, then, that Yahweh's appraisal of motives is normative, and there is no echo of the mythological representation of judgement associated with Thoth, according to which the god weighs the hearts of men at death. *tōkēn rūḥōt* cannot be translated 'he who weighs spirits' (cf. Gemser; contrary to H. Gressmann, *Spruchweisheit*, pp. 43f., Barucq and Scott).

I have indicated that vv. 2 and 9 set limits to human activity and assert that he has to reckon ultimately with Yahweh. [1] The question which I now raise is whether v. 1 does not also have the same type of structure. If it has, the meaning of v. 1b is different from what it is sometimes taken to be. One interpretation of this verse is that man has to do his own thinking and to order his thoughts systematically, but that having done this he has to count on Yahweh for the power of effective utterance, and that, in this sense, 'the reply of the tongue comes from Yahweh'. Thus Toy supposes that 'the reply of the tongue' means 'the final outcome of one's reflections and purposes' and Ringgren comments that the knack of giving the right answer, that is, of finding the apt word for every occasion, is a gift of God. This assumes (as also Scott's translation) that the man who orders his thoughts (v. 1a) is identical with the one who does the speaking. A more meaningful antithesis and one which conforms to the type of vv. 2 and 9 can be had if it is supposed that v. 1b refers to Yahweh's answer. Ringgren considers this possibility but departs from it. Barucq takes the point correctly ('But the decision comes from Yahweh'), and suggests that we are to think of Yahweh's creative word, which is the final answer and determines the shape of the future. This makes v. 1 more or less synonymous with v. 9, and I believe that this is the right understanding of it. A man can expect his plans to be implemented only if they coincide with what Yahweh has determined for him. It is this state of affairs which the obscure recommendation of v. 3 takes for granted.

[3] The difficulty here resides in the phrase 'Roll your actions towards Yahweh', which is usually rendered 'Commit your actions to

Yahweh' (Toy, Ringgren, RSV), or, 'Confide your actions to Yahweh' (Barucq). The idiom is an odd one and the metaphor awaits elucidation. If this difficulty is by-passed and it is assumed that 'confide' approximates to the meaning, Scott is to be followed in his supposition that 'actions' are 'projected actions' or 'projects'. 'Reveal your projects to Yahweh' (Pesh., Targ., V, *gal* for *gōl*) requires no change in the consonantal text and makes good sense. The sentence would then recall Isa. 29.15: 'Woe to those who are secretive so as to conceal their policy from Yahweh, whose activities are in the dark and who say: "Who sees us or is cognizant of us?" ' (*PWM*, p. 70). A fatal objection to this emendation is the *scriptio plena* in Ps. 37.5 (*gwl*), which indicates *gll* and not *glh*; also the sense of Ps. 22.9 which confirms the idiom 'rolling to Yahweh'. The Instruction would seem to be consonant with what is stated in vv. 1, 2 and 9. To confide one's projects to Yahweh implies an element of resignation to Yahweh's will, a willingness to give up anything which clashes with Yahweh's resolve and so a quest for attunement and harmony. This is the way for a man to proceed if he wishes to ensure that his plans will not be nullified by Yahweh's veto and so fail of implementation.

The doctrine of theodicy is evident in two sentences (vv. 4f.). **[4]** In v. 4, *ma'ane* is not 'goal', 'purpose', 'design' (contrary to Toy, Gemser, Ringgren, Barucq, Dahood, p. 35, RSV), but 'answer', and so the suffix (*l^ema'^anēhū* should be read, cf. GK §127.i) refers to *kōl* not to *YHWH*. Yahweh has made everything in relation to what answers to it ('with its counterpart', Scott), and so a wicked man for an evil day. LXX's paraphrase of MT (v. 9 in the Greek text) gets the right sense of the verse: 'All the works of the Lord are with justice and he will keep the impious man for an evil day.' The sentence 'Yahweh has made everything in relation to its counterpart' suggests a self-contained, self-regulating order rather than theodicy in the strict sense, i.e., a government which is enforced by repeated forensic interventions made by Yahweh either to 'justify' or 'condemn'. It approximates to von Rad's notion that the act is pregnant with its consequences, so that we have a process of action and reaction rather than an effect separable from a cause and produced by a forensic intervention (see on 1.20–33, above, pp. 272f.).

[5] There can be no doubt, however, that v. 5 reintroduces the typical vocabulary of theodicy; *lō' yinnāqe* (cf. 11.21a, above, p. 437) is the passive equivalent of *yaršīa'*, and *rāṣōn* and *tō'ēbā* are descriptive of Yahweh's emotive stance and are associated with acquittal and condemnation respectively (see above, p. 448 on 12.2). Pride in a context of piety is a sin rather than an intellectual flaw (see above on v. 18, p. 490). The phrase *yād lᵉyād* has already been explained (see on 11.21a, above, p. 437).

[6] Mention of the fear of Yahweh occurs in v. 6, and v. 6a betrays a 'spiritualizing' tendency in relation to cultic procedures similar to that of 15.8 (see above, p. 486). That this is a deliberate reinterpretation is indicated by the use of *kpr*, which is priestly terminology (cf. G. von Rad, *Old Testament Theology* i, p. 262: 'Of the ninety-one instances of this verb, sixty are found in the priestly texts') and regularly indicates making atonement by a sacrificial rite. It is therefore hard to resist the conclusion that v. 6a is anti-cultic in tone and that in assigning priority to loyalty and steadfastness, i.e., to a complete inward and outward assent to Yahweh's word and demands, it approximates to the prophetic polemic against mere externalism (see on 15.8, above, p. 486). The words 'In the fear of Yahweh is the avoidance of evil' could just possibly mean that when Yahweh is feared, evil is relinquished (cf. Scott), but the meaning, in view of the parallelism, is almost certainly that by fearing Yahweh one will not suffer evil or injury (Toy, Gemser, Ringgren, Barucq, see on v. 17, below, p. 500). 'The fear of Yahweh' corresponds with *ḥesed weʾᵉmet* and 'security' with 'atonement'.

[20] There is a question whether v. 20a belongs to the same frame of Yahwistic piety as v. 20b ('Happy is he who trusts in Yahweh'; on the form see 3.13, above, p. 294). If it does, the *maśkīl* is one whose illumination is the product of piety rather than one who has achieved intellectual grasp, and *dābār* can be equated with the prophetic *dābār*, the word of Yahweh, which plays a crucial part in the pro-prophetic reinterpretation of old wisdom (*PWM*, pp. 65f.; cf. Barucq). Gemser suggests that the reference is probably to the instruction of the wisdom teacher, in which case the *maśkīl* is the pupil who is quick to take the point that his teacher has made and whose intellectual keenness augurs well for his career (cf. LXX συνετὸς ἐν πράγμασιν 'knowledgeable in affairs'). One would then have to say that the verse envisages a partnership of intellectual competence and trust in Yahweh as constituting a whole man. Or, perhaps, the parallelism is antithetic and the point then is that the blessedness which Yahweh gives is a greater good than the prosperity of the man with a keen and disciplined intellect.

[19] Verse 19 illustrates the ambivalence of *ʿᵃnāwīm* (Q.) or

ʿanīyīm (K.), to which I referred in commenting on 15.16 (see above, pp. 486f.). Poverty and humility are natural allies, and impious pride goes with ill-gotten gain. **[8]** Another sentence which has the same form as 15.16 and 16.19 ('better . . . than'), and which is probably informed by the same conviction, is 16.8. The assumption here is that large revenues are hardly reconcilable with righteousness (*ṣᵉdāqā*) or justice (*mišpāṭ*). Although I am persuaded that this is how vv. 8 and 19 should be taken and that they establish an equation of poverty and piety, an interpretation such as I have placed on v. 16 (above, p. 489) is not absolutely excluded. The concern will then be to set wealth in a framework of values, the significant antithesis of v. 8 will be justice and injustice, and of v. 19 humility and pride. This makes a positive attitude to wealth still possible, and what is condemned is not wealth *per se* but wealth with inequity and *hubris*.

There is one certain reference to the machinery for consulting Urim and Thummim (v. 33), and another possible reference (v. 10a, *qesem*, see below). **[33]** Verse 33 observes that although the decision is reached by what is apparently an arbitrary procedure (on the operation of Urim and Thummim see my *I and II Samuel*, on I 14.41f.), it has all the authority of Yahweh's decision and is inerrant. The *ḥēq* (LXX, *κόλπους*, 'folds') is to be equated with the *ḥōšen*, the breast pocket in the priestly garment where the lots lay (Ex. 28.30; Lev. 8.8). I have noted elsewhere (*PWM*, pp. 55f.) that in I Samuel both Saul and David are represented as relying on Urim and Thummim for a right decision and that Saul's perplexity is consequent on his slaughter of the priests of Nob and the defection of the survivor, Abiathar, with the oracle to David. An apologetic concern is evident in v. 33 – an awareness that there is a need to assert that it is indeed Yahweh's will which finds expression in so mechanical and chancy a process as that of Urim and Thummim. But the defence consists in bare assertion, and no attempt is made to explain how this result can come about (see *PWM*, pp. 55f.).

[10] Is the puzzling *qesem* (v. 10a) – a word used elsewhere in the Old Testament pejoratively of heathen divination, as Gemser notes – to be explained as a reference to the king's use of Urim and Thummim in making crucial decisions, thereby avoiding error? The difficulty about this assumption is that *mišpāṭ* in v. 10b indicates that the sentence has precisely the king's infallible *legal* judgement in mind, rather than the safe guidance assured by Urim and Thummim over the entire field of military and political decisions. Cazelles draws attention to this when he says that the verse echoes the sentiments of the woman of Tekoa who says that David is as wise as the messenger (or 'angel') of God to hear good and evil (II Sam. 14.17, 20), where 'hear' has an exact legal significance (H. Cazelles, *VT* viii, 1958, p. 324; cf. II Sam. 19.28, *PWM*, pp. 58–60). On the other hand, *qesem* is correctly translated 'oracle' (LXX *μαντεῖον*, Toy, Gemser, Barucq, Cazelles; KB², 'decision produced by oracle'; Ringgren, 'divine decision'). But, if the verse has to do with the kind of legal acumen attributed by the woman of Tekoa to David, it is not concerned with a decision produced by oracular machinery, but with an ability to sift the evidence, to get at the truth and to arrive at a fair verdict. I would suggest that the significance of *qesem* may be explained on the analogy of II Sam. 14.27 (cf. 19.28), where the point that David's legal acumen is impeccable is made by comparing his decision to the utterance of a 'messenger of God', i.e., to a revealed and so infallible communication (see *PWM*, pp. 58f.). Or again, on the analogy of II Sam. 16.23, where a statement about the unerring political judgement of Ahithophel takes the form of an equation of his *ʿēṣā* with the *dābār* of God, where the reference may be to the prophetic *dābār* or to the decision of the priestly oracle (*PWM*, pp. 13, 55f.). Verse 10 then says that a legal judgement given out by a king has the quality of inerrancy which attaches to an oracular decision (*qesem*), just as the woman of Tekoa asserts that in his judgement of a legal case David is as wise as a messenger of God.

[11] *mōʾzenē mišpāṭ*, 'fair scales', are the opposite of *mōʾzenē mirmā* (11.1). Yahweh holds himself responsible for the accuracy of the balance and scales and makes it his business to see that the weights which are used conform exactly to standard (cf. *šelēmā*, 11.1b). I have noted (see 11.1, above, pp. 438f.) that this is a concern of international wisdom, but have suggested that it is perhaps more rewarding to relate such sentences to specific Old Testament references to the same subject in law and prophets. This is so because, as Gemser observes, the comparison with Egyptian wisdom can only be of a very general character, since the thought that God is the guarantor of the order is so typical of it. Moreover, the agreement with *Amenemope* xvii.18–xix.9 is formally slight.

[17] Verse 17 is about the way of life along which upright men are conducted. The contrast is not wisdom and folly, intellectual discipline and indiscipline, but piety and impiety, uprightness and crookedness, righteousness and unrighteousness. The upright man who walks along a road with an even surface, built up from a good foundation, keeps out of harm's way (the meaning of *sūr mērā'* is the same as in 16.6 and the allusion is not to the probity of the *yāšār* but to his safety; cf. Gemser on 16.17). The emphasis is on the security of the road and the expeditious progress which can be made along it, and this is complemented by the observation in v. 17b that he who watches his route (i.e., takes care not to deviate from the *mᵉsillā*) keeps his life (*nepeš*). Life is conceived dynamically; it is a journey along a road and to lose one's way is to lose one's life.

I have discussed the quantitative aspect of a full life or of 'wholeness' in connection with 10.27 (see above, p. 425). According to that verse the foreshortening of life is what the *rᵉšā'īm* may expect, just as 16.31 associates a grey head (a life which attains a fitting climax in an honourable seniority) with righteousness. **[31]** It is remarkable that old age is viewed so exclusively in its aspect of fulfilment – it is a crown of glory – and that nothing of the sadness and despair of old age is allowed to emerge, the failing of strength and the withering away of powers. The estimate reflects life in a society where the status of greybeards was assured, where 'knowledge' was a conservative concept, where wisdom was correlated with a long experience of life and the elders had weight in counsel and power in affairs.

Chapter 17

It can be observed in this chapter that with the reduction of antithetic parallelism (only in vv. 9, 17?, 22, 24) there goes a tendency towards looser form. Some of the sentences are devoid of parallelism of any kind and are of the type described by Toy as 'a continuous sentence' (vv. 2, 11, 13, 14, 15, 16, 18, 25). Others have parallelism of a kind which is called synthetic (vv. 5, 6, 8, 19, 20, 26, 27) or synonymous (vv. 4, 21, 28), although the distinction between these two types is sometimes a very fine one and difficult to draw. I do not attach much importance to it. There are a few examples of comparison; 'better . . . than' (v. 1), 'more . . . than' (v. 10) and 'rather . . . than' (the lesser of two evils, v. 12). In v. 3 the form 'as . . . so' is probably implicit (cf. Toy); v. 7 has an *a fortiori* construction (*'ap kī*) and v. 23b is a final clause.

Class A: vv. 2, 6, 7, 8, 10, 12, 14, 16, 17, 18, 21, 22, 24, 25, 26, 27, 28.
Class B: vv. 1, 4, 9, 11, 13, 19, 20.
Class C: vv. 3, 5, 15, 23.

Class A

Three sentences illustrate that old wisdom crystallizes into competence and mastery of affairs, that it is concerned with practical effectiveness and results, in a word, with success rather than with agonizing over matters of principle and points of conscience (vv. 2, 8, 18).

[8] If a bribe will smooth the way, then it is wisdom to employ a bribe. Toy discusses whether 'its possessors' refers to those who employ the bribe or those who receive it. The first alternative gives a much superior sense (so Gemser, Ringgren, p. 71, n.3, Barucq, RSV), but Scott prefers the second. 'A bribe works like magic' would be a fair paraphrase, since the *'eben ḥēn* is the stone with magical properties or the amulet. 'Many a pilgrim and tourist in Palestine will have noted the string of blue beads – almost the favourite amulet. Today they are hung over the driving wheel of a car; in the days not so far past they were round the donkey's neck' (E.F.F.B.). The bribe acts like a charm and the person who knows how to use it judiciously makes a success of everything to which he addresses himself. LXX has apparently reacted against the opportunism of MT. What is achieved by bribery according to MT is, according to LXX, the product of παιδεία (*mūsār*), 'discipline', and the reference to a lucky stone is absent from the text. Discipline is a μισθὸς χαρίτων to those who employ it, i.e., a gift or talent which wins them favour and recognition and ensures them success. Again, there is little doubt that the subject in v. 8b is the briber and not the bribe (cf. Toy), and the transition from *beʿālāw* to the singular verbs is not grammatically difficult (each of the bribers).

[2] Whoever makes himself competent and becomes a masterful man of affairs is able to overcome disadvantages of birth and to supplant those born into better estate but lacking in ability and character. The son who is the black sheep of the family and brings his father into contempt is to be envisaged as the member of the household which the *ʿebed maśkīl* serves. The 'sons' are members of the same family, and what the sentence then says is that the worthless son will be disinherited (see on 23.13, above, p. 386; also G. von Rad, *Old Testament Theology*, i, p. 151, on Deut. 21.18f.), while the able slave will inherit as if he were a son of the family.

[18] The counsel of v. 18 inculcates cautiousness and a hard-headed assessment of financial risk in the same terms as 6.1–5 (above, pp. 321f.). The sealing of a (rash) bargain by striking the hands (see on 11.21, above, p. 437; 16.5, above, pp. 497f.), or going surety for another person – a risk which cannot be measured and which cannot be accepted – is a mark of deficient acumen. Gemser translates *lipne rēʿēhū* 'on behalf of his neighbour', which is probably the correct general sense, but the phrase must be translated 'in the presence of his neighbour' (Ringgren, Scott, Barucq, RSV), or, perhaps, 'with respect to his neighbour', with a weakened sense of *lip^e nē* (cf. *l^e* in 6.1a, above, p. 321). The neighbour is in all likelihood the one on whose behalf financial liability is incurred, and the phrase indicates that he would be present at the proceedings of going surety. There is another possibility, more remote but not to be excluded entirely. If the translation 'in the presence of his neighbour' is pressed, the neighbour may be the one to whom the guarantor will be liable, should a third party for whom he has assumed financial responsibility be in default of his obligations.

[6] More is intended by v. 6a than that old men like to have their grandchildren playing about their feet. The generality that the very old derive pleasure from the company of the very young is indicated, but the sentence is perhaps also a more precise reflection of the values of the society out of which it comes. Young children give proof of the vigour of the family and assure its continuance; they are therefore an aspect of the crown (climax, fulfilment) of old age (cf. 16.31a, above, p. 501). They are 'subjects' of the *zāqēn*, who reinforce the power of his domestic empire, for he is not a valetudinarian who has surrendered authority in his house to his sons, but one to whom they defer and give precedence and in whom they experience an enhancement of their own dignity and status.

[21, 25] Since the family is an indispensable social unit in which corporate experience attains its most concentrated expression, it is a great denial and deprivation if for any reason a man is unable to found a family. Childlessness constitutes absolute deprivation, and little satisfaction is to be had in sons of poor calibre. A son who is a fool will never give pleasure to his father. Instead of watching him grow to maturity and the full exercise of his powers, and enjoying a peculiar sense of satisfaction, he will derive nothing but grief from his son. All his days he will suffer the pain of disappointment; a fool is vexation for his father and bitterness for his mother (vv. 21, 25). It is in the son that the father might expect to experience a prolongation of his own life, but a father does not see any continuance of himself in a son who is a fool.

The incapacity of the fool for the discipline of wisdom is the topic of three sentences (vv. 10, 16, 24). **[10]** A word of reproof makes a deeper impression on a perceptive man than does one hundred stripes on a fool. The *mēbīn* is ready to believe that he has erred and to learn from his mistakes by assimilating each rebuke of his teacher and making the necessary adjustments in his intellectual attitudes. He reacts sensitively to what he recognizes as a word of wisdom, and acknowledges the justice of the discipline to which he is made to submit. But the fool has no awareness of his need to learn; he is satisfied with his own wisdom and so is incapable of benefiting from instruction or submitting to an intellectual discipline. Whatever corporal punishment may be administered and however much physical pain he may suffer, the shell of his incorrigibility will remain intact and he will be inaccessible to education.

[24] In similar vein v. 24 states that the perceptive man keeps Wisdom in sight, while the eyes of the fool are on the ends of the earth. The contrast is between vigilance and concentration in the tasks of learning and the lack of these virtues. The *mēbīn* does not let Wisdom out of his sight for an instant (so Gemser), i.e., the personified Wisdom who is the source of knowledge as in 1.20f., 8.1f., 9.1f. (see above, pp. 272f., 344f., 360f.). The eyes of the *mēbīn* are riveted on the teacher, for he is fascinated by her instruction and is a picture of unbroken concentration. The *k^esīl* has the wandering eye and the vacant distracted mind, and his condition is expressed by a hyperbole. As a student who is hearing nothing of what his teacher says might let his eyes rove to every corner of the classroom, so the fool who is inattentive to the instruction of Wisdom is said to have his eyes on the ends of the earth. Toy, 'The goal of the man of understanding is wisdom', does not take the point of v. 24a correctly, while the meaning of the verse is hardly (see Toy) that the fool supposes wisdom is only to be found at the ends of the earth, but the perceptive man knows that it is at his door.

[16] Oesterley held that there was a reference in v. 16 to school fees, and this opinion is repeated by Scott (p. 111, n.16), but the suggestion is discounted by Toy and Gemser. It is not entirely clear what Gemser has in mind when he says that 'money' and 'buying' are to be understood metaphorically. Presumably he means that the representation of the fool with the fee in his hand coming to the wisdom teacher is just a picturesque way of saying that money cannot buy learning, i.e., it can only be acquired by strenuous intellectual effort (so Toy and Ringgren). I am inclined with Oesterley to believe that this sentence is a comment on *mores* and not just an imaginative construction which can be reduced to a generalization. One has to visualize a *k^{e}sīl* coming to a wisdom teacher with a fee in his hand and supposing that his money is an open sesame and his career as a sage assured, and then the biting comment of the shrewd observer: 'Why then does the fool have a fee in his hand? To buy wisdom, when he has no brains?'.

[12] A fool is a danger to others as well as being his own worst enemy (see on 13.20b, above, p. 456), and is to be avoided at all costs (see on 14.7, above p. 464). It is a lesser evil to be waylaid by a bear enraged by the loss of her cubs than to be embroiled with the folly of a fool.

[14] In v. 14, there is a lively awareness of the danger of allowing a quarrel to get under way. It may begin as a very small disagreement, but if the processes of conciliation are not brought to bear on it at once, it may get out of hand and acquire the dimensions of a major breach. It is like a small seepage of water from a dam (Gemser, p. 112, *pōṭēr* an abstract of the form *qōṭēl*; cf. G. R. Driver, *Biblica* 32, p. 196), which, if it is not mended in time, will destroy the construction. The dam will burst and the trickle will become an avalanche. There may be a special reference to litigation here, as in 15.18, where *mādōn* and *rīb* are also coupled. Thoughts of having recourse to the courts should be nipped in the bud, for at the beginning of a legal action the end is never in sight, and the consequences of embarking on litigation can never be foreseen. In any case, this is the way to perpetuate a quarrel, for the quest for legal victory implies the will to confer permanence on a disagreement, to give it a form which will endure for ever, and to accept a state of permanent estrangement from another person without making an effort to understand and effect a reconciliation.

[17] The meaning of v. 17 is affected by a decision about the parallelism, which is generally taken to be synonymous or synthetic (Gemser, Ringgren, Scott). Gemser holds that there is no distinction to be drawn between 'friend' and 'brother' – they are synonymous. If the parallelism is indeed synonymous, the sense of the sentence turns on the virtue of constancy in a friend and v. 17b specifies the condition of distress in which his constancy is seen to burn with a particularly bright flame. Friendship is a stable relationship which excludes fickleness, which is stronger than the severest strains which may be placed on it, and whose qualities are seen at their best when most is required of it. If the parallelism is antithetic, as Barucq supposes (*mais*), the meaning is rather that friendship is to be distinguished from a blood relationship. Friends are chosen for their personal qualities and a man spends his life with his friends because their company is congenial to him. On the other hand, brothers may not be naturally drawn to each other and may not see a great deal of each other, but yet there is a bond of kinship which they feel, and it creates peculiar obligations which they acknowledge. They are joined in an elemental solidarity, and while a brother may not be the chosen companion of his brother, he can be counted on for support and help in a time of extremity – this is a brother's office.

[22] Verse 22 is to be understood in the same way as 14.30 (above, p. 472), and is a statement on psycho-somatic relations, whether *gēhā* is translated 'healing', 'health' (Toy, Ringgren, Barucq, Scott, KB³, *ghh* 'to heal'), or 'face' (so G. R. Driver, *Ephem. Theol. Lovan.* 1950, p. 344, after Arabic *jihatu* 'face'; cf. 15.13), or is emended to *gᵉwīyā* 'body' with Pesh. and Targ. (Gemser and KB²). Although *gēhā* is a *hapax legomenon*, it should be read. The force of Driver's suggestion derives from the assumption that 17.22 is to be approximated to 15.13 (above, p. 480), but since admirable parallelism can be had by rendering *gēhā* 'health', this consideration should not be regarded as decisive (cf. Toy). According to the one rendering of *gēhā*, the meaning of the verse is that high morale or even mental health (*lēb śāmēaḥ*) improves or promotes physical health (or 'healing [of the body]'), whereas low morale (a broken spirit) produces physical debility (dries up the bone). According to the other rendering, the meaning is that high morale is reflected in the set of a man's face, while low morale destroys vitality (see on 15.13).

[26] The *gam* at the beginning of v. 26 may indicate that there was a previous statement on the topic of this verse which has not been preserved. The topic is apparently certain legal abuses, and *ṣaddīq* has a forensic sense – he is an innocent man who ought to have been acquitted (*hiṣdīq*; *lᵉ* with the direct object an Aramaism?; or 'with respect to', as Gemser and Ringgren suppose). It is questionable whether the argument from the parallelism ought to be pressed so as to support the conclusion that *nᵉdībīm* is to be understood in a moral sense (cf. Scott, Barucq, 'honourable people'). It is more probable that it has its usual reference to rank and status, and that moral excellence is not intended. The verse then simply contains two random samples of bad penal practice. It is bad to fine an innocent man, and it is improper to degrade noblemen by punishing them with scourging. *ʿal yōšer*, which I have paraphrased as 'improper', is difficult. I have taken it to mean 'contrary to what is right', i.e., bad practice. Toy emends to *bal yāšār*, 'is not right', on the basis of LXX οὐδὲ ὅσιον, and Kamphausen (also BH, Gemser; cf. Ringgren, p. 72, n.2) to *ʿal yeter* 'excessively'.

[27f.] An important aspect of intellectual discipline, as we have seen from the Egyptian Instruction, is economy of utterance and such certainty of self-control that speech is neither impulsive nor compulsive, but always a matter of careful timing and judiciously chosen words. This restraint and capacity for cool appraisal are marks of the knowledgeable and perceptive man (v. 27). When the clarity of the processes of thought in others is clouded by temper or tension, and their speech runs to excess, he maintains a calm front and weighs every word he speaks. His capacity to keep silent and eschew hot, angry words is also part of this self-mastery, and Grollenberg notes that in the Egyptian Instruction passion is opposed both to coolness and taciturnity (L. Grollenberg, *RB* lix, 1952, pp. 42f.). Even a fool may hide his intellectual deficiencies from others if only he has enough wit to keep his mouth shut. It is his speech which will betray him, and his wisdom is to conceal his defects as best he can and to permit others to put a profound interpretation on his silence. They will suppose that his are the intellectual habits of a *ḥākām* and a *nābōn*, and they will credit him with powers which he does not possess (v. 28). *qar rūaḥ* (v. 27b, K.) is certainly to be preferred to *yeqar rūaḥ* (Q.), 'of rare spirit' (see Toy); the man of cool temper (*qar rūaḥ*) is alternatively described as *'erek 'appayim*, 'even tempered', in 14.29; 15.18; 16.32. In the last-mentioned passage, this is associated with self-mastery. The opposite of *qar rūaḥ* or *'erek 'appayim* is *'īš ḥēmā* (15.18) or *qeṣar 'appayim* (14.17, 29; see on 14.17, 29, above, pp. 468f.; 15.18, 23, above, pp. 482, 477f.).

[7] In v. 7, the point should be sought in the second half of the verse and v. 7a is illustrative of v. 7b. Choice or elegant diction (speech which has a quality of distinction; BDB, 'arrogant speech') is not in character for a fool, and still less does lying become a person of breeding and rank. *nādīb* is not one who is morally excellent (cf. v. 26b, above, p. 506), but a gentleman with a code of honour, to whom truthfulness is second nature; if this is so, the emendation of *yeter* to *yōšer* (BH, Gemser, Toy, KB², Scott), for which LXX πιστά gives slight support, loses its force. The sentence is not moralistic in tone.

It simply describes one kind of activity which is out of character in a fool and another which is even more out of character in a gentleman.

Class B

The common denominator of the sentences in this block is the social concern to which they give expression and the antithetic social attitudes, creative and destructive, which they formulate.

[4] There is the man whose ambition in life is to hurt other people as much as he can and who is practised in the art of lying and misrepresentation (reading *šaqqār*; Gemser explains *šeqer* as a case of abstract for concrete). He has a ready ear for malicious gossip which will further his malevolent mission in life; any word which will do harm to others is his stock in trade; he will snap it up when he hears it and subsequently use it to promote faction and ill-will. He is dedicated to the destruction of concord and wholeness in his community. Gemser sees the point of this sentence not so much in what it says as in what it does not say but implies; i.e., this is the worst kind of social disease, a misanthropic stance which is fatal to the well-being of the community and which must at all costs be renounced.

[9] Both positive and negative aspects of the matter are explicit in v. 9, which contrasts one who serves love by keeping a charitable silence about another's misdemeanour with another who deliberately sets out to break up a friendship by circulating a damaging or defamatory report (see on 11.13, above, p. 429). The only question of interpretation which arises is whether it is magnanimity in the face of a hurt or affront to oneself, or whether it is rather a generosity of spirit in relation to another's indiscretion, as I have suggested. Most commentators suppose that there is no reference to a third party in the sentence, and that it is about the man who bears a personal injury in silence and desists from retaliatory action. He buries the wrong which has been done to him for the sake of love. He is then contrasted with the person who repeats a story which is damaging or hurtful to his friend and thereby severs the bond of friendship (Gemser, Toy, Scott, Barucq). I take *maprīd 'allūp* to mean the same here as in 16.28b, 'severs friends' (so Ringgren) and I suppose that v.9a refers to the benevolent overlooking of another's foibles and not response to a personal affront. This provides a better antithesis; on the one hand the person who believes that love is better served by a charitable silence than by a campaign of exposure and, on the other, the person who breaks up friendships – other men's friendships not his own – by scandalous gossip. Even if this is done with a kind of zeal for the welfare of the community, the means are not justified by the end, for it is an activity which will destroy love and trust and so destroy what it sets out to preserve. And those who begin as crusaders will be degraded by what they supposed to be their mission in life and will become common informers and persecutors.

[19] Verse 19a is about the person who likes to give offence, to pick a quarrel and to engender bitterness. He has this settled aim in life to hurt others and to precipitate a painful rupture of understanding and regard. He is a defective human being whose response to a social situation is aggressive and destructive. The phrase *magbīa pitḥō*, 'heightens his door' (19b), is obscure. It has been thought to refer to pride and ostentation finding expression in a pretentious style of house-building, and LXX, 'who makes his house high', could bear this interpretation (cf. Toy). This would yield the meaning that pride comes before a fall (cf. 16.18, above, p. 490; 18.12a, below, p. 521); in that case, *m^ebaqqēš šeber* refers to one who seeks his own ruin and not to one who seeks (social) disintegration (the latter is what 19a would lead us to expect). Scott thinks in terms of the inaccessibility of the entrance – a precaution which invites attack – but this is improbable. Gemser and Ringgren suppose that 'door' is a picturesque substitute for 'mouth', and Toy would read 'his mouth' (*pīw*). It would then be the braggart, the person who is excessively self-assertive and makes exaggerated claims for himself, who seeks his own ruin or, alternatively, who is a disruptive influence in the community. I have taken *m^ebaqqēš šeber* in conjunction with *magbīa pitḥō* to mean 'asks for a crash', i.e., seeks his own ruin, although this leaves 19b unrelated in topic to 19a.

[1] Again in v. 1 there is the contrast between concord (*šalwā*) and contention (*rīb*). Dahood (p. 37) cites Ugaritic *dbḥ dnt*, 'a banquet of contention' (*Baal* II iii.18f., *CML*, pp. 94f.). *dnt* is similarly explained by J. Aistleitner (p. 80, no. 766). Driver (*CML*, p. 154, n.15) connects it with Arabic *danā* and renders 'wickedness', Gordon with Arabic *dāna* (p. 386, no. 684), 'baseness'. Elaborate hospitality and practised civility do not necessarily indicate a desire for friendship, and a banquet may be a tense, unhappy occasion with dislikes and rivalries just below the surface and with a climate of insincerity, where men affect goodwill, but are, in fact, probing for weaknesses in their opponents, engaged in a delicate but deadly form of verbal fencing. Here there is no love of other men (see on 15.17, above, p. 484), only jealousy, suspicion, hostility, bad faith, and no deep, social experience can be had. But if there is a will for such experience, it can be had in the breaking of bread. A very simple meal will suffice to make brothers of those who seek each other out in sincerity, desiring to enrich others and to be enriched themselves. The mention of sacrifices is to be explained, as Gemser suggests, by the circumstance that any elaborate meal would have a cultic connection in that the meat to be eaten would first be slaughtered sacrificially (cf. Barucq, p. 148, n.27).

There are three sentences (vv. 11, 13, 20) in which the identity of self-interest and benevolence is the theme. **[11]** The evil man who is bent on faction and sedition and who strikes at the roots of the community of which he is a member will come to a bad end. He sets out to destroy law and order and to promote social disintegration, but the likelihood is that society will prove stronger than he, and that because it will not tolerate seditious behaviour it is he himself who will be destroyed. The 'ruthless messenger' who will be sent against him should be compared with 'the messenger of death' in 16.14a. Society will pass its sentence, and when this is 'officially' conveyed to him he will realize that no mercy is shown to one who seeks the death of his own community (see my comments on Absalom's rebellion, *I and II Samuel*, on II Sam. 19).

[13] Verse 13 describes one who is innately misanthropic and who has not even the elementary sense of gratitude which moves a man to repay good with good. When kindness has been shown to him, he does his benefactor an injury. Such a person is his own worst enemy, for he makes his own position in society an impossible one. He excommunicates himself and works himself into a corner where the disease from which he suffers will rage within him until he is destroyed. Moreover, his fate is inseparable from that of his family; they are bound up together in the bundle of life and he destroys them, too.

[20] In v. 20, the connection between this identity of self-interest and benevolence and the doctrine of theodicy is more evident. The man who deliberately twists the facts and engages in misrepresentation in order to create social havoc suffers from a deep inner disturbance and perversion. He is hostile to other men, and this hostility is evidence of a deep derangement, of a fundamental maladjustment which makes him less than a human being. There is an intrinsic connection between a twisted mind and a twisted tongue, i.e., speech which is directed towards injuring others and damaging human relationships. This malevolence will boomerang on himself. He purposes evil and attacks social integrity and wholeness. But this is an 'order' which cannot be opposed effectively and he will be visited with punishment ('He will fall into evil').

Class C

The theme of theodicy is taken up by three sentences (vv. 3, 5, 15) which declare Yahweh's will for justice and the investigation in depth which he makes before arriving at his verdict. **[3]** He is a judge who misses nothing (see on 15.3, above, p. 484), and who submits men to a process of testing which reveals all that is in them. Two images are constructed as similitudes of the activity of Yahweh in trying or ascertaining the quality of men. As silver and gold are tried for genuineness and purity in a furnace, so Yahweh is the Assayer who tries human motives, separating the spurious from the genuine and ascertaining what a man is as opposed to what he professes to be (see on 16.2, above, pp. 495f.).

The remaining two sentences contain forensic vocabulary and indicate that Yahweh upholds a rule of righteousness. **[5]** He who sneers at a poor man insults his (i.e., the poor man's) Maker (see on 14.31a, above, p. 473), and a verdict of 'Not Guilty' will not be brought in for one who makes fun of another's calamity. Driver observes that the parallelism (*rāš*) and LXX ἀπολλυμένῳ (which points to *le'ōbēd*, 'one who is perishing', who is being submerged in his misfortunes) suggest that *'yd* should be read as a participle. He notes that several Hebrew manuscripts read *'d*, which he points as *'ēd* and connects with Arabic *'āda*, 'bent', 'inclined', 'weighed down'; Hebrew **'ōd* (cf. *mōt*, *mēt*). Driver postulates formations from this root also in Job 31.23 and Ps. 31.12 (*Biblica* 32, p. 182). This would make the translation of v. 5b: 'He who finds pleasure in one who is burdened with troubles will not be acquitted'. There is weight in this argument, but 'calamity' should be retained despite the defective parallelism which it yields.

[15] Verse 15 alludes to corrupt legal procedures, to the acquittal of a guilty person and the condemnation of an innocent one – both are an abomination to Yahweh. I have shown that Yahweh's disapproval (*tō'ēbā*) is to be correlated with his verdict of 'Guilty' and his approval (*rāṣōn*) with a verdict of 'Not Guilty'; the one is for the *rāšā'* and the other for the *ṣaddīq*. I have hinted (above, p. 448) that this mode of expression may represent a free adaptation of declaratory formulae spoken in a cultic context by means of which the priest indicated to the worshipper Yahweh's attitude of approval or disapproval of himself or of his offering (see on 12.2, above, p. 448; cf. 11.20, above, p. 438, and 15.8f., especially 15.8, where the context is cultic; above, pp. 486f.).

[23] The pejorative attitude to bribery in v. 23 accords with the estimate of 15.27b (above, p. 485) which, however, views the transaction from the other end. There the acceptance of bribes is a form of cupidity, and it is the refusal to accept them which is commended. Here it is the *rāšā'* who employs the bribe in order to make a judge acquiescent and thereby conspires to defeat the ends of justice. He carries it about in his breast pocket and slips it to the corrupt official at the opportune moment. In v. 8 a very different estimate of bribery appears – it is a way of getting things done, of eliminating bottlenecks. I have suggested that the change of attitude towards bribery is an aspect of the reinterpretation of old wisdom which involved the superseding of hard-headed, pragmatic attitudes by a stringent Yahwistic ethic in which righteousness and wickedness were sharply differentiated (*PWM*, p. 65).

Chapter 18

The observation made in ch. 17 that there is a correlation between the reduced number of sentences with antithetic parallelism and a general loosening of form is equally applicable to this chapter. Beside the sentences which certainly have an antithetic construction (vv. 12, 14, 23, 24), there are two others admitted by Toy to this class which do not fulfil its formal criteria. Verse 2 is a continuous sentence with the same subject throughout, and although *kī 'im* is adversative, one can hardly speak of parallelism. In v. 17 it is perhaps legitimate to speak of 'implied parallelism' (Toy), but here again the formal articulation of the antithetic parallelism is defective. Again, the sentences which can be described rather loosely as exhibiting synthetic parallelism are somewhat heterogeneous (vv. 1, 3, 4, 5, 6, 7, 8, 10, 11, 15, 16, 18, 19, 20, 21, 22) and there are two verses in which there is no trace of a balancing of halves and so no parallelism (vv. 9, 13). Here we have simply a continuous sentence, not one shaped by the parallelism of two halves. In vv. 4, 8, 10, the synthetic parallelism amounts to explication of figures of speech which appear in the first half of each of these verses. Thus v. 4b is explication of 'deep waters', v. 8b of the simile in v. 8a and v. 10b of the metaphor in v. 10a (on the opinion that v. 4 has antithetic parallelism – an opinion which affects the interpretation of the verse – see below).

Class A: vv. 2, 4, 5, 6, 7, 9, 11, 13, 14, 15, 16, 17, 20, 21, 23, 24.
Class B: vv. 1, 8, 19.
Class C: vv. 3, 10, 12, 18, 22.

Class A

The importance of speech and its effects for good or ill is the theme of one group of sentences (vv. 2, 4, 6, 7, 13, 20, 21). [4] The suggestion that the parallelism of v. 4 is antithetic and that the intention is to contrast a cistern whose store of water is exhaustible with a spring which is inexhaustible is discussed by Toy and rightly rejected (contrary to Gemser, who says: 'The two stichoi probably stand in an antithetic or climactic relationship to one another'; also Scott; cf. Ringgren, p. 76, n.1). Barucq has the right sense of the verse: 'The words of a man's mouth are deep waters, a bubbling brook, a spring of wisdom.' This, as Barucq points out, has the support of LXX, except that it reads 'fountain of life' (so 10 Hebrew manuscripts). Toy adopts this and conjectures 'the words of the wise' for 'the words of a man's mouth'. MT should be retained and then we have to assume that it implies what Toy would make explicit by emendation.

This view of MT is in accord with the metaphorical language which it uses (deep waters, a bubbling brook, a spring of wisdom), which only fits the words of a wise man. 'Deep waters' is indicative of profundity and the other figures of ampleness. The speech of a wise man has a quality of depth; it is a perceptive, well-considered utterance free from superficiality and rashness. Moreover, he is never at a loss for words and draws again and again from a copious store of words, meeting every occasion with a well-chosen and weighty expression of the fine qualities of his mind which assume form and substance in his speech. Scott supposes that 'deep waters' indicates obscure rather than profound speech and his rendering of v. 4b, 'the well of wisdom is a flowing stream' (similarly Gemser and Ringgren), produces an odd association of images which Ringgren explains as a representation that the words of the wise, issuing from the depths of a spring of wisdom, flow away as a fructifying stream. The interpretation would then be that those who pay attention to the teaching of the wise men will have life and happiness, but the verse should rather be interpreted on the basis of the translation of v. 4b which I have discussed above.

[20] The phrase 'the fruit of a man's mouth' has already occurred in 12.14a and 13.2a (see above, pp. 448, 459), and the meaning of vv. 20 and 21 hinges on the interpretation that is put on it. In v. 20 a supplementary consideration is the degree of literalness which is to be attached to *beṭen* and *tiśbaʿ*. Both Toy and Ringgren reduce v. 20 to the generalization that words have consequences and that a man must be prepared to bear the consequences of his speech. Hence Ringgren is consistent in applying the same interpretation to v. 21b, which is then an observation on the liabilities of the person who likes to speak a lot; the more words spoken, the greater the effects for good or evil, depending on the quality of his speech. Against this I would urge that the metaphors of v. 20 have to be taken more seriously and understood more exactly, and that 'fruit' here as in 12.14a and 13.2a means 'good fruit', and is the antithesis of absence of fruit. It is not therefore an ambivalent expression which can be taken to represent consequences good or bad; the reference is to fruitful speech as opposed to barren speech.

The literal meaning of v. 20 would then be that there is a kind of speech which has economic value and which contributes to a man's livelihood. It is fruitful and productive (cf. *t^{e}bū'ā*) in the sense that it is a factor in his earning power. It is unlikely, however, that this is what is intended by v. 20, and the references to the satisfaction of the stomach and the output of the lips should be understood metaphorically. The verse is then connected with a particular view of the function of speech (see on 15.1, above, p. 477), namely, that it should be productive, and with the belief that this is the criterion by which its value should be judged. Speech may be clever or barbed, but if it is no more than an exercise in rhetoric or polemic and is not fruitful in the sense of being directed towards constructive ends, it will not give satisfaction to the speaker. Satisfaction is to be experienced not in articulateness as an end in itself, but in the productive issue towards which speech is directed, whatever this may be.

[21] Speech is an important aspect of a man's weight or effectiveness, and so much depends on a judicious and timely use of words that life and death are in the power of the tongue; it is those who have a proper regard for the power of words whose speech will bear fruit. Such men are in love with language; they use it fastidiously, they search for chaste expression and precise meaning, and they have an end in view which they will reach because they know what language is for and how it can best be used to achieve its purpose. In short, language is a political instrument, using that word broadly, and satisfaction is to be had in the political goals which can be reached through mastery of its potentialities.

[6] Contrariwise, the fool misuses words so that they become socially mischievous and work to his own detriment. A fool's lips enter upon controversy (G. R. Driver, *VT* i, 1951, p. 249) or lead (him) into controversy (reading *yābī'ū* with LXX and Targ.), and he speaks so provocatively as to appear to call out for a beating. Those who listen to him judge his words to be disruptive and inflammatory, and the effect of his speech is always to alienate himself from public sympathy and to attract feelings of hostility. **[7]** His speech is his ruin; it is the snare in which he is trapped and loses his life (*nepeš* = 'life', so Ringgren, contrary to Toy, Gemser, Barucq, Scott, who translate 'self' and suppose that *napšō* is parallel to *lō* in v. 7a). The fool's words have a socially destructive intent, and he thereby draws on himself the disapproval and retaliation of the community and condemns himself to isolation, ineffectiveness, loss of vitality and ultimately death. The thought that there is a harmony of self-interest and social responsibility (see on 14.21, 22, above, p. 473; 17.11, 13, 20, above, pp. 456f.) is here formulated with special reference to speech. Since I wanted to bring out especially the point of the abuse of language, I have put these sentences in class A rather than class B, which would have been equally appropriate.

[13] There is the flaw of speaking impulsively and of acquiring the bad habit of not listening to what the other man says. This is an aspect of folly, and the person guilty of such practice will suffer disrepute. It is impossible to speak to the point if the point has not been taken, and effective speaking is inseparable from high relevance and a sensitive regard for all views which are being expressed. The self-opinionated bore will never make a telling intervention, nor will the man who is so anxious to speak that he does not have the patience and self-control to listen to the case which he takes it on himself to answer. To blurt is to be guilty of intellectual indiscipline, and a compulsive speaker is soon written off and disregarded.

[2] It is the same foible which is indicated in v. 2. The fool has no pleasure in perceptiveness (*t^ebūnā*), but only in spewing out his opinions. He is not in love with knowledge (cf. v. 15), but with his own ideas, and is so absorbed in the business of seizing every opportunity of expressing them that he has no inclination to weigh other men's opinions or for the objective of intellectual clarity. [15] He is the opposite of the *nābōn*, who is bent on the acquisition of knowledge, or the pupil who listens to his teachers and searches incessantly for knowledge. The one man has so many opinions of his own and is so satisfied with them that he is unteachable, while the other submits himself to discipline and acquires the knowledge and acumen which will make his opinions weighty when he begins to hold them (see on 12.23, above, pp. 442f. and 13.16, above, p. 456).

Two verses (vv. 5, 17) are concerned with judicial procedures, one with the procuring of an injustice and the other with the contribution of cross-examination to the process of arriving at a fair verdict. [5] In v. 5, *rāšā'* and *ṣaddīq* are precise forensic terms; the first is the man who is in the wrong but is pronounced in the right, and the second is the one in whose favour the verdict (*mišpāṭ*) should have gone and who is denied justice. There is a miscarriage of justice because the judge is partial to one of the parties without regard to the merits of the case (see on 17.15, above, pp. 511f.). The expression 'to lift up the face' is probably derived, as Toy suggests, from the practice of raising the face of a prostrate suppliant in token that his plea has been granted. Dahood (p. 39) cites Isa. 10.2, *l^ehaṭṭōt middīn dallīm*, 'to deny justice to the poor', and suggests that *b* in v. 5, as in Ugaritic, means 'from', i.e., 'to deny justice to a righteous man'. [17] The first speaker in v. 17 is, as Driver points out, the plaintiff or pursuer, whose speech appears to show that he is in the right and that his case is unanswerable. Then the legal perspective is restored when the defendant submits him to a searching interrogation, thereby enabling the judge better to assess the issues at stake and to determine the evidential value of his submissions (G. R. Driver, *Biblica* 32, p. 183). The exact point of v. 17 is not that the judge should listen to both parties (Ringgren), but that cross-examination brings out the truth or, at least, facilitates the sifting of the evidence and the doing of justice.

[9] The one envisaged in v. 9 is slack and lazy in his business. He does not act as if he expected to be successful and his half-hearted, unconvincing efforts are ruinous. He is a brother to a wrecker in the sense that although he does not ruin himself by wild insensate behaviour which is devoid of self-interest and self-destructive, yet the end of his lethargy coincides with that of recklessness. [11] Verse 11

takes up the thought of 10.15 that wealth affords security, v. 11a reproducing exactly the metaphor of 10.15a (see above, p. 416). The rich man envisages his wealth as a high wall in which he is enclosed and given protection from the chanciness and dangers of life. While his safety is not absolute, he is not naked and defenceless before the whims and caprice of circumstance in the same degree as the poor man. His wealth is a buffer (see 10.15b, above, p. 416). To read *bimᵉśukkātō*, literally, 'in his being enclosed' (cf. Ringgren, p. 74, n.3) for *bᵉmaśkītō* is not an improvement, but, if it were adopted, v. 11b would mean that wealth encloses and protects him who possesses it like a high wall (cf. Scott).

[14] The influence of morale on physical health (see on 14.30, above, p. 472; 17.22, above, p. 506) is further commented on in v. 14. It is a man's spirit which enables him to 'contain' his illness, that is, to impose a measure of control on it, to cope with it in such a way that it is not permitted to deter him from life and its responsibilities. Hence he does not permit his infirmity or disease to tyrannize over him or to dictate its terms to him. He has to live with it, but he enjoys a real freedom, even within the limitations which it may impose on him, and it does not coerce him to abdicate from life and wait passively for death. It is a sickness of spirit which is mortal, for when this inner citadel of resistance has been crushed and all zest for the warfare of life has departed, no man can endure. Frankenberg's emendation (*mᵉḥallēhū* for *maḥᵃlēhū*), which is noted by BH and Ringgren (p. 75, n.1), 'He who soothes a man controls his anger', introduces an idea which is foreign to the verse (cf. Toy).

[16] Verse 16 takes up the same pragmatic attitude towards bribery as 17.8 (see above, p. 502). Toy supposes that it is not precisely bribery which is in view here, but rather the gift which is offered to an influential superior with a view to winning his favour and soliciting his assistance. The gift makes room for the giver in the sense that it gives him the *entrée* to those circles of high society to which he aspires. The verse should be understood rather as a more general recommendation of the bribe for the clearing of bottlenecks and the unlocking of doors. The ambitious man who desires to rise to the top and mix socially with the great will find that the judicious use of the bribe facilitates his progress. There is no reason to conclude (contrary to Ringgren) that it is specifically the bribing of judges which is envisaged. The possibility that *mattān* could mean 'intellectual endowment' is rightly dismissed by Toy.

[23] Verse 23 is an acute observation on an aspect of human behaviour. A poor man is in no position to do other than speak ingratiatingly, and it is the role of the rich man to harden his heart against appeals for charity. Speech for the poor man is an instrument to relieve his misery and to awaken pity for his distress in the person who is addressed. Civility, deference and even flattery are second nature to him; they are numbered among the conditions of his survival. The remark that the rich man replies roughly is factual rather than condemnatory. This is just the way of the world, and the rich man's response is as natural to his situation as is the poor man's to his. The wealthy man is always hearing these hard-luck stories, and his brusqueness is part of his defensive mechanism, for there are limits to what his wealth can do to allay poverty and he is not prepared to allow pity to sear his soul too frequently. His uncouth rebuff is a reflection of his consciousness of the pressures which are on him by reason of the existence of poverty and the unrelenting demands which it makes on his generosity. I take this to be a quite general statement, and not one which is bounded by a particular historical period or can be assigned to one (contrary to Toy, 'probably the Greek period').

[24] The various possibilities for the interpretation of v. 24 hinge on textual and linguistic judgements. Driver (*Biblica*, 32, pp. 183f.) derives *hitrōʿēaʿ* from *rūaʿ* 'to shout', used here like Syriac *rāʿ* in the weakened sense 'to chatter', and cites in support the Greek of the Hexapla, ἀνὴρ ἑταιριῶν τοῦ ἑταιρεύασθαι, 'a man of companionships (is a man) for getting companions', i.e., according to Driver, social flair goes with superficial personal relationships (Field, *Orig. Hex*, ii, p. 349). The contrast of v. 24 would then be between the person who is an adept at social chatter – who has innumerable acquaintances but no friends – and the very different kind of person who is not a social success in this sense, but who is capable of a deep spiritual engagement with another and who makes his friends for life. This meaning is also had if Pesh. and Targ. are followed (MT: *'īš* = *yēš*?; cf. Aramaic *'īt*), and *hitrōʿēaʿ* emended to *hitrāʿōt* (Toy: 'There are friends who only seek society'; RSV: 'who pretend to be friends').

Alternatively *hitrōʿēaʿ* may be derived from *rʿʿ* = *rṣṣ* and *le* may then indicate 'is likely to' (G. R. Driver, *Biblica* 32, p. 196): 'There are companions who are likely to break each other in pieces' (cf. Gemser, '*wird wahrscheinlich*'). The reference is then to an association with appearances of social warmth in which there is no brotherhood nor sacrificial friendship. Such an association has no enduring bond; it is riven by destructive tensions and contains within itself the seeds of faction and internecine conflict. Over against this *bonhomie* which is vulnerable to jealousy, hatred and feud there is the friendship which is nothing less than the discovery of a brother – a kindred soul. It is this which endures (see on 15.17, above, p. 484, and 17.1, above, pp. 509f.). A decision is difficult and cannot be made with assurance. I accept Driver's explanation of 24a and translate: 'There is a companion who does nothing but chatter.'

Class B

[1] In v. 1, LXX translates: 'A man who wants to separate himself from his friends seeks pretexts, but on every occasion he will be culpable.' There are two respects in which this might serve to elucidate MT. 'Pretexts' (*προφάσεις*) has been thought to point to *tō'^{a}nā*, 'occasion' (for a quarrel), as against MT *ta'^{a}wā*, 'desire', and *b^{e}kol tūšīyā* has apparently been translated 'on every occasion' (*ἐν παντὶ δὲ καιρῷ*), which is then supposed to give some slight support to the translation 'by every means' (Frankenberg, cf. Toy), or 'with all power' (Gemser, Ringgren). The verse then means that the social misfit (*niprād*) whose aggressiveness and hostility alienates him from other men and makes him an 'outsider' is always seeking an occasion for a quarrel; he is ready to fulminate, to be bitterly contentious with all the strength of his being.

But *b^{e}kol tūšīyā* means 'against all sound and effective policy' (cf. *PWM*, p. 80) and not 'with all (destructive) power' – *tūšīyā* is not pejorative. Further, I am not persuaded that *ta'^{a}wā* (MT) is inapposite. The *niprād* (Scott, 'unsociable man') seeks only the satisfaction of his anti-social impulses, and so he dissents (destructively) from every sound policy (cf. Barucq and Scott).

[8] The slanderer's wares are tit-bits (literally, 'food which is gorged') which go down into the inner compartments of the stomach. Slander is hospitably received and welcomed for a long stay. This is an observation on a human flaw – the appetite for evil gossip and the relish with which it is savoured and devoured. People like to hear evil of their fellows and whatever they may forget they will recollect slander without any effort of memory; it is remembered, and in all probability it will be transmitted by a damaging whisper. The *ḥad^{e}rē beṭen* are the storerooms from which words issue when they are spoken (see on 22.18, above, pp. 374f.; cf. *Amenemope* xiv.2f.: 'God hates him who falsifies words; his great abomination is the contentious of belly', *ANET*, p. 423).

[19] In v. 19, the text of MT is obscure and the extensive emendations of Toy and BH amount to an admission that nothing can be made of it as it stands. LXX reads: 'A brother saved by his brother is like a town fortified and elevated; he is as strong as a royal rampart.' BH (cf. Barucq) suggests that LXX (also Pesh., Targ., V) may have read *nôšāʿ* and not *nipšāʿ*, but this is doubted by Toy ('improbable in the connection'). Again, *keqiryat ʿōz* is easier than *miqqiryat ʿōz*, but this may indicate that the principle *lectio difficilior potior* should apply, although considerations of parallelism (*kiberîaḥ*) point to the former. A beginning can be made by asserting that *nipšāʿ* is a person who feels that he has been snubbed or wounded and has taken offence (Barucq and Scott), rather than one who has been deceived (Gemser and Ringgren). *miqqiryat ʿōz* may mean 'more inaccessible than a fortified city' (Gemser, Barucq, Scott) or 'more formidable than a fortified city' (Ringgren), although either way one is conscious of straining after sense.

Ringgren supposes that what is indicated is the changing of a close friend into an implacable enemy through abuse of his friendship. With the other rendering, the emphasis is on the difficulty of penetrating the barriers of estrangement and effecting a reconciliation. *keqiryat ʿōz* could also bear this interpretation, and v. 19b can be similarly construed. Gemser argues that the originality of *midyānîm* (v. 19b) is shown by the circumstance that it is the stitch-word which explains the contiguity of vv. 18 and 19. The quarrels and misunderstandings which divide men are as hard to break down as the bar (on the gate) of a palace. The person who has quarrelled with his fellows and has cut himself off from them with a deep sense of personal injury is not easily reached with a view to conciliation. He has taken what seems to him an irrevocable step, and he consciously strives to be invulnerable to every conciliatory approach. The friend who seeks an estranged friend embarks on an arduous task; it is a scaling of fortifications and a breaking down of bars which would obstruct his passage to the person he once knew, and deny him the rediscovery of the friend whom he has lost. It is on the other side of the defences which the estranged one has erected that there exists the possibility that confidence will be re-established, injuries forgiven and friendship renewed.

Class C

A group of sentences reflect different aspects of the doctrine of theodicy (vv. 3, 10, 12, 22). **[3]** Contempt follows hard on the heels of wickedness (reading *reša'* for MT *rāšā'*, Toy, BH, Gemser, Ringgren, Scott) and insult on disrepute. I have pointed out (see on 13.18, above, p. 456) that *qālōn*, 'disrepute', means literally 'lightness', i.e., lack of social esteem, and so is the opposite of *kābōd* 'heaviness', i.e., status, recognition, honour. **[12]** According to v. 12, *'anāwā*, pious submission to Yahweh, precedes *kābōd*, whereas an impious *hubris* (see on 16.18, above, p. 490) will precipitate a collision with Yahweh of such violence as to cause disintegration (*šeber*). This verse may embody a reinterpretation of old wisdom akin to the prophetic one (*PWM*, pp. 65f.), in which case *lēb* is precisely 'acumen', 'intellectual capacity'; the point then is that the man who acts on the assumption that the world can be bent to the shape of his plans will experience a moment of 'shattering' (on *yigbah lēb*, see *PWM*, pp. 73–78). **[10]** Verse 10 deals with the security of the righteous man (see on 10.2, 9, 24, 25, 29, 30, above, pp. 422f.; 11.4, 6, 8, 21, above, pp. 430f.; 12.3, 7, 12, above, p. 449; 13.6, above, p. 461) and says that Yahweh's name is a strong tower into which the *ṣaddīq* runs and is inaccessible to those who would hurt him. The particular aspect of Yahweh's name or nature in view is that which is expressed in the theodicy. By its enforcement, Yahweh makes the *ṣaddīq* safe and exposes the *rāšā'* to punishment.

[22] When v. 22 declares that he who finds a wife finds a good thing, we have to assume that wife in question is an *'ēšet ḥayil* (31.10–30, see below, pp. 665f.) and not a trollop or a shrew (*mebīšā*), who is described in 12.4b as maggots in the bones (see above, p. 443). A good wife is a mark of Yahweh's *rāṣōn*; I have noted the correlation of *ṣaddīq* and *rāṣōn*, *rāšā'* and *tō'ēbā* (see on 12.2, above, p. 448; 14.9, above, pp. 475f.; 15.8, above, p. 486; 17.15, above, pp. 511f.) and have shown that this is the vocabulary of theodicy. It is uncertain whether *rāṣōn* has this full theological import here. The verse may not mean any more than that any man who finds a good wife has been favoured by Yahweh, but there may be the further implication that it is the *ṣaddīq* who deserves a good wife and, with her, assured domestic peace and prosperity as the basis of *kābōd*.

[18] When legal proceedings have been interminable and indecisive, the quest for a legal verdict may be deserted and an appeal made to the lot which is Yahweh's decision (see on 16.33, above,

p. 499). Albright has suggested that *yašbīt* is a technical term for the termination of a process of litigation (W. F. Albright, *VTS* iii, p. 10), and Driver emends *ʿaṣūmīm* to *ʿōṣemīm*, 'litigants', postulating **ʿāṣam* on the basis of Syriac *ʿṣam*, with which he connects *ʿaṣūmōt*, 'pleas', in Isa. 41.21. I am not persuaded that the rendering 'powerful opponents' is 'obviously unsuitable to the context' (G. R. Driver, *Biblica* 32, p. 183). I take the point to be – it is confirmed by the litigious habits of some wealthy people in our own society – that only those who are not unduly worried by considerable expense will engage in a long drawn out legal contest for the pleasure of the taste of victory. The meaning of v. 18b may be that the decision of the lot is a way of separating powerful parties who are locked together in legal contest.

Chapter 19

Evidences of disintegration of form to which I have referred in the chapters immediately preceding this can again be detected here. As I have already suggested, this can, to some extent, be correlated with the diminution of antithetic parallelism, since all other types of parallelism lack the tightness of form which characterizes a precise antithesis. Apart from the sentences with synthetic or synonymous (vv. 2, 5, 6, 8, 9, 11, 13, 15, 22?, 23, 28, 29) and antithetic (vv. 4, 12, 14, 16, 21) parallelism, there are some which are devoid of any parallelism (vv. 3, 17, 24, 26). These are continuous sentences which do not divide into two *stichoi*. Special constructions are the *a fortiori* (*'ap kī*, vv. 7, 10) and the 'better . . . than' (v. 1) types.

Another indication of slackening of form is the fact that some verses approximate formally to the Instruction rather than to the wisdom sentence, as is evidenced by the presence of the imperative rather than the indicative, and by the subordinate clauses which belong to the Instruction but are inimical to the parallelism of a wisdom sentence. Thus v. 18 has two imperatives, one with a motive clause; v. 20 has two imperatives with a final clause, and v. 19b is a motive clause. That v. 27 is a fragment of Instruction is shown by the address 'my son', whose presence argues the originality of the imperative *ḥadal*, even if it is used in a weakened sense (see below, p. 525). All these examples depart from the form of the wisdom sentence in that they are not factual observations in the third person, and this is true also of v. 25, although with regard to parallelism it has some affinity with the wisdom sentence. There is no doubt that the *we* of

v. 25b is adversative and that the verse does have antithetic parallelism of a kind, but in other respects it has the shape of Instruction rather than of the wisdom sentence. The imperfect *takke* (v. 25a) almost has the force of an imperative, and *hōkīaḥ* (v. 25b) is an imperative, so that each *stichos* consists of an imperative followed by an 'and so' clause (asyndetic in the case of v. 25b) in the manner of the Instruction.

Class A: vv. 2, 4, 5, 6, 7, 8, 9, 10, 11, 12, 13, 15, 16, 18, 19(?), 20, 24, 25, 26, 27, 28, 29.
Class B: v. 22.
Class C: vv. 1, 3, 14(?), 17, 21, 23.

Class A

A group of sentences converges on the theme of discipline (vv. 16, 18, 20, 25, 27, 29). Teachability leads to life and incorrigibility to death (vv. 16, 18). **[16]** Verse 16, like 13.13 (see above, pp. 454f.), is probably to be referred to the authoritative sayings (*miṣwā*) of the wisdom teacher. He who pays attention to them will keep his life, and he who despises them will die (so Q.; K., 'will be put to death'). The latter case is a supercilious disregard of the teaching given and a consequent incapacity for education – a stance associated with the *lēṣ* (see below, p. 525, on vv. 25 and 29) rather than simply a lack of attentiveness to what is said (Ringgren and Scott). The phrase 'his ways' in v. 16b is obscure. The emendation of *derākāw* to *dābār* (Toy, BH, Gemser, BJ) removes the difficulty (cf. 13.13a) without dealing faithfully with it. Barucq follows Dahood (p. 40) in connecting *derākāw* with Ugaritic *drkt* and translates 'his authority', but the plural form in Hebrew makes difficulties for this suggestion. If MT is retained, 'ways' has to be equated with 'instructions', and if the sentence is taken to refer to educational discipline rather than the discipline of piety ('the fear of Yahweh'), 'his ways' will mean the instructions of the wisdom teacher. It would seem to me, however, that the phrase 'his ways' could be understood more easily of Yahweh than of a wisdom teacher (cf. Barucq, 'perhaps ways of Yahweh'), and if this were thought to be a decisive consideration, one would have to think of the *miṣwā* of Yahweh also in v. 16a. The verse would then be representative of the new discipline of piety rather than of the educational discipline of old wisdom, and would belong to class C.

[18] In v. 18, the rather quaint motive clause which is attached to the imperative ('for there is hope') is apparently intended to reassure a father that parental discipline, if it is sustained, will take effect, and that a son is not so incorrigible or intractable as he may appear. If the father keeps it up, he will eventually be knocked into shape. The phrase *'al tiśśā' napšekā* (v. 18b) is troublesome. LXX translates, 'But do not rouse your soul to excess' (εἰς δὲ ὕβριν), which suggests that the Hebrew phrase refers to a loss of temper, and this is how Gemser and Barucq translate it. εἰς δὲ ὕβριν could translate *we'el ḥēmōt*, which Gemser substitutes for *we'el hamītō* ('But do not be carried off in a rage'). Nevertheless, the correct translation of *nś' nepeš* is probably 'contrive' or 'aspire' (cf. KB2; Toy, 'Set not thy heart'; Ringgren, 'Do not undertake'), and v. 18 is a replica of 23.13. 'Do not contrive to kill him' does not mean 'Do not chastise him excessively' (contrary to D. Winton Thomas, *VTS* iii, p. 288), but 'Do not bring about his death by failing to discipline him' (see on 23.13, above, p. 386). Although Scott paraphrases rather than translates, he gets the sense right: 'And do not indulge him to his own destruction.' The thought is the characteristic one that indiscipline leads to death, and the other side of this appears in v. 20.

[20] The pupil must listen to his teacher's advice (*'ēṣā*) and accept it as mandatory. His business is to listen and remember, not to criticize or dissent. Where he is remiss, he must be prepared to acknowledge that reproof is salutary and that one must accept *mūsār* (i.e., this rigorous educational discipline in all its aspects) in order to become wise. Verse 20b ('in order that you may be wise in your *'aḥarīt*') does not mean 'that you may eventually be wise' (Toy, Ringgren, Barucq, Scott), although this is a suitable sense for the final clause in relation to the preceding imperatives, but rather 'that your *'aḥarīt* may be that of a *ḥākām*'. Since the *'aḥarīt* of a *ḥākām* is life, this implies a steadfast perseverance in the path of life and the gathering up of this sustained discipline into a fitting climax of maturity and recognition. On the meaning of *'aḥarīt* and the framework of interpretation appropriate to it, see on 14.12 (above, p. 467). There and in 16.25 the *'aḥarīt* of the self-opinionated man is 'the ways of death' – the opposite of the *'aḥarīt* of the *ḥākām*. The reading of Pesh., 'that you may be wise in all your paths', would refer to the ordering of affairs or to modes of behaviour, but it is weaker than MT.

The Instruction is concerned with educational discipline, and so we can say of the two sentences just considered that they have the form and content of this genre (vv. 18, 20). **[27]** Verse 27 almost falls into this category, except that the imperative does not appear to communicate a plain instruction. 'Cease, my son, to attend to *mūsār*', is not really a command to neglect discipline, but a rhetorical device for enforcing the lesson that such neglect will have serious consequences. In order to accommodate the construction of v. 27b it is necessary to suppose that the weapon of irony is being employed (cf. Gemser). The construction is that of imperative and final clause – characteristic of the Instruction – but the intention, contrary to the meaning which lies on the surface, is to enter a dissuasive against the neglect of *mūsār*. 'Cease, my son, to listen to instruction, that you may stray from words of knowledge,' really means: 'You can only acquire knowledge if you submit to the discipline imposed by a teacher.' Or, formulated negatively: 'If you neglect discipline, you will not become knowledgeable.' But it cannot be said that v. 27a with the imperative is grammatically equivalent to a conditional clause (cf. Gemser, GK §110f.; cf. the translations of Gemser, Ringgren and Scott), since v. 27b cannot be construed with a protasis. Gemser, Ringgren and Scott are all in difficulty here. Gemser and Ringgren translate *liśgōt* 'you will err', and Gemser suggests improbably that it means literally 'since it leads to error'. Scott's translation of v. 27b is too involved to be convincing and Barucq, who translates *ḥadal* as an imperative, supplies *ce sera* in order to make sense of v. 27b. Barucq would seem to me to paraphrase aptly ('Cease, my son, to attend to discipline; that will be to stray from words of knowledge'), but not to indicate correctly the construction of v. 27b.

Another possibility is that LXX should be followed (*υἱὸς ἀπολειπόμενος*), *ḥdl* vocalized as a participle and *b^enī* emended to *bēn* (Toy, cf. BH). In that case *liśgōt* may mean 'is likely to err' (cf. Gemser, see on 16.30, above, pp. 494f.): 'A son who ceases to attend to discipline is likely to stray from words of knowledge.' I have already indicated, however, that *b^enī* and the imperative belong together and that form-critical considerations confirm the correctness of MT.

The two remaining sentences of this group touch on the incorrigibility of the arrogant person (see on 9.7f., above, pp. 368f.; 13.1b, above, p. 453); **[25]** one has the form of Instruction (see above, pp. 522f.) and the other (v. 29) of the wisdom sentence. Chastisement will have no effect at all on the *lēṣ*, yet it should be administered for the salutary effects which it will have on the *petī* (the untutored youth who comes to learn from the wisdom teacher; see on 1.4, above,

p. 265). The impressionable *petī* will observe and will learn the lesson which escapes the *lēṣ* himself. If the *lēṣ* is beaten for the sake of the *petī*, the correction administered to a perceptive man is for the sake of that *nābōn* himself, for it has the effect of enhancing his intellectual grasp and clarity. **[29]** Verse 29 observes that penalties (literally, 'judgements', cf. Barucq) are ready for the arrogant and blows for the backs of fools. Even if they are incapable of learning from punishment, their behaviour invites it and they do not escape. The emendation of *š^{e}pāṭīm* to *š^{e}bāṭīm*, 'rods' (LXX *μάστιγες*, 'scourges', 'lashes') improves the parallelism and is adopted by Toy, Gemser, Ringgren and Scott. Dahood (p. 43) suggests that *š^{e}pāṭīm* is a dialectal variant of *š^{e}bāṭīm*, 'rods'. I translate *š^{e}pāṭīm*, 'penalties'.

The thought that many companions flock around a rich man, and that association with him makes no demands but rather confers benefits, reappears in vv. 4 and 6 (see on 14.20, above, pp. 471f.). **[4]** Wealth multiplies friends, whereas the poor man is alienated from his companion who comes to resent the sacrificial demands made on him by the relationship, until the feeling that it is an intolerable burden which must be laid down masters him, and he cuts off his friend in order to be free. **[6]** Verse 6 points to the dubious character of a rich man's companions and the difficulty which he has in separating the wheat from the chaff, of distinguishing between those who want him for his own sake and those who are sycophants and flatterers bent on using him for their own ends. The latter category will be numerous, and the man of wealth, whose influence counts for much and who has preferment in his gift, will be swamped by a sea of affability. Men will make studious efforts to say the right things to him, they will play skilfully on his moods and compete strenuously to induce the sun of his favour to shine on them. The metaphor of stroking the face in v. 6a aptly represents this process of deliberately cultivating a nobleman's favour, of inducing a mood in which he will be serviceable to the person who wants to use him, for, as v. 6b acutely observes, everyone is the companion of the man who has something to give away.

[7] The opposition of brothers and friends (*m^{e}rē'ēhū* = *mērē'ēhū*, a collective) in v. 7 may be similar in character to that in 17.17 (see above, p. 505). Brothers resent having a brother who needs to be supported, but the obligations of blood are so primary and inescapable that they may have to do their duty whatever their feelings. How much more will those who are not constrained by any bond of blood drop a friend who has become an inconvenience and a burden, and set about erecting barriers which will keep him at a distance from them and destroy the old intimacy. Nothing can be made of the additional *stichos* in MT ('He who pursues words, not they'), and one can only agree with Toy that it 'appears to be a corrupt remnant of a lost couplet, but it is hardly possible with our present means of information to recover the original form.' There is no case for reconstructing a Hebrew text on the basis of the longer Greek text as Gemser does ('All the brothers of a poor man hate him and much more do his friends hold themselves aloof from him. Good sense is near to those who are acquainted with it and a perceptive man will find it. He who talks a great deal brings evil to a head and he who pursues words will not escape'), because in the distich where MT and LXX can be compared the correspondence is very imperfect (LXX: 'He who hates a poor brother will alienate himself from friendship'), and in these circumstances the enterprise of using the additional Greek text to reconstruct a non-existent Hebrew one has little value. V translates the additional *stichos*, 'He who pursues only words will have nothing', and connects it with v. 8.

[2] In v. 2, *nepeš* means 'vitality', 'drive' (cf. Gemser, Ringgren, Scott; Barucq, 'zeal') rather than 'desire' (Hitzig, van der Ploeg) or 'resolve' (BH, cf. Gen. 23.8; II Kings 9.15). The verse is directed against a busyness which is an end in itself and has no clearly thought-out and well-defined objectives. There is the feverish activist who is always doing but who does not know what he is doing and, at the other pole, there is the man who is so fastidious in perfecting his plans and who so agonizes over their niceties that he is permanently inhibited from acting. The *ḥākām* steers skilfully between this Scylla and that Charybdis; he is a master of *ʿēṣā* and lays his plans carefully, but when the time for action comes he acts incisively. The activist who does not know where he is going but is in a hurry to get there will go astray, for drive without a clear awareness of the ends which are being pursued is not an asset. If *npš* is pointed as a niphal participle (*nāpōš*) and derived from *pōš*, 'one who dashes about without knowledge is a menace' (Tur Sinai, *Job*, 1957, p. 167, n.1), the effect is the same as translating *nepeš* 'drive'.

[10] Verse 10, which discusses fitness for power, has some connection with the topic of v. 2. It is formally identical with 17.7, and from the *a fortiori* construction we should probably conclude that here, as there (see above, pp. 507f.), the emphasis falls on the second half of the verse. The first half has then the character of a self-evident proposition whose acceptance can be taken for granted, and then the real point of the sentence is established *a fortiori* ('If you grant the truth of this, much more you must admit the truth of that'). Consequently the parallelism of *taʿanūg* and *mešōl beśārīm* is not necessarily desiderated, although there is such a parallelism in the case of 17.7 ('fine speech', 'false speech'), and Winton Thomas's suggestion that *taʿanūg* means 'administration' is attractive (cognate with Arabic *ʿanaja* rather than *ġanija*. The noun *ʿināju(n)* 'rope', 'cord', 'management' suggests a semantic development similar to *taḥbūlōt* 'ropes', 'procedural skill', 'political and administrative dexterity'.) See D. W. Thomas, *JTS* xxxviii (1937), pp. 400f.; cf. G. R. Driver, *VTS* iii, p. 84, 'control'.

The meaning would then be that if it is inappropriate for one lacking acumen to hold a position of power and responsibility, it is even more inappropriate for a slave to wield authority over high-ranking statesmen (on *śārīm*, see *PWM*, pp. 18f.). The implication of this would seem to be that if it is incongruous that a *kesīl* should preside over affairs, it is unthinkable that a slave, who is not even a fully entitled member of a community, should ever leap the formidable social and constitutional barriers which block his path to advancement and power. If *taʿanūg* means 'luxury' (LXX τρυφή), the two halves of the verse contain separate instances of incongruity, the one self-evident and the other *a fortiori*, as I have suggested above. Luxury ill becomes fools who will mistake vulgarity and ostentation for style and gracious living, which presuppose intelligence and discrimination, but the times would be even more out of joint if an *ʿebed* were to impose his authority on *śārīm*.

[8] According to v. 8, the man of acumen (*qōne lēb*, cf. *PWM*, p. 15), loves his life, and he who has regard to (intellectual) discrimination will find what is good (on the construction of *limṣō'* see 16.30, above, pp. 494f. The parallelism (*nepeš–ṭōb*) indicates that 'life' is to be understood qualitatively and that this, rather than 'self', is the correct translation of *nepeš* (so Gemser, Ringgren; contrary to LXX, Toy, Scott, Barucq). The point is not that the person with a good mind consults his own interest ('self') or that his instincts of self-preservation are highly developed ('life'), but rather that he is in love with life, a love which is expressed by his undeviating progress along the path of life and the consequent enhancement of his vitality.

Three verses (vv. 5, 9, 28), two of them almost identical **[5, 9]**, are on the subject of perjured evidence in a law court. *y^e^pīaḥ k^e^zābīm* is parallel to *ʿēd š^e^qārīm* in vv. 5 and 9 (see on 12.17; 14.5, 25; above, pp. 445, 469). The witness who deliberately falsifies the facts will not be acquitted, i.e., perjury may not be committed with impunity. Since *yinnāqe* is certainly legal terminology, the same may also be true of *yimmālēṭ*, and *yōʾbēd*, may indicate the imposition of capital punishment. **[28]** The *ʿēd b^e^līyaʿal* of v. 28 is either a witness whose testimony is destructive or one who wilfully distorts the facts (see on 6.12, above, pp. 325f.; cf. A. Guillaume, *JTS* xiii, 1962, p. 321). Such a person is guilty of contempt of court and deliberately perverts the course of justice (he scoffs at *mišpāṭ*). The *r^e^šāʿīm* (v. 28b) are so named precisely because their lack of candour in relation to judicial processes defeats the ends of justice. According to MT, they 'devour evil', i.e., they have an insatiable appetite for evil (van der Ploeg and Barucq), but the metaphor cannot stand in connection with *pī r^e^šāʿīm*, which must be followed by a reference to 'output', i.e., speech, and not 'input'. Toy, BH, Gemser, Ringgren and Scott follow Frankenberg and read *yabbīaʿ*, 'the mouth of wicked men gushes evil' (as water gushes from a spring); and Driver (see Gemser) retains MT, which he explains in connection with Arabic *balaġa* (2nd form, 'to communicate information', 'to express'): 'And the mouths of *r^e^šāʿīm* enunciate evil.' I follow Driver.

[19] Although v. 19 is obscure, the vocabulary indicates that a forensic situation is envisaged (*nōśēʾ ʿōneš*, 'pay a fine'; *taṣṣīl*, 'save from legal consequences', cf. *yimmālēṭ*, v. 5). *g^e^dol ḥēmā* (Q.) describes the same person as *q^e^ṣar rūaḥ* (14.29) or *q^e^ṣar ʾappayim* (14.17) or *ʾīš ḥēmā* (15.18). His tendency to respond impulsively and with ungovernable passion makes his behaviour irrational, and he is a type of fool who makes trouble for himself and creates mischief for others (see on 14.17, 29, above, pp. 468f.; 15.18, above, p. 482). The man who acts in heat and whose excesses get him into trouble with the law should be left to pay the consequences of his foibles. If you relieve him of the legal consequences of his display of temper once, you will be involved again and again in similar rescue operations (Toy, Ringgren, RSV). On this understanding of v. 19b, its intention is to state that the *g^e^dol ḥēmā* is incorrigible, that kindness cannot teach him a lesson and that if you once begin to rescue him from scrapes you will spend your life bailing him out of prison. Or – and this seems to me more likely – v. 19b is concerned rather with the bad effect of misplaced kindness on the *g^e^dol ḥēmā* himself; it will aggravate his condition and encourage him to further excess (Gemser, Scott, Barucq).

[11] The opposite of *q^e^ṣar 'appayim* is *'erek 'appayim*. According to MT it is a man's good sense (*śēkel*) which makes him even-tempered. If Pesh., Aquila and Theodotion are followed and *ha'^a^rīk* is read (Toy, BH), *śēkel* consists in having an even temper. Either way it is evident that an even temper is an aspect of a disciplined person; it amounts to a toughness of intellectual and temperamental make-up which enables one to remain calm and unflurried even when subject to intense pressure or provocation (see on 14.29, above, pp. 468f.; 15.1, above, p. 477; 18, above, p. 482). Associated with tranquillity and coolness as a crowning achievement is magnanimity. The virtue which is indicated here is more than a forgiving temper; it includes also the ability to shrug off insults and the absence of a brooding hypersensitivity. It is the ability to deny to an adversary the pleasure of hearing a yelp of pain even when his words have inflicted a wound, of making large allowances for human frailties and keeping the lines of communication open. It contains elements of toughness and self-discipline; it is the capacity to stifle a hot, emotional rejoinder and to sleep on an insult (see on 17.9, above, pp. 508f.; 18.19, above, p. 520).

Two verses describe the languor and fecklessness of the lazy person (vv. 15, 24). **[15]** In view of the connection which is established between laziness and sleepiness in 6.9–11, there is little doubt that *tardēmā* means 'deep sleep', and Gemser's suggestion that it may be a feminine singular collective meaning 'useless person' ('Laziness overcomes a worthless character') can be discounted (Gemser, p. 112). The other thought, that laziness is a condition associated with poverty and hunger, is also present in 6.9–11 (see above, pp. 324f.). Laziness induces sleep, and since a man must work to eat, the appetite (*nepeš*) of the lethargic person (*r^e^mīyā*, cf. 12.27, above, pp. 444f.; see BDB) will go unsatisfied. **[24]** Verse 24 conjures up the humorous picture of the person so lacking in will and energy that, having put his hand into the communal dish in the middle of the table, he is too tired to raise it to his mouth in order to eat. Perhaps we are to think of him as dozing off with his hand in the dish, so fond of sleep that he cannot stay awake to eat. D. Winton Thomas (*VT* xv, 1965, p. 272f.) notes that LXX, Pesh., Arabic version, some Jewish commentators and AV render *ṣallaḥat* 'bosom'; that Aquila,

Symmachus, Targ. and V render 'armpit'. He suggests that *ṣallaḥat* means something scooped out or cut out, that 'bosom' is a possible rendering, but that the rightness of 'dish' is established by the context.

[12] Since the king is a fountainhead of preferment, his favour is like dew on the grass – it refreshes and fructifies the recipient. But then if he can bestow patronage without any man saying to him, 'What are you doing'?, he can express his disfavour and mete out punishment with equal freedom. When his voice is raised in anger, he does not make empty noises. He is as capable of dismembering the object of his wrath as is the lion its prey. In both cases the snarl is a cry for blood. Gemser (p. 112) notes Ehrlich's proposal that *kakkᵉpīr* should be emended to *kakkᵉpōr* and *naham* deleted as a secondary intrusion, attributable to the change of *kakkᵉpōr* to *kakkᵉpīr*. This would produce the antithetic parallelism of 'dew' and 'frost', the refreshing, fructifying effect of the king's favour on the one hand, and the cold hand of his disfavour on the other; a disfavour which destroys a man's prospects as frost kills natural growth (cf. J. L. Seeligman, *VTS* i, 1953, p. 64). I retain MT.

[13] The sentiments of v. 13a are those of 10.1b (see above, p. 418) and 17.21 (see above, p. 503), while v. 13b is a cry from the heart of the same kind as 12.4b (see above, p. 443). To beget a son who is a fool is an unmitigated disaster, and to have a querulous wife who niggles and nags perpetually is as unendurable as inhabiting a house with a leaking roof and being tormented by a drip which never lets up. A *delep ṭōrēd* is literally a leak which harries or pursues, i.e., which is so unrelenting that one has either got to run away from it or go mad, and this is just the situation of a man with a nagging wife (cf. Arabic *ṭarada*, 'repel', 'pursue', see L. Kopf, *VT* viii, 1958, pp. 175f., 'incessantly dripping eaves', which invites the pun 'incessantly dripping Eves').

[26] Verse 26 describes the scandalous behaviour of the son who is a wastrel, seen in his callous treatment of father and mother. Winton Thomas suggests that *mᵉšaddēd* should be derived from Ethiopic *sadada*, 'expel', 'reject', in which case *mᵉšaddēd* is synonymous with *yabrīaḥ* and what is envisaged is apparently the forcible eviction of (aged) parents from the family home (*VTS* iii, p. 289; a similar result is obtained by emending *mᵉšaddēd* to *mᵉnōdēd*). Driver also supposes that the two terms are synonymous, but he explains the first in terms of Arabic *sadda*, 'to silence (by striking on the mouth)' and the second in terms of Arabic *barraḥa*, 'to afflict'. It is then the contempt of parents and their maltreatment which are the disgraceful features of the son's behaviour (*yabrīaḥ* might then equally well be derived from Arabic *baraḥa* 'to bruise'; cf. G. R. Driver, *ThZ* 11, 1955, pp. 372f.). Driver construes: 'He who silences his father (by striking him on the mouth) distresses his mother (like) a son who shames and disgraces his parents.' Of all these attempts to explain the two verbs in v. 26a as synonyms, Winton Thomas's is the most convincing (it is improbable that *yabrīaḥ* has a meaning other than 'expel', 'evict'), but there is no compelling reason why they must be synonymous. They may point to two different aspects of disgraceful behaviour, violence done to a father and the forcible eviction of a mother (so Toy, Gemser, Ringgren, Barucq).

Class B

[22] The best starting place for the discussion of the difficult textual questions which are raised by v. 22 is LXX, which reads: 'Compassion is fruit to a man, and a poor man who is righteous is better than a wealthy man who is perfidious.' The addition of 'righteous' and 'wealthy' is connected with the effort to produce a clear-cut moralistic antithesis, and it is the type of expansion in LXX which has no textual significance. The important textual considerations are that LXX has translated *ḥasdō* and *kāzāb*, thereby confirming MT in these particulars, and that it has apparently read *t*ᵉ*bū'at* or the like instead of MT *ta'*ᵃ*wat*. Any attempt to make sense of the verse by emending either *ḥasdō* or *kāzāb* goes against the testimony of LXX. For this reason the suggestions of Ringgren (*saḥrō*, following BH) and Scott (*ḥosnō*), although they produce attractive antithetic parallelism, do not deserve credence: 'The desire of a man is for his (own) gain, but a poor man is better than a false one.' The same objections can be made to Gemser's proposal that *kāzāb* should be emended to *'akzār* or *'akzārī*. Some weight must be attached to the fact that *'īš ḥesed* is contrasted with *'akzārī* in 11.17, but, on the other hand, the emendation assumes that LXX was already translating a corrupt Hebrew text. Gemser renders: 'It is his kindness which is a man's productivity (*t*ᵉ*bū'at*, with LXX), and a poor man is better than a cruel one.' Barucq attempts the translation of MT unaltered, but *ta'*ᵃ*wat 'ādām* can hardly be rendered 'what is desiderated in a man' (similarly RSV, BJ; cf. Gemser). LXX must therefore be followed in this particular and the verse then reads: 'A man's productivity is his loyalty and a poor man is better than a false one.' I take *ḥesed* to mean 'loyalty' rather than 'kindness' (cf. 11.17, above, p. 433), so that *'īš ḥesed*, 'a loyal man', is the opposite of *'īš kāzāb*, 'a perfidious man'. Productivity should be measured in terms of loyalty rather than wealth, and a poor man with a will for social wholeness is better than a treacherous man whose behaviour destroys society, however great his worldly success. Output or productivity is correlated with integrity and benevolence in personal relationships, for this is what truly enriches a society.

Class C

[1] In v. 1 the text of Pesh. is easier than MT and approximates to the variant of this sentence in MT of 28.6 (Pesh. is followed by BH and Gemser). In Pesh. we have the metaphor of the two ways, probably in a framework of piety rather than in the setting of the school and educational discipline. The poor man whose conduct is blameless – who keeps his integrity in every situation and encounter – is in better case than the wealthy man whose ways are twisted. On the one hand, there is a single-minded sincerity – a wholeness of word and action – while on the other, there is a basic moral confusion and untruthfulness. Although *d^erākāw* appears in 50 Hebrew manuscripts (cf. BH), and 10.9b as well as 28.6b gives support to the reading of the Pesh. in 19.1b, MT *mē'iqqēš ś^epātāw* is, nevertheless, a perfectly good reading (cf. 8.8; also with *lēb* in 11.20, 17.20) and is retained by Toy, Ringgren, Barucq and Scott. Toy and Scott substitute *'āšīr* for *k^esīl*, following Pesh., while Ringgren and Barucq retain MT here also. The poor man speaks and acts with simplicity, sincerity and benevolence, whereas the *k^esīl* or *'ašīr* speaks in such a way as deliberately to confuse the issues; he is the master of half-truths, or else he lives on discord and creates it for its own sake. If *k^esīl* is retained it is the folly of moral confusion rather than of intellectual ineptness which must be envisaged. In the antithesis of 'poor' and 'rich' (if *'āšīr* is read), something of the correlation of poverty with piety and wealth with impiety may be implied (see on 16.8, 19, above, p. 498), but this is not directly given by the form of the verse (cf. Toy). All that is said is that the poor man who is *tāmīm* is better off than the wealthy man who is perverse. I retain MT.

[3] Verse 3 similarly speaks of the man whose way is twisted, and it attributes this misdirection to folly, which, in the light of v. 3b, is again seen to be impiety and a deep-seated wrongness of motive and

attitude. He is also a rebel who fulminates against Yahweh and whose defiance is associated with a poisoning of motivation and ethical deformity, so that the course on which he embarks will provoke a fatal collision with Yahweh.

[23] According to v. 23, the fear of Yahweh makes for life (see on v. 20, above, p. 524; also 14.12, above, pp. 467f.; 15.24, above, pp. 479f.; 23.18, above, pp. 387f.), and a man (who fears Yahweh) passes the night replete, undisturbed by any visitation of evil. Verse 23b is difficult to construe and its relationship with 23a is obscure. Dahood (p. 41) supposes that the parallelism is antithetic and renders: 'But he who sleeps to satiety will surely be visited by calamity.' The antithesis is that of the frugal saint and the impious one who is a glutton and a winebibber. There is also an antithesis in LXX: 'The fear of the Lord is life to a man, but the man without fear lodges in places where knowledge does not keep watch.' But *bal* is more probably negative than asseverative and, in any case, *śābēaʿ* can hardly be pejorative. The man who fears Yahweh has a right to be *śābēaʿ* – this is his proper condition according to the doctrine of theodicy. A statement like that contained in this verse cannot be dissociated from the opposition of life and death which is attached to a pupil's attitude to his teacher. Life and death which depend on intellectual discipline and indiscipline are here set in a framework of piety in which respect for the authority of the teacher is replaced by the fear of Yahweh which constitutes the new discipline (see on v. 16a, above, p. 523). The hours of the night are the time when men feel themselves particularly exposed to attack from dark and malignant forces and when the security afforded by Yahweh is particularly precious.

[21] Another aspect of this process of reinterpretation is that wisdom is held to stem from religious illumination and not from a rigorous intellectual discipline. Men have many plans in their mind, but it is Yahweh's policy (*ʿēṣā*) which stands (the test of implementation) and, as I have shown elsewhere, it is the prophets, as bearers of the revealed *dābār*, who claim to be the official exponents of this *ʿēṣā* (*PWM*, pp. 65f.).

[17] The language of theodicy is used in v. 17 of one who has compassion on the poor. Such practical social concern is a form of lending to Yahweh and so of putting Yahweh in debt. This is a credit of righteousness which Yahweh will honour in full (*yᵉšallem lō*) by paying the compassionate man his due (*gᵉmūl*). In *The Dialogue of*

Pessimism (*BWL*, pp. 146f., *ll.* 56f.), the man who sacrifices to his god is described as one 'who is making him loan upon loan' and 'is satisfied with the bargain', i.e., perhaps with the rate of interest (cf. *BWL*, p. 326). In our verse it is compassion, not cultic zeal, which is described as a form of lending to Yahweh.

[14] Toy is probably right in saying of the belief that a good wife comes from Yahweh that it is popular rather than theological. It should not perhaps be construed too strictly as an expression of the doctrine of theodicy, although I have tended to do this in 18.22, in view of the presence of the theological term *rāṣōn* (see above, p. 521). Rather than an explicitly formulated doctrine, this may simply express the awareness that choosing a wife is a chancy business and that there are no assured means of knowing beforehand how it is going to work out. It is always something of a leap into the dark, so that when a man discovers that he has been blessed with a competent and reasonable wife, he is not disposed to take all the credit for this happy state of affairs. The nature and extent of one's patrimony is determined by circumstances of birth, and these are not matters about which a difficult personal decision has to be taken or can be taken. A person may inherit domestic stability and affluence, but he has to take a chance on his own marriage and, when it turns out well, he is inclined to believe that a higher wisdom had a hand in the match.

Chapter 20

Evidences of formlessness or of disintegration of form in this chapter can be seen in the lack of parallelism (vv. 7, 8, 10, 11, 12, 14, 20, 21, 25, 26, 28) and in the intrusion of features of the Instruction (vv. 13, 16, 18, 19, 22). Precise antithetic parallelism occurs in vv. 3, 6, 15, 17, 29, and there is an antithetic element in v. 5. Verse 15 is taken by Toy as a continuous sentence, whereas only Toy (cf. LXX δὲ) supposes that v. 29 is a case of antithetic parallelism (contrary to Gemser, Ringgren, Scott, Barucq). The less well-defined synthetic or synonymous parallelism is found in eight sentences (vv. 1, 2, 4, 9, 23, 24, 27, 30). In vv. 1 and 27 it consists of the elucidation of the metaphors in the first half of these verses, and it is difficult to know how v. 9 should be described, whether as having synthetic parallelism or being a continuous sentence.

As for the verses which have the form of the Instruction, v. 13

consists of an imperative with a 'lest' clause, followed by two imperatives which probably have the function of imperative and final clause ('Open your eyes, so that you may have enough bread'). Verse 16 is made up of two imperatives, one followed by a motive clause (*kī*) and the other by an imperfectly formed motive clause (*ūbe'ad nokrīyīm* = *wekī 'ārab be'ad nokrīyīm*). Toy supposes that *hākēn* (cf. BH *tekōn*) should be read for *tikkōn* in v. 18a, in which case there would be an imperative in each half of the verse, but the rightness of MT is confirmed by v. 19, since both verses have exactly the same structure, and the force of *ū* at the beginning of vv. 18b and 19b is 'therefore' or 'and so'. What we then have is a statement followed by a consequential demand. In v. 22 two imperatives, the first negative and the second positive, are followed by a consequential clause.

Class A: vv. 1, 2, 3, 4, 5, 6, 8, 11, 13, 14, 15, 16, 17, 18, 19, 20, 21, 25, 26, 29, 30.
Class B: v. 28.
Class C: vv. 7, 9, 10, 12, 22, 23, 24, 27.

Class A

Two verses (vv. 5, 18) deal explicitly with the character and function of *'ēṣā*, and others (vv. 3, 19, 25) which recommend certain intellectual attitudes and modes of behaviour may be regarded as formulations of policy (*'ēṣā*). [5] The point of the deep waters in v. 5 is usually taken to be the natural secretiveness of men and their unwillingness to divulge what is in their minds to an outsider (cf. Toy). Even their speech does not disclose the cast of their mind and the tendency of their thinking with respect to the matter under discussion. There are inner depths in every person in which the formation of opinion and the shaping of intellectual judgements are concealed. The eliciting of *'ēṣā* from another is a skilful operation which only a perceptive person with power of intellectual penetration can perform. It is as if a bucket had to be lowered into a deep well and then skilfully manoeuvred to the surface filled with water.

In 18.4a, however, I have argued that 'deep waters' is a figure for profundity of thought rather than for secretiveness (see above, pp. 513f.), and the same would seem to me to be the case here. The skill of the perceptive man does not reside in his knack of wheedling secrets out of another, but rather in a Socratic function of clarification. He is a kind of midwife who brings *'ēṣā* to the birth. The profound

ʿ*ēṣā* of whose value an individual is convinced, but which remains inchoate below the level of articulation and which he struggles unsuccessfully to bring to completion, is elicited by the *ʾîš tᵉbūnā*.

[18] I have already argued that the form of v. 18 in MT is to be preserved. Plans are prepared and perfected by ʿ*ēṣā*, and, if this is so, war should be conducted in accordance with a pre-determined strategy and tactics worked out with such detail as to leave nothing to chance (cf. the modern notion of 'contingency planning'). Here, as in 15.22 (see above, p. 482), ʿ*ēṣā* is probably envisaged as a consensus – as a consequence of men taking counsel together and one mind being sharpened against another. The common wisdom of a group of able men is thought to have a quality of maturity and comprehensiveness which none of them could have achieved by himself (on *taḥbūlōt* as another item of the vocabulary of old wisdom see 1.5, above, pp. 265f.).

[3] Verse 3 returns to the thought (see on 17.14, above, p. 505; 18.1, above, p. 519) that the provoking of violent quarrels and the use of words (however dexterous and devastating be the polemic) in order to engender heat and bitterness and to start a slanging-match is a manifestation of unwisdom. A man enhances his standing when he shows that he has qualities of restraint and moderation which enable him to stop short of undignified and unedifying wrangling. There is the question whether *šebet* is to be derived from *yšb* (KB²) or *šbt* (BDB, Dahood, p. 41). The forensic sense of *šbt* is established by Prov. 18.18 (cf. W. F. Albright, *VTS* iii, 1955, p. 10), i.e., the termination of litigation, but a derivation from *yšb* yields equally good sense. If the latter derivation were followed; *yšb min* would be analogous to Arabic *qaʿada ʿan*, 'to desist from, (L. Kopf, *VT* ix, 1959, p. 258). The community will set a high value on the person who avoids such explosions, who has the capacity of preserving a working arrangement with even the most difficult people and of keeping the lines of communication open. It is to this end that the wise man employs language, and not in order to feed the passions and precipitate crises.

[19] The tale-bearer and inveterate gossip is not the one with whom confidences should be reposed, for he will betray them (v. 19, see on 11.13, above, p. 429). The emphasis is not so much on calculated and malicious slander as on the indiscipline and weakness of garrulity. There is the person who is constitutionally incapable of holding his tongue and who lacks the steadiness and taciturnity (cf.

11.13b) which is desiderated in a confidant. The sentiments are almost exactly those of *Amenemope*:

Empty not thy belly to everybody,
Nor damage (thus) the regard for thee.
Spread not thy words to the common people,
Nor associate to thyself one (too) outgoing of heart.
Better is the man whose talk (remains) in his belly,
Than he who speaks it out injuriously. (xxii, *ANET*, p. 424).

[25] Impetuosity is a major intellectual flaw and is incompatible with a proper regard for *ʿēṣā*, i.e., for the carefully considered and well-balanced judgement and the nicely calculated response. The man who acts impulsively and without regard to his ability to fulfil obligations which he incurs is like someone who devises a snare for himself. Such is he who speaks irresponsibly with an element of braggadoccio (KB², *s.v. lʿʿ*, Arabic *laġā*, 'to talk wildly') in earmarking money or property for sacred uses. His gesture is generous, but ill-considered, and out of touch with his resources. After he has made his pledges he finds himself scratching his head and asking how he can possibly honour them (or, perhaps, wriggle out of them). The latter of these two interpretations is indicated by LXX: 'It is a snare to a man hastily to consecrate property, for after (such) vowing comes a change of mind'. 'And after vows to seek' (the literal rendering of v. 25b) does not mean, 'And after vows to seek means of evading them', but, 'And after vows to begin enquiring how they can be honoured' (cf. Toy). *bqr* is not 'reflect' (contrary to Gemser, Ringgren, Scott, Barucq), but 'seek ways and means'. The subject of rash, ill-considered vows is dealt with at greater length in Eccles. 4.17–5.6: 'When you make a vow to God, do not delay paying it; for he has no pleasure in fools. Pay what you vow. It is better that you should not vow than that you should vow and not pay' (5.5f.). Our verse, too, is concerned with the unrealistically onerous vow which cannot be honoured, rather than with the calculated evasion of vows. The point in the Gospels is evasion – the misuse of vows in order to avoid responsibility for one's parents, i.e., financial obligations towards them (Matt. 15.4–6; Mark 7.10–13).

Three sentences are occupied with the relation of wealth to the good life which is enjoyed by the wise man (vv. 15, 17, 21). **[15]** Verse 15 establishes an order of priority or perhaps a parity as between knowledge and wealth. Gold and abundance of precious stones do exist; the glamour of searching for them and the achievement of possessing them has been enjoyed by men in every age, but lips of knowledge are even more precious (or, are no less precious). It is as if lips of knowledge were envisaged as a costly work of art (*k*ᵉ*lîy*ᵉ*qār*), unique in kind. As in 3.14f.; 8.10f.; and 16.16 (see above, pp. 295f., 346f., 489), the intention is not to disparage the possession of wealth but to set it in a framework of values within which the wise man lives. Wealth is the proper condition of the man who has fulfilled himself and is an ingredient of *kābōd*, but if it is divorced from the discipline of wisdom and the virtues of intellect and character with which it should co-exist, it becomes an evil (vv. 17, 21). **[21]** The flaw which is described in v. 21 is essentially that of 13.11 and 15.27, i.e., a ruthless determination to get rich quickly and a stopping at nothing in order to achieve this end. *m*ᵉ*bōhelet* (Q.) is supported by LXX ἐπισπουδαζομένη, and *naḥ*ᵃ*lā* has to be translated 'patrimony' or 'inheritance' rather than 'fortune'. This is not the person who makes a fortune quickly by unscrupulous means, but the one who lays hands on the family fortune prematurely.

This would suggest that there is an intrinsic connection between the topics of v. 20 and v. 21, and that the latter deals with another case of filial infidelity. Such base gratitude and unnatural greed will not lead to a blessed sequel or climax (on *'aḥ*ᵃ*rît* see on 14.12, above, pp. 467f.), and herein lies the difference between this aberration and the possession of wealth in the context of a life which has achieved maturity and fulfilment along the path indicated by wisdom. Gemser's suggestion that *naḥ*ᵃ*lā* may mean 'palm tree' (Arabic *naḫlat*) assumes that vv. 20 and 21 make up a single unit. The son of v. 20 is then likened to a palm-tree which bears unripe (and unpalatable) fruit. But this is not a figure which is particularly apposite to the son of v. 20, for it is not obvious why a son who curses father and mother is like a palm-tree which bears fruit prematurely. Moreover, where the 'context' is so regularly the single sentence it is a large assumption that here we have a unit consisting of two sentences.

[17] Verse 17 says that the acquisition of easy money by dishonest means is a dead-end occupation. The bread of falsehood tastes good to begin with, but ultimately it turns to sand or gravel in the mouth. The meal which seemed so delightful a prospect proves loathsome in the long run, and instead of satisfaction there is revulsion and vomiting. Here again the acquisition of wealth has been divorced from the comprehensive concept of fulfilment to which it contributes, so that it is no more than an instinct of rapacity. There comes a time when one can no longer live with such sharp practices and grasping greed; one loathes them and vomits them up and then nothing remains but emptiness.

[30] According to v. 30, corporal punishment is an effective instrument of education and reform. Weals rub away evil (K. *tamrīq*), or are a massage for evil (Q. *tamrūq*, a noun). Q. accords better with v. 30b if the assumption is made that *ūmakkōt ḥadrē bāṭen* = *ūmakkōt tamrūq b^{e}ḥadrē bāṭen*: 'Weals are a massage for evil, and strokes for the chambers of the belly'. This is preferable to Delitzsch's suggestion that *makkōt* is a participle agreeing with *ḥabbūrōt*, 'reaching to the chambers of the belly'. LXX reads: 'Blows and contusions befall evil men, and stripes (penetrate) the inward parts.' LXX 'evil men' (*κακοῖς*) is in all probability an inaccurate rendering of *rāʿ* and so confirms MT. The conjecture *rēaʿ*, 'will', 'intention' (Gemser, Ringgren, p. 81 n.4; KB[2] *s.v.* III **rēaʿ*) is a good parallel to 'chambers of the belly', whose significance is discussed in 18.8 (see above, p. 519). The belly is the repository of thoughts and motives and so the seat of words and action. A person who dissimulates is 'contentious of belly', and one who affects affability when he is terrified has terror in his belly (*Amenemope* xiii.10f., *ANET*, p. 423); a garrulous person is incapable of keeping words in his belly (*Amenemope* xxii.15, *ANET*, p. 424, see below, p. 547 on Prov. 20.27b). Both 'will' and 'chambers of the belly' are indicative of the core of personality. This is the point at which the truth about an individual is to be found, so that to touch him at this deepest of all levels is to effect the most radical education or reform. The metaphor, as was observed by Rashi (cf. Toy) is a medical one (cf. Accadian *marāqu*, 'to rub with medicinal herbs'; the meaning 'rub' explains 'polish', 'furbish' in II Chron. 4.16; Jer. 46.4; Lev. 6.21), and corporal punishment is conceived as a remedial deep massage which reaches down to the roots of perversion and is a radical therapeutic agency. This meaning can be had from MT without emending *rāʿ* to *rēaʿ*. The verse then turns on the eradication of evil and 'the chambers of the belly' are identified as its seat which can be reached by the deep massage of corporal punishment.

Two verses have to do, in different ways, with youth and age (vv. 20, 29). **[20]** The lamp of the son who curses father and mother will go out at the approach of darkness (Q. *'^{e}šūn*, so Ringgren), or, better, in pitch darkness (K. *'īšōn*; Gemser, 'thickest darkness'; Toy, 'midnight darkness', see on 7.9, above, p. 336), i.e., he will be left in pitch darkness as a consequence of his lamp going out (for the elucidation of the metaphor of the extinguished lamp see on 13.9b, above, p. 461). It has been pointed out that the legal punishment for this offence was death (Ex. 21.17; Lev. 20.9; Deut. 27.16), but it is likely that the verse comes from a period when the law had become a dead letter and had been replaced by a theological threat. Such a son will be judged by Yahweh, cut off prematurely from the land of the living and consigned to the darkness of Sheol. The curse which he utters against his parents will be answered by Yahweh's curse on him (so Ecclus. 3.16). Here, too, legal sanctions have been superseded by theological condemnation and exhortation; cf. 3.11; 41.7; and 7.28: Your parents gave you life, and how can you repay them?

[29] In v. 29, the statement that the glory of young men is their physical strength is true of young men at any time and in any society, but the assessment of old age as also a time of glory and fulfilment is much more remarkable, and is explicable only in relation to the pre-eminence enjoyed by the old in the society out of which the verse comes (see on 16.31, above, p. 501). Old age is affirmed without hesitation and sadness for the years which the locusts have eaten. Grey hairs are not a symbol of decrepitude or unwantedness, for the greybeards are in the saddle; their wisdom is exercised and their authority undisputed. They are not over the top of the hill, but securely established at the summit of self-fulfilment and political influence.

A group of sentences may be generally described as prudential, being concerned with drunkenness (v. 1), sloth (vv. 4, 13), commercial practice (v. 16) and stratagems (v. 14). **[1]** Wine is personified as a Scorner and liquor as a Roisterer. The first could mean that wine mocks at the person under its influence and brings him into contempt, but the analogy of the second would suggest that it is the arrogant behaviour of the inebriated person which is indicated. He brags and sneers, rants and roars. The second half of the verse is ambiguous. It could mean: (*a*) it is not wise to get drunk, or: (*b*) the person who has had too much to drink is incapable of wise behaviour. Since v. 1a describes the idiotic behaviour of the drunk man, it is perhaps (*b*) rather than (*a*) which is intended in v. 1b. Drink destroys whatever gumption a man may possess, and under its influence he acts like an imbecile (see on 23.29, above, pp. 393f.).

[13] The association of laziness and sleep reappears in v. 13 (see on 19.15, above, p. 530). Love of sleep brings loss of patrimony (*pen tiwwārēš*), and you have to wake up (early) and set to work if you want to win a livelihood.

[4] The lazy chap does not do his ploughing in the autumn, and, although he expects crops at harvest time, he gets nothing. Verse 4b reads literally: 'He asks at harvest and there is nothing', and RV supposes that 'asks' is equivalent to 'begs' (following V) and that the lazy man is represented as begging unsuccessfully from others what he has not grown for himself. Associated with this is the suggestion that he is deterred by cold (*mēḥōrep*: RV, 'by reason of the winter'; cf. Scott, 'at the onset of winter'). Rather, it is the lazy man's blithe expectation of a crop when he has not done the work at the right time ('in the autumn') to bring it about which is being taken off in this verse. This is what lazy people are like, not only in this particular situation but in any situation, and so this is a 'proverb' because it has a representative potential. In our different but related idiom, the lazy man is not willing to do the spade-work, but he expects to get as good a result as someone who has. He may sow the seed after a fashion in unprepared soil, but this is not good enough and will not produce a crop. He is clear about the goal which he wants to achieve, but he hopes to get there without doing any work. He is all for excellence without endeavour.

[14] Verse 14 mirrors with wonderful accuracy and humour the climate and devices associated with the striking of a bargain in a commercial context where fixed prices have no place. Haggling is a dour economic contest, but it is also a social occasion with civilities and courtesies, as the Westerner can still discover in parts of the Near East today. It is a war of attrition, for which the buyer is fortified with coffee, and which can be conducted at a leisurely pace and in a civilized fashion. The buyer protests that he is having the worst of the bargain; when he has made it he goes off to congratulate himself on a good stroke of business. I have seen a seller performing just this piece of ritual in the old city of Jerusalem when he complained that the price which was being offered for a carpet was 'Bread without cheese', but I have no doubt that in fact he had the better of the deal.

[16] I have indicated (see above, p. 536) how v. 16 ought to be construed. There are two motive clauses, identical in content, which show why the instruction conveyed by the imperatives should be attended to. There is, however, some ambiguity as to the situation which these injunctions are addressed to. Toy supposes (also L. A. Snijders, pp. 85f.) that a debtor has defaulted and that the instruction

is: 'Make the man who went surety for the debtor pay up his debts.' This gives the instruction an *ad hoc* character untypical of the genre, whereas what I should expect here is a general rule of commercial practice. I suppose the meaning, rather, to be: 'Do not have commercial dealings with him unless he gives you security on the spot, because he is liable as surety for the debts of foreigners (K. *nokrīm*) and will be in serious financial trouble if they default.' The allusion is to his risky and speculative financial transactions with foreigners, and *zār* is not to be translated 'another' (contrary to Toy, Gemser, Ringgren), nor can *zār* and *nokrīm* (K.; or Pesh. *nokrī* which agrees in number with *zār*) refer to 'outsiders', i.e., socially ostracized Israelites, as Snijders holds (see on 6.1f., above, pp. 321f.). I take the gist of the instruction to be this: if you are to have dealings with a person who is a bad risk and is liable for dubious debts, secure yourself immediately.

M. Dahood (*Biblica* 42, 1961, pp. 362f.) reads *nokrīyā* (Q.), which is the reading in the almost identical 27.13. Dahood establishes the association of harlots, garments and pledging from the Marisa graffito. He translates: 'Take his garment when a stranger has offered it in pledge and pawn it for a harlot.' This is unacceptable for the following reasons: (*a*) *kī* almost certainly introduces a motive clause (see above, p. 536); (*b*) *ʿārab zār* cannot be translated 'a stranger has given it in pledge'; (*c*) Aquila and Theodotion (περὶ ξένης) do not give any indication that they understood *nokrīyā* as 'harlot'. What they were attempting was a literal rendering of MT; (*d*) the verse should be taken as serious, straightforward advice, not as an ironical invitation to a fool to commit two crimes, namely, to retain overnight a garment given in pledge (Ex. 22.26) and to pawn the garment for the services of a prostitute.

[2] In 19.12a, the rage of a king is likened to the roar of a lion, but this is not a sufficient reason for emending *'ēmat* to *ḥᵃmat* in 20.2a (contrary to Frankenberg, Toy, BH, Barucq). LXX ἀπειλή, 'threat', is no nearer to the one than the other (contrary to Barucq). The king, like the young lion, has destructive power and does not issue empty threats, so that he, too, inspires awe and dread (see on 19.12, above, p. 531). Verse 2b is variously translated, *mitʿabbᵉrō* being the main source of difficulty: 'He who draws on himself his (the king's) anger forfeits (literally, 'misses') his life' (Gemser, Ringgren). 'He who irritates him (the king) sins against himself' (Barucq; cf. LXX: 'He who irritates him sins against his own soul'). BH (also KB², *s.v.*, II

ʿbr) reads *mitʿabbēr weḥōṭē*', and this is translated by Driver: 'He that is negligent is as (*wāw adequationis*) one that sinneth in respect of his life' (G. R. Driver, *JTS* xli, 1940, p. 174; cf. Gemser, p. 112: *nepeš* is 'life' rather than 'self'). Driver connects *mitʿabbēr* with the ithpeel of Syriac *ʿbr* and with Arabic *ġabara*, whereas KB² has in mind some such translation as: 'He who loses his temper is as one who forfeits his life.' According to Driver, the danger lies in the consequences of incompetence and neglect, while, according to KB², it lies in loss of self-control. No one can afford to vent his temper on a king, however much he may have been provoked. If he wishes to survive, he has to maintain a front of courtesy and deference. The rendering of Gemser and Ringgren (see above) recalls the description of the king's anger in 16.14 as 'messengers of death', which it is the concern of the wise man to cover over (see on 16.14, above, p. 488). This accords better with *ḥamat* than with *'ēmat* in v. 2a. LXX^A, 'he who mixes himself up (in the affairs of a king)', which points to *mitʿārēb*, introduces the thought of meddling or intrigue, and this is also apposite in relation to v. 2a (cf. Gemser, p. 112). I retain MT, acknowledging the obscurity of *mitʿabberō*.

[8, 26] Although v. 26b is obscure and perhaps corrupt, the measure of identity between v. 26a and v. 8b establishes that both verses are comments on the judicial functions of a king, and there is evidence elsewhere that this was a sphere where his wisdom was especially manifested (II Sam. 14.17; I Kings 3.16f., *PWM*, pp. 58f.). The metaphor implied by *mezāre* is probably that a wise king (v. 26a), by virtue of his legal acumen and ability to identify evil and evil-doers, is like one who separates the chaff from the wheat by a winnowing process (LXX, v. 26a, 'a winnower of the impious'). When he sits in the judge's seat and hears a case, nothing evades his penetrating scrutiny, and there is no possibility of a miscarriage of justice. The *rāʿ* will not escape punishment with whatever forensic skill he may present his case, nor will the *ṣaddīq*, however innocent of legal procedures, be the victim of injustice. Verse 26b, 'and he has brought back a wheel upon them', is difficult. As Driver has observed, the verb 'brought back' does not fit the thought that the wheel is an instrument of torture, nor is this what the intelligible part of the verse requires (cf. Gemser). The substitution of *'ōnām* for *'ōpān* ('and he has recompensed their evil', or, 'that he may recompense their evil': BH, *weyāšīb*) is unsupported by the versions, but it does supply the forensic reference which is desiderated and is an idiom found elsewhere (Ps. 94.23). Driver's proposal, 'and brings back (the) wheel (of fortune against them)', i.e., turns the tables on them, is speculative (G. R. Driver, *Biblica* 32, p. 184). Barucq suggests that LXX ('and casts a wheel upon them') may have envisaged the wheel as a winnowing machine, and that the king is likened to a winnower who causes the wheel to pass over the grain so as to throw it into the air and effect the separation of the wheat from the chaff. A similar but more exact solution is offered by D. Winton Thomas (*JJS* xv, 1964, pp. 155f.). He translates MT, 'and brings the wheel over them'. The wheel is that of the threshing cart, *ʿagālā*, whose rollers were fitted with sharp iron wheels (cf. *ʾōpan ʿagālā*, parallel to *ḥārūṣ* in Isa. 28.27). Verse 26b refers to the process of threshing, of separating grain from straw. Hence in v. 26b, as in 26a, it is the king's powers of discrimination to which reference is made.

The thought which is common to vv. 6 and 11 is the dichotomy of profession and practice, of seeming and being, of appearance and reality. **[6]** The reading indicated by the versions (Pesh., Targ., V), 'Many a man is called an *ʾīš ḥesed*', is attractive, since *ʾīš ḥesed* is exactly paralleled by *ʾīš ʾemūnā* in v. 6b. Nevertheless, MT should be retained, with *ʾīš* distributive: 'many a man proclaims (each) his loyalty'. The antithesis is between the frequent and eloquent protests of loyalty which men make and the rarity of a friend with rock-like qualities of steadfastness and integrity. Utterly loyal and reliable friends are hard to come by, but there is no dearth of declamations of *ḥesed*. **[11]** Verse 11 (MT) is awkward; Toy transposes *gam* before *naʿar* and reads *rāšāʿ* for *yāšār* (Even a youth is known by his deeds, according as his conduct is good or bad). Verse 11a can hardly bear this rendering without the transposition of *gam*, but MT can be retained in v. 11b ('if his action be pure and upright', i.e., depending on whether his action is pure and upright). The intention of the verse is broadly the same as that of the dominical saying: 'That is why I say you will recognize them by their fruits' (Matt. 7.20). Deeds speak louder than words. The way to ascertain the quality of a youth is to observe his behaviour. His calibre is not established by what he says about himself or what others say about him, but by the purity and uprightness of his deeds. If MT is read in v. 11a, *gam* means either 'moreover' (see on 17.26, above, pp. 506f.) or 'just' (Gemser, Ringgren). In the latter case, the meaning is that one has no need to do any more than to observe behaviour in order to assess the character of a youth (cf. Barucq, 'by his very deeds'). All the evidence that is required is furnished by overt action ('It is in what he does that a youth reveals himself', i.e., divulges his true nature). The acid test of his character is how he behaves.

Class B

[28] BH's tentative proposal that *yiṣṣōr* should be read for *yiṣṣ*^{e}*rū* makes the king subject of both halves of v. 28 and simplifies its sense. The meaning is then simply that a king promotes, or should promote, the cohesiveness of his community, and that so long as it is his prime aim to guard the wholeness of the common life from divisive forces of any kind, his throne will rest on sure foundations. MT, however, should be retained (cf. LXX), and then the thought of the verse is somewhat more complicated. Gemser suggests that Loyalty and Stability are personified as guardian angels of the king (cf. Ps. 61.8). This would point to Yahweh's *ḥesed* and *'*^{e}*met* assured to the Davidic king as the member of a dynasty with whom Yahweh has sworn an everlasting covenant (II Sam. 7.12f.; 23.1f.; Ps. 89.21f.) and the occurrence of *ḥsd* and *'mn* in two of these passages may be significant. In II Sam. 7.15f. Yahweh says of David: 'I will not take my *ḥesed* from him', and says to him: 'Your house (dynasty) and kingdom will be stable (*ne'*^{e}*mān*) for ever.' In Ps. 89.34 Yahweh says of the Davidic king: 'I shall not abrogate my *ḥesed* in respect of him nor default in my *'*^{e}*mūnā*.' The king is himself sustained by Yahweh's loyalty (*ḥesed*) and by the steadfastness and stability (*'*^{e}*mūnā*) which Yahweh contributes to the covenant relationship, and he in turn mediates *ḥesed* to his community by constituting himself a focus of loyalty and working for its ever fuller corporate realization. The emendation of *ḥesed* to *ṣedeq* (LXX δικαιοσύνη; Toy, Gemser, BH) would obliterate the twin reference of *ḥesed*.

Class C

[24] The intention of v. 24 is to set limits to man's ability to pick his way through life without faltering or going astray, and is the same kind of riposte to the claims of old wisdom as I have already discussed in 16.9 and 19.21 (see above, pp. 495, 534). Such guidance and mastery are not to be had by a rigorous educational discipline, and *t*^{e}*būnā* is consequently transferred from the sphere of educational striving and attainment to that of piety and religious illumination. No man can walk with enlightened assurance along the path of life by reason of a well-cultivated nicety of judgement and power of intellectual penetration. He is dependent at every step of the way on Yahweh, and without this light on his path his journey is deprived of safe guidance and enlightened purposiveness.

[27] The thought of divine illumination is also present in v. 27, not the thought that guidance for the road of life comes from Yahweh, nor yet that nothing is hidden from his scrutiny, but that he lights up the deepest and darkest recesses of the mind and knows what is in man (see on 15.11, above, p. 484). The emendation of *nēr* to *nōṣēr* which is linked with the appeal to 24.12 ('he who watches over you will know', see above, pp. 400f.) is unnecessary, and weakens the sense of the verse (contrary to BH, Gemser, Ringgren). MT, which is confirmed by LXX *φῶς*, envisages Yahweh's lamp as within man and equates it with the breath *n*ᵉ*šāmā* which was breathed into him at his creation. 'The chambers of the belly' are the locus of his thoughts and motives, and so the place where the truth about him is to be found (see on v. 30, above, p. 540). The sentence is not directed against man's capacity for pretence and hypocrisy as a warning that God sees him as he is and not as he seems, but is rather a confident assertion that he need not be a victim of self-deceit, since he has this inner light on which he can rely. He has the power of introspection by which he can examine the depths of his self and see clearly in Yahweh's light what is there. Something more than the voice of conscience is indicated, or, at any rate, a discovery of truth which is inward and yet not merely subjective (cf. Toy, 'the inward moral and intellectual being').

[12] A confidence in the evidence of eyes and ears which is similarly grounded is expressed in v. 12. The assertion that Yahweh made ear and eye is taken by Toy, Gemser and Ringgren as an oblique way of saying that they should always be used to his glory and in obedience to his will. Gemser declares that the moral of the sentence is that they should be used for the purposes for which they were created, and Toy states: 'The suggestion is that he (Yahweh) is greater than they, that he watches them and that they must be used in obedience to him.' The meaning which lies much nearer to hand is that the evidence of eye and ear can be trusted, that their reliability is guaranteed by their maker and that men can take for granted the precision of these instruments. They are not given to him by Yahweh to be a source of deception and error, but in order to give him access to knowledge and wisdom by his hearing, seeing and reading.

[9] Over against this, v. 9 appears to throw doubts on man's ability to come to reliable conclusions about his own motives and moral state and it suggests, after the manner of 16.2 ('All of a man's conduct is pure in his own eyes, but it is Yahweh who weighs up motives', see above, pp. 495f.), that if he does assert his purity, there will almost certainly be a discrepancy between his estimate and Yahweh's definitive judgement. The verse is usually understood differently and is thought to be a confession of moral impotence and bondage to sin (Toy, Gemser, Ringgren). Gemser cites a Sumerian sentence: 'Never has a sinless child been born to its mother' (S. Kramer, *VTS* iii, p. 179), and Ps. 51.7 then comes to mind: 'Behold I was brought forth in iniquity, and in sin my mother conceived me.' Ringgren observes that this thought of congenital corruption and moral incapacity is untypical of the sentence literature, and this suggests the need to question such an interpretation of v. 9. I take the question ('Who can say: "I am pure and without alloy of sin"?') to point to man's inability to know himself and to reach certitude about his moral condition. He can never be certain that his mind is pure and that he is without alloy of sin. Even when he has no good reason to believe otherwise, and might draw such a conclusion in good faith, he cannot be certain that he is not self-deceived and has failed to plumb unsuspected depths of duplicity and perversion which Yahweh will take into account (see on 15.3, 11, above, p. 484).

[22] Although there are passages in *Amenemope* (v. 15–17; xxii.1–8, *ANET*, p. 424) and *Ahikar* (xii.174; Cowley, p. 218) which can be compared with v. 22, it is probably to be understood as a precise expression of a Yahwistic doctrine rather than as the taking up of a motif of international wisdom. The *ṣaddīq* has no need to take the law into his own hands, since he can rely on Yahweh to avenge evil and should await his retributive action. The words *wᵉyōšaʿ lāk* may indicate a process of legal vindication with Yahweh as the *mōšiaʿ* whose powerful advocacy avails to 'justify' the *ṣaddīq*. This would support the view that *mōšiaʿ* is, among other things, a title for a legal official (cf. J. Sawyer, *VT* xv, 1965, pp. 475f.).

[7] According to v. 7, the consequences of the blamelessness or the probity of the *ṣaddīq's* way of life are seen in the blessedness of his children. The thought is that of the solidarity of the home for weal or woe. The children are drawn so completely into the sphere of their father's life that the doctrine of theodicy can be stated in terms of the *bayit*. The *ṣaddīq* transmits a blessing to his children, and the *rāšaʿ* a curse (see on 13.22, above, p. 462; 14.11, above, p. 474; 14.26, above, p. 474).

[10, 23] Verses 10 and 23 condemn an aspect of commercial sharp practice, the giving of short measure and weight, either by using a measure or weight which deviates from the standard or by a falsification of the scales (see on 11.1, above, p. 438, and 16.11, above, p. 500). The statement that it is loathed by Yahweh places the offence in the context of theodicy, and furnishes a doctrinal expression of it. Yahweh's *tōʿēbā* is reserved for the *rāšāʿ* as his *rāṣōn* is for the *ṣaddīq* (cf. 11.1, above, pp. 438f.; see on 11.20, above, p. 438; 12.2, above, p. 448; 15.8, 9, above, p. 486; 17.15, above, pp. 511f.).

Chapter 21

In this chapter, the trend which set in with ch. 16 is reversed and the predominance of antithetic parallelism over synthetic or synonymous parallelism which was marked in chs. 10–15 is reasserted. Ten sentences have antithetic parallelism (vv. 2, 5, 8, 11, 15, 20, 26, 28, 29, 31), and six synthetic parallelism (vv. 1, 10, 12, 14, 17, 18). Against this, the absence of parallelism in ten sentences (vv. 3, 4?, 6, 13, 16, 21, 22, 23, 24, 30) constitutes an affinity with the immediately preceding chapters. The motive clause in v. 7b and v. 25b is a formal element of the Instruction imported into the wisdom sentence, and there are examples of the 'better . . . than' (vv. 9, 19) and *a fortiori* (*'ap kī* v. 27) type of formulations.

Class A: vv. 5, 6(?), 9, 11, 14, 16, 17, 19, 20, 22, 23, 24(?), 25, 28.
Class B: vv. 10, 13, 21, 26.
Class C: vv. 1, 2, 3, 4, 7, 8, 12, 15, 18, 27, 29, 30, 31.

Class A

The topics of several sentences (vv. 5, 11, 22, 23, 24, 25?) correspond with characteristic concerns of the educational tradition of old wisdom. [5] Verse 5 strikes a balance between impetuosity and dilatoriness or indecision. There is the Hamlet whose intense intellectual activity is never translated into decision and action and so runs to neurosis, and there is the person who acts with speed but whose haste is undirected or misdirected. Careful planning combined with executive nerve (*maḥšᵉbōt ḥārūṣ*) is profitable, but activism (i.e. activity for the sake of activity) or ill-conceived and misdirected action will not pay dividends. The contrast is between a calculated expeditiousness and an unproductive haste. There is thus no need to emend v. 5b so as to obtain the more pedestrian antithesis of diligence and laziness (contrary to Toy, who reads *darkē ʿāṣēl*).

Nevertheless, the commoner thought in these sentences is that it is laziness rather than haste that leads to want (cf. 6.9f., above, pp. 324; 19.15, above, p. 530), and this idea is present in v. 25. **[25]** 'His hands refuse to act' recalls the picture of the *ʿāṣēl* who lacks the energy to raise food to his mouth from the communal dish which lies on the table (19.24, above, p. 530). The difficult phrase in v. 25a, 'The desire of an *ʿāṣēl* kills him', suggests death by frustration rather than starvation, and the verse may have the same kind of ambivalence as 13.4 (see above, pp. 457f.). Desire which is disproportionate to, or disengaged from, solid attainment is illusion, or neurosis and bondage. It is a dream world which is inhabitated after a flight from reality and from the possibility of life through struggle and achievement. The *ʿāṣēl* who is swamped by desire, but who lacks the character to engage with the real world and to strive after attainment, is one who has refused life and is journeying towards death (cf. Ringgren, 'killed by unfulfilled desire').

[11] The inflicting of a penalty on the intellectually supercilious person is justified in v. 11 in exactly the same manner as in 19.25 (above, p. 525). The unteachability of the *lēṣ* is taken for granted; yet he is to be called to account, for the *petī* may learn the lesson which he himself cannot assimilate. The wise man never ceases to be a learner; he is amenable to instruction and open to the reception of new knowledge. The contrast is between the discipline administered to the *lēṣ* for the sake of the *petī*, and the instruction of a *ḥākām* which is immediately and not mediately salutary (see on 19. 25, above, p. 525).

[24] The intellectual pride, or *hubris*, which stultifies an apprenticeship in wisdom and is destructive of educational discipline, is the topic of v. 24. Toy suggests that this verse offers a formal definition of *lēṣ* (also Gemser) and argues that it points to 'the existence of a precise, philosophical form of instruction in the schools'. The sentence is susceptible of different translations, and it is not certain that it is intended as a formal definition of *lēṣ*, although this is how it is understood by Gemser, Ringgren, RSV and Barucq. Scott, on the other hand, supposes that *zēd*, *yāhīr* and *lēṣ* are synonyms lying side by side, so that *šᵉmō* refers to any one of them and not just to *lēṣ*. Gemser and Ringgren translate *yāhīr* adverbially: 'He who is excessively arrogant, *lēṣ* is his name, one who acts with excess of *zādōn*' (cf. G. R. Driver,

Biblica 32, p. 185). Another possible rendering is: 'He whose name is *zēd, yāhīr, lēṣ*, is one who acts with *hubris*.' There is no good reason why this sentence should be thought to refer to the pride of impiety rather than to intellectual arrogance as an aspect of intellectual indiscipline (contrary to Toy; cf. Ringgren, 'one who despises wisdom'). Consequently I locate it in the context of old wisdom, not that of Yahwistic piety. In the one, pride is a lack of intellectual humility and an unwillingness to serve an apprenticeship in wisdom under the authority of a teacher; in the other, it is the lack of the humility of piety and a refusal to submit to the sovereignty and revealed will of Yahweh.

[22] The theme of v. 22 is that of 16.32 and 24.5f. (see above, pp. 488, 397f.). Brains are more important in war even than picked troops and fortified positions. Tactics can be devised to scale (*ʿālā*, so KB²) a walled city and defeat a garrison of soldiers who are an *élite*; a 'Maginot Line' mentality (*mibṭeḥāh*, the suffix should be read) is vulnerable to an enterprising and talented tactician. This, rather than the bare antithesis of intellectual power and physical strength, is probably what is intended (see on 24.5–6, above, pp. 397f.). The use of the *wāw* consecutive imperfect as a gnomic present is unusual.

[23] Verse 23 expatiates on the virtue of taciturnity in a manner reminiscent of 15.23; 18.13; and especially 13.3. *nepeš* is to be translated 'life' (so Gemser, Ringgren), and not 'himself' (Toy, RSV, Scott), nor 'soul' (Barucq). Economy of speech, and the ability to remain silent when silence is the most judicious response to a situation, are aspects of the intellectual discipline of old wisdom, which is designed to direct those who are shaped by it along the way of life. This will keep a man from being trapped in perilous 'narrows', where his very life is at stake. Otherwise, he may find himself through unguarded speech in a situation where he is hemmed in on all sides, and where the pressures on him are so insistent and powerful that he is conscious of his life being squeezed out of him. This is how distress is envisaged and the taciturn man guards his life from such sinister possibilities of strangulation.

[6] In v. 6, LXX reads: 'He who acquires riches through a false tongue pursues vanities into the snares of death.' Hence Gemser substitutes *pōʿēl* for *pōʿal*, *rōdēp* for *niddāp*, and *bᵉmōqᵉšē* for *mᵉbaqqᵉšē* (metathesis of *b* and *m*; cf. 13.14; 14.27). Alternatively, Gemser (p. 112) suggests that *hebel* is adverbial, 'are aimlessly driven into the snares of death'. The form of the emendation proposed by BH and

Ringgren (*ūmōqᵉšē*) is unsatisfactory, because it does not account for the *bēt* in the (*ex hypothesi*) corrupt *mᵉbaqqᵉšē* and because 'pursuing snares of death' is not a particularly credible metaphor. There is little doubt that *mōqᵉšē māwet* should be read (contrary to Barucq, who translates MT: 'It is a fleeting vanity of people who seek death') and, if so, it is difficult to make sense of *hebel niddāp*. It cannot mean 'fleeting breath' (Toy), but is rather a vanity (or, emptiness) which is driven (as by the wind) among the snares of death. The sense, whether or not *rōdēp* is adopted, is that ill-gotten wealth is insubstantial and unreal, and he who has it is not a man of weight, firmly anchored in the esteem of his community, with an assured hold on life, but one who is being borne at speed, without the ability to resist, towards the snares of death (or, with *rōdēp*, one who is pursuing emptiness among the snares of death). The contrast is then between wealth as an index and aspect of harmonious self-fulfilment, associated with fulness of life, and wealth divorced from intrinsic worth of character which is evidence of a flaw that accelerates progress towards death. The person whose main aim in life is to get rich quickly, and who uses deceit to serve the ends of his avarice, will never know what it is to possess wealth as an ingredient of *kābōd* and *šālōm*.

[20] Wealth in the possession of a wise man is the subject of v. 20. The allusion is apparently partly to his thriftiness, since he is contrasted with the fool who devours or squanders wealth. LXX translates: 'Precious treasures rest on the mouth of a sage, but the fool devours them', and this interpretation is favoured by Gemser and Ringgren, who suppose that the verse refers, on the one hand, to the costliness of wisdom and, on the other, to the incorrigibility of the fool – the words of the wise are wasted on him (Gemser follows LXX, reading *yiškōn* for *wāšemen* and *bᵉpī* for *binᵉwē*). More probably LXX, here as elsewhere, has interpreted so as to expunge the earthiness of the Hebrew text, and so it is unsound to rely on it as a guide to the meaning of the original (cf. Toy). The verse, rather, says that the *ḥākām* is wealthy and shows good taste (*neḥmād*) as a collector of precious objects, whereas a *kᵉsīl* allows money to run through his fingers and does not use it to create the material environment for gracious living. *wāšemen*, if it is read (cf. Toy and Ringgren), would, as Toy remarks, have to be explained as another reference to gracious living, namely, the use of oil for anointing the body on festive occasions (cf. v. 17b). Scott suggests that *'ōṣār neḥmād* may be a gloss on 'oil'. I. Eitan (pp. 62f.) equates *šmn* with Arabic *ṯmn* and vocalizes *šāmīn* (Arabic *ṯamīn*, 'dear', 'expensive'): 'Desirable and rare wealth are in the home of a wise man.' Verse 20b accords ill with Scott's suggestion. Surely the fool is not said to swallow oil. MT is hardly credible. Eitan's proposal is speculative, but I accept it. **[17]** In v. 17 the phrase 'wine and oil' is explicative of *śimḥā*, 'a good time', and is pejorative. Feasting and drinking are recipes for poverty, and the man who has a fondness for the extravagances of high living is always short of money and by way of becoming a pauper.

[16] Verse 16, with its implied contrast of the two ways of life and death, also connects with v. 6. Everyone is a traveller, and the journey involves either an increase or a diminution of life. Whoever is informed by wisdom travels safely and effectively, and lays hold on life with an ever surer grasp, but he who wanders from the path of understanding (i.e., who has not served his apprenticeship with a wisdom teacher and been shaped by the discipline of wisdom) will end his journey among the assembly of the shades in the realm of the dead (for *r^epā'īm* see on 2.18, above, pp. 287f.; 9.18, above, p. 367). It is the direction of the journey which is the exact point of the verse – towards death and not life – rather than the aspect of premature death (Toy, Gemser and Ringgren), although this is not excluded.

[9, 19] The topic of the nagging wife (see on 19.13, above, p. 531) is resumed in vv. 9 and 19. The meaning of v. 19 is clearly that it is better to accept solitariness and discomfort or even privations (to live in a desert), than to be vexed by a nagging wife. Verse 9, which is formally identical with v. 19, has the same general import, although certain of its details are less easily elucidated. Gemser has argued that *pinnat gāg* is a cramped attic such as a guest might use in an emergency (cf. II Kings 4.10, *ʿ^alīyat qīr*; I Kings 17.19, *hāʿ^alīyā*; I Sam. 9.25) or to which a widow might withdraw (Judith 8.5). Toy and Barucq take the meaning to be that it is better to be perched precariously and uncomfortably on the corner of a roof (cf. LXX ὑπαίθρου, 'in the open air') than to endure a nagging wife. I follow Gemser here (cf. M. Noth, *The Old Testament World*, 1966, p. 153: 'The roof could support an upper chamber, Hebrew *ʿ^alīyā*, probably built at a *corner* (italics mine) of the roof'). *ʿ^alīyat qīr*, 'walled upper chamber' (II Kings 4.10) indicates that it was a properly built room and not a temporary booth, and so implies that an *ʿ^alīyā* might be no more than a temporary booth (Judith 8.5, 'a tent on the roof of her house') erected for makeshift accommodation. To live in primitive conditions on the roof of the house is better 'than a contentious wife and a *bēt ḥāber*'. Barucq renders: 'Than to make common house with a contentious woman', and this supplies the contrast which is needed (similarly Gemser and Ringgren; cf. LXX ἐν οἴκῳ κοινῷ). Toy and BH emend to *ūbayit rāḥāb*, producing an antithesis between the cramped conditions on the roof and the spaciousness of the house. The appearance of *bt ḫbr* in Ugaritic has been noted by Albright and Driver. The passage in question (*Keret* I iv.8–10, G. R. Driver, *CML*, pp. 32f.) is translated by Albright:

> And Keret shall go down from the roof thrones,
> Make ready grain from the granaries (*qryt*),
> Wheat from the breweries (*bt ḫbr*) (W. F. Albright *VTS* iii, pp. 11f.).

Driver translates:

> With his (offering of) game Keret did come down
> from the roofs, did make ready food from the granary,
> and wheat from the inn.

Gordon translates *qryt* 'city', and *bt ḫbr* 'community':

> And let Krt go down from the roofs,
> Prepare food for the city,
> Wheat for the community.

(C. H. Gordon, *Ugaritic Literature*, 1949, p. 69; *Ugaritic Textbook*, *An. Or.* 38, 1965, p. 400, no. 924.) In a similar passage (*Keret* I ii.26–29, *CML*, pp. 30f.), Driver translates *qryt* 'inn' and *bt ḫbr* 'storehouse', and gives Gordon's rendering of *lqryt*, 'for the city', in a note (p. 31, n.4). *qryt*, 'granary', is associated by Driver (*CML*, p. 31, n.5; p. 144, n.4) with Accadian *qārītu*, and *bt ḫbr* is rendered 'house of vats', 'brewery', 'alehouse' in agreement with Albright (Middle Assyrian *bīt ḫubūri*).

The parallelism 'city – community' is at least as probable as 'granary – alehouse', so that the evidence of the Ugaritic texts cannot be regarded as decisive for Prov. 21.9. Further, it is not at all clear what relevance this reference to an alehouse is supposed to have in Albright's translation: 'Dwelling in a roof corner is better than a quarrelsome woman and a public-house.' This has to be understood as an allusion to two separate evils to which discomfort and solitariness on the roof are to be preferred. The one is a nagging wife, and the other the din and brawling of an alehouse. A comparison with the form of v. 19b (*me'ēšet midwānīm wakā'as*) suggests that the right sense is more probably 'to share a house with a nagging wife', a meaning which has some support from LXX (ἐν οἴκῳ κοινῷ). J. J. Finkelstein has suggested (*JBL* lxxv, 1956, pp. 328–31) the translation: 'It is better to live on the edge of a roof than with a contentious wife and a noisy household.' He connects *ḥāber* with Accadian *ḫabāru*, 'to be noisy'; Arabic *ḫbr* II and IV 'to inform'; Syriac *ḥbārā*, 'noise', 'discordant sound'. LXX moralizes: 'It is better to live in a corner in the open air than within walls plastered with lime, in a common house, with injustice.' All reference to the nagging wife who is the occasion of the sentence in MT is expunged.

[14] In v. 14, where the bribe is recommended as an effective way of deflecting anger and bad temper, the pragmatism of 17.8 and 18.16 is again in evidence (cf. the condemnatory attitude of 15.27b and 17.23). The bribe is carried in a breast pocket (on *ḥēq* see 17.23, above, p. 512), and is to be discreetly conveyed so as to improve the climate of the negotiations which are contemplated. Verse 14a (MT) reads: 'A clandestine gift deflects (*yikpe*) rage.' BH emends to *yekappēr*, 'covers anger' (cf. 16.14b). Symmachus, Targ., point to *yekabbeh*, 'extinguishes anger', and Gemser suggests 'satisfies anger' (*yekabbeh* cognate with Arabic *kafā*, rather than *kafa'*, p. 113). MT can stand; of the emendations suggested, Gemser's is the least apt and *yekabbeh* the most attractive and best attested.

[28] Verse 28 begins in the same way as other sentences of a similarly forensic kind, but the manner in which the antithesis is worked out in v. 28b differs from the normal forms of expression (cf. 14.5, 25; 19.5, 9, which have synthetic parallelism). Toy argues that the connection between the two halves is defective (cf. Barucq) and that no satisfactory antithesis can be constructed out of v. 28b. Gemser elucidates *'īš šōmēa'* in connection with the demand for receptivity and unbroken concentration which is made in the Instruction. One must listen hard in order to become wise, and a good listener with the ability to remember and to reproduce exactly what he has heard will give a good account of himself in the witness-box and will speak with lasting effect. Such an interpretation is contemplated by Toy, but rejected. Driver cites *šōmēa'* in Judg. 11.10, which he describes as a Gileadite word for 'witness' and with which he compares Assyrian *šāmeānu*, 'ear-witness', and Ethiopic usages. In Job 23.7, *lāneṣaḥ* is a juristic phrase meaning 'successfully', 'rightly', and this is its sense in v. 28 (cf. Pesh., 'rightfully', Targ., 'truthfully', and the phrase in Talmudic Aramaic *tešūbā niṣṣeḥā*, 'convincing answer'). The meaning then is that the lying witness will perish, i.e., will be debarred from successfully concluding his evidence and so lose his case, while the truthful or effective witness will speak (on), i.e., speak to the end without being refuted or put down (similarly Ringgren, who posits an antithesis of hearsay, and evidence which stands up to legal scrutiny). Yet, even so, the difficulties indicated by Toy are not entirely overcome, and Driver has had to work very hard to establish an antithesis. Thus 'perish' has to bear a specialized juristic sense, as also has 'speak', and the straining after sense is so laborious that Toy perhaps has the last word (G. R. Driver, *ZAW* 50, 1932, p. 145).

Class B

[10] There is no constructive social aspect to the behaviour of the *rāšāʿ*, and he is untouched by the desire to enlarge his own life by living in a human community which is constituted by compassion and brotherliness. Humanity consists in the willingness to go out towards other men and to contribute towards social enrichment; the man who cannot transcend his own self-assertiveness is in a prison and is dehumanized. The *rāšāʿ* is incapable of loving his neighbour, and is unable to make the positive social responses which establish his status as a human being. Within him there is a festering hatred of all men, and his humanity is so deeply tainted that his capacity for encountering others with goodwill and benevolence is destroyed. He is a hater of men with an insatiable desire to hurt others, whose neighbour is always the object of his malice and never of his compassion.

[13] Such a person will inevitably cut himself off from the social support which he might otherwise enjoy and will lay up for himself a store of trouble. He has stopped up the springs of mercy within himself, and has long since been deaf to the appealing cry of the poor. There will come a day when he needs help, and then he will appear before his fellows as if he had always been one of them, but they will reject him, and his pleas will meet with a stony silence. (This, rather than that his prayer is a cry to God, as is indicated by Pesh. and Targ.) He whose consistent aim in life has been to destroy concord between man and man will appeal in vain in his evil day to the generous humanity of others.

[21] With isolation and death is to be contrasted integration and life. The pursuit of *ṣᵉdāqā wāḥesed* is evidence of a high regard for the commonweal. By such behaviour a man proves himself to be a loyal citizen and constructively affirms his oneness with his brethren; he promotes social cohesiveness (*ḥesed*), and maintains the quality of corporate life (*ṣᵉdāqā*, 'social health'). Such a person will find life both quantitatively and qualitatively (*kābōd*; *ṣᵉdāqā* in v. 21b should be deleted with LXX. So Toy, BH, Gemser, Ringgren, Scott; contrary to Barucq, who retains it and translates 'fruit of justice', i.e., prosperity). He will enjoy length of days (see on 10.27, above, p. 425) and 'weight', i.e., reputation, influence, wealth and self-fulfilment (see on 3.2, 16, above, pp. 290, 295f.; 11.31, above, p. 437; 12.28, above, pp. 450f.).

[26] The *ṣaddīq* is a generous benefactor, who gives without grudge or stint (v. 26b). One would expect in v. 26a an antithetic comment on the *rāšā'* who is mean and hardens his heart against the need of his brother. Verse 26a (MT) is obscure and, as Toy observes, it presents apparently insoluble problems. The presence of *ta'ᵃwā* in v. 25 and *hit'awwā ta'ᵃwā* in v. 26 explains why the two verses have been placed side by side, but the arrangement may arise simply from the occurrence of *ta'ᵃwā* in both verses and does not show that there is any intrinsic connection between them (cf. Toy). Driver renders 'All the day long he coveteth greedily' (cf. Ringgren 'avaricious desire'), assumes a continuity between v. 25 and v. 26, and takes *'āṣēl* as the subject of v. 26a. The contrast is then between the lazy man who is potentially greedy but is impotent to realize his desires and is a man of straw, and the *ṣaddīq* who is a man of substance and a benefactor (G. R. Driver, *JTS* xli, 1940, p. 174). LXX reads: 'The impious man has evil desires all the day', but it is difficult to decide what textual significance should be attached to this in view of the tendency of LXX to moralize on MT. Thus *ta'ᵃwā*, 'desire', has apparently been rendered by ἐπιθυμίας κακάς, 'evil desires', and ἀσεβής does not therefore show that the Greek translator had before him a Hebrew text with *rāšā'* or the like in it, although the support of LXX is claimed for such emendations (BH, Gemser, Scott, Barucq; cf. Ringgren, p. 84, n.3). ἀσεβής (v. 26a) may have no significance for textual criticism, since it is the type of moralizing expansion which would be encouraged by *ṣaddīq* (v. 26b). Even if LXX were followed, the antithesis is imperfectly articulated (Toy), but one would have to suppose that it lies in the contrast between the *rāšā'* who is constantly consumed with self-centred desire and the *ṣaddīq* who gives liberally to help others (cf. v. 10).

Class C

I have already discussed several sentences which appear to challenge the claims of old wisdom along the lines of the prophetic critique (see on 16.2, 9, above, pp. 495f.; 19.21, above, p. 534; 20.24, above pp. 546f.; cf. *PWM*, pp. 50, 65f.), and there are a few sentences of a similar character in this chapter (vv. 2, 4, 30, 31). The language of the *ḥakāmīm* by which they give expression to their belief in the strength of their intellects and the effectiveness of their policies is here called in question, and the dependence of men on Yahweh for truth and guidance is stressed. **[2]** Verse 2 states, in terms almost identical with those of 16.2, that a man's own appraisal of his way of life is in the very nature of the case unreliable and at variance with Yahweh's estimate (on *tōkēn* see 16.2, above, pp. 495f.). Even if self-criticism assumes its most rigorous forms, there is necessarily a discrepancy between this crude and unreliable measurement and Yahweh's norm, so that even the most judicious man should not conclude that he is pursuing a safe course along the road of life. The implication of this is that it does not lie in man to know the truth about himself and his conduct, unless his mind is illumined by Yahweh and safe guidance is granted him.

[30] Verse 30 and, especially, v. 31 are directed against the political pretensions of old wisdom in a way reminiscent of the prophetic polemic. 'Wisdom', 'discernment', 'policy', this is the jargon of the sages, who represent themselves as an intellectual *élite* who alone have the acumen and the equipment to deal with the complex and delicate matters of statesmanship and diplomacy. But the sages do not in fact possess the prescience and control which are indicated by these high-sounding words; their vocabulary and claims make shipwreck on Yahweh, to whom alone the vocabulary which the wise men use of themselves and their intellectual powers really applies (*PWM*, pp. 65f.). **[31]** Another feature of the prophetic attack on old wisdom is paralleled in v. 31, namely, the antipathy to reliance on weight of armament and so on foreign alliances, as opposed to trust in Yahweh (*PWM*, pp. 65f., 113f.). As in the experience of Holy War in days of old, Yahweh's people must look to him alone for victory (G. von Rad, *Old Testament Theology*, ii, pp. 159f.).

[4] This critical reassessment of old wisdom is again nicely illustrated by the pejorative use of *rōḥab lēb* in v. 4. *rōḥab lēb* (to which *reḥab lēb* should be emended) is breadth of intellect, and so is descriptive of mental power and capacity, not of a flaw in a person's make-up (cf. I Kings 5.9, where it is used with *ḥokmā* and *tebūnā* of Solomon's intellectual endowment). Hence *rōḥab lēb* is the opposite of *ḥasar lēb*, which is used of a person of low intelligence (cf. 6.32; 7.7; 9.4, 16; 10.13; 11.12; 12.11; 15.21; 17.18). Here, however, as in Ezek. 28.2f.

(*PWM*, pp. 73f.), *rōḥab lēb* is not the native acumen which will respond to education and is the reservoir of all intellectual attainment; it is a megalomaniac aberration which can be equated with intellectual pride or *hubris*; it is man behaving as if he were God and not observing his creaturely limits. Thus pride and breadth of *lēb* are synonymous in v. 4a. Toy has questioned whether there is any connection between v. 4a and v. 4b, and Gemser supposes that two lines may have been lost. LXX reads: 'The lamp of the wicked is sin', and Ringgren suggests that 'lamp' may be a metaphor for fortune or well-being (see on 13.9, p. 461), but the expression, 'the lamp of the wicked is sin', is both lame and obscure. Barucq renders v. 4b, 'a light for the wicked – rather a sin!', an exclamation which alludes to the *hubris* of v. 4a, but v. 4b cannot be so translated. If MT is retained in v. 4b, the reference may be to the incorrigibility of the wicked, as Gemser suggests. The *r^ešā'îm* cannot be cultivated, they are not amenable to educational discipline. The relation of v. 4a and v. 4b would then consist in the connection between arrogance and incorrigibility as in 13.1, 10; 15.12; 17.10; 19.25; 21.11, and *ḥaṭṭā't* would then be misdirected effort rather than sin, unless v. 4b is to be translated: 'The tilth of the *r^ešā'îm* (produces only) sin.' Sin is the crop, and so education is a waste of time. As the pejorative use of *rōḥab lēb* shows, pride is impiety rather than a lack of intellectual humility (see on 15.12, above, p. 480; 17.10, above, p. 504; 19.25, above, p. 525; 21.11, above, p. 550). What is in view is not the *lēṣ* who will not learn at the feet of a wisdom teacher, but the *rāšā'* who will not submit to Yahweh (see above, pp. 550f., on v. 24).

[1] Another sentence which conflicts with the presuppositions of old wisdom is v. 1. The king is not dependent on the expertise of *śārîm* or *ḥ^akāmîm* or *yō'^aṣîm* for guidance in state matters or for the formulation of policy (cf. *PWM*, pp. 15f.). His mind (*lēb*) is not shaped by their deliberations and advice; it is directly influenced and controlled by Yahweh. Just as the farmer leads water along the irrigation channels in pursuance of his agricultural projects, Yahweh directs the mind of the king and makes him the agent of his designs. 'These are channels that can be directed to where they will do most good. It is very easy to do this by damming up the stream and turning it in another direction, just as the verse puts it' (E.F.F.B.). The shape of the king's rule derives directly from Yahweh and is not determined by the policy-making of a cabinet of *ḥ^akāmîm*, and, if so, the well-being of the community is independent of the nice calculations of diplomacy and hinges only on the king's willingness to respond to Yahweh's leading (cf. *PWM*, pp. 113f.).

The prophetic attitude to sacrifice is reproduced in two verses (vv. 3, 27; see on 15.8, above, p. 486). **[3, 27]** The doing of justice and righteousness is higher than sacrifice in Yahweh's order of priorities (v. 3). Neither this statement nor that of v. 27 amounts to a repudiation of sacrifice, as Ringgren observes, but both subordinate it to morality, and v. 27 says that the sacrifice of *rᵉšāʿīm* is an abomination (*tōʿēbā, tōʿᵃbat YHWH* according to LXX). I have commented already (see on 12.2, above, p. 448; 17.15, above, pp. 511f.) that *tōʿēbā* and *rāṣōn* were formulae which communicated decisions about cultic matters, so that both this verse and 15.8 are illustrations of the original cultic *Sitz* of these declaratory formulae (cf. G. von Rad, *Old Testament Theology*, i, pp. 197, 247, 261). Toy is mistaken in supposing that *bᵉzimmā* means 'to pay for a crime' (*bēt pretii*; RSV margin, 'as an atonement for a crime'). The *a fortiori* construction is directed towards a special intention of deceit or malevolence connected with the bringing of the sacrifice (cf. LXX παρανόμως). The established character of the man (*rāšāʿ*) makes his sacrifice *tōʿēbā*, but the case is worse if he brings it as a cloak for the attainment of a nefarious end (cf. Matt. 15.5; Mark 7.11).

Several sentences inculcate the doctrine of theodicy (vv. 7, 12, 15, 18). **[15]** In v. 15, the antithetic parallelism is a guide to the meaning of v. 15a which must be rendered 'Doing what is right brings joy to the righteous man' (so Toy, Gemser, Ringgren, Scott) and not, 'It is a delight to a righteous man to do justice' (so Barucq). *śimḥā* is not so much indicative of the feelings of the *ṣaddīq* as of the well-being which accrues to him in consequence of the operation of *mišpāṭ*. When *mišpāṭ* is effective, both the welfare of the *ṣaddīq* and the 'shattering' or ruin of evil-doers are assured. *śimḥā* is a correlate of justification and *mᵉḥittā* of condemnation.

[7] In v. 7, the metaphor indicated by *yᵉgōrēm* can best be assessed in relation to Hab. 1.15, which supplies a context helpful for the elucidation of *grr*. In that passage, the prophet describes how Yahweh catches men like fish, pulling them up on a hook or taking them in nets. *yᵉgōrēhū bᵉḥermō*, 'he drags him in his net', would seem to have in mind the operation of dragging the net through a stretch of water in order to make a catch of fish. The thought that the wicked are netted or snared by their own deeds of violence can be compared with the same metaphor in 12.13; 13.14; 14.27.

[12] Verse 12 also touches on the destruction of the *rᵉšāʿîm*, but its details are obscure and it is difficult to elucidate. LXX, καρδίας, points to the consonants *lbwt* (MT *lbyt*). This is adopted by Scott ('thoughts of evil men'), but it does nothing to mitigate the difficulties of the verse which are associated with *maśkîl* and *ṣaddîq* rather than *bēt rāšāʿ* – in itself a perfectly credible phrase (cf. 3.33a, above, p. 302). Hitzig emends *rāšāʿ* to *rešaʿ* and alters the punctuation of MT so as to read: 'The righteous man considers his household, but wickedness hurls the wicked to ruin.' Apart from the general consideration whether such an alteration of MT is justifiable, there are two particular reasons for rejecting this emendation: (*a*) the correctness of *bēt rāšāʿ* is almost certain (see above), (*b*) the probability is that Yahweh is the subject of *mᵉsallēp* (cf. 22.12b). If *ṣaddîq* (v. 12a) means 'righteous man', one would have to suppose that he is credited with keeping the household of the *rāšāʿ* under review and of toppling it (so Ringgren, Barucq, Scott). There is no satisfactory explanation of v. 12a, but in view of what I have said under (*b*), I regard it as a lesser evil to assume with Gemser that *ṣaddîq* refers to Yahweh (cf. *ṣaddîq* – *kabbîr* used of God in Job 34.17b). Yahweh exercises effective control (for this sense of *maśkîl* see *PWM*, p. 68) over the household of the *rāšāʿ*, and he topples the wicked to their ruin.

[18] Verse 18 gives a curious account of the relationship of *ṣaddîq* to *rāšāʿ* which should, however, be regarded as an aberrant statement of the doctrine of theodicy (see on 11.8, above, p. 436). In legal parlance, *kōper* is the sum of money by which liability to a legal penalty is discharged, as in Ex. 21.30, where the death penalty may be commuted to a money payment, which is the *kōper*. Barucq suggests that the intention of the verse is to indicate such a relation of reciprocity between wicked and righteous that the punishment of the one is the *kōper* of the other, but Toy is probably correct in his insistence that the exact legal notion of *kōper* is not to be pressed in this verse. If it were, it would, strictly understood, be inconsistent with the doctrine of theodicy, according to which the *ṣaddîq* enjoys well-being and success on his own merits and has no need of a *kōper*. The emphasis should rather fall on the alternatives implied by the double-sided nature of theodicy, namely, reward or retribution, and the verse should be understood as a novel way of making this point (see on v. 15, above, p. 560) which is not to be pressed with legal exactitude. The righteous man's meat is the wicked man's poison.

Verses 8 and 29 contain contrasts of straightness and crookedness, pretence and reality, in association with the metaphor of the road of life. **[8]** The meaning of *wāzār* in v. 8 is uncertain. If it is to be connected with Arabic *wizru(n)* 'crime', the *'īš wāzār* is a criminal (a crook). Gemser favours the emendation *'īš kāzāb*, 'a liar', and Driver and Snijders would emend v. 8a to read *'īš hapakpak darkō zār*, which Driver translates: 'The man whose way is crooked is false', deriving *zār* from Arabic *zawira*, 'inclined'; II *zawwara*, 'falsified'; *zūru*, 'falsehood' (*Biblica* 32, p. 185). Snijders takes *zār* to mean 'outsider', 'deviating (untrustworthy) man' (p. 69, n.96; see on 2.16, above, pp. 285f.). Apart from this particular obscurity, the general sense is not in doubt. The *zak* is the candid person who is transparently sincere and is without taint of deviousness or duplicity. He is a man of upright character who keeps a straight course in contrast with the labyrinthine route of the *'īš wāzār*.

[29] The *rāšā'* (v. 29a) is the brass-faced person who believes that he can extricate himself successfully from every situation by a combination of bluff and resolute impudence. The upright man will have nothing to do with such bogus posturing, and concentrates on laying sound foundations for his life. Gemser prefers *yābīn* (Q.) to *yākīn* (K.) and *darkō* (Q.) to *derākāw* (K.). The meaning would then be that the upright man discerns his way, i.e., picks his steps with discernment. This does not seem to me to sustain so well the antithesis of fraud and genuineness; from this point of view, *yābīn*, if it is to be read, goes better with *derākāw* ('discerns his ways' means that his conduct is regulated by nice moral discrimination; so Toy). The contrast is then between the spurious and unprincipled behaviour of the *rāšā'* and the integrity of the *yāšār*. Gemser, despite his preference for *yābīn*, makes the alternative suggestion that the intention may be to oppose the hardening of the face to the reinforcement of the road. This is how the verse is taken by Reuss: 'a wicked man fixes his face, an upright man his conduct' (*darkō*='way of life'). The *rāšā'* is concerned to keep up appearances and to gain his ends by bluff and effrontery, but the *yāšār* founds his life on truth rather than a lie. He prepares a road with solid foundations and a good surface along which he can make safe and sure progress (Scott, 'is sure of his way').

Chapter 22.1–16

Again in this chapter there is formal diversity and a paucity of precise parallelism. There is one certain case of antithetic parallelism in v. 3, and it is probably also intended in v. 16, which is then asyndetic (see below). Verse 12 is construed by Toy, Gemser, Barucq and RSV as a case of antithetic parallelism, but the question of form is here inseparable from that of meaning and, following Frankenberg, I suppose that the parallelism is synthetic (cf. Ringgren; see below). Another sentence (v. 15) is understood as an instance of (asyndetic) antithetic parallelism by Toy and RSV, who supply 'but'. It is not certain, however, that an antithesis is intended (Scott: '[Only] the teacher's cane will rid him of it'; cf. Gemser, Ringgren, Barucq), and I suppose it to be the less well-defined synthetic parallelism which is in evidence here. These are interesting examples of how decisions respecting form have an important bearing on exegesis (see below). Other verses with synthetic parallelism are 2, 5 (implied antithesis according to Toy, see below, p. 565), 7, 8, 14. Verses 4 (emended), 11, 13 are continuous sentences with no trace of parallelism. A fragment of Instruction appears in v. 6 (imperative with asyndetic motive clause?) and v. 10 (imperative followed by two 'and so' clauses); v. 9b is a motive clause – a formal element of the Instruction. Verse 1 has a 'more . . . than' type of construction in both its stichoi.

Class A: vv. 1, 3, 5, 6, 7, 10, 11, 13, 15.
Class B: v. 9.
Class C: vv. 2, 4, 8, 12, 14, 16.

Class A

[3] The task of the wisdom teacher is to impart *'ormā* to the *petī* (see on 1.4, above, p. 265), so that the contrast of *'ārūm* and *petī* has educational significance. The *petī* is the credulous, uncritical, unwary youth who is the raw material to be shaped into a wise man by a strenuous educational process. In his untutored state the *petī* is not equipped to survive in a dangerous world. He is an innocent abroad, insufficiently thoughtful and perceptive to apprise himself of danger and to take the necessary evasive action. With his uncritical, naïve ways he blunders into trouble and has to pay the penalty of his ignorance of the world. The forensic meaning of *'nš*, 'fine', which is evident in 17.26 and 19.19, is generalized here and in 21.11a (cf. Toy). The *'ārūm* is the product of education, the graduate of the wisdom school, who has the acumen to take the measure of a developing situation, and knows how to edge away from it into inconspicuousness (Q. *wenistār*, cf. 27.12). Dahood's suggestion (pp. 45f.) cited

by Barucq, that *yistār* should be derived from *sūr*, gives the required sense ('takes evasive action'), but a formation from *str* is more probable. If Dahood were followed, *yistār* would have to be explained on the analogy of the imperfect of the Arabic 8th form (*yaḫtār* from *ḫyr*). The only point of contact with normal practice in Hebrew hithpael would be the infixed *t* with the sibilant (e.g. *'eštammēr* from *šmr*); hithpael forms, however, are not found in Hebrew ayin waw and yod verbs. LXX reinterprets rather than misunderstands (Gemser) MT. πανοῦργος, 'clever knave' or 'versatile fellow', is recognizably a translation of *'ārūm*, but what is then attributable to the πανοῦργος has no discernible connection with the deftness and intellectual flexibility denoted by the word. The sentence is given a moralistic twist and is made to turn on the ability of the πανοῦργος to learn from the severe punishment which is meted out to the evil man (πονηρός).

[6] The importance of education for the young is also stressed in v. 6. This is the age when impressionability can be taken for granted and when change for the better is possible. The task of education is to enable the youth to raise his capabilities to the highest pitch of effectiveness and to set him undeviatingly on the right road by disciplining his habits and enlightening his attitudes. Once he is set in this mould, he will be essentially the same person to the end of his days. 'According to his way' does not mean 'according to his aptitudes', as Ringgren appears to suggest, but rather 'according to the way he ought to go'. The thought that the educational process must be tailored to the requirements of the individual is not at all what is intended. There is only one right way – the way of life – and the educational discipline which directs young men along this way is uniform. The wise man is a type who is identifiable by the texture of his mind and the style and orientation of his life. Barucq translates 'at the entrance of his way' (*pī* 'mouth'; cf. Frankenberg, 'at the beginning of his way'). This is improbable.

[15] An insight into the presuppositions of these educators is given by v. 15, which indicates how the *petī* is viewed by his teachers. 'Folly is tied to the mind of a youth' is an indication that they do not underestimate the difficulties of their task and are aware that they do battle with an innate recalcitrance and perversity. There is more to education than making manifest what is already there or hastening the maturity of the seed which already contains all the possibilities of growth and nothing that would hinder it. The educator's task is both to tear down and to build up; he has to eradicate as well as to implant. There are elements of chaos in the mind of the youth and order has to be restored; his innate tendency is towards folly rather than wisdom, and only the *šēbeṭ mûsār* will put a distance between him and folly. This is not just a reference to corporal punishment, though it includes this. It is an indication of a theory of education which comes down strongly on the side of discipline, but the most important application of this is not corporal punishment. It is rather the emphasis on the intellectual authority of the teacher and the duty of unbroken attentiveness and unquestioning acceptance which is laid upon the pupil.

[5] The way of the wrong-headed man is the opposite of that along which the youth should be directed (v. 6). The parallelism is not strictly antithetic, since the function of v. 5b is not so much to contrast *ʿiqqēš* with *šōmēr napšō* as to indicate that the *ʿiqqēš* is not the one who keeps his life. Consequently v. 5b is explanatory of v. 5a and the parallelism may be described as synthetic. *nepeš* should certainly be translated 'life' (Gemser and Ringgren) and not 'himself' (Toy, RSV, Barucq). The implication is that the *ʿiqqēš* is on the path of death, and so we again have the opposition of the two ways. 'Thorns and (LXX and versions) snares' are an improbable combination, so attention is focussed on the obscure *ṣinnîm*. It is supported by LXX τρίβολοι, 'prickly plants', whereas both Pesh. (*nešbe'*) and Targ. (*nyšb'*) indicate 'trap' or the like. Hence Toy suggests *ṣammîm*, which is parallel to *paḥ* in Job 18.9 (cf. BH). In Amos 4.2 *ṣinnōt* means 'hooks', which is not appropriate here, but a form akin to *ṣinnîm*, namely *ṣᵉnînîm*, means 'thorns' in Num. 33.55 and Josh. 23.13. MT is retained by Gemser, Ringgren, Barucq and Scott, and 15.19, where the way of the sluggard is said to be overgrown with thorns, is cited. Dyserinck's emendation (*ṣᵉpûnîm*), 'Concealed are the snares in the way of the crooked man', is noted by Toy and BH. Driver postulates **ṣēn*, Targumic Aramaic *ṣinna*, 'basket', and Arabic *ṣinnu*, 'basket'; cf. Hebrew *ṣinṣenet*, 'receptacle'. Hebrew **ṣen*, 'basket', 'trap' would show the same semantic development as Arabic *quffa*, 'basket', 'bird-cage'. 'Traps and snares are in the way of the *ʿiqqēš*' gives the required sense. The *ʿiqqēš* is the incurably wrong-headed and perverse person who is the despair of educators and to whose mind folly will be bound (cf. v. 15, above, pp. 564f.) till the end of his days. He treads a perilous road, infested with traps and snares, and his destruction will come sooner or later. He has no firm hold on life, for the man who keeps his life walks along a safe road, differently orientated.

[1] Verse 1 should not be understood as a polemic against wealth, but rather as supplying a framework of values within which material prosperity can make its contribution to a full life. Divorced from this frame of reference and order of priorities, the possession of wealth may be a snare and a delusion (see on 20.17, 21, above, pp. 539f.; 21.6, above, pp. 551f.). Wealth should be an index of worth, but it may degenerate into a mere consequence of rapacity. Reputation (on *šēm* see 10.7, above, pp. 422f.) is to be given preference over great wealth, and engaging personal qualities (on *ḥēn* see 11.16, above, p. 430) are better than silver and gold.

[7] A frank recognition of the power of wealth appears in v. 7. Gemser sees this as a warning of what may happen in a society where the supply of credit is a regular feature of commercial operations (see on 6.1, above, pp. 321f.). The verse, however, does not have the form of a warning and must be regarded simply as a factual statement about the power of money. Toy suggests that the reference to slavery is not to be taken literally, and so not to be associated directly with such passages as Ex. 21.2–7 and Amos 2.6. However this may be, the general character of the verse is illustrated by the law and the prophets, which enable us to see how a close observer of Israelite society might have arrived at such a conclusion. We know that a man might have to sell himself or his children into slavery, if he could not otherwise pay his debts, and that a creditor might enslave a debtor (Ex. 21.2–7; II Kings 4.1; Amos 2.6; Neh. 5.5). This bondage in which the rich hold the poor is capable of wider expression, as appears from the prophetic protest. The poor man inevitably borrows from the rich, and in doing so he tightens the noose around his own neck. Debt is itself a form of slavery, and by a remorseless logic it deprives the poor man of all that is independent and distinctive in the pattern of his life, until he becomes a mere pawn in the rich man's game. As the prophets saw it, the power of the mortgage secured the eviction of the peasant and destroyed a style of life which was indispensable to the social well-being of the community (Micah 2.2, 8f.; 3.1f.; Isa. 5.8).

[10] The proposal of Wolfson (*JQR* 37, 1946–7, p. 87) and Driver (*Biblica* 32, p. 186), that LXX ἐν συνεδρίῳ should be followed in v. 10b and *qālōn* emended to *weyaqlennū* (Driver) or *yaqlō* (*yaqlēhu*, *yaqle*, Wolfson), should not be adopted, because it rests on risky assumptions. The text which would result in v. 10b is as follows: *weyēšēb bēt dīn weyaqlennū*, 'And, if he sits in the law-court, he dishonours it'. *weyēšēb bēt dīn* would become *weyišbōt dīn* by haplography of *b*, but *weqālōn* is not easily explained as a corruption of *w^e^yaqlennū* or *yaqlō* or the like (contrary to Wolfson: 'The confusion of *w^e^qālōn* with *yaqlō* or *yaqlēhū* or simply *yaqle* is quite understandable'). The question of the validity of this emendation principally hinges on whether the degree of reliance on the text of LXX which it implies can be justified in all the circumstances of this particular case. Thus in v. 10a the additional words ἐκ συνεδρίου appear in LXX (Wolfson, 'an interpretative gloss'), and λοιμός 'trouble-maker', 'pest', is an inaccurate translation of *lēṣ*. If ἐκ συνεδρίου is an interpretative addition in v. 10a, might not the same be true of ἐν συνεδρίῳ in v. 10b? If so, what is happening is that a paraphrase of MT is being employed in order to reconstruct an 'original' Hebrew text which never existed.

The argument that there has been a haplography of *b* would have carried more conviction if *w^e^yišbot dīn* (MT) had been unintelligible. As it is, we have to assume that this is a corruption which fortuitously makes sense. In other words, we seem to be gratuitously seeking a reason for emending a perfectly satisfactory Hebrew text rather than explaining how a corruption has arisen in a text which makes no sense. The only objection which might be made to MT is the pejorative use of *dīn* which it requires. This may be accounted for by the fact that the word which might have been expected in v. 10b (*mādōn*) had already been used in v. 10a. But there is no reason why *dīn* should not be used in this way. The Greek translator believed that the verse had a legal context in view, and litigation can deteriorate into litigiousness. Toy, however, is right in saying that the verse has wider aspects of strife and discord in mind. The arrogant, supercilious person has a genius for creating dissension and is a master of invective and denigration (*qālōn*). He is a divisive agent who destroys harmony and mutual respect in any association of men, and there will be no peace until he is expelled. Gemser correctly says that v. 10b of MT follows on more naturally from v. 10a than does Driver's emendation.

[11] Again, v. 11 raises the question of whether LXX may be used to reconstruct the Hebrew text. LXX reads: 'The Lord loves the pure in heart, all who are blameless in their ways are acceptable to him.' On the basis of this, BH and Gemser read: *'ōhēb YHWH ṭ^e^hōr lēb ūr^e^ṣōnō kōl t^e^mīmīm*, 'Yahweh loves the pure in heart, all who are blameless meet his approval'. But it is more probable that κύριος is interpretation than that the Greek translator read *YHWH* in the Hebrew which he was translating. In v. 11b, the lack of correspondence between LXX and MT is so complete that it is doubtful whether there is any value in incorporating the longer Greek text and then assuming that a *stichos* (v. 11c) has fallen out and, finally, preferring MT to LXX for v. 11d (with *śᵉpātāw* emended to *śᵉpātayim* and *rēʿēhū* to *rᵉṣōn*): 'Grace of utterance is what wins a king's approval' (cf. Toy, *wᵉḥēn śᵉpātayim rᵉṣōnō*, 'and grace of utterance is approved by him', i.e., by the king, since Toy inserts *melek* after *'ōhēb* in v. 11a). Gemser's reconstruction, which is the one indicated above, reads: 'Yahweh loves the pure in heart and all who are blameless win his acceptance. . . . Grace of utterance is what wins a king's approval.' In what is v. 11d according to Gemser, LXX reads: 'The king shepherds his flock with his lips.'

Driver's earlier proposal for this verse was that *reʿā* should be taken as a denominative of *rēaʿ* (*rēʿeh*), 'friend', and that *rēʿēhū melek* should be translated 'makes him friendly with a king', on the analogy of *šiḥᵃrō mūsār*, treats him early with discipline' (13.24): 'He who loves purity (Q. *ṭᵉhor*, construct of *ṭōhar*) of mind, the charm of his speech makes him friendly with a king' (G. R. Driver, *JTS* xli, 1940, p. 174). Driver now proposes, following Rashi and Toy, that *melek* should be transposed to v. 11a and the verse rendered: 'The king loves the pure of heart, the grace of his speech wins his (i.e., the king's) friendship.' Driver supposes that the insertion of 'Lord' in LXX and Pesh. represents an attempt to make sense by supplying a subject from v. 12a, consequent on the misplacement of *melek*, which fell out of its proper place, was put in the margin and then added *contra sensum* to the end of the line (*Biblica* 32, pp. 186f.). The sense of v. 11b is then the same as that which results from Toy's emendation (*rᵉṣōnō* for *rēʿēhū*). Driver retains MT, but has to assume a denominative from *rēaʿ*. It is unlikely that *rēʿēhū* means other than 'his friend'.

Ringgren endeavours to translate MT, 'Whoever loves purity of heart, whose lips are gracious, his friend is the king' (similarly Barucq), but v. 11b cannot be so translated. There is therefore no satisfactory solution to the problem of this verse, but it is, at any rate, improbable that Yahweh is its subject, and the interpretation of LXX and Pesh. should be discounted. It is rather, as Toy and Driver suppose, about the type of man who commends himself to a king, and it is likely that its theme is precisely that of 16.13 (see above, p. 493; cf. 20.28). Purity of motive, single-minded loyalty, elegance and persuasiveness of speech – these are the qualities which the king looks for in a confidant. I transpose *melek* to 11a and emend *rēʿēhū* to *rᵉṣōnō* (cf. Toy).

[13] Verse 13 indicates in an ironic and even comic way to what absurd lengths a lazy man will go in rationalizing his laziness. There is, of course, an element of caricature and exaggeration in the rationalization which is put in his mouth. In fact the excuses of the *ʿāṣēl* will never be so manifestly absurd as this. This is intended as the *reductio ad absurdum* of all his rationalizations. No one would believe a man who said that he could not go to his work because he was afraid of being mauled by a lion in the streets. This is the tallest of tall stories, but none of the accounts which the *ʿāṣēl* gives of his behaviour, however plausible and refined they may be, deserve any more credence. They are all evasive devices, attempts to hide the truth from himself that he has a character defect and is a kind of cripple. LXX: 'There are murderers in the streets' is a translation which may be due to the circumstance that *rṣḥ* is elsewhere used only of death by human hands.

Class B

[9] The *ṭōb ʿayin* has a benevolent disposition, a keen social conscience and a concern for the poor which finds practical expression. The paradox is that because he does not live to himself and is not the prisoner of selfish desires and ambitions, he achieves the highest degree of self-fulfilment. As in 21.21 ('He who pursues righteousness and loyalty finds life and honour'), a harmony of self-fulfilment and social involvement is postulated. Blessedness is not to be found in a context of selfish aspiration, where there is lack of love for the neighbour and a repudiation of responsibility for his well-being. It is the state of the man who is one with his brothers, who acknowledges that he is their keeper and who believes that wherever their welfare is diminished, his own humanity suffers loss.

Class C

All of the sentences in this class have some bearing on the doctrine of theodicy. **[2]** In v. 2 *nipgᵉšū* can indicate no more than that rich and poor are found side by side in every community, that social structures everywhere have this polarity of wealth and poverty. Ringgren (p. 87, n.3) notes the suggestion of van der Ploeg (who follows Torczyner) that *nipgᵉšū* means 'are equal to one another', but this sense is foreign to *pgš*. Even those exegetes who do not adopt it, try to accommodate their exegesis to the thought of the equality of rich and poor in the eyes of Yahweh (Toy), or they suggest that there is an implied demand here for compassion towards the poor (Ringgren). The verse does not attempt to explain how the co-existence of rich and poor is compatible with Yahweh's rule, but it does assert that both are contained within the order which he has created and upholds. 'Yahweh is the maker of them all' (LXX, 'The Lord is the maker of them both').

[4] The content of 'life' in v. 4b is the same as in 21.21 (see above, p. 556). In the context of old wisdom, access to this life was had by those who submitted to the authority of a wisdom teacher, who were shaped by his discipline and whose guidance along the right road was then assured by the wisdom which they had acquired. Here 'life' – and it is still a this-worldly concept – is the consequence of piety, not of educational discipline. Reverence for Yahweh is the new discipline, replacing the authority of the wisdom teacher, and *ʿanāwā* is humble submission to Yahweh, not intellectual humility (reading *wᵉyirʾat YHWH*).

[8] Verse 8a contains a typical expression of the doctrine of theodicy – the person who sows iniquity will reap evil. *ʿebrā* is *hubris* (so Gemser and Ringgren) as in 21.24, and not 'anger' (Barucq); it is the opposite of *ʿanāwā* (v. 4). The sense of MT in v. 8b is defective and various emendations have been suggested. BH and Gemser propose *yakkēhū* for *yikle*: 'The rod of his excess smites him.' Ringgren reads *yᵉkalle* following LXX συντελέσει and translates: 'and the rod makes an end of his arrogance'. It is doubtful whether the word order permits this rendering. Toy, on the basis of LXX ἔργων, reads *ʿabōdātō* and adopts *šeber* from Frankenberg: 'And the produce of his work will come to an end.' This is weak and, moreover, the meaning 'produce' is not attested for *šeber*. Gemser's emendation gives the required sense. *hubris* brings down punishment on the man who is guilty of it.

[12] In v. 12, both Gemser and Ringgren suppose that *daʿat* is abstract for concrete (Gemser, 'the one who possesses knowledge'; Ringgren, 'the wise'). Toy asserts that the eyes of Yahweh cannot be said to guard knowledge, and he proposes *baṣṣaddīqīm* for *nāṣᵉrū dāʿat* ('The eyes of Yahweh are on the righteous'). There is no particular merit in this emendation and, in any case, Toy's grounds for rejecting MT are ill-considered. There is no doubt that LXX διατηροῦσιν αἴσθησιν is a translation of MT, and it is not clear to me that Gemser and Ringgren improve on this by assuming that *daʿat* is abstract for concrete. The meaning of v. 12a, as Frankenberg maintained, is that Yahweh's vigilance is infallible and that, as a consequence, he never fails to act so as to vindicate truth and destroy lies. The sentence supplies a basis for belief in the operation of a theodicy in much the same way as 15.3: 'The eyes of Yahweh are in every place, observing the evil and the good' (see above, p. 484). Yahweh, as the guardian of *daʿat* ('knowledge' in the sense of what is true or real), is the destroyer of falsehood. D. Winton Thomas (*JTS* xiv, 1963, pp. 93f.) connects *daʿat* with Arabic *daʿā* 'sought', 'demanded', and translates 'law-suit'. He suggests that *bgd* may also be legal terminology; the setting of the sentence is then forensic. Yahweh sees that justice is done in court despite the efforts of perjurers (see on 29.7, below, pp. 641f.).

[14] The *zārōt* are not 'immoral women in general' (Ringgren), but foreign women who are thought to have promiscuous propensities and the opportunity of indulging them (see on 2.16; 23.27, above, pp. 285f., 391f.). What is indicated by v. 14a is that the honeyed words of the *zārā* are an important part of the seductive charm with which she lays siege to her victim (see on 5.3, above, p. 314; 6.24, above, pp. 327f.; 7.5, 14–20, above, pp. 334f.). To succumb to her wiles is both sin and punishment (on 'deep pit' see 23.27, pp. 391f.), for those who fall into that pit are accursed of Yahweh (*zeʿūm YHWH* has the same force as *tōʿabat YHWH*, see on 12.22, above p. 448; 17.15, above, pp. 511f.). They have made themselves abhorrent to Yahweh, and the pit into which they have fallen is the punishment consequent on his condemnation or curse.

[16] The ambiguities of v. 16 are noted by Toy: in v. 16a the 'him' who is enriched may be either the oppressor or the poor man, and in v. 16b the one who suffers want either the rich man or the person who gives to him. If *lō* in v. 16a is referred to the *ʿōšēq*, the verse has to be translated as a continuous sentence. Thus Scott: 'One who oppresses the poor to aggrandize himself will have to yield to the rich and will end in poverty' (cf. Toy). This is a forced translation of the verse, and should not be adopted. Barucq urges that v. 16b does not say that the rich man will be impoverished, but rather that it is pointless to impoverish oneself by giving to a rich man what he does not need. If, however, v. 16a means (as Barucq maintains) that the poor man who is the victim of oppression and extortion will be compensated by Yahweh, the appositeness of v. 16b as an antithesis (on his interpretation of it) is not obvious. The meaning would presumably be that the theodicy operates to protect the poor, but that it is no part of Yahweh's order to intervene in the case of the man who lets money run through his fingers because of his own idiocy (i.e., giving money to a person who is already rich is an example of squandermania).

Another sense is taken by Ringgren, who sees v. 16b as also a reference to the operation of theodicy, the reverse of v. 16a. The *l*[e] of *l*[e]*harbōt* may mean 'is likely to' (see on 16.30, above, pp. 494f.). He who extorts money from a poor man is likely to (cf. Barucq, *tend à*) enrich him, but he who gives to a rich man will produce only impoverishment. Yahweh creates plenty for the poor man when his oppressor intends to make him destitute, and produces want in a situation where wealth is being added to wealth. In both cases he makes nonsense of men's intentions and achieves what from their point of view can only be regarded as a freak result. The verse betrays a tendency to correlate poverty with piety and wealth with impiety. Gemser agrees with this in respect of v. 16a which he illustrates by citing Joseph's words to his brothers in Gen. 50.20 ('as for you, you meant evil against me, but God meant it for good'). On the other hand he offers a rational explanation of v. 16b. To give more money to a rich man is to encourage further extravagances and so, in the end, he will not have enough.

B. CHAPTER 24.23–34

The introduction, 'These also are to be attributed to the sages,' probably takes up the reference to 'the words of the sages' in 22.17, in which case 24.23–34 is envisaged as an appendix to 22.17–24.22. Unlike 22.17–24.22, it is not consistently Instruction, although this is represented in vv. 27–29. Otherwise it consists of two sentences without parallelism (vv. 23, 26), and two pieces which transcend the limits of sentence literature (vv. 24–25, 30–34). In vv. 24–25, the antithetic parallelism is between the two sentences, not the stichoi of a single sentence, and the unit may be regarded as a short poem. A longer poem with formal features foreign both to the sentence and the Instruction is found in vv. 30–34. In setting out by reporting an observation in the first person singular (vv. 30–31), it recalls the style of 7.6f. (see above, pp. 334f.). The personal character of the poem is continued in v. 32, where the author tells us that he pondered the significance of what he had seen and took its lesson to heart. Here is a new way of accepting *mūsār* – not by paying attention to the authoritative instruction of a teacher and acting on his advice, but by direct observation, followed by reflection, then conviction (cf.

Gemser). Consequently, the imperatives of the Instruction are replaced by first person singulars which autobiographically describe the progress towards enlightenment and discipline (*mūsār*). The subjective, personal style of the poem is not maintained to the very end, for the discovery which has been made is communicated in a maxim which is to be regarded as a quotation (vv. 33–34; cf. 6.10–11). Rather than express the conclusion which he has reached in his voyage of discovery in his own words, the poet prefers to incorporate a 'canonical' saying.

The orientation of the verses concerned with legal matters is that of the class B material. Social considerations and consequences are here paramount (cf. Ringgren, who speaks of the anthropocentric grounding of vv. 24–25). **[23]** A judge must not extend favouritism to one of the two litigants in giving his verdict, but strive to be fair to both and to administer the law objectively. The phrase *hakkēr pānīm* conjures up a situation where personal factors influence the verdict, whether the judge's previous acquaintance with one of the parties or the circumstance that he takes a liking to one and is antipathetic to the other. Both Gemser and BH assume an original distich, which Gemser would restore by inserting a line similar to 18.5b or 28.21b.

[24] To obstruct the course of justice and defeat its ends is social subversion in one of its deadliest forms, and merits the curse of the community (*z'm* is synonymous with *qbb*, see on 22.14, above, p. 571). Where the guilty man is acquitted and the innocent man condemned, confidence in the integrity and impartiality of the judiciary can be destroyed, and the basis of common life in equality before the law is called in question. **[25]** The corrupt judge earns the curse of the community, but those who administer the law without fear or favour (*mōkīḥīm*; cf. Gemser and Ringgren, 'those who pass the right sentence') will be acclaimed as benefactors and enjoy true prosperity. Society blesses those who bless it and curses those who curse it. This is just another way of expressing the conviction that concern for the community's true weal coincides with the best interests of the individual (here *qua* judge and so a particularly crucial application of the principle). Cf. 11.17, 24, 25, 26, 27 (above, pp. 433f.).

[28] In v. 28, interest switches from the corrupt judge to the malicious or perjured witness. If MT is retained in v. 28b ('and will you deceive with your lips'?, cf. BH), the question is rhetorical and expects an emphatic 'No' as an answer. It is then tantamount to a prohibition (cf. v. 28a), and this is how it is taken by LXX, unless we suppose that the Greek translator read *w^{e}'al t^{e}pat* and that MT should be emended accordingly (Toy and Gemser). Driver supposes that μηδὲ πλατύνου, 'do not exaggerate', indicates II *pātā*, 'make spacious' (KB^{2}) rather than I *pātā*. Driver (*Biblica*, p. 189), following Pesh. (*la tpatptiw*(*h*)*y*; palpel, 'to tear a reputation to pieces', Payne Smith), would derive from *ptt*, 'to break in pieces', 'to slander', 'to tear one's character to pieces' (also two Hebrew manuscripts read *h^{a}pittōtā* 'you have smashed'). He maintains that an object is desiderated and that the verb should be a qal imperfect. By a transposition of the consonants of MT (*whptyt*) and by substituting *w* for *y* he reads *wtpthw* (*ūt^{e}puttēhū*), 'and do (not) slander him with thy lips' (carrying over the negative from the first to the second clause as in Ps. 75.6). But this operation can hardly be described as a 'mere transposition' of the consonants. *t* is transposed from the end to the beginning and *h* from the beginning to the end, while *y* is ignored. Yet *y* is important, because it points to *pth*, not *ptt*. I follow MT with one small emendation—the deletion of the initial *w*. MT *ḥinnām*, 'gratuitously' (Barucq), makes perfectly good sense, and LXX ψευδής, 'false', should not be preferred to it (cf. Ringgren, p. 99, n.2; *ḥinnām* does not mean 'false', contrary to Gemser). The *'ēd ḥinnām* is the informer, the exponent of public denunciation who specializes in giving damning testimony against his neighbour. Or he is the person who abuses the legal processes by going into the witness box in order to incriminate another as a means of paying off an old personal grudge. In this case, he is a spiteful (Scott) or revengeful witness. In order to achieve his ends he is prepared to commit perjury (this is what v. 28b amounts to, whether the verb is *pth* or *ptt*); *pth* indicates the lie and *ptt* the iconoclastic fury with which the *'ēd ḥinnām* sets to work on the reputation of those whom he denounces and traduces. The meaning of *'ēd ḥinnām* is well illustrated by a Babylonian Instruction which issues a warning against loitering in the courts and becoming involved with other people's litigation. 'For in the dispute they will have you as a testifier. Then you will be made their witness and they will bring you to a law-suit not your own to affirm' (*BWL*, p. 100, *ll.* 31–35).

[29] The same Babylonian text has some light to throw on v. 29, which is most probably to be interpreted in association with v. 28, and so the words which are reproduced can be regarded as an expression of the spirit of revenge. On this, '*Precepts and Admonitions*' gives the following advice: 'Do not return evil to the man who disputes with you. Requite with kindness your evil-doer. Maintain justice to your enemy. Smile on your adversary' (*BWL*, p. 100, *ll.* 41–44). As Gemser points out, the question of the propriety of the *lex talionis* as a legal principle is not being raised here and, further, it seems to me unlikely that v. 29 rests on any theological presuppositions such as the leaving of punishment to God. This is the motivation of *Amenemope* xxii.1–9 (*ANET*, p. 424) and Prov. 20.22, where the prohibition is coupled with the assertion that Yahweh will enforce his theodicy. Here the matter is conceived rather in terms of what is socially desirable and beneficial. Even when a man has been wronged and feels a deep sense of personal injury, he should not permit a spirit of revenge to dictate his responses. He is not to say: 'I shall do to him as he has done to me, I shall repay a man according to his deed.' He is not to be consumed with a passion to get even with his adversary or to become involved in interminable litigation, winning a legal victory but losing his humanity, destroying all possibilities of conciliation and diminishing rather than adding to the well-being of the community of which he is a member.

[26] Verse 26 is also on the subject of socially constructive behaviour, of which speaking the truth in love is an example. A kiss is the salute of a friend, and it is hideous when, as with the kiss of Judas, it becomes an instrument of betrayal. The man who gives straight answers to the questions which his friend addresses to him and is a model of candour and frankness is a friend indeed, whose kiss is not counterfeit (so Toy and Gemser, who proposes tentatively the insertion of *kᵉmērēaʿ*, 'he who kisses the lips as a friend'). Ringgren, on the other hand, supposes the point to be that a kiss and candid speaking are aesthetically comparable. To receive an honest reply is an experience which gives pleasure comparable to that bestowed by a kiss.

[27] The only textual question in v. 27 concerns *lāk*. Scott (also Gemser) would emend to *lēk*, 'go', with the *athnach* transposed to *baśśāde*. Alternatively Gemser suggests that *lēk* should be inserted after *'aḥar*. BH tentatively proposes the restoration of two distichs instead of a tristich by inserting *tiqqaḥ lᵉkā 'iššā* after *'aḥar*. Ringgren and Scott are aware of the 'proverbial' character of v. 27 and the consequent openness of its meaning. It has different levels of intelligibility, and its interpretation requires the recognition of this rather than the acceptance of one meaning and the rejection of another. Although 'build a house' is certainly an idiom for 'found a household', this does not exclude the literal meaning of building a house, and the exegesis of the verse must begin there. Cultivation of the fields takes precedence over house-building, and it is essential to observe the correct order of operations. This is an economic necessity, since the fields produce wealth which is required to support life and to furnish the materials for building a house. The house, on the other hand, will consume wealth both in its building and its upkeep.

'Building a house' in the sense of founding a family is a well-established idiom which is not to be dissociated from the task of construction, since a man cannot begin to raise a family until he knows that they will have a roof over their head. The expression is found in *Ptahhotep* ('found thy household', *ANET*, p. 413), *Hor-Dedef* ('build thy house for thy son', *ANET*, p. 419) and in the Babylonian *Dialogue of Pessimism* (the text is broken, but is restored by Lambert to read: 'The man who sets up a home', [*ba*]*nu bīti*, *BWL*, p. 144, *l*. 31). In Deut. 25.9 and Ruth 4.11 it is used of the duty of levirate marriage, and the sense of founding a family is supposed by Rudolph in Neh. 7.4 (W. Rudolph, *HAT*, 1949, p. 140) and by Horst in Ezek. 11.3 (F. Horst, *VT* iii, 1953, p. 340). The other instances noted by Horst (p. 340, n.4) show *bayit* with the specialized sense of 'dynasty' (II Sam. 7.27; I Kings 11.38; I Chron. 17.10), and the Samuel and Chronicles passages turn on a particular ambivalence of *bayit*, temple and dynasty (II Sam. 7.5, 27; I Chron. 17.4, 10).

Toy notes that the verse has been taken to refer to the founding of a home from Rashi onwards and, while this is a perfectly proper exegesis (on *bayit* meaning 'household' see 3.33, above, p. 302), it does not exhaust the possibilities of interpretation. Its 'proverbial' essence is that no task should be begun until the resources which are necessary to its successful completion are assured and effectively present. A correct sequence of operations is indicated, and it is implied that the reversing of the sequence is economically disastrous. Wealth must be produced before it is consumed. Scott appositely cites the dominical saying about the man who had begun to build a tower before he had counted the cost of the total operation and whose unfinished building drew the scorn of those who saw it. 'This man began to build and was not able to finish.' Here it is the cost of discipleship which has to be estimated in advance of commitment (Luke 14.28–30).

[30–34] The poem on the sluggard describes his unkempt and derelict property, polluted with thistles and chick-weed (*ḥarullīm*, so KB²), the stone dyke which marks its boundaries in a ruinous state of disrepair (probably a dry stone dyke, cf. KB³). The lazy man is deficient in good sense; laziness is an aspect of folly. The poet ponders the significance of this spectacle and its lesson is salutary. He accepts *mūsār*, i.e., recognizes its necessity, and is convinced that indiscipline in the form of laziness is disastrous. His conclusion is expressed in the words of 6.10–11 (see above, p. 324; the connection between sleep and laziness is also made in 20.13).

C. CHAPTERS 25–29

Chapter 25

With this chapter there begins a new section of sentence literature (25–29), and according to v. 1 the transmission and editorial arrangement of its contents are due to the literary activity of a royal scribal establishment. The ascription of authorship to Solomon here, as at 10.1, indicates that he was regarded as the founder and arch-patron of the wisdom literature, and that the beginnings of this genre in Israel have a special connection with the emergence of a learned class created to serve the diverse needs of a state which had been formed on international models (*PWM*, pp. 13f.). This is not to say that the sentence literature in the book of Proverbs is royal or vocational in character. For the most part this is not so, but in all its diversity it is regarded as wisdom, and Solomon is designated as the fountainhead of the wisdom tradition in Israel.

[1] The notice in v. 1 may have historical importance in so far as it points to a particular phase of editorial activity in the reign of Hezekiah (cf. R. B. Y. Scott, *VTS* iii, p. 273), but again it has to be said that it is the sentences one by one, irrespective of when or how they were arranged, which can tell us most about the direction of the wisdom tradition in Israel. The most significant feature of this chapter as compared with the wisdom sentences which have preceded it is the marked increase in imagery. There are two sentences similar in character to those which up till now have been most common, one with antithetic parallelism (v. 2) and the other with synthetic parallelism (v. 15). There is one instance of a 'better . . . than' type of formulation (v. 24) and several examples of Instruction. Verses 6–7 consist of two prohibitions followed by a motive clause (*kī*) with a 'better . . . than' form, and vv. 7c–8 are made up of a prohibition

with a motive or 'lest' clause (see below). In vv. 9f. an imperative and a negative imperative are linked to a 'lest' clause. Verse 16 consists of a conditional clause ('you have found honey' = 'if you have found honey'), an imperative, a 'lest' clause' and an 'and so' clause. In v. 17, an imperative is joined to a 'lest' clause. The pattern of vv. 21f. is a conditional clause, an imperative, a conditional clause, an imperative, two motive clauses.

The description of the remaining sentences turns on the way in which imagery is used in them. Apart from one exception (v. 13), these sentences are not fully-formed similes; they have an asyndetic character. The pictorial elements appear in the first half of the sentence adjacent to the application or interpretation in the second half (see above, pp. 138, 141, 185f.). The two constituents lie side by side without formal connection, although it is evident that the verse functions as a simile or metaphor. In some sentences the imagery constitutes a single, simple or complex, picture (vv. 11, 13, 14, 20?, 23, 25, 27, 28); in others a succession of individual pictures with a cumulative effect (vv. 3, 12, 18, 19, 26). These verses are not 'proverbial' in the full sense, just because the imagery is bounded by a particular interpretation or application, whereas the 'proverb' is so organized that its concreteness is always open to future interpretation.

Special mention has to be made of vv. 4f., 16f., in which this arrangement of imagery and interpretation is based on the quatrain rather than the couplet, so that the picture extends over one verse and the interpretation follows in the next. Although the infinitive absolute (*hāgō*) in vv. 4f. is rightly translated as an imperative, these verses are not Instruction. 'Take away dross from silver' is equivalent to 'If you take away dross from silver', and similarly in v. 5. On the other hand, vv. 16f., which correspond formally to Instruction (see above), are organized as a quatrain (although Toy doubts this; cf. Ringgren) in terms of imagery and application. It is difficult to believe that vv. 16 and 17 were originally quite independent of each other and have been associated solely for the reason that *śbʿ* occurs in both.

Verse 3 has been described as a *Priamel* by Delitzsch (cf. Toy) and Boström (see Gemser), i.e., 'unsearchable' is the common factor and the verse gives three examples of the unsearchable. I take the verse rather to have the same organization as the others, the first half containing two separate pictures which illustrate the unsearchability of a king's mind.

Class A: vv. 2, 3, 6–7, 7c–8, 9–10, 11, 12, 13, 14, 15, 16–17, 18, 19, 20, 23, 24, 25, 27, 28.
Class B: vv. 4–5.
Class C: v. 26.

Verses 21–22 present a special difficulty. One motive clause (22a) points to class B and the other (v. 22b) to class C.

Class A

[2] Verse 2 catches the antithesis of God and king, of religion and statecraft, of residual mystery and exhaustive investigation. It is the glory of God to conceal a matter, in the sense that religion becomes ordinary, flat and facile if the worshippers are not aware of a boundary beyond which explanation cannot go and an area of mystery which is unexplored and unexplorable. When it is supposed that everything is known about God, it is no longer possible to worship him. The numinous in God is inexplicable and inaccessible to research, and it is this dimension which fascinates, and awakens awe. The status of a king is differently regulated, and success in politics requires a determination to get to the bottom of every affair of state on which a decision has to be taken. Every piece of evidence which is available must be produced and examined, so that every decision taken will be the best possible decision and the king will never be seen to be ignorant or badly informed or unwilling to take the trouble to get at the truth, however complicated or vexatious the process of discovery. A king like this will earn respect and no man will presume to take him for a fool.

[3] The next verse is also concerned with the calibre of a king; the verses are contiguous for this reason and, more especially, because formations from *ḥqr* are common to both. The king whose glory it is to press investigations of affairs with the utmost rigour and resolution is himself unsearchable. The heavens are so high that their ceiling is beyond human reach and the earth is inaccessible by reason of its depths. A king's mind has its heights and depths, with a range and subtlety and complexity which baffle those who would study it as an object to be described, analysed and definitively explained. This is interesting as an indication of the kind of person a king was expected to be and of what was desiderated in a king. He is immensely resourceful and mobile in his thinking, so that his mind cannot be catalogued and his responses predicted; and he is splendidly inscrutable, so that he does not give away the direction of his thinking and

keeps others guessing as to what his next move will be. These qualities enhance his power and tighten his grip on affairs.

[6f.] In vv. 6f., the king in person does not occupy so central a place, since they have to do rather with the kind of behaviour which is to be avoided at court and on state occasions when notables are assembled (see above, p. 60). A man should not parade himself ostentatiously before the king, i.e., on some formal court occasion, or otherwise be guilty of bumptious behaviour, giving himself airs and representing himself to have a dignity and rank which are not in fact generally accorded to him. Nor should he stake his claim to precedence in the ranks of the notables, for nothing damages esteem and reputation more than to outreach the limits of one's dignity and to suffer a rebuff to which no rejoinder can be made. The person who is demoted from a place of precedence in full view of the court – a place which he has presumed to occupy – suffers a grievous loss of face. It is better deliberately to occupy a place in the procession which is lower than your entitlement and then to have your prestige boosted by a request from the marshal, which everyone hears, that you move up to a higher order. The verb *ʿmd* 'stand' is against the view that the verses refer to the order of seats at a banquet, but Luke 14.7–11, which reproduces exactly the ideas of vv. 6f. in the context of a marriage feast, may owe something to this passage (so Ringgren).

[7c–8] Verses 7c–8, 9f. are perhaps directed against indiscreet and injurious gossip rather than litigiousness and, if so, elements of vocabulary which might seem to be forensic have to be understood in a more general sense. According to MT, v. 7c is to be taken with what precedes, but the versions are to be followed in their attaching it to v. 8. Symmachus reads: 'What your eyes have seen, do not bring out to the multitude quickly', and this points to *tōṣēʾ* for *tēṣēʾ* and *rōb* for *rīb* (Bickell, Toy, Gemser). A circumstance which could encourage the vocalization of *rb* as *rīb* is the occurrence of *rīb* in v. 9a. Otherwise, if MT is retained, *rīb* must refer to a legal process (Ringgren, Scott, Barucq), but it is not clear why something which has merely been witnessed should be the occasion of precipitate litigation, unless the thought is that of 24.28 (see above, pp. 573f.) that one should not become a 'professional' witness and make a practice of intervening in other people's law suits by giving evidence on one side or the other (cf. G. R. Driver, *Biblica* 32, p. 190, who paraphrases: 'Do not blurt out what you have seen too hastily in court'). On balance I incline to Gemser's view that this is a demand for taciturnity in the character of international wisdom and comparable to the directive in *Amenemope* xxii.11f.: 'Empty not thy belly to everybody, nor damage (thus) the regard for thee. Spread not thy words to the common people, nor associate to thyself one (too) outgoing of heart. Better is a man whose talk (remains) in his belly than he who speaks it out injuriously' (*ANET*, p. 424). It is particularly applicable to those who move in the circles of government and court, who see and hear things which must not be generally disclosed and where looseness of tongue would make a man a bad risk and a potential betrayer of confidences. We are therefore to assume the courtly context of vv. 6–7b (so Gemser).

There is, however, some doubt whether *lārōb* can be translated 'to the multitude'. Its meaning elsewhere is 'in abundance', and except in such adverbial expressions it is always defined by a noun (cf. Toy). If the adverbial sense is assumed here, the meaning of *'al tōṣē' lārōb mahēr* might be, 'Do not be in a hurry to broadcast'. Driver maintains the forensic sense of the verse and also the 'lest' clause in v. 8b, which is transformed into a motive clause by BH, Gemser, Ringgren and Scott by emending *pen* to *kī*. Driver's translation of v. 8b ('lest thou do aught at the end of it at the cost of thy neighbour putting thee to shame') is awkward (*Biblica* 32, p. 190). This is almost certainly a motive clause and the necessary emendation should be made (Dahood, pp. 53f., explains *pen* as *pa* 'and' with affixed *n*. He translates 'for'). Again, in my judgement, the argument which the clause contains is more apposite to reckless gossip and broken confidences than to rash and ill-considered legal action. What is depicted is the moment when the consequences of gossip have worked themselves out and have had damaging effects on the victim, who then comes to confront his friend (or colleague) and to reproach him for his weakness and disloyalty. The reproach is well deserved and he is put to confusion.

[9f.] The question has again to be raised whether *rīb* in v. 9a refers to a legal process. If it does, v. 9b, which urges that the confidence of another should not be betrayed, is somewhat inconsequential, whereas one would expect that the two directives in v. 9 are intended to be cumulative in their effect and deal with the same topic. The difficulty is increased by the character of the 'lest' clause, which is a warning against the possible evil consequences of gossip and broken confidences, and has nothing in it that requires a strictly legal interpretation of 'Fight your (own) case with your neighbour'. I am not therefore inclined to think that Barucq is right in saying that *rēaʿ* in v. 8b and v. 9a means a legal opponent. Rather, I would take v. 9a to mean that where your own interests are directly involved you should press your case with all the energy and skill that you can muster and that you should carry the fight to the neighbour or friend with whom you have your disagreement. The point would then be that others should not be involved in your dispute and their personal relationship with your opponent compromised or impaired. There should be a direct and honourable confrontation, and resort should not be had to devious and cowardly manoeuvres in which others are used as cats' paws. The converse would then be that you should not consent to being so used, thereby divulging the confidence which another has reposed in you (v. 9b).

It is possible to arrange the argument about the sense of vv. 9f. differently by treating v. 9a separately from v. 9b and holding that the 'lest' clause in v. 10 depends only on v. 9b. In this case v. 9a would be elucidated by 24.28a (see above, pp. 573f.), which utters a warning against interference in other people's litigation. The gist of the instruction is then that you should confine your interest in legal proceedings to what is your direct concern and not become a habitual witness for the prosecution in the law courts. That v. 9b, however, does not have such activities in mind is clear from v. 10a, since the words 'lest he who hears you puts you to shame' must refer to what has been overheard in a private or semi-private context and not to evidence given in public which is necessarily given in order to be heard. In breaking faith with a friend and divulging what is injurious to him, a man is personally discredited and acquires the reputation of disloyalty and unreliability – a stigma which sticks and will not easily be eradicated. To revise the estimate of others and restore their confidence in him so as to rehabilitate his reputation will be a long and difficult operation.

[23] Verse 23 also deals with the effects of slander on friendship, although its precise interpretation is debatable and, in particular, the statement that the north wind brings rain does not suit Palestinian climatic conditions. This difficulty is met by commentators in different ways. Toy (also G. R. Driver, according to Gemser, p. 113) suggests that north is to be equated with north-west (the west wind brings rain in Palestine, I Kings 18.41–44) and so disposes of the difficulty. Just as this wind produces (lit., gives birth to) the rain (cf. P. Reymond, *VTS* vi, 1958, p. 202, n.2), so slander secretly disseminated enrages the person whose reputation is being assaulted, once he is aware of its circulation. On the other hand, Gemser and Barucq suggest that the reference to the north wind as a rain-bearing wind may be an indication that the saying is of foreign, probably Egyptian provenance. Gemser (p. 113) takes up the point of Morenz (S. Morenz, *ThLZ* 78, 1953, col. 191) that while rain is a source of fructification and blessing in a Palestinian context, it has a negative rather than a positive evaluation in Egypt, where the source of fertility is the inundation of the Nile, and so is an apposite metaphor for slander. Otherwise, on Toy's interpretation, one has to suppose that the verse turns merely on the relation of cause and effect which is common to v. 23a and v. 23b, irrespective of the circumstance that rain is a blessing and slander an evil, unless with Ringgren one discovers the link between figure and application in 'darkness'. As rain clouds darken the sky, slander darkens the face.

The explanation in terms of the foreign provenance of the saying is contested by van der Ploeg (J. van der Ploeg, *VT* iii, 1953, pp. 189–191), who argues that it is difficult to credit, since it would imply its currency in a milieu where it made no sense. He notes the suggestion of G. Dalman (*Arbeit und Sitte*, I. i, 1928, p. 246) that *t*ᵉ*ḥōlēl* means '*setzt in Angst*', i.e., emphasizing the aspect of 'pain' rather than 'birth' (cf. *ḥīl* 'labour pains', 'birth throes'). The north wind distresses the rain i.e., inspires fear in the rain and inhibits it (cf. Sa'adya's Arabic translation: 'The north wind repels the rain'). This would mean that evil consequences are described in both v. 23a and v. 23b, but the translation can hardly be right. Van der Ploeg also considers Torczyner's translation: 'Hold (*ṣ*ᵉ*pōn*) your anger (*rūaḥ*) (and) you will give birth to rain (i.e., you will be blessed); your enraged countenance betrays your thought' (literally, 'is a silent (or 'secret') tongue', i.e., it speaks without words). In taking 'enraged face' as the subject of v. 23b, Torczyner has the support of LXX and V. van der Ploeg himself renders: 'The wind which comes from a hidden source (*ṣāpūn*) gives birth to rain.' Just as a cause, secret, unknown, invisible, has concrete and visible effects, so slander whose origin is unknown has an effect which is seen on the face of its victim. I am not, however, convinced that *rūaḥ ṣāpōn* means anything other than 'north wind', and I have already discussed the difficulties raised by this reference and the suggested solutions.

[18] In v. 18, the disloyalty which is envisaged is perpetrated by the giving of perjured evidence. One who so testifies falsely against his neighbour makes a savage assault on his reputation and inflicts grievous bruises and wounds. He is a club or hammer (reading *mappēṣ*, LXX ῥόπαλον, 'club'), a sword, a sharp arrow; one who does not engage in crude physical violence but is an adept assassin of character and whose work of mutilation is fundamental.

Two verses expatiate on the power of the spoken word (vv. 11, 15). **[11]** *ʿal ʾopnāw* is obscure. The form is a dual from *ʾ*ōpen*; there are several suggested explanations. KB² associates it with Arabic *fannu(n)* 'manner', 'mode' and translates 'at the right moment' (i.e., a well-judged intervention). Toy infers this sense from *beʿittō* (15.23b), and Gemser (also Ringgren), who translates similarly, suggests that the literal meaning is 'according to its circumstances'. None of these suggestions deals adequately with the difficulty created by the dual form. KB² suggests that *ʾopnāw* is a dual from *ʾōpan* 'wheel' (the suggestion is not repeated in KB³). In that case the form would be *ʾōpannāw*, but no change in the consonantal text is involved. The reference is then to the compact elegance of expression produced by the balancing halves of a wisdom sentence. This is a proposal which has some attractiveness. The *stichos* is a wheel, and the sentence, consisting of two wheels, is a 'well-turned' expression (cf. Barucq; also the opinion of Boström, noted by Gemser, that *ʾ*ōpen* is a special type of *māšāl*). An obscure line in Ben Sira (50.27) contains the words *wmwšl ʾwpnym*, which should perhaps be emended to *wmšl ʾwpnym*, 'and a *māšāl* of two wheels'. The text is cryptic and fragmentary, but one could speculate that in the line *mūsar śēkel ūmešal ʾōpannayim* the first phrase refers to the content (sensible instruction) and the second to the form of the wisdom sentence.

Verse 11a contains a complex image rather than two images (Ringgren), and there is no difficulty in MT, although BH and Scott read *pittūḥē* ('engravings' or 'inlay') for *tappūḥē* ('apples'). The point is that the most precious part of these objects of art worked in silver is the apples of gold embodied in them and it is to this centre of supreme value that words well-turned or well-timed are compared.

[15] By patience (in negotiation) a prince or a judge (Arabic *qāḍī* 'judge' = Hebrew *qāṣīn*, cf. Gemser and Barucq) can be gulled (literally, 'made to act like a *petī*', a youth who is untutored and innocent of affairs), and by a gentle persuasiveness and advocacy the backbone of a man's resistance can be broken. Both *Ahikar* 105f. and Ecclus. 28.17 (Greek), which are cited as illustrative of v. 15b, in that both refer to words which break bones, are in fact using the expression in senses different from 25.15 and from each other. In

Ahikar we read: 'Soft is the tongue of a king, but it breaks the ribs of a dragon like death which is not seen' (Cowley, p. 216). The contrast here is between the soft tones in which the king speaks and the power which his word commands. When he speaks softly, he enlists irresistible and lethal forces to implement his commands. He has no need to shout his orders, and the quietness of his voice increases the terror of his authority. The breaking of the bones is therefore near to a literal breaking of bones, but this is not true either of Prov. 25.15 or of Ecclus. 28.17, which reads:

The blow of a whip makes weals,
But the blow of a tongue crushes the bones.

The point here is precisely in the comparison of the power of physical violence with the power of the barbed word. The lash of a whip makes weals on the skin, but the lash of the tongue reduces the victim to pulp. The injuries inflicted by the tongue on self-esteem and honour are more deadly than those resulting from strokes with a whip. The soft tongue of v. 15 is neither the terrible quietness of a king's voice not the barbed tongue of a polemicist, but the conciliatory and persuasive advocacy which succeeds in the end over against the most determined and studied recalcitrance.

[12] Verse 12 describes an ideal teacher-student relationship by comparing it to two items of jewellery which go together and enhance each other. They are a good match and an effective combination; so, too, it is when a wise teacher exerts discipline over a receptive pupil. The two are complementary to each other; the skill of the teacher has its reward in that he effectively communicates his wisdom and asserts his authority; the application of the pupil is not misplaced, since his attention is given to a teacher whose calibre earns his deference and confidence.

[13] In v. 13, LXX^{A} and LXX^{ℵ} render: 'As a fall of snow in harvest helps in the heat' (*šeleg* is not translated by LXX^{B} from which χιόνος has apparently fallen out). Scott would read *b*^{e}*ḥōm*, following LXX, while Toy, Ringgren and Barucq retain MT (*b*^{e}*yōm*). κατὰ καῦμα is perhaps to be regarded as a free rendering of MT, rather than as evidence that the Greek translator read *b*^{e}*ḥōm*. The reference to a fall of snow is an erroneous paraphrase of MT. What is indicated by *ṣinnat šeleg* is not a fall of snow, but the application of ice-cold water to hot foreheads or the slaking of a fierce thirst with 'living water' marvellously refrigerated in its underground course and arriving at the spring in prime condition. The theme is that of refreshment and restoration, and this is underlined by v. 13c which is probably an explanatory gloss (so Toy, Barucq; cf. BH and Gemser). Just as the cold water revives the stamina of the harvesters, banishing their fatigue and giving them new zest for their work, so a messenger who is completely trustworthy puts new life (*nepeš*) into his master. The knowledge that he can count unreservedly on the loyalty of this man and on the accuracy of his representations in any mission on which he is employed lightens his burden and fortifies him to carry his responsibilities. The reliable envoy is a spring of living water to his principal.

[14] A different kind of person – a man of straw rather than of steel – is described in v. 14. This is the man who poses as a great benefactor and who promises munificent gifts to others, but whose undertakings bear no relation to his resources. He is the eternal *poseur* whose projected beneficence is as insubstantial as a bubble (*šeqer*), and whose affectation of generosity is a form of playing to the gallery and of egotistical inflation. In the end, after all his fair promises, nothing happens. His words are empty, and in this respect he is like the clouds and wind which bring no rain. 'Everyone knows how deceptive the clouds can be in Palestine, especially when, in the wake of a scorching summer, people long for the rains. The clouds can be red and lowering, betokening a storm, but time and again it does not come off' (E.F.F.B.).

[19] In v. 19, which describes another kind of worthless individual, LXX has the appearance of a moralizing paraphrase which asserts that the theodicy is operative and that retribution will fall on evildoers. 'The tooth of the wicked and the foot of the impious will be destroyed in an evil day.' It should not therefore be supposed that LXX can be used to emend MT, either in the change of *rōʿā* to *rāʿā* or in the deletion of *mibṭāḥ*. LXX in fact does not give any textual support to these emendations (contrary to Gemser), since its form is explicable as paraphrase rather than as the translation of a different Hebrew text. The two figures employed in v. 19a are those of the crumbling, decaying tooth (reading *rōʿaʿā*) and the palsied foot (reading *mōʿādet*). Both are incapable of performing their functions, and so what is indicated by them is ineffectiveness and impotence. Food cannot be chewed by a tooth which is crumbling away (the the fact that in such circumstances one may suffer toothache is an aspect of the matter not considered here), and a man cannot walk with a palsied foot. Both tooth and foot are useless, and equally useless is a false sense of security in a period of acute difficulty.

Toy's translation, 'Such is a bad man's ground of hope', requires the pointing *mibṭaḥ* as also does the rendering 'confidence in a liar' (RV, RSV, Ringgren, Barucq, Scott). If *mibṭāḥ* is deleted (BH and Gemser), it is the *bōgēd* himself who is the crumbling tooth and palsied foot. The support of LXX cannot, however, be claimed for this emendation. It is a simplification which is convenient and not an emendation for which good textual reasons can be given.

[16f.] The clause 'if you find honey' indicates that it is wild honey, upon which one comes accidentally (cf. I Sam. 14.26f.) or after a search, which is envisaged. As is clear from 24.13 (see above, pp. 402f.), it is just because honey is a nourishing food which has medicinal virtues and promotes the health of the body that it serves illustratively to sharpen the point of vv. 16f. Honey is a health-giving food, but you can have too much of it and a surfeit produces sickness and vomiting. Honey is wholesome, provided it is taken in moderation and a sufficiency is not exceeded. In the same way, your company is good for your friend provided that you do not over-cultivate the relationship and foist yourself upon him. If you are never away from his door, a point will be reached where your presence is intrusive on his privacy and his desire to have leisure in order to be a person in his own right, and instead of enriching his life you will take away from it. He will have had more than enough of you and will resent your interference. The right thing to do is to avoid the temptation of seeking him out too frequently. This may require an effort of self-control, but it will ensure that the friendship will flourish. Winton Thomas's proposal (*JTS* xxxviii, 1937, p. 402) that *hōqar* should be associated with Arabic *waqara*, 'Make heavy thy foot (in keeping away) from thy friend's house' can be accommodated to the above exegesis, but I take the meaning of v. 17a to be: 'Use your feet sparingly so as not to be always on your neighbour's doorstep.'

[27] In v. 27, honey has exactly the same illustrative function ('To eat honey in excess is not good'), but the second half of the verse is unintelligible and the application of the illustration cannot be ascertained. Verse 27a, as Driver observes, says that the over-eating of honey is bad, but the implication is that honey eaten in the right quantities is good, and Driver is wrong in supposing that v. 27b 'must denote something the reverse of that', i.e., of the badness of over-eating honey. What v. 27b should deal with is a good analogous to honey, which becomes an evil if it is sought immoderately. Hence the emendation which Driver constructs on the basis of the reading of Symmachus ('to seek out honour is glory in itself') is not what is desiderated (*wᵉḥēqer kābōd mᵉkubbād*, 'but the search for honour is honourable', *Biblica* 32, pp. 190f.). On the analogy of vv. 16f. one would expect a statement that *kābōd* is good as honey is good, but not in excess, and this is the effect which is achieved by the emendations of Frankenberg (also Toy and Gemser), BH and Barucq. Frankenberg suggests *wᵉhōqar dibrē kābōd*, 'so be sparing with eulogizing words' (cf. LXX: 'It is needful to honour eulogizing words'). BH reads *ūdᵉḥōq kābōd mikkābōd*, 'nor that honour throngs upon honour'. Barucq reads *wᵉḥēqer kābōd mikkābōd*, 'nor the searching for honour after honour'. I follow Frankenberg.

[20] The textual problems associated with v. 20 are formidable and cannot be finally resolved. LXX reads: 'As vinegar is bad for a wound, so a pain which afflicts the body afflicts the heart. As moth in a garment and worm in wood, the pain of a man wounds the heart.' The only fragment of this longer text which is recognizable in MT is the clause 'as vinegar is bad for a wound' (*ḥōmeṣ ʿal nāter*, Arabic *natratu*, 'a deep wound') and, in these circumstances, there are insufficient grounds for reconstructing MT by adopting this longer text, which is the procedure of Gemser, Ringgren and Driver (G. R. Driver, *VT* iv, 1954, pp. 241f.). In other words, the character of the longer Greek text is such that it affords no evidence to support the opinion that an 'original' Hebrew text is its basis.

Gemser supposes that v. 20 (*maʿᵃde beged bᵉyōm qārā* is a corrupt dittograph of v. 19b (*bōgēd bᵉyōm ṣārā*). So also Barucq ('a variant') and Ringgren (p. 101, n.2). Gemser then inserts *ʿal neteq kᵉmayim* after *ḥōmeṣ* (on *neteq* 'scab', cf. BH and Toy) and translates: 'Like vinegar on a scab, like water on soda, so is one who sings songs on a sad heart.' This is identical with Bickell's proposal noted by Toy, except that *neteq* is substituted for *peṣaʿ*. The singing of songs on a sad heart is then the same type of expression as marching on an empty stomach, and one would think by way of illustration of the celebrated case of the clown whose audience is in tears laughing at his performance, while he, below his expertise, can hardly stifle tears of sorrow. So it is with one who has to sing (perhaps joyful songs) for the entertainment of others, while he is in the grip of a great sorrow. This is like vinegar on a wound, i.e., it exacerbates and inflames a wounded heart; it is like water on soda, i.e., it has only bad effects, just as water destroys the soda by dissolving it and the soda ('natron', bicarbonate of soda, cf. Toy and Driver) in turn makes the water undrinkable (so Driver). The second figure is not so naturally wedded to the application as the first.

Driver's reconstruction hinges on the assumption that the stylistic device of two homonyms (*neter*) is employed in this verse and that one of them has been accidentally omitted by vertical haplography. He restores the text as follows:

[mayim ʿal neter] maʿade beged beyōm qārā
ḥōmeṣ ʿal neter šār baššārīm ʿal lēb rāʿ

Water (poured) on soda,
taking off one's clothes on a cold day.
Vinegar on a wound,
A singer in a choir with a sad heart.

This has the merit of incorporating *maʿade beged beyōm qārā* and making it intelligible. Taking off one's garment on a cold day, like pouring water on soda, is bad in all its effects, in the cold which is suffered and in the possible ill consequences of exposure. Driver's conjecture (*baššārīm*, following Wildeboer) conjures up a different picture from *šār baššīrīm*. It is that of an individual who sings in a choir without gusto or conviction, because there is no song in his heart and he feels sadly disconcerted. Driver makes too large a claim when he says that the differences in the texts of the ancient versions support his hypothesis of vertical haplography. The fact that LXX reads 'wound', while Symmachus, V, Targ., and Pesh. read 'soda', is explicable in terms of the ambiguity of *neter*, i.e., the homonyms *neter* 'wound' and *neter* 'natron'. This does not, however, show that there was an 'original' text in which both appeared; it only shows that *ḥōmeṣ ʿal neter* was understood in one way by LXX (ὄξος ἕλκει) and in another by Symmachus (ὄξος ἐπὶ νίτρῳ), V, Targ. and Pesh. I follow MT and suppose that the verse contains two images which conjure up extreme discomfort and pain (taking off one's clothes on a cold day and having vinegar applied to a wound). These are used to illumine an experience involving inward discomfort and pain – singing songs with a sad heart.

[24] Verse 24, on the nagging wife, is identical with 21.9 (see above, pp. 553f.), **[25]** and v. 25, whose figure is cold water on a tired throat, is a more explicit expression of what I have taken to be a possible meaning of v. 13a (see above, pp. 585f.). 'Throat' (Ringgren,

Barucq; cf. Gemser) is to be preferred to 'soul' or 'man' (Toy, Gemser, RSV, Scott) as a translation of *nepeš* (see on 1.12, above, pp. 269f.). Gemser has suggested (p. 113) that *nepeš ʿayēpā* may mean 'thirsty throat' and has pointed to LXX διψώσῃ (also Pesh. and V), but the expression 'tired throat' is idiomatic English and gives the required sense. Thirst and dust make the throat tired and it becomes the centre where fatigue is most acutely experienced, so that the relief produced by a drink of cold water is not just local, but amounts to a total revitalization. So it is with good news from a far country – where the reference to the far country perhaps hints that its receipt is unexpected, out of the blue, and the sense of pleasure and well-being deriving from it thereby enhanced. It puts new heart into the man who receives it, and changes his whole outlook on life for the better.

[28] According to v. 28, the person who has no self-control has no defences, and is as exposed and vulnerable and foredoomed to disaster as the city which has been breached by an enemy and has no wall around it on which it can organize effective resistance. With self-control, which comprises disciplined and clear thinking, an even temper, restraint and economy of utterance, and judicious, well-considered action, a man is well-equipped to take care of himself and to make his way safely and successfully in a dangerous world. If he is unable to exercise this comprehensive control over himself and is deficient in any aspect of it, he is always in imminent danger of becoming a casualty and will come to grief sooner or later. As Ringgren observes, self-control is an indispensable adjunct of the wise man (see on 16.32, above, p. 488).

Class B

[4f.] KB[2] (cf. Gemser) suggests that *sīg*, which has to be separated from the silver, is oxide of lead used as a flux in the process of smelting it. The meaning of the verse is that silver must be one hundred per cent pure and entirely free from any base admixture. The raw material with which the craftsman works must have the hallmark of purity and be worthy of the consummate skill which he lavishes on it. Verse 4b (MT) is obscure. *wᵉyikkōn* (v. 5b) indicates that *wᵉyēṣēʾ* (MT *wayyēṣēʾ*), 'and it will come out', should be read in 4b, and this is supported by LXX, Pesh., V, Targ. But 'and so there will emerge from the silversmith a vessel (work of art)' is not very intelligible, unless it means that the purity of the silver is absolutely necessary for the finished work of art. If the smith does not have quality material to work with, the product will not be perfect, however much skill he may lavish on it. In v. 4b, LXX reads: 'It will emerge purified, entirely pure', and on the basis of this MT is emended to read *wᵉyēṣē' niṣrāp kullō*, 'and it will come out entirely purified' (Dyserinck, Wildeboer, Toy, BH). D. Winton Thomas (*VT* xv, 1965, pp. 274f.) suggests that LXX ἅπαν may translate *kālīl* as in Lev. 6.15 (EVV 22). He reads *wᵉyēṣē' niṣrāp kālīl*, 'so that it may come forth completely purified'. *kālīl* occurs as an adverbial accusative in Isa. 2.18, 'and the idols will completely disappear'. G. R. Driver (*Biblica* 32, p. 190) reads *liṣrōp* or *lᵉṣōrēp* and associates *yṣ'* with Accadian *aṣū*, 'to go out', used in a Sumerian-Accadian word list as a synonym of *namāru* 'shine'. He thus seeks to establish that Hebrew *yṣ'* has the meaning 'shine'. 'So that it may shine (in its purity) for the fashioning of (or 'for the fashioner of') a work of art' (cf. LXX καθαρισθήσεται). Dahood (p. 52) supposes that Ugaritic *yṣů* means 'lights up' in *Keret* II.i.52f., but Driver translates *pnh tġr yṣů*, 'he peeped by the gate', literally, 'he put forth his face (at) the gate' (*CML*, pp. 40, 41 n.13). I retain MT despite its obscurity and I take *yṣ'* in its usual sense: 'Take away dross from silver and the smith will produce a work of art.'

[5] A body politic should be a harmonious whole like a work of art, and righteousness is the creative principle which affords structure and stability. The king whose rule is not vitiated by evil counsellors and who has weeded out all *rᵉšā'īm* from places of influence will establish his throne on enduring foundations and create a community in which *ṣedeq* is realized. This will mean that solidarity is not simply imposed from the top, but is also the consequence of the free resolve of the members of the community to be incorporated and to find social enrichment in a society where every man respects the rights of his neighbour (see on 16.12, above, p. 491; 20.28, above, p. 546).

[21f.] The motivation which connects vv. 21f. with the doctrine of theodicy ('and Yahweh will requite you') may, as Gemser suggests, (p. 113) be secondary, and in that case, the verses might more properly belong to class B than to class C. The advice which is given is then justifiable in humanist terms without resort to a theological dogma of reward and retribution, and this is what the first motive clause ('for you will heap live coals on his head') indicates. To show kindness and magnanimity to an enemy by satisfying his hunger and thirst is to deal with him in a salutary way and to bring on a punishment which is self-inflicted (cf. 'Precepts and Admonitions', *BWL*, p. 100, *ll.* 41f.):

Do not return evil to the man who disputes with you,
Requite with kindness your evil-doer.

Kindness shown to an enemy, because it is undeserved, awakens feelings of remorse. When the enemy has steeled himself to meet hate with hate and is impervious to threats of revenge, he is vulnerable to a generosity which overlooks and forgives, and capitulates to kindness. If his need had been made an occasion for crowing or gloating, he would have remained unbowed, but bread and water have accomplished more than was in the power of the most bitter invective. The food and drink which his enemy gave him not only put an end to his hunger and thirst; they also put an end to his enmity. The pain of contrition purifies and recreates; it is the birth pangs of a new brotherhood. Hence this is how to deal with an enemy and to punish him in the most constructive way. He is to have pain inflicted on him by his experience of the magnanimity and generous forgiveness of the one from whom he expected enmity. In this way he will be punished and, at the same time, reinstated as a brother.

Morenz argues (*op. cit.*, cols. 187–91) that the figure itself is derived from an Egyptian penitential ritual in which live coals on the head of the penitent one were endured as a mark of contrition. He thinks that the rite was probably confined to Egypt, but that the metaphor as it exists in a Palestinian context is to be elucidated on this ritual basis. Certainly there is little doubt that it is the penitence of the enemy which is indicated by the use of this imagery in v. 22a.

Class C

[26] The *maʿyān nirpāś* is the spring which is fouled as a consequence of having been trampled over by animals, and the *māqōr mošḥāt* one that has been polluted by unspecified causes, so that it is useless for drinking or cooking. 'To befoul a water-hole on a track across the desert is one unforgiveable sin among the Bedouin' (E.F.F.B.). The image in both cases is that of a wasted asset. What should have been a perennial source of living water, and so a fountainhead of vitality and abundance, has been made unproductive and even noxious. The difficulty in this verse lies in determining how precisely this image is to be applied to the *ṣaddīq* of v. 26b. LXX translates: 'Thus ἄκοσμον is it for a righteous man to fall before an impious man', i.e., if this were to happen the world would be out of joint, things would have gone awry, just as they have done when the bounty of nature is frustrated by accident or design. LXX has taken

v. 26b correctly and we have to connect the use of *mwṭ* here with those passages to which Toy has called attention, which assert that the righteous or godly man will never be moved (Prov. 10.30; 12.3; Pss. 15.5; 16.8). These are expressions of confidence in the operation of a theodicy; the righteous man believes that by virtue of Yahweh's enforcement of a rule of righteousness, his safety and success are assured and he lives in the best of all possible worlds. 'Tottering' does not therefore refer to ethical faltering, but to the inability of the *ṣaddīq* to maintain himself against the *rāšāʿ*, which is a scandalous and contradictory state of affairs. It is *ἄκοσμον*, since it makes nonsense of the principle of order posited for human existence by a theodicy, and a *ṣaddīq* who cannot withstand a *rāšāʿ* is as perplexing a phenomenon as a wasted spring. He, too, should be an unfailing source of vitality, but the wholeness and abundance of his life have been impaired by the ascendancy of the wicked man over him.

Ringgren (following Strack and Wildeboer, see Toy) supposes that 'totters before a *rāšāʿ*' means 'stumbles morally in the presence of a *rāšāʿ*'. The righteous man's lapse will encourage the wicked; they will use it to justify their own behaviour, and so it is a catastrophe. Such an interpretation cannot be placed on v. 26b (cf. Toy). The closest approximation to this which is feasible is to take v. 26b as a reference to a loss of nerve or lack of moral fibre on the part of the *ṣaddīq*. If he really believes in the operation of a theodicy, he will not allow himself to be intimidated by a *rāšāʿ*. This would imply a criticism of the *ṣaddīq*, or even the placing of a question mark against his righteousness; this is not, in my judgement, what is intended by v. 26b, which rather depicts a situation constituting an affront to the doctrine of theodicy.

Chapter 26

As in ch. 25, most of the sentences in this chapter are artistically produced similes in which a figure has been selected in order to make a particular point, which then becomes the interpretation and usually constitutes the second stichos of the verse. Thus snow in summer and rain at harvest are two figures of incongruity which illustrate that honour does not befit a fool. These similes are quite obviously engineered – they are literary products – and are articulated with varying degrees of explicitness. The fullest construction is with *kᵉ* in the first half of the verse and *kēn* in the second (vv. 1, 2, 8). In vv.

18f., the construction extends over two verses with *k*^{e} in v. 18 and *kēn* in v. 19. In vv. 11 and 23 *kēn* is absent, and the simile is indicated by the initial *k*^{e} only. A different device is followed in vv. 3, 7, 9, 10?, 14, 20, 21, 24, where the simile is indicated by *w*^{e} in the second half of the verse. There is a special feature in v. 21a, namely, that it has two images instead of the normal single image. The least explicit simile is the type which appears in vv. 6 and 17 and which predominated in ch. 25, where the figure and its application are simply placed side by side. Verse 22 deviates from the pattern of the image in the first stichos and the explication in the second, since here the simile is complete in v. 22a, and v. 22b adds such details as are thought necessary to underline the appositeness of the image.

There are three verses which are 'proverbial' in the more exact sense, vv. 13, 15 and, especially, 27. The significant difference between v. 27 and the similes is that the images of v. 27 are not directed towards one particular point or given one specific interpretation. The verse contains two pictures, and it is up to us to judge the situations to which they can be appropriately applied. In respect of this element of openness to interpretation, vv. 13 and 15, because they are less imaginative than v. 27, are 'proverbial' to a lesser degree, but they do have a special kind of concreteness which is also the mark of the truly proverbial. Thus v. 13 reproduces an actual, wildly improbable, excuse of an indolent person in order to say in a striking way that there are no limits to his powers of self-deception. In rationalizing his behaviour he will stick at nothing. Similarly v. 15 says that the *ʿāṣēl* is incurably lazy, but it does this by picturing him as having put his hand into a dish of food and not having the energy to feed himself.

The remainder of the chapter is made up of wisdom sentences of a more pedestrian kind (vv. 12, 16, 24, 26, 28) and fragments of Instruction (vv. 4, 5, 25). Verse 12 is a continuous sentence without parallelism, there is antithetic parallelism in vv. 24 and 26, synthetic parallelism in v. 28, and a 'more . . . than' type of construction in v. 16. Verses 4 and 5 consist of an imperative with a 'lest' clause and v. 25, which is continuous with v. 24, is made up of adverbial clause, imperative and motive clause.

The notable feature with respect to content is the complete absence of any religious interest or emphasis throughout the chapter, with the possible exception of v. 2. The sentences describe human flaws, whether of an intellectual or a more general kind, and they also give hard-headed advice on how to deal with a fool (vv. 4f.) and a malicious person (v. 25). They describe and analyse acutely and objectively without recourse to moralism or piety. Verses 1–19 are to be allocated to class A, and vv. 20–28, because they are concerned with anti-social behaviour and its adverse consequences for the community, as well as for the malicious person himself, to class B. The editorial grouping of sentences which have a common theme is more than usually evident in this chapter. The continuity of the theme 'folly' in vv. 1–12 is broken only by v. 2, whose concern appears to be somewhat different. Verses 13–16 have to do with the lazy person and vv. 20–28 with malevolent, anti-social behaviour. It is a question whether vv. 17–19 should also be attached to vv. 20–28, or whether it is the foolishness of the agent rather than his malicious intent on which the emphasis falls in these sentences. I am inclined to opt for the latter, for, even in the case of vv. 18f., the point is not so much that the man wilfully deceives his neighbour as that his joke is in the worst possible taste and is an act of idiocy.

Class A

vv. 1–12 *The Ways of the Fool*

[1] If snow fell in the summer or rain at harvest, it would be a sign that the world was topsy-turvy and that the times were out of joint (cf. I Sam. 12.17, where rain at harvest constitutes a miracle, an interruption of the normal course of nature). 'The country is rainless from March to October. If a shower of rain did occur in June, it would only be of the slightest duration' (E.F.F.B.). So it is if a man acquires reputation, stature and influence which are disproportionate to his intrinsic worth. We have to reckon here, as Gemser observes, with the twin reference of *kābōd*. It refers to the intrinsic qualities which give a man weight and also to the external recognition of his worth. It is right that the inner and outer aspects should be in balance and that the *'îš kābōd* should be a man of property and reputation who commands general respect and has power over affairs. This situation cannot obtain in the case of the *k^e^sîl*, who has no weight nor worth and who is an impostor if he erects himself as an object of public esteem. Indeed he is palpably a fraud, and his pose is so utterly incongruous with his worthlessness, that it cannot be sustained.

[3] A horse has to be whipped and an ass bridled, for this is the only language which they understand, and they are not amenable to any more refined kind of discipline. So with a fool whose hallmarks are unteachability and incorrigibility (see on 9.8a, above, p. 368, 15.12, above, p. 480), it is a waste of time to appeal to reason or to pursue a path of persuasion, and all that can be done is to restrain and subdue him by corporal punishment. Any more elevated or humane concept of education for a *kᵉsīl* will be barren of results.

[4, 5] On the relation between v. 4 and v. 5, Gordis observes that the sages quote one proverb and then register their disagreement in another diametrically opposed to it (R. Gordis, *JQR* xxx, 1939, p. 137). Although ἀλλά of LXX indicates an antithetical relationship, this has probably a more subtle character than Gordis's remarks would lead us to suppose. The two verses have to be held together and then, as Barucq suggests, they constitute a paradox or dialectic. The intention is not to deny the validity of v. 4 by asserting v. 5, but to say that both verses contain aspects of the truth and that an approximation to the whole truth can only be achieved by taking both together. Or one might say with H. H. Schmid (p. 172) that wisdom is always wedded to a particular situation, and that v. 4 is the right advice for one kind of situation and v. 5 for another. The same technique is used by St Paul in Gal. 6.2, 5. In dealing with a fool, the best policy in certain circumstances is to say nothing by way of rejoinder or to say as little as possible. If he is allowed to go on and on, he will condemn or discredit himself out of his own mouth, and this is the most complete and bloodless victory that can be achieved. There are certain dangers in becoming involved in a debate with a fool which are thereby avoided, for it is difficult to take on a man whose mind is indescribably confused without being tainted by his confusion. In such an encounter there is a levelling-down process, and you are reduced to his level and made to look like a fool. Nevertheless, in a certain situation it may be a lesser evil to speak than to keep silent; it may be more important that he should be disabused of his illusions than that you should pursue a course which has the least risk for yourself. Nothing worse is conceivable than that a fool should become self-opinionated and behave as if his advice were valuable.

[12] This is the point of v. 12, that the fool who has a high opinion of his own wisdom is at the furthest reach of folly. Less hope can be held out for him than for a fool of any other kind, no condition of folly is more incurable. To stave off such an eventuality, it is right to accept the risk of replying to a fool, since trenchant speech may prove to be a therapy with salutary effects.

[6] The folly on which v. 6 discourses is that of employing a *k^e^sīl* on a mission where it is a matter of importance that the point of view of a principal should be accurately represented, and his position and interests adequately maintained, in any negotiations which may ensue. Anyone who relies on a fool to do all this is himself the personification of unwisdom. He is like one who cuts off (his) feet and drinks violence. It is the obscurity of these images in v. 6a which makes the verse difficult. Gemser records Delitzsch's suggestion that instead of putting another pair of legs into service on his behalf, the man in question is really cutting off his own legs by entrusting his affairs to a fool. The other phrase, 'drinking violence', will then mean tasting or suffering violence. He will come to a sticky end through relying on a fool in a matter which touches his own interests and safety. Gemser (p. 113), following Tur Sinai (*Job*, 1957, pp. 259f.), emends to *ḥōmēs šētō(h)*, *ḥōmēs* 'bare' (*neḥm^e^sū* parallel to *niglū* in Jer. 13.22) and *šētō(h)* 'posterior', 'buttocks' (II Sam. 10.4; Isa. 20.4). Gemser also presumably intends that *mqṣh* should be pointed as a pual. The person who employs a fool in his service is like one whose legs are cut short (who is crippled or deformed) and whose buttocks are bare. The latter phrase refers to his contorted walk and to the baring of his buttocks as a consequence of the grotesqueness of his limp. To entrust important business to a fool is to make of oneself a helpless and ludicrous cripple. But the emendations are improbable, especially *ḥōmēs* 'bare', and, even if they are conceded, the interpretation is farfetched. It has to be acknowledged that the MT of v. 6a is obscure and cannot be satisfactorily elucidated.

[7] The situation is similar with v. 7, in that the application of the image is again clear, whereas the image itself (in a lesser degree than v. 6a) is obscure. Barucq cannot be right in retaining MT *dalyū* and translating it as an imperative from *dlh* (cf. LXX: 'Take away mobility from the lame'), because there is no doubt that 'and' in v. 7b indicates a simile, as it does in the other verses where it occurs in the same position (above, p. 594), and Barucq's imperative, which does not in any case make particularly good sense of the verse, has the effect of giving v. 7 a different form from vv. 3, 9, 14, 20, 24. *dalyū* is perhaps a composite form (*dālyū* from *dlh* and *dallū* from *dll*, cf. Gemser). Driver vocalizes *dillūy* (Delitzsch) and redivides *šōqayim mippisséaḥ* into *šōqē m^e^pass^e^ḥīm*, 'the loose hanging of the legs of those who limp'. Driver urges (*Biblica* 32, p. 191) that *k^e^sīlīm* (v. 7b) favours the plural participle. This is the correct elucidation of the figure, but I would retain MT, except that I would vocalize *dlyw* as *dālyū* (*dlh* with the same sense as *dll*, 'to dangle'). 'Legs hanging limp from a lame man, a proverb in the mouth of a fool.' An aphorism spoken by a fool limps; it lacks fluency and authority. It is impotent, like dangling, emaciated legs.

[8] According to v. 1, *kābōd* does not befit a fool, and I take the point of v. 8 also to be that there is a strong incongruity, even absurdity, in bestowing status and reputation on a fool. I am consequently in disagreement with Delitzsch's view (cf. Gemser) that it is the cheapening of *kābōd* which is indicated by the verse; and I would not seek an elucidation of the image in v. 8a along the line of Toy, who also shares Delitzsch's assumption. One can see that, if this is really what the verse is about, it makes sense to suggest that *'eben* (v. 8a) may mean 'precious stone' and then to say with Toy: 'The proverb may have had some such form as: "Like him who puts a jewel on a swine's snout is he who gives honour to a fool." ' My assumption is rather that the point of the verse is the absurdity of according *kābōd* to a fool, and I seek to understand v. 8a on this premise. The possibilities for v. 8a are then narrowed. It has to be translated either 'Like tying a stone in a sling' (Gemser, Scott), or, 'Like fixing a stone on a cairn', i.e., a heap of loose stones (Ringgren, cf., however, p. 103, n.2). The first rendering is to be preferred for the following reasons: (*a*) the *hapax legomenon margēmā* is translated σφενδόνη, 'sling', by LXX. Another word for sling, *qela'*, occurs seven times in biblical Hebrew. *rgm* means 'to stone', and *margēmā* is then an instrument for hurling stones (BDB), rather than a heap of stones (KB²); (*b*) *ṣ^erōr* is more apt in the first than in the second; (*c*) even if the second translation can mean 'making fast a stone on a heap of loose stones', this is not so palpably impossible or absurd as tying a stone in a sling, and the latter is the figure which is demonstrably apt to convey the idea of absurdity. It is not necessary to emend to *k^eṣōrēr*, 'like one who ties', although this is the sense of LXX (ὃς ἀποδεσμεύει), and the participle would furnish a more exact parallel to *nōtēn* in v. 8b. It is a nonsense and an absurdity to tie a stone in a sling, for a stone is put in a sling so that it may be ejected, and the same degree of incoherence and contradiction attaches to the act of according *kābōd* to a fool (cf. v. 1).

[9] In v. 9b, as in v. 7b, the function of the image is to illustrate what an aphorism in the mouth of a fool is like. In v. 7b, the point was the lameness or ineffectiveness of the aphorism, while here it seems to be the aspect of comic absurdity (so Toy), although the sense of v. 9a is uncertain. RSV translates: 'A thorn has gone up into the hand of a drunk man' (Better: 'A thorn which pierces a drunk man's hand'). This conjures up a picture of a person who is so drunk that he is incapable of looking after himself in the normal way, and who will stagger and fall upon hazards which he would avoid were he sober. The application might then be that the fool has no more control over an aphorism than a drunk man has over his movements, and will probably employ it to his own hurt. This sense cannot be achieved without straining after it, and it is not really a very convincing solution. If *ʿālā bᵉ* can mean 'has come into the hand (possession) of' (cf. Toy), the picture is rather that of the inebriated reveller who has torn a branch from a tree or uprooted a bush, and who goes on the rampage waving it in his hand (Gemser, Ringgren, Scott, Barucq). He is a comic and absurd figure, and so is a fool who affects the form of speech of a wise man.

[10] The text of v. 10 has a corrupt appearance, and it cannot be reconstructed with any degree of assurance. The numerous attempts at translation and emendation are noted by Toy. The proposal to translate *rab* 'archer' (cf. Job 16.13; Jer. 50.29), made by Bickell and noted by Toy, has been widely adopted (BH?, Gemser, Ringgren?, Barucq); the other elements of Bickell's reconstruction (the transposition of *ʿōbᵉrīm* to the end of v. 10a and the emendation of the second *śōkēr* in v. 10b to *šikkōr*) are adopted by Gemser, Renard (cf. Barucq) and Scott. The archer who shoots passers-by at random has gone berserk, and the man who takes a fool and a drunkard into his service exhibits a similarly advanced degree of unreason.

[11] Verse 11 returns to the well-worn theme of the unteachability of the fool (see on vv. 3, 4, above, pp. 595f.), and makes its point by constructing an image of a dog returning to its own vomit. There are moralizing additions in LXX, 'and becomes odious' in v. 11a and in v. 11b the rendering 'Thus the fool who by virtue of his wickedness turns back to his sin'. LXX has an additional couplet (also found in Ben Sira 4.21) which is in the same moralizing vein: 'There is shame which leads on to sin, but there is shame which is glory and grace.' The dog is so utterly lacking in discretion that it eats again what it has vomited; the fool is equally incapable of learning the most elementary lessons from his experience of life. Not only is the fool incapable of learning from a wisdom teacher (cf. 15.12, above, p. 480); neither can he learn from experience.

[2] Verse 2 deals with quite a different topic, namely, the curse which is groundless or unjustified. *lō' tābō'* should be taken as a relative clause with the particle suppressed, and so the same kind of construction as *'ālā bᵉyad šikkōr* in v. 9a. The simile has then a greater fluency than when these words are translated 'it does not alight', after a comma or a colon (Gemser, Ringgren), or when v. 2b is translated in some such way as: 'The curse that is groundless does not strike' (Toy; similarly LXX, Scott). What is really being likened to a sparrow on the wing and a swallow in flight is the undeserved curse, and it is on this that the emphasis rightly falls when v. 2b is translated, 'so is the undeserved curse which does not alight'. While, therefore, the theological point is made that a curse does not have objective reality or certain efficacy, irrespective of its merits, it is not made so directly as is commonly supposed. Verse 2b does not contain a direct assertion that an undeserved curse does not alight (on the one against whom it is directed). The verse observes, rather, that an undeserved curse which does not alight is like a sparrow on the wing and a swallow in flight. It does not then teach a new doctrine, but takes for granted that an undeserved curse is inoperative, and describes this state of affairs by likening it to a sparrow on the wing and a swallow in flight, with these birds envisaged as remaining airborne and not alighting.

Barucq reads too much into the simile when he supposes the point of the verse to be that birds in flight will not enter a house unless attracted to it, and likewise a curse is not a blind force and will not enter the house against which it is directed if there is no good reason for its utterance.

vv. 13–16 *The Ways of the Sluggard*

[13, 15] Verse 13 approximates to 22.13 (above, p. 569), and v. 15 is almost identical with 19.24 (above, p. 530). **[14]** In v. 14, the lazy man who turns in his bed is likened to a door turning on its hinge or mortise. Gemser (also Toy) suggests that the simile points to the immobility of the sluggard; he turns (again and again) in his bed without making any progress towards rising. Just as a turning door has a stationary aspect in that it is anchored to its hinge, so the sluggard is anchored to his bed. The thought that a door moves easily and naturally on its hinge may also be present. The function of a hinge is to facilitate movement from a fixed point, and the point of having a door is that it should be able to move in this way. The sluggard turns in his bed as naturally as a door turns on its hinge, and this is the greatest degree of movement to which he aspires. Where another man would put his feet on the floor and get up as a matter of routine and habit, the lazy man habitually turns in his bed.

[16] Complacency and self-deceit make the worst kind of fool (v. 12), and the sluggard is also vulnerable to them. Laziness is a form of escapism, for the lazy man lives in the little world constituted by his bed and his dreams. Since he is incapable of striving and enduring hardness in the real world, he is all the more prone to nourish his illusions in bed, and as long as he stays there he will never be disabused of the high opinion which he has of his own wisdom. This is expressed concretely by saying that he is wiser in his own eyes than 'seven *mešībē ṭaʿam*'. 'Seven' has no precise numerical significance and means something like 'any number of'; *mešībē ṭaʿam* are those who have a flair for the *mot juste*, who speak well and judiciously and whose rejoinders exemplify intellectual discrimination (on *ṭaʿam* see 11.22, above, p. 430) of the highest degree.

This would seem to me to be the meaning of the verse, rather than Toy's suggestion that it gives expression to a form of Epicureanism, namely, that lying in bed is, in the opinion of the sluggard, a higher form of wisdom than that displayed by those who bring trained minds to bear on the affairs of the world. His idleness and detachment is a superior wisdom to their striving and involvement.

vv. 17–19 *Further Aspects of Folly*

[17] There is the folly of becoming involved in the quarrels of others by an act of gratuitous and blatant interference. If the *athnach* is transposed to *ʿōbēr* (Gemser, Ringgren and Barucq), the effect is to emphasize that the dog was minding its own business and that the person who grabbed its ears (LXX, 'tail') committed an act of unprovoked aggression. Since he has made trouble for himself, he has no ground for complaint if he gets bitten. According to the punctuation of MT, *ʿōbēr* belongs to v. 17b, in which case it is the meddler who is the passer-by and who, since he is that kind of person, pokes his nose into some dispute on which he chances to alight (RV, cf. Toy). Either way the meaning of the verse is not significantly changed, and *ʿōbēr* may be redundant, as Toy suggests, for the verse seems complete without it. The professional busybody throws himself with enthusiasm into disputes which are none of his business and works himself up to a fine pitch of frenzy (*mitʿabbēr*). He spoils for a quarrel and invites himself to other people's quarrels, where he does duty for them in the matter of vituperation. If *mitʿārēb* is read (Pesh., V), it is simply gratuitous interference which is indicated (so Toy, Gemser, cf. Ringgren, p. 104 n.2). Whoever gets himself involved in a quarrel which has nothing to do with him provokes retaliation and will suffer damage and injury. It is unlikely that *rīb* here refers to legal contest, but if it did, the folly described would be a particularly virulent kind of litigiousness, that of the man who makes himself a party to the legal disputes of others.

[18f.] The general sense of vv. 18f. is clear, although there is some doubt about the exact meaning of *mitlahlēah*. It is translated 'madman' by Toy, Gemser and Ringgren, but *meśaḥēq* in v. 19 suggests that the meaning may rather be 'one who indulges in horse-play' or 'one who plays the fool' (Barucq). It is possible, though not certain, that this sense is supported by Ben Sira 32(35).15, where *mtlhlh* is the antithesis of *dwrš*, and where the intention may be to contrast the earnest seeker after the *tōrā* with the trifler: 'He who seeks the law will obtain it, but he who plays the fool will be ensnared by it.' Kopf has suggested that the meaning to be attached to *mtlhlh* here is 'neglects' on the basis of Arabic *lahā ʿan* (*VT* viii, 1958, pp. 180f.). The person whose idea of a joke is to deceive his friend and then to say to him, 'I was only having a bit of fun', is like the practical joker whose rags run to lunacy and whose lethal toys, such as firebrands and arrows, can inflict death and produce tragedy. Liberties cannot be taken with dangerous weapons, nor can they be taken with the confidence of a friend. When this is betrayed it is the death of friendship, for the damage done is irreparable and the old relation of trust and openness cannot be resuscitated. Deceit is no less deceit, nor are its tragic consequences for friendship relieved by the subsequent pleas that it was done for a laugh.

Class B

vv. 20–28 *Malice in Action*

[20] Slander is the fuel which stokes the fires of dissension. The slanderer's role in society is a divisive and destructive one, and he speaks with malice aforethought to destroy the trust and regard which produce solidarity and concord and to create instead suspicion and contempt, alienation and bitterness. The hardening of misunderstanding into ever more implacable enmity is facilitated by gossip, and if only the slanderer's voice were quietened, room would be made for more sober reflection and mature consideration; the flames of controversy would die out and the process of reconciliation be set in motion.

[21] The same thought and imagery are present in v. 21, and the *'îš midyānîm* who stokes the flames of dissension is indistinguishable from the *nirgān* of v. 20. He, too, adds fuel to the flames of controversy at every opportunity and is a professional saboteur of human relationships. Wherever he finds a trace of a difference of opinion or of misunderstanding, he works on it assiduously to magnify its dimensions, to invent sinister implications and to raise the temperature of the dispute to boiling point. Verse 21a appears to envisage two different kinds of fuel ('as charcoal is to embers and wood to fire'), but some difficulty has been felt with *peḥām*. LXX reads ἐσχάρα, 'hearth', but it is doubtful whether this can be said to lend any support to Wildeboer's *mappūaḥ* 'bellows' (so Barucq), although it is adopted by Gemser (cf. Toy, Ringgren, p. 104, n.3). The change has little effect on the interpretation of the verse. The slanderer fans and feeds the flames of dissension. He is a perverse creature dominated by malice and incapable of positive social experience. His aim in life is to wreck the regard of man for man which is the basis of corporate life and to produce disruption, feverish instability and chaos. **[22]** His technique is further described in v. 22, which is the same as 18.8 (above, p. 519) and requires no further comment.

Verses 23–26 are all concerned with the thought that an attitude of deep, settled malice may be cloaked by a cultivated civility of speech and charm of manner. **[23]** If MT: 'silver dross' (RV), 'impure silver' (Toy), 'unpurified silver' (Barucq) is retained in v. 23, the ingratiating manners which accompany an evil disposition are described as an admixture of dross. The polished exterior is not all that it seems to be; it is not itself genuine and it effectively conceals the real man. In this respect it is like debased silver covering a piece of earthenware. This gives us a somewhat complicated simile and has the effect of deflecting the emphasis from where it might be expected to fall. The contrast which is desiderated is simply between the outer covering or veneer and what lies concealed beneath it. Moreover, the phrase *kesep sîgîm*, which occurs only here, is difficult and the rendering 'debased silver' is dubious. KB^2 supposes that it means oxide of lead (used in glazing pottery), and BH deletes it as a gloss of *kesep*. Ginsberg (*BASOR* 98, 1945, p. 21, n.55; cf. G. R. Driver, *Biblica* 32, p. 191) arranges the consonants to form *kspsg*. *spsg* occurs in Ugaritic with the sense 'glaze' (a noun). Albright (*BASOR* 98, 1945, p. 24) and Driver cite Hittite *zapzaga(y)a* with the same meaning (cf. G. R. Driver, *CML*, p. 54, *Aqhat* II vi.35, where the white hair which covers the head of an old man is likened to glaze on pottery. See also Driver, *CML*, p. 55, n.8 and p. 147, n.11). The combination of lips which are hot or ardent (Gemser p. 113, 'rash', on the basis of Arabic *dalaqa* does not give the required sense) with protestations of friendship and a mind of settled malevolence are likened to a glaze or enamel (*kspsg*) spread over a piece of earthenware. The surface is pleasing, smooth and brilliant and it obliterates the nature of the material over which it is coated. Since this appears to be the point of the figure in v. 23a, the simile is improved if *ḥᵃlāqîm* is read for *dōlᵉqîm* with LXX (λεῖα, so Toy, Gemser, Ringgren). Smoothness of speech, superficial charm and polished manners cover an evil disposition and hostile intent. The corruption of *sg* into *sygym* will have been consequent on the failure to recognize *spsg* and the identification of *ksp* with *kesep*.

[24] Verse 24 is a pedestrian repetition of the sentiments of v. 23. I retain *dolᵉqîm* and accept *kspsg*. **[25]** Verse 25 proffers advice on how to deal with one who beneath his veneer of civility is a dangerous enemy of society, and v. 26 expresses the confidence that he will be found out and publicly discredited. He has no respect for words, and language as used by him is always prostituted to evil ends and made the servant of deceit and fraud. He has no interest in using language constructively or benevolently; he has no desire to communicate his thoughts to others and to explain himself to them so that the possibilities of common understanding and action may be enlarged. His use of language is determined by his basic malevolent motivation. He hates his fellows and this is the truth about him. He speaks only to conceal and deceive and implement his destructive hostility. When he turns on his charm, he is not to be believed in or relied on, for he is hatching any number (on 'seven' see v. 16b, above, p. 601) of villainies in his mind (v. 25). He is a master of the art of dissimulation, but his viciousness will be uncovered and he will be branded by society as a danger to its health and vitality (v. 26).

[26] Toy's suggestion that the *qāhāl* of v. 26b is a judicial body, and that a formal sentence of condemnation is indicated, would seem to me to be unlikely. All that is meant is that society will see through the postures of the malicious person and will be armed against his malice. He may expect short shrift from those whose common life he is bent on destroying.

[27] The 'proverbs' of v. 27 (cf. Ecclus. 27.25–27; Eccles. 10.8f.; Pss. 7.16f.; 9.16f.; *Onchsheshonqy*, above, p. 135) have probably such a troublemaker in mind, but they can be applied to any situation where a person who creates mischief or sets in motion a dangerous train of events is overtaken and engulfed by his own villainy:

For 'tis the sport to have the enginer
Hoist with his own petar (*Hamlet* III.iv.207).

What happens to Haman (Esther 7.10) and Daniel's enemies (Dan. 6.24f.) is a transformation of the proverb into a *motif* of narrative art, and also a theological expression of the exactness of God's act of retribution. Haman is put to death on the gallows which he had erected for Mordecai, and Daniel's enemies are mutilated by the lions which were to have devoured him. Here it is the exact working-out of a theodicy which is envisaged, whereas the proverbs themselves in the context of Prov. 26.20–28 see the end as produced inexorably by an immanent, self-destructive process rather than as contrived by an act of judicial interference (cf. Ps. 9.17, where both aspects are stressed, Yahweh's judicial act and the self-destructive activity of the *rāšā'*).

A man digs a pit to cause injury to his neighbour or his livestock, and he is so wrapped up in his malicious plan that he fails to make a mental note of where he has dug the pit and to take adequate precautions against falling into it himself. Or he starts a landslide with evil intent without considering how he can ensure his own eventual safety. The proverbs point to a myopic aspect of malice and indicate how the deep-seated corruption of character which unfolds carefully laid plans to injure others will eventuate in self-destruction. The hater of men who is consumed with the urge to injure and destroy others is in the process of destroying himself.

[28] The general question which has to be raised in v. 28 is whether, like v. 27, it dwells on the self-destructive tendencies of the malicious and accomplished liar or whether, like vv. 20–26, it describes rather his evil disposition towards others. The efforts which are made to deal with the obscure *dakkāw* (v. 28a) are influenced by the broad understanding of the verse which is assumed. Thus Gemser takes v. 28b to refer to the self-ruin of the slanderer, and so he follows

Ewald in emending *dakkāw* to *'ᵃdōnāw*; alternatively he suggests *bᵉʿālāw*. The false tongue is its owner's worst enemy (cf. Scott, who supposes that this sense can be had by emending *dakkāw* to *dᵉrākāw*).

Toy reckons with both possibilities, and he emends *yiśnā' dakkāw* to *yābī' šeber* ('a lying tongue brings destruction'), thereby leaving the meaning of the verse open (similarly Ringgren, p. 105 n.1, who reads *dᵉkī* 'collapse', 'anarchy', and cites *dᵉkī* = 'crashing (of the waves)' in Ps. 90.3). Toy says: 'The couplet may refer to the ruin brought by the false tongue either on others or on its possessor; the latter interpretation is suggested by the sense of the preceding couplet; the former is the more natural suggestion of the words.' LXX, which translates 'A lying tongue hates truth and a chatter-box creates anarchy', clearly points to the evil effects of a slanderer's activities on others, and v. 28b of MT is more naturally susceptible of such a translation (i.e., 'makes ruin for others' rather than 'works his own ruin').

RV: 'hateth those whom it hath wounded' is the general sense which is needed, but, as Toy and G. R. Driver have observed, it can hardly be got out of *dakkāw* ('its? oppressed ones'). Driver, noting LXX ἀλήθειαν and *midḥe* of v. 28b, has suggested that *dakkāw* may be a corruption of **dikyū*, 'purity' (cf. Syriac *dakwātā*). This would be an Aramaism, and the masculine gender of *lāšōn*, reflecting the gender of Aramaic *liššānā*, would be further evidence of the Aramaic provenance of the saying (G. R. Driver, *JTS* xli, 1940, pp. 174f.). This has been superseded by a more attractive suggestion that an Aramaism **dikkūy*, 'acquittal', should be read (Aramaic *dakkī*, Hebrew *zikkā*, 'declared innocent'). This makes good sense, but the meaning of v. 28b is not just, as Driver supposes, that 'a flatterer brings about the ruin of anyone whom he praises' (G. R. Driver, *JRAS* 75, 1948, p. 168, n.3). It might then be thought that he does it by ineptitude or extravagance, inadvertently rather than by design, but the point of *ḥālāq* here as in the emended v. 23b is that he does it by design. It is his facility for slander and the smooth civility which may conceal his deadly malevolence that are indicated by *pe ḥālāq*, and this is more malignant than flattery. A practised and malicious liar hates to see innocence established and reputation vindicated, since this spells defeat for his own efforts to smear and traduce. He works with a malign dedication for the ruin of individuals and for social anarchy.

Chapter 27

The simile, constructed variously as in chs. 25 and 26, is again a prominent feature in this chapter, in vv. 8 and 19 with *kᵉ* . . . *kēn*, and in vv. 9, 17, 18, 20, 21 with 'and' in the second stichos. The use of *ništāwā* (or *nišwātā*, BH, KB²; cf. GK §75x; Dahood, p. 54; *t* may be transposed for reasons of euphony, but probably *nišwātā* should be read) is a further variation which occurs here (v. 15) for the first time. The 'more . . . than' type of sentence appears in vv. 4, 5?, 10c and in v. 3 with figurative elements. Verses 6, 7, 12 have antithetic parallelism, and v. 7 is a 'proverb' in the full sense. There is an increase in the incidence of the Instruction genre over the preceding chapters, and ch. 27 has a higher proportion of Instruction than any other chapter classified as sentence literature. In particular, vv. 23–27 is a continuous piece comprising imperatives (v. 23) and extended motivation (vv. 24–27), with synonymous parallelism in v. 24 and v. 26. Other fragments of Instruction are v. 1 (imperative and motive clause), v. 2 (imperatives with synonymous parallelism), v. 10ab (imperatives), v. 11 (imperatives, with 'my son' and a final clause) and v. 13 (imperatives with motive clauses; see on 20.16, above, pp. 542f.). Verses 14 and 22 are continuous sentences without parallelism. If v. 16 is continuous with v. 15, as is commonly supposed (the position is obscure), it contains two motive clauses which reinforce the position adopted in v. 15.

All of the verses fall into class A except for v. 14. If the thoughts of v. 1 are coloured by religious considerations, as is almost certainly the case, it might be put into class C (see below), and the difficult v. 14 has perhaps the social emphasis of the class B material. This is another chapter without God-language, marked by shrewd observations and a tough, empirical concept of wisdom as advice for the business of life. The special emphasis of vv. 23–27 is discussed below.

Class A

[1] The thought of v. 1 is almost certainly that of the precariousness of man's existence and the uncertainty of his tenure of life. He must live from day to day, grateful for the life which he has from God, with the awareness that it may be withdrawn at any time and that he must not speak nor plan as if he himself had full disposal of his destiny and power over his future. According to *Amenemope*, tomorrow is God's province and not man's (xix.13; xxii.5–8; xxiii.8–12, *ANET*, pp.

423f.), and Ben Sira observes: 'There is a man who is rich through his diligence and self-denial and this is the reward allotted to him. When he says: "I have found rest and now I shall enjoy my goods", he does not know how much time will pass until he leaves them to others and dies' (RSV; Greek, Ecclus. 11.18f.; cf. Hebrew 11.16f.). This is a kind of folly, because whatever virtues a man may have (Ecclus. 11.18, 'diligence and self-denial'), he is living in a fool's paradise if he speaks confidently about his future. The folly in Ben Sira consists in taking a long and comfortable retirement for granted (v. 19), and when Jesus resumes this theme in a parable, he thinks of a man who is so engrossed with plans for building his own empire and amassing his fortune that he has overlooked the unpredictability of his future. It is God who commands his tomorrow: 'But God said to him: "Fool, this night your soul is required of you" ' (Luke 12.20). It is wisdom to live in the present and to grasp what God now gives; it is folly to use the present as a means to a comfortable and assured future, for man may not presume on God's future.

[2] Verse 2 contains quite a different thought from v. 1, but the two verses are associated on the stitch-word principle (*tithallēl*, *y^e^hallel^e^kā*). Self-praise does not have the significance of praise given by others and does not establish reputation (cf. *mah^a^lāl*, v. 21). The wise man's strength lies in silence and reticence, and the loud person who specializes in self-advertisement and self-recommendation is really uncovering his flaws before the world and cheapening whatever status he happens to possess. **[21]** Men will not take him seriously, for a community has processes for putting a man to the test and trying him thoroughly before it accords him acclaim and preference and entrusts him with power. Ringgren has remarked (p. 107, n.2) on the laconic character of v. 21b, and has suggested that one would expect the verse to say that the critic's judgement tries a man's reputation in the same way as a furnace tests the genuineness of silver and gold. However, v. 21b can simply be translated, 'a man with respect to his reputation', and the point of the simile then is that the processes at the disposal of the community for testing a man's reputation are as rigorous and reliable as those employed for testing silver and gold, and that consequently no one may hope to succeed by pretence or affectation. A man will enjoy such public esteem as he deserves. Scott's translation of v. 21b, 'Flattery will show you what a man is', is improbable. The suggestion that flattery is envisaged as a criterion for testing a person's worth is itself hard to credit, but, in any case, *mah^{a}lāl* cannot be translated 'flattery'. If flattery were the criterion, it would be exclusively a negative one – it would invariably discredit – whereas the furnace not only discloses the spuriousness of what purports to be precious metal, but also confirms its genuineness, where it is genuine.

[3] The provocation offered by a fool is an intolerably heavy burden. The carrying of a boulder or a sandbag can impose an immense strain on a man's physical resources and cause intense discomfort and misery. With the bearing of such weights is associated aching and strained muscles, inhibition of free movement, and general physical depression and exhaustion. All this is a real discomfort and lack of well-being, but it is less wearing and exhausting than to carry the burden of a fool's provocation. The fool imposes on those who have to endure his company a kind of spiritual malaise, and this is harder to bear than physical fatigue. The mind is more delicate than the body and cannot suffer mental confusion and chronic wrongheadedness.

[22] The fool in himself, rather than in his effects on others, is the subject of v. 22 which is yet another expression of his incorrigibility. The suggestion of 26.3 (above, p. 595) is that the only language which the fool can understand is that of corporal punishment, and this verse is even more despairing of his reformation. The figure employed is that of (the mortar and) the pestle – an apparatus to pulverize material. Even if the most drastic methods of discipline and chastisement are used, even if he is pulverized, there will be no salutary effects. He is incapable of learning sense by any process of education, and nothing will make him turn aside from his folly. The original text of v. 22a may have been 'If you pulverize a fool with a pestle', and the words 'in a mortar among powder(?)' are then a heavy-handed expansion or gloss – an unnecessary underlining of the point (so BH and Gemser). Toy supposes that the words which should be omitted are 'among bruised corn (?) with a pestle', but no appeal should be made to the LXX in support of this (cf. Barucq). No textual conclusions can be drawn from LXX, which has the appearance of a pedestrian paraphrase of MT without the imagery of mortar and pestle: 'If you were to flog a fool in the assembly, thereby dishonouring him, you would not remove his folly.' Koehler (*ZAW* 40, 1922, p. 17) conjectures that *ḥ^{a}rīpōt* should be read for *hārīpōt* here and in II Sam. 17.19, and that it means 'grains of sand' (so Ringgren, who otherwise retains MT; cf. Barucq who translates *rīpōt*, 'grains'). Gemser (pp. 113f.) emends to *hār^{e}pōt* from Arabic *rafata*, 'to be broken', 'to be crushed', *rufāt* 'an object broken into small pieces', Hava, 'crumbs', 'decayed bones' (cf. Scott 'fragments').

[12] In v. 12 it is inexperience and an untutored condition rather than inveterate folly that are contrasted with shrewdness and acumen. The *p^etā'īm* who blunder into danger and evil, and have to suffer the hurtful consequences, are raw youths who have not yet been exposed to the educational process (see on 22.3, above, pp. 563f.).

Both v. 5 and v. 6 are concerned with a process of salutary reproof, but both have obscure elements. **[5]** In v. 5, the antithesis of 'open reproof' should be 'simulated love', and then the meaning would be that speaking the truth in love, even where it may injure the self-esteem of the other, is more genuine evidence of regard than a show of affection and a desire to please which is cultivated rather than spontaneous, affected rather than real, and which consequently has a sycophantic taint or the suspicion of toadying attached to it. But *m^esuttāret* means 'concealed' rather than 'simulated', and the contrast is perhaps that of love which expresses its concern effectively and love which is mute and impotent in relation to the other's welfare. Toy is then right to reject the suggestion that doubt is being cast on the sincerity of this hidden love. It is not that it does not give proof of its genuineness in deeds, but that it is lacking in ruggedness. If it is the antithesis of 'open reproof', the 'concealed love' remains concealed for fear of straining or breaking the tie of friendship. The friend is too timid, or else the relationship is too precious, and the two do not know each other well enough or trust each other sufficiently to admit reproof as an element of love. BH's suggestion that 'hidden enmity' should perhaps be read does give a possible antithesis to 'open reproof' – benevolence with hard words is better than hostility with silence – but there is no reason for doubting the originality of *mē'ah^abā*.

[6] The difficulty in v. 6 stems from the obscurity of *na'tārōt*, rendered by RV as 'profuse' (cf. Barucq 'de trop'; *'tr* is then an Aramaism = Hebrew *'šr*, cf. *'ōšer* 'wealth'). It is possible to make some sense out of the verse with this rendering, although, as Toy observes, it does not furnish an exact antithesis of 'trustworthy' (unless 'profuse' implies 'insincere', 'sycophantic') and is, moreover, lexicographically dubious. The best of the emendations in relation to the requirements of the parallelism is that proposed by Gemser (cf. Ringgren, p. 106 n.1): **n^e'ōtōt* (niphal participle of *'wt*), 'treacherous'. If a friend wounds by speaking the truth, the wound is salutary and he inflicts it out of a concern for the deepest welfare of the other. The truth may hurt, but it is evidence of a friendship which can be relied on through thick and thin. Over against the word which wounds for no other reason than that it is the truth are the kisses which are false and insincere. They are the kisses of a Judas; the enemy wears the badges of love in order to achieve the ends of enmity; he makes the sign of friendship into a lie and puts it to work in the service of malice. KB² suggests that *n^erā^ʿōt* 'corrupt' (*r^ʿʿ*) should be read, and Scott follows the tentative proposal of BH, 'The kisses of an enemy are like knives' (*katte^ʿ ārōt*). The latter gives a similar sense to **n^e ʿōtōt*, but considerations of parallelism would suggest that the original was a niphal participle (cf. *ne'^emānīm*). Driver points to the readings of Symmachus and Theodotion. (*τεταραγμένα*, 'disturbed', 'agitated', 'disordered'), and connects *naʿtārōt* with Arabic *ʿatara*, 'unruly', 'turbulent', 'wanton'. He would translate *w^ehaʿtartem ʿālay dib^erēkem*, in Ezek. 35.13, 'and you spoke unruly words against me'. The enemy's kisses are given with hardy or brazen wantonness (the basic sense of the root, according to Driver, is that of quivering into rigidity), but this is not quite what is needed as an antithesis to *ne'^emānīm* (G. R. Driver, *JTS* xli, 1940, p. 175). I retain MT and translate v. 6b, 'but the kisses of an enemy are effusive'.

[4] The form of v. 4, which is the same as that of v. 3, is obscured if it is translated: 'Anger is ruthless and rage torrential, but who can stand before jealousy' (Toy, Barucq). The structure is not simply antithetic as might seem from this translation, but is rather a kind of simile in which the destructive violence of jealousy is indicated by comparing its operation with that of anger: 'Ruthless anger and flood-waters of rage, but who can stand before jealousy' (cf. Gemser, Ringgren and Scott). Anger is a destructive flood, but jealousy a consuming fire. Jealousy is a raging emotion which clouds reason, destroys humanity and fulfils itself in destructive violence. Here it is the effects of jealousy on others which are described, whereas 14.30b (see above, p. 472) was concerned with the disintegration which is brought about by the fever of jealousy in the jealous person himself.

[7] In v. 7, *nepeš* should perhaps be translated 'person' (Toy, Gemser, Ringgren and Scott) rather than 'appetite' (Barucq 'throat'). The latter would be preferable were it not that the verb *tābūs* requires the assumption that there is a personification of appetite; *tābūz* tentatively conjectured by BH removes this impediment (cf. Scott) and makes very good sense of the verse. The appetite which is surfeit despises even such a delicacy as honey, but the appetite sharp with hunger enjoys anything edible and does not discriminate nicely with respect to taste, cf. *Ahikar* 188; 'Hunger sweetens what is bitter' (Cowley, pp. 218, 247). MT should be retained, although either way the general sense of the verse is not affected. Even the most tempting food is rejected (with loathing) by the man who is sated, but a hungry person can make an enjoyable meal of the coarsest food. This is a 'proverb' with an unlimited scope for interpretation, with a province as wide as the possibilities of our human situation. Our appropriation or rejection of what is offered us and the value judgements inherent in this response are regulated by the kind of persons we are as well as by the nature of our world. Our consequent experience is as illuminating with respect to ourselves as it is to the world which we encounter, but it is an irreducible compound which cannot be separated off into its parts.

[8] Verse 8 is to be understood as a comment on the malaise of rootlessness. One may speculate on the occasions which may have necessitated a pulling up of roots and a feeling of alienation from the natural social context of existence. The travels of sages in search of learning, wars, exile, trade and commerce have all been suggested as facets of experience out of which this comment might have emerged (Gemser, Barucq). The statement that a man who flies off from his home is like a bird flying from its nest is not just an expression of the insecurity or vagrancy of a life lived away from home, but also includes the thought that when an individual cuts himself off from his family and community, he diminishes his own life in essential respects. He loses the social support of his existence and in doing so cuts himself off from his history and suffers a loss of identity. Historical existence in depth he can only have so long as he lives in the community whose history he shares. If he leaves it, he leaves behind the presentness of his past and belongs nowhere. He becomes a wanderer on the face of the earth.

There is a group of sentences which touches on different aspects of friendship (vv. 9, 10, 17, 19). **[9]** Verse 9b is obscure, and even if sense can be had from MT, it is not the sense to which v. 9a seems to point. Driver (also Gemser, p. 113) has suggested that *rēʿēhū* is a corruption of *raʿᵃwā*, 'friendship' (Aramaic *raʿᵃwā* 'acceptance', a form similar to Hebrew *gaʾᵃwā* 'pride'). The cause of the metathesis of *h* and *w* is the rarity of the form. Driver's further suggestion is that *mēʿᵃṣat nāpeš* should be rendered 'more (than that) of fragrant wood' (cf. Kamphausen, *mēʿᵃṣē nāpeš* 'more than scented trees'; see Toy,

Ringgren and Dahood p. 54). In Isa. 3.20, *bāttē hannepeš* means 'perfume boxes' (Symmachus σκεύη τῆς ἐμπνοίας; Jerome *olfactoriola*). Alternatively Driver suggests that *mē*ʿ*ᵃṣat nāpeš* should be rendered 'More than (that of) the counsel of the soul', i.e., it is sweeter to be able to rely on a friend's advice than to be thrown back on one's own judgement (so Barucq; G. R. Driver, *ZAW* 52, 1934, p. 54; *ZAW* 55, 1937, pp. 69f.). Driver remarks that the translation of *ʿēṣā* as 'tree' assumes the existence of a unique *nomen unitatis*, i.e., **ʿēṣā* feminine, referring to a piece of wood (cf. Arabic *ʿiḍatu*, 'thorny tree'). He also takes account of von Soden's suggestion (*ZAW* 53, pp. 291f.) that the phrase 'houses of the neck' in Isa. 3.20 refers to ruffs or the like. He notes that *nepeš*, 'scent', is a natural development from *nepeš*, 'breath', and is evidenced by Accadian *nipšu* and Arabic *nafasu*. He concludes: 'Although *nepeš*, 'scent', cannot be proved for and may not be admitted in either of these passages (Prov. 27.9; Isa. 3.20), I am still inclined to think that such a word did actually exist on the strength of the Ancient Versions which have often preserved genuine words, even where their translations are demonstrably wrong.' But the form of v. 9b which is desiderated in relation to v. 9a is neither 'more than a scented tree' nor 'more than one's own counsel'. What is required to balance v. 9a is not an element of comparison but a verbal form (cf. *yᵉśammaḥ* in v. 9a). Nor is it any help to follow LXX in v. 9b, as Gemser does, since this too produces an inept second-half of the verse, 'But the soul is rent by affliction' (similarly Frankenberg, see Toy). All that can be done in the face of these difficulties is to suggest that Reuss's conjecture *ūmeteq rēʿēhū mᵉʾammēṣ nepeš* should be modified to *ūmeteq raʿᵃwā mᵉʾammēṣ nepeš*, 'The sweetness of friendship strengthens the spirit' (similarly Scott; cf. Toy, 'The sweetness of advice (*ʿēṣā*) strengthens the spirit'). D. Winton Thomas, *VT* xv, 1965, p. 275, suggests *waʿᵃṣat rēaʿ mamtīqā nepeš*, 'and the counsel of a friend makes sweet the soul'. The verse is then a type of simile. Great social and, perhaps, religious occasions have an exhilarating effect on those who participate in them. Oil and incense have these associations of joy and social enrichment. Less public and thrilling, but no less wholesome and profound, is the experience of friendship in a more ordinary or private context. Alternatively it may be supposed with Toy that it is simply the physical well-being associated with anointing and the smell of incense to which v. 9a alludes, and then the contrast is between this and friendship which produces a sense of spiritual well-being.

[10] Verse 10 is Instruction, and the third stichos might have been taken as an asyndetic motive clause but for the fact that it does not seem to have this relationship to either v. 10a or v. 10b or both. Hence the deletion of v. 10b (Gemser, cf. Scott) does not improve the coherence of the verse, because the injunction not to neglect an old friend of the family has no intrinsic connection with the observation that a neighbour who is on the doorstep is a bigger help than a brother who is at a distance. This (v. 10c) has to be taken as an independent aphorism (Toy), and its point is easily grasped. It is to his brother that a man naturally turns when he needs help, for this is the office of a brother (cf. 17.17, above, p. 505). When the brother is far away, distance makes his goodwill impotent and thwarts the effective expression of his concern. He can watch and wait anxiously and he can even give some tangible proofs of his will to help, but it is the neighbour on the doorstep who is contiguous with the point of need, and who can insert himself into the situation out of which it arises and help to bear the burden. Moreover, the small kindnesses which constitute neighbourliness and which touch daily life in many places can only be received from a neighbour.

The difficulty which is felt with v. 10b is occasioned by the discrepancy between it and 17.17 (cf. Toy). To help his brother in trouble is what a brother is there for; why, then, should a man not go to his brother's house when he is in deep trouble (so Toy)? It is just a possibility that this may be another example of a dialectic relationship between two apparently conflicting points of view (see on 26.4f., above p. 596), in which case both have to be asserted in order to produce a balanced expression of opinion. The meaning here would then be: Do not abuse your brother's solicitude for you, a solicitude which you can take for granted just because of the strength of family solidarity. Do not make a practice of paying him a visit only when you have a hard-luck story to tell him. I do not make this suggestion with any great degree of conviction, for it does amount to special pleading and does violence to the plain sense of v. 10b. If we are left with this, it makes puzzling reading, as Toy has remarked. BH tentatively rewrites the verse (*tābūz* for *tābō'* and *dayyekkā* for *'ēdekā*), 'Do not despise your brother when you are prosperous'.

[17] There can be little doubt that the versions are right in deriving *yḥd* from *ḥdd* and translating 'sharpen' (LXX, Pesh., V, Targ.). The pointing in v. 17a should perhaps be *yuḥād* (hophal) and in v. 17b *yāḥēd* (hiphil), as Gemser and KB[2] have proposed. Barucq notes the attempt to justify the Masoretic vocalization by the assumption that the first *yāḥad* is a stative qal and the second a hiphil with *pataḥ* instead of *ṣērē* because of the medial guttural. The application of the simile in v. 17b is not altogether clear and it is difficult to decide between the possibilities. The reference to the 'face' of one's neighbour is puzzling, but this is hardly an adequate reason for deleting 'face' (Toy), although this makes v. 17b easier. The question which has to be answered is what can be meant by a man sharpening the face of his neighbour. The thought may be that a man acquires polished manners through the experience of social intercourse (Gemser, Ringgren, Barucq). If this is so, v. 17a apparently envisages some kind of buffing or polishing process in which an iron tool (a file?) is used in order to shape a piece of iron and make it a highly-finished object. But v. 17a would more naturally refer to a sharpening process in which 'a steel' is used to sharpen knives or swords or the like. In this case the application which is required in v. 17b is to sharpened wits and not polished manners, and this is probably the meaning, although 'sharpening the face' is a difficult expression for 'sharpening the wits'. I am inclined to follow Scott, who renders: 'So a man sharpens the perception of his companion'. It is by such a dialectic, by the sharpening of one mind on another, that a man's thinking becomes as keen as a razor blade.

[19] Verse 19 is cryptic, and v. 19a presents formidable difficulties. It is commonly taken to mean 'as the face is mirrored in water' (Gemser, Ringgren, Barucq, Scott, G. R. Driver, *ZAW* 50, 1932, pp. 146f.). Kopf argues that *mayim* is a possible construct form, and cites the Arabic idiom 'water of the face' (*mā'ul-wajhi*), meaning 'shame', 'reverence'. He interprets ingeniously; as a face is not really human without the appearance of shame or modesty, so a man without a mind or heart (*lēb*) is not a human being in the full sense (L. Kopf, *VT* ix, 1959, pp. 260f.). But *mayim* as a construct form cannot be justified, and sense has to be made out of v. 19b on the assumption that v. 19a means something like 'as a face is reflected in water' (cf. Arabic *māwiyatu*, 'mirror', 'looking-glass'). Driver illustrates v. 19a from Plato's *Thaetetus* (206D), 'into a mirror or (into) water', and v. 19b from *Phaedrus* (255D), 'seeing himself (reflected) in his lover as in a mirror', and Aeschylus, *Agamemnon* 838–40, 'mirror of companionship'. Driver paraphrases: 'As a man sees his own and no other face reflected in water, so he will see only his own nature reflected in his companion's heart.'

Driver's interpretation of v. 19b has this much in common with Toy, Gemser and Ringgren ('through the observation of other people a man can know himself') that it presupposes a reference to a second man. Scott ('so a man's thoughts are reflected in the man') and Barucq ('so a man's thoughts are a mirror for the man') assume that only one person is in view. One can see that it is appropriate to represent the beloved as the lover's mirror in which he sees his essential self. This is an expression of the transparency of true love, and the enhancement of self-understanding which is produced by the interpenetration of kindred spirits, but is not clear to me (contrary to Driver) that this is the particular thought of v. 19b, which is concerned only with the face of a single person, a face which is reflected in water. Verse 19b has to do only with one man whose self is mirrored in his *lēb*, and the meaning, as Barucq has indicated by his translation, is that it is through introspection, through self-examination in depth, that a man acquires self-knowledge.

[11] Verse has the form of Instruction, but not the intention normally associated with this form. The father or, more probably, the teacher commands the 'son' to be wise, but it is his own welfare and justification which he consults, and the final clause which would normally describe the salutary consequences to the 'son' which follow upon obedience to the teacher's directives return rather to the teacher himself. When the teacher is denigrated or vilified, or when the value of his work is otherwise called in question, he can point to the pupil whose mind he shaped and whose acumen he raised to the highest pitch of excellence. The wise man whom he brought into the world by his maieutic skill is his joy and vindication and the proof that he has not laboured in vain.

[13] Verse 13, whose subject is imprudence, is almost the same as 20.16 (above, pp. 542f.; *nokrīm* should be read as in 20. 16), **[15]** and v. 15 on the contentious woman is similar to 19.13b (above, p. 531). LXX offers an exegesis rather than a translation of the verse: 'Drips drive a man out of his house on a wintry day; similarly a railing woman (drives him) out of his own house.' *yōm sagrīr* means 'a day of downpour', not 'a wintry day'; on *delep ṭōrēd* and the application of the figure to the contentious woman see on 19.13b (above, p. 531).

[16] Verse 16 is wrapped in obscurity, unless the assumption is made that it is continuous with v. 15 (V, Gemser, Ringgren, Driver, Barucq), and the 'her' of *ṣōpᵉnehā* is the shrew of that verse. Driver translates: 'He that would keep her safe keepeth safe the wind, and oil will meet (*yīqrā'=yiqrāh*) his right hand' (so also Gemser and Ringgren). To keep her in safe custody is an impossible task. It is like trying to put the wind under lock and key or holding oil in a firm grasp. Like oil she runs through the fingers. Driver (*JTS* xli, 1940, p. 175) cites Hos. 13.12: 'Ephraim's iniquity is tied up, his sin is kept safe' (*ṣᵉpūnā ḥaṭṭā'tō*). Driver supposes that the figure implied by the use of *ṣpn* here is that of the record kept in the ledger which is under lock and key, so that the entries are inviolate and safe from falsification until the time comes for the ledger to be brought out and the account settled. This supports and illustrates the translation of *ṣōpᵉnehā* in v. 16, 'he that would keep her safe'. Barucq's free translation, 'Whoever wishes to keep her in check wishes to detain the wind and to seize oil with the right hand', apparently assumes that *yᵉmīnō* is the subject ('his right hand encounters oil'). This gives the sense suggested by Driver, Gemser and Ringgren more naturally than 'Oil meets his right hand', but is precluded by the feminine gender of *yāmīn*.

[18] If BH's tentative emendation were accepted in v. 18 (*'adᵉmātō* for *'ᵃdōnāw*), the topic would be akin to that of vv. 23–27 and the verse would embody Boström's 'agricultural ideal' (see on vv. 23–27, below, pp. 618f.). The emendation is, however, to be rejected, not only because it is gratuitous, but also because it does not do justice to the form of v. 18, which is a simile of the same type as vv. 9, 17, 20, 21. In other words, v. 18 is not just a wisdom sentence with synonymous or synthetic parallelism, but this is what it becomes if *'ᵃdōnāw* is emended to *'adᵉmātō*. Rather it begins with what is regarded as axiomatic, that good husbandry will have its reward. The farmer who lavishes care and time on the cultivation of a fig tree will enjoy its fruit, and, in the same way, the man who takes care of his master and his master's interests will be honoured for his years of loyal service. The honest servant need not fear that his years of constancy will go without reward and recognition and that at the end of the day he will have nothing to show for his work. He, too, no less than the skilful and hard-working farmer, will have *kābōd*, material reward and a general recognition of his worth.

[20] Behind v. 20 there is the mythological portrayal of Mot (Death), the god with the gaping throat by whom life is swallowed up in death (see on 1.12, above, pp. 269f.). His appetite is insatiable and there is no end to the descent of the living into the shadowy world of the dead. Here the old mythology is used to cast light on man's psychological make-up, on the drives and urges which will not let him be at peace. It is the eye which informs and awakens desire (cf. Toy, Gemser), and as there is no end to what he sees, so he cannot set limits to his desires and is the slave of a raging appetite. He lives in a chaos of unrealized and unrealizable desire and this is a kind of underworld, a state of death. One may speak here of a psychologizing or interiorizing of mythology. LXX has a moralizing addition which is not particularly related to the point of the simile: 'He who fixes his eye is an abomination to the Lord and the incorrigible have unruly tongues.'

[23–27] The meaning of vv. 23–27 is tolerably clear, though the text is obscure in one or two places. MT is retained in v. 24b by Barucq, but the sense ('a crown does not pass from generation to generation') is not very good. Even then it is doubtful whether *we'im* can be so translated, although it is retained by Toy, who emends *nēzer* to *'ōṣār*, 'wealth' (cf. Jer. 20.5, where *ḥōsen* and *'ōṣerōt* are associated) and reads *ledōr wādōr* (Q.). Gemser and Scott follow Toy except that they additionally emend *we'im* to *we'ēn* (cf. LXX οὐδὲ). Verse 27 appears to be too long, and *leleḥem bēteḵā* is perhaps a secondary expansion, but LXX ('My son, within earshot of me you have words which are effective for your life and for the lives of those who serve you') gives no indication one way or the other (contrary to Toy, BH, Gemser). I follow Gemser in v. 24b.

Barucq observes that vv. 24–27 (LXX) are a mixture of fidelity to MT and paranetic gloss. Flocks and herds are a basic and stable form of wealth and one which is self-perpetuating. If they are fed and cared for properly, and full benefit is obtained from recurring increments of natural increase, they should, in the ordinary course of things, never become a wasting asset. Verse 24 is not a warning against improvidence, but rather the contrasting of a different kind of wealth with wealth in flocks and herds (Boström, p. 64, Gemser, Ringgren). Money quickly made in trade and commerce is dissipated with equal rapidity, whereas flocks and herds establish a 'tradition' of wealth in a family, a kind of wealth which is consolidated by each succeeding generation and faithfully conveyed to the next (cf. *le'ōlām* and *dōr wādōr* in v. 24). These verses embody not so much Boström's 'agricultural ideal' as a 'pastoral ideal'. The hay is to be taken off (*gālā*) a field at the right time, so that the benefit of a second growth of hay may be had, and the hill grasses are to be cut and gathered as fodder. The sheep will provide wool for clothing and the goats milk for the sustenance of the household, including the servants (*ḥayyīm*, 'maintenance'; Toy; D. Winton Thomas *JTS* xv, 1964, p. 295; Dahood, p. 55). Hence what is described is not just a form of wealth but a self-contained way of life. Whether the field (*śāde*) which the goats provide the capital to purchase is envisaged as arable land or not is unclear. Perhaps the thought is rather that another field will augment the production of hay and this in turn will support larger flocks and herds. That is to say, it is this kind of expansion in a pastoral context rather than an element of arable farming which is being described.

Class B

[14] The words 'rising early in the morning' in v. 14 are absent from one Hebrew manuscript and are omitted by Toy, BH and Gemser. If they are to be retained (so Barucq), they will have some such force as 'at the crack of dawn' and indicate that this man leaves no stone unturned in his endeavour to present himself to the other as the very soul of benevolence and goodwill. He blesses, or perhaps simply greets (Gemser, Ringgren), his fellow with a loud voice and this is part of his affectation of friendship. It is, as Gemser remarks (p. 113), a forced heartiness, a boisterous but hollow camaraderie which is designed to disarm the other against his malicious intent. LXX takes the sense of v. 14b correctly with its paraphrase 'differs in nothing from him who launches curses'. The person who goes to such extravagant lengths to create an impression of aimiability is to be reckoned as a curse to the one to whom he is excessively civil. This is the significance of his behaviour, and, like the man described in 26.24f. (above, pp. 604f.), his words and gestures bear no relationship to his intentions which are evil. He wears the badges of a friend too ostentatiously, and from this it may be gathered that he plans the work of an enemy (see above, p. 107, on *Amenemope* xii.10–xiv.3, especially, 'Do not say to him "Hail to thee" falsely', *ANET*, p. 423).

Chapter 28

The contrast in respect of form between this chapter and those immediately preceding is most striking. The simile, prominent in chs. 25–27, is found only in two verses (3, 15), and the dominant feature is the sentence with antithetic parallelism (1, 2?, 4, 5, 7, 11, 12, 13, 14, 16?, 18, 19, 20, 25, 26, 27, 28). There is one sentence with synonymous (or synthetic) parallelism (v. 21), another with a 'better . . . than' construction (v. 6), and several which are continuous sentences without any suggestion of being constituted by balanced stichoi (8, 9, 10, 17, 22, 23, 24).

To this change of form and marked reduction of imagery there corresponds an equally significant change of content. Most of the sentences are to be allocated to class C, and the chapter leaves behind the world of old wisdom with its emphasis on educational discipline and has to be interpreted, for the most part, in the framework of a legal piety of theodicy. The remainder of the sentences belong to class B, since they take up matters of social concern, whether commenting on the consequences of misrule (2, 3, 15, 16) or discriminating between social benefit and the reverse (19, 21, 23, 24).

Class B: vv. 2, 3, 15, 16, 19, 21, 23, 24.

Class C: vv. 1, 4, 5, 6, 7, 8, 9, 10, 11, 12, 13, 14, 17, 18, 20, 22, 25, 26, 27, 28.

Class C

There are various ways of taking the pulse of this chapter and characterizing its ethos. One is to notice the way in which the vocabulary of wisdom is reinterpreted to bring it into accord with a particular style of piety. **[5]** Thus we read in v. 5 that evil men do not discern (*yābīnū*) justice (*mišpāṭ*) but those who seek Yahweh are all discerning. Dahood (p. 56) suggests that *mišpāṭ* has the meaning 'due limits', 'restraint' and that a form **kōl*, 'moderation' (from *kwl*), should be postulated. Evil men have no insight into the boundaries prescribed by moderation, but those who seek Yahweh are masters of moderation. The suggestion has some attractiveness, but there is no need to postulate a form **kōl*, 'moderation', when *kōl*, 'everything', gives good sense. In this context, *bīnā* or *tᵉbūnā* is not intellectual clarity but moral discernment, and its possession hinges on a correct religious attitude. This is akin to the prophetic reinterpretation of the vocabulary of wisdom which I have described elsewhere (*PWM*, pp. 65f.).

[26] The same presuppositions are present in v. 26, where the person who relies on his own intellect (*lēb*) is declared a fool and is contrasted with the man who walks in wisdom. There are several sentences which oppose the security of the *ṣaddīq* to the insecurity of the *rāšāʿ* (vv. 1, 10, 14, 18), and I have no doubt that this is the antithesis which is intended by v. 26. Here the wise man is the *ṣaddīq* whose security is guaranteed by Yahweh (he will escape harm). The person who relies on his own intellect is not necessarily a fool in the context of old wisdom. He is a fool only if he is self-opinionated and incorrigible, wanting in intellectual humility and unwilling to learn from a teacher. Yet the end of the educational process is none other than to make him rely on his own intellect once it has been informed and disciplined. Not educational indiscipline, but impiety, is presupposed by the form of the statement in v. 26a; *ḥokmā* is redefined so that even the ideal of intellectual discipline becomes a kind of folly, smacking of arrogance and a lack of pious acquiescence.

[11] In v. 11 the contrast of rich and poor, which is a prominent feature of the chapter (vv. 6, 8, 11, 20, 22, 25, 27), is associated with a reinterpretation of *mēbīn*. In these verses, wealth is synonymous with impiety and poverty with piety, so that the *mēbīn* of v. 11b is the seeker after Yahweh who keeps the *tōrā*, while the *ḥākām beʿēnāw* of v. 11a is the same kind of person as the *bōṭēaḥ belibbō* of v. 26a. Hence *ḥākām beʿēnāw* does not mean the same here as it does in 26.12 (above, p. 596). This is a new definition of a fool; not a man who refuses to submit to the *tōrā* (authoritative instruction) of a wisdom teacher, but one who will not submit to Yahweh and his *tōrā* (directives or Law).

Another pointer in the same direction is the use of the wisdom sentence as an instrument of dogmatic teaching to give expression to the doctrine of theodicy, whether it is the security of the *ṣaddīq* which is contrasted with the insecurity of the *rāšāʿ* (vv. 1, 10, 14, 18), or whether the antithesis of *ṣaddīq* and *rāšāʿ* is otherwise expressed or implied (vv. 4, 5, 7, 9, 12, 17, 28). **[1]** Thus the *rāšāʿ* has the mentality of a fugitive and is under the impression that he is being hunted, driven from pillar to post, even though his pursuers are the product of his own imagination (v. 1). Toy suggests that it is the bad conscience of the *rāšāʿ* which is portrayed, and this may be accepted as a legitimate comment on the verse, but not a sufficient explanation of it. It is not just that the impious man feels insecure and the pious man secure, but that by virtue of a theodicy this is the actual state of affairs. The safety of the *ṣaddīq* is guaranteed and he is not mistaken in feeling as secure as a lion, while the *rāšāʿ* is in reality doomed to punishment and disaster. It is the inevitability of judgement which makes him conjure up imaginary pursuers and live like a fugitive (BH, Gemser and Ringgren regularize the grammar by reading *nās* in v. 1a and *weṣaddīq* in v. 1b).

[10] In v. 10, the same figure is used as in 26.27 (above, p. 605), but it has to be interpreted in the context of belief in a theodicy. The figure in 26.27 amounts to an empirical observation that aggressive anti-social behaviour is self-destructive, but here it illustrates the dogma that those who are morally blameless will inherit what is good. This is just another way of saying (cf. v. 1) that for righteous or pious men this is the best of all possible worlds, since God sees to it that they are secure and successful. Even if v. 10c is a gloss (Toy, BH, Gemser), it is none the less correct exegesis of the preceding part of the verse. The person who sets out to entice and seduce the upright, and to lead them astray, to their hurt will himself fall into the pit (probably *šaḥtō* should be read) which he digs for the pious. God will take care of his own. **[14]** Hence the man who fears (Yahweh) continually is blessed, while he who hardens his heart (in impiety) will fall into evil, i.e., will suffer hurt. This is an antithesis of piety and impiety; on the one hand, the man who fears Yahweh and keeps his *tōrā* and is thereby safe and successful; on the other, the man who confronts him with unbending defiance and who suffers for his impiety and indiscipline (so Gemser and Scott; contrary to Toy, who urges that the contrast is between a fear of transgressing Yahweh's *tōrā*, a fear of 'sin' in that sense, and the absence of such a fear).

[18] The same theme is resumed in v. 18. The man whose way of life is blameless (cf. v. 10c) will be safe, while he who is crooked in his ways (reading *d^erākīm* here and in v. 6) will fall into a pit (reading *šaḥat*, cf. v. 10b). Barucq retains MT and translates: 'He who perversely follows two ways will fall into one of them.' A reference to the two ways (of life and death, of security and insecurity) is not the antithesis which is required in v. 18b. The way of safety in which the *tāmīm* walks is described in v. 18a, and so v. 18b should describe the unsafe way in which the *ne'qāš* (cf. *'ikkēš*, v. 6) goes. Hence a *ne'qāš d^erākīm* is one whose conduct is perverse because of a basic crookedness of motivation and attitude which expresses itself in impiety and malevolence. *b^e'eḥāt* at the end of the verse is highly suspect (Toy simply deletes it), and *b^ešaḥat* (so Lagarde, p. 88, Dyserinck, Bickell, Gemser, Ringgren) is probably the correct reading, but, in any case, *yippōl b^e'eḥāt* can hardly be translated 'will fall into one of them' (Barucq).

I have discussed the effect of the context of piety on the meaning of formations from *byn*, and similar observations have to be made about *tōrā* in vv. 4, 7, 9. Its theological significance in these verses has to be brought out by some such rendering as 'Law', even if the strict accuracy of this may be called in question. The reference is to Yahweh's directives, and so to his demands, which must be met by the pious man (Barucq translates 'Law'; Toy 'law' in v. 4, 'instruction' in vv. 7, 9; Gemser and Ringgren translate 'instruction' in all three verses). The rendering 'instruction' is an interesting illustration of the kind of problem which I am raising when I speak about the reinterpretation of the vocabulary of wisdom, since *tōrā* was certainly an item of this vocabulary, having a well-defined meaning within the framework of the Instruction in Proverbs 1–9, namely, that of parental or scholastic instruction. The reinterpretation of *tōrā* observable in the verses before us and others which have preceded them in class C is associated with a new concept of discipline in which the directives of Yahweh ('the Law of Yahweh') are substituted for the authoritative instruction of the wisdom teacher. In brief, educational discipline is replaced by the discipline of piety. **[4]** The *rāšāʿ* is the one whose impiety consists in his contempt for the Law, and so those who share his attitude to it (who neglect or condemn it) are full of praise for him. His attitude commends itself to them, whereas it has the opposite effect on those who piously observe the Law – they are incensed against him (reading *bō* for MT *bām*). The latter might be thought to assume a collective use of *rāšāʿ*, but it is more probable that the plurals *ʿōzᵉbē tōrā*, *šōmᵉrē tōrā* have caused the lapse.

[9] The coupling of *tōrā* with *tᵉpillā* in v. 9 betrays the intention to establish the place of Law observance in any scheme of piety. Even prayer, which is a classic and undisputed trait of piety, becomes an abomination (to Yahweh) if it is associated with inattention to Yahweh's directives. I have shown earlier (above, p. 448 on 12.22) that these words belong to the context of a theodicy. Yahweh's *rāṣōn* is enjoyed by the *ṣaddīq*, and his *tōʿēbā* is incurred by the *rāšāʿ*. Hence one who fails to attend to Yahweh's *tōrā* is a *rāšāʿ*, even if he is a man of prayer.

[7] In v. 7, on the other hand, the element of ambiguity attaching to *tōrā* has to be acknowledged. Were it not for the prevailing climate of piety in this chapter, it would be reasonable to argue that *tōrā* here means 'parental instruction' rather than 'Yahweh's directives'. This would seem to be borne out by the nature of the antithesis in v. 7b, 'the companion of profligates puts his father to shame'. The verse would then say that one who pays attention to his father's advice is a perceptive son, whereas one who ignores it and so becomes the companion of profligates puts his father to shame. He does this not only because of his disgraceful way of life, but also because his father is thereby confronted with irrefutable evidence that he has failed to exercise a proper parental authority and influence over his son.

This may have been the original significance of the sentence, but in the setting of the chapter I think it probable that what is intended by *tōrā* is not the wisdom of seniority and experience which is imparted with a natural, parental authority, but the Law of Yahweh, just as *mēbīn* here refers to religious illumination rather than intellectual clarity (see above, pp. 620f.). The pious son who has the *tōrā* as a lamp for his feet is contrasted with the wastrel who covers his father with shame. There is then the implication in v. 7a that such a pious son is his father's pride and joy; he covers him with honour and not with shame.

[12, 28] Two verses of related content, in both of which there is an antithesis of *r*ᵉ*šā*ʿ*īm* and *ṣaddīqīm*, are 12 and 28. In view of the near identity of vv. 12b and 28a it is not unreasonable to suppose that *vissātēr* (v. 28a) may afford some indication of the meaning of the obscure *y*ᵉ*ḥuppaś* (v. 12b). At any rate, it would seem to me that since *str* normally means 'hide' in Biblical Hebrew, and since *ḥpś* means 'search' (which is related to 'hide'), it is improbable that the correct solution to the difficulties of these verses will be found by ignoring these indications and postulating homonyms in both cases. This is what G. R. Driver does, but while there is a need for elucidation in the case of v. 12b (*y*ᵉ*ḥuppaś*), there seems no good reason for doubting that *yissātēr* in v. 28a has its usual meaning. In v. 12b, Driver connects *y*ᵉ*ḥuppaś* with Arabic *ḫafaša*, 'prostrated', 'trampled upon', 'pulled down (a building)', and renders 'but when the wicked arise, (ordinary) men are trampled down'. In v. 28a he equates *yissātēr* with Accadian *satāru*, 'demolish', Aramaic *s*ᵉ*tar*, 'destroyed': 'but when the wicked arise, (ordinary) men are destroyed' (*Biblica* 32, pp. 192f.; cf. *JTS* xliv, 1943, p. 17; *HTR* 29, 1936, p. 186). The MT of v. 12b, 'when impious men have the upper hand, the (ordinary) man is sought out' could mean that a community in which the *r*ᵉ*šā*ʿ*īm* hold the reins of power is a bad place for the ordinary man to live. He will be harried and exploited and will hide himself away (so v. 28a explicitly). This thought of the ordinary man making himself inconspicuous or scarce can be made explicit in v. 12b, if *yitḥappēś* is read (so Gemser and KB²) for the rare pual (only here and in Ps. 64.7). The emendation of *ba*ʿ*ᵃlōṣ* to *ba*ʿ*ᵃlōt* (Gemser, Scott) is unnecessary, although it would be a good match for *b*ᵉ*qūm* (v. 12b).

Ringgren supposes that *ʿlṣ* can be translated 'triumph', and this is certainly involved in the rejoicing of the *ṣaddīqīm*. They are in good heart and their morale is high, because they have achieved power in their community and made righteousness effective in it. From this order of righteousness great lustre and decorum derive. Hence the increase of the righteous mentioned in v. 28b is probably an increase in power and social effectiveness, rather than in numbers. This is the sense which is needed, but Toy doubts whether it can be had from *yirbū* (cf. Scott 'flourish' and Ringgren 'come to power'). Gemser notes Kuhn's emendation *yērā'ū*, 'come into prominence'. The special contribution of these verses is that they carry the doctrine of theodicy beyond the *ṣaddīqīm* and *rešāʿīm* themselves and indicate its social consequences. They thus touch on the concern which is characteristic of the sentences in class B. It is not just that the *saddīq* will be rewarded and the *rāšāʿ* punished, but that the life of the community will be influenced for good or evil depending on which class has the upper hand.

[17] Driver supposes that *ʿāšūq* makes a difficulty in v. 17, and that the thought of being burdened with bloodshed or oppressed (in one's conscience) with bloodshed 'goes beyond anything that can fairly be extracted from the Hebrew verb'. Driver suggests either *ʿōśēq* (Aramaic *ʿasaq* 'busied himself') or *ʿōšēq* (Arabic *ʿasiqa* 'clung to', 'was devoted to'); 'a man who is given to shedding blood' or 'a man who makes a habit of shedding blood' (*Biblica* 32, p. 192). The principal question of interpretation is whether this is legal demand or whether it is a theological statement about the efficacy of theodicy. Toy suggests the former and detects a possible reference to the *lex talionis*. 'If a man charged with homicide flees to a city (?), let no one seize (or protect) him.' Toy adds: 'The sentence (which is prose) perhaps belongs in a law book and was here inserted by mistake.' Such a forensic context is suggested by LXX, whose sense is, however, far removed from that of MT ('He who goes surety for a man on a charge of murder will be obliged to flee and will not find security'). I take the verse as a theological statement that a man who has committed murder is sentenced to death by Yahweh and that the theodicy will take effect inexorably, so that it is futile to try by any human action to stay its execution. 'Let them not stop him' means 'Let them not suppose that they can deflect the course of Yahweh's judgement'. The psychological concomitant of this sentence of death is the draining away of the murderer's vitality and in this sense he is oppressed with bloodshed – his own life is burdened with another's lifeblood (*dam nepeš*). Toy wrongly asserts that the pit is not the grave; there is not the slightest doubt that what is indicated here as in 1.12 (see above, pp. 269f.) is the entrance to the shadowy world of the dead. The murderer will be a fugitive until he dies, but however hard he may endeavour to run away from death, he is being borne irresistibly towards the place where life will be swallowed up in death.

Those sentences in which wealth is associated with impiety make up another distinctive group within the general framework of belief in a theodicy (vv. 8, 20, 22, 25, 27). **[8]** Wealth is not necessarily a mark of impiety, for it is not incompatible with compassion and generosity. Only the person who uses his wealth with such responsibility and generosity will be allowed to hold on to it (v. 8b). There is a tendency for wealthy men to be ruthless and greedy; they sacrifice their humanity to an insatiable appetite for money and are careless of the social consequences of their rapacity. They pile up wealth by means of *nešek* and *tarbīt* (v. 8a), 'commission' and 'interest' according to Gemser (p. 114). Gemser identifies *nešek* with the practice of giving a borrower, say, £90, when he is borrowing £100, and retaining the residue as 'commission', while *tarbīt* is 'interest', that is, requiring a borrower of £100 to repay £110. *nešek* and *tarbīt* are forbidden in Lev. 25.36 and *nešek* in Ex. 22.24 and Deut. 23.20. To levy interest is a sin against Yahweh and the needy members of the community. It is incompatible with 'righteousness' (Ezek. 18.8, 13) and is an affront to brotherhood. The poor are to be helped, but their need is not to be made the occasion for commercial gain.

[20] The *'īš 'emūnōt* (v. 20a) is of the same breed as the *ḥōnēn dallīm* of v. 8b. He has sufficient integrity and humanity to enable him to possess wealth without being corrupted by it. It does not destroy his solidarity with his brothers, but rather enables him to give effective expression to his sense of social responsibility. Only the wealthy man who has the insight to interpret his social role and the character to implement it is truly prosperous and blessed. Where wealth is simply the consequence of rapacity, it will prove to be evanescent (v. 20b). Here the vocabulary of a theodicy is employed (*lō' yinnāqe*). Such a person is subject to (Yahweh's) infallible review and will be found guilty; he has no hope of a 'not guilty' verdict, for he is a *rāšā'*, not a *ṣaddīq*.

[22] The phrase *ra' 'ayin* occurs only in one other place (23.6 above, pp. 383f.), and there I have suggested that it may denote one who has no natural benevolence and who is actuated by ill-will rather than good-will towards others. Since, however, the connection of the phrase here with a policy of getting rich quickly at all costs points to the more precise meaning 'avaricious', 'grasping', 'stingy', this may also be what is intended in 23.6, where the advice is given not to eat food with one who is *ra' 'ayin* (cf. 22.9, the *ṭōb 'ayin* is he who gives bread to the poor, i.e., the one who responds generously to need). On the other hand, 'misanthropic' can be defended in 23.6 and 28.22 on the ground that greed for money is just one expression of misanthropy, and 'philanthropic' in 22.9 because generosity towards the poor is an instance of a general philanthropic attitude. The *ra' 'ayin* is unfit for the responsibility of wealth and want will overtake him (v. 22b). This in all probability implies that Yahweh will see to it that only men of character and compassion hold wealth in his community. **[27]** Thus, according to v. 27, he who gives to the poor will never suffer want, whereas whoever hides his eyes (from need) will be the recipient of many a curse (cf. v. 20a). Blessing and hardness of heart are incompatible.

[25] The *reḥab nepeš* is the inordinately greedy person whose appetite for self-gratification (perhaps money or wealth is intended) is insatiable. The phrase may indicate primarily a glutton for food (Barucq) but it undergoes a metaphorical extension of meaning. This is a form of impiety, and so the *reḥab nepeš* is contrasted with the *bōṭēaḥ 'al YHWH*, the man who trusts in Yahweh and who thereby sets proper limits to his desires and ambitions. The *reḥab nepeš* is like the person who will always barge to the front of the queue, standing on the toes of others and jabbing them with his elbows in the process. He is utterly selfish and inconsiderate, and so he brings out the worst in other men; they reciprocate with a self-assertive temper and strife ensues. Hence the *reḥab nepeš* will not get the wealth and prosperity with which he is obsessed for the very reason that he pushes too hard and other men will resist his ambitions. In Yahweh's community he is unacceptable, because he has flaws of character which show him to be unfitted to hold wealth and exercise influence. The man who trusts in Yahweh – who has the basic stance and discipline of piety – will have the responsibility of holding wealth and will enjoy true prosperity (on *yeduššān* see 11.25, above, p. 437).

In vv. 6 and 11 there is a simple contrast between the impious rich and the pious poor. **[6]** Even if the impious man does not lose his wealth or the pious man acquire it (as the foregoing verses maintained), poverty with spiritual wholeness and integrity is better than wealth with radical depravity. The estate of the poor man whose way of life is morally blameless is better than that of the wealthy man who is sick with a moral turpitude (on *ʿiqqēš dᵉrākīm* see v. 18, above, p. 622). **[11]** In v. 11 (see above, p. 621), all that remains for me to comment on is the meaning of *yaḥqᵉrennū*. The poor man with his religious insight (*mēbīn*) searches out the flaws of the wealthy man who has a high opinion of his intellectual powers and his ability to carve out an empire for himself by his own efforts. The *dal mēbīn*, as Toy's translation suggests, probes the chinks in his armour and effectively takes the measure of him. Winton Thomas's suggestion that *ḥqr* is here cognate with Arabic *ḥqr* (II 'despise') tends to make the verse more pedestrian (*JTS* xxxviii, 1937, pp. 402f.; followed by L. Kopf, *VT* ix, 1959, p. 256 and Barucq; cf. Ringgren, p. 109 n.3).

[13] Oesterley remarks that v. 13 is the only sentence in Proverbs which contains a reference to the confession of sin, and that *hōdā* has the sense of confessing sin only here and in Ps. 32.5. The verse is concerned to establish in what prosperity or well-being consist, and finds it in confession of sin and amendment of life. He who conceals his sins (from Yahweh) is pretending that he has no cause for penitence or is seeking to evade it through a sinful pride. He will not humble himself before Yahweh nor discover the truth about himself through submission to the discipline of penitence. Because he does not confess his sin and forsake it, he does not find the mercy of Yahweh in which resides his true prosperity. This verse has affinities with the spirit of prophetic preaching and has to be numbered with the few verses of Proverbs in which the prophetic emphasis is detectable.

Class B

Verses 3, 15, 16, which describe the consequences of misrule, seem to me to observe rather than to dogmatize, and for this reason I have placed them in class B rather than class C. They place on record the conclusions reached as a consequence of the careful observation of misrule and its effects, but, for the most part (the exception is v. 16b), they do not assert that those who abuse power will be brought down and that only the righteous ruler will prosper. Even v. 16b is perhaps better explained as an empirical judgement that probity in politics is the best policy than as a dogmatic assertion which assumes a theodicy (see below, pp. 629f.).

[3] In v. 3a, *geber rāš* = 'poor man' does not give the required sense, and another meaning has to be sought for *rāš* or else the text has to be emended. BH indicates that *rāšā'* (Frankenberg's emendation, cf. Toy) has the support of LXX, but this does not accord with the facts. LXX reads: 'A courageous (perhaps here 'masterful') man oppresses (or 'accuses') the poor with impieties'. *ἐν ἀσεβείαις συκοφαντεῖ* is exegesis of *'ōšēq* and *ἀνδρεῖος* renders *geber*. Hence *rāšā'* has no textual support and, in any case, is not a happy proposal. Barucq translates 'a powerful man' and connects *rāš* with Mishnaic Hebrew *ršy*, *ršh*, Aramaic *rš'*, *ršy*, 'to have power' (cf. Jean-Hoftijzer, *ršy*[4], Palm., adj., 'principal', 'supreme'). This is the sense which is needed, but I would suggest that *rāš* should be vocalized *rōš* (= *rō'š*), 'principal'. This is also the meaning of *rā'šîm* (cf. Gemser, p. 114) in 13.23 (see above, pp. 462f.) and is to be compared with *rō'š*, 'chief' (Deut. 20.9 *et al.*, see KB[2]). Cf. GK §131b for the construction. Perhaps *kōhēn hārō'š* in II Kings 25.18 means 'the priest (who is) the chief man', i.e., apposition rather than the construct relationship.

The *geber rāš* is in a position of authority and can be a force either for good or evil. If he slides into irresponsibility and abuses his power, he will be a blight on the life of the community. His oppressive measures will bear most heavily on those in the community who are least able to take care of themselves and so he will be an exploiter of the poor. Such an administrator or executive is like the hard, driving rain which lays and spoils the crops and fruit and is the harbinger of famine (or, perhaps, like the torrential rain which washes away the soil and brings on famine). The latter is favoured by KB[2], Gemser, Ringgren.

[15] Such a ruler is like a roaring lion or a prowling bear. In the one case the appetite for prey is indicated by ferocity of sound, and in the other by predatory movements. The poor are as much at the mercy of a *mōšēl rāšā'* as are the potential victims of a lion on the hunt or a bear on the prowl.

[16] Although there are minor textual dubieties in v. 16, the only important decision which has to be taken concerns *w^erab*. The requirements of parallelism indicate that there should be a verb to correspond with *ya'^arîk* in v. 16b. For this reason, the suggestion that *w^e* should be deleted and v. 16a read 'a prince who is an oppressor is lacking in intelligence' (cf. Toy, Gemser) or 'a prince lacking intelligence is a great oppressor' (cf. Scott) is not entirely satisfactory. *yereb* (hiphil of *rbh*) should be read (Dyserinck, *yārēb*, hiphil of *rbb*; cf. Toy and Ringgren): 'An undiscriminating ruler piles oppression upon oppression'. *nāgīd* may be a gloss (Toy, Gemser, Scott), in which case it may be explained as a consequence of the assimilation of v. 16 to the theme of v. 15 (*mōšēl rāšā'*). The singular *śōnē'* is indicated by Q., and Gemser reads *w^eśōnē'* with the versions. There is not much at stake exegetically in these emendations. The oppressor lacks perceptiveness, and the abuse of power is a form of stupidity and proof of an incapacity for responsibility which will not be tolerated for long. It is the honest and honourable man who does not stoop to corruption that will have a long and successful tenure of office. If *nāgīd* is a gloss, the meaning of the sentence may simply have been that the practitioner of graft and oppression is not the clever fellow he supposes himself to be. He is really stupid and short-sighted, for wisdom is inseparable from probity; it is the man who will have nothing to do with sharp practice, and to whom every form of injustice and dishonesty is anathema, that will enjoy a long (and successful) life.

[2] Verse 2 is so full of obscurities that one can only hazard a number of guesses as to what may be intended by it. LXX has been thought to provide some clues to the original Hebrew text (cf. Barucq). It reads: 'Because of the sin of impious men disputes arise, but a resourceful man will extinguish them.' Thus *'ereṣ* has been emended to *'ārīṣ* (Frankenberg, Gemser, Driver), *rabbīm* to *rībīm* (Jäger, Gemser, Driver), *śārehā* to *yē'ōrū* (Gemser) and *yōdēa' kēn* to *yid'ākūn*, with *ya'^arīk* deleted as a dittography of *yōdēa' kēn* (Bickell, Gemser, cf. BH). The verse then reads: 'Through a violent man's transgression disputes are awakened, but they are extinguished by a perceptive man.' Such an elucidation of the sentence is in accord with Driver's suggestion (*Biblica* 32, pp. 191f.) that **yirše* should be read for *śārehā* (**ršh*, Aramaic *rš'*, 'to bring a case against', A. E. Cowley, p. 104, 28[8]; Jean-Hoftijzer, *ršy*[1], 'to raise an action against'). Verse 2a then reads: 'Through a violent man's transgression legal actions are raised', and v. 2b contrasts a peacemaker with this trouble-maker. The *'ārīṣ* is the insensitive, aggressive person who has a genius for making enemies and driving others into the law courts to get legal satisfaction. The *mēbīn* damps down the flames of controversy and deflects men's thoughts from litigation to reconciliation.

The other main possibility is to leave MT as it stands (Scott deletes *yōdēa'* as a gloss on *mēbīn*) and to take *kēn* as 'order', i.e., political and social order. Toy's suggestion that *ṣārehā*, 'its adversaries', or *ṣārōtehā*, 'its calamities', should be substituted for *śārehā* does not help very much. Gemser supposes that the MT of v. 2a may allude to the instability with which the Northern Kingdom was plagued. In this case, the meaning is that a land gets the kind of statesmen which it deserves. When violence begets violence and rulers come and go, this is a reflection of a deep-seated and widespread social indiscipline and disorder. Such a community will not raise knowledgable and perceptive statesmen, and no tradition of stable rule and judicious management of affairs will be established within it. This is how I have translated the verse.

[19] Verse 19 is almost identical with 12.11 (see above, p. 444), and may be taken as an expression of Boström's 'agricultural ideal' (see on 27.23–27, above, pp. 618f.). It is concerned to discriminate between agriculture and other 'empty' pursuits in terms of satisfaction and profit. The empty pursuits which are condemned as profitless are perhaps mercantile and financial transactions, and the verse probably contains no more than a warning against occupations which are bad economic risks. It is not just that a farmer will always have enough to eat, whereas a speculator may starve, but that the one occupation has a hinterland of social value and makes a basic contribution to the stability and health of the community, while the other is socially valueless and even pernicious.

[21] Another social problem is touched upon in v. 21, namely, the employment of the bribe to defeat the ends of justice. Any deviation from strict judicial impartiality is a grave social evil, and the problem is made all the more acute by the circumstance that a man is prepared to commit perjury for a very small consideration. This suggests that it is the suborning of witnesses rather than the corrupting of the judge which is envisaged (cf. 24.24, above, p. 573).

[23] The thought of v. 23 is similar to that of 27.5 and 27.14 (above, pp. 610, 619). Plain speaking may subject a friendship to great strain and appear to be a false step. Silence, it may be argued, would have been a better response (27.5), or even words of reassurance designed to please and flatter (cf. 27.14). But whoever takes the risk of speaking the truth in love is the kind of person who is worth having as a friend and ultimately this will be recognized. His words which seemed to wound will be seen to have had salutary effects, and he will rise in the regard of the one who has benefited from his integrity and courage. Complete honesty is the cement of friendship. The meaning of *'aḥ^{a}ray* is uncertain. Toy deletes, and Gemser, Ringgren, Scott and Barucq translate 'finally', 'in the long run'. G. R. Driver (*ZAW* 50, 1932, p. 147) suggests that *'aḥ^{a}ray* is an adjective with an Aramaizing ending (*ay*) having the same meaning as Accadian *aḫur(r)u*, i.e., 'back-standing', used of an ordinary person who does not stand out from the mass of his fellows. He translates: '(As) a rebuker a common man shall find more favour than (as) a flatterer.' BH, following Bickell (cf. KB³), suggests that *'aḥ^a^rāw*, transposed after *lāšōn*, should be read, i.e., the person who reproves honestly will be more highly regarded than the one who tries to efface the impression of his plain speaking by subsequent flattery. LXX *ὁδούς* points to *'^o^rāḥōt*. *'orḥō* makes sense and may have been the original.

[24] Toy is to be followed in his view that v. 24 has a general, moral rather than a specifically legal character. It is not based on a particular legal demand and has more the character of ethical reflection on a type of behaviour which, because it is so unnatural, is especially abhorrent and reprehensible. For it might be supposed that one place where the legal draftsman need not intrude is the home, where all the conditions of solidarity of interest are fulfilled. Where there is a filial relationship affection should run in the blood and there should be no occasion to legislate for justice. Whoever plunders his parents and makes out that he is entitled to do it is an unnatural son – an associate of murderers (Scott, 'the next thing to a parricide'). The measure of his perversion is not that he robs them, but that he does it without any sense of shame or guilt ('there is no wrong in it').

Chapter 29

The dominant formal feature is antithetic parallelism (vv. 2, 3, 4, 6, 7, 8, 10, 11, 15, 16, 18?, 23, 25, 26, 27). There is one instance of synonymous or synthetic parallelism (v. 22), one of Instruction (v. 17, imperative followed by two final clauses) and the remaining verses are continuous sentences (vv. 1, 5, 9, 12, 13, 14, 19, 20, 21, 24). The chapter is almost devoid of imagery; v. 5, which is the only instance of its employment, is metaphor rather than simile. The motive clause in v. 19, which is associated with a statement and not the characteristic imperative, may be regarded as a formal element of the Instruction transferred to the wisdom sentence. Verse 20 ('You have seen') has the same form as 22.29 and 26.12.

Class A: vv. 1, 3, 8, 9, 11, 15, 17, 19, 20, 21, 22, 23.
Class B: vv. 4, 5, 10, 12, 14.
Class C: vv. 2, 6, 7, 13, 16, 18, 24, 25, 26, 27.

Class A

The general theme is wisdom and unwisdom, and this is discussed particularly in its relationship to educational discipline and indiscipline. In the sentences with antithetic parallelism (vv. 3, 8, 11, 15, 23), the constrast is present within the scope of a single verse. **[1]** The well-worn topic of incorrigibility is resumed in v. 1. The person who is not amenable to correction is simply made more recalcitrant by repeated doses of discipline. He has the fatal flaw of incorrigibility, and, as a consequence, what ought to be salutary in its effects is fatal for him. It hardens him in his wilfulness and wrong-headedness. A point in this process is reached when his own blind stubbornness will break him to pieces and this will be the end. This is a moment of disintegration from whose effects there is no cure; the pieces of life cannot be gathered up again and the wholeness of his life is no longer a realizable possibility. He has willed his own destruction.

[23] Pride is a constituent of this attitude which produces sclerosis and then disintegration. Pride is a way of death, for the proud man must always know everything even if he knows nothing; so he is never in need of a teacher and is the worst of learners. Because he cannot sit down at another man's feet, he must suffer the consequences of his ignorance. In view of this major flaw he will be a stranger all his life to discrimination and well-proportioned behaviour, and will come to grief. He will be reduced to the level at which the arrogant man must eventually settle, for pride is a way of descent to mediocrity or worse, and the road to recognition and attainment is that taken by the modest learner. Others will say of him who has become wise through unremitting intellectual humility that this is a man of weight who deserves reputation and is fit to exercise power. Hence he will be able to grasp *kābōd*. *Be intellectually humble, curious to learn.*

An aspect of indiscipline which looms large in Prov. 1–9 is sexual promiscuity. The prostitute is seen as the largest single threat to the young man; this is an all too familiar way of death and her house can be described as the very entrance to the realm of death. **[3]** In v. 3 such behaviour is described as ruinous, and, in view of the antithetic parallelism, the implication is that nothing is more calculated to break a father's heart than that his son should make himself a pauper through his fondness for prostitutes. Such behaviour here, as in Prov. 1–9, is a paradigm of unwisdom which can be contrasted with that of the son who loves wisdom and rejoices his father's heart

(Gemser's suggestion, p. 114, that *rōʿe zōnōt* should be translated 'one who practises fornication', is not an alternative which commends itself to me).

[15, 17] Verses 15 and 17 are also concerned with matters of parental discipline and represent that corporal punishment is an indispensable element of discipline and education. Corrections administered by the rod produce wisdom, but the youth who is not under discipline is running to waste. Apparently free as the wind, he is in fact abandoned to the chaos of destructive impulses whose slave he is, and he will bring shame on his mother. Hence the advice of v. 17: Discipline your son so that he may be a source of comfort (or satisfaction) and pleasure to you.

[19] A servant is appropriately disciplined by corporal punishment rather than verbal reproof. It is not that he is too ignorant or stupid to understand what is being said to him. He completely grasps the terms of the reproof, but he is deliberately unresponsive. The implication is that a servant will not be made to change his ways by words, however hard, for words do not hurt him and the only way of teaching him a lesson is by making clear to him that you will inflict pain until he does what you want.

[21] Verse 21 is also concerned with the right management and disciplining of a servant, this much being clear despite the obscurity of *mānōn* (v. 21b). LXX, which takes a different sense from the verse, can only be regarded as an incorrect paraphrase ('He who is pampered from childhood will be a servant and in the end will come to grief'), and it is dubious whether one can draw the exact textual inference that LXX (also a passive in Pesh. and Targ.) read *mᵉpunnāq* as Reider does (J. Reider, *VT* iv, 1954, pp. 285f.). Reider follows the broad lines of LXX, reading *ʿebed* instead of *ʿabdō* (dittography of *wāw*) and explaining *mānōn* as 'weakling' on the basis of Arabic *naʾna*, 'to be weak', *munaʾna*', 'weak', 'feeble'. Even if *mᵉpunnāq* were read, 'he who is pampered from his youth is a slave' can only be had from *mᵉpunnāq minnōʿar ʿebed* by some stretching and straining of these words. MT should be retained in v. 21a ('He who pampers a servant from youth') and then the 'his' of *ʾaḥᵃrītō* could refer either to the one who pampers his servant or to the servant who is pampered. In the long run he will become a *mānōn*, a word which is still unelucidated. Gemser, Ringgren and Scott make the guess 'refractory', following V, and thus refer 'his' to the servant. Similarly with Barucq's rendering, 'will end up by having him as his heir' (*nīn*, 'offspring', 'posterity'). The same derivation is implied in Delitzsch's rendering which, however, refers 'his' to the master: 'He will finally become a nursery', i.e., his house will be overrun by the offspring of the servant whom he has spoilt. I follow Gemser.

Wisdom is associated with a calm bearing and measured words; unwisdom with impulsive, passionate behaviour (vv. 8, 11, 20, 22; cf. especially the quiet or tranquil man in *Amenemope*, above, pp. 106f.). **[8]** Supercilious and arrogant men fan the flames of dissension (so Toy and Gemser), and exacerbate every difficult and delicate situation in a city, but wise men seek to neutralize the irrational gestures of overheated tempers as a necessary preparation for a cool and reasonable appraisal of the issues. **[11]** Irascibility is a mark of folly; the wise man keeps control of his temper. The fool is the slave of impulse and is at the mercy of every moment when he chances to feel irritation. The wise man cannot avoid feeling irritation but he does not show it. He is characterized by self-mastery and composure, so that his irritation does not explode into anger. He reimposes an inward calm on his mounting anger, and stifles it before it comes to the surface in injudicious words or other ill-considered overt behaviour. He is never driven by passion into foolish responses. I agree with Ringgren (p. 111, n.1) that no emendation of MT is required here. The construction may be pregnant, as is supposed by RV ('keepeth it back and stilleth it') and Barucq, or we should simply translate *beʾāḥōr yešabbeḥennā*, 'restrains it' (Ringgren, cf. LXX ταμιεύεται, 'has self-control').

One aspect of the provocative behaviour of *ʾanšē lāṣōn* (v. 8) or the explosive behaviour of the *kesīl* (v. 11) is the way in which they speak. The misuse of language, whether it is the liability to a passionate outburst of speech or the malevolent design to set men against each other with words which wound self-esteem and inflame passions, is an extreme expression of folly. Words are a political instrument in that they should always make a positive and beneficial contribution to human relationships. Whoever is carried away by the cleverness of his polemic, even if it is in fact devastating in its effects, is misusing language, because there is no constructive intent in what he is doing. The wise man always speaks in order to dispel misunderstanding or solve problems of social relations. He has these social objectives in view and directs his words towards them. **[20]** In v. 20 it is the ill-considered, rash and hasty utterance which comes under fire. Whoever speaks before he has had leisure to think, and to weigh carefully the form of words which is most judicious and effective, is a fool of the worst kind (cf. 26.12b, above, p. 596).

[22] In v. 22, the effects of ungovernable anger (cf. v. 11) are described. The volcanic temper creates havoc when it erupts. It engenders heat and changes the debate into strife. Thoughtless speech gives offence and is a source of social injury. It produces the explosive moment when understanding and communication break down and disagreements harden into factions or become festering vendettas.

[9] Verse 9 apparently confines itself to description, and simply indicates the behaviour which a wise man has to be prepared to tolerate, if he has the misfortune to become involved in litigation with a fool. He must reckon with unreasonable and objectionable behaviour and a complete lack of moderation and proportion. The fool will go on interminably, now raging and ranting, now laughing and sneering (with an affected superiority). Or perhaps *wᵉʾēn nāḥat* indicates that with this involvement the wise man must resign himself to bedlam and accept a temporary estrangement from his tranquil and reasonable existence (Gemser). Eissfeldt (see Ringgren, p. 110, n.4) suggests the translation 'and there is no reconciliation', in which case the sentence transcends description and points to the futility of exposing oneself to the irritations and frustrations of such a legal process. However, the judge decides, and even if a legal victory is scored, the fool will not be persuaded of his unreason. If the effect is not to make an end of personal estrangement and misunderstanding and to restore a right relation between man and man (and what process of litigation can do that), the whole enterprise is mistaken. Barucq follows V in supposing that v. 9b refers to the wise man, 'whether he vexes himself or laughs he will have no more peace' (cf. Toy). There is little doubt that it is the behaviour of the fool which is described in v. 9b.

Class B

Two verses are concerned with aspects of misanthropy (vv. 5, 10) and the other three state that righteousness is the sure foundation of a throne (vv. 4, 12, 14). **[5]** The sycophant is not to be trusted, for words which are too smooth and too obviously designed to gratify are a form of premeditated malice and a cloak for evil intent. They disarm the person to whom they are addressed, and while he savours the pleasure of hearing them and lowers all his defences, a net is being spread about his feet. This is the object of the exercise, and he is disarmed and trussed up while the glow of pleasure is still within him (cf. 26.28, above, pp. 605f.; 27.14, above, p. 619; 28.23, above, pp. 631f.).

[10] The anti-social behaviour of v. 10 consists in violence and a carelessness for the sanctity of human life. Such persons hate the man of integrity, the one who is free from deficiencies, excesses and distortions in his social behaviour and who, in every respect, has a due regard for the well-being of his neighbour. The *tām* wills the well-being of those with whom he has relations, and not their injury. The second half of the verse is more difficult, since the usual meaning of *y^{e}baqq^{e}šū napšō* (cf. Barucq) is 'seek to take his life' and not 'seek to preserve his life', which is the sense desiderated. Barucq suggests that *biqqēš nepeš* is here to be equated with *biqqēš pānīm*; the meaning is then that upright men seek out the company of the *tām* – as an expression of the high regard in which they hold him. Another possibility is that *bqr* should be read for *bqš*; then the sense will be that upright men will place a high value on the life of the *tām* and will be concerned to protect it from all injury and outrage (Gemser, Scott, cf. Ringgren who takes this sense out of *y^{e}baqq^{e}šū*). G. R. Driver's translation (*JSS* xii, 1967, p. 108), 'The upright amply esteem his life', associating *y^{e}baqq^{e}šū* with Accadian *baqāšu* (see on 11.27, above p. 434), yields this sense. The upright make much of his life, i.e., hold it in high regard. My translation, however, assumes that the sense 'have regard for' is derived from 'seek', i.e., 'seek the welfare of'.

[4] It is by establishing justice (*mišpāṭ*) in his land that a king confers on it a massive stability. This is a comprehensive social justice which implies the absence of oppression and despotic abuse and the according to every man a truly human worth. Such a community does not need to be coerced or held together by external constraints because it possesses an inner unity which expresses itself in the general will to give to every man his due and always to leave room for the working of compassion. This creates a social solidarity which will last. A ruler who is interested only in levying taxation and bending the backs of his people with ever more swingeing financial imposts is ignorant of the conditions of stability. He will create a division between his regime or establishment and the people at large and this will be the beginning of the end. Whenever his relation with his people ceases to have a truly human character, he has begun to demolish his community. When his people are degraded to being pawns in his game, chattels at his disposal, means to his self-aggrandizement, the process of disintegration is under way and the country will fall to pieces (*'īš t^e^rūmōt*, 'one eager for contributions', i.e., taxes [KB²]). Gemser connects *t^e^rūmōt* with Arabic *rāma*, 'to long after' (so also D. Winton Thomas, *JTS*, xxxviii, 1937, p. 403) and translates the phrase 'a greedy man' (cf. V *vir avarus*). This would make little difference to the exegesis. Barucq thinks that the reference is to bribery; a king who is amenable to bribes is the opposite of one who rules with *mišpāṭ*. This is less likely. **[14]** To be steadfast in the determination that the poor will have justice is to do *mišpāṭ* (v. 14, cf. v. 7, below, pp. 641f.), and the king who is so resolved need have no fear for the stability of his throne (cf. 16.12, above, p. 491).

[12] A ruler will get the kind of officials which he deserves, and if he is not himself a stickler for truth and probity, he will not attract men of such calibre into his service. 'Paying attention to a false word' means accepting it as true and acting on it without investigating the affair and getting to the bottom of it. It is therefore the king's slackness and irresponsibility, rather than any vicious addiction to untruth, which is indicated. Men who love the truth will not tolerate this lack of rigour and probity and will not serve him, but those who want uninterrupted peace and liberty to do evil, and to poison the life of the community with lies for their own ends will seize the opportunity of serving such a master.

Class C

The familiar collocation of righteousness and well-being, fear of Yahweh and security, reappears in a group of verses (vv. 6, 16, 25, 26). **[6]** G. R. Driver argues that sense can be had from v. 6 only if *mōqēš* and *yārūn* of MT are emended to *mūqāš* and *yādōn* respectively. The first is supported by Pesh. and Targ., and the second by two Hebrew manuscripts (Arabic *dāna*, *yadānu*, 'continued'): 'In transgression the evil man is snared, but the righteous man remains (in security and well-being) and rejoices' (*Biblica* 32, pp. 193f.). MT of v. 6a is not, however, impossible, and it has been translated by Gemser, Ringgren and Scott, who have adopted Pinsker's emendation (*yārūṣ* for *yārūn*) in v. 6b: 'There is a snare in the wicked man's transgression, but the righteous man runs on rejoicing.' The minimum alteration of MT required would be *yārūn* to *yārōn* ('the righteous man exults and rejoices', so Barucq). I emend to *yārūṣ*; 'exults and rejoices' might be *hendiadys*, i.e., 'is deliriously happy'. Verse 6a may mean that the evil man is snared by his own wrong-doing (so Driver). I take it to refer to his unsuccessful attempts to snare the righteous man.

[16] The suggestion has been made (Gemser, p. 114) that *birbōt* *rᵉšāʿīm* means 'when the wicked are in authority' (Jewish Aramaic *rᵉbū*, *rᵉbūtā*, 'high office'). In 29.2 *rbh* and *mšl* are parallel, and there is a good case for translating *yirbū* 'come to power' in 28.28. This sense can be had out of Hebrew *rbh*, 'to increase', i.e., increase in power and influence, and I adopt the translation 'come to power' in 28.28 and 29.2. 29.16, however, is most naturally rendered, 'When wicked men are on the increase, wrong-doing increases.' To translate, 'When wicked men come to power, wrong-doing increases', would give the impression that *rbh* is deliberately being used with two different senses in 16a and I do not believe that this is so. Verse 16b asserts that righteous men look on (with pleasure) at their downfall. Yahweh enforces his theodicy.

[2] In v. 2, as in 28.12, 28 (see above, pp. 624f.), theodicy does not focus on the well-being of righteous individuals, but on the effect which they have on the society where they attain to influence and power. They preside over a community whose keynote is joy, and which contrasts with one over which a *rāšāʿ* rules (the versions have a plural, LXX ἀρχόντων δὲ ἀσεβῶν), where only the groans of the oppressed are heard.

[25] To cringe in fear before men (in authority) will only prove a snare, but he who relies on Yahweh will be inaccessible to the assaults of his enemies (cf. v. 26). The antithesis is between servility or cowardly fear and trust in Yahweh, and this is apparently missed by Kopf, who urges that *ḥerdat ʾādām* means 'to seek refuge in men' (*VT* ix, 1959, p. 257). Trust in Yahweh, if it is thoroughgoing and comprehensive, is incompatible with fearfulness, because whoever relies for safety on Yahweh is safe indeed.

[26] It is the way of men to suppose that their merits are not acknowledged and that society undervalues their worth, and they seek to repair this supposed injustice by cultivating the favour of the ruler who has the power of patronage and preferment and who can advance their cause. But then they are asking for privileged treatment, and they cannot have this without committing an injustice against those who live side by side with them. If a man really wants justice (*mišpāṭ*) and not favours, he need not lay siege to a ruler in order to have it. He will get it by waiting in trust for Yahweh to give it to him, and not by lobbying a ruler.

[27] *tōʿēbā* is the repugnance which accompanies Yahweh's verdict of guilty on the *rešāʿīm*, and *rāṣōn* is the approval which is the inward concomitant of his acquittal of the *ṣaddīqīm* (see on 12.22, above, p. 448). This repugnance also exists between *ṣaddīq* and *rāšāʿ* (v. 27); the one has an intense antipathy for crookedness and the other for uprightness.

[13] Verse 13 says much less than those verses which confidently assert a theodicy. It observes that the poor man and the person who exercises (oppressive) power over him exist side by side in every society, and that both are contained within an order which Yahweh created and upholds ('Yahweh illumines the eyes of both' means much the same as 'Yahweh is the maker of them all', 22.2b). The verse does not explain how the co-existence of the poor man and his oppressor is compatible with Yahweh's rule; it simply says that all social structures contain this polarity of wealth and poverty, power and weakness (cf. Toy, 'there must be social classes, but God governs all'). There would seem to be here some accommodation of the doctrine of theodicy to the hard facts of life (see on 22.2, above, p. 569). LXX translates: 'When creditor and debtor have a meeting with each other, the Lord has both of them under surveillance.' This brings the thought of the verse more into line with theodicy. Yahweh knows what is going on, so let the creditor bear that in mind and not bring inhuman pressure to bear on the man who owes him money.

[18] Two verses which are off the beaten track are 18 and 24. In v. 18 it is not clear why the cessation of prophecy (which must be the meaning of *beʾēn ḥāzōn*, cf. I Sam. 3.1) should be contrasted with keeping the Law (*tōrā* has this definitive sense, as Barucq and Scott suppose, rather than 'instruction', the translation of Gemser and Ringgren; see above, pp. 622f.). Nor is it obvious why the indiscipline or disorder of a community consequent on the cessation of prophecy should be set in antithesis to the blessedness of the *individual* who keeps the Law (of Yahweh). It is just possible that this shift of emphasis from community to individual is deliberate and provides a clue to the intention of the sentence. The age of prophecy is past, and there is now no word of God addressed in the prophetic manner to the *nation* with clarity and authority. In these circumstances it is vulnerable to indecision and indiscipline, but the remedy lies in the Law, response to whose demands is the affair of the *individual* (cf. LXX: 'There is certainly no guide for a lawless nation, but blessed is he who keeps the Law'). The world of blessing and curse is now the world of the individual and if he chooses the righteousness of the Law he chooses blessing.

It seems to me unlikely that v. 18a means anything else than 'when there is no (prophetic) vision, a people are indisciplined' (cf. LXX). G. R. Driver (*Welt d. Orients*, 1948, p. 235) connects *ḥāzōn* with Accadian *ḫaziān*, 'magistrate' (cf. Gemser, p. 114, Mishnaic Hebrew *ḥāzān*, *ḥazzān*, 'superintendent'), and notes that it was taken by LXX as referring to a person (ἐξηγητής 'guide'): 'Without a magistrate people are indisciplined, but a guardian of the Law keeps it on the right course' (*yeʾaššerēhū*). The effective rule of law is essential to the well-being of a community. This disposes of the reference to prophetic vision which I retain, although it is the solitary reference to *ḥāzōn* in the book of Proverbs.

[24] Verse 24 hinges on belief in the power of the curse. Toy makes heavy weather of this verse. This man has compromised himself by accepting a share of a thief's loot, but he is not 'called into court as a witness' (so Toy). This would imply the general knowledge that he was a witness, which is just the thing that he conceals. He is not free to come forward as a witness because he is implicated in the theft. The situation is that which is envisaged in Lev. 5.1 (cf. Judg. 17.2) where it is said that if any person who has seen or heard anything in connection with a crime does not volunteer as a witness when the whole community is confronted with this obligation by public intimation, he must bear his iniquity. The entire community, in view of this public ceremony, hears the curse and it is this curse which the thief's accomplice also hears. He cannot come forward because he shares guilt for the crime, but in remaining silent he exposes himself to the power of the curse and chooses the way of death (*śōnēʾ napšō* means 'hates his life' [Gemser and Ringgren] rather than 'is an enemy to himself' or 'hates himself' [Toy, Barucq and Scott]).

[7] Verse 7 is another (cf. 28.13, above, p. 628) of the few examples of a wisdom sentence which is an instrument of prophetic teaching. The key to understanding it is the awareness that 'know' and 'knowledge' are being used in the prophetic sense, and that we have to reckon here with a prophetic reinterpretation of the vocabulary of wisdom (this applies also to *yābīn*). To 'know' what constitutes justice for the poor includes the acknowledgement that this is so, and the doing of justice to the poor. It is in these terms that Jeremiah defines knowledge of Yahweh in his address to Jehoiakim: 'Did not your father eat and drink and do justice (*mišpāṭ*) and righteousness (*ṣᵉdāqā*)? Then it was well with him. He did justice (*dān dīn*) to the poor and needy, then it was well. Is not this to know me, says Yahweh?' (Jer. 22.15f.). Consequently I do not believe that v. 7b presents any problem of interpretation. When Toy says that *lō' yābīn dā'at* indicates lack of intellectual clarity and vigour and that this reference is out of place, he is not reckoning with the reinterpretation of this vocabulary which is intended. Nor are Scott and Barucq correct in supposing that v. 7a merely speaks of a particular item of knowledge and that *da'at* in v. 7b shares this limitation (cf. Gemser). This is also what is involved in the suggestion of Winton Thomas (cf. Gemser, p. 114), that *da'at* should be derived from **d'h* (Arabic *da'ā*, 'sought', 'asked', 'demanded'), and understood as (legal) claim (*JTS* xxxviii, 1937, pp. 401f.). Caring for the poor and defenceless in the community is not a bit of knowledge but actually constitutes knowledge (of Yahweh). In view of his active social concern (i.e., because he 'knows' what is required in order to give justice to the poor), the *ṣaddīq* has this knowledge of Yahweh, but the *rāšā'* has no grasp of it. 'Grasp' is used, not in the sense of intellectual grasp, but of an understanding which is open only to one inside the social situation who out of his concern and participation wills to give justice to the poor and needy.

VII

POEMS AND NUMERICAL SAYINGS

A. CHAPTER 30

vv. 1–4 *The Words of Agur*

The problem of ascertaining the extent of the words of Agur is made more severe by the insuperable difficulties of v. 1. It may be that they consist only of vv. 1b, 2, 3, which are in the first person, and they certainly do not go beyond v. 4 (so Toy). Although Gemser describes vv. 1–14 as 'the words of Agur' (also Ringgren), he recognizes that these verses are not an original unity and that their arrangement is editorial and depends on the catchword principle or on affinity of theme.

Scott supposes that vv. 1–9 contain a dialogue with a sceptic who is answered in vv. 5f. by a believer who then appends a prayer in vv. 7–9. Barucq, who makes the same division (also C. C. Torrey, 'Proverbs, chapter 30', *JBL* lxxiii, 1954, p. 95), takes v. 4 as the reply of God in view of which nothing more is to be said (vv. 5f.). He acknowledges that the connection of vv. 7–9 with what precedes is not very evident.

There is some virtue in Scott's suggestion, but vv. 1–9 are not formally a dialogue and vv. 5f. are to be regarded as subsequent corrective comment whose intention is not so much to disavow vv. 1–4, as to put the matter in a proper perspective, by noting that the hidden God is nevertheless one who has made himself known by his word (so Toy). There is therefore no original artistic unity between vv. 1–4 and 5–6. Moreover, vv. 7–9 are concerned with quite different matters and are probably attached to v. 6 only because *kzb*, which occurs in v. 6, is also present in v. 8. This is a superficial link, since v. 8 is not concerned with falsehood in the same sense as v. 6. It is a prayer for honesty and integrity linked with another for enough to eat, and is far removed from v. 6, which warns against tampering with the word of God (see below).

In v. 1, MT reads: 'The words of Agur, the son of Yaqeh, the oracle, the saying of the man to Ithiel, to Ithiel and Ucal.' In such a verse, where there is hardly a glimmer of light, one feels powerless to make even the first move towards its elucidation. If *hammaśśā'ī* is read for *hammaśśā'* (Ringgren, Scott), Agur stems from the same area as Lemuel, perhaps a north Arabian locality (Gen. 25.14), but this may be a false lead, for *hammaśśā'* and *n*^{e}*'ūm* are both terms of prophetic vocabulary and may be parts of the same problem. The words which follow are a confession of human failure (vv. 2f.), and not *maśśā'* in the prophetic sense; moreover, the phrase *n*^{e}*'ūm haggeber* is very odd, if *haggeber* is Agur. The best that can be done is to read *hammaśśā'ī* and to suggest that the change of text has been brought about by the proximity of *hammaśśā'ī* to *n*^{e}*'ūm* (the two associated as items of prophetic vocabulary).

The words of Agur are then thought to begin after *n*^{e}*'ūm haggeber* and the text is vocalized *lā'ītī 'ēl lā'ītī 'ēl w*^{e}*'ēkel*: 'I am weary O God, I am weary O God and exhausted' (cf. Barucq for variants of this emendation), or *lū 'ittī 'ēl lū 'ittī 'ēl*: 'O that God were with me, O that God were with me' (BH). Gemser (cf. Bickell) proposes *lō'e 'ēt hā'ēl lō'e 'ēt hā'ēl wayyūkāl*, 'who has exerted himself much with God, who has exerted himself much with God and triumphed.' The first of these emendations has the merit that it keeps to the consonantal text, but it does not produce a very impressive line with the repetition of 'I am weary' and 'O God'. Torrey urges that 'O God' requires *hā'ēl* and that the emendation does not fit the context. Since the context is so problematical, the value of his second observation is doubtful.

Torrey's other point has more substance. He maintains that if 'I am weary O God, I am weary O God and exhausted', or, 'O that God were with me, O that God were with me that I should have power' (*w*^{e}*'ūkāl*), has been changed into 'To Ithiel, to Ithiel and Ucal', it is impossible to believe that this can have happened by accident. It can only be explained as a deliberate process of mystification, in which case one has to look for a motive. Why should such a riddle be constructed? There seems nothing objectionable or dangerous about either of the conjectural reconstructions which would make it appear expedient in the interests of orthodoxy to conceal them. If, then, we are to think in terms of deliberate mystification, we should look for an original which has the appearance of being theologically scandalous. This original, according to Torrey, was *lō' 'ānōkī 'ēl lō' 'ªnī'ēl we'ūkāl*: 'I am not God, I am not God that I should have power', or, 'I am not a god, I am not a god that I should have power'.

The Jewish editor did not like the association of the human 'I' and God, while, on the other hand, he had conscientious scruples about suppressing the text, so he solved the problem by rendering the Hebrew into Aramaic and grouping the characters in such a way that the two names Ithiel and Ucal were indicated. The Aramaic would read *lā' 'ītay'ēl lā' 'ītay'ēl we'ūkāl* (*JBL* lxxiii, pp. 93–96). Torrey's other contention that the dislocation of ch. 30 in LXX is connected with the dubious theology of its opening verse is not so well made. Torrey supposes that the chapter was suppressed in the Hebrew text and that this explains its absence in LXX between 29 and 31. The Greek translator, however, found the two halves of the chapter separated and inserted them in 24, vv. 1–14 (of ch. 30) after v. 22 and vv. 15–33 after v. 34. The reading in LXX is to be explained as an attempt to render the offending verse harmless ('These things says the man to those who trust in God and I cease'), and when the scandal in v. 1 of the Hebrew had been suitably concealed, the entire chapter was subsequently restored to its original place in the Hebrew Bible. This tortuous argument makes the dislocation of ch. 30 and 31.1–9 in LXX consequent on the theological aversion felt towards 30.1, and then it has to make the assumption that the Hebrew text of chs. 30 and 31.1–9 was suppressed and subsequently restored. Chapter 30.1 is not capable of explaining so much, and there are enough difficulties already without making more.

With respect to Torrey's translation of the Aramaic which he posits, there is some doubt whether *lā' 'ītay* can mean 'I am not'. The form does not appear in Jewish Aramaic, since the objective and not the pronominal suffix is used in the first person singular. Dalman notes that the longer form of *'īt* (*'ītay*) in Old Testament Aramaic and Nabataean is often assumed to be the ground form (G. Dalman, *Grammatik des jüdisch-palästinischen Aramäisch*², 1905, p. 108). Scott's translation, 'There is no God, there is no God', is preferable (cf. Dan. 3.29, 'There is no God [*lā' 'ītay 'elāh*] who is able to save like this God'). See F. Rosenthal, *A Grammar of Biblical Aramaic* (1961), p. 41, par. 95. The final part of Scott's translation, 'and I can (not know anything)', strains *we'ūkāl* impossibly.

There is little doubt that *kī* (v. 2) introduces a motive clause (LXX γάρ; so Ringgren, Torrey, Scott; cf. Toy, Gemser) and that there is a logical connection between vv. 2f. and the original form of v. 1 (whatever that may have been). Since v. 1 constitutes so vexatious a problem, every clue which might alleviate it has to be followed up, and it is worthwhile enquiring whether vv. 2f., as motive clauses, are consistent with the reconstructions of v. 1 which have been hazarded. Is it possible to work backwards from vv. 2f. in order to form some idea what the sentiments of v. 1 may have been? Obviously this is not an operation which can be carried through with any precision or high degree of certainty.

In vv. 2f., Agur says that he is an animal rather than a man, and that he does not have the discernment or intellectual grasp (*bīnā*) which most men claim to possess. What is intended here by *bīnā* becomes more evident in v. 3, where the synonymous parallelism indicates that *ḥokmā* (v. 3a) is characterized as knowledge of the Holy One (assuming that the plural *q*ᵉ*dōšīm* means this, as most commentators suppose; cf. *'*ᵉ*lōhīm* 'God'). The negative of v. 3a has to be carried over to v. 3b (cf. Toy), or else v. 3b is to be understood as a final clause, 'so that I might have knowledge of the Holy One' (Ringgren). LXX catches the meaning of v. 2 cleverly: 'I am the most stupid of all men and I do not possess human wisdom.' It then goes on to establish an antithesis in v. 3; Agur, who lays no claim to wisdom *qua* man, is taught of God and has knowledge of the Holy One. It is unlikely that v. 3b (LXX) represents the original text, although it is adopted by Gemser. Rather, it has the characteristic marks of a reinterpretation of the vocabulary of wisdom dictated by piety. *bīnā* and *ḥokmā* are not taught by a wisdom teacher through an educational discipline; they are conditional on piety, on illumination of the mind by God.

It is difficult to believe that this is what Agur is saying, and it accords ill with any of the attempted reconstructions of v. 1. One who is weary with seeking after God or who has given up the quest in despair is not to be identified with the saint who has God himself for a teacher and who has found a way to him which bypasses the labours of unaided research. The sentiments of v. 3 (LXX) are more in harmony with vv. 5f., but these are not to be attributed to Agur (see above, pp. 642f.). In so far as any judgement can be made about the enigma of these opening verses, Agur's tone in vv. 2f. appears to be ironical. With a mock ruefulness he observes that others seem to know all about God and to have him completely in their grasp, whereas he, poor fellow, is apparently sub-human, since for him God is shrouded in mystery. He has never been able to penetrate this domain of knowledge in which others seem to move with great familiarity and assurance. If this is what is indicated by vv. 2f., it is compatible with the weary or despairing searcher after God who has been created by the reconstructions of v. 1. Even the translation 'There is no God, there is no God and I am at the end (of my resources)' is not ruled out, only it must be taken as a cry of despair and not as a militant dogmatic atheism. It is the cry of one who has searched to the furthest limits of his powers and has found nothing; for whom God, as he says in v. 4, is wrapped in a mystery which no human mind can penetrate.

Thus I am inclined to suppose that Agur is still speaking in v. 4 and that Barucq is wrong in assuming that this is God's reply. The suggestion is not entirely misplaced, and one can see its force. God in effect tells Agur that he is not unique in his perplexity, and that his condition reflects faithfully the transcendence and hiddenness of God who is inaccessible to the researches of men. The verse is more impressive if it is a comment from Agur himself on the inaccessibility of God to human enquiry. The knowledge of God which is taught with such confidence and ranks as wisdom has no empirical basis; it is empty speculation and vain imagining. If any man has been up to heaven where God is and has come down again to report what he found, he deserves to be listened to, but there is no such wisdom teacher. Has any man held the wind in his fists or the waters in his garment (God's garment is the clouds, cf. Job 26.8a), or established (i.e., created, brought into existence) the furthest limits of the earth? If there is such a man (Agur is sceptical of his existence; this is the force of *kī tēdāʿ*, cf. Ringgren *du weisst es ja wohl*), or anyone taught by him ('his son' is perhaps 'his pupil'), Agur wants to know his name. There is an emphasis here on the hiddenness and unknowability of God which recalls Ecclesiastes. Against those who speak about God as if he were familiar to them and the subject had no difficulties, Agur says that nothing at all is known by men about God. There is an unbridgeable gulf between men and a Being whose dominion is so vast, who collects the wind in his fists, and whose clothing is the clouds.

vv. 5–9 *The Counsel and Prayer of a Sage*

The wise man who emerges in vv. 5–9 is fully integrated into the fold of Yahwism. He is no longer the bearer of an international tradition, but a scholar of sacred learning entrusted with the preservation and transmission of the Jewish scriptures. I have argued that this transformation began in the late pre-exilic period (*PWM*, pp. 102f.); that it gathered pace in the post-exilic period is evident from the example of Ben Sira, who clearly stands in the succession of the pre-exilic *ḥakāmīm* but who is also a master of biblical learning. The form-critical corollary of this has been discussed by Baumgartner, who has shown that Ben Sira utilizes *Gattungen* and themes which lie outside the strict province of wisdom literature and belong to psalmody and prophecy (*ZAW* 34, 1914, pp. 161f.; *Israelitische und Altorientalische Weisheit*, 1933, p. 29). Mowinckel envisages him as one who composes psalms as suitable models for his pupils and composes prayers in order to show them how to give shape to their expressions of pious aspiration (*VTS* iii, pp. 213f.; *Psalms in Israel's Worship* ii, pp. 111f.).

It is this late stage in the wisdom tradition, when the wisdom literature has begun to lose its formal identity and when the wise man as the pious scholar takes the whole of the scriptures as his province and dedicates his learning to the adornment of piety, that is reflected in vv. 5–9. Verses 5f. are written in defence of the word of Yahweh and in such a way as to display biblical learning, since v. 5 is a quotation of Ps. 18.31 (II Sam. 22.31) and v. 6a is perhaps dependent on Deut. 4.2. Verses 7–9 are a model prayer in which a decent and modest style of piety is cultivated. The use of *ne'ūm* in v. 1 may be due to late editorial activity, reflecting a time when the wise man had become as well acquainted with prophetic terminology as he was with the vocabulary of wisdom. Toy suggests that the emphasis on the completeness of God's word may assume the three-fold division of the Jewish Scriptures into Law, Prophets and Writings which is first expressly mentioned in the preface to Ben Sira (132 BC). He adds: 'This paragraph (i.e., vv. 5f.) may have been written not far from that date.' It is doubtful whether as much can be inferred from the injunction: 'Do not add to his words' (cf. Deut. 4.2). It would, however, seem to point to a situation where an authoritative text of the written scriptures was taking shape, and this would be an important aspect of the work of those engaged in sacred learning (cf. *PWM*, pp. 102f.).

The word of God (*'imrat YHWH* in Ps. 18.31) is of proved authenticity and preciousness, like gold which has been tried by fire. God is a shield to those who take refuge in him. It may be, as Agur has said, that God is shrouded in mystery, but there is a knowledge of him which is granted to men, although it is different in character from that whose absence is lamented by Agur. For God has given men his word, and this is a revelation which Agur leaves out of account. It is not for man to endure mental weariness and despair seeking the God who is past finding out. Let him submit to God, make him his refuge and live by the light of his word. The command not to add to God's words may be intended as a warning against the dangers of pursuing the way of speculation in seeking after God. Is not Agur in danger of adding to his words? But this is a grave presumptuousness and indiscipline. It is now the discipline of piety and not the discipline of education which is important; it is to God and not to the wisdom teacher that the wise man submits. Those who substitute their own words for God's word will be subject to correction and be proved liars.

Verses 7–9 appear among Roth's 'Reflective Numerical Sayings' (W. M. W. Roth, *Numerical Sayings in the Old Testament*, *VTS* xiii, 1965, pp. 69f.), and this analysis affords form-critical corroboration that a late stage of the development of the wisdom tradition is represented here. Roth observes that the extremes of poverty and wealth mentioned in v. 8b are taken up in the 'lest' clauses of v. 9. He makes no comment on the circumstance (cf. Toy) that the cautionary comments of v. 9 follow only on v. 8bc and take no cognizance of v. 8a. The possibility that v. 8c is superfluous and is to be regarded as a secondary expansion of v. 8b is mentioned by Gemser and Barucq. At any rate, the first petition is stated *simpliciter* and the second elaborated with 'lest' clauses.

'Do not deny (them) to me before I die' is an odd expression, but it must mean 'Do not deny them to me as long as I live'. Keep me until death from perfidy, and from the extremes of wealth and poverty. Let my life never become a lie. Put far away from me falsehood and speech which lacks integrity. Do not give me either poverty or wealth, but let me have a fair portion of bread to eat. If I am too well-fed, I shall become self-satisfied and deny God. I shall say: 'Who is God?' i.e., who is this God of whom men speak as if they were dependent on him? God will be declared redundant. A life which is too easy and spacious will create the illusion of self-sufficiency and lead to apostasy. But if I lose my wherewithal and am reduced to poverty, a desperate state of destitution will drive me to sin and sacrilege. I shall break the commandment by becoming a thief and I shall 'take hold of' the name of God. The meaning of *tāpaśtī* is uncertain. The name of God will be roughly grasped, i.e., his holiness will be infringed. Or perhaps the meaning is that his name will be brought into disrepute (Toy, cf. Gemser and Ringgren, 'I shall take the name of my God in vain'). G. R. Driver's suggestion (see Gemser) that *tāpaštī* should be read (Arabic *tafiṯa* 'to stain') is attractive: 'And I besmirch the name of my God.'

[10] Verse 10 is a fragment of Instruction, made up of an imperative and a 'lest' clause, which has no connection with what precedes it and only a superficial link with v. 11 (*qll* occurs in both). It is unwise to pass on to a master damaging gossip about a domestic servant, even if the slander or denunciation has some basis. There is something improper and nasty about carrying such tales, and it is implied that the servant has the right to feel aggrieved that the relation between himself and his master has been subject to such interference. If a servant is leading his master a merry dance, the master should be able to find this out for himself and put his own house in order. Each man must be left to manage his own domestic affairs and deal directly with his servants, and even the well-intentioned informer full of zeal to correct abuses and expose malpractices, will make matters worse by his intervention and draw to himself the invective of the servant about whom he has gossiped. I am not inclined to suppose that the objective power of the curse is the point of v. 10b (Toy) or that 'and you have to make amends' is a good translation of w^{e}*'āšāmtā* (Gemser, Ringgren). A weakened sense of *qll* is indicated here. The servant will lay about the informer with the rough edge of his tongue and will make him look small – subject him to indignity – and expose the wrong of his gratuitous interference. The question of whether there is any substance in the gossip or not is not raised. It is wrong in any event to intervene between a master and his servant and this in itself is enough to merit verbal abuse and to put one in the wrong.

vv. 11–14 *Contemporary Sins*

[11–14] Roth (pp. 38f.) supposes that this is a numerical saying whose title-line has accidentally fallen out; and this he restores following C. F. Kent and Millar Burrows (*Proverbs and Didactic Poems*, 1927, p. 109): 'There are three kinds of men whom Yahweh hates and four that are abhorrent to him.' According to Roth, vv. 11–14 (v. 14cd a gloss, so also Toy; Georg Sauer, *Die Sprüche*

Agur; *BWANT* v. 4, 1953, pp. 103f.) is a reflective numerical saying which engages itself with observation of society. This may be questioned as a judgement on both the form and contents of vv. 11–14. With respect to form, it could be asked whether these verses are an original series or whether they have been associated by an editor because they all began with the same word (*dōr*). The more probable answer is that they are originally a series, but then there is no decisive indication that they constitute a numerical saying. The distinctive stylistic feature may rather be the use of the same word to begin each verse.

As for content, Roth has observed that there is a didactic and hortative emphasis in vv. 11–14, but he still maintains that they have a reflective character and make observations on society. On the other hand, he notes a similarity in content and tone between vv. 11–14 and certain 'prophetic condemnations'. The word 'condemnations' is significant, for the tone of these sentences is condemnatory rather than reflective, and in this they approximate to the prophetic reprimand (*Scheltrede*). I do not gather the impression that a thoughtful observer of human foibles expresses himself here; it is rather the voice of a preacher or prophet denouncing the sins of his contemporaries (*dōr*, cf. Jer. 2.31; 7.29). Only, it has to be conceded that there is no direct address here and that one may say that these are observations rather than condemnations or rebukes, in so far as they are communicated in the third rather than the second person. It is worth noting that when Jesus speaks in this way it is in the context of direct address to an audience, whether this is indicated by the vocative, 'O generation of vipers' (Matt. 3.7; 12.34; 23.33; Luke 3.7) or, as is more usual, by the phrase 'this generation' (Matt. 11.16; Luke 7.31 *et al.*) or variants (Matt. 12.45 *et al.*). Where he says, 'An evil and adulterous generation seeks for a sign' (Matt. 12.39, 16.4), the form is apparently that of a statement in the third person, but the intention to address an audience is still clear (on *dōr*, 'group' or 'circle', see P. R. Ackroyd, *JSS* xiii, 1968, pp. 3–10). Whether the element of address is present with the use of *dōr* in the third person in vv. 11–14 is impossible to say (Ewald, 'O generation that curses'). If the verses are exclamatory, as Toy supposes, the implication of condemnation is unmistakable and they are nearer to direct denunciation than to the form of wisdom sentences (cf. RV: 'There is a generation who'; Scott: 'There is one kind of man'). I am prepared to accept Roth's view that these verses are observations in so far as they have the form of wisdom sentences, but it must be recognized that their formulation in the third person barely conceals their character as denunciatory preaching directed towards contemporaries.

The sins which are condemned range over wide areas of conduct and have no inner relationship. The catalogue consists of cursing or reviling of parents (see on 20.20, above, pp. 540f.), hypocritical self-righteousness, pride symbolized by haughty eyes and proud glances (see on 4.25, above, p. 311 for *ʿapʿappāw*), and merciless rapacity (men with teeth as sharp as swords and butchers' knives). The final metaphor indicates that those condemned as rapacious wreak havoc in the community. They are as barbarous in their ways and as destructive in their effects as invading soldiers with their swords. They are responsible for carnage and butchery. The gloss (v. 14cd) correctly interprets the figure, with its reference to the poor and defenceless. BH proposes *'ᵃdāmā* for *'ādām*. Dahood postulates **'ādām*, a masculine variant of *'ᵃdāmā*. This supplies exact parallelism to *'ereṣ*: 'and the needy from the land'. It is among these that the slaughter will be most severe when the men with sharp teeth set to work. There are ways other than war in which a society can be mutilated, as when the poor are devoured by oppressive and greedy men who are members of the same community.

vv. 15b–16 *Four which are never satisfied*

[15b–16] Both Gemser and Ringgren associate v. 15a with vv. 15b–16, but this is to be rejected on formal grounds (it produces a type of numerical saying for which no parallel can be adduced) and also because of the interpretation which has to be put on v. 15a in order to sustain the connection with what follows. Gemser renders, 'There are two greedy things which lick and lap' (*lāʿū laqqū* for *laʿᵃlūqā*), literally, 'two daughters of Give, Give (reading *bᵉnōt hab hab*) which lick and lap'. Ringgren takes *ʿᵃlūqā* as a proper name and renders: 'Ascribed to *ʿᵃlūqā*: Two daughters (say) "Give Give".' The same objection applies to J. J. Glueck's reconstruction (*VT* xiv, 1964, pp. 367–70). Glueck connects *ʿᵃlūqā* with Arabic *ʿalāqā*, 'copulation', and *habhab* with Arabic and Aramaic *ḥbb*, Ethiopic *hbb*. He renders: 'As for erotic passion, two girls of burning desire'. Also F. S. North (*VT* xv, 1965, pp. 281f.) who rejects Glueck's lexical proposals, but who postulates the sequence 2, 3, 4.

Roth has shown that the numerical sequence x/x+1 was a

characteristic device of Ancient Near Eastern literature and that it is to be understood as a kind of parallelism (W. M. W. Roth, *VT* xii, 1962, pp. 304f.). Since the arrangement of the text proposed by Gemser and Ringgren disturbs this pattern and produces a numerical saying with the form x/x+1/x+2, it should be rejected. Moreover, of the other specimens which lie nearer to hand in Prov. 30, three are of the 'three . . . four' type (vv. 18f., 21f., 29f.), while the other simply specifies the number four (vv. 24f.). Hence the numerical saying consists of vv. 15b–16 and v. 15a is a separate unit (so Toy, Barucq and Scott). Its attachment to what follows can be readily understood, both because the number two does suggest the sequence two, three, four and also because the thought of insatiability accords with the contents of vv. 15b–16 (see W. M. W. Roth, *VTS* xiii, p. 28 n.3; also H. Schneider, *Lex tua veritas, Festschrift für Hubert Junker*, 1961, pp. 257–64. Schneider argues that 'leech' is a paradigm for 'greed' and hence v. 15a was placed after v. 14, whose subject is greed for land. It was followed by vv. 15b–16, because of the apparent numerical sequence and the slight affinity in content, but was originally independent of vv. 15b–16).

[15a] Verse 15a is based on observation of nature, and the two grasping daughters are the suckers of the leech. I would quarrel with Roth here and also in respect of the other sayings in ch. 30 which he classifies as observations of nature (vv. 18f., 24f., 29f.), in so far as this descriptive category gives the impression that the interest focuses on the scientific or zoological facts – that it is the curiosity of a naturalist and the desire to record observations accurately and systematically that constitutes the point of departure of these sayings (cf. Roth, *VTS* xiii, pp. 20f.). Roth agrees with Alt (*K.S.* ii, pp. 90–99) that the numerical saying in Prov. 30.15–31 is employed to formulate a kind of natural science (pp. 2f.), and he describes this as an illuminating interpretation of Prov. 30.15–31 in particular and of the genre of the numerical saying in general (p. 99). Roth maintains that these formulations have an encyclopaedic character, although he does not postulate any onomasticon-like *Vorlage* for the numerical saying in Prov. 30 (p. 25). The reference to Solomon's knowledge of trees and animals (I Kings 5.10f.) is thought to be significant, and it is suggested that the awakening of an interest in nature (of which the numerical sayings are taken as evidence) is to be associated with the intellectual climate of the age of Solomon – an interest which was sustained in later periods (pp. 3, 25). With this should be compared the contention of Gese that collections of proverbs represent an ordering, scientific activity and are intended to demonstrate the structural unity of human life (*Lehre und Wirklichkeit*, pp. 66f.; cf. his article in *Journal for Theology and the Church*, i, 1965, pp. 52f. on Sumerian lists of plants, animals, etc.). However, the centre of interest in the numerical sayings of Prov. 30 is not nature but the field of human behaviour, and attention is directed towards nature with the intention of discovering there 'parables' which will serve as effective comments on human traits (cf. J. Hempel, *BZAW* 77, 1958, p. 74, who notes this transition from nature to man). As for v. 15a, in the two suckers of the leech which never have enough, the observer discerns a parable of grasping greed in human society.

Verses 15b–16 are what Roth calls a graded numerical saying (*VTS* xiii, p. 6) and he has supplied many examples of these from Ancient Near Eastern literature. In most of these the sequence x/x+1 indicates an indefinite numerical value, and only two of Roth's examples have strict appositeness in relation to the graded numerical sayings of Prov. 30, where an exact number (four) is indicated. One is an Ugaritic text (*Baal* II iii.16–19, G. R. Driver, *CML*, pp. 94f.), and the other from *Ahikar* (vii.92f.; Cowley, pp. 215, 223). Roth, however, has done enough to demonstrate that the graded numerical saying is a studied stylistic device, and that the two numbers are distributed over two halves of a line of poetry as a mode of parallelism, whether synonymous, synthetic or antithetic (*VT* xii, pp. 306f.). This was suggested much earlier by Wünsche (A. Wünsche, *ZDMG* 65, 1911, p. 59) and rejected by Stevenson (W. B. Stevenson, *TGUOS*, ix, 1938/9, pp. 26–38). Stevenson argued that while the development of this numerical sequence into a stereotyped literary form was assisted by the analogy of parallelism, parallelism alone cannot account for the creation or emergence of the usage. He supposes it to originate in the mannerism of an influential teacher as a corrective adjustment in connection with extempore comment: 'There are three points I want to make – no four'. Stevenson's 'psychologizing explanation' is rejected by Roth (*VT* xii, p. 311 n.1). The fact that x/x+1 is used to indicate indefinite numerical value as well as a precise number would seem to show that Stevenson's explanation is too narrow, since it is unlikely that the two usages are entirely separate.

On the other hand, the distinction between the indication of indefinite numerical value and precise numerical value which

Stevenson has made may be significant. When this type of parallelism is used to indicate a precise number, is not this a particular didactic or mnemonic application of a more generalized stylistic feature? In other words, the transition from indefinite to exact numerical value may be an indication that this element of poetic style has been taken over by the teacher in the interests of didactic efficiency. The didactic motive in the numerical saying (whether simple or graded) has been stressed by Wünsche (*op. cit.*, pp. 57–61) and Hempel (*BZAW* 77, p. 73; cf. A. Bentzen, *Introduction to the Old Testament*[5], 1959, p. 176).

Another remark made by Stevenson was that the common factor of the items of the numerical saying is given in the title line. This is the starting-point of Torczyner's argument that the numerical saying is derived from the riddle. He supposes that the three or four things of the graded saying are different solutions which have been offered for the one riddle. The numerical saying contains only the solutions, and the title-line may originally have had the form of the question. In the case of 30.18, this would be: What are three or four things that leave no trace?, and the riddle would be: What goes and leaves no trace? Torczyner adds: 'A question which has reference to a definite number of things need not, of course, always be a riddle. Very often such a question may be a numerical aid which helps the student to remember' (*HUCA*, 1, 1924, pp. 135f.).

Torczyner's reconstruction of the original riddle in 30.18 is unsatisfactory, since he misinterprets *derek* (see below, cf. Toy). That the four things leave no trace of their movement cannot be the point, because it makes no sense in relation to the fourth item. A more general criticism of Torczyner's hypothesis is that it does not explain the peculiar form of the graded numerical saying. If four solutions to the one riddle are to be given, why should they be introduced with the formula, 'Three things are too wonderful for me and of four I have no knowledge'? Wünsche's remark that the final item of the graded numerical saying is the particularly significant one (p. 59) does not bear close examination, but is not entirely mistaken. For example, in vv. 15b–16 is it an error to enquire whether the saying has a particular point? This would seem to me to be the element of truth also in Torczyner's contention that all four items relate to a single riddle. Is there one particular observation which the other items subserve, or is the list just a random one? Here Roth remarks: 'Nature observation was not always confined to phenomena which are grouped together in modern science' (*VTS* xiii, p. 28). Again: 'However, the spirit in which these observations were made is important, because here nature phenomena are taken for what they are and an attempt is made to categorize them' (p. 30).

But the reference to Sheol is not an observation of nature (in the sense intended by Roth which is 'the province of the naturalist'), nor is that to the womb which has never opened to produce a child. There are two genuine observations of nature, the one about the land which never has enough water and the other about the insatiable appetite of the fire for fuel. A third is discovered by D. Winton Thomas (*VTS* iii, p. 290), who revives Hodgson's suggestion that *rāḥam* refers to a bird and translates *'ōṣer* 'voracity' (Arabic *'aẓira*). The 'voracity of the carrion-vulture' is then the example of insatiability which is listed. One may say that the reference to Sheol is based on the observation that there is no end to people dying. The thought of the insatiability of death derives, however, from mythology; it is a reference to the gaping throat and insatiable appetite of the god Mot (see on 1.12, above, pp. 269f.) and Roth is aware of this. I would hazard the suggestion that the interest of this numerical saying focuses on the barren woman, and that insatiable death, the thirsty land and the greedy fire are all metaphors of her appetite for sexual intercourse, for the fierce urge to remove the reproach of her barrenness (cf. Toy). If this is so, Dahood's proposal (p. 59), which would eliminate the reference to the unopened womb, misses the point. From the portrait of Hannah (I Sam. 1f.) it can be gathered that such a woman had the makings of a tragic figure and that she attracted interest and comment. To have fulfilment and blessing in her grasp and yet to remain unblessed; to have a husband and yet to be barren of children; this is the cruel irony of her situation. It is a fate to which she will not resign herself; she will give herself to her husband with abandon.

v. 17 *Dishonouring of Parents*

[17] This is a quatrain with synonymous parallelism in both couplets. It is quite separate in form and tone (cf. Toy) from what precedes or follows, but its topic is akin to that of v. 11. It is a kind of silent contempt which is envisaged, a sneering with the eye rather than the tongue, the look which communicates scorn as surely as words. The reference of v. 17b, as Toy correctly states, is to the denial of burial – the ultimate disgrace and disaster. The bodies of such unnatural children will be exposed, and the offending eye will be picked out and eaten by birds of carrion (an allusion to the *lex talionis*), by ravens and vultures (or, eagles). Cf. the Rizpah story in II Sam. 21 (especially v. 10). Verse 17b, 'and scorns a mother's obedience' (see KB² for *y^eqāhā* in Gen. 49.10), is an awkward expression which is explained by Gemser and Barucq as 'scorns the obedience due to a mother'. G. R. Driver has suggested that *lah^aqat hann^ebī'īm* (I Sam. 19.20) should be translated 'seignory of the prophets', observing that *lhq*, 'old', occurs frequently in Ethiopic (*JTS* xxix, 1928, p. 394). Winton Thomas has noted that Prov. 30.17 (LXX) reads *γῆρας* and has suggested such a form as *l^ehāqā* or *l^ehīqā* (so also J. C. Greenfield, *HUCA* xxix, 1958, pp. 212f., who, on the basis of LXX *γῆρας*, argues that *lhq*, 'to be white of hair', was known to the Greek translators). This is a smaller emendation than *l^eziqnat* (Toy, KB²), and it grapples more seriously with the problem of MT. The corruption of *lhyqt* into *lyqht* is understandable: 'The eye that mocks a father and despises an aged mother' (D. W. Thomas, *JTS* xlii, 1941, pp. 154f.; similarly Ringgren and Scott). LXX, Pesh. (*sybwt'*) and Targ. (*qšyšwt'*) appear to have read *lhq* and I accept their testimony.

vv. 18f. *Four which are incomprehensible*

[18f.] Again I question whether it is a truly scientific interest which is reflected in these verses. Toy says that they give a lesson in natural history and physics, and Roth remarks that this saying 'extends the field of observation beyond zoology into the area of *general science*' (*VTS* xiii, p. 21). The saying is a confession of defeat and one would not expect a naturalist to make a class of phenomena which he does not understand. Roth meets this objection by suggesting that the intention is to list phenomena which lie beyond the boundary of rational observation, and that the title line indicates that an unsuccessful reflective effort has been made to classify them positively (p. 22). I am not convinced by this – all the more so, since the fourth item has to do not with nature in Roth's sense but with human nature. Here is a case where Wünsche's contention that the fourth item is the significant one appears to work out. The change which takes place in the sense of *derek* points in the same direction.

Wonderful and mysterious is the flight of an eagle, the gliding of a snake over a rock and the passage of a ship over the seas. The common element is the marvel and grace of these different forms of movement and all this is nearer to the way in which a poet or painter sees than to a scientist's observations. Surely one is not to suppose that in the fourth item *derek* refers to the graceful and mysterious way in which a man moves in his advances towards a woman; or yet to the circumstance that he knows his way, has a sure instinct how to proceed, and that this sense of direction is a mystery in so far as it is not taught. On the contrary, the fourth is linked to the first three through a utilization of the ambivalence of *derek* as well as by the common element of mystery. Here again the key lies in the recognition that the first three are parables of the mystery of man's desire for a woman or perhaps rather for the irresistible and inexplicable attraction which draws together the man and the woman. The first three have more in common with each other than they together have with the fourth and this, too, sets the final item apart. The subject of reflection is the mystery of sexuality, and other mysteries are suitable parables because the ambivalence of *derek* fastens them to the centre of reflective interest. The Hebrew word used for woman (*ʿalmā*) is none other than the celebrated crux of Isa. 7.14 rendered by LXX as παρθένος 'virgin'. Here LXX renders νεότητι 'young woman'. There is no doubt that *ʿalmā* in both passages means 'young woman' and not 'virgin'. It is the way of a man with a woman and not with a virgin which is the topic of Prov. 30.19 (see my article in *VT* xvii, 1967, pp. 213f.).

v. 20 *The Adulteress*

[20] The suggestion that v. 20 is a gloss on vv. 18f. (Toy, BH, Gemser) goes back to Hitzig, but it should be rejected. The association of v. 20 with v. 19 is explicable on the catchword principle (*derek*, so Barucq), and there is no reason why the reference of *kēn* should not be forward rather than backward. Scott translates correctly: 'This is how the adulteress acts.' The verse might mean that adultery is all in a day's work for her, and that afterwards she enjoys her food quite unconcerned about questions of morality. More probably the verse has a metaphorical character and refers to the act of sexual intercourse. So far as she is concerned, it is as innocent of moral issues as the eating of food, where you eat, wipe your mouth and that is an end to it. As Toy observes, the portrayal has a comic character and it is not entirely out of place to smile at such behaviour. It is beside the point to direct moral censure at such a creature who is amoral rather than immoral. One who has no moral sensibilities cannot be described in ethical terms; what would be immorality in others is just animal spirits in her.

Another possibility is that moral sclerosis is indicated by the figure, in which case the words, 'I have done nothing wrong', would be attributable to the relics of a conscience which the hardened adulteress has all but strangled. Such moral twinges as are still felt are momentary and swiftly pass.

vv. 21–23 *Four Earth-shaking Occurrences*

[21–23] Roth takes the title line quite literally and supposes that the intention is to classify occurrences which disturb and threaten fixed orders of society and that this classification, once achieved, would serve to undergird traditional values and institutions, and so promote stability (*VTS* xiii, p. 36). I find it very difficult to believe that the saying has such high sociological significance as Roth attaches to it. It does not read like the outcome of mature reflection on the causes of social instability and disorder. If a slave became a king, the foundations of society might be shaken, but the other cases are too paltry to sustain Roth's interpretation. Roth assumes a chiastic arrangement; then there is a correspondence between the slave who becomes a king and the maidservant who enters into the inheritance of her mistress (so Barucq; cf. LXX *ἐκβάλῃ* which suggests *tōrîš* 'disinherits' (Gemser), unless the qal can mean 'disinherit', 'supplant'). It may be that the reference is to the transference of a husband's affections from his wife to her maid, as Roth suggests (p. 35). This may be associated with the barrenness of the wife and the pregnancy of the maid. I am dubious about the chiastic arrangement which Roth posits, and I doubt whether there is any implication that such a supplanting of the wife threatens the stability of the home which is a basic order of society. The impression which I get from the four occurrences mentioned is that they are a quite random selection, and that they are not significantly selective in relation to the upholding of the social order, as Roth maintains.

Toy's remark that the intention is humorous or whimsical is more to the point. The saying is a species of satire on the theme that there are some situations in which certain people are unbearable. When the title line declares that a land shudders in the presence of these events and finds them unbearable, this is a hyperbole which means no more than that men in society cannot endure them. It is hard to see how it can have the significance which Roth attaches to it. An unattractive woman who gets a husband is not a danger to society, nor is a fool filled with food. Roth argues that the *nābāl* is not a fool but an outcast from society who has not the right to eat and live (*VT* x, 1960, pp. 401–4), and that the *śᵉnū'ā* is the wife who remains in her husband's household but is relegated permanently to the status of a female slave with no hope of ever recovering honourable marital status, i.e., finding another husband (*VTS* xiii, p. 36). The evidence which Roth cites does not bear out this contention. It appears from Deut. 21.14 and 24.4 that a husband's dislike of a wife is a sufficient ground for divorce, and from Deut. 21.15f. that an unloved wife may retain the status of a wife and her children suffer no disadvantages in relation to their right to inherit (cf. Gen. 29.30f.). There is therefore some substance in the contention that the *śᵉnū'ā* is a divorcee (G. R. Driver, see Gemser), although the evidence indicates that a woman could lose her husband's affection without ceasing to be his wife. Since, however, loss of affection leads naturally to divorce, the past participle may have become a technical term for a divorcee. Toy thinks rather of the unattractive woman who has a long record of failure in her efforts to get a man and who eventually succeeds.

A slave who has been subject to authority and who comes to exercise great authority is insufferable. There is no tyrant so unbearable as the one who has known servitude. The unattractive woman who at last gets a husband, or the divorcee who finds another one, will parade her feelings of achievement and self-satisfaction in a manner not to be endured. So it is also with the maid visibly gloating with triumph at having replaced her mistress in the master's affections. The odd man out in this set is the *nābāl*, since there appears to be no contrast in this case between a former and present condition. It is hardly the difference between a hungry fool and a well-fed one which is intended (cf. Roth). All that is meant is that a fool is hard to thole at any time, but if he is replete with food (and drink) and becomes expansive, to share his company is extreme agony.

VV. 24–28 *Four small but accomplished Creatures*

[24–28] Roth cites Toy with approval: 'The proverb is simply descriptive of the habits of the animals, a bit of natural history, without expressed reference to human life, but perhaps with the implied suggestion that success is not confined to bigness.' The original purpose of this numerical saying, according to Roth, is to fix a newly discovered order of nature, although the derivation of a 'moral' may have been a secondary factor which assisted its preservation (*VTS* xiii, pp. 20f.).

These assessments are valuable in so far as they point to the element of keen and exact observation of nature which can be detected in vv. 24–28. It would be fair to say that the person who was responsible for these verses had a flair for careful observation and accurate description of the habits of these creatures, and that he was consequently something of a naturalist. It is this factor which marks off this saying so decisively from a fable like that of Jotham (Judg. 9.7–21, a contest fable, cf. *BWL*, pp. 150f.), where the trees strike human attitudes and speak and act like men, so that an interest in the trees *qua* trees exists only in so far as this is necessary to make the point that there is no role for a king in the ordered world of men since Yahweh is king. In such a fable the interest in natural history is minimal, and it has to be recognized that the piece is primarily social comment rather than observation of nature. But this would seem to me to be still true of vv. 24–28, and I question whether Toy and Roth are right in ascribing a scientific intention to this classification. Rather, the author's activities as a naturalist are orientated by his search for 'parables' of human life and it is this, and not natural history as an end in itself, which is reflected in this classification of creatures which are competent and effective despite their physical insignificance. The theme is that severe physical limitations can be compensated for by strength of mind.

The creatures are spoken of as if they were human beings, and while this might be used as an argument that the centre of interest is society rather than nature, it is not a point of which I make too much, since it might be that it reflects a limitation of vocabulary more than anything else. That is, even if the author were a naturalist and nothing more how else could he have expressed himself? I do not, however, regard this consideration as an entirely adequate explanation. These four creatures are the wisest of the wise (reading *mēḥᵃkāmīm* for MT *mᵉḥukkāmīm* with the versions; LXX σοφώτερα τῶν σοφῶν). The ant which makes provision for the winter by storing food in the summer is a model of foresight and industry. The badger which, despite its lack of physical strength, is able to make a house for itself in the rocks is a model of technical ingenuity and application. It is particularly vv. 27f. which are not credible as observations which a naturalist would make. Verse 27a itself does not correspond to the first *stichoi* of the other verses, since there is no reference in it to the minuteness and frailty of the locust. The main point, however, is this. What naturalist, ancient or modern, would think it relevant to remark that locusts do not have a king? This is a sure indication, so far as I can see, that the verse focuses on society and not on nature. It is principally social comment rather than natural history. The locusts are well-organized and disciplined; they are viewed by this observer on the analogy of a well-governed community. By observing that they have no king he can only intend to raise the question whether the institution of kingship is an indispensable condition of order and strength in a community. This is perhaps no more than a query, and need not be construed as a polemic against kingship, but the point of view is not entirely divorced from that which finds expression in the fable of Jotham (above, p. 179).

D. Winton Thomas (*VT* xv, 1965, p. 276) explains *ḥōṣēṣ* on the basis of Arabic *ḥaṣṣa*, 'cut', 'severed'. He points *ḥṣṣ* as *ḥāṣāṣ* (an adverbial accusative) – the locusts go out in 'divisions'. *g^edūd*, another military term, is formed from *gdd*, 'cut'. This, rather than 'destroy', 'annihilate' (N. Tur Sinai, *Job*, pp. 329f.) is the right kind of solution for the obscure *ḥōṣēṣ*. The military imagery used of the locusts in Joel 2.4f. is instructive. The statement in v. 8 that they maintain perfect marching order and do not jostle one another is an apt elucidation of the LXX translation of *ḥōṣēṣ* in Prov. 30.27 (*εὐτάκτως*, cf. KB³). As Winton Thomas points out, *yṣ'* is also military terminology.

As for v. 28, I can see no scientific reason for associating an observation that lizards are fragile (they have no dangerous sting or bite and so can be clutched and destroyed with impunity) with another that they make their way into kings' palaces (*tittāpēś* should be read). The intention of this association is artistic and not scientific, and the 'parable' means that there are those who despite their weakness and vulnerability make such good use of the resources which they have that they attain to eminence of the first rank – to the circle of the court.

vv. 29–31 *Four which move regally*

[29–31] Roth (*VTS* xiii, p. 20) describes this as a codification of an order in the world of zoology which has been discovered and fixed in the form of a numerical saying. He can make this statement because he expunges from v. 31b the reference to a king, and follows

Toy's suggestion that the name of an animal originally stood in the text (he apparently reads *w*^{e}*'aqqō qām 'el-ʿammō*). Otherwise he follows LXX and renders:

Three there are which are stately in their stride,
four which are stately in their tread:
the lion, the ruler of the four-footed animals
(and he does not turn back from anything),
the rooster lifting himself over the hens,
the he-goat walking before the herd,
and the mountain-goat standing up in front of his people.

The reason why these animals move with stately step is that they are leaders of their kind and are supreme within their sphere of influence.

A similar approach to the saying is made by Winton Thomas (*VTS* iii, p. 291), who is more concerned than Roth to grapple with the formidable difficulties of MT rather than simply opting for LXX as Roth does, and whose suggestions are consequently more tentative. He does, however, follow Toy (as Roth also does) in the assumption that because three of the four things mentioned are animals, it is probable that the fourth is also an animal. This is not an assumption with which I agree, as will be gathered from my treatment of the preceding numerical sayings in this chapter. The transition from these animal models or parables to a human subject is just what I would expect here, and this is a case where Wünsche's observation that the first three exist for the sake of the fourth works out. Winton Thomas suggests that *w*^{e}*tayiš* should be read for *'ō tayiš*, which has arisen through *tayiš* being taken as an explanatory gloss on the obscure *zarzīr motnayim*.

Bewer's reconstruction (*JBL* lxvii, 1948, pp. 61f.) suffers from the assumption that LXX reflects, for the most part, the 'original' Hebrew text. It is more probable that LXX is a free paraphrase of a Hebrew text with the same difficulties as MT now has. Bewer conjectures *mitnaśśē'* (of which *motnayim 'ō* is a corruption) on the basis of ἐνπεριπατῶν . . . εὔψυχος, and *mōlīk* for *melek* on the basis of ἡγούμενος αἰπολίου, 'a strutting cock and a leading he-goat'. *'alqūm* is explained as *'l* = *'ayil* 'leader' and *qedem* 'in front of', a corruption of *m*^{e}*qaddēm*, 'a leader preceding his people' (*ʿammō*).

zarzīr motnayim ('girt at the loins') is quite obscure, and is variously translated 'starling' (Mishnaic Hebrew, Arabic, Syriac), 'cock' (versions, LXX ἀλέκτωρ, cf. KB^{3}), 'greyhound' (RV), 'war-horse'

(RV margin). *motnayim* may be a corruption; Toy suggests *magbe* and Gemser (following Bewer) *mitnaśśē'*, both indicating the proud deportment of an animal. Bewer and Gemser follow LXX in supposing that it is a cock. For the corrupt *'alqūm 'immō*, Driver (*Biblica* 32, p. 194) conjectures either *'immō lō' qām* (cf. Barucq *lō' qāmū 'immō*), 'against whom there is no rising up', i.e., who is irresistible (so Scott), or *qām 'el 'ammō* (*'el* = *'al*), 'standing over his people', 'at the head of his people' (cf. LXX, 'a king haranguing his people'). Gemser adopts Driver's latter suggestion and Ringgren reads *kᵉ'ēl qām bᵉ'ammō*, 'and the king who like a god stands among his people'. I read *mitnaśśē'* with Bewer and *qām 'el 'ammō* with Driver. This is not a solution of the problem of MT. It is a conjectural reconstruction which makes a translation possible. The acceptance of *mitnaśśē'* involves the deletion of *'ō*. The three animals (whatever was the second) were apparently selected as supreme in their own realms, and this is clearly how the lion is portrayed. He is the king of the animals and yields to none, and so he carries himself regally. As in v. 27, a reflection on kingship is grounded in the world of nature. The king, too, is supreme in a human realm and when he makes a public appearance his presence and deportment befit his royalty.

vv. 32f. *Misconduct and its Consequences*

[32f.] These verses are most intelligible as a fragment of Instruction, in which case an imperative is implied after the two conditional clauses of v. 32 and is then followed by three motive clauses. Scott supposes that 'Beware!' (*hiššāmer lᵉkā*) is implied. Gemser and Ringgren indicate an anacolouthon, with v. 32 exclamatory, but the effect is still that of Instruction with motive clauses. Barucq (so RSV) finds the imperative concealed in the phrase 'hand to mouth', which is translated 'put your hand to your mouth', i.e., keep silent. The phrase 'hand to mouth' is more probably to be taken with *zammōtā* (Gemser, Ringgren, Scott); the alternatives then are brash and voluble self-assertiveness and silent intrigue. Toy observes that a verbal form of *nbl* is not used elsewhere in the sense of 'acting foolishly', and that similarly this would be the only instance where a verbal form of *zmm* had a pejorative sense. One can only say that these are the meanings which seem to be demanded by the context, and that nouns formed from *nbl* and *zmm* do have these senses (for *mᵉzimmā* see *PWM*, p. 80).

Altercation results from either of these forms of misconduct, whether it is pushing other people out of the way in order to get to the top or scheming in an underhand way to get the better of them. If one of the *stichoi* of v. 33 is an addition, it would be v. 33c (a variant of v. 33b, so BH, Scott) rather than v. 33a (Toy). Verse 33a is the figure by means of which the point is made. When sour, whole milk is twisted tighter and tighter in a cloth, curds are produced, and if sufficient pressure is applied to the nose, blood is produced (here Scott misses the point). If anger is pressed beyond certain limits (*'appayim*, 'anger', echoing *'ap*, 'nose') the result is strife. The consequences of giving extreme provocation to others are that you get a bloody nose or that you awaken a volcanic anger and are involved in protracted and bitter strife.

B. CHAPTER 31 vv. 10–31

A Wife of many Parts

This poem, which appears in LXX after 29.27, jumps from one topic to another in a manner which might be ascribed to the author's whim, were it not obvious that it is rather dictated by the acrostic form (cf. M. B. Crook, *JNES* xiii, 1954, pp. 137f.). There is no evidence of separate themes such as would justify a division into stanzas (contrary to Toy). Rather, where there are verses dealing with cognate matters these may occur at intervals, separated from each other by intervening material. So with vv. 13, 19, 24, and, as Crook has noticed, the spinning process (v. 19) is described after the 'manufacturing' one (v. 13).

The author had enough on his hands with the acrostic principle to work out, and as he tackled the verses one by one he took no thought for what had gone before or what was to come after, except in so far as he was guided by the overall subject of the poem and had a mental picture of the woman whom he intended to portray. Toy divides the poem into six stanzas of three distichs and two of two distichs, and in the process makes the acrostic defective by removing *mēm* and inserting an additional *šīn* before *nūn*. The entire poem does make a cumulative impression, and the poet succeeds in constructing a recognizable and credible portrait of a particular kind of woman. There is thus a unity belonging to the poem as a whole in so far as it has a subject ('A Wife of many Parts'), but the randomness deriving from the strain imposed by the acrostic principle is none the less marked. The uneven progress of the work is enough to show this.

A good wife is of inestimable worth (v. 10); her husband relies on her and derives good from her (vv. 11f.). She makes garments of wool and flax (v. 13); she brings food from afar (? v. 14); she rises early and feeds (?) the household (v. 15). She examines a field and acquires it (v. 16a); with her earnings she plants a vineyard (v. 16b). She steels herself for work and makes the most of good trading conditions (vv. 17f.). She spins (v. 19); she gives to the poor (v. 20); she clothes her household well (v. 21). Her own wardrobe is made up of magnificent clothes (v. 22). Her husband is distinguished in the municipality (v. 23). She sells garments to merchants (v. 24). She is well-equipped for the uncertain future (v. 25). She is a wise and reliable counsellor (v. 26). She keeps a tight control over all domestic affairs and misses nothing (v. 27). She earns the praise and gratitude of her sons and husband (vv. 28f.). She has a worth which transcends physical attractiveness and deserves credit for her accomplishments (vv. 30–31).

Crook (pp. 139f.) supposes that the poem is a paradigm for brides-to-be rather than a description of a wife of quality. She suggests that it is a memorandum such as a young woman of rank might take home with her from a school where she had been groomed for marriage with a man of influence, and so a feminine counterpart of the Instruction, especially in its Egyptian setting. It does not, however, have the form of the Instruction and the scholastic setting postulated by Crook is bare conjecture.

[10] Gemser remarks that the question in v. 10a is not pessimistic in intent, but is rather a rhetorical device. This may be granted in so far as its implication is not that the *'ēšet ḥayil* is an unobtainable ideal, while, nevertheless, it does indicate the rarity and so the value of a wife so variously gifted, as is suggested by the allusion to precious stones in v. 10b. Part, at any rate, of the value of pearls derives from their scarcity, and the even higher worth of the *'ēšet ḥayil* is not unconnected with the difficulty of finding her.

[11f.] Her husband relies on her and has complete confidence in her abilities and judgement, nor has he ever any reason to change his mind on these matters, for she is a model of benevolent constancy and brings him nothing but good and gain. 'Gain' (v. 11b) is an unusual sense of *šālāl*, which elsewhere means 'booty', and G. R. Driver (see

Gemser) suggests 'offspring' (Arabic *salīl*). This weakens the force of v. 11b, where, in agreement with the general tendency of the poem, a reference to the wife's skill as a domestic economist rather than to her fertility is desiderated. Winton Thomas (*VTS* iii, pp. 291f.; *VT* xv, 1965, pp. 277f.) cites the Arabic proverb 'a clever woman is never without wool' (Arabic, *ṯalla* 'wool'), i.e., she fills in every spare moment working with wool. He equates *šālāl* with *ṯalla* and inserts *lāh* (LXX ἡ τοιαύτη): 'Wool is not lacking to her'. The idea is in accord with the poem's portrait of a woman who improves every shining hour. LXX makes the *'ēšet ḥayil* the subject of v. 11b, but this is perhaps to be regarded as an interpretation of MT rather than evidence of a Hebrew text containing *lāh*. I retain MT, recognizing that *šālāl* 'gain' is difficult.

[13] Her raw materials are wool and flax which she makes up into finished articles of different kinds. The precise significance of the phrase 'with the pleasure of her hands' is difficult to determine, but I incline to Toy's view that *ḥēpeṣ* does not refer directly to 'hands' and is not an anthropopathism. Too much cannot be made of this, and such translations as 'with her willing hands' (Köhler), 'with merry hands' (Gemser), 'with inspired hands' are legitimate. Nevertheless, *ḥēpeṣ* refers to the pleasure which the woman derives from her unfettered artistic freedom as the possessor of a pair of skilful hands rather than to the hands themselves (so Toy). Dahood (pp. 60f.), following Ehrlich, supposes that *kappehā* is subject of *watta'aś*, 'which her hands turn into a work of beauty'. He argues that the lack of congruence between subject and verb can be tolerated. But an object has also to be supplied, 'and her hands make (them) into a thing of beauty'. Also a change of subject in v. 13b as compared with 13a has to be assumed.

[14] If v. 14 is taken literally, it apparently means that she does not rely only on local supplies (so Toy), but this does not give particularly good sense. A freer interpretation of the simile is demanded, and the words 'she brings her bread from afar' indicate that she explores and exploits the further possibilities of producing wealth on the basis of the husbandry of her household. Her husband is a farmer and she manufactures and trades in the produce of fields and animals. In becoming a secondary producer and trader, she can be likened to merchant ships; she explores beyond the immediate domestic, wealth-producing context to bring bread from afar.

[15] In v. 15, *ṭerep*, 'prey', is even more embarrassing than *šālāl*

(v. 11), and the translation usually offered ('food') cannot be justified. The obscurity of v. 15b may be the reason why it has been glossed, if v. 15c is indeed a gloss (so Toy, BH, Gemser, Ringgren). Even then it is uncertain whether *ḥōq* means 'rations' or 'duties'. If the mistress gets up before daylight to see that her maids are fed, this might be indicative of her concern for their welfare, while, on the other hand, it might rather be associated with her desire to supervise the distribution of the rations and to ensure that there there will be no wastage nor extravagance. The more probable portrayal is of her rising early to allot her servants their duties for the day and in this case *ṭerep* may be a corruption of *ṭōraḥ* 'work', 'duties' (Kuhn, BH). She is there to set the work of the household in motion at the beginning of each working day, to make sure that everyone has something to do and all fit into her co-ordinated plan.

[16–19] In the *'ēšet ḥayil*, application and tenacity are happily joined to good judgement and acumen. Her capacity for sustained work is expressed metaphorically by the statement that she has strength as a girdle about her loins. She gathers up her dress for prolonged effort and she strengthens her arms (for work, so LXX). She knows how to spin wool and flax (v. 19, *kīšōr* is obscure. KB² thinks it is a whorl for turning the distaff; *pelek* is usually rendered 'spindle'). She has a sharp eye for business opportunities (v. 16), and having weighed up the value of a field which has come on the market, she decides to acquire it. The profit which she earns from her skill as a dressmaker (cf. v. 13b) furnishes the capital for the planting of a vineyard (reading *nāṭeʿā*, with Q.). I take v. 18 to mean: she adjudges that trading conditions are good and so she burns the midnight oil to make the most of them while they last. Toy (following Wildeboer, also Gemser) objects that this is not the sense of v. 18b, and that the lit lamp here as in 13.9 (above p. 461), is symbolic of a prosperous household rather than of the woman's industry. In support, Gemser cites the proverb 'He sleeps in the dark' which means 'He has not another penny in the house'. The interpretation which I have offered binds v. 18b more closely to v. 18a. **[20]** She is as virtuous as she is competent and has a generous care for the poor.

[21f.] The *'ēšet ḥayil* provides warm clothing for her household and her own wardrobe contains nothing but the best. It is usual to emend *šānīm*, 'scarlet', to *šᵉnāyim*, 'double' (BH, Gemser, Ringgren, Barucq, Scott). No alteration of the Hebrew consonantal text is involved and the vocalization is supported by V, *duplicibus*, and LXX, *διασάς* (which is at the beginning of v. 22, but clearly should be attached to the end of v. 21). G. R. Driver (*BASOR* 105, 1947, p. 11) has drawn attention to the difficulty of the form *šānīm* (plural?, cf. Isa. 1.18) and has restored *Baal* IV.iii.24 to read *wtksynn bṯnm*, 'and he covered him with two coverings' (*CML*, p. 118; cf. Dahood, p. 62). Nevertheless, I am not convinced that this is a very probable sense for the verse. Is this really the way in which the *'ēšet ḥayil* would keep her family warm in winter? Would they have to put on two of everything? It could be argued that this is just a way of saying that there is no shortage of good clothing in her household. But the emphasis in both verses is on quality rather than quantity, and for this reason I would retain 'scarlet', which, as Toy and Gemser note, indicates the very best, the clothing of kings. It is the quality of the clothes which they wear which keeps them warm, and she, too, has a magnificent wardrobe made up of fine linen and purple.

[23] Such a woman makes a notable contribution to her husband's success in public life, for he has no domestic worries and can build his reputation on the basis of an honourable and prosperous household. By virtue of her character and genius for sound management he is well set to exert his influence on the life of the community and make a name for himself as a counsellor and man of weight. The gates of the town are the places of assembly where deliberations of public moment take place, where legal and political matters are settled. Dahood (pp. 62f.) argues on the basis of Phoenician evidence that *'ereṣ*, can mean 'city', 'city-state'. **[24]** Verses 24f. revert to economic activities and considerations. She trades in the garments which she makes. The meaning of *sādīn* is uncertain. KB^2 suggests 'underskirt'; LXX *σινδόνας*, 'muslin', is apparently the same word (cf. Toy, who derives *sādīn* from Accadian *sudinnu* 'garment' and supposes that *σινδών* is a Semitic loan word with *n* inserted). Gemser suggests tentatively that *sādīn* may be equated with 'satin'. *The Oxford Dictionary of English Etymology* derives 'satin' from Arabic *zaitūnī*, pertaining to the town Tseutung in China.

[25] The suggestion that her being clothed in strength and majesty (v. 25a) alludes to her nobility of spirit (Ringgren) is not borne out by v. 25b, which suggests rather an allusion to the economic strength of her household (so Toy). She can laugh at the uncertainty of the future because she has built up ample reserves and is confident that no tide of adversity will be able to swamp and undermine her prosperity.

[26f.] She is equally adept at instruction and management. Alert and energetic, she has her finger on the pulse of her household and nothing escapes her scrutiny and control. Whatever she has to say ranks as wisdom and reliable advice. **[28f.]** Her husband and sons sing her praises and testify to her superlative worth. Physical beauty and charm are treacherous and worthless, because there is no constancy and continuance in them. They depart like an unfaithful friend and make way for wrinkles and blemishes, but the woman who fears Yahweh (*yir'at* feminine participle, Gemser, Ringgren, Barucq) deserves praise.

[30] The emphatic religious note in v. 30b contrasts strongly with the tendency in the remainder of the poem to define *ḥayil* in terms of mundane competence (cf. Crook, p. 137). The only exception is v. 20, where her care of the poor could be regarded as the fulfilment of a religious duty. On the other hand, *tōrat ḥesed* (v. 26b) is not necessarily moral or religious instruction, and perhaps rather points to the sound and expert advice which she gives to those whose activities she controls within the context of her domestic economy. Crook urges that v. 30b is a late emendation. **[31]** 'Give her the fruit of her hands' (v. 31a) means 'give her credit for her achievements', as is confirmed by the second half of the line which urges that her deeds should be publicly acknowledged and acclaimed. She deserves a good reputation and a high standing in the community. G. R. Driver (cf. Gemser) suggests *tannū* for *tᵉnū*: 'Give her praise for the fruit of her hands.'

HOYT SHERWIN

THE PORTABLE MBA IN ENTREPRENEURSHIP

The Portable MBA Series

The Portable MBA, Eliza G. C. Collins and Mary Anne Devanna

The Portable MBA in Marketing, Alexander Hiam and Charles D. Schewe

The Portable MBA in Finance and Accounting, John Leslie Livingstone

The Portable MBA in Management, Allan R. Cohen

The Portable MBA in Entrepreneurship, William D. Bygrave

The Portable MBA Desk Reference, Paul Argenti

Real-Time Strategy: Improvising Team-Based Planning for a Fast-Changing World, Lee Tom Perry, Randall G. Stott, W. Norman Smallwood

New Product Development: Managing and Forecasting for Strategic Success, Robert J. Thomas

Total Quality Management: Strategies and Techniques Proven at Today's Most Successful Companies, Stephen George and Arnold Weimerskirch

THE PORTABLE MBA IN ENTREPRENEURSHIP

William D. Bygrave

John Wiley & Sons
New York • Chichester • Brisbane • Toronto • Singapore

This text is printed on acid-free paper.

Copyright ©1994 by John Wiley & Sons, Inc.
All rights reserved. Published simultaneously in Canada.

Reproduction or translation of any part of this work beyond that permitted by Section 107 or 108 of the 1976 United States Copyright Act without the permission of the copyright owner is unlawful. Requests for permission or further information should be addressed to the Permissions Department, John Wiley & Sons, Inc.

This publication is designed to provide accurate and authoritative information in regard to the subject matter covered. It is sold with the understanding that the publisher is not engaged in rendering legal, accounting, or other professional services. If legal advice or other expert assistance is required, the services of a competent professional person should be sought. *From a Declaration of Principles jointly adopted by a Committee of the American Bar Association and a Committee of Publishers.*

Library of Congress Cataloging-in-Publication Data

Bygrave, William D., 1937–
The portable MBA in entrepreneurship / William D. Bygrave.
p. cm.—(Portable MBA series)
Includes index.
ISBN 0-471-57780-4 (acid-free paper)
1. New business enterprises. 2. Small business–Management.
3. Venture capital. 4. Entrepreneurship. I. Title. II. Series.
HD62.5.B94 1994
658.02′2—dc20 93–9024

Printed in the United States of America

10 9 8 7 6 5 4 3 2 1

Contents

Introduction

I am at INSEAD in France on sabbatical leave from Babson College. As I write this introduction, it is a glorious spring day. The nearby Fontainebleau forest is teeming with life. Everything is budding and sprouting. Fresh green shoots are everywhere. Nature is busily renewing herself, unaware that the economy lies in deep winter, frozen in an economic recession. Unemployment, already too high, is on the rise. In Europe entrepreneurial springtime, with its green shoots of economic growth, seems a long way off.

What a contrast with the United States. Across the Atlantic the East Coast is paralyzed by the "storm of the century," but entrepreneurial spring is in the air. New jobs are being created. Productivity is at a 20-year high. Stock prices of small companies are the highest they have ever been. Long-term interest rates are falling. And the cost of capital is the lowest in the industrial world.

Entrepreneurship is what America does best, bar none. No other advanced industrial nation comes close. In the United States entrepreneurial companies created the personal computer, biotechnology, fast food, and overnight package delivery industries; transformed the retailing industry; overthrew AT&T's telecommunications monopoly; revitalized the steel industry; invented the integrated circuit and the microprocessor; founded the nation's most profitable major airline; and the list goes on. Indeed, every sector of the economy feels the influence of entrepreneurs.

Just to keep up with population growth, the U.S. economy must generate about 10,000 jobs every working day. That amounts to 2.5 million new jobs each year. Just to keep level with the number of births, let alone the number of new immigrants, the United States will need to generate something like 20 million new jobs between now and the year 2000. Where are those jobs going to come from? If the trend of the 1980s continues, small, entrepreneurial firms will generate most of the new jobs. Projecting present trends on the birth, survival, and job creation rates of startup firms, we estimate that the nation will need at least 15 million new entrepreneurs between now and the end of the century.

Consider these employment statistics produced by David Birch, the MIT business demographer: The U.S. economy created 21 million jobs in the 1980s. Just 5% of the young and rapidly growing companies accounted for 77% of those jobs, and 15% accounted for an astonishing 94%. There were approximately 500,000 small companies growing by 20% per year. But while small businesses were putting

Americans to work in the 1980s, giant corporations were laying them off in droves. *Fortune* 500 companies eliminated more than 3.5 million jobs in the 1980s. In one year alone, 1988, 3.6 million new jobs were added, while 400,000 jobs were eliminated by the *Fortune* 500. And the pace continues unabated into the 1990s: *Fortune* 500 companies are laying off 400,000 workers annually. Nowhere has the carnage been more bloody than in the manufacturing sector, where almost one million jobs were lost between 1988 and 1990. In contrast, small manufacturers with fewer than 20 workers added more than 200,000 jobs. Today only 5% of the U.S. work force are employed in *Fortune* 500 manufacturing plants.

It is not just blue-collar workers who have been hit hard by unemployment. In the five years ended January 1992, 2.8 million white-collar workers lost their jobs. And since January 1992, four pillars of the *Fortune* 500—Citicorp, Digital Equipment, Sears Roebuck, and IBM—have laid off 100,000 white-collar workers. Small wonder that increasing numbers of recent MBAs are unable to find management positions commensurate with their qualifications: large corporations that traditionally hired new MBAs have fewer openings.

Never before in the history of business schools has there been such a demand from students for entrepreneurship education—a demand that most business schools have not met satisfactorily. True, 317 four-year or graduate U.S. institutions (304 of them business schools) reported having entrepreneurship courses, according to Karl Vesper's survey; and virtually every ranked business school now offers courses in entrepreneurship or related fields, according to another survey. However, the quality or depth of coverage of most programs is thin. A survey of entrepreneurship education in America's major universities found that only 31% of undergraduate and 13% of graduate schools teaching entrepreneurship offer courses beyond the introductory level. And less than half of those schools (44%) have any full-time entrepreneurship faculty. It seems to me that a business education without entrepreneurship is as incomplete as medical training without obstetrics. After all, without the conception, birth, and growth of new enterprises, there would be no businesses.

The Portable MBA in Entrepreneurship is a book for would-be entrepreneurs, people who have started small firms and want to improve their entrepreneurial skills, and others who are interested in entrepreneurship, such as loan officers, lawyers, accountants, and consultants—indeed, anyone who wants to get involved in the birth and growth of an enterprise. The chapters are written by leading authorities on new business creation. They include professors, consultants, and entrepreneurs with extensive experience in teaching the art and science of starting a business. These authors practice what they teach. They have started businesses, served on boards of venture capital funds, been directors of high-growth businesses, raised startup and expansion capital, filed patents, registered companies, and, perhaps most important of all, have created new products and many new jobs. What's more, they are tireless champions of entrepreneurship. They believe that entrepreneurs are America's best hope for an eternal economic springtime.

1 THE ENTREPRENEURIAL PROCESS

William D. Bygrave

This is the entrepreneurial age. Entrepreneurs are driving a revolution that is transforming and renewing economies worldwide. Entrepreneurship is the essence of free enterprise because the birth of new businesses gives a market economy its vitality. New and emerging businesses create a very large proportion of innovative products that transform the way we work and live; products such as personal computers, software, biotechnology drugs, and overnight package deliveries. They generate most of the new jobs. According to some estimates a thousand new businesses are born every hour of every working day in the United States. During the 1980s, small, growing firms generated more than 20 million new jobs in the U.S. economy, whereas the largest firms destroyed 4 million. In central and eastern Europe as many as 7 million entrepreneurs are striving to transform the command economies of the postcommunist nations into free markets. Even China, the last major bastion of communism, is encouraging entrepreneurs. The People's University of Beijing is dropping its Marxist courses and replacing them with courses dealing with free enterprise and entrepreneurship.

There has never been a better time to practice the art and science of entrepreneurship. But what is entrepreneurship? Early this century, Joseph Schumpeter, the Moravian-born economist writing in Vienna, gave us the modern definition of an entrepreneur as the person who destroys the existing economic order by introducing new products and services, by creating new forms of organization, or by exploiting new raw materials. According to Schumpeter, that person is most likely to accomplish this destruction by founding a new business but may also do it within an existing one.

Very few new businesses have the potential to initiate a Schumpeterian "gale" of creation-destruction as Apple computer did in the computer industry. The vast majority of new businesses enter existing markets. In *The Portable MBA in Entrepreneurship,* we take a broader definition of entrepreneurship than Schumpeter's. Ours encompasses everyone who starts a new business. Our entrepreneur is the person who perceives an opportunity and creates an organization to pursue it. And the entrepreneurial process involves all the functions, activities, and actions associated with perceiving opportunities and creating organizations to pursue them. Our entrepreneur's new business may, in a few rare instances, be the revolutionary sort that destroys the global economic order. But it is much more likely to be of the incremental kind that enters an existing market.

- An *entrepreneur* is someone who perceives an opportunity and creates an organization to pursue it.
- The *entrepreneurial process* involves all the functions, activities, and actions associated with perceiving opportunities and creating organizations to pursue them.

But can the art and science of entrepreneurship be taught? Or is the birth of a new enterprise just happenstance and its subsequent success or demise a haphazard process? Although ten years ago—even as recently as five—many business school gurus maintained that entrepreneurship could not be taught, entrepreneurship is today the fastest-growing subject in the business school curriculum. That transformation has come about because a whole body of knowledge about entrepreneurship has developed during the past decade or so. The process of creating a new business is well understood. Yes, entrepreneurship can be taught. However, we cannot guarantee to produce a Bill Gates or a Liz Claiborne any more than a physics professor can guarantee to produce an Albert Einstein or a tennis coach a Martina Navratilova. But give us students with the aptitude to start a business, and we will make them better entrepreneurs.

CRITICAL FACTORS FOR STARTING A NEW ENTERPRISE

We will begin by examining the entrepreneurial process (see Exhibit 1.1). What we are talking about here are the factors—personal, sociological, and environmental—that give birth to a new enterprise. A person gets an idea—an *innovation*—for a new business—either through a deliberate search or a chance encounter. Whether or not he decides to pursue that idea depends on

EXHIBIT 1.1. A model of the entrepreneurial process.

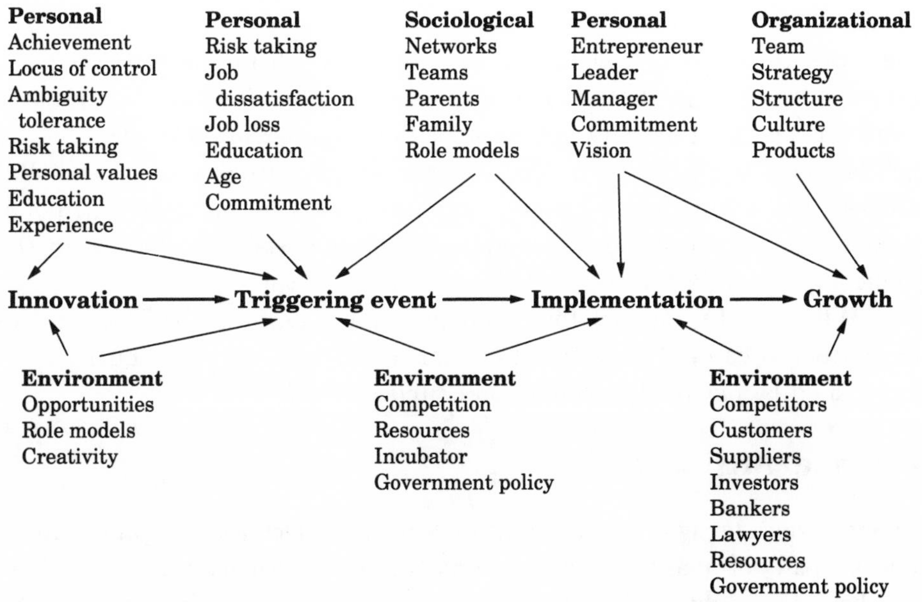

Source: Based on Carol Moore's model, presented in "Understanding Entrepreneurial Behavior," in J. A. Pearce II and R. B. Robinson, Jr., eds., *Academy of Management Best Papers Proceedings,* Forty-sixth Annual Meeting of the Academy of Management, Chicago, 1986.

factors such as his alternative career prospects, family, friends, role models, the state of the economy, and the availability of resources.

There is almost always a *triggering event* that gives birth to a new organization. Perhaps the entrepreneur has no better career prospects. For example, Melanie Stevens was a high school dropout who, after a number of minor jobs, had run out of career options. She decided that making canvas bags in her own tiny business was better than earning low wages working for someone else. Within a few years she had built a chain of retail stores throughout Canada. Sometimes the person has been passed over for a promotion, or even laid off or fired. Howard Rose had been laid off four times as a result of mergers and consolidations in the pharmaceutical industry, and he had had enough of it. So he started his own drug packaging business, Waverly Pharmaceutical. And Tim Waterstone founded Waterstone's book stores after he was fired by W. H. Smith.

For other people, entrepreneurship is a deliberate career choice. Sandra Kurtzig was a software engineer with General Electric who wanted to start a family and work at home. She started ASK Computer Systems Inc., which is now a $400 million-a-year business.

Where do would-be entrepreneurs get their ideas? More often than not it is through their present line of employment or experience. It has been estimated that 90% of all new businesses are founded in industries that are the same as, or closely related to, the one in which the entrepreneur has previous experience. That is not surprising because it is in their present employment that they will get most of their viable business ideas. Some habitual entrepreneurs do it over and over again in the same industry. Bill Poduska was a founder of Prime Computer, which he left to form Apollo, from which he retired and subsequently formed Stellar—all firms in the minicomputer industry.

What are the factors that influence someone to embark on an entrepreneurial career? As with most human behavior, entrepreneurial traits are shaped by *personal attributes* and *environment*.

Personal Attributes

About a decade ago, at the start of the entrepreneurial eighties, there was a spate of magazine and newspaper articles that were titled "Do you have the right stuff to be an entrepreneur?" or words to that effect. The articles described the most important characteristics of entrepreneurs and, more often than not, included a self-evaluation exercise to enable readers to determine if they had the right stuff. Those articles were based on flimsy behavioral research into the differences between entrepreneurs and nonentrepreneurs. The basis for those exercises was the belief, first developed by David McClelland in his book *The Achieving Society,* that entrepreneurs had *a higher need for achievement* than nonentrepreneurs, and that they were moderate risk takers. One engineer almost abandoned his entrepreneurial ambitions after completing one of those exercises. He asked his professor at the start of an MBA entrepreneurship course if he should take the class because he had scored very low on an entrepreneurship test in a magazine. He took the course, however, and wrote an award-winning plan for a business that was a success from the very beginning.

Today, after more research, we know that there is no neat set of behavioral attributes that allow us to separate entrepreneurs from nonentrepreneurs. It turns out that a person who rises to the top of any occupation, whether it be an entrepreneur or an administrator, is an achiever. Granted, any would-be entrepreneur must have a need to achieve, but so must anyone else with ambitions to be successful.

It does appear that entrepreneurs have a *higher internal locus of control* than nonentrepreneurs, which means that they have a higher desire to be in control of their own fate. A recent survey of a broadly representative

EXHIBIT 1.2. The 10 Ds.

Dream	Entrepreneurs have a vision of what the future could be like for them and their businesses. And, more importantly, they have the ability to implement their dreams.
Decisiveness	They don't procrastinate. They make decisions swiftly. Their swiftness is a key factor in their success.
Doers	Once they decide on a course of action, they implement it as quickly as possible.
Determination	They implement their ventures with total commitment. They seldom give up, even when confronted by obstacles that seem insurmountable.
Dedication	They are totally dedicated to their business, sometimes at considerable cost to their relationships with their friends and families. They work tirelessly. Twelve-hour days, and seven-day work weeks are not uncommon when an entrepreneur is striving to get a business off the ground.
Devotion	Entrepreneurs love what they do. It is that love that sustains them when the going gets tough. And it is love of their product or service that makes them so effective at selling it.
Details	It is said that the devil resides in the details. That is never more true than in starting and growing a business. The entrepreneur must be on top of the critical details.
Destiny	They want to be in charge of their own destiny rather than dependent on an employer.
Dollars	Getting rich is not the prime motivator of entrepreneurs. Money is more a measure of their success. They assume that if they are successful they will be rewarded.
Distribute	Entrepreneurs distribute the ownership of their businesses with key employees who are critical to the success of the business.

sample of small businesses owners in Britain found that more than 50% said independence was their main motive for running their own businesses. Only 18% said their main reason was to make money, and 10% mentioned other reasons that included enjoyment, challenge, more room for creativity, personal satisfaction. And according to another recent study, more than 80% of 121 Russian entrepreneurs surveyed said they started a business so as to be their own boss, and that having their own business reinforced feelings of autonomy and freedom.

By and large, we no longer use psychological terms when talking about entrepreneurs. Instead we use everyday words to describe their characteristics. The most important characteristics of successful entrepreneurs are shown in Exhibit 1.2.

Environmental Factors

Perhaps as important as personal attributes are the external influences on a would-be entrepreneur. It's no accident that some parts of the world are more entrepreneurial than others. The most famous region of high-tech entrepreneurship is Silicon Valley. Because everyone in Silicon Valley knows someone who has made it big as an entrepreneur, role models abound. This situation produces what Stanford University sociologist Everett Rogers called Silicon Valley fever. It seems as if everyone in the valley catches that bug sooner or later and wants to start a business. To facilitate the process, there are venture capitalists who understand how to select and nurture high-tech entrepreneurs, bankers who specialize in lending to them, lawyers who understand the importance of intellectual property and how to protect it, landlords who are experienced in renting real estate to fledgling companies, suppliers who are willing to sell goods on credit to companies with no credit history, and even politicians who are supportive.

Role models are very important because knowing successful entrepreneurs makes the act of becoming one yourself seem much more credible. Would-be entrepreneurs see role models primarily in the home and at work. Indeed, if you have a close relative who is an entrepreneur, it is more likely that you will have a desire to become an entrepreneur yourself, especially if that relative is your mother or father. At Babson College, more than half of the students studying entrepreneurship come from families that own businesses. But you don't have to be from a business-owning family to become an entrepreneur. Bill Gates, for example, was following the family tradition of becoming a lawyer when he dropped out of Harvard and founded Microsoft. He was in the fledgling microcomputer industry, which was being built by entrepreneurs, so he had plenty of role models among his friends and acquaintances. The chairman of the British Venture Capital Association recently observed that one of the reasons his nation has relatively few early-stage high-tech startups is that Britain has a scarcity of visible role models compared with the United States, where high-tech entrepreneurs such as Steve Jobs, Bill Gates, and Ken Olsen are household names. One of them, Ross Perot, is so well known that he was the presidential candidate preferred by one in five American voters in 1992.

Some universities are hotbeds of entrepreneurship. For example, Massachusetts Institute of Technology has produced numerous entrepreneurs among its faculty and alums. Companies with an MIT connection transformed the Massachusetts economy from one based on decaying shoe and textile industries into one based on high technology. According to a 1989 study by the Bank of Boston, from the end of the Second World War through 1988, 636 businesses had been established in Massachusetts alone by MIT alums, creating 300,000 jobs and a total income of $10 billion for Massachusetts residents. Annual worldwide sales of those companies totaled about $40 billion in 1988. The neighborhood of East Cambridge adjacent to MIT was termed "The Most Entrepreneurial Place on Earth" by *Inc.* magazine. According to that article, roughly 10% of Massachusetts software companies and 25% of the state's 140 biotechnology companies are headquartered in that square mile.

It is not only in high-tech that we see role models. Consider these examples:

- It has been estimated that half of all the convenience stores in New York city are owned by Koreans.
- It was the visibility of successful role models that spread catfish farming in the Mississippi delta as a more profitable alternative to cotton.
- The Pacific Northwest has more microbreweries than any other region of the United States.
- In the vicinity of the town of Wells, Maine, there are a half-dozen second-hand book stores.

One of the major reasons for a relative lack of entrepreneurship among inner city African-Americans compared with Asian-Americans is the scarcity of African-American entrepreneurs, especially store owners, to provide role models. A similar problem exists among Native Americans. Lack of credible role models is also one of the big challenges in the formerly communist European nations as they strive to become entrepreneurial.

Other Sociological Factors

Besides role models, entrepreneurs have other sociological factors that influence them. *Family responsibilities* play an important role in the decision whether to start a company. It is, relatively speaking, an easy career decision to start a business when a person is 25 years old, single, and without many personal assets and dependents. It is a much harder decision when a person is 45 and married, has teenage children preparing to go to college, a hefty mortgage, car payments, and a secure, well-paying job. A recent survey of European high-potential entrepreneurs, for instance, found that on average they had 50% of their net worth tied up in their businesses. And at 45 plus, if you fail as an entrepreneur, it will not be easy to rebuild a career working for another company. But despite the risks, plenty of 45-year-olds are taking the plunge; in fact, the typical CEO of the 500 fastest-growing small companies, the *Inc.* 500, is a 50-year-old.

Another factor that determines the age at which entrepreneurs start businesses is the trade-off between the *experience* that comes with age and the *optimism* and *energy* of youth. As you grow older you gain experience, but sometimes when you have been in an industry a long time, you know so many pitfalls that you are pessimistic about the chance of succeeding if you decide to go out on your own. Someone who has just enough experience to feel confident as a manager is more likely to feel optimistic about an entrepreneurial career. Perhaps the ideal combination is a beginner's mind with the experience of an industry veteran. A beginner's mind looks at situations from a new perspective, with a can-do spirit.

Robert Swanson was 27 years old when he hit upon the idea that a company could be formed to capitalize on biotechnology. At that time he knew almost nothing about the field. By reading the scientific literature, Swanson identified the leading biotechnology scientists and contacted them. "Everybody said I was too early—it would take ten years to turn out the first microorganism from a human hormone or maybe twenty years to have a commercial product—everybody except Herb Boyer." Swanson was referring to Professor Herbert Boyer at the University of California at San Francisco, coinventor of the patents that, according to some observers, form the basis of the biotechnology industry. When Swanson and Boyer met in early 1976, they almost immediately agreed to become partners in an endeavor to explore the commercial possibilities of recombinant DNA. Boyer named their venture Genentech, an acronym for genetic engineering technology. Just seven months later, Genentech announced its first success, a genetically engineered human brain hormone, somatosin. According to Swanson, they accomplished ten years of development in seven months.

Before leaving secure, well-paying, satisfying jobs, would-be entrepreneurs should make a *careful estimate of how much sales revenue* their new businesses must generate before they will be able to match the income that they presently earn. It usually comes as quite a shock when they realize that if they are opening a retail establishment, they will need annual sales revenue of at least $400,000—to pay themselves a salary of $50,000 plus fringe benefits such as health care coverage, retirement pension benefits, long-term disability insurance, vacation pay, sick leave, and perhaps subsidized meals, day-care, and education benefits. Four hundred thousand dollars a year is about $8,000 per week, or about $1,333 per day, or about $133 per hour, or $2 per minute if they are open 6 days a week, 10 hours a day. Also they will be working much longer hours and bearing much more responsibility if they become self-employed. A sure way to test the strength of a marriage is to start a company that is the sole means of support for your family.

When they actually start a business, entrepreneurs need a host of *contacts,* including customers, suppliers, investors, bankers, accountants, and lawyers. So it is important to understand where to find help before embarking on a new venture. A network of friends and business associates can be of immeasurable help in building the contacts an entrepreneur will need. They can also provide human contact because opening a business can be a lonely experience for anyone who has worked in an organization with many fellow employees.

Fortunately, today there are more organizations than ever before to help fledgling entrepreneurs. Often that help is free or costs very little. The SBA has Small Business Development Centers in every state; it funds Small Business Institutes; and its Service Core of Retired Executives provides free assistance to entrepreneurs. Many colleges and universities also provide help. Some are particularly good at writing business plans, usually at no charge to the entrepreneur. There are more than 400 incubators in the United States where fledgling businesses can rent space, usually at a very reasonable price, and spread some of their overhead by sharing facilities such as copying and FAX machines, secretarial help, answering services, and so on. Incubators are often associated with universities, which provide free or inexpensive counseling. There are numerous associations where entrepreneurs can meet and exchange ideas. In the Boston area, for example, the 128 Venture Forum provides a place where entrepreneurs, financiers, accountants, lawyers, and other professionals meet each month for a two-hour breakfast.

EVALUATING OPPORTUNITIES FOR NEW BUSINESSES

Let's assume you believe you have found a great opportunity for starting a new business. How should you evaluate its prospects? Or, perhaps more importantly, how will an independent person such as a potential investor or a banker rate your chances of success? The odds of succeeding appear to be stacked against you, because according to small business folklore, only one business in ten will ever reach its tenth birthday. This doesn't mean that nine out of ten of the estimated two million businesses that are started every year go bankrupt. We know that even in a severe recession, the number of businesses filing for bankruptcy in the United States has never yet surpassed 100,000 in any year. In an average year, the number is about 50,000. So what happens to the vast majority of the ones that do not survive 10 years? Most just fade away: They are started as part-time pursuits and are never intended to become full-time businesses. Some are sold. Others are liquidated. Only 700,000 of the two million are legally registered as corporations or partnerships, which is a sure sign that many of the remaining 1.3 million never intended to grow. Hence, the odds that your new business will survive may not be as long as they first appear to be. If you intend to start a full-time, incorporated business, the odds that the business will survive at least eight years with you as the owner are better than one in four; and the odds of its surviving at least eight years with a new owner are another one in four. So the eight-year survival rate for incorporated startups is about 50%.

But survival may not spell success. Too many entrepreneurs find that they can neither earn a satisfactory living in their businesses nor get out of them easily because they have too much of their personal assets tied up in them. The happiest day in an entrepreneur's life is the day doors are opened for business. For unsuccessful entrepreneurs, an even happier day may be the day the business is sold—especially if most personal assets remain intact. What George Bernard Shaw said about love affairs is also apt for business: Any fool can start one, it takes a genius to end one successfully.

How can you stack the odds in your favor, so that your new business is a success? Professional investors, such as venture capitalists, have a talent for picking winners. True, they also pick losers, but a startup company funded by venture capital has, on average, a four in five chance of surviving five years—better odds than for the population of startup companies as a whole. By using the criteria that professional investors use, entrepreneurs can increase their odds of success. Very few startup businesses—perhaps no more than one in a thousand—will ever be suitable candidates for investments from professional venture capitalists. But would-be entrepreneurs can learn a lot by following the evaluation process used by professional investors.

There are three crucial components for a successful new business: the opportunity, the entrepreneur (and the management team, if it's a high-potential venture), and the resources needed to start the company and make it grow. They are shown schematically in Exhibit 1.3, the basic Timmons framework that will be developed further in the next chapter. At the center

EXHIBIT 1.3. Three driving forces.

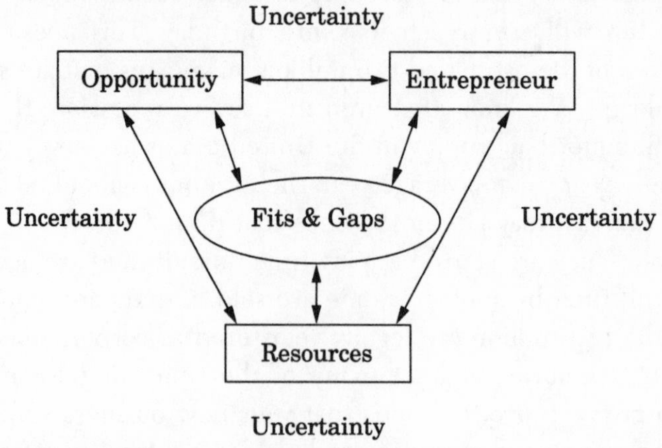

Source: Based on Jeffry Timmons's framework, as presented in Jeffry A. Timmons, *New Venture Creation* (Homewood, IL: Richard D. Irwin, 1990).

of the framework is a business plan, in which the three basic ingredients are integrated into a complete strategic plan for the new business. The parts must fit together well. It's no good having a first-rate idea for a new business if you have a second-rate management team. Nor are ideas and management any good without the appropriate resources.

Georges Doriot, the founder of modern venture capital, used to say something like this: "Always consider investing in a grade A man with a grade B idea. Never invest in a grade B man with a grade A idea." He knew what he was talking about. Over the years he invested in about 150 companies, including Digital Equipment Corporation (DEC), and watched over them as they struggled to grow. But Doriot made this statement about business in the 1950s and 1960s. During that period there were far fewer startups each year; U.S. firms dominated the marketplace; markets were growing quickly; there was almost no competition from overseas; and most entrepreneurs were male. Today, in the global marketplace with ever shortening product life cycles and low growth or even no growth for some of the world's leading industrial nations, the crucial ingredients for entrepreneurial success are a superb entrepreneur with a first-rate management team and an excellent market opportunity.

> The crucial ingredients for entrepreneurial success are a superb entrepreneur with a first-rate management team and an excellent market opportunity.

Frequently I hear the comment that success in entrepreneurship is largely a matter of luck. That's not so. We do not say that becoming a great quarterback, or a great scientist, or a great musician, and so on, is a matter of luck. There is no more luck in becoming successful at entrepreneurship than in becoming successful at anything else. In entrepreneurship, it is a question of recognizing a good opportunity when you see one and having the skills to convert that opportunity into a thriving business. To do that, you must be prepared. So in entrepreneurship, just like any other profession, *luck is where preparation and opportunity meet.*

In 1982, when Rod Canion proposed to start Compaq to make personal computers, there were already formidable established competitors, including IBM and Apple. By then literally hundreds of companies were considering entering the market or had already done so. For instance, in the same week of May 1982 that DEC announced its ill-fated personal computer, four other companies introduced PCs. Despite the competition, Ben Rosen of the venture capital firm Sevin Rosen Management Company, invested in Compaq. Started initially to make transportable PCs, it quickly added a complete range of high-performance PCs and grew so fast that it soon broke Apple's record for the fastest time from founding to listing on the *Fortune* 500.

What did Ben Rosen see in the Compaq proposal that made it stand out from all the other personal computer startups? The difference was Rod Canion and his team. Rod Canion had earned a reputation as an excellent manager at Texas Instruments. Furthermore, the market for personal computers topped $5 billion and was growing at a torrid pace. So Rosen had found a superb team with a product targeted at an undeveloped niche, transportable PCs, in a large market that was growing explosively.

> In entrepreneurship, as in any other profession, luck is where preparation and opportunity meet.

The Opportunity

Perhaps the biggest misconception about an idea for a new business is that it must be unique. Too many would-be entrepreneurs are almost obsessed with finding a unique idea. Then, when they believe they have it, they are haunted by the thought that someone is just waiting to steal it from them. So they become super secretive. They are reluctant to discuss it with anyone unless that person signs a nondisclosure agreement. That in itself makes it almost impossible to evaluate the idea. For example, many counselors who provide free advice to entrepreneurs refuse to sign nondisclosure agreements. Generally speaking, these super-secret, unique ideas are big letdowns when the entrepreneur reveals them to you. Among the notable ones I have encountered were "drive-through pizza by the slice," "a combination toothbrush and toothpaste gadget," and "a Mexican restaurant in Boston." One computer programmer telephoned me and said that he had a fantastic new piece of software. Eventually, after I assured him that I was not going to steal his idea, he told me his software was for managing hairdressing salons. He was completely floored when I told him that less than a month previously another entrepreneur had visited my office and demonstrated a software package for exactly the same purpose. Another entrepreneur had an idea for fluoride-impregnated dental floss. Not three months later, on a visit to England, I found the identical product in Boots—Britain's largest chain of drug stores and a major pharmaceutical manufacturer.

I tell would-be entrepreneurs that almost any idea they have will also have occurred to others. For good measure I point out that some of the most revolutionary thoughts in the history of mankind occurred to more than one person almost simultaneously. For instance, Darwin was almost preempted by Wallace in publishing his theory of evolution; Poincaré formulated a valid theory of relativity about the same time Einstein did; and the integrated circuit was invented in 1959 first by Jack Kilby at Texas Instruments, and then independently by Robert Noyce at Fairchild a few months later. So the idea per se is not what is important. In entrepreneurship, ideas really are a dime a dozen. Developing the idea, implementing it, and building a successful business are the important things. Alexander Fleming discovered penicillin by chance but never developed it as a useful drug. About 10 years later Ernst Chain and Howard Florey unearthed Fleming's mold. They immediately saw its potential. Working in England under wartime conditions, they soon were treating patients. Before the end of World War II, penicillin was saving countless lives. It was a most dramatic pharmaceutical advance and heralded a revolution in that industry.

The idea per se is not what is important. In entrepreneurship, ideas really are a dime a dozen. Developing the idea, implementing it, and building a successful business are the important things.

Customer Need

Many would-be entrepreneurs call me up and tell me that they have an idea for a new business and can they come to see me. Unfortunately, it is impossible to see all of them, so I have developed a few questions that allow me to judge how far along they are with their idea. By far the most telling question is, "Can you give me the names of prospective customers?" Their answer must be very specific. If they have a consumer product—let's say it's a new shampoo—I expect them to be able to name buyers at different chains of drug stores in their area. If they are unable to name several customers immediately, they simply have an idea, not a market. There is no market unless customers have a real need for the product—a proven need rather than a hypothetical need in the mind of a would-be entrepreneur. In a few rare cases it may be a revolutionary new product, but it is much more likely be an existing product with improved performance, price, distribution, quality, or service. Simply put, customers must perceive that the new business will be giving them better value for their money than existing businesses.

Would-be entrepreneurs who are unable to name customers are not ready to start a business. They have only found an idea and have not yet identified a market need.

Timing

Time plays a crucial role in many potential opportunities. In some emerging industries, there is a definite window of opportunity that opens only once. For instance, about 10 years ago, when VCRs were first coming into household use in the United States, there was a need for video stores in convenient locations where viewers could pick up movies on the way home from work. Lots of video retail stores opened up in main streets and shopping centers. They were usually run by independent store owners. Then the distribution of videos changed. National chains of video stores emerged. Supermarket and drug store chains entered the market. Today, the window of opportunity for starting an independent video store is closed. There are simply too many big competitors in convenient locations.

In other markets, high-quality restaurants for example, there is a steady demand that, on average, does not change much from year to year, so the window of opportunity is always open. Nevertheless, timing can be important, because when the economy turns down, those kinds of restaurants are usually hit harder than lower-quality ones, so the time to open one is during a recovering or booming economy.

If the window of opportunity appears to be very brief, it may be that the idea is a consumer fad that will quickly pass away. It takes a very skilled entrepreneur indeed to make money out of a fad. When Lucy's Have A Heart Canvas of Faneuil Hall Market in Boston introduced shoe laces with hearts on them, they flew off the shelves. Children and teenagers could not get enough of them for their sneakers. The store ordered more and more of them. Then demand suddenly dropped precipitously. The store and the manufacturer were left holding huge inventories that could not be sold. As a result the store almost went under.

Most entrepreneurs should avoid fads or any window of opportunity that they believe will only be open for a very brief time, because it inevitably means that they will rush to open their business, sometimes before they have time to gather the resources they will need. Rushing to open a business without adequate planning can lead to costly mistakes.

The Entrepreneur and the Management Team

Regardless of how right the opportunity may seem to be, it will not make a successful business unless it is developed by a person with strong entrepreneurial and management skills. What are the important skills?

First and foremost, entrepreneurs should have experience in the same industry or a similar one. Starting a business is a very demanding undertaking indeed. It is no time for on-the-job training. If would-be entrepreneurs do not have the right experience, they should either go out and get it before starting their new venture or find partners who have it.

Some investors say that the ideal entrepreneur is one who has a track record of being successful previously as an entrepreneur in the same industry and who can attract a seasoned team. Half of the CEOs of the *Inc.* 500 high-growth small companies had started at least one other business before they founded their present firms. When Joseph Crugnale acquired his first ice cream shop in 1977, he already had almost 10 years in the food service industry. Six years later, when he sold Steve's Ice Cream, it was a 26-store operation. He opened his first Bertucci's Brick Oven Pizzeria in 1981 and began expanding it into a chain in 1985. By 1991, he and his management team, with a total of more than 100 years experience in the food industry, had built Bertucci's into a rapidly growing chain with sales of $30 million and net income of $2 million. When the company went public in June 1991, it had a market value of $63 million.

Without relevant experience, the odds are stacked against the neophyte in any industry. An electronics engineer told me that he had a great idea for a chain of fast-food stores. When asked if he had ever worked in a fast-food restaurant, he replied, "Work in one? I wouldn't even eat in one. I can't stand fast food!" Clearly, he would have been as miscast as a fast-food entrepreneur as Crugnale would have been as an electronics engineer.

True, there are examples of people who have succeeded with no prior industry experience. But they are the exceptions that definitely do not prove the rule.

Second to industry know-how is *management experience*, preferably with responsibility for budgets, or better yet, accountability for profit and loss. It is even better if a would-be entrepreneur has a record of increasing sales and profits. Of course, we are talking about the *ideal* entrepreneur. Very few people measure up to the ideal. That does not mean they should not start a new venture. But it does mean they should be realistic about the size of business they should start. Five years ago, two 19-year-old students wanted to start a travel agency business in Boston. When asked what they knew about the industry, one replied, "I live in California. I love to travel." The other was silent. Neither of them had worked in the travel industry, nor had anyone in either of their families. They were advised to get experience. One joined a training program for airline ticket agents; the other took a course for travel agents. They became friends with the owner of a local Uniglobe travel agency who helped them with advice. Six months after they first had the idea, they opened a part-time campus travel agency. In the first six months they had about $100,000 of revenue and made $6,000 of profit but were unable to pay themselves any salary. In that way, they acquired experience at no expense and at low risk. Upon graduation, one of them made it his full-time business. In 1993, the business was expecting sales revenue of $3 million.

Resources

It's hard to believe that Olsen and Anderson started DEC with only $70,000 of startup capital and built a company ranked in the top 25 of the *Fortune* 500 companies. "The nice thing about $70,000 is that there are so few of them, you can watch every one," Olsen said. And watch them he did. Olsen and Anderson moved into a 100-year-old building that had been a nineteenth-century woollen mill. They furnished it with second-hand furniture, purchased tools from the Sears catalog, and built much of their own equipment as cheaply as possible. They sold $94,000 worth in their first year and made a profit at the same time—a very rare feat indeed for a high-tech startup.

Successful entrepreneurs are frugal with their scarce resources. They keep overheads low, productivity high, and ownership of capital assets to a minimum. By so doing they minimize the amount of capital they need to start their business and make it grow. One quarter of the *Inc.* 500 small business stars began with less than $5,000 of capital, half with less than $25,000, and three-quarters with less than $100,000. Fewer than 5% began with more than $1 million.

Entrepreneurial frugality is:

- Low overhead
- High productivity
- Minimal ownership of capital assets

Determining Resource Needs and Acquiring Resources

In order to determine the amount of capital that a company needs to get started, an entrepreneur must determine the minimum set of essential resources. Some resources are more critical than others. The first thing an entrepreneur should do is assess what resources are crucial for the company's success in the marketplace. What does the company expect to do better than any of its competitors? That is where it should put a disproportionate share of its very scarce resources. If the company is making a new high-tech product, technological know-how will be vital. Then its most important resource will be engineers and the designs they produce. Therefore, the company must concentrate on recruiting and keeping excellent engineers, and safeguarding the intellectual property that they produce, such as engineering designs and patents. If the company is doing retail selling, the critical factor is most likely to be location. It makes no sense to choose a site in a poor location just because the rent is cheap. Choosing the wrong initial location for a retail store can be a fatal mistake, because it's unlikely that there will be enough resources to relocate.

When Southwest Airlines started up 20 years ago, its strategy was to provide frequent, on-time service at a competitive price between Dallas, Houston, Austin, and San Antonio. To meet its objectives, Southwest needed planes that it could operate reliably at low cost. It was able to purchase four brand-new Boeing 737s—very efficient planes for shorter routes—for only $4 million each because the recession had hit the airlines particularly hard and Boeing had an inventory of unsold 737s. From the outset, Southwest provided good, reliable service and had one of the lowest costs per mile in the industry. Today, Southwest is the most successful domestic airline, while two of its biggest competitors when it started out, Braniff International and Texas International, have gone bankrupt.

Items that are not critical should be obtained as thriftily as possible. The founder of Burlington Coat, Monroe Milstein, likes to tell the story of how he obtained estimates for gutting the building he had just leased for his second store. His lowest bid was several thousand dollars. One day he was at the building when a sudden thunderstorm sent a crew of laborers working at a nearby site to his building for shelter from the rain. Milstein asked the crew's foreman what they would charge for knocking down the internal structures that needed to be removed. The foreman said, "Five." Milstein asked, "Five what?" The foreman replied, "Cases of beer."

A complete set of resources includes everything that the business will need. A key point to remember when deciding to acquire those resources is that a business does not have to do all its work in-house with its own employees. It is often more effective to subcontract the work. That way it need not own or lease its own manufacturing plant and equipment. Nor does it have to worry about recruiting and training production workers. Often, it can keep overhead lower by using outside firms to do work such as payroll, accounting, advertising, mailing promotions, janitorial services, and so on.

Even startup companies can get amazingly good terms from outside suppliers. An entrepreneur should try to understand the potential suppliers' marginal costs. Marginal cost is the cost of producing one extra unit beyond what is presently produced. The marginal cost of the laborers who gutted Milstein's building while sheltering from the rain was virtually zero. They were being paid by another firm, and they didn't have to buy materials or tools.

A small electronics company was acquired by a much larger competitor. The large company took over the manufacturing of the small company's products. Production costs shot up. An analysis revealed that much of the increase was due to a rise in the cost of purchased components. In one instance, the large company was paying 50% more than the small company had been paying for the same item. It turned out that the supplier had priced the item for the small company on the basis of marginal costs and for the large company on the basis of total costs.

Smart entrepreneurs find ways of controlling critical resources without owning them. A startup business never has enough money. It should not buy what it can lease. It must be resourceful. Except when the economy is red hot, there is almost always an excess of capacity of office and industrial space. Sometimes a landlord will be willing to offer a special deal to attract even a small startup company into a building. Such deals may include reduced rent, deferral of rent payments for a period of time, and building improvements at low cost or even no cost. In some high-tech regions, there are landlords who will exchange rent for equity in a high-potential startup.

When equipment is in excess supply, it can be leased on very favorable terms. A young database company was negotiating a lease with IBM for a new minicomputer when its chief engineer discovered that a leasing company had identical secondhand units standing idle in its warehouse. It was able to lease one of the idle units for one-third of IBM's price. About 18 months later, the database company ran out of cash. Nevertheless, it was able to persuade the leasing company to defer payments, because by then there were even more minicomputers standing idle in the warehouse, and it made little economic sense to repossess one and add it to the idle stock.

Startup Capital

You have reached the point where you have developed your idea; you have carefully assessed what resources you will need to open your business and make it grow; you have pulled all your strategies together into a business plan; and now you know how much startup capital you will need to get you to the point where your business will generate a positive cash flow. How are you going to raise that startup capital?

There are two types of startup capital: debt and equity. Simply put, with debt you don't have to give up any ownership of the business, but you have to pay current interest and eventually repay the principal; with equity you have to give up some of the ownership to get it, but you may never have to repay it or even pay a dividend. So you must choose between paying interest and giving up some of the ownership.

What usually happens, in practice, depends on how much of each type of capital you can raise. Most startup entrepreneurs do not have much flexibility in their choice of financing. If it is a very risky business without any assets, it will be impossible to get any bank debt without putting up some collateral other than the business's assets—most likely that collateral will be personal assets. Even if entrepreneurs are willing to guarantee the whole loan with their personal assets, the bank will expect them to put some equity into the business, probably equal to 25% of the amount of the loan.

The vast majority of entrepreneurs start their businesses by leveraging their own savings and labor. Consider how Apple, one of the most spectacular startups of all time, was funded. Steven Jobs and Stephan Wozniak had been friends since their school days in Silicon Valley. Wozniak was an authentic computer nerd. He had tinkered with computers from childhood, and he built a computer that won first prize in a science fair. His SAT math score was a perfect 800, but after stints at the University of Colorado, De Anza College, and Berkeley, he dropped out of school and went to work for Hewlett-Packard. His partner, Jobs, had an even briefer encounter with higher education: After one semester at Reed College, he left to look for a swami in India. When he and Wozniak began working on their microcomputer, Jobs was working at Atari, the leading video game company.

Apple soon outgrew its manufacturing facility in the garage of Jobs's parents' house. Their company, financed initially with $1,300 raised by selling Jobs's Volkswagen and Wozniak's calculator, needed capital for expansion. They looked to their employers for help. Wozniak proposed to his supervisor that Hewlett-Packard should produce what later became the Apple II. Perhaps not surprisingly, he was rejected. After all, he had no formal qualification in computer design; indeed, he did not even have a college degree. At Atari, Jobs tried to convince founder Nolan Bushnell to manufacture Apples. He too was rejected.

However, on the suggestion of Bushnell and Regis McKenna, a Silicon Valley marketing ace, they contacted Don Valentine, a venture capitalist in the fall of 1976. In those days, Jobs's appearance was a hangover from his swami days. It definitely did not project the image of Doriot's grade A man, even by Silicon Valley's casual standards. Valentine did not invest. But he did put them in touch with Armas Markkula, Jr., who had recently retired from Intel a wealthy man. Markkula saw the potential in Apple, and he knew how to raise money. He personally invested $91,000, secured a line of credit from Bank of America, put together a business plan, and raised $600,000 of venture capital.

The Apple II was formally introduced in April 1977. Sales took off almost at once. Apple's sales grew rapidly to $2.5 million in 1977 and $15 million in 1978. In 1978, Dan Bricklin, a Harvard business student and former programmer at DEC, introduced the first electronic spreadsheet, VisiCalc, designed for the Apple II. In minutes it could do tasks that had previously taken days. The microcomputer now had the power to liberate managers from the data guardians in the computer departments. According to one source, "Armed with VisiCalc, the Apple II's sales took off, and the personal computer industry was created." Apple's sales jumped to $70 million in 1979 and $117 million in 1980.

In 1980, Apple sold some of its stock to the public with an initial public offering (IPO) and raised more than $80 million. The paper value of their Apple stock made instant millionaires out of Jobs ($165 million), Markkula ($154 million), Wozniak ($88 million), and Mike Scott ($62 million), who together owned 40% of Apple. Arthur Rock's venture capital investment of $57,600 in 1978 was suddenly worth $14 million, an astronomical compound return of more than 500% per year, or 17% per month.

By 1982, Apple IIs were selling at the rate of more than 33,000 units a month. With 1982 sales of $583 million, Apple hit the *Fortune* 500 list. It was a record. At five years of age, it was at that time the youngest company ever to join that exclusive list.

Success as spectacular as Apple's has seldom been equaled. Nonetheless, its financing is a typical example of how successful high-tech companies are funded. First, the entrepreneurs develop a prototype with sweat equity and personal savings. Sweat equity is ownership earned in lieu of wages. Then a wealthy investor—sometimes called an informal investor or business angel—who knows something about the entrepreneurs, or the industry, or both, invests some personal money in return for equity. When the company is selling product, it may be able to get a bank line of credit secured by its inventory and accounts receivable. If the company is growing quickly in a large market, it may be able to raise capital from a formal venture capital firm in return for equity. Further expansion capital may come from venture capital firms or from a public stock offering.

Most new firms will never be candidates for formal venture capital or a public stock offering. Nevertheless, they will have to find some equity capital. In most cases, after they have exhausted their personal savings, entrepreneurs will turn to family, friends, and acquaintances (see Exhibit 1.4). It can be a scary business. Entrepreneurs often find themselves with all their personal net worth tied up in the same business that provides all their income. That is double jeopardy, because if their businesses fail, they lose both their savings

EXHIBIT 1.4. Sources of seed capital for the *Inc.* 500.

Personal savings	78.5%
Bank loans	14.4%
Family members	12.9%
Employees/partners	12.4%
Friends	9.0%
Venture capital	6.3%
Mortgaged property	4.0%
Government guaranteed loans	1.1%
Other	3.3%

Source: *Inc.*, October 1992.

and their means of support. Risk of that sort can be justified only if the profit potential is high enough to yield a commensurate rate of return.

Profit Potential

The level of profit that is reasonable depends on the type of business. On average, U.S. companies make about 5% net income. Hence, on one dollar of revenue, the average company makes five cents profit after paying all expenses and taxes. A company that consistently makes 10% is doing very well, and one that makes 15% is truly exceptional. Approximately 50% of the *Inc.* 500 companies make 5% or less; 13% of them make 16% or more. Profit margins in a wide variety of industries for companies both large and small are published by Robert Morris Associates. Hence it is possible for entrepreneurs to compare their forecasts with the actual performance of similar-sized companies in the same industry.

Any business must make enough profit to recompense its investors (in most cases that is the entrepreneur) for their investment. It must be profit after all normal business expenses have been accounted for, including a fair salary for the entrepreneur and any family members who are working in the business. A common error in assessing the profitability of a new venture is to ignore the owner's salary. Suppose someone leaves a secure job paying $50,000 per year plus fringe benefits and invests $100,000 of personal savings to start a new venture. That person should expect to take a $50,000 salary plus fringe benefits out of the new business. Perhaps in the first year or two, when the business is being built, it may not be possible to pay $50,000 in actual cash; in that case, the pay that is not actually received should be treated as deferred compensation to be paid in the future. In addition to an adequate salary, the entrepreneur must also earn a reasonable return on the $100,000 investment. A professional investor putting money into a new, risky business would expect to earn an annual rate of return of at least 40%, which would be $40,000 annually on a $100,000 investment. That return may come as a capital gain when the business is sold, or as a dividend, or a combination of the two. But remember that $100,000 compounding annually at 40% grows to almost $2.9 million in 10 years. When such large capital gains are needed to produce acceptable returns, big capital investments held for a long time do not make any sense unless very substantial value can be created, as occasionally happens in the case of high-flying companies, especially high-tech ones. In most cases, instead of a capital gain, the investor's return will be a dividend, which must be paid out of the cash flow from the business.

The cash flow that a business generates is not to be confused with profit. It is possible, indeed very likely, that a rapidly growing business will have a negative cash flow from operations in its early years even though it may be profitable. That may happen because the business may not be able to generate enough cash flow internally to sustain its ever-growing needs for working capital and the purchase of long-term assets such as plant and equipment. Hence, it will have to borrow or raise new equity capital. So it is very important that a high-potential business intending to grow rapidly make careful cash-flow projections so as to predict its needs for future outside investments. Future equity investments will dilute the percentage ownership of the founders, and if the dilution becomes excessive, there may be little reward remaining for the entrepreneurs.

Biotechnology companies are examples of this; they have a seemingly insatiable need for cash infusions to sustain their R&D costs in their early years. Their negative cash flow, or *burn rate*, sometimes runs at $1 million per month. A biotechnology company can easily burn up $50 million before it generates a meaningful profit, let alone a positive cash flow. The expected future capital gain from a public stock offering or sale to a large pharmaceutical company has to run into hundreds of millions of dollars, maybe into the billion-dollar range, for investors to realize an annual return of 50% or higher, which is what they expect to earn on money invested in a seed-stage biotechnology company. Not surprisingly, to finance their ventures biotechnology entrepreneurs as a group have to give up most of the ownership. A recent study of venture-capital-backed biotechnology companies found that after they had gone public, the entrepreneurs and management were left with less than 18% of the equity, compared with 32% for a comparable group of computer software companies.

As has already been mentioned, the vast majority of businesses will never have the potential to go public. Nor will the owners ever intend to sell their businesses and thereby realize a capital gain. In that case, how can those owners get a satisfactory return on the money they have invested in their businesses? The two ingredients that determine return on investment are (1) amount invested, and (2) annual amount earned on that investment. Hence, entrepreneurs should invest as little as possible to start their businesses and make sure that their firms will be able to pay them a "dividend" big enough to yield an appropriate annual rate of return. For income tax purposes, that "dividend" may be in the form of a salary bonus or fringe benefits rather than an actual dividend paid out of retained earnings. Of course, the company must be generating cash from its own operations before that dividend can be paid. For entrepreneurs, happiness is a positive cash flow. The day a company begins to generate cash is a very happy day in the life of a successful entrepreneur.

For entrepreneurs, happiness is a positive cash flow.

INGREDIENTS FOR A SUCCESSFUL NEW BUSINESS

The great day has arrived. You found an idea, wrote a business plan, and gathered your resources. Now you are opening the doors of your new business for the first time, and the really hard work is about to begin. What are the factors that distinguish winning entrepreneurial businesses from the also-rans? Rosabeth Kanter prescribed Four Fs for a successful business, a list that has been expanded into the Nine Fs for entrepreneurial success (see Exhibit 1.5).

First and foremost, the founding entrepreneur is the most important factor. Next comes the market. This is the "era of the other," in which, as Regis McKenna observed, the fastest-growing companies in an industry will be in a segment labeled "others" in a market share pie-chart. By and large, they will be newer entrepreneurial firms rather than large firms with household names; hence specialization is the key. A successful business should focus on niche markets.

The rate of change in business gets ever faster. The advanced industrial economies are knowledge based. Product life cycles are getting shorter. Technological innovation progresses at a relentless pace. Government rules and regulations keep changing. Communications and travel around the globe keep getting easier and cheaper. And consumers are better informed about their choices. To survive, let alone succeed, in business, a company has to be quick and nimble. It must be fast and flexible. It cannot allow inertia to build up. Look at retailing: The historical giants such as Sears are on the ropes, while nimble competitors dance around them. Three of the biggest retailing successes are Les Wexner's The Limited, the late Sam Walton's Wal-Mart,

EXHIBIT 1.5. The Nine Fs.

Founders	Every startup company must have a first-class entrepreneur.
Focused	Entrepreneurial companies focus on niche markets. They specialize.
Fast	They make decisions quickly and implement them swiftly.
Flexible	They keep an open mind. They respond to change.
Forever-innovating	They are tireless innovators.
Flat	Entrepreneurial organizations have as few layers of management as possible.
Frugal	By keeping overhead low and productivity high, entrepreneurial organizations keep costs down.
Friendly	Entrepreneurial companies are friendly to their customers, suppliers, and workers.
Fun	It's fun to be associated with an entrepreneurial company.

and Anita Roddick's The Body Shop. Entrepreneurs such as those know that they can keep inertia low by keeping the layers of management as few as possible. Tom Peters, an authority on business strategy, likes to point out that Wal-Mart has three layers of management, whereas Sears has ten. "A company with three layers of management can't lose against a company with ten. You could try, but you couldn't do it!" says Peters. No wonder Ferdinand Piëch, the new boss of Volkswagen, wants to eliminate seven or eight levels of management as part of his effort to revive the profits of Europe's largest automobile manufacturer. So keep your organization flat. It will facilitate quick decisions and flexibility, and keep overhead low.

Small entrepreneurial firms are great innovators. Big firms are relying increasingly on strategic partnerships with entrepreneurial firms in order to get access to desirable R&D. It is a trend that is well under way. Hoffmann-La Roche, hurting for new blockbuster prescription drugs, purchased a majority interest in Genentech and bought the highly regarded biotechnology called PCR (polymerase chain reaction) from Cetus for $300 million. Eli Lilly purchased Hybritech. In the 1980s, IBM spent $9 billion a year on research and development, but even that astronomical amount of money could not sustain Big Blue's technological leadership. As its market share was remorselessly eaten away by thousands of upstarts, IBM entered into strategic agreements with Apple, Borland, Go, Lotus, Intel, Metaphor, Microsoft, Novell, Stratus, Thinking Machines, and other entrepreneurial firms for the purpose of gaining computer technologies.

> Just 10 years ago, IBM stood astride the computer industry like a big blue giant. According to one survey, it was the most respected company in the world. Two suppliers to its personal computer division were Intel and Microsoft. In comparison to IBM, Intel was small, and Microsoft was a midget. Six years ago, IBM's market value was almost $100 billion—handily surpassing the gross domestic product of nations such as Ireland, Portugal, and New Zealand. Today, the market values of IBM, Intel, and Microsoft are about equal in the $25 billion range. And Microsoft's founder, Bill Gates, who was mistaken for an office boy when he first visited IBM in 1981 as a possible vendor of the operating system for IBM's PC, has a personal net worth of $6.5 billion, making him the richest man in America.

When it comes to productivity, the best entrepreneurial companies leave the giant corporations behind in the dust. For example, in the computer industry in 1990, Apple and Compaq ranked first and second with productivity per employee of $451,600 and $317,500, compared with IBM's $184,600 (no wonder John Akers recently stepped down as IBM's CEO). They put even the Japanese and Germans to shame. Their nearest Japanese competitor, NEC, was at $198,200, and their only significant German competitor, Siemens-Nixdorf, trailed far behind at $106,700. True, Apple and Compaq subcontract more of their manufacturing. Even so, it does not explain all the difference. Whether you hope to build a big company or a small one, the message is the same. Strive tirelessly to keep productivity high.

But no matter what you do, you probably won't be able to attain much success unless you have happy customers, happy workers, and happy suppliers. That means you must have a friendly company. It means that *everyone* must be friendly, especially anyone who deals with customers. I recently went to a Sears store to purchase a chain saw that was advertised in the newspapers. I couldn't find it on display. Eventually, I found a salesman who told me curtly that the particular model was not in stock and he didn't know when it would be in stock. "Trucks arrive here every hour of the day," he said offhandedly. He didn't offer a rain check. Nor did he suggest that I look at an alternative model. He did not even apologize. I went to Wal-Mart and found a model on display that met my needs. Unfortunately, it was not in the stock on the shelf. An attentive salesman asked if he could help. He offered to go to the stock room to check the inventory—and returned smiling with what I wanted. The Sears salesman was not to blame. He was clearly a nonmotivated worker. It is not much fun to work for a company that is on the ropes, that is in the news for its failures rather than its successes, and that is closing down stores and laying off workers. Entrepreneurial companies pay attention to the happiness of their workers. They are fun to work for. Could you imagine the president of Sears parading down Wall Street in a grass skirt as Sam Walton once did to celebrate record earnings?

Most new companies have the Nine Fs at the outset. Those that become successful and grow pay attention to keeping and nurturing them. The key to sustaining success is to remain an entrepreneurial gazelle and never turn into first a lumbering elephant and finally a dinosaur, doomed to extinction.

2 OPPORTUNITY RECOGNITION: THE SEARCH FOR HIGHER-POTENTIAL VENTURES

Jeffry A. Timmons

I was seldom able to see an opportunity until it had ceased to be one.

Mark Twain

A majority of the new businesses started each year are traditional, very small businesses employing one or two people who are willing to sacrifice income for the life-style they are afforded. These firms are called *mom-and-pop businesses, marginal firms*, or *life-style firms*.[1] The idea of *value creation and distribution* is implicit in the definition of entrepreneurship, however, so these life-style firms do not succeed in this way.

If we separate life-style firms from the pool of new businesses, two other types of firms remain. First, there are *high-potential firms*, that is, firms with the potential for significant capital gain. The second type includes *foundation firms*, or attractive small companies that generate enough income to fully compensate those involved.[2] These two types of firms—the higher-potential ventures—have sales of at least $500,000 to $1 million and grow at a rate of at least 10% per year. It is interesting to note that, according to government data, only about one business in five had annual sales in 1980 of over $1 million, one in ten over $2 million, one in eighty over $10 million, and sixty-seven in one thousand greater than $25 million.[3] Further, the 500 largest service companies earned, in 1988, net income as a percent of sales typically in the 3% to 5% range, and these companies outperformed the 500 largest companies in the industrial group.[4]

This chapter was excerpted and modified from Jeffry A. Timmons, L. E. Smollen, and A. L. Dingee, *New Venture Creation*, 3rd ed. (Homewood, IL: Richard D. Irwin, 1990).

CHARACTERISTICS OF HIGHER-POTENTIAL VENTURES

Success, rather than the 90%+ failure rate among most new enterprises, is the rule among higher-potential ventures and attractive small companies. They are driven by talented and experienced founders who are pursuing attractive opportunities and are able to attract both the right people and the necessary resources to make the venture work.

Threshold Concept: How the Size of a Firm Affects Its Success

There appears to be a minimum threshold size of at least 5 to 10 employees—20 is even better—and sales of $500,000 to $1 million. Exhibit 2.1, based on a cross-section of all new firms, shows that the one-year survival rate for new firms jumps from approximately 78% for those with up to 9 employees to approximately 95% for those with between 20 and 99 employees. Exhibit 2.2 shows that after four years, the survival rate jumps from approximately 37% for firms with fewer than 19 employees to about 54% for firms with 20 to 49 employees. Although any estimates based on sales per employee vary considerably from industry to industry, this minimum threshold translates roughly to $50,000 to $100,000 of sales per employee annually. But highly successful firms can generate much higher sales per employee. Take Apple Computer, for instance, which, by 1988, had sales per employee of $329,000, well above IBM's figure of $127,000.[5]

Promise of Growth

The definition of entrepreneurship implies the promise of expansion and the building of long-term value and durable cash flow streams as well. But, as discussed later in this chapter, it takes a long time for new companies to become established and grow. Exhibit 2.3 shows the results of a recent

EXHIBIT 2.1. One-year survival rates by firm size.

Firm size (employees)	Survival percentage
0–9	77.8
10–19	85.5
20–99	95.3
100–249	95.2
250+	100.0

Source: Michael B. Teitz et al., "Small Business and Employment Growth in California," Working Paper No. 348, University of California at Berkeley, March 1981, p. 42.

EXHIBIT 2.2. Four-year survival rates by firm size.

Firm size (employees)	D&B study (1969–76)	California study (1976–80)
0–19	37.4%	49.9%
20–49	53.6	66.9
50–99	55.7	66.9
100–499	67.7	70.0

Sources: David L. Birch, *MIT Studies, 1979–1980*; and Michael B. Teitz et al., "Small Business and Employment Growth in California," Working Paper No. 348, University of California at Berkeley, March 1981, Table 5, p. 22.

Small Business Administration study, covering the period from 1976 to 1986; two of every five small firms founded survived six or more years, but few achieved growth during the first four years.[6] The study also found that survival rates more than double for firms that grow, and that the earlier in the life of the business that growth occurs, the higher the chance of survival.[7]

Other data also confirm this exception to the rule cited earlier. A study done by *Inc.* shows that, between 1982 and 1987, the average growth in sales of the *Inc.* 500 was 96% per year. The study also finds that, of the 7 million corporations in the United States, approximately 7% (or just under 500,000 firms) grew over 20% per year, and just over 1% (or approximately 80,000 firms) grew 50% per year.

EXHIBIT 2.3. Percentage of new small firms surviving six or more years.*

Industry	All classes (percent)	Zero growth 0%	Low growth 1–4%	Medium growth 5–9%	High growth 10%+
Total, all industries	39.8	27.5	66.3	75.5	78.4
Agriculture, forestry, fishing	43.1	35.0	74.7	80.7	82.8
Mining	39.1	27.1	67.8	61.5	57.0
Construction	35.3	24.1	65.0	72.2	74.3
Manufacturing	46.9	27.0	66.9	73.5	76.0
Transportation, utilities, communications	39.7	25.7	68.5	72.4	75.6
Wholesale trade	44.3	28.3	66.5	74.9	77.2
Retail trade	38.4	27.1	62.7	74.4	76.8
Finance, insurance, real estate	38.6	28.7	68.7	76.4	78.5
Services	40.9	28.7	69.1	79.4	83.5

* Ranked by number of jobs created from 1976–86.

Source: U.S. Small Business Administration, August 29, 1988; B. D. Phillips and B. A. Kirchhoff, "An Analysis of New Firm Survival and Growth." In *Frontiers in Enterpreneurship Research: 1988*, B. Kirchhoff et al. (eds.) (Babson Park, MA: Babson College, 1988), 266–267.

Venture Capital Backing

Another notable pattern of exception to the failure rule applies to businesses that have attracted startup financing from private venture capital companies. Instead of the 70% to 90% *failure rate* shown among all types of new firms, these new ventures enjoy a *survival rate* nearly that high. Studies of success rates of venture capital portfolios show that in the portfolios of experienced professional venture capital firms, about 15% to 20% of the companies will typically result in total loss of the original investments. Furthermore, it is unusual for the loss rates for portfolios of experienced venture capital firms to exceed 30% to 35% and fall below 10%.[8]

Another study, which analyzed 218 investments made by five prominent venture capital firms during the 1970s, found that 14.7% of those portfolio companies resulted in complete losses and another 24.8% experienced partial losses.[9] Thus, about 40% of the portfolio involved losses of some kind. It is interesting to note that offsetting these losses were spectacular successes. Among the 218 investments in the 10-year period of the study, 3.8% returned 10 times the original investment after taxes, or more, and another 8.3% returned 5 to 10 times, again after taxes. This translates into about 25% compounded return on investment after taxes.

Even higher returns have been achieved by such spectacular successes as Apple Computer, Lotus, Digital Equipment, Intel, and Compaq. These compelling data have led some to conclude that there is a *threshold core* of 10% to 15% of new companies that will become the winners in size, job creation, profitability, innovation, and potential for harvesting (and thereby realizing a capital gain). And, eventually, from among these 10% to 15% of all new firms emerge the "winning performers."[10] The top 25% among all medium-sized companies achieved records of growth from 1978 to 1983 that exceeded the growth of the top quarter of the economy, the top quarter of the *Fortune* 500, and firms classified as excellent companies.

DETERMINANTS OF ENTREPRENEURIAL SUCCESS: THREE DRIVING FORCES

What is going on here? What do talented entrepreneurs and companies backed by successful venture capital do differently? What accounts for this exceptional record? Are there some lessons here for aspiring entrepreneurs? Certain central, fundamental forces do indeed drive the entrepreneurial process and account for these success rates. Granted, there are almost as many different approaches, philosophies, and nuances to the art and craft of new venture creation as there are entrepreneurs, private investors, and venture capital companies. Yet time and again, central themes rise to the surface.

Successful venture capital investors follow a unique approach in their businesses, and successful entrepreneurs who grow multimillion-dollar firms, often from scratch and sometimes with little money, also understand that *entrepreneurial achievement is driven by people who search for and shape superior opportunities.*

Most importantly, an understanding of these fundamental forces is not the monopoly of venture capitalists or the entrepreneurs they back. Thousands of examples confirm the universal nature of the forces driving the entrepreneurial process.

Consider the following examples:

- Tony Harnett came to this country from his native Ireland as a young high-school dropout. He had a lot of ambition and was in search of opportunity. In 1976, he and his wife, Susan, bought a small natural foods store in Brookline, Massachusetts, with annual sales of a meager $110,000 per year. By paying a lot of attention to the critical driving forces, those that venture capitalists also seem to concentrate on, they built Bread And Circus into a multistore venture whose annual sales in 1988 exceeded $35 million. Interestingly, they did this without having to raise a dime of venture capital. They sold the company in 1992 for over $25 million.
- Another entrepreneur without venture capital started and built a small company that became the leading firm manufacturing and selling metal picture frames. By 1983, the company had about 70% of the North American market, yet did only $15 million in very profitable sales. The company was acquired by a European firm for over $20 million in cash.

In analyzing new entrepreneurial ventures, it is not useful to rely solely on traditional models (such as a psychological model or a competitive strategy model) for the following reasons. First, any unidimensional model that attempts to distill the common basis for the collective successes of entrepreneurial ventures can tell only part of the story. Second, systematic research into the characteristics of successful ventures has only recently begun, and research in economics and strategic management has barely begun to focus on new venture development and performance. Third, entrepreneurship typically occurs in a "real-world" environment that lacks certainty, predictability, stability, and smoothness. Risk and uncertainty, paradoxes and contradictions, market imperfections, and asymmetries and vacuums are the rules rather than the exceptions. Consequently, confusing and often chaotic change and turbulence in markets, technology, and availability of resources is "business as usual." (It is no wonder that large, multilayered organizations have such a dismal record competing and innovating in this domain.)

Instead, the analytical framework illustrated in Exhibit 2.4 isolates the three primary driving forces behind new venture creation:

EXHIBIT 2.4. Real-world environmental context and central driving forces of entrepreneurship.

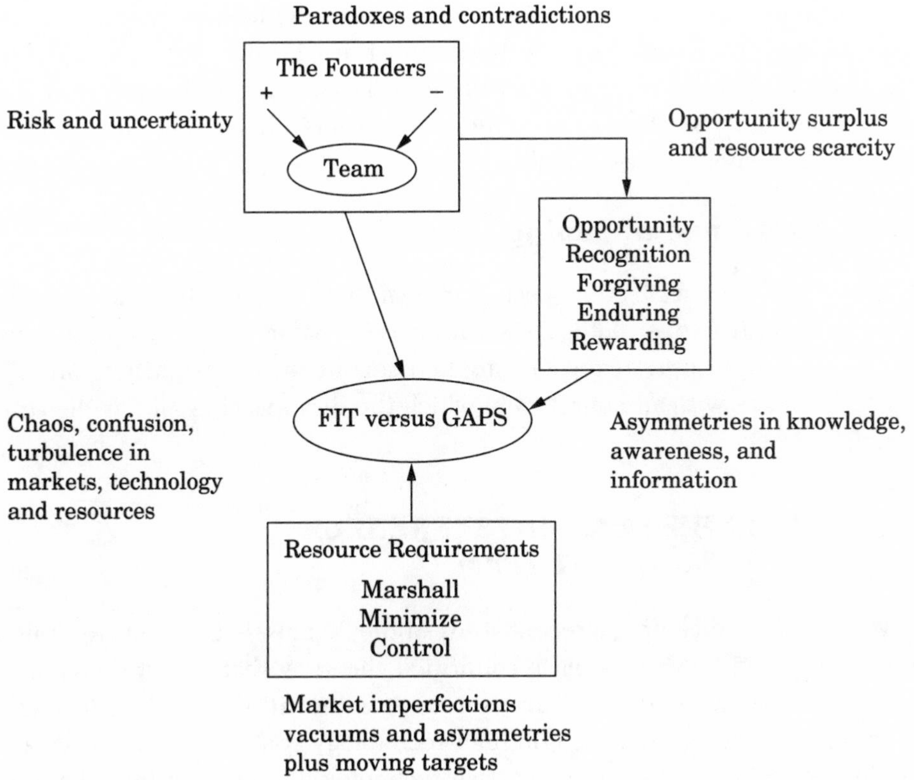

- Founders
- Opportunity recognition
- Resource requirements

Experience shows that these forces can be assessed and influenced to improve the chances of succeeding. The key to success in creating a new venture is a continual, careful, and realistic assessment of these driving forces and the real time in which they occur.

The Importance of Fit

The building of a business is a trial-and-error, iterative process of finding out how to shape a good *fit*. The key elements of successful new ventures (i.e., the founders, the opportunity, and the resources) fit one another—rarely perfectly, but reasonably so—within the context of the "real world." The potential of the venture will depend on how well the lead entrepreneur and her management team (the founders) fit together and on how well the lead entrepreneur and the management team fit with the opportunity. A question that should be answered, then, is, For whom is the opportunity desirable? Entrepreneurs should recognize that their personal values and life-styles enter heavily into whether there is a fit. In turn, the lead entrepreneur, the management team, and the opportunity must fit with the venture's ability to marshal and control the necessary resources. Thus, realistically evaluating the merits and deficiencies of each element and accurately judging the potential fit of each element are essential.

The Importance of Timing

Every entrepreneurial event occurs in *real time,* where the clock can be either enemy, friend, or both. Thus, timing is crucial in every entrepreneurial situation. The process of recognizing and seizing an opportunity is often a precarious race with an hourglass in which the disappearing sand is the cash running out.

THE FOUNDERS: LEAD ENTREPRENEUR AND THE MANAGEMENT TEAM

Several studies, including a recent study of the 50 most active venture capital firms in the United States, have confirmed the view that one of the central forces driving the entrepreneurial process is the firm's founding management team.[11] Recent research on high-technology companies formed in this country since 1967—highly innovative technological ventures in which one would expect the elegance of the technology to have special importance—shows that *the founders are more important than the technology.*[12] Of course, the high-tech game cannot be won without innovative technology, but venture capitalists (who are among the most active and prominent investors in the country in this area) still insisted that they placed greatest weight and emphasis on the quality and proven track record of the management team.

That the team is a driving force of the entrepreneurial process is demonstrated in the responses of venture capitalists when they are asked to list the five most important factors that determine if a new venture will be successful. Venture capitalists will state plainly and simply:

- The lead entrepreneur and the quality of the team
- The lead entrepreneur and the quality of the team
- The lead entrepreneur and the quality of the team
- The lead entrepreneur and the quality of the team
- Market potential

A good example of this is the philosophy of Burr Egan Deleage & Company of Boston, one of the largest and most successful venture capital firms with over $200 million under management and investments in over a hundred emerging companies. Partner Bill Egan, who has been centrally involved in such successes as Continental Cablevision, Federal Express, and Tandon, states his strong preference for high-quality management this way:

> The management team must have quality, depth and maturity. It must be experienced in the industry in which the company competes. The top manager should have had prior profit center responsibility. Management must possess intimate knowledge of the market for its products and have a well thought out strategy for the penetration of this market. The strength of the management team is the most important consideration in the investment decision.

Ideally, having a top-notch idea or innovation and a first-rate entrepreneurial team is the best of all worlds. But this does not happen very often. General Georges Doriot's preference for a Grade A entrepreneurial team with a Grade B idea to a Grade B team with a Grade A idea[13] is one of the standard operating axioms of the venture capital industry today.[14] Another famous entrepreneur who has expressed such a position is Arthur Rock, founder of a firm that was the lead venture capital investor in such new enterprises as Fairchild Semiconductor, Teledyne, Scientific Data Systems, Intel, and Apple Computer. He put it this way: "If you can find good people, they can always change the product. Nearly every mistake I've made has been I picked the wrong people, not the wrong idea."[15] Furthermore, the management team is critically important to the chances of survival and expansion of new ventures, whether or not they are candidates for venture capital. As was seen earlier, those firms that managed to grow beyond 20 employees and roughly $1 million in sales were most likely to survive and prosper. In a large majority of cases, it is quite difficult to achieve this size without a team of at least two key contributors.

A Word about Solo Entrepreneurs

A substantial amount of research and practical experience confirms that *a team grows a business,* whereas *a solo entrepreneur makes a living.* If an entrepreneur's aspirations include growing a business large and profitable enough to realize a capital gain, then he or she needs to think *team.* However, teams are not for everyone. Numerous solo entrepreneurs have carved out small niches for themselves, earning substantial six-figure incomes, and building wealth by wise financial planning and investing.[16] In these instances, the fundamental driving forces are at work without a team.

RECOGNIZING THE DIFFERENCE BETWEEN IDEAS AND OPPORTUNITIES[17]

If there is any single spark that ignites an entrepreneurial explosion, it is opportunity. There is certainly no lack of ideas for new or improved products or services. Entrepreneurs, inventors, innovators, and college students abound with new ideas. However, there are far more ideas than good business opportunities. This is because *an idea is not necessarily an opportunity.* Although at the center of an opportunity is always an idea, not all ideas are opportunities. To understand this crucial distinction, it is necessary to understand that entrepreneurship is a market-driven process. An opportunity is *attractive, durable,* and *timely* and is anchored in a product or service that *creates or adds value* for its buyer or end-user. Opportunities are created because there are changing circumstances, inconsistencies, chaos, lags or leads, information gaps, and a variety of other vacuums in the market and because there are entrepreneurs who can recognize and take advantage of these imperfections. In addition, successful new ventures are invariably anchored in opportunities with *rewarding, forgiving. and durable gross margins and profits.*

The challenge, then, is recognizing an opportunity buried in often contradictory data, signals, and the inevitable noise and chaos of the marketplace, since the more *imperfect* the market, that is, the greater the gaps, asymmetries, and inconsistencies of knowledge and information, the more abundant the opportunities. A skillful entrepreneur can shape and create an opportunity where others see little or nothing—or see it too early or too late. After all, if recognizing and seizing an opportunity were simply a matter of using available techniques, checklists, and other screening and evaluation methods, we might have far more than the one in five businesses that had sales in 1990 of over $2 million. Why? Because the literature on techniques for screening and evaluating ideas indicates that over two hundred such methods have been developed and documented.

Another Look at Fit and Timing

Recent work has lent further support to the hypothesis that an opportunity is situational and depends on the mix and match of the key players and on how promising and forgiving the opportunity is, given the team's strengths, advantages, and shortcomings. Furthermore, the vast majority of those founding new businesses run out of money *before* they find enough customers for their good ideas. Thus, for entrepreneurs, timing can be everything.

Another critical question is, therefore, If there really is a business opportunity (rather than just a product or two), is there time to seize the opportunity? If an opportunity does exist, whether an entrepreneur can seize it in time depends on movements in technology and competitors' thrusts, among other factors. Thus, an opportunity is also a constantly moving target, and there exists a *window of opportunity.*

Ideas as Tools

It is worth emphasizing again that *a good idea is nothing more than a tool in the hands of an entrepreneur.* Finding a good idea is only the first step in the task of converting an entrepreneur's creativity into an opportunity. The importance of the idea is most often overrated, usually with the result that the need for products or services that can be sold in enough quantity to real customers is underemphasized. Furthermore, the new business that simply bursts from a flash of brilliance is rare. What is usually necessary is a series of trial-and-error iterations, or repetitions, before a crude, promising product or service fits with what the customer is really willing to pay for. For example, Howard Head made a total of 40 different metal skis before he finally made one that worked consistently. In fact, with surprising frequency, major businesses are built around products totally different from those originally envisioned. Consider these examples:

- F. Leland Strange, the founder and president of Quadram, a maker of graphics and communications boards and other boards for microcomputers, told the story of how he developed his marketing idea into a company with $100 million in sales in three years.[18] He stated that he had developed a business plan to launch his company and that the company even hit projected revenues for the first two years. He noted, however, that success was achieved with completely *different products* from those in the original plan.
- In the 1930s, Dr. Edwin H. Land developed and patented *Polaroid,* a plastic substance that reduces glare by polarizing light. Polaroid Corporation was founded to sell polarized headlamps, which, it was reasoned, would have the compelling safety feature of reducing head-on collisions caused at night by drivers "blinded" by oncoming lights. Conceivably, such polarized lamps could be installed by car manufacturers in each of their vehicles. However, the company grew to its present $2-billion-plus size through a quite *different application* of the original technology—instant photography.
- IBM began in the wire and cable business and later expanded to time clocks. Sales in the 1920s were only a few million dollars a year. Its successful mainframe computer business and then its successful personal computer business emerged much later.

The Great Mousetrap Fallacy

Perhaps no one did a greater disservice to generations of would-be entrepreneurs than Ralph Waldo Emerson in his oft-quoted line:

> If a man can make a better mousetrap than his neighbor, though he builds his house in the woods the world will make a beaten path to his door.

What can be called the *great mousetrap fallacy* was thus spawned. Indeed, entrepreneurs often assume that success is possible if they can just come up with a new idea. And in today's rapidly changing world, if the idea has anything to do with technology, success is certain, or so it would seem. The truth of the matter is that ideas are inert and, for all practical purposes, worthless. Further, the flow of ideas is really quite phenomenal. Venture capital investors, for instance, during the investing boom of the 1980s, received as many as one hundred to two hundred proposals and business plans each month. Only 1% to 3% of these actually received financing, however.

Yet the fallacy persists despite the lessons of practical experience noted long ago in the insightful reply to Emerson by O. B. Winters:

> The manufacturer who waits for the world to beat a path to his door is a great optimist. But the manufacturer who shows this "mousetrap" to the world keeps the smoke coming out his chimney .

This fallacy has been perpetuated for several reasons. One is the portrayal in oversimplified accounts of the ease and genius with which the founders of such ventures as Xerox, IBM, and Polaroid have become wealthy. Unfortunately, these exceptions do not provide a useful rule to guide aspiring entrepreneurs.

Another reason is that inventors seem particularly prone to *mousetrap myopia*. Perhaps they are (as Emerson was) substantially sheltered in viewpoint and experience from the tough, competitive realities of the business world. Consequently, they underestimate the importance of what it takes to make a business succeed. Frankly, inventing and brainstorming tend to be a lot more fun than the careful, diligent observation, investigation, and nurturing of customers that are often required to sell a product or service.

Also contributing to the great mousetrap fallacy is the tremendous psychological ownership attached to an invention or, later, to a new product. This attachment is different from attachment to a business. The intense and highly involved personal identity and commitment to an invention or new widget tends to weaken, or preclude entirely, realistic assessment of the other crucial aspects of the business. While an intense level of psychological ownership and involvement is certainly a prerequisite for creating a new business, the fatal flaw in attachment to an invention or product is the narrowness of focus. The focal point needs to be the building of the business, rather than just one aspect of it, the idea.

Another source of mousetrap myopia lies in a technical and scientific orientation; that is, a desire to "do it better." For example, a Canadian entrepreneur founded, with his brother, a company to manufacture truck seats. The brother had developed a new seat for trucks that was a definite improvement over other seats. The entrepreneur knew they could profitably sell this seat, and they did so. When they needed more manufacturing capacity, the brother was not as interested in manufacturing more of the first seat as he was in the several ideas he had on how to improve the seat. The first brother stated, "If I had listened to him, we probably would be a small custom shop today, or out of business. Instead, we concentrated on making seats that would sell at a profit, rather than just making a better and better seat. Our company has several million dollars of sales today and is profitable."

The Best Idea Does Not Always Lead to Success

Consider the following examples, which drive home the point that having the best technology or idea often does not make the critical difference in success:

- UNIVAC had the early elegance and technology lead over IBM in computers, but it was never able to seize the emerging, significant opportunities in the computer industry.
- In 1967 and 1968, a prominent investor, Fred Adler, received over 50 business plans from entrepreneurs who proposed to start minicomputer firms. Several of the other minicomputer companies started at that time actually had a "better idea" in the form of more advanced technology than the one that most attracted Adler's attention. Data General's lead entrepreneur and his team had an entrepreneurial flair and market focus that Adler bet on.[19] In 1988, the company had sales of $1.3 billion.
- In 1969, the fledgling Cullinet, Inc., raised $500,000 in a then-hot new issues market. Two years later the firm had spent this initial capital and, according to its founder, John Cullinane, still had a payroll of $8,500 to meet. Cullinane said the money had been spent unwisely through "programmer anarchy." He turned the company around by firing his programmers since, he said, they did not understand what happiness was. "Happiness," Cullinane said, "is a satisfied customer."[20] He then developed customer-anchored software products and a plan for growth that led to a substantial venture capital investment during a time in which such capital was hard to come by.
- A final example is Lotus, whose Lotus 1-2-3 was the first integrated package for the personal computer to include spreadsheet, graphics, and database management capabilities. Critics and reviewers have since

reported that some new software products are indeed more elegant and sophisticated than Lotus 1-2-3, but new entrants probably require $5 million and up to fund the marketing necessary to launch new software products and gain attention and distribution in this tumultuous marketplace.

Being There First Is No Guarantee

Furthermore, having the best idea first by no means guarantees success. Again, just ask Adam Osborne, who introduced the first transportable PC, or Dan Bricklin, who was first with the spreadsheet software VisiCalc. Also, unless having the best idea first includes the capacity to preempt other competitors by capturing a significant share of the market or erecting insurmountable barriers to entry, being there first can mean proving to the competition that the market exists to be snared.

The Experience Factor

However, since ideas are building tools, one cannot build a successful business without them, as one could not build a house without a hammer. In this regard, experience is vital in the evaluation of new venture ideas. Time after time, experienced entrepreneurs exhibit an ability to quickly recognize a pattern—and an opportunity—while it is still taking shape. Thus, the process of sorting through ideas and recognizing a pattern can also be compared to the process of fitting pieces into a three-dimensional jigsaw puzzle. It is impossible to assemble such a puzzle by looking at it as a whole unit. Rather, one needs to see the relationships between seemingly unrelated pieces and be able to fit them together before the whole is visible. The ability to recognize ideas that can become entrepreneurial opportunities stems from a capacity to see what others do not—that one plus one equals three, or more.

Consider the following examples of the common thread of pattern recognition and the creation of new businesses by linking knowledge in one field or marketplace with quite different technical, business, or marketing know-how:

- A middle manager employed by a large company was on a plant tour of a small machinery manufacturer, a customer, in the Midwest. A machinist was mechanically cutting metal during a demonstration of a particular fabricating operation. Shockingly, the machinist accidentally sliced his hand in the cutting machine, removing two fingers. Instantly, the manager recognized that the new laser technology would make it possible to eliminate such horrible accidents. He subsequently built a multimillion-dollar company. Here the ability to link knowledge of the capabilities of lasers to an old, dangerous metal-cutting technology yielded an opportunity.

- During travel throughout Europe, the eventual founders of Crate & Barrel frequently saw stylish and innovative products for the kitchen and home that were not yet available in the United States. When they returned home, they decided to offer these products, for which market research had, in a sense, already been conducted in Europe. This knowledge of consumer buying habits in one geographical region was thus applied to a previously untapped consumer market in another country.
- Howard Head had been an aeronautical design engineer working with new light metal alloys to build more efficient airfoils during World War II. Head transferred knowledge of metal-bonding technology from the aircraft manufacturing business to a consumer product, metal skis, and then to another, tennis rackets. Although he had limited skiing experience, he concluded that, if he could make a metal ski, there would be a significant market as a result of the limitations of wooden skis. His company dominated the ski industry for many years. In talking about his decision to develop the oversized Prince tennis racket after he saw a need for ball control among players learning tennis, Head said, "I saw the pattern again that had worked at Head Ski. . . . I had proven to myself before that you can take different technology and know-how and apply it to a solution in a new area."[21] He set about learning enough about the physics of tennis rackets and surfaces and developed the oversized Prince racket.
- In Texas, a young entrepreneur launched a modular home sales business in the late 1970s. First, he parlayed experience as a loan officer with a large New York City bank into a job with a manufacturer of mobile and modular homes in Texas. This enabled him, over a three-year period, to learn the business and to understand the market opportunity. He then opened a sales location in a growing suburb about 25 miles from a booming larger city. By studying his competitors and conducting an analysis of how customers actually went about purchasing new modular homes, he spotted a pattern that meant opportunity. Customers usually shopped at three different locations where they could see different models and price ranges before making a purchase decision. Since his market analysis showed that there was room in the city for three or four such businesses, he opened two additional sites, each with a different name and different, but complementary, lines. Within two years, despite record high interest rates, his business had nearly tripled to $17 million in annual sales, and his only competitor was planning to move.

Good Ideas Are Not Necessarily Good Opportunities

If a good opportunity is not just a good idea, what is it?[22] A *good opportunity* is attractive, durable, and timely; it is anchored in a product or service that creates or adds value for its buyer or end-user. For an opportunity to have these qualities, the "window of opportunity" must be opening rather than closing and it must remain open long enough. Furthermore, entry into a market with the right characteristics must be feasible (and the management team must be able to achieve it). The venture must have been or must be able to achieve a competitive advantage, that is, to achieve leverage. Finally, the economics of the venture must be rewarding and forgiving and must offer significant profit and growth potential. The most successful entrepreneurs, venture capitalists, and private investors are focused on just such opportunities. They start with what customers and the marketplace want and do not lose sight of this objective.

The Real World

Opportunities are created on a foundation of ideas and entrepreneurial creativity. Yet the process by which this occurs is less like the work of the carpenter than it is like the collision of particles in the process of a nuclear reaction or like the spawning of hurricanes over the ocean. Ideas interact with real-world conditions and entrepreneurial creativity at a point in time. The product of this interaction is an opportunity around which a new venture can be created.

The business environment in which an entrepreneur launches a venture is usually given and cannot be altered significantly. And, with the exception of perhaps some businesses established as social or nonprofit organizations, businesses in the United States operate in a free enterprise system characterized by private ownership and profits.

In a free enterprise system, opportunities are spawned in circumstances of change, chaos, confusion, inconsistency, lags or leads, knowledge and information gaps, and a variety of other vacuums in an industry or market. Changes in the business environment, and anticipation of these changes, are so critical in entrepreneurship that constant vigilance for changes is a valuable habit. It is thus that an entrepreneur with credibility, creativity, and decisiveness can seize an opportunity while others study it.

Opportunities are situational. Some conditions under which opportunities are spawned are entirely idiosyncratic, whereas, at other times, they are generalizable and can be applied to other industries, products, or services. In this way, cross-association can trigger in the entrepreneurial mind the crude recognition of existing or impending opportunities.

Consider the following broad range of examples that illustrate the phenomenon of vacuums in which opportunities are spawned:

- Deregulation of telecommunications and airlines led to the formation of tens of thousands of new firms in the 1980s.
- Microcomputer hardware in the early 1980s far outpaced the development of software, on which the development of the industry depended. This discrepancy led to aggressive efforts by IBM, Apple, and others to encourage software entrepreneurs to close this gap.
- Many opportunities exist in fragmented, traditional industries that may have a craft or mom-and-pop character and little appreciation of or know-how in marketing and finance. Consider such possibilities as fishing lodges, inns, and hotels; cleaners/laundries; hardware stores; pharmacies; waste management plants; flower shops; nurseries; tents; and auto repair shops.
- In our service-dominated economy (where, today, 70% of businesses are service businesses versus 30% just 25 years ago), customer service, rather than the product itself, can be the critical success factor. One recent study by The Forum Corporation in Boston showed that 70% of customers leave because of poor service and only 15% leave because of price or quality.
- Sometimes existing competitors cannot, or will not, increase capacity to keep pace with the market. The tent industry was characterized by this capacity stickiness in the mid-1970s. In the late 1970s, when some steel had a 90-week delivery lag, with the price to be determined, foreign competitors certainly took notice.
- There has been a tremendous shift to offshore manufacturing of labor-intensive and transportation-insensitive products in Asia and Mexico, such as computer-related and microprocessor-driven consumer products.
- In a wide variety of industries, entrepreneurs sometimes find that they are the only ones who can perform. Such fields as consulting, software design, financial services, process engineering, and technical and medical products and services abound with examples of know-how monopolies. Sometimes a management team is simply the best in an industry and irreplaceable in the near term, just as is seen with great coaches with winning records.

Real Time

Opportunities exist, or are created, in real time and have what is called a *window of opportunity.* For an entrepreneur to seize an opportunity, the window must be opening, not closing, and it must remain open long enough to be used.

EXHIBIT 2.5. The window of opportunity.

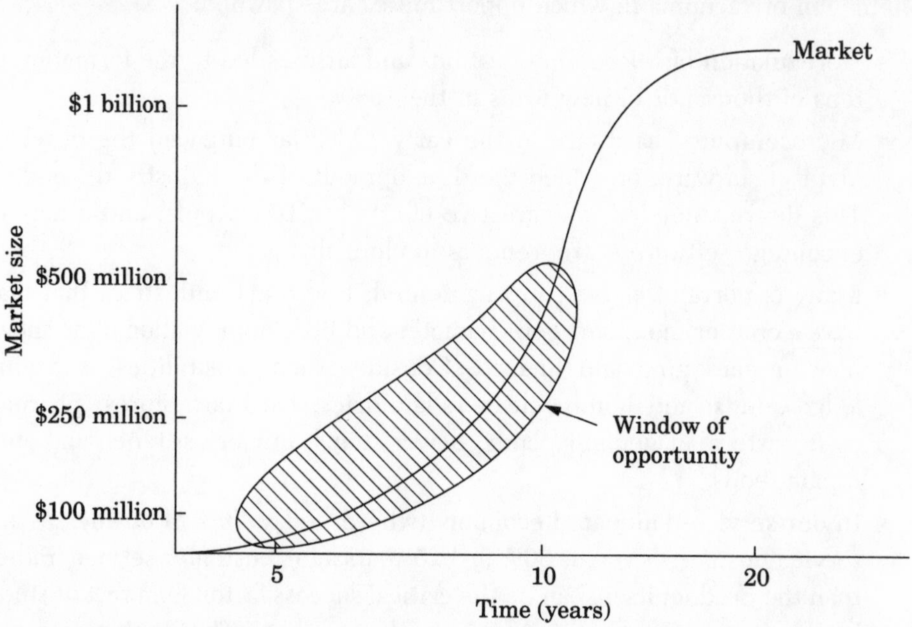

Exhibit 2.5 illustrates a window of opportunity in a generalized market. Markets grow at different rates over time, and as a market quickly becomes larger, more and more opportunities are possible. But when the market becomes even larger—and established—conditions are not as favorable. Thus, when a market starts to become sufficiently large and structured (that is, at 5 years in Exhibit 2.5), the window opens. The window begins to close as the market matures—that is, at 15 years in Exhibit 2.5.

The curve shown describes the rapid growth pattern typical of such new industries as microcomputers and software, cellular car phones, quick oil changes, and biotechnology. For example, in the cellular car phone industry, most major cities first began service between 1983 and 1984. By 1989 there were over 2 million subscribers in the United States, and the industry continued to experience significant growth. In other, mature, industries, where growth is not so rapid, the slope of a curve is less steep and the opportunities fewer.

Finally, the length of time that the window of opportunity will be open is important. It takes a considerable length of time to determine whether a new venture is a success or a failure. And, if it is to be a success, the benefits of that success need to be harvested. This does not happen overnight. It is said in the venture capital industry that the lemons (that is, the losers) ripen in about two and a half years, while the pearls (that is, the winners) take seven or eight years. An extreme example of the length of time it can take for a pearl to be harvested is the experience of a Silicon Valley venture capital firm that invested in a new enterprise in 1966 and was finally able to realize a capital gain in early 1984.

The process of creating and seizing an opportunity in real time can also be seen in terms of selecting objects, opportunities, from a conveyor belt moving through an open window, the window of opportunity. The speed of the conveyor belt changes, and the window through which it moves is constantly opening and closing, as in the volatile and dynamic marketplace where timing is of utmost importance. For an opportunity to be created and seized, it must be selected from the conveyor belt before the window closes.

The ability to recognize a potential opportunity when it appears and the sense of timing to seize it as the window is opening rather than slamming shut are critical. That opportunities are a function of real time is illustrated in a statement made by the president and founder of Digital Equipment Corporation in 1977: "There is no reason for any individual to have a computer in their home."

Finally, it is important to remember that, once recognized, successful opportunities fit with the other forces of new venture creation. This iterative process of assessing and reassessing the fit among the central driving forces in the creation of a new venture was shown in Exhibit 2.4. Especially important in opportunity recognition is the fit between the lead entrepreneur and management team and the opportunity they encounter. Good opportunities are those that are *desirable* to the team and *attainable* by the team with available resources.

SCREENING AND EVALUATING OPPORTUNITIES[23]

Opportunity focus is also the most fruitful place for the founders to begin as they screen opportunities. The screening process should not begin with strategy (which derives from the nature of the opportunity), with financial and spreadsheet analysis (which flow from the former), or with estimations of how much the company is worth and who will own what shares. These starting points, and others, usually place the cart squarely before the horse.

Perhaps the best evidence of how the cart is often placed before the horse comes from the tens of thousands of tax-sheltered investments that turned sour in the mid-1980s. Also, as has been noted, a good number of entrepreneurs who start businesses—particularly those for whom the ventures are their first—run out of cash faster than they bring in customers and profitable sales. There are many reasons why this happens, but one thing is certain: *These entrepreneurs have not focused on the right opportunity.*

Over the years, those with experience in business and in specific market areas have developed rules of thumb to guide them in screening opportunities. One such rule was used by a firm with approximately $1 billion in sales in evaluating startups in the minicomputer industry in the mid-1980s. This firm analyzed performance data relating to 60 computer-related startups in the United States from 1975 to 1984 and concluded that one leading indicator of the progress of new firms and a good boundary measure of positive performance and a healthy start was *sales per employee of $75,000 or more*. To this firm, sales of less than $50,000 per employee signaled serious trouble. Although there is always the risk of oversimplification in using rules of thumb, it is true also that one can miss the fundamentals while searching for subtleties.

Screening Criteria

Venture capitalists, savvy entrepreneurs, and investors all use this rule of boundaries in screening ventures. Exhibit 2.6 summarizes criteria used by venture capitalists to evaluate a select group of opportunities that tend to have a high-technology bias. As will be seen later, venture capital investors reject 60 to 70% of the new ventures presented to them very early in the review process, depending on how the entrepreneurs satisfy these criteria.

However, these criteria are not the exclusive domain of venture capitalists. They are based on plain good business sense that is used by successful entrepreneurs, private investors, and venture capitalists.

The point of departure here is opportunity and, implicitly, the customer, the marketplace, and the industry. Exhibit 2.6 shows how higher- and lower-potential opportunities can be placed along an attractiveness scale. The criteria provide a quantitative way for an entrepreneur to make judgments about the industry and market, competitive advantage, economic issues and harvest potential, management team, and any fatal flaws. These add up to a compelling opportunity. For example, *dominant* strength in any one of these criteria can readily translate into a winning entry, whereas a flaw in any one can be fatal.

As outlined in Exhibit 2.6, business opportunities with the greatest potential will possess many of the criteria described in the following sections—or they will so dominate in one or a few that the competition cannot come close.

Industry and Market Issues

Market

Higher-potential businesses can identify a market niche for a product or service that meets an important customer need and provides high value-added or value-created benefits to customers. Customers are reachable and receptive to the product or service, with no brand or other loyalties. The user or customer of a given product or service will receive the potential payback through cost savings or other value-added or value-created properties in one year or less. This payback is identifiable, repeatable, and verifiable. Furthermore, the product or service life exists beyond the time needed to recover the investment, plus a profit. And the company is able to expand beyond the limits of a single product.

For example, consider the growing success of cellular car phone service. At prevailing rates, one can talk for about $25 an hour, and many providers of professional services can readily bill more than the $25 an hour for what would otherwise be unproductive time. If benefits to customers cannot be calculated in such dollar terms, the market potential is far more risky and difficult to ascertain.

Lower-potential opportunities are unfocused in regard to customer need; customers are unreachable or have conflicting brand or other loyalties. A payback to the user of more than three years and a low value added or value created also make an opportunity unattractive. A company's inability to expand beyond a single product can also make for a lower-potential opportunity. The failure of one of the first portable computer companies, Osborne Computer, is a good example of this.

Market structure

Market structure is characterized by:

- The number of sellers
- The size distribution of sellers
- The differentiation of products
- The conditions of entry and exit
- The number of buyers
- The cost conditions
- The sensitivity of demand to changes in price

All these factors are significant.

A fragmented, imperfect market or emerging industry often contains vacuums and asymmetries that create unfilled market niches—for example, markets where resource ownership, cost advantages, and the like, can be achieved. Also attractive are markets in which information or knowledge gaps exist and competition is profitable but not overwhelming.

Here is an example of a market with an information gap. A Boston entrepreneur encountered a large New York company that wanted to dispose of a small, old office building in downtown Boston. The book value of this building was about $200,000, and it was therefore viewed by the financially oriented firm as a "low-value asset." The company wanted to dispose of it so

EXHIBIT 2.6. Criteria for evaluating venture opportunities.

Criterion	Attractiveness: Higher potential	Attractiveness: Lower potential
Market issues		
Market:		
Need	Identified	Unfocused
Customers	Reachable; receptive	Unreachable or loyal to others
Payback to user	Less than one year	Three years plus
Value added or created	High	Low
Product life	Durable; beyond time to recover investment plus profit	Perishable; less than time to recover investment
Market structure	Imperfect competition or emerging industry	Perfect competition or highly concentrated or mature industry or declining industry
Market size	$100 million sales	Unknown or less than $10 million sales or multibillion
Market growth rate	Growing at 30% to 50% or more	Contracting or less than 10%
Gross margins	40% to 50% or more; durable	Less than 20%; fragile
Market share attainable (year 5)	20% or more; leader	Less than 5%
Cost structure	Low-cost provider	Declining cost
Economic/harvest issues		
Profits after tax	10% to 15% or more; durable	Less than 5%; fragile
Time to:		
Break even	Under 2 years	More than 3 years
Positive cash flow	Under 2 years	More than 3 years
ROI potential	25% or more/year; high value	15%–20% or less/year; low value
Value	High strategic value	Low strategic value
Capital requirements	Low to moderate; fundable	Very high; unfundable
Exit mechanism	Present or envisioned harvest options	Undefined; illiquid investment

the resulting cash could be put to work for a higher return. The buyer, who had done more homework than the out-of-town sellers, bought the building for $200,000 and resold it in less than six months for over $8 million.

Typically, unattractive industries include those that are:

- Highly concentrated
- Perfectly competitive
- Mature or declining

EXHIBIT 2.6. ***(Continued)***

	Attractiveness	
Criterion	**Higher potential**	**Lower potential**
Competitive advantages issues		
Fixed and variable costs:		
Production	Lowest	Highest
Marketing	Lowest	Highest
Distribution	Lowest	Highest
Degree of control:		
Prices	Moderate to strong	Weak
Costs	Moderate to strong	Weak
Channels of supply/resources	Moderate to strong	Weak
Channels of distribution	Moderate to strong	Weak
Barrier to entry:		
Proprietary protection/ regulation advantage	Have or can gain	None
Response/lead time advantage in technology, product, market innovation, people, location, resources, or capacity	Resilient and responsive; have or can gain	None
Legal, contractual advantage	Proprietary or exclusivity	None
Contracts and networks	Well-developed; high-quality; accessible	Crude; limited; inaccessible
Management team issues		
Team	Existing, strong proven performance	Weak or solo entrepreneur
Competitor's mind set and strategies	Competitive; few; not self-destructive	Dumb
Fatal flaw issue		
Fatal flaws	None	One or more

The capital requirements and costs to achieve distribution and marketing presence can be prohibitive, and behavior such as price cutting and other competitive strategies in highly concentrated markets can be a significant barrier to entry. (The most blatant example is organized crime and its life-threatening actions when territories are invaded.) Yet revenge by "normal" competitors who are well-positioned through product strategy, legal tactics, and so on, can also be punishing to the pocketbook.

Since deregulation, the airline industry has been an example of a perfectly competitive market, one in which many of the new entrants did not survive. The unattractiveness of such industries is captured by the comment of one prominent Boston venture capitalist, William Egan, who put it this way: "I want to be in a non-auction market."[24]

Market size

An attractive new venture sells to a market that is large and growing, one where a small market share can represent significant and increasing sales volume. A minimum market size of over $100 million in sales is attractive. In such a market, it is possible to achieve significant sales by capturing roughly 5% or less and not threaten competitors.

For example, to achieve a sales level of $1 million in a $100-million market requires capturing only 1% of the market. Thus, a recreational equipment manufacturer entered a $60-million market that was expected to grow at 20% per year to over $100 million by the third year. The founders were able to create a substantial smaller company without obtaining a major market share and possibly incurring the wrath of existing competitors.

However, a market of this type can be too large. A multibillion-dollar market may be too mature and stable, and such a level of certainty can translate into competition from *Fortune* 500–type firms or, if the market is highly competitive, lower margins and profitability. Furthermore, a market that is unknown or has less than $10 million in sales is also unattractive. To understand the disadvantages of entering a large, more mature market, consider the entry of a firm into the microcomputer industry today versus the entry of Apple Computer into that market in 1975.

Growth rate

An attractive market is large and growing, that is, one where capturing a good share of the increase is less threatening to competitors and where a small market share can represent significant and increasing sales volume. A market with an annual growth rate of 30% to 50% creates new niches for new entrants. This is a thriving and expansive market rather than a stable or contracting one where competitors are scrambling for the same niches. Thus a $100-million-plus market growing at 50% per year has the potential to become a $1-billion industry in a few years, and if a new venture is able to capture just 2% of sales in the first year, it can attain sales in that year of $2 million. If, over the next few years, it just maintains its market share, sales will grow significantly.

The microcomputer industry was just such a market, with plenty of room for innovative entrants targeting sales of $50 million to $100 million. Compaq, the portable microcomputer firm, achieved sales of $110 million in its first year and, by 1988, reached nearly $2 billion in sales. Sun Microsystems, a 1983 startup in CAD/CAM workstations, grew to $1.2 billion by 1988.

Conversely, a market that is growing at less than 10% or contracting is unattractive.

Gross margins

The potential for high and durable gross margins (the unit selling price less all direct, variable costs) is important. Gross margins exceeding 40% to 50% provide a tremendous built-in cushion that allows for more error and more opportunity to learn from mistakes than do gross margins of 20% or less. High and durable gross margins, in turn, mean that a venture can reach breakeven earlier, an event that preferably occurs within the first two years. Thus, for example, if gross margins are just 20%, for every $1.00 increase in fixed costs (for example, insurance, salaries, rent, and utilities), sales need to increase $5.00 just to stay even. If gross margins are 75%, however, a $1.00 increase in fixed costs requires a sales increase of just $1.33.

The cushion provided by high and durable gross margins is illustrated by an entrepreneur who built the international division of an emerging software company to $17 million in highly profitable sales in just five years (when he was 25 years of age). He emphasizes that there is simply no substitute for outrageous gross margins, by saying, "It allows you to make all kinds of mistakes that would kill a normal company. And we made them all. But our high gross margins covered all the learning tuition and still left a good profit."[25]

Gross margins of less than 20%, particularly if they are fragile, are unattractive.

Market share

The potential to be a leader in the market and capture at least a 20% share of the market is important because it can create a very high value for a company that might otherwise be worth little more than book value.

For example, one such firm, with less than $15 million in sales, became the dominant factor in its small market niche, with a 70% market share. Consequently, the company was acquired for $23 million in cash.

A firm that can capture less than 5% of a market is unattractive to most investors seeking a higher-potential company.

Cost structure

A firm that can become the low-cost provider is attractive, whereas a firm that continually faces worsening cost conditions is less so. Attractive opportunities exist in industries where economies of scale are either insignificant or advantageous to the new venture. Attractive opportunities boast the low costs of learning by doing. Where costs per unit are high when small amounts of the product are sold, existing firms that have low promotion costs can face attractive market opportunities.

Economic and Harvest Issues

Profits after taxes

High and durable gross margins usually translate into strong and durable after-tax profits. Attractive opportunities have potential for durable profits of at least 10% to 15% and often 15% to 20% or more. Those generating after-tax profits of less than 5% are quite fragile.

Time to breakeven and positive cash flow

As mentioned, breakeven and positive cash flow for attractive companies is possible within two years. Once the time to breakeven and positive cash flow exceeds three years, the attractiveness of the opportunity diminishes accordingly.

ROI potential

An important corollary to forgiving economics is reward. Very attractive opportunities have the potential to yield a return on investment of 25% or more per year. After all, during the 1980s, many venture capital funds achieved only single-digit returns on investment. High and durable gross margins and high and durable after-tax profits usually yield high earnings per share and high return on stockholder's equity, thus generating a satisfactory harvest price for a company. This is likely to be true whether the company is sold through an initial public offering or privately or whether it is acquired. Given the risk typically involved, a potential return on investment of less than 15% to 20% per year is unattractive.

Value

New ventures that are based on strategic value, such as valuable technology, are attractive, whereas those with low or no strategic value are less attractive. For example, a product technology of compelling strategic value to Xerox was owned, in the mid-1980s, by a small company with about $10 million in sales and a prior-year loss of $1.5 million. Xerox purchased the company for $56 million.

Opportunities with extremely large capital commitments, whose value on exit can be severely eroded by unanticipated circumstances, are less attractive. Such an example would be nuclear power.

Capital requirements

Ventures that can be funded and that have low to moderate capital requirements are attractive. Realistically, most higher-potential businesses need significant amounts of cash—several hundred thousand dollars and up—to get started. Accordingly, businesses that can be started with little or no capital are rare, but they do exist. One such venture, which was launched in Boston in 1971 with $7,500 of the founder's capital, grew to over $30 million in sales by 1989. In today's venture capital market, the first round of financing is typically

$1 million to $2 million or more for a startup.[26] Some higher-potential ventures, such as those in the service sector or "cash sales" businesses, have lower capital requirements than do high-technology manufacturing firms with continual large research and development expenditures.

If the venture needs too much money or cannot be funded, it is unattractive. An extreme example is a satellite-repair venture that a team of students recently proposed. The students believed that the required startup capital was in the $50-million to $200-million range. Projects of this magnitude are in the domain of the government and the very large corporation rather than that of the entrepreneur and venture capitalist.

Exit Mechanism

Businesses that are eventually acquired or sold—privately or to the public—are usually started and grown with a harvest objective in mind. Attractive companies that realize capital gains from the sale of their businesses have, or envision, a harvest or exit mechanism. Unattractive opportunities do not have an exit mechanism in mind. (Chapter 13 covers exit mechanisms in detail.)

Competitive Advantages

Variable and fixed costs

An attractive opportunity is potentially the lowest-cost producer, with the lowest costs of marketing and distribution. It should certainly not have the highest costs. For example, Bowmar was unable to remain competitive in the market for electronic calculators after the producers of large-scale integrated circuits, such as Texas Instruments, entered the business. The inability to achieve and sustain a position as a low-cost producer shortens the life expectancy of a new venture.

Degree of control

Attractive opportunities have potential to exercise a moderate to strong degree of control over prices, costs, and channels of distribution. Fragmented markets with no dominant competitor—no "IBM"—have this potential. These markets usually have a market leader with 20% or less of the market share. For example, a new venture with sole control of the source of supply for its product or of channels of distribution can achieve market dominance even if it is weak in other areas.

Lack of control over such factors as product development and component prices can make an opportunity unattractive. For example, when suppliers could not produce several needed semiconductors at low enough prices, Viatron was unable to make an inexpensive computer terminal that it had extensively publicized.

A major competitor with a market share of 40%, 50%, or, especially, 60% usually has sufficient power over suppliers, customers, and pricing to create a serious barrier for a new firm. An enterprise starting up in such a market will have little freedom. Nevertheless, if a dominant competitor is at full capacity, is slow to innovate or to add capacity in a large and growing market, or routinely ignores or abuses the customer (remember "Ma Bell"), there may be an entry opportunity. Rarely, however, do entrepreneurs find such sleepy competition in dynamic, emerging industries dense with opportunity.

Entry barriers

Having a favorable window of opportunity is important. Having or being able to gain proprietary protection, regulatory advantage, or other legal or contractual advantage, such as exclusive rights to a market or with a distributor, is attractive. Having or being able to gain an advantage in response/lead times is also important since these can create barriers to entry or expansion by others.

For example, advantages in response/lead times in technology, product innovation, market innovation, people, location, resources, or capacity make an opportunity attractive. It is also advantageous to have well-developed, high-quality, accessible contacts that are the products of years of building a top-notch reputation and cannot be acquired quickly. In fact, there are times when this competitive advantage may be so strong as to provide dominance in the marketplace, even though many other factors are weak or average.

Examples of how quickly the joys of startup may fade if others cannot be kept out can be found among firms in the hard disk drive industry that were unable to erect entry barriers in the United States in the early to mid-1980s. By the end of 1983, some 90 hard disk drive companies were launched, and severe price competition led to a major industry shakeout.

If a firm cannot keep others out or if it faces existing entry barriers, it is unattractive. An easily overlooked issue is a firm's capacity to gain distribution of its product. As simple as it may sound, even companies backed by venture capital fall victim to this market issue. Air Florida apparently assembled all the right ingredients, including substantial financing, yet was unable to secure sufficient gate space for its airplanes. Even though it sold passenger seats, it had no place to pick the passengers up or drop them off.

Management Team Issues

Entrepreneurial team

An opportunity is attractive if there is a strong team that contains industry superstars. This team should have proven profit-and-loss experience in the same technology, market, and service area, as well as complementary and compatible skills. An opportunity is unattractive if there is no qualified team, or no team at all.

Fatal Flaw Issues

Basically, attractive ventures have no fatal flaws; one or more fatal flaws render an opportunity unattractive. Usually, these flaws relate to one of the criteria described. In many instances, markets are too small, competition is overpowering, the cost of entry is too high, an entrant is unable to produce at a competitive price, and so on. An example of an entry barrier that acted as a fatal flaw was the inability of Florida Air to get its flights listed on reservation computers.

Personal Criteria

One of the most challenging aspects in the screening of opportunities is the application of personal criteria, as discussed in the following sections.

Upside/Downside Issues

An attractive opportunity does not have excessive downside risk. The upside and the downside of an opportunity are not linear, nor are they on the same continuum. The upside is easy, and it has been said that success has a thousand sires. The downside is quite another matter, since it has also been said that failure is an orphan.

An entrepreneur needs to be able to absorb the financial downside in a way that permits a rebound without excessive debt obligations. If the financial exposure involved in launching a venture is greater than the entrepreneur's net worth, the resources that can reasonably be drawn upon, and the alternative disposable earnings stream if the venture does not work out, the deal may be too big. Although today's bankruptcy laws are extremely generous, the psychological burdens of living through such an ordeal are infinitely more painful than the financial consequences. The owner of an existing business needs to consider whether a failure will be too demanding to the firm's reputation and future credibility, aside from the obvious financial consequences.[27]

Opportunity Cost

Any venture opportunity entails opportunity costs. An entrepreneur who is skilled enough to grow a successful multimillion-dollar venture has talents that are highly valued by medium to large firms as well. While assessing benefits that may accrue in pursuing an opportunity, an entrepreneur needs to take a serious look at other alternatives, including potential "golden handcuffs," and account honestly for any "cut" in salary that may be involved in pursuing a certain opportunity.

Furthermore, pursuing an opportunity can shape an entrepreneur in ways it is hard to imagine. It will probably be possible for an individual to execute between two to four multimillion-dollar ventures between the ages of 25 and 50. Each of these experiences will position the entrepreneur, for better or worse, for the next opportunity. Since it is important in one's early years to gain relevant management experience and since building a venture (either one that works out or one that does not) takes a lot more time than is commonly believed, it is important to consider alternatives while assessing an opportunity.

Desirability

A good opportunity is not only attractive but also desirable; that is, a good opportunity *fits*. An example of an intensely personal criterion would be the desire for a certain life-style. This desire may preclude certain opportunities, that is, certain opportunities may be opportunities for someone else.

For example, the founder of a major high-technology venture in the Boston area was asked why the headquarters of his firm were located in downtown Boston, whereas those of other such firms were located on the famous Route 128 outside the city. His reply was that he wanted to live in Boston because he loved the city and wanted to be able to walk to work. He said, "The rest did not matter."

IN CONCLUSION: GET THE CHUNKS

Nobel prize-winner Herbert Simon of the Department of Psychology at Carnegie-Mellon University described the recognizing of patterns as a creative process that is not simply logical, linear, and additive; he says, rather, that the process is often intuitive and inductive, involving the creative linking, or cross-association, of two or more in-depth "chunks" of experience, know-how, and contacts.[28] His research on creativity has some significant implications for your search for the right business opportunity for you. He describes world-class creativity as a process whereby people get what he calls the "50,000 chunks" of diverse experiences, know-how, and exposure to different tasks, ideas, and situations that enable them to be highly creative and to develop the ability to recognize patterns. He contends that it takes 10 years or more for people to accumulate these "50,000 chunks" that enable them to be highly creative and recognize patterns—familiar circumstances that can be translated from one place to another.

The message is clear. Most ideas for higher-potential ventures will come after you have accumulated those 10 to 15 years of experience and "chunks." That means learning an industry and specific markets and getting the know-how and contacts to enable you to make some profits for someone else before you try it on your own. Even Steven Jobs, co-founder of Apple Computer at age 25 had those chunks. Few people realize that he had been working with homemade computer kits from the time he was 10 years old.

3 ENTRY STRATEGIES

Karl H. Vesper

INTRODUCTION

Setting up a new business collides with the wishes of established competitors, who want all the customer dollars they can get. To get those dollars, they try to give good service, look for new customers and new ways to serve them, take care in pricing not to drive too many customers away, and advertise to remind customers that they are there and anxious to serve. If a competitor comes up with a better offering for customers, they try to match or beat it.

To established companies, a new competitor means any number of unattractive things, such as lost potential sales, lower margins from price cutting, longer hours, loss of key employees, and buildup of inventory that is not moving. At the very least, competitors add worries, keep profits down, and threaten complete displacement from the market; at worst, new competitors can cause bankruptcy. Airlines have gone through such nightmares repeatedly. When deregulation was introduced, entrepreneurs seized the opportunity to start new airlines. Prices dropped. Some major carriers, such as Branniff, failed. The big lines fought back. Most of the entrepreneurs (for example, People's Express and Laker) failed. Then big lines, such as Pan Am, failed. For them the pain from competition has been easy for the whole public to see. At a less visible level competition means discomfort for other companies as well, even when they do not totally fail.

When a new competitor enters, established companies usually fight back. The response may be quick. When Preston Tucker introduced his new automobile in the late forties, the established interests ran him out of business before he had made more than a few dozen cars. Interestingly, they did it not by cutting prices or introducing superior products, but rather by using political influence to bring the government down on him. His company died while he was defending himself from litigation.

Sometimes the response is slower. IBM let Control Data get started and become a well-established mainframe competitor before it struck back. Then it was again slow in responding when Digital Equipment introduced minicomputers, so slow that it had still not caught up after decades. Finally, it let the microcomputer startups get ahead of it by about five years before it finally introduced its PC and started catching up. But then it did so with a vengeance, and scores of microcomputer entrepreneurs were put out of business.

Of course, the entrepreneurs were also putting each other out of business in the meantime. More features, better designs, lower prices, better service, higher reliability, bundled software promotions, and more effective advertising all made entry progressively more difficult as the industry developed. Both capital and customers became harder to get. Consequently, the number of startups that survived became smaller, and the number of attempts to start up also declined. There were just too many competitors, and some of them, such as IBM, Tandy, Apple, and a host of small, low-overhead IBM cloners, had become very tough.

But the startup attempts in microcomputer manufacturing kept on, and some of them became highly successful. One relatively late entrant was IBM, which enjoyed the advantages of its well-established brand name and image of dependable high quality in both products and service. Another late entrant was Compaq, which managed to make headway even against IBM by being equal in quality but higher in performance. Still another was Dell Computer, which found a way to bypass the established channels of distribution, namely computer retailers, by selling direct at low prices both to large single customers and, through mail order, to small ones.

Thus, there was an interplay between the defensive advantages built up by those companies already in business and the *entry wedges* used by new entrepreneurs to crack through those defenses and break into the competitive arena. Such interplay is constantly going on in virtually all industries, with established companies trying to kill each other off and keep new competitors out while entrepreneurs look for entry wedges that will enable them to break in.

Such entrepreneurial entry wedges can be grouped into six types:[1]

- Developing a new product or service
- Developing a similar product or service—that is, the "better mousetrap"
- Buying a franchise

- Exploiting an existing product or service
- Sponsoring a startup enterprise
- Acquiring a going concern

This chapter discusses each of these entry strategies in detail.

DEVELOPING A NEW PRODUCT OR SERVICE

The first auto, airplane, radio, life insurance policy, jet engine, TV, plastic plumbing pipe, color TV, microwave oven, microchip, and microcomputer were clearly new products. Some were introduced by existing companies. Others were the basis for forming new companies. Sometimes the products lasted but the startups did not. For example, the first pocket calculator (by Bomar) and the first microcomputer kit (by MITS) were clearly winning products, but the companies they formed the bases for did not have what it took to continue with them.

Dramatically new services are not so easy to name. Some, however, arose to serve markets created by new products. For instance, the microcomputer created opportunities to start repair businesses, disk-copying firms, data-salvaging companies, trade shows, and companies to collect and sell data on the industry. Cellular telephones created similar service startup opportunities. Opportunities for service startups in such things as occupational safety and environmental management were created by new government regulations.

What it takes to start a company around a new product or service includes, most importantly, the discovery of an intersection between the market for that product or service and a way to create one. Sometimes the right person for this is someone working on a technical frontier who discovers a way to accomplish something worthwhile physically or an inventor with a "better idea." Other times it may be a person who comes in contact with a potential market through work or hobbies and either finds a way to satisfy it or teams up with another person capable of solving the product or service design problem.

What Are the Risks?

Risks in applying the new product or service entry wedge include a number of possibilities:

- The design task may be practically impossible for the entrepreneur to accomplish in time.
- The new venture may err in the design.
- Another company with stronger resources may follow and wipe out the startup.

- The startup may not be able to persuade enough people to buy the new product or service either fast enough or at a high enough price to make a profit.

How easy it can be to succeed with a truly new product was illustrated by the experience of Osborne Computer, which was immediately swamped with orders when its product, the first "compact" microcomputer, was introduced. The same company also illustrated how easy it is to fail by doing so within two years of its takeoff as it bungled on design, deliveries, and costs while competitors surpassed it with better designs. Even a company with strong resources and an entrepreneur with a proven successful track record can fail with a startup, as was illustrated by the total failure of Fred Smith's Zap Mail venture.

Most companies with new products that last probably succeed, although nobody has made a count of that particular approach. Among high-technology startups, for instance, the success rate appears to have been about 80% on a five-year time span.[2]

CREATING PARALLEL COMPETITION BY DEVELOPING A SIMILAR PRODUCT OR SERVICE

Across a shade of gray from new products and services are those that are not really new but are just different enough to allow a startup to accomplish competitive entry with them. The clones of IBM's PC provide examples of this. They ranged from those that were dramatically cheaper to those of Compaq, which were somewhat more expensive than IBM's but were also a bit higher in performance though not fundamentally different in design. These products, which were similar, but sufficiently differentiated to succeed, enabled entry via what might be termed *parallel competition*, a term coined by Professor Arnold Hosmer of Harvard.

Examples of parallel competiton include a restaurant that starts with nearly the same location but a different menu or price structure, another job machine shop, cabinet shop, construction contractor, or advertising agency; these are all types of firms that continually enter competition in parallel. Every city has them. Most are small, but some, such as recent startups in warehouse stores (such as Price Savers and Costco) or home improvement stores (Builders' Emporium, Home Club, and Eagle Hardware, for example), can be quite large. Eagle Hardware, for instance, started out with public financing made possible by the credibility of its founding entrepreneur, who had previously developed another hardware store chain. Interestingly, the prior chain, Pay 'N Pak, had been sold to a larger firm that proved unable to sustain it; shortly after Eagle opened, Pay 'N Pak went out of business.

Parallel competition is often fierce. By definition it involves firms that lack strong differentiation and therefore tend to compete on price, which drives margins down. A curious exception, up to a point, seems to be local microbreweries, which seem to do better when they have local competitors. Evidently, only then do local beer drinkers take an interest in them.

To succeed in parallel competition certainly requires some degree of differentiation, however. It may be based on price. Filling stations often start with a lowered price. It may also be a different use of advertising, service, personality or contacts of the owner, style of presentation, or convenience features. The toughness of such competition will likely force the entrepreneur to be good at performing the functions of the business. The margin for error in learning and acquiring skill may be vanishingly small. Thin capitalization may also not be tolerable, since margins are thin and competitors may lower prices to keep the new company out of contention.

What Are the Risks?

Risks in applying parallel competition as an entry wedge include the possibilities that the startup's financing may not be sufficient to carry it to profitability and that the owner may simply not be capable of competing with "pros" in the business, who already have their routines polished and their names established. An easy risk to overlook is that competitors will likely take retaliatory action to counter whatever features the new parallel startup attempts to use for differentiating itself. Also easy to underestimate may be the gap in credibility that the new firm will have with customers it is attempting to take from established firms and the strength of customer habits in buying from existing firms.

BUYING A FRANCHISE

Help from an already-established business can be bought through a contract that grants some sort of franchise, usually for a particular geographical territory. This help may include permission to use the established business's name and logo, to sell its products, or to use its methods. The already-established business, called the franchisor, may provide training, accounting services, performance evaluations, assistance in choosing locations and arranging financing, as well as annual meetings where those who have bought franchises—the franchisees—meet and exchange information about what has been working well and what has not in their operations.

Examples of businesses started with the help of franchisors are easy to find in any community or yellow pages. They include fast-food outlets, car dealers, dry cleaners, filling stations, many types of retail stores, real estate offices, insurance offices, tax services, mailing firms, ice cream shops, printing businesses, and other services. One simple way to learn what franchising is like is to visit such firms and ask their owners. Some will likely be very satisfied that they chose franchising as a wedge for competitive entry, and others will be less so. Some franchisees have become very wealthy by building their own chains of outlets, whereas others have gone broke trying to make their franchises work. Countless lawsuits have been conducted by franchisees who claimed that their franchisors did not deliver as promised. One result of these suits has been the enactment of many state laws and regulations to control franchisors.

Customarily, the franchisee begins with a cash payment or a promise to pay a royalty to the franchisor. These, plus capital to equip and operate the franchise, are requisites for the franchisee to get started in business. Usually prior experience in the same line of work is not required, which sometimes makes franchising an attractive way to enter business in a new line of work. Many franchisees are people who have retired from some other job, such as the military.

Some franchisees have become very prosperous by obtaining franchises from franchisors that are just beginning and selling them cheaply to prove themselves, or by obtaining franchises for large territories, where it is possible to develop chains of them and earn large profits from multiple outlets. More often, however, it is the franchisors who make the large profits.

What Are the Risks?

Risks include failure by the franchisor to tell the truth about how likely the franchise is to be successful or to live up to its part of the bargain, such as providing the sorts of help mentioned above. For checking out a franchise there are lists available from the Small Business Administration and in books on franchising. Other risks are that the franchisee will start with too little capital to sustain operations until breakeven occurs and that the franchisee simply may not like the work. Compared to investing the capital required in securities that pay interest or dividends and taking a job that pays a salary, the franchisee may not be ahead financially at all. So a franchisee can end up simply providing the investment for a franchisor to expand and working long hours at routine tasks for low pay.

EXPLOITING PARTIAL MOMENTUM FROM AN EXISTING PRODUCT OR SERVICE

Sometimes situations arise in which the potential for profit is generated by events outside the control of the entrepreneur. Then what is needed is simply to notice that the potential is there and take advantage of it. There are three types of such circumstances: transferring a product or service to a new location, meeting a supply shortage, and capitalizing on unused resources.

Transferring to New Locations

The underlying principle of chains in such businesses as stores, restaurants, and filling stations is that the same type of business is needed in many places. When a new kind of business is created to which this same principle applies, an opportunity exists to transfer that kind of business to many other places. This transfer can be accomplished by independent entrepreneurs as well as chains and franchisors, and it often is. Recent examples of such new businesses have been instant photo shops, copy centers and microcomputer retailers.

Sometimes such startups are subsequently acquired by larger chains as a way of expanding faster. This can generate a substantial cash-out profit to the entrepreneur who spots the geographical transfer opportunity and takes advantage of it early.

What Are the Risks?

To accomplish such a transfer, the entrepreneur must first notice the potential and then either have or be able to recruit the capital and talent to introduce the new type of firm in a new setting. The risk is that the entrepreneur will not have enough of these two advantages to get the new firm started or to sustain it once competition develops.

Meeting a Supply Shortage

There may be a period of time before the sources of supply recognize shortages of desired goods or services that occasionally crop up in the economy. Shortages of housing, for example, may arise in areas with rapidly expanding populations, such as certain areas in the Sun Belt and in areas hit by such calamities as fires and hurricanes. Shortages of water, such as those that occurred in Seattle in 1990, give rise to entrepreneurs who truck in water from other areas to be used for watering lawns when it is prohibited to use city water for doing so.

What Are the Risks?

At the outset, there is usually little risk in undertaking to relieve such shortages, though attempting to gouge on prices can generate hostility and contempt. With time, however, the risk is that the shortage will go away because other sources will be better equipped to supply the needs; competition must be anticipated.

Capitalizing on Unused Resources

The other side of the supply shortage picture is an availability of resources that are not being used. Harvesting industries such as mining and forestry are built on such circumstances. A more recent example of such entrepreneurial opportunity has been the collection and processing of recyclable materials. Another is to process surplus grain and make it into ethanol for use as a gasoline substitute.

Requisite for making a venture in unused resources are to discover them, to see how they might be exploited to make a sale, and to act to bring that about. Devices sometimes used in doing so include buying an option on the resources or obtaining an agency agreement for selling them. These approaches may be able to circumvent the need to invest capital in the resources.

What Are the Risks?

The biggest risk is investing time and capital to take control of resources that turn out not to be salable at a profit after all. The entrepreneur needs to ask himself why the resources were unutilized in the first place. Was it because nobody else could see the opportunity that they contained, or was it because everybody could see that in fact there really was not an opportunity? What is it that the entrepreneur knows that others do not? Such activity inevitably involves speculating, and in speculation there is always risk of loss.

FINDING SPONSORSHIP

A safer bet as an entry wedge may be to take advantage of the willingness of someone to help sponsor the startup in some manner. Typically, the sponsor is a customer, a supplier, or an investor in the startup venture.

- *Customer sponsors.* A potential customer who strongly wants to obtain what the new venture will offer may be willing to provide sponsorship through a substantial purchase order, a contract to buy goods over time, or a cash advance on some purchase.
- *Supplier sponsors.* A supplier who strongly wants to see the venture develop as a user of what she offers may be willing to advance inventory or labor as a way of helping the venture get started.
- *Investor sponsors.* Someone who thinks the prospective venture will become highly successful may advance cash to it as an investor. The purpose usually includes making a profit, but sometimes people advance cash to ventures simply because they like the entrepreneur, think the venture is a "good cause," or want to participate in the adventure of a startup. Less

encouraging investor motivations can include the investor's hope that he will be hired by the venture or will be taken on as a director.

A prime requisite for all these types of sponsorship is that the entrepreneur and the venture be regarded by the sponsor as credible and likely to succeed. The strongest basis for this is usually a track record of prior accomplishment and a demonstration that the entrepreneur possesses the capacity to perform the critical tasks of the venture. How good the venture idea looks is also crucial, and it may be helpful for the entrepreneur to develop in writing a clear description of just how it works and how it will be implemented.

What Are the Risks?

Credibility is also important for the entrepreneur to assess personally, because the risk is that sponsorship may be lost if the venture fails, and that can make it much harder to pull off a venture the next time. Even when direct sponsorship is not involved, the entrepreneur requires help from other people in venturing. Suppliers, customers, employees, banks, and government agencies are usually all involved to some degree. The more confidence they have in the entrepreneur and what he is trying to do, the more they are likely to help the venture.

ACQUIRING A GOING CONCERN

The final main entry strategy is to acquire a going concern. This can tremendously simplify the process of getting into business. A business can be viewed as basically a bundle of habits—customers buying, suppliers supplying, employees doing their jobs. In a going concern, those habits are already present. The premises are set up, any necessary permits are in effect, and the cash flow should be giving a fairly clear picture of what the financial needs are. In a startup business, there will likely be a negative cash flow that is hard to predict while the company struggles to break even. Two important needs can be circumvented by the entrepreneur through entering business via acquisition: the need for expertise and the need for capital.

Expertise in a going concern should already be present in employees of the business. Even if it is not, the buying entrepreneur should be able to obtain education and operating help from the selling owner to fill in the expertise needed. Consequently, it is fairly common to find businesses owned by entrepreneurs who bought them with no prior experience in that particular line of work and nevertheless succeeded. This is in stark contrast to a startup. Those who start companies and succeed usually do so with the benefit of prior related business experience unless the business is either such a new type that nobody has such experience or, alternatively, it is so straightforward that little expertise is required. Examples of such simple types are small retail stores and restaurants or services such as housecleaning, painting, or hedge trimming.

The need for capital in acquisition entry is often circumvented by having the selling owner help with financing through leveraging the buyout. The purchaser may be able to borrow against assets of the business to provide for a down payment to the seller and some working capital to continue operations. The seller takes a note for the balance owed, which the buyer pays off over time from earnings of the business. Thus the buying entrepreneur may be able to enter an independent business in a line of work new to her and to make a salary and profit from it right away without putting up any cash at all. There will, of course, be a debt obligation for the buyer, but the odds of succeeding with a buyout of a business, provided it has a history of profitability and is in reasonably good shape, historically appear to have been very high. It is often the most effective way to enter independent business.

Negotiation of price and terms may be the most discussed part of the acquisition, but that may not be the really hard part. Finding a suitable buyout and establishing credibility with the seller are. But it is still necessary and therefore worth thought and possibly some study.

One task that certainly should be part of this process is to develop a checklist of criteria to use in deciding whether to buy the business or not. A general list for this task appears in the more extensive discussion of acquisition entry in *New Venture Strategies*, chapters 9 and 10.[3] Some questions to be asked and answered are:

- What is the real reason that the seller is willing to sell?
- What assets are to go with the business?
- How much would be required to replicate the business rather than to buy it?
- What elements in the business are key to its survival?
- If the former owner drops out, how would this affect decisions by customers and the conduct of operations in the business?

Another key task is to develop a projected cash flow for the business during takeover and subsequent operations of the business. Consider the following:

- How much cash will the buyer have to have and when?
- How fast will the cash come back in, and what net inflow will occur over time?
- What will be the discounted present value of this flow, and how will that compare to the price of the business?

To answer the last question some sort of discount rate will have to be assumed. Several should be tried, ranging from the interest rate on a secure investment to a much higher rate characteristic of a high-risk investment. Presumably, the appropriate figure will be somewhere in between.

Another assumption, usually critical, will concern the cash drawdown to be taken by the buyer as salary. An appropriate figure here might be the estimated salary appropriate for a manager who might be hired to run the business.

Each of these assumed figures can be adjusted in size to assess the impact of error in estimating the financial future of the buyout. Such adjustments should probably be tried with the help of a personal computer spreadsheet program to generate "what if" scenarios and assess possible consequences of going through with the buyout.

What Are the Risks?

There are two main catches in attempting this method of entry. The first arises from the fact that the approach is so effective. As a consequence, there are far more people who would like to acquire a business than there are opportunities to do so. This tends to make available buying opportunities scarce. They tend to be grabbed up quickly, and they tend to drive the prices of buyouts up, sometimes to the point of financial unfeasibility. To deal with this problem, the entrepreneur should try as many approaches as possible for locating buying opportunities. These include using such lead sources as:

- Classified advertisements ("Business Opportunities")
- Business and commercial real estate brokers
- Professionals (bankers, accountants, attorneys)
- Cold calling

The second major problem with accomplishing a buyout is to appear adequately credible to the seller. The "ideal" seller is most often a person who is getting older and wants to sell a business *not* because it has problems but rather in order to retire. Such a person will likely care not only that the full purchase price will be paid on time but also that the business, its employees, its name, and its facilities will be well maintained.

To provide this assurance, a buyer is likely to benefit from having developed a reputation for demonstrating high-quality performance in whatever she did, being an honorable person who keeps promises, being competent in controlling costs and managing finances, and being able to set and follow effective priorities. Personal agreeability and compatibility with the nature and idiosyncrasies of the seller may also be important. Sellers sometimes compromise on price and terms for the sake of the comfort they feel in dealing with the buyer and the peace of mind they think they will derive from having that particular person as a debtor and a steward of their business.

CONCLUSION

Which of these entry wedges will fit best for a given entrepreneur has to be decided by the individual. Any of them can work. At a particular point in time none of them may work. At other times it may be possible to combine more than one. Having them in mind and searching continually until something works out may be the most effective individual strategy.

4 MARKET OPPORTUNITIES AND MARKETING

Gerald E. Hills

Entrepreneur R. David Thomas opened the first Wendy's restaurant because he saw an unfilled need in the marketplace.[1] Thus, he started with a *market orientation.* Realizing that many customers wanted more choice and a fresher hamburger than they received at McDonald's, he decided to sell his four Kentucky Fried Chicken franchises and open Wendy's (after his daughter's nickname). Thomas said, "I like a hamburger with mustard, pickle, and onion, and you didn't have a choice at a McDonald's or Burger King. I thought the other ones were . . . just giving you what they wanted to and not what you really wanted." This kind of customer orientation is the foundation for modern marketing. "No one else was doing a very good job, and I wanted a hamburger that was different, made to order so you could choose whatever you wanted to put on it and get out of the heat-lamp and heat-bin syndrome." Thomas did not use frozen patties but ground his hamburger fresh daily, and he let the customers select their own condiments. That provided customers with 256 possible combinations of condiments. The market perceived Wendy's products to be of higher quality and better taste than those of the competition, and Thomas grabbed a piece of the market not exploited by McDonald's and Burger King. Wendy's went on to successfully offer the restaurant industry's first drive-up windows.

When Thomas started, McDonald's had 1,298 restaurants. Two years after he started, he had 2 restaurants. He opened 2 more the year after that, then 4 more, then 12 more. In 1973 he sold his first franchise for $5,000;

The author wishes to acknowledge the contributions of Dr. Robert B. Woodruff and Dr. David W. Cravens to this chapter as previous coauthors with me of *Marketing Management* (Homewood, IL: Richard D. Irwin, 1987).

in 1976 there were 300 Wendy's restaurants, and the company went public. Today, Wendy's restaurants number nearly 4,000 with sales over $3 billion, and, as Chairman of the Board, R. David Thomas is still the largest stockholder and the centerpiece of their promotional strategy. He demonstrated once again what an entrepreneur can do by perceiving market opportunity and using sound marketing fundamentals.

Marketing is the process of planning and executing the conception, pricing, promotion, and distribution of ideas, goods, and services to create exchanges that satisfy individual and organizational objectives.[2] The Wendy's operation illustrates the definition of marketing. Through convenient distribution of quality goods and services at the right price, Wendy's has created millions of mutually beneficial exchanges that satisfy individuals and attain company objectives. This chapter discusses the critical importance of marketing within entrepreneurship—both as a philosophy and orientation, and as a set of management tasks that together form the marketing plan for a business.

MARKETING AS A PHILOSOPHY

The foundation for contemporary marketing management and entrepreneurial success is the "marketing concept," which provides an orientation for conducting business, a way of thinking, and a basic approach to business problems. Although the marketing concept may seem obvious, a surprising number of entrepreneurs still fail to grasp its far-reaching implications. The *marketing concept* is a customer-oriented philosophy that is implemented and integrated throughout the business to serve customers better than competitors and achieve specified goals.

> Marketing requires separate work and a distinct group of activities. But it is, first, a central dimension of the entire business. It is the whole business seen from the point of view of its final result, that is, from the customer's point of view.[3]

As Exhibit 4.1 shows, the marketing concept is made up of three components. Starting with *customer needs and wants,* a business owner develops an *organizationally integrated marketing strategy* to accomplish its *goals*. The concept begins with the customer: "The principal task of the marketing function . . . is not so much to be skillful in making the customer do what suits the interests of the business as to be skillful in conceiving and then making the business do what suits the interests of the customer."[4]

Identifying Customer Needs or Desires

Since no businesses have the skills and resources to be all things to all people, entrepreneurs must identify which customer needs and wants can

EXHIBIT 4.1. The marketing concept.

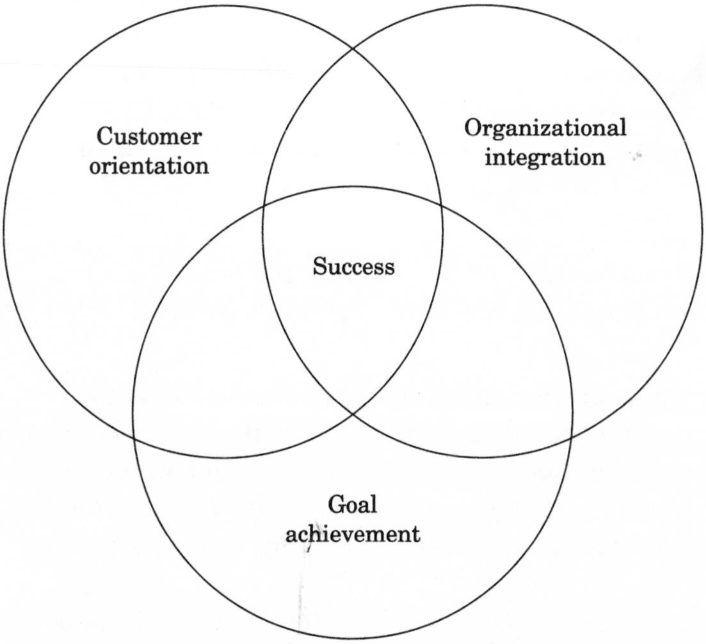

and should be met. Deciding which preferences and potential customers to serve is crucial, given any entrepreneur's limited resources and competitive strengths. A *target market* is a group of existing or potential customers within a particular product market toward which the business directs its marketing efforts. Selectively choosing target markets is an integral part of the philosophy suggested by the marketing concept. The alternative is to try to serve all potential customers in a mediocre fashion and thus to fall short in providing customer satisfaction.

Entrepreneurs who are not market oriented are often technology or product oriented, production oriented, or sales oriented. A *technology or product orientation* often exists in firms that have had a highly successful product. Where such an orientation exists, management implicitly believes that if "you build a better mousetrap, the world will beat a path to your door." It is true that, given enough publicity, a glamorous technological innovation may, for a time, seem to create its own market. Texas Instruments has been accused of being a technology-oriented company because when it was founded, its high-tech products seemed almost to sell themselves. In later years, however, competition and the company's failure to adapt spelled trouble for its entry into new markets.

Entrepreneurs with nontechnical products and services may also fall into the product orientation trap. A lawyer, for example, may strive for a

Wilkinson Library
Telluride, CO 81435

"perfect, risk-free" agreement for a client, a beautiful "product," but destroy a valuable deal for the client. Communicating the reasons to buy a product requires adopting the role of a buyer, not that of an engineer, inventor, or developer. There is obviously a very real need for the development of quality technologies, products, and services. But these should not be developed for their own sake. Peter Drucker captured the essential difference between a product orientation and a customer orientation:

> True marketing starts . . . with the customer. . . . It asks, "What does the customer want to buy?" It does not say, "This is what our product or service does." It says, "These are the satisfactions the customer looks for, values, and needs."[5]

Another orientation that sometimes develops in entrepreneurial businesses is a *production orientation*. Professional service firms such as dentists or accounting firms can become so enamored with how they deliver a service that they lose a focus on the customers' wishes. A cost-cutting efficiency focus in manufacturing operations may also hinder efforts to deliver customer satisfaction.

Finally, an entrepreneur with a *sales orientation* is one who assumes that effective selling can "push" its output into the hands of customers. Even first-rate personal selling, however, is at most one element in a total marketing program. A sales orientation is geared toward converting an existing product into cash rather than beginning with customer needs and responding to those needs. Pushing products is less necessary if a business's products and services fill customer needs better than those of competitors. A new office furniture producer learned this truth because his furniture, prices, and distribution channels were the same as most other firms in the industry. The business owner believed that the key to success was a better group of furniture brokers and more salespeople. The firm went bankrupt within a year, having fallen victim to a sales orientation. For a business to succeed it must, of course, have good products and services, good production, and good selling. But these revolve around creating customer satisfaction in a target market—that is, marketing!

Integrating the Customer Focus throughout the Organization

The second major component of the marketing concept philosophy is *organizational integration* (refer to Exhibit 4.1). Whether an entrepreneur owns a startup company of three people or a rapidly growing firm of 200, she can encounter hurdles as she tries to integrate a customer focus as a philosophy for all people in the company. The technical genius who develops exciting products and services may be rude or incompetent in answering telephone calls from customers. Or a conservative accountant may alienate potential customers in reviewing their credit rating. Or the marketing leader in the entrepreneurial team may not be given equal influence in decisions or, worse yet, may not even be a marketer but rather a salesperson with a narrow perspective. Virtually all the people in a company directly and indirectly affect how customers perceive the firm. There is an opportunity in a new, small firm for everyone to act in an integrated, consistent way toward customers. This early-stage philosophy, then, provides the foundation for developing customer-oriented guidelines and organizational structures as the company grows.

Marketing to Achieve Your Goal

The third part of the marketing concept illustrated in Exhibit 4.1 refers to *goal achievement*. Marketing is oriented toward sales volume as a success measure, but it is essential to strive not just for sales, but also for *effective* marketing that contributes to *profitable* sales. Other goals often exist as well, such as developing an image for the new business or taking over significant market share from existing firms. For example, Marketplace Business, an entrepreneurial mailing list firm, decided to offer some unique "product" features to potential business clients. Marketplace Business's user-friendly mailing lists are creating a differentiated image in a highly comparative and saturated market, which will likely result in some significant market share gains.[6]

EXHIBIT 4.2. Indicators of customer and marketing orientation.

1. What information do you carefully collect about the exact needs of your customers?
2. Could you consider custom designing your services or products for smaller groups of customers? How?
3. Are your (nonsales) employees specifically trained to represent your company to customers? How?
4. Are customers contacted after the sale to determine their level of satisfaction? How?
5. How do you convert unsatisfied customers to satisfied customers? Do you have any strategy?
6. Is your top marketer in the company a top-level, equal team member?
7. To what extent do you build your strategies around an in-depth understanding of your customers?
8. To what extent are activities of different people (or departments) coordinated to ensure customer satisfaction?

Business owners can look reflectively in the "mirror" shown in Exhibit 4.2 and the questions there can help answer the question "How customer-oriented and marketing-oriented is my business?"

MARKETING MANAGEMENT: CREATE A MARKETING PLAN

Marketing management requires analyzing the environmental situation and the market opportunities, setting marketing objectives, formulating marketing strategies and tactics, and then creating an action plan to implement the marketing practices. Exhibit 4.3 illustrates how marketing is based on the entrepreneur's vision and *mission*. And the macroenvironment—encompassing broad economic, governmental, social, natural, and technological changes—constantly provides new business opportunities as well as threats. For

EXHIBIT 4.3. Marketing management and entrepreneurship.

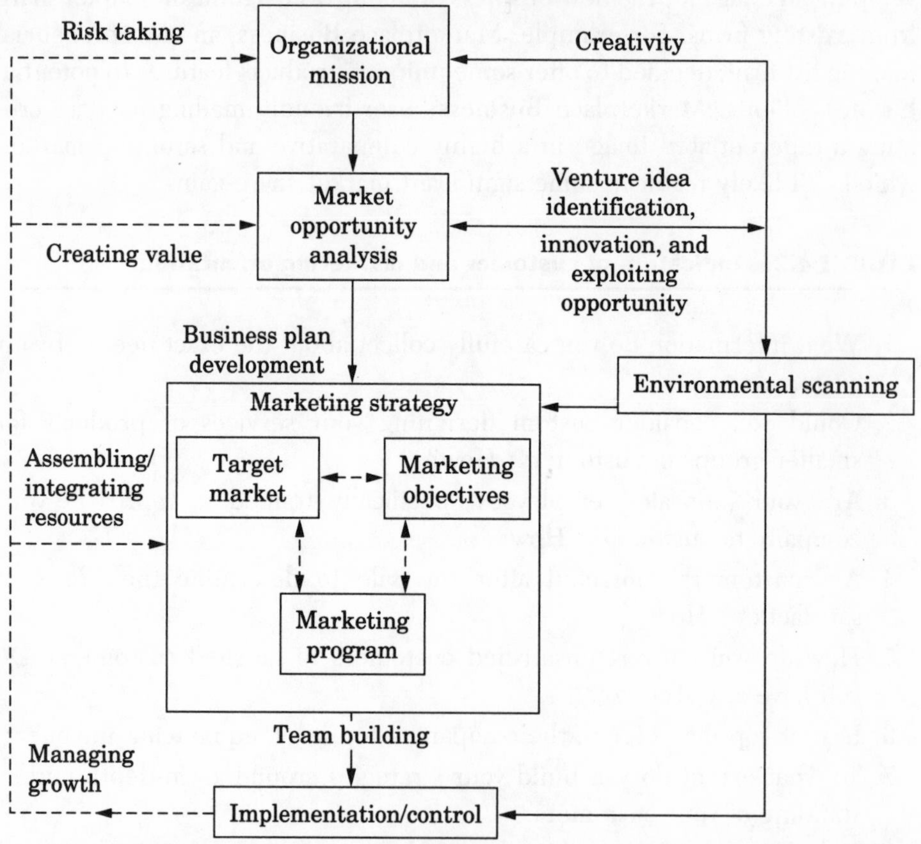

Source: Gerald E. Hills and Raymond W. LaForge, "Marketing and Entrepreneurship: The State of the Art." In *The State of the Art of Entrepreneurship,* Donald L. Sexton and John D. Kasarde (eds.) (Boston, MA: PWS-Kent Publishing Company, 1992), 164–190.

example, the recreational vehicle (RV) industry has been impacted over the past two decades by interest rates, varying levels of consumer confidence, changing gasoline prices, and even gasoline shortages. The author observed the opening of two RV retailers one mile apart a few years ago, but one soon failed. The successful retailer, anticipating substantial gasoline price hikes and consumer uncertainty, minimized the initial investment in facilities and inventory. The unsuccessful retailer ignored the signals from external forces and purchased land, constructed a building, and offered a large RV inventory and a full array of services. The changing environment reduced consumer demand for RVs, and the second retailer was forced to liquidate. The surviving entrepreneur gradually expanded into newly constructed facilities, largely financed from internal cash flow, and still operates successfully today.

Marketing management, as shown in Exhibit 4.3, also captures the elements of a *marketing plan*. The marketing plan is part of a *business plan*, or *strategic plan*. The marketing plan includes a situation analysis that in large part comprises a market opportunity analysis and an assessment of the existing or potential businesses' strengths, weaknesses, threats, and opportunities in the marketplace. Other major elements of a marketing plan include developing specific marketing objectives, determining which target markets to serve, and formulating a marketing program for each target market. Together, the objectives, target market selection, and marketing programming decisions form the marketing strategy for the business. The last portion of a marketing plan is to outline specific actions and a timetable. To summarize, the marketing plan outline is as follows:

1. Analyze the environmental situation and the market opportunity
2. Develop marketing objectives
3. Formulate a marketing strategy
4. Create an action plan

Entrepreneurs are often immersed in the marketplace, meeting customers every day. "My marketing plan is in my head" is a common statement by successful business owners. Yet the rigor of being more systematic and of casting words to paper nearly always clarifies entrepreneurs' thinking and leads to profitable changes and longer-run strategies. A good marketing plan is "intensive thinking on paper." The rest of this chapter discusses in detail the four steps for creating a marketing plan.

ANALYZING THE ENVIRONMENTAL SITUATION AND THE MARKET OPPORTUNITY

Situation analysis consists of identifying and evaluating uncontrollable external influences, customers, and competition, as well as company capabilities,

EXHIBIT 4.4. The five steps to analyzing market opportunity.

1. Identify the business environmental forces.
   - Economic conditions and trends
   - Legal and regulatory situation and trends
   - Technological positioning and trends (state of the art; related R&D)
   - Relevant social changes
   - Natural environment (shortages? vulnerabilities?)
2. Describe the industry and its outlook.
   - Type of industry
   - Size—now and in 3–5 years
   - Types of market segments
   - Industry marketing practices
   - Major trends
   - Implications for opportunity
3. Analyze the key competitors.
   - Product description
   - Market posititioning (relative strengths and weaknesses, as seen by customers)
   - Market practices: channels, pricing, promotion, service
   - Estimated market share (if relevant)
   - Reactions to competition
   - Implications for opportunity
4. Create a target market profile.
   - Levels: generic needs, product type, specific brands
   - End-user focus; also channel members
   - Targeted customer profiles
     - Who are my potential customers?
     - What are they like as consumers/businesspeople?
     - How do they decide to buy/not buy?
     - Importance of different product attributes?
     - What outside influences affect buying decisions?
   - Implications for opportunity?
5. Set sales projections.
   - As many formal or intuitive approaches as possible
   - Comparison of results
   - Go/no go

to determine opportunities, threats, strengths, and weaknesses. This information is then used in preparing and implementing the marketing strategy. A significant part of the situation analysis required for developing a marketing plan is a market opportunity analysis (MOA). *Market opportunity* refers to a situation in which a combination of factors creates the potential for selling the company's product or service. In some ways, conducting an MOA is similar to putting together a jigsaw puzzle. An entrepreneur gathers pieces of information from many sources. Each piece describes some aspect of the customers, the competition, or the environmental forces influencing them. The challenge lies in putting all of the information together to form a picture of the nature and extent of market opportunity. This picture becomes the foundation for building a marketing strategy to tap the opportunity.

We need an approach for conducting an MOA that can be used to guide the analysis, particularly in situations where we start with little or no advance understanding of product markets. Exhibit 4.4 provides such an approach.

Because markets exist only for particular products and services, MOAs and marketing plans should be done on a product-by-product, market-by-market basis. This means that an MOA can begin only after the entrepreneur decides on the product for which markets are to be analyzed. Exhibit 4.5 shows typical sources of information for MOAs. Published sources are the place to start because they are easily accessible and relatively inexpensive. Interviews with experts, personal observation, and primary marketing research are used to fill in the gaps with information not found in published sources. The costs and time required for an analysis rise dramatically when primary marketing research is used, so other sources are usually exhausted before a decision is made on whether to conduct such research.

One of the first steps is to define the product-market boundaries. In some industrial markets, customers can be listed by name. More typically, customers must be classified by various characteristics to give entrepreneurs

EXHIBIT 4.5. Sources of information for MOAs.

Published sources	Personal observation
Periodicals and newspapers	Of customers
Trade association reports	Of competitors
Standardized information service reports	Of macroenvironmental influences
Government documents	
Company reports	
Interviews with experts	**Primary marketing research**
Managers of suppliers	Cross-sectional surveys
Managers of trade companies	Longitudinal panels
Managers of trade associations	Experiments
Consultants	
Salespersons	

insight into who makes up product markets. An MOA must sort from the population those people who are most likely to buy and use the products and services. Then the analysis can look for specific groups or market segments. Many characteristics of people have been used to define the makeup of markets. Among the more frequently used are geographic area, demographic characteristics, life-styles, importance of product benefits, rate of product use, and product preferences.

Analyzing the Customer Profile

Whatever the characteristics, such as demographics, used to define markets, these characteristics provide only a glimpse into the real people. The next task is to build a customer focus to help entrepreneurs understand customers well enough to anticipate their market requirements. *Customer profiles* are intended to describe what these customers are like as people, how they decide what product/brand to buy, and what outside influences affect their buying decisions.

Customer profiling concentrates on learning why demand exists by describing the underlying needs and wants. Here, profile information helps the entrepreneur understand which customers are likely to buy a product. Activities, interests, opinions, decision processes, and demand factors affecting customer preferences for one product type over others are described. The challenge for entrepreneurs is to create a marketing program that effectively appeals to targeted customers in these product markets. The marketing strategy must demonstrate to customers how the company's marketing, including the products and services, meets their requirements.

Discovering What Customers Are Like

Many factors are used for this purpose, including activities, interests, attitudes, experiences with the product, personal tastes, values, and personality. Which ones are best depends on the product and market being analyzed. Learning more about the makeup of customers helps business owners visualize how a product fits into life-styles (or work styles) and how customers might react to marketing strategies. Already knowing the customer benefits of the company's products, entrepreneurs can search profiles for clues to the customer requirements that the products can best meet.

Discovering How Customers Decide What to Buy

Learning how customers make choices among products reveals customer requirements. The decision processes that customers go through help them determine how product benefits match their requirements for purchase. Only a careful search through entire customer profiles will reveal all the market requirements that customers have.

Discovering What Outside Influences Affect Buying Decisions

Demand factors are influences on customer buying decisions that come from outside the market and the industry serving the market and are largely uncontrolled by customers or competitors. Important categories of demand factors that show up in many MOAs are economic, legal, technological, natural, and social influences coming from the macroenvironment. For example, government moves to protect national forests have encouraged customers to consider alternative building materials. Rivenite Company products are lumber, extruded from dirty waste plastic that is heated and mixed with sawdust. One major customer, the Florida Department of Transportation, estimates it can replace a hardwood post, which costs $65 and lasts 5 years, with Rivenite, which costs only $1.50 more and will last 44 years.[7]

Attracting Customers to Innovative Products or Services

Entrepreneurs who offer innovative new products and services encounter special challenges in the marketplace. There is evidence that the customer profile of those who first buy innovative products may be different from those who buy the product after it is generally accepted. And the rate of acceptance by customers depends on a number of factors, some of which the entrepreneur can control. The product or service must be adopted (purchased) and diffused throughout the markets and, usually, the faster this happens, the better. *Adoption* is the decision of an individual to use the product. *Diffusion* is the collective spread of individual adoption decisions throughout a population or market. Both pertain to *innovative* new products and services, the result of entrepreneurial efforts. There is usually a limited window of opportunity for new products. Venture capitalists often indicate that their projected sales for a product are more accurate than their timing. It often takes longer than expected to attain projected sales levels. This rate of acceptance often differentiates a tremendously successful product from a disaster. So how can the *rate* of acceptance be increased?

First, consumers usually go through a process of deciding to buy a product. The usual steps in the adoption process, the buying decision process for new products, are

Awareness ⟶ Interest ⟶ Evaluation ⟶ Trial ⟶ Adoption

EXHIBIT 4.6. Types of adopters by adoption time required.

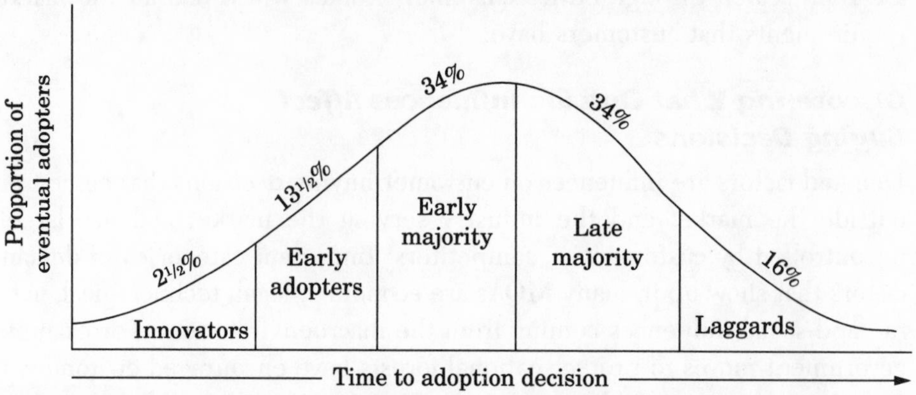

Source: Reprinted with permission of The Free Press, a division of Macmillan, Inc., from *Diffusion of Innovations* (3rd ed.), by Everett M. Rogers. Copyright © 1971 by The Free Press.

Marketing in the introduction and early growth stages must be oriented toward facilitating the rapid movement of as many customers as possible through this process. The timing of various marketing tactics (informative advertising, coupons, or incentives to try a product, and so forth) becomes critical.

Second, some customers adopt products more quickly than others, which has strategy implications. Individual customers may be labeled according to how quickly they adopt a product, ranging from *innovators* to *laggards*, as shown in Exhibit 4.6. If possible, marketing should be initially directed to the innovators and early adopters, both to develop an early cash flow and to encourage a faster rate of diffusion into the majority of the market. Unfortunately, research has found little consistency of innovator and early adopter demographic or psychographic characteristics across different types of products. Marketers should, however, seek to find common characteristics for early purchasers in their particular product category and, if possible, target their marketing strategy accordingly. Some evidence exists for the general innovator profile (depicted in Exhibit 4.7), but again, those results should be viewed cautiously with respect to specific products.[8]

For example, consider the glow-in-the-dark Nitelite golf balls. Because there are 25 million golfers, Corky Newcomb, cofounder of Pick Point Sports thought, "Some should be selling for me." But in 1989, retailers would not stock his innovative ball. So Newcomb designed a campaign aimed at amateur golfers, by offering a $100 reward to amateur golfers who could persuade their clubs to sponsor a Nitelite tournament. By 1992, sales of the Nitelite golf ball were $10 million. He succeeded in enlisting innovator consumers not only to buy but to help him with his marketing campaign.[9]

EXHIBIT 4.7. Comparative profiles of the consumer innovator and the later adopter.

Characteristic	Innovator	Noninnovator (or later adopter)
Product interest	More	Less
Opinion leadership	More	Less
Personality		
Dogmatism	Open-minded	Closed-minded
Social character	Inner-directed	Other-directed
Category width	Broad categorizer	Narrow categorizer
Venturesome	More	Less
Perceived risk	Less	More
Purchase and consumption traits		
Brand loyalty	Less	More
Deal proneness	More	Less
Usage	More	Less
Media habits		
Total magazine exposure	More	Less
Special-interest magazines	More	Less
Television	Less	More
Social characteristics		
Social integration	More	Less
Social striving (e.g., social, physical, and occupational mobility)	More	Less
Group memberships	More	Less
Demographic characteristics		
Age	Younger	Older
Income	More	Less
Education	More	Less
Occupational status	More	Less

Third, many diffusion studies have demonstrated that a product's characteristics as *perceived* by potential buyers are extremely important. Marketing activity can be partially directed toward helping to minimize misperceptions and enhancing product strengths. Important perceived product characteristics include the following:

- *Relative advantage* is the extent to which potential customers perceive a new product as superior to existing substitutes.
- *Compatibility* is the extent to which potential customers consider a new product to be consistent with their values, needs, and behavior.
- *Complexity* is the degree to which an innovation is difficult to understand or use.

- *Testability* is the extent to which a new product or venture is capable of being tried on a limited basis by customers.
- *Observability* or communicability, is the ease with which a product's benefits can be seen by, imagined by, or described to potential consumers.

Exhibit 4.8 suggests marketing actions related to each of these perceived product characteristics. Although each of these product characteristics borders on being intuitively obvious, paying systematic and creative attention to them can be critical to the design of effective marketing strategies for new products. Apple Computer's Macintosh personal computer was a good example of a product designed with the above characteristics in mind. Compared to IBM's PC, at the time, the relative price/quality advantage of the Macintosh was assumed to be favorable, and its compatibility and lack of complexity were major advantages.

EXHIBIT 4.8. Marketing implications of important product venture characteristics.

Characteristic	Marketing action
Relative advantage	Clearly and credibly communicate the product's advantage. Obtain third-party/professional/objective endorsements. Price the product to compare favorably with others. Construct the product to "deliver" benefits quickly.
Compatibility	Develop an understanding of customer life-styles, behavior, etc., to minimize the required adaption. Make the product fit in with related products. Make the product/brand fit customer's social situation.
Complexity	Make the product readily understandable. Strive to make the product user friendly. Make the product at a complexity level not exceeding that of substitutes.
Testability	Offer money-back guarantee (reduce the cost/risk of trial). Make small quantities free or at low price. Provide incentives to encourage trial. Offer special incentives for durable items (test drives for autos, etc.).
Observability	Encourage visible use by customers. Make it easy for others to perceive the product/brand. Create incentives for customers to encourage friends to consider trial.

Source: Leon G. Schiffman and Leslie Lazer Kanuk, *Consumer Behavior,* 4th ed. (Englewood Cliffs, NJ: Prentice Hall, 1991).

Analyzing the Industry and the Competition

Opportunity in product markets is influenced as much by competition as by customer characteristics and demand factors. Gaining an advantage over the competition is crucial to a successful marketing plan. So that entrepreneurs can determine what the advantage over the competition should be, an MOA profiles and evaluates the capabilities and actions of competitors serving the same product markets.

When competition comes from only a very few firms, analyzing each of these firms is possible. Typically, however, there are many competitors in the industry, so that analyzing each of them is unnecessarily time-consuming and expensive. So, first, the industry is analyzed. Then key competitors are singled out for in-depth evaluation.

Industry Analysis

Competitors serving the same market can be grouped together into an industry so that conclusions can be drawn about the similarities and differences in the way in which a market is served. Because business owners are concerned with the most direct competition, an industry can be restricted to those firms that sell the same product or service, operate at the same level in a channel of distribution, and sell in the same geographic area. For example, a wholesale wine distributor serving Chicago considers its industry to be all of the wine distributors serving the same area. In contrast, a national wine producer, such as Gallo, views its industry as all the wine producers selling to the nation's markets.

An industry analysis begins with accumulating an information base, or profile. First, the size, growth, and structure of the industry are described. Next, information is obtained on the marketing practices of the industry, including target market coverage, key marketing objectives, and marketing mix strategies and tactics. Entrepreneurs use industry information to draw conclusions about probable changes in industry size, structure, and marketing practices. They also evaluate industry practices to look for weaknesses or problem areas that can be exploited. For example, Unity Forest Products proclaims that it "is thriving in an industry threatened by a severe shortage of raw material—timber—and depressed by a downturn in housing starts. Yet . . . the company has never had an unprofitable month." One observer says that Enita Nordeck, the principal owner, "runs the company with tactics that are nothing less than revolutionary in the hidebound, unhurried lumber business. . . . What she has is a theory of inventory management and sales and marketing that hasn't found its way into this industry yet."[10]

Key Competitor Analysis

Key competitors are those companies in, or predicted to enter, an industry that are expected to have the most effect on a venture's success. Key competitor analyses begin with the construction of a profile describing the size, growth, objectives, management, technical capabilities, and marketing practices of each key competitor. As noted in Exhibit 4.4, attention should also be given to the market positioning and practices of key competitors, their estimated market share, and their likely responses to our competitive moves. This information is used to predict future changes in the competitor's marketing actions and to evaluate how well the competitor is meeting customer requirements. Through published sources, interviews with those familiar with each competitor, and observation, a picture can be pieced together of the marketing strategies, tactics, and management styles of each key competitor. The crucial factors that influence the marketing strategies and tactics of key competitors are shown in Exhibit 4.9. The purpose of key competitor analyses is to describe these factors and to evaluate their effects on the marketing decisions of key competitors.

As a first step in conducting such an analysis, entrepreneurs should construct a financial picture of each key competitor. There are independent published sources of financial information, such as Dun & Bradstreet, Standard & Poor's, and Moody's. More creative means may sometimes have to be employed to estimate financial strength—counting the number of advertisements run in a certain time period or keeping track of the number of sales personnel in overlapping sales territories. The resulting financial profile can be invaluable as an indicator of a key competitor's ability to sustain a marketing strategy in target markets.

EXHIBIT 4.9. Factors influencing the marketing strategy of key competitors.

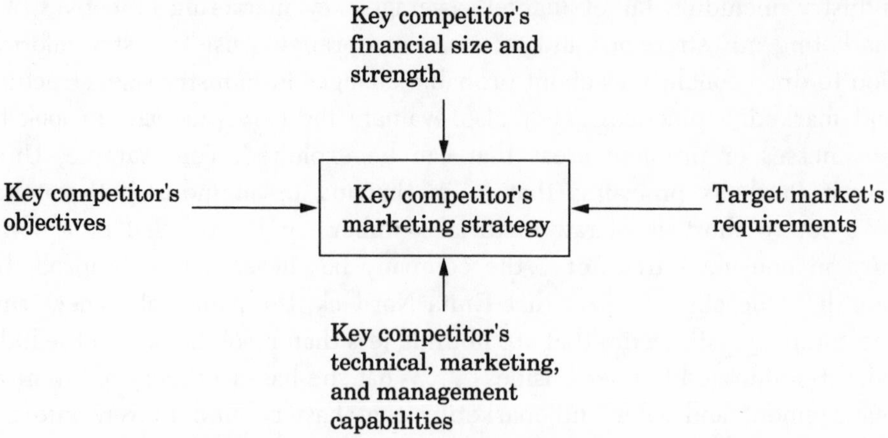

Source: Dr. Robert B. Woodruff, The University of Tennessee.

Second, entrepreneurs should pay close attention to key competitors' objectives and capabilities. Competitor characteristics that are ideally profiled are the following:

- Mission and business objectives
- Market position and sales trends
- Management capabilities and limitations
- Target market strategies
- Marketing objectives
- Marketing strategies and tactics

The result is a picture of the way in which a key competitor strives to reach markets and positions itself against competition. The information gathered allows an entrepreneur to evaluate a key competitor's strengths and weaknesses. The entrepreneur considers both the competitor's coverage of market segments and its success in meeting customer requirements. The evaluation of key competitors' respective abilities to meet or exceed customer requirements is concerned with the quality of each key competitor's marketing program. Customer profiles are examined to identify customers' important requirements and then the strategy and tactics used by each key competitor are scrutinized to see how they meet each customer requirement. Judgments can then be formed about how well or poorly each of these requirements is satisfied. This analysis helps entrepreneurs uncover the strengths and weaknesses of each key competitor's technical and marketing strategy and tactics.

Finally, entrepreneurs should predict changes in key competitors' marketing strategies and tactics. But entrepreneurs should not place too much reliance on trend analysis. Other methods include the following:

- Analyzing key competitors' probable responses, given their management styles, to anticipated changes in market conditions
- Interviewing key competitors' suppliers, distributors, and customers
- Hiring away key competitors' executives

One expert comments on the efforts of some companies to familiarize themselves with the key competitors:

> What appears to be vital to effective intelligence activities is that the emphasis be focused on anticipating expected behavior by key competitors.... Several firms have successfully institutionalized this emphasis on anticipating behavior or responses by key players by assigning to line managers the role of a "shadow" competitor.... In strategy meetings, it is expected of these "shadow" executives that they be able to present their best judgment as to how their particular "shadow" will respond to strategic moves being considered.[11]

Clearly, to be successful, a new venture's marketing strategy must meet customers' requirements and also effectively position itself against competition. In fact, the essence of planning marketing strategy is to effectively position a company against the competition in the minds of customers. *Positioning* refers to the use of marketing strategy to match the strengths of competition and to exploit its weaknesses, thereby giving customers a reason to buy from your company rather than another. Entrepreneurs can achieve positioning through target market selection by exploiting competitive weaknesses in market coverage. From the industry and key competitor analyses the entrepreneur looks for "holes" in the competitive coverage across the market. A hole is evident when there is more demand in the market, or in a specific market segment, than is being met by competition.

But selecting target markets is only a start toward effective positioning. The marketing strategy must also be creatively employed to build a differential advantage over competition in the minds of customers. Being different from the competition is not enough. The difference must represent an advantage to customers by meeting at least some important customer requirements better than other sellers.

Careful analyses of both customer requirements and competitor strengths and weaknesses in meeting those requirements are the cornerstone for differential advantage strategies. The payoff from an MOA comes when the entrepreneur:

- Reviews the information and target market options
- Determines important customer requirements
- Reviews competitive strengths and weaknesses for building a differential advantage
- Forecasts the sales expected from marketing strategy

Customer groups or segments in which buyers have similar customer requirements are identified and separated from segments in which buyers have different requirements. Each segment becomes a target market option. The sales generated by a marketing strategy depend to a great extent on how well buyers' expectations are met. Matching company strengths (and not exposing weaknesses) to the market requires understanding exactly what customers want—their requirements. Customer profile information must be examined to develop a list of requirements reflecting the benefits and services that customers want. The entrepreneur should consider the relative importance of each of these requirements. For example, President Michael Harris of Deck House, Inc., said, "We felt that forcing standardized homes on customers was infringing on their freedom.[12] But in reality the variety of choices was overwhelming. This was a conclusion based on customer survey responses. As a result, Deck House designed a new line of standardized homes that met most customers' requirements without needing a lot of customization. We are seeing an uptick in business even though the housing market is still flat." For those target markets in which the entrepreneur believes that a strong position can be developed or maintained, the company must position itself against the strengths and weaknesses of the competition. Ultimately, success in markets comes from finding a unique advantage over key competitors.

The final step in evaluating market opportunity is forecasting the sales return for the planned marketing strategy. Aggregate and market forecasts provide a starting point for the evaluation of sales opportunity in the target markets. Having selected markets as candidate targets, the entrepreneur plans a marketing program to tap sales from these markets. The plan will show the extent to which a company's strengths can be brought to bear on meeting customer requirements and providing an advantage over the competition. Only then can a sales forecast be made to estimate the sales return from the marketing program. The sales forecast is used, in turn, to estimate profits, return on investment, cash flow, and other financial indicators of the worth of alternative target markets.

Target markets are finally selected based on all of these indicators as well as other considerations, such as consistency with the firm's mission, legal constraints, and available resources. Several sales-forecasting methods may be considered for use, and although beyond the scope of this chapter, it is noteworthy that without historical sales data in a new venture, many of the traditional methods are not helpful to the entrepreneur.[13] The market opportunity analysis is essential to the situation analysis as the first step toward developing a marketing plan. With this understanding in hand, the entrepreneur can move on to the second step—setting the marketing objectives for a particular product market.

SETTING MARKETING OBJECTIVES

The next step in developing a marketing plan is to set marketing objectives. Objectives should be stated for each target market in terms of sales, profit contribution, and other qualitative aims, such as building an image. Objectives are sometimes divided into two groups: market performance objectives and marketing support objectives. *Market performance objectives* pertain to specific outcomes such as sales and profits. *Marketing support objectives* pertain to tasks that precede final performance outcomes such as building customer awareness and engaging in educational efforts.

Objectives help shape the marketing strategy for each target market. For example, an entrepreneur seeking to increase sales in a target market by 6% for the coming year would probably make only limited changes in the existing marketing program. Alternatively, starting a new business requires developing an entirely new marketing strategy.

Objectives must, at least to some degree, be measurable; otherwise, identifying progress toward their achievement is impossible. But in marketing, this is no easy task. A support objective could include creating an image in the minds of potential customers—and progress toward that objective could be measured by surveying (even informally) customer perceptions. Objectives should be worded very carefully, with the intention of developing measurable and attainable standards. For example, the following marketing performance and support objectives were used in an early-stage personal computer education business:

- To increase (over last year) the number of student/class hours (unit = one student for one class hour) by 36%
- To increase class size to an average of 28 (despite a 6% price increase) and thereby to increase profits by 20%
- To increase awareness of our services to at least 50% of our targeted customers
- To develop, over the next year, three new class offerings, with high-quality instructors, to serve the personal computer user
- To develop a targeted, systematic, and coordinated advertising program

The first two objectives are oriented toward market performance, whereas the last three are market support objectives.

FORMULATING A MARKETING STRATEGY

Marketing strategy is the set of guidelines and policies used for effectively matching marketing programs (products, distribution, prices, and promotion) with target market opportunities in order to achieve the venture's objectives. This is the third step in developing a marketing plan. The development of an overall marketing strategy helps ensure that mutually beneficial exchanges occur, which is part of the definition of marketing. It is oriented toward the long run, composed of fundamental decisions (not day-to-day adjustments), and developed with an eye to competition as well as markets. Developing a marketing strategy includes deciding which customers to target and how to position products and the business relative to competitors in the minds of existing and potential customers.

Developing marketing programs involves identifying alternative combinations of marketing variables (for example, Wendy's higher-quality, higher-priced hamburgers) and then judging how well these combinations match the market opportunity. The key to such matching is forecasting potential customer response to the mix of marketing variables. Then, a program with great potential is implemented!

For example, in starting a new venture targeted to wealthy customers, the guidelines and policies that constitute a strategy could be oriented toward creating the highest-quality image possible. They might include the following:

- A high, narrow pricing range to convey an image of price exclusiveness
- Products that offer exceptionally high quality and service standards and excellent warranty coverage
- Advertising media and messages that impart an exclusive, high-quality image

These guidelines and policies (marketing strategy) narrow the range of marketing actions that are appropriate given the overall marketing objectives (quality image). Basically, a marketing strategy guides how marketing objectives will be achieved. Marketing objectives, part of marketing strategy, were discussed in a previous section of this chapter. Objectives, target market selection, and determination of the marketing program together form the marketing strategy. A target market may consist of all end-users or one or more subgroups in a product market. Making decisions about target markets is one of management's most important tasks. For example, Wendy's decision to go after a subgroup of the population—young adults—with a particular food service was a *target market decision.*

A firm's marketing must consist of an integrated strategy aimed at providing customer satisfaction. To develop a strategy, a firm uses demand-influencing variables that make up the "marketing mix." The marketing mix, like a puzzle, has numerous pieces that must be appropriately combined for a successful result (see Exhibit 4.10). It includes the following:

- The products (or services) offered by the firm
- The distribution channels the firm uses (wholesalers, distributors, retailers) to make the product available to customers
- The prices the firm charges
- The promotion (advertising, personal selling, sales promotion, and publicity)

Other terms used to describe the components of the marketing mix are the marketing program, the marketing offer, and the Four Ps (product, place, price, and promotion). Each of these four elements in the marketing mix is discussed in detail in the subsections that make up the rest of this chapter.

EXHIBIT 4.10. Marketing mix variables.

Product	Distribution	Price	Promotion
Features Quality Packaging Branding Services Guarantees Assortment	Types of channels/ middlemen Store/distributor location Storage Transportation and logistics Service levels	List price Credit terms Discounts Selection and allowances Flexibility	Promotion blend Advertising Media Copy Timing Personal selling Training Motivation Allocation Sales promotion Publicity

These variables must be consistent with one another, and ideally they complement one another for a synergistic result. Building a high-quality, prestigious product and combining it with inconsistent mix ingredients such as heavy price discounting would yield a poorly integrated, internally inconsistent marketing program. The mix ingredients would conflict with one another in the minds of customers.

The creative role that entrepreneurial management must play in moving from knowledge of the market to the formulation of marketing programs is both a major challenge and an opportunity. For instance, Mallards clothing specialty store for men in Chicago provides an excellent example of the development and implementation of a unique marketing mix for a firm's target market. Started in the 1980s, Mallards offers updated versions of classic Ivy League and sportswear-oriented clothing for men, which, because of its traditional styling, avoids quick outdating. The target market is ambitious and active, career-oriented individuals, 25- to 45-year-old college graduates, mostly professionals, with above-average incomes. Yet Mallards customers still value a good buy. The clothing is mostly private label, obtained directly from high-quality producers. This departure from traditional industry practices enables the firm to offer reasonable prices for the quality it provides. The store location projects a quality image and is convenient for the targeted customers. The company engages in limited advertising, relying primarily on location, window displays, and a quality reputation to attract customers. All Mallards employees also project a quality image. They are fully trained in selling techniques, fitting, garment care, fabrics, and styles, allowing them to deal with discriminating buyers. Mallards offers an appealing blend of marketing mix elements.

Building a marketing program for a target market consists of the following:

- Determining how large the marketing budget should be
- Allocating the budget to the marketing mix variables of the firm
- Determining the best use of the resources for each marketing mix variable

Given the myriad of possible marketing programs that could be developed and the difficulty of estimating the likely revenue and cost results of each alternative program, these are complex decisions. Management must determine the emphases and combination of marketing variables that will yield the most favorable profit contribution, after subtracting marketing costs. Estimating the responsiveness of target markets to alternative marketing mixes is perhaps the key uncertainty in all of marketing management.

Finally, the terms *strategy* and *tactics* are often used in marketing discussions. *Strategy* (or strategic) *decisions* provide a broad, long-term framework (a year or usually more) for marketing action. They are fundamental decisions that guide the day-to-day actions. *Tactical decisions* determine how marketing strategies are to be carried out on a day-to-day basis. For Mallards, strategy includes placing an emphasis on quality, private brands, and reasonable prices. The strategy of a company is implemented by day-to-day tactical decisions, such as setting the exact prices, deciding whether or not to include prices in advertising copy, and deciding how frequently to offer sale prices.

Product Decisions

Each of the marketing mix elements should be discussed as part of the marketing plan. First, the *product* is anything that is potentially valued by a target market for the benefits or satisfactions it provides, including objects, services, organizations, places, people, and ideas. Making product decisions requires grouping the various meanings of the term *product* into three levels (see Exhibit 4.11). Level 1 comprises the basic *benefits* or *satisfactions* that a particular product delivers. The same product may provide different benefits to different people. For example, to one person a Cadillac is a means of enhancing status; to another it is a source of comfortable, quiet, and reliable transportation.

Marketers must also understand the linkages between objective, tangible *product attributes* (level 2 in Exhibit 4.11) and subjective satisfactions. The Cadillac brand name, quality, and styling enhance the satisfactions that customers feel. Tangible attributes, however, sometimes receive a disproportionate amount of attention in product decision making.

Finally, the *extended product* (level 3 in Exhibit 4.11) comprises marketing elements that go beyond the specific product itself but are valued by

EXHIBIT 4.11. Customer perception hierarchy.

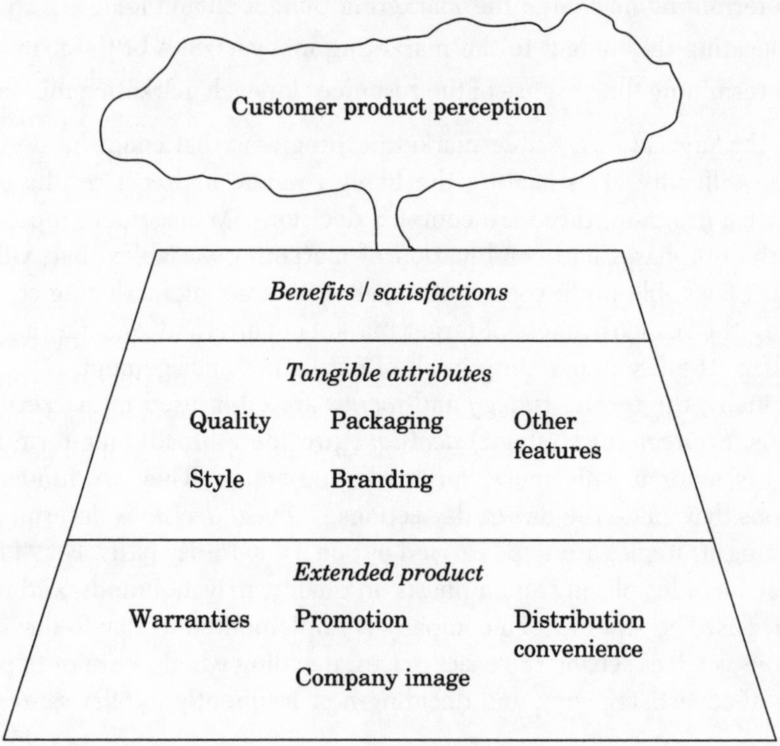

customers. The extended product is the broader set of marketing elements within which the product exists. For a Cadillac, it includes such things as warranty service, status-oriented promotion, and delivery arrangements.

These three levels—the extended product, product attributes, and benefits/satisfactions—together create the customer's overall *perception* of a product. The entrepreneur's task is to blend the three levels in a consistent, synergistic manner to meet the needs and wants of well-defined target markets. The levels imply that product perceptions in the marketplace are hierarchical; such perceptions are affected most by the customer benefits derived from products, second by the specific attributes of products, and last by the other marketing elements associated with products. Business owners can adopt this customer-oriented perspective in attempting to create product images for target markets. This is also true for the huge service sector of the U.S. economy. Services are intangible; they blend production and consumption; and they often involve unorthodox distribution channels. Yet the delivery of services involves attributes (e.g., pleasant, smiling personnel) that contribute to the perception shown in Exhibit 4.11.

New Product Development Process

New products and services provide new life for otherwise aging organizations and propel entrepreneurs to the top of new industries. Few decisions in a business are as fundamental, pervasive, and long lasting as those concerning products. *New* products are those whose degree of change *for customers* is sufficient to require the design or redesign of marketing strategies. A business is usually created with one product or service or, if a retailer or distributor, with one location and one target market. But products eventually die, and without product/service improvements and new products the business will eventually die.

Booz-Allen & Hamilton's research of 700 U.S. companies involved with 13,000 products concluded that most companies use a formal new-product-planning process as shown in Exhibit 4.12. It must be emphasized, however, that they studied few new or smaller businesses and that not all companies

EXHIBIT 4.12. New product development process.

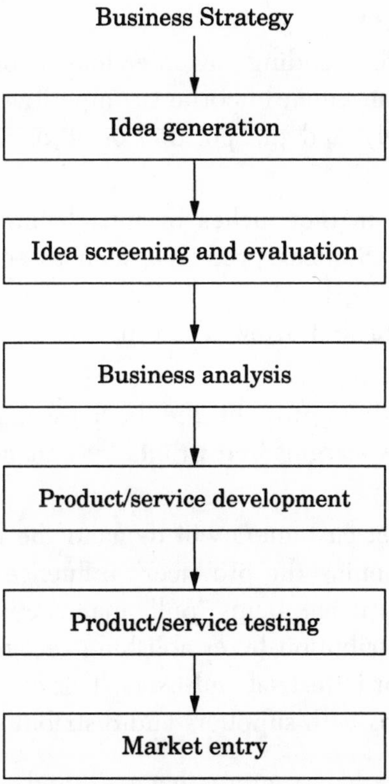

Source: Adapted from Booz-Allen & Hamilton, *New Product Management for the 1980s* (New York: Booz-Allen & Hamilton, 1982), 11.

use a systematic new-product-planning process. Indeed, Feldman and Page concluded that it is a myth that companies use a new-product-planning process that is orderly, logical, and sequential.[14] Yet they also stated that use of a strategic new-product-planning process is important to success. Entrepreneurs can benefit from knowing what the steps are in a formal new product development process.

Whether the entrepreneur wants to familiarize the public with the name of an entire entrepreneurial business, a group of products, or a single product, he should consider building a "brand" image. There are several important reasons:

- To create a market identity. A brand helps position a business's product offering in terms of price level, quality, service, prestige, and other factors that are important to buyers in the firm's target markets. Consumers often use brand image as a proxy for quality and dependability, particularly if they find it difficult to evaluate a product because of its newness or complexity.
- To legally protect a name or symbol for which major promotional expenditures may be made.
- To create a basis for building customer loyalty for a successful business or brand, which can be an important competitive strategy. Repeat sales become more likely, and the position of other company products may also be enhanced.
- To serve different market niches by introducing different brands as a business expands. Similiar products, such as soft drinks, with different brand names (Pepsi, Mountain Dew, Orange Crush, Mr. Pibb) can help provide a sufficient array of alternatives to increase sales in many markets.
- To create a brand identity of the business and/or products, which may itself increase margins and profits by enhancing the perception of quality.
- To help ensure that customers will demand the product from distributors, thus strengthening the producer's influence in the channel of distribution. A strong image helps "pull" manufacturers' products through the channel of distribution by establishing recognition and preferences among consumer or industrial end-users. This can also establish powerful bargaining positions with suppliers and distributors.

The entrepreneur should be aware that a "brand" image, at least of the business, is being created in the minds of customers in any event. Careful attention to the creation of a strong image can be critical to success.

Distribution Decisions

Another important part of the marketing plan involves distribution decisions. The marketing system is made up of a vast configuration of organizations and individuals, linked together by flows of information, products, negotiations, risks, money, and people. A *channel of distribution* is "an organized network [system] of agencies and institutions which, in combination, perform all the activities required to link producers with users and users with producers... to accomplish the marketing task."[15] Each organization in the distribution channel performs particular activities in connecting end-users with desired goods and services.

For example, consider the firms, functions, flows, and relationships involved in transforming a steer on an entrepreneur's Texas ranch into a roast on the dinner table of a family in Washington, D.C. The animal is sold by the rancher to a feedlot operator for fattening and then purchased by a meat packer for processing. The hindquarter of the carcass, or bulk packaged portions, are sold to a large retail food chain, transported from a regional warehouse of the food chain to a supermarket in Washington, D.C., and processed by the supermarket butcher into steaks, roasts, and ground beef that are finally placed in the meat display case.

Marketing intermediaries are organizations that perform the various channel-of-distribution functions necessary to connect producers with end-users. Intermediaries drastically reduce the number of buyer-seller transactions. Suppose 10 customers each wanted to buy a Gant Oxford button-down shirt, a pair of Calvin Klein jeans, an Aigner belt, and Bass loafers. Each person dealing directly with each manufacturer would have to conduct 4 transactions, for a total of 40. Now place a retailer between the 4 manufacturers and the 10 consumers, and the number of transactions is reduced from 40 to 14. By taking advantage of the economies obtainable through specialization and by greatly reducing the number of transactions needed to bring end-users and producers together, middlemen perform functions that are often not possible for manufacturers or end-users.

Companies in the distribution channel perform various functions—procurement, storage, packaging, financing, transportation, and counseling. A substantial portion of the price paid by consumers for products and services is frequently accounted for by activities performed by these companies. For example, 69¢ of each dollar spent for food is used to pay for distribution and processing activities.[16] The entrepreneur who assumes, without study, that direct distribution will lower costs usually misunderstands the efficiencies offered by distribution systems.

Over time, inefficient intermediaries are eliminated from the marketing system. The competitive marketplace generates new distribution alternatives when entrepreneurs see better ways to provide cost-effective services to buyers and when buyers are willing to consider different levels of customer service. For example, one of the most rapidly expanding distribution concepts today is nonstore marketing, including mail, telephone, vending machines, and door-to-door selling.

Middlemen may be classified by their level in the channel of distribution. Exhibit 4.13 illustrates alternative vertical channels. Closest to consumers and organizational end-users are retailers. Manufacturers may employ salespersons for contacting wholesalers and distributors and sometimes own their own sales offices and branches. If sales personnel cannot be economically justified by a new venture's sales volume, manufacturers may use agents or brokers on a commission basis.

There are sometimes important relationships between marketers at a given level of distribution. Marketers may join together for mutual advantage in voluntary groups and retailer cooperatives. For example, pooled buying groups include independent, entrepreneur grocers who work cooperatively to lower the costs of goods purchased from wholesalers.

Actually deciding which method of distribution to use may be obvious, or it may be a very complex decision process. Michael Dell, in starting Dell Computer, decided to advertise directly to customers and eliminate intermediaries. Dell is now leading a rapidly growing *Fortune* 500 company. His distribution strategy has been a huge success!

As business owners consider different distribution alternatives, and selection of intermediaries, they should consider the decision criteria shown in Exhibit 4.14.

Pricing Decisions

Pricing is often used by entrepreneurs to enhance the image of a product or business, to increase sales through discount pricing, or, in combination with promotion, to build future sales. At times, however, price is an inactive element of the marketing mix, with business owners using traditional markups over cost or following industry leaders. The use of price as a competitive tool, particularly by new, smaller companies, is often avoided because of fear of retaliation and price wars. But whether pricing is an active or inactive element, it is an integral part of the overall marketing program.

Price is used in different ways by different companies, depending on the role it plays in the overall marketing program. For example, Service Merchandise, a catalog showroom discounter (and entrepreneurial success story), uses low prices on name brands as its major basis for appealing to customers. In return for low prices, customers are willing to complete an order form and wait until their purchase is obtained from the warehouse. Through

EXHIBIT 4.13. Alternative marketing channels.

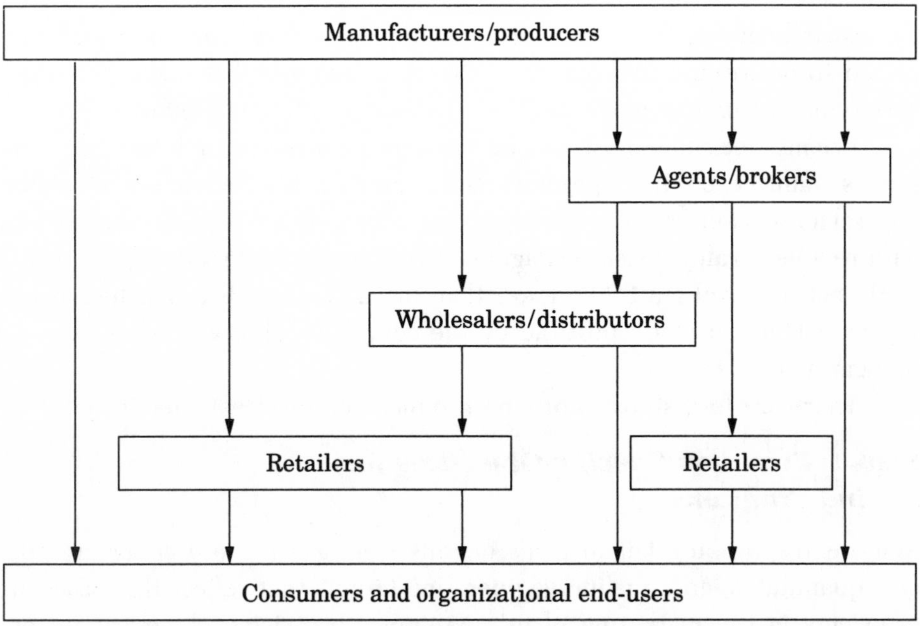

EXHIBIT 4.14. Channel design decisions and decision criteria.

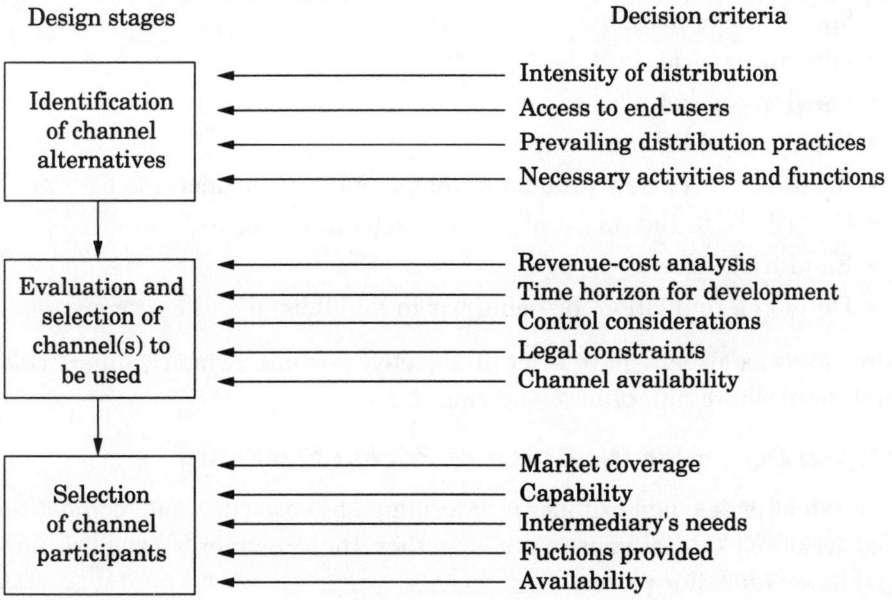

Source: Dr. David W. Cravens, Texas Christian University.

operating efficiencies, reduction in customer service, and high volume, catalog showrooms are able to compete with other retailers by using low prices. Exclusive, high-end furniture stores assign price a very different role. High-priced furniture and fixtures allow attractive margins that make possible a variety of customer services and help support promotional efforts.

Pricing decisions must also be made in light of channel/distributor interests. Palm Beach, Inc.'s pricing strategy for its Evan-Picone line of tailored apparel for women was developed, in part, as a way to strengthen relationships with retailers. Palm Beach management promised retailers designer-quality clothes at prices at least 30% lower than those of other distinguished labels, a price reduction made possible by the company's ability to mass-produce fine garments.

There are four steps to pricing products (or services) effectively.

Step 1: Establish Specific Objectives for Pricing Programs

Many entrepreneurs fail to focus on this step. *Pricing objectives* are specific quantitative and qualitative operating targets that reflect the basic role of pricing in the marketing plan.[17] Examples of pricing objectives for entrepreneurs might include:

- Increase sales or profit growth
- Maximize short- and long-run profits
- Discourage entrants
- Speed exit of marginal competitors
- Discourage price cutting
- Stabilize market prices
- Rapidly establish market position
- Rapidly recover new product development costs or increase cash flow
- Contribute to the image of the product and the firm
- Build traffic
- Develop a reputation for being fair to middlemen and customers

Organizations usually have a set of objectives—some primary, others collateral; some short run, others long run.

Step 2: Determine the Extent of Pricing Flexibility

The extent of pricing flexibility is determined by costs, demand, competition, and legal and ethical constraints. Together, these elements establish upper and lower limits for prices.

The writer once consulted for a business owner who, after study, was found to be pricing under cost—hardly a long-term strategy. We joked that he could set prices below cost and make it up on volume! Costs often vary at different volume levels and may not allocate fixed costs appropriately. Hands-on involvement with the financial whiz of the new venture is essential for determining the *floor* for setting prices.

Demand and competition set the *ceiling* for prices, and the expression "what the market will bear" goes to the heart of evaluating demand. The range between the cost floor and the demand and competition ceiling defines the flexibility in pricing available to the entrepreneur. A critical demand consideration is price elasticity; that is, the percentage change in sales (based on the number of units) divided by the percentage change in price. If an entrepreneur reduces a price from $20 to $15 (a 25% cut) and sales volume jumps from 100,000 to 200,000 units (100%), the elasticity is greater than 1, and we say that the demand is price elastic. Conversely, a Chicago entrepreneur who manufactures furniture says, "If it sells well, raise the price!" If he raises the price of a certain model of sofa 25% and demand drops by 20%, the elasticity is less than 1 and we say that the demand is price *in*elastic. The more that customers know of competitive products, the less flexibility the business owner possesses with pricing strategy. Determining the likely behavior of customers in either buying less or more, or in buying competitor's products is essential to determining the price ceiling.

Step 3: Develop Price Strategies

Price strategies are the guidelines and policies used to effectively guide pricing decisions to match target market conditions. Price strategies determine, among other things, the following factors:

- The day-to-day variability of prices
- Overall price levels
- The use of price lining
- Price stability
- Pricing relative to stages of the product life cycle
- The use of psychological pricing

For example, in a new venture, it could be decided to minimize day-to-day changes in prices, to set prices slightly above the competition, not to set prices at different levels within a product line, and to use a psychological pricing premium (such as a high price for a difficult-to-evaluate product, such as a sound system) to enhance the perceived value of the product.

Step 4: Establish Prices

Setting pricing objectives, determining the extent of pricing flexibility, and selecting price strategies provide considerable direction to management for setting specific prices. But how are prices for specific products actually set? Again, a sound approach to pricing must incorporate cost, competition, and demand factors. Costs establish the floor for a possible price range. Thus, cost-plus pricing often involves simply adding a percentage of the cost to set the price. However, there are many other strategies to setting prices.

Markup pricing

This is a variation of cost-plus pricing in that markups are calculated as a percentage of the selling price rather than as a percentage of the cost. Successful new ventures are sometimes founded on innovative, low-margin pricing, in the hope that high volume selling will provide a good return. For example, in the 1930s, supermarkets shook up the food distribution business using this approach, and in the 1980s the health care industry experienced similar changes. Traditional hospitals and HMOs (health maintenance organizations) are facing increased competition from major brand name health care providers, such as Humana, Inc.

Break-even pricing

This is another cost-oriented method; it determines the level of sales needed to cover all of the relevant fixed and variable costs. If fixed costs are $100,000, unit variable costs are $2, and the price per unit is $4, then the firm must sell 50,000 units to break even [$100,000/($4 − 2)].

Target return pricing

Whereas break-even prices typically just set a pricing floor, target return pricing sets prices at a desired percentage return over and above the break-even point. The obvious weakness of this and other cost-oriented pricing methods is that prices determined according to these methods are without regard to market demand. The actual quantity sold at the determined price could easily be greater or less than the quantity required. Yet using costs helps ensure that prices exceed all costs and therefore contribute to profit.

Going-rate pricing

This method involves setting prices equal to or a certain percentage above or below competitors' prices. Whether or not this method is appropriate depends on several factors:

- The firm's pricing objectives
- The structure of the industry (for example, oligopoly)
- Whether there is excess production capacity (so the added cost of more production is low)
- The relative production, selling, and administrative costs of competitors
- Customers' perceptions of the firm's products compared with those of competitors

Entrepreneurs often use competitive pricing when retaliatory price changes are likely and when price changes by competitors can have a substantial effect on company sales. Retailers often employ competition-oriented pricing methods in conjunction with the cost markup method. Retailers hire comparison shoppers who survey competitors' prices on selected items, and individual store managers are given the authority to adjust prices.

Demand-modified break-even pricing

This strategy involves setting prices to achieve the highest profit (over the break-even point) in consideration of the amount demanded at alternative prices. Demand-modified break-even pricing requires estimates of market demand at each feasible price; break-even points and expected levels of total sales revenue can then be calculated. The primary challenge in demand-oriented pricing (particularly for new ventures) is obtaining accurate estimates of the price/quantity relationships. One approach is to conduct direct customer interviews, asking respondents within a target market a series of questions to measure their likely response at different price levels. This approach is complicated by customers who find it difficult to judge how they would actually respond.

Although it may often seem an insurmountable task, particularly for firms with new products, some new firms have been successful in gaining a better understanding of their markets' responsiveness to price changes. For example, Approach Software, a startup firm whose only product is a database software for "non-techies," tested three introductory prices for their product on five mailing lists of 50,000 prospective customers. The result provided "statistical proof—sales came in almost as high at $149 as at $129." A price of $199 "crossed a threshold of what people would spend to try a new product through the mail," according to Jaleh Bisharat, Approach's marketing director.[18]

Perceived-value pricing

This strategy is sometimes used to set the prices of industrial products. The price of an industrial (versus consumer) product is probably determined somewhat more by the exact potential benefit that the product offers the buyers. This is especially true when an industrial product faces little direct competition.

For example, one new manufacturer developed a new electronic temperature measurement instrument, and the owner was unsure about how to price it. The variable costs were about $1200. Management usually set a selling price of about four times the variable costs to cover other costs and contribute to profits, but the fixed costs were to be proportionately lower for the new product. Management estimated that a price of $3600 for the new product would cover costs and meet the profit objectives. But then several potential users were asked to rate the new product and key competitive products on product attributes. Management learned that less accurate competitive instruments were available at $3200. After assessing the product's potential benefit to users and the willingness of users to purchase the product at different price levels, management set the price at $4500. Demand factors ultimately dictated the appropriate price.

Perceived-value pricing is also applicable to consumer products, often being based on a psychological pricing strategy. For instance, branded shirts are priced in part on consumers' perception of their value. This pricing method underscores the behavioral foundation underlying pricing. The willingness of customers to pay a higher price depends on their perception of the fairness of the price and the quality they get for the price they pay. Perceptions sometimes stray from reality, and conducting market research on perceptions as they affect demand can be very useful.

Skimming and penetration pricing strategies

Approaches to new product pricing are also particularly relevant to entrepreneurs entering new markets. Pricing objectives for new products have more latitude than those for existing products and pricing flexibility is also greater for new products. For products in the growth, maturity, or decline stages of the product life cycle, there is usually growing competition and a smaller number of acceptable prices. The prices of such products often have to be reduced. New products with little competition usually offer the option of a skimming or penetration strategy.

A *skimming pricing strategy* sets introductory prices at a high level relative to costs so as to "skim the cream" off the market. With price-insensitive customers (in the absence of immediate competition), firms often consider it safe to set initial new product prices high relative to costs and to lower the prices gradually as market conditions dictate. Skimming profits allows sellers to recover their investment rapidly, though the high margins tend to attract competition. For example, makers of personal computers charged high prices in the early years, but there has been competitive price warfare in recent years.

In contrast to the skimming strategy, a *penetration pricing strategy* sets new product prices low relative to costs. This strategy is usually employed to rapidly acquire a large share of a potential market. Relatively low margins discourage the entry of competitors. The appropriateness of a penetration strategy depends on the firm's ability to retain its desired market share once competition develops.

Establishing the Price Floor

Setting specific new product prices within the strategies selected, given limited competition, normally involves first establishing a price floor through break-even analysis. Unit costs may be high at first, so a long-run viewpoint may be essential in deriving cost estimates. Cost and demand uncertainties are high, so building in alternative cost assumptions and using *sensitivity analysis* to determine important cost thresholds can be very important. Sensitivity analysis answers such questions as:

- What *if* production costs are 10% higher than anticipated?
- What happens to the break-even point?
- What are the odds of achieving the required, higher sales level?

The uncertainty that accompanies new products cannot be totally eliminated, and monitoring new product prices is therefore particularly critical.

Nonprice competition is often emphasized in marketing strategies by entrepreneurs, in part because price changes are easy for competitors to counter. It is far more difficult to directly counter a strong brand image with unique product features than to counter a price change. Marketing strategies comprise an array of marketing mix variables, of which the price variable is sometimes best left alone. Yet promotion is virtually always an active part of the marketing plan.

Promotion Decisions

Promotion is considerably more than just advertising. In fact, an entrepreneur can draw on four major tools:

- *Sales Promotion* is communicating with an audience through a variety of nonpersonal, nonmedia vehicles such as free samples, gifts, and coupons.
- *Advertising* is communicating with an audience through nonpersonal, paid media.
- *Publicity* is communicating with an audience by personal or nonpersonal media that are not explicitly paid for delivering the messages; the audience is likely to perceive the media rather than the business as the source of messages.
- *Personal Selling* is communicating directly with an audience through paid sales personnel of the organization or its agents.

Together, these tools make up the *promotion mix*. The promotion mix is the combination of promotion tools used by a company to communicate with its audiences.

Each major promotion tool includes a wide variety of activities, some of which are listed in Exhibit 4.15. Business owners use all four of these tools to achieve promotional objectives, but place different weights on each of the tools. For example, industrial companies typically spend more for personal selling than for advertising or publicity. In contrast, consumer products

EXHIBIT 4.15. Promotion mix tools.

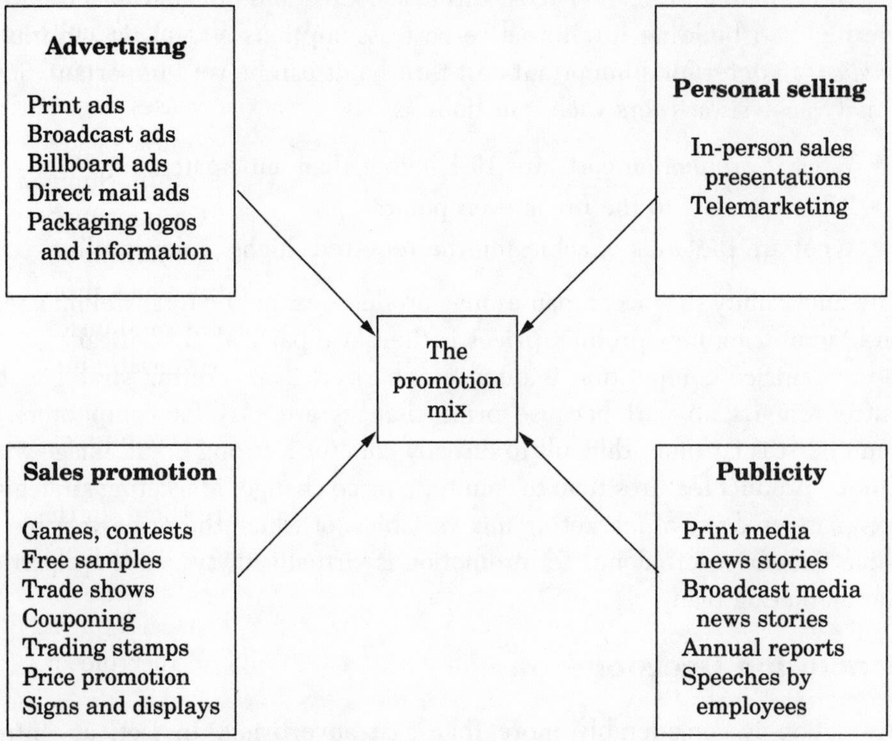

Source: Dr. Robert B. Woodruff, The University of Tennessee.

companies are likely to place heavy weight on advertising and sales promotion to reach customers.

The use of *publicity* affords an opportunity for entrepreneurs to receive valuable exposure without spending a penny. A business startup is often very newsworthy. Newspapers and the trade press, particularly in smaller cities or neighborhoods of large cities, are often eager to receive such news items. The keys to success are to (1) try to benefit the media writer and (2) be creative. A cure for cancer would require little more than publicity to be a success. It would be a rare exception and the world would beat a path to the entrepreneur's door. The more innovative and revolutionary the new product or service, the easier it is to obtain publicity. But media writers often *need* stories. The business owner, thinking in terms of the *writer's* needs, can provide a one-page story of 200 to 300 words that helps to make the writer's job easier. Creativity can transform a boring announcement of a new restaurant to that of a "unique restaurant concept with exciting dimensions." The announcement can be mailed to as many outlets as possible. (Use the library and other sources to find lists of media.) Radio or even TV interviews are also possible. The print media often find a high-quality, glossy photograph appealing, particularly if taken creatively. And once the articles appear, copies of a highly credible outlet may be used in other ways to enhance the exposure. What is written or said must be of interest to the media outlet's audience. If this requirement is satisfied, the writers are likely to be interested. A telephone follow-up to letters and news releases often increases the chances of exposure. Even after a business opens and there are no new products or services being offered, creative efforts may yield a great return. Supporting a charitable drive (e.g., offering a free service) can add a noncommercial appeal to gain entry to the media. A now-deceased, famous entrepreneur who started 30 food stores in the Southeast, for example, many times threw live chickens from the roof of a new store to an eager crowd of rural customers. Imagine the free media exposure! Using creative (and appropriate) means to "make news" is often an important entrepreneurial talent.

The entire promotion program—objectives, creative content of messages and format, selection of delivery vehicles, and the budget—should follow directly from marketing objectives and help achieve them. In this way the marketing plan ensures that promotion is coordinated with marketing strategy.

Firms rarely rely on only one of the four tools of promotion. Entrepreneurs can use the following five criteria to determine the role of each promotional tool:

- Cost of reaching an audience member
- Ability to reach target audiences with little leakage to persons not included in them
- Ability to deliver a complicated message
- Ability to engage in interchanges with the target audiences
- Credibility

Exhibit 4.16 summarizes how well the four tools compare on these criteria.

Upon consideration of the four promotion tools, it is evident why promotion managers must use a mix. There are clear trade-offs to be made between the tools. A comparison of advertising and personal selling illustrates such trade-offs. Advertising reaches far larger audiences than personal selling for a given total cost. But personal selling is better able to target a particular audience and can develop an interchange with customers, responding to their questions and refuting their objections. Further, complicated messages, such as explaining how a technical product works or how a product may be applied in an unusual way, are much better presented in person than by advertising. Finally, because salespeople can build rapport with customers over time, personal selling has the potential to build much greater credibility with audiences.

EXHIBIT 4.16. Promotion tools' strengths and weaknesses.

Criteria	Advertising	Sales promotion	Publicity	Personal selling
Cost per audience member	Low	Low	Very low	Very high
Confined to target markets	Poor to good	Good	Moderate	Very good
Deliver a complicated message	Poor to good	Poor	Poor to good	Very good
Interchange with audiences	None	None	Low to moderate	Very good
Credibility	Low	Low	High	Moderate to high

Source: Dr. Robert B. Woodruff, The University of Tennessee.

Sales Promotion

Sales promotion can be aimed at target markets, but also at channel-of-distribution companies (called "the trade") and at the company's own sales force. Usually, the trade or the sales force is a target when business owners want to encourage cooperation in a company's total marketing effort. Offering a free vacation to the person with the highest sales volume is a sales promotion activity of this type. Sales promotion aimed at the trade or the sales force acts as an incentive to increase the selling effort directed at target markets. For example, grocery manufacturers use price promotions (price discounts to stores) to encourage retailers to lower prices to consumers, arrange special displays of products, and give products a featured position in advertising. Similarly, many manufacturers periodically offer gifts (appliances, vacations) to motivate sales personnel to push particular brands or models.

If there are several target audiences, a company may use a number of sales promotion activities at the same time. A real estate developer selling houses, condominiums, or lots for a development project uses sales promotion tactics that are aimed directly at constumers, as well as sales promotion activities directed at real estate brokers who might steer consumers to the project. The developer's promotion could include the following:

- Special events to draw consumers' attention to the development; these events include family barbecues and picnics.
- Price promotions on slow-moving property.
- Attractive signs at the development site.
- Prizes and other incentives for high-selling real estate brokers.

Sales promotion is usually intended to promote overt actions in target audiences, and well-formulated promotion objectives state exactly what these actions are for each target audience. The objectives differ somewhat for different audiences. An entrepreneur may want customers to:

- Try the product
- Switch brands
- Stock up on the product
- Visit a dealer's showroom
- Make an inquiry about the company's product

Sales promotion is a catchall category that encompasses a wider variety of activities than do the other promotion tools. One way to organize these many activities is by the way they reach audiences:

- *In-store promotions* are activities aimed at communicating with customers while they are shopping in a store; they include in-store signs, displays, and brochures.
- *Audience-direct sales promotions* are activities aimed at reaching audiences directly, through the mail, through advertising media, or through delivery by sales personnel; they include samples, gifts, contests, and cents-off coupons.
- *Trade shows* are events in which a number of companies display their wares in exhibits at a central location and invite dealers or customers to visit the exhibits.

Emphasis on sales promotion varies considerably among organizations. Some firms do very little sales promotion, whereas others spend more on sales promotion than on advertising. Sales promotion budgets in the United States have been increasing rapidly in recent years, owing to a new recognition of its effectiveness and the rising cost of other media.

Advertising

A central part of the advertising mission is communicating with specific audiences. One important audience for advertising is the trade (resellers in a company's channel of distribution). This audience is reached through trade advertising intended to enlist wholesaler or retailer cooperation in selling the new venture's products. For instance, retail stores may be encouraged to stock the advertiser's product, to participate in a cents-off price promotion, or to buy larger quantities of the product.

How entrepreneurs split budgets between trade and end-user advertising depends on the type of marketing strategy used. A *push strategy* that emphasizes placing products into the distribution channel requires relatively more trade advertising. In contrast, a *pull strategy* to build a strong preference for a company's brands among end-users must have a higher proportion of consumer advertising. Of course, many marketing strategies fall somewhere in between push and pull and have more balanced allocations.

The primary purpose of advertising is to convey to audiences information about a company and its products. On the basis of this information, customers form beliefs, likes and dislikes, predispositions, and intentions that later influence purchase decisions. In this way, advertising contributes to the total selling effort of a marketing strategy but does not carry the entire burden of generating sales.

The most creative part of advertising is planning an *advertising campaign*. The campaign determines what to say to target audiences and how to say it so that people will listen to and understand the messages and remember them when they make buying decisions.

A marketing plan should provide a "position statement" explaining how a company's product (or service) is to be differentiated from those of key competitors. A position statement helps advertising managers plan a *selling proposal*. A selling proposal is a statement describing the important facts, images, and persuasive arguments to be communicated to target audiences. This is illustrated in Exhibit 4.17.

EXHIBIT 4.17. Advertising for a selling proposal.

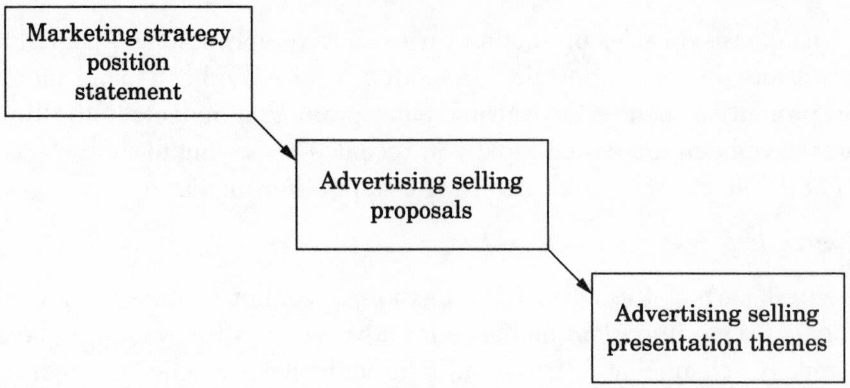

The next stage is to develop media strategy and tactics. Developing media strategy is complicated by the fact that many different vehicles are available, each having its advantages and disadvantages. Typically, no one vehicle reaches an entire target audience. Consequently, media planners must evaluate the many alternatives so as to construct a *media mix* that will meet objectives. The media mix is the combination of vehicles (for example, magazines, newspapers, TV, radio, direct mail, billboards) that will carry advertisements to target audiences.

Further, the timing of advertisements—a *media schedule*—must be determined so that they are properly sequenced when the advertising campaign is run. The media schedule is the combination of specific times (for example, by day, week, month) when advertisements are inserted into media vehicles and delivered to target audiences. The media plan lists the media to be used, the times or issues in which each advertisement is to be carried by each vehicle, and the cost of the media mix. It serves as a blueprint for implementing the delivery of an advertising campaign.

Exhibit 4.18 describes important advantages and disadvantages of various media types. Choosing the best combination of these vehicles and deciding the number and size of advertisements to place in each of them requires careful attention.

Business owners can deal with this complexity by setting criteria for comparison to ensure that the vehicles selected meet advertising objectives and budget constraints. Three particularly important criteria are:

- Overlap of vehicle audience with target audiences
- Media communication capabilities
- Cost

The success of new ventures depends in part on the availability of cost-effective promotional vehicles to reach the particular market.

Personal Selling

Annual expenditures for personal selling in the United States currently exceed advertising expenditures by as much as 50%. Selling includes:

- Locating prospective customers
- Planning calls
- Making sales presentations
- Interacting with customers (for example, overcoming objections)
- Closing sales

EXHIBIT 4.18. Advantages and disadvantages of major advertising media.

Media	Advantages	Disadvantages
Television	Reaches large audiences Has visual and audio capabilities Provides great flexibility in getting attention Short lead time needed to place ad	Not easy to reach specific target markets Total cost is high relative to other media Requires production specialists Short exposure time
Magazines and journals	Reach of issues is high for demographic and geographic segments High-quality production Ad lasts as long as magazine or journal is kept Issues are often read by more than one person Credibility of magazine or journal can benefit ad	Must place ad well in advance of publication Provide limited flexibility in gaining attention Provide incomplete control over location of ad in issue
Outdoor advertising	Relatively inexpensive Many repeat exposures	Only very limited message possible Cannot reach well-defined target markets Very short exposure time
Radio	Audio capability Low cost relative to costs of the other media Short lead time needed to place ad Can reach demographic and geographic segments Reaches large audiences Reaches audiences in cars	No visual capability Short exposure time Provides little flexibility in gaining attention
Newspapers	Reach large audiences Can reach segments by locale Short lead time needed to place ad Credibility of newspaper can benefit ad	May be relatively expensive Provide little flexibility for use of creativity Limited reproduction quality (e.g., little or no use of color) Short life carries over to ad
Direct mail	Provides great flexibility in reaching target market segments No clutter from competing ads Easy to personalize copy and layout	Easily thrown away as "junk mail" Obtaining appropriate mailing lists can be expensive

Source: Dr. Robert B. Woodruff, The University of Tenessee.

In addition, salespeople collect information on competitive products, price, customer reactions to product use, stock levels, and service and delivery problems. Customer service can encompass a variety of responsibilities, including delivery, marketing assistance (for example, promotional and display advice), credit evaluation, product application assistance, and repair of products. The importance of these job components varies with different sales positions.

The size and characteristics of each target market help determine how personal selling will be used in a firm's marketing mix. When the number of customers is very large, as in mass markets, and the size (in dollars) of the purchase is relatively small, personal selling costs become prohibitive. A sales call is expensive, although its cost is influenced by the salesperson's qualifications, the degree of customer concentration, the size of the territory, waiting time, and the time spent with the customer. The average cost of an industrial sales call exceeds $200. In contrast, a minute of national television advertising during prime viewing time costs less than $10 per thousand viewing homes. Yet television is often not available to the entrepreneur because of its high cost.

The sales force forms a major part of the marketing mix when customer needs can best be met through personal selling efforts and when there are sufficient margins between the purchase price and the costs to cover sales force expenses. Personal selling is often used in industrial markets since the number of customers and prospects is relatively small (compared to most consumer markets) and the dollar amounts of purchases are sufficient to support salespeople. The same characteristics may exist in some consumer markets, for example, in encyclopedia sales. In other situations, the marketing of consumer products may combine personal selling to channel intermediaries with heavy use of advertising at the consumer level.

The task of the entrepreneur is to select the best combination of marketing mix elements to obtain the desired responses from target markets. The role of personal selling should be determined in conjunction with that of the other marketing mix components. Several characteristics of marketing programs that may indicate a relatively important role for personal selling are shown in Exhibit 4.19.

Most studies of salespersons' performance have failed to identify factors that are always good predictors of performance. Predicting sales performance is an elusive task, and in the absence of research findings a great deal of reliance is typically placed on the entrepreneur's judgment and experience. A major problem is pinpointing relevant influences on sales performance, since a number of influences are involved, some of which are interrelated, and the impact of each is often impossible to estimate. Possible determinants fall into the following categories:

EXHIBIT 4.19. Conditions suggesting personal selling as a major element of the marketing mix.

Mix area	Characteristics
Product or service	Complex products requiring customer application assistance (computers, pollution control systems, steam turbines) Major purchase decisions, such as food items purchased by supermarket chains Features and performance of the product requiring personal demonstration and trial by the customer (private aircraft)
Channels	Channel system relatively short and direct to end-users Product and service training and assistance needed by channel intermediaries Personal selling needed in "pushing" product through channel Channel intermediaries available to perform personal selling function for supplier with limited resources and experience (brokers or manufacturer's agents)
Price	Final price negotiated between buyer and seller (appliances, automobiles, real estate) Selling price or quantity purchased enable an adequate margin to support selling expenses (traditional department store compared to discount house)
Advertising	Advertising media do not provide effective link with market targets Information needed by buyer cannot be provided entirely through advertising and sales promotion (life insurance) Number and dispersion of customers will not enable acceptable advertising economies

Source: Dr. David W. Cravens, Texas Christian University.

- *Aptitude* includes physical factors, such as appearance; mental abilities, such as education and past experience; and personality characteristics, such as empathy, ego strength, and sociability.
- *Skill level* is a learned proficiency at performing the requirements of the job. It includes salesmanship and the interpersonal and technical skills needed in the selling environment.
- *Motivation* is the amount of effort that the salesperson chooses to expend on each of the activities associated with the job.
- *Role perceptions* are the salesperson's perceptions of the activities or behaviors necessary to meet the expectations, demands, and pressures communicated by management, customers, and family.
- *External and constraining factors* are factors that may directly facilitate or constrain performance or interact with other performance determinants. Among such factors are the intensity of competition, the quality of management, and the market potential.

The lead entrepreneur in a new venture is often the lead salesperson, but aptitude and skill-level factors are often used in selecting salespeople when the company expands. Here, the difficulty is that factors in the other three areas may also affect eventual performance. Although some of the determinants of sales performance can be controlled or influenced by training, supervision, and motivational tools, others are uncontrollable. Considering the variety of the possible influences on sales performance and the meagerness of the available research findings, it is not surprising that sales force management places heavy reliance on experience and judgment.

CREATING AN ACTION PLAN TO IMPLEMENT THE MARKETING PRACTICES

The final step in developing a marketing plan is to take the important decisions that have been made and turn them into an action framework. Based on analysis of the environment and the market opportunity, the entrepreneur has developed a marketing strategy that targets well-defined markets, sets quantitative and qualitative marketing objectives, and specifies which elements should form the marketing program. The products and services to offer, the prices, the channels of distribution, and the promotion elements, when combined, will portray the new venture or entrepreneurial firm to the eyes of customers. Customers' preceptions of this mix of marketing elements will contribute to success or failure.

To convert the many marketing decisions into a plan, the final step is to delineate numerous tasks and develop a detailed timetable and budget with an assignment of responsibilities. Although maintaining flexibility is essential, particularly once market feedback begins to flow, it is helpful to identify the major tasks required to implement the marketing plan and establish a timeline to achieve various milestones. Certain tasks, such as advertising, may require detailed scheduling as a subpart of the overall marketing plan.

Too often, entrepreneurs place little emphasis on monitoring and control as the business grows. There is often a tendency to fight intensely through the startup phase, but then place too little detailed attention on marketing control as the enterprise grows. When the business becomes so large that it is beyond the capacity of the founding entrepreneur to manage all of the major elements, it is often necessary to develop a team with the marketing expertise to reach the next development stage.

CONCLUSION

To conclude, marketing is the home for entrepreneurship, and vice versa. In a study of venture capitalists, the importance of marketing management to venture success, was rated 6.7 on a 7.0 scale.[19] They further agreed that venture failure rates could be reduced, by as much as 60%, through better preventure market analysis. Finally, they agreed that entrepreneurs face several unique marketing-related challenges, such as the inability to spread advertising costs, poor access to good-quality distributors, and lack of access to retail shelf space.[20] Several volumes have now been published that provide an in-depth look at many of these issues.[21] But even more important, in a study of highly successful entrepreneurs, the factors cited by business owners as most responsible for their success were high-quality products and services, development of a good customer reputation, and responsiveness to customer desires.[22] This requires adopting the marketing concept as a business philosophy and developing and implementing effective marketing strategy.

5 CREATING A SUCCESSFUL BUSINESS PLAN

David E. Gumpert

When I write about management issues, I try as much as possible to begin on a positive note. That way, even if there are negative points to make, at least I will have gained the interest and involvement of readers, increasing the likelihood that they will be receptive to the inevitable unpleasant matters.

When it comes to the subject of business plans, though, I have come to believe that it is best to make an exception and start with a negative slant. Otherwise, I run the risk of being misleading and, more significantly, of discouraging you from completing the task at hand—creating a successful business plan. By giving you the bad news first, I hope to clear a path for you to get on with what you need to do, which is to write a business plan that will attract the support your business requires.

So here is the straight dope: Writing a business plan is no fun. For many entrepreneurs, the mindset associated with writing a business plan is akin to that associated with root canal surgery or periodontal work. It's not something you look forward to. It's something that goes on for a long while with repeat sessions of agony. The dentist tries to relieve the pain with Novocain.

In one sense, this chapter serves the role of the dentist and relieves the pain. But, fortunately, this chapter is designed to do something much more positive than the dentist does.

When you are finished with the dentist, you breathe a sigh of relief because everything is back to normal, at least until the next visit. But as you complete your business plan, you'll actually begin feeling excited. I know because I've been through the process many times—with my own business and with that of other entrepreneurs—and it's truly exhilarating. The psychological benefits alone are worth the effort. They include a feeling of confidence and a sense of control over your own destiny.

Now that you have the straight story, let's deal with the task at hand. My goals in this chapter are threefold:

1. To get you off on the right foot in writing a business plan
2. To provide you with a process that makes the writing seem less forbidding
3. To give you an overview of the information requirements of a successful business plan

THE BUSINESS PLAN AS A SELLING DOCUMENT

To get off on the right foot, you need to understand the task at hand. How you define the business plan affects your approach to writing it. If you view it as a very complex and boring task, your plan will come across that way—to the detriment of your business.

Indeed, there's a tendency to define a business plan as a roadmap, a statement of strategy, or some other conceptual label. As a result, too many business plans are rambling, dry, and technical, because the entrepreneurs see them as some sort of formal academic exercise.

In my view, the business plan is best defined as a selling document, not unlike sales literature you pass out to customers or a sales pitch you give to prospective employees. Except with the business plan you're not just selling a product or a work environment, *you're selling the entire company as a package.*

If you're really excited about your company, it should come through in the business plan. If you approach the business plan as a document designed to convey, and support, your sense of excitement about the company, you will avoid the dry, convoluted document that too many entrepreneurs produce.

This is not to say that the business plan should consist of a lot of puffery or exaggeration. You need supporting evidence in the form of solid research and experience to back up the excitement and the sales pitch. The point is that the business plan should convey to readers the *excitement* and *promise* that you feel.

DEFINING A BUSINESS PLAN

A good definition: A business plan is a document that convincingly demonstrates the ability of your business to sell enough of its product or service to make a satisfactory profit and be attractive to potential backers.

A better definition: A business plan is *a selling document* that conveys the excitement and promise of your business to any potential backers or stakeholders.

EIGHT REASONS FOR WRITING A BUSINESS PLAN

Why write a business plan? This is a legitimate, indeed essential, question to ask yourself before you plunge in.

If you write a business plan in a vacuum—because you feel it is something you are "supposed" to do—you run the risk of engaging in a painful process of conceptualizing and in the end conveying a sense of aimlessness. But if you write the business plan with one or more specific purposes and audiences in mind, you will likely feel a greater sense of commitment and produce a more focused and practical document.

Your audience most fundamentally consists of those individuals or organizations with a stake in your company's success—those I refer to as *stakeholders*. Here are eight of the most important reasons for writing a business plan, with a description of the stakeholders associated with each:

1. To sell yourself on the business. This is a "sanity check." The most important stakeholders in any business are its founders. First and foremost, you need to *convince yourself* that starting the business is right for you—both from a personal viewpoint and an investment viewpoint.

The case of Fred Gibbons helps illustrate this point. Back in the early 1980s when he was considering leaving Hewlett-Packard to start Software Publishing, he was a rising star at the computer giant. Moreover, he would need to take a second mortgage on his house and borrow money from his family to make it work.

Gibbons decided he needed to write a business plan to serve as a "sanity check," to convince himself he was doing the right thing. In other words, he needed to sell himself on committing so deeply to his idea.

2. To obtain bank financing. Up until the late 1980s, writing a business plan to obtain bank financing was an option left up to the entrepreneur. Bankers usually took the approach that a business plan helped you make a better case, but wasn't an essential component in the banks' decision-making process.

The bank failures of the late 1980s and early 1990s changed all that. Banks are under greater scrutiny by federal regulators and, as a consequence, are requiring entrepreneurs to include a written business plan with any request for loan funds. Getting bank money is tougher than it has ever been, and a business plan is an essential component of any campaign to sell banks on your company.

3. To obtain investment funds. For many years now, the business plan has been the "ticket of admission" to the venture capital evaluation process. Now, though, whether you are seeking venture capital or so-called informal capital from private investors, you will need a written business plan. Rare is the private investor—typically a successful entrepreneur or other well-heeled individual—who will make a financial commitment based entirely on your oral presentation. Even if you get in the door to sell your idea, you will be asked to send along something in writing, namely a business plan. If you attempt a private offering under Securities and Exchange Commission rules and exemptions, you will need a business plan to enable your lawyer to write a private placement or offering memorandum.

4. To arrange strategic alliances. Joint research, marketing, and other efforts between small and large companies have become increasingly common in recent years. These efforts, which have come to be known as strategic alliances, have resulted from the need of small and large companies for each other. Small companies need financial support and large companies need innovation.

Despite the mutual needs, though, many more small early-stage companies seek out alliances with corporations than the corporations can ally with. To help them in their selection process, the corporations usually want to see the business plans of prospective small company alliance partners. Indeed, the large companies are more likely to be attracted to a company that volunteers a plan early in the negotiating process, without being asked for one.

5. To obtain large contracts. When small companies are seeking substantial orders or ongoing service contracts from major corporations, the corporations often respond (somewhat arrogantly): "Everyone knows who we are. But no one knows who you are. How do we know you'll be around in three or five years to provide the parts or service we might require for your product?"

If, at this point in the conversation, entrepreneurs can pull out their business plans, the corporate representatives will be immediately impressed that the entrepreneurs have thought about the future. More important, the corporate representatives will see that the small company fully expects to be around in three or five years, bigger and stronger than it is now. This can be a powerful argument in the selling process. And in today's selling environment, in which corporations are increasingly looking toward their suppliers as partners, the business plan helps convey that feeling of partnership.

6. To attract key employees. One of the biggest obstacles that small, growing companies face in attracting key employees is convincing the best people to take the necessary risk—that the company will thrive and grow during the coming years. Even in today's uncertain job environment, the best executives are still attracted to large corporations. A small company must be as convincing as the corporate officials can be. A written business plan can assure prospective employees that the entrepreneurs have thought through the key issues facing the company and have a plan for dealing with them.

A business plan does something more, though. It helps the prospective employee understand the company's culture and rationale for doing business.

Conveying such fundamentals helps ensure that the most compatible people will take the job.

7. To complete mergers and acquisitions. No matter which side of the merger process you are on, a business plan can be very handy. If you want to sell your company to a large corporation, a business plan helps you stand apart from the crowd. Corporations searching for acquisition candidates typically examine hundreds of companies. The business plan says to the potential acquirer that you have thought about the future and know where the business is headed.

Similarly, if you are seeking to acquire a company, your business plan can help convince a reluctant seller that your company would be a suitable partner. The business plan in these situations serves almost as an extended company résumé.

8. To motivate and focus your management team. As smaller companies grow and become more complex, a business plan becomes an important component in keeping everyone focused on the same goals. Frank Carney, a founder of Pizza Hut, points out that in the late 1970s, when his company was showing signs of foundering, a business plan helped it resume its fast growth. The process of developing and writing a plan helped get everyone thinking about the company's long-range goals. And the final document served as a roadmap over the next year, until the plan was updated.

Beginning to Write: The Bite-Size Approach

The hardest part about trying to write a business plan is getting started. You look at that blank piece of paper or computer screen and you have no idea where to begin. Then you begin thinking about coming up with 30 or 40 pages, and you are understandably discouraged. In such a state of mind, it is easy to move on to a more immediate business task and put off writing the plan.

There is a way around the inevitable anxieties that come up when you are faced with such a seemingly overwhelming task. My approach involves two facets:

1. Posing the right questions or subjects
2. Providing bite-size answers to those questions

In my experience, it is a lot easier to write a few paragraphs or even a few pages in answer to specific questions or requests than to begin writing in the abstract. It is also important to keep in mind that the questions need not be completely answered all at once. It is all right to jot down some notes about things that occur to you immediately and think further about other matters that the question suggests. Even in answering focused questions, you often gain insights into additional research you need to do.

With that in mind, let's consider specific questions or issues that should be dealt with in writing a plan.

HOW LONG SHOULD THE BUSINESS PLAN BE?

It often helps psychologically when beginning a writing project to have some sense of the task's scope. So it is with business plans.

From a practical organizing perspective, it helps to have some idea ahead of time about how much written material is expected. That way, discipline can be exerted early rather than later after much work has been done. Too often, business plans are much longer than is necessary or appropriate. As in most areas of writing, it is more difficult to write a concise business plan than to write a long one.

To provide guidance about the size of the task, I categorize business plans broadly into three types: the summary business plan, the full business plan, and the operational business plan. Each type is discussed in the following sections.

The Summary Business Plan: 10 Pages

Summary business plans—running about 10 pages or so—have become increasingly popular and accepted in recent years. This is considerably shorter than the 40 or so pages traditional for business plans. Summary plans obviously require less data and research to complete, so, in some cases, they can be written more quickly than a traditional plan.

Summary plans also tend to be most appropriate for early-stage businesses for the simple reason that they don't have as much history or as many product lines to explain as more mature businesses.

Here are some of the situations in which a summary business plan works best.

Bank Loan

Though bankers are increasingly demanding written business plans as part of any application for loan funds, the summary business plan will usually serve the purpose. The business plan is often a supplement to some other application and documentation asking for personal financial information, asset valuations, and other such data that wouldn't normally be included in a business plan.

Well-Known Founders

If the founding entrepreneurs are well known in their industries or as celebrities, a shorter plan is likely to be acceptable to investors or bankers. Thus, Fred Gibbons, who was well known in computer circles, was able to raise venture capital based on a business plan of fewer than 10 pages.

Lifestyle Business

This is the term I apply to the bulk of the nation's businesses—those that tend not to seek outside financing, which are intended to provide a nice living to the owners while employing a handful of people. Lifestyle businesses range from the corner dry cleaner and hardware store to the small graphic design and consulting firm. Because these businesses are most likely to want a business plan to help focus the owners on the most important business issues, a summary plan may be the most effective way to get the task completed.

Gauge Investor Interest

Before sending a lengthy business plan to venture capitalists and private investors, entrepreneurs may want to try out their ideas. A summary plan can serve that purpose, enabling them to obtain feedback that can then be applied to a lengthier plan.

And, indeed, venture capitalists increasingly say they prefer to see a shortened version of a plan initially. After all, it saves them reading time as well.

The Full Business Plan: 10 to 40 Pages

This is the traditional plan. It covers all the key subjects in enough depth to allow a full exploration of the key issues, yet it doesn't go on much beyond 40 pages. For a well-established business, dealing with its key issues in 40 pages or less can be a real challenge.

The full business plan is most appropriate in the following two situations:

Seeking a Substantial Amount of Financing

For companies trying to raise several million dollars, a full business plan will likely be required at some point in the fund-raising process, even if a summary plan was used to get in the door. A summary plan unfortunately just doesn't allow entrepreneurs to provide the depth of discussion that professional investors typically demand.

Looking for a Strategic Partner

A small company in search of a corporate partner should likewise expect to complete a full business plan. Because major corporations have so many more such opportunities than they can possibly take advantage of, the corporations understandably want to scrutinize promising candidates as closely as possible. A full business plan allows that process to take place.

The Operational Business Plan: 40+ Pages

I used to feel strongly that executives should do everything possible to keep their business plans from exceeding 40 pages. Plans that extended much beyond that ideal, in my view, were likely to lack focus and discipline.

Once I saw the business plans of some highly successful companies like Celestial Seasonings and Pizza Hut, though, my viewpoint changed. A Celestial Seasonings plan, for example, extended just beyond 100 pages, and, in reading it through and discussing it with Mo Siegel, the company's founder, I realized that the plan actually did a very effective job in accomplishing what needed to be done.

Basically, there are two reasons to have such a long plan:

Company Growing Quickly

For companies that are already complex and are growing quickly, a business plan must cover quite a few issues to be truly complete. Such was the case with Celestial Seasonings in the early 1980s.

Part of an Annual Process

Equally important in fast-growing companies, the management team must be focused on the same issues. It is easy in such situations for the executives to lose their focus. For the business plan to be effective in keeping everyone on track, though, it must contain a level of detail not necessary in either a summary or full plan. An operational plan must get into the details of distribution, production, and other areas that are essential to making certain everyone understands what is expected. Indeed, managers often welcome such detail so they know clearly what they need to work toward.

WHAT SHOULD THE BUSINESS PLAN COVER?

Once you've decided which type of plan is right for your company, you need to organize it. In my experience, there is no completely right or wrong way to organize the plan, but in general, it includes the following features:

1. Cover Page. This may seem like an insignificant detail, but in fact, a cover page serves several purposes. It is the place where you include not only the company's name and address, but the name of the main contact (usually the president) and a phone number. You want to avoid the situation in which an investor or banker becomes excited by the plan and then discovers that the phone number is nowhere to be found, except by searching out directory assistance.

The cover page should also warn readers that the material in the plan contains private information and is not to be copied or otherwise transmitted. It can also include a copy number, to convey the message that you keep track of each plan. (For details on composing and handling confidentiality statements and other related matters, consult a lawyer.)

If your company has a product that is especially interesting visually, such as computer graphics or a new type of machinery, your cover could include a photo. If your company's product is a low-cost consumer item, like food, you might want to consider including a sample with the plan you send to outside stakeholders.

2. Table of Contents. This should be as detailed as possible, with the page numbers of each section included. Some bankers or investors have a preferred way of reading business plans that may not involve starting at the beginning. Some like to begin at the executive summary, while others seek out the marketing section or the financial section. For this reason, you don't want to frustrate readers by failing to include page numbers.

3. Executive Summary. This is the single most important section of the business plan because most readers turn to it early in their reading for a sense of the entire plan. The executive summary is the heart of the plan and requires much attention; I provide more detail about the executive summary a little later.

4. The Company. In this section you discuss the company's strategy and its management team. These matters must be evaluated from the perspective of the company's history and current situation.

5. The Market. Who are the potential buyers? How many of them exist? This section identifies the prospective customers and provides evidence of how many are likely to become real customers.

6. The Product/Service. This is the section of the business plan that most entrepreneurs find the easiest to do. Because most feel strongly about the quality and utility of their product or service, they love to describe its attributes. Here is where such discussion is most appropriate.

7. Sales and Promotion. Here you explain how sales will be completed. Will there be an in-house sales force? Or manufacturers' representatives? Or will mail order be used? And how will the product/service be promoted? Via advertising? Or public relations?

8. Finances. This is the section for the nuts-and-bolts financial issues to be considered and financial results/projections to be included. Generally speaking, three types of financial statements are necessary: cash flow, income/loss, and balance sheet.

9. Appendix. Here you can include items that don't fit well within particular sections of the plan—items like executive résumés, product literature, and endorsement letters from customers.

Sample Cover Page

copy number 5

The Company

Chris Smith, President
123 Lincoln Way, Suite B
Chicago, IL 60606
(312) 222-2222

The material in this plan is private information and is not to be copied or transmitted.

Sample Table of Contents

THE EXECUTIVE SUMMARY: YOUR GUIDING LIGHT

What is the executive summary? It is *not* an abstract, an introduction, a preface, or a random collection of highlights. It is much more than those things. Quite simply, it is *the business plan in miniature*. As such, it should stand alone as a document, almost as a kind of "business plan within the business plan." It should capture the excitement and essence of the business. Someone who has finished reading your executive summary should be able to say, "So that's what these people are up to."

If you have hopes of obtaining any financing from the plan, the executive summary has to keep potential investors or bankers interested. Otherwise, those individuals will not bother to spend time with the rest of the plan.

Writing the executive summary in its final form is an enormous task because it must carry out its duties in *at most two pages*. Any executive summary that goes on longer than two pages dilutes the impact of this segment of the plan simply because the longer it gets, the less of a summary it becomes.

Because the executive summary is of necessity such a concise document, it offers entrepreneurs an important initial writing opportunity. You can begin writing the executive summary, knowing that it shouldn't be longer than two pages. You can also take comfort in the fact that this initial draft can be revised later, after other parts of the plan are completed.

In writing the initial executive summary draft, you will likely make an important discovery. You will begin to see gaps or holes in your knowledge and ideas. This discovery provides direction for the challenge of researching and writing the rest of the plan.

THE COMPANY: WHAT'S YOUR IDENTITY?

The section on the company should address two primary matters: your business strategy and your management team.

Describing Your Business Strategy

Strategy is one of those words that gets misused because it is applied to so many different aspects of business life. It is really a buzzword for your company's overall approach to producing and selling its products/services—and its goals for maximizing success. In describing your company's strategy, though, there needs to be a logical consistency between what you say you plan to do and what the rest of the plan will support.

For example, take the case of a bearings manufacturer that had been in business nine years and had achieved inconsistent results—sales would rise 8% one year and decline 3% the next; one year it would be profitable and the next it would lose money.

In its business plan, though, the company said it had devised a strategy based on new product innovations that would increase sales and profits 15% annually in each of the coming three years. The obvious question a reader might have about this plan was how the company would suddenly change a nine-year pattern of operations. If the strategy had included replacing one or more top managers by someone with a proven record of helping companies achieve such growth, it might have been more believable. As it was, a discrepancy existed between what had happened in the past and what the company projected for the future.

In describing the strategy, therefore, entrepreneurs need to directly address three main areas: the past, the present, and the future.

Analyzing the Company's Past Successes and Problems

For mature companies, the past must be explained as directly and honestly as possible, in both its positive and negative aspects. This may be painful, but it assures stakeholders that the executives are realistic about themselves and their company.

For startup companies, the past can only be dealt with in terms of individual executives. What have they accomplished in managerial terms? Ideally, one or more have been through startup situations that required the sorts of skills that are needed in this venture.

Describing the Company's Current Status

The discussion of the company's current status should answer the following questions:

- Is the company operating profitably or at a loss?
- What have been the recent sales and earnings trends?
- What recent important changes have taken place in the product or service mix?
- Are there any other significant changes?

Note that here the plan may touch on areas considered in greater detail later in the plan, like product or marketing issues, as they relate to overall strategy.

Outlining the Company's Future Goals

At this point, the plan can move on to the future. Of course, this part of the plan is likely to be optimistic. That is fine, but it is essential that the plan's description of future strategy and goals be in keeping with what has happened before. And if there will be significant changes in direction, explain forthrightly how they will occur.

Describing the Management Team

The key issue is whether the people running the company have what it takes to enable the company to fulfill its strategy. Professional investors are fond of saying that they would rather invest in a company with a mediocre product and top people than the reverse.

How do you demonstrate that your company has top people? By bringing aboard individuals with a track record of past accomplishment. Preferably, these accomplishments will have occurred at your company; if you have new managers, determine their track record from what they have accomplished in the past in other positions.

Try to avoid the common management team traps. One trap is putting too much responsibility into the hands of a single leader, which I refer to as "the one-man-band syndrome." Another problem is choosing managers who all have the same background. For example, in high-technology companies, it is common for all the founders to be engineers. This worries professional investors, who want to see expertise in marketing and finance as well.

Describe the management team members in just a paragraph each, if possible. But be sure you are making the most of your resources—using everyone's experience and capabilities to their fullest in your descriptions. This includes listing consultants or part-timers who are key players.

MARKETING ISSUES: WHO ARE THE BUYERS?

Marketing tends to get confused with selling. The two functions are, however, quite distinct, which explains why they are treated separately in the business plan. Quite simply, *marketing* is identifying your customer prospects and determining how best to reach them. *Selling* is convincing those prospects to buy from you.

One way to begin identifying prospective customers is by demographics. For example, if you have a cosmetics store on the north side of Chicago, your prospects may be all of the women ages 16 to 40 with annual incomes above $25,000 living in a two-mile radius. Once you understand those parameters, your choices about trying to reach them become clearer; if you are inclined toward advertising, you might want to select a neighborhood newspaper rather than a citywide daily that reaches lots of people who are not potential customers.

Selling the Benefits of Your Product or Service

An important part of the task of identifying your customer prospects is determining what your company is *really* selling. Entrepreneurs tend to view their companies in terms of the products or services they sell. For example, they think of their companies as selling high-quality pizzas or high-quality graphic design services.

In writing this section of the plan (and in running a business), you must think about your company in terms of the *benefits* you sell to customers. The best benefits are those that help customers make money, save money, or feel good. As much as possible, try to *quantify* the benefits—the amount of money made or saved. Moreover, determine how long it takes for that money to pay for your product or service.

An example helps illustrate this point. When you buy insulation for your home, one of the first questions that you most likely want answered is how much energy it will save you each year. If insulation costs $800 and saves $200 in heating bills annually, it will take four years to recover the cost of the product. Thereafter, the savings are all gravy.

That information is valuable on two counts. First (and most obviously), it helps in *developing a promotional theme* to sell the product. But it also helps in *identifying prospective customers*. What kind of people are most likely to be interested in that kind of benefit? Perhaps better-educated individuals who tend to have a longer time horizon than poorly educated individuals. But also individuals who expect to stay in their homes for many years as opposed to those who plan only a short stay. Additional conclusions are certainly possible, based on the company's location, energy price trends, and so forth. The key point is that looking at your company's products or services from a *benefits* perspective provides important marketing insights.

Of course, customer benefits are not as obvious for many products as they are for home insulation. But by thinking creatively, you can often come up with similar benefits. If a computer software company's $500 package reduces a $25,000-a-year bookkeeper's time expenditure by one-fifth, the system saves the owner $5,000 per year and pays for itself in less than two months. The promise of improved productivity is behind the success of many personal computer software companies.

An interior designer specializing in servicing businesses may be able to save its corporate clients 10% to 15% in space requirements through efficient design. For a corporation paying $200,000 a year in prime city center office rent, saving 10% would be equal to $20,000. If the design fee is $20,000, the corporation would pay for its design in one year and then pocket the $20,000 savings for years into the future.

Not surprisingly, the more quickly your product or service can pay for itself in money saved or made, the more attractive it is to buyers. The calculations you come up with should be clearly spelled out in the business plan.

When a clear financial benefit doesn't exist, there should be other compelling benefits. Many mail-order companies selling everything from clothing to food to flowers have capitalized on the growing desire for convenience. People who can save a trip to a shopping mall have more time to spend with their families.

Simplifying Market Research

Market research is one of those terms that sounds intimidating, conjuring up images of statistical analysis and complex formulas. But it is really quite straightforward. It is a matter of determining, first, whether there are enough potential customers to achieve the growth you want and, second, whether they are increasing or decreasing in number.

Here are some of the key questions that need to be answered:

- What is the market, precisely? Is it all restaurants, or just fast-food restaurants, gourmet restaurants, or wine bars? The more specific you can be, the better off you usually are.
- Is the market growing or shrinking? Obviously, you'll want a growing market rather than a declining market, and the faster it's growing, usually the better off you'll be. (Declining markets can be attractive if you are strong enough financially to outlast competitors falling by the wayside.)
- Is it worth your while? You may have identified a niche market that is growing, but it may not achieve a size that makes it worthwhile. Keep in mind that no matter how good your product or your promotion, you are unlikely ever to capture more than a significant minority of a total market. Competitors will see to that.

Market research need not be a complicated matter. For example, take the case of two entrepreneurs who owned a stationery wholesaling business and were investigating the possibilities for selling office products directly to large-scale users in the Rochester, New York, area—corporations, midsize businesses, universities, and nonprofit organizations.

The first thing they did was look through a corporate guide and tally up the number of companies that had more than $50 million in annual sales in their region. They also looked through the Yellow Pages and determined how many universities existed and contacted an association of nonprofit organizations for a tally on such organizations in the area.

Then they looked at U.S. Commerce Department statistics along with those from some office products trade associations to determine annual sales of office supplies in their region. From those statistics, they could begin calculating the expected size of purchases per business, university, and nonprofit organization.

To validate such raw data, though, they conducted some telephone interviews to determine not only the actual volume of purchases, but how purchases were being made. Such real-life research enabled the entrepreneurs to determine that corporations were buying a growing percentage of supplies directly from paper and other suppliers. This discovery reduced the entrepreneurs' estimate of the potential market.

Assessing the Competition

Entrepreneurs are quick to minimize the significance of competitors. In the entrepreneurs' view, the competitors are flawed in important ways—producing an inferior product or providing poor service. The fact is, if competitors are attracting customers, it is for a good reason.

For a business plan to have credibility, it must analyze the competitors objectively—not just in terms of their weaknesses, but in terms of their strengths. The best business plans I have seen include a complete competitor assessment; they carefully evaluate each competitor on several criteria including sales, number of employees, product or service, and future plans.

Effective business plans demonstrate a willingness to learn from competitors. In an early business plan, Ben & Jerry's, the ice cream maker, pointed out that the success of a competitor's ice cream plant forced the company to abandon its focus on several regional plants and conclude that a national plant could indeed serve its needs. Most competitors offer at least a few potential lessons in how to improve your business.

Equally important, an objective analysis of competitors in your business plan helps convince stakeholders that your company is serious in its overall analysis.

Facing the Pricing Dilemma

This is one of the toughest issues any business faces, and I wish I had a magic formula to help deal with it. Unfortunately, I don't, because none exists. Most fundamentally, the pricing decision is the outcome of your marketing research and testing of what your target market is willing to pay for your product or service. Pricing is also partly a function of what the competition is charging, as well as what your costs and margins are.

But in the final analysis, pricing comes down to basic planning issues—balancing your goals on margins versus market share and the attractiveness of your benefits versus those of the competition.

As you agonize over prices, remember that they aren't engraved in stone. You are free to raise and lower your prices and to test out new pricing structures on prospects or certain existing customers. Just try not to lose sight of the ramifications of your changes or testing. If you lower your prices for prospects, you may irritate existing customers who learn about the change. If you adjust your prices downward too often, you may find it difficult to raise them. For example, the auto companies and many large mass-market retailers relied so heavily on rebates or sales during the late 1980s and early 1990s that they eventually found it difficult to sell their products at regular prices.

The business plan should include a well-articulated rationale for your company's overall pricing strategy.

Just as the description of the issues that must be dealt with in the marketing plan constitute the longest single segment of this chapter, so should the marketing section of your business plan be the longest single section of the plan. In general, it should be twice as long as the section that follows, on the product or service.

PRODUCT/SERVICE ISSUES: WHAT ARE YOU SELLING?

This is the area of the business that most entrepreneurs love to talk about. They tend to be wrapped up in the details of their product or service—its uniqueness, high quality, or innovativeness. In this section of the business plan, all important aspects of the company's products or services should be dealt with in detail. The following sections describe some of the most important product/service issues.

How Many Bells and Whistles?

Entrepreneurs tend to get wrapped up in the details of product or service performance. Thus, they want to have as many features and options as possible. They are urged on by product designers, engineers, and salespeople who want the same things.

All the recent attention to quality issues has only added to this tendency. Quality is associated with providing as many attributes that the customer could want as possible.

In reality, though, some attributes are more important than others to customers. And some features that rank lowest on the customer priority list may be among the most expensive to include.

I suggest as part of the planning process that you make a list of all the features you expect your product or service to include. That in itself is often revealing. Then go through the list with an eye to *costs* versus *benefits*. You may find that some low-cost features, like a simplified instruction sheet, may give you more bang for the buck than some expensive electronically controlled accessory that most customers have little need for.

This section of the plan should assess your key product or service features and justify their existence.

Can You Deliver?

One of the worst things any company can do is announce a new product or service and then be unable to provide it when promised. It is equally bad when the company ships the product before all the bugs have been worked out, and initial purchasers are irritated. These have been big problems for producers of computer software, hardware, and accessories.

Such *delivery* problems then become *marketing* problems. Customers have developed an image of the company as having uneven quality or as being untrue to its word.

The business plan should address these delivery issues, especially for new products or services. It should provide not only a schedule of events, but an explanation of steps that will be taken to ensure that deadlines are met.

Who Will Provide Ongoing Service?

It's popular for companies of all sizes to offer guarantees and warranties to attract customers. But how will such offerings be administered and who will pay for them? Once again, the answers may become marketing-related issues. Having a more attractive warranty than competitors may help bring in more customers, assuming that they consider warranties a high-priority item. But an attractive warranty can also eat into profit margins. Some companies have turned after-sales service into a separate profit center.

Whatever decision is made, it should be listed in this section, and the rationale for the decision should be explained.

SALES AND PROMOTION: HOW DO YOU SELL?

Now that you have sketched out your marketing and product/service approaches, you are ready to tackle sales. This is the make-or-break issue for any business. As good as your marketing and product/service strategies may be, they will all be for naught if you can't convince prospective customers to buy.

In my experience, selling is the most difficult single task associated with business success. That helps explain why salespeople are usually the most highly paid individuals in most companies. Enlightened executives understand that salespeople bring in the business and don't mind if they earn even more than the president.

To help you map out the sales section of your business plan, the following sections describe the key issues to address.

What Is Your Selling Approach?

There are many ways to sell products and services—via an in-house sales force, sales representatives, executives, or direct mail. If you sell a consumer product, you may have a *multistage selling approach*. That is, your in-house sales force sells to wholesalers, who in turn sell to retailers. Not only must you be on top of the first stage, but you must find ways to influence the second stage, to ensure that your product is purchased by the retailers and displayed and promoted in the retail outlet for maximum sales.

In this section of the business plan, you need to explain and justify your selling approach or approaches. Different selling approaches entail different costs and other demands. Generally speaking, an in-house sales force costs more to support than outside representatives. But because outside representatives are selling several products or services, your company won't get the same level of attention it would get from its own salespeople.

Increasingly, products and services are being sold via more than one sales vehicle. For example, book publishers sell through retail bookstores and direct mail.

Many companies are tied to particular selling approaches because of tradition. Plumbing supplies are sold through wholesalers because they have always been sold that way. Today's most successful growing companies, though, are open to unconventional ways of selling and distributing their products. The high-flying retailers in stationery supplies, hardware, consumer wholesale clubs, and computer products are testimony to the new possibilities.

Alternative approaches are expanding for two reasons. First, for most products or services, *selling costs* are rising dramatically. Second, *competitive pressures* make it difficult to rely on a single approach, especially if competitors are using two or three approaches. Thus, if you use an in-house sales force, you may want to experiment with direct mail. Or if you use only direct mail, you may want to get into retail outlets.

The sales section of your business plan should explain the rationale for a particular sales approach. It should also provide an assessment of costs. And it should evaluate any alternative sales approaches you may be considering to relieve cost and competitive pressures.

How Will You Motivate Your Sellers?

Because selling is so difficult, salespeople need to be trained, supported, and, above all, motivated. They need sales literature, administrative support to send out promotional material, and presentation graphics. They also need *incentives* that work—the right combination of commissions, prizes, stock, and whatever else you might dream up. What are you doing in these areas and what do you plan for the future to upgrade your selling efforts?

If you plan to use new sales approaches, the motivation becomes even more important because it is difficult to know in the early stages which approaches will work best—commissions, bonuses, prizes, or increased vacation time.

Generally speaking, though, a good rule to follow is that when you find something that works, stay with it, even if it means paying what seems to be obscene amounts of cash. The best salespeople should earn top dollar.

How Will You Promote Your Product or Service?

The real issue here is, how will you identify prospective customers? Your sales force can, of course, make calls to individuals in your target market. But beyond that effort, you will likely want a larger-scale approach to generating sales leads and referrals, based on *advertising* and/or *public relations*. Neither choice is either right or wrong, and some companies choose both advertising and public relations. Generally speaking, advertising provides companies with greater control over the message that goes out to the target market but costs more than public relations.

Public relations involves convincing the media to cover your company and/or its executives. Newspaper articles and radio interviews have more credibility than advertising and may thus be more effective than advertising in convincing prospective customers to buy. Equally impressive, such coverage is free. Of course, there is a cost involved in communicating with the media and obtaining its interest. (Chapter 4 provides a detailed discussion of advertising, publicity, and other approaches to promoting your product or service.)

For service companies, in particular, public relations is especially attractive. A big part of selling services involves *creating an image*. This is a tricky issue because the image for many services must be one of trustworthiness and professionalism that advertising tends to work against.

Fortunately, the public relations opportunities for such businesses are tremendous. For example, consultants can serve as experts to be quoted by the press on their area of expertise. Or they can write their own articles for publication in magazines catering to a specific target market. Editors are often in great need of such articles to fill up space, especially if the writer does not have to be paid. The beautiful thing about public relations for service companies is that you can be a one-person business and give the impression of being a national or international firm.

None of this is meant to minimize the public relations opportunities for manufacturers, retailers, and other sellers of products. Companies involved in everything from futuristic technologies to more mundane businesses like machine tools or groceries can obtain publicity—provided they are imaginative and tuned in to the needs of the media.

Once you get mentioned in the press, try to use that success to gain additional publicity. For example, you may be able to leverage magazine articles into radio and television interviews.

The key point here is that *media exposure brings in prospective customers*. The right article or radio mention can generate dozens of leads for salespeople to follow up on. For maximum effectiveness, though, companies must leverage any media exposure.

For example, in telemarketing efforts, it helps a lot after making a cold call if you can offer to send some newspaper or magazine clippings as a follow-up. You can also follow up with existing prospects by using articles that quote the company or its executives. Send them out to individuals who are in a position to recommend customers or to become customers. You can also use such articles in the business plan you intend for investors or lenders, to convince them of your credibility (although the actual article texts are usually best included in the appendix of your business plan).

Whichever promotional choice you make, though, you need a budget. This section of the business plan should explain how much you plan to spend on advertising or public relations.

"Love Letters" and Other Evidence of Success

Another useful promotional tool is a letter of thanks or praise from a customer—commonly referred to as a "love letter." Ideally, you already have some love letters, but if you don't, you can encourage customers to write them. Or you can even write the letters and simply ask customers to sign them.

These can be used to great effect. For example, a Los Angeles store specializing in custom-made men's shirts had a wonderful application of the love letter concept in its store window. Along with displays of shirts were inscribed photos of movie stars. One of Burt Reynolds read, "Thanks always for a perfect fit." Another one of Sylvester Stallone said, "Brilliance!" And a third one of Kirk Douglas had a similar complimentary inscription. That was a brilliant use of love letters.

Another similar tactic, though a bit more tricky, is to use a partial list of clients to give yourself credit. It's tricky because some customers don't take kindly to having their names used publicly, so you have to approach them gingerly.

While love letters and client lists can be excerpted in this section of the business plan, the full texts or lists belong in the appendix.

FINANCIAL ISSUES: HOW ARE YOU DOING?

This section of the business plan covers your financial history and your projections. Ideally, you should look back and ahead between three and five years. You do this with three different types of financial analyses: the cash flow statement, the profit/loss statement, and the balance sheet.

But this section of the plan should also include an explanation or analysis of the numbers. If there have been losses, what do they really signify? If there is much existing debt, how will it be dealt with?

Assembling financial projections has become much easier with the advent of computer spreadsheet programs like Lotus 1-2-3 and Excel. But their very ease of assembly has made many bankers and investors nervous about the projections that entrepreneurs come up with. Some are put off by many pages of such projections, feeling that the numbers have simply been plugged in rather than seriously analyzed.

In any case, this section of the business plan should conform to generally accepted financial and accounting principles. There is no room for creativity. The next sections provide details about the three finance areas entrepreneurs should cover.

Cash Flow: The Business Lifeline

A useful way to learn about cash flow is to view the business as a person. Cash is the nutrient that runs through its arteries and veins.

A famous but unnamed economist once put it aptly when he said, “Cash flow is more important than your mother.” A T-shirt that became popular a few years back reads, “Happiness is positive cash flow.”

Because your business is an organism with cash for blood, insufficient cash flow leads to death; the thriving organism becomes a skeleton. The point here is basic but often overlooked. Cash flow is different from profit, and, for a smaller business, much more important. It’s possible to run out of cash and go broke even as you’re making a major sale that will give the business a profit.

Besides being vitally important, cash flow can be used as a planning tool. By monitoring cash flow on a regular basis as cash comes in and goes out, you develop a record that enables you to plan into the future.

That becomes very important, especially if you want to expand or go after new markets: you can quickly calculate the effect of such actions on the flow of cash and determine whether you’ll need to seek out a bank loan or other financing, or whether you can support the new activity from internally generated funds.

Technically, cash flow is a record of cash available at different points in time. It’s usually monitored on a monthly basis. A cash flow statement may seem complicated when you first look at it, but it's really very simple, and it's extremely important as a planning tool, once you get the hang of it.

You start with the cash on hand at the beginning of the month.

To that you add the receipts during the month from customer payments and any other sources.

From that you subtract the actual disbursements, the cash going out each month in what are generally categorized as fixed and variable expenses. *Fixed expenses* are recurring items that can't easily be changed, such as rent, debt, salaries. *Variable expenses* include advertising, office supplies, promotion, consulting, and other such expenses that can more easily be increased or decreased from month to month.

The result is the amount of cash available at the end of the month. The cash flow is the difference between what the business started and ended with.

The Income Statement: The Bottom Line

The income statement is the one that, for public companies at least, gets all the attention for showing the company's profit or loss.

Actually, it's similar to the cash flow statement. You start with the company's revenues, less any commissions.

From that you subtract direct labor and materials.

The result is a subtotal that is your gross profit or loss. Just as a side note, the percentage of gross profit to revenues can be a very useful number. It's your gross margin, and it can help you to compare yourself to others in your industry, because it immediately tells you whether your labor costs are appropriate.

Next, you subtract from the subtotal indirect labor, administrative labor, and expenses (general and administration), along with depreciation.

The result is another subtotal that is the company's pretax net profit or loss.

From that you subtract a provision for taxes, and the result is, at long last, net income, or the net increase (or decrease) in retained earnings.

The main difference between the cash flow and income statements is one of timing. The cash flow statement is a more accurate barometer of cash on hand at any particular moment.

The Balance Sheet: A Statement of Business Health

The balance sheet is the financial statement bankers like to focus on because they believe it offers the most revealing clues about basic business health by highlighting the state of assets and liabilities at a particular point in time.

On one side of the balance sheet are the company's assets—in terms of *current assets* like cash and accounts receivable, and in terms of *fixed assets* like furniture and computers.

On the other side of the balance sheet are the liabilities—the *current liabilities* in the form of accounts payable and notes payable, and *long-term liabilities* in the form of equity held by investors.

The assets and liabilities add up to the same number.

The balance sheet tends to assume greater importance for manufacturing and other product companies than for service companies because the service companies tend not to have traditional assets like machinery and real estate. Indeed, a balance sheet can be misleading for a service firm, since its primary assets are its people, and it's difficult to measure that in balance sheet form.

Unfortunately, bankers often rely heavily on the balance sheet, using ratios of various assets and liabilities to decide whether a company is creditworthy. Bankers are gradually changing their attitudes, though, as the economy becomes increasingly service oriented.

TARGETING AND WRITING THE PLAN

By this time, you should actually have a fair amount of written material. You should have written a first draft of the executive summary. You should have notes in answer to questions and issues raised about your company, marketing, product, and selling approaches.

Now the challenge is to put it all together into the selling document that is an effective business plan. Two issues need to be addressed in putting together a draft you can begin showing around: targeting and writing.

Who Are the Readers?

As I pointed out early in this chapter, the business plan is meant to influence various stakeholders to support your business. Thus, your business plan should ideally be *targeted at specific stakeholders* most important to your business.

Different stakeholders have different priorities in evaluating businesses; these need to be addressed in the business plan. Sometimes, though, the priorities conflict. For example, bankers tend to be scared by fast growth, while venture capitalists love it.

Taking the targeting need a step further, there is nothing that says you can't have *several* business plans, each targeted to a particular group of stakeholders. These plans need not differ on the basic facts, only in the

EXHIBIT 5.1. Business plan targeting summary.

Stakeholder	Issues to emphasize	Issues to deemphasize	Length
Banker	Cash flow, assets, solid growth	Fast growth, hot market	10–20 pp.
Investor	Fast growth, potential large market, management team	Assets	20–40 pp.
Strategic partner	Synergy, proprietary products	Sales force, assets	20–40 pp.
Large customer	Stability, service	Fast growth, hot market	20–40 pp.
Key employees	Security, opportunity	Technology	20–40 pp.
Merger & acquisition specialist	Past accomplishments	Future outlook	20–40 pp.

presentation of the company's needs. To obtain venture capital, a company may say that it will use the money to stimulate fast growth. To obtain a bank loan, however, that same company may say that it will use the money to improve quality and productivity, with a somewhat slower growth rate.

Exhibit 5.1 summarizes the key targeting issues associated with different stakeholders.

How Can You Write an Effective Plan?

Entrepreneurs often get bogged down in the actual mechanics of writing. The material often comes out too conceptual or disorganized, and they don't know how to fix it. Here are some suggestions to smooth the writing process:

Support Your Goals and Claims

One key to effective writing is the use of examples to back up general statements. This is especially true for business plans.

Supporting evidence should include *statistics, studies*, and *examples*. If you say the market is growing by 12% annually, provide evidence for that statement such as market studies or prior history. Feel free to use anecdotal evidence, but in moderation.

Place One Person in Charge

Another way to ease the writing process is to get as many written inputs as possible from partners or subordinates. You may then have one person write the entire plan or several people each write a section or two.

Whatever your approach, place one person in charge of overseeing the process: setting deadlines, reading drafts, and rewriting material. Otherwise, the process can easily get bogged down. People have a way of avoiding deadlines that they do not perceive as very important. Emphasize that this particular deadline is of the highest priority. The person in charge should then set a deadline for getting the material into a readable format for everyone to review.

Designate an Outside Reader/Editor

As a company's executives get ever more deeply involved in writing the plan, they tend to lose perspective and objectivity. They will use industry buzzwords and shorthand expressions that outsiders won't understand.

The solution to this problem is to get an outsider with some editorial expertise to look at the plan critically—a business school professor, another business owner, or an accountant or lawyer. Try for someone who will be candid. The plan is bound to have problems, and you want to learn about them from someone you designate rather than from a banker or venture capitalist.

This person may even have the skills to rework and reorganize the plan, if necessary. It's all right to have an outsider do some writing, as long as the ideas and supporting evidence come from the company.

Rewrite, Rewrite, Rewrite

I always stress that very few people can write finished prose on their first or even second tries. The secret to successful writing is rewriting. Do a small chunk, leave it for a day or two, and come back to it. Rewrite it, fill it in, and add to it. You'll be surprised at how it will change shape over time.

Set some limits, though. Beyond a certain point—and that varies from person to person—the rewriting process becomes counterproductive. When you sense that is happening, give the plan to the designated outsider for reaction.

At some point, you need to declare the plan complete, for now. But keep in mind that the business plan is never really complete. The business is always changing, so the plan must struggle to keep up. To help in that process, I suggest reviewing the plan at least annually, and preferably more often. As market changes speed up, so does the need to adjust the plan.

And that's all there is to it. Good luck.

6 FINANCIAL PROJECTIONS: HOW TO DO THEM THE RIGHT WAY

Bob Ronstadt

Harold Geneen, the former chairman of IT&T, once said that "to be good at your business, you have to know the numbers—cold." Geneen's advice sounds simple and straightforward. If only it were that simple. Unfortunately, business decision makers need to respond to change and unforeseen events. The numbers change because *nothing* ever turns out precisely the way it is planned.

That doesn't mean you should stop planning or ignore the numbers. Quite the contrary, you need to better understand the numerical dimensions of your business so you can respond as best you can to change when it occurs.[1]

Although Geneen's words are oversimplified, they are nevertheless true for both planning new businesses and managing ongoing operations. In all businesses—whether they are new ventures or established smaller businesses or larger corporations—superior management means having a sense for the *future financial implications* of decisions that must be made today. Geneen knew that to ignore the numbers was dangerous. If you ignore the numbers, particularly the numbers that relate to the future, pretty soon your business will begin to ignore you.

WHAT ARE FINANCIAL PROJECTIONS?

Numbers that relate to the future are called financial projections or financial pro formas. These future-oriented numbers differ greatly from accounting numbers, that is, numbers based on past performance. Financial projections differ from accounting numbers in why, how, and by whom they should be constructed.

At the minimum, a good set of financial projections should include a pro forma income statement, balance sheet, and cash flow statement, along with a detailed explanation of the assumptions that underlie the projections.[2] A comprehensive set of financial projections will also provide a separate sales forecast that will include considerable detail about how the sales numbers are derived. Finally, you should use the data in your projections to compute selected key measures, standard financial ratios, and projected breakevens. The latter are necessary for several reasons, but chiefly to see if your projections are fairly accurate. For instance, a set of projections may look fine until you see that the derived current ratio is simply absurd for a startup in your industry.

The purpose of financial projections is to show what a business will realize in sales, gross profits, net profits, net worth, cash flows, and several other measures associated with the income statement, balance sheet, and cash flow. But more specifically, you usually want to know the answers to several questions. Given your assumptions about 50 to 100 different variables (sales growth rates, receivable collections, rent, wage levels, salaries, interest rates, and so on), you need to ask the following questions:

- How much money will my business need to maintain a positive cash flow?
- When exactly will I need this money?
- What kind of money (debt or equity or both) should it be?

Answering these questions is almost impossible when you use a simple set of *stand-alone projections* because venturing is a *dynamic* process. Things change—often quite rapidly. Yesterday's financial projections are often out-of-date today, and creating a new set simply becomes too time-consuming.

The answer to these realities is a set of financial projections that represents a valid financial model of your business. Instead of a stand-alone income statement, balance sheet, and cash flow statement, you need to *link* these different statements together so that they change when the underlying assumptions and their values change. The fact that all the numbers are related or tied to one another is why these linked financial projections are called *integrated financial statements*.

For the record, financial projections are linked, or *integrated*, when your projected income statement, balance sheets, cash flows, and the assumptions underlying these financial projections are linked by formulas. To be valid, these formulas must be consistent with accepted accounting principles. Your statements also should *tie out*, that is, your balance sheet should still balance whenever you change the assumptions that drive your financial projections.

But you may ask, "Can't I get by with a pasted-up set of stand-alone projections?" The answer is "probably yes." Many investors and bankers don't understand or require integrated financial projections. You may be able to satisfy them with stand-alone projections. But the sharper ones will require linked financials because they know that a new set of conditions will emerge almost as soon as you are out the door. What will you do then? Ignore or misread the financial implications? No, the savvy investor or banker wants to be sure you understand how the numbers in your business are interconnected. They also want to be sure you have the ability to determine the financial implications of unforeseen changes that are likely to occur.

This chapter explains how financial projections should be constructed and why the leaders of a business need to understand these projections if they are ever to take control of their financial decision making. But first the chapter shows:

- Why financial projections are actually quite difficult to construct.
- Why financial projections are rarely constructed properly, even when spreadsheets are used.
- Why financial projections should be constructed by the principal decision makers of a business, despite the difficulty involved.

Although these observations probably sound like a lot of bad news, the good news is that linked financial projections have an ongoing business use. Unlike the one-use, misleading stand-alone projections, linked financial projections stay with you, once they have been created, and can help you make better management decisions.

WHY FINANCIAL PROJECTIONS ARE DIFFICULT TO PRODUCE

"What happens" when "what if" happens? The future is concerned with "what if." As you change basic assumptions about sales growth, wage levels, product costs, and so on, you need to know more than their profit-and-loss (P&L) effect. You also need to understand their effect on cash flow, on your balance sheet, and on a variety of other derived measures (for example, breakevens on selected financial ratios).

In other words, to play "what if" appropriately, you need to know what happens not just to sales, wages, and product costs but also to operating cash flow. For example, how are inventory levels, accounts receivable and accounts payable affected? What happens to profitability, breakeven, and owner's equity? Before long, implementing this "simple" process gets detailed, downright complicated, and, for lack of better words, "intensely muddy."

It also gets exhausting. The point is that before you can simplify your numbers and know them cold, you must first produce literally thousands of numbers. It's an arduous job, even with an electronic spreadsheet. Then, to add insult to injury, you should know that most of the numbers are wrong.

Why does this happen? It happens because of technical errors. First, you need to realize that the real problems associated with producing good financial projections aren't *forecasting errors* of one kind or another. For instance, sales have always been difficult for most ventures to predict, and always will be. No one has a crystal ball, and plans rarely, if ever, work out the way intended because actual sales and cost numbers rarely match budgeted or forecasted numbers. No, the real problem lies in *technical errors;* specifically, the implicit, incomplete, and misleading financial models that most people create when putting together their financial projections, whether they use paper, pencil, and calculator, or an electronic spreadsheet.

WHY FINANCIAL PROJECTIONS ARE RARELY CONSTRUCTED PROPERLY

Why do people serious about making good decisions rely on faulty financial models? There are two reasons, and they reside in two myths:

- *Myth #1:* Most people, especially those schooled in business, believe that they can develop technically correct financial projections.

  The Reality: Most people, including most MBAs, cannot develop anything more than crude, generally misleading, financial projections.
- *Myth #2:* Spreadsheets alone (or with financial templates) make it possible for most people to create technically correct financial projections that can be used for business planning and budgeting purposes, that is, financial decision making.

  The Reality: Only a tiny percentage of spreadsheet users are capable of putting together integrated financial projections, and even they are prone to commit spreadsheet errors. They are a select group who are very advanced in both their spreadsheet skills and their accounting/finance skills. A rare breed indeed.

Consequently, most people don't really "know the numbers," cold or otherwise; they only think they know them. This lack of knowledge isn't simply a failure to "push the numbers." That used to be a problem when calculations were done with paper, pencil, calculator, and eraser. Fortunately, the proliferation of spreadsheets helped to overcome the pure tedium of number pushing. Unfortunately, spreadsheets compounded the problem by giving people the idea that financial projections were now easier than ever to produce. Spreadsheets certainly allow people to push numbers. But, unfortunately, when it comes to financial projections, the folks using spreadsheets rarely derive the correct numbers and only rarely understand the numbers they create so plentifully.

The hard cold fact you must learn to accept is that deriving correct business numbers is impossible when working with financial models that are incomplete more often than not, and that also contain accounting or mathematical errors. To use some software lingo, the resulting financial projections are *internally corrupted.* The numbers are wrong because the implicit models people adopt are technically wrong. To use another software expression, it's classic GIGO: Garbage in, garbage out. And because the underlying assumptions aren't explicit in nine out of ten spreadsheet models, the garbage is nicely hidden from view.

What's So Important about Integrated Financials Anyway?

In life, especially business life, good ideas aren't much help if you can't execute them. And the quality and accuracy of your execution is everything. For planning and budgeting, quality and accuracy means translating your assumptions about different alternatives into a set of financial projections that are linked together into a financial model that reflects your business.

Why is this unique financial model needed? It's needed because everything you know about the first part of Geneen's advice, that is, "to be good at your business," points to understanding the interconnected totality of your decisions. Just as a business is a web of interconnected individuals and resources where every decision impacts everyone to some degree, so the various statements of your financial projections need to be interconnected because they impact one another.

For instance, let's suppose you want to add several employees, buy a piece of expensive equipment, or start or end a sales campaign. In each of these instances, you need to see the likely financial impact of your decisions. And you need to see how these decisions affect not only your income statement, but also your cash flow, balance sheet, and numerous financial measures, including breakevens.

In short, financial projections must be tied together, or *integrated*, to have much utility—not just for strategic purposes but for everyday financial decision making.

Without this total picture, disaster can occur. For instance, projected P&Ls that show healthy profits can mask *negative operating cash flows* and *weak balance sheets* that literally drive a business into the ground. Business leaders need a full representation of their businesses, not an isolated snapshot of an individual projection that shows only part of the story.

Integrated financial projections are especially needed when a business takes a nose dive. Good times can mask all kinds of errors. But when the bad times come, and we all see them at one time or another, there is no room for error. At these difficult moments, integrated financial models are nearly priceless. Hard decisions must be made. What projects get axed? What equipment, property, or other assets must be sold? Which vendors must wait to be paid? How much should salaries be cut? Who gets a pink slip? How soon should these actions and others be taken?

Decisions like these are never easy to make, but it helps immeasurably to know the impact of each decision on the "ending cash balance" of your cash flow projection. Many businesses that will fail in the future can be saved if they have but one tool: a financial model that produces integrated financials.

WHO SHOULD PRODUCE YOUR FINANCIAL PROJECTIONS?

The short answer is that you need to produce and understand your financial projections. The problem, however, with the short answer is that it doesn't reflect the realities of existing deficiencies in your awareness about and skills for developing integrated financials.

A wise friend once told me that the road to truth and knowledge begins by becoming aware of the things you don't know you don't know. If you are aware that you don't know something, that's 80% of the battle. It's those things about which you are totally oblivious that are the real snares of life. Integrated financials represents one such snare.

So first, *you need to recognize that significant obstacles exist when it comes to developing meaningful financial projections.* Despite intellectual muscle flexing by "spreadsheet power users," business consultants, and even some business school professors, the reality is that most people can't put together a valid and useful set of financial projections in a reasonable period of time. The reason is that for mere mortals, they are actually quite difficult to prepare.

Second, *you need to understand the concept of integrated financials and realize its importance for doing everyday financial decision making.* Fudging your financials, or putting together with a set of unlinked or stand-alone projections (for example, the income statement isn't linked to the cash flow or balance sheet) simply won't do. A financial model that truly reflects your business is a tremendous decision-making asset. In fact, I have found that it can be the difference between success and failure—not just for occasional planning and budgeting exercises, but, when necessary, for running your venture from day to day.

Given the real difficulties involved, *you will probably need to find someone who will help you to build these financial decision-making models.* The person may be a CFO, financial analyst, or accountant within your own organization. Also, there are financial business consultants who do understand integrated financials and how to implement them, and most importantly how to teach you to modify and use the model.

HOW TO PRODUCE INTEGRATED FINANCIAL PROJECTIONS

The traditional way to produce financial projections is to do the following:

1. Build a sales forecast.
2. Use the projected sales revenue as a basis for deriving a projected income statement—for example, the income statement is produced either by using historical percentage analysis or by simply making assumptions about the relationship of each cost item as a percentage of total sales. For instance, you can assume that future cost of goods sold will be 70% of projected total sales if, for one reason or another the historical cost of goods sold has been 70% of past sales (for the industry, or for other startups during their first year, or based on your own company experience if you have prior history). If forecasted sales are projected to be $1,000,000, then cost of goods sold will be 70% of this total, or $700,000. The same procedure is then used for all other expense items, calculating them individually as a percentage of total sales.
3. Use a similar approach to generate a balance sheet—for example, each balance sheet item can be derived by using its historical relationship to total assets. An alternative method is to use historical ratios (such as the accounts receivable turnover period or the inventory turnover period) to derive the projected balance sheet.
4. Build a cash flow statement using one of several approaches, including:
   - Do a rough approximation of the *net* cash flows by taking profit after tax and adding back depreciation and other accounting items that are not real cash outflows. (I don't recommend this approach.)
   - Calculate changes in beginning and ending balance sheets to derive the net change in cash. (This approach is ok, but it is tough for most practitioners to do.)
   - Actually track cash inflows and cash outflows over a *relevant time period*.(For most startups, a relevant time period is a month. For other startups, and most turnaround situations, the relevant time period is often a week. Avoid quarterly and especially annual cash flows since these longer time periods can mask all sorts of potential cash flow disasters.)

This traditional approach for generating financial projections is fine for "quick & dirty" analysis, that is, to get a fast but rough idea about what a business will be like in numerical terms. But the traditional approach has four major deficiencies:

- It generally fails to be explicit about the assumptions that are producing the numbers.
- The individual statements aren't linked together, so the real picture isn't being produced, only (at best) a close likeness.
- Most practitioners don't understand the implications of the numbers, principally because they aren't linked together and because they aren't linked to other measures (ratios, breakevens, industry-specific measures, and business valuations) that help us to understand their implications.
- Major alternatives and unforeseen changes in your business are very difficult to quickly incorporate into these partial models without almost completely redoing them.

Using the traditional approach is a little like riding a bicycle on a freeway. The bicycle is okay for academic off-road games, but it won't do for real world applications. Instead I recommend you travel your business highways in a real automobile, that is, take the time to build an integrated financial model of your business. To build one, you must do the following:

1. **Be explicit about your assumptions by first building an assumptions statement.** (A sample assumptions statement is presented later in Exhibit 6.3 for a retail business.)[3] Remember, an assumptions statement is no less important than your income statement, balance sheet statement, or cash flow statement. It's what produces them. List your sales assumptions, your P&L assumptions, your balance sheet assumptions, your cash flow assumptions, plus other assumptions as they relate to supporting budgets or output analysis such as breakevens; for instance, what percentage of cost of sales is a variable cost?

2. **Make certain you understand the general interrelationships between your assumptions and the sales revenue projection, the income or P&L projection, the balance sheet projection, and the cash flow projection.** In other words, you need to know how your projected financial statements are related to one another as a group.

3. **Make certain you understand the specific relationships between line items within and across the different statements.** Such knowledge will enable you to make better venture decisions by knowing:

   How the individual components or line items of each financial statement are linked together *within* the same statement;

   How the individual components of each financial statement are linked to components with the same or similar names on different statements; for example, how is "cash" on the balance sheet linked to "cash" on the cash flow statement; and

EXHIBIT 6.1. A specific relationship between financial statements.

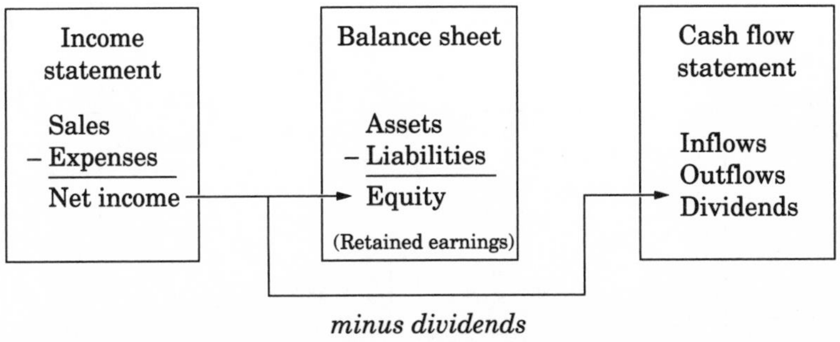

How the individual components of each financial statement are linked to different components in other financial statements.

In the latter two cases, you especially want to know the number of items involved in each linkage and the direction of the association. For example, net income from the income statement and retained earnings from the balance sheet are linked. However, you also need to know that retained earnings is derived from net income, not vice versa. Exhibit 6.1 illustrates these linkages. And you need to know what other variables, if any, are involved (or could be involved) in the calculation; for example, if dividends were declared, they would have to be subtracted from net income and subtracted from ending cash on the cash flow statement.

Once you understand how these specific linkages work, you will better understand not only what it takes to balance your balance sheet, but also how to obtain answers about how much money your business will need, when it will need this money, and what kind of money it can or should be.

GENERAL RELATIONSHIPS BETWEEN THE PROJECTED FINANCIAL STATEMENTS

Now examine how projected financial statements are linked together as a group. A diagram helps you to visualize these general linkages. Graphically, the relationships between the statements are shown in Exhibit 6.2.

After providing information for an assumptions statement (including optional data for a beginning balance sheet for Period #0), Exhibit 6.2 traces how this information flows to produce the values in the sales forecast, the income statement, the balance sheet, and the cash flow statement. Here's how it works:

- Selected values that are produced in the sales forecast (such as net sales) based on data taken from the assumptions statement flow directly into the income statement for Period #1.

EXHIBIT 6.2. General linkages between core statements.

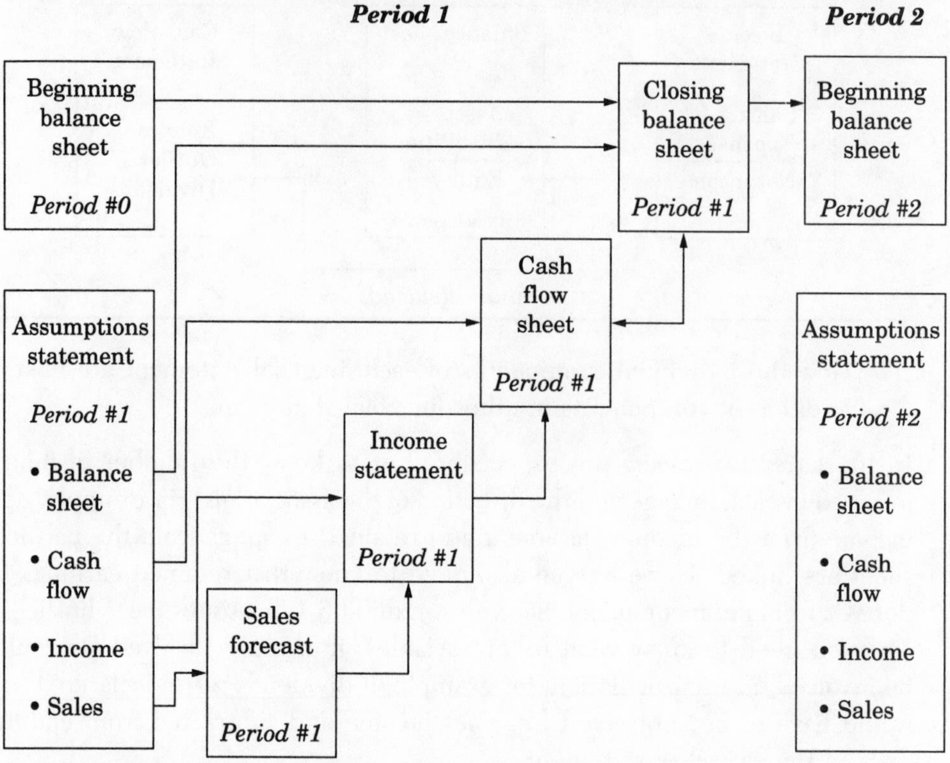

- Beginning balance sheet values for Period #0 (if you have listed them under the *base period* in the balance sheet statement) are combined with information for Period #1 from the assumptions statement, the income statement, and the cash flow statement to create the values shown in the closing balance sheet for Period #1. [*Note:* The closing balance sheet for Period #1 becomes the beginning balance sheet for Period #2, and the process continues for the total number of time periods being projected. In Exhibit 6.2, the beginning balance sheet (sometimes called the opening, or base period, balance sheet) is shown as part of the balance sheet statement because this positioning is conventional; however, the base period items and values are effectively assumptions that can be listed in the assumptions statement and linked by formulas to Period #1 of the balance sheet.]
- Certain information is also flowing from the closing balance sheet into the cash flow statement. This information is supplemented with data drawn from the assumptions statement and the income statement to produce the values shown in the cash flow statement.
- Then, the process is repeated for Period #2, Period #3, and so on.

SPECIFIC RELATIONSHIPS BETWEEN THE PROJECTED FINANCIAL STATEMENTS

Although *general relationships* exist between projected financial statements, there are many specific ways to configure projected financial statements, perhaps as many as there are different ventures. Some obvious differences exist between industries. However, differences in projected financial statements can also exist within the same industry. Sometimes these differences are minor and at other times they are quite significant in the number of individual items and the way individual items are derived and linked together. Consequently, there are unlimited specific kinds of financial statements and multiple ways to derive the specific linkages across statements. What follows represents but one way. Yet, because many of the variations can be minor, it serves as a blueprint for building and linking together the components of financial projections.

Case Study

Because actual numbers help trace the linkages, let's assume you are planning to expand a small retail venture you recently started. Assume you've just finished completing the assumptions statement shown in Exhibit 6.3. You've also filled out the base period, or beginning, balance sheet column on the balance sheet statement. Your program should then compute your monthly revenue statement, income statement, balance sheet, and cash flow for the next 12 months. (Each of these statements is presented and discussed in the following sections.) The assumptions made in Exhibit 6.3 can be summarized as follows:

- Annual sales are $300,000 for Store A (eventually, you hope to start two or three more stores).
- The spread of sales shows a strong seasonality factor with 20% and 26% of total sales realized respectively in November and December. *Note:* The sales formula multiplies $300,000 by each month's seasonality factor, which projects monthly sales; thus, the $300,000 shown in January is not simply replicated across all 12 months for total sales of $3,600,000.
- A 10% annual growth rate is used to calculate 1989 sales, which are used to figure certain 1988 items (for example, purchases) that need to "look into" January and February of 1989 to calculate and derive November and December values.
- Cost of goods is projected at 45% of total sales based on prior experience.
- Operating expenses include the addition of a store manager (so we can subsequently start Store B). Advertising is increased to 3% (from 0%).
- Assets are depreciated over seven years.

EXHIBIT 6.3. Sample assumptions statement for a retail company.

	1/31/88 Retail	2/29/88 Retail	3/31/88 Retail	4/30/88 Retail	5/31/88 Retail	6/30/88 Retail	7/31/88 Retail	8/31/88 Retail	9/30/88 Retail	10/31/88 Retail	11/30/88 Retail	12/31/88 Retail
Revenue forecast assumptions:												
Annual sales, Store A	$300,000											
Percent of sales allocated / month	4.0%	5.5%	3.5%	5.0%	9.0%	7.0%	5.0%	2.0%	4.0%	9.0%	20.0%	26.0%
Should sum to 100%	100.0%											
Growth rate next year:												
Growth rate Store A	10%											
Income statement assumptions:												
Cost of goods as a percent of sales												
Store A	45.00%											
Store A: Monthly operating expenses												
Store A manager's salary	$2,500											
Salespeople salaries:												
Base salaries	$750											
Commission rate	5.00%											
Advertising and promotion, Store A	3.00%											
Rent, Store A	$1,500											
Supplies, Store A	3.00%											
Telephone, utilities, and insurance	$1,000											
Store payroll tax and benefit rate	18.00%											
Balance sheet assumptions:												
Inventory purchases:												
Enter minimum purchasing lead time, in months to receive inventory	2											
Please review your inventory. You may want to increase or decrease your inventory.												
Enter your adjustments below:												
Inventory adjustments Store A	$6,300	$7,000	$0	$0	$0	$0	$0	$0	$0	$0	$0	$0
Fixed assets purchased:												
Fixed assets Store A	$25,000	$0	$0	$0	$0	$0	$0	$0	$0	$0	$0	$0
Depreciation schedule:												
Store fixed assets (in years)	7											

EXHIBIT 6.3. *(Continued)*

	1/31/88 Retail	2/29/88 Retail	3/31/88 Retail	4/30/88 Retail	5/31/88 Retail	6/30/88 Retail	7/31/88 Retail	8/31/88 Retail	9/30/88 Retail	10/31/88 Retail	11/30/88 Retail	12/31/88 Retail
Cash flow assumptions:												
Base period accounts receivable received	100%	0%	0%	0%	0%	0%	0%	0%	0%	0%	0%	0%
Monthly sales collected:												
% collected 0–30 days	80%											
% collected 31–60 days	10%											
% collected 61–90 days	5%											
% collected 90+ days	5%											
Total monthly sales collected	100%											
Base period accounts payable paid	40%	50%	10%	0%	0%	0%	0%	0%	0%	0%	0%	0%
Monthly expenses paid:												
% paid 0–30 days	70%											
% paid 31–60 days	30%											
% paid 61–90 days	0%											
% paid 90+ days	0%											
Total monthly expenses paid	100%											
Vendor deposits required	$1,250	0%	0%	0%	0%	0%	0%	0%	0%	0%	0%	0%
Line of credit:												
Annual line of credit interest rate	12.00%											
Maximum line of credit	$50,000											
Notes payable:												
Annual note interest rate	11.50%											
Term of note in months	60											
Minimum cash balance	$5,000											
Additional funding:												
New equity	$15,000	$0	$0	$0	$0	$0	$0	$0	$0	$0	$0	$0
New debt (notes payable)	$20,000	$0	$0	$0	$0	$0	$0	$0	$0	$0	$0	$0
Projected breakeven assumptions:												
Variable portion of cost of goods	50.0%											
Variable portion of store salaries	20.0%											
Variable portion of advertising and promotions	30.0%											

- Payroll taxes and benefits have been increased to 18% due to a new employee benefits package.
- Purchases need to be made two months in advance of actual delivery, on average. *Note:* The formula related to the two-month lead time won't show any inventory purchases until Month #3; consequently, you need to enter your assumed inventory purchases for January and February ($6,300 and $7,000, respectively).
- Cash flow assumptions show that 100% of your *prior* accounts receivable will be collected in January. These were a few known customers, who were allowed to charge their purchases. However, you've decided to liberalize your policy to allow more store accounts. You believe collections will be slower (represented by the 80%, 10%, 5%, 5% spread of accounts receivable over 90+ days), but will be more than offset by greater sales compared to last year.
- *Prior* year's payables will be paid over a three-month period with 40% paid in January, 50% in February, and 10% in March.
- Accounts payable incurred in 1988 will be paid faster (70% within 30 days and 30% within 60 days) to improve credit ratings with suppliers so that good terms can be obtained when Store B is started.
- An additional $25,000 in fixed assets will be purchased in January to improve Store A. Some vendor deposits ($1,250) have been made for various deposits.
- Remaining long-term debt ($20,000) is payable over five years or 60 months at 11.50%. You also have a $50,000 line of credit at 12% with your bank where you must maintain a minimum cash balance of $5,000.
- Additional funding is set at zero for both new equity and new debt, so you can determine the minimum cash balance (to be shown in the cash flow statement). This figure will tell you if you need additional funding, and how much you need. The monthly ending cash balance will indicate when you will need these funds. You can then experiment with injecting different amounts of equity or debt into the venture to see what kinds of financial projections are associated with different combinations of debt and equity.

In order to calculate the amount of sales the store needs to break even for different assumptions and financial projections, you also need to make rough estimates to what extent monthly costs are totally variable (100% means these costs vary directly with each incremental sale, that is, the cost is not incurred until the sale is made) versus totally fixed (0% means these costs must be paid even if nothing is sold). For example, salaries (0%) must be paid each month even if there are no sales. Thus, salaries are totally fixed costs. However, advertising and promotion is 30% variable because the promotions portion (30%) is paid *only* when someone buys something. Advertising is 70% of the budget, and it is fixed because you must pay your advertising bill even if you sell nothing.

The Revenue Statement (or Sales Forecast)

The better business plans I've read over the last decade usually did a fairly good job of forecasting their costs. Though it is sometimes tedious, you can generally obtain good ballpark estimates of R&D, marketing, production, and administrative expenses. If these "better plans" had a flaw, it was their estimates of sales revenues or the *top line*.

Before startup, the top line is the most important line for nearly all entrepreneurial enterprises. After startup, other lines may assume greater importance. For instance, a materials-intensive manufacturing enterprise may need to monitor inventory and purchasing of certain materials much more closely than sales (once these are known for some relevant period of time). The reason is that slight variations in materials costs can have a devastatingly negative or incredibly positive impact on profits compared to slight changes in sales.[4] But before venture launch, the top line is usually the hardest line to forecast accurately. (That's why I've separated sales from the income statement and given it the status of a separate statement.)

Unexpected sales growth or sales decline can cause an increase in cash needs that pushes you above the upper limit of your venture's required capitalization. For instance, you need to know the *maximum sales increase* for which you have sufficient cash to cover related increases in costs and cash outflows that may suddenly begin increasing faster than cash inflows. Conversely, you need to know the *maximum sales declines* for which you have sufficient cash to cover decreases in cash inflows that may be occurring faster than the decline in costs and cash outflows.

Exhibit 6.4 illustrates the capital you'll need in different sales scenarios. The shaded portion represents a range of sales. Your ultimate task (in terms of entrepreneurial finance) is to discover what is the appropriate amount of capital that will finance not just likely sales, but the entire range of sales possibilities between pessimistic and optimistic sales forecasts.

The Components of the Sales Revenue Statement

There can be one or many items in a sales revenue statement. There may be no more than a single line (for example, net sales) if you are doing a quick feasibility analysis as is the case for the retail venture described in the case study. Exhibit 6.5 provides a sample retail revenue statement. Of course, many additional line items can be involved for a more detailed forecast of sales. For instance, a slightly more complicated sales forecast

EXHIBIT 6.4. Capital needed for a range of sales.

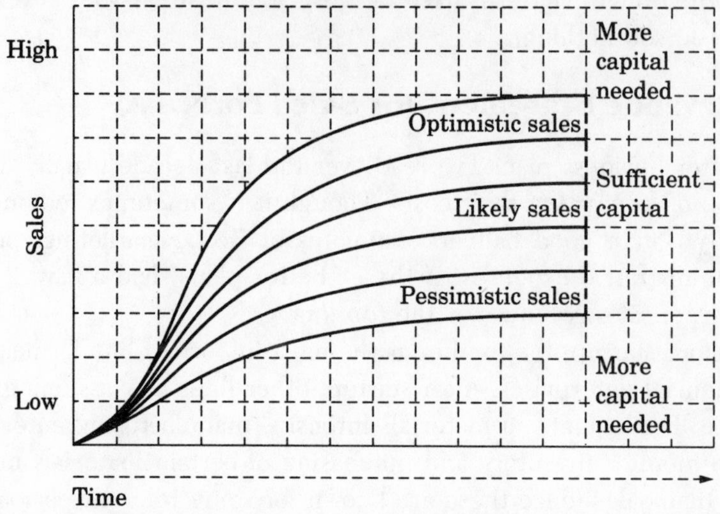

may break out sales discounts, deductions, and/or returns. More extensive calculations of sales may show units and prices for different products and services. Detailed sales forecasts may disaggregate sales by location (Store A, Store B, and so on), channel of distribution, or many other ways.

The Derivation of the Sales Forecast's Components

For the retail venture, the analysis is fairly simple for the first cut to see if the venture expansion is feasible. The analysis can be refined later. Based on some preliminary work, $300,000 in annual sales represents a realistic top line. The assumptions statement assumes a seasonality spreading of these sales based on discussions with other retailers in related businesses. Consequently, monthly sales in Exhibit 6.5 are derived in the revenue statement simply by multiplying the annual sales assumption by the percent of sales allocated per month (both found in the assumptions statement).

The Income Statement

The income statement presents your venture's performance over a specified period of time (be it a month, quarter, or year) in terms of sales, costs, and profits or losses. A projected income statement's main purpose is to show how much profit (or loss) you hope to earn based on when you make your sales and legitimately incur your costs, as opposed to when you actually collect the cash for the sales or pay for the costs you are obligated to pay.

EXHIBIT 6.5. Sample revenue forecast for a retail company.

	1/31/88 Retail	2/29/88 Retail	3/31/88 Retail	4/30/88 Retail	5/31/88 Retail	6/30/88 Retail	7/31/88 Retail	8/31/88 Retail	9/30/88 Retail	10/31/88 Retail	11/30/88 Retail	12/31/88 Retail	Year 1 Retail
Sales, Store A	$12,000	$16,500	$10,500	$15,000	$27,000	$21,000	$15,000	$6,000	$12,000	$27,000	$60,000	$78,000	$300,000
Net sales	$12,000	$16,500	$10,500	$15,000	$27,000	$21,000	$15,000	$6,000	$12,000	$27,000	$60,000	$78,000	$300,000
Monthly increase/decrease in sales	0%	38%	(36%)	43%	80%	(22%)	(29%)	(60%)	100%	125%	122%	30%	N/A

EXHIBIT 6.6. Sample income statement for a retail company.

	1/31/88 Retail	2/29/88 Retail	3/31/88 Retail	4/30/88 Retail	5/31/88 Retail	6/30/88 Retail	7/31/88 Retail	8/31/88 Retail	9/30/88 Retail	10/31/88 Retail	11/30/88 Retail	12/31/88 Retail	Year 1 Retail
Net sales	$12,000	$16,500	$10,500	$15,000	$27,000	$21,000	$15,000	$6,000	$12,000	$27,000	$60,000	$78,000	$300,000
Cost of goods	5,400	7,425	4,725	6,750	12,150	9,450	6,750	2,700	5,400	12,150	27,000	35,100	135,000
Gross profit	6,600	9,075	5,775	8,250	14,850	11,550	8,250	3,300	6,600	14,850	33,000	42,900	165,000
Operating expenses:													
Payroll, taxes, and benefits	4,543	4,809	4,455	4,720	5,428	5,074	4,720	4,189	4,543	5,428	7,375	8,437	63,720
Occupancy	2,500	2,500	2,500	2,500	2,500	2,500	2,500	2,500	2,500	2,500	2,500	2,500	30,000
Advertising and promotion	360	495	315	450	810	630	450	180	360	810	1,800	2,340	9,000
Supplies and other	360	495	315	450	810	630	450	180	360	810	1,800	2,340	9,000
Depreciation	714	714	714	714	714	714	714	714	714	714	714	714	8,571
Total operating expenses	8,477	9,013	8,299	8,834	10,262	9,548	8,834	7,763	8,477	10,262	14,189	16,331	120,291
Operating profit (loss)	(1,877)	62	(2,524)	(584)	4,588	2,002	(584)	(4,463)	(1,877)	4,588	18,811	26,569	44,709
Interest expenses/income	288	476	486	621	665	597	524	496	587	775	920	733	7,168
Net income before taxes	$(2,165)	$(413)	$(3,010)	$(1,205)	$3,922	$1,405	$(1,108)	$(4,959)	$(2,464)	$3,812	$17,890	$25,835	$37,540

The Derivation of the Income Statement's Components

In the retail store example, several items (gross profit, total operating expenses, operating profit, and net income before taxes) are calculated internally from other income statement items. Also, you've already seen how one item, net sales, has simply been copied from the revenue statement. The actual values are shown in Exhibit 6.6. The remaining items are all derived as follows:

Note: The source of each item in the following list is shown in brackets when it comes from a statement other than the income statement.

- *Cost of goods* is calculated by multiplying net sales by 45% (the Cost of goods as a percentage of sales for Store A [assumptions statement]).
- *Payroll, taxes, and benefits* is calculated by adding payroll to taxes and benefits. First, payroll is derived by adding the store manager's salary [assumptions statement] to the product of net sales on the income statement times the 5% commission rate [assumptions statement]. Then, taxes and benefits are calculated by multiplying base salaries [assumptions statement] by the 18% store payroll tax and benefit rate [assumptions statement].
- *Occupancy* is calculated by adding monthly rent [assumptions statement] plus monthly telephone, utilities, and insurance [assumptions statement].
- *Advertising and promotion* is calculated by multiplying net sales on the income statement by the 3% monthly advertising and promotion rate [assumptions statement].
- *Supplies and other* is calculated by multiplying net sales by the 3% monthly supplies rate [assumptions statement].
- *Depreciation* is calculated by using a straight line depreciation function that is equivalent to rounding the figure for total property and equipment at cost [balance sheet] for Period #1 to $60,000 and dividing it by seven years, the store fixed assets depreciation rate [assumptions statement], and then dividing this total ($8,571) by 12 months to arrive at the $714 of monthly depreciation shown on the income statement.
- *Interest expense/income* is calculated by multiplying the beginning principal balance [cash flow statement] times the 11.5% annual interest rate [assumptions statement] divided by 12 months *plus* the previous period's line of credit [balance sheet] times the 12% annual line of credit interest rate [assumptions statement] divided by 12 months.

The Balance Sheet

A balance sheet is a statement of a venture's financial position at a specific point in time. It gives a snapshot of the venture's financial position at this time, expressed in terms either of historical costs for an accounting statement or future costs when a balance sheet is used for financial projections. Often the date of a balance sheet coincides with the ending date of an income statement; however, you should remember that the income statement is showing sales, expenses, and profit activity *over a specified period*, whereas the balance sheet is showing the venture's financial position *exclusively as of the ending date.*

Actually, there are at least two balance sheets you need to consider when generating a set of linked financial projections: one is the opening balance sheet, and the other is a closing balance sheet. The *opening balance sheet* contains all prior transactions, and is sometimes called the base period, or beginning, balance sheet. The *closing balance sheet*, as the name suggests, shows the status of your assets, liabilities, and equities at the end of a specified period.

One reason you need two balance sheets on the balance sheet statement is that the other projected financial statements encompass or cross some period of time. However, the balance sheet is different. It shows the status of an enterprise at a specific point in time, for example, on January 1, 1990, when you first committed some significant dollar resources to your venture. It's vital to recognize at least two balance sheets because the comparison of the two statements allows us to understand how an organization changed the size and deployment of its assets and liabilities during the time period.

The opening balance sheet is unique because it represents either:

- A statement of historical fact, for example, I've started working on this venture and here are the assets I've allocated and the liabilities I've incurred, and the equity I've invested up to this point in time; or
- An assumption about the future set of assets, liabilities, and equity I will bring to the initiation of the venture.

If the latter, you may ask, "Then why isn't the opening balance sheet part of the balance sheet assumptions in the assumptions statement?" The answer is that it could be included in the assumptions statement. However, convention and convenience require us to show the opening balance sheet (or at least some base period) on the balance sheet statement so it can be compared easily with other projected balance sheets.

What the initial time point of an opening balance sheet should be for a new venture is a matter of judgment. To be informative, the opening balance sheet should be prepared after some assets have been obtained and deployed. The key point is that every venture has an opening balance sheet. Even if you aren't explicit about its existence, an implicit balance sheet exists. Theoretically, one exists from the time you first had the idea for your venture, even if you had zero assets invested and zero liabilities incurred at that point.

Obviously, listing a balance sheet with zero assets and liabilities is not very informative; consequently, it usually pays to select a base period to mark the beginning point of your business for comparative purposes. The fact that the base period is not necessarily the first balance sheet does not matter for our purposes since a balance sheet captures all that has transpired financially up to that time.

For instance, Base Period #5 in Exhibit 6.7 incorporates all prior balance sheet transactions, covering a 60-day prestartup period for a venture. See if you can explain the transactions that have occurred by the end of each period shown in Exhibit 6.7:

- *Period #1:* The end of Day 1 marks the birth of your venture idea. No financial transactions have taken place yet, but an implicit balance sheet already exists.
- *Period #2:* As of Day 15, the following transactions have occurred: $10,000 has been invested in the venture as *equity* and appears as $10,000 in cash on the asset side of the balance sheet.
- *Period #3:* As of Day 30, an additional $10,000 has been borrowed as long-term debt, raising total liabilities and equities to $20,000. Cash is increased to $20,000 on the asset side of the balance sheet.
- *Period #4:* As of Day 45, $5,000 of trade payables have been incurred to finance the buildup of $5,000 worth of Inventory.
- *Period #5:* As of Day 60, no charges occur on the liabilities and equities side of the balance sheet. However, $5,000 is used to purchase (for cash) some fixed assets.

EXHIBIT 6.7. Opening balance sheet or base period.

	Idea for venture	Prestartup period (no sales)			60 days later
	Day 1 Period #1	Day 15 Period #2	Day 30 Period #3	Day 45 Period #4	Day 60 Period #5
Cash	$ 0	$10,000	$20,000	$20,000	$15,000
Inventory	0	0	0	5,000	5,000
Fixed assets	0	0	0	0	5,000
TOTAL ASSETS	$ 0	$10,000	$20,000	$25,000	$25,000
Trade payables	0	0	0	5,000	5,000
Long-term debt	0	0	10,000	10,000	10,000
Equity	0	10,000	10,000	10,000	10,000
TOTAL LIABILITIES AND EQUITY	$ 0	$10,000	$20,000	$25,000	$25,000

Although these transactions are simple, they reveal two important things about the balance sheet:

- The size of your balance sheet in terms of total assets can increase (as it did in Period #3 and #4) if you simply increase long-term or short-term debt.
- Shifts in assets and liabilities can occur that will have a definite impact on the amount of cash you end up with.

The Derivation of the Balance Sheet's Components

The retail venture's balance sheet is shown in Exhibit 6.8. The numbers for the opening balance sheet come from either historical data or assumed data that are entered directly into each line item of the base period, just as sales, income, and cash flow assumptions are entered directly into the assumptions statement. [*Note:* In the present model, the only requirement is that the amount of total assets you enter in the base period must equal total liabilities and equities. There is no discretionary balancing, or "plug," figure that automatically equalizes these totals for the base period. The formulas for this model are written to start at Period #1, so you do not necessarily have to enter an opening balance sheet since the equalizing precondition is still satisfied in the base period when zero assets equals zero liabilities and equities.]

The derivation of the numbers for the closing balance sheet is described in the following lists, with the source statement for variables shown in brackets if the variable comes from a statement other than the balance sheet.

Current assets are derived as follows:

- *Cash and equivalents* is derived from the ending cash balance [cash flow statement] for the period in question.
- *Accounts receivable* is derived from the previous period's accounts receivable plus the current period's net sales [income statement] *after* subtracting total cash receipts [cash flow statement].
- *Inventories* is derived by adding purchases [cash flow statement] to the previous period's inventories and then subtracting cost of goods [income statement].

Fixed assets are derived as follows:

- *Net property and equipment at cost* is calculated by adding the previous period's fixed assets at cost plus fixed assets purchased [assumptions statement] minus accumulated depreciation.
- *Accumulated depreciation* is calculated by adding the previous period's accumulated depreciation plus the current period's depreciation [income statement].

EXHIBIT 6.8. Sample balance sheet for a retail company.

	Base period	1/31/88	2/29/88	3/31/88	4/30/88	5/31/88	6/30/88	7/31/88	8/31/88	9/30/88	10/31/88	11/30/88	12/31/88
Assets													
Current assets:													
Cash and equivalents	$24,700	$34,893	$5,000	$5,000	$5,000	$5,000	$5,000	$5,000	$5,000	$5,000	$610	$5,000	$19,197
Accounts receivable	12,500	2,400	4,500	4,350	4,875	7,425	7,650	6,450	3,750	3,750	6,900	15,300	22,950
Inventories	7,250	12,875	19,200	26,625	29,325	23,925	17,175	15,825	25,275	46,875	69,825	48,765	21,833
Total current assets	44,450	50,168	28,700	35,975	39,200	36,350	29,825	27,275	34,025	55,625	77,335	69,065	63,979
Property and equipment, net	33,500	57,786	57,071	56,357	55,643	54,929	54,214	53,500	52,786	52,071	51,357	50,643	49,929
Other assets	2,500	3,750	3,750	3,750	3,750	3,750	3,750	3,750	3,750	3,750	3,750	3,750	3,750
Total assets	$80,450	$111,704	$89,521	$96,082	$98,593	$95,029	$87,789	$84,525	$90,561	$111,446	$132,443	$123,458	$117,658
Liabilities and equity													
Current liabilities:													
Accounts payable	$32,456	$31,247	$8,418	$4,584	$3,855	$3,261	$1,938	$2,640	$4,503	$9,066	$11,766	$3,612	$4,604
Accrued expenses	1,850	1,850	1,850	1,850	1,850	1,850	1,850	1,850	1,850	1,850	1,850	1,850	1,850
Current portion of long-term debt	10,000	14,000	14,000	14,000	14,000	14,000	14,000	14,000	14,000	14,000	14,000	14,000	14,000
Line of credit	0	0	1,676	15,702	20,775	14,516	7,835	5,622	15,406	34,852	50,000	31,950	0
Total current liabilities	44,306	47,097	25,944	36,136	40,480	33,627	25,623	24,112	35,759	59,768	77,616	51,412	20,454
Long-term debt	20,000	35,628	35,012	34,390	33,762	33,129	32,489	31,843	31,191	30,533	29,868	29,197	28,519
Stock-holders' equity:													
Contributed capital	20,000	35,000	35,000	35,000	35,000	35,000	35,000	35,000	35,000	35,000	35,000	35,000	35,000
Accumulated earnings	(3,856)	(6,021)	(6,434)	(9,444)	(10,649)	(6,727)	(5,322)	(6,430)	(11,389)	(13,854)	(10,041)	7,849	33,684
Total equity	16,144	28,979	28,566	25,556	24,351	28,273	29,678	28,570	23,611	21,146	24,959	42,849	68,684
Total liabilities and equity	$80,450	$111,704	$89,521	$96,082	$98,593	$95,029	$87,789	$84,525	$90,561	$111,446	$132,443	$123,458	$117,658
Does the balance sheet balance?	Yes	Yes	Yes	Yes	Yes	Yes	Yes	Yes	Yes	Yes	Yes	Yes	Yes

EXHIBIT 6.9. Calculation of accounts payable.

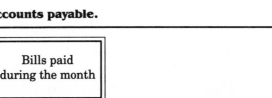

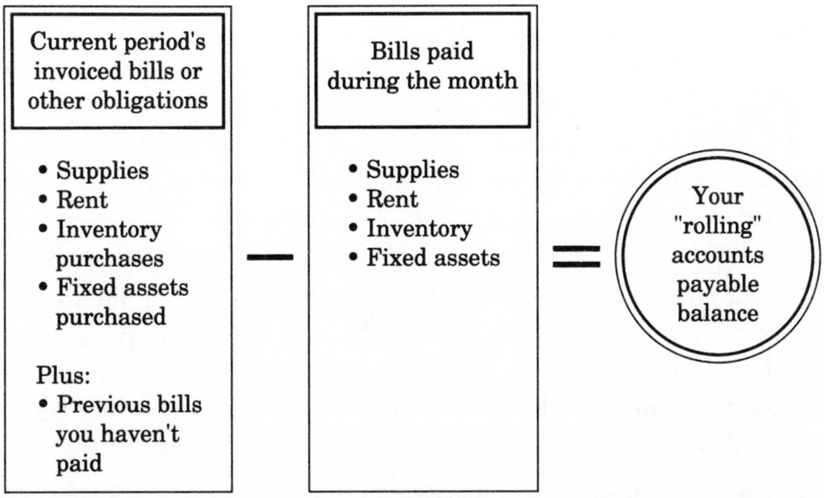

- *Other assets* is calculated by adding the previous period's other assets plus vendor deposits required [assumptions statement].

Current liabilities are derived as follows:

- *Accounts payable* is calculated by taking all the previous payables that have not been paid and adding all the new bills or obligations incurred in operating expenses [income statement] *plus* inventory purchases [inventory purchasing statement, not shown here] *plus* fixed assets purchased [assumptions statement] *minus* the bills or obligations that are paid during the month (for example, payroll, taxes, and benefits [income statement]) *minus* noncash expenditures included in operating expenses (for example, depreciation, [income statement]). Exhibit 6.9 illustrates the calculation of a rolling accounts payable balance.

  Unfortunately, the formulas used to project your balance sheet are often the most complicated among those in your financial projections. For instance, the specific formula for *accounts payable* for our retail store is calculated by adding the previous period's accounts payable on the balance sheet *plus* inventory purchases [inventory purchasing statement] *plus* fixed assets purchased [assumptions statement] *plus* operating expenses [income statement] *minus* payroll, taxes, and benefits [income statement] *minus* depreciation [income statement] *minus* accounts payable paid from 1987 expenses [cash flow statement] *minus* monthly expenses, inventory, and fixed assets paid [cash flow statement].
- *Accrued expenses* for the retail store are assumed to equal the previous period's accrued expenses. In other situations, you may wish to include new

items that are obligations you have incurred legally but have not yet received an invoice or are not yet obligated to pay. If so, the process is similar to accounts payable in which old and new accrued expenses are combined and then subtracted from accrued expenses actually paid during the current period to arrive at a net accrued expenses balance. For example, income taxes are incurred legally for each day you operate. However, you are not invoiced daily or even monthly but are expected to pay quarterly. Perhaps a better example is services you have received from a lawyer or consultant, who will not send a bill or invoice for three or four months.

- *Current portion of long-term debt* is calculated by taking the previous period's current portion of long-term debt plus the current period's current portion of long-term debt on the balance sheet minus the notes payable principal payment [cash flow statement] *until* long-term debt becomes a zero balance.

Equities are derived as follows:

- *Contributed capital* is derived from the previous period's contributed capital on the balance sheet plus new equity [cash flow statement] from the current period.
- *Accumulated earnings* is derived from the previous period's accumulated earnings on the balance sheet plus net income before taxes [income statement] *minus* dividends [cash flow statement] for the current period.

How to Get the Balance Sheet to Balance

If you have ever tried to put together a set of financial projections, you probably experienced some trying moments attempting to discover why your balance sheet didn't balance. Don't worry. You're not alone. I've seen experienced CPAs spend hours trying to figure out why a particular set of projections didn't *tie out*, that is, produce a balanced balance sheet.

Despite what people may say, getting your balance sheet to balance isn't easy. You may also wonder, since we're dealing with imprecise future projections, why you need to have a balance sheet that balances. The answer relates to the *interdependent nature of all the statements*. Because the balance sheet is tied to the cash flow and ultimately all other statements, a balance sheet that is out of balance can provide the wrong answers about how much cash your venture needs, when it needs this cash, what form the cash should take, and where you should try to raise the needed funds.

In short, an incorrect balance sheet can mess up your cash flow statement, your ratios and profitability measures, your sales breakeven, and any other analysis that is derived directly or indirectly from the balance sheet. That means just about everything, since the linkages between the statements ensure that errors ripple through all of your projections. In addition, you can't ignore or rationalize away a small error in your balance sheet. Flagging potential errors is important here. It's why Exhibit 6.8 asks a simple "Yes" or "No" question at the bottom of the statement: "Does the balance sheet balance?" Remember, a small error in your balance sheet often gets bigger with each new round of calculations for each successive time period.

The Cash Flow Statement

The income statement and the balance sheet have dominated the attention of stockholders, and, consequently, many managers in the past. The reasons for this domination include the facts that:

- Both statements are important indicators of the organization's past performance and current position; and
- Accountants can reduce and consolidate a great deal of information from other statements into these two statements for presentation purposes.

Both the income statement and the balance sheet also satisfy the needs of managers and stockholders of larger corporations for a relatively accurate picture of an enterprise's future health, especially when these people can focus on a few financial ratios drawn from these statements. For instance, the amount of debt your venture has incurred relative to total equity (the debt/equity ratio) shows the financial commitment of the owners compared to that of outside creditors and bankers. Where nearly all debt is used with very little equity, this shows little financial reason for the owners to stick with the venture when it experiences difficult times. They personally have little to lose by selling the business. They also have little or no further ability to use debt to help the venture through difficult times.

Over the last decade, a third statement—the cash flow statement—has garnered increasing attention among entrepreneurs, and especially owner/managers of smaller businesses. The reason is simple. Cash is what keeps ventures alive and functioning. The cash flow statement tracks the *actual flow of cash into and out of the venture*. The income statement and balance sheet can be misleading about the true existence of cash, and this is especially likely if a venture is new, small, or rapidly growing. For example, at some point *within* an accounting period, a venture may not have sufficient cash to continue operating, even though the income statement shows a substantial projected profit and the balance sheet projects a positive net worth and positive cash for the end of the accounting period (some months away).

This possibility is more likely to have a devastating impact when the accounting period or the projection period is relatively long, (for example, a quarter or especially a year). Annual income and balance sheet projections have been known to show entrepreneurs rich and famous at the end of the year although their ventures actually run out of funds six months before that time. For instance, monthly cash flow projections in the exhibit on page 167 show big negative cash flows in August, September, and October followed by large positive cash flows in November and December. Unfortunately, the venture never sees November unless it raises additional funding of $4,390 in October.

Consequently, the cash flow statement is an extremely important statement for new enterprises. It shows not only *how much* money you need to launch the venture but also *when* you will need it.

The cash flow statement tracks when you actually receive cash and when you pay it out over some specified period of time. In short, its basic purposes are to tell you if you have sufficient cash to continue present and future operations, and, if not, how much cash you will need and when you will need it to keep the venture operating at some designated level.

The cash flow statement is important because it prevents you from equating sales with cash flow unless sales are actually cash sales. It also tells you what your minimum cash point will be over the time period in question. From a projections perspective, the cash flow statement tells you how to manage the cash you have. It gives you the insight and time to react, to decide how to spend (or not spend) cash under a variety of circumstances.

For example, your ending cash position for any particular month can be positive or negative, depending on whether you've received more cash (including your starting cash position) than you've spent. If you cannot offset negative cash flows with additional capital (debt or equity), someone will go unpaid. You may be able to live with this condition for some period of time depending on your creditors. But eventually you will be forced to take action to turn cash flow positive in the future. This action can include a reduction in expenditures as shown on the income statement—that is, reducing wages, salaries, rent, utilities, travel, and so on. Or it can include changes in balance sheet items that free up cash: selling fixed assets, reducing your accounts receivables faster (that is, increasing your collections), increasing your accounts payable (that is, extending the average time you pay vendors and other creditors), or reducing the amount of cash tied up in inventory. Should these and other possible actions prove insufficient to turn cash flow positive, you may have no other choice but to sell or discontinue the venture.

The critical point, however, is that you can use an integrated financials model to test the effects of these actions *before* they happen. This capability allows you to manage financial decisions by evaluating numerous options quickly, using a true "what if" approach to find a viable, if not the best, option available to you.

EXHIBIT 6.10. Timing of cash flows.

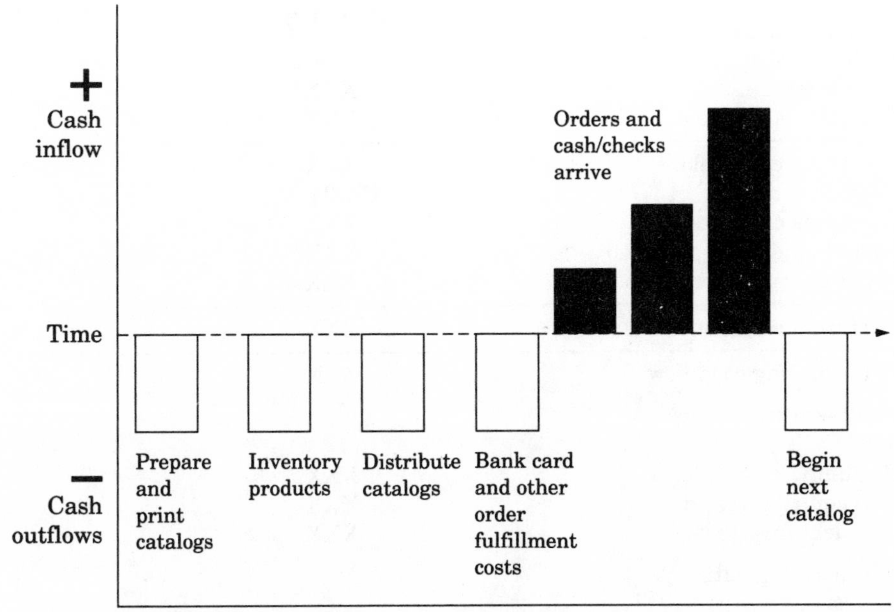

This chart illustrates the timing of cash flows in the mail-order business.

Many new and fairly new ventures show negative net cash flows from their operations because entrepreneurs and other investors have to spend money to build up the business. These negative positions should be covered by the initial capital invested in the venture and other debt and equity financings that prove necessary. Eventually, however, a venture needs to earn a positive *operating* cash flow so the business can not only stand on its own feet but presumably begin providing a return to investors from the operations of the venture. For instance, Exhibit 6.10 illustrates the typical situation for a mail-order venture at startup where operating cash flows are negative at first.

Components of the Cash Flow Statement

Cash flow statements are arranged in many different ways. These can be categorized into three basic types in terms of complexity:

1. *The simple cash flow statement*, so called because all items are arranged into only two categories: cash inflows (including your starting cash position) and cash outflows.
2. *The operating cash flow statement*, so called because cash inflows and outflows are limited initially to the cash flows that stem from the venture's ongoing operations, as opposed to the cash flows needed to finance the venture.

EXHIBIT 6.11. Operating cash flow statement.

	Period #1	Period #2
Cash received:	(Inflows)	
Cash sales	XXX	
Receivables collected	XXX	
Operating cash inflows	XXX	
Cash disbursed	(Outflows)	
Purchases paid	XXX	
Payroll paid	XXX	
Other operating expenses paid	XXX	
Operating cash outflows	XXX	
Net operating cash flow	XXX	
Nonoperating inflows		
Add:		
Beginning cash balance	XXX	
New equity invested	XXX	
New debt invested	XXX	
Nonoperating outflows		
Minus:		
Debt principal payments	XXX	
Interest payments	XXX	
Income taxes paid	XXX	
Fixed assets paid	XXX	
Dividends paid	XXX	
Ending cash balance	XXX	
Cumulative cash flow	XXX	

3. *The priority cash flow statement*, so called because cash inflows and particularly cash outflows are further classified into any number of priority or discretionary groupings.

Priority cash flow statements are very useful. However their increased utility is often offset by their greater complexity. For our purposes, the operating cash flow statement offers a better trade-off. A slight decrease in complexity is worth the advantage of knowing whether a positive cash flow for a particular month, quarter, or year is being produced from the venture's operations, from financial inflows, or from operating inflows from *prior* periods.

Because of this advantage, I've chosen to use the operating cash flow model with only some slight variations. The fundamental model is shown in Exhibit 6.11, followed by the projected cash flow statement for our retail venture in Exhibit 6.12.

EXHIBIT 6.12. Cash flow statement for a retail company.

	1/31/88	2/29/88	3/31/88	4/30/88	5/31/88	6/30/88	7/31/88	8/31/88	9/30/88	10/31/88	11/30/88	12/31/88
Cash received (inflows)												
Accounts receivable collected from 1987 sales	$12,500	$0	$0	$0	$0	$0	$0	$0	$0	$0	$0	$0
Monthly sales collected	9,600	14,400	10,650	14,475	24,450	20,775	16,200	8,700	12,000	23,850	51,600	70,350
Total cash receipts	22,100	14,400	10,650	14,475	24,450	20,775	16,200	8,700	12,000	23,850	51,600	70,350
Cash disbursed (outflow)												
Payroll paid	4,543	4,809	4,455	4,720	5,428	5,074	4,720	4,189	4,543	5,428	7,375	8,437
Accounts payable paid from 1987 expenses	12,982	16,228	3,246	0	0	0	0	0	0	0	0	0
Monthly expenses, inventory, fixed assets paid:												
1–30 days paid	27,472	12,068	10,696	8,995	7,609	4,522	6,160	10,507	21,154	27,454	8,428	10,743
31–60 days paid	0	11,774	5,172	4,584	3,855	3,261	1,938	2,640	4,503	9,066	11,766	3,612
61–90 days paid	0	0	0	0	0	0	0	0	0	0	0	0
90+ days paid	0	0	0	0	0	0	0	0	0	0	0	0
Vendor deposits	1,250	0	0	0	0	0	0	0	0	0	0	0
Total cash disbursement	46,247	44,878	23,568	18,299	16,892	12,857	12,818	17,336	30,200	41,948	27,569	22,792
Operating cash surplus (deficit)	(24,147)	(30,478)	(12,918)	(3,824)	7,558	7,918	3,382	(8,636)	(18,200)	(18,098)	24,031	47,558
Less: interest payments:												
Interest on debt (notes payable)	288	476	470	464	458	452	446	439	433	427	420	414
Interest on line of credit	0	0	17	157	208	145	78	56	154	349	500	320
Less: notes payable principal payment	372	616	622	628	634	640	646	652	658	665	671	677
Add: beginning of month cash balance	24,700	34,893	5,000	5,000	5,000	5,000	5,000	5,000	5,000	5,000	610	5,000
Cash balance before funding	$(107)	$3,324	$(9,026)	$(72)	$11,259	$11,681	$7,212	$(4,784)	$(14,446)	$(14,538)	$23,050	$51,147
Line of credit principal payments	0	0	0	0	6,259	6,681	2,212	0	0	0	18,050	31,950
Dividends	0	0	0	0	0	0	0	0	0	0	0	0
Additional funding:												
New equity	15,000	0	0	0	0	0	0	0	0	0	0	0
New debt (notes payable)	20,000	0	0	0	0	0	0	0	0	0	0	0
Line of credit borrowings	0	1,676	14,026	5,072	0	0	0	9,784	19,446	15,148	0	0
Ending cash balance	$34,893	$5,000	$5,000	$5,000	$5,000	$5,000	$5,000	$5,000	$5,000	$610	$5,000	$19,197
Is additional funding required?	No	No	No	No	No	No	No	No	No	Yes	No	No
If Yes, please enter your amount in the "new equity" or "new debt" (notes rows on the assumptions statement)												
Your minimum cash requirement was	$5,000											
The cash to fund your venture is	$4,390											

The Derivation of the Cash Flow's Components

The components of retail store's cash flow are derived from several sources. Some items come directly from the assumptions statement. Others come from the balance sheet or income statement. Again, the source statement is shown in brackets.

The formulas for certain cash flow items are very complex for legitimate technical reasons. In these instances, I've chosen to demonstrate how the calculation works; however, the reader should realize that computing a number in your head or even with a calculator is very difficult. In one or two instances, such calculations are even impossible because they require access to some intermediary calculations that are not shown.

Operating cash inflows are derived as follows:

- *Accounts receivable collected from 1987 sales* are taken directly from the amounts estimated in the assumptions statement.
- *Receivables collected from 1988 sales* are calculated from the sum of the following:

  Receivables collected 30 days after sale, which is derived by multiplying the previous month's net sales [income statement] by the assumed percentage collected in 30 days [assumptions statement].

  Receivables collected 60 days after sale, which is derived by multiplying the net sales [income statement] realized two months ago by the assumed percentage collected in 60 days [assumptions statement].

  Receivables collected 90 days after sale, which is derived by multiplying the net sales [income statement] realized three months ago by the assumed percentage collected in 90 days [assumptions statement].

  Receivables collected over 90 days after sale, which is derived by multiplying the net sales [income statement] realized four months ago by the assumed percentage collected after 90 days [assumptions statement]. Note: In this set of projections, bad debts are part of deductions and subtracted from gross sales. An alternative calculation would be to make receivables collected add up to something less than 100% in the assumptions statement with receivables collected over 90 days incorporating the shortfall (for example, a cumulative receivables collected percentage of 98% gives a 2% bad debt rate).

In some instances, cash sales are assumed to be any sale where cash is received within the first 1 to 30 days. When this assumption is made, cash sales are simply combined with receivables collected instead of being listed as a separate item.

EXHIBIT 6.13. Accounts receivable spreading.

	Actual		Projected					
Month	F	M	A	M	J	J	A	S
Sales	300	200	100	100	200	300	400	400
Cash receipts								
1–30 days (20%)	60	40	20	20	40	60	80	80
31–60 days (50%)	150	150	100	50	50	100	150	200
61–90 days (30%)	120	90	90	60	30	30	60	90
Total receipts from sales	330	280	210	130	120	190	290	370

Source: Adapted from Leon Haller's excellent book, *Making Sense of Accounting Information* (New York: Van Nostrand Reinhold, 1985), 41 (with the author's permission).

Exhibit 6.13 shows how receivables are spread over time.

Operating cash outflows are derived as follows:

- *Payroll paid* is taken from payroll, taxes, and wages and benefits [income statement].
- *Accounts payable paid* [from 1987 expenses] is calculated by multiplying the '87 accounts payable of $32,456 [base period of balance sheet] by the base period accounts payable paid [assumptions statement].
- *Monthly expenses, inventory, fixed assets paid* is calculated by *multiplying* operating expenses [income statement] *minus* salaries and wages, *minus* depreciation, *plus* any inventory purchases and any fixed assets purchased [assumptions statement] by a monthly expenses paid rate that is spread over 90+ days.
- *Vendor deposits* is taken from vendor deposits required [assumptions statement].
- *Interest part of debt (notes payable) payment* is calculated by multiplying the beginning principal balance [memo item or cash flow statement, not shown] times the annual interest rate [assumptions statement] and divided by 12 months.

- *Principal part of debt (notes payable) payment* is calculated by subtracting the interest part of payment from the monthly payment amount [memo item or cash flow statement, not shown].
- *Interest on line of credit* is calculated by multiplying the previous period's line of credit [balance sheet] times the line of credit interest rate [assumptions statement] and dividing by 12 months.
- *Add: beginning of month cash balance* is taken from the previous period's cash and equivalents [balance sheet].
- *Line of credit principal repayments* occur when the cash balance before funding [cash flow statement] is above the $5,000 minimum cash balance [assumptions statement]. The exact amount paid is either the total principal due on line of credit borrowings or the maximum amount that will still leave an ending cash balance of $5,000.
- *New equity* is taken directly from new equity [assumptions statement] and is held at zero initially in order to determine incremental cash needs.
- *New debt* is taken directly from new debt [assumptions statement] and is held at zero initially in order to determine incremental cash needs.
- *Line of credit borrowings* are calculated when the cash balance before funding plus new equity and new debt are less than the $5,000 minimum cash balance [assumptions statement]. The amount calculated is whatever amount is needed to make the ending cash balance $5,000 without exceeding the maximum line of credit [assumptions statement] of $50,000.

YOUR ULTIMATE GOAL: POSITIVE OPERATING CASH FLOWS

If happiness is a positive cash flow, then venture ecstasy is a *positive operating cash flow*. One can finance a venture forever and show a positive cash flow by injecting new debt or equity. Yet your business may never be profitable in either an accounting or economic sense because you haven't produced a positive cash flow from the operations of the business.

Under certain conditions, a conscious decision may be made to subsidize a venture (for example, some nonprofit ventures) through donations and other fund-raising activities. For instance, many symphonies and museums operate on this basis in order to keep admission prices affordable. Although they operate in the red every year, a positive cash flow is produced by annual gift giving or periodic capital campaigns.

Most ventures, however, do not fit these nonprofit profiles. The goal of most for-profit entrepreneurs, though it may be unappreciated and unstated, is to earn a positive *operating* cash flow. Only as these operating cash flows increase over time can true wealth be created and equity increased in a venture so that the venture is worth something substantial to you because others place value on it.

KNOWING YOUR NUMBERS COLD MEANS NEVER GUESSING ABOUT THEM UNLESS YOU MUST

This chapter has shown how the initial assumptions you make will produce an interrelated set of projections. These projections start with a revenue statement and culminate in a cash flow statement. Don't worry if you don't understand every interrelationship perfectly at this time. With experience, these linkages will become clearer. For now, it's enough to understand how every element of your financial projections are related to all other elements. There's a saying in business that a change in any part of an organization finds a way of eventually rippling across the entire venture. Your financial projections are no different.

Today's entrepreneurs need to understand how accounting statements and financial projections are created and evolve. Practically speaking, they need this knowledge to plan and execute the startup of their ventures. They also need it for their own peace of mind. The experience of one entrepreneur speaks for many:

> Numbers may be the language of commerce, but it's a dialect few of us speak when we first go into business. That can make for some very anxious moments. I recall being at the mercy of my bookkeeper for seven long years. She was oracular, and I would wait nervously for her to deliver each month's profit-and-loss statement. It took about 15 years before I actually understood the double-entry method of accounting. As much as I pretended to read, comprehend, and comment on P&Ls and balance sheets, I was operating under a thick film of ignorance that I was too embarrassed to admit. It was only later—after I got over both my ignorance and my embarrassment—that I fully appreciated the role numbers should play in the management of a successful business.[5]

What's true about understanding historical accounting statements is doubly true for future-based financial projections. Most entrepreneurs need to control their environments as much as possible given the uncertainty that confronts them. Fortunately, reduction of uncertainty in the area of financial projections is attainable, and you shouldn't have to wait years to experience it. For venturing to be truly a calculated risk, you should be *calculating* likely cash flows, not *guessing* about them. As someone once said, "Never guess . . . unless you have to. There is enough uncertainty in the universe."

Creating a set of integrated financial projections allows you to take calculated risks. It allows you to limit your guessing. With integrated financial projections you can test and retest your basic assumptions about your business. You can understand the impact of changing many variables simultaneously. As this process evolves, you begin to see the forest, not just the trees, and eventually you truly understand your numbers, as Harold Geneen would say, "cold."

7 VENTURE CAPITAL

William E. Wetzel, Jr.

During the late 1980s, venture capital funds left their traditional role as early-stage investors in young companies. Fund portfolios now include large, later-stage deals, management/leveraged buyout financing, private placements for public companies, and, in some cases, investments in the stock of public companies. For a history of the venture capital industry and a provocative discussion of recent trends, see *Venture Capital at the Crossroads.*[1]

This chapter focuses exclusively on traditional, or classic, venture capital. *Classic venture capital* is distinguished by the following characteristics:

- It requires early-stage equity or equity-linked financing.
- It involves high risk.
- There is a lack of liquidity or marketability.
- Investment returns are primarily from capital gains.
- It is typically provided by patient investors equipped to offer value-added advice.

Classic venture investors are in the business of financing and building businesses that will be worth five to ten or more times the capital invested in five to ten years. *These investors look for long-term capital gains* on their portfolios and typically invest their financial and managerial know-how as well as their capital. In a very real sense, the decision to bankroll a new

For their critique of this chapter the author extends a special "thank you" to Patricia M. Cloherty (Alan Patricoff Associates, Inc.), Robert J. Crowley (Massachusetts Technology Development Corp.), Peter D. Danforth (Kearsarge Ventures, L.P.), Robert C. McCray (private investor), P. Andrews McLane (TA Associates), Richard E. Morley (private investor), and Stephen G. Woodsum (Summit Partners).

venture is the ultimate capital investment decision. It involves finding and funding investment opportunities that are expected to be worth substantially more than they cost.

Venture capital is expensive. Extreme uncertainty surrounding investment outcomes, coupled with the absence of investment liquidity, accounts for the high cost of venture capital. Consequently, the number of investment opportunities attractive to venture investors is limited. This chapter unravels some of the mystery surrounding the exciting but arcane world of venture capital.

WHEN *NOT* TO LOOK FOR VENTURE CAPITAL

Time runs a close second to *cash* on every entrepreneur's list of scarce resources. Don't waste valuable time thinking about raising venture capital until you have convinced yourself that your venture will generate substantial wealth for yourself and your investors. Your goal must be more than self-employment. You must have a burning desire to build an enterprise that will seize every opportunity for *profitable growth* and, ultimately, provide *liquidity for your investors*. Furthermore, the venture must be positioned in markets that provide such opportunities.

In practical terms, that means your vision and your business plan must support expectations that within five years your venture will be generating revenues of at least $10 million and growing by at least 20% per year with a pretax profit margin of at least 15%. Ventures below these thresholds may provide a comfortable income and perks for the entrepreneur, but the prospects for capital gains for investors are unattractive. At the other extreme, entrepreneurs will have the least trouble raising venture capital when their vision and financial projections support expectations of revenues in excess of $50 million within five years, growing at 30 to 50% or more per year and bringing down pretax profit margins of 20% or more.

Reread the previous paragraph. From a venture investor's perspective there are three types of entrepreneurial ventures:

1. *Life-style* ventures have five-year revenue projections under $10 million. These are fine for entrepreneurs driven by life-style motives, but they are of no interest to investors. Life-style ventures account for more than 90% of all startups.
2. *Middle-market* ventures have five-year revenue projections from $10 million to $50 million. These are also fine for entrepreneurs, but they may need venture financing. They can, if properly structured, offer capital gains and cash-out opportunities for investors. These ventures make up the backbone of our entrepreneurial economy. Most will remain

privately owned or will be sold. They rely heavily on *bootstrap* financing and financing from individual investors.

3. *High-potential* ventures have five-year revenue projections in excess of $50 million. These are the potential big winners for both entrepreneurs and investors. They typically require several rounds of six- or seven-figure financing. Such ventures should expect to be publicly traded or acquired within five years. They are the next generation's Apple, Federal Express, and Genentech. They are candidates for financing from venture capital funds. High-potential ventures make up less than 1% of startups.

This chapter will be of interest to entrepreneurs trying to raise early-stage and growth financing for middle-market and high-potential ventures.

TAPPING THE VENTURE CAPITAL MARKETS

There are no hard data on the number of startup and high-growth middle-market and high-potential ventures or their annual capital requirements. Educated guesses place the number of companies growing at rates in excess of 20% per year at about half a million. Companies on the *Inc.* 500 list of fastest-growing private companies are leading examples. The number of startups with attractive capital gains potential is in the neighborhood of fifty thousand per year. The annual equity financing requirements of these high-growth and startup ventures are estimated to total some $60 billion per year.

There are two primary sources of venture financing for these entrepreneurs: one visible and one invisible.

Venture Capital Funds

The *visible* venture capital market is composed of over 500 venture capital funds that manage about $35 billion—not a lot of capital in the grand scheme of things. It is equivalent to the total assets of one good-sized bank, such as the Bank of Boston. *Pratt's Guide to Venture Capital Sources* is a comprehensive directory of venture capital funds in the United States.[2]

In the early 1990s, venture capital funds were investing about $2 billion annually in entrepreneurial ventures. Two billion dollars per year sounds like a lot of money to all of us, but keep in mind that more than $2 billion changes hands before noon every day on the floor of the New York Stock Exchange. IBM's R&D budget is in the neighborhood of $5 billion per year. Here are two more sobering statistics: Venture capital funds bankroll fewer than 2,000 companies per year, and two-thirds of these financings are for ventures already in their portfolios. Furthermore, all venture fund portfolio companies started life in the *high-potential* category.

A typical round of financing from a venture capital fund is a later-stage deal in excess of $1 million. If your venture is looking for equity financing, you are on the wrong side of 100-to-1 odds that you will be able to raise it from institutional venture capital investors. To save time knocking on the wrong doors, test your business plan against the high-potential venture criteria discussed in Chapter 2. If it flunks, take a close look at the invisible venture capital market.

Business "Angels"

The *invisible* venture capital market is also the oldest and the biggest. It is made up of about two million individuals, each with a net worth in excess of $1 million, excluding their personal residences. The majority of these individuals are self-made millionaires (first-generation money)—individuals with substantial business and entrepreneurial experience. They are often referred to as business "angels." Best estimates of the scale of this informal venture capital market suggest that about 250,000 angels invest $10–$20 billion every year in over 30,000 ventures.

For ventures with competent and committed management and a convincing business plan, the odds of raising angel financing are much higher than the odds of raising capital from venture capital funds. A typical angel deal is an early-stage round in the $100,000 to $500,000 range raised from six or eight investors. These co-investors usually are trusted friends and business associates. Find one angel and you have found five or ten.

The better odds are offset by the fact that angels are not easy to find. For obvious reasons, angels keep low profiles. There is no *Pratt's Guide to Angels*, and there are no public records of most angel deals. The resources closest to a *Pratt's Guide* are regional venture capital networks. The original, Venture Capital Network, Inc. (VCN), was founded in 1984 as a not-for-profit corporation affiliated with the Center for Venture Research at the University of New Hampshire. VCN moved in 1990 to MIT, where it is now affiliated with the MIT Enterprise Forum of Cambridge. It was renamed Technology Capital Network (TCN) in 1992. There are six or eight similar organized networks in other regions of the country. These networks have proven to be effective in connecting angels and entrepreneurs. However, they are all relatively young and still minor players in the angel market.

Entrepreneurs need to depend on ingenuity and tenacity in their pursuit of angel financing. Here are some tips on how to find prospective angels:

- Look close to home—most angels invest in ventures they can reach in a half-day's drive.
- Look for individuals familiar with your markets or technology—they are the most likely to be interested in your venture.

- Many angels are active in charitable and civic affairs—look for their names in the local press and on the boards of directors and sponsors of such organizations.
- Most angels are risk-takers in their avocations as well as their professions—many are private pilots and sailors, and private aircraft and yachts must be registered with the FAA or the U.S. Coast Guard; these registrations are public information.
- Although it sounds bizarre, use your state motor vehicle department to find the owners of expensive performance cars.
- Use "gatekeepers"—lawyers, patent attorneys, accountants, venture capitalists, and bankers who specialize in serving early-stage and high-growth ventures.
- Above all, start building a roster of potential investors at least six months before you start your search for money.

"Bootstrap" Financing

If your search for financing from venture capital funds or from angels comes up empty, and, realistically, the odds are not in your favor, *don't quit*. Interviews with the founders of 100 companies on the 1989 *Inc.* 500 list attest to the prevalence of *bootstrap* financing. From these interviews it was estimated that more than 80% of the *Inc.* 500 fastest-growing private companies were financed *solely* by founders' personal savings, credit cards, second mortgages, customer advances, extended terms from vendors, and a multitude of other bootstrap techniques. The founders revealed that the median startup capital of the 100 companies was about $10,000. Less than one-fifth of the *Inc.* 500 raised outside equity capital during the five or more years that they had been in business.[3]

A Comparison of the Three Venture Capital Markets

A study of the financial histories of 284 new technology-based firms (NTBFs) founded in New England between 1975 and 1986 sheds light on the role of bootstrap financing,[4] angels, and venture capital funds:

- One hundred seven firms (38%) raised no outside financing.
- The remaining one 177 firms (62%) raised $671 million in 445 rounds of financing.
- Angels financed 120 firms.
- Venture capital funds financed 90 firms.

EXHIBIT 7.1. Size and source of rounds invested in new technology-based firms.

Size of financing round	Private individuals		Venture capital funds	
<$250,000	102	(58%)	8	(5%)
$250,000–$499,999	43	(24%)	14	(8%)
$500,000–$999,999	15	(8%)	31	(18%)
≥$1,000,000	17	(10%)	120	(69%)
Total	177	(100%)	173	(100%)

- Thirty-three firms used both sources.
- The distribution of angel versus venture capital fund financing according to the size and stage of the venture is illuminating: See Exhibits 7.1 and 7.2.

The median size of a round of seed, startup, and later-stage financing provided by angels was $150,000, $150,000, and $200,000, respectively. The median size of a round of seed, startup, and later-stage financing provided by venture capital funds was $450,000, $1,500,000, and $2,000,000, respectively.

The data contrasting angel and venture capital fund financing suggest that these two sources of capital complement each other. The complementary relationship is a function of the size and the stage of the deal. Angels are the most likely source of small amounts of early-stage financing, whereas venture capital funds are more likely to provide larger amounts of later-stage financing.

OBTAINING FINANCING: START EARLY

A successful hunt for angel financing or financing from a venture capital fund normally will take at least six months from start to finish. The Center for

EXHIBIT 7.2. Stage and source of rounds invested in new technology-based firms.

Stage of financing	Private individuals		Venture capital funds	
Seed	52	(29%)	11	(6%)
Startup	55	(31%)	38	(22%)
First stage	29	(16%)	56	(32%)
Second stage	26	(15%)	46	(27%)
Third stage	10	(6%)	19	(11%)
Bridge	5	(3%)	3	(2%)
Total	177	(100%)	173	(100%)

Venture Research at the University of New Hampshire asked entrepreneurs who had raised venture financing how long it took to raise funds. The fund-raising process was divided into two stages:

- Stage 1—the elapsed time between the decision to raise funds and the first meeting with an angel or managing partner of a venture capital fund
- Stage 2—the elapsed time between the first meeting and the receipt of funds

In *Stage 1*, the median elapsed time was one month to find and meet the first angel and 1.75 months to find and meet the first managing partner or senior investment professional of a venture capital fund. This result seems counterintuitive, given the relative obscurity of angels. However, although venture capital funds are easier to find, it may take more persistence to arrange an appointment with a venture capitalist than with an angel. One venture capitalist tests an entrepreneur's persistence by never returning the first three or four telephone calls.

A more significant difference was reported in the elapsed time between the first meeting and the receipt of funds (*Stage 2*). The median elapsed time was 2.5 months for angels and 4.5 months for venture capital funds.

The shorter deliberation time for angels may be due to the fact that angel deals typically involve a close group of co-investors led by a successful entrepreneur who is familiar with the venture's technology, products, and markets. Typically, the lead investor will vary from deal to deal, and each angel's piece of the deal tends to be a relatively small percentage of her total assets.

Venture capital funds, on the other hand, typically are involved in larger deals that represent a significant fraction of fund assets. As managers of other peoples' money, venture capital funds have a fiduciary responsibility to their investors. Their organizational structure and decision-making authority involve more people in the approval process.

Entrepreneurs reported that, from start to finish, raising funds from angels consumed about four months compared to six months for capital raised from venture capital funds. In his critique of this section of the chapter, one battle-scarred entrepreneur/angel commented: "I do not believe this is correct. I believe this is revisionist hindsight. I would suspect nine to twelve months from the concept to the check is much more realistic."

BUSINESS PLANS ARE CRITICAL WHEN OBTAINING VENTURE CAPITAL

A comprehensive, investor-oriented business plan will not guarantee success in raising funds, but *the lack of a business plan will ensure failure.*

Preparing a winning business plan is a painful, but essential, exercise for two reasons:

1. The discipline of the process forces you to articulate your vision and how and when you expect to achieve it. Anticipate weeks of hard work to do the job right.
2. A clearly written and attractively packaged business plan will raise the odds of getting the attention of serious investors. Because the business plan speaks for the venture, it must speak loud and clear. The ability to articulate goals, objectives, and a strategy for achieving them is characteristic of successful entrepreneurs. Investors look for entrepreneurs who can manage limited resources by objectives as well as by instinct.

GET PROFESSIONAL ADVICE

This chapter makes many generalizations that are necessary to cover complex issues in limited space. If you are launching a venture that will be looking for outside investors, you can't afford less than the best legal, accounting, banking, financial, and management advice. One word of caution: don't confuse legal and accounting advice with business advice. Early-stage companies sometimes make the mistake of looking to attorneys to shape their businesses.

Be cautious about whom you choose for advisors. Ask for and check references. Here are some general guidelines on what to look for in each advisor:

- Attorneys—Your attorney should be experienced in negotiating, pricing, and structuring venture financing and must also be familiar with state and federal securities regulations.
- Bankers—Picking the right banker is as important as picking the right bank. A commercial loan officer who has been through the financing of emerging companies more than once can be an invaluable source of financial advice and contacts. The right banker knows the difference between cash flow and profit. Your banker will be there when it counts if you maintain frank and frequent contact. A brief status report once a month is sufficient.
- Accountants—Pick a respected CPA with a firm that specializes in the design of accounting and management information systems for emerging companies. The cost is high, but the sooner you have a full audit of your financial statements, accompanied by an unqualified opinion, the better.

Finally, you should know that successful entrepreneurs are the best single source of advice. Use several you respect on a working board of directors and pay them if you can. The benefits are certain to exceed the costs.

FINDING THE RIGHT INVESTORS

Think of fund raising as a process of *buying capital* rather than *selling stock.* The difference is subtle but important. Venture capital is a commodity. It is available from a variety of sources on a variety of terms. For every venture, some combination of sources and terms will be more appropriate than others and will exert a powerful influence on the future of the venture. Besides the price, the following factors will influence the choice of sources:

- Investors' exit expectations
- The availability of future financing
- The quality of management assistance available from investors
- Investors experience in dealing with illiquid, high-risk investments

The final deal should be a partnership of professionals with *complementary resources* and *shared goals.*

As a fund-raising strategy, entrepreneurs should always look for knowledgeable investors. They are the most likely to be attracted to your venture, and whether you ask for it or not, they will provide you with the benefit of their know-how—most of which they acquired by making their own mistakes in business, the way entrepreneurs learn their most valuable lessons. The right investors are *value-added investors.* For first-time entrepreneurs, the know-how available from battle-tested investors can be more valuable than their capital.

Your best investor prospects will be familiar with your markets, products, and technologies. Often these investors have managed or financed a successful startup in a similar field. For your sake as well as theirs, these investors will stay in close touch with your venture. However, there is a fine line between meddling and a productive relationship. Your investors' professional qualifications are necessary but not sufficient for a healthy relationship. Interpersonal chemistry will determine the quality of the relationship. The fit must *feel* right as well as *look* right.

Attention to chemistry and shared goals is especially important when dealing with individual investors. The following comments paraphrase the thoughts of one successful angel. For him success is more than the numbers; it has to do with *values* and *commitment to a shared vision.* While he sits on the boards of directors of his portfolio companies, he describes his role as a *coach* and *mentor*, someone with whom the entrepreneur can share doubts, fears, and vulnerabilities. Creating a company that is so successful that he can sell his shares back to the founders at a reasonable profit is his idea of the ultimate achievement.

Create a compatible structure for the relationship: a seat on a working board of directors, an informal consulting role, or full or part-time employment. Maintain frequent contact with all your investors. Quarterly financial statements accompanied by status reports from the CEO are bare minimums. Contact can mean a simple telephone call or faxed message. Investors like to be touched by short but frequent contacts.

The right investors will be aware of the risks involved in your venture and should be emotionally, as well as financially, able to bear those risks. You don't have time to deal with impatient, inexperienced investors while trying to cope with the inevitable delays and problems that plague all entrepreneurs. Murphy (of Murphy's Law fame) will be your constant companion.

Unless your margins are truly exceptional (more than 20% after-tax), your venture will develop an insatiable appetite for cash if it succeeds. Ideally, your original investors should be prepared and able to provide the additional funds required to finance growth. If not, be sure that they anticipate the need and are realistic about the cost (dilution) of second- and third-round financing. Your pro forma financial statements provide the basis for discussing these issues with your initial investors.

BE PREPARED FOR THE DUE DILIGENCE PROCESS

Once you and your prospective investors have reached a preliminary agreement, your investors will begin what is known as *due diligence*. Due diligence is the homework investors complete before a final investment decision is reached. The process typically includes background checks on the management team, industry studies, analysis of your competition, identification of major risks and other reasons, often intangible, why the investment should or should not be made. In essence, due diligence is a detailed evaluation of your business plan. Expect six to eight weeks to pass before the due diligence is complete.

The most important variables in an investor's decision to finance a venture are the integrity, competence, and commitment of the entrepreneur and his or her management team. But due diligence is a two-way street. Entrepreneurs should be equally concerned about the qualifications of their investors. Ask for the names of your investors' bankers, accountants, and attorneys. Then have your banker, accountant, and attorney check their professional reputations. If they don't have impeccable reputations, you may want to look for other investors. Guilt by association is not conclusive, but it does raise warning flags. If you are dealing with angels, ask for references and résumés describing their professional and educational backgrounds. Talk to each of the references.

Remember that you will be living with your investors through stressful times. Finding the right investors is worth the effort! The most valuable homework you can do is to talk to other entrepreneurs that your potential investors have bankrolled. Ask your investors for a list of their portfolio companies, including those that failed. Contact a random sample. Here are some key questions to discuss with the founders of these ventures:

- Are your investors trustworthy and predictable?
- Do you consider them fair and reasonable?
- Were they difficult to deal with?
- How long did it take to get your money?
- What are your investors like to work with on a consistent basis?
- How active are they in your business?
- Do you consider them meddlesome or helpful?
- What have they done for you besides invest money?
- How have they been helpful?
- Do they act like your partners or your adversaries?
- How did your investors behave during periods of difficulty?
- Who were the investors' representatives on your board of directors?
- If you had to do it all over again, would you raise money from the same investors?

All of these questions focus on the relationship between investors and the management they bet on. They are designed to help you decide whether your investors will make good partners. Satisfying yourself on these issues is part of the subtle distinction between buying capital and selling stock.

One entrepreneur/angel took exception to the list, reacting to these questions as follows: "The key questions seem to be adversarial. Sometimes it's better to have money and excellent advice, and good experience from investors than have them nice people to deal with. Fair and reasonable fall by the wayside when compared to good advice and patient money." Although this experienced investor makes a useful point, "fair and reasonable" are not imcompatible with "good advice and patient money."

THE COST OF VENTURE CAPITAL

Deal pricing is the central mystery of venture capital. Pricing venture capital is part art, part science, and part Yankee horse trading. Risk and, consequently, the cost of venture capital vary substantially over the developmental stages of a new venture. The following generally accepted definitions of the stages of financing are taken from *Pratt's Guide to Venture Capital Sources*.

Early-Stage Financing

Seed Financing

This is a relatively small amount of capital provided to an inventor or entrepreneur to prove a concept and to qualify for startup capital. If the initial steps are successful, this may involve product development and market research as well as building a management team and developing a business plan.

Startup Financing

This money is provided to companies completing product development and initial marketing. Companies may be in the process of organizing, or they may already have been in business for one year or less but not sold their product commercially. Usually such firms will have made market studies, assembled the key management, developed a business plan, and become ready to do business.

First-Stage Financing

This is provided to companies that have expended their initial capital (often in developing and market-testing a prototype) and require funds to initiate full-scale manufacturing and sales.

Expansion Financing

Second-Stage Financing

This financing provides working capital for the initial expansion of a company that is producing and shipping and has growing accounts receivable and inventories. Although the company has made progress, it may not yet be showing a profit.

Third-Stage, or Mezzanine, Financing

This is provided for major expansion of a company that has an increasing sales volume and that is breaking even or profitable. These funds are used for marketing, working capital, further plant expansion, or development of an improved product.

Bridge Financing

This type of financing may be needed when a company is between stages and when it plans to go public in six months to a year. Bridge financing is often structured so that it can be repaid from the proceeds of the next round or a public underwriting. It may involve restructuring of major stockholder positions through secondary transactions.

Estimating the Return on Various Types of Financing

Despite every entrepreneur's confidence in his "sure thing," more new ventures fail than succeed. Investors need a few big winners to offset the losers. Depending on the stage of the financing and, therefore, the risks involved, compound rates of return from 25 to 50% or more are not unreasonable expectations. A typical range of risk/return expectations is shown in Exhibit 7.3.

Keep in mind that the figures in Exhibit 7.3 are *anticipated* returns. Seasoned investors know that, no matter how thorough their due diligence, only one venture in five or ten will meet or exceed their expectations. There is no average deal. Investors are fond of saying (with tongue in cheek) that they never made a bad investment—all their losers went bad after the deal was made. In other words one or two big winners are required to offset the inevitable losers.

The rates in Exhibit 7.3 are also *rough approximations*. The unique characteristics of each venture and investor will determine the appropriate rate. The lesson for entrepreneurs is that you must recognize that the lower your investors' *perceptions of risk*, the lower will be their required return on investment (ROI), that is, the lower the share of equity an entrepreneur will have to give up to obtain any given amount of capital. Put another way, the longer an entrepreneur can survive on founders' capital, sweat equity, and bootstrap financing, the lower will be the cost of venture capital.

Investors give value-added advice and accept risk and lack of liquidity, yet realized returns on a successful investor's portfolio of venture deals will seldom be more than five to ten points above the returns on a diversified portfolio of quality common stocks, that is, venture portfolio ROIs of 20 to 25%. Entrepreneurs should keep in mind that if a venture fails, investors typically incur bigger losses than the founders—and if the venture succeeds, the founders typically are bigger winners than their investors. For this reason alone, losing potential investors by quibbling over a few percentage points of ownership seldom makes sense.

EXHIBIT 7.3. Risk-adjusted cost of venture capital.

Stage (risk)	Expected returns
Seed	80%
Startup	60
First-stage	50
Second-stage	40
Third-stage	30
Bridge	25

EXHIBIT 7.4. Capital gain/ROI conversion table.

	Exit year				
Multiple	**3**	**4**	**5**	**7**	**10**
3 times	44%	32%	25%	17%	12%
4 times	59	41	32	22	15
5 times	71	50	38	26	17
7 times	91	63	48	32	21
10 times	115	78	58	39	26

Investors tend to think in terms of capital gains multiples rather than rates of return. The conversion is simple and can be done on most hand calculators. Exhibit 7.4 illustrates conversion relationships.

To use Exhibit 7.4, select the exit year (that is, the expected holding period between investment and cash-out). In the *Exit year* column, select the required ROI appropriate for the risk perceived by investors. Risk, and therefore ROI, primarily reflects the stage of the financing. The multiple expected by investors can be found in the *Multiple* column.

EMPHASIZE THE NONFINANCIAL PAYOFFS OF INVESTMENT IN YOUR VENTURE

The influence of *nonfinancial payoffs* is another distinction between the venture capital fund and angel markets. Individual investors frequently look for nonfinancial as well as competitive financial returns from their venture investments.

Nonfinancial considerations fall into several categories. Some reflect a sense of social responsibility, and some are forms of *psychic income* (so-called hot-buttons) that motivate many individuals. The list of influential considerations includes whether your venture can:

- Generate jobs in areas of high unemployment
- Develop socially useful technology (for example, medical, energy, and environmental technology)
- Assist in the economic revival of urban areas
- Support female and minority entrepreneurs
- Provide personal satisfaction derived from assisting entrepreneurs who build successful ventures in a free enterprise economy

In addition to bringing a certain missionary zeal to the deal, angels (especially cashed-out entrepreneurs) typically look for fun in their investments.

Entrepreneurs sensitive to the match between the characteristics of their ventures and the *personal tastes* of investors should be able to raise funds on terms that are attractive to both parties.

PRICING THE DEAL: THINK LIKE AN INVESTOR

Based on projected revenues, profits, growth rates, and future financing requirements (dilution), entrepreneurs and investors should arrive at a *shared vision* of the venture's value five to ten years after financing, or at whatever exit date they agree on, and its exit strategy. Think in terms of *dollars* and *value* as opposed to ownership percentage. A business plan based on realistic assumptions is an entrepreneur's best friend at this point in the negotiations.

Four basic principles are involved in the pricing decision:

1. The division of ownership between founders and outside investors is determined by the *expected future value* of the venture and the *share* required to compensate investors at competitive rates—not by the relative dollar investments of the two parties.
2. The longer the track record of a new venture, the lower the risk to an investor, the lower the cost of capital, and the lower the share of equity required to purchase any given amount of capital. Exhibits 7.3, 7.4, and 7.5 illustrate this principle.
3. The more a venture is expected to be worth at any point in the future, the lower the share of equity required to purchase any given amount of capital. Exhibit 7.5 illustrates this principle.
4. The shorter the waiting period to cash out (that is, to harvest), the lower the share of equity required to purchase any given amount of capital. The time to liquidity is very important to investors. This is also illustrated in Exhibit 7.5.

Exhibit 7.5 illustrates how future values and holding periods affect percentage of a venture's equity required to yield a 40% return on a $1 million investment. The impact is dramatic: In a venture expected to be worth $25

EXHIBIT 7.5. Percentage of ownership required to yield a 40% rate of return on a $1 million investment.

Exit year (holding period)	Future value of the company (in millions)				
	$5	$10	$15	$20	$25
2	39%	20%	13%	10%	8%
3	55	27	18	14	11
4	77	38	26	19	15
5	N/A	54	36	27	22
7	N/A	N/A	70	53	42
10	N/A	N/A	N/A	N/A	N/A

N/A = Not applicable; investment would not be made.

million in two years an 8% stake would be required, whereas in a venture expected to be worth $15 million in seven years a 70% stake would be required. The lower left-hand corner of Exhibit 7.5 illustrates the fact that over 100% of the equity would be required if holding periods are too long or future values too small.

Most venture investors do not want to own a controlling interest in your venture or tell you how to run the business. Some investors argue that no one should own 50%, and no one should own control, that it should take at least two people to effect a major change in the company's goals, direction, or financing. As Exhibit 7.5 reveals, investors seek more than 50% of a company *only* when they need that much to justify the amount of money invested. Investors expect you and your management team to run the company profitably. Beware of investors who are "control freaks," including former operating managers who assume that they can run the company better than its management.

Take a look at a common approach to pricing a deal. *Pricing* refers to the fraction of the equity your investors will receive for the capital they provide. By focusing on the pricing models and assumptions that determine values in the capital markets, you can avoid some of the emotional biases that creep in during negotiations when the stakes are high or when human relationships are involved. A discussion of the pricing model (that is, its assumptions and probabilities) is bound to reveal differences between entrepreneurs' and investors' perceptions. Reconciling these discrepancies will be useful to both parties. The pricing model is a powerful tool for negotiating and reaching agreement on the appropriate pricing of an investment.

The following simple example employs traditional discounted cash flow techniques, except that it focuses on future values rather than present values using the risk-adjusted rates of return given in Exhibit 7.3.

DEVELOPING A PRICING MODEL: A CASE STUDY

Assume that we are dealing with a startup venture, Goforit, Inc., that needs a single round of financing of $1 million (an unrealistic assumption for a high-potential venture). The venture expects to generate $20 million in revenues after five years with a 10% after-tax net profit. Assume that after five years, the company expects to be growing at 20% or more and plans to go public. Stocks of companies with comparable size and growth rates trade at a price that is 15 times earnings.

Given these numbers and the investors' target ROI of 60% (ten times the investment in five years), the founders will have to provide investors with 33% of the company. See the *Most Likely* scenario in Exhibit 7.6.

The pricing model unfolds as follows: $20 million of revenues with a 10% margin yields after-tax profits of $2 million. Using a P/E ratio of 15 for a young, growing company with a thin market for its shares, the equity will have a market value of $30 million. To earn their 60% ROI, investors need 10 times their initial investment of $1 million, that is, $10 million. For their investment to be worth $10 million, they will need to own 33% of the company's total equity value of $30 million.

As shown in the last row of Exhibit 7.6 (which shows premoney valuation), these numbers imply that, before the investor's money goes in, the venture has a value of $2 million. This value is the result of the entrepreneur's recognition of a market opportunity and the capital and sweat equity invested to create a venture positioned to capitalize on that opportunity. If the founders' investment one year prior to startup was $200,000, they have generated a return of 900%, on paper, 10 times their investment in one year.

Exhibit 7.6 also contains *best case* and *worst case* scenarios. Both scenarios can be thought of as those outcomes or assumptions for which the probability of occurrence is one chance in ten. By focusing and agreeing on the range of possible outcomes and their probabilities, entrepreneurs and investors can accomplish the most difficult task of venture capital with a minimum of subjective debate and hard feelings. Both parties should feel that the pricing outcome is fair and openly arrived at. Recognize, however, that, because of entrepreneurs' optimism and investors' pessimism, it is unlikely that real agreement will be reached on your projections. Most investors assume that an entrepreneur's *worst case* is, in fact, the *best case*.

Computer spreadsheets are indispensable tools for examining the implications of alternative assumptions. But beware of spreadsheet diarrhea. Investors are more interested in sales/marketing, management, production,

EXHIBIT 7.6. Goforit, Inc. pricing model.

	Worst case	Most likely	Best case
Assumptions			
Investment	$1 million	$1 million	$1 million
Exit year	7	5	3
Revenue	$10 million	$20 million	$30 million
Net margin	5%	10%	15%
Growth rate	10%	20%	30%
P/E multiple	10×	15×	20×
Total equity value	$5 million	$30 million	$90 million
Investor multiple	15×	10×	5×
ROI	47%	58%	71%
Investor equity value required	$15 million	$10 million	$5 million
Results			
Investor %	N/A	33%	6%
Premoney valuation	None	$2 million	$17 million

and technology. Financial projections are the result of the vision, not vice versa.

For examples of other pricing models see "The Pricing of a Venture Capital Deal" in *Pratt's Guide to Venture Capital Sources* and *OED Report on Venture Capital Financial Analysis.* [5] A lot of homework on the application of these principles will pay big dividends. The booklets published by national accounting firms are useful summaries. Recommended books include *New Venture Creation* by Jeffry Timmons (Richard D. Irwin, Inc.) *Venture Capital Handbook* by David Gladstone (Prentice Hall) and *Venture Capital: Law, Business Strategies, and Investment Planning* by Joseph Bartlett (John Wiley & Sons).

STRUCTURING THE DEAL—TERMS AND CONDITIONS

If you are dealing with a venture capital fund, once you have reached an oral agreement, but before the legal documents are drafted, you will receive a nonbinding commitment letter and a term sheet setting forth the following terms of the deal:

- The amount of the investment
- The form of the investment
- The share of the equity represented by the investment
- The terms and conditions to which you will be asked to agree

You are, in effect, your investors' agent—"a person empowered to act for another." The terms and conditions are legal obligations designed primarily to protect investors from management behavior incompatible with investor interests. The term sheet is useful for identifying issues that could turn into deal killers if they are not addressed and resolved.

Everything in this life is negotiable, including the terms and conditions governing a venture investment. Don't go shopping for capital until you are familiar with the terms and conditions typically demanded by investors. These will be spelled out in the term sheet. Go over a sample term sheet with your legal counsel and financial advisors before you start the negotiations. Concessions made under pressure to raise cash can lead to ruinous conflicts later. Since most terms are negotiable, it is essential that you understand the terms, identifying those that are most important to investors and those that are and are not acceptable to you. Pay special attention to voting rights, antidilution provisions, board seats, and stock restriction agreements. The ultimate contract should be one in which both parties feel that they have been treated fairly.

Before going over the sample term sheet, do your homework! Never underestimate the wisdom to be found in interviews with other venture founders or the value of libraries, books, and seminars. "The Legal Process of Venture Capital Investment," one of the essays in *Pratt's Guide to Venture Capital Sources,* is an excellent place to start. Other sources include *Start-Up Companies: Planning, Financing and Operating the Successful Business* by Richard D. Harroch (Law Journal Seminars-Press, New York) and *Venture Capital: Law, Business Strategies, and Investment Planning* by Joseph W. Bartlett (John Wiley & Sons, New York).

The types of equity-linked securities used by venture investors range from common stock (typical of angel deals) through convertible preferred (typical of venture capital fund deals) to subordinated debt with conversion features or warrants (typical of Small Business Investment Company—SBIC—deals). (SBICs are privately owned but chartered by the U.S. Small Business Administration.) Angel deals typically are less tightly structured than venture fund deals. Some angels won't do a deal if their agreement with an entrepreneur can't be captured in two pages. Venture fund deals often involve agreements that require 15 pages or more to cover everything the investors (and their well-paid attorneys) insist on reducing to written agreements.

The sample term sheet provided in Exhibit 7.7 (see pp. 192–193) summarizes the terms and conditions of a $1 million convertible preferred stock financing placed by Goforit, Inc. with a venture capital fund. The text under each heading identifies principal features, but it is not a complete description.

The outline in Exhibit 7.7 is far from a complete enumeration of all the terms and conditions that investors and entrepreneurs might wish to impose on a venture investment. At best, the outline is an agenda of issues to be explored with your attorney, financial advisors, and other entrepreneurs who have raised venture capital.

DETERMINING THE HARVEST STRATEGY

Venture capital is "patient money." Returns to investors take the form of long-term capital gains realized after an extended period during which the investment has little or no marketability (liquidity). Because expectations about *timing* and *method* of exit influence investment decisions significantly, be prepared to discuss these issues early in your negotiations with investors. A harvest mentality based on the creation of substantial wealth for founders and investors is central to the fund-raising process.

Successful companies typically require several years to launch and build (although each venture is unique and each industry is unique). The harvest strategy should reflect this fact of life by contemplating a medium-to-long time frame, at least three to five years for a high-potential venture and as long as seven to ten years for a middle-market company. A public stock offering, merger, or outright sale of the company are common exit strategies for high-potential ventures. Management and Employee Stock Ownership Plan (ESOP) buyouts are common harvest strategies for investors in middle-market companies.

Patience and shared exit expectations are particularly critical for middle-market ventures, that is, ventures with limited prospects for a public offering or an acquisition by a larger firm within the five-to-ten-year exit horizon of venture investors. If an investor expects to cash out by selling shares back to your venture or its management, be sure that the terms and conditions of the sale are tied to the operating performance and cash flow of the venture and not to some arbitrary multiple of the original investment. For example, if the investors in Goforit, Inc. own 33% of the common stock, the "put" option might read as follows:

> There shall be a "put" provision whereby anytime after five years the holders of the convertible preferred shares may require the Company to purchase the preferred shareholders' equivalent common shares at the higher of the following:
>
> 1. $1,000,000 cash.
> 2. Book value times 33% ownership.
> 3. Five times pretax earnings for the year just ended times 33% ownership.
> 4. Fifty percent of sales for the year just ended times 33% ownership.
> 5. Ten times operating cash flow times 33% ownership.
> 6. Appraised value times 33% ownership.

Your legal and financial advisors can help design acceptable "put" arrangements.

LESSONS FROM LOSERS

Most entrepreneurs learn lessons the hard way—by making mistakes. However, entrepreneurs can learn some financial lessons from the mistakes of others. For example, the reasons cited by investors for rejecting investment proposals can be instructive. The most common reasons are:

- Lack of confidence in management
- Unsatisfactory risk/reward ratios
- Absence of a well-defined business plan
- The investor's unfamiliarity with products, processes, or markets
- In the case of angels, the business's unattractiveness to the investor.

EXHIBIT 7.7. Sample term sheet for *Goforit, Inc.*

December 31, 1993
Memorandum of principal terms and conditions

Amount: $1,000,000

Type of Security: Series A convertible preferred stock

Price: $1,500,000 premoney valuation. This will result in the following stockholdings after the fully diluted effect of the investment and the addition of management options:

Preferred stock:	40%
Founders stock:	35%
Management options and stock:	25%

Closing: On or before March 1, 1994.

Rights and Preferences

Dividends:

Dividends at the rate of 7.5% per share per annum, cumulative after third anniversary of the closing. No dividends payable on common stock unless first paid on the Series A shares.

Liquidation preference:

Original issue price per share plus all accrued but unpaid dividends. Participation in remaining assets on a pro rata basis with common shares. Merger or sale shall be deemed a liquidation.

Conversion rights:

Each Series A share shall be convertible at any time at the option of the holder into one share of common stock. Automatic conversion if voted by a two-thirds majority of the preferred stockholders. Automatic conversion on public offering at a price exceeding three times the purchase price of the preferred, where at least $5 million is raised.

Redemption:

At investor discretion between years 5 and 7 at original issue price plus 6% interest compounded annually plus accrued and unpaid dividends.

Antidilution protection:

Weighted average antidilution protection. Proportional adjustments for splits, stock dividends, recapitalizations, and similar events.

Voting rights:

Voting rights equal to common equivalent shares. Holders of Series A shares can elect a majority of the board of directors in the case of certain events:

a. Default in two annual dividend payments
b. Default in redemption
c. A loss of $25,000 or more in two consecutive quarters
d. Company net worth falls below $2,000,000

EXHIBIT 7.7. (*Continued*)

Registration rights:

a. Two demand registrations at Company's expense.
b. Unlimited piggyback registrations at Company's expense.
c. Rights may be transferred.

Restrictions:

Consent of a majority of Series A shares required to:
a. Issue any equity security or security convertible into equity
b. Approve merger or sale of all or substantially all the assets of the Company
c. Approve any liquidation of the Company
d. Approve the acquisition of or investment in another company

First refusal rights:

a. Preferred shareholders will have a right to maintain their pro rata interest in the Company on a fully diluted basis on any subsequent offering of stock prior to an effective public offering.
b. Preferred shareholders will have a right of first refusal with respect to any employee's shares proposed to be resold to a third party, which rights will terminate upon a public offering.

Information rights:

a. Audited annual financials within 90 days of year end and unaudited quarterly financials comparing actual results to budget within 30 days of quarter close. Annual budgets shall be supplied prior to the commencement of each fiscal year.
b. All other reports prepared by management for the board of directors.
c. Inspection rights. No more often than once a month, with four days notice.

Board of directors:

The board shall initially consist of five directors. The Series A preferred holders shall have the ongoing right to elect two members of the board of directors. Management limited to two board seats.

Stock restriction agreement:

All present holders of common stock of the Company who are employees of the Company will execute a stock restriction agreement pursuant to which the Company will have an option to buy back at cost the shares of common stock held by such person in the event that such shareholder's employment with the Company is terminated prior to the expiration of 48 months from the date of employment.

Special conditions:

a. Management shall have entered into two-year noncompetition agreements.
b. The company shall have obtained key person life insurance on the life of the Chief Executive Officer in the amount of $1,000,000. The policy shall be owned by and payable to the preferred shareholders.
c. Founders' shares shall vest over five years through nominal price buy-back arrangement.

Expenses:

Company shall pay all fees and expenses of counsel to the preferred shareholders up to a specified amount. Expenses in excess of that amount will be subject to written approval by the preferred shareholders and the company.

The following comments from private investors reflect the range of reasons that investment proposals are rejected:

- "We need to see market dominance. Never invest in 1% of any market. We will invest in 100% of a yet undiscovered market segment."
- "In most cases management did not seem adequate for the task at hand."
- "Simply not interested in the proposed businesses. Saw no socioeconomic value in them."
- "Risk/return ratio was not adequate."
- "Unable to agree on price."
- "Too much wishful thinking."
- "One of two key principals not sufficiently committed—too involved with another activity."
- "Unfamiliar with business."
- "Spouse refused."

CONCLUSION

Entrepreneurs and venture investors are at the heart of the free enterprise system. Just as the 1980s brought financial engineering and the leveraged buyout, the 1990s are bringing the downsizing of large corporations and the emergence of the entrepreneur. Employment of the *Fortune* 500 peaked at 16 million in 1979 and has fallen since then by 25%—a loss of 4 million jobs. In the meantime, *entrepreneurs and their investors have created 20 million jobs*. All these signs point to an acceleration of this "sea change" in the structure of the U.S. economy. This chapter has been written for the next generation of entrepreneurs with the *integrity, competence*, and *commitment* to build ventures that will create wealth for themselves and their investors as well as the jobs, innovative products and services, export trade, and tax revenues of the future.

Business history in the United States is the history of equity financing. Raising equity is arduous. Multiple rejections are part of the process. But business history and the stock market pay tribute to the entrepreneurs who stuck it out.

8 DEBT AND OTHER FORMS OF FINANCING

Joel M. Shulman

Entrepreneurs at small, growing firms, unlike finance treasurers at most *Fortune* 500 companies, do not have easy access to a variety of inexpensive funding sources. In the entire world, only a handful of very large firms have access to funding sources such as asset-backed debt securitizations, A-1 commercial paper ratings, and below-prime lending rates. Most financial managers of small- to medium-size firms are constantly concerned about meeting cash flow obligations to suppliers and employees and maintaining solid financial relationships with creditors and shareholders. Their problems are exacerbated by issues concerning growth, control, and survival. Moreover, their difficulty in attracting adequate funds exists even when firms are growing rapidly and bringing in profits (this is explored later in the chapter).

This chapter describes various financing options for entrepreneurs and identifies potential financing pitfalls and solutions. It also discusses how these issues are influenced by the type of industry and life cycle of the firm and how management should plan accordingly.

GETTING ACCESS TO FUNDS—START WITH *INTERNAL* SOURCES

Entrepreneurs requiring initial startup capital, funds used for growth, and working capital generally seek funds from *internal* sources. This contrasts with managers or owners of large, mature firms that have access to profits from operations as well as funds from external sources. I distinguish internal from external funds because internal funding sources do not require external analysts or investors to independently appraise the worthiness of the capital investments before releasing funds. Moreover, since external investors and lenders do not share the entrepreneur's vision, they may view the potential risk/return trade-off in a different vein and may demand a relatively certain return on their investment after the firm has an established financial track record.

Exhibit 8.1 shows a listing of funding sources and the approximate timing of the firm's usage. In the embryonic stages of the firm's existence, much of the funding comes from the entrepreneur's own pocket. For example, in the beginning entrepreneurs will consume their personal savings accounts, credit cards, and other assets such as personal computers, fax machines, in-home offices, furniture, and automobiles.

Soon after entrepreneurs begin tapping their personal fund sources, they may also solicit funds from relatives, friends, and banks. Entrepreneurs would generally prefer to use other people's money (OPM) rather than their own because if their personal investment turns sour, they still have a nest egg to feed themselves and their families. The nest egg phenomenon may be particularly acute if the entrepreneur leaves a viable job to pursue an entrepreneurial dream on a full-time basis. The costs to the entrepreneur in this case include the following:

- The opportunity cost of income from the prior job
- The forgone interest on the initial investment
- The potential difficulty of being rehired by a former employer (or others) if the idea does not succeed.

After adding to this the embarrassment of having to beg for a new job while paying off old debts, the prospective entrepreneur quickly realizes that the total cost of engaging in a new venture is very high.

Family and friends may "volunteer" to fund the entrepreneur's project in the early stages, and often will do so without a formal repayment schedule or specified interest cost. However, the funds are far from free. Total

EXHIBIT 8.1. Sources of outside funding.

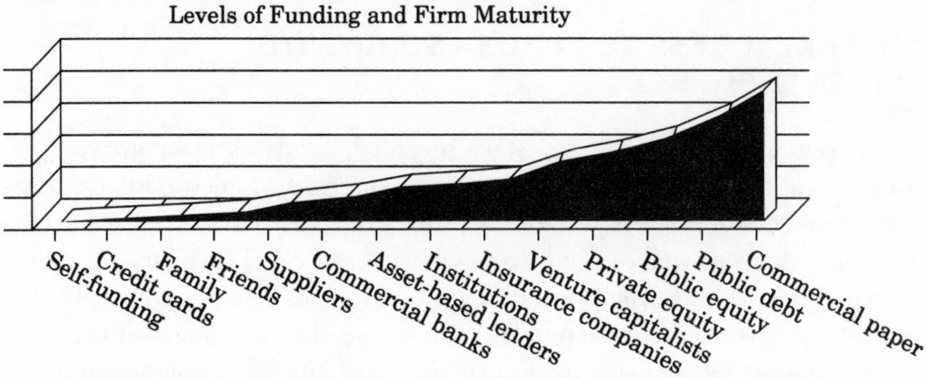

costs, including nonfinancial indirect costs—such as family pressure, internal monitoring, and strained relations—are probably extremely high. Moreover, family and friends make poor financial intermediaries since they have limited financial resources, different repayment expectations, and narrow loan diversification. This will contribute to the entrepreneur's desire to get outside funding from a traditional source as soon as possible. The question is, where can entrepreneurs go before banks will give them money?

WORKING CAPITAL—GETTING CASH FROM RECEIVABLES AND INVENTORIES

The timing of receivables collection and payment of accounts payable are key determinants in whether a firm is cash rich or cash poor. For example, an increase in net working capital (that is, current assets minus current liabilities) does not necessarily translate into an increase in liquidity. One reason for this is that increases in net working capital often result from increases in operating assets, net of increases in operating liabilities. These operating assets, such as accounts receivable or inventory, are usually tied up in operations and are not commonly liquidated (prematurely) to pay bills. Bills are typically paid with liquid financial assets, such as cash and marketable securities. Thus, only the liquid financial assets can be used to assess a firm's liquidity. Furthermore, corporate insolvency usually results when the firm fails to service debt obligations or callable liabilities in a timely manner. Consequently, corporate liquidity can be estimated fairly accurately by taking the difference between liquid financial assets and callable liabilities. This is referred to as the *net liquid balance*.

Exhibit 8.2 shows how the net liquid balance is actually a part of net working capital. *Net working capital* is easily calculated in one of two ways:

- Take the difference between current assets and current liabilities (as described earlier).
- Take the difference between long-term liabilities, including equities, and long-term assets (such as fixed assets).

The first formula is often misinterpreted to be the difference between two liquid components, whereas the second definition suggests that the residual of long-term liabilities minus long-term assets is used to finance current assets, some of which may be liquid. The second definition also enables us to analyze the current assets and liabilities as consisting of both liquid financial/callable components and operating components.

Net working capital is actually the sum of working capital requirements (current operating assets minus current operating liabilities) and the net liquid balance. This suggests that only a part of net working capital is liquid. Clearly, as a small firm grows, current operating assets will increase. If current operating liabilities do not increase at the same rate as the increase in current operating assets (which is true when an entrepreneur pays suppliers before receiving payment from customers), then the entrepreneur will find that the firm's net liquid balance will decrease (assuming the firm does not increase its long-term funding arrangements). This may be true even though the firm is generating paper profits. As long as the increase in working capital requirements *exceeds* the increase in profits (note: profits are included in the long-term liabilities part of Exhibit 8.2 due to increase in stockholders' equity), then the firm will find itself reducing its liquidity levels.

This highlights one of the fundamental weaknesses of the traditional liquidity ratios, such as the current ratio or quick ratio. These ratios include both liquid financial assets and operating assets in their formula. Since operating assets are tied up in operations, inclusion of these assets in a liquidity ratio is not very useful from an ongoing concern perspective. Note the difference between a liquidity perspective and a liquidation perspective. A *liquidation*

EXHIBIT 8.2. Integrative approach to working capital management.

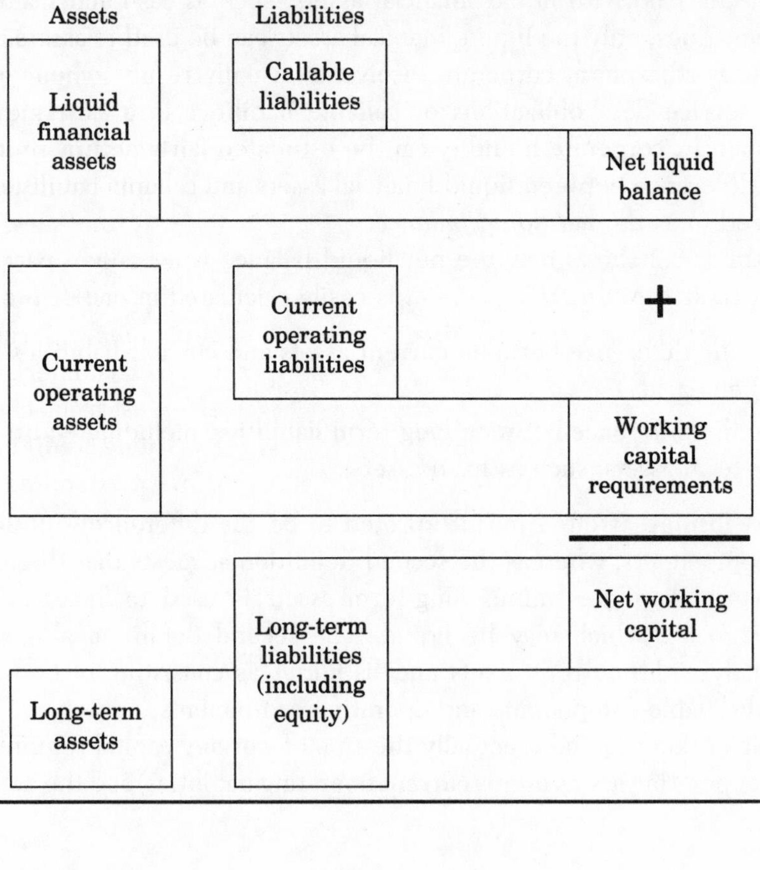

perspective assumes that in the event of a crisis assets may be sold off in order to meet financial obligations, while a *liquidity perspective* assumes the firm's financial obligations are met without impairing the viability of future operations. From an ongoing perspective, a new ratio—*net liquid balance* to *total assets*—may be more indicative of liquidity than either the current ratio or the quick ratio.

USING ACCOUNTS RECEIVABLE AS WORKING CAPITAL

Accounts receivable, that is, the money owed to the company as a result of sales made on credit for which payment has not yet been received, are a major element in working capital for most companies. And they are one of the items that gave us reason to assert that *working capital* is not the same as *available cash,* and that the timing of short-term flows is vitally important.

If a company is selling a major part of its output on credit and giving 30 days' credit, its accounts receivable will be about equal to sales of 30 days, that is, to one-twelfth of its annual sales, if sales are reasonably stable over the year. And if the company's collection policies are so liberal or ineffective that in practice customers are paying on an average, say, 45 days after they are billed, accounts receivable are no less than one-eighth of annual sales. Investment in accounts receivable is a use of funds. The company has to finance the credit it is giving to its customers by allowing its money to be tied up in this way instead of being available for investment in productive uses. Therefore, accounts receivable, like cash, have an opportunity cost.

But a company that does not give credit will obviously lose sales, particularly if its competitors offer generous credit. Here, again, there is a trade-off to be made between the cost of *giving credit* and the cost of *restricting credit.* In other words, there are two possible errors that a firm can make. It can incur the cost of being *too conservative* (deny credit to a good customer), or risk being *too aggressive* (grant credit to a poor customer). Most firms choose to exercise caution in granting credit, since the cost of extending credit to a customer who doesn't pay can far exceed the profits lost by not extending credit.

The magnitude of a company's accounts receivable obviously depends upon a number of factors:

- The level and the pattern of sales
- The breakdown between cash and credit sales
- The nominal credit terms offered
- The way these credit terms are enforced through a collection policy

Each of these factors is discussed in detail in the following sections.

The Sales Pattern

The basis of all receivables and collections is clearly *actual net sales,* that is, items sold minus any returns. From actual sales come the assumptions about receipts from future cash sales and collections of future credit sales. These are the key inputs in forecasting cash flow, as discussed later in this chapter.

Techniques for forecasting future sales fall into two broad groups:

- Techniques that use external or economic information
- Techniques based on internal or historical data from the company's own past sales

Most managers are more familiar with the techniques in the second group than they are with the techniques of economic forecasting. The methods for forecasting from historical data range from the very simple (such as straightforward moving average) to fairly sophisticated models. For instance, variations on exponential smoothing make it possible to take into account both long-term trends in the company's sales and seasonal variations. Simply put, although the more sophisticated techniques are useful, no forecasting method based *only* on historical sales data is completely satisfactory. You cannot be sure that either total industry sales or the company's share of the sales will be the same as they have been. There are a variety of external factors that an entrepreneur must also consider.

Methods of forecasting environmental change also fall into two broad groups. One group is primarily concerned with *forecasting the future performance of the economy as a whole,* particularly future levels of the gross national product and the national income. These GNP models, as they are called, are highly complex, computer-based models. Their construction may be beyond the capabilities of most entrepreneurs, but their output can readily be purchased. The other group is more concerned with *forecasting sales for individual industries and products*. One way to do this is to identify economic time series that can be used as leading indicators to signal changes in the variable being forecast. Again, this technique is best used by an experienced economist with a computer. The important point for the entrepreneur is that forecasting techniques are becoming progressively less of an art and more of a science.

Cash versus Credit Sales

The relative proportions of cash sales and credit sales may make an important difference to expected cash flows. Unfortunately, this is a variable over which most entrepreneurs have little control. For example, a company in retail sales can certainly take steps to increase its cash sales, either by banning credit entirely or by offering a discount on cash sales. But a company selling primarily to other corporate organizations—other manufacturing companies, wholesalers, distributors, or retail chains—has few cash sales. Its best hope is to set its credit terms to encourage prompt payment; but the sales will still be credit sales, not cash sales.

Credit Policies

Credit policies can be summarized into two general questions:

- To whom should credit be given?
- How much credit should be given?

But the two questions are closely interconnected. Most potential credit sales need to be evaluated on their own merits, and this is costly and time-consuming. In fact, the salaries and overhead of the credit analysts are likely to be the largest single item in the cost of giving credit to customers.

How much freedom a company has in setting the terms on which it will grant credit depends very much on its *competitive position*. For example, an organization in a monopolistic position has considerably more flexibility than one that faces aggressive competition. But real monopolies are rare. Most companies approach such a position only during very short periods, after they have introduced radically new products and before their competitors have had time to introduce similar products. A company in such a position may be tempted to take advantage of it through product price, but it is unlikely to tighten up its credit policy as well. The advantage will be fairly short-lived, but the damage to customer relations arising from a restriction of credit would continue for a long time.

Nevertheless, economic factors do play an important part in credit policy. The key issue is *elasticity of demand* for the entrepreneur's product. This assumes that the credit terms offered to customers are a component of the overall price as the customer sees it and that customers will resist a reduction in credit, just as they will resist a price increase. If demand for a product is *inelastic*—that is, if an increase in price or restriction in the terms of credit will produce a relatively small drop in demand, with the result that net sales revenues actually increase—then there is some potential flexibility in the terms of sale. Even here, however, it will be the industry as a whole that enjoys this flexibility; individual companies will probably have to accept whatever is general industry practice. If demand for a product is *elastic*, on the other hand, there will be little room to change the terms of the sale, either at company or at industry level.

Finally, an entrepreneur's credit policies may be influenced by the length of the company's order backlog and whether or not the company is working at full output capacity. A company operating below full capacity or below its optimum output may well be tempted to offer unusually generous credit terms in order to stimulate demand. The key question then will be whether the cost of the additional funds tied up in accounts receivable will be more than offset by the additional sales and reduced operating costs. Alternatively, a company working at full capacity, with its product back ordered, is in a position to tighten up on its credit policies to reduce its investment in receivables.

Setting Credit Terms

The terms of credit include both the *length of time* given before payment is due and the *discount* given for prompt payment. Terms expressed as "2/10, net 30" mean that payment is due within 30 days (from the date of invoice) and that 2% may be deducted from the bill if payment is made in 10 days or less. Some companies, on the other hand, set their net terms as payment by the end of the month following the month in which the sale is invoiced. Obviously, this latter policy is considerably more generous than "net 30" and is likely to result in a much larger investment in receivables.

An entrepreneur's failure to take advantage of cash discounts available on its accounts payable may be a very expensive mistake, equivalent to borrowing short-term funds at 36%. Therefore, is it an equally serious mistake for a company to offer the same terms to its customers? The answer is that it depends on whether giving a cash discount really does speed up collections, and whether the *opportunity cost* of the funds that would otherwise have been locked up in receivables justifies the reduction in net sales revenues.

For example, assume that an entrepreneur's terms are 2/10, net 30 and that 25% of its customers actually take advantage of this discount. Annual sales are $36 million, of which $9 million are discounted, and the company recognizes profits when the sales are made. The discount cost is, therefore, 2% of $9 million, or $180,000. Assuming that 25% of the customers pay in 10 days and the rest pay in 30, the average collection period, (including both discount and nondiscount sales) is 25 days, giving average accounts receivable of $2.5 million, as shown in the following equation:

$$\$36{,}000{,}000 \div 360/25 = \$2{,}500{,}000$$

If the company did not give a discount, none of its customers would pay within 10 days, and the average collection period would fall from 25 to 30. In that case, average accounts receivable would be $3 million:

$$\$36{,}000{,}000 \div 360/30 = \$3{,}000{,}000$$

The question is, then, whether the added return the company makes on the $500,000 by which the discount policy has reduced the average accounts receivable exceeds $180,000, the cost of the discount policy. As this represents a return on investment of more than 36%, the answer is probably no.

A change in the net terms, however, is likely to make a greater difference to the average accounts receivable balance than giving or withholding a discount for prompt payment. Even if terms of 2/10, net 30 are given, you may assume that a relatively small percentage of the company's customers will take advantage of the discount. But if the net terms are changed from 30 days to 45, doubtless a high percentage of customers will take advantage of this change. Going back to the previous example and assuming that 25% of customers pay within 10 days and the rest at the end of 45 days, the average payment period now becomes approximately 36 days [(10 × .25) + (45 × .75)], and the average accounts receivable will now be $3.6 million, as shown:

$$\$36{,}000{,}000 \div 360/36 = \$3{,}600{,}000$$

This example, however, has assumed that if the net terms are set at 30 or 45 days, everyone who does not take advantage of the discount for prompt payment will pay by the end of the net period. This is unrealistic. Many entrepreneurs and the companies they do business with make a practice of reducing their requirements for funds by paying all their bills late. True, the most commonly offered terms are 2/10, net 30, but a recent survey revealed that the actual experience of U.S. companies is that their average receivables run between 45 and 50 days. A company's accounts receivable depend not only on the terms of credit offered, but on how well those terms are enforced through the company's collection policy.

Collection Policies

Some of a company's accounts receivable will be paid some time after the theoretical time limit has expired. Others will never be paid at all and will have to be written off as bad debts. Neither of these variables is completely within the company's control. But both can be controlled to some extent through the company's collection policy.

There are many kinds of collection policies. The collection techniques of companies selling directly to the ultimate consumer are often highly standardized and even automated. Master records of customers are stored in computer data files. Periodically a search is made to identify overdue accounts. Each customer whose account has been outstanding for more than the net terms is sent a polite letter asking for payment, and the fact that such a letter has been sent is recorded in the file. If, on the next search, the customer is still found to be delinquent, a more strongly worded letter goes out, though the tone is still more in sorrow than anger. The third letter is quite harsh, the fourth threatens legal action, and so on. Such a system provides little opportunity to match the collection technique to the particular customer and situation. The average amount owed is probably small, however, and more individualized techniques are hard to justify in such circumstances.

When an entrepreneur's firm sells primarily in the industrial market and its customers are businesses, a different approach is in order. It becomes necessary to look at each individual case and determine how best to collect. If the other company is believed to be able to pay, the entrepreneur should rigorously attempt to secure payment before the situation becomes any worse. The methods open include:

- Refusing any further supplies or supplying only for cash
- Threatening legal action
- Actually undertaking legal proceedings
- Using a specialized collection agency

Where the other company is already in serious financial trouble, however, a different approach is often required. An all-out collection attempt may simply force the customer into insolvency, followed by liquidation or reorganization. In this event the debt may be repaid only in part, after many months of delay, or not at all. The wisest approach in this case may be to continue to give credit, or at least not to try to collect existing receivables, in the hope of keeping the other company in business. But a note of caution is in order here: If the company with the outstanding receivable is one of a number of creditors, it will gain nothing by being generous unless the other creditors are willing to do the same. Otherwise, it is simply subordinating its claims to those of others and increasing the chance that it will never be paid at all.

One generalization that can safely be made is that collection procedures are expensive, and their use is justifiable *only when the expected results exceed the cost*. Collection operations, in fact, are an excellent demonstration of the economists' law of diminishing returns. For a given volume of overdue accounts, the first few thousand dollars spent on collection will probably produce worthwhile results. But further expenditure is likely to yield less and less return.

How much should an entrepreneur be willing to spend on collection? The answer depends on the expected reduction in accounts receivable and the return that could be expected if these additional funds were available for reinvestment in productive operations. Assume that an entrepreneur decides that he can reduce his overdue accounts receivable $250,000 by hiring an assistant for $25,000. To cover the salary of his asistant, the entrepreneur would need to earn at least 10% return on the funds released from accounts receivable. This represents a fairly reasonable rate of return and should be attainable. However, the entrepreneur needs to consider all other nonwage costs of hiring an assistant, including FICA taxes, healthcare, and benefits, which could easily push the costs of the assistant another $10,000, or 40%. Consequently, whenever the entrepreneur considers reducing excess receivables, he needs to examine the size and scope related to the collection attempts and judge whether or not the costs justify the expenditure.

Setting Credit Limits for Individual Accounts

Entrepreneurs have another method of reducing overdue accounts and limiting bad debts: setting limits to the credit allowed on individual accounts. This is often a job that takes up much of the credit department's time. Again, as in collections, entrepreneurs need to distinguish between *sales to individual consumers* and *sales to corporate buyers*. An entrepreneur selling directly to consumers clearly cannot afford to undertake a thorough credit investigation of each one (unless the product being sold is a very expensive item, such as a boat or an automobile) and will set fairly arbitrary limits on the basis of limited information. But if the customers are business organizations, the setting of credit limits requires more thorough analysis. Such analysis is needed whenever a new customer is added to the company's files and whenever a customer's circumstances are suspected to have deteriorated.

The work of the credit department is simplified to some extent by the fact that reports of credit ratings are available from a number of professional agencies. The best known of these agencies is Dun & Bradstreet. This organization publishes a reference book, revised every two months, that lists more than 3 million U.S. businesses and gives a credit rating for most of them. These ratings range from "high" to "limited" and include an estimate of the company's financial strength, usually based on net worth. If more detail than this is needed, Dun & Bradstreet and other agencies sell reports that include information on a company's principal officers, any past bankruptcies, and, most important, the company's credit history in relation to its existing suppliers.

There are a number of other sources of information:

- Some industry associations operate credit advisory services for the benefit of their members.
- Companies selling directly to the consumer can get information from local credit bureaus.
- Commercial banks are also a useful source of credit information—an entrepreneur considering an extension of credit to a customer can ask his bank to carry out a credit investigation, which the bank will do by approaching the customer's bank for information about the customer's financial strength.

When none of the available services proves adequate or when the entrepreneur providing credit is concerned about a very recent or impending development in the customer's affairs that has not yet come to the notice of the information services (for example, a rumor picked up by the company's own salespeople that the customer is in trouble), then the credit department will have to do the analysis itself. This probably involves approaching the customer directly, which often means incurring substantial expense.

Much of the work appraising the creditworthiness of new customers can be cut short by using external sources of information; but the work of monitoring accounts receivable and deciding whether to increase credit limits or ban further credit is a continuing task that must be done by the entrepreneur's own staff. The decisions to be made are often difficult. No company likes to turn down orders. Once again, there is a trade-off to be made: the potential profit on the sale versus the cost of financing increased receivables and the probability of bad debt.

The evaluation of creditworthiness is slowly evolving from an art to a science, with all sorts of computerized packages used to perform the analysis. However, the two major determinants of the credit decision are the character of the individual creditor or management of the creditor firm and the capacity of the firm to repay the loan. In other words, what is the likelihood that management will be willing to pay according to the terms of the agreement, and what is the ability of the firm to repay the loan out of future cash flows? Entrepreneurs will find that the same simple set of guidelines that they use in extending credit to customers will be used by banks extending credit to entrepreneurs. The guidelines are known as the Five Cs of credit:

- *Character* refers to the customer's integrity and willingness to repay the financial obligation.
- *Capacity* addresses the borrower's cash flow and ability to repay the debt from ongoing business operations.
- *Capital* is the borrower's financial net worth—consequently, a wealthy borrower may be a desirable customer even if her annual cash flows are relatively low.
- *Collateral* refers to the resale value of the product in the event the repossession becomes necessary.
- *Conditions* refer to national or international economic, industrial, and firm-specific prospects during the time period of the credit.

One of the most difficult decisions that an entrepreneur has to make as a credit manager is whether or not a prospective customer is to receive credit. Two potential problems can occur: A good customer can be denied credit, in which case the entrepreneur loses out in potential profit; or the entrepreneur can extend credit to a poor credit risk and thus lose her investment in the sold merchandise. Since the cost of the latter far exceeds the cost of the former, most entrepreneurs are very careful about granting credit.

However, the credit-granting decision is only part of the entrepreneur's concern. Another important task is the monitoring of accounts receivables balances. Since receivables tied up in operations may represent a large opportunity cost, either in lost investment returns or in greater borrowing balances, entrepreneurs are careful not to let the accounts receivable balances get too large.

Although the opportunity costs for accounts receivable may be quite large, the largest current asset balances are usually in inventories. Accordingly, as the entrepreneur's business grows, inventory balances rise, and resulting operating cash flows decline. Consequently, the entrepreneur needs to monitor both accounts receivable and inventories and keep the levels as low as possible without interfering with profitable sales. This is especially true if the entrepreneur has a shortage of capital or credit limitations.

INVENTORY

Inventory represents the most important current asset of most manufacturing and trading companies. Indeed, for many entrepreneurs, inventories account for an important part of total assets. Yet money invested in inventory does not earn a return. In fact, it costs money to maintain inventories. They must be stored, moved about, insured, and protected from theft and deterioration. Records must be kept, and clerks must be paid to keep those records. In addition, some inventory will be devalued or become a total loss because it deteriorates or becomes obsolete before it can be used or sold. These costs can easily add up to 20% or more annually of the inventory value. Since the money tied up in inventory might otherwise be invested profitably, the real costs plus the opportunity costs of carrying inventory may add up to 30%, 40%, or even more. As with accounts receivable, the dollar amount of inventory depends on when the entrepreneur chooses to recognize profit: Is it at the time of production or the time of sale? A strong argument can be made for valuing inventories at cost or market, whichever is lower. With inventories, there may be a lot of uncertainty as to how much cash flow will actually be generated, so a conservative approach to valuation is recommended.

Entrepreneurs usually want to keep inventory levels as low as possible. Although they are not likely to be directly interested in the more detailed and lower-level decisions (which are usually made by production or purchasing personnel), they must be able to evaluate and influence overall results. Not only does keeping inventory at a minimum reduce inventory carrying charges such as storage costs and insurance, but it also ensures that as little as possible of the entrepreneur's capital is tied up in inventory.

But carrying too little inventory also incurs heavy costs. These include:

- The costs of too frequent reordering
- Loss of quantity discounts
- Loss of customer goodwill or plant efficiency due to items being unavailable when needed

Entrepreneurs must be able to weigh these costs against those of carrying excessive inventory in order to be able to judge what is an optimum inventory level.

The control of investment in inventories is particularly important to *the management of working capital*. Inventories are likely to represent the entrepreneur's largest current investment, and they are likely to be the least liquid of his current assets. Marketable securities can be turned into cash in a matter of hours, and most accounts receivable will usually be collected within the next 30 days. But three months' supply of inventory will take three months to turn into cash, if forecasts of demand or usage prove to have been accurate. If forecasts prove to have been optimistic, even more time than this may be required. The alternative—an immediate forced sale—is hardly attractive. Marketable securities can be sold for their market value, and receivables can usually be sold, or factored, for something like 80% of their face value. But inventories, other than some raw materials for which a ready market always exists, traditionally sell for little more than 10% of their acquisition cost in a forced sale. Thus, controlling a company's investment in inventory is of critical importance to the management of working capital.

SOURCES OF SHORT-TERM CASH—MORE PAYABLES, LESS RECEIVABLES

Entrepreneurs usually do not have all the cash they need all the time. Very often, an entrepreneurial firm needs to build up its inventory, thus reducing cash levels. Or an entrepreneur's customers may place unusually large orders, thus increasing accounts receivable financing or reducing company cash levels. This section describes the many ways entrepreneurs obtain additional short-term cash to restore their cash balances to the required levels.

As a rule, entrepreneurs look for short-term cash at the lowest possible rates. If they cannot obtain cash at no cost or at a very small cost, they begin to explore more expensive sources of cash. For example, an entrepreneur faced with a cash shortage might look first to her company's suppliers and her customers. She would look to suppliers because they extend credit to the company by collecting for goods and services after those goods and services are supplied. The entrepreneur can enlarge this credit by paying bills more slowly. The entrepreneur may also obtain additional cash by collecting from her company's customers more quickly.

Cash from Short-Term Bank Loans

If these relatively low-cost options are unavailable (or if their cost is too high because of the ill will generated), the entrepreneur may next turn to the company's bank for a short-term loan. Entrepreneurs faced with a severe cash shortage may also try to convert into cash two of their working capital assets—accounts receivable and inventory. An entrepreneur may pledge her accounts receivable to a finance company in exchange for a loan, or she may sell them to a factoring company for cash. Similarly, an entrepreneur may pledge her inventory (often using a warehousing system) in exchange for a loan.

Cash from Trade Credit

Trade credit is one important and often low-cost source of cash. Nearly all entrepreneurs make use of trade credit to some degree by not paying suppliers immediately for goods and services. Instead, companies bill the entrepreneur, and the entrepreneur pays in 10 days, 30 days or more. From the time when the supplier first provides the goods or services to the time when the customer finally pays for them, the supplier has, in effect, loaned the entrepreneur money. The sum of all these loans (bills) represents an entrepreneur's trade credit. By paying bills more slowly, an entrepreneur can increase the amount of these loans from his suppliers.

One way an entrepreneur can take more time to pay for his bills (or stretch his payables) is to stop taking discounts. For example, if his company normally takes advantage of all prompt-payment discounts, such as 2% for payment within 10 days, he can increase his company's cash by passing up the discount and paying the bill in the expected 30 days. Of course, this is an expensive source of cash. If he loses a 2% discount and has the use of the funds for 20 more days, he has paid approximately 36% interest (annual rate) for using the money.

However, he might argue that, in practice, the interest cost would not really be 36% because by forgoing discounts and aggressively stretching payables the company would not pay the bill in 30 days. Instead, such a company would stretch out this payable as long as possible and perhaps attempt to pay in 60 days. Now, the equivalent interest rate is only about 15% (50 days' extra use of the money for 2%).

This brings up the subject of late payments. Many entrepreneurs do not consider 30 days (or any other stated terms) a real deadline. Instead, they try to determine the exact point at which further delay of payment will have a penalty. For example, if a company pays too slowly, the supplier may take one of the following actions:

- Require payment in full on future orders
- Report the company to a credit bureau, which would damage the company's credit rating with all suppliers
- Bring legal action against the company

Many cash managers believe, however, that as long as they can pay company bills just before incurring any of these penalties, they maximize their company's cash at little or no cost. The *hidden costs* of this approach include such risks as damaged reputation, lower credit limit from suppliers, higher prices from suppliers to compensate for delayed payment, and the risk of exceeding the supplier's final deadline and incurring a penalty.

Cash Obtained by Negotiating with Suppliers

If an entrepreneur wants more credit and would like to stretch out her payables, she does not always have to incur the risks described above. Very often, she can negotiate with her suppliers for more generous credit terms, at least temporarily. If she and her supplier agree on longer credit terms (say 60 or 90 days), she can get the extra trade credits she needs without jeopardizing her supplier relations or credit ratings. It's important to bear in mind that suppliers are trying to build up their businesses and must compete with other similar suppliers. One way these suppliers compete is through credit terms, and that fact can be used to the entrepreneur's advantage. Just as the entrepreneur solicits several price quotes before placing a major orders, she may also want to encourage competition among suppliers for credit terms.

Some suppliers use generous terms of trade credit as a form of sales promotion. This is especially likely where a distributor is trying to enter a new geographical area and is faced with the need to lure customers away from established rivals. In such circumstances, generous credit may well be more effective than an intensive advertising campaign or a high-pressure sales team. The credit may be a simple extension of the discount or net terms, or it may take a modified form such as an inventory loan.

Cash Available Because of Seasonal Business Credit Terms

If the entrepreneur is in a highly seasonal business, such as many types of retailing, he will find large differences in credit terms in different seasons. For example, as a retailer, he might be very short of cash in the fall as he builds up inventory for the Christmas selling season. Many suppliers will understand this and willingly will extend their normal 30-day terms.

Furthermore, some suppliers will offer exceedingly generous credit terms in order to smooth out their own manufacturing cycle. Consider a game manufacturer that sells half its annual production in the few months before Christmas. Rather than produce and ship most of the games in the late summer, this manufacturer would much rather spread out its production and shipping schedule over most of the year. To accomplish this, the manufacturer may offer seasonal dating to its retail store customers. Seasonal dating provides longer credit terms on orders placed in off-peak periods. For example, the game manufacturer might offer 120-day terms on May orders, 90-day terms on June orders, and so on. This will encourage customers to order early, and it will allow the game manufacturer to spread out production over more of the year.

Advantages of Trade Credit

Trade credit has two important advantages that justify its extensive use. The first advantage is convenience and ready availability; because it is not negotiated, it requires no great expenditure of executive time and no legal expenses. If a supplier accepts a company as a customer, the usual credit terms are automatically extended even though the maximum line of credit may be set low at first.

The second advantage (which is closely related to the first) is that the *credit available from this source automatically grows as the company grows.* Accounts payable are known as a spontaneous source of financing. As sales expand, production schedules increase, which in turn means that larger quantities of materials and supplies must be bought. In the absence of limits on credit, the additional credit becomes available automatically simply by placing orders for the extra material. Of course, if the manufacturing process is long and the supplier's payment is reached before the goods have been sold, some additional source of credit will also be needed. But the amount required will be much less than it would have been if no trade credit had been available.

Cash Obtained by Tightening Up Accounts Receivable Collections

Rapidly growing accounts receivable tie up a company's money and can cause a cash squeeze. However, these same accounts receivable become cash when they are collected. Some techniques—such as lockboxes and wire transfers—enable firms to collect receivables quickly and regularly. However, the question is: How can the rate of collection of receivables be increased temporarily during a cash shortage?

The most effective way to collect receivables quickly is simply to *ask for the money.* If the entrepreneur just sends a bill every month and shows the amount past due, the customer may not feel a great pressure to pay quickly. But if the entrepreneur asks for the money, either with a handwritten note on the statement of account, a phone call, or a formal letter, the customer will usually pay more quickly. To take an extreme case, a customer receiving several calls a week from an aggressive entrepreneur may pay the bill just to get the entrepreneur to stop bothering him. Of course, these more aggressive collection techniques also have costs, such as loss of customer goodwill, scaring away new customers, loss of old customers to more lenient suppliers, and the generation of industry rumors that the company is short of cash and may be a poor credit risk.

Stretching out accounts payable and collecting accounts receivable more quickly are really two sides of the same issue. Most entrepreneurs attempt to stretch out their bill payments as long as is reasonably possible and to collect their own bills as quickly as competitively possible. The entrepreneur's objective is to maximize company cash, using both techniques, without antagonizing either suppliers or customers so much that his working relationship with them suffers.

Although the fastest way to collect receivables is to ask for the money regularly, the entrepreneur can also *change his sales terms* to collect cash more quickly. The entrepreneur has several options, including:

1. *Introduce discounts.* A company can initiate a discount for prompt payment (for example, a 2% discount for payment within ten days). Similarly, a company with an existing discount may increase the discount (for example, increase discount from 1% to 2%).
2. *Reduce credit terms.* If competitively possible, an entrepreneur may require payment in full in 15 days, a deposit when the order is placed, COD orders (in which the customer must pay for goods on delivery), or even full payment with the order. Companies will have difficulty instituting these measures if competitors offer significantly more lenient credit terms.
3. *Emphasize cash sales.* Some entrepreneurs, particularly those selling directly to consumers, may be able to increase their percentage of cash sales.
4. *Accept credit cards.* Sales made on bank credit cards or on travel or entertainment cards are convertible within a couple of days into cash. The credit card companies charge 3% to 7% of the amount of the sale for this service.

5. *Impose a penalty for late payment.* Some companies now charge 1.0 or 1.5% of the unpaid balance per month as a penalty for late payment. Again, competitive conditions may make this approach unlikely.

OBTAINING BANK LOANS THROUGH ACCOUNTS RECEIVABLE FINANCING

One approach an entrepreneur can take to free up working capital funds is to convert his accounts receivable into cash more quickly through aggressive collection techniques. However, when the entrepreneur fears that aggressive collection may offend customers and cause them to take their business to competitors, the entrepreneur may decide to convert his accounts receivable to cash through a financing company. In this form of financing, the entrepreneur can choose between two methods: pledging and factoring. The following sections describe both methods. In practice, finance companies or banks offer many variations on these two financing methods.

Pledging

Pledging means using accounts receivable as collateral for a loan from a finance company or bank. The finance company then gives money to the borrower, and as the borrower's customers pay their bills, the borrower repays the loan to the finance company.

With this form of accounts receivable financing, the borrower's customers are not notified that their bills are being used as collateral for a loan. Therefore, pledging is called *nonnotification financing*. Furthermore, if customers do not pay their bills, the borrower (rather than the finance company) must absorb the loss. Thus, if the customer defaults, the lender has the right of recourse to the borrower.

In general, a finance company will not lend the full face value of the accounts receivable pledged. In determining what fraction of the face value of receivables to lend, the finance company considers three factors:

1. The credit rating of the borrower's customers (because bills that may be paid slowly, or not at all, obviously do not make good collateral).
2. The quantity and dollar value of the accounts receivable (because a small number of large dollar-value receivable is easier to control).
3. The borrower's credit rating (because the finance company prefers having the loan repaid to taking possession of the collateral).

Typically, a company can borrow 75% to 90% of the face value of its accounts receivable if it has a good credit rating and its customers have excellent credit ratings. Companies with lower credit ratings can generally borrow 60% to 75% of the face value of their receivables.

Pledging receivables is not a cheap source of credit. In recent years, when the commercial bank lending rate was between 8% and 15%, the cost of pledging receivables was almost 20%. Moreover, an additional charge is often made to cover the lender's expenses incurred in appraising credit risks. Therefore, this source of financing is used mostly by smaller companies that have no other source of funds open to them.

Pledging with Notification

Another form of pledging is called *pledging with notification,* in which the borrower instructs its customers to pay their bills directly to the lender (often a bank). As checks from customers arrive, the bank deposits them in a special account and notifies the borrower that money has arrived.

With this approach, the lender controls the receivables more closely and does not have to worry that the borrower may collect pledged accounts receivable and then not notify the lender. The company loses under this system, however, because it must notify its customers that it has pledged its accounts receivable, which can reduce the company's credit rating.

Factoring

Factoring is defined as selling accounts receivable at a discount to a finance company (known as the *factor*). There are many variations of factoring, but the following example covers the main points. With factoring, a company usually transfers the functions of its credit department to the factor. That is, the factor takes over credit checking and collection. If the factor rejects a potential customer as an unacceptable credit risk, the company must either turn down the order or insist on cash payment.

An example will demonstrate how this process works. Suppose the W. Buygraves Inc. company (buyer) orders $10,000 worth of exotic wood and marble from the Saleman company (seller). The Saleman company calls its factor to report the order. The factor checks the credit rating of the Buygraves company and, if all is satisfactory, calls the Saleman company with an approval. The Saleman company then ships the goods and sends an invoice to the Buygraves company. The invoice instructs the Buygraves company to pay the factor. At the same time, the Saleman company sends a copy of the invoice to the factor, and the factor sends approximately 85% of the invoice amount ($8,500 in this case) to the Saleman company. The factor must now collect the $10,000 from Buygraves. When the factor actually collects the bill, it may send the Saleman company a small additional amount of money to recognize collections being higher than original estimates.

The fees that factors charge vary widely. These fees include:

- An interest charge, usually expressed on a daily basis (for the time the bill is outstanding) and equivalent to a 15% to 30% annual interest rate
- A collection fee, usually in the range of an additional 6% to 10% annual rate
- A credit checking charge, either a percentage of the invoice or a flat dollar amount

The factor keeps a hold-back amount (which is not immediately paid to the Saleman company) to more than cover these various fees and charges, deducts the total from the hold-back amount, and sends the remainder to the Saleman company.

Recourse

Factoring may be with or without recourse. In the previous example, factoring without recourse means that if the Buygraves company does not pay its bill (that is, is a true deadbeat), the factor must absorb the loss. Factoring with recourse, on the other hand, means that if the Bygraves company does not pay the bill within a prenegotiated time (for example, 90 days), the factor collects from the Saleman company. The Saleman company must then try to collect from the Buygraves company directly.

Naturally, a factor charges extra for factoring without recourse. Typically, a factor adds 6% to 12% (on an annual basis) to the interest rate it charges the Saleman company. For factoring without recourse, factors generally come out ahead because they minimize bad-debt expense by carefully checking each customer's credit. Nevertheless, the Saleman company might prefer factoring without recourse for two reasons:

- The Saleman company does not have to worry that any bills will be returned. In this way, factoring without recourse is a form of insurance.
- The factor expresses the extra charge for factoring without recourse as part of the daily interest rate. This daily interest rate may look very small.

Most factoring is done with notification. This means that the customer company is notified and instructed to pay its bill directly to the factor. Occasionally, factoring is done without notification. In this case, the customer sends his payment either directly to the supplier or to a post office box. In general, factoring is more expensive than pledging. On the other hand, factors provide services, such as credit checking and collection, that a company would otherwise have to carry out itself. For a small company using the factor is often less expensive than providing the services on an internal basis.

OBTAINING LOANS AGAINST INVENTORY

An entrepreneur's inventory is an asset that can often be used as collateral for a loan. In this way, entrepreneurs can get the cash they need while still retaining access to their inventory. There are four basic ways to use inventory as security for a loan, depending on how closely the lender controls the physical inventory. These four ways are:

1. *Chattel mortgage*, in which specific inventory is used to secure the loan.
2. *Floating* (or blanket) lien, in which the loan is secured by all the borrower's inventory.
3. *Field warehousing*, in which the lender physically separates and guards the pledged inventory right on the borrower's premises.
4. *Public warehousing*, in which the lender transfers the pledged inventory to a separate warehouse.

Each method is discussed in the following sections.

Chattel Mortgage

A *chattel (or property) mortgage* is a loan secured by specific assets. For example, a borrower might pledge 5,000 new refrigerators as collateral for a loan. To guarantee the lender's position as a secured creditor (in case of bankruptcy), a chattel mortgage must precisely describe the items pledged as collateral. In the case of the refrigerators, the loan agreement would include the serial numbers of the specific refrigerators pledged by the borrower. If the borrower sells some of these refrigerators or receives a new shipment of refrigerators, the chattel mortgage must be rewritten to include these changes specifically.

Because the chattel mortgage describes the collateral so specifically, it offers fairly high security to a lender. Lenders further reduce their risk by lending only a fraction of the estimated market value of the collateral. This fraction depends on how easily the assets can be transported and sold. In the case of refrigerators, which are easy to sell, a borrower might obtain as much as 90% of their wholesale cost. But a borrower with a highly specialized inventory, such as bulldozer scoops, might get 50% or less of their fair market value because the lender would have difficulty selling the bulldozer scoops to recover the money. Because chattel mortgages describe the collateral so specifically, lenders limit their use to high-value items.

Floating Lien

Instead of naming specific items of inventory to secure a loan, borrowers may pledge all of their inventory. This is a *floating, or blanket, lien.* Because such an arrangement does not describe specific items of inventory, it does not have to be rewritten each time the borrower sells an item from inventory or receives new items into inventory. However, this flexibility makes it extremely difficult for the lender to maintain the security for the loan. For example, the borrower might sell most of the inventory and not leave enough to secure the loan. For this reason, banks and finance companies will usually lend only a small fraction of the inventory's market value when using a floating lien.

Field Warehousing

Field warehousing was invented to fully protect the lender's security. Under a field warehousing arrangement, the borrower designates a section of the premises, often a room or a specific area of the regular warehouse, for the use of the finance company. The finance company then locks and guards this field warehouse area and stores in it the actual inventory that the borrower is using as collateral. The finance company gives the borrower the agreed-on fraction of the fair market value of the inventory and receives in return a warehouse receipt, which gives the finance company title to the inventory. Companies use field warehousing when the inventory is especially bulky or valuable, such as structural steel, bulk chemicals, or diamonds.

Whenever the borrowing firm needs some of the inventory, it repays part of the loan, and the finance company releases part of the inventory. In this way, the finance company guarantees that there is sufficient collateral at all times to secure the loan.

Public Warehousing

Public warehousing is similar to field warehousing except that the actual inventory is moved to an independent warehouse away from the borrower's plant. As with field warehousing, the finance company releases inventory as the borrower repays the loan. Again, this ensures that the collateral is always sufficient to cover the loan.

There are many variations of warehousing. For example, some bonded warehouses accept checks in payment for loans and then forward these checks to the finance company while releasing the appropriate amount of inventory to the borrower. If such an arrangement is acceptable to all parties, it helps the borrower regain title to the inventory more quickly.

Costs of Warehousing

Warehousing companies collect both a service charge and interest. The service charge is usually a fixed amount plus 1% to 2% of the loan itself. This service charge covers the cost of providing field warehousing facilities or of transferring inventory to a public warehouse. In addition, the warehouse company charges interest, usually 10% or more. Because of the high fixed costs of setting up a warehousing system, this form of financing is practical only for inventories larger than about $500,000.

OBTAINING "FINANCING" FROM CUSTOMER PREPAYMENTS

Some companies are actually financed by their customers. This situation typically occurs on large, complex, long-term projects; it includes defense contractors, building contractors, ship builders, and management consulting firms. These companies typically divide their large projects into a series of stages and require payment as they complete each stage. This significantly reduces the cash these companies require, compared to firms that finance an entire project themselves and receive payment on completion. In some companies, customers pay in advance for everything they buy. Many mail-order operations are financed this way.

CHOOSING THE RIGHT MIX OF SHORT-TERM FINANCING

The entrepreneur attempts to secure the required short-term funds at the lowest cost. The lowest cost usually results from some combination of trade credit, unsecured and secured bank loans, accounts receivable financing, and inventory financing. Though it is virtually impossible to evaluate every possible combination of short-term financing, entrepreneurs can use their experience and subjective opinion to put together a short-term financing package that will have a reasonable cost. At the same time, the entrepreneur must be aware of future requirements and the impact that using certain sources today may have on the availability of short-term funds in the future.

In selecting the best financing package, the entrepreneur should consider the following factors:

- The firm's current situation and requirements
- The current and future costs of the alternatives
- The firm's future situation and requirements

For small firms, the options available may be somewhat limited, and the total short-term financing package may be less important. On the other hand, larger firms may be faced with a myriad of possibilities. Clearly, the short-term borrowing decision can become quite complex, but the selection of the right combination can be of significant financial value to the entrepreneur's firm.

TRADITIONAL BANK LENDING: SHORT-TERM BANK LOANS

After an entrepreneur has fully used her trade credit and collected her receivables as quickly as competitively possible, she may turn to a bank for a short-term loan. The most common bank loan is a *short-term, unsecured loan made for 90 days*. Standard variations include loans made for periods of 30 days to a year and loans requiring collateral. Interest charges on these loans typically vary from the prime rate (the amount a bank charges its largest and most financially strong customers) to about 3% above prime.

Very often, an entrepreneur doesn't immediately need money but can forecast that she will have a definite need in, say, six months. The entrepreneur would not want to borrow the required money now and pay unnecessary interest for the next six months. Instead, the entrepreneur would formally apply to its bank for a *line of credit*—that is, an assurance by the bank that, as long as the company remains financially healthy, the bank will lend the company money (up to a specified limit) whenever the company needs it. Banks usually review a company's credit line each year. A line of credit is not a guarantee that the bank will make a loan in the future. Instead, when the company actually needs the money, the bank will examine the company's current financial statements to make sure that actual results coincide with earlier plans.

Banks also grant *guaranteed lines of credit*. Under this arrangement, the bank guarantees to supply funds up to a specified limit, regardless of circumstances. This relieves the company of any worries that money may not be available when it is needed. Banks usually charge extra for this guarantee, typically 1% a year on the unused amount of the guaranteed line of credit. For example, if the bank guarantees a credit line of $1 million and the company borrows only $300,000, the company will have to pay a commitment fee of perhaps $7,000 for the $700,000 it did not borrow.

In return for granting lines of credit, banks usually require that an entrepreneur maintain a *compensating balance* (that is, keep a specified amount in its checking account without interest). For example, if an entrepreneur receives a $1 million line of credit with the requirement that she maintain a 15% compensating balance, the entrepreneur must keep at least $150,000 in her demand account with that bank all year. The bank, of course, does not have to pay interest on this demand account money; so the use of this money is the bank's compensation for standing ready to grant up to $1 million in loans for a year. Of course, when the bank actually makes loans during the year, it charges the negotiated rate of interest on the loan.

Maturity of Loans

The most common time period, or maturity, for short-term bank loans is 90 days; however, an entrepreneur can negotiate maturities of 30 days to one year. Banks often prefer 90-day maturities, even when the entrepreneur will clearly need the money for longer than 90 days, because the three-month maturity gives the bank a chance to check the entrepreneur's financial statements regularly. If the entrepreneur's position has deteriorated, the bank can refuse to renew the loan and, therefore, avoid a future loss.

Entrepreneurs, on the other hand, prefer maturities that closely match the time they expect to need the money. A longer maturity, (rather than a series of short, constantly renewed loans) eliminates the possibility that the bank will refuse to extend a short-term loan because of a temporary weakness in the entrepreneur's operations.

Interest Rates

The rates of interest charged by commercial banks vary in two ways:

- The general level of interest rates varies over time.
- At any given time, different rates are charged to different borrowers.

The base rate for most commercial banks traditionally has been the *prime rate,* which is the rate that commercial banks charge their very best business customers for short-term borrowing. It is the rate that the financial press puts on the front page every time it is changed. Congress and the business community speculate about the prime's influence on economic activity because it is the base line for loan pricing in most loan agreements.

Historically, the prime was a base line for loan pricing; "prime plus two" or "2% above prime" was a normal statement of interest rate on many loan contracts. However, as the banking industry has begun to price its loans and services more aggressively, the prime is becoming less important. Along with the change in the prime, *compensating balances* (that is, the borrower's agreeing to hold a certain percentage of the amount of the loan in a noninterest-bearing account) are becoming less popular.

The current trend in loan pricing is *to price the loan at a rate above the marginal cost of funds* as typically reflected by the interest rates on certificates of deposit. The bank then adds an interest rate margin to the cost of funds, and the sum becomes the rate charged to the borrower. This rate changes daily in line with the changes on money market rates offered by the bank. As liability management becomes more of a way of life for bankers, the pricing of loans will become a function of the amount of competition, both domestic and international, that the banker faces in securing loanable funds. As a result of this competition for corporate customers and enhanced competition from the commercial paper market, large, financially stable corporations are often able to borrow at a rate below prime.

Interest represents the price that borrowers pay to the bank for credit over specified periods of time. The amount of interest paid depends on several factors:

- The dollar amount of the loan
- The length of time involved
- The nominal annual rate of interest
- The repayment schedule
- The method used to calculate the interest

The various methods used to calculate interest are all variations of the simple interest calculation. *Simple interest* is calculated on the amount borrowed for the length of time the loan is outstanding. For example, if $1 million is borrowed at 15% and repaid in one payment at the end of one year, the simple interest would be $1 million times 0.15, or $150,000.

When the *add-in interest* method is used, interest is calculated on the full amount of the original principal. The interest amount is immediately added to the original principal, and payments are determined by dividing principal plus interest by the number of payments to be made. When only one payment is involved, this method is identical to simple interest. However, when two or more payments are to be made, the use of this method results in an effective rate of interest that is greater than the nominal rate. In the example above, if the $1 million loan were repaid in two six-month installments of $575,000 each, the effective rate is higher than 15% because the borrower does not have the use of funds for the entire year.

The *bank discount method* is commonly used with short-term business loans. Generally, there are no immediate payments, and the life of the loan is usually one year or less. Interest is calculated on the amount of the loan, and the borrower receives the difference between the amount to be paid back and the amount of interest. In the example, the effective interest rate is 17.6%. The interest amount of $150,000 is subtracted from the $1 million, and the borrower has the use of $850,000 for one year. If you divide the interest payment by the amount of money actually used by the borrower ($150,000 divided by $850,000), the effective rate is 17.6%.

If the loan were to require a compensating balance of 10%, the borrower does not have the use of the entire loan amount; rather, the borrower has the use of the loan amount less the compensating balance requirement. The effective rate of interest in this case would be 20%—the interest amount of $150,000 divided by the funds available, which is $750,000 ($1,000,000 minus $150,000 interest and minus a compensating balance of $100,000). The effective interest cost on a revolving credit agreement includes both interest costs and the commitment fee. For example, assume the TBA Corporation has a $1 million revolving credit agreement with a bank. Interest on the borrowed funds is 15% per annum. TBA must pay a commitment fee of 1% on the unused portion of the credit line. If the firm borrows $500,000, the effective annual interest rate is 16% [(0.15 × $500,000) + (0.01 × $500,000) divided by $500,000].

Because many factors influence the effective rate of a loan, when evaluating borrowing costs, only *the effective annual rate* should be used as a standard of comparison to ensure that the actual costs of borrowing are used in making the decision.

Collateral

To reduce their risks in making loans, banks may require collateral from entrepreneurs. Collateral may be any asset that has value. If the entrepreneur does not repay the loan, the bank owns the collateral and may sell it to recover the amount of the loan.

Typical collateral includes both specific high-value items owned by the company (such as buildings, computer equipment, or large machinery) and all items of a particular type (such as all raw materials or all inventory). Banks use blanket liens as collateral where individual items are of low value, but the collective value of all items is large enough to serve as collateral.

The highest level of risk comes in making loans to small companies, and it is not surprising to find that a high proportion of loans made to small companies—probably 75%—is secured. Larger companies present less risk and have stronger bargaining positions; only about 30% of loans made to companies in this class are secured.

One aspect of protection that most banks require is *key person insurance* on the principal officers of the company taking out the loan. Because the repayment of the loan usually depends on the entrepreneur or managers running the company in a profitable manner, if something should happen to the entrepreneur or key managers, there may be some question about the safety of the loan. To avoid this uncertainty, a term insurance policy is taken out for the value of the loan on the life of the entrepreneur or key managers.

If the officer or officers die, the proceeds of the policy are paid to the bank in settlement of the loan.

When making loans to very small companies, banks often require that the owners and top managers personally sign for the loan. Then, if the company does not repay the loan, the bank can claim the signer's personal assets, such as houses, automobiles, and stock investments.

Applying for a Bank Loan

To maximize the chances of success in applying for a bank loan, an entrepreneur should maintain good banking relations. Personal visits by the entrepreneur and other senior officers, as well as quarterly delivery of income statements, balance sheets, and cash flow statements, are useful means of sustaining such relations.

The actual process of obtaining bank credit (whether a line of credit or an actual loan) must be conducted on a personal basis with the bank loan officer. The loan officer will be interested in knowing the following information:

- How much money the company needs
- How the company will use this money
- How the company will repay the bank
- When the company will repay the bank

Entrepreneurs should be able to fully answer these questions and support their answers with past results and realistic forecasts; if so, they stand an improved chance of obtaining the line of credit or loan that they need.

Restrictive Covenants

Bank term loans are negotiated credit, granted after formal negotiations take place between borrower and lender. As part of the terms agreed to in these negotiations, the bank usually seeks to set various restrictions, or *covenants,* on the borrower's activities during the life of the loan. These restrictions are tailored to the individual borrower's situation and needs; thus, it is difficult to generalize about them. This section introduces some of the more widely used covenants and their implications. All of these covenants are (at least to some degree) negotiable; it is wise for the financial executive to carefully review the loan contract and to attempt to moderate any overly restrictive clause a bank may request.

The restrictive covenants in a loan agreement may be classified as:

- *General provisions*—these are found in most loan agreements and are designed to force the borrower to preserve liquidity and limit cash outflows. They typically vary with the type of loan.

- *Routine provisions*—these are also found in most loan agreements and are normally not subject to modification during the loan period.
- *Specific provisions*—these are used according to the situation and are used to achieve a desired total level of protection.

The following sections describe these restrictions in more detail.

General Provisions

Most common of all general provisions is a requirement relating to the *maintenance of working capital*. This may simply be a provision that net working capital is to be maintained at or above a specified level. Alternatively, when the company is expected to grow fairly rapidly, the required working capital may be set on an increasing scale. For example, the bank may stipulate that working capital is to be maintained above $500,000 during the first twelve months of the loan, above $600,000 during the second, above $750,000 during the third, and so on. If the borrower's business is highly seasonal, the requirement for working capital may have to be modified to reflect these seasonal variations.

The provision covering working capital is often set in terms of the borrower's current ratio—current assets divided by current liabilities—which must be kept above, for example, 3 to 1 or 3.5 to 1. The actual figure is based on the bank's judgment and whatever is considered a safe figure for that particular industry.

Working capital covenants are easy to understand and very widely used. Unfortunately, they are often of rather doubtful value. As discussed in this chapter, a company may have a large net working capital and still be short of cash.

Another widely used covenant is *a limit on the borrower's expenditures for capital investment*. The bank may have made the loan to provide the borrower with additional working capital and does not wish to see the funds sunk into capital equipment instead. The covenant may take the form of a simple dollar limit on the investment in capital equipment in any period. Alternatively, the borrower is often allowed to invest up to, but not more than, the extent of the current depreciation expense. Such a provision may prove to be a serious restriction to a rapidly growing company. And clearly, any company will find such a covenant damaging if the maximum expenditure is set below the figure needed to maintain productive capacity at an adequate and competitive level.

Most term loan agreements include *covenants to prevent the borrower from selling or mortgaging capital assets without the lender's permission*. This may be extended to cover current assets other than the normal sale of finished goods, in which case the borrower is prohibited from factoring accounts receivable, selling any part of the raw-material inventory, or assigning inventory to a warehouse finance company without the bank's express permission.

Limitations on additional long-term debt are also common. The borrower is often theoretically forbidden to undertake any long-term debt during the life of the term loan, though in practice the bank usually allows new debt funds to be used in moderation as the company grows. The provision is often extended to prevent the borrower from entering into any long-term leases without the bank's authorization.

One type of covenant that clearly recognizes the importance of cash flows to a growing company is a *prohibition of or limit to the payment of cash dividends*. Again, if dividends are not completely prohibited, they may be either limited to a set dollar figure or based upon a set percentage of net earnings. The latter approach is obviously the less restrictive.

Routine Provisions

The second category of restrictive covenants includes routine provisions found in most loan agreements that usually are not variable. The loan agreement ordinarily includes the following requirements:

- The borrower must furnish the bank with periodic financial statements and maintain adequate property insurance.
- The borrower agrees not to sell a significant portion of its assets. A provision forbidding the pledging of the borrower's assets is also included in most loan agreements. This provision is often termed a negative pledge clause.
- The borrower is restricted from entering into any new leasing agreements that might endanger the ability to pay the loan.
- The borrower is restricted from acquiring other firms unless prior approval has been obtained from the lender.

Specific Provisions

Finally, a number of restrictions relate more to the borrowing company's management than to its financial performance. For example:

- Key executives may be required to sign employment contracts or take out substantial life insurance.
- The bank may require the right to be consulted before any changes are made in the company's top management.
- Some covenants prevent increases in top management salaries or other compensation.

Restrictive covenants are very important in borrowing term loans. If any covenant is breached, the bank has the right to take legal action to recover its loan, probably forcing the company into insolvency. On the other hand, it may be argued that the covenants protect the borrowing company as well as the lender, in that their intention is to make it impossible for the borrower to get into serious financial trouble without first infringing on one or more restrictions, thus giving the bank a right to step in and apply a guiding hand. A bank is very reluctant to force any client into liquidation. In the event that a restriction is infringed on, however, the bank may use its very powerful bargaining position to demand even tighter restrictions—and some control over the borrower's operations—as the price of continuing the loan.

OBTAINING TERM LOANS FROM INSURANCE COMPANIES

Term lending by insurance companies is much less common than bank term lending. It does, however, offer an unusual range of maturities that span both intermediate- and long-term credit.

Insurance companies—especially life insurance companies—have a particularly stable and predictable business. Their cash inflows (which consist primarily of premium payments on insurance policies) can be forecast accurately. Their principal cash outflows (that is, payment of claims on policies) are also predictable on the average because the unpredictability of individual cases is effectively smoothed out by large numbers. Insurance companies, then, do not have any of the potential problems of liquidity of commercial banks. They can lend funds for a relatively long term.

The shortest-term loans made by insurance companies are for about five years. Ten years is probably about the average, and 15 years is not uncommon. During the 1950s some companies moved heavily into long-term financing and made loans that were virtually permanent capital: a number of term loans with maturities of more than 40 years were granted, and one major company made some 100-year loans. This trend has been reversed, however, and 10- to 15-year loans may be considered typical.

The preferred maturities of banks on the one hand and insurance companies on the other are obviously complementary, and some companies have been able to match term loan funds to their needs very effectively by putting together a package of bank and insurance funds. In such a case the bank advances funds for the first five years; then the insurance company takes over the loan for perhaps a further ten years. The borrower negotiates with representatives of both the bank and the insurance company at the same time, and the restrictive covenants are set at this time to apply to both phases of the loan.

OBTAINING TERM LOANS FROM PENSION FUNDS

The very rapid growth in pension funds has been one of the most striking developments in the financial world in recent years. At the same time, pension funds have a somewhat greater degree of flexibility in the ways they can be invested, and many pension-fund managers have aggressively looked for ways of maximizing their rates of return. One result of this has been an increasing interest in term loan lending. However, availability of loans from this source for very small dollar amounts is limited.

Pension funds have much the same stability and predictable cash flows as life insurance companies, and their managers also prefer the same kinds of longer-maturity loans. The characteristics of pension fund lending, in fact, are almost the same as those for insurance term loans.

It should be added that, when borrowing from both pension funds and insurance companies, the borrower does not usually approach the lender directly. Typically, the first move is for the entrepreneur or key officer of the firm to approach the company's commercial bank. If the bank is not able to supply the company's needs—probably because the funds are needed for a longer period than the bank's maximum maturity—the bank itself may then invite a life insurance company or pension fund to participate in the loan. Alternatively, the commercial bank may introduce the borrower to an investment banker, who will discuss the company's needs and facilitate the private placement of paper through a pension fund or life insurance company.

EQUIPMENT FINANCING

Capital equipment is often financed by intermediate-term funds. These may be straightforward term loans, usually secured by the equipment itself. Both banks and finance companies make equipment loans of this type. The non-bank companies charge considerably higher interest rates; they are used primarily by smaller companies that find themselves unable to qualify for bank term loans.

As with other types of secured loans, the lender will evaluate the quality of the collateral and advance a percentage of the market value. In determining the repayment schedule, the lender ensures that the value of the equipment exceeds the loan balance. In addition, the loan repayment schedule is often made to coincide with the depreciation schedule of the equipment.

One further form of equipment financing that should be considered is the *conditional sales contract*, which normally covers between two and five years. Under such a contract, the buyer agrees to buy a piece of equipment by installment payments over a period of years. During this time the buyer has the use of the equipment, but the seller retains title to it until the payments are completed. Companies that are unable to find credit from any other source may be able to buy equipment on these terms. The lender's risk is small because the equipment can be repossessed at any time if an installment is missed.

Equipment distributors who sell equipment under conditional sales contracts often sell the contract to a bank or finance company, in which case the transaction becomes an interesting combination of equipment financing for the buyer and receivables financing for the seller.

The credit available under a conditional sales contract is less than the full purchase price of the equipment. Typically, the buyer is expected to make an immediate down payment of 25% to 33% of the full cash price, and only the balance is financed. The cost of the credit given may be quite high. Equipment that is highly specialized or subject to rapid obsolescence presents a greater risk to the lender than widely used standard equipment, and the interest charged on the sale of such specialized equipment to a small company may exceed 15% to 20%.

USING EQUIPMENT LEASING AS A FINANCING STRATEGY

Leasing has become popular in recent years because there has been a trend emphasizing the ability to use property over the legal ownership of property. Other reasons often mentioned include the sharing of tax benefits between lessors and lessees. But the big incentive for leasing continues to be the nontax attributes such as flexibility, a hedge against obsolescence and inflation risk, service and maintenance contracts, convenience, lower costs, and off-balance-sheet financing. These advantages are discussed in the following sections.

Use versus Ownership

Many entrepreneurs have come to realize that the use of a piece of equipment is more important to the production of income than the possession of a piece of paper conveying title to the equipment. In fact, if people can use equipment for most of its economic life without having the full legal responsibilities, risks, and burdens of ownership, why should they ever desire to own it? Even farmers, who may have traditionally valued land ownership, now readily acknowledge that the use of land is more important than ownership of it. Many farmers and ranchers lease tracts of land to increase production of cattle or crops.

Tax Considerations

A big boost to leasing over the years has been the sharing of large tax benefits created through accelerated depreciation and investment tax writeoffs. This advantage may become even more valuable through the Clinton administration's proposals mentioned in early 1993. For example, the reenactment of the investment tax credit would be a tremendous boost to low-income capital/property users. Lessees in low or negative tax positions may not be able to enjoy the full tax benefits of asset ownership and thus look to lessors in high tax positions to share some of the tax benefits through competitive lease pricing.

Nontax Attributes

Although in the past leasing may have gained from the investment credit and other tax benefits, it doesn't depend on the tax code for its survival. Much of the growth in leasing of late has been a result of nontax attributes. Many lease and tax experts generally agree that some companies, especially nonfinancial companies that did leveraged leasing primarily for the tax advantage, will leave the market. They also point out that a principal purpose of leasing is asset use, not ownership.

Leasing provides 100% financing, flexibility in usage requirements and terms, fixed rates, and convenience. Furthermore, from the lessee's perspective, leasing is a source of off-balance-sheet financing, a hedge against obsolescence and inflation risks, and often a cheaper financing source than borrowing. These attributes are particularly useful to lessees, which are often cash-poor companies.

Flexibility of Leases

Flexibility is a major factor in the recent growth of leasing. A short-term cancelable lease offers a firm flexibility, particularly if the leased asset is in an industry undergoing rapid technological advances. If a superior product comes to market, the lessee can cancel the current lease and enter into a new lease with the new product. Many managers mention the ability to specifically structure the financial and usage terms of the lease agreement as one of the major benefits of leasing.

In addition to allowing flexibility provisions, leases seldom contain the restrictive covenants usually found in loan agreements. For example, some loan agreements prohibit future financing of equipment until the loan is paid down significantly; leasing allows further expansion without restrictions.

Obsolescence of Equipment

Another reason use of equipment has been emphasized is that penalties are attached to the ownership of equipment (such as computers) that is developed by high-technology industries undergoing rapid growth. Some computers have even become obsolete between the order date and the delivery date—and who wants to own an outmoded piece of equipment? Short-term, cancelable leases permit firms to avoid the pitfalls of owning obsolete equipment.

If a piece of equipment becomes outdated, the lessee cancels the lease and orders updated equipment. In fact, automatic replacement of obsolete equipment is written into an upgrade lease agreement. A renewable operating lease enables a lessee to transfer the obsolescence risk to the lessor, who presumably is in a better position to resell a product and to forecast the residual value of a piece of equipment. Some lessors, such as Equitable Life Leasing, even specialize in equipment where the risk of technological obsolescence is great.

Cost and Convenience

Some entrepreneurs are attracted to leasing because of lower costs, fewer down payment restrictions, and convenience. Leasing companies generally require down payments lower than other financial institutions. The typical lease requires the first and last rental payments in advance (representing 2% to 4% down), whereas many banks require 10% to 20% as a down payment. In addition, other incidental costs of acquiring the asset—such as sales tax and installation charges—can be included as part of the lease payments rather than (as required by other financial institutions) paid in advance along with the large down payment. Frequently, the opportunity cost of tying up cash in equipment acquisitions is high enough that it almost necessitates leasing as an alternative. This is especially true for small, rapidly growing companies, where available funds are tied up in accounts receivables and inventories. (For example, if a small, growing firm needs a piece of equipment that it cannot afford to buy from funds generated internally, it may be able to lease the equipment immediately.)

Economies of Scale

Certain leasing companies, because of their large size, can effect savings in the form of quantity discounts received from volume purchasing. Such savings can be partially passed on to the entrepreneur. Additional savings from economies of scale may be obtained through the service lease, in which the cost of maintaining the leased equipment is included as part of each rental payment.

Autos, trucks, computers, and office copiers are examples of equipment often accompanied by a maintenance and service contract. Many lessees believe that leasing companies, because of familiarity with the equipment and large size, may be more proficient in servicing the equipment and will therefore pass along any savings. It does not always follow that large size and efficiency go hand in hand, however. Therefore, savings must be ascertained by comparing lease rates charged by competing companies.

Large leasing companies usually have access to secondary markets in which returned equipment may be resold. Since operating leases tend to be short-term, a great reliance is placed on the resale or salvage value. Lessors assume the risk of the resale value and are often willing to wait until the end of the lease term to realize their return objective. Thus, they are able to reduce their front-end cost to the entrepreneur and may charge a lower lease payment.

Off-Balance-Sheet Financing

Operating leases that meet certain accounting criteria are not capitalized on the balance sheet of the entrepreneur. Thus, the entrepreneur can acquire the use of equipment without showing the lease as a payable liability on his balance sheet. This attribute is not as significant as it once was because of stricter reporting requirements and more sophisticated creditors. However, some creditors may not consider leases as debt if they are properly structured. This may enlarge the firm's overall debt capacity.

When examining long-term projects, the entrepreneur needs to make important decisions about the financing of major assets. One obvious choice is to purchase the desired asset with either corporate cash or borrowed funds. Leasing provides an alternative. Leasing is designed to be a flexible financing vehicle. This may someday be helpful to the entrepreneur who anticipates future problems, and presents alternative and flexible strategies.

OBTAINING EARLY FINANCING FROM EXTERNAL SOURCES

The Small Business Administration

During much of the 1970s and 1980s the Small Business Administration (SBA) provided billions of dollars to small business owners and entrepreneurs through the SBA direct and guaranteed loan programs. However, the direct loan program—in which the SBA works in concert with banks or local agencies to provide loans directly to borrowers—has been strongly curtailed.

The more common approach is for the entrepreneur to receive an SBA-guaranteed loan from the local bank. The SBA can guarantee up to 90% of the loan (not exceeding $750,000) once a local bank has rejected the loan application. With the SBA guarantee the local bank has less risk; however, the bank must also forfeit part of the interest rate that it might normally charge. Prospective borrowers should recognize that the SBA, as well as SBICs, venture capitalists, and angels, have specific guidelines that they follow in lending money to new business operations.

Business borrowers should be advised to thoroughly prepare for their meeting with their (prospective) bankers. Bankers are likely to demand the following information and documents:

- Pro forma financial statements
- Personal balance sheet and credit history
- A list of all equipment/assets and pledged collateral
- A description of how loan proceeds are being used
- A description of shareholder and creditor interests
- Personal business disclosures
- A detailed business plan

In addition, entrepreneurs should be able to respond to questions regarding their own salary, spending habits, and willingness to personally cosign a note on any borrowed funds. Moreover, as explained later in this chapter, it's also important for the entrepreneur to avoid the appearance of commingled personal and corporate assets and liabilities.

SBICs

The SBA licenses and regulates SBICs (Small Business Investment Companies). The SBA mandates SBIC investments be made to businesses with a net worth less than $6 million and with an average net income after taxes less than $2 million. Moreover, SBICs may not exceed a 20% capital interest in a single business nor more than 33% in a portfolio of real estate investments. These investment restrictions result in many relatively small investments in small companies. For example, from their inception through 1990, SBICs invested almost $9 billion in over 90,000 small firms including such success stories as Apple Computer, Cray Research, Federal Express, Teledyne, and Midway Airlines. At year end 1990, there were approximately 380 SBICs with assets of $3.1 billion.

SBICs draw their initial capital from private sources such as individuals, corporations, and banks and borrow funds from the government or from private financial institutions through government-guaranteed loans. The SBA guarantees enable the SBIC to attract more capital for investment and capital at more favorable rates than it could commercially. As such, SBICs are able to leverage their capitalization by a factor up to three or four.

SBICs make either *equity investments* or *long-term subordinated or unsecured loans* to companies with significant profit potential that otherwise could not qualify for long-term funding from banks or the private equity market. SBICs are regulated under the 1940 Investment Company Act and are required to pay out at least 90% of their net income, exclusive of capital gains, each tax year. Any income retained within the 10% limit is subject to the corporate income tax. Capital gains may be retained or paid out. If retained, they are subject to the corporate income tax. The result of this policy is that the company can only retain a small fraction of its earnings, so that the only manner in which the firm can grow is to either raise new equity capital or increase the firm's financial leverage.

Unfortunately, despite the fact that SBICs have provided original seed money to a number of extremely successful startups, the SBA, with encouragement from the U.S. Senate, has placed a moratorium on granting new SBIC licenses. Moreover, due to perceived fund mismanagement, at least some senators have suggested that the misguided SBICs could lead to "a mini S&L bailout." Consequently, the SBA—concerned about potential government losses exceeding $800 million—has threatened the existence of the SBIC government-assisted program. These government actions have not only sparked debate over the continued usefulness of SBIC financing but have also rekindled interest in the advantages and disadvantages of investments in publicly traded SBICs and other related venture capital funds.

CASH FLOWS AND FUNDING NEEDS

The management of working capital involves more than just monitoring liquidity balances. It also includes managing accounts receivable and inventories, as well as acquiring appropriate levels of financing from suppliers and creditors. In order to forecast the amount and timing of its funding requirements, an entrepreneur usually needs to develop a detailed cash forecast. The cash forecast is also useful in determining the appropriate maturity of funding sources.

Some level of current assets, such as accounts receivable and inventories, will always be required for corporate needs. These *permanent levels of current liabilities,* such as accounts payable, will always be on hand. If the firm pays its suppliers before it receives payment, then the firm will generally be in a borrowing situation due to its permanent layers of current assets. The firm's needs will increase even more during stages of growth. How fast the firm grows and how easily it can obtain funding from institutional sources will affect the amounts and types of funds it should pursue. For example, permanent layers of accounts receivable and inventories should be financed by long-term sources if management is concerned about exposure to refinancing risk (that is, rising interest rates or the possibility of funding becoming unavailable). This is consistent with the matching principle, which states that long-term or permanent assets should be financed by long-term or permanent sources, and short-term assets should be financed by short-term sources.

However, management may choose not to be conservative and decide to finance permanent needs with short-term debt because it believes that short-term debt is generally less expensive than long-term debt. This would be considered an aggressive management approach because the firm would be subject to the risk of rising interest rates and to problems with refinancing retiring debt. Nevertheless, some studies suggest that management quite often attempts to minimize short-term interest rates in spite of increasing refinancing risks.

PLANNING CASH FLOW AND PLANNING PROFITS

Although there is a relationship between them, cash flows are not the same as profit. *Profit* is an accounting concept designed to measure the overall performance of the company. It is a somewhat nebulous concept, open to various measurement techniques and accounting conventions, each of which produces somewhat different results, which are then open to different interpretations.

In contrast, *cash flows* are not always a direct measure of a company's performance. For example, take two opposite extremes: a young, profitable company sinking as many funds as it can get into a new venture; and an old, unprofitable company heading for bankruptcy. The results in terms of cash flow are likely to be the same: *declining cash balances*. A company can show a handsome profit and a net cash outflow in the same month, if it chooses to pay for new capital equipment in that month. It can equally well show a substantial loss and an increased cash balance in one month, if the results of new financing or the proceeds from the sale of substantial fixed assets are received in that month.

Moreover, the concept of *cash* is not nebulous. Either the company has a certain amount of cash or it has not. And a lack of cash is critical. A company can sustain losses for a time without suffering permanent damage, but a company that has no cash is insolvent and in imminent danger of bankruptcy, no matter what its profit picture may be.

Thus, many financial transactions that do not enter into the calculation of profit—such as buying new fixed assets, getting additional financing, and paying dividends—enter into cash flows. Similarly, some transactions that enter into the determination of profit—notably, the deduction of depreciation and amortization expenses—do not directly enter into cash flows (although there are cash flow benefits related to taxes) because they are noncash transactions with no effect on cash balances.

Many entrepreneurs and bankers are becoming increasingly interested in a concept called "free cash flow." Free cash flow is equal to the firm's cash flow from operations minus investments in capital expenditures that are required to maintain the company's competitiveness. For example, a firm that has $1,500,000 in cash from operations that spends $2,000,000 in property, plant, and equipment, has a *negative* free cash flow of $500,000 ($1,500,000–$2,000,000). This implies that the firm does not have surplus funds from operations, as it is in fact borrowing in order to maintain appropriate levels of capital investments.

Another term that is becoming more common is "pretax undedicated cash flow." Undedicated cash flow is equal to free cash flow plus tax plus interest expense. Undedicated cash flow, or "raider" cash flow, is emerging as an important variable in appraising the investment attraction of engaging in leveraged buyouts, restructuring and mergers of publicly owned companies. Prospective buyers (raiders) often add back interest and taxes so that they can get the broadest possible picture of the company's available cash. Then the investors determine how they could redirect the cash flows. Since the prospective buyers are going to be owners and not passive shareholders, they are more concerned about having control of the cash than about operating profits. Often, much of the operating cash flow is devoted to servicing debt after the transaction. As the firm begins to service the debt arrangement, the equity in the company automatically grows.

SUMMARY OF WORKING CAPITAL ISSUES

Working capital is often misinterpreted as being synonymous with *firm liquidity*. In fact, only a part of net working capital is liquid; the balance of net working capital is tied up in firm operations. *Liquidity* is largely a function of a firm's growth and the timing of receipts and payments. In situations where payments are made to suppliers before customers pay, growth in sales generally results in lower liquidity.

Preparing a cash flow forecast assists entrepreneurs in assessing the timing and maturity of funding needs. With a cash forecast, the entrepreneur can more easily determine the type of funding to procure and the small, growing firm's ability to grow with available funds. This includes efficiencies in accounts receivable, inventories, payables, and accruals. To the extent that entrepreneurs can successfully negotiate with customers and suppliers, they will be able to manage future growth.

However, small firms are rarely afforded the benefits associated with growth funded exclusively through internal cash generation. The more common occurrence includes external debt sources, leasing, cash innovations, and small firm/governmental programs. Such is the fate for the small business entrepreneur. Early, growth stages offer large funding requirements and huge risks to those that can't meet payroll and supplier demands. However, once an entrepreneur has negotiated a level of external sources of funds, including bank financing, privately placed debt, leasing options, or other financing innovations, that entrepreneur has a better chance for long-term corporate survival.

9 EXTERNAL ASSISTANCE FOR STARTUPS AND SMALL BUSINESSES

Elizabeth J. Gatewood
Keiron E. Hylton

There is a wealth of external assistance out there that you have probably never heard of. Federal, state, and local governments and nonprofit institutions together offer a bewildering array of helpful resources. This chapter offers a map for the varied terrain of entrepreneurial assistance.

WHY YOU SHOULD CONSIDER EXTERNAL ASSISTANCE PROGRAMS

External sources of assistance are certainly useful and probably necessary for almost all entrepreneurs because the successful creation of a startup company is a highly complex, time-consuming, and difficult process. You may need all the help you can get.

The stereotypical entrepreneur—the so-called rugged individualist who doesn't need help—may still wince at the thought of government assistance. Some entrepreneurs believe that government regulations (especially in the areas of taxation, employee benefits, and environmental controls) may hinder small business. Nevertheless, many agencies of the government are committed to assisting entrepreneurship, usually because of the potential of small businesses to create jobs.

According to the U.S. Small Business Administration, small businesses create two out of every three new jobs, produce about 40% of the gross national product, and invent more than half of the nation's technological innovations. Over 20 million small companies (constituting 99% of all businesses in the United States) provide work and income for 57% of the private U.S.

work force, and inspire further entrepreneurial activity. Small businesses are central to the U.S. economy, despite the dominance in the business and general press of the corporate giants that make up the *Fortune* 500.

Not all successful companies have required external assistance in their early stages. But many successful entrepreneurs have built their companies with government-guaranteed startup loans, lucrative government contracts, or government-sponsored advice on business plan development. Here are some recent prominent examples:

- Electronic Data Systems (EDS), built by Ross Perot—Some of EDS's early contracts were with the state of Texas and the federal government's Medicare programs.
- Apple Computer, Inc., and Cray Research, Inc., received Small Business Investment Companies capital during their early stages.
- Nike, Federal Express, Compaq Computer, Winnebago Industries, T.J. Cinnamons, and Godfather's Pizza were all assisted by SBA-sponsored programs.

External assistance programs have helped entrepreneurs at all phases of small company growth, in all sectors of industry, at all income levels, of all races, and of both genders.

You should consider external assistance programs because they are available, free, or inexpensive, and often effective in delivering useful services. They can also give you a competitive advantage in the difficult and complex project of starting up a new company or building a small company.

EXTERNAL ASSISTANCE AVAILABLE NATIONWIDE TO ANYONE IN THE UNITED STATES

Getting Advice: Business Development Programs

Most small business owners or would-be entrepreneurs begin with a need for business development assistance. This may involve managerial or technical assistance, for example, identifying and accessing relevant business and technical information, or using such information to evaluate new products, business concepts, and business plans. Many turn to the U.S. Small Business Administration.

The U.S. Small Business Administration (SBA)

Recognizing the importance of entrepreneurial initiative, Congress in 1953 created the Small Business Administration, an independent federal agency, to promote small business. The SBA is the primary federal agency charged with aiding, counseling, assisting, and protecting the interests of small business, although other federal agencies also provide services to this diverse economic constituency. Since 1953, the SBA has delivered more than 9 million loans, contracts, counseling sessions, and other forms of assistance to businesses across the nation. The agency has 110 offices covering every state, the District of Columbia, Guam, Puerto Rico, and the Virgin Islands, and annual loan guarantee authorization of $4 billion.

A small business must meet certain size criteria to be eligible for the SBA's services. These services include not only business development programs carried out by the SBA's Resource Partners (discussed later in this chapter), but also loans, procurement assistance, and international trade assistance. The Small Business Administration Act of 1953 defines a small business as "one which is independently owned and operated and not dominant in its field of operation." For statistical purposes, the SBA defines a small business as one with fewer than 500 employees. For business development assistance, loans, and other services, the SBA defines eligibility either by employment size or annual revenue criteria that vary by industry and change periodically.

The SBA uses the Standard Industrial Classification (SIC) manual to define industries, and it periodically reorganizes and clarifies eligibility criteria. Another major overhaul took effect in early 1993. This established an alternative eligibility standard based on net worth of less than $6 million and average annual after-tax income of less than $2 million over the past two years. The SBA predicts that this change will allow another 47,000 small businesses, mainly in the service and retail industries, to qualify for SBA help.

The current SBA sales and employment size criteria are as follows:

- *Services and retailing*—Small if annual sales are not over $2.5 to $13.5 million, depending on the specific industry.
- *Wholesaling*—Small if number of employees does not exceed 100.
- *Manufacturing*—Small if average employment in the preceding four calendar quarters did not exceed 500, including employees of any affiliates; large if average employment was more than 1,500. If employment is between 500 and 1,500, the SBA decides based on a size standard for the particular industry.
- *Construction*—Small if average annual sales for three years preceding application did not exceed $17.0 million, except for specialty contractors, for whom sales may not have exceeded $7 million.
- *Agriculture*—Small if average annual sales range from $0.5 to $7.0 million, depending on the industry.

The SBA has gradually reduced its provision of management and technical assistance to small business firms via its own field representatives. Technical and management assistance is now primarily provided through several innovative partnerships, collectively called the SBA's Resource Partners, described in the next sections of this chapter. The SBA still provides a comprehensive set of useful brochures and sponsors conferences and training programs on a full range of management topics. In 1991 the SBA distributed more than 3 million SBA publications and videotapes. In 1992 the SBA introduced SBA On-Line, an electronic bulletin board that allows anyone with a computer and modem to browse through detailed descriptions of the SBA's services and publications.

WHERE TO FIND THE SBA

For your district SBA office, look in the Blue Pages, under the U.S. Government listing headed "U.S. Small Business Administration." Or call the 24-hour SBA answer desk at 800-8-ASK-SBA. The SBA On-Line access numbers are 800-859-INFO (for a 2,400 bps modem) and 800-697-INFO (for a 9,600 bps modem). For the hearing-impaired, the TDD number is (202) 205-7333.

As mentioned, the SBA also supports business development efforts through the following "Resource Partners":

- The Small Business Development Center (SBDC) program
- The Service Corps of Retired Executives (SCORE) program (into which the former Active Corps of Executives (ACE) program was merged in 1982)
- The university-based Small Business Institute (SBI) program

These SBA Resource Partners counseled or trained almost 900,000 prospective and existing business owners in fiscal year 1992 alone. That's still less than 5% of the 20 million small businesses in the country—clearly, they're waiting to hear from you!

Small Business Development Centers (SBDCs)

Congress initiated the Small Business Development Center program as a pilot program in 1977 to make management assistance and counseling more widely available to present and prospective small business owners. Congress enacted the SBDC program into law in 1980 and granted the SBA oversight for the program.

SBDCs offer one-stop assistance to small businesses and startups by providing a wide variety of information and guidance in central and easily accessible locations. They offer free counseling services and reasonably priced seminars and workshops to new and existing businesses. There are now more than 700 service locations organized into 57 SBDC territories—one or more in each of the 50 states, the District of Columbia, Puerto Rico, and the Virgin Islands.

In each state there is a lead organization (often within a state university and sometimes within the state government itself), endorsed by the governor, which sponsors the SBDC and manages the program. The lead organization coordinates program services offered to small businesses through a network of subcenters and satellite locations in each state. Subcenters are located at colleges, universities, community colleges, vocational schools, chambers of commerce, and economic development corporations.

SBDC assistance may be divided into two main areas: free one-on-one counseling and inexpensive classroom-style training. Customized counseling services range from informal detailed evaluations of business plans by an industry-experienced counselor to advising growing companies on expansion plans for new territorial or product markets.

SBDCs sometimes supplement their free counseling services by making referrals on specialized accounting, legal, or technical subjects to professional business services. One SBDC, at the University of Houston, has negotiated a reduced-fee program for these services. The service also offers referrals to potential advisory board members for the small business owner.

SBDC training seminars are usually priced at substantial discounts off commercial rates (for example, $30–60 for a four-hour minicourse on how to write a business plan). They are offered by recognized local experts. Training seminars cover topics such as:

- Strategic planning
    - Business planning
- Market analysis and strategy
    - Marketing to the government
    - International trade
- Product feasibility and development
    - Technology access
- Organizational analysis
- Financial control
    - Loan assistance
    - Cash management
    - Bookkeeping and accounting

Some SBDCs also feature specialized centers that provide assistance in the following areas:

- Government contracting (procurement)
- International trade (for existing businesses looking for international expansion, or startups focused on international trade)
- Technology transfer and product development—Guidance in commercializing new products or services may include advice on royalty agreements, patent research, and new product evaluations.

Each SBDC center has full-time and part-time employees and recruits qualified volunteers from professional and trade associations, the legal and banking communities, academia, and chambers of commerce to counsel clients. Many SBDCs also use paid consultants, consulting engineers, and testing laboratories from the private sector to help clients who need specialized expertise.

SBDCs maintain strict client confidentiality. Only counselors directly working with you learn details of your company's operations. All advisors—whether staff, paid consultants, or volunteers—have to sign a conflict-of-interest agreement. This prohibits disclosure of information about any client to any non-SBDC personnel or any other client, solicitation or acceptance of gifts from clients, or investment in SBDC clients.

The SBA provides 50% or less of the operating funds for each state SBDC. The matching-fund contributions come from state legislatures, private sector foundations and grants, state and local chambers of commerce, state-chartered economic development corporations, public and private universities, vocational and technical schools, and community colleges. The success of SBDCs is reflected in the increasing tendency of sponsors' contributions to exceed the minimum 50% matching share. Unlike the SCORE and SBI programs (described in the next sections of this chapter), which are totally funded by the SBA, SBDCs are more free to develop programs and services independently of the SBA.

WHERE TO FIND SBDCS

For a local office, look in the Blue Pages under the U.S. Government listing. The Association of Small Business Development Centers (ASBDC) is located at

1313 Farnum, Suite 132
Omaha, NE 68182
(402) 595-2387

Service Corps of Retired Executives (SCORE)

SCORE, a volunteer organization founded in 1964, numbers more than 13,000 retired and active executives who volunteer their professional management expertise to help current and future business owners and managers. Most SCORE volunteers are retired, but about 18% are still in the work force. SCORE provides business information and management help through confidential counseling, training, and workshops.

SCORE provides the following information and advisory services:

- Short-term startup counseling
- Longer-term counseling for established clients
- Team counseling, when several experts are desirable

SCORE counseling may occur at a SCORE office or at the client's place of business. Its clients have included a wide variety of businesses—for example, graphic arts companies, archaeological consulting firms, and security systems stores. Nearly 40% of SCORE's clients are referrals from former clients.

SCORE offers a monthly prestartup seminar, one of many topics covered in the 3,808 workshops SCORE provided nationwide for more than 100,000 people in 1992. A new SBA/SCORE initiative is the development of Business Information Centers (BICs). There are now five BICs nationwide: in Seattle, Los Angeles, Houston, St. Louis, and Atlanta. These include a video library; computer services, including on-line research capabilities and applications software; and other business library services for entrepreneurs. BICs in Denver, Chicago, Boston, New York City, and Washington, D.C., are expected to open in 1993.

SCORE has helped more than 2.5 million people since 1964. In fiscal year 1992 its $2.9 million budget supported 800 counseling locations, providing assistance to almost 300,000 Americans through its network of 400 chapters.

WHERE TO FIND SCORE

For your district SBA office, look in the Blue Pages, under the U.S. Government listing headed "U.S. Small Business Administration." Or call the 24-hour SBA answer desk at 800-8-ASK-SBA. For the hearing impaired, the TDD number is (202) 205-7333. The National SCORE Office (NSO) is located at

409 Third St., S.W., Suite 5900
Washington, DC 20024
(202) 205-6762

Small Business Institutes (SBIs)

The Small Business Institute program, sponsored by the SBA, provides customized consulting services to the small business community through selected graduate and senior undergraduate business students, guided by a faculty advisor. Students typically provide assistance in business plan preparation, marketing research, market planning, and accounting. Small Business Institutes do not provide emergency advisory services or advice on demand. They offer long-term company analysis, structured as term projects, in which students will write the business or marketing plans after many weeks, averaging 100 hours per student, of primary and secondary research. SBIs are operated on over 500 college campuses in every state around the nation, and consult to 6,000 small business clients each year.

WHERE TO FIND SMALL BUSINESS INSTITUTES

For your district SBA office, look in the Blue Pages, under the U.S. Government listing headed "U.S. Small Business Administration." Or call the 24-hour SBA answer desk at 800-8-ASK-SBA. For the hearing-impaired, the TDD number is (202) 205-7333. You may also try graduate and undergraduate schools of business at your local colleges and universities.

Summary of SBA, SBDC, SCORE, and SBI Programs

Exhibit 9.1 clearly shows that of the SBA and its Resource Partners, the SBDCs and SCORE do the bulk of classroom training (the SBA's large total of training hours reflects its format of relatively long and well-attended two-day conferences, as useful for networking with contacts as for transferring knowledge). SBDCs do the bulk of counseling. SCORE has the shortest counseling hours per client, whereas SBIs have the longest counseling hours per client.

EXHIBIT 9.1. Business development programs: A profile of the SBA and the SBA's resource partners (fiscal year 1992).

	SBA	SBDCs	SCORE	SBIs	Professional/ trade*	Total
Counseling						
Clients counseled	N/A	222,497	171,518	6,661	1,707	402,383
Counseling hours	N/A	1,130,948	375,571	683,542	8,942	2,199,003
Hours/client	N/A	5.08	2.19	102.62	5.24	5.46
Training units	1,438	15,041	3,645	N/A	N/A	20,124
Attendees	67,574	319,535	108,896	N/A	N/A	494,005
Training hours	2,600,414	1,281,750	429,674	N/A	N/A	4,311,838
Attendees/unit	47	21	30	N/A	N/A	25

*"Professional/trade" refers to private consultants contracted by the SBA under the 7(j) Minority Contract cooperative agreement to provide business development services to 8(a) certified minority procurement firms, and includes any other counseling services contracted for by the SBA.

Getting Money: Financial Assistance from the SBA

Debt fuels growth. The entrepreneur promoting a new business venture through a well-prepared business plan and the successful small business proprietor both face the challenge of finding money for startup operations, for working capital, and for expansion and growth. A variety of institutions respond to these needs.

The SBA's financial assistance programs for small companies and startups complement its business development programs. Financial assistance programs may be divided into guaranteed loans, direct loans, and other loans. Many SBA loan programs are targeted to specific groups and needs. Borrowers can use different SBA financial assistance programs simultaneously, up to the SBA's statutory loan guarantee limit of $750,000.

Loan Guarantees

The 7(a) general loan guarantee

This is the SBA's principal way of financially promoting small business creation and growth. (The 7(a) name refers to a section of the original SBA law.) It represents more than 90% of the agency's total loan effort. 7(a) loans are made by private lenders to small businesses that cannot obtain credit without an SBA guarantee and are then guaranteed by the SBA for up to 90% of the amount provided by the commercial lender.

The maximum loan guarantee is $750,000; however, the average loan amount is $230,000. The maximum repayment period for loans is 25 years. The repayment period, which depends on loan use, averages 11 to 12 years. Funds can be used for working capital; to construct, expand or convert facilities; to purchase machinery or equipment; or to buy land and buildings. In some cases the loan may be used for refinancing certain types of debt. In fiscal year 1992 the SBA provided guarantees on 22,459 loans, for a total value of $5.62 billion. Between 1980 and 1990 the SBA provided guarantees for 180,000 loans worth more than $31 billion.

A recent study by Price Waterhouse reports that businesses that get these loan guarantees show higher growth than comparable businesses. Perhaps only companies with very strong business plans and founding teams can pass the screens of a primary lender and the SBA guarantee evaluation.

The Small Loan Program

This program has extended the SBA's guaranteed lending efforts to loans that most banks previously would have been reluctant to make because they would have considered them too small to be profitable. The Small Loan Program encourages conventional lenders to make loans of $50,000 or less by enabling the lenders to keep half of the guarantee fee (see the discussion of the SBA interest rate policy in the next section of this chapter) and charge an interest rate higher than that allowed under the 7(a) program. Although in some cases this results in higher rates for borrowers, it may make lenders more willing to make smaller, previously less profitable loans.

The Green Line Program

This program is designed to improve small business access to working capital. SBA will provide guarantees up to 85% on lines of credit extended by commercial lenders for up to five years. The maximum loan amount is $750,000. Interest rates are capped at 2.75 percentage points above prime. In 1993 the program was available in Alabama, Arkansas, Florida, Georgia, Kentucky, Louisiana, Mississippi, New Mexico, North Carolina, Oklahoma, South Carolina, Tennessee, and Texas.

The 502/504 Development Company Loan Program

This program finances fixed assets with long-term, low-interest funds through certified development companies (CDCs). The typical structure for a CDC funding project would include 50% conventional bank financing, 40% CDC second mortgage, and 10% owner's equity. CDCs are nonprofit economic development agencies, certified by the SBA and licensed by the state to operate in designated counties only. They raise their funding by selling 100% SBA-guaranteed debentures to private investors.

These loans are available up to $750,000 at 10- to 20-year maturities. Funds can be used for purchasing land; constructing, renovating, or expanding buildings; or buying machinery or equipment. Collateral and personal guarantees are required. Interest rates are based on 5- and 10-year U.S. Treasury issues plus an increment. CDCs consider jobs generated or jobs saved in choosing projects to fund. In fiscal year 1992 the SBA made 2,062 loans under the 502/504 program for a total value of $655.3 million. The 502/504 program has produced over $5 billion in investments and more than 301,000 jobs since its start in 1980.

Targeted guaranteed loan programs

These programs are divided into six categories:

- *Small general contractor loans* assist small construction firms with short-term financing for constructing or renovating residential or commercial property that will be offered for sale. The loan maturity cannot be more than 36 months plus a reasonable project time.
- *Seasonal line-of-credit guarantees* provide short-term financing for small firms with loan needs caused by seasonal increases in business. These guarantees are limited to 12 months.

- *Energy loans* are granted to firms engaged in manufacturing, selling, installing, servicing, or developing specific energy measures.
- *Pollution control financing* is offered to small businesses requiring long-term fixed interest financing for planning, designing, and installing pollution control facilities and equipment.
- *Contract loans* are short-term loans available to businesses more than one year old to finance the estimated cost of labor and materials needed to perform a specific contract, for which the proceeds are assignable. Loan maturity is usually 12 months or less from the time the first disbursement is made. In larger projects the loan maturity may increase to 18 months.
- *Qualified employee trust loans* are made to employee trusts to allow the trust to reloan funds to the employer company for growth and development or to permit the employees to purchase the employer company in leveraged buyouts.

Other Loans

Direct loans

Although SBA brochures advertise their availability, the number of direct loans made by the SBA has decreased over the years. Direct loans are available only to:

- Vietnam-era veterans
- 30% disabled veterans from any era
- Handicapped persons
- Persons living in economically distressed areas
- 8(a) program participants (see the section on procurement for more information about the 8(a) program)

Generally, recipients of these loans must have had loan requests denied by two conventional lenders for reasons other than credit factors.

Loan money is allocated quarterly from a limited pool of funds at the SBA's central office. When these rare direct loans are made, they are made up to $150,000. Only 608 direct loans for approximately $50 million were made in 1992. Loan proceeds can be used for the establishment, acquisition, or operation of a small business. Interest rates for loans to veterans and persons living in distressed areas are set at the rate for regular loans. Loans to the handicapped or handicapped veterans have 3% interest rate.

Disaster loans

The SBA offers two types of loans for businesses of all sizes located in disaster areas designated by the president or the SBA administrator. Businesses suffering property damage or economic losses from the disaster can obtain long-term recovery loans at low interest rates. Property damage (physical disaster) loans of up to $500,000 are available to businesses damaged in a disaster. Loans of up to $500,000 for economic losses are for operating capital to meet the business obligations that could have been met had the disaster not occurred. Businesses in Florida and Louisiana were beneficiaries of SBA loans in the wake of Hurricane Andrew in September 1992.

Micro-Loans

The SBA's experimental Micro-Loan Program was distributed through 45 nonprofit organizations (for example, community service and church groups) in over 30 states in 1992. The SBA expects to add 50 to 65 nonprofit organizations as participants in the program in 1993 for a total of $80 million. These micro-loans are targeted at women, low-income, and minority entrepreneurs, especially those in areas that have suffered economic downturns. They help entrepreneurs form or expand small, often home-based, enterprises. Individuals should have the skills but not the capital needed to operate a small business.

Micro-loans may range from a few hundred dollars up to $25,000. There are incentives to keep the average loan below $7,500. Funds may be used for working capital, inventory, supplies, furniture, fixtures, machinery, and equipment. Borrowers seeking more than $15,000 must demonstrate that they cannot obtain credit from other sources at comparable rates. The maximum term of the loan is six years. The SBA requires the nonprofits to secure larger loans with collateral but allows them to accept character references and personal guarantees for smaller loans. The interest rate on these loans is close to market rates.

The Surety Bond Guarantee Program

The SBA provides guarantee bonds for qualified small contractors who are unable to obtain surety bonds through regular bonding markets. For a contractor to be eligible for the program, average annual revenues for the last three fiscal years cannot exceed $3.5 million.

The SBA guarantees bonds for contracts up to $1.25 million. The guarantees are for 80% or 90%, depending on the amount of the contract or the minority status of the contractor. Approved minority contractors receive a 90% guarantee for contracts regardless of the contract size; nonminority contractors receive a 90% guarantee for contracts not exceeding $100,000 and an 80% guarantee for those over $100,000.

The small business pays the SBA a guarantee fee of six dollars per thousand of the contract amount, and when the bond is issued, it pays the surety company's bond premium. In fiscal year 1992 the SBA provided surety bond guarantees to 7,262 contractors with construction contracts worth more than $1 billion.

SBA Interest Rate Policy

Interest rates on guaranteed loans are negotiated between borrowers and lenders, although rates cannot be higher than levels set by SBA regulations. Except where noted in specific descriptions of particular SBA programs, SBA maximum rates are 2.25 percentage points above prime for a loan greater than $50,000 with maturity less than seven years, and 2.75 percentage points above prime for loans from seven to 25 years. Rates on loans under $50,000 may be higher. All guaranteed loans require payment of a guarantee fee, which varies with the type of loan guaranteed.

How to Apply for an SBA Loan Guarantee

The SBA has the following general credit requirements:

1. The applicant must be of good character and have a good credit history.
2. The applicant must have experience in business management and demonstrate the commitment necessary for a successful operation.
3. The applicant must have enough funds—including the SBA-guaranteed loan plus personal equity capital—to operate the business on a sound financial basis. If the company is a new business, this means enough cash to fund startup expenses and sustain expected losses during the early stages of operation.
4. If the company is an existing business, it must have a past earning record and future prospects to show repayment ability.
5. If the company is a new business, the startup entrepreneurs must provide at least one-third of the total startup capital needed. Therefore, the loan requested should be no more than twice the value of the owner's equity capital in the business.

Borrowers must fully secure the loan with collateral and provide personal guarantees. The SBA normally takes about two weeks to process a request.

Finding an SBA-Approved Lender

About 8,000 lenders nationwide have made at least one SBA loan in the past five years. Some 600 of these lenders have been designated as either SBA-preferred or SBA-certified lenders. It is worth your while to identify SBA-preferred lenders in your area because they are empowered to apply an SBA loan guarantee to a loan without consulting the SBA in advance. The benefit of dealing with an SBA-certified lender is that the SBA will decide whether to guarantee a bank loan within three days. To find out which lenders are preferred or certified, call your SBA district office.

WHERE TO FIND THE SBA

For your district SBA office, look in the Blue Pages, under the U.S. Government listing headed "U.S. Small Business Administration." Or call the 24-hour SBA answer desk at 800-8-ASK-SBA. The SBA On-Line access numbers are 800-859-INFO (for a 2,400 bps modem) and 800-697-INFO (for a 9,600 bps modem). For the hearing-impaired, the TDD number is (202) 205-7333.

Selling to the Government: The Art of Procurement

The federal government is a big customer. It buys $200 billion worth of goods and services every year from U.S. businesses. The government buys about $43 billion directly from small business and another $30 billion through federally mandated subcontracts between small business and large prime contractors. Nearly 98% of all procurement contracts are for $25,000 or less, although this composes only 20% of all spending.

Procurement Assistance Programs Sponsored by the SBA

The Small Business Act provides for preferential treatment to be granted to small business concerns in the award of government procurement contacts. The SBA has developed cooperative programs with major government purchasing agencies under which proposed purchases are reviewed by purchasing officials and suitable items are set aside, wholly or partially for small business bidders. This system of preferences in contract awards is known as "set-asides." They are aimed at small businesses, disadvantaged and minority-owned small businesses, and small businesses owned by women.

The law also requires large prime government contractors to subcontract work to small businesses. The SBA accordingly develops subcontracting opportunities by negotiating the amounts to be subcontracted to small business concerns by prime contractors undertaking major federal projects.

To achieve these goals the SBA maintains the *Procurement Automated Source System (PASS)*, a computerized database that lists small firms and their contracting or subcontracting capabilities. Using remote terminals at SBA regional offices and the offices of major federal procurement officials, government agencies and major corporations attempt to match their needs to the profiles submitted by participating small businesses. In 1991 the SBA made more than 900,000 referrals to procuring officials from the more than 236,000 small firms registered in PASS.

SBA field officers provide counseling and other services to small business owners seeking to do business with the federal government. Procurement specialists at SBA district offices can help:

- Identify the government agencies that are prospective customers
- Instruct small businesses about inclusion on bidders' lists
- Obtain drawings and specifications for specific contracts

The SBA has its own procurement center representatives (PCRs) stationed at major military and civilian procurement installations. The SBA also provides an appeal procedure when the ability of a low-bidding small firm to perform a contract is questioned.

The SBA also provides surety bonds, whereby it guarantees up to 80% of losses incurred under bid, payment, or performance bonds issued to contractors on government contracts valued up to $1.25 million. The Surety Bond Guarantee Program (described earlier in this chapter) has provided more than 236,000 surety guarantees for small businesses that have won $19 billion in government and other contracts since 1976.

Doing business with the federal government has the following advantages:

- Variety—the federal government has a wide range of purchasing needs
- Creditworthiness
- The potential for long-term contracts
- Detailed bidding procedures designed to ensure fairness

On the other hand, disadvantages include the facts that the competitive nature of the bidding process may reduce profit margins, and its bureaucratic aspects require painstaking attention to involved procedures.

The SBA and minority subcontracting

The SBA is authorized under Section 8(a) of the Small Business Act to enter into contracts with other federal agencies for goods and services and then to subcontract the work to firms owned by socially and economically disadvantaged persons. The 8(a) program is a business development program that helps socially and economically disadvantaged individuals enter the economic mainstream partially through access to federal contracts. The firms must be approved to participate in the 8(a) program by the SBA after demonstrating the nature and source of their disadvantage. The maximum period of eligibility is nine years from initial program certification.

More than half of all federal procurement through minority firms is channeled through the 8(a) program. In fiscal year 1992 more than 4,000 contracts were awarded for a total value of $4.3 billion. In addition the SBA is authorized under Section 7(j) of the act to provide management and technical assistance to 8(a) clients and small businesses in areas of high unemployment (see Exhibit 9.1 for details on the type of assistance offered by various programs).

Procurement Assistance Programs Sponsored by the U.S. Department of Defense (DOD)

Congress has created a national policy stating that a fair proportion of the products and services used by the DOD be purchased from small businesses and small disadvantaged businesses. This policy is grounded in the need to maintain a strong, diversified industrial base and increase competition in defense-related procurement. Defense purchasing officials therefore maintain contact with small business firms, small disadvantaged business firms, and small business firms owned by women.

The Department of Defense accordingly supports various procurement counseling services under the *Defense Procurement Technical Assistance (PTA) program.* The PTA is a cooperative program in which the DOD shares the cost of the services with state and local governments and nonprofit organizations. These services (which go by different names in different states) can help entrepreneurs seeking to sell goods and services to the DOD. They also help small businesses identify government agencies—federal, state, county, and municipal agencies that may buy their goods and services—and identify bid opportunities that are currently or prospectively available.

PTAs may offer procurement assistance in the form of technical data, drawings, and the counseling know-how to complete a bid package. They may maintain a library of relevant government specifications, standards, and regulations, including the *Federal Acquisition Regulations* (which describes the basic contracting rules for all federal agencies) and key supplements, plus military specifications and standards. PTAs may access technical data and generate pricing histories on parts, help the client develop quality control manuals, and match by computer the client's business capabilities and products with the millions of items and services purchased by government agencies. PTAs may use computer software to scan the *Commerce Business Daily,* which lists many government bid requests, contract awards, and leads on subcontracting, and the *U.S. Government Purchasing and Sales Directory,* which lists the military and civilian agencies that tend to buy particular products and services.

HOW TO GET SBA AND DOD PROCUREMENT HELP

For your district SBA office, look in the Blue Pages, under the U.S. Government listing headed "U.S. Small Business Administration." Or call the National SBA answer desk at 800-8-ASK-SBA (827-5722). For the hearing-impaired, the TDD number is (202) 205-7333.

To find whether a PTA program is available in your area, call the nearest Defense Contract Management District (DCMD), administered by the DOD's Defense Logistics Agency.

Mid-Atlantic: 2800 South 20th Street
P.O. Box 7478
Philadelphia, PA 19101-7478
Telephone: (215) 737-4006/4007
Toll-free (PA): 800-843-7694
Toll-free (MI, OH, DE, KY, MD, NJ, VA, WV, DC): 800-258-9503

Northeast: 495 Summer Street
8th Floor
Boston, MA 02210-2184
Telephone: (617) 451-4317/4318
Toll-free (MA): 800-348-1011
Toll-free (ME, NH, VT, CT, RI, NY): 800-321-1861

North Central: 10601 West Higgins Road
P.O. Box 66926
Chicago, IL 60666-0926
Telephone: (312) 825-6020
Toll-free (MI, IL, IN, WI, IA, MN, SD, ND, CO, NB, KS, VT, MO, WY): 800-637-3848

West: 222 North Sepulveda Boulevard
El Segundo, CA 90245-4394
Telephone: (310) 335-3260
Toll-free (CA): 800-624-7372
Toll-free (AK, AZ, HI, ID, MT, NM, NV, OR, WA): 800-624-7372

South: 805 Walker Street
Marietta, GA 30060-2789
Telephone: (404) 590-6196
Toll-free: 800-932-3560
Toll-free (GA): 800-551-7801
Toll-free (AR, OK, TX, TN, NC, SC, MS, AL, LA, FL): 800-331-6415

International: 209 Chapel Drive
Navy Security Group Activity
Sabana Seca, PR 00952
Telephone: (809) 795-3202

Selling Abroad: International Business in the Global Village

According to the SBA, every billion dollars in U.S. exports generates about 25,000 jobs. Small firms account for almost a quarter of all exporters. Because of the importance of small business in export, the SBA, the SBA's Resource Partners, the U.S. Department of Commerce, the U.S. Export-Import Bank, and the Overseas Private Investment Corporation (OPIC) have business development and financial assistance programs to help companies involved in exporting.

Export Business Development Programs

The SBA's Office of International Trade (OIT) and the U.S. Department of Commerce cosponsor export training programs and conferences. These teach owners and managers of small businesses how to apply practical export methods and provide opportunities to meet international trade specialists.

The Small Business Automated Trade Locator Assistance System (ATLAS)

ATLAS, sponsored by the OIT, provides a computerized service useful to exporters. ATLAS provides international marketing and trade information by scanning several large databases. ATLAS can identify the largest markets for specific products ranked by unit sales and dollar volume, five-year trends within those markets, and major sources of foreign competition.

ATLAS is available free of charge through SBA regional and district offices, SBDCs, SCORE, and SBI offices. Under an agreement between the SBA and the Federal Bar Association, the Export Legal Assistance Network (ELAN) offers free initial consultations with an experienced international trade attorney on topics ranging from contract negotiation to agent/distributor agreements, export licensing requirements, and credit collection procedures.

International Trade Centers

The SBA's Resource Partners have a special mission in international trade. SBI projects can focus on international trade. Six hundred SCORE members have international trade experience. Many SBDCs offer international trade assistance through their International Trade Centers. These centers can help the client:

- Evaluate the potential for company and product exports
- Analyze and research potential export markets
- Define market entry strategies
- Select distribution networks
- Manage the logistics of export

The International Trade Administration

The U.S. Department of Commerce (USDOC) also helps companies expand their international trade capabilities through the International Trade Administration. ITA operates domestic and overseas programs designed to stimulate the expansion of U.S. exports. Major programs include export counseling and assistance.

Through ITA a U.S. business can tap into a worldwide network of:

- Trade specialists who can provide export counseling on a variety of products and industries
- Country specialists versed in international economic policies and specific markets
- Industry specialists who help develop trade promotion programs
- Import trade specialists who can advise domestic industries with regard to unfair trade practices

The ITA's U.S. and Foreign Commercial Service (USFCS) can access a network of some 2,500 trade experts located in 67 countries, 68 U.S. cities, and Commerce Headquarters in Washington, D.C. This network covers 95% of the global markets for U.S. goods and services.

The following services are available through your local USFCS offices. These services are not free: They range from $35 for the National Trade DataBank disc to $500 to $4,000 per country for the Comparison Shopping Service.

- Developing export expertise:

  —The *Export Qualifier Program* helps firms evaluate their readiness to export through a computerized diagnostic questionnaire.

- Identifying target markets:

  —The *National Trade DataBank* includes 100,000 trade-related documents, product-specific market research reports, and trade statistics. Information is collected by 15 agencies, updated monthly, and issued on one CD-ROM.

  —The *Comparison Shopping Service* can assess the competitiveness of your product in a specific market. It involves intensive custom research involving product-specific interviews or surveys.

- Finding potential partners:

  —The *Agent/Distributor Service* can help you locate up to six foreign representatives who, after looking at your product literature, may be interested in marketing your product.

—A *World Traders Data Report* will help you evaluate potential partners overseas, in terms of reliability, creditworthiness, and standing in the local business community.

—*Commercial News USA* is a catalog of new U.S. products and services sent to 110,000 potential overseas buyers, agents, and distributors.

—The *Foreign Buyer Program* brings delegations of overseas buyers from around the world to your exhibit at participating U.S. trade shows.

—The *Trade Opportunities Program* identifies timely sales leads overseas and provides them to U.S. business.

—*Catalog and video/catalog exhibitions* are organized every year for certain industries in selected markets. The Department of Commerce shows U.S. exporter catalogs and videos to potential agents, distributors, and other buyers in each market. Participating exporters often receive up to 50 leads from each exhibition.

—*Trade mission/trade shows* organized with state, local, or private groups help U.S. companies that have representatives visiting their targeted overseas export market to introduce and market their products there.

—*Matchmaker delegations* are introductory missions for firms entering export markets. The Matchmaker program visits more than 15 countries each year. Matchmaker organizers evaluate a product's potential for a market and make introductions to potential buyers or licensees. This program is also for entrepreneurs who are visiting their export market.

—The *Gold Key Service* provides the following services to U.S. businesspeople who are visiting their export market:

Market orientation briefings

Specialized market research

Introductions to potential partners

Interpreter for meetings

All services are organized by commercial officers located at overseas posts.

The Department of Commerce's Bureau of Export Administration issues licenses for the shipment of controlled exports, especially in the areas of computers, electronics, communications, and biotechnology.

Export Financial Assistance

The SBA offers two types of export loan guarantees that protect the lender from default by the exporter. Both must be collateralized with U.S.-based assets. The SBA guaranteed over 600 loans to exporters, supporting $241 million in exports in fiscal year 1992.

International trade loan guarantees

These are guaranteed long-term loans through private lenders that help U.S.-based facilities to develop or expand export markets or recover from the effects of import competition. The maximum guaranteed loan is $1 million for fixed assets such as facilities and equipment (for a maximum of 25 years) and an additional $250,000 for working capital (for up to 3 years). Proceeds may not be used for debt refinancing. The SBA's guarantee may not exceed 85% of the loan.

Export revolving line-of-credit loan guarantees

These are short-term loan guarantees available to small businesses that are at least one year old. Loans provide working capital to finance labor and materials for manufacturing or wholesaling of products, to develop foreign markets, or to finance insured foreign accounts receivable. The SBA can guarantee up to 90% of a bank line of credit up to $155,000. For larger ERLC loans, up to the maximum amount of $750,000, the maximum guarantee is 85% of the commercial loan. Loan maturities are generally for 12 months, with options to renew up to the maximum term of three years.

Traditional SBA 7(a) guaranteed loans

These loans are also available and may be more appropriate if the primary purpose is to develop foreign markets, that is, if the funds are to be used for export marketing advice, foreign business travel, or trade show participation. The contract line of credit program and the 502/504 programs can also be used for exporting.

The Export-Import Bank of the United States (EximBank)

EximBank has four major export finance programs: loans, guarantees, working capital guarantees, and insurance. The loan program provides competitive, fixed-interest-rate financing for businesses.

EximBank guarantees provide repayment protection for private sector loans to creditworthy foreign buyers of U.S. commercial goods and services. The guarantees provide coverage for both political and commercial risks. Under the working capital guarantee program for U.S. exporters, EximBank will guarantee 90% of the principal and some of the interest on loans or revolving lines of credit extended to eligible exporters. The funds may be used for preexport activities such as buying raw materials or foreign marketing. EximBank and the SBA also participate in a coguarantee program for small business exporters and export trading companies. The coguarantees apply to loans ranging from $200,000 to $1,000,000 per borrower and cover 85% of the loan.

To manage the risk of a foreign buyer defaulting on payment for goods sold or services rendered, U.S. exporters may insure their foreign receivables. EximBank insures overseas receivables against commercial and political risk. A variety of policies are available.

The Overseas Private Investment Corporation (OPIC)

In general, OPIC insures U.S. investments in foreign countries against political and currency risks. The *Small Contractor's Guarantee Program* will guarantee an eligible financial institution for up to 75% of an on-demand standby letter of credit or other form of payment guarantee issued on behalf of a small construction or service firm.

WHERE TO FIND INTERNATIONAL TRADE ASSISTANCE

For your district SBA office, SCORE, and SBI, look in the Blue Pages, under the U.S. Government listing headed "U.S. Small Business Administration," or call the toll-free hotline at 800-8-ASK-SBA. For a local SBDC office, look in the Blue Pages, under the U.S. Government listing.

The Department of Commerce's 800-USA-TRAD is a clearinghouse of international trade sources.

You can find Department of Commerce industry and country desk officers at

U.S. Department of Commerce
International Trade Administration
14th and Constitution Avenue, N.W.
Washington, DC 20230
(202) 482-3022

Contact the Export-Import Bank of the United States at
811 Vermont Avenue, N.W.
Washington, DC 20571
(202) 289-2703
Export Finance Hotline: (800) 424-5201

Contact the Overseas Private Investment Corporation at
1615 M Street, N.W.
Washington, DC 20527
(202) 457-7091

EXTERNAL ASSISTANCE FOR SPECIAL GROUPS, LOCATIONS, AND INDUSTRIES

Business Assistance Programs for Women

According to the SBA, between 1982 and 1987 the number of businesses owned by women increased 58%, to more than 4.1 million. Women continue to open businesses at twice the rate of men. The SBA estimates that by the year 2000, more than 40% of all businesses will be owned by women.

Despite this explosive growth, few special support programs are aimed solely at women. This has fueled a debate about whether women need special programs or whether they are better served by accessing business assistance programs aimed at the general population.

All SBA offices have a staff member designated as a Women's Business Ownership Representative, whose duty it is to discuss resources that are available for women and to provide assistance for accessing those resources. A relatively new program available in all 50 states, designated the *Women's Network for Entrepreneurial Training (WNET)*, provides mentoring for small business owners. The mentoring program matches a successful woman business owner with at least five years experience to a woman business owner who has been in business for at least one year and has shown potential for growing her business. The mentoring relationship is for one year.

Another relatively new program for women, called *the Demonstration Projects*, has established centers for potential or current women business owners in a few states. The centers offer counseling and training in management, marketing, and finance. Although open to all women, the program was developed for women who might not normally use services provided through traditional channels.

WHERE TO FIND SBA HELP FOR WOMEN

For your district SBA office, look in the Blue Pages, under the U.S. Government listing headed "U.S. Small Business Administration." Or call the 24-hour SBA answer desk at 800-8-ASK-SBA for your district SBA office. Speak to a Women's Business Ownership Representative. For the hearing-impaired, the TDD number is (202) 205-7333.

Assistance Programs for Minority-Owned Businesses

Recent statistics on minority business ownership show the changing face of small business in America (see Exhibit 9.2). The national average for

EXHIBIT 9.2. Growth in minority businesses, 1982–1987.

	1982	1987	Increase (%)
African-American-owned	308,000	424,000	38
Hispanic-owned	234,000	422,000	81
Asian-American-owned	188,000	355,000	89

nonminority business ownership is 67.1 per 1,000 persons. Two minority groups exceed this national nonminority average: Korean-Americans, with 102.4 per 1,000 (1 in 10 Korean-Americans is a business owner), and Asian-Indian Americans, with 75.7 per 1,000. Other minority groups participating in business ownership at a rate near the nonminority average are Japanese-Americans (66.1 per 1,000), Chinese-Americans (63.5 per 1,000), and Cuban-Americans (62.9 per 1,000).

The Minority Business Development Agency (MBDA), an agency of the U.S. Department of Commerce, is the only federal agency specifically created to establish policies and programs to develop the U.S. minority business community. The MBDA sponsors a network of approximately 100 *Minority and Indian Business Development Centers* (MBDCs/IBDCs), located throughout the country in areas with the largest minority populations.

Each center develops and maintains a listing of existing minority-owned firms for inclusion in the agency's *Automated Business Enterprise Locator System* (ABELS). The ABELS system is used by government and private industry purchasing officials to identify minority vendors qualified to supply the goods and services they need. To qualify for ABELS, you must certify that your firm is a nonretail business that:

- Is at least 51% owned, controlled, and actively managed by minority persons
- Can provide products or services to other businesses, private organizations, and government agencies

The centers cannot make or underwrite loans because the MBDA has no loan-making authority. MBDCs/IBDCs do engage in business development counseling for a fee. Clients with gross sales of $500,000 or less pay $10.00 per hour. Those with gross sales in excess of $500,000 pay $17.50 per hour. Services typically offered include business planning, marketing, financial analysis, accounting, and loan packaging.

The maximum federal funding of each MBDC/IBDC represents not more than 85% of the total cost of the project. Each center is expected to provide the other 15% through private sources of support.

(Other minority assistance programs are discussed in the section on procurement.)

WHERE TO FIND THE MBDA

The U.S. Department of Commerce
Minority Business Development Agency
14th and Constitution Avenue, N.W.
Room 5073
Washington, DC 20230

To locate the nearest MBDA office, call (202) 482-1936. A recorded message will provide the address and telephone number of a regional MBDA office.

Business Assistance Programs for Veterans

The SBA has a special mission to help veterans get into business and stay in business. In each local SBA office, there is a staff person designated the *Veterans Affairs Officer,* specially trained to guide the veteran seeking business assistance. In addition to SBA Resource Partners' normal business development counseling and training courses (which veterans are welcome to attend), the SBA and its resource partners conduct special business training conferences for veterans.

For example, during the Persian Gulf war, SCORE set up workshops to teach businesspeople called up by the Reserves how to cope with sudden and long absences from their businesses. SCORE members also mentored family members and others chosen to manage businesses during the reserves' absences. About 1,200 training conferences were held for prospective and established veteran business owners in fiscal year 1991.

(Information on special loans for veterans was provided earlier in this chapter, in the SBA direct loans.)

WHERE TO FIND SBA HELP FOR VETERANS

For your district SBA office, look in the Blue Pages, under the U.S. Government listing headed "U.S. Small Business Administration." Or call the 24-hour SBA answer desk at 800-8-ASK-SBA for your district SBA office. Speak to the Veterans Affairs Officer. For the hearing-impaired, the TDD number is (202) 205-7333.

Business Assistance for the Physically Challenged

SBA Handicapped Assistance loans are offered to physically handicapped small business owners and to private nonprofit organizations that employ handicapped persons or operate in their interests. For special loans for the handicapped, see the earlier section in this chapter on direct loans.

WHERE TO FIND SBA HELP FOR THE PHYSICALLY CHALLENGED

For your district SBA office, look in the Blue Pages, under the U.S. Government listing headed "U.S. Small Business Administration." Or call the 24-hour SBA answer desk at 800-8-ASK-SBA. For the hearing impaired, the TDD number is (202) 205-7333.

Business Assistance for Rural and Agricultural Entrepreneurs

Before describing programs for this group, it should be pointed out that *rural* is not synonymous with *agricultural*. Not all rural entrepreneurs are engaged in the traditional rural occupation of agriculture. Consider different potential sources of assistance based on your location *and* your line of business. For example, the U.S. Department of Agriculture offers programs that provide management and technical assistance, guaranteed and other loans, and grants and cooperative agreements in areas not limited to traditional agricultural enterprises.

The Cooperative Extension Service

This is the outreach arm of the Department of Agriculture. Although the Cooperative Extension Service has agents in all land-grant universities and nearly all the nation's 3,150 counties, services of interest to businesses vary dramatically by location. It sometimes provides management and marketing assistance to rural businesses, including agricultural and natural-resource-based enterprises, manufacturers, retail businesses and service businesses. The services are aimed at increasing the profitability and growth of existing businesses, as well as identifying neglected market segments.

HOW TO FIND THE COOPERATIVE EXTENSION SERVICE

To find what services are available in your area, look under the Blue Pages (U.S. Government) for "U.S. Department of Agriculture" or the Blue Pages (County) for "County Extension Office."

The U.S. Department of Agriculture's Rural Development Administration (RDA) Business and Industry Loan Program

This program offers loan guarantees similar to the SBA's for businesses located in cities with a population of less than 50,000. Most loans are made in towns with populations of 25,000 or less. Funds can be used for working capital; equipment purchases; improvement, construction, or acquisition of fixed assets (including land and buildings); and, in some cases, debt refinancing.

The maximum loan amount is $10 million, and the average is slightly over $1 million. The maximum for alcohol fuel production facilities is $20 million. A minimum of 10% of total capital is required in the form of equity for existing businesses (20% to 25% for startups). The terms are 30 years for land and building, 15 years for machinery and equipment, and up to 7 years for working capital. RDA loan guarantees do not require that you prove your inability to get credit without the guarantee. Interest rates are at competitive banking rates.

The RDA's Intermediary Relending Program

This program makes loans to nonprofit organizations, which in turn lend funds to small businesses in their service area. The nonprofit organization may provide up to 75% of each project's cost up to $150,000. The RDA has the following requirements:

- Projects must create new jobs or retain old jobs.
- Funds must be used in towns of 25,000 or fewer people.
- Applicants must have been turned down from at least two other sources before applying for this program.

Funds may be used to start a new business or expand an existing one. The interest rate to intermediaries is 1% for up to 30 years. Intermediaries charge interest at a rate to cover their operating costs, typically around 7% to 9%.

The Alternative Agricultural Research and Commercialization Center (AARC)

This new program of the Department of Agriculture, announced in 1992, provides grants and cooperative agreements for the development of nonfood, nonfeed products made from agricultural and forestry materials (for example, starches and carbohydrates, fats and oils, fibers, forest materials, animal products, and other plant materials). The grants or cooperative agreements are to fund precommercial development activities such as:

- Identifying viable market needs
- Designing equipment
- Scaling up prototypes to commercial scale
- Obtaining regulatory clearances
- Conducting precommercial runs

Private firms, individuals, public or private educational or research organizations, federal agencies, cooperatives, nonprofits, or combinations of the above are eligible to receive funding. Funding is on a competitive basis. More than 400 proposals requesting a total of $200 million were submitted for the October 30, 1992, deadline. Ten million dollars was available for distribution, although this is expected to increase in the future.

Selection of projects to be funded is based on the likelihood that the projects will result in commercially viable products or processes. Some examples of proposals submitted are:

- Attic insulation from low-grade cotton fibers
- Biodiesel fuel from waste fat collected by restaurants
- Ethanol from cellulose material in straw, cornhulls, and grasses

The program requires matching funds from program recipients. Although the match percentage is not specified, the program requires that AARC funding not exceed two-thirds of the total cost of the project.

FOR MORE INFORMATION

Alternative Agricultural Research and Commercialization Center
14th and Independence Avenue, S.W.
342 Aerospace Center, Suite 342
Washington, DC 20250-2200
(202) 401-4860

HOW TO FIND HELP FOR RURAL AND AGRICULTURAL ENTREPRENEURS

Look under the Blue Pages (U.S. Government) for "U.S. Department of Agriculture" or the Blue Pages (County) for "County Extension Office."

Business Assistance for Urban Entrepreneurs

The U.S. Department of Housing and Urban Development (HUD) offers a *Community Development Block Grant (CDBG) Entitlement Program* that awards grants annually to entitled metropolitan cities and urban counties. Cities designated as central cities of metropolitan statistical areas (MSAs), other cities with populations of at least 50,000, and qualified counties with populations of at least 200,000 (excluding the population-entitled cities) are eligible to receive grants. The amount of grants for each community is determined by a formula using several measures of community need, such as the poverty level.

Communities receiving grants are free to develop programs that meet local needs in housing, public works, economic development, public services, acquisition, clearance or redevelopment of real property, or administration and planning concerning urban needs, as long as the activities meet the national objectives of the program. The national objectives are to benefit low- and moderate-income persons, to prevent or eliminate slums or blight, or to meet other urgent community needs. Some communities establish revolving loan pools that may be accessible by startups and small businesses.

Total funds available for the program in fiscal year 1991 were $2.2 billion; however, only about 10% of these funds were used for economic development projects, and an even smaller percentage of funds directly benefited for-profit businesses.

> **WHERE TO FIND HUD**
>
> Businesses should contact their city or county planners to determine whether a CDBG revolving loan pool exists or could be started for funding their projects. City or county planners should contact HUD (look in the Blue Pages under "U.S. Government") for more information.

Business Assistance for Entrepreneurs in Distressed Areas

The U.S. Department of Commerce, through its Economic Development Administration (EDA), aims to decrease unemployment and underemployment in economically distressed areas.

> **FOR MORE INFORMATION**
>
> Businesses should contact their city or county planners to determine whether a Title IX revolving loan pool exists or could be started for funding their projects. City or county planners should contact EDA for more information.
>
> U.S. Department of Commerce
> Economic Adjustment Program
> Hoover Building, Room 7327
> 14th and Constitution Avenue N.W.
> Washington, DC 20230
> (202) 482-2659

The Economic Adjustment (Title IX) Program (EAP) provides funds to communities that have suffered from long-term economic decline (chronic distress) or from a sudden and severe event, such as a hurricane or plant closing, that has undermined the economic stability of the community. In either case, to be eligible for Title IX funding, the community must demonstrate very high unemployment or very low per capita income. The EAP funding to the community must be used for planning or implementing economic rebuilding.

Some communities have chosen, as part of their rebuilding efforts, to establish revolving loan pools. The funds are then available for targeted small business startups and expansions, business and job retention projects, and the redevelopment of blighted land and vacant facilities.

Business Assistance for High-Tech or Technologically Oriented Startups

According to the SBA, U.S. small businesses in the twentieth century have invented the airplane, the aerosol can, double-knit fabric, the heart valve, the optical scanner, the pacemaker, the personal computer, the soft contact lens, and the zipper. Although building a better mousetrap may not automatically trigger a stampede to your door, technological innovation is a valuable competitive advantage. Recognizing this, a variety of federal initiatives have promoted technological innovation. Unfortunately, these federal technological assistance programs are highly fragmented, the result of many different initiatives over many years.

The federal government provides both business development programs and financial assistance programs. Development programs for technologically oriented businesses include the following:

- Small Business Development Centers
- National Innovation Workshops
- Manufacturing Technology Centers
- Shared Flexible Computer-Integrated Manufacturing
- The Federal Laboratory Consortium for Technology Transfer
- NASA Regional Technology Transfer Centers
- National Technology Transfer Center
- The National Technical Information Service
- A catalog of government inventions available for licensing
- Federal Research in Progress Database

Financial assistance programs for technologically oriented businesses include:

- The Small Business Innovation Research Program
- The Advanced Technology Program

All of these programs are discussed in detail in the following sections.

Small Business Development Centers (SBDCs)

SBDCs provide technical services to startups and small businesses. These services provide assistance in product licensing or small business formation based on new product development. Several SBDCs around the nation provide innovation assessments designed to determine a new product idea's potential for commercialization.

More than 80% of SBDCs provide assistance to small businesses in developing Small Business Innovation Research proposals (discussed in the next section). All SBDCs provide links to federal, state, and local sources of technology and technical information. In 1992 six SBDCs (in Maryland, Missouri, Oregon, Pennsylvania, Texas, and Wisconsin) were selected to participate in a pilot project sponsored by the National Institute of Science and Technology (NIST). This Technology Access Program (TAP) improves small businesses' access to scientific, technical, and business information and expertise through on-line services. Access to these on-line services is subsidized through the program.

National Innovation Workshops

The Departments of Energy and Commerce, in partnership with SBDCs, sponsor five to six innovation workshops each year around the country. The two-day workshops are targeted at inventors and technology-based businesses. The workshops provide information on:

- The availability of federal R&D funding through Small Business Innovation Research and other programs at the federal or state level
- Technical assistance available through federal laboratories
- Federal and state sources of technical information

They also provide more generic business assistance information.

FOR MORE INFORMATION

To find the times and places of the next National Innovation Workshops, contact:

The Association of Small Business Development Centers (ASBDC)
1313 Farnum, Suite 132
Omaha, NE 68182
(402) 595-2387

Manufacturing Technology Centers (MTCs)

The Department of Commerce and the National Institute of Science and Technology (NIST) fund regional Manufacturing Technology Centers to support small and mid-sized manufacturers in their drive to improve quality, efficiency, and productivity. In 1993 regional centers were located in Torrance, CA; Minneapolis, MN; Cleveland, OH; Albany, NY; Columbia, SC; Ann Arbor, MI; and Overland Park, KS.

The centers are sponsored by nonprofit organizations that contribute at least 50% of funding for the first three years. The centers must be self-supporting after six years. The centers act as bridges between companies and sources of manufacturing technologies such as vendor companies, professional organizations, universities, or federal government organizations.

Services vary depending upon the local client base and regional needs. In general, they provide:

- An in-depth assessment of manufacturing and technology needs
- Assistance in selecting appropriate technology and processes and integrating those technologies into company operations
- Specialized employee training

MTCs have large databases of computer-aided design (CAD) and computer-aided manufacturing (CAM) software packages, as well as PC-based hardware systems.

Since 1989 more than 6,000 firms have received assistance ranging from factory floor layout to invoice-handling procedures.

FOR MORE INFORMATION

Manufacturing Technology Center Programs
National Institute of Standards and Technology
8212 Chemistry Building
Gaithersburg, MA 20899
(301) 975-3414

Shared Flexible Computer-Integrated Manufacturing (SFCIM)

This is a program of the Department of Commerce aimed at introducing advanced manufacturing technologies to small and medium-sized businesses. The program consists of a network of manufacturing service centers, usually associated with universities or community colleges. The service centers lease manufacturing time on their state-of-the-art, off-the-shelf Flexible Manufacturing Systems (FMS) to businesses. This technique was used in the 1950s and 1960s by mainframe computer companies to introduce computers to a wider market.

FOR MORE INFORMATION

U.S. Department of Commerce
Technology Administration
Hoover Building, Room 824
14th and Constitution Avenue N.W.
Washington, DC 20230
(202) 482-1575

The Federal Laboratory Consortium for Technology Transfer (FLC)

Federal research and development laboratories received approximately $25 billion in fiscal year 1992 (which was about 35% of total federal R&D investment for that year). More than 700 federal laboratories employ more than 100,000 scientists and engineers. Federal laboratories may enter into agreements with individuals or companies to conduct cooperative research. The U.S. government also holds thousands of patents available for licensing. The key to entrepreneurial success may be deciding how to access these resources given the number of federal laboratories and the complexity of their technological resources.

Many individual federal laboratories, such as Los Alamos and Sandia, have ad hoc outreach programs to help small and medium-sized manufacturers. These programs are subject to annual budget reauthorizations, but they are part of a trend to increase the laboratories' budgets to provide enhanced outreach services. This trend has reached its fullest development in the FLC, formalized in 1986, which recognizes the need for technology transfer to the private sector from the large number of federal laboratories that are potential sources of technology. Consortium members include all major federal R&D laboratories and their parent organizations, comprising some 500 laboratories belonging to 17 federal departments and agencies.

The FLC provides access for entrepreneurs and small businesses to technology, top-notch scientists and engineers for problem solving, and state-of-the-art laboratory equipment and facilities. FLC members devote 5% of their total laboratory budget to transferring technology out of the laboratories.

FOR MORE INFORMATION

Federal Laboratory Consortium
P.O. Box 545
Sequim, WA 98382
(206) 683-1005

A request for assistance flows from the entrepreneur or small business person to an FLC regional coordinator to a laboratory representative, and then to the actual technologist who can solve the problem or supply the resource. There is no cost for any of the services.

NASA Regional Technology Transfer Centers (RTTCs)

These are a network of six regional centers that are linked to the NASA field centers. The centers are affiliated with universities and provide access to approximately one million documents in the NASA data bank and to more than 400 other computerized databases. The databases include selected contents for some 15,000 scientific and technical journals.

The RTTC mission is to transfer to the private sector and assist in the commercialization of NASA technology and other federal technology. RTTC consultants assist in the identification, evaluation, acquisition, and adaptation of technology to meet specific business needs. They also provide assistance in commercialization of technology.

FOR MORE INFORMATION

To contact your RTTC, call 800-472-6785.

National Technology Transfer Center (NTTC)

The NTTC helps businesses access federal technologies resources by matching specific needs of the business with the appropriate federal resource. The NTTC will search federal databases and will expedite communication with a federal laboratories expert who may assist with solutions.

The NTTC has recently created a national electronic bulletin board service for the public and private sectors. The free service includes announcement of new technologies, answering of questions on technical problems, and notices of technology transfer conferences and meetings. The bulletin board will also include a number of searchable databases.

FOR MORE INFORMATION

To contact NTTC, call 800-678-NTTC.

The National Technical Information Service (NTIS)

This is an agency of the U.S. Department of Commerce. NTIS is a national and international information system for technical, engineering, and business-related information. NTIS serves as the central source for federally generated computerized data files, databases, and software, and for the licensing of U.S. government-owned patents. The on-line database system is accessible by modem.

> **FOR MORE INFORMATION**
>
> Call the National Technical Information Service at (703) 487-4650.

Catalog of Government Inventions Available for Licensing

This annual catalog includes approximately 1,200 entries divided into 43 subject areas. Each entry includes a detailed summary, inventor information, and information on obtaining supplementary materials. The cost for the 1991 catalog is $59. Catalogs from prior years are also available.

> **TO ORDER**
>
> National Technical Information Service
> 5285 Port Royal Road
> Springfield, VA 22161
> (703) 487-4650

Federal Research in Progress Database (FEDRIP)

FEDRIP is a program of the Department of Commerce. The database contains summaries of the U.S. government-funded research projects currently in

> **FOR MORE INFORMATION**
>
> On-line access for a fee can be obtained by calling:
>
> Dialog Information Services
> Marketing Department
> 34650 Hillview Avenue
> Palo Alto, CA 94304
> 800-334-2564
>
> Knowledge Express
> 613 South Valley Forge Road
> P.O. Box 8301
> Rodnor, PA 19087
> 800-248-2469

progress. In 1992 it included some 120,000 project summaries. Each FEDRIP entry includes title, starting date, principal investigator, performing and sponsoring organization, detailed abstract, project objectives, and sometimes intermediate findings and funding amount. The summaries provide up-to-date research progress in specific technical areas before technical reports or journal articles are published. Updates to the database are done monthly.

The Small Business Innovation Research (SBIR) Program

Many high-technology companies started up with a government research and development (R&D) contract. If your company has the ability to do technological research and development, you should consider applying to the SBIR program.

The SBIR program is a multiagency federal research and development grant program coordinated through, but not managed by, the SBA. The SBIR program began in 1982 with the enactment of the Small Business Innovation Development Act. The act required agencies of the federal government with budgets for externally contracted R&D in excess of $100 million to establish SBIR programs. Funding for the program is derived from a fixed percentage of each agency's R&D budget. Under the SBIR program, federal agencies set aside 1.5% (to be raised to 2.0% in fiscal year 1995–1996 and 2.5% after fiscal year 1996) of certain research and development funds for use by small firms.

The SBIR program aims to fund scientifically sound research proposals that will, if successful, have "significant public benefit." SBIR's threefold objectives are:

- To increase small firm participation in federal R&D
- To foster commercial applications from applied federal research
- To encourage innovation for public benefit

The SBIR program involves a competitive three-phase award system that provides qualified small business concerns with opportunities to propose innovative studies that meet the specific R&D needs of the various agencies of the federal government:

- Phase 1: SBIR awardees receive up to $100,000 to evaluate the scientific merit and technical feasibility of an idea. The period of performance normally does not exceed six months. Only Phase 1 awardees are eligible for consideration in Phase 2.
- Phase 2: Awardees receive up to $750,000 to develop prototypes, finalize products, and further expand on the research results of Phase 1. The period of performance normally does not exceed two years.

- Phase 3: Firms try to commercialize the results of Phase 2. Despite its classification as Phase 3, this stage requires the use of private or non-SBIR federal funding. No SBIR funds are utilized in Phase 3. However, Phase 3 may involve production contracts with a federal agency for future use by the federal government.

From the start of the SBIR program in 1982 through fiscal year 1991, the participating federal agencies have made 21,400 competitive awards totaling $2.7 billion to qualified small business concerns. Many firms of 10 or fewer employees have won funding for their proposals. In fiscal year 1992 small business concerns successfully competed for 2,553 Phase 1 awards and 788 Phase 2 awards under the SBIR program, for a total of 3,341 awards worth $483 million.

The end of the Cold War and the associated reduction in defense spending has implications for the SBIR program, especially for the Department of Defense SBIR awards. The Office of Technology Assessment has suggested that the SBIR program may be especially useful to small defense companies in the conversion process to dual-use (military and civilian) manufacturing capability.

The master schedule of SBIR solicitations for fiscal year 1993 shows 11 agencies participating at the following levels:

Department of Defense—$400 million

Department of Health and Human Services—$115 million

National Aeronautics and Space Administration—$99 million

Department of Energy—$55 million

Nuclear Regulatory Commission—$15 million

Department of Agriculture—$6.5 million

Environmental Protection Agency—$4.8 million

Department of Education—$2.7 million

National Science Foundation—$2.7 million

Department of Commerce—$2.2 million

Department of Transportation—$2 million

SBIR proposals should be 25 pages or less and should follow the specified agency format. Proposals should demonstrate:

- A hypothesis that rests on sufficient evidence
- Clear use of technical information
- Familiarity with recent literature or methods

- Adequate experience or training
- A realistic proposed effort
- Technological innovation
- Good potential commercial application

HOW TO APPLY FOR AN SBIR GRANT

Although the SBA sponsors various SBIR conferences and seminars in every state, the agency does not distribute copies of SBIR solicitations. The participating federal agencies responsible for generating SBIR topics and conferring awards release their own solicitation announcements. However, the SBA's SBIR Pre-Solicitation Announcement (PSA), a guide to upcoming SBIR R&D grant opportunities, is published quarterly, in March, June, September, and December of each year. PSAs provide the following information:

- The research topics of current interest to each participating agency
- The opening and closing dates of each solicitation
- The approximate number of awards to be made under each solicitation
- Whom to contact for a copy of the agency solicitation.

To get on the mailing list for SBIR PSAs contact

U.S. Small Business Administration
SBIR Program
409 Third Street, S.W.
Washington, DC 20416
(202) 205-7777

Technical abstracts of past SBIR awards are available through an on-line service of the U.S. Department of Commerce National Technical Information Service (NTIS) known as the Federal Research in Progress (FEDRIP) database (described earlier in this chapter). FEDRIP is also accessible through DIALOG or Knowledge Express, the private information services. About 10,000 projects are currently listed in this database.

Information on each past SBIR project includes:

- Company name, address, and telephone number
- Sponsoring federal agency
- Funding awarded for Phase 1 and Phase 2
- A 200-word abstract describing the technical work
- Commercialization potential

Free copies of the FEDRIP Search Guide are available by calling (703) 487-4650. For information on DIALOG, call 800-3-DIALOG; on Knowledge Express, call 800-248-2469.

Awards have covered a broad range of scientific research, from human habitability and biology in space to airborne datalink cockpit management, and from neural-network-based speech identification to aquacultures.

To be eligible to compete, a business concern must be at least 51% owned and controlled by individuals who are citizens of, or lawfully admitted permanent residents of, the United States, and, including affiliates, may not have more than 500 employees.

The Advanced Technology Program (ATP)

The Department of Commerce and the National Institute of Standards and Technology also make awards to businesses or industry-led joint ventures of businesses, universities, government organizations, and independent research centers. These awards are for innovative research and development of cutting-edge, generic technologies. Generic technologies underlie a wide range of potential applications for a broad range of products or processes. The technologies can be from any scientific area.

Past awards have ranged from ceramics to metal processing, from refrigeration technology to tissue engineering. The awards support the development of laboratory prototypes and proof of technical feasibility, not commercial prototypes or proof of commercial feasibility.

Awards to individual firms are limited to $2 million over three years to cover direct R&D costs. Awards to joint ventures are for five years, and the dollar amounts are limited only by available funding. However, NIST funding to joint ventures is capped at less than 50% of total R&D costs. Support for the ATP program has increased over time from a 1990 appropriation of $10 million to appropriations of $36 million in 1991, $44 million in 1992, and $68 million in 1993.

HOW TO FIND ATP

Proposals must be submitted to specifically dated solicitations. To get your name on the mailing list for solicitation announcements contact:

Advanced Technology Program
A430 Administration Building
National Institute of Standards and Technology
Gaithersburg, MD 20899
(301) 975-2636

To reach the ATP Hotline for the latest program update call (301) 975-2273.

The awards are based on scientific and technical merit and the potential benefit to U.S. industry. They are highly competitive. Only 59 awards have been made from 659 proposals as of the end of 1992. However, two-thirds of the 21 awards that were announced in December 1992 were garnered by small businesses.

EXTERNAL ASSISTANCE AVAILABLE PRIMARILY TO STATE AND LOCAL RESIDENTS

State Resources

State, local, and regional development agencies imitate, support, and expand federal efforts to help startups and small businesses. Like the federal agencies, their services target business development, startup and small business financing, procurement, and international trade. Their clients include women, minorities, entrepreneurial ventures in rural or depressed areas, and technologically oriented startups.

Your first stop should be your *state department of commerce*, a useful starting place for finding other resources, such as those national programs described in this chapter, and other state, regional, and local-sponsored management assistance and financial support programs. This management and technical assistance may range from business planning to licensing, helping firms locate capital, and finding state and federal procurement opportunities. They typically offer state certification programs for businesses owned by minorities and women.

Local Resources

Chambers of Commerce

These are city-based groupings of local businesses that often provide assistance for firms wishing to relocate or start operations in the city. Chambers often provide information packages on local regulations and taxes. They also work closely with economic development organizations to lobby the city government for more favorable business conditions. They have traditionally provided a setting for business leaders, including entrepreneurs, to network and discuss common problems.

Incubators

These organizations nurture several fledgling firms that share services and equipment and occupy building space at a reduced rate. Nationwide there are about 500 incubators, with an average of one added each week. Businesses starting out in incubators have an 80% success rate, which is higher than the average startup success rate. In addition to low-cost shelter and services, one of the biggest benefits provided by incubators is the support and counsel provided by other tenants and in-house professional counselors.

WHERE TO FIND INCUBATORS

National Business Incubation Association
153 S. Hanover Street
Carlisle, PA 17013
(717) 249-4508

University Libraries

Athough they have no direct charter to assist startups, many university business libraries, particularly those at public universities, are dedicated to serving the information needs of business. They offer reasonably priced information services, including:

- Photocopies or book loans
- Government publications
- Company reports—annual or 10K
- Scientific or technical information
- Business management information
- Market or product studies
- Reviews of computer hardware or software
- Tax or legal information searches
- Patent and trademark searches
- Technical standards and specifications
- Consumer profiles and census data
- Corporate financial information
- Mailing labels
- Other search help

Public Libraries

The business sections of city-funded public libraries also provide useful resources.

FOR FURTHER READING

Delphos, William A. *The World Is Your Market: An Export Guide for Small Business*. Washington, D.C.: Craddock Communications, 1990.

Dorgan, Charity Anne, ed. *Small Business Sourcebook*. Detroit: Gale Research Inc., 1989.

Lesko, Matthew. *Government Giveaways for Entrepreneurs*. Kensington, Md.: Information USA, 1992.

U.S. Department of Commerce, International Trade Administration. *A Basic Guide to Exporting*. Washington, D.C.: U.S. GPO, 1992.

U.S. Department of Commerce, Trade Promotion Coordinating Committee. *Export Programs: A Business Directory of U.S. Government Resources*. Washington, D.C.: U.S. GPO, 1992.

U.S. Small Business Administration. *The States and Small Business*. Washington, D.C.: U.S. GPO, 1989.

10 LEGAL AND TAX ISSUES

Richard Mandel

Tony and Jennifer had both worked for the same manufacturer of computer disk drives since their college graduations some five years ago. Their employer manufactured and sold a variety of drives that were powered by the company's own proprietary software. These products sold fairly well, but the company regularly received complaints regarding the slow response time of these drives relative to the computers to which they were linked.

Tony worked in sales at the company and was acutely aware of these complaints. He had often spoken about this problem with Jennifer, who was employed in engineering. After considering the problem for some time, Jennifer was convinced she could solve the problem through new software that could be loaded into these or any company's drives by the end-user.

One night, after work, the two budding entrepreneurs decided to establish their own company to develop and sell this software. Jennifer estimated it would take her six months to develop and perfect the software, and Tony thought he could develop significant sales volume within eight months after that. Tony was additionally convinced he could obtain enough money from his wealthy uncle Max to keep them going until then. However, they both recognized that when it became time to market and distribute their product on a large scale, they would probably need both bank and investor financing. Furthermore, although the two of them could probably perform all necessary tasks in the short run, they expected that additional programmers, sales professionals, and packing and shipping personnel would be necessary in the long run. Both of them knew of fellow employees who would be perfect for these positions. Excited about their plans, Jennifer and Tony prepared to submit their resignations.

This chapter covers legal issues that an entrepreneur must consider before leaving a position to start a new venture (for example, whether the new firm can legally compete with the former company). The chapter then discusses issues that need to be resolved before initiation of the new venture, including how to choose the legal form of the business (such as a corporation or partnership), how to name the business, and how to avoid potential tax pitfalls related to the initial founders' investment (such as how to negotiate stockholder agreements and handle the disposition of stock). The legal and tax issues involved in hiring employees is covered, as are insurance considerations and tax issues related to financing the venture.

LEGAL ISSUES INVOLVED IN LEAVING A POSITION

Enthusiastic entrepreneurs may be so excited about where they are going that they forget to consider where they have been. Many are surprised to learn that serious limitations arising out of their former employment may be imposed upon their freedom of action. Some of these limitations may be the result of agreements the entrepreneur signed while in the former position. Others may be imposed as a matter of law, without any agreement or even knowledge on the part of the employee.

The Corporate Opportunity Doctrine

The corporate opportunity doctrine is an outgrowth of the traditional obligation of loyalty owed by an agent to a principal. In its most common form, *it prohibits an officer or director of a corporation, a partner in a partnership, or a person in a similar position from identifying a business opportunity that would be valuable to his company and using that information for his own benefit or the benefit of a competitor.*

Thus, a corporate director who discovers that one of the corporation's competitors may shortly be put on the market cannot raise money and purchase the competitive company himself. To discharge his legal obligation to the corporation of which he is a director, he would be required to disclose the opportunity to his board and allow the board to decide (without his participation) whether the corporation will make the purchase. Only after the corporation has been fully informed and has decided not to take advantage of the opportunity may the director use that information for himself. Even then, as the new owner of a competitor, he would be required to resign from his former corporation's board.

The scope of this *duty of loyalty* is normally adjusted by the law to reflect the individual's position within the business. Although the president and members of the board may be required to turn over knowledge of all opportunities that may be in any way related to the business of the company, lower-level employees probably have such an obligation only with regard to opportunities that are directly relevant to their positions. Thus, arguably, a sales manager may be required to inform her company of any sales opportunities she may encounter that are relevant to the company's products. She may not be required to inform the company of a potential business acquisition.

Tony and Jennifer must consider the corporate opportunity doctrine because the opportunity to create a product that more quickly drives the devices made by their employer is directly relevant at least to Jennifer's job. Yet both Jennifer and Tony probably have positions low enough in the company hierarchy that their obligations in this regard are very limited. In addition, the slow pace of the company's disk drives and the fact that such a problem might be solved by more sophisticated software appears to be well known by the company's officers, who have shown little interest in the software side of the business.

Recruitment of Employees from the Former Employer

As Jennifer and Tony delved more deeply into their dreams, they began to identify certain fellow employees who might wish to join their company sometime down the road. This, too, can in some circumstances be problematic.

Another aspect of the duty of loyalty owed by an employee to an employer is the legal requirement that *the employee cannot knowingly take action designed to harm the employer's business*. This is, perhaps, pure common sense. After all, the employee is collecting a paycheck to perform tasks that advance the employer's interests. We would not expect the law to countenance a paid salesperson's regularly recommending that customers patronize a competitor, nor would we expect the law to endorse an engineer's giving his best ideas to another company. Similarly, courts have held that it is a breach of the duty of loyalty to solicit and induce fellow employees to leave their jobs.

Once again, the likelihood that a court would enforce this obligation depends to some extent on the nature of the employee's activities and her position in the company. Neither Tony nor Jennifer need fear reprisals for their having convinced each other to leave. Nor would there be much likelihood of liability if they convinced another employee to leave with them, especially if these conversations took place after working hours.

However, if either Tony or Jennifer worked in the human resources department, where their job descriptions would include recruiting and retention of employees, this activity might well expose them to liability. Furthermore, if their plan included the wholesale resignations of a relatively large number of employees, *such that the company's ability to continue to function efficiently might be compromised,* a court would be more likely to intervene with injunctive or other relief. This is especially true if the defendants' job descriptions included maintaining the efficient operation of the departments they were involved in destroying.

Use of Proprietary Information

Another potential complication involves Tony and Jennifer's use of information or technology belonging to their former employer. Such information need not be subject to formal patent or copyright protection to be protected. *Any information that the company has successfully kept confidential, and that is not otherwise known to outsiders, is likely to be protected by law as a trade secret.* Such information may include inventions and technology, but it may also include such other valuable information as customer lists, pricing strategies, and unique operating methods.

In this case, if Jennifer had developed the software concept that solves the speed problem as part of her job, that concept might well belong to the company and be unavailable to Jennifer and Tony for their new enterprise. Of course, it is not enough for the concept to be developed by or for the company; the concept must be unique and unknown to other software engineers, and the company must have taken steps to keep it that way.

Thus, the company should label any physical manifestations of the information as "confidential" and should restrict its distribution to those who have either a legal or contractual obligation to keep such information private. If, on the other hand, the company had deliberately or carelessly allowed the distribution of the information to outsiders, it has likely lost the right to restrict its use.

Many companies require employees to sign agreements that spell out the employees' obligation to protect trade secrets. This has led some employees to believe that such an obligation applies only to those who have signed such an agreement, which is a misconception. *The obligation to respect an employer's trade secrets and keep them confidential is imposed by law and is not dependent upon contract.* Furthermore, that obligation continues after the employment relationship has been terminated, for whatever reason, and continues indefinitely until the information makes its way into the public domain.

Employers who require a confidentiality agreement from their employees are generally not misinformed about the general applicability of the law but are simply making sure that the employees are aware of their responsibilities in this regard. After all, if an employee, under a mistaken belief about his rights, releases proprietary information to outsiders, it is small comfort to the employer to have the right to sue the employee for damages.

Fortunately for Jennifer and Tony, they appear to have merely identified a need that is known generally to the industry; they have not begun to develop the specific software solution to the problem. On that set of facts, it is extremely doubtful that their new enterprise will make use of any information that legally belongs to their former employer.

Protecting Proprietary Information in the New Business Venture

By the time Jennifer and Tony have developed a product that meets the identified need, they will have created a body of proprietary information of their own. At that point they will be forced to consider the variety of means at their disposal to protect that information from use by competitors and end-users who have failed to pay for the privilege.

A measure of protection is available from the copyright laws and, depending upon the nature of their product, from a patent. Both of these options require disclosure of the information in exchange for the protection granted by the government; thus, they present the risk that others may engineer around the patent or reconfigure the software around the copyright. In such a case, Tony and Jennifer would be unlikely to have resources adequate to bring the necessary lawsuits to protect their rights.

Thus, they may choose to forgo statutory protection and protect their asset by a policy of nondisclosure as a trade secret, accompanied by very tight licensing agreements with customers. Further discussion of these issues and of the relative advantages and risks of these various modes of intellectual property protection is contained in Chapter 11.

Noncompetition Obligations to the Former Employer

Related to the obligation not to disclose proprietary information is *the obligation not to compete with one's employer.* Like most of the obligations discussed already, this is derived from the fiduciary relationship between employer and employee, specifically, the duty of loyalty. How can an entrepreneur justify accepting a paycheck from her employer when she is simultaneously establishing, working for, or financing a competing business?

The law imposes this duty not to compete upon all employees, officers, directors, partners, and so on, while their association with the employer remains in effect. Unlike the obligation to protect proprietary information, however, this obligation does not extend to the period after termination of the relationship. Extension of this obligation requires the contractual promise of the employee. Thus, in the absence of a contract, as soon as Tony and Jennifer quit their present jobs (but not before), they are free to go into direct competition with their former employer, so long as they do not make use of any of the employer's proprietary information.

Noncompetition agreements can be analyzed using many different measurements. To begin with, the scope of the obligation must be examined. In an extreme case, an employee may have agreed not to engage in any activity that competes with any aspect of the business his former employer engaged in, or planned to engage in, at the time of the termination of the employee's association with the company. At the other end of the spectrum, the employee may have agreed only to refrain from soliciting any of the former employer's customers or (somewhat more restrictively) from dealing with any of them no matter who initiated the contact. Such agreements also may be measured based on the length of time they extend beyond the termination of employment and by the size of the geographic area they cover.

Such measurements are important because, in the employment context, many states take the position that such agreements contravene basic public policies, such as encouraging competition and allowing each individual to make the best use of her talents. A few such states actually refuse to enforce noncompetition agreements. Most, however, purport to enforce only those agreements that are deemed reasonable under the circumstances. Thus, these public policies are balanced against the employer's recognized interest in protecting its business and goodwill. Only those restrictions intended to prevent harm to the employer's legitimate interests will be enforced.

For example, a medical practice that does business only with customers located within a 25-mile radius would probably not be able to enforce a noncompetition agreement that extends much beyond that geographic area. Furthermore, although a manufacturer may be able to enforce such an agreement against an officer, salesperson, or engineer who has either direct contact with customers or knowledge of the company's processes and products, it might not be able to enforce the same agreement against a bookkeeper, whose departure would have little effect upon the company's goodwill. Even the officer, salesperson, or engineer might be able to resist an agreement that purports to remain in effect beyond the time the employer might reasonably need to protect its goodwill and business from the effects of new competition.

Another factor that may affect the enforceability of a noncompetition agreement is whether the employer agrees to continue part or all of the former employee's compensation during the noncompetition period. In addition, a noncompetition agreement that might be unenforceable against an employee might nonetheless be enforceable against the seller of a business or a major stockholder having his stock redeemed. Finally, employers in some states can take comfort in the fact that some courts that find the scope or length of a noncompetition agreement objectionable, nonetheless enforce the agreement to the maximum extent they deem acceptable. Others take an all-or-nothing approach.

Since in Tony and Jennifer's case there is no indication that they have signed a noncompetition agreement, they need only resign from their current positions before taking any affirmative steps to establish their new enterprise. After resigning, they are under no further noncompetitive restrictions.

CHOOSING AN ATTORNEY AND ACCOUNTANT

There is a natural reluctance to incur what are perceived to be unnecessary expenses in beginning a new venture, and many people perceive engaging an attorney and accountant as just such expenses. However, as may already be evident from the discussion so far, the earlier these professionals can be consulted, the more likely the business will be to avoid costly mistakes. One is tempted to repeat the old cliche "either pay me now or pay me later," the latter alternative being much more costly.

Choose a Lawyer Who Is Experienced in Small Business Startups

The choice of an appropriate attorney is complicated by the fact that American law does not officially recognize legal specialties. Thus, in virtually all states, there is only one form of licensing, and, once licensed, an attorney can practice in all areas of the law. In practice, however, the American legal profession has become highly specialized, with many attorneys confining their practices to one or two areas of expertise. Thus, most patent attorneys do very little else, and most good litigation attorneys concentrate on litigating. Few very good corporate attorneys know their way around a courtroom. Just as these legal areas are practiced mainly by specialists, the representation of startups and small businesses is becoming a specialty as well.

Tony and Jennifer would do well to ask their prospective attorney to describe her experience in representing small businesses. The local generalist may not be sufficiently aware of the many technical matters identified in this chapter (and elsewhere in this book). Also, an attorney experienced in the problems of startups will be familiar with the unique cash-flow problems of such ventures. A business's need for legal services may never be so great in comparison with its ability to pay than at the outset. The attorney may be willing to work out installment payments or other arrangements to avoid postponing essential early planning.

Unfortunately, many attorneys practicing in this area have adopted a policy of accepting equity in the new business as part of the fee arrangement. Interestingly, many such attorneys do not lower their fee in exchange for equity but justify taking equity as the price of accepting the risk that their fee may not be paid if the business does not succeed. Such an arrangement may lead to dangerous conflicts of interest in the future, when legal advice affects the value of the company's stock. For example, how can an entrepreneur be confident of an attorney's advice regarding the suitability of the company for a public offering when such an offering would have the effect of creating a market for the same attorney's stock? Tony and Jennifer may wish to avoid such an arrangement.

Choose a Small, Local Accounting Firm

Many of the same considerations inform the choice of an accountant. Although the level of expertise in the national and international firms is unmatched, most of them have little experience with startups such as that proposed by Tony and Jennifer, since their fee structures are inappropriate for the size of such businesses. Many local firms have all the skills necessary to serve the startup and can be sensitive to the cash-flow issues mentioned earlier.

It is important to engage the accountant as early as possible so he can establish the information management systems and recommend the computer software that will get the company's records off on the right foot. This gives the entrepreneur the tools necessary to gauge the success of her efforts against her budget before it is too late to adapt, and it prevents the expensive and frustrating task of reconstructing the company's results from fragmented and missing records at the end of the year.

CHOOSING THE LEGAL FORM OF YOUR BUSINESS

Business Forms

One of the first issues Jennifer, Tony, and their attorney will confront, after weaving their way through the thicket of issues associated with leaving their current jobs, is what legal form they should choose for their new venture. Many choices are available.

The Sole Proprietorship

The most basic business form (and the one that will apply unless an entrepreneur chooses otherwise) is the sole proprietorship. This is a business owned and operated by one individual, who is in total control. No new legal entity is created; the individual entrepreneur just goes into business, either alone or with employees, but without any co-owners. This is the simplest of entities but one that will not be attractive to Jennifer and Tony unless one of them chooses to forgo ownership and act only as an employee.

The Partnership

The default mode for Tony and Jennifer is the partnership. This is the legal form that results when two or more persons go into business for profit, as co-owners, sharing profits and losses. Since Tony and Jennifer clearly contemplate sharing ownership and control, they will find themselves in a partnership unless they choose otherwise.

A Corporation

Another choice available to our subjects is the corporation. This form is created by state government, as a routine matter, upon the entrepreneur's filing an application and paying a fee. It is a separate entity, with legal existence apart from its owners, the stockholders. Jennifer and Tony might well choose to form a corporation, dividing its stock betweeen them.

The Subchapter S Corporation

A variation of the corporate option is the so-called subchapter S, or small business, corporation. If a corporation passes a number of tests, it may elect to be treated as such. However, it is essential to understand that such election affects only the tax status of the corporation. In all other respects, a subchapter S corporation is indistinguishable from a standard corporation. For reasons discussed later in this chapter, Jennifer and Tony may also find this business form attractive.

The Professional Corporation

This is another variation of the corporate form. This choice is typically available only to business-people who intend to render professional services, such as medical or legal practitioners, accountants, architects, and social workers. It was created primarily to allow these professionals to take advantage of certain tax opportunities available only to corporations, without granting them the limited liability afforded to normal business corporations.

Over time, however, many of the tax advantages formerly available only to corporations have been extended to sole proprietorships and partnerships, and some of the limited liability formerly associated with business corporations has been extended to professional corporations. Thus, the differences between these forms have narrowed considerably. In any case, Tony and Jennifer will not be practicing a profession, so this business form will not be available to them.

The Limited Partnership

Another possible legal form is a hybrid of the corporate and partnership forms known as the limited partnership. Such a business has one or more general partners (who conduct the business) and one or more limited partners (who act as passive investors, similar to stockholders with no other interest in the business). Because both Tony and Jennifer intend to be actively involved in the business, neither would qualify as a limited partner. But Uncle Max may well qualify if he is willing to fade into the background once he has made his investment.

The Nonprofit Entity

A summary of available business forms should not omit the nonprofit entity. Typically, such a business will take the form of a corporation or trust and will elect nonprofit status as a tax matter. Although many startups do not make a profit, nonprofit (or, more accurately, *not-for-profit*) status is available only to certain types of entities, such as churches, educational institutions, social welfare organizations, and industry associations. If an organization so qualifies, its income is exempt from taxation (as long as it doesn't stray from its exempt purpose), and if certain additional tests are met, contributions to it may be tax-deductible. However, since Tony and Jennifer do not intend to operate a qualifying business, they need not explore this option.

Choosing the Form

Faced with all these choices, the budding entrepreneur will want to compare these various business forms in terms of a number of issues relevant to the needs of his business. Both the attorney and accountant for the business can be extremely helpful at this juncture.

Although these forms may be compared on the basis of an almost endless list of factors, those normally most relevant include control issues, exposure to personal liability, tax factors, and administrative costs. Thise issues are discussed in detail in the following sections, and Exhibit 10.1 provides an overview of the issues and how they affect each business form.

Control Issues

The *sole proprietorship* is the simplest and most direct with regard to the subject of control. Since there is only one principal in the business, this individual wields total control over all issues. However, that option is not available to Tony and Jennifer.

The simplest option available to them is the *partnership*. In that form, control is divided among the principals in accordance with their partnership

EXHIBIT 10.1. Comparison of various business forms.

	Control	Liability	Taxation	Administrative obligations
Sole proprietorship	Owner has complete control	Unlimited personal liability	Not a separate taxable entity	Only those generic to businesses
Partnership	Partners share control	Joint and several unlimited personal liability	Not a separate taxable entity	Only those generic to businesses
Corporation	Control distributed among shareholders, directors, and officers	Limited personal liability	Separate taxable entity unless subchapter S election	Some additional
Limited partnership	General partners control, limited partners do not	General partners: joint and several unlimited personal liability, limited partners: limited personal liability	Not a separate entity	Some additional

agreement. Although a written agreement is normally not legally required, this issue and many of the others that arise in a partnership argue for a written agreement to encourage specificity. The parties may decide that all decisions must be made by unanimous vote, or they may adopt a majority standard (making Uncle Max the swing vote). More likely, they may require unanimity for a stated group of significant decisions and may allow a majority vote for others. In addition, Jennifer and Tony may delegate authority for certain types of decisions to one or both of the active partners.

Regardless of how this power is allocated in the partnership agreement, however, third parties are allowed to rely on the authority of any partner to bind the partnership to contracts relevant to the ordinary course of the partnership's business. Thus, no matter what may have been agreed among them, Uncle Max will have a free hand with third parties, subject only to the consequences of his breaching his agreement with the others. This is also true for the consequences of torts committed by any partner acting in the course of partnership business. The looseness of this arrangement may well be enough to discourage Jennifer and Tony from choosing the partnership option.

A *corporation*, whether professional or business, and regardless of whether it has elected subchapter S status, is controlled by three levels of authority. Broadly speaking, the stockholders' vote, in proportion to the number of shares owned, on the election of the board of directors, sale or dissolution of the business, and amendments to the corporation's charter. In virtually all cases, these decisions are made either by the majority or by two-thirds of the shares. Thus, if Tony, Jennifer, and Uncle Max each owned one-third of the issued stock, Tony and Jennifer (if they voted together) could elect the entire board and sell the business over the objections of Uncle Max. Uncle Max would not even be entitled to a minority position on the board. He would, however, be the swing vote should Jennifer and Tony ever disagree, perhaps prompting them to consider nonvoting stock or some similar device for him.

The board of directors, in turn, makes all the long-term and significant policy decisions for the business, as well as electing the officers of the corporation. Votes are virtually always decided by majority. The officers, consisting of a president, treasurer, and secretary at minimum, run the day-to-day business of the corporation and, as such, are the only level of authority that can bind the corporation by contract or in tort.

In this case, one would expect either Tony or Jennifer to be president and the other, perhaps, to be executive vice president and treasurer. Other commonly used titles are chief executive officer, chief operating officer, and vice president of finance. It is not uncommon for the corporation's attorney to act as secretary, since the attorney presumably has the expertise necessary to keep the corporate records of the company in an accurate manner. We might also expect that Tony and Jennifer would convince Uncle Max not to insist upon a title, thus eliminating his power to deal with third parties on the corporation's behalf.

The *limited partnership* concentrates all control in the general partners, who exercise that control as set forth in the limited partnership agreement (just as such control is allocated in a partnership agreement). Limited partners have virtually no control, unless the limited partnership agreement has granted them some influence over very significant issues such as sale of the business or dissolution. Only the general partners have the apparent authority to bind the partnership in contract or tort with third parties. Since the limited partnership is required to file the names of its general partners with the state, third parties are deemed to know that limited partners (whose names do not appear) cannot have such authority.

Based upon control issues alone, therefore, Tony and Jennifer would likely be leaning away from a general partnership and toward either the limited partnership or the corporation. Their decision will, however, be greatly affected by considerations of personal liability.

Personal Liability Issues

If the business should ever incur current liabilities beyond its ability to pay, must the individual owners make up the difference? If so, this could easily result in personal bankruptcy for the owners on top of the loss of their business. And this unhappy result need not occur as a result of poor management or bad business conditions. It could just as easily be brought about by an uninsured tort claim from a buyer of the product or a victim of a delivery person's careless driving.

For both the *partnership,* and the *sole proprietorship,* the business is not recognized as a legal entity separate from its owners. Thus, the debts of the business are ultimately the debts of the owners if the business cannot pay. This unlimited liability is enough to recommend avoidance of these forms for virtually any business, with the possible exception of the one-person consulting firm, for which all liability will be the direct result of the wrongdoing of its owner in any case.

If this unlimited liability is uncomfortable for Jennifer and Tony, imagine what it means to Uncle Max, who apparently has significant assets to lose and who will likely be excluded from meaningful control over the business. This is made even worse by the fact that all partnership liabilities are considered joint and several obligations of all partners. Thus, Uncle Max will be responsible for full payment of all partnership liabilities if Tony and Jennifer have no significant assets of their own.

Uncle Max can gain solace from the fact that in trading away his influence over the operation of the business in a limited partnership, he is granted limited liability for its debts. Thus, if the limited partnership cannot meet its obligations, Uncle Max will lose his investment, but his personal assets will not be exposed to partnership creditors except to the extent that he made promises of future investment.

However, the limited partnership does not afford this protection to the general partners. They retain unlimited exposure. Tony and Jennifer may believe they can afford to take this risk, especially if they have no significant assets. Yet even if that is so today, it may not be the case at the time liability is incurred.

The solution to all this seems to be the *corporation,* which affords limited liability to all stockholders. None of the three stockholders of our enterprise would have personal liability for its debts. If the corporation ultimately becomes insolvent, its creditors will look only to the corporation's assets for payment and will absorb any shortfall.

Of course, this solution is not quite as simple as it sounds. To begin with, creditors know these rules as well as the entrepreneurs. Thus, large or sophisticated creditors, such as banks and other financial institutions, will insist upon personal guarantees from the stockholders before extending credit. In addition, the law has developed a number of theories that allow creditors to "pierce the corporate veil" and go after the stockholders of a failed corporation under certain conditions. Generally, these fall into one of two categories.

The first of these covers corporations that were initially underfunded, or "thinly capitalized." A corporation should start out with a combination of capital and liability insurance adequate to cover the claims to which it might normally expect to be exposed. As long as the capital was there at the outset and has not been depleted by dividends or other distributions to stockholders, the protection of the corporate form survives, even after the capital has been depleted by unsuccessful operation.

The second situation that may result in the piercing of the corporate veil is the failure of the stockholders to respect the corporate form by treating the corporation as an entity separate from themselves. This may be manifest by the entrepreneurs acting in one or more of the following ways:

- Failing to use "Inc.," "Corp.," or a similar legal indicator when dealing with third parties
- Commingling corporate and personal assets in a personal bank account or allowing personal use of corporate assets
- Failing to keep corporate records and to hold regular directors and stockholders meetings

After all, why should creditors be required to respect the difference between the corporation and its owners when the owners themselves have not?

Assuming, however, that Tony and Jennifer will avoid conduct that would expose them to such personal liability, the corporate form should look rather attractive to them. No significant business decision should be made, however, without a look at the tax consequences.

Taxation Issues

Once again, the business form that is simplest to understand in regard to taxation is the *sole proprietorship*. The financial results of the business are calculated, and the profit or loss appears on the tax return of the sole owner. He can eliminate much of the profit by taking it out of the business as salary, but that has no tax effect, as it simply increases taxable wages by the exact amount that it lowers profit. The tax rate applied to any profit would be the maximum marginal rate to which the taxpayer is exposed by the combination of this profit and all other taxable income. If there is a loss, the results of the business act as a sort of tax shelter by offsetting an equal amount of other taxable income, if any.

As one might expect, the *partnership* acts in a manner very similar to that of the sole proprietorship. Since a partnership is not recognized as a separate legal entity, it pays no taxes itself (although in many cases it is required to file an informational return). Its profit or loss is reported by its partners. The only complication is allocating the percentage of this profit or loss to be reported by each partner. This is normally determined by the allocations of profit and loss set forth in the partnership agreement by the partners themselves, so long as that allocation reflects a "substantial economic reality."

The *limited partnership* is taxed in exactly the same way as the partnership, with profit and loss allocated among *all* partners, both general and limited, in accordance with the limited partnership agreement. Since the business contemplated by Jennifer and Tony is likely to lose money at the outset, the tax-sheltering aspects of both the partnership and limited partnership may be attractive to Uncle Max, who surely has other sources of income he would like to shelter.

Of the two, the limited partnership would be preferable, since by accepting limited partner status, Uncle Max can have his shelter without being exposed to personal liability. He may be tempted to request that the agreement allocate 99% of the losses to him, since he likely needs the shelter more than Jennifer and Tony do. However, unless he is contributing 99% of the capital and will receive a similar percentage of profit (both operating and capital gain), such an allocation might fail the "substantial economic reality" test.

A further obstacle to Uncle Max's taking advantage of the possible tax shelter of early losses is presented by the recently enacted passive loss rules. Simply stated, if Uncle Max is not actively involved in the business (which would, by definition, be the case if he were a limited partner), any losses distributable to him from the business could be used to offset income generated only by other passive activities (such as investments in other limited partnerships). The losses could not shelter income from salaries, interest, or dividends from traditional portfolio investments.

Were the business to be organized as a *corporation*, Tony and Jennifer would doubtless be warned about the bugaboo of "double taxation." This fear results from the fact that a corporation is recognized as a separate legal entity for tax purposes, and it thus pays a separate corporate level of income tax. Double taxation arises when the corporation makes a profit, pays tax on it, and distributes the remainder to its stockholders as a dividend. The stockholders must then pay income tax on the dividend, resulting in double taxation of the same money.

The same would be true if the corporation paid tax on its profit and then retained the remainder for operations. When the corporation was eventually sold, the increased value caused by that retention of earnings would be taxed to the selling stockholders as a capital gain.

In reality, however, double taxation is more a myth to the small business than a legitimate fear. In fact, in most cases, it presents an opportunity for significant economic savings. To begin with, most small corporations reduce or even eliminate profit by increasing salaries and bonuses for their owners. This can be done up to the point where the compensation of these individuals is deemed unreasonable by the Internal Revenue Service. If profit is eliminated in this way, the owners will have removed their money from the corporation and will pay only their own individual income tax on it.

On the other hand, if it is necessary to retain some of these earnings, the corporation will pay income tax at a *lower* rate than the stockholders would have, since tax will be imposed at the lowest marginal corporate rate, rather than the stockholders' highest rate. When the corporation is later sold, the stockholders will be taxed at favorable capital gain rates, and the corporation will have had the use of the money in the meantime to create greater value. Thus, it is the rare small corporation that will actually pay the much-feared double tax.

Furthermore, if the corporation meets certain eligibility requirements, it can elect (under subchapter S of the Internal Revenue Code) to be taxed essentially as if it were a partnership. Whatever profit or loss it generates will appear on the tax returns of the stockholders in proportion to the shares of stock they own, and the corporation will file only an informational return. To take advantage of this option, the corporation must have 35 or fewer stockholders, all of whom are individuals and either resident aliens or citizens of the United States. The corporation cannot have any subsidiaries, and it can have only one class of stock.

The *subchapter S* election can be very useful in a number of circumstances. For example, if the business is expected to be profitable and Uncle Max insists on a share of those profits, Tony and Jennifer could not avoid double taxation by increasing salaries and bonuses. Since Uncle Max performs no services for the business, any compensation paid to him would automatically be deemed unreasonable. But under subchapter S, since there is no corporate tax, a dividend to Uncle Max would only be taxed at his level.

If the business were to become extremely successful, Tony and Jennifer could reap the rewards without fear that their salaries might be attacked as unreasonable, since, again, there are no corporate compensation deductions to disallow. Furthermore, if the business is expecting losses in the short term, Uncle Max can use his share of the losses (determined by his percentage of stock) as a shelter (subject to the passive loss considerations described previously). Even Tony and Jennifer could use their losses against the salaries from their former jobs earlier in the year. An early subchapter S election can also avoid double tax should the corporation eventually sell all its assets and distribute the proceeds to the stockholders in liquidation.

At this point in the analysis, it is likely that Tony and Jennifer are favoring a subchapter S corporation for the conduct of their business. Such an entity would shield them from personal liability and allow them to exercise control free from undue influence from Uncle Max. In addition, all three of them would have the advantage of short-term losses on their tax returns. Only an undue administrative burden seems sufficient to reverse this decision.

Administrative Obligations

Certain administrative obligations will be required no matter which business form Jennifer and Tony choose. For example, upon entering business, they should obtain a federal identification number for their business. This will facilitate interaction with the federal government, including the filing of tax returns (real or informational) and the withholding of income and payroll taxes.

On the state level, the business should obtain a sales and use tax registration number, to facilitate reporting and collection of such taxes and to qualify for exemption from such taxes when it purchases items for resale. A nonprofit entity has 18 months to file for and secure nonprofit status from the Internal Revenue Service. Furthermore, as described earlier, all business entities will incur a certain amount of additional accounting expense, specifically for the calculation and reporting of taxable profit and loss.

Corporations, however, bring some additional administrative burden and expense. A corporation (as well as a limited partnership in most states) must file an annual report with the state government in addition to its tax return. This document usually reports only the corporation's current address, officers, directors, and similar information, but it is accompanied by an annual maintenance fee. The fee, which is in addition to any minimum income tax that the state may levy, must be paid to avoid eventual involuntary dissolution by the state.

In addition, it is often the case that a corporation is formed under the laws of one state while operating in another. In particular, the state of Delaware has acquired the reputation of having a corporate law that is particularly sympathetic to management in its dealings with stockholders. Although this is a questionable advantage in the context of a small business, many corporations nonetheless form in Delaware merely for the appearance of sophistication. In such cases, the corporation must pay initial fees and annual maintenance fees not only to the state of Delaware (or whichever state is chosen for formation) but also to each state in which it actually operates.

Many large, national businesses pay these fees in virtually all 50 states. Although Jennifer and Tony could avoid these fees by operating as a partnership, it is likely they will conclude that corporate advantages are worth the price. They will be well advised, however, to incorporate in the state in which they operate in order to save duplicate fees.

CHOOSING A NAME FOR THE BUSINESS

The choice of a name for a business may at first seem to be a matter of personal taste, without many legal ramifications. However, since a business's name is ultimately the repository of its goodwill, the entrepreneur must take care to choose a name that will not be confused with the name of another business. If she does not exercise such caution, the entrepreneur may discover sometime in the future that she has expended considerable money and effort enhancing the goodwill of another entity. Worse yet, she may be sued for infringement of another's rights.

Even apart from these concerns, an entrepreneur choosing to operate in the corporate or limited partnership form must clear her choice of name with the state of organization. Although partnerships and sole proprietorships need not do so, corporations and limited partnerships obtain their existence by filing charters with the state. As part of this process, each state will check to see if the name chosen by the potential new entity is "confusingly similar" to a name used by another entity currently registered with that state. This includes entities formed under that state's laws and foreign entities qualified to do business there. Some states will also deny the use of a name they deem misleading, even if it is not similar to the name of another entity.

Passing this test is far from sufficient for the protection of goodwill, however. The fact that no other corporation is using your name in your state does not mean that others are not using it in other states. Furthermore, passing the corporate or limited partnership name check doesn't guarantee that no one is using or will use your name for a partnership, sole proprietorship, or product name, in your state or elsewhere.

Fortunately, it is possible to discover whether your chosen name is being used by others and to protect it from later use. A number of companies have compiled databases that contain the names of a wide range of entities and products. Virtually all such services contain all corporate and limited partnership names from all U.S. jurisdictions. Others add trade and service mark registrations from around the country. Most lawyers have access to a particularly comprehensive data base that includes the preceding lists as well as names from major trade directories, big-city telephone directories, and similar sources. Once a name has passed this test, you can be relatively sure that it is yours if you protect it.

A limited form of protection can be obtained relatively inexpensively by filing the name (and any associated logo or slogan) with the *state trademark registry* in any state in which you intend to use the name, logo, or slogan. If your business provides a service rather than sales of goods, the same protection can be provided by the state's *service mark registry*. The protection provided by these registries extends only throughout the state and will be preempted elsewhere by any federal registration existing or later obtained. Thus, at best, state registration is merely evidence of your prior use of a mark, resulting perhaps in a later federal registrant's being required to allow your continued use of the mark in a limited market area.

The most effective form of protection is a *federal registration*. Such a registration bars future use of the mark within the relevant class of goods or services anywhere in the United States by anyone who has not established rights through prior use. Since this protection is rather draconian, it is not granted without serious examination by the U.S. Patent Office. Registration can be denied, of course, if the name or mark is already in use by others. Protection can also be denied if the name is excessively generic, such that it describes all goods or services in a particular class instead of identifying the goods and services of a particular market participant. Thus, the name Disk Drive Software would likely be denied protection in the case of Jennifer and Tony's business. (Other legal doctrines relevant to trademark registration are described in Chapter 11.)

Once Jennifer and Tony have chosen a name for their business and product and have selected a level of protection with which they are comfortable, they can turn their attention to the initial funding of their enterprise.

POTENTIAL TAX PITFALLS RELATED TO THE INITIAL INVESTMENT OF THE FOUNDERS

Left to their own devices, Tony and Jennifer would likely arrange the issuance of their stock in the corporation for no tangible investment whatsoever. After all, they intend to look to Uncle Max for working capital in the short run, and their investment will be the services they intend to perform for the corporation in the future.

Historically, such a plan would have run afoul of some rather anachronistic corporate legal restraints that required consideration for stock issuances to take the form of present property or cash and to at least equal the par value of the stock issued. These requirements were based upon a theory of protection for corporate creditors, who could be assured that the corporation had assets at least equal to the aggregate par value of the shares of its stock that had previously been issued. Stock issued for less than par value was considered "watered stock" and exposed the holder and the directors issuing it to personal liability for the shortfall.

Much of the protection provided by these rules has been eroded over the years, however, by a number of developments. For example, it has long been commonplace to authorize stock with minimal par value (such as $0.01 per share) or even no par value at all. The corporation then issues stock for what it believes to be fair value without risk of failing to cover the aggregate par. In addition, it has long been possible to issue stock in exchange for intangible assets such as past services rendered. However, stock issuance for future services remains illegal under most corporate statutes, although many proposals have been made to legitimize it.

Of more practical concern than these corporate problems, however, is the fact that any property (including stock) transferred to an employee in exchange for services is considered *taxable income* under the Internal Revenue Code. Thus, even were it possible for Tony and Jennifer to be issued stock in exchange for future services under corporate law, they would face an unexpected tax liability as a result.

The solution to all this may be to require Tony and Jennifer to reach into their limited resources and contribute some minimal cash amount to the corporation in exchange for their stock. So long as the cash amount exceeds the par value (which will be minimal or nonexistent), this would avoid the corporate and tax problems associated with issuance for future services. However, as noted above, if their minimal investment was the full extent of the corporation's initial capitalization, the corporate veil might well be in danger.

Of course, Jennifer and Tony have no reason to fear exposure to personal liability since, at the same time they will be making their minimal investment, Uncle Max will be putting in the real money. Yet the participation of Uncle Max exposes Jennifer and Tony to a danger they may believe they have successfully avoided. Since Uncle Max will be paying substantially more for his stock than Jennifer and Tony are paying for theirs, the Internal Revenue Service will likely take the position that they are being afforded the opportunity for a bargain purchase in exchange for the services they are providing to their employer. Thus, once again, Tony and Jennifer may face an unexpected income tax on the difference between the price of Uncle Max's stock and the price of theirs.

One way to solve this problem is to postpone Uncle Max's investment until a time sufficiently remote from the date of Tony and Jennifer's investment that an argument can be made for an increase in the value of the corporation's stock. However, in addition to the essentially fictional nature of this approach, Jennifer and Tony cannot wait that long. To solve this problem, the parties must design a vehicle other than common stock for Uncle Max's investment.

It may seem immediately advisable to create some sort of senior security for Uncle Max, such as *preferred stock* with a liquidation preference of approximately the amount he invested. In fact, assuming for a moment that the initial plan was to split the common stock equally among the parties, Uncle Max may well insist on such a security; otherwise, Tony and Jennifer could dissolve the corporation immediately after its formation and walk away with one-third of Uncle Max's investment. In addition to having a preference upon liquidation, Uncle Max might insist that his stock share in the company's growth, but this could be accommodated by allowing the preferred stock to participate in profits remaining for distribution after dividend and liquidation preferences have been paid.

Demonstrating the sometimes frustrating interrelated character of tax and corporate law, however, is the fact that the issuance of preferred stock to Uncle Max would render the corporation ineligible for subchapter S status, because it would then have more than one class of stock. As discussed previously, the likelihood of initial losses by the corporation makes subchapter S status very attractive, especially for Uncle Max.

The solution appears to lie in the *utilization of debt securities*. If Uncle Max pays for his stock the same price per share as Jennifer and Tony paid, and if he injects the remainder of his investment in the form of a loan, his fellow stockholders will not face taxable compensation income, and he will retain the opportunity to benefit from subchapter S.

Even were the corporation not to choose subchapter S status, investment as debt affords Uncle Max the potential for future nontaxable distributions from the company in the form of debt repayment, and he gains priority as a creditor should the corporation be forced to liquidate. All the while, he protects his participation in growth through his additional ownership of common stock.

Of course, as with all benefits, it is possible to get too much of a good thing. Too high a percentage of debt may expose all the stockholders to the accusation of thin capitalization, resulting in the piercing of the corporate veil. And abusively high debt/equity ratios or failure to respect debt formalities and repayment schedules might induce the Internal Revenue Service to reclassify the debt as equity, thus imposing many of the adverse tax results described earlier.

NEGOTIATING STOCKHOLDER AND PARTNERSHIP AGREEMENTS

The results of the negotiations among Jennifer, Tony, and Uncle Max regarding their respective investments would normally be memorialized in a stockholders' agreement. In the unlikely event that this business were to be organized as a partnership or limited partnership, very similar provisions allocating equity interests and rights to distributions of profit and cash flow would appear in a partnership agreement. In either case, however, the parties would be well advised to go beyond these subjects and reach written agreement on a number of other potentially thorny issues at the outset of their relationship.

Negotiating Employment Terms

For example, Tony and Jennifer should reach agreement with Uncle Max as to the extent of their *commitment to provide services* and the *level of compensation* for doing so. It would be very unusual for persons in the position of Tony and Jennifer to forgo compensation solely to share the profits of the business with their investor. For one thing, what would they live on in the interim? For another, the profits of the business are properly conceived of as the amount left after payment of the costs of capital (interest on Uncle Max's note) and the expenses of the business (including reasonable compensation to its employees). Thus, Jennifer and Tony should negotiate *employment terms* into the stockholders' agreement, setting forth their responsibilities, titles, compensation, and related issues.

This is especially important in this case, since each of the three stockholders holds only a minority interest in the corporation. Both Tony and Jennifer may wish to foreclose the possibility that Uncle Max may ally with one of them and employ a majority of the shares to remove the other as a director, officer, and employee of the company. Given the lack of any market for the shares of this corporation, such a move would essentially destroy any value the shares had for the holder in the short run.

Although a concise description of each party's obligations and rewards is still advisable to avoid dispute, the negative scenario just outlined would be illegal in a *partnership* (in the absence of serious misconduct by the party being removed) since the majority partners would be violating the fiduciary duty of loyalty of each partner toward the others imposed under partnership law. Although no such duty formally exists among stockholders in a *corporation,* many states have recently extended the fiduciary duties of partners to the relationship among founders of a closely held corporation. Thus, in many states, were Jennifer to be removed without cause from her employment and corporate positions by Tony and Uncle Max, she would have effective legal recourse even in the absence of a stockholders' agreement.

Negotiating Disposition of Stock

As for other items that might be covered in the stockholders' agreement among Jennifer, Tony, and Uncle Max, many such agreements address the disposition of stock held by the stockholders under certain circumstances.

Transfer of Stock

To begin with, it is probably not contemplated by any of these persons that their stock will be freely transferable, such that new "partners" may be imposed upon them by a selling stockholder. Although sale of stock in a closely held corporation is made rather difficult by federal and state securities regulation and the lack of any market for the shares, transfers are still possible under the correct circumstances. To avoid that possibility, stockholders' agreements frequently require that any stockholder wishing to transfer stock to a third party must first offer it to the corporation or the other stockholders, who may purchase the stock, usually at the lower of a formula price or the amount being offered by the third party.

Disposition of Stock upon the Stockholder's Death

Stockholders' agreements should also address the disposition of each party's stock in the event of death. Again, it is unlikely that each stockholder would be comfortable allowing the stock to fall into the hands of the deceased's spouse, children, or other heirs. Moreover, should the corporation's business succeed over time, each stockholder's stock may well be worth a significant amount at the time of death. If so, the Internal Revenue Service will wish to impose an estate tax based upon the stock's value, regardless of the fact that it is an illiquid asset. Under such circumstances, the stockholder's estate may seek the assurance that some or all of such stock will be converted to cash so that the tax may be paid. If the agreement forbids free transfer of the stock during one's lifetime and requires that the stock be redeemed at death for a reasonable price, the agreement may well be accepted by the IRS as a binding determination of the stock's value, preventing an expensive and annoying valuation controversy.

Any redemption provision upon the death of the stockholder, especially one that is mandatory at the instance of the estate, immediately raises the question of the availability of funds. Just when the corporation may be reeling from the loss of one of its most valuable employees, it is expected to scrape together enough cash to buy out the deceased's stock. To avoid this disastrous result, many of these arrangements are funded by insurance policies on the lives of the stockholders. This would be in addition to any key person insurance held by the corporation for the purpose of recovering from the effects of the loss. In structuring such an arrangement, however, the parties should be aware of two quite different models.

The first, and traditional, model is referred to as a *redemption agreement*. Under such an agreement, the corporation owns the life insurance policies and is obligated to purchase the stockholder's shares upon his death. The second model is referred to as a *cross-purchase agreement* and provides for each stockholder to own insurance on the others and to buy a proportional amount of the deceased's shares. Exhibit 10.2 illustrates the primary differences between the two agreements.

The second arrangement poses some serious mechanical problems, but it may be quite advantageous. To begin with, the cross-purchase agreement becomes quite complicated if there are more than a few stockholders, since each stockholder must own and maintain a policy on each of the others. There must be a mechanism to ensure that all these policies are kept in force and that the proceeds are actually used for their intended purpose. Complicated escrow arrangements are often necessary to accomplish this. In addition, if the ages of the stockholders are materially different, some stockholders will be paying higher premiums than others. One might ignore this difference on the basis that those who pay most are most likely to benefit from this arrangement, since their insureds are likely to die sooner. An alternative is to equalize the impact of the premiums by adjusting the parties' compensation from the company.

If these complications can be overcome, however, the cross-purchase agreement provides some significant benefits over the redemption agreement. For example, if Uncle Max were to die and the corporation purchased his stock, Tony and Jennifer would each own 50% of the corporation's stock, but their cost basis for a later sale would remain at the minimal consideration originally paid for their stock. In a cross-purchase arrangement, they would purchase Uncle Max's stock directly. This would still result in 50-50 ownership, but their cost basis for later sale would equal their original investment plus the amount of the insurance proceeds used to purchase Uncle Max's

EXHIBIT 10.2. Comparison of stock redemption agreement and stock cross-purchase agreement.

	Effect on tax basis	Effect on alternative minimum tax	Need for adequate corporate surplus
Redemption agreement	No stepped-up basis	Risks accumulated current earnings preference	Need adequate surplus
Cross-purchase agreement	Stepped-up basis	No effect	Surplus is irrelevant

stock. Upon later sale of their stock, or the company as a whole, the capital gain tax would be significantly lowered.

Another benefit of the cross-purchase agreement is the fact that although the receipt of life insurance proceeds is exempt from income taxation, it can result in a *tax preference item* for a corporation not electing subchapter S treatment. This would expose the corporation to the alternative minimum tax. This tax preference item does not apply to individuals and is thus avoided by use of the cross-purchase model.

Finally, the cross-purchase model eliminates the possibility that the corporation will not have sufficient surplus to fund a buyout upon the death of a stockholder. It would be highly ironic if the stockholder's life insurance merely funded an earnings deficit and could not be used to buy his stock.

Disposition of Stock upon Termination of Employment

Of course, stockholders' agreements normally also address disposition of stock upon events other than death. Repurchase of stock upon termination of employment can be very important for both parties. The former employee, whose stock no longer represents an opportunity for employment, would like the opportunity to cash in the investment. The corporation and other stockholders may resent the presence of an inactive stockholder, who can capitalize on their subsequent efforts. Thus, both partnership and stockholders' agreements normally provide for repurchase of the interest of a stockholder or partner who is no longer actively employed by the company. This, of course, applies only to stockholders or partners whose efforts on behalf of the company were the basis of their participation in the first place. Such provisions would not apply to Uncle Max, for example, since his participation was based entirely upon his investment.

This portion of the agreement presents a number of additional problems peculiar to the employee-owner. For example, the company cannot obtain insurance to cover an obligation to purchase stock upon termination of employment. Thus, it may encounter an obligation to purchase the stock at a time when its cash position cannot support such a purchase. Furthermore, in addition to the requirement of adequate surplus, courts uniformly prohibit repurchases that would render the corporation insolvent. Common solutions to these problems involve committing the corporation to an installment purchase of the stock over a period of years (with appropriate interest and security) or committing the remaining stockholders to make the purchase personally if the corporation is unable to do so for any reason.

Furthermore, these agreements frequently impose penalties upon the premature withdrawal of a stockholder or partner. In our example, Uncle Max is relying on the efforts of Tony and Jennifer in making his investment, and Tony and Jennifer are each relying on the other's efforts. Should either Tony or Jennifer be entitled to a buyout at full fair market value if he or she simply decides to walk away from the venture? Often, these agreements contain so-called *vesting provisions* that require a specified period of service before repurchase will be made at full value. For example, a vesting provision might state that unless Tony stays with the venture for a year, all his stock will be forfeited upon his departure. After a year, one-fifth of his stock will be repurchased for full value, but the rest will be forfeited. Another 20% will vest at the end of each ensuing year.

Such provisions, in addition to providing incentive to remain with the company, have complicated tax implications. As discussed earlier, if an employee receives stock for less than fair market value, the discount would be considered taxable compensation. The Internal Revenue Code provides that compensation income with regard to unvested stock is not taxed until the stock is vested. But at that time, the amount of income is measured by the difference between the price paid for the stock and its value *at the time of vesting*. The only way to avoid this result is to file an election to pay the tax on the compensation income measured at the time of the purchase of the stock, even though the stock is not then vested. For Tony and Jennifer, this provision acts as a trap. Although they have arranged the initial investments of the parties such that there is no compensation income at the time the stock is purchased, if it is not then fully vested, their taxable income will be measured at the end of each future year as portions of the stock vest. Thus, they must file the election to have their income measured at the time of purchase to avoid a tax disaster, even though there is then no income to measure. And that election must be filed within 30 days of their receipt of the stock, not at the end of the year, as they might think.

Some stockholders' agreements go beyond vesting provisions and give incentive to the founders by imposing further penalties on stockholders who leave voluntarily or are terminated for cause. Thus, the agreement applicable to Jennifer and Tony might provide that vested stock be repurchased for full fair market value if they are terminated involuntarily (including as a result of disability or death) and for only half of fair market value if they leave for any other reason. Of course, involuntary termination without cause is a somewhat remote possibility due to the expansion of the concept of fiduciary loyalty mentioned earlier.

Negotiating Distributions of Company Profits

Stockholders' and partnership agreements may also include numerous other provisions peculiar to the facts and circumstances of the particular business. Thus, partnerships and subchapter S corporations often provide for mandatory distributions of profit to the partners or stockholders, at least in the amount of the tax obligation each will incur as a result of the profits of the business. If Uncle Max had agreed to accept nonvoting stock, the stockholders' agreement might include provisions to resolve deadlocks between Tony and Jennifer on significant issues; otherwise, the 50-50 split of voting stock might paralyze the corporation. Various types of arbitration provisions might be employed to prevent this problem.

Negotiating Repurchase of Stock

Further, some stockholders' agreements provide an investor like Uncle Max with the right to demand repurchase of his stock at some predetermined formula price at a designated future time, so that he will not be forever locked into a minority investment in a closely held corporation. Conversely, some agreements provide the corporation with the right to repurchase such stock at a predetermined price (usually involving a premium) should the capital no longer be needed. The presence or absence of these provisions depends, of course, on the relative negotiating strength of the parties.

LEGAL AND TAX ISSUES IN HIRING EMPLOYEES

From the beginning of this venture, Tony and Jennifer have known that if they are successful, they will have to hire employees for both the engineering and the marketing and sales functions. Thus, they should consider some of the issues raised by the presence of employees.

Obligations of Employees as Agents of the New Company

It should be understood that employees are agents of the company and as such are governed by many of the agency rules that define the relationships of partners to the partnership and officers to the corporation. Thus, employees have the previously described duty of loyalty to the company and obligations to respect confidentiality, to account for their activities, and not to compete.

Yet Jennifer and Tony are probably more interested in the potential of their employees to affect the business's relationships with third parties, such as customers and suppliers. Here the rules of agency require that a distinction be drawn between obligations based on contractual liability and those resulting from noncontractual relationships such as tort actions. Exhibit 10.3 provides an overview of these employee obligations.

Employees can bind their employers to contracts with third parties if such actions have either been expressly or implictly authorized. Thus, if Tony and Jennifer hire a sales manager and inform him that he has the authority to close any sale up to $50,000, he may wield that authority without further consultation with his principals. He also has the implied authority to do whatever is necessary to close such deals (such as sign a purchase order in the company's name, arrange delivery, and perhaps even alter some of the company's standard warranty terms).

However, the employee's authority often extends beyond that expressly or implictly given him. To illustrate this, suppose Tony and Jennifer's sales manager decides to close a sale for $100,000 worth of goods. This goes beyond his express authority and is not within his implied authority, since it was expressly prohibited. Yet from the point of view of the customer, the company's sales manager appears to have the authority to close all sales transactions. A customer who has not been informed of the limitation imposed upon the employee has no reason to think that anything is wrong. The law vindicates the customer in this situation by providing that the employee has apparent authority to conclude contracts within the scope of authority he appears to have. Since he was put into that position by his employer, and the employer has not informed the customer of the limits imposed upon the employee, the employer is bound by the employee's actions.

Outside of the contract arena, the employee's power to bind the employer is based on similar considerations. Under the doctrine of *respondeat superior* (or *vicarious liability*), the employer is responsible for any actions of the employee occurring within the scope of his employment. Thus, if the sales manager causes a traffic accident on the way to a sales call, the employer is responsible for damages. This imposition of liability is in no way

EXHIBIT 10.3. Comparison of employee obligations based on contractual liability and tort action.

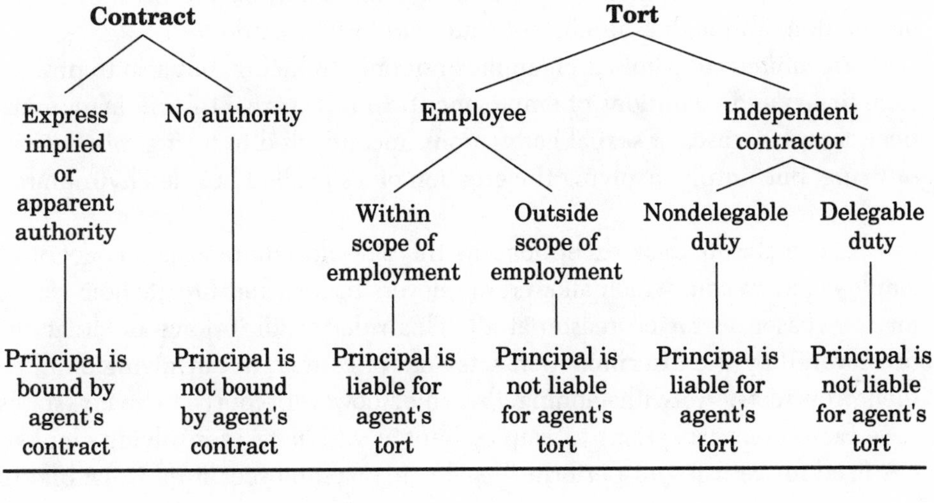

based on the employer's fault; it is *liability without fault,* imposed as a result of the economic judgment that employers are better able to spread losses among customers and insurance companies. Consistent with this approach, employers are normally not liable for the torts or criminal actions of employees outside the scope of their employment, such as actions occurring after hours or while the employee is pursuing her own interests. Furthermore, an employer is normally not liable for the torts or criminal actions of agents who are not employees (so-called independent contractors) since they are more likely to be able to spread these costs among their own customers and insurance companies.

However, employers should not take this as an invitation to avoid all liability by wholesale hiring of independent contractors. To begin with, the labeling of a potential employee as an independent contractor is not necessarily binding on the courts. They will look to the level of control exerted by the employer and other related factors to make this determination. In addition, many activities of employers are considered nondelegable (such as disposal of hazardous waste). Employers cannot escape the consequences of such activities by hiding behind independent contractors.

Laws Prohibiting Employment Discrimination

In addition to these common law considerations, there are, of course, a number of statutory rules of law that govern the employer-employee relationship. Perhaps the most well known of these are the laws prohibiting employment discrimination. These laws, which include Title VII of the Civil Rights Act of 1964, the Age Discrimination in Employment Act, and laws protecting disabled and pregnant employees, collectively prohibit employment discrimination on the basis of sex, race, national origin, religion, age, and handicap. Interestingly, they do not yet prohibit discrimination on the basis of sexual orientation, although a number of state and local laws do.

Prohibited discrimination applies not only to hiring, but also to promotion, firing, and conditions of employment. In fact, sexual discrimination has been found in cases of sexual harassment unconnected to hiring, promotion, or firing, but simply involving the creation of a so-called hostile environment for the employee.

These statutes are exceptions to the age-old common law concept of *employment at will,* which allowed employers to hire and fire at their whim, for any reason or for no reason at all. This rule is still in force in situations not covered by the discrimination acts and, of course, not involving employment contracts. Notwithstanding the rule, however, courts in many states have carved out exceptions to employment at will in cases involving employees fired for refusing to perform illegal acts or employees fired in bad faith, resulting in windfalls to the employer. Furthermore, courts in some states have been willing to discover employment contracts hidden in employee manuals or personnel communications that employers may not have thought legally binding.

Other Employment Statutes

When they begin taking on employees other than themselves, Tony and Jennifer will encounter a variety of other statutes that regulate the employment relationship and the workplace itself. For example:

- ERISA and the Internal Revenue Code closely regulate the form and amounts of any tax-qualified pension, profit-sharing, or welfare plans that employers may wish to maintain, generally prohibiting discrimination in favor of owners and highly paid employees.
- OSHA and the regulations adopted under that act closely regulate safety and health conditions in the workplace, imposing heavy fines for violations.
- The Fair Labor Standards Act provides minimum wages and overtime pay for employees in nonexempt (generally nonexecutive) positions, as well as prohibiting child labor and other practices.
- Social security and unemployment compensation—The corporation will find itself contributing to both these funds for each of its employees, as well as withholding social security and income taxes from its employees' wages. With regard to unemployment compensation, the amount of the contribution may depend on the number of employees laid off over the years, causing Jennifer and Tony to contest claims from employees who may have left voluntarily or been fired for cause.
- Worker's compensation—The corporation will probably be required to carry worker's compensation insurance to cover claims under that system. Although the premiums may seem burdensome, worker's compensation was, at the outset, a welcome compromise between the interests of employers and those of employees. In exchange for avoiding the costs and uncertainties of litigation, employees were assured payment for job-related injuries but lost the opportunity to sue for increased amounts based on pain, suffering, and punitive damages. Employers gave up many common law defenses that formerly could be used against employees but were able to avoid the disastrously high judgments available under common law.

Employment Agreements

In addition to the common law and statutory considerations common to the hiring of all employees, the hiring of persons for professional positions in engineering, marketing, and sales presents a new set of issues. Such persons are likely to demand employment agreements and a piece of the action in some form.

Negotiating the Term of Employment

The attractiveness of employment agreements stems, in the main, from their protection against *firing without cause*. Thus, a major item of negotiation will likely be the term of the contract. Although one might think that, for the employee, the downside of such a provision is that she must make a commitment to stay with a company she may come to dislike, courts have universally held that an employee cannot be forced to work for an employer against her will. Any contrary ruling would, it has been said, amount to a form of slavery! Thus, an employment contract is essentially a one-way street. The employee is promised employment for a period of time, with accompanying salary, bonus, and incentive provisions; but she can leave the company at any time without consequence. As a result, Tony and Jennifer would be well advised to *avoid* employment agreements whenever possible and, if forced to grant one, at least obtain some benefit for the company.

Negotiating Employee Obligations

Such benefit usually comes in the form of the *noncompetition* and *proprietary information covenants* discussed at the beginning of this chapter. For example, an engineer may promise, in exchange for a two-year employment agreement, not to work in the software industry for a year after termination of his employment. Yet, as mentioned earlier in the context of Tony and Jennifer's former employment, proprietary information obligations exist quite apart from any employee agreement, and it is quite possible that courts would refuse to enforce noncompetition provisions against the employee. Although one could make the argument (in a state that will listen) that the company needs some protection against a former sales manager soliciting the company's customers for a competitor, the argument appears more difficult when applied to a software engineer. This is especially true when one realizes that such an engineer's use of proprietary information learned or developed under a former employer would in any case be prohibited by common law and by contractual prohibitions on the use of proprietary information.

Negotiating Equity Sharing with Employees

In addition to demands for job security, higher-level employees will frequently ask to share in the company's success. This can be easily accomplished by a grant of stock, but Jennifer and Tony would be well advised to resist such a demand, which could upset the corporate balance of power and expectations of economic return among the major stockholders. These demands can often be satisfied by an incentive bonus plan tied to the success of the company or, more effectively, to the accomplishment of individual goals set for the employee.

If this is unacceptable to the employee, his return could be tied to the fortunes of the company by the use of *phantom stock* or *stock appreciation rights*, which simulate the benefits of stock without requiring actual stock ownership. These plans grant the employee bonuses equal to any distributions that would have been made if he had owned a certain number of shares of stock, while also rewarding him through payment of any increase in value such shares would have experienced. However, even this type of plan might not be acceptable to an employee with significant negotiating leverage, because it does not give him voting rights. In addition, because the employee does not actually own stock (a capital asset), he cannot report the increase in value as capital gain at lower federal income tax rates. Thus, in certain cases it may be necessary to grant the employee stock in some form.

As previously mentioned, a direct grant of stock to an employee is considered a taxable event. The employee pays income tax on the difference between the value of the stock and the amount paid for it, if any. However, as previously described, the imposition of tax can be postponed if the stock is forfeitable, for example, upon the employee's leaving the employ of the company before the passage of a designated period of time. No doubt Tony and Jennifer would condition the grant of stock to any employee on his remaining employed for a substantial period, so this rule would apply.

The negative side of this rule, of course, is that when the stock is finally vested, the taxable income is measured by the difference between the amount paid, if any, and the value of the stock *at the time of vesting*. Worse yet, this tax will be payable before the employee has received any cash with respect to this transaction. Cash will be available upon sale of the stock; but typically, the employee will not wish to sell at this time, and there will be no market for stock in a closely held corporation in any case.

Offering Stock Options to Employees

The issuance of stock options is often thought of as a solution to the tax problem. The employee is given the right to purchase stock in the corporation at a fixed price for a significant period of time. Thus, without investing any money, the employee can watch the value of this right increase as the value of the stock increases relative to the amount he would have to pay to purchase it. This right would be much less valuable, of course, if the grant of the option to the employee were a taxable event, but, unless the option is transferable and there is a recognized market for it (which is extremely unlikely in a case like the one used here), the grant of the option is not taxable.

Unfortunately, however, when the employee ultimately exercises the option and purchases the stock, the Internal Revenue Code requires recognition of income in the amount of the difference between the amount paid and the value of the stock at that time. Again, this occurs at a time when the employee has received no cash and likely has little desire or ability to sell.

Recognizing this problem, Congress has provided more favorable tax treatment for an employee stock option that meets a number of requirements:

- Incentive stock options (ISOs) must be issued pursuant to a stock option plan approved by the corporation's stockholders.
- The exercise price must be the fair market value of the stock at the time of issuance.
- Each option cannot last more than 10 years, and no more than $100,000 of exercise price may become exercisable in any one year.
- Perhaps most significant, the employee must hold any stock purchased pursuant to the option for the longer of one year after exercise or two years after the grant of the option.

If these requirements are met, the employee is not taxed until he actually sells the stock acquired under the option (and has cash to pay the tax), and the income is taxed at favorable long-term capital gain rates.

The corporation can still require the employee to sell such shares back to the corporation upon termination of employment. The only drawback is that the corporation loses any deduction that would otherwise be available for compensation paid to employees. Tony and Jennifer may find this plan to be an attractive way to grant the requested incentive to their key employees.

Exhibit 10.4 compares various ways of handling equity sharing with employees.

INSURANCE

The expenses associated with beginning a business are considerable. The fees demanded by the state and the costs associated with retaining attorneys and accountants have already been described. As employees are added to the organization, social security, unemployment compensation, and other costs increase. As previously mentioned, worker's compensation insurance is required by many states. But this is not the only insurance that should be considered.

EXHIBIT 10.4. Comparison of equity sharing methods.

	Date of grant	Risk removed	Sale of stock
Vested stock	Ordinary income	×	Capital gain
Risk of forfeiture	No income	Ordinary income	Capital gain
Risk of forfeiture Sec. 83(B) election	Ordinary income	No income	Capital gain
	Date of grant	**Date of exercise**	**Sale of stock**
Nonqualified stock option with readily ascertainable value	Ordinary income	No income	Capital gain
Nonqualified stock option with no ascertainable value	No income	Ordinary income	Capital gain
Incentive stock option (ISO)	No income	No income	Capital gain

Property Insurance

To begin with, Tony and Jennifer should consider property insurance for any equipment or inventory that they may have on hand. In fact, should they ever obtain a loan for their business, the lender will likely take inventory and equipment as collateral and insist that it be insured (with the proceeds payable to the lender).

Liability Insurance

Tony and Jennifer should also consider purchasing liability insurance to cover claims against them for product liability and other possible tort claims. As mentioned before, the presence of such insurance often mitigates against claims of undercapitalization by plaintiffs attempting to pierce the corporate veil. Automobile liability insurance is required by many states as a condition for registration of a car. And the dangers of tort liability caused by employees have been discussed earlier.

Key Person Life Insurance

The advisability of purchasing life insurance to cover stock redemptions under cross-purchase or redemption agreements has been discussed. Yet this is not the only role for life insurance in a business. Consider what would result from Tony's untimely death. Not only may Jennifer or the corporation be required to repurchase his stock, but the operations of the corporation would likely grind to a standstill while it searched for a new sales manager. If the corporation owned additional insurance on Tony's life (known as "key person" insurance), it would have funds to tide it over during this business slowdown as well as money to apply to the search for and compensation of Tony's successor.

Business Interruption Insurance

Similar in effect to key-person insurance, is so-called business interruption insurance, which, in many cases of catastrophic business shutdown, will replace some of the company's cash flow. Such a policy is usually quite expensive, however, and may not be within the reach of a typical startup.

Group Life, Disability, and Health Insurance for Employees

As the company grows and adds employees, there will be increasing demand for insurance as part of the employee benefit package. Many corporations provide group life insurance or group disability insurance for its employees. The latter can help the business avoid the moral dilemma caused by an employee who is too sick to work. Cutting off his salary may seem unthinkable, but paying another full salary for a long-term replacement may be more than the company can afford. Purchasing a policy with a significant deductible (such as 90 to 180 days) may solve this problem at very reasonable cost. Furthermore, in many industries it has become routine for the employer to provide health insurance as an employee benefit. According to certain predictions, this provision may soon become law.

These three group policies may be provided to employees tax-free, and the corporation may deduct the costs of premiums. The only exceptions to this favorable tax result are for the partner in a partnership and the significant shareholder of a subchapter S corporation, both of whom must report these benefits as taxable income. Thus, one negative aspect of the choice of subchapter S for Tony and Jennifer is that any group life, disability, or health insurance provided to them by the corporation would be included in income. Only 25% of this expense is then deductible.

RAISING MONEY

Thoughts of future hirings will inevitably bring Tony and Jennifer to consider another challenge to the company. Although Uncle Max's money may be sufficient for the short term, other sources of investment will eventually have to be identified. Although financing new business is discussed in detail in Chapters 5 through 9, this section describes potential legal and tax implications.

Loans

One source of financing that leaps to mind is debt financing from a commercial bank or other institutional lender. Although these institutions are notoriously loathe to advance loans to startup companies, such a loan may be possible if sufficient collateral or guarantees are available. The loan may take the form of a term note, a line of credit, or some sort of revolving credit plan, depending upon the circumstances. It will almost certainly be the case, however, that the lender will insist upon security for the loan.

Liens

At a minimum, this security will consist of an interest in all of the borrower's assets. In Jennifer and Tony's case, the lender will perfect a lien under Article 9 of the Uniform Commercial Code on the company's property, including:

- Machinery and equipment (computers, filing cabinets, desks, and so on)
- Inventory (copies of their software as well as blank disks, paper, pencils, and so on)
- Accounts receivable
- All intangible property (copyrights, patents, and trade secrets relating to their product)

Notice of such security interest will be filed under the Code wherever appropriate to perfect this interest such that no future potential lender or purchaser will be misled.

Under the provisions of the Code, such filing will perfect the lender's lien on any new property, including:

- New machinery or equipment purchased after the loan is made, unless such new items are purchased on credit and a lien is granted to the seller or lender
- Accounts receivable that arise later
- All new inventory, but any inventory sold to customers in the ordinary course of business will be automatically freed from the lien
- Any further amounts advanced by the lender to the company in the future

If the loan ultimately goes into default, the lender may take possession of the collateral and arrange its sale. The proceeds are then applied to the costs of repossession and sale and the amount unpaid under the loan. Any additional amounts would be turned over to any lower-priority secured creditor and ultimately to the borrower.

Although such a lien might seem to provide adequate security to the lender, most lenders will insist upon guarantees from additional parties. In some cases, guarantees from governmental agencies such as the Small Business Administration may be available (see Chapter 9 for information on how to obtain such guarantees). However, in almost every case, the lender will insist upon personal guarantees from the major stockholders of the borrower. In our case, this will certainly include Tony and Jennifer, and probably also Uncle Max due to his large share of the company's equity and obviously deep pockets. In many cases, the lender further demands that such guarantees be backed by collateral interests in the private property of the guaranteeing stockholders. Thus, Uncle Max may find that his signature is required both on a personal guarantee and on a second mortgage on his home. Or he may be required to pledge securities held in his personal brokerage account.

It should be noted that these personal guarantees circumvent the limited liability that entrepreneurs hope to achieve through use of the corporate form. The abandonment of this protection is unavoidable, however, and extends only to the particular lender. The stockholders remain protected against other trade creditors and tort plaintiffs.

Tax Effects

As a matter of strategy, the form in which a guarantee is given can have serious negative tax effects if insufficient care is given to structuring the loan transaction. For example, if Tony, Jennifer, and Uncle Max were to approach a small, local bank, they might find that the bank is reluctant to lend to a corporation under any circumstances. Under these conditions, the three stockholders may choose to borrow the money personally and invest the proceeds in the corporation themselves. Repayment of the loan would then be made out of the company's profits when they are distributed to its stockholders. As a result of this arrangement, however, the stockholders would receive taxable distributions from the corporation (in the form of either salary or dividends) but would receive no compensating deduction for the repayment of a personal loan.

It would be better if they could convince the bank to lend to the corporation and take personal guarantees. Then the corporation could repay the loan directly (deducting the interest as a business loan), and the money would never pass through the hands of the stockholders. Alternatively (but with some additional risk), the stockholders could borrow directly from the bank but grant it a second mortgage as collateral, thereby rendering the interest deductible for them as mortgage interest.

Ironically, if the corporation elects subchapter S treatment, strategy considerations may point in the opposite direction. Since Uncle Max, especially, will wish to see the corporation's short-term losses appear on his personal return, he will be concerned that the amount of loss he may use is limited to his tax basis in his subchapter S investment. Such basis consists of the amount he paid for his stock, plus any amount he has loaned directly to the corporation. If the corporation were to borrow from the bank and Uncle Max were merely to guarantee the loan, the amount of the loan would not increase his basis (or his allowable loss). Were he to borrow the money from the bank and lend it to the corporation himself, his basis would be increased. Of course, in either event, the amount of loss he can use may be limited by the passive loss rules discussed earlier.

Legal Issues in the Sale of Securities to Outside Investors

As an alternative to institutional lending, Jennifer, Tony, and Uncle Max may turn to outside investors. Although it may be difficult to attract venture capitalists to such a small startup, other sources of capital, in the form of neighbors, friends, doctors, lawyers, dentists, and other individuals or entities with an interest in ground-floor investing, may be available. If they choose this route, it is crucial that they take note of two common misconceptions.

Although most businesspeople are aware that both federal and state law regulates the offer and sale of securities, most believe that these statutes apply only to the offerings of large corporations, and that small companies are exempt. This is one of the dangerous misconceptions held by many people like Tony, Jennifer, and Uncle Max. In fact, these laws (specifically, the federal Securities Act of 1933, the federal Securities Exchange Act of 1934, and state "Blue Sky" statutes) apply to all issuers.

Further, even many businesspeople who are aware of the scope of these acts believe that they apply only to issuers of equity securities, mainly stock. This, too, is a misconception. These statutes apply to all issuers of "securities," not just issuers of stock. Securities include, in addition to stock, most debt (other than very short term loans), options, warrants, and all other forms of investment in which the investor buys into a common enterprise and relies on the efforts of others for the investment's success. Thus, such disparate items as orange groves, Hawaiian condominiums, and even worms have been held to be regulated securities under the circumstances of their respective cases.

The wide scope of these statutes led some to assert that they include the offering of *franchise opportunities*. Those offering franchises argued that the success of a franchisee is not normally determined solely by the efforts of the franchisor, but requires significant effort on the part of the franchisee. This debate has been rendered moot, however, by the adoption by the

Federal Trade Commission of regulations requiring disclosure by franchisors of virtually the same range of information as is required under a securities registration statement. Many states have enacted similar franchise registration laws, requiring dual federal and state registration in most franchise offerings. (Further discussion of franchising can be found in Chapter 12.)

In general, then, the securities laws prohibit the offering of securities to the public without prior (and very expensive) registration with an appropriate government authority such as the federal Securities and Exchange Commission. They also punish fraudulent activities in connection with such offerings, including not only affirmatively false statements, but also mere nondisclosure of material facts about the investment. Because of the complexity and expensiveness of registration, these laws allow exceptions to the registration requirement in specific circumstances, but even these are subject to the antifraud provisions of the laws. Thus, the challenge to our three entrepreneurs is to identify provisions in the securities laws that will offer them an *exemption from registration*, with the understanding that they must still provide sufficient disclosure to potential investors (in the form of a so-called offering circular) to avoid antifraud liability.

One such exemption contained in the Securities Act of 1933 is the *intrastate offering exemption*. Based on the general principle that the federal government can constitutionally regulate only *interstate* commerce, the statute necessarily exempts offerings that are purely local. However, the scope of this exemption is relatively narrow. Not only must all persons who purchase the securities reside in one state, but all offerees must be resident there as well. Furthermore, the company offering the securities must be incorporated under the laws of that state and do most of its business there. Due to these restrictions, this exemption may be useful only for the smallest of offerings. Besides, the exemption excuses the offering only from registration with the Securities and Exchange Commission (SEC). The state's securities laws may still require expensive and time-consuming state registration.

The more popular exemption from registration under the federal act is the *private placement exemption*, which excuses transactions "not involving a public offering." Over the last decade, the SEC has relied on this exemption to issue regulations designed to facilitate the raising of capital by small businesses in small offerings. Thus, as of this writing, Regulation D under the act exempts from registration any offering of under $1 million worth of securities. Above that amount, the regulation requires increasing levels of disclosure (still short of full registration, however) and limits the number of offerees to 35 plus an unlimited number of so-called accredited investors. For these purposes, accredited investors include certain institutions, as well as individuals with net worth or annual income levels that indicate a need for less protection. Even apart from the regulation, however, issuers can argue that offerings made to relatively sophisticated investors with prior relationships to the issuer qualify as transactions "not involving a public offering."

Of course, exemption from registration under the federal act does not grant exemption under a state act. In fact, offerings made to investors in a number of states require adherence to the Blue Sky statutes of each state. Fortunately, however, virtually all state statutes allow similar exemptions for private placements, typically excusing offerings to 25 or fewer persons.

Thus, Tony and Jennifer will likely be able to seek out the investment they will need without having to register with the federal or state government. However, it cannot be overemphasized that they remain subject to the *anti-fraud provisions* of these acts. Thus, they will be well advised to seek professional assistance in drawing up a comprehensive offering circular disclosing all that an investor would need to know about their company to make an intelligent investment decision. (See Chapter 7 for further discussion of venture capital.)

CONCLUSION

Considering all the legal and tax pitfalls described in this chapter, one is tempted to ask whether Tony, Jennifer, or any other entrepreneur would choose the road of the startup if she were fully aware of all the potential complications lying in wait. Yet not to be aware of these matters is to consciously choose to play the game without knowing the rules. These issues are there whether one chooses to prepare for them or not. Surely, Tony and Jennifer are much more likely to succeed in their venture for having taken the time to become aware of the legal issues facing the entrepreneur.

11 INTELLECTUAL PROPERTY

Joseph S. Iandiorio

One of the most valuable and fundamental assets of a new small business is its intellectual property. Intellectual property is defined as a business's intangible assets, including patents, trademarks, copyrights, and trade secrets. The rights to such property can be used to prevent competitors from entering your market and can represent a separate source of revenue to the business. All too often, however, they are overlooked or misunderstood, and they are nearly always undervalued. To fully protect and utilize these assets, every entrepreneur, small business owner, and manager, as well as advisers such as management, financial and technical consultants, lawyers, accountants, bankers, and venture capitalists, must be aware of what these rights are and how they are protected and preserved. This awareness is becoming even more critical in a world of global competition and international markets where ideas and information are fast becoming more valuable than products and things.

THE BASICS: WHAT IS PROTECTABLE AND HOW SHOULD IT BE PROTECTED?

When a new idea is conceived or a new product or method is designed, one of the first questions that arises is: Can I protect this? Can I keep competitors from copying this? There are very practical reasons for protecting a new idea. Investors are loathe to put money into a venture that cannot establish a unique product niche. Stockholders will challenge a corporation's investment of its resources in a program that can be easily copied once it is introduced to the market. All the time, effort, and money invested in perfecting the idea, as well as advertising and promoting it, may be wasted if imitators can enter the market on your heels with a product just like yours. Moreover, the imitators can cut prices because they have not incurred the startup expenses you had to endure to bring the idea from conception to a mass-producible, reliable, and appealing product or service.

Here are some examples of things that may be protected:

- A new product
- A new method
- A process
- A new service
- A new promotional or merchandising scheme or approach
- New packaging
- A new design

Once it has been determined that a new idea, product, or method is eligible for one or more forms of protection—a patent, trade secret, trademark, or copyright—the rights should be secured as quickly as possible. Each form of protection is obtained in a different manner and provides a different set of rights. The various forms are discussed in the following sections.

For example, consider a typical modern product—a computer on a stand. The computer has a disk with software on it. The computer includes the usual circuitry, including memory, CPU, and ancillary circuits. It bears the name of the manufacturer and the brand name and is accompanied by a user's manual and a label or tag. What is protectable, and how should you protect it? The next sections provide information to help answer these questions.

Patents

There are three kinds of patents: utility, design and plant. *Utility patents* are the kind commonly considered when one seeks to protect an invention. They are granted for any new and useful process, machine, manufacture or composition of matter, or improvement thereof, including new uses of old devices or new combinations of well-known components. *Design patents* cover only the new design of an object—its ornamental appearance. *Plant patents* are available for inventions or discoveries in asexual reproduction of distinct and new varieties of plants. This area of patents has become much more important with the growth of biotechnology inventions in the last few years, especially regarding the protection of human-engineered life forms. Most of the following discussion focuses on utility patents, though some special considerations of design patents are also provided.

Utility Patents

Utility patents cover three classes of inventions:

- *Chemical inventions* include new compounds, new methods of making old or new compounds, new methods of using old or new compounds, and new combinations of old compounds. Biological materials and methods, drugs, foodstuffs, drug therapy, plastics, petroleum derivatives, synthetic materials, pesticides, fertilizers, and feeds are all protectable.
- *General/mechanical inventions* include everything from gears and engines to tweezers and propellers, from zippers to fur-lined keyhole appliqués to Jacque Cousteau's scuba regulator. For example, complex textile-weaving machines, space capsule locks and seals, and diaper pins are all protectable.
- *Electrical inventions* include everything from lasers to light switches, from the smallest circuit details to overall system architectural concepts.

Computer software is patentable in various forms:

- Application programs, such as the software that runs in a computer used to control a chemical-processing plant or a rubber-molding machine, are patentable.
- Software for running a cash management account at a brokerage house or bank is patentable.
- The microcode in a ROM that embodies the entire inventive notion of a new tachometer is patentable.
- Internal or operations programs that direct the handling of data in the computer's own operations are patentable.

Obtaining a utility patent

The basic requirement for a utility patent is that the idea be new and that it be embodied in a physical form. The physical form may be a thing or a series of steps to perform.

Patent protection is established only upon the issue of a patent on the invention. From the date of issue forward for 17 years, the owner of the patent has the right to exclude others from making, using, and selling the patented invention. Prior to issue there are no rights under a patent.

The effort begins when the inventor or inventors conceive the invention. They or a registered patent attorney on their behalf prepare a patent application and file it in the U.S. Patent and Trademark Office. From the date that the application is filed there is a "patent pending," but this confers no rights or protection. Protection applies if and when the Patent and Trademark Office agrees that the invention is patentable and issues the patent.

The patent application must contain a complete and understandable explanation of the invention. It does not have to be a nuts-and-bolts instruction manual. It is enough to convey the inventive concept so that a person skilled in the art to which the invention relates can make and use the invention without undue experimentation. Further, the explanation must contain a full description of the best mode known by the inventor for carrying out the invention. For example, the inventor cannot use the second best embodiment of the invention as an illustration for the patent application disclosure and keep secret the best embodiment. That will make the resulting patent invalid.

The *timing* of the filing of the patent application is critical. It must be filed within one year of the first public disclosure, public use, sale, or offer for sale of the invention, or the filing will be barred and the opportunity to obtain a patent forever lost. This is known as the one-year period of grace. This may change in the near future to a system in which there is no period of grace (the application must be filed before any activity listed above), to conform with practice in most other countries.

A description of the invention in a printed publication constitutes a public disclosure. A mere announcement is not sufficient, unless it contains an explanation of the invention. It matters not that only a few copies of the publication were made available, so long as it was an unrestricted distribution.

Market testing, exhibitions, or even use by the inventor himself is a public use sufficient to activate the one-year period. An exception is a public use for experimental purposes. The test for whether a public use was an excepted experimental use is rigorous. The inventor must show that it was the operation and function of the invention that was being tested, not the appeal or marketability of the product employing the invention. Further, some evidence of the testing should be established. For example, if samples were sent to potential customers for evaluation, it would be good to show that the customers returned filled-out evaluation forms and that the inventor considered and even made changes based on those evaluations.

A sale will bar a patent even if the invention is embedded so deeply within a larger system that it could not ever be discovered. If the device containing the invention is sold, that is enough. The idea is that an inventor should be given only one year in which to file his patent application after he has begun to commercially exploit or to attempt to commercially exploit his invention. Thus, for an invention embodied in a production machine installed in a locked, secure room, the one-year period for filing a patent application begins the first time a device produced by that machine is sold, even though the machine may never be known to or seen by anyone other than the inventor. And it is not just a sale that triggers the one-year period. An offer for sale is enough, even if the sale is never consummated.

Criteria for obtaining a utility patent

A patent application contains three basic parts:

- Drawings showing an embodiment of the invention
- A written description of the embodiment referring to the drawings
- One or more claims

Sometimes (often, in chemical cases), the drawings are omitted. The definition of the patented invention, the protected property, is not what is disclosed in the drawings and specification portion of the application; this is only the description of one specific embodiment. The coverage of the patent is defined by the third part of the application, the claims.

To qualify for a patent, the claims must be novel and unobvious. *Novelty* is a relatively easy standard to define: either a single earlier patent, publication, or product shows the entire invention, or the invention is novel. *Obviousness* is somewhat more difficult to grasp. Even though an invention may be novel, it may nevertheless be obvious and therefore unpatentable. The test for obviousness is fairly subjective: Are the differences between the invention and all prior knowledge (including patents, publications, and products) such that the invention would have been obvious to a person having ordinary skill in the art to which the invention pertains at the time the invention was made? If so, the invention is not patentable even if it is novel.

The meanings of "novelty" and "unobvious" in the area of patentability can be better understood with an example. Suppose a person is struggling to screw a wood screw into hard wood, and he realizes that the problem is that he cannot supply enough twisting force with the blade of the screwdriver in the slot in the head of the screw. So he gets the bright idea of making the slot a little deeper, so that the screwdriver blade can bite a little deeper and confront more surface area of the slot, thus applying more force to turn the screw. This is a good idea, but it creates another problem. The deeper slot extends much closer to the sides of the screw head. There is less support, and fatigue lines develop, which eventually cause the screw head to crack. The inventor then gets the idea to use a new screwdriver with two shorter, crossed blades, which will give increased surface area contact with two crossed slots in the head of the screw.

But a problem still exists. Although the twin blades do not require such deep slots, there are now twice as many slots, and the screw head is seriously weakened. Now the inventor sees another path: keep the double-blade configuration, but chop off the corners, so that the slots need not extend out so close to the edge of the new screw head.

The result: he has invented the Phillips head screwdriver, for use with a Phillips head screw. Certainly the invention is "novel": no one else has made that design before. It is also "unobvious" and thus patentable. The addition of the second blade and elimination of the corners has resulted in a wholly new screwdriver concept. The concept is patentable.

Now suppose another party, seeing the patent issued on this double-blade Phillips head, comes up with an improvement of her own. Her invention is to use three crossed blades (cutting the head of the screw into six equal areas), with their corners removed. This design is not patentable. Certainly it is novel, but is it unobvious? Not likely. Once the first inventor has originated the idea of increasing the number of blades and eliminating corners, it is obvious to simply add more blades.

Drafting the patent claims

Once it is decided that a patentable invention exists, it must be protected by properly drafted patent claims. It is the claims that the U.S. Patent and Trademark Office examiner analyzes and accepts or rejects in considering the issuance of the patent. It is the claims that determine if someone has infringed on a patent. It is the claims that define the patent property.

Claims are clearly, then, the most important part of a patent. It is no good to have claims that cover the invention yet do not protect your product or process from being copied by competitors. Does this sound contradictory? Study the following example and you will understand.

Suppose an inventor meets with a patent attorney and shows the attorney a new invention for carrying adult beverages on the slopes while skiing. The invention eliminates the risk of smashing glass, denting metal, or squashing a wineskin, and it also eliminates the need to carry any extra equipment: It's a hollow ski pole. The ski pole has a shaft, a chamber, and a handle. The handle has a threaded hole that communicates with the hollow shaft. Partway down the inside of the hollow shaft is a plastic liner that creates a chamber for holding liquids; this plastic liner is sealingly attached to the shaft. The chamber is closed by a threaded plug, which engages the threaded hole. The inventor wants to patent the pole, so he assists the patent attorney in writing a description of the ski pole. They write the following claim:

"A hollow ski pole for carrying liquids, comprising:

- a hollow shaft;
- a liner sealingly engaging the hollow inside of the shaft to define a chamber for containing liquid;
- a handle on the shaft;
- a threaded hole in the handle communicating with the chamber in the hollow shaft; and
- a threaded plug for engaging the threaded hole."

The patent application is filed. The U.S. Patent and Trademark Office examines the application and issues the patent with that claim. The inventor is happy. But not for long, because a competitor comes out with a similar hollow ski pole that doesn't use a liner. The competitor simply welds a piece of metal across the inside of the shaft to make a *sealed* chamber. The competitor has avoided infringing the patent, because there is no liner, which was one of the specifications of the first patent claim. Another competitor replaces the threaded plug with an upscale mahogany cork. Again the patent is not infringed, because there is no threaded plug.

To infringe a patent, a competitor must infringe a claim of the patent. In order to infringe a claim of the patent, the infringing process or product must include *every* element of the claim.

This problem can be avoided by exploring the various ways in which the product can be built. This may require input from sales, marketing, engineering, and production people as well as the inventor. After a thorough study, a better claim might emerge as follows:

"A hollow ski pole for carrying liquids, comprising:

- a hollow shaft;
- a chamber formed in said hollow shaft for containing a liquid;
- a handle on the shaft having a hole communicating with the chamber in the hollow shaft; and
- a means for closing the hole in the handle."

Someone could still design around this claim by leaving out the means for closing the hole; the skier could use her thumb and hope she doesn't fall. Practically speaking, however, the claim would be good enough to keep others from making a meaningful competing product without infringing. There is a limit to how broadly the claim can be worded, however. Eventually, if the claim becomes broader and broader, and does not specify the ski pole or hollow shaft, it will apply to a bottle or a pot with a cover, and the patent will not be obtainable. Careful claim drafting is critical.

Inventorship

Another important area is inventorship. In the United States a patent must be filed by the inventor(s) and no one else. The inventor is the originator of the inventive concept. A project leader is not by his supervisory position alone an inventor of an invention. Neither is a technician or engineer who may have built the first working model. The inventor may have sold or assigned the patent application to someone else—his employer, a partner in some enterprise, a company he has newly formed, or another inventor. Thus, the original inventors may not be the owners of the patent, but it must still be filed in their names.

Design Patents

Hockey uniforms, ladies' dresses, computer housings, automobile bodies, buildings, shoes, and game boards are all protectable with design patents. But this type of patent covers only the *appearance*, not the idea or underlying concept. What you see is what you get. Design patents are generally less expensive than utility patents and in some cases are the only protection that is needed or obtainable.

Design patents have a life of only 14 years but are otherwise generally subject to the same rules as other patents. That is, the new and original ornamental design to be patented must be novel and unobvious and must be filed within one year of the first public use, publication, sale, or offer for sale.

Trade Secrets

Trade secrets cover everything that patents cover, and much more. A trade secret is knowledge, which may include business knowledge or technical knowledge, that is kept secret for the purpose of gaining an advantage in business over one's competitors. Customer lists, sources of supply of scarce material, or sources of supply with faster delivery or lower prices may be trade secrets. Certainly, secret processes, formulas, techniques, manufacturing know-how, advertising schemes, marketing programs, and business plans are all protectable.

There is no standard of invention to meet as there is with a patent. If the idea is new in this context, if it is secret with respect to this particular industry or product, then it can be protected as a trade secret. Unlike patents, trademarks, and copyrights, there is no formal procedure for obtaining trade secret protection. Protection is established by the nature of the secret and the effort to keep it secret.

A trade secret is protected eternally against disclosure by all those who have received it in confidence and all who would obtain it by theft for as long as the knowledge or information is kept secret. In contrast to patent protection, there are no statutory requirements for novelty or restrictions on the subject matter.

The disadvantage of trade secrets compared with patents is that *there is no protection against discovery by fair means,* such as accidental disclosure, independent inventions, and reverse engineering. Many important inventions, such as the laser and the airplane, were developed more or less simultaneously by different persons. Trade secret protection would not permit the first inventor to prevent the second and subsequent inventors from exploiting the invention as a patent would.

The distinction between patents and trade secrets is illustrated in a case in which a woman who designed a novel keyholder immediately filed a patent application. It was a simple design and could be easily copied. While the patent was still pending, she licensed it to a manufacturer for a 5% royalty, with the agreement that if the patent didn't issue in five years, the royalty would drop to 2½%. The patent never issued, and the royalty was dropped to 2½%. Over the next 14 years, on sales of $7 million, the manufacturer's edge eroded as others freely copied the design. The manufacturer repudiated the royalty contract on the ground that it required payment forever for the small jump that the manufacturer got on its competitors, whereas the patent, had it issued, would have allowed only 17 years of exclusivity. The Court held the manufacturer to its requirement to pay. The ruling allowed the inventor to receive 2½% royalty for as long as the manufacturer continued to sell the keyholder. Had the patent issued, royalties would have lasted only 17 years.

Many companies use both approaches, filing a patent application on a trade secret. When the patent is ready to issue, the company reevaluates its position. If the competition is close, they pay the fee and let the patent issue. If not, they don't pay the fee, allowing the patent application to go abandoned, and preserve the trade secret.

Certain trade secrets have been appraised at many millions of dollars, and some are virtually priceless. For example, the formula for Coca-Cola is one of the best-kept trade secrets in the world. Known as Merchandise 7X, it has been tightly guarded since it was invented 100 years ago. It is known by only two persons within the Coca-Cola Company and is kept in a security vault at the Trust Company Bank in Atlanta, Georgia, which can be opened only by a resolution from the company's board of directors. The company refuses to allow the identities of those who know the formula to be disclosed or to allow them to fly in the same airplane at the same time. The company elected to forgo producing Coca-Cola in India, a potential market of 550 million people, because the Indian government requires the company to disclose the secret formula as a condition for doing business there. While some of the mystique surrounding the Coca-Cola formula may be marketing hype, it is beyond dispute that the company possesses trade secrets that are carefully safeguarded and are extremely valuable.

Secrecy is essential to establishing trade secret rights; without it there is no trade secret property. There are four primary steps for ensuring secrecy:

1. Obtain confidential disclosure agreements with all employees, agents, consultants, suppliers, and anyone else who will be exposed to the secret information. The agreement should bind them not to use or disclose the information without permission.

2. Take security precautions to keep third parties from entering the premises where the trade secrets are used. Sturdy locks, perimeter fences, guards, badges, visitor sign-in books, escorts, and designated off-limits areas are just some of the ways that a trade secret owner can exercise control over the area containing the secrets.
3. Stamp specific documents containing the trade secrets with a confidentiality legend and keep them in a secure place with limited access, such as a safe or locked drawer or cabinet.
4. Make sure all employees, consultants, and others who are concerned with, have access to, or have knowledge about the trade secrets understand that they are trade secrets, and make sure they recognize the value to the company of this information and the requirement for secrecy.

Trade secret owners rarely do all of these things, but enough must be done so that a person who misappropriates the secrets cannot reasonably excuse his conduct by saying that he didn't know or that no precautions were ever taken to indicate that something was a trade secret. This is important because, unlike patents, trade secret protection provides no "deed" to the property.

Since there is no formal protection procedure, the necessary steps for establishing a trade secret are often not taken seriously until a lawsuit is brought by the owner against one who has misappropriated them. In each specific case the owner must show that the precautions taken were adequate.

Trade secret misappropriations generally fall into one of two classes: someone who has a confidential relationship with the owner violates the duty of confidentiality, or someone under no duty of confidentiality uses improper means to discover the secret.

Trade secret theft issues frequently arise with respect to the conduct of ex-employees. Certainly, a good employee will learn a lot about the business during his employment. And some of that learning he will take with him as experience when he leaves. That cannot be prevented. The question is, did he just come smart and leave smarter, or did he take certain information that was exclusively the company's?

For example, in one case a company that had been making widgets for the government for many years did not get its annual contract renewal. When the company questioned the loss of the contract, it was explained that a competitor was supplying widgets of equal quality at a lower price. Upon investigation the company determined that the competitor was located in the same town, that the competitor's widgets were uncannily identical in every dimension, and that the competitor was owned by an ex-employee of the company who had left over a year before. Amicable approaches failed, and a lawsuit was instituted during which the company discovered that the ex-employee had copied their detailed engineering drawings to make the widgets; this eliminated all engineering and design costs and enabled the competitor to sell the widgets to the government at a much lower price. But the ex-employee had not stolen anything. It seems the man knew that every year his ex-employer reissued important engineering drawings that had become torn and tattered or that needed updating, and he threw out the old ones. The ex-employee testified that while driving by one day, he saw the old drawings sticking out of the dumpster. He drove in, took them out of the dumpster, put the ones he wanted in his car, and chucked the rest back in the dumpster. That's how he got a widget with identical dimensions. The court held him liable for misappropriation of trade secrets. He had trespassed to obtain the drawings, and he had learned of the ex-employer's practice of disposing of old drawings while an employee with a duty of confidentiality to the company. The court granted an injunction preventing the ex-employee from selling widgets for a period of months equal to the jump he got by not having to develop his own engineering drawings.

But what if the ex-employee had not trespassed to obtain the drawings from the trash? What if he had waited for the trash collector to remove them and then asked if he could pore over the trash? Or what if he had gone to the dump and picked the drawings out of the mud? When does the owner part with ownership of trade secret materials dumped in the trash?

Trade secrets are extremely valuable, often more so than patents, and can form the basis for lucrative licensing programs. Care should be taken to identify and protect them early and consistently.

Trademarks

Trademark protection is obtainable for any word, symbol, or combination thereof that is used on goods to indicate their source. Any word—even a common word such as "look," "life," or "apple"—can become a trademark, so long as the word is not used descriptively. "Apple" for fruit salad might not be protectable. Apple™ for computers certainly is.

Common forms such as geometric shapes (circles, triangles, squares), natural shapes (trees, animals, humans), combinations of shapes, or colors may be protected. Even the single color pink has been protected as a trademark for building insulation. Three-dimensional shapes such as bottle and container shapes and building features (for example, McDonald's golden arches) can also be protected.

While people generally only speak of trademarks, that term encompasses other types of marks. A trademark is specifically any word or symbol or combination of the two that is used on goods to identify its source. However, a *service mark* is a word or symbol or combination used in connection with the offering and provision of services. Blue Cross/Blue Shield, Prudential Insurance, and McDonald's are service marks for health insurance services, general insurance services, and restaurant services, respectively. Ownership is established by advertising the mark in conjunction with the service, as opposed to trademarks, where advertising is insufficient—the mark must be used on the goods in commerce.

There are also other types of marks. A *collective mark* indicates membership in a group, such as a labor union, fraternity, or trade association. A *certification mark* is used to indicate that a party has met some standard of quality; Quality Court motels, Underwriter's Laboratory, and Good Housekeeping's seal of approval are familiar examples.

If you use any such name or feature to identify and distinguish your products, then think trademark protection. Ownership of a trademark allows you to exclude others from using a similar mark on similar goods that would be likely to confuse consumers as to the source of the goods. This right applies for the duration of ownership of the mark.

Trademarks can be more valuable to a company than all of its patents and trade secrets combined. Consider the sudden appearance and abrupt increase in the worth of trademarks such as Cuisinart, Häagen-Dazs, and Ben & Jerry's. Consider also the increased value that a trademark name such as IBM, Kodak, or GE brings to even a brand new product.

A trademark, unlike a patent, is established without any formal governmental procedure. Ownership of a trademark is acquired simply by being the first to use the mark on the goods in commerce. And it remains the owner's property as long as the owner keeps using it.

The mark should not be descriptive of the goods on which it is used, although it may be suggestive of the goods. However, it is best to select a mark that is arbitrary and fanciful with respect to the goods. This is because every marketer, including a competitor, has the right to use a descriptive term to refer to its goods. Therefore, exclusive rights to such a mark cannot be secured.

A trademark owner should also take care to prevent the mark from becoming generic, as happened to Aspirin, Cellophane, Linoleum, and other product names. Thus, it is not proper to refer to, for example, simply a Band-Aid, Jello, or Kleenex. The correct form of description is Band-Aid adhesive bandages, Jell-O fruit-flavored gelatin dessert, or Kleenex facial tissues.

It is wise to have a search done for a proposed new mark to be sure that the mark is clear to adopt and use on the goods, that is, to verify that no one else is using the same or a similar mark on the same or similar goods. It is confusing to customers and expensive to change a mark and undertake the costs of all new printing, advertising, and promotional materials when you discover that your new mark has already been used by another.

Registering a Mark

Although there is no need to register a mark, there are benefits associated with registration that make it worthwhile. Registration may be made in individual states, or a federal registration may be obtained. A state registration applies only in the particular state that granted the registration and requires only use of the mark in that state. A federal registration applies to all 50 states, but to qualify, the mark must be used in interstate or foreign commerce. A distinct advantage of federal registration is that even if a mark is used across only one state line, that is, if goods bearing the mark are in commerce only between one state and another state or country, that is enough to establish federal protection in all 50 states. Thus, if you are using your mark in Massachusetts, New Hampshire, and Rhode Island, for example, but do not register it federally, you may later be blocked from using your mark in all other states if a later user of the same mark, without knowledge of your use of the mark, federally registers it. That later user would then have the rights to the mark in all other 47 states even though its actual use may have been only in Oregon and California!

While your common law rights to a trademark or service mark last as long as you properly use the mark, registration must be periodically renewed. Federal registrations extend for 20 years (10 years for registrations filed after November 16, 1989); terms for states vary, but 10 years is typical.

Over the history of trademark law in the United States, registration in the U.S. Patent and Trademark Office followed the common law. That is, to establish ownership of a trademark one had to use the mark on the goods in commerce, and to register the mark in the U.S. Patent and Trademark Office one had to establish that the mark was indeed in use.

That has changed somewhat. Now an application can be filed to register a mark that is not yet in use but is intended to be used. After the U.S. Patent and Trademark Office examines the application and determines that the mark is registrable, the applicant is required to show actual use within six months. The six-month period can be extended if good cause is shown. Nevertheless, before registration, even before actual use, the mere filing of the application establishes greater rights over others who actually used it earlier but did not file an application for registration.

Ownership of a Mark

Care must be taken with trademark properties. A trademark cannot simply be sold by itself or transferred like a desk or car, or a patent or copyright. A trademark must be sold together with the business or goodwill associated with the mark, or the mark will be abandoned. Further, if a mark is licensed for use with a product or service, provision must be made for quality control of that product or service. That is, the trademark owner must require the licensee to maintain specific quality levels for products or services with which the mark is used, under penalty of loss of license. And the owner must actually exercise that control through periodic inspection, testing, or other monitoring that will ensure that the licensee's product quality is up to the prescribed level.

Ownership of a mark is most important in a business. When Cuisinart started selling its food processors, it promoted them vigorously under the trademark Cuisinart. A good part of the business's success was due to the fact that the machines were sturdily made by a proud, quality-conscious French company, Robot Coupe, who had been making the machines for many years before they became popular among U.S. consumers under the mark Cuisinart. When price competition reared its head, Cuisinart found cheaper sources. Robot Coupe owned no patents and had no other protection. When Cuisinart began selling brand X under the name Cuisinart, a wild fight ensued through the courts and across the pages of major newspapers in the United States, but to no avail. The whole market had been created under the name Cuisinart, and Cuisinart had the right to apply its name to any machine made anywhere by anyone it chose. Robot Coupe, whose machine had helped create the demand for food processors, was left holding its chopper.

Copyright

Copyrights cover all manner of writings, and the term *writings* is very broadly interpreted. It includes books, advertisements, brochures, spec sheets, catalogs, manuals, parts lists, promotional materials, packaging and decorative graphics, fabric designs, photographs, pictures, film and video presentations, audio recordings, architectural designs, and even software and databases. Software and databases are protected not only in written form but also as stored in electronic memory.

A utilitarian object such as a hypodermic needle, a hammer, or a lamp base cannot be the subject of a copyright. Yet stained glass windows, software, piggy banks, and a sculpture useful as a lamp qualify for copyright protection.

It is said that a copyright does not protect a mere idea; it protects the *form* of the expression of the idea. But this is broadly interpreted. For example, one can infringe a book without copying every word; the theme is protected even though upon successive generalizations the theme will devolve to one of seven nonprotectable basic plots. This is apparent in the software area, where using the teachings of a book to write a program has resulted in copyright infringement of the book by the computer program. In another case a program was infringed by another program even though the second program was written in an entirely different language and for an entirely different computer. The form of the expression protected was not merely the actual writing, the coding, but the underlying concept or algorithm—the flow chart. The copyright is a very strong and readily achievable source of protection.

A copyright has a term extending for the life of the author plus 50 years. For corporate "authors" or works made for hire, the period is 75 years from first publication or 100 years from creation, whichever is shorter. During the life of the copyright the owner has the exclusive rights to reproduce, perform, and display the work.

Establishing Copyright

Historically, under law a copyright was established by publishing the work—a book, painting, music, software, instruction manual—with copyright notice, typically "Copyright," "Copr.," or © followed by the year of first publication and the name of the owner. The notice may appear on the back of the title page of a book, on the face of a manuscript or advertisement, or on the base of a sculpture. It had to be visible and legible, but it could be placed so as not to interfere with the aesthetics of the work. If more than a few copies of the published work appeared without the notice, the copyright was forfeited forever. Works that were unpublished did not need notice. They were protected by virtue of their retention in secrecy. Publication with notice was all that was required; registration with the Copyright Office was not always immediately necessary.

Under the laws enacted in 1976, publication without notice can be rectified if the notice is omitted from only a small number of copies, registration of the work with the Copyright Office is effected within five years, and an effort is made to add the notice to those copies published without it. Notice must be on the work in all its forms. For example, for software the notice should appear on the screen, in the coding, on the disk, and on the ROM, wherever the software is resident or performing. In one case an infringer got away with reading out copyrighted software from a ROM because there was no notice on the ROM, although there was notice elsewhere.

Presently, under an amendment to the current law effective March 1989, no notice is required at all. In order to become a member of an international copyright treaty known as the Bern Convention, the United States had to abolish all formalities required to establish copyright in a work. Now the simple fact that a work was created, whether published or not, is enough to establish the copyright. It is not clear that this removal of the need for notice is retroactive. Thus, new works after March 1989 need not have notice, but those that were required to bear notice before the amendment should, in the exercise of prudence, continue to bear the notice.

Although notice is no longer compulsory, it is a valuable and worthwhile practice since it enables the pursuit of innocent infringers. That is, an infringer who did not have actual notice that the work copied was copyrighted is nevertheless liable if the work bore copyright notice.

Registering a Copyright

Registration also is noncompulsory, but it, too, bestows valuable additional rights. If the copyright owner has registered the copyright, statutory damages of up to $500,000 can be recovered without proof of actual damages. This can be a real advantage in copyright cases where actual damage can be difficult and expensive to prove.

Registration requires filling out the proper form and mailing it to the Copyright Office with the proper fee and a deposit of two copies of the work for published works, or only one copy if the work is unpublished. Accommodations are made for filing valuable or difficult deposit copies: Deposit for three-dimensional works can be effected using photographs, and deposits for large computer programs can be effected using only the first and last 25 pages. Further, if the program contains trade secrets, there is a provision for obscuring those areas from the deposit.

Summing Up

Now consider the question posed at the beginning of this chapter: What parts of a computer on a stand are protectable, and how can they be protected? The computer memory, circuits, and CPU, as well as its architecture, could be protected by patents or trade secrets. The software could be protected by patent, too. The software could also be protected by copyright and trade secret. (Software protection is discussed in detail later in this chapter.) The user's manual could also be protected by copyright and trade secret. The company name and the brand name could be trademarks. The housing of the computer as well as the stand could be protected by design patents. The contents or form of the label may be protected by trademark or copyright.

INTERNATIONAL PROTECTION FOR INTELLECTUAL PROPERTY

Obtaining protection for patents, trademarks, and copyrights in the United States alone is no longer sufficient in the modern arena of international competition and global markets. International protection often needs to be extensive and can be quite expensive, but there are ways to reduce and postpone the expense in some cases. Protection must be considered in countries where you intend to market the new product or where competitors may be poised to manufacture your product.

A patent in one country does not protect the invention in any other country: A novel product or method must be protected by a separate patent in each country. In addition, each country has different restrictions that must be met, or no patent protection can be obtained. The first and most important restriction is the *time* within which you must file an application to obtain a patent in a country or else *forever lose your right to do so*.

Patent Filing Deadlines

Not all countries are the same with respect to filing deadlines. For example, as previously noted, in the United States an inventor may file an application to obtain a patent on an invention up to one year after the invention has become public through a publication explaining the invention, a public use of the invention, or the sale or offer for sale of the invention. This one-year period is known as the *period of grace*.

There is no period of grace in many other countries, such as Great Britain, West Germany, Sweden, France, Italy, Switzerland, Belgium, Austria, the Netherlands, Australia, and Japan. And each country has a slightly different view of what constitutes making an invention public. In Japan, for example, public use of an invention before the filing of an application bars a patent only if the public use occurred within Japan, but in France any public knowledge of the invention anywhere bars the patent.

Thus, whereas the United States allows a business *one full year* to test market its new product, most other countries require that the patent application be filed *before any public disclosure*, that is, before the owner can even begin to determine whether the new product will be even a modest success. And meeting this requirement is not inexpensive, especially when the U.S. dollar is down against the currencies of other major countries.

How to Extend Patent Filing Deadlines

However, there are ways around having to file immediately, as provided for by the treaty known as the *Paris Convention*. If you file in the United States and then file in any country that is a party to the convention within one year of the date on which you filed in the United States, the U.S. filing date applies as the filing date for that country. In this way, by filing one application for the invention in the United States, you can preserve your initial U.S. filing date for up to one year. This means that you can file an application in the United States, and then immediately make the invention public by advertising, published articles, and sales. If within one year the product appears to be a success, you can then file in selected foreign countries, even though the prior public use of the invention would ordinarily bar your filing in those countries.

There are other options by which you can postpone the cost of foreign filings while preserving your right to file. Another, more recent treaty known as the *Patent Cooperation Treaty* (PCT) permits a delay of up to 20 or even 30 months before the costs of filing in individual countries are incurred. The PCT option is available if you file and request PCT treatment within one year of your U.S. filing date.

Thus, by filing a PCT application in a specially designated PCT office within one year of your U.S. filing, and by designating certain countries, you can preserve your right to file in those countries without further expense for 20 or 30 months after the U.S. filing date. That will provide an additional 8 or 18 months for test marketing the product. This does introduce the extra cost of the PCT application filing, but if you are considering filing in, say, six or more countries, the extra PCT filing may be well worth the cost for two reasons:

- It delays the outflow of cash that you may not presently have or may require for other urgent needs.
- If the product proves insufficiently successful, you can decide not to file in any of the countries designated under the PCT and save the cost of all six national application filings.

Another cost-saving feature of international patent practice is the *European Patent Convention* (EPC), which is compatible with the Paris Convention and the PTC and which enables you to file a single European patent and designate any one or more of 17 European countries in which you wish the patent to issue.

There are a number of international treaties that affect trademark rights and copyrights as well.

LICENSING AND TECHNOLOGY TRANSFER

A license is simply a special form of contract or agreement. Each party promises to do or pay something in return for the other party doing or paying something. Contracts that deal with the transfer of technology, or more broadly, intellectual property—patents, trade secrets, know-how, copyrights, and trademarks—are generally referred to as licenses. The licensed property can be anything from the right to use Mickey Mouse on a T-shirt or to make copies of the movie *Star Wars*, to the right to operate under the McDonald's name, to use a patented method of making a microchip, or to reproduce, use, or sell a piece of software. Software licenses are just one of the many types of licenses. The basic considerations are the same as for any other license, but specific clauses and language are tailored to the software environment.

Common Concerns and Clauses

The term *license* is typically used to refer to a number of different types of contracts involving intellectual property, including primarily an assignment, an exclusive license, and a nonexclusive license. And this broad reference will be used in this section.

An assignment is an outright sale of the property. Title passes from the owner, the assignor, to the buyer, the assignee. An assignment can take a number of forms:

- It can cover an entire patent, including all the rights under the patent.
- It can apply to an undivided fractional portion of all the patent rights (such as 30% undivided interest).
- It can include all the rights embraced by a patent limited to any geographical part of the United States.

A license is more like a rental or lease. The owner of the property, the licensor, retains *ownership*; the buyer, the licensee, receives the *right to operate* under the property right, be it a patent, trade secret, know-how, copyright, or trademark. An *exclusive license* gives the licensee the sole and exclusive right to operate under the property to the exclusion of everyone else, even the licensor. A *nonexclusive license*, in contrast, permits the licensee to operate under the licensed property but without any guarantee of exclusivity. The licensor can try to find more licensees and license them, there may be others who are already licensed, and the licensor can also operate under the property.

By definition, an assignment is exclusive since the assignee acquires full right and title to the property. Many licensees prefer an assignment or exclusive license because they want a clear playing field with no competitors in order to maximize their revenue from the property and justify the license cost.

Within either of these forms—exclusive license or nonexclusive license—may be included a right to *sublicense*, which is the right of the licensee to license others. This removes part of the licensor's control over the property and extends the licensee's liability to the conduct and payment of all sublicensees. A sublicense is an important and valuable right that is not automatically conveyed with the primary license right; it must be expressly granted. The term *transferable* in a license means that the license can be transferred as a whole along with the part of the licensee's business to which the license pertains; it does not confer the right to sublicense.

Licensors often prefer a nonexclusive license because it spreads their royalty income over a number of diverse licensees, increasing the chances of a successful return. In addition, if the property is freely available to all credible businesses, no one is left out or disadvantaged. All have an equal chance to compete, and the chances are reduced of a lawsuit from a rejected potential licensee.

Defining the Property Being Licensed

Great care must be exercised to clearly define the property being licensed. For example, consider the following questions:

- Is it more than one patent, just one patent, or only a part of one patent?
- Is it just the trademark, or the entire corporate image—names, advertising, and promotional scheme and graphics?
- If it concerns copyright, does it cover just the right to copy a book or other printed material in the same print form, or does it include any of the following rights?

    —Translation into another language

    —Adaptation for stage, screen or video

    —Creation of derivative works

    —Merchandising its characters and events on T-shirts and toys?

- If it involves know-how or trade secrets, where are they defined?

Licensees must be sure that they are getting what they want and need. And a licensor must make clear the limits of the grant. In a software license if the grant is only to use the software, not to modify it or merge it with other software, that must be expressly stated.

Limitations on Licenses

A license may have numerous, different limitations, including time, the unit quantity, and the dollar value of products or services sold. The license can also be limited geographically. Field-of-use limitations are quite common, too. This limitation restricts the licensee to exploit the licensed property only in a designated field or market.

Assigning Value to a License

Perhaps the most universal concern in negotiating a license is, how do you assign a dollar value to intellectual property? First, determine what it *cost* to acquire that property, to build that property. For example, all of the following are hard costs that go into creating a property:

- The research and development cost involved in coming up with a new invention
- The design cost of coming up with a new trademark or copyrighted work
- The cost of commercializing the invention
- The cost of advertising and promoting the trademark or copyrighted work, which can run into millions of dollars a year
- Incidental costs, such as legal costs, engineering costs, and accounting costs

Second, determine how this intellectual property affects the *profitability* of the product or the business. Can you charge more because the product has a famous name or because of the new features the invention has bestowed on the product? Can your costs be cut because of the new technology of the invention? If so, determine dollar values for those figures.

You might also determine how much the intellectual property increases gross revenues by opening new markets or by acquiring a greater percentage of established markets. All of these figures can be converted into dollar amounts for valuation.

Royalty Rates

A "typical" royalty rate for a nonexclusive license to a patent, trade secret, or know-how is universally stated to be 5%, but that rule is breached as often as it is honored. Nonexclusive license royalty rates in patent licenses can be 10%, 20%, 25%, or even higher. And exclusive license royalty rates tend to be higher because the licensee receives total exclusivity and the licensor is at risk if the licensee does not perform. Exclusive licensors generally demand initial payments for the same reason. In determining a reasonable royalty as a damage award in an infringement suit, courts have considered the following factors:

- The remaining life of the patent
- The advantages and unique characteristics of the patented device over other, prior devices
- Evidence of substantial customer preference for products made under the patent
- Lack of acceptable noninfringing substitutes
- The extent of the infringer's use of the patent
- The alleged profit the infringer made that is credited to the patent

Negotiating License Agreements

In any commercial agreement in which the consideration promised by one party to the other is a percentage of profits or receipts or is a royalty on goods sold, there is nearly always an implied promise of diligent, careful performance and good faith. But licensors generally seek some way to ensure that the licensee will use its best efforts to exploit the property and maximize the licensor's income. One approach is simply to add a clause in which the licensee promises to use its "best efforts." Another approach is to compel certain achievements by the licensee. The license may require a minimum investment in promotion and development of the property, which may be expressed in dollars, human labor hours, or even specific stated goals of performance or sales. Or the simpler approach of a minimum royalty can be employed: The licensee pays a certain minimum dollar amount in running royalties annually, whether or not the licensee's sales actually support those royalties—not a pleasant condition for the licensee but one that provides a lot of peace of mind for the licensor.

Perhaps the best insurance of performance is a competent, enthusiastic licensee. A little preliminary investigation of the licensee (in terms of net worth, credit rating, experience, reputation, manufacturing/sales capability, and prior successes/failures) can assuage a lot of fears and eliminate risky licensees. A *reverter clause*, which evicts the licensee and returns control to the licensor in the event of unmet goals, is the ultimate protection. Often the licensor's greatest concern is that the licensee might now or later sell one or more competing products, leading to a plain conflict of interest. A *noncompetition clause* can prevent this, but antitrust dangers are raised by such clauses, and licensees do not like this constraint on their freedom. Other approaches are safer, such as specified minimum performance levels.

Confidential disclosure clauses are necessary in nearly all license agreements, especially those involving trade secrets, know-how, and patent applications. Such clauses are necessary to protect not only the property that is the subject of the license, but also all of the technical, business, financial, marketing, and other information the parties will learn about each other during the license term, and even during negotiations before the license is executed.

Foreign Licenses

The aforementioned clauses and concerns pertain generally to all licenses, domestic U.S. as well as foreign. In addition, there are other clauses more peculiarly suited to foreign agreements.

Geographic divisions are important because of the somewhat different treatment of intellectual property in each country. The manufacture and use of the product related to the patent, trade secret, or know-how may be limited to the United States, but sales may be permitted worldwide. Payment must be defined as to the currency to be used as well as to who will pay any taxes or transfer charges. The parties must provide for government approval of the transfer of royalties and repatriation of capital.

A license agreement is a special form of contract in which each party promises to do something in exchange for promises by the other party. It is based on a business understanding between the parties and common sense applied to the attainment of business goals. But it is more complex than a normal contract because of the uniqueness of its subject matter, intellectual property—patents, trademarks, copyrights, trade secrets, and know-how. These properties require special action for their creation and maintenance. And great care is necessary in licensing such properties to maximize their returns and prevent their loss.

SOFTWARE PROTECTION

Protection for computer software has been the subject of debate for many years. At one time there was strong opposition to the awarding of patents for inventions embodied in or involving software. That is no longer the case: Now software is commonly patented. Copyright protection had been considered only for the coding, but that too has changed: Now it is clear that copyright protection covers not only the coding (the literal aspects of a computer program), but also aspects such as the sequence and flow, organization and structure, user interface, and menus. Trade secret protection was formerly available, but only if you kept the software secret, which made it awkward to embrace copyright. Now the Copyright Office has a procedure whereby software copyrights can be registered yet trade secrets contained in the software can be specifically preserved.

Patents for Software

Broad patent protection is available for software. The scope of patent protection extends beyond the coding or routines, beyond the structure and organization, beyond the user interface and menus of the program, to the broad underlying concept or algorithm. All manner of software is protectable by patent regardless of how it is perceived—as controlling industrial equipment or processes, as effecting data processing, or as operating the computer itself.

For example, software implementation of steps normally performed mentally may be patentable subject matter. Thus, while a method of doing business is not patentable subject matter, the software to effect a business activity may be. In one case, the software implementation of a system that automatically transferred a customer's funds among a brokerage security account, several money funds, and a Visa/checking account automatically upon the occurrence of preset conditions, was held to be patentable subject matter. Also, a software method of translating from one language to another (Russian to English) was found to be protectable.

Many patents have been issued on data processing software; following are some examples:

- A system for registering attendees at trade shows and conventions
- A securities brokerage cash management system
- An automated securities trading system
- An insurance investment program for funding a future liablity
- Software for managing an auto loan
- Software for optimization of industrial resource allocation
- Software for automatically determining and isolating differences between text files (word processing)
- Software for returning to a specified point in a document (word processing)
- Software for determining premiums for insurance against specific weather conditions.

Software that operates the computer itself is patentable, too. For example, patents have issued on:

- Software for converting a source program to an object program
- Programs that translate from one programming language to another
- A cursor control for a pull-down menu bar
- Software that displays images in windows on the video display
- A computer display with window capability

The software may be composed of old routines as long as they are assembled in a different way and produce a different result, for it is well established in patent law that a combination of old parts is patentable if the resulting whole is new. Indeed, most inventions are a new assembly of well-known parts or steps.

Design patents too have been used to protect software. Design patents have been issued for visual features produced on the screen by the computer software, such as various display icons; one example is an icon for a telephone display.

Software Copyrights

Copyright protection for software, though not as broad as patent protection, is nevertheless quite broad. As stated earlier, a copyright protects not just against the copying of the coding but also against the copying of the organization and structure—its "look and feel." If a subsequent developer creates software that "looks and feels" like earlier copyrighted software, there is infringement, whether or not the coding is similar. But courts do differ on the breadth of copyright protection.

All forms of programs are protectable by copyright—flow charts, source programs, assembly programs, object programs. And it makes no difference whether the program is an operating system or an applications program. No distinction is made concerning the copyrightability of programs that directly interact with the computer user and those that, unseen, manage the computer system internally. Protection is also afforded microcode or microprograms that are buried in a microprocessor, and even programs embedded in a silicon chip.

Databases too are protected by copyright. The input of a copyrighted database results in the making of a copy, so there is copyright infringement. It makes no difference if the data copied from indices and graphs or maps is rearranged not as another book or visual aid but as an electronically stored database: It is infringement. And this is so even if new and different maps, graphs, and text are produced from a database by the computer.

Even more subtle copyright problems have occurred regarding databases. The purveyor of a computer program that permits users to access and analyze the copyrighted database of another was found liable for copyright infringement because in order to analyze the data, the program had to first copy portions of the database.

Software Trade Secret Protection

Software may also be protected through a trade secret approach, separately or in conjunction with patent and copyright protection. Normally, all information disclosed in a published copyrighted work is in the public domain. However, the U.S. Copyright Office fully recognizes the compatibility of copyright and trade secret protection, and its rules provide special filing procedures to protect trade secrets in copyrighted software.

HOW TO AVOID THE PRELIMINARY PITFALLS OF PROTECTING INTELLECTUAL PROPERTY

Frequently, when a person thinks of protecting a new idea or product, the thoughts turn to patents, trade secrets, and copyrights. But the game can be won or lost long before one has the opportunity to establish one of those forms of protection. That is why the fundamental forms of protection—confidential disclosure agreements, employment contracts, and consultant contracts—are so important. Whether or not an idea or product is protectable by an exclusive statutory right such as a patent or copyright, there still is a need at an early stage, before such protection can be obtained, to *keep the basic information confidential* in order to prevent public use or disclosure, which can result in the loss of rights and inspire others to seek statutory rights before you.

Confidential disclosure agreements, employment agreements, and consultant agreements have some things in common. They define the obligations of the parties during the critical early stages of development of a new concept, product, or process. They are usually overlooked until it's too late, after the relationship is well under way and a problem has arisen. For proper protection of the business, there must be agreements with employees, consultants, and, in some cases, suppliers and customers to keep secret all important information of the business and to assign to the business all rights to that information.

It is commonly thought that only technical information can be protected. This is not so. All of the following can be protectable information:

- Ideas for new products or product lines
- A new advertising or marketing program
- A new trademark idea
- The identity of a critical supplier
- A refinancing plan

And all of these can be even more valuable than the technical matters when it comes to establishing an edge over the competition and gaining a greater market share.

Employment contracts, consultant contracts, and confidential disclosure agreements all should be in writing and signed before the relationship begins, before any work is done, before any critical information is exposed, and before any money changes hands. A business must not be in such a rush to get on with the project that it ends up without full ownership of the very thing it paid for. And the employees, consultants, or other parties must not be so anxious to get the work that they fail to understand clearly at the outset what they are giving up in undertaking this relationship.

Preparing Employment Contracts

Employment contracts must be fair to both parties and should be signed by all employees, at least those who may be exposed to confidential company matters or may contribute ideas or inventions to the business. They should also be short and readable.

Employment contracts, like all agreements, must have considerations flowing both ways. If I agree to paint your house for $1,000, my consideration to you is the painting of your house. Your consideration to me is the $1,000. In an employment contract, the consideration from the employee includes all promises to keep secrets and assign ideas and inventions; the consideration from the business is to employ the employee. Thus, it is best to present these contracts to the prospective employee well before she begins work.

After the job has begun, the consideration will be the employee's "continued" employment, and that sounds a bit threatening. Although "continued" employment is certainly proper consideration, in construing these contracts courts can easily see that the employer usually has the superior bargaining position, and so they generally like to know that when the contract was offered for signature, the employee had a fair opportunity to decline without suffering severe hardship. It is not a good idea to present the employment contract in a packet of pension, hospitalization, and other forms to be signed the day the employee shows up to begin work after having moved the entire family across the country in order to take the job.

Transfer of Employee Rights to Company Innovations

One of the most important clauses in an employment contract is the agreement by the employee to transfer to the company the entire right, title, and interest in and to all ideas, innovations, and creations. These include designs, developments, inventions, improvements, trade secrets, discoveries, writings, and other works, including software, databases, and other computer-related products and processes. The transfer is required whether or not these items are patentable or copyrightable. They should be assigned to the company if they were made, conceived, or first reduced to practice by the employee. This obligation should hold whether the employee was working alone or with others and whether or not the work was done during normal working hours or on the company premises. So long as the work is within the scope of the company's business, research, or investigation or it resulted from or is suggested by any of the work performed for the company, its ownership is required to be assigned to the company.

This clause should *not* seek to compel transfer of ownership for everything an employee does, even *if it has no relation to the company's business*. For example, an engineer employed to design phased array radar for an electronics company may invent a new horseshoe or write a book on the history of steeplechase racing. An attempt to compel assignment of ownership of such works under an employment agreement could be seen as overreaching and unenforceable. The same may be true of a clause that seeks to vest in the employer ownership of inventions, innovations, or other works made for a period of time after employment ends or before employment begins.

Ancillary to this transfer or assignment clause is the agreement of the employee to promptly disclose the inventions, innovations, and works to the company or to any person designated by the company, and to assist in obtaining protection for the company, including patents and copyrights in all countries designated by the company. The employee at this point also agrees to execute:

- Patent applications and copyright applications
- Assignments of issued patents and copyright registrations
- Any other documents necessary to perfect the various properties and vest their ownership clearly in the company

If these activities are called for after the employee has left the company, she is still obligated to perform but must be paid for time and expenses.

How Employee Moonlighting Might Compromise Confidentiality

Another important concern is moonlighting. While a company that sells CAD/CAM workstations doesn't care if its programmers drive fish delivery trucks on their own time, there are extremely sensitive situations that the company as well as the employee must take care to avoid. In one case a CAD/CAM company discovered huge telephone charges for various lengthy periods from 3:00 P.M. to 8:00 P.M. on most days of the week, including Saturdays and Sundays. The company challenged the telephone bill and found that the calls were indeed made from the company's own phones to a major computer manufacturer many miles away. The computer manufacturer claimed ignorance. But after a lengthy investigation it was discovered that an employee of the company had been hired on a consulting basis by a middle manager at the manufacturer to develop a software system. The employee had been doing his consulting for the computer manufacturer over the telephone lines from his computer terminal while sitting at his desk in his company office. The employee was not shortchanging the company as far as hours were concerned; he was working long hours to make up for his moonlighting, and the software he was developing was not in the company's CAD/CAM area. But the revelation was chilling. The mere awareness that an information line existed between this giant computer manufacturer and the company, and what might have transpired over that line, haunted the company's officers and managers for some time afterward.

To prevent this, the employee should agree in the employment contract that during employment by the company there will be no engagement in any employment or activity in which the company is now or may later become involved, nor will there be moonlighting on the company's time or using the company's equipment or facilities.

Noncompetition Clauses

A closely related notion is a noncompetition provision whereby the employee agrees not to compete during his employment by the company and for some period after leaving the company's employ. This is a more sensitive area. It may be perfectly understandable that a company does not want its key salesperson, an officer, a manager, or the head of marketing or engineering to move to a new job with a competitor and have the inside track on his ex-employer's best customers, new product plans, manufacturing techniques, or new marketing program. But the courts do not like to prevent a person from earning a livelihood. Courts do not compel a lifelong radar engineer, for example, to turn down a job with a competitor in the same field and instead take a job designing cellular phones. A person who has spent a lifetime marketing and selling drapes and curtains cannot be made to sell floor coverings or used cars.

However, the higher up and more important a person is in the operation of the company, the greater is the probability that that person will be prevented from competing if the employment agreement provides for it. Officers, directors, founders, majority stockholders, and other key personnel have had such provisions enforced against them, but even then the scope of the exclusion must be fair and reasonable in terms of both time and distance. A few months, a year, or even two years could be acceptable, depending on how fast the technology and market is moving. Worldwide exclusion might be acceptable for a salesperson who sells transport planes. In the restaurant business, a few miles might be all that is necessary. A contract that seeks to extend the exclusion beyond what's fair will not be enforced.

One way to ensure that an ex-employee does not compete is to allow the company to employ the person on a consultant basis over some designated period of time. In this way the employee's involvement in critical information areas can gradually be phased out, so that by the time the employee is free to go to a competitor there is no longer a threat to the company, and at the same time the employee has been fairly compensated.

Bear in mind, however, that even if ex-employees are free to compete, they are not free to take with them (in their memories or in recorded form) any trade secrets or any information confidential or proprietary to the company or to use it or disclose it in any way. To reinforce this the employment contract should provide that the employee will not, during employment by the company or at any time thereafter, disclose to others or use for her own benefit or for the benefit of others any trade secrets or any confidential or proprietary information pertaining to any businesses of the company—technical, commercial, financial, sales, marketing, or otherwise. The restriction could also protect such information pertaining to the business of any of the company's clients, customers, consultants, licensees, affiliates, and the like.

Along with this the employment contract should provide that all documents, records, models, electronic storage devices, prototypes, and other tangible items representing or embodying company property or information are the sole and exclusive property of the company and must be surrendered to the company no later than the termination of employment, or at any earlier time upon request of the company. This is an important provision for both the employer and employee to understand. In some states the law imposes serious criminal sanctions and fines for the removal of tangible trade secret property.

Preventing Employee Raiding

Another potential area of conflict is employee raiding, the hiring away of employees by an ex-employee who is now employed by a competitor or who has founded a competing business. This is a particularly sensitive situation when the ex-employee holds a position of high trust and confidence and was looked up to by the employees she is now attempting to hire. And it is particularly damaging when the employees being seduced are critical to operations either because of their expertise or their sheer numbers. In all circumstances such an outflow of employees is threatening because of the potential loss to a competitor of trade secrets and know-how. This can be addressed by a clause prohibiting an employee, during her employment period and for some period thereafter, from hiring away fellow employees for another enterprise.

Employee Ownership of Copyright

One of the most hazardous areas of ownership involves the title to copyrights. If a copyrighted work is created or authored by an employee, the company automatically owns the copyright. But the employee must be a bona fide employee. That is, there must be all the trappings of regular employment. If a dispute arises over ownership between the company and the author, the courts will seek to determine whether the author was really an employee. Was this person provided a full work week, benefits, withholding, unemployment insurance, worker's compensation, and an office or workspace? If the author was anything less than a full employee, the copyright for the work belongs to the person. It does not belong to the company!

This means that if the company hires a part-time employee, a consultant, a friend, or a moonlighter, that person may end up owning the copyright for the work. Thus, when that nonemployee completes the software system that will revolutionize the industry and bring income cascading to the enterprise, the employee, not the company, will own the copyright. The company will own the embodiment of the system that the employee developed for the company, but the employee will own the right to reproduce, copy, and sell the system over and over again. It has happened. A company that spent hundreds of thousands of dollars to develop a software system owned the finished product but not the copyright in the product. The nonemployee owned the copyright and had the right to reproduce the product without limit and sell it to those who most desire it—typically the company's competitors and customers.

This is a chilling scenario but one that is easy to avoid with a little forethought. The solution is easy: Simply get it in writing. Before any work starts, payment changes hands, or plans are revealed, *have the proposed author sign a written agreement* specifying that, whether or not the author is subsequently held to be an employee or a nonemployee, all right, title, and interest in any copyrightable material is assigned to the company. The lack of such a clear understanding in writing can wreck great dreams, ruin friendships and partnerships, and hamstring businesses to the point of insolvency while the parties fight over who owns the bunny rabbit, the book, the software, the poster, or the videotape on how to be a successful entrepreneur.

Moral Rights of Authors or Artists

Another area that must be considered is the moral rights of authors in their works. Under a law effective June 1, 1991, in the United States, moral rights of artists in their visual works are protected. Moral rights are variously defined as the rights of attribution and integrity, or the rights of paternity and integrity. What this means is that an artist has a right to insist that his name be associated with the work, or to refuse to have his name associated with the work if it is mutilated in the artist's opinion, and also to insist that the work not be mutilated; that is, the integrity of the work must be maintained. The moral rights doctrine has been invoked, for example, in an attempt to prevent the removal of a wall containing a painted mural.

The law in the United States that established the moral rights doctrine provides that the artist's moral rights may not be transferred, but may be waived by the artist in a written statement that specifically identifies the work and the uses to which the waiver applies.

Therefore, in every agreement dealing with copyrights it is prudent to include a clause in which the artist in writing specifically refers to the work or works and waives the moral rights for all uses of all the works. It probably would also be wise to refer to Section 106(a) of the Copyright Act, which embodies the moral rights doctrine.

Rights of Prior Employees

There is another issue to consider under employment contracts. When a new employee is to be hired, obtain a copy of the employment contract with the last employer or the last few employers to determine whether this employee is free to work for this company now, in the capacity the employee seeks. Prior employers have rights, too, that can conflict, rightly or wrongly, with the employee's new employment.

Consultant Contracts

Consultant contracts should contain provisions similar to those in an employment contract, along with some additional provisions. A consultant agreement should clearly define the task for which the consultant is hired—for example, to research a new area; to analyze or solve a problem; design or redesign a product; set up a production line; or assist in marketing, sales, management, technical, or financial matters. This is important to show:

- Why the consultant was hired
- What the consultant is expected to do
- What the consultant may be exposed to in the way of company trade secrets and confidential and proprietary information
- What the consultant is expected to assign to the company in the way of innovations, inventions, patents, and copyrights

Clearly, a company hiring a consultant wants to own the result of whatever the consultant was hired to do, just as in the case of an employee. But a consultant's stock in trade is the expertise and ability to solve problems swiftly and elegantly in a specific subject area. Sharp lines must be drawn as to what the consultant will and will not assign to give both parties peace of mind.

Consulting relationships by their nature can expose each of the parties to a great deal of the other party's trade secrets and confidential and proprietary information. The company can protect itself with clear identification of the pertinent information and by employing the usual safeguards for trade secrets. It also must limit disclosure to the consultant to what is necessary to do the job, and also limit the consultant's freedom to use the information in work for others and to disseminate the information. Consultants must protect themselves in the same way to prevent the company from misappropriating the consultant's special knowledge, problem-solving approaches, and analytical techniques.

An often overlooked area is the ownership of notes, memos, and failed avenues of investigation. False starts and failures can be as important as the solution, especially to competitors. Related to this is the question of the ownership of the raw data. Raw data may be extremely valuable in their own right but also may be used to easily reconstruct the end result of the consultant's work, such as a market survey.

Confidential Disclosure Agreements

Whenever an idea, information, an invention, or any knowledge of peculiar value is to be revealed, a confidential disclosure agreement should be signed by the receiving party to protect the disclosing party. The disclosure may be necessary for any of the following reasons:

- To interest a manufacturer in taking a license to make and sell a new product
- To hire a consultant to advise in a certain area
- To permit a supplier to give an accurate bid
- To allow a customer to determine whether or not it wants a product or wants a product modified
- To interest investors to invest in the business

Domestic agreements are important not only to protect the knowledge or information itself, but also to preserve valuable related rights such as *domestic and foreign patent rights*. These agreements should be short and to the point.

Basically, the receiver of the disclosure should agree to keep confidential all information disclosed. Information is defined as all trade secrets and all proprietary and confidential information, whether tangible or intangible, oral or written, and of whatever nature (for example, technical, sales, marketing, advertising, promotional, merchandising, financial, or commercial).

The receiver should agree to receive all such information in confidence and not to use or disclose the information without the express written consent of the discloser. It should be made clear that no obligation is incurred by the receiver for any information that it can show was in the public domain, that the receiver already knew, or that was told to the receiver by another party.

The receiver should be limited to disclosing the information to only those of its employees who need to know in order to carry out the purposes of the agreement and who have obligations of secrecy and confidentiality to the receiver. Further, the receiver should agree that all of its employees to whom any information is communicated are obligated under written employment agreements to keep the information secret. The receiver should also represent that it will exercise the same standard of care in safeguarding this information as it does for its own, and in no event less than a reasonable standard of care. This latter phrase is necessary because some businesses have no standard of care or a very sloppy attitude toward even their own important information.

Provision should be made for the return of all tangible embodiments of the confidentially disclosed information, including drawings, blueprints, designs, parameters of design, monographs, specifications, flow charts, sketches, descriptions, and data. A provision could also be included preventing the receiving party from entering a competing business or introducing a competing product or service in the area of the disclosed information. Often a time limit is requested by the receiver, after which the receiver is free to disclose or use the information. Such a time period could extend from a few months to a number of years, depending on the life cycle of the information, tendency to copy, competitive lead time, and other factors present in a particular industry. Strong, clear language should be used to establish that no license or any other right, express or implied, to the information is given by the agreement.

While such confidential disclosure agreements between the discloser and receiver are the ideal, they are not always obtainable. The receiver may argue that no such agreement is necessary, saying in effect, "Trust me." Or the receiver may flatly refuse on the grounds that it is against its policy. Some large corporations turn the tables and demand that their own standard *non*confidential disclosure agreement be signed before the disclosure of any information.

Under a nonconfidential disclosure agreement, often referred to as *idea submission agreements*, the discloser gives up all rights to the information except as covered by a U.S. patent or copyright. Outside of those protections the receiver is free to use, disclose, or do whatever it wishes with the information. This is not due simply to arrogance or orneriness. A large corporation has many departments and divisions where research and development of new ideas are occurring unknown to other areas of the corporation. In addition, in a number of cases courts have held corporations liable for misappropriation of ideas and information when no written agreement existed, and even where a *non*confidential disclosure agreement purported to free the receiver from any restriction against dissemination and use of the idea.

If no agreement can be reached or if the nonconfidential disclosure agreement counteroffer occurs, the discloser must decide whether to keep the idea under the mattress or take a chance on the honesty of the receiver; however, in such a case it is wise to reduce the initial disclosure to a minimum to cut the losses should a careless or unscrupulous receiver make public or misappropriate the idea.

A middle ground that courts have recognized is an implied confidential relationship evidenced by the actions of the parties. In one case a letter soliciting a receiver's interest in a particular field and indicating that the matter was confidential, resulted in a face-to-face meeting between the discloser and receiver, where the full idea was revealed. Later, when the receiver came out with a product using the idea, the discloser sued and won. The letter set up a confidential relationship which the receiver did not reject, but rather accepted by meeting with the discloser and accepting the idea without any comment or exclusion. The letter was not signed by the receiver, but it bound the company nevertheless under the totality of the circumstances.

Summing Up

These basic forms of protection—employment contracts, consultant contracts, and confidential disclosure agreements—need not be complex or lengthy, but they are essential at the earliest stages of idea generation to protect and preserve for the business some of its most valuable and critical property.

12 FRANCHISING

Steve Spinelli

In the United States in 1990, some 540,000 franchised outlets had total sales of over $750 billion, accounting for 35% of all retail sales.[1] The International Franchise Association believes that number will rise to $1 trillion by 1994. There are another 62,000 franchised outlets internationally. Franchising experienced a 127% growth in the 1980s. Between 1972 and the present, franchising has shown real growth in every year. The sheer size of what is called franchising makes it worth investigating.

WHAT IS FRANCHISING?

Over the years franchising has been much maligned as anything from a pyramid scheme to just another form of employment. Robert T. Justis, Professor of Franchising at the University of Nebraska, defines franchising in general as

> a business opportunity by which the owner, producer, or distributor (franchisor) of a service or trademarked product grants exclusive rights to an individual (franchisee) for the local distribution of the product or service, and in return receives a payment or royalty and conformance to quality standards.

Business format franchising is defined as a contractual, ongoing business relationship between a franchisor and franchisee. The business format concept includes a marketing plan, documented and enforced procedures, process assistance, and business development and innovation. Business format franchising is an overall method of doing business and is a more complex relationship than franchising solely for the purpose of product distribution. The relationship in a business format franchise must be as dynamic as the marketplace to survive.

HISTORICAL BACKGROUND

Few business practitioners or students have not heard about the McDonald's story and its founder, Ray Kroc. Although their contribution to franchising is monumental, the history of franchising dates much further back.

The extensive "pub" network in the United Kingdom may be the oldest franchise system in the world. During the Roman occupation of Britain, the major supplier of food, drink, and accommodations for the traveler was the Church. Religious tenets of the time dictated that two days' food and lodging be supplied free to any traveler. Abuses of these privileges resulted in the growth of commercial enterprises around 740–750.

By 957 King Edgar decided there were too many alehouses and decreed a limit of one per village. As a part of that decree some common standards were instituted. The business format required a standard measure, limited quantities, and a prohibition of sales to priests. A monitoring system was established and fines levied against violators. Franchising was born.

The population steadily grew, and evolving consumer and economic realities forced consolidation of the industry. The national brewers recognized a need to secure market share. "Publicans grappled with the difficulty of keeping pace with fast moving events and the ever-increasing demands of various kinds."[2] More and more pub owners allied with brewers. By the early nineteenth century, half of all alehouses were tied by some form of agreement. The House of Commons Committee on Public Breweries in 1818 noted that tied houses were "of much higher order" than free houses.[3] Franchising was here to stay.

Franchising in the United States began in the 1840s and continues to grow today.[4] Two distinct types of franchises have developed. The first, *product franchising*, was created by makers of complex durable goods who found existing wholesalers either unwilling or unable to market their products. These manufacturers built their own distribution systems and created franchise systems as alternatives to the high cost of company-owned outlets. The second type, *business format franchising*, was created in the 1950s when it became evident that the outlet itself could be a vehicle for entrepreneurial activity.

A franchise system can be a combination of franchisor-operated outlets and franchisee-operated outlets or only franchisee-operated outlets. Eighty-seven percent of the outlets in U.S. franchise systems are operated by franchisees. Types of businesses generally included in business format franchising are restaurants, food and nonfood retailing, and business services. Not included in business format franchising are gas stations and soft drink bottlers, for example. Midas and Dunkin' Donuts are two examples of business format franchises. A consumer electronics retailer of Sony would be a product franchise.

BECOMING A FRANCHISEE VERSUS STARTING A STAND-ALONE BUSINESS

The issues pertinent to success in a franchise are the same as for any other business. The difference is that the array of factors responsible for a franchise's success are tried and true, and there is a proven ability to transfer this system of excellence to varied and dispersed locations. Therefore, the franchise model is predicated on the assumption that *value has been developed* through the careful operation, testing, and documentation of a commercially viable idea. Given that this has been accomplished (which your own diligence must verify), the initial success of the system lies in the ability of the franchisor to communicate this system to qualified franchisees. The long-term success of the system is uniquely tied to the franchisor's ability to receive and assimilate process feedback from the franchisees and use this feedback to modify the system.

The choice of becoming a franchisee or starting a stand-alone business hinges on your answers to two important questions:

- Is risk sufficiently mitigated by the trademark value, operating system, economies of scale, and support process of the franchise to justify a sharing of equity with the franchisor (vis-à-vis the franchise fee and royalty payments)?
- Is my personality and management style amenable to sharing decision-making responsibilities in my business with the franchisor and other franchisees?

For those who need to quantify the choice between a franchise and a stand-alone business, I offer the following:

$$\text{Franchise fee} + \text{PV of royalty} = \text{PV of the increased net income from the value of the franchise trademark}$$

where PV is the present value of a sum of money. (For an explanation of PV, see Chapter 13 and the glossary.) If your analysis reveals this equation to be true, or if the right-hand side of the equation is greater than the left-hand side, the franchise decision is appropriate.

Much of this chapter focuses on the quantity and quality of the services and systems that a franchise offers. The choice of a franchise versus stand-alone startup is a question of due diligence, of evaluating the competitive advantages offered by the franchise. Those advantages must exist in sufficient quantity to justify the cost in franchise fees, royalties, and management encumbrances. The foundation for due diligence lies in the contract between the franchisee and franchisor.

THE FRANCHISE CONTRACT

The most refined franchise relationship develops into a partnership between the franchisor and the franchisee, and among the franchisees. However, a contract is necessary to ensure an understanding between the parties of their rights and obligations and the associated costs. In franchising, this contract is usually called a license agreement or a franchise contract. Because of the degree of regulation of franchising in the United States, the license agreement has become the definitive statement if litigation occurs.

In a mature franchise the trade name and trademark are the most valuable assets owned by the franchisor. In the business format franchise the documented operating system is integral to the trade name and trademark. Together they are responsible for the market value of the franchise. In some cases building specifications, equipment design, and secret formulas or recipes may be important parts of the franchisor's assets. (For example, the Colonel adamantly believed his "secret recipe" was integral to the product and image of Kentucky Fried Chicken.) Some assets may be patented or copyrighted.

Consideration of franchising by a company or due diligence by a franchise prospect requires an intimate understanding of the license agreement. Franchising is a legal specialization, and some firms concentrate their entire practice in this field. An attorney's review of the license agreement is a necessary cost of franchising. As a part of the legal review, the attorney should prepare a lay-language brief of the license agreement. In the development or review of a license agreement, business issues will be woven into the legalese. The more practical the detail in the license agreement, the better the chance for a healthy long-term relationship. However, implementing the license agreement will require the franchisor to incur monitoring costs, which must be considered along with other costs of the relationship such as litigation expense and quality concerns.

This chapter focuses primarily on the license agreement, or franchise contract. Understanding the terms of the license agreement is an integral part of the risk management process vital to all franchise endeavors. The following sections highlight the normal operating parameters in a franchise contract with special attention to the pitfalls. Proper evaluation of the franchise opportunity rests in assessing the value and cost of the franchise in relation to expected profits from going it alone.

Services Provided by the Franchisor

This section of the contract is invariably briefer than that detailing the franchisee obligations. However, a few key references will be sufficient to indicate the franchisor's positive intent and obligation. The services provided by the franchisor are separated into initial and continuing services. The type of business will heavily influence the services the franchisor supplies. As a rule of thumb, the prospective franchisee should discount any personal knowledge or experience in the industry and then ask the question, will the magnitude of the initial services establish the franchisee business in a manner appropriate to efficient operation on the day of opening?

Real Estate Development

Because many business format franchises include a real estate ingredient, site selection and construction specification and supervision are extremely important. Such slogans as "Location, location, location," "Just around the corner from success," and "a 'B' site will get you an 'F' in profitability" are not exaggerations. The real estate on which an outlet is located is often the point of sale and usually cannot be changed without severe economic stress. Most franchisors will approve the location, but not all will actually search for a site. Even fewer will take *responsibility* for finding a site.

The key aspects of site location include a thorough understanding of the primary target audience (PTA), your most likely customer, and the propensity of the PTA to patronize your franchise under varying environmental conditions. An important part of the franchisor's value lies in the accumulation and processing of data from the operating units. Although the franchisor cannot and should not give out information regarding specific stores, compilations with analysis are usually available. This is how the PTA information is gathered. If it is the franchisee's responsibility to locate a site, there must be clearly documented processes linking the PTA to the location specifics. General location parameters include cost, population, traffic volume, traffic patterns, visibility, zoning and permits, and ingress and egress; each of these factors is discussed in the following sections.

Cost

A Holiday Inn franchise requires at least a $2,000,000 investment, much of which is in the real estate. A long-established retail venture may decide to franchise, and a thorough analysis of the site characteristics will reveal certain location standards for successful expansion. A problem can soon surface, however, if the current real estate's market value is not known or is calculated on the existing operation's occupancy cost.

A franchised location under the current market values may not be viable. Contact a large commercial real estate broker and review the site specifications. Gather examples of recently sold or leased property with comparable specifications. Do the property or occupancy costs correlate with the franchisor guidelines? This process should also be followed by the franchisor, especially when expansion into new geographic territories is contemplated. Even if purchase prices are the same, lease terms and conditions can vary over time and among regions. Make sure that the "cap rates" used in calculating lease cost are comparable. The capitalization rate is the percentage return the landlord can expect her property to yield on the value of the asset (in this case, land and building) that is being leased. The term of a lease, the amount of time the lessee contractually holds the property, should match the term of the license agreement.

Population

How many PTA members—not members of the general population—in how wide a market area are prescribed by the franchisor? For example, ServiceMaster lawn care tracks dual-income homes in their trade areas. Cross the minimum PTA number with the franchisor pro forma market share and sales projection:

3-mile radius

50,000 population, 20,000 PTA

10% market share

2,000 PTA × 3 visits per year = 6,000 customers

Franchisor's sales projections/6,000 = Average ticket price

Do a spreadsheet analysis ramping up volume to equal these sample numbers. Are your projections reasonable and in line with the numbers projected by the franchisor? Will existing outlets' performance validate these projections?

Traffic Volume

Volume is quoted as pedestrians or vehicles per day. Many franchisors will prescribe a minimum volume, usually quoted on a 12- or 24-hour basis. Take note of the outlets the franchisor has singled out or the outlets of franchisees who have expressed satisfaction with their sales volume. Most state departments of motor vehicles, registry, or public works have traffic flow information.

Traffic Patterns

Corner location, the home-bound versus work-bound side of the road, and speed of traffic are but a few of the critical issues related to traffic patterns. A donut franchise may require the work-bound side of the road. Customers are less likely to stop for morning coffee if they must cross traffic when rushing to their jobs. This is an example of the fine distinction between a marginal return and a substantial return—or worse, the difference between failure and success.

Visibility

Visibility is especially important for products bought on impulse. When it is noon and you are hungry, you may act on impulse in reaction to a fast-food sign. Finding a preschool (a growing area of franchising) is probably a more considered choice and not an impulse purchase.

Visibility is a three-prong issue, including the elements of sign, building, and property entrance. At the top speed of the vehicles traveling the road of the proposed location (not to be confused with the posted speed), how many feet and seconds pass from the first view of each of these criteria to the entrance of the site? Is there sufficient time from the initial sighting of the location variable for a driver to comfortably turn into the location? A location that provides adequate turning time with respect to all three visibility variables has the highest ranking in this area.

Seasonality has an impact on visibility. A site as viewed in the winter may yield dramatically different results from the same site in the spring, with trees in full leaf.

Zoning and Permits

The cost and time requirements relating to zoning can vary dramatically from state to state and among local municipalities. Often a land use attorney is required for the process, as well as architects, surveyors, civil engineers, and traffic specialists. Increasingly, environmental impact studies are mandated by state regulation. Estimate the cost of these professionals as a part of due diligence.

Usually the franchisee is required to bear these costs up front. If the franchisor bears the costs, they are often capitalized in the real estate development expense and will be reflected in the outlet rent. In particularly complicated zoning affairs the cost may inflate the project well beyond the ultimate market value and potentially beyond the occupancy cost projected in the franchisor's financial pro forma.

Ingress and Egress

This is real estate jargon for entrance to and exit from the site. Checkers drive-in restaurant, launched in 1986, requires most site plans to have two drive-through windows in the flow of ingress and egress. Planning boards frequently modify a site plan even at the last minute. A quick change in entrance and exit layout can dramatically alter site acquisition criteria.

Summing Up: Don't Ignore Location Success Factors

If franchising is the vehicle chosen by a currently operating firm for expansion, it is critical to match the existing location success factors to the business format developed for sale to a franchisee. To neglect this is a fatal flaw, especially if the franchisee is responsible for finding the new location. It is extremely difficult to overcome location flaws and often impossible to change them.

In rapidly growing franchise systems there is a greater propensity to compromise on the development of individual stores in a rush to gain market share. Often the decision to franchise is made as a result of the desire to grow quickly. This cannot be allowed to dominate good business practice if long-term stability is an objective.

It is mutually beneficial to the franchisor and franchisee to have franchisor professionals provide detailed input in the real estate development. Some franchises typically locate in a mall—T-Shirt *plus*, for example. The same attention to location and demographic issues applies. A successful outlet will yield profit for the franchisee and capital for expansion. The franchisor will gain larger royalty payments. If the franchise is operated poorly and it ultimately fails, the franchisor can turn over the unit quickly, operate it as a company store, or sell the property to an unrelated third party only if the real estate has been carefully acquired and developed.

Investing in the real estate is a separate business venture from the franchise for both the franchisor and the franchisee. In evaluating the franchise opportunity, calculate the occupancy cost on a *market rental rate*. This can be done by multiplying the market square footage rental cost by the size of the proposed project. Alternatively, use the *market lease factor*—8% in a depressed market (August 1992 in New England), 12% in an expansive market (New York, 1987)—applied to the total project cost. The market lease factor is the rate the landlord will charge based on the current demand in the marketplace.

A franchisor who wishes to be the realty holder or lessor will need to negotiate the rental relationship. Some franchisors use what is called "percentage rent" to calculate the occupancy cost for the franchisee. There are a number of methods to implement percentage rents. The simplest is to charge a constant percentage of top-line sales. This can be beneficial in the startup phase but can result in above-market rents for the exceptionally performing location. This is particularly true for businesses with rapidly escalating costs and pricing, and can result in squeezed franchisee margins. This rental formula may seem attractive at the outset but could become burdensome. The variations in the use of percentage rents are limitless. Other methods include charging base rent, a minimum amount each month plus a smaller amount of top-line sales, or an amount slightly less than market rent plus a percentage of top-line sales over the projected break-even sales volume. Some franchisors will offer a variety of options; some will not. The franchisee should negotiate the options as a result of pro forma analysis and in congruence with risk mentality.

Established expertise in interpreting crucial real estate variables is included as part of the franchise purchase. Therefore, the franchisee must be sufficiently convinced that the necessary expertise is in place, available, and utilized.

Construction Specification and Supervision

Upon preliminary qualification of the site, the franchisor should integrate its construction department into the process. The franchisor usually has a standard set of blueprints. Most states require modification to meet state building code with the stamp of an architect from that state. Further modification may be required by local municipalities. Some franchisors modify plans even to the local level, but most do not. The level of sophistication of the model plans will greatly impact modification cost and efficiency. Very general plans leave much room for architectural inventiveness, resulting in diminished standardization, loss of efficiency, and reduced market value of the real estate.

Beyond the physical blueprints, the franchisor may provide construction supervision. Bidding contracts, draw approvals, construction monitoring, and final punch list are the categories of construction supervision. Beware of the franchisor who controls the construction process without independent bidding. There is nothing wrong with construction as a profit center if it also accrues benefits to the franchisee. This is best monitored through the marketplace of contractors. The franchisee should be involved in the construction process even if it is totally supervised by the franchisor. The franchise operator will understand the building better and live with it in greater harmony. Minor examples of building aspects the operator must be familiar with include the heating, ventilation and air conditioning, and basement sump pump operation.

Training

Training is a vital initial service and is also helpful on a continuing basis. The license agreement must define the *specific* form in which this franchisor responsibility will be carried out. It should extend significantly beyond a manual and the classroom. Training will vary with the specifics of the franchise but invariably should include organized and monitored on-the-job experience. Well-established and stable franchise systems require operational experience in the system for as long as a year prior to the purchase of a franchise. However, this is not the norm. Once the franchise is operational, the franchisee may be expected to do much or all of the onsite training. Manuals, testing, training aids such as videos, and certification processes are often provided by the franchisor.

As discussed previously, the trade name and mark are the most valuable assets in a franchise system. This is the result of delivery of the product on a consistent basis to consumers who acknowledge the value through paying a price that includes a profit margin. A poor training regimen will inevitably dilute the standardized, consistent delivery of the product and reduce trade name value.

Preopening Support

The foundation of the support services program is the level and sophistication of preopening support. Preopening support is a concentrated, multifunctional program to launch the new franchise. Inventory and equipment purchase and setup, staff hiring and training, and startup marketing are key variables. Built upon a sound location program, preparedness at launch can create the momentum for success. The franchisor who has the expertise in place to provide sophisticated startup assistance likely has the capability to provide the contractually required continuing services. A poor opening experience is an ominous sign concerning the quality of the franchise.

Continuing Services

Many license agreements define royalties as payment for the use of intellectual property. However, the continuity of the franchise relationship often rests on the cost/value rationalization of the royalty payment by the franchisee to the franchisor. Not only must the franchisor create a marketplace basket of services, but in the provision of services the system must be sustained and nurtured.

The actions of each franchisee affect the value of the trademark and thus the value of each individual franchise. The actions of the franchisor also affect franchise value. Both parties are necessarily interdependent and have a vested interest in actively supporting the system. A franchise agreement that acknowledges and addresses this interdependence is advantageous. The franchisee's performance is somewhat dependent on the quantity and quality of franchisor support. Conversely, the degree of franchisor support is usually inversely related to franchisee performance; more attention is usually provided the underperforming franchisee. Although this is a reasonable response to a threat to trademark value, balance in the application of franchisor resources is a key ingredient for success.

Performance and Standards Monitoring

By developing an array of statistical and financial monitoring devices, the franchisor can identify both the exceptional performer and the potential failure. Application of resources against identified problems maintains a stable system. Operational systems or marketing programs are often changed in a franchise system because of the exceptional performer. The best franchise systems not only compile data but analyze and efficiently distribute the information to franchisees for feedback. Does the contract provide for this informational conduit role?

Field Support

The license agreement should provide for scheduled visits to the franchisee's place of business with prescribed objectives. An efficient agenda might include performance review, field training, facilities inspection, local marketing review, and operations audit. The reality is that some franchisors use their field role as a diplomatic or pejorative exercise. The greater the substance of the field function, the easier it is for the franchisee to justify the royalty cost. Additionally, in a litigious environment a well-documented field support program will mute franchisee claims.

One means of understanding the franchisor's field support motive is to investigate the manner in which the field support personnel are compensated. If field staff are paid commensurate with franchisee performance and ultimate profitability, then politics will play a diminished role. Warning signals are bonuses for growth in the number of stores versus individual store sales growth and pay or bonus for franchisee product usage. Tying arrangements will be discussed later. However, the field support system is a part of the practical application of the influence strategy the franchisor has chosen.

Operational Research and Development

Economies of scale for research and development is a principal benefit in franchising. These economies are best achieved through the centralized, monitored, and standardized franchisor. Research of a franchise should track operations-level changes in franchised stores over a period of two to four years. How are changes in the system encouraged, cultivated, harvested, and communicated? A practical mechanism should be referred to or specifically outlined in the license agreement.

This is a difficult and delicate area for the franchisor. The franchisor must ensure standardization but also must encourage change. This paradox is resolved by realizing that change will occur but must be managed. Franchising provides the mechanism for the efficient management of change. Customer needs, the legal environment, competition, and most of all the entrepreneurial fervor of franchisees will stretch the envelope of standardization.

Recognizing this, the franchise must provide rules in the license agreement for optimizing efforts in the search for betterment of the system. In franchise systems where the franchisor does not operate a number of company-owned stores, the existing franchise body or representative group should play a part in reviewing and approving issues of product or operational change. These kinds of changes are sometimes covered in the marketing services section of the license agreement.

Marketing, Advertising, and Promotion

This is one of the most sensitive areas in the ongoing franchise relationship. Marketing imprints the trade name and mark in the mind of the consumer. If delivery of the product validates the marketing message, the value of the franchise is enhanced. Store growth increases budgets and spreads marketing costs, optimizing the marketing program for the system.

There are a number of mechanisms to fund and implement a marketing program. Typically, a national advertising fund is controlled by the franchisor. Each franchisee contributes a percentage of top-line sales. The franchisor then produces materials (television, radio, and newspaper ads; direct mail pieces; and point-of-sale materials) and, depending on the size of the fund, buys media time or space. As it is virtually impossible to allocate these services on an exactly equal basis among franchisees, the license agreement will specify the use of "best efforts" to approximate equal treatment, or some such language. "Best efforts" invariably leave some franchisees with a little more and others with a little less advertising. Over time, this should balance but must be carefully monitored.

The second level of marketing, advertising, and promotion in franchising is regional. This is often structured on the basis of an "area of dominant influence," or ADI. All the stores in a given ADI—Greater Hartford, Connecticut, for example—would contribute a percentage of top-line sales to the ADI advertising cooperative. The cooperative's primary function is usually to buy media using franchisor-supplied or -approved advertising and to coordinate regional promotions. If the franchise has a regional advertising cooperative requirement in the license agreement, it should also have standardized ADI cooperative bylaws. These bylaws will outline such things as voting rights and define expenditure parameters. A single-store franchisee can be disadvantaged in a poorly organized cooperative. Conversely, a major contributor to the cooperative may find voting rights disproportionately low.

The final level of advertising is typically dubbed local advertising or local store marketing. At this level the franchisee is contractually required to make direct expenditures on advertising. There is a wide spectrum of permissible advertising expenditures, depending on the franchisor guidelines. However, the license agreement will probably not be specific. Franchisors will try to maintain discretion on this issue for maximum flexibility in the marketplace. Company-owned stores should have advertising requirements equal to those for the franchised units to avoid franchisor free-riding. Historical behavior is the best gauge of reasonableness.

It is important that the franchisor monitor and enforce marketing expenditures. A customer leaving one ADI and entering another will have been affected by the advertising of adjacent regions. Additionally, advertising expenditures not made are marketing impressions lost to the system. The marketing leverage inherent in franchising is thus suboptimized.

Product Purchase Provision

In many franchise systems, a major benefit is bulk buying and inventory control. There are a number of ways to account for this in a license agreement. Most franchisors will not be bound to best-price requirements. Changing markets, competitors, and U.S. antitrust laws make it impossible for the franchisor to ensure this. The franchise should employ a standard of best efforts or good faith to acquire both national and regional product contracts.

Depending on the nature of the product, regional deals might make more sense than national ones. Regional contracts may provide greater advantages to the franchisee because of shipping weight and cost or service needs. The clever franchisor will recognize this. When this is true and the franchisor doesn't act, the franchisees will fill the void. The monthly ADI meeting then becomes an expanded forum. The results of such ad hoc organizations can be reduced control of quality and expansion of franchisee associations outside the confines of the license agreement. Advanced activity of this nature can fractionalize a franchise system or even render the franchisor effectively obsolete. In some cases the franchisor and franchisee-operated buying coops peaceably coexist, acting as competitors and lowering the costs to the operator. However, dual buying coops usually reduce economies of scale and dilute system resources, as well as providing fertile ground for conflict.

For purposes of quality control, the franchisor will reserve the right to publish a product specifications list. The list will very clearly establish the quality standards of raw materials or goods used in the operation. From those specifications a subsequent list of approved suppliers is generated. This list can evolve into a franchise "tying arrangement," which occurs when the business format franchise license agreement binds the franchisee to the purchase of a specifically branded product. This varies from the product specifications list because brand, not product content, is the qualifying specification. The important question here is, does the tying arrangement of franchise and product create an enhancement for the franchisee in the marketplace? If so, then are arm's-length controls in place to ensure that pricing, netted from the enhanced value, will yield positive results? This is impossible to quantify exactly. However, if the tying arrangement is specified in the license agreement, the prospective franchise owner is advised to make a judgment before purchasing the franchise. A franchisor should make a clear distinction of value or abandon the tying arrangement.

Less overt tying arrangements occur when the license agreement calls for an approved suppliers list that ultimately lists only one supplier. If adding suppliers to the list is nearly impossible, there is a de facto tying arrangement. Another tying arrangement occurs when the product specification is written so that only one brand can possibly qualify. A franchisor should disclose any remuneration gained by the franchisor or its officers, directly or indirectly, from product purchase in the franchise system. The market value enhancement test is again proof of a credible arrangement.

The Operations Manual

The business format is documented in a manual or series of manuals. The fact that it is documented should be noted in the license agreement. The operations manual is the heart of the franchise asset, as it delineates the manner in which the trade name and mark are to be delivered to the customer. The franchise purchase should be made on the basis of the business's effectiveness in the marketplace. However, to remain viable, the operations manual must be a dynamic instrument. In 1984 Ray Kroc said, "I don't know what we'll be serving in the year 2000, but I know we'll be serving more of it than anybody else."

The research and development previously discussed must be documented in the operations manual before being implemented. The method of change is crucial to the health of the system, again emphasizing the delicate line between standardization and change. Some license agreements will contain a clause stating that the franchisee must adhere to the operations system as outlined in the "current operations manual," which may change from time to time. Given that the system should change to maintain a competitive advantage, the franchisee must be comfortable that this change will take place for valid commercial reasons and be willing to live with less personal control of the operational techniques.

Specialist Support

The franchisor's organizational design must be congruent with franchisee support needs. If real estate is a system variable, there must be sufficient real estate expertise in the franchisor organization to meet the demand created by the sale of franchises. This should occur in all management disciplines.

Territorial Rights

It is very difficult to establish a protected geographic area that is fair to both the franchisee and the franchisor. Demographics are a constantly evolving factor, and hence the true market area will inevitably change. A territory suitable for one site today may support three sites tomorrow because of a road change or mall development. The newer the franchise system, the more pronounced the problem.

If likely market penetration cannot be judged, then how can geography or customers be allocated? On the sale of a single franchise the address is sometimes the only protected territory. This allows the franchisor to ensure that the market is fully developed, but it provides little protection for the franchisee. When the individual outlet reaches a preestablished market share (measured by sales dollars, customers, or units of output), the franchisor will conclude that customer demand is not being fully met. Its concern is that unfilled customer needs create an opportunity for competition. Because of the market leader's advertising and promotion, a "copycat" operation can propel its startup through the leader's market exposure. Indeed, this is a viable market strategy for some franchisors. Fast-food operators have been known to purposefully locate directly adjacent to the market leader.

One way to handle this problem is to formalize the criteria for market share in an individual location to give the operator the opportunity for a return commensurate with existing franchisees. Penetration within the agreed band of market share for a given period of time triggers the creation of another location for development. The franchisee in the first location has the right of first refusal of the second location. This right may be qualified based on balance sheet and operational standards. This solution allows for the full exploitation of the marketplace, with the performing franchisee having an equally exciting upside.

Related to the territorial issue is the "relocation clause." This item may be separate or contained within the exclusive territory clause, or operations clause. It may give the franchisor the right to compel a franchisee to relocate the business under specific economic or demographic conditions. Typically, a relocation clause is not found in a franchise contract when the franchisee is required to make a real estate investment.

European franchising has considerably different legal considerations. If the franchise company is large enough to affect trade between nations, the European Community competition laws may come into effect. These laws were established to regulate contracts or practices that may be anticompetitive. Exclusive territory agreements are generally barred in the EC. However, block exemptions can be granted, and a properly structured franchise exclusive territory will likely qualify for this exemption.

Term of the Agreement

Generally, the franchise relationship is established on a long-term basis. A 15- or 20-year agreement is normal, but some can be as short as 5 years. The key is renewal rights. If the terms of the agreement have been met, the franchisee may reasonably expect the relationship to continue. In some states the renewal right is legislated, and in others there is legal precedent for court-enforced renewal.

A franchise prospect should be wary of an agreement that does not address renewal. It may be an indicator that the franchisor is predisposed not to grant renewals. Legally enforced renewal will be expensive, or the franchisor may impose substantial renewal fees as a condition for continuing the relationship. Many franchise systems do not have a long history, and renewal is not an easily researched issue. Therefore, it should always be contractually stipulated.

Sale of the Business

The good franchisor spends considerable time establishing the basis for choosing franchisees. It is understandable that they want to have some control over who their partners will be. The franchisee is motivated by the ownership of a business and accruing the benefits of that ownership and, at the end of the experience, a capital gain. All issues regarding control of the sale of the existing franchisee company should be covered in the license agreement. Additionally, the procedure by which the controls are implemented must be clearly defined.

Three other clauses will affect the franchisee's ability to sell the business.

1. Right of first refusal—Some license agreements give the franchisor this right. If so, the price should be equal to or a premium of the bona fide third-party offer. A right of first refusal will typically hinder a sale. The prospective buyer may not be willing to spend time or money on a deal that might be pulled out from under him by the franchisor—hence the premium requirement.

2. Buyout formula—At the beginning of the franchise relationship the franchisor has an advantage in understanding the ultimate value of a successful franchisee company. Franchisors have been known to set a buyout formula in the license agreement.
3. License agreement—Some agreements call for the buyer of an existing franchise to sign the "then current form of license agreement." Of course, the new franchisee has no way of knowing what future changes will be incorporated, and the franchisee is not bound to modify his license. Therefore, the value of the franchisee company in the marketplace can be significantly altered by a unilateral decision of the franchisor. The value will, of course, be diminished if the new form of agreement changes the fee structure, institutes tying arrangements, or modifies the protected territory or term.

Death or Incapacity of the Franchisee

Most license agreements are signed personally. This generally means that the franchisee must devote all or a majority of her professional life to operating the franchise. Also, the economics of the relationship are guaranteed by the individual(s) who sign the license agreement. Usually, the personal attention of the franchisee is impossible to monitor. However, upon death or disability the franchisee or his estate may be forced into an uneconomic sale of the company or even the loss of the franchise rights. The proper stipulation is for the franchisor to render short-term assistance in operating the franchise (for a fee) until it is sold or transferred to a qualified heir.

Arbitration

The cost of litigation is often too high for a single-outlet operator to bear. The franchisor will sometimes exclude an arbitration clause because it may afford a small franchisee the opportunity to air a grievance and receive redress she otherwise might not be granted. Conversely, such a clause reduces the likelihood of petty arguments. Arbitration is done in private proceedings with an issue judged by an individual who usually has special knowledge of the subject in dispute. Arbitration can be binding or nonbinding. It is usually to the advantage of the smaller franchisee but is gaining support among franchisors also.

License Agreement Termination

Issues of default must be specifically delineated in this section. Important is a reasonable right to remedy a default, provided the breaches are not recurring. Termination means that the franchisee must cease using the trade name and mark, and other property rights of the franchisor. Practically, this means taking down the sign, changing the name of the operation, and returning all manuals and marketing and promotional materials.

In some cases, the franchisor will tie the property lease to the license agreement. Termination of one can mean voiding of the other. This tie can occur even when the franchisor does not own the property vis-à-vis an "assignment and assumption" agreement. This agreement is signed as an addendum to the lease and states that the termination of the license agreement triggers the right, but not obligation, of the franchisor to assume the franchisee's position in a lease. The lessor must be a party to the assignment for it to be valid.

NONCONTRACTUAL CONSIDERATIONS OF BUYING A FRANCHISE

Financial Analysis

The dream of entrepreneurship can become a nightmare if your financial well-being is threatened. An advantage of franchising is a track record that can be scrutinized. The prospect can and should make an in-depth analysis of the offered franchise. The franchisor is wise to package the offering in a manner that assists this due diligence. The franchisor who demonstrates a keen financial understanding gains a pricing advantage in the franchise sales marketplace, attracts a more sophisticated franchisee, and offers that franchisee an advantage in the capital marketplace.

U.S. law requires franchisors to disclose pertinent details of the offering. The federal requirement is fulfilled through the Uniform Franchise Offering Circular (UFOC), which is filed with the Federal Trade Commission and is a matter of public record. The UFOC must be given to the franchisee the sooner of 10 days prior to the franchisor's accepting a fee or the first personal meeting. Many states have similar but usually more stringent disclosure requirements.

A vast majority of franchisors adhere to disclosure laws. A franchise search that reveals the slightest deviation from FTC or state rules should be abandoned. The disclosure will have pro forma financials based on actual franchisee experience. These are not designed to apply to any individual investment; they are an average of the composite operations. Assuredly, the new operator will find variances in the actual statements from the disclosure pro formas. The next sections focus on the areas of likely variance.

Estimating Startup Costs/Initial Investment

If there is a real estate component to the franchise, it is often treated as a lease or rental and not included in the startup calculation. If owning the real estate is a part of the franchisee's strategic plan, it must be accounted for separately from the franchise investment. The basics included in this section are leasehold improvements, furniture and fixtures, machinery and equipment, and tools. Even so-called turnkey arrangements will have some startup expense associated with the leasehold interest. Equipment can sometimes be leased also. This is especially true in restaurant franchises.

Low initial investment may dramatically affect operating expenses. A lease is simply a way to leverage your startup cost. Startup losses should be funded in the initial capitalization but are not always included in the disclosure. Assume a worst-case scenario. Even in franchising, undercapitalization is a major reason for failure.

Calculating Profit and Loss/Income Statement

All the numbers should be adjusted by the prospective franchisee to reflect the realities of the area where operation is planned. For example, New York City will be more expensive to operate in than Pocatello, Idaho, but income will probably be higher also. Decisions about owner's compensation should be incorporated into the pro forma (or into the cash-flow projections, discussed later). The disclosure will typically show the average manager's compensation, and not any remuneration to the franchisee. The franchisor will assume the franchisee is the manager. If the ownership of the franchised company is spread over more than one individual, the issue of compensation is best answered up front.

Remember the discussion of lease versus buy. If leasing is the leverage decision, its costs should be incorporated here. Also, a disclosure pro forma may not include interest payments. The franchisor takes the position that capitalization methods vary so dramatically as to render an average impractical.

Another item sometimes neglected in pro forma projections is depreciation and amortization. These noncash items represent the cost to the business of the decreasing value of fixed assets. Understanding depreciation and amortization will allow for better pricing decisions and more accurate calculation of profit margins.

Pro forma income statements are often annualized. The ramping up of sales and the accrual of expenses on a *monthly* basis will prove invaluable in the first year of operation. Many financial institutions require 36 months of pro forma statements. Although some franchisors will generate or help generate the additional monthly projections, many will reasonably avoid this out of fear of misleading a franchisee and incurring some liability. What a franchisee sees as help in the startup may be remembered as a promise years later, especially in a courtroom setting.

Constructing a Balance Sheet

The long-term health of a franchisee company can be significantly aided by constructing a strong opening balance sheet. Too often small businesses focus solely on the income statement and ignore the balance sheet. Business format franchises are heavily weighted in the service and particularly retail segments of the economy. Strong understanding of working capital management in a retail environment, depending on the business, can mean advantageous supplier terms along with cash payments from customers. This may provide you with significant short-term leverage. As with the income statement, franchising gives you the unique opportunity to use pertinent historical data in the balance sheet to lay a sound foundation in your company through proper capitalization.

There is a whole series of financial ratios that should be constructed for the ideally positioned franchisee company. In general, everyone should be aware of liquidity, capital, debt, and trade ratios as they apply to the franchisee requirements. In theory, liquidity is measured to assess a company's ability to generate operating capital or meet sudden credit demands. The level of optimal liquidity varies dramatically by industry. Franchising allows you to know the details and risks prior to startup, and the astute franchisor will make this analysis readily available. The Initial Investment section of the UFOC, modified for your specific needs, will define your capital requirement but will not specify the form of capital. Use historical numbers from the franchisor to generate stability ratios to help answer this question. This is particularly important if there is a tying arrangement in the franchise, even if the arrangement is informal. Also, when the franchisor is a key supplier, inventory estimates will be very precise. However, conflicts of interest by the franchisor should be carefully avoided, such as excessive startup inventory requirements.

Cash-Flow Projections

Happiness is a positive cash flow no matter what commercial vehicle you choose. However, profitability does not equate to positive cash flow; a profitable business can suffocate and fail due to insufficient cash flow. Cash-flow projection should also be done on a 36-month basis to match the income statement and balance sheet pro forma. Often omitted in the franchisor's cash-flow projection will be the prospect's franchise search cost, professional consultant expense, and the site search and acquisition costs. Failure to consider these will strangle cash flow even before startup.

Financing a Franchise

Financing requirements for a franchise are no different than for any other business startup. Acquisition or alteration of business premises, fittings and fixtures, machinery and equipment, and working capital are all included in the list. Cash flow shortages due to business cycle may be added later. The advantage of franchise financing is the added variable of the franchisee. The franchisor packages a proven product and business methods. The franchisee is a "partner" in the deal who brings additional capital and entrepreneurial commitment. This should provide greater comfort to the financing institution. Properly exhibiting the transferability of the success factors is the principle function of the loan request. Existing operations that are profitable makes access to a lender's ear easier.

A franchisor will systematically meet with large banks to help build confidence in the concept and clear initial hurdles for franchisees. Structuring a debt proposal should utilize much of the due diligence included in the franchise search. In general, the franchise system and the outlets operating in it should be presented both as an integrated organization and as a stand-alone operation. This will promote the franchisee as one who is independently capable of success but whose prospects are dramatically enhanced by being a part of a system. A banker will likely define the long run as the amount of time debt is outstanding. If the successful operation of the franchise system exceeds the term of the loan, the lender will have a higher comfort level.

From the franchisee's perspective, a franchise is a risk management tool. The increased prospects for success will allow for a more secure loan for the bank. Examples of the franchise system's changing to meet the demands of the marketplace will be helpful in projecting future success. The franchisor's organizational chart and support role is appropriate material to review with a banker. It gives depth to the not-as-yet-operating franchisee organization, an advantage the solo startup doesn't have. Pressing the franchise advantage at startup might yield a more competitive loan and more serviceable debt, compounding the advantage over the nonfranchised competitor. Even with these advantages, the personal commitment of the franchisee in the form of cash invested in the business is inevitably required. The financial analysis done in the investigative stage will be helpful in the search for capital. For the purposes of securing debt, add the proposed loan and subsequent debt service to the projections.

The terms in the loan will vary by specific business, franchisor strength, franchisee strength, and general economic conditions. Loans for the substantiated initial investment can run as high as 80%, but 50% to 67% is more likely. Machinery and equipment will have a 3- to 7-year term with a corresponding amortization. The franchisor can help boost the loan-to-value ratio if a market for used machinery and equipment can be demonstrated. Real estate will likely have a 3- to 5-year term with a 15- to 20-year amortization. A few franchisors will provide some financing, and a few more will assist in placing debt. However, a franchisor should not be expected to be a vehicle for acquiring capital.

A problem the franchisor must be cognizant of is franchisee underinvestment. Many franchisees are required to invest a substantial portion of their wealth in the franchise. Theoretically, this could result in a burdensome risk perspective that might cause the franchisee to pass on a favorable opportunity. Franchisee underinvestment is interwoven with the issue of protected territory and expansion rights. Some franchisors include expansion requirements where rights are given. This is especially true when a geographic territory is sold to a franchisee. Often a development schedule is agreed on in advance. Failure of the franchisee to build out the territory under the terms of the agreement (sometimes called an "area development agreement") results in loss of the exclusivity.

HOW SELLING A FRANCHISE IS REGULATED

The United States has an extensive statutory regulatory system governing franchising. In essence, the sale of a franchise is subject to the same scrutiny as the sale of a security. On the federal level, the government mandates extensive disclosure through the Uniform Franchise Offering Circular, developed by the American Securities Administrators Organization. The document must include a copy of the license agreement, an area development agreement if applicable, and a laundry list of standard disclosure items.

Details of the costs and ongoing payments and product tying arrangements follow. Typically, the document opens with a narrative description of the franchise. The franchisor must also list details concerning litigation, bankruptcy and store transfer, acquisition, and termination. There is also a summary of the franchisee's responsibilities and the services provided by the franchisor. There is usually a pro forma compilation of financial statements taken from franchise operating histories. If the UFOC does not present financial information, any statement about the economics of the franchise by the franchisor must be disclosed to the prospective franchisee in an "earnings claim document." If the claims are made in a public fashion, such as in the newspaper, then the earnings claim document is required regardless of UFOC content and use.

The franchisor is required to file the UFOC with the Federal Trade Commission. Any change to the license agreement or any executory document must be filed at least five days prior to signing. The prospective franchisee is asked to sign a receipt for the UFOC, which the franchisor keeps on file. Although the FTC dictates disclosure requirements, it does not editorialize or approve the quality of the content.

A number of state governments have passed legislation specific to franchising that also requires a disclosure document. Financial and termination disclosure is often more extensive than under federal requirements. Franchisors face a morass of complicated laws and must be mindful of the legal costs when contemplating a national expansion program.

LIMITATIONS OF FRANCHISING

The franchisor must recognize that "equity" in the business is being sold when a franchise is sold. Rapid growth and a highly motivated management team are born, but a partner, not an employee, is created. That partner, the franchisee, will risk time, energy, and capital and will expect a return. Because of the long-term nature of the license agreement, the franchisor is bound to this partnership for many years. Anyone who considers expansion through franchising must understand that the benefits of a "system" must endure the test of time.

Sources of Conflict

As a part of understanding the implications of franchising, one should note the potential sources of conflict in the relationship. As discussed, the franchisor builds a prototype operation, completes system documentation, establishes support overhead, complies with regulatory requirements, and then sells the first franchise. Typically, a large amount of capital has been used before any franchise fees or royalties are received. Therefore, a high percentage of the franchisor's costs are necessarily fixed. As the system of franchisees and outlets grow, the franchisor's costs are spread over an increasing base. The average cost to the franchisor for providing services per franchisee decreases as the number of outlets increases.

On the revenue side, the franchisor is motivated to maximize system sales. The franchisor's continuing income is derived from franchisee royalty payments, a percentage of top-line outlet sales paid to the franchisor. System growth in terms of the number of outlets and individual outlet sales results in higher franchisor revenue applied against lower per-unit support costs.

The franchisee, on the other hand, aspires to achieve optimal unit sales (not necessarily maximum sales) to maximize profit. An important aspect of optimal sales is the optimal number of outlets in the market (again, not necessarily the maximum). The franchisee's operating model has more variable expense than the franchisor's. The implication is that there may be sensitive discussion in the areas of pricing, promotion, and the development of outlets. The potential for conflict is exacerbated by the phenomenon of larger, more sophisticated franchisees. With today's heightened level of competition in the marketplace, franchisees are necessarily more educated, with more capital, entrepreneurial drive, and organizational skills, and are capable of building fully integrated companies.

Inefficient Investment

Especially in single-outlet franchise systems, the franchisee is investing a high proportion of personal wealth in the venture. This is opposed to the large operation, where one additional store does not consume a majority of ownership capital. Therefore, such a franchisee might be excessively risk-averse when facing a large capital outlay. The investment might be forgone, creating an opportunity for the competition or simply suboptimizing the system potential.

SUMMARY

Franchising might best be described as the combination of a unique association of corporate organizations and a unique form of raising capital. For franchising to work best, the franchisor and franchisee goals must be congruent. The relationship must be highly interactive and dynamic. Although the license agreement is the focal point of franchising, if it is strictly interpreted, the probability of conflict being resolved through litigation is heightened. The franchise system that understands that interdependence is a reality has a higher probability of optimizing return.

13 HARVESTING

William Petty

The year was 1981. It had been 15 years since Bill and Frances Griffin had started their single restaurant establishment. They now had a chain of 84 restaurants throughout Texas, Oklahoma, Arkansas, and Colorado; the one in Colorado had revenues exceeding those of any other restaurant in the state. Amazingly, all 84 units were profitable. Bill and Frances had started the company largely on borrowed money to finance one small restaurant in Texas. For the first seven years, the couple worked seven days a week to make a go of the business. By 1981 revenues were in excess of $50 million.

On several occasions they had been approached by other companies or individuals interested in buying the Griffins' business. Bill was always willing to listen, saying that he invariably learned something about his company in the process. However, he had no interest in selling. In 1981 a firm from England approached him about selling his company. After several meetings, they offered the Griffins $32 million for the company, and they asked Bill to stay on as president to run the company for at least five more years. Faced with such an offer, the Griffins decided to sell their company. The date was set for the closing. The Griffins went to London, signed the papers, and collected their money.

The day after the sale, the Griffins flew back to the States. On the return trip, Bill began having some regrets for selling his business. By the time he arrived in New York, he was convinced that he had made a big mistake. Instead of continuing the trip home to Texas, the Griffins stayed in New York for the night. The next day they caught the first flight to England for the purpose of buying back their company. They offered to pay $1 million for the buyer to cancel the contract, but the acquiring company had no interest in selling. The Griffins returned home, but instead of feeling a sense of accomplishment, they felt mostly disappointed for no longer owning their business.

Today, over 10 years later, the Griffins still regret selling their company. They feel it is the greatest mistake they have ever made. They had spent 15 years developing and growing the company into what they wanted it to be, only to lose it. The money, though nice, became a burden in one way. Managing the money was not nearly as enjoyable to them as managing the company. Although they had envisioned the good they could do with the money, they had not fully realized how much good they were doing through their company. In their eyes, they had lost their "base" for accomplishing many things they wanted to do, both within and outside of the company. To make matters even worse, they soon discovered that they had significant philosophical differences with the buyer in terms of how to run a business—differences that to them were not merely opinion or judgment, but matters of principle. Within two years, the Griffins left the firm in search of a new opportunity, which they eventually found, but still with deep regrets for having abandoned their "child."

Another entrepreneur, the owner of a successful sunglasses company, had the opportunity to sell his firm but decided not to do so. At the time, he did not believe the offering price was adequate. Since that time, the industry has become increasingly competitive, almost to the point of being brutal, and he now regrets not selling. He no longer finds running the company to be fun, and there are other things he would like to do. However, because the industry is in a slump, there is not the opportunity to sell on terms as favorable as had existed earlier. The window of opportunity appears to have closed, at least for the time being.

Both of these stories, which were real events, have something to say to us in our study of entrepreneurship. They occur more frequently than you might expect. There is a real chance that an entrepreneur will be disappointed with the final phase of the investment process, which comes when he tries to harvest the venture. In the first case, the Griffins did achieve the harvest, and in a way many of us would consider totally successful. However, for them, the outcome proved to be a disappointment. The second entrepreneur failed to realize the harvest opportunity when it was within reach, and later regretted letting it slip through his hands. The moral of the story: An entrepreneur needs to understand the *why* and *when* of the harvest. For the venture to be ultimately successful in the eyes of the entrepreneur, there must be an effective and rewarding end. Stated a bit differently by some anonymous wizard, "Getting into a deal is a cinch, compared to getting out."

This chapter is devoted to an examination of the final outcome, often called the harvest. The chapter covers three issues:

- The need for a *strategy* in harvesting the opportunity
- The *financial value* of the harvest
- *Options available* for harvesting a company

THE NEED FOR A HARVEST STRATEGY

In formulating a strategy for harvesting a business opportunity, we should first clarify exactly what is meant by the term *harvest*. The harvest is the owners' and investors' strategy for achieving the terminal after-tax cash flows on their investment. It does not necessarily mean that the entrepreneur will leave the company; it merely defines how she will extract some or all of the cash flows from the investment to be used for other purposes. Nor should it totally disregard the personal and nonfinancial aspects of the transaction.

The harvest could involve selling the company for cash, or it could mean intentionally not growing the firm and instead using the cash flows generated by the business for personal needs. Likewise, a harvest can provide some of the managers who have been impact players in the venture with the opportunity to buy all or part of the founder's ownership in the company. Thus, harvests come in many forms, allowing the entrepreneur and the investors to achieve their respective goals.

Steven Covey, in his book *The Seven Habits of Highly Effective People*, says that one of the keys to being effective in life is "beginning with the end in mind."[1] According to Covey, we should visualize the end and then develop a plan to make it happen. Although Covey is speaking of one's personal life, the statement is also true with respect to a venture. If the entrepreneur is to take full advantage of an investment opportunity, it is essential not only to evaluate the merits of the opportunity at the outset, but also to anticipate the options for exiting the business. If the entrepreneur's goal with the venture is only to provide a living, then the exit or harvest strategy is of no concern. But if the goal is to create value for the owners and the other stakeholders in the company, a harvest strategy is absolutely mandatory. Then the exit becomes more than simply leaving a company; it is the final piece necessary in creating the *ultimate value to all the participants in the venture*, especially the owners, managers, and employees.

Harvesting the venture brings both excitement and trepidation to most entrepreneurs, particularly if it takes the form of going public or being acquired by another firm or a private investment group. Few events in the life of the entrepreneurial firm, as well as in the life of the entrepreneur, are more significant. Even so, many entrepreneurs refuse to think about the harvesting of their company. They simply choose to ignore the issue, assuming that there will be ample time to make such decisions later on. Besides, who can predict how it will all end? They contend that attention needs to be focused on the daily operations and growing of the company, not on some distant event that may or may not occur. Despite such an attitude, the fact remains that few events will have a greater personal and financial effect on the entrepreneur's life as the harvesting of the company. Thus, an understanding of the different aspects of a harvest is no small matter for the entrepreneur.

The harvest is also of prime importance to outside investors. Such investors typically have a priori expectations about their investment that include the firm's either going public or being acquired by other investors.[2] The investors, be they professional venture capitalists or private informal investors, have an obvious interest in the exit mechanism used to liquidate their investment. Though the harvest will not have the same personal significance to the firm's investors as it does to the entrepreneur, its effectiveness will in large part determine the after-tax cash flows to be received, which in turn determine the return earned on their investment. For an investor there is no issue more important than the rate of return. This rate is the driving force for most, if not all, of the investor's decisions.

Whatever the final decision by the entrepreneur and others regarding the harvest strategy, several words of advice and caution are appropriate.

Set Personal Goals and Objectives

For most entrepreneurs, the company is a dominant part of their lives. Thus, the decision to harvest a venture cannot effectively be made apart from the entrepreneur's personal goals and objectives. Without an understanding of what is important in his life, the entrepreneur is apt to make a bad decision when it comes to harvesting a firm.

Plan Your Exit and Harvest Strategy

The time will come when the entrepreneur will need to harvest the venture. The circumstances will differ from case to case, but it will happen, sooner or later. Ignoring this eventuality will most likely cause problems, either for the entrepreneur or for other family members. Mistakes will be made either because of a lack of forethought or because of lost opportunities.

Work to Anticipate the Consequences of Decisions Made Today on the Ability to Harvest the Firm in the Future

In the event the firm is successful, thereby creating value for its owners, you want to maximize the chance that the value created can be effectively harvested. For example, you would not want to make any decision today that might preclude harvest options in the future. Sahlman illustrates this point well:

Some startup companies raise capital from a major participant in the industry. Although doing so may provide necessary capital and some expertise or marketing, it may also mean that no other large competitor of the original founder will even consider an offer later on. A startup can thus lose the option to market the company to the highest bidder in the industry.[3]

Keep in Mind that the Window of Opportunity for Harvesting a Venture Can Open and Close Quickly

Opportunities to sell or take the company public come and go with the conditions of the economy and the industry. One of the most striking examples of the window of opportunity closing occurred in the late 1980s. A young entrepreneur specializing in land speculation in the northern part of the Dallas metropolitan area developed a net worth exceeding $30 million. Only 28, he had accomplished this feat in a matter of four years. He had started with a small amount of capital but with a willingness to take risks and work hard. However, his business depended totally on the ability to borrow the money to do the deals. He had developed good relationships with several savings and loan institutions that were ready to loan him money. A single event changed everything. One afternoon the federal regulators told the S&Ls they were not to make any more real estate loans. The debt markets that provided the financing for these deals evaporated in a matter of hours. The market for land speculation was killed instantly. The young man lost all of his holdings in a matter of months, barely avoiding bankruptcy.

Don't Harvest Too Soon

Although it is good to be sensitive to the opening and closing of a window of opportunity, it is also wise to be patient. It usually requires at least 7 to 10 years for a company to develop to a point that allows the founders and early investors to realize attractive returns on their investment. Rarely does a company allow the entrepreneur the opportunity to get rich quickly. It generally takes longer than expected to develop the sales base needed to create sustainable firm value, which is the key for an attractive harvest opportunity.

Beware of the "Experts"

Advisors, especially those whose income depends on your firm being sold or taken public, can develop biased perspectives, sometimes to your detriment. These advisors provide a useful service in the right situation, but their advice needs to be balanced with that of others who have been through the same process. Seek out other entrepreneurs who have gone through the "rapids" of harvesting a venture. Also, where possible, use advisors whose fee is not based on a deal being consummated, but who get paid regardless of the outcome.

Make Certain that All the Players in the Venture Have the Same Vision for the Harvest Strategy

One entrepreneur who had raised $5 million in venture capital had always conceived of "his" company being acquired by one of the larger players in the industry. The only problem was his failure to convince the venture capitalists of the merits of an acquisition. They believed a public offering would be in their best interest. The entrepreneur was unrelenting in the matter. He was determined to be acquired. Without a word of warning, the venture capitalists appeared at the business one morning, informing the entrepreneur that he was no longer in charge. They were exercising their right to remove him as president. He had antagonized them one too many times. Even though they did not own a majority of shares in the business, the terms of their agreement specified that they could replace the president at will.

Plan Your Harvest Carefully

In conclusion, let there be little doubt as to the importance of achieving an effective harvest strategy. Ignoring the issue or making bad decisions in this regard can have significantly detrimental consequences, both financially and personally. Much of the strategy for harvesting a venture depends on the assessment of the value of the company. Thus, we will next consider some of the basics in valuing a firm.

VALUING THE HARVEST OPPORTUNITY

Valuing a firm is a difficult assignment, especially when the stock is not traded in the marketplace. The academic community assumes that markets are efficient, meaning that the price of a company's stock reflects all available information about the company. Although market efficiency has been the source of much disagreement between the academician and the practitioner, it is not an issue here. When it comes time to develop a harvest strategy for the entrepreneur and the early investors, there is seldom an established market for the firm's securities. Consequently, you will be trying to value an asset for which a great amount of incomplete and conflicting information exists. Nevertheless, the effectiveness of the harvest strategy depends to a significant extent on your valuation of the opportunity.

The Internal Revenue Service is one of several government agencies interested in the valuing of businesses. Frequently the need arises to value a company for tax purposes. Based on its experience at the task, the IRS believes that the value of a company is affected by a combination of factors, including the following:

- The history and nature of the business
- The economic outlook for the company, as well as for the specific industry
- The book value of the equity and the financial condition of the business
- The firm's earning capacity
- The company's dividend-paying capacity
- The value of intangible assets, such as goodwill
- Any prior sales of the firm's stock
- The market value of firms in the same or a similar line of business, whose stocks are traded actively in a free and established market
- Whether the stock being valued represents a majority or a minority interest in the firm

Although the preceding information may provide insight in a general sense, it provides no framework for actually estimating a firm's value. The possible approaches for determining a company's value are legion. For example, one accountant at a big six accounting firm, whose job it is to value companies, suggested that over 300 possible configurations can be used in valuing a company. Obviously, this chapter could not begin to describe each wrinkle and twist that can be used in valuing a firm. Instead, the following sections describe the basic ways to study the problem, because all 300 techniques (or however many there are) come from one of four fundamental perspectives, or some combination thereof:

- Asset-based valuation
- Market-comparable valuation
- Earning-capitalization valuation
- The present value of the firm's future cash flows

Asset-Based Valuation

The asset-based approach assumes that the value of a firm can be determined by examining the value of the underlying assets of the business. Automobile dealerships, for example, are often valued using an asset-based approach, which essentially lists the accounts receivable, inventories, and plant and equipment and assigns a value to each.

There are three variations of this approach:

- Modified book value—This method uses the book value of the asset, as shown in the balance sheet, and adjusts this value to reflect any obvious differences between the historical cost of an asset and its current value. For instance, for marketable securities held by the firm, market value may be totally different from the historical book value. The same may be true for real estate.

- Replacement value—This method attempts to determine what it would cost to replace each of the firm's assets.
- Liquidation value—This method estimates the amount of money that could be received if the firm ended its operations and liquidated the individual assets. One entrepreneur who had the opportunity to acquire a competing firm valued the company based solely on a conservative estimate of the liquidation value of the accounts receivable and inventories. However, he was interested not so much in knowing the firm's value as he was in acquiring product at a bargain price.

The asset-based approaches are not particularly attractive from a conceptual basis, nor are they very accurate on a practical basis. *Historical costs* from the balance sheet typically bear little relationship to the *current value* of the assets. The book value of an asset was never intended to measure the firm's current value. Making some adjustments may be better than no recognition at all of the inherent weakness of asset-based valuation, but it is still building an estimate of value on a bad foundation. Also, all three techniques fail to recognize the firm as a going concern. The use of asset-based valuation is similar to using the conventional payback period in capital budgeting. We know its weaknesses, but we still calculate it just to be "comfortable." It's like an old habit that is hard to break. The only possible exceptions to this criticism are firms in the natural resources industry or the securities industry.

Market-Comparable Valuation

The market-comparable approach uses the market prices of "comparable" companies as the basis for valuing the equity of a given firm that is not traded publicly. After comparable companies are found (which is no easy task in itself), the price-earnings ratios or the market-to-book-value ratios for these companies are computed. These ratios are then applied to the earnings and equity book value of the firm to be valued.

The reliability of this approach depends in part on the frequency and amount of shares being traded in the "comparable" firms and the extent to which the trades are arm's-length transactions. Market quotes of thinly traded shares can be misleading, as can trades between insiders of closely held firms. More often, you must look at the market prices of "similar" companies and then subjectively adjust the price estimate, given the uniqueness of the situation. Also, the mere fact that you are comparing companies that are traded publicly with one that is not tells you that the situations are not fully comparable. Thus, it is common practice to discount the nontraded stock for its lack of marketability, sometimes by as much as 50%, which suggests that there is considerable subjectivity in the process.

Also, you may need to make some adjustment depending on whether you are valuing a controlling interest of the business or only a minority share of the firm. Because minority shares cannot control the firm's policies, a discount is often assigned to these shares vis-à-vis majority shares.

The issues of marketability and controlling interest aside, this approach can rarely be applied with total confidence. Even in the best of situations, you will probably have difficulty isolating a company that is comparable in every way. It is not enough simply to find a firm in the same industry, although that might provide a rough approximation. You need to find a company that is in the same or a similar type of business and that has similar growth rates, financial structure, asset turnover ratios, and operating profit margins. All too frequently, you just have to do your best and use a lot of judgment.

Case Study

Let's look at an example of this valuation approach. Assume that the Aberdeen Corporation has earnings after tax of $80,000 and its equity book value is $440,000. There are 40,000 shares outstanding. Also, the company has $400,000 in outstanding debt. You are interested in knowing a fair price for the company in anticipation of choosing among several alternative harvest strategies. You have located a comparable firm that sells publicly for $20 per share with earnings per share of $2.50. It has an equity book value per share of $12. Given this information, you would estimate Aberdeen's equity value, both in total and on a per-share basis, and the firm's total value, which equals the value of the debt plus the value of the equity. The process is as follows:

1. Calculate the price-earnings ratio and the market-to-book-value ratio for the comparable company:

$$\text{Price-earnings ratio} = \frac{\$20}{\$2.50} = 8$$

$$\text{Market-to-book} = \frac{\$20}{\$12} = 1.6667$$

2. Use the price-earnings ratio of the comparable company to calculate Aberdeen's equity value:

$$\text{Price-earnings ratio} = \frac{\text{Price per share} \times \text{Number of shares}}{\text{Earnings per share} \times \text{Number of shares}}$$

$$= \frac{\text{Total equity market price}}{\text{Total earnings}} = 8$$

Given Aberdeen's earnings of \$80,000,

$$\frac{\text{Total equity market price}}{\$80,000} = 8$$

Thus,

$$\text{Total equity market price} = \$80,000 \times 8 = \$640,000$$

The equity value per share would then be \$16:

$$\frac{\text{Total equity value}}{\text{Number of shares}} = \frac{\$640,000}{40,000} = \$16$$

3. Compute the total value of the firm:

$$\begin{aligned}\text{Total value of the firm} &= \text{Total equity value} + \text{Value of debt}\\ &= \$640,000 + \$400,000\\ &= \$1,040,000\end{aligned}$$

4. Alternatively, use the market-to-book-value ratio to compute Aberdeen's equity value:

$$\frac{\text{Total equity market price}}{\text{Total equity book value}} = 1.6667$$

Given Aberdeen's equity book value of \$440,000,

$$\frac{\text{Total equity market price}}{\$440,000} = 1.6667$$

Thus,

$$\text{Total equity market price} = \$440,000 \times 1.6667 = \$733,333$$

The equity value per share would then be \$18.33:

$$\frac{\text{Total equity value}}{\text{Number of shares}} = \frac{\$733,333}{40,000} = \$18.33$$

5. Compute the total value of the firm:

$$\begin{aligned}\text{Total value of the firm} &= \text{Total equity value} + \text{Value of debt}\\ &= \$733,333 + \$400,000\\ &= \$1,133,333\end{aligned}$$

Thus, Aberdeen's firm value would be approximated at \$1,040,000 using the price-to-earnings ratio of a comparable firm and \$1,133,333 if you use the market-to-book relationship of the comparable firm. These values would be the starting point for determining your firm's value; you would then have to make adjustments for such things as the lack of marketability of the Aberdeen stock.

Earnings-Capitalization Valuation

Different procedures are used in capitalizing a company's earnings to find its value, but the underlying concept is the same: Determine "normalized earnings" and capitalize this amount at some rate of return, called the *capitalization rate.* Typically, this rate is determined by some rule of thumb based on conventional wisdom and the experience of the person doing the valuation. For instance, if you believe that the "normal earnings after tax" for a company are $100,000, and you use a 12.5% capitalization rate, you would value the firm's equity at $800,000, calculated as follows:

$$\text{Firm value} = \frac{\text{Normalized earnings after taxes}}{\text{Capitalization rate}}$$

$$= \frac{\$100{,}000}{.125} = \$800{,}000$$

In using the earnings-capitalization technique, there are two essential questions to answer:

1. What earnings should you use?
2. How do you determine the appropriate capitalization rate?

In selecting the earnings to capitalize, all kinds of approaches are taken.

- Some use the most recent earnings.
- Others take next year's expected earnings.
- Others compute the average earnings of the last five years.
- Still others use a weighted average of the last five years, where the more recent years receive the greater weights.

Whatever convention is used, the objective is to use some figure that is representative of the firm's expected earnings.

Using the earnings-capitalization technique also requires that you decide on a capitalization rate befitting the situation. Some think of the capitalization rate as a discount rate. Although it may seem like a discount rate used to find the present value of future cash flow streams, it is not. It is true that a similar equation is used when you value a stream of equal cash flows, each year (an annuity) expected to continue in perpetuity. However, a discount rate is used to value a *stream of future cash flows*, whereas a capitalization rate is used for a *single-point estimate of earnings* to determine value.

Despite some concern regarding the earnings-capitalization approach to valuation, it is popular with practitioners. As such, you should understand the rationale for how the capitalization rate is determined. Here are some general principles.

- There is an inverse relationship between value and the capitalization rate—that is, given the earnings to be capitalized, the higher (lower) the capitalization rate, the lower (higher) the value. In that regard, it is like a discount rate.
- You would increase the capitalization rate, and therefore lower value, as the riskiness of the income stream is perceived to be greater—as you would with a discount rate.
- The capitalization rate is reduced, and value is increased, as growth prospects in future earnings are greater. That is, you would use a lower capitalization rate for a high-growth firm than for a low-growth company.

In this way, you may think of the capitalization rate as equivalent to the discount rate less the expected growth rate in the future income stream, which is similar to valuing a cash flow stream that is expected to grow at a constant rate in perpetuity.

The fundamental problem with this approach lies in using *earnings* as the item to be valued rather than *cash flows*. Despite conventional wisdom in the popular press, the marketplace values a firm based on future cash flows, not on reported earnings. The valuation of a firm is just too complex to be captured in a single earnings figure. For one thing, there are simply too many ways that a firm's earnings can be affected favorably through generally accepted accounting techniques, but that have no effect on future cash flows or, even worse, may result in reduced cash flows. Thus, the market much prefers to think of a firm's value as the present value of its future cash flows, and not as some multiple of earnings. The next section considers how you would value a firm based on future cash flows.

Free Cash Flow Valuation

The present value of a firm's cash flows represents the heart of its intrinsic or economic value. This method of valuation may be stated as follows: Find the present value of the firm's expected "free cash flows," using the company's cost of capital as the discount rate.

Measuring Free Cash Flows

Free cash flows are those generated from a firm's operations that are available for distributing to all the firm's investors, both debt and equity.[4] Free cash flows are important because it is these cash flows that may be used to satisfy the investor's rates of return.

You would measure a firm's free cash flows in year t, FCF_t, as follows:

Free cash flows = Operating income
− Taxes on operating income (tax rate × operating income)
+ Depreciation and other noncash charges
− Increase in net working capital during the year
− Capital expenditures for the year, both for replacement investments and for investments required to support growth in the company's sales

Determining the Value of the Free Cash Flows

To value a firm's future free cash flows (and thereby value the firm itself), you project future cash flows and then determine the present values of these flows. You could conceivably do as one Japanese firm reportedly does: Develop a strategic plan for 250 years, estimate the expected cash flows, and then find the present value of these amounts. Alternatively, you should:

1. Decide on a planning period, preferably one that approximates the expected duration of any competitive advantage that the firm enjoys. Within this time period, the firm should expect to earn rates of returns from its investments in excess of its cost of capital.
2. Make assumptions about the cash flow stream beyond the planning horizon, such as assuming that the cash flows will continue in perpetuity, either as an annuity or increasing at a constant rate each year.
3. Assume that there is a relationship between future growth in sales and increasing asset requirements. To project future asset requirements as sales increase, you might rely on the historical relationships of assets to sales.

You then find the present value of the free cash flows during the planning period and the present value of the cash flows beyond the planning horizon (the residual value), and then sum these two values to estimate the present value of all future free cash flows. That is, the present value of the free cash flows from operations would be the sum

Present value of Planning-period cash flows + Present value of Residual value

where the present value, PV, of the planning-period cash flows (FCF_t) through year T is

$$PV = \sum_{t=1}^{T} \frac{FCF_t}{(1 + K)^t}$$

where K is the discount rate, or the firm's cost of capital.

To find the value of the residual cash flow stream beginning in year $T + 1$ and continuing in perpetuity, you must make an assumption about the growth rate of these future cash flows. If you assume that the cash flows beginning in year $T + 1$ will increase at a constant growth rate g, the present value of this cash flow stream as of year T may be reduced to the following equation:[5]

$$PV_T = \frac{FCF_{T+1}}{K - g}$$

You would then find the present value of PV_T effective today as follows:

$$PV = \frac{PV_T}{(1 + K)^T}$$

Thus, the present value, PV, of the combined free cash flows, for both the firm's planning period and the residual, may be expressed as follows:

$$PV = \sum_{t=1}^{T} \frac{FCF_t}{(1 + K)^t} + \frac{PV_T}{(1 + K)^T}$$

Let's look at an example of free cash flow valuation.

Case Study

The Griggs Corporation had sales last year of $5 million; its operating profit margin (operating profits divided by sales) has been 10%, which should continue into the future. You expect sales to grow at 12% for four years and at 5% thereafter. The firm's tax rate is 30%. Typically, fixed assets as a percentage of sales is 25%, and current assets to sales is 15% net of any "spontaneous financing," such as accounts payable. Also, the amount of the firm's depreciation has approximated the cost of replacement equipment. The firm's outstanding debt is $1,200,000. The company's cost of capital is 15%.

Given these assumptions, the free cash flow value of the firm would be determined as follows:

1. Estimate the firm's free cash flows for each year in the planning horizon—in this case, four years. Next, compute the free cash flow in the first year only of the residual period (year 5). These computations are shown in Exhibit 13.1 and are based on the following logic:

EXHIBIT 13.1. Measuring free cash flows.

	Planning horizon (T = 4)				Beginning of residual period
Year:	**1**	**2**	**3**	**4**	**5**
Sales	$5,600,000	$6,272,000	$7,024,640	$7,867,597	$8,260,977
Operating profits	$560,000	$627,200	$702,464	$786,760	$826,098
Taxes	168,000	188,160	210,739	236,028	247,829
Profits after taxes	$392,000	$439,040	$491,725	$550,732	$578,268
Incremental investments in:					
Net working capital	90,000	100,800	112,896	126,444	59,007
Fixed assets	150,000	168,000	188,160	210,739	98,345
Total investments	$240,000	$268,800	$301,056	$337,183	$157,352
Free cash flows	$152,000	$170,240	$190,669	$213,549	$420,916

- Sales are assumed to increase at 12% for four years and then at 5% in year 5.
- Operating profits are 10% of sales.
- Taxes equal 30% of operating profits.
- Since depreciation is assumed to equal replacement assets, do not add back any depreciation, but neither should you subtract for any cash flow used to purchase replacement equipment. Given the assumption, they would be a wash. Thus, the cash outflows for assets (incremental investments) would only be the increases in assets corresponding to sales increases.
- The incremental investment in assets equals the change in sales times the relationship of assets to sales. For example, in year 1, sales have increased $600,000 from the prior year. The increase in net working capital is therefore $90,000 ($600,000 × 15%).
- The free cash flows in any year are then computed as

$$\text{Operating income} - \text{Taxes on operating income} - \text{Incremental investments}$$

The resulting amount of free cash flows may be distributed to the firm's investors.

2. Compute the present value of the free cash flows. First, find the present value of each year's free cash flows for years 1 through 4 and sum them. The answer is $508,365, estimated as follows:

$$\text{Present value} = \frac{\$152{,}000}{(1+.15)^1} + \frac{\$170{,}240}{(1+.15)^2} + \frac{\$190{,}669}{(1+.15)^3} + \frac{\$213{,}549}{(1+.15)^4}$$
$$= \$132{,}174 + \$128{,}726 + \$125{,}368 + \$122{,}097$$
$$= \$508{,}365$$

Then find the value of the free cash flows beginning in year 5 and continuing in perpetuity at a 5% growth rate. The value as of year 4, the end of the planning horizon, would be

$$PV_4 = \frac{FCF_5}{K - g} = \frac{\$420{,}916}{.15 - .05} = \$4{,}209{,}160$$

The present value today of an amount worth $4,209,160 in year 4 would be

$$PV = \frac{\$4{,}209{,}160}{(1+.15)^4} = \$2{,}406{,}603$$

3. Compute the total value of the firm, which equals the present value of the free cash flows during the planning horizon (years 1 through 4) plus the present value of the residual value:

$$\text{Total firm value} = \$508{,}365 + \$2{,}406{,}603 = \$2{,}914{,}968$$

4. Calculate the value of the firm's equity:

$$\text{Equity value} = \text{Total firm value} - \text{Value of outstanding debt}$$
$$= \$2{,}914{,}968 - \$1{,}2000{,}000 = \$1{,}714{,}968$$

The Free Cash Flow Valuation: A Commentary

Valuing a firm is not easy, but it is an important issue to an entrepreneur for a number of reasons, one of which is the development of an effective harvest strategy. Although the free cash flow method for estimating value may be hard to apply in some cases, it gives the best framework for approaching the issue. As an entrepreneur, you should be more concerned about the *cash flows* generated from the business than with *profits*. Only by receiving after-tax cash flows do you receive a return on your investment. It is no different than a savings account at a bank. The rate of return on your savings account depends on the cash that accrues in the account, not on some reported earnings based on generally accepted accounting principles. Valuing a firm is the same in principle, although the application is harder.

The discussion of the free cash flow method illustrates what matters in determining the value of an investment (in this case, a business). The driving forces of *value* include the following items:

- The beginning sales
- The estimated rate of growth of sales, both for the planning period and beyond
- The time duration of the sales growth
- The expected operating profit margins
- The firm's tax rate
- The projected ratio of operating assets to sales
- The firm's weighted average cost of capital

These variables have come to be known as the *value drivers,* in that the value of a firm is driven by changes in these items.

Al Rappaport provides an excellent graphical representation of what determines a firm's value. See Exhibit 13.2. Beginning at the bottom of Exhibit 13.2, management makes certain operating, investment, and financing decisions. These decisions affect the firm's value drivers, which in turn determine the firm's free cash flows and the cost of capital (discount rate). If effective decisions are made by management, the consequence is the creation of shareholder value; however, if bad decisions are made, value could be destroyed. The value created then determines the availability of cash flows to

EXHIBIT 13.2. Firm valuation.

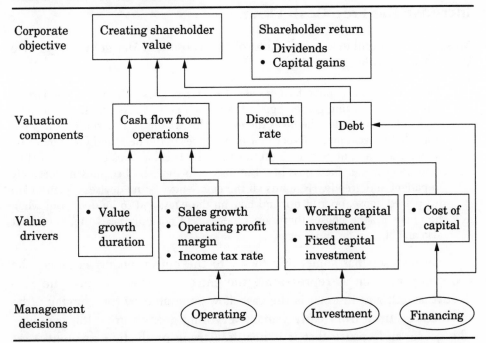

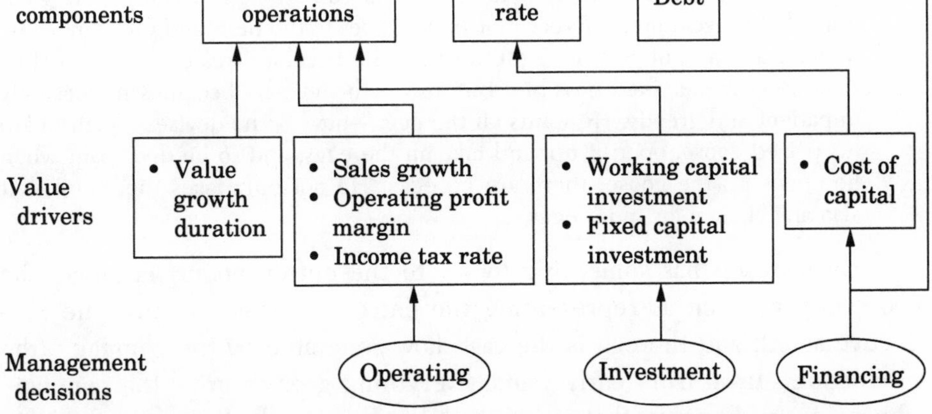

Source: Adapted from Alfred Rappaport, *Creating Shareholder Value* (New York: The Free Press, 1989), 76.

the stockholders in the form of dividends and capital gains. The final result also dictates the options and the eventual outcome of the harvest strategy. If no value is created, there will be no meaningful harvest.

You should now have a basic understanding of firm value, which has serious implications on an entrepreneur's harvest strategy. The next section looks at some of the choices for implementing the harvest strategy.

THE OPTIONS FOR HARVESTING

The structuring of a harvest strategy depends to a significant extent on the set of feasible options available to the entrepreneur. Not all options will be available to all firms. The following presentation looks at the more common options, beginning with the most likely and continuing to the least likely. The strategies to be presented are as follows:

- Increase the free cash flows
- A management buyout (MBO)
- An employee stock ownership plan (ESOP)
- Merging or being acquired
- An initial public offering (IPO)

Increase the Free Cash Flows

Most of us remember Aesop's fable of the goose and the golden egg. The story went something as follows:

> There was once a poor farmer who had a pet goose. One day the farmer discovers a glittering golden egg in the goose's nest. At first, he thinks it to be a trick. However, when he takes the egg to the assayer, he is told it is pure gold, much to his excitement. Every morning he goes to the nest, and every morning he finds a beautiful golden egg. Over time, he becomes wealthy, more wealthy than he ever imagined possible. But also with time, he becomes increasingly impatient and greedy. He wants all the eggs—now. So he devises a plan to kill his prized goose, open it up, and take all the eggs; and so he does. But when he opens up the goose, there are no eggs. He not only loses the goose, but also any chance for more eggs.

Even Aesop has something to say to the entrepreneur (farmer). The goose may be seen as representing the entrepreneur's company (the productive asset), and the egg is the cash flow generated by the company (the production). In a firm's early years, everything goes to grow the company (the goose) and ensure that it is healthy (strong production capability). As much cash as possible is reinvested in the company to increase sales and, it is hoped, generate additional future cash flows.

At some point, however, the entrepreneur may use discretion about the amount of cash to retain within the business. Rather than reinvesting all the cash flows back into the company, the owner could begin taking some cash out of the business for personal needs and desires. Then only the amount of cash required to maintain the firm (the goose) in reasonably good health would be retained within the company; the rest of the cash flows would be harvested. Of course, if the entrepreneur is interested only in the short term, he or she would run the plant at full capacity while reducing maintenance expenses to a minimum and eliminating employee training and other such "discretionary" expenses, choosing instead to go for all the cash (eggs) now. However, doing so could well kill the goose (liquidation or even bankruptcy of the firm).

Enough of Aesop. Let's restate the case in the language of the twentieth century. The golden goose analogy illustrates one means of harvesting the company. In the discussion of the free cash flow valuation approach, the case study assumed that the Griggs Corporation could increase the company's sales at 12% per year (see Exhibit 13.1). To accomplish this, the firm had to make sizable investments in new assets, both working capital and fixed assets. Then, in year 5, the growth rate is reduced from 12% to 5%; the result is a significant decrease in investment requirements and an equivalent increase in free cash flows. Specifically, free cash flows increased from about $214,000 in year 4 to almost $421,000 in year 5. As a result of the reduction in the firm's growth rate, the firm's free cash flows almost doubled in one year. Thus, restricting a company's growth can be a viable strategy for harvesting the venture, given, of course, you have some time. *The strategy is one of retaining within the firm only the amount of cash necessary to maintain current markets* and not trying to grow the present markets or expand into new markets.

Advantages

Increasing the firm's free cash flows has two real advantages:

- You retain the ownership of the company if you are not ready to sell. The story of the Griffins at the beginning of the chapter might have been different had they chosen this strategy instead of selling their restaurant chain.
- The strategy does not depend on finding an interested buyer and going through the time-consuming and at times energy-draining experience of negotiating the sale. In this regard, it can be less risky.

Disadvantages

There are, however, some disadvantages as well:

- Negative tax implications—In harvesting the business, you want to maximize the after-tax cash flows to the company's owners and investors. If the firm simply distributes the cash flows as dividends, the income will be taxed as *corporate income* and again as *personal dividend income* to the stockholders. Preferably, the cash should be distributed so that it is taxed only as corporate income or as personal income, but not both. There are ways, within limits, to accomplish this objective, but it may not provide the entrepreneur with as much discretionary cash flow as an outright sale would. Here the entrepreneur needs the counsel of a good tax accountant or attorney, and well in advance of the harvest.

- Shrinking competitive advantage—Another disadvantage of this strategy is the chance that you may not be able to sustain your competitive advantage while you are harvesting the venture. It is common for an entrepreneur to hold on to the business too long. The conditions that made the venture attractive at the outset may cease to exist, or the competition may become so intense that the rates of return on the investment are unacceptable. The entrepreneur tries to ride the same horse too long and ends up having to shoot it (a Texas euphemism here). The computer industry is an apparent example of this danger.
- Patience and time are required—Finally, for the entrepreneur who is simply tired of the journey, harvesting the venture by siphoning out the free cash flows over time may take too much patience. Unless there are individuals within the company who are qualified to provide the needed managerial leadership, the strategy may be emotionally infeasible.

Management Buyout

The 1980s will long be remembered, not so favorably by some managers and employees, as the decade of the raiders and takeover artists, including such notables as Carl Icahn and T. Boone Pickens. These paragons (or parasites, some might say) popularized financial engineering. They would attempt to buy a company for the purpose of restructuring it and selling it off in pieces to the highest bidder. To finance the deal, they used heavy amounts of debt, with as much as 90% being high-yield debt. But they knew that the servicing of the debt could not be sustained by the company for the long haul. Their usual strategy was to sell off some of the firm's assets to reduce the debt and then rely on the firm's free cash flows to pay down the remaining debt—thus the name *leveraged buyout* (LBO).

On some occasions the leveraged buyout was performed by a small group of the managers within the company. Such a transaction came to be called a *management buyout* (MBO). When the managers had little in the way of capital, which was usually the case, they had to borrow the money to buy the company's stock, just as the raiders did.

Advantages

The leveraged buyout, and often the management buyout, came to be perceived by many in the financial community in a negative context. There is, however, considerable evidence that some good came from these financing arrangements, namely, a new incentive structure for the managers to act more like owners.[6] Also, it probably brought increased attention to using the MBO as an exit mechanism for an entreprenurial firm's founders and investors.

Disadvantages

As already noted, the MBO generally involved a lot of debt financing. Moreover, for MBOs that were designed to buy out the entrepreneur and some of the investors, this debt came from two sources: private investors brought into the deal by financial institutions and the sellers themselves. Thus, in these situations the entrepreneur was at times exposed to considerable risk—the risk that the lenders may call the debt if the new owners should fail to abide by the terms of the loan, and the risk that the new owners may not be able to pay the money owed to the seller.

Although the 1980s, or the decade of the deals, is now over, the use of MBOs is still a possible strategy for harvesting an entrepreneurial venture. The managers within many entrepreneurial businesses often have a strong incentive to buy the firm. However, the use of large proportions of high-yield debt is no longer an option in most situations. The debt markets for this purpose have, for all practical purposes, disappeared. If the MBO is to be used, the managers buying the firm must have a large proportion of the money available personally, or the selling parties must be willing to accept debt as full or partial payment of the purchase price.

When the entrepreneur accepts debt in consideration for the company, an added complication must be resolved. The deal must be structured to minimize any agency problems. Specifically, if the new owners have placed little or none of their own money in the deal, they may be inclined to take risks that are not in the best interest of the selling entrepreneur; they have nothing to lose if the company fails. Also, if the terms of the deal include an earnout, where the final amount of the payment depends in part on the subsequent profit performance of the company, the buying owners have an incentive to do things that will lower the firm's profits during the earnout period. Thus, the entrepreneur needs to take great care in structuring the deal; otherwise, there will most likely be some disappointment with the outcome. Some good advice here could be well worth the money.

Employee Stock Ownership Plan (ESOP)

The owners of small and middle-sized firms are increasingly turning to employee stock ownership plans, or ESOPs, when they are ready to sell their firms. At least half of all ESOPs are used to create a market for the shares of departing owners of closely held companies. The remaining ESOPs are created either to provide a supplemental employee benefit plan or as a way for a company to borrow money. As noted by one tax accountant, "ESOPs often work best in circumstances where the owner is getting out of the business or where there already is the expectation or reality of some level of public ownership within the company."[7]

An employee stock ownership plan is designed primarily to provide a retirement plan for the firm's employees. At the same time, however, an ESOP can facilitate the financing of the company, as well as provide the entrepreneur with a vehicle for harvesting the company. Whereas most other retirement plans *limit* the amount of an employer's stock that can be bought by the plan, an ESOP is intended to allow employees to *invest primarily* in such stock. The combination of being able to invest in employer stock and take advantage of some significant tax savings not available with other plans makes the ESOP potentially attractive as a way to harvest the venture.

If the primary purpose of the ESOP is to provide a retirement plan for the employees, the arrangement usually takes the form of an *unleveraged ESOP*. In this case, the company makes an annual contribution to the ESOP for the employees' retirement; the ESOP then uses the money to buy stock from the company and, on frequent occasions, from some of its stockholders. With the unleveraged ESOP, the amount of stock purchased in any year is limited to the company's annual contribution to the ESOP. As a result, an unleveraged ESOP is not particularly attractive for the entrepreneur who wants to sell a sizable number of shares within a short period.

A *leveraged ESOP* better fits the needs of an entrepreneur wanting to harvest a venture. With this type of ESOP, money is borrowed to buy the company's stock. With access to borrowed money, the leveraged ESOP can make large purchases of the stock at one time. In fact, the ESOP could conceivably purchase the entire company, which means buying all the shares of the current owners.

Exhibit 13.3 presents a flow chart of the sequence of events in the use of a leveraged ESOP to provide an employee retirement plan and, in conjunction, to allow the present owners to sell their stock. First, the firm establishes an ESOP and guarantees any debt borrowed by the ESOP for the purpose of buying the company's stock. Next, the ESOP borrows money from a lender, and the cash is used to buy the owner's stock. The shares are

EXHIBIT 13.3. Owner stock sale using leveraged ESOP.

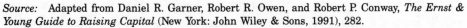

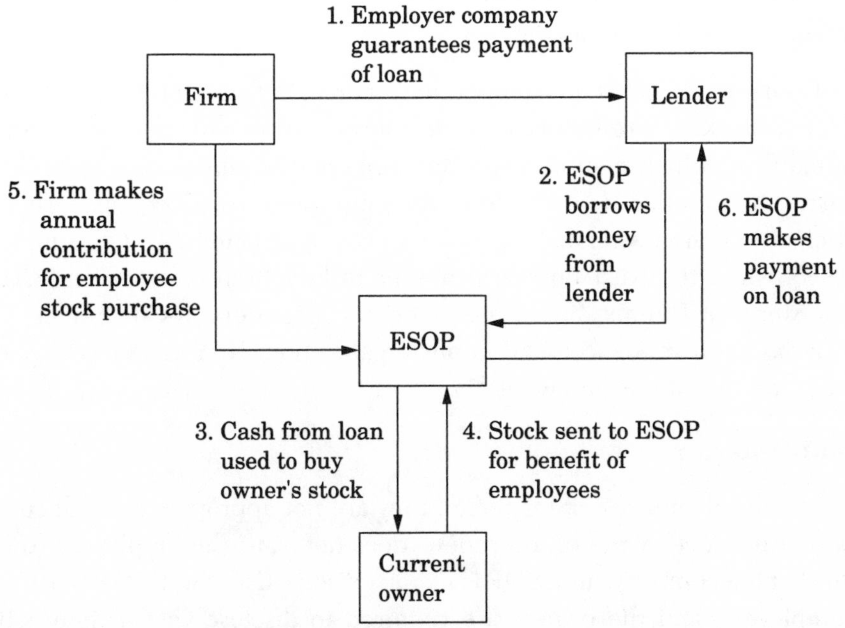

Source: Adapted from Daniel R. Garner, Robert R. Owen, and Robert P. Conway, *The Ernst & Young Guide to Raising Capital* (New York: John Wiley & Sons, 1991), 282.

held by a trust, and the company makes annual tax-deductible contributions to the trust so it can pay off the loan. As the loan is paid off, shares are released and allocated to the employees.

Advantages

Although an ESOP benefits the owner by providing a market for selling stock, it also carries some tax advantages that make the approach attractive to owner and employee alike. Some of the benefits are as follows:[8]

- A company can deduct both principal and interest payments on an ESOP loan.
- If the ESOP owns at least 30% of the firm after purchasing the shares, the seller can avoid current tax on the gain by using the proceeds to buy stocks or bonds of another U.S. industrial company.
- If the ESOP owns more than 50% of the company, those who lend money to the ESOP are taxed on only 50% of the income received on such loans. Thus, the lender can afford to offer a lower interest rate, usually about 1½ percentage points below a company's normal borrowing cost.

- The dividends that a business pays on the stock held by the ESOP are allowed as a tax-deductible expense; that is, they are treated like interest expense when it comes to taxes.

ComSonics, Inc. is an example of owners using an ESOP as a means to sell their stock. Warren Braun was the former owner of the Harrisonburg, Virginia firm, which manufactures and repairs equipment for the cable TV industry. Braun offered an ESOP to the employees in 1975 to allow them to participate in the ownership of the company. The purchase was completed in 1985, when the trust borrowed money to buy Braun's remaining shares. In the words of Dennis Zimmerman, the new president of ComSonics, "The ESOP has been very successful in our organization. It empowers the person on the line to work as an owner."[9]

Disadvantages

Despite the advantages ESOPs offer, they are not appropriate for all companies. For instance, if the entrepreneur does not want the employees to have control of the company, an ESOP is not an option. Also, the ESOP must cover all employees, and the owners are required to disclose certain information about the company, such as its performance and its key executives' salaries, which for some entrepreneurs is not palatable. Finally, using an ESOP can place the employee in double jeopardy, where both her job and her retirement fund depend on the success of a single business. However, even with these potential negatives, an entrepreneur should give serious consideration to an ESOP when crafting a harvest strategy.

Merging or Being Acquired

As commented earlier, the 1980s was a time of unfriendly takeovers, which many instinctively felt to be wasteful and harmful. (There is remarkably little evidence either to support this view or to refute it.) The "merger mania" has come and gone. Between 1989 and 1990 alone, the number of transactions was down 12%, with the value of the transactions falling a far greater amount, 50%; and the trend is continuing into the 1990s. Thus, fewer and smaller deals are being done in the early 1990s. Exhibit 13.4 shows the activity of mergers and acquisitions of privately held firms during the latter part of the 1980s and 1990 that were sold at a value between $5 million and $100 million. Along with the overall trend, Exhibit 13.4 shows the decline in the number of privately held companies acquired, along with a modest decrease in the average price per transaction. Also, the seller's value relative to earnings has decreased in recent years, coming more in line with the price-earnings ratios of the buying firms. However, the selling price relative to the firm's book

EXHIBIT 13.4. Mergers and acquisitions transactions of privately held firms with sale prices between $5 and $100 million.

Year	Number	Price ($ millions)	Price-earnings Seller	Price-earnings Buyer	Seller market-to-book
1984	128	35.0	19.3	16.5	3.3
1985	165	30.8	19.4	16.0	2.8
1986	141	38.0	24.4	18.7	2.9
1987	91	43.2	23.0	18.9	2.4
1988	162	39.1	27.3	18.2	3.1
1989	101	41.4	21.4	16.0	3.8
1990	78	34.0	19.6	20.0	3.9

Source: The data in this table is taken from the 1984 through 1990 annual reports of *Mergerstat Review,* Chicago, Ill.: W.T. Grimm & Co.

value actually increased, an encouraging fact for the entrepreneur wanting to sell a company.

The turmoil in the financial markets during the latter 1980s and early 1990s, including the collapse of the junk bond market, eliminated the primary source of high-debt financing frequently used in acquiring other companies. Financial buyers were frozen out of the credit markets in more recent years. Yet not all was bad in the 1980s. The merger and acquisition activity of the decade allowed shareholders of a significant number of privately held companies to realize the value locked up in their companies via a market-based transaction.

In the 1990s *debt* is out and *equity* is in when it comes to financing a company acquisition. Also, practice has moved away from financial strategies designed to turn a quick profit and from purchasing a company in a different industry. Instead, the 1990s are witnessing more *strategic corporate consolidation of close-fitting companies.* One lesson of the 1980s is now clear: Buying a big company is one of the riskiest things a management can do.

There have been a significant number of studies trying to explain the rationale for mergers and acquisitions and to examine the financial consequences of the transaction on the respective buying and selling shareholders.[10] Most of these studies ask the question, "Is there any value created by a firm's management acquiring another company?" In other words, can management do anything that the stockholders could not do for themselves, possibly even more easily? Although such studies may be of interest to acquisitive managers and their shareholders, they offer little to the entrepreneur attempting to sell a company. The purpose of merging with another company or being acquired makes perfect sense—to capture the value that has been created through the venture.

Advantages

Although the idea behind harvesting the venture ought to be about releasing the value locked up in the firm for the benefit of the owners and investors, the specific impetus for doing so will understandably vary. In the case of merging with another company or being acquired, the most prevalent reason relates to estate planning and the need and opportunity to diversify one's investments. A second reason is the need for financing growth, where the firm or the owner does not have the capacity to provide the needed funds. Many others simply want a change, mostly for personal or family reasons.

Pitfalls

The financial issues related to selling a firm are basically the same for any exit strategy:

1. How should the company be valued for the purpose of the sale?
2. How is the payment to be structured?

However, the financial matters, though not insignificant by any means, are not the only issues of importance when it comes to selling the firm, and they may not even be the primary concern. What the enterpreneur believes to be important when going into the acquisition process is often not what is important after the sale. Most entrepreneurs lack experience in negotiating the sale of their firm and are a bit naive in their expectations about the eventual outcome. Although selling the company does provide the long-sought-after liquidity, there may be some negative consequences during and after the sale.

What can go wrong during the process of selling a company? Several possible entrapments come to mind. First, sellers are often disappointed in the advice they receive from "experts" during the negotiations. After the fact, they may wish they had talked more with other entrepreneurs who had been through the experience of a company sale.

A second problem occurs when significant energy and resources have been committed to selling the firm, and the bidder walks out in the final negotiations. Entrepreneurs describe, with some emotion, the difficulties resulting from failure to consummate the sale. The negotiations may extend over a six-month period, during which time management's focus shifts from company operations to completing the sale. Also, some members of the existing management may expect to be promoted after the acquisition. When the deal is canceled, they have difficulty recapturing their enthusiasm for the existing firm; some eventually leave. When all is said and done, it can take several months for the firm to regain its prior momentum.

To avoid some of these pitfalls, consider the following pointers from an entrepreneur who sold his company:[11]

- You only sell your firm once. Whoever is acquiring your company may buy businesses repeatedly. Therefore, prepare thoroughly and leave nothing to chance.
- Selling your company is a personal affair. You cannot delegate the responsibility to someone else, including a business broker. A family company is you.
- If you want liquidity and you do not want your assets tied up in someone else's company, sell for cash.
- Negotiate with two or more willing buyers at the same time. However, approach potential buyers discreetly to avoid tainting the company with a shopped-around image.
- Carefully select those companies that your firm will appeal to most, and then develop a substrategy for contacting them.
- Plan on 18 months to complete the sale, especially if you must locate the buyer.
- Once you negotiate the framework of the deal, select a lawyer who will negotiate the details in a style compatible with your own personality.
- Stay alert and healthy. The process is stressful.
- Avoid becoming complacent about the transaction. After you have reached an agreement in principle, the hard work has really just begun. A company is not sold until the money is in your bank account.

Once the firm has been sold, there may still be some unresolved issues for the entrepreneur. If stock was accepted in the trade, the entrepreneur's fortunes are linked directly to the successes and failures of the acquiring company. Until the stock can be sold, the entrepreneur is still exposed to considerable risk—a position that can only be improved through diversification of the portfolio of risky assets. For the risk-averse person, which includes even most entrepreneurs, there is merit in diversifying as soon as feasible.

Also, if the entrepreneur continues in the management of the company after the sale, but under the supervision of the acquiring owners, disillusionment may eventually occur. Some selling entrepreneurs perceive a real change on the part of the buyer after the sale—mostly for the worse, in their eyes. Also, the differences in corporate culture can become a significant problem for both companies involved in the transaction, but more so for the entrepreneur.

The next section looks at the option for harvesting the venture that most entrepreneurs would love to attain, but few do.

The Initial Public Offering (IPO)[12]

Conventional wisdom tells us that going public is generally the preferred choice for harvesting a firm, if at all possible. The rationale for going public, vis-à-vis other exit mechanisms, rests largely on the contention that IPOs provide higher valuations than what an entrepreneur could expect from other avenues. If a better price can be realized from going public rather than from being acquired or merging, the IPO is obviously the logical choice. Such a position is particularly popular in times of "hot" IPO markets, and it is hard to argue with the successes experienced during these periods.

Although IPOs are attractive in many ways for a firm needing access to the equity markets, the fact remains that many privately held firms will never find themselves in a position to go public. They simply will not qualify, because of their size, because they are not in the right industry, or because they lack the requisite management. Also, if liquidity is a important issue, it may be several years before an entrepreneur could sell any of the newly issued public shares, owing to legal restrictions placed on such stock. Nevertheless, an IPO is a possible alternative and one of considerable appeal for many an entrepreneur who aspires to take the company public, and as such it deserves our attention here.

Understanding the IPO Process[13]

Taking a firm public appears on the surface to be a logical process. Here's a brief but factual description of this process:

> The entire process can take as little as six months to complete, but some companies take eighteen months or longer to go public. In some cases, where the corporate structure is poorly organized and additional financing is required to position the company for a more beneficial public offering, the process can take two years.
>
> During that time, a minimum of one and preferably two or more officers of the corporation will spend much of their time interfacing with attorneys, auditors, underwriters, and financial printers, collecting information for the reams of documentation that need to be submitted.
>
> As the effective date approaches, roadshows—a means for showing off the company and of improving the potential price performance in the after-market—will have to be prepared and then executed. The CEO will spend a fair amount of time making presentations to brokers and institutional investors. Slide shows, product brochures, and possibly videos will have to be produced and distributed. Trips must be planned to make the presentations nationally and, possibly, internationally.[14]

During this process, the firm's owner and managers will be answering such questions as

- What do we need to do in advance of going public?
- What are the legal requirements?
- Who should be responsible for the different activities, and how should we structure our "team" to make it all happen?
- How do we choose an investment banker?
- How do we determine an appropriate price for the offering?
- How will life be different after we are a public company?

Although the preceding description cannot be faulted for being factually inaccurate, it does not capture the essence of the journey. Taking a company public is one of the most exhilarating, frustrating, stimulating, and exhausting experiences owners and managers will ever encounter. They are exposing themselves to the vicissitudes of the capital markets and to the world of investment bankers, which few entrepreneurs understand, much less appreciate. The cost of the process seems excessive and exorbitant. The owners find themselves having little influence in the decisions being made, which becomes most disconcerting to them. Disillusionment with the investment bankers, and with much of the entire process itself, may develop for the company's owners. At some point the owners may wonder where they lost control of the process. Although it may be of little comfort, these feelings are not unique but are shared by many who have participated in a public offering.

Exhibits 13.5 and 13.6 provide an overview of the IPO process, first as most entrepreneurs expect it to be, and then more as it really is. Exhibit 13.5 presents the chronology of the IPO events, beginning with an entrepreneur's decision to begin the process. The entrepreneur then selects an investment banker to serve as the underwriter, who in turn brings together a group of investment houses to help sell the shares. With the help of the underwriter and a host of other experts, the entrepreneur prepares a prospectus, the legal document used to satisfy the SEC that he is telling the whole truth and nothing but the truth to prospective investors. The managers, along with the investment banker, go on the road to tell the firm's story to the brokers who will be selling the stock. At the very end—actually, the day before the offering is released to the public—the decision is made as to the actual offering price. To this point, any discussion of the price of the stock has been tentative. Then all the work, which by now has been months, comes to fruition in a single event—offering the stock to the public and waiting for the consequence.

Exhibit 13.5 does not provide the complete story. A missing element that needs to be anticipated is the shift in power that occurs during the process. Exhibit 13.6 shows what really occurs. When the chain of events begins, the company's management is in control. They can dictate whether

EXHIBIT 13.5. The initial public offering process: A partial view.

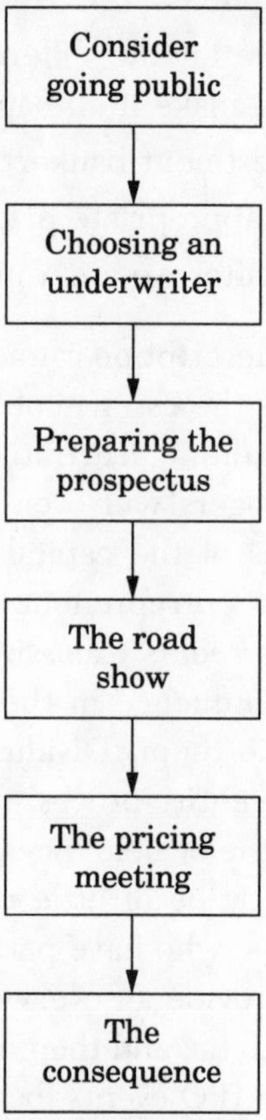

Source: "Teaching Notes, CML (B) and (C)," Copyright 1985 by the President and Fellows of Harvard College (Boston: Harvard Business School, 1985).

or not to go public and who the investment banker will be. However, after the prospectus has been prepared and the road show is under way, the firm's management, including the entrepreneur, no longer has primary responsibility for decision making. Now the investment banker has control. Finally, the marketplace, in complement with the investment banker, begins to take over, and ultimately it is the market that dictates the final outcome. So it behooves the entrepreneur to understand this loss of power as the events play out; otherwise, total frustration will occur.

In addition to the issue of who controls the events and decisions in the IPO process, one other matter is important. Whenever you are negotiating, it is always good to know the underlying motivation for the other side. In this case, you need to understand the investment banker's incentives for assisting with an IPO. For instance, who is the investment banker's primary customer here? Clearly, the issuing firm is rewarding the underwriter for the services

EXHIBIT 13.6. The inital public offering process: The complete view.

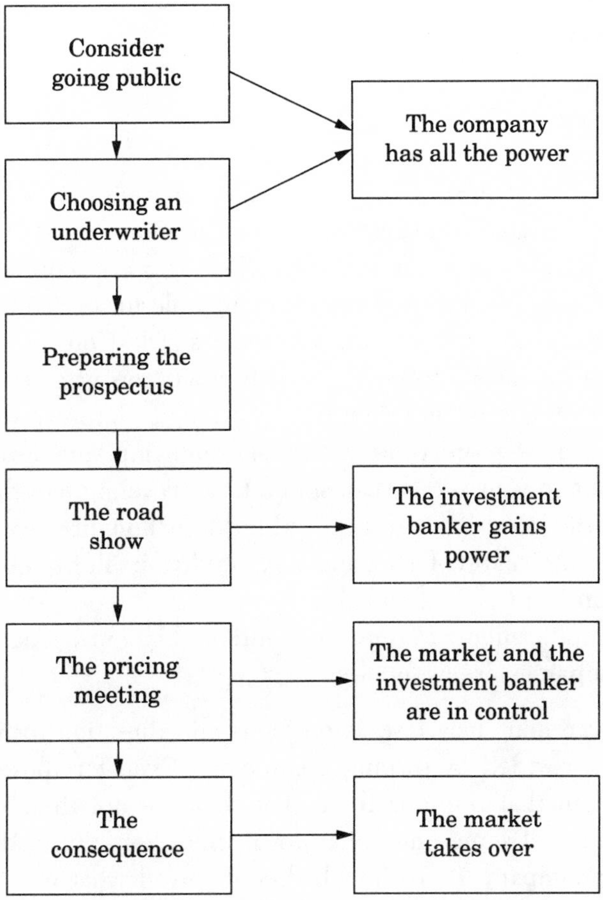

Source: "Teaching Notes, CML (B) and (C)," Copyright 1985 by the President and Fellows of Harvard College (Boston: Harvard Business School, 1985).

performed through the fees paid and a participation in the deal. But the economics for helping with an IPO is not as rewarding as other activities performed by investment bankers, such as their involvement with corporate acquisitions. The banker is also selling securities to its customers on the other end of the trade. There is some strong evidence that investment bankers tend to underprice new offerings.[15] Is this being done to benefit their customers buying the stock? This ongoing debate will not be resolved soon, but regardless of its outcome, unless you understand how the investment banker and others in the process are compensated, your expectations as to what they will do for your firm may be grossly exaggerated.

Even with the negative aspects associated with the initial public offering, it is a dream come true for most entrepreneurs. I would not advise against pursuing such a dream, as long as the entrepreneur comes into the deal with realistic expectations and asks candidly and honestly, "Does it really make sense?" If so, go for it!

WHAT NEXT?

Once the firm has been sold, taken public, or merged with a larger corporation as part of a strategic alliance, and once the money or stock has changed hands, the entrepreneur is a free person. No longer are there concerns about losing market share, being sued, or not being able to service the firm's debt. The unending and at times chaotic schedule is at last put in order. You now have the financial means to do essentially what you want to do when you want to do it. You can begin relentlessly working to improve your golf game; you can spend a lot more time at the lake enjoying your favorite pastime, fishing; or you and your spouse can spend time traveling. On the other hand, you may find the *good life* is not everything you thought it would be. There may even be some regrets for having separated yourself from something that was such a dominant part of your life.

Two disappointments frequently mentioned by entrepreneurs who have sold their companies are as follows:

- The entrepreneur may lose some focus and direction in life, focus that had been provided by owning a company. Even for those with a basic value system that reminds them that they are not their work, there is a real chance of some emotional down time. Some wish they had never sold their company, even though they received what was to them a fair price. They came to realize that the firm served as the base for much of what they did, both in and out of the business arena.
- Managing the liquidity resulting from the company sale becomes a burden for some. They find managing money more difficult and less enjoyable than they had expected, and less rewarding than operating their own company.

If the loss is too great, chances are you will soon be back working to build a company, either on your own or as a private investor supporting a son or daughter or some other aspiring entrepreneur. Whatever the decision, the key is knowing what is important to you; this was true when you began the entrepreneurial process, and it is equally true in the harvest.

SUMMARY

Harvesting a business venture is both an economic and emotional decision. While the goal is to build and harvest a business to create value for its founders and investors, the business also is a way of life. The entrepreneurial dream is as much about an ideology as it is about making a living.

A rewarding harvest can come only if you have built a company of value. If the business has provided a good life-style but not created value, there will be no harvest. The only option then is liquidation, or even possibly bankruptcy. That is, the only option is no harvest, which will not be particularly attractive when the time comes to leave the business. Thus, contrary to what you might be inclined to do, anticipating and even planning for the harvest is the only viable choice. Making this decision effectively is, to a large extent, dependent on an understanding of what you value and what is important to you—a deep and genuine understanding. Otherwise, you will be disappointed with the end result. So make a good decision for you and enjoy the fruits.

14 ENTREPRENEURSHIP ECONOMICS

Bruce A. Kirchhoff

The 1980s are often referred to as the "decade of entrepreneurs." But who are the entrepreneurs? To some, entrepreneurs are those who form new businesses that prosper and create new employment. Examples are Bill Gates at Microsoft, Steve Jobs and Steve Wozniak at Apple Computer Co., and Mitch Kapor at Lotus Development, Inc. But others view entrepreneurs as unscrupulous business owners and managers who cheat America out of millions of dollars. The Wall Street mogul Michael Milken and California savings and loan promoter Charles Keating are well-known examples. A third perspective is that entrepreneurs are corporate managers who achieve outstanding success with their firms. For example, Lee Iacocca with Chrysler Corporation and Jack Welch with General Electric are frequently mentioned as entrepreneurs.

With such a broad definition, the 1980s was surely the decade of entrepreneurs, but then so were the 1970s, the 1960s, and every decade before and after the 1980s. Clearly, if the 1980s were somehow a unique period of entrepreneurial activity, not all of these definitions can be correct. Not every businessperson who draws media attention can be an entrepreneur. Sorting out the uniqueness requires the application of some systematic thought about what makes entrepreneurship special to the U.S. economy.

Economic theory provides a basis for systematic thought and a definition of entrepreneurship that clarifies its special importance. The economic theory definition gives entrepreneurs a sense of purpose and accomplishment. And economics provides the explanation for why the 1980s became the decade of entrepreneurs. As will be demonstrated in this chapter, the economics of entrepreneurship are surprisingly important to the economic development, market competition, and social welfare of the United States.

ENTREPRENEURSHIP ECONOMICS

Economic theory is concerned with two major questions about society:

- How does a society *create new wealth*? Without new wealth, as population increases, per-capita wealth declines. Thus, any society that wants to improve its standard of living must find ways to continuously increase its overall wealth.
- How does a society *distribute wealth* among its members? Unless there is some form of equitable wealth distribution, less fortunate members of the society will be dissatisfied, and the society will not be stable.

Obviously, wealth creation and distribution are fundamental to social progress. And, as will be shown here, entrepreneurship is a major mechanism for ensuring both wealth creation and distribution.

To understand entrepreneurial economics, it is useful to look back to the early development of capitalist economic theory. After all, entrepreneurship is not new in economics. The term has been used for at least 150 years, and the concept goes back over 200 years. Looking back to early observations will provide a perspective on the experience of the 1980s and help to explain the sudden surge in attention that entrepreneurship has received worldwide since 1980. Following this look backward is a description of the newly emerging economic theory of entrepreneurship. This leads into a discussion of the social contributions of entrepreneurs during the 1980s, followed by a discussion of the economic options that aspiring entrepreneurs face as they choose their directions.

How Classical Capitalism Spawned Entrepreneurship

Capitalism is an economic system characterized by the private ownership of property—not only land and buildings, but also machinery, telephone cables, transportation equipment, patents, information, and so forth—that is used by owners *to create profits for themselves*. In a pure theoretical sense, capitalism is also a system where opportunities to exchange goods and services exist in open, uncontrolled markets accessible to all buyers and sellers. The capitalism concept was first formulated in a relatively complete theory by Adam Smith in his book *The Wealth of Nations*, published in 1776. Smith perceived the "capitalist" as an owner-manager who combined basic resources—land, labor, and capital—into a successful industrial enterprise. Smith described how capitalists were essential ingredients to the growth and distribution of wealth in society. Smith's book is the foundation of "classical" capitalist economic theory.

The next 100 years saw a bevy of economic theorists expand and modify Smith's original theories. Sometime during the middle of the nineteenth century, the French word *entrepreneur* (meaning "to undertake") began to be used to identify the owner-manager of a new industrial enterprise. Later, around the turn of the twentieth century, the role of the entrepreneur and the term's definition became more succinct. This further refinement actually arose from the development of another body of theory, called "neoclassical economic theory."

Neoclassical Theory's Deletion of the Entrepreneur

Neoclassical theory owes its development to the work of Walras and Marshall in the late nineteenth century. Following Sir Isaac Newton's development of logical and mathematical analysis, Leon Walras (in 1874) and Alfred Marshall (in 1890) separately developed similar models of capitalist economics that incorporate a rigorous logical framework and provide a foundation for mathematical description. The key component of this theory is the specification that markets consist of many buyers and many sellers who interact so as to ensure that supply equals demand. When supply equals demand, the market is said to be in "equilibrium." Equilibrium is achieved by fluctuations in prices. If demand rises but supply does not, prices will rise so that demand will be discouraged by higher prices, the available supply will suffice, and equilibrium will be attained. Economists call neoclassical markets "perfectly competitive," meaning that such markets perfectly match the theoretical definition.

Economists note that commodity markets operate much like perfectly competitive markets. For example, the Chicago Board of Exchange operates with many buyers and sellers who meet on the trading floor with offers to buy and sell. Prices fluctuate to reflect the variations in supply and demand for various commodities. Since these markets are nearly "perfectly competitive," economists refer to them as "efficient" or nearly perfect.

Expressions such as "free markets" derive from this neoclassical formulation of market characteristics. Ideas such as the equating of supply and demand in markets where prices are free to move up and down stem from this theory. Several characteristics of the neoclassical definitions of markets are essential to achieving "equilibrium" market operations:

- There must be many buyers and many sellers;
- no single buyer or seller can influence market price.
- Prices are set by the operation of the market—not by buyers or sellers, but by transactions or sales.

- Products and services must all be equivalent in content so that they differ only in price.
- All buyers and all sellers must know of all transactions that take place.

Perfect competition is the mathematically precise, theoretical model of equilibrium markets.

The practical application of market equilibrium economic theory emerges from its ability to predict the outcome of economic events. With predictive ability, economists can recommend actions on the part of government to encourage positive or avoid negative economic effects. Neoclassical theory has been developed into a useful body of knowledge, called "general equilibrium theory," for such prediction and recommendations. General equilibrium theory is the mainstream economic theory in America.

But the neoclassical model, unlike the classical model, does not incorporate the owner-manager as an active cause of economic activity. The neoclassical perfect market cannot allow any supplier to create a product different from all other products. No supplier is allowed to control or set market prices. Instead, suppliers (owner-managers) must behave as passive, responsive participants as the market sets prices and determines demand. As prices rise, suppliers produce more; as prices fall, they produce less. So, although the perfect market provides a solid foundation for economic predictability, it achieves this sophisticated capability *by eliminating the unpredictable behavior of entrepreneurial owner-managers* who thrive on upsetting market activities by introducing innovative products and services. Entrepreneurship, then, is assumed to be only a minor occurrence in an otherwise equilibrium-dominated market. This assumption allows general equilibrium theorists to predict overall market behavior (or overall economic performance).

An example of the importance of product-service uniformity may help here. The Chicago Board of Trade (which, as noted, is a reasonable representation of the neoclassical market) would not operate very well if one trader suddenly introduced a new commodity. What if some trader unilaterally decided to trade rhinoceros horn contracts? The contracts may be of interest to other traders, and there might be a surge in trading activity. But the trading floor would be tossed into confusion as word of the new commodity caused other traders to shift their buying and selling habits. Still others would demand clarification of the characteristics and size of the horns. Very quickly, the offending innovative trader would be removed from the floor.

New commodities are introduced at the Board of Trade only after careful examination and analysis by the Board. Individualistic behavior, where one trader brings in a new commodity, is forbidden here and in all equilibrium (perfect) markets. In fact, commodities are traded with very detailed and explicit standards for their composition so that price is the only variable at the time of a transaction. For example, the moisture content of grain is defined in trading standards so that all grain is of a standard quality. Thus, all grain is equal in every way, and price alone is the market variable. It is important for the Chicago Board of Trade to ensure a nearly perfect market where price serves as the market-equilibrating factor so that trade is carried out in an orderly fashion.

Government policies designed to discourage inflation, stimulate economic activity, and reduce the deficit all have their roots in the neoclassical theory of perfect markets. And general equilibrium theorists argue that their theory works "pretty well," even though they recognize that it is flawed. These flaws became glaring faults when entrepreneurship emerged as a major factor in economic growth. As such, the 1980s represent a turning point in the character of the U.S. economy and a serious challenge to mainstream economic thought. This radical departure from general equilibrium theory is the reason the 1980s stand out as the decade of the entrepreneur.

How Neoclassical Theory Views Wealth Distribution and Creation

Neoclassical theory is carefully crafted to demonstrate that capitalism—characterized by perfect markets and unfettered by outside interference—will equitably distribute wealth among buyers and sellers through the intricate operations of markets that adjust fluctuations in demand and supply by variations in prices. The process of wealth creation and distribution is, of course, a major component of this economic theory. The wealth distribution function of the neoclassical equilibrium market theory is described by tracing the flow of income that occurs with the creation of new demand for a product. The increase in demand becomes an increase in product manufacturing activity as suppliers expand production to satisfy the new demand and earn more profit. As suppliers' revenues and profits increase, they add more workers, thereby increasing overall employment and total wages paid. Workers spend their increased wages, and owners spend their increased profits. The net result is that an increase in sales of products causes an increase in suppliers' and workers' income. Thus, the overall level of economic activity rises because of a rise in the demand for goods and services, driven by the increased spending of workers and suppliers. Since wealth is defined as the storage of income, the increase in economic activity adds to the overall wealth of society as some of the increased income is saved.

Thus, the neoclassical model shows that the market mechanism of many buyers and many suppliers operating so that prices are set by the functioning of the market as supply and demand fluctuates, results in the equitable distribution of income among suppliers and buyers, owners and workers. Although the explanation here is overly simplistic, neoclassical theory is logically consistent and demonstrates that capitalism equitably distributes income within society.[1]

But neoclassical theory does not postulate the origin of "new demand." The theory simply assumes an increase in demand without detailing how such new demand occurs. Yet new demand is the source of new wealth creation. It is the absence of a specific mechanism for creation of new demand that many economists perceive as neoclassical theory's greatest weakness. Another group of theorists, the Austrian school, contend that the entrepreneur is the source of new demand.

Schumpeter's Reaffirmation of the Entrepreneur

Neoclassical theory has always had its critics. Around the turn of the twentieth century, many classical economists (especially those associated with educational institutions in Austria) objected to the absence of entrepreneurship from the neoclassical model. Austrian economists argued that entrepreneurship was far too important a part of capitalism to ignore for the sake of achieving predictability through logical and mathematical rigor.

The Austrians advanced their arguments in theoretical terms. In the meantime, neoclassical theorists developed more and more useful mathematical prediction tools and accumulated hard, statistical evidence to demonstrate the value of their theory. The scientific nature of neoclassical theory was particularly appealing to the emerging American economic discipline, so neoclassical theory grew to dominate American economic thinking.

Joseph Schumpeter was a student of the Austrian school who came to the United States early in his career and wrote most of his books here. He saw innovation—the use of an invention to create a new commercial product or service—as the driving force for creating new demand for goods and services. An innovation is a new idea brought to the market, where buyers find it so appealing that they expand their purchases to include this new product or service. Every innovation successfully introduced by business firms, large or small, new or old, creates new demand for goods and services and therefore creates new wealth.

But Schumpeter disagreed with neoclassical theory about the mechanism of wealth distribution. He argued that neoclassical perfect markets with many buyers and many sellers do not exist. All but a trivial few markets are dominated by a few sellers, who often collude to control the market functions. The concept of free exchange is unreal, he states; instead, suppliers control the market for their own benefit, not the buyers' benefit.

Instead of neoclassical competitive markets functioning systematically to achieve equilibrium between supply and demand, Schumpeter observed *chaotic markets* driven by the regular appearance of entrepreneurs who enter the markets using innovations that challenge the established few suppliers who dominate the markets. Entrepreneurs, by definition, are owner-managers who start new, independent businesses to exploit innovations. Entrepreneurs begin their firms with little personal wealth and the ambition to create wealth for themselves. They develop innovations and struggle to achieve success in the market. If successful, they expand the overall market as buyers increase their purchases to include the new product or service offered. As overall demand increases, new wealth is created. The entrepreneurs gain market share and new wealth for themselves.

But, at the same time, their innovations destroy the structure of existing markets and cause established firms with older products or services to decline. The entrepreneurs acquire thc market shares once held by the older firms, thereby acquiring some of the older firms' wealth. The older firms lay off employees, and some declare bankruptcy. Their creditors, employees, and shareholders lose some of their wealth. At the same time, the entrepreneurs hire new employees, pay increased dividends to their shareholders, and increase their purchases from suppliers. New wealth is created through new demand, and both new and old wealth is distributed to the entrepreneurs and their employees, shareholders, and suppliers.

Entrepreneurs, Schumpeter argues, are the mechanism of wealth creation and distribution in capitalism. Schumpeter called this process *creative destruction* because entrepreneurs create new wealth through the process of destroying existing market structures.

Schumpeter derived his theory of creative destruction through observations of the real world during the first half of the twentieth century, but it is still evident in the United States. Examples are easy to find in the highly innovative computer markets. Apple Computer Company brought the microcomputer to markets that were dominated by a few manufacturers of minicomputers and mainframes. Within 15 years the structure of these markets was irrevocably changed. Minicomputer companies such as Digital Equipment Company and Data General Corporation have declined. Still others have disappeared; Prime Computer was acquired, and Wang Computer went into bankruptcy.

But creative destruction did not stop with the microcomputer innovation. Another wave of marketing and distribution innovations surged through this industry in the late 1980s as Dell Computer Company brought direct mail sales to a microcomputer industry dominated by retail sales outlets. Even "big blue," IBM Corporation, has experienced loss of market share to these "mail-order techies" and experienced declining profits in response to this new form of competition. In the meantime, once-small firms with minimal resources have become giant firms with many wealthy shareholders, employees, and suppliers.

An especially important aspect of Schumpeter's economic theory is that *innovations create new demand* and *entrepreneurs bring innovations to the market.* This means entrepreneurs are central to wealth creation and distribution. Entrepreneurs are owner-managers of new, independent firms that bring innovations into existing markets. They destroy the existing markets as their innovations increase demand and create new wealth. And entrepreneurs distribute wealth as a new set of shareholders, workers, and suppliers experience increases in income and an old set experiences declines. Once entrepreneurial firms become large and wealthy, they become prey for new entrepreneurs.

Good examples of this process are again found in the computer industry. Digital Equipment Company was formed as an entrepreneurial venture in 1957. Data General was formed by entrepreneurs in 1968. Both manufactured minicomputers that gradually took over the market share of several mainframe computer manufacturers. General Electric and RCA exited the computer hardware business in the late 1960s and early 1970s. But both DEC and Data General became victims of the next wave of innovative computers: microcomputers introduced by Apple Computer Company. The cycle of creative destruction goes on endlessly.

Schumpeter's theory of creative destruction, with innovative entrepreneurs as central actors in creating market chaos, stands in sharp contrast to neoclassical theory, with its systematically operating markets with passive, reactive buyers and sellers responding to price fluctuations to adjust demand and supply and achieve equilibrium. The two theories defy systematic comparison. Neoclassical theory depicts the market as *static*, with changes occurring only as movement from one equilibrium condition to another. In Schumpeter's theory the market is *dynamic*, depending upon continuous change in buyer and supplier behavior. But, the scientific appeal of neoclassical theory with its predictive power overwhelmed the theories of Schumpeter and emerged as the dominant theory in American economic thought—until the decade of the entrepreneur.

Entrepreneurship prior to 1980

If Schumpeter is correct and entrepreneurs play such an important role in society, why wasn't this recognized prior to 1980? The answer lies in America's popular belief systems. After World War II American society was dominated by the belief that large corporations were the source of wealth creation and distribution. In 1956 William Whyte observed the emergence of this popular perspective in American society in his book *The Organization Man.* He suggested that the widespread exposure of Americans to poverty during the depression and military training during World War II created a behavioral norm of accepting employment within and obedience to bureaucracies. Thus, America had become conditioned to believe in the large corporation as a preferred source of employment.

This admiration of large corporations led to a theory of how society would eventually come to be dominated by these corporations. In 1967 John Kenneth Galbraith published *The New Industrial State*, wherein he expressed the belief that large corporations would work in coordination with big government and large labor unions to run the nation. This would occur because large organizations, with their large-scale, efficient production, had professional managers who held similar values centered upon organization life. Entrepreneurs are notably absent from Galbraith's "new industrial state."

Views of society as being dominated by large corporations are consistent with neoclassical theory, which includes *economies of scale* as a necessary component. "Economies of scale" means that as the size of a firm increases, the cost of production per unit declines.[2] This is due to the increase in specialization of labor and machinery that evolves as production organizations become larger. Henry Ford's invention of the assembly line to produce low-cost automobiles is a familiar example of production cost reduction through increasing the size of production plants. Ford's low-cost production of the Model T allowed it to dominate the automobile market for 20 years.

The principle of economies of scale specifies that larger firms have lower costs of production than smaller firms. This is a very practical, intuitively appealing principle of economics. Neoclassical theory proceeds further by arguing that large firms are more profitable than small firms because large firms have lower production costs. This conclusion is logically consistent for perfect markets, where all suppliers sell at the same price.

Thus, both social observers and mainstream economists find society's respect for large firms to be consistent with their theories and a logical condition for society.

Growing Dissatisfaction with Neoclassical Economics

Researchers have had great difficulty finding evidence that economies of scale exist. Few economists doubt the existence of economies of scale because considerable production management information exists to validate the theory. Most engineers can run through calculations that show larger manufacturing plants are more cost-efficient than small plants.

But researchers have difficulty finding real-world examples to demonstrate that larger producers are *more profitable*. Neoclassical theory requires not only that firms have lower costs of production but also that market prices be equal for all producers. Only when prices are equal does the lowest-cost producer earn the greatest profit. If market prices are not equal and products are differentiated, then smaller, less efficient firms can have higher prices and be more profitable.

Furthermore, large manufacturing plants that take advantage of specialization of labor and machinery in order to lower production costs become somewhat inflexible. Thus, when entrepreneurs enter markets with new technologies, existing large-scale plants may have difficulty adjusting and can actually fail as they lose market share. Manufacturing costs are a small part of market dynamics in an entrepreneurial economy, and production efficiency does not directly translate into profitability. In other words, *equilibrium markets do not exist, and economies of scale is not a dominant economic factor.*

Still, throughout the post-World War II era, discussions of entrepreneurship's role in American capitalism were relegated to a few academics involved in the study of "small business." The dominant perception of entrepreneurs is summed up in the joke "Entrepreneurs are people who start their own business to avoid getting a job." Then, in 1979, David Birch published results of an economic analysis demonstrating that *small firms dominate job creation and economic growth in the United States.* Economic theory and society's perceptions of entrepreneurs were irrevocably changed.

EMERGING THEORY OF ENTREPRENEURSHIP ECONOMICS

In 1979 David Birch created a furor in the economic establishment by publishing the results of research based on a data file of all U.S. firms and their employment from 1969 through 1976. His research concluded that small firms, those with 100 or fewer employees, created 81% of the net new jobs in the United States. ("Net new jobs" is defined as total new jobs added minus total jobs lost during the time period.) Since net new job creation is a widely accepted measure of economic growth, Birch's findings mean that small firms created most of the economic growth. In 1987 Birch provided a more complete assessment of his findings in a book entitled *Job Creation in America.*

Birch's work was largely discounted by mainstream economists at the time because it is counter to the conclusions reached using methods derived from neoclassical theory. But economists who replicated his work in the United States and other nations have verified his conclusions. In response to Birch's work, the U.S. Small Business Administration (SBA) established a long-term project to create and maintain a data file similar to Birch's beginning with 1976. The SBA continued his dynamic analytical methodology and has provided further evidence that small firms do indeed create new jobs in excess of their share of overall employment.

Evidence that Small Firms Dominate Economic Growth

The SBA's database includes all firms in the United States over the period from 1976 to 1990. The SBA calculates the respective shares of jobs created by small and large firms on a biennial (two-year) basis and publishes these statistics in the annual report *The State of Small Business*. A summary of Birch's and the SBA's findings on the small-firm share of net new jobs is shown in Exhibit 14.1.

Exhibit 14.1 shows that small firms do not produce the majority of the net new jobs in every biennial period. Period-to-period variations in small-firm share are due to fluctuations in the overall economy. During periods of economic recessions (1981–82, 1989–90) and in the first period after such recessions (1977–78, 1983–84), small firms demonstrate substantial contributions to net job creation. Late in the periods of expansion following recessions (1979–80, 1985–88), the small-firm share falls to lower levels.

Interestingly, these wide swings in employment growth shares are due primarily to variations in the hiring/firing practices of the 15,000 firms that have more than 500 employees and constitute 50% of the private-sector work force. During recessions, large firms frequently experience overall net declines in employment (job losses exceeding job additions) or only minimal net gains. Small firms, on the other hand, continue to show net gains in

EXHIBIT 14.1. Small firms' share of net new jobs: Comparison of Birch and SBA results.

Period	Birch	SBA	Static share
1969–72	82%		
1973–74	53		
1975–76	65		
1977–78		57%	36%
1979–80		37	35
1981–82		92	36
1983–84		65	36
1985–86		44	35
1987–88		33	35
1989–90		100	44

Small firm: ≤100 employees

Source: Bruce A. Kirchhoff, *Entrepreneurship and Dynamic Capitalism*, ©1994 by Bruce A. Kirchhoff, Figure 1, Quorum Books, an imprint of Greenwood Publishing Group, Inc., Westport, CT. Reprinted with permission.

employment during recessions and therefore account for a much larger share of net new employment. In fact, the stable, regular net job creation of the small-firm sector regardless of the condition of the overall economy is an important strength of the U.S. economy.

Statistics for longer-term net job creation (four to eight years) show that, on average, small firms create more net new jobs per employee than large firms, and they typically produce more than half of the total. These data make it clear that small firms are the primary job creators in the United States.

Entrepreneurial Growth and Neoclassical Theory

The impact of these findings on neoclassical economic theory (and general equilibrium theory) is profound. First, the results provide convincing evidence that economies of scale do not dominate economic growth since small firms, not large firms, create most of the growth. Second, it suggests that Schumpeter's theory of creative destruction offers a better description of the overall economy. These findings cast doubt on neoclassical theory as an appropriate model for American capitalism. Without economies of scale and with entrepreneurial suppliers as active participants in the economy, general equilibrium theory is without a solid foundation and without predictive powers.

Since 1979 the job creation research has made entrepreneurs into heroes:

- Entrepreneurs are the creators of wealth through innovation.
- Entrepreneurs are at the center of job and economic growth.
- Entrepreneurs provide a mechanism of wealth distribution that depends on innovation, hard work, and risk taking. This is widely respected as an appropriate basis for wealth distribution. Thus, entrepreneurs provide a "fair and equitable" method of wealth redistribution.

Michael Milken and Charles Keating are not entrepreneurs. Nor is Lee Iacocca or Jack Welch. These men did not form new firms with innovations and destroy existing market structures as they created new demand and new wealth.

Entrepreneurs are now recognized as important components of U.S. society. Employment in a large corporation is no longer considered the preferred objective of all who seek gainful work. Galbraith's "new industrial state" is no longer perceived as the ultimate form of society. "Going it alone" has a uniquely American, individualistic appeal, and with success the "loner" becomes wealthy while contributing to the nation's overall economic progress. To become economically independent through one's own efforts—entrepreneurship—is the ultimate expression of the American ideal of individualism.

The economics profession is now in a state of theoretical turmoil as the dominant neoclassical theory is experiencing increasing pressure to accommodate entrepreneurship. But the neoclassical perfect market cannot incorporate entrepreneurs.

A new economic theory explaining capitalism with such clarity that it allows prediction is now needed. Schumpeter's theory of creative destruction does not meet this need. It cannot be modeled mathematically or used to predict economic events. Rather, it describes capitalism as directionless, driven by the random, unpredictable phenomena of entrepreneurship. Creative destruction offers no methods to forecast the next innovation, the next successful entrepreneur, or the next economic expansion or recession. The theory's absence of predictive power leaves economics without a substitute for neoclassical economics. Much work is required to build a new theory.

A TYPOLOGY OF ENTREPRENEURS: DEFINING SURVIVAL AND SUCCESS

Economists are now working to construct a new theory to incorporate entrepreneurs into capitalism. Typology development is one step toward the development of a new theory. *Typologies* organize existing knowledge into categories that help explain relationships and guide theory development. Furthermore, typologies can provide guidance to policy development and entrepreneurial choices even in the absence of full theory development. This is important because the absence of a fully developed theory does not remove society's need to identify entrepreneurial opportunities and design economic policy to promote entrepreneurial activity. And, given the nonentrepreneurial policy prescriptions emanating from general equilibrium theory, development of a new basis for guiding pro-entrepreneurial activity is desperately needed to ensure the continued vitality of an entrepreneurial economy.

Business firms, including small businesses, have long been classified for decision analysis. Traditional classification criteria are business size, industry type (product or service produced), ownership type, age, and location. None of these provides adequate information to identify the few creative destroyers among the millions of small businesses that exist. Creative destroyers emerge from all industries, all sizes, all ownership types, all ages, and all locations.

To develop a new theory or typology for entrepreneurs, economists need to:

- Identify creative destroyers
- Determine where innovative market entry opportunities exist
- Clarify what the entrepreneurs need
- Guide economic policy so as to improve entrepreneurs' success

So far, research has established that small firms excel in job creation and innovation. There are millions of small firms,[3] and most of these stay small while producing only one or a few innovations and contributing little or only modest economic growth per firm. Birch observed that small firms create most of the net new jobs, but the vast majority of the new jobs are created by less than 10 to 12% of all small firms. This observation suggests that a small percentage of the small firms are the creative destroyers.

Furthermore, by Schumpeter's definition, entrepreneurship means new firm formation and growth, whereas the job generation statistics measure the job creation of *all* small firms—old, middle-aged, and new. Statistics show that approximately 500,000 to 700,000 new small firms are formed every year. In a small-business sector that includes 7 to 9 million firms, this amounts to an 8 to 10% annual increase. Creative destroyers are among these new firms, as well as among the existing firms, especially the ones that are still young. But not all newly formed or young firms are, or are intended to be, *high-growth firms* that challenge the giants in their markets. Most of these firms have limited growth ambitions. The owner forms and grows the business to the point where it provides a satisfactory standard of living and allows time to enjoy the benefits.

It is useful to describe and understand the phenomenon of new firm formation. Of all the important dynamics that occur in a capitalist system, *firm formation* is paramount. The more firm formations, the greater the potential economic growth. Firm formation is also the phenomenon of greatest interest to aspiring entrepreneurs. Entrepreneurs want to know:

- What are the chances of survival, failure, and growth?
- How can the chances of success be improved?
- What are the odds of achieving huge success such as that experienced by Microsoft, Apple Computer, or Dell Computer?

Economists are beginning to answer these questions. But this requires putting entrepreneurs into categories, categories that are related to theory—into a typology.

The following paragraphs present a useful typology and report the results of analysis of one group of new firms as they age and grow. But first it is necessary to dispel the "fiction of firm failure" that dominates the thinking about new small firms.

Survival Rates of Entrepreneurial Firms

Economists and politicians often quote a widely believed statement about small firm failure; "Four out of five small firms fail in their first five years."

Administrators (CEOs) of the SBA have used this alliteration to express their concern about the health of small firms, and mainstream economists have used it to express their disdain for small firms. However, this claim has no basis in fact; no statistical sources or analyses report such high failure rates. In fact, there is good evidence that *more than half*—rather than one-fifth—*of all new small firms survive for eight or more years.*

These failure statistics are especially important to aspiring entrepreneurs concerned about their future success. A description of failure is necessary for a full understanding of the survival statistics for new small firms. There is considerable difference between death and failure.

The Difference between Death and Failure of an Entrepreneurial Venture

Every year between 8% and 10% of all businesses terminate operations. Large corporations terminate as large a percentage of their plants and offices every year as do small firms. The difference is that most small firms have only one plant or office, so the termination of a small firm's only plant means the termination of the firm. Large firms, on the other hand, have multiple plants and offices, so the termination of a plant does not eliminate the firm.

Examination of the net effect of closings on employment reinforces this evidence. Over a period of several years, the large- and small-firm sectors lose the same percentage of their total employment because of plant and office closings.

Whereas large firms are required to announce plant and office closures six months in advance, small firms are not. Thus, small firms terminate operations without an announced or recorded rationale. This makes identification of small-firm deaths far more difficult. There is limited research on the reasons for small-firm closures, but one source of information, Dun & Bradstreet Corporation (D&B), records when firms fail for financial reasons. D&B operates the nation's largest commercial credit rating service, so it promptly notes a firm's default on debts to creditors.

D&B defines business "failure" as business termination with losses to creditors. This is an appropriate definition because it distinguishes the firms that fail because of financial distress and the firms that terminate operations by the choice of the owners. Those familiar with small-firm owners will not be surprised to learn that most firms terminate operations *voluntarily.* In fact, D&B reports that only 20% to 25% of all small-firm terminations are failures as defined by closure with losses to creditors.

The other 75% to 80% of small-firm terminations are due to reasons other than failure:

- Some small-firm owners simply grow tired of the business, pay the creditors, and close the doors. They retire, obtain employment elsewhere, or move on to another business.
- Other owners sell their businesses to new owners.
- Still others change their type of business. For example, an owner of a photo shop may decide to convert it to a videotape rental store.

Here are some statistics substantiating these statements. There were 814,000 new small firms formed in 1977 and 1978. Eight years later, 28% of these firms were still in existence with their same owners. U.S. Department of Labor statistics show that, on average, every year 3.3% of all businesses change ownership. For reasons that originate in data collection methods, ownership changes are largely recorded as *terminations* (sale of a firm) and *subsequent formations* (new owner acquisition of an existing firm) in the statistical data used to calculate survival rates. Thus, we need to add back 8 times 3.3%, or 26%, to the survival percentage. This gives an eight-year survival rate of 28% plus 26%, or a total of 54%. In other words, over half of all small firms formed in 1977–78 survived for eight years. (We do not have data beyond eight years.)

Of those firms that were recorded as being terminated during their first eight years (72%, including ownership changes), D&B states that *only 20% to 25% of these were failures*. Twenty-five percent of 72% is 18%. Thus, of the 814,000 firms formed in 1977–78, *only 18% terminated with losses to creditors* within eight years. A pie chart summarizing the destinies of these new firms after eight years is provided in Exhibit 14.2.

These statistics clearly show that new small firms are far more resilient and capable than is popularly believed. The chances of success for an

EXHIBIT 14.2. Eight-year destinies of all small firms formed in 1977–78 (814,000 firms).

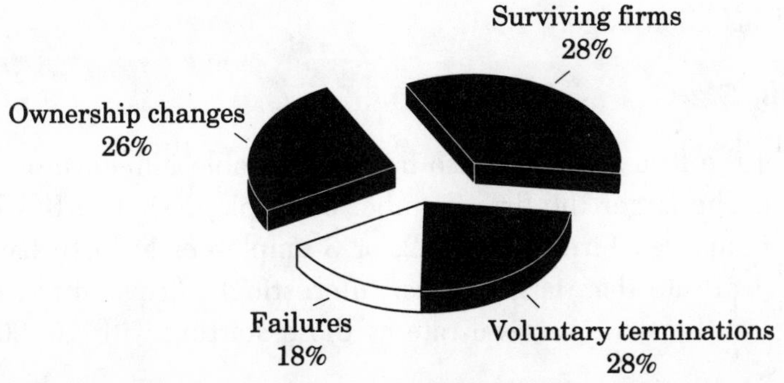

Source: Bruce A. Kirchhoff, *Entrepreneurship and Dynamic Capitalism*, ©1994 by Bruce A. Kirchhoff, Figure 2, Quorum Books, an imprint of Greenwood Publishing Group, Inc., Westport, CT. Reprinted with permission.

entrepreneur starting out in the United States are surprisingly good. Certainly, from a lender's perspective, the probability of losses from lending to new businesses is far less than that implied in the statement "four out of five (80%) fail in five years." The survival rate of the small firm, including ownership changes, is one out of two, and 28% survive with their original owners.

Factors Affecting Survival Rates of Entrepreneurial Ventures

By relating a variety of demographic factors to firm survival rates, research has determined which factors are most likely to influence survival. The factors examined are:

- Type of business activity (industry)
- Geographical area (state) where the firm is located
- Size of the firm at birth
- Degree of growth experienced by the firm
- Extent of competition in the region (state) where the firm operates

Results of this research are very encouraging for aspiring entrepreneurs.

Type of Business Activity

This factor is very important in determining survival. For example, manufacturing firms have a greater survival rate than construction firms. In fact, manufacturing firms have the greatest survival rate of all types of business.

Firms that change their business activity during the first eight years are more likely to survive. This is especially interesting because it means that business experience teaches startup entrepreneurs what is right and wrong with their business, and survivors are able to adapt their products/services based on this knowledge.

Company Size

The size of the firm at startup also has considerable influence on its chance of survival. The larger the firm (number of employees) at birth, the greater its odds of survival. Firms with 1, 2, or 3 employees at birth have a much lower survival rate than larger firms. Interestingly, firms with 4 employees at birth have the same survival rate as those starting with 10, 20, or more employees.

For reasons as yet unknown, only firms with fewer than four employees at birth experience lower survival rates. It is probable that the number of employees at birth is actually a surrogate measure for the extent of *resources* at birth. In other words, a firm beginning with four or more employees is likely to also have more startup capital and a wider variety of knowledge and skills available than a firm with only one or two employees.

Degree of Growth

Growth of the firm greatly increases its survivability. The degree of growth need not be large; the addition of only one employee after birth makes a great difference in survival rate. It is interesting to note, however, that the majority of firms show no growth for the first six years. Slightly more than 50% of surviving firms show growth after six years. Thus, growth takes much longer to achieve than most entrepreneurs expect at the time of the firm's birth.

Competition

Several of the factors examined have no effect on survival rates. The extent of competition (whether there are many competitors or only a few) makes no difference to survival. The neoclassical economic competition theory suggests that the existence of competitors will make the success of a new firm more difficult. However, Schumpeter's theory says that new firms enter with innovations that provide the opportunity for growth. Thus, Schumpeter's theory, not neoclassical theory, is supported by this finding. Entrepreneurs can rest assured that with the right innovation, they can achieve success in spite of the number of competitors.

Geographical Location

Geographical area also has no effect on survival. In other words, the chances of a small firm's survival are as good in one state as in any other. This is not good news for the state economic development specialists who busy themselves with recruiting firms from other states on the grounds that their state is a better place to be. It is good news, however, for entrepreneurs because it means that they can start their businesses where they live.

However, an important relationship exists between location and type of business. Firms in the *same type of business* tend to locate near each other. For example, computer manufacturing firms tend to cluster in California, Texas, and the Northeast. Thus, locating a computer firm in Kansas may increase your risk of termination since the clusters of computer-knowledgeable and experienced personnel and investors are not in Kansas. Of course, exceptions prove the rule, as evidenced by the success of Gateway 2000 Corporation, a major manufacturer of microcomputers located in South Dakota.

Entrepreneurs' Control over Potential Survival of the Firm

Overall, the general pattern revealed by this survival analysis is that entrepreneurs largely control the factors that influence their chances of survival. The type of business (and changes thereto) and size of firm are decisions made by the entrepreneur. Entrepreneurs may not have complete control over the growth of their firms, but they can influence growth.

Therefore, to ensure survival, entrepreneurs need to carefully pick their type of business, adjust the type according to market needs, define birth size, and work hard to achieve growth. And they need not move out of state or away from competitors to survive. If you are interested in starting a firm, remember these rules. Also remember that more than half of all new firms will survive for at least eight years.

DYNAMIC CAPITALISM TYPOLOGY: UNDERSTANDING ENTREPRENEURSHIP'S CONTRIBUTIONS TO ECONOMIC GROWTH

Survival is not itself indicative of success or economic contribution. Most business owners measure success in terms of *survival and growth*. As mentioned earlier, of those 814,000 firms formed in 1977–78, less than half of the survivors (with their original owners) experienced any growth in employment during the first six years. Growth comes slowly, not during the first year, as most entrepreneurs hope, but in six to eight years.

In a dynamic capitalist economy, entrepreneurs enter existing markets using innovations. Thus, it is logical to expect that the number of innovations created by a firm will be related to the firm's growth rate. On the other hand, it is apparent that the direct relationship proposed by Schumpeter between innovation and firm growth through creative destruction is not correct. Not all innovations are successful, so some firms that create a large number of innovations will not experience high growth. And some innovations are far more successful than others, so some firms with only a few innovations will achieve high rates of growth. This complex relationship between the rate of innovation and the rate of firm growth can be expressed in a matrix called the *dynamic capitalism typology,* illustrated in Exhibit 14.3.

The typology matrix is divided into four main categories: economic core, constrained growth, glamorous, and ambitious. Each category designates businesses with common characteristics that reflect their creative destruction capability. The matrix represents a simplification of the real world, because it lists only the extreme cases registering either high or low on each scale. As noted later in this chapter (in the discussion of the statistical evidence),

EXHIBIT 14.3. Dynamic capitalism typology.

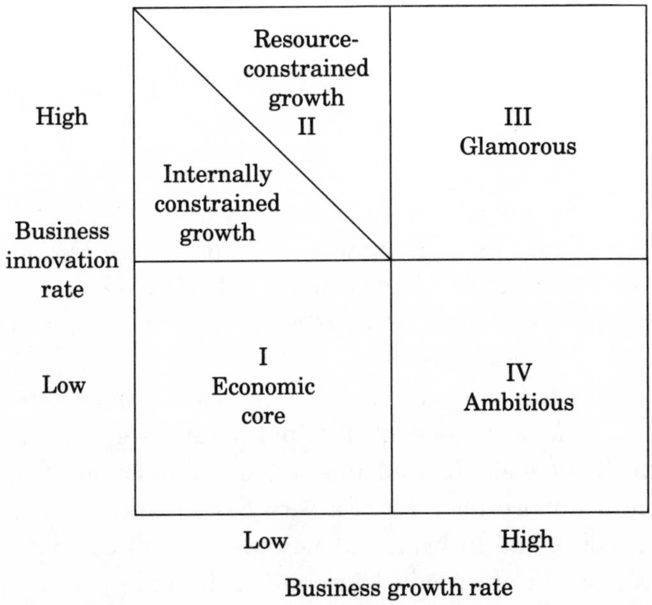

Source: Bruce A. Kirchhoff, *Entrepreneurship and Dynamic Capitalism,* ©1994 by Bruce A. Kirchhoff, Figure 3, Quorum Books, an imprint of Greenwood Publishing Group, Inc., Westport, CT. Reprinted with permission.

the vast majority of businesses lie in the middle ground, between the extremes. Still, the matrix describes categories that add to our understanding of entrepreneurship's contributions to economic growth.

Economic Core Firms

Economic core firms dominate in total numbers. There are more low-innovation and low-growth firms in the small-firm sector than any other kind. Most of these firms satisfy their owners' needs and therefore continue to successfully operate and fulfill their functions in the marketplace without achieving significant growth. No doubt, these firms achieve a degree of growth shortly after their formation, but once they achieve a size that meets the owners' needs, growth stops. Small, independent retail stores, service firms, and repair shops are economic core firms. Such firms are truly ubiquitous—there are probably 5 to 6.5 million of them—and they provide a bevy of goods and services necessary to the functioning of the U.S. economy.

The economic core also includes hundreds of thousands of firms that are small temporarily. Owners of these firms are ambitious; they want to grow into big businesses. But, to the outsider, these firms look like all other economic core firms—small, independently owned, and struggling. For example, Sam Walton's first Gibson Discount Store looked like most rural discount stores until he found the right formula for growth, changed the name to WalMart, and became the world's largest retailer. To some degree, the massiveness of the economic core hides the ambitious entrepreneur until success causes the growing firm to leap into the realm of ambitious firms.

Ambitious Firms

Ambitious firms achieve high rates of growth with one, or a combination of a few, initial innovations. A single new product or service can provide growth for many years, especially in a large market such as the United States. Growth comes as the innovative product or service takes over the market share of older, established competitors.

Examples of this type are easy to find. Dell Computer Company developed an innovative method of distributing and servicing microcomputers, through direct mail. It used this initial combination of innovations to gradually acquire more than 5% of a very large market within eight years. Of course, it continued to bring out new versions of computers, but none of these was a significant product innovation, because microcomputers had become essentially standardized. Its distribution innovation worked best because of this standardization.

So high growth can be achieved without high rates of innovation. However, an ambitious firm's growth will eventually decline *unless it develops additional innovations*, because markets do not remain static. New entrepreneurs will enter the market with product or service innovations, and the once-ambitious firm will experience loss of market share. A good example of this is Wendy's International, founded in 1968. Its original innovation—"hot and juicy hamburgers"—was extremely successful. But after 10 years, its growth rate slowed, and it searched for additional innovations in fast food to continue its growth. Unfortunately, it has never found another innovation that would allow it to achieve the high growth rates of the 1970s.

Glamorous Firms

High growth rates can be achieved over the long term only with high rates of innovation. I call firms with these characteristics *glamorous* because they attract news media attention and receive local and national awards for their successes. Most of these firms are rooted in technology-based product businesses, products that lend themselves to continuous development and spawn innovation after innovation. Microsoft is a good example of a product-manufacturing firm that has created an endless stream of innovations in the software business. It began with the now universal operation system called

Microsoft DOS. Then it expanded to include a spreadsheet program, word processor, graphics, and other features, and today it is the world's largest software company.

Constrained-Growth Firms

Many glamorous firms emerge only after a period of *constrained growth.* Lacking the proper resources, these firms have high rates of innovation but do not achieve high growth. Unless revenues grow rapidly to support the expensive innovation efforts, these firms experience financial failure. Owners of such firms fall into two classes: those who make decisions that constrain their firm's growth and those who choose growth but are unable to acquire the needed resources.

Internally Constrained Firms

Owners of these companies deny that they choose to constrain their growth, insisting that growth is constrained by the reluctance of the providers of resources to supply the firm. But, in truth, these owners place such burdens on the suppliers of resources that they are unable to cooperate. Thus, the inventor who refuses to sell more than 10% of her firm's stock in order to raise a million dollars is to blame for her lack of capital. And the owner who refuses to offer a key manager a significant share of the firm's stock to keep the manager constructively employed is also constraining the firm's growth.

Resource-Constrained Firms

Other entrepreneurs are willing to give up reasonable shares of ownership, but they are unable to find or attract the capital or personnel necessary to grow the business. These are the truly resource-constrained businesses. Such business represents a major problem in the United States because there is a lack of capital for investment in early-stage, highly innovative small firms. Without early-stage capital, many constrained-growth firms never have the opportunity to demonstrate the value and contribution of their innovations. Because innovation is expensive, such firms do not last very long. They either cease innovation and become economic core firms or they terminate.

A greater danger threatens constrained-growth firms' continued existence. Innovations (especially patented inventions) are easy prey for better-financed competitors. Highly innovative firms that do not pursue high growth may find their innovations copied and markets devoured by competitors that gobble up market share for themselves. Inventors believe that patents will protect them from such competition, but this belief is false. An issued patent actually exposes the technology to all competitors. If a competitor copies the technology, it is assumed that the courts will punish the offending firm. But the cost of bringing a patent infringement case can be afforded only by firms with good revenue and profit streams. And even if the infringement suit is successful, the courts rarely require offending firms to remove their products from the market and give up their market share. Instead, such firms pay a fine and are awarded licenses to the patent, so they continue their products and maintain their market shares. The inventor owns the patent rights, but the competitor owns the market.

Because of these forces, the constrained-growth category of firms is small in comparison to the economic core. Either firms grow or they die.

Entrepreneurs Can Apply This Typology to Classify Their Own Firms

What is interesting about these four classes of firms is that they do not depend on industrial sector, business size, age, or location. For example, ambitious manufacturing firms share many problems, needs, and opportunities with ambitious construction firms and service firms of different sizes and in different locations. At the same time, ambitious firms have little in common with economic core firms in the same industry or state. The typology also makes it clear that firms in the same industry are not the same in terms of their ambitions and goals. This is true regardless of age, since firm ownership changes sufficiently often that a firm's age tells nothing about the ambitions and goals of the owners. Even the transfer of ownership among family members (for example, parent to child) may create a new set of ambitions. This typology identifies the firm behaviors that indicate the true ambitions and goals of the owners and defines their contribution to economic growth.

Aspiring entrepreneurs need to realistically assess their personal ambitions and where they wish to be in this typology. Not everyone wants the traumas and chaos of starting and running an ambitious firm. Once a modicum of growth is achieved, many formerly ambitious owners suddenly discover that achievement of their ambitions is too costly to their personal lives, and they decide to settle for less. For example, many local retail and restaurant chains have the potential for national growth but choose to remain local. The owners decide that the costs in money and time necessary to achieve national growth are simply more than they want to commit.

Few aspiring entrepreneurs have the drive for innovation and growth that is required to build a glamorous firm. Many inventors have an initial interest in becoming the next Microsoft or Apple Computer Company, but they lack the necessary business savvy or capital.

This leaves the *economic core as the bastion of entrepreneurs* who have moderate ambitions and those who had greater ambitions but decided to settle for less. Some constrained-growth firms reduce their innovation rates and settle for low growth, thereby becoming a part of the economic core. This does not mean, however, that the economic core is a refuge for failed ambitious and glamorous entrepreneurs. These entrepreneurs find niche markets where they provide goods and services that are preferred by a variety of buyers. The very existence of so many small firms in all industrial sectors demonstrates their success in meeting market needs. Their contribution to overall economic activity and growth is considerable because even a small rate of growth among 5 million businesses creates a lot of new jobs annually.

This contribution to growth is not just a belief. It can be measured and, as shown in the next section, it is considerable.

Measuring Growth Contributions of Entrepreneurs

The dynamic capitalism typology provides a basis for measuring the relative contributions of the four types of entrepreneurs to overall economic growth. In Schumpeter's original theoretical formulation, new small firms that have been formed to exploit innovations create economic growth. Therefore, measurement of dynamic capitalism focuses on newly formed firms. This approach understates the total contributions of all small firms because it considers growth attributable to only a small group of newly formed firms. The approach does, however, isolate the dynamics of new firms in a direct test of the dynamic capitalism typology and creative destruction.

To accomplish this task, Bruce Phillips and I identified all firms formed in the United States between December 31, 1976, and December 31, 1978. For practical purposes, this includes all firms formed during 1977 and 1978. This cohort of firms was followed for the next six years, until the end of 1984. Measures of the number of employees in each firm were taken at the time of birth and at the end of 1984.

The cohort consists of 814,190 small firms formed during 1977 and 1978. Of these, 312,804 survived with the same ownership through 1984. We divided these firms into the four typology classes. We calculated the growth in employment of all firms and defined *high growth* to include the 10% with the greatest growth rates. *Low growth* included the 10% of all firms with the smallest growth rates.

We defined *high innovation* as comprising all firms in a selected gr
of industries where business activity is characterized by above-ave
ployment of scientists, engineers, and technical professionals
tries also display above-average expenditures in research
(This is a common research definition of "high-tech
We selected another group of industries with the oppo
and defined firms in these industries as *low innovation* (

Success of High-Innovation Firms

Growth rates differed significantly among typology classes. As suggested earlier, glamorous firms showed the greatest growth of all classes. More than 16% of the high-innovation firms became high-growth firms. But only 9% of the high-innovation firms survived as low-growth firms (constrained growth). As discussed earlier, growth is essential for the survival of high-innovation firms because of the cost of innovation. Overall, however, the survival rate of high-innovation firms was as good as that for low-innovation firms. These statistics are shown in Exhibit 14.4.

Success of Low-Innovation Firms

Not surprisingly, only 9% of the low-innovation firms achieved high growth to become ambitious firms. This is significantly lower than the 16% reported for high-innovation firms. But, more than 10% of the low-innovation firms reported low growth. These statistics are shown in Exhibit 14.5.

EXHIBIT 14.4. Six-year destinies of high-innovation firms formed in 1977–78 (58,714 total births).

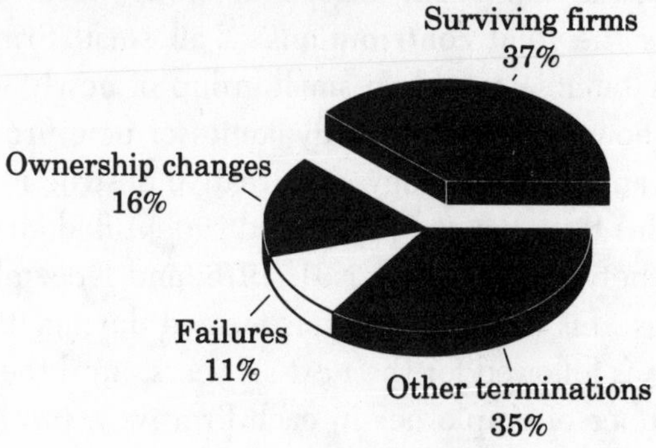

All High-Innovation Firms

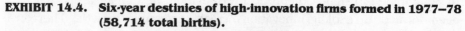

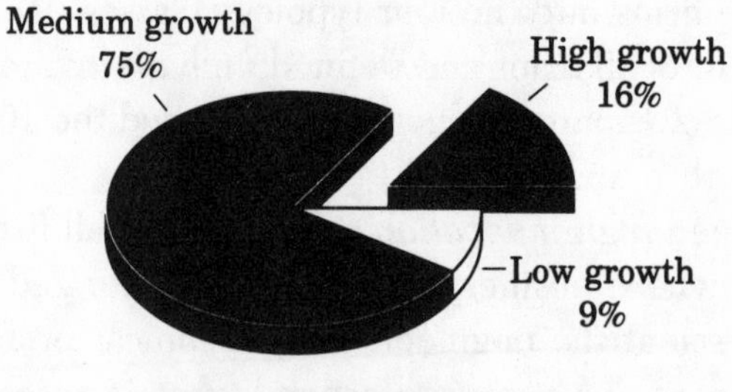

Surviving Firms

Source: Bruce A. Kirchhoff, *Entrepreneurship and Dynamic Capitalism,* ©1994 by Bruce A. Kirchhoff, Figure 4, Quorum Books, an imprint of Greenwood Publishing Group, Inc., Westport, CT. Reprinted with permission.

EXHIBIT 14.5. Six-year destinies of low-innovation firms formed in 1977–78 (number of firms formed = 280,305).

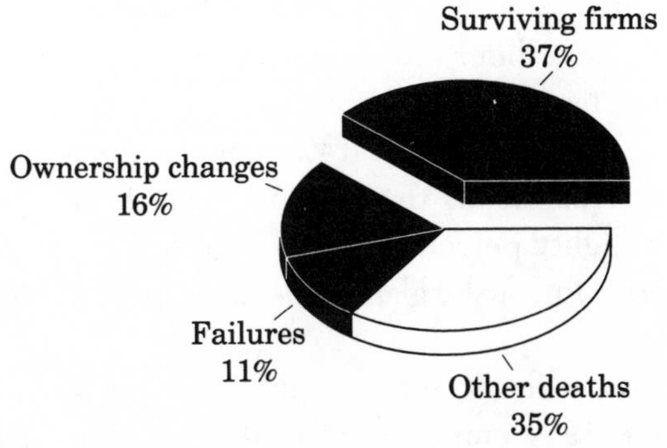

All Low-Innovation Firms

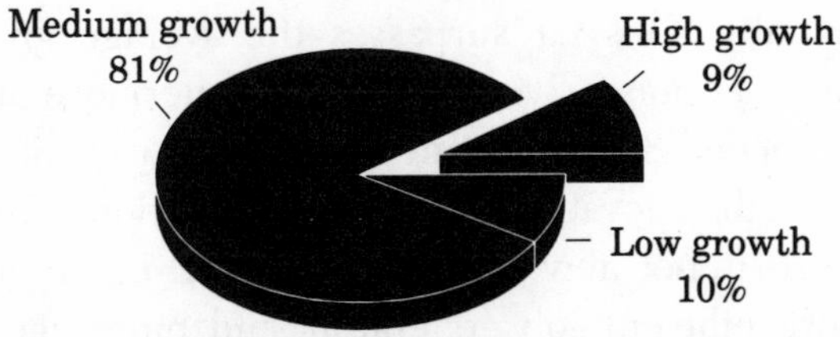

Surviving Firms

Source: Bruce A. Kirchhoff, *Entrepreneurship and Dynamic Capitalism,* ©1994 by Bruce A. Kirchhoff, Figure 5, Quorum Books, an imprint of Greenwood Publishing Group, Inc., Westport, CT. Reprinted with permission.

Overall Survival of Entrepreneurial Ventures

In summary, it is apparent that overall survival of newly formed small firms does not depend on innovation rates. Thus, the risk of starting a high-tech firm is no greater than that of starting a low-tech firm. However, the chances of achieving high growth are almost twice as great for high-tech firms as for low-tech firms. Still, among high-tech firms, terminations take a greater toll, as low-growth firms are unable to hang on for as long as low-tech firms.

Given these statistical results, it is somewhat surprising that so few high-tech firms are formed relative to low-tech firms. Low-tech firm formations outnumbered high-tech formations 5 to 1. This fact has significant import concerning the overall job creation contribution of the two-year cohort of newly formed firms. The total employment of the 312,804 surviving firms at the end of 1984 was actually 25% less than the birth employment of the 814,190 firms in 1978. In 1978 the total cohort employment was 4.5 million. By 1984, this had declined to 3.4 million. This is due largely to the departure of 502,000 firms during the six years. Among the 312,804 surviving firms, total employment increased 75% over birth employment. However, some of the surviving firms also suffered declining employment.

Employment changes differ considerably among typology classes. Among high-innovation firms, total employment increased by 14%. That is, the 21,603 surviving firms employed 14% more workers than the entire birth cohort of 58,714. This means that the surviving firms increased their employment by 169%. Eighty percent of this job growth occurred within the glamorous class of firms. Obviously, glamorous firms are the big job creators among new small firms.

Among low-innovation firms, total employment decreased by 31%. A comparison of birth and 1984 employment of the survivors showed an employment increase of 67%. Seventy percent of this job creation activity was concentrated in the ambitious firms. Although not spectacular, 67% growth in employment over a six-year period is an average of more than 9% compounded annually. This far surpasses the average growth in the employment, which is at most 3% annually. Furthermore, these low-innovation survivors produced 380,000 net new jobs. Because there are so many more of these than high-innovation firms, low-innovation firms outproduced high-innovation firms in net new jobs by over 2 to 1. In summary, high-innovation firms are more efficient job generators and more aggressive growers than low-innovation firms, at least during their first six years. But so many more low-innovation firms are started that these firms produce more net new jobs.

It is likely that few of these firms achieved full growth in their first 6 years. Only after analyzing their performance for 10 to 20 years can we identify the full job creation potential of these firms.

These firms had a significant net impact on the U.S. economy. Between the end of 1976 and the end of 1984, the formation and growth of this cohort of firms added 3.5 million net new jobs.[4] Since the total private-sector employment during this time was about 90 million, these firms increased total employment by nearly 4%.

We have examined only one two-year cohort of newly formed firms. Another 800,000 firms were formed in 1979–80, another 800,000 in 1981–82, and so on. If each of these two-year cohorts contribute 4% of the net new jobs, then the average effect is a 2% contribution annually to new employment in an economy that creates 3% to 3.5% new jobs annually. This is how small firms create the largest percentage of net new jobs in America.

ECONOMIC ADVICE FOR ASPIRING ENTREPRENEURS

The typology and research data and their implications for the economic theory of dynamic capitalism provide some advice for aspiring entrepreneurs.

Be Innovative

There are no a priori economic reasons for not starting a new firm using an innovation. In spite of dire warnings from mainstream economists, economies of scale are easily overcome by innovations. But be sure your innovation is significant enough to overcome any economies of scale that exist within the markets you are entering.

For example, small retailers are being ravaged by large firms entering with computerized inventory control systems. These systems allow firms to track daily sales to determine what items are and are not selling. With such control, they can ensure adequate stock on their retail shelves while maintaining a minimum of backup stock in their warehouses. This reduces the cash invested in inventory and frees it for use in advertising, store refurbishing, or salary increases for successful sales personnel. Unless you have a retailing innovation that overcomes this computer advantage, entering retailing is a high-risk venture. On the other hand, there may be entrepreneurial independent wholesalers who are willing to link their warehouses to their small retailers' computerized cash registers to give these retailers the advantages now possessed by larger firms. This may be the innovation the small retailers need. Perhaps you are the entrepreneur capable of developing and marketing this innovation.

Don't Worry about Location

Location is not an impediment to entrepreneurial success. You can start your firm in any location regardless of tax rates, living conditions or other touted advantages. One state is as good as another, although few state and local departments of economic development will agree with that statement. If you like where you live, stay there. Do not let someone convince you to move to start your business. If you really have doubts about this, I have the telephone number of a successful small computer firm in Spalding, Nebraska (population 635). Try to find Spalding on a map.

Choose Your Business Type Carefully

Highly innovative firms have greater chances for high-growth success but less staying power if early success is not achieved. You do not have to be a scientific genius to start a highly innovative firm. The list of highly innovative firms includes many services such as business consulting and environmental consulting.[5]

Furthermore, high innovation is not the only route to success. Firms with low rates of innovation can and do succeed. The restaurant business has seen a host of successful innovations in the last 20 years, and restaurants basically serve the same food. Most restaurant innovations have been in marketing. For example, Domino's Pizza is home-delivered, hot and on time. Little Caesar's Pizza is pickup and inexpensive. Both are highly successful and definitely low-technology innovations. With a good marketing gimmick and a willingness to work, you can become a national restaurant franchisor.

Join with Three or More Partners to Start Your Firm

The larger your business is at startup, the better your chances of survival. It takes a wide variety of skills to start a new firm, and few individuals possess all the skills needed. So round up some partners to round out your skills—and to provide the early-stage startup capital.

Don't Be Intimidated by Competitors' Size and Proximity

A good innovation finds an initial small market segment and grows it into a major market share. Large competitors are especially slow to respond to an innovation. One firm I started entered a market where there was one dominant competitor with over 75% market share. And this firm had a history of copying all new products that entered the industry. But it rarely copied a product until five to seven years after its successful introduction. That is a long enough time for a new firm to start up and earn enough money to fund a patent suit.

Be Proud of What You Are Doing

It has been said that an entrepreneur is someone who starts a business because he cannot keep a job. This is not true. Most entrepreneurs want to achieve success through their own efforts. And successful entrepreneurs are very important to America's economic growth. Every new firm creates new jobs. Every successful, growing new firm creates lots of new jobs and new wealth and redistributes wealth. Entrepreneurship is America.

Furthermore, it is becoming more obvious that large firms cannot guarantee lifetime employment. Younger Americans are beginning to recognize that dependence on one's own abilities through owning and managing a business is an attractive option to being booted out when the large corporation begins to experience market share decline, decline that is often attributable to entrepreneurial activity.

Be Ever Alert for Other Entrepreneurs

Once your firm becomes established in an attractive market environment, some entrepreneur is going to take aim at you. With any luck, the entrepreneur's attack and your positive response will result in a growing market big enough for both of you. Remember, even IBM earned considerable profits initially from Apple Computer's introduction of the personal computer by rapidly creating its own competing standard in the market. Unfortunately for IBM, it was unable to sustain its dominant market share in the face of a variety of entrepreneurial attacks from Compaq, Dell, and Gateway 2000. A well-planned "me too" response to an entrepreneurial entry can ensure your continued involvement in the market.

Keep Your Eye on Foreign Firms

Entrepreneurs are not always independent small American firms. Foreign corporations are equally powerful in entering and gobbling up market shares. This is especially evident in automobiles and home electronics, where Japanese corporations have entered and now dominate. When this happens, the U.S. economy suffers losses of jobs and wealth. Thus, the decline of the domestic automobile and home electronics industries can be viewed as a failure of U.S. entrepreneurship: If U.S. entrepreneurs had entered these industries before the Japanese entrepreneurs, these industries might still be U.S.-dominated. Prior to World War II, nations had relatively closed market borders. But today, creative destruction travels easily across national boundaries.

CONCLUSION

It is now apparent that entrepreneurial entry benefits buyers by providing products and services with lower prices, better quality, and more features than were previously available. In fact, it is these characteristics of entrepreneurial innovation that make the entrepreneurs so successful. People do not buy entrepreneurs' new products or services because they like entrepreneurs; they buy these innovations because they provide greater buyer satisfaction. *Buyer satisfaction drives the success of entrepreneurs.*

For this reason, entrepreneurship is now recognized as the engine of competition and economic growth. It is the mechanism by which new products and services enter the economy and create growth. A logical extension of this reality is that the more entrepreneurship an economy produces, the better are its chances of remaining competitive in domestic and world markets.

SUGGESTED READINGS

David Birch, *Job Creation in America* (New York: The Free Press, 1987).

Bruce A. Kirchhoff, *Entrepreneurship and Dynamic Capitalism* (Westport, CT: Quorum Books, 1994).

GLOSSARY

Accounts payable: Money the company owes to vendors who supplied it with goods or services on credit. A measure of the average time taken to pay suppliers is the number of days payable, which is (accounts payable/annual credit purchases) × 365.

Accounts receivable: Money owed to a company by customers who have bought goods or services on credit. Accounts receivable are a current asset on the balance sheet. They are a liquid asset inasmuch as they are converted to cash in a relatively short time. If payment terms are net 30 days, then in principle every account receivable will be paid in 30 days or sooner. In practice, customers take longer. A measure of the average time taken is the number of days receivable, which is (accounts receivable/annual sales on credit) × 365.

Acid-test (quick) ratio: Current assets minus inventories divided by current liabilities. This ratio indicates a company's ability to meet its current liabilities with its most liquid (quick) assets.

Additional paid-in capital: Money received by a company from the sale of common stock that is in excess of the par value of the stock. If the par value of a share of common stock is $0.10 and investors purchase stock from the company at a price of $1.00 per share, the additional paid-in capital is $0.90 per share. (See *par value.*)

Adjusted book value (of a company): The book value on the balance sheet after assets and liabilities are adjusted to market value (synonymous with modified book value).

Agency costs: An agency relationship occurs where one party (the principal) rewards another (the agent) for taking decisions on its behalf. Contract design plays an important role in ensuring that the agent acts in the interest of the principal. Agency costs occur because contracts are costly to write and enforce. They include the costs of structuring, monitoring, and bonding a set of contracts among agents with conflicting interests, plus the residual loss incurred because the cost of the full enforcement of contracts exceeds the benefits.

Agency theory: A branch of economics dealing with the behavior of principals (for example, owners) and their agents (for example, managers).

American Stock Exchange (Amex): Stock exchange located in New York, listing companies that are generally smaller and younger than those on the much larger New York Stock Exchange.

Angel: Wealthy individual who invests in private companies. (See *invisible venture capital.*)

Antidilution (of ownership): The right of an investor to maintain the same percentage ownership of a company's common stock in the event that the company issues more stock. (See *dilution.*)

Asked: The price level at which sellers offer securities to buyers.

Asset acquisition: Means of effecting a buyout by purchase of certain desired assets rather than shares of the target company.

Audited financial statements: A company's financial statements prepared and certified by a certified public accounting firm that is totally independent of the company.

Balance sheet: Summary statement of a company's financial position at a given point in time. It summarizes the accounting value of the assets, liabilities, preferred stock, common stock, and retained earnings. Assets = Liabilities + Preferred stock + Common stock + Retained earnings. (See *pro forma statements.*)

Basis point: One-hundredth of a percent (0.01%), typically used in expressing yield differentials (7.50% − 7.15% = 0.35%, or 35 basis points). (See *yield.*)

Bear: A person who expects prices to fall.

Bear market: A period of generally falling prices and pessimistic attitudes.

Best efforts offering: The underwriter makes its best efforts to sell as much as it can of the shares at the offering price. Hence, unlike a firm commitment offering, the company offering its shares is not guaranteed a definite amount of money by the underwriter.

Bid: The price level at which buyers offer to acquire securities from sellers.

Big Board: See *New York Stock Exchange.*

Blue sky: Refers to laws that safeguard investors from being misled by unscrupulous promoters of companies with little or no substance.

Book value (of an asset): The accounting value of an asset as shown on a balance sheet is the cost of the asset minus its accumulated depreciation. It is not necessarily identical to its market value.

Book value (of a company): The common stock equity shown on the balance sheet. It is equal to total assets minus liabilities and preferred stock (synonymous with net worth and owners' equity).

Break-even point: The sales volume at which a company's net sales revenue just equals its costs. A commonly used approximate formula for the break-even point is Sales revenue = Total fixed costs/Gross margin.

Bridging finance: Short-term finance that is expected to be repaid relatively quickly. It usually bridges a short-term financing need. For example, it provides cash needed before an expected stock flotation.

Burn rate: The negative real-time cash flow from a company's operations, usually computed monthly.

Business plan: Document prepared by entrepreneurs, possibly in conjunction with their professional advisors, detailing the past, present, and intended future of the company. It contains a thorough analysis of the managerial, physical, labor, product, and financial resources of the company, plus the background of the company, its previous trading record, and its market position. The business plan contains detailed profit, balance sheet, and cash flow projections for two years ahead, and less detailed information for the following three years. The business plan crystallizes and focuses the management team's ideas. It explains their strategies, sets objectives, and is used to monitor their subsequent performance.

Call: A contract allowing the issuer of a security to buy back that security from the purchaser at an agreed-upon price during a specific period of time.

Capital gain: The amount by which the selling price of an asset (for example, common stock) exceeds the seller's initial purchase price.

Capitalization rate: The discount rate K used to determine the present value of a stream of future earnings. PV = (Normalized earnings after taxes)/(K/100), where PV is the present value of the firm and K is the firm's cost of capital. (See page 387.)

Carried interest: A venture capital firm's share of the profit earned by a fund. In the United States, the carried interest (carry) is typically 20% of the profit after investors' principal has been repaid.

Cash flow: The difference between the company's cash receipts and its cash payments in a given period.

Cash-flow statement: A summary of a company's cash flow over a period of time. (See *pro forma statements.*)

Chattel mortgage: A lien on specifically identified property (assets other than real estate) backing a loan.

Collateral: An asset pledged as security for a loan.

Common stock: Shares of ownership, or equity, in a corporation.

Compensating balance: A bank requires a customer to maintain a certain level of demand deposits that do not bear interest. The interest forgone by the customer on that compensating balance recompenses the bank for services provided, credit lines, and loans.

Conversion ratio: The number of shares of common stock that may be received in exchange for each share of a convertible security.

Convertible security: Preferred stock that is convertible into common stock according to a specified ratio at the security holder's option.

Corporation: A business form that is an entity legally separate from its owners. Its important features include limited liability, easy transfer of ownership, and unlimited life.

Cost of capital: The required rate of return of various types of financing. The overall cost of capital is a weighted average of the individual required rates of returns (costs).

Cost of debt capital: The interest rate charged by a company's lenders.

Cost of equity capital: The rate of return on investment required by the company's common shareholders (colloquially called the hurdle rate).

Cost of goods sold: The direct cost of the product sold. For a retail business, the cost of all goods sold in a given period equals the inventory at the beginning of the period plus the cost of goods purchased during that period minus the inventory at the end of the period.

Cost of preferred stock: The rate of return on investment required by the company's preferred shareholders.

Covenant: A restriction on a borrower imposed by a lender. For example, it could be a requirement placed on a company to achieve and maintain specified targets such as levels of cash flow, balance sheet ratios, or specified capital expenditure levels in order to retain financing facilities.

Cumulative dividend provision: A requirement that unpaid dividends on preferred stock accumulate and have to be paid before a dividend is paid on common stock.

Current ratio: Current assets/Current liabilities. This ratio indicates a company's ability to cover its current liabilities with its current assets. (See *acid-test ratio.*)

Deal flow: The rate at which new investment propositions come to funding institutions.

Debenture: A document containing an acknowledgment of indebtedness on the part of a company, usually secured by a charge on the company's assets.

Debt service: Payments of principal and interest required on a debt over a given period.

Deep pockets: Refers to an investor who has substantial financial resources.

Default: The nonperformance of a stated obligation. The nonpayment by the issuer of interest or principal on a bond or the nonperformance of a covenant.

Deferred payment: A debt that has been incurred and will be repaid at some future date.

Depreciation: The systematic allocation of the cost of an asset over a period of time for financial reporting and tax purposes.

Dilution (of ownership): This happens when a new stock issue results in a decrease in the preissue owners' percentage of the common stock.

Discounted cash flow (DCF): Methods of evaluating investments by adjusting the cash flows for the time value of money. In the decision to invest in a project, all future cash flows expected from that investment are discounted back to their present value at the time the investment is made. The discount rate is whatever rate of return the investor requires. In theory, if the present value of the future cash flows is greater than the money being invested, the investment should be made. (See *discount rate, internal rate of return, net present value,* and *present value.*)

Discount rate (capitalization rate): Rate of return used to convert future values to present values. (See *capitalization rate, internal rate of return,* and *rate of return.*)

Doriot, General Georges: Founder of the modern venture capital industry, Harvard Business School professor, and one of the creators of INSEAD.

Double jeopardy: The case where an entrepreneur's main source of income and most of her net worth depend on her business.

Due diligence: The process of investigation by investors into a potential investee's management team, resources, and trading performance. This includes rigorous testing of the business plan assumptions and the verification of material facts (such as existing accounts).

Dun & Bradstreet (D&B): The biggest credit-reporting agency in the United States.

Early-stage financing: This category includes seed-stage, startup-stage, and first-stage financing.

Earnings: This is synonymous with income and profit.

Earnings before interest and taxes (EBIT): See *operating income.*

Earnings per share (EPS): A company's net income divided by the number of common shares issued and outstanding.

Elasticity of demand: The percentage change in the quantity of a good demanded divided by the percentage change in the price of that good. When the elasticity is greater than 1, the demand is said to be elastic, and when it is less than 1, it is inelastic. In the short term, the demand for nonessential goods (for example, airline travel) is usually elastic, and the demand for essentials (for example, electricity) is usually inelastic.

Employee stock ownership plan (ESOP): A trust established to acquire shares in a company for subsequent allocation to employees over a period of time. Several possibilities are available for structuring the operation of an ESOP. Essentially, either the company makes payments to the trust, which the trust uses to purchase shares; or the trust, having previously borrowed to acquire shares, may use the payments from the company to repay loans. The latter form is referred to as a leveraged ESOP and may be used as a means of providing part of the funding required to effect a buyout. A particular advantage of an ESOP is the possibility of tax relief for the contributions made by the company to the trust and on the cost of borrowing in those cases where the trust purchases shares in advance.

Employment agreement: An agreement whereby senior managers contract to remain with the company for a specified period. For the investing institutions, such an agreement provides some measure of security that the company's performance will not be adversely affected by the unexpected departure of key managers.

Equity: See *owners' equity.*

Equity kicker (or warrant): An option or instrument linked to the provision of other types of funding, particularly mezzanine finance, which enables the provider to obtain an equity stake and hence a share in capital gains. In this way, providers of subordinated debt can be compensated for the higher risk they incur.

Exit: The means by which investors in a company realize all or part of their investment.

Expansion financing: Working capital for the initial expansion of a company that is producing and shipping products and has growing accounts receivable and inventories.

Factoring: A means of enhancing the cash flow of a business. A factoring company pays to the firm a certain proportion of the value of the firm's trade debts and then receives the cash as the trade debtors settle their accounts. Invoice discounting is a similar procedure.

Filing: Documents, including the prospectus, filed with the SEC for approval before an IPO.

Financing flows: Cash flows generated by debt and equity financing.

Firm commitment offering: The underwriter guarantees to raise a certain amount of money for the company and other selling stockholders at the IPO.

First-round financing: The first investment made by external investors.

First-stage financing: Financing to initiate full manufacturing and sales.

Five Cs of credit: The five crucial elements for obtaining credit are character (borrower's integrity), capacity (sufficient cash flow to service the debt), capital (borrower's net worth), collateral (assets to secure the debt), and conditions (of the borrowing company, its industry, and the general economy).

Fixed and floating charges: Claims on assets pledged as security for debt. Fixed charges cover specific fixed assets, and floating charges relate to all or part of a company's assets.

Floating lien: A general lien against a group of assets, such as accounts receivable or inventory, without the assets being specifically identified.

Flotation: A method of raising equity financing by selling shares on a stock market, and often allowing management and institutions to realize some of their investment at the same time. (See *initial public offering*.)

Franchising: An organizational form in which a firm (the franchisor) with a market-tested business package centered on a product or service enters into a continuing contractual relationship with franchisees operating under the franchisor's trade name to produce or market goods or services according to a format specified by the franchisor.

Free cash flow: Cash flow in excess of that required to fund all projects that have a positive net present value when discounted at the relevant cost of capital. Conflicts of interest between shareholders and managers arise when the organization generates free cash flow. Shareholders may desire higher dividends, but managers may wish to invest in projects providing a return below the cost of capital. (See *cost of capital* and *net present value*.)

Future value: The value at a future date of a present amount of money. $FV_t = PV \times (1 + K/100)^t$, where FV_t is the future value, PV is the present value, K is the percentage annual rate of return, and t is the number of years. For example, an investment of $100,000 must have a future value of $384,160 after four years to produce a rate of return of 40%, which is the kind of return that an investor in an early-stage company expects to earn. (See *net present value*, *present value*, and *rate of return*.)

Gearing: British term of leverage. (See *leverage*.)

Going concern: This assumes that the company will continue as an operating business as opposed to going out of business and liquidating its assets.

Golden handcuffs: A combination of rewards and penalties given to key managers to dissuade them from leaving the company. Examples are high salaries, paid on a deferred basis while employment is maintained, and stock options.

Goodwill: The difference between the purchase price of a company and the net value of its assets purchased.

Gross margin: Gross profit as a percentage of net sales revenue.

Gross profit (gross income, gross earnings): Net sales revenue minus the direct cost of the products sold.

Guarantee: An undertaking to prove that a debt or obligation of another will be paid or performed. It may relate either to a specific debt or to a series of transactions such as a guarantee of a bank overdraft. For example, entrepreneurs are often required to provide personal guarantees for loans borrowed by their companies.

Harvest: The realization of the value of an investment. (See *exit*.)

High-potential venture: A company started with the intent of growing quickly to annual sales of at least $30–50 million in five years. It has the potential to have a firm-commitment IPO.

Hurdle rate: The minimum rate of return that is acceptable to investors. (See *return on investment*.)

Income statement: A summary of a company's revenues, expenses, and profits over a specified period of time. (See *pro forma statements*.)

Initial public offering (IPO): Process by which a company raises money, and gets listed, on a stock market (See *flotation*.)

INSEAD: The European Institute of Business Administration located in Fontainebleau, France.

Interest cover: The extent to which periodic interest commitments on borrowings are exceeded by periodic profits. It is the ratio of profits before the deduction of interest and taxes to interest payments. The ratio may also be expressed as the cash flow from operations divided by the amount of interest payable.

Internal rate of return (IRR): The discount rate that equates the present value of the future net cash flows from an investment with the project's cash outflows. It is a means of expressing the percentage rate of return projected on a proposed investment. For an investment in a company, the calculation takes account of cash invested, cash receipts from dividend payments and redemptions, percentage equity held, expected date of payments, realization of the investment and capitalization at that point, and possible further financing requirements. The calculation will frequently be quoted in a range depending on sensitivity analysis. (See *discount rate, present value, future value,* and *rate of return*.)

Inventory: Finished goods, work in process of manufacture, and raw materials owned by a company.

Investment bank: A financial institution engaged in the issue of new securities, including management and underwriting of issues as well as securities trading and distribution.

Investment flows: Cash flows associated with purchase and sales of both fixed assets and business interests.

Invisible venture capital (informal venture capital): Venture capital supplied by wealthy individuals (angels), as opposed to visible venture capital, which is supplied by formal venture capital firms that make up the organized venture capital industry.

Junior debt: Loan ranking after senior debt or secured debt for payment in the event of a default.

Junk bonds: A variety of high-yield, unsecured bonds tradeable on a secondary market and not considered to be of investment quality by credit-rating agencies. High yield normally indicates higher risk. Michael Milken, the king of the U.S. junk bond industry in the 1980s, served time in federal jail after pleading guilty to several felonies relating to the junk bond market.

Key person insurance: Additional security provided to financial backers of a company through the purchase of insurance on the lives of key managers who are seen as crucial to the future of the company. Should one or more of those key executives die prematurely, the financial backers would receive the insurance payment.

Lead investor: In syndicated deals, normally the investor who originates, structures, and subsequently plays the major monitoring role.

Lemons and plums: Bad deals and good deals, respectively.

Leverage: The amount of debt in a company's financing structure, which may be expressed as a percentage of the total financing or as a ratio of debt to equity. The various quasi-equity (preference-type shares) and quasi-debt (mezzanine debt) instruments used to fund later-stage companies means that great care is required in calculating and interpreting leverage or gearing ratios.

Leveraged buyout (LBO): Acquisition of a company by an investor group, an investor, or an investment/LBO partnership, with a significant amount of debt (usually at least 70% of the total capitalization) and with plans to repay the debt with funds generated from the acquired company's operations or from asset sales. LBOs are frequently financed in part with junk bonds.

Lien: A legal claim on certain assets that are used to secure a loan.

Line of credit (with a bank): An arrangement between a bank and a customer specifying the maximum amount of unsecured debt the customer can owe the bank at a given point in time.

Line of credit (with a vendor): A limit set by the seller on the amount that a purchaser can buy on credit.

Liquidation value (of an asset): The amount of money that can be realized from the sale of an asset sold separately from its operating organization.

Liquidation value (of a company): The market value of the assets minus the liabilities that must be paid of a company that is liquidating.

Liquidity: The ability of an asset to be converted to cash as quickly as possible and without any price discount.

Listing: Acceptance of a security for trading on an organized stock exchange. Hence, a stock traded on the New York Stock Exchange is said to be listed on the NYSE.

Loan note: A form of vendor finance or deferred payment. The purchaser (borrower) may agree to make payments to the holder of the loan note at specified future dates. The holder may be able to obtain cash at an earlier date by selling at a discount to a financing institution that will collect on maturity.

Management buyout (MBO): The transfer of ownership of an entity to a new set of owners in which the existing management and employees are a significant element.

Market capitalization: The total value at market prices of the securities in issue for a company, a stock market, or a sector of a stock market, calculated by multiplying the number of shares issued by the market price per share.

Mezzanine financing: Strictly, any form of financing instrument between ordinary shares and senior debt. The forms range from senior mezzanine debt, which may simply carry an interest rate above that for senior secured debt, to junior mezzanine debt, which may carry rights to subscribe for equity but no regular interest payment.

Middle-market company: A company that has sales revenue of $5–20 million and modest growth. In contrast to a high-potential company, it does not have the potential to float an IPO, but it may be a candidate for an acquisition, LBO, MBO, or ESOP.

Multiple: The amount of money realized from the sale of an investment divided by the amount of money originally invested.

Murphy's Law: What can go wrong, will go wrong. An unexpected setback will happen at the most inconvenient moment.

National Association of Securities Dealers (NASD): Organization for brokers and dealers in OTC stocks.

National Association of Securities Dealers Automated Quotation (NASDAQ): An electronic system set up by NASD for trading stocks. It is commonly referred to as the OTC market.

Net income (net earnings, net profit): A company's final income after all expenses and taxes have been deducted from all revenues. It is also known as the bottom line.

Net income margin: Net income as a percentage of net sales revenue. In a typical year an average U.S. company has a net income margin of about 5%.

Net liquid value: Liquid financial assets minus callable liabilities.

Net present value: The present value of an investment's future net cash flows minus the initial investment. In theory, if the net present value is greater than 0, an investment should be made. For example, an investor is asked to invest $100,000 in a company that is expanding. He expects a rate of return of 30%. The company offers to pay him back $300,000 after four years. The present value of $300,000 at a rate of return of 30% is $105,038. Thus, the net present value of the investment is $5,038, so the investment should be made. (See *free cash flow, future value, present value,* and *rate of return.*)

Net profit: See *net income.*

Net worth: See *book value.*

New York Stock Exchange (NYSE): The largest stock exchange in the world, located in New York. Also known as the Big Board.

Offering circular: See *prospectus.*

Operating cash flows: Cash flows directly generated by a company's operations. The cash flow from operating activity equals net income plus depreciation minus increase in accounts receivable minus increase in inventories plus increase in accounts payable plus increase in accruals. (See *financing flows* and *investment flows.*)

Operating income: Earnings (profit) before deduction of interest payments and income taxes, abbreviated to EBIT. It measures a company's earning power from its ongoing operations. It is of particular concern to a company's lenders, such as banks, because operating income demonstrates the ability of a company to earn sufficient income to pay the interest on its debt. (See *times interest earned.*)

Out of cash (OOC): A common problem with entrepreneurial companies. The OOC time period is cash on hand divided by the burn rate.

Over the counter (OTC): The purchase and sale of financial instruments not conducted on a stock exchange such as the New York Stock Exchange or the American Stock Exchange. The largest OTC market is the NASDAQ.

Owners' equity: Common stock plus retained earnings. (See *book value of a company.*)

Paid-in capital: Par value per share times the number of shares issued. Additional paid-in capital is the price paid in excess of par value times the number of shares issued.

Partnership: Legal form of a business in which two or more persons are co-owners, sharing profits and losses.

Par value: Nominal price placed on a share of common stock.

Piggy-back registration rights: The right to register unregistered stock in the event of a company having a public stock offering.

Pledging: The use of a company's accounts receivable as security (collateral) for a short-term loan.

Portfolio: Collection of investments. For example, the portfolio of a venture capital fund comprises all its investments.

Pratt's Guide to Venture Captial Sources: Annual sourcebook for the venture capital industry.

Preemptive rights: The rights of shareholders to maintain their percentage ownership of a company by purchasing a proportionate number of shares of any new issue of common stock. (See *antidilution, dilution,* and *pro rata interest.*)

Preference shares: A class of shares that incorporate the right to a fixed dividend and usually a prior claim on assets, in preference to ordinary shares, in the event of a liquidation. Cumulative preference shares provide an entitlement to a cumulative dividend if in any year the preference dividend is unpaid due to insufficient profits being earned. Preference shares are usually redeemable at specific dates.

Pre-money valuation: The value of a company's equity before additional money is invested.

Prepayment: A payment on a loan made prior to the original due date.

Present value (PV): The current value of a given future cash flow stream, FV_t, after t years, discounted at a rate of return of $K\%$ is $PV = FV_t/(1 + K/100)^t$. For example, if an investor expects a rate of return of 60% on an investment in a seed-stage company, and she believes that her investment will be worth $750,000 after five years, then the present value of her investment is $71,526. (See *discount rate, future value, net present value, present value,* and *rate of return.*)

Price-earnings ratio (P/E ratio): The ratio of the market value of a firm's equity to its after-tax profits (may be calculated from price per share and earnings per share).

Prime rate: Short-term interest rate charged by a bank to its largest, most creditworthy customers.

Private placement: The direct sales of securities to a small number of investors.

Profit: Synonymous with income and earnings.

Pro forma statements: Projected financial statements: income and cash-flow statements, and balance sheets. For a startup company, it is unusual to make pro forma statements monthly for the first two years and annually for the next three years.

Pro rata interest: The right granted the investor to maintain the same percentage ownership in the event of future financings. (See *antidilution* and *dilution.*)

Prospectus: A document giving a description of a securities issue, including a complete statement of the terms of the issue and a description of the issuer, as well as its historical financial statements. Also referred to as an offering circular. (See *red herring.*)

Put: A contract allowing the holder to sell a given number of securities back to the issuer of the contract at a fixed price for a given period of time.

Rate of return: The annual return on an investment. If a sum of money, PV, is invested and after t years that investment is worth FV_t, the return on investment $K = [(FV_t/PV)^{1/t} - 1] \times 100\%$. For example, if $100 is invested originally, and one year later $108 is paid back to the investor, the annual rate of return is 8%.

Realization: See *exit.*

Redeemable shares: Shares that may be redeemable at the option of the company or the shareholder or both.

Red herring: Preliminary prospectus circulated by underwriters to gauge investor interest in a planned offering. A legend in red ink on its cover indicates that the registration has not yet become effective and is still being reviewed by the SEC.

Registration statement: A carefully worded and organized document, including a prospectus, filed with the SEC before an IPO.

Retained earnings: The part of net income retained in the company and not distributed to stockholders.

Return on investment: The annual income that an investment earns.

Running returns: Periodic returns, such as interest and dividends, from an investment (in contrast to a one-time capital gain).

SBA: Small Business Administration.

SBDC: Small Business Development Centers (supported by the SBA).

SBI: Small Business Institutes, run by universities and colleges with SBA support.

SBIC: Small Business Investments Companies.

SBIR: Small Business Innovation Research Program.

Schumpeter, Joesph A.: Moravian-born economist whose book *The Theory of Economic Development*, written in Vienna in 1912, introduced the modern theory of entrepreneurship, in which the entrepreneur plays the central role in economic development by destroying the static equilibrium of the existing economy. Excellent modern examples are the roles played by Steve Jobs, Bill Gates, and Dan Bricklin in creating the microcomputer industry in the late 1970s. By the beginning of the 1990s, microcomputers (personal computers) were the principal force shaping the computer industry, and the old companies manufacturing mainframe and minicomputers, which dominated the computer industry until the mid-1980s, were in distress, ranging from outright bankruptcy to record-breaking losses.

SCORE: Service Core of Retired Executives, sponsored by the SBA to provide consulting to small businesses.

Second-round financing: The introduction of further funding by the original investors or new investors to enable the company to grow or deal with unexpected problems. Each round of financing tends to cover the next period of growth.

Securities and Exchange Commission (SEC): Regulatory body for investor protection in the United States, created by the Securities Exchange Act of 1934. The supervision of dealers is delegated to the self-regulatory bodies of the stock exchanges and NASD under the provisions of the Maloney Act of 1938.

Seed financing: A relatively small amount of money provided to prove a concept; it may involve product development and market research but rarely involves the initial marketing of a product.

Sensitivity analysis: Examination of how the projected performance of the business varies with changes in the key assumptions on which the forecasts are based.

Short-term security: Generally an obligation maturing in less than one year.

Sole proprietorship: A business form with one owner who is responsible for all the firm's liabilities.

Startup financing: Funding provided to companies for use in product development and initial marketing. Companies may be in the process of being organized or may have been in business a short time (one year or less), but have not sold their product commercially. Generally, such firms have assembled the key management, prepared a business plan, made market studies, and completed other preliminary tasks.

Stock option plan: A plan designed to motivate employees, especially key ones, by placing a proportion of the common stock of the company under option at a fixed price to defined employees. The option may then be exercised by the employees at a future date. Stock options are often introduced as part of the remuneration package of senior executives.

Subchapter S Corporation: A small business corporation in which the owners personally pay the corporation's income taxes.

Subordinated debt: Loans that may be unsecured or, more commonly, secured by secondary charges and that rank after senior debt for repayment in the event of default. Also referred to as junior debt or mezzanine debt.

Sweat equity: Equity acquired by the management team at favorable terms reflecting the value to the business of the managers' past and future efforts.

Syndicate: A group of investors that act together when investing in a company.

Term loan: Debt originally scheduled to be repaid in more than one year, but usually in 10 years or less.

Term sheet: Summary of the principal conditions for a proposed investment by a venture capital firm in a company.

Times interest earned: Earnings before interest and taxes, divided by interest (EBIT/*I*). The higher this ratio, the more secure the loan on which interest is paid. It is a basic measure of the creditworthiness of a company.

Underwrite: An arrangement under which investment banks each agree to buy a certain amount of securities of a new issue on a given date and at a given price, thereby assuring the issuer of the full proceeds of the financing.

Underwriter: An institution engaged in the business of underwriting securities issues.

Underwriting fee: The share of the gross spread of a new issue accruing to members of the underwriting group after the expenses of the issue have been paid.

Unsecured loans: Debt that is not backed by a pledge of specific assets.

Valuation (of a company): The market value of a company. (See *market capitalization.*)

Value-added (by investors): Many venture capital firms claim that they add more than money to investee companies. They call it value-added, which includes strategic advice on such matters as hiring key employees, marketing, production, control, and financing.

Venture capitalist: A financial institution specializing in the provision of equity and other forms of long-term capital to enterprises, usually to firms with a limited track record but with the expectation of substantial growth. The venture capitalist may provide both funding and varying degrees of managerial and technical expertise. Venture capital has traditionally been associated with startups; however, venture capitalists have increasingly participated in later-stage projects.

Vesting period: The time period before shares are owned unconditionally by an employee who is sold stock with the stipulation that he must continue to work for the company selling him the shares. If his employment terminates before the end of that period, the company has the right to buy back the shares at the same price at which it originally sold them to him.

Visible venture capital: The organized venture capital industry consisting of formal firms, in contrast to invisible venture capital or informal venture capital.

Vulture capital: A derogatory term for venture capital.

Waiver: Consent granted by an investor or lender to permit an investor or borrower to be in default on a covenant.

Warrant: An option to purchase common stock at a specified price. (See *equity kicker.*)

Warranty: A statement of fact or opinion concerning the condition of a company. The inclusion of warranties in an investment agreement gives the investor a claim against the company if it subsequently becomes apparent that the company's condition was not as stated at the time of the investment.

Yield: Annualized rate of return on a security.

CHAPTER NOTES

CHAPTER 2: OPPORTUNITY RECOGNITION

[1]Patrick R. Liles, *New Business Ventures and the Entrepreneur* (Homewood, IL: Richard D. Irwin, 1974), 4–5.

[2]Ibid., 10.

[3]The State of Small Business: A Report of the President (Washington, D.C.: U.S. Government Printing Office, 1989), 47.

[4]*Fortune,* 11 June 1984, 170–194.

[5]From annual reports to shareholders.

[6]Bruce D. Phillips and Bruce A. Kirchhoff, "An Analysis of New Firm Survival and Growth," in *Frontiers in Entrepreneurship Research: 1988,* ed. B. Kirchhoff et al. (Babson Park, MA: Babson College, 1988), 266–267.

[7]This confirms this exception to the failure rule noted above and in the original edition of J. A. Timmons, L. E. Smollen, and A. L. Dingee, *New Venture Creation* (Homewood, IL: Richard D. Irwin, 1977).

[8]Ibid., 10–11.; C. Taylor, Starting-Up in the High Technology Industries in California (Wells Fargo Investment Company, 1969); R. B. Faucett, "The Management of Venture Capital Investment Companies," master's thesis, Sloan School of Management, MIT, 1971; and R. B. Faucett, "Venture Capital: Fact and Myth," Foothill Group, 1972.

[9]T. Dehudy, N. D. Fast, and S. E. Pratt, *Venture Economics,* Wellesley Hills, MA, 1981.

[10]Donald K. Clifford, Jr., and Richard E. Cavanagh, *The Winning Performance* (New York: Bantam Books, 1985), 3.

[11]J. A. Timmons and D. E. Gumpert, "Discard Many Old Rules for Raising Venture Capital," *Harvard Business Review* 60 (January–February 1982): 152–156.

[12]Jeffry A. Timmons, Norman D. Fast, and William D. Bygrave, "The Flow of Venture Capital to Highly Innovative Technological Ventures," in *Frontiers of Entrepreneurship Research: 1983,* ed. J. A. Hornaday et al. (Babson Park, MA: Babson College, 1983), 316.

[13]In 1946 General Doriot, a retired Harvard Business School professor noted for encouraging entrepreneurship among his students, founded the American Research and Development Corporation in Boston, the first institutional U.S. venture capital firm. The company put venture capital on the map when its investment of about $70,000 in 1957 in four young MIT engineers with an idea for a new computer grew to about $350 million—as shares in Digital Equipment Corporation, today America's second-largest computer firm.

[14]J. A. Timmons, N. D. Fast, S. E. Pratt, and W. D. Bygrave, "Venture Capital Investing in Highly Innovative Technological Ventures," published by *Venture Economics* (March 1984) for the National Science Foundation.

[15]Arthur Rock, "Strategy vs. Tactics from a Venture Capitalist," *Harvard Business Review* (November–December 1987): 63–67.

[16]Sources of information about solo entrepreneurs and small enterprises include the following magazines: *Entrepreneur, In Business,* and *Home-Based Business.*

[17]Opportunity recognition was originally identified as a driving force in new venture creation in the 1977 edition of this text. The conceptual framework developed by Howard H. Stevenson at the Harvard Business School, and his helpful suggestions have both reinforced and refocused this identification of opportunity recognition as central. See also Howard H. Stevenson, "A New Paradigm for Entrepreneurial Management," in *Entrepreneurship: What It Is and How To Teach It,* ed. John J. Kao and Howard H. Stevenson (Boston: Harvard Business School, 1984). Empirical research bearing on the question of opportunity screening and evaluation and any common characteristics of successful entrepreneurial ventures is documented in a paper by Jeffry A. Timmons, Daniel F. Muzyka, Howard H. Stevenson, and William D. Bygrave, "Opportunity Recognition: The Core of Entrepreneurship," in *Frontiers of Enterpreneurship Research: 1987,* ed. Neil Churchill et al. (Babson Park, MA: Babson College, 1987), 409.

[18]Keynote address at the 1984 Babson Entrepreneurship Research Conference, cosponsored by the School of Management, Georgia Institute of Technology, April 23–25, 1984, Atlanta, GA.

[19]The story of the entrepreneurial culture at Data General was told in a best-seller, *The Soul of a New Machine* by Tracy Kidder (Boston: Little, Brown, 1981).

[20]Speaking at his induction in 1984 into the Babson College Academy of Distinguished Entrepreneurs.

[21]Keynote address at the first annual Entrepreneur's Night of UCLA Graduate School of Business, April 18, 1984, Westwood, CA.

[22]Jeffry A. Timmons, *New Business Opportunities* (Acton, MA: Brick House Publishing, 1989).

[23]See Timmons, Muzyka, Stevenson, and Bygrave, "Opportunity Recognition: The Core of Entrepreneurship."

[24]Comments made during a presentation at Babson College, May 1985.

[25]R. Douglas Kahn, President, Interactive Images, Inc., speaking at Babson College about his experiences as international marketing director at McCormack & Dodge from 1978 through 1983.

[26]Jeffry A. Timmons, William D. Bygrave, and Norman D. Fast, "The Flow of Venture Capital to Highly Innovative Technological Ventures," in *Frontiers of Entrepreneurship Research: 1984,* ed. J. A. Hornaday et al. (Babson Park, MA: Babson College, 1984).

[27]This point was made by Willard Marriott at Founder's Day, Babson College, 1988.

[28]Described in a working paper by Herbert A. Simon, "What We Know About the Creative Process" (Carnegie-Mellon University, 1984).

CHAPTER 3: ENTRY STRATEGIES

[1]Karl H. Vesper, *New Venture Strategies* (Englewood Cliffs, NJ: Prentice Hall, 1990).

[2]Arnold C. Cooper et al., *New Business in America* (Washington, DC: The NFIB Foundation, 1990), 16.

[3]Vesper, *New Venture Strategies.*

CHAPTER 4: MARKET OPPORTUNITIES AND MARKETING

[1]This discussion is based on *Annual Report*, Wendy's International Inc., 1991; and John Gorman, "Wendy's: A Made to Order Hamburger Empire," *Chicago Tribune*, 10 March 1986, Business section, 1, 5, 6.

[2]"AMA Board Approves New Marketing Definition," *Marketing News*, 1 March 1986, 1. Published by the American Marketing Association.

[3]Peter F. Drucker, *Management: Tasks, Responsibilities, Practices* (New York: Harper & Row, 1974), 63.

[4]J. B. McKitterick, "What Is the Marketing Management Concept?" in *The Frontiers of Marketing Thought and Science*, ed. Frank M. Bass (Chicago: American Marketing Association, 1957), 78.

[5]Drucker, *Management: Tasks, Responsibilities, Practices*, 64.

[6]Susan Greco, "Desktop Target Marketing," *Inc.* (April 1992): 118.

[7]Andrea Trank, "From Animal Feed to Lumber," *In Business* (Summer 1991): 28–29.

[8]Leon G. Schiffman and Leslie Lazer Kanuk, *Consumer Behavior*, 4th ed. (Englewood Cliffs, NJ: Prentice Hall, 1991), 680.

[9]Susan Greco, "Users Get Sales on Course," *Inc.* (November 1992): 29.

[10]Jay Finnegan, "Against the Grain," *Inc.* (November 1992): 116.

[11]Ian C. MacMillan, "Seizing Competitive Initiative," *Journal of Business Strategy* (Spring 1982): 45.

[12]Teri Lammers, "The Smart Customer Survey," *Inc.* (November 1992): 133–135.

[13]Donald R. Lehmann and Russell S. Winer, *Analysis for Marketing Planning*, 2nd ed. (Homewood, IL: Richard D. Irwin, 1991).

[14]Laurence P. Feldman and Albert L. Page, "Principles versus Practice in New Product Planning," *Journal of Product Innovation Management* (January 1984): 44.

[15]Reavis Cox and Thomas F. Schutte, "A Look at Channel Management," in *Marketing Involvement in Society and the Economy*, ed. Philip R. McDonald (Chicago: American Marketing Association, 1969), 100.

[16]"What Keeps Food Prices High and Rising," *Citibank* (June 1980): 4.

[17]Alfred R. Oxenfeldt, "A Decision-Making Structure for Price Decisions," *Journal of Marketing* 37 (January 1973): 48–53.

[18]Susan Greco, "Smart Use of 'Special Offers,'" *Inc.* (February 1993): 23.

[19]Gerald E. Hills, "Market Analysis in the Business Plan: Venture Capitalists' Perceptions," *Journal of Small Business Management*, vol. 22 (Jan. 1985): 5.

[20]Gerald E. Hills and Alvin D. Star, "Marketing Strategy Elements for New Venture/Early Stage Firms as Perceived by Venture Capitalists," in *Frontiers of Entrepreneurship Research*, eds. John Hornaday, Edward B. Shils, Jeffry A. Timmons, and Karl H. Vesper, (Wellesley, MA: Babson College, 1985), 215.

[21]These volumes are all published annually by the University of Illinois at Chicago. Each volume is entitled *Research at the Marketing/Entrepreneurship Interface*, and the year of publication is also included in the title. Editors of the volumes are 1987, Gerald E. Hills; 1988 (no publication); 1989, Hills, Raymond W. LaForge, and Beverly J. Parker; 1990, Hills, LaForge, and Harold P. Welsch; 1991, Hills and LaForge; 1992, Hills and LaForge; 1993, Hills, LaForge, and Daniel F. Muzyka.

[22]Gerald E. Hills and Chem L. Narayana, "Profile Characteristics, Success Factors and Marketing in Highly Successful Firms," in *Frontiers of Entrepreneurship Research*, ed. Robert H.

Brockhaus, Sr., Neil C. Churchill, Jerome A. Katz, Bruce A. Kirchhoff, Karl H. Vesper, and William E. Wetzel, Jr. (Wellesley, MA: Babson College, 1989), 23.

CHAPTER 6: FINANCIAL PROJECTIONS

[1]Portions of this article and Exhibits 6.1–6.12 have been excerpted with permission from Robert Ronstadt, *Entrepreneurial Finance: How to Take Control of Your Financial Decision Making* (Wayland, MA: Lord, 1989).

[2]This chapter makes the assumption that the reader is familiar with the basic purpose and components of an income statement, balance sheet, and cash flow statement. If the reader needs to review these statements, please refer to Chapter 5 of Eliza Collins and Mary Anne Devanna, eds., *The Portable MBA* (New York: John Wiley & Sons, 1990).

[3]The integrated model used as an example in this chapter was produced using *Ronstadt's Financials* (Wayland, MA: Lord, 1989), Version 2.0, which is DOS-based software for the IBM PC and compatibles with minimum 640k of RAM, or internal operating memory. Models for nonretail businesses accompany the software for manufacturing, contract service, professional service, wholesale distribution, real estate, and other businesses.

[4]See Chapter 5 of Robert Ronstadt, *Entrepreneurship: Text, Cases, & Notes*, (Wayland, MA: Lord, 1984), specifically the discussion of high-variable-cost ventures versus high-fixed-cost ventures.

[5]Paul Hawken, "Mastering The Numbers," *Inc.* (October 1987): 19.

CHAPTER 7: VENTURE CAPITAL

[1]W. D. Bygrave and J. A. Timmons, *Venture Capital at the Crossroads* (Boston: Harvard Business School Press, 1992).

[2]J. Morris, S. Isenstein, and A. Knowles, eds., *Pratt's Guide To Venture Capital Sources* (New York: SDC, 1992).

[3]Amar Bhide, "Bootstrap Finance: The Art of Start-ups," *Harvard Business Review* 70(6): 109.

[4]J. Freear and W. Wetzel, "Who Bankrolls High Tech Entrepreneurs?" *Journal of Business Venturing* 5(2): 77.

[5]James L. Plummer, *QED Report on Venture Capital Financial Analysis* (Palo Alto, CA: QED Research, 1987).

CHAPTER 12: FRANCHISING

[1]International Franchise Association and Horwath International, *Franchising in the Economy 1990* (Evans City, PA: IFA Publications, 1991), 1.

[2]H. A. Monckton, *The History of the English Public House* (London: Bodley House Publishing, 1969), 87.

[3]Ibid., 88.

[4]International Franchise Association and Horwath International, *Franchising in the Economy 1990*.

CHAPTER 13: HARVESTING

[1]Steven R. Covey, *The Seven Habits of Highly Effective People* (New York: Simon & Schuster, 1989), 95.

[2]See J. Freear, J. A. Sohl, and W. E. Wetzel, Jr., "Raising Venture Capital: Entrepreneurs' Views of the Process," *Frontiers of Entrepreneurship Research* (Wellesley, MA: Babson College, 1990).

[3]William Sahlman, "Aspects of Financial Contracting in Venture Capital," *Journal of Applied Corporate Finance* (Summer 1988): 33.

[4]For a complete presentation on the free cash flow valuation approach, see Alfred Rappaport, *Creating Shareholder Value* (New York: The Free Press, 1986); and Bennet Stewart III, *The Quest for Value* (New York: Harper Business, 1991).

[5]For a more complete explanation of the logic of this equation, see a corporate finance text, such as J. William Petty, David Scott, Arthur Keown, and John D. Martin, *Basic Financial Management* (Englewood Cliffs, NJ: Prentice-Hall, 1993).

[6]For example, see Amar Bhide, "The Causes and Consequences of Hostile Takeovers," *Journal of Applied Corporate Finance* (Summer 1989): 36–59.

[7]Joan C. Szabo, "Using ESOPs to Sell Your Firm," *Nation's Business* (January 1991): 50.

[8]Ibid.

[9]Ibid.

[10]P. Asquith and E. H. Kim, "The Impact of Merger Bids on the Participating Firms' Security Returns," *Journal of Finance* (December 1982): 1209–28; and K. Aiginger and G. Tichy, "Small Firm's and the Merger Mania," *Small Business Economics* 3, no. 2 (June 1991): 83–101.

[11]Michael G. Berolzheimer, "The Financial and Emotional Sides of Selling Your Company," *Harvard Business Review* (January–February 1980): 6–11.

[12]Many of the ideas in this section come from Roger G. Ibbotson, Jody L. Sindelar, and Jay R. Ritter, "Initial Public Offerings," *Journal of Applied Corporate Finance* (Summer 1988): 37–45.

[13]For a relatively complete presentation of the process of going public, see David P. Sutton and M. William Beneddetto, *Initial Public Offerings* (Chicago: Probus, 1990).

[14]Ibid., 21.

[15]See Ibbotson, Sindelar, and Ritter, "Initial Public Offerings."

CHAPTER 14: ENTREPRENEURSHIP ECONOMICS

[1]Aside from having important implications for society, neoclassical theory offered an important response to the growing popularity of Marxist theory around the turn of the century.

[2]This discussion focuses on product production, as does neoclassical theory. Whether the principle of economies of scale applies to services is another subject which I will not discuss since my objective here is to show that, even in its simplest form, the "economies of scale" argument is flawed.

[3]There is no agreement among statistical sources concerning the number of small firms that exist. The counts vary from as few as 4 million to as many as 21 million. I will use a count of 7 to 9 million, based on my own estimates. For a description of the various counts, see Bruce A. Kirchhoff, *Entrepreneurship and Dynamic Capitalism* (Greenwood, CT: Quorum Books, 1994).

[4]The cohort includes firms not included in either the high- or low-innovation class. In total numbers, this is the largest group, and it creates the greatest number of jobs. However, this

class is not described here because it adds immense complexity to the analysis. See Kirchhoff, *Entrepreneurship and Dynamic Capitalism.*

[5]For a complete list of the industries included in the high-innovation class, see Kirchhoff, *Entrepreneurship and Dynamic Capitalism.*

BIBLIOGRAPHY

J. C. Van Horne, *Fundamentals of Financial Management*, 8th ed. (Englewood Cliffs, NJ: Prentice Hall, 1992).

L. J. Glitman, *Principles of Managerial Finance* (New York: Harper Collins, 1991).

ABOUT THE AUTHORS

William D. Bygrave is the Frederic C. Hamilton Professor for Free Enterprise and Director of the Center for Entrepreneurial Studies at Babson College, and visiting professor at INSEAD (The European Institute for Business Administration). As a practitioner, he founded a Route 128 venture-capital-backed high-tech company, managed a division of a NYSE-listed high-tech company, cofounded a pharmaceutical database company, and was a member of the investment committee of a venture capital firm. His company won an *IR100* award for introducing one of the 100 most significant new technical products in the United States in 1977. As an academic, he teaches and researches entrepreneurship. He and Jeffry Timmons are the authors of *Venture Capital at the Crossroads*, which examines the venture capital industry and its role in the economy. It was published by the Harvard Business School Press in August 1992. He serves on the review boards of two entrepreneurship journals. He was the academic coordinator for the European Foundation for Entrepreneurship Research's 1992 Conference *Realizing Enterprise Value: IPOs, Trades Sales, Buybacks, MBOs*. He holds doctorate degrees from Oxford University and Boston University, an MBA from Northeastern University, and an MA from Oxford University.

Elizabeth (Betsy) Gatewood is Director of the University of Houston Small Business Development Center, an organization that provides training and consulting services to small businesses in the greater Houston region. Dr. Gatewood is also a research professor in the Department of Management at the University of Houston's College of Business Administration. Previously, Dr. Gatewood served as Director of the Center for Business and Economic Studies at the University of Georgia, a position she held from 1983 to 1989. Dr. Gatewood currently serves as chair for the Entrepreneurship Division of the Academy of Management. Additionally, she is a member of the editorial review boards for *Entrepreneurship: Theory and Practice* and the *Wisconsin Small Business Forum*. Dr. Gatewood has written over 40 articles, papers, and book sections on entrepreneurship, innovation, strategic management, and financial analysis. She received her doctorate and master's in business administration from the University of Georgia and her bachelor's in psychology from Purdue University.

David E. Gumpert is an expert on entrepreneurship, marketing, and other areas of business management. His company, David E. Gumpert Communications, Inc., of Needham, Massachusetts, specializes in marketing communications services, providing newsletters, booklets, and brochures on the management of small and midsize companies. He is former senior editor of *Inc.* Magazine and associate editor of the *Harvard Business Review*. His articles on business management have appeared in the *Harvard Business Review* and many other publications. He is also the author of three recent business books—*How to Really Start Your Own Business, How to Really Create a Successful Business Plan,* and *How to Really Create a Successful Marketing Plan*—all from Inc. Publishing. In addition, Mr. Gumpert has spoken extensively on business planning and management. He received his BA in political science from the University of Chicago and his MS in journalism from the Columbia University Graduate School of Journalism.

Gerald E. Hills is holder of the Coleman/Denton Thorne Chair in Entrepreneurship and Professor of Marketing at the University of Illinois at Chicago. His doctorate is from Indiana University. Dr. Hills has written and edited seven books and written more than 70 articles in such journals as the *Journal of Marketing, Business Horizons, Journal of Technological and Social Change, Entrepreneurship: Theory and Practice, International Journal of Small Business,* and the *Journal of Business Venturing.* He is past president of the International Council for Small Business, was first president of the United States Association for Small Business and Entrepreneurship, and recently served as the elected head of the education/professor division of the American Marketing Association.

Keiron Hylton is Managing Director of Scenarios, headquartered in Houston, Texas and has been a management consultant and entrepreneur for 10 years. He has consulted to a North American clientele of *Fortune* 500 companies on strategic planning issues for two large Boston-based international consulting firms: The Monitor Company and Temple, Barker and Sloane (now Mercer Management Consulting). He was the founding general manager of KLAS-FM, an adult-contemporary format radio station in Kingston, Jamaica, which exemplified the trend toward entrepreneurship and privatization in the developing world. KLAS-FM goes public in 1993. Mr. Hylton has also been a consumer marketing analyst for the Jamaica Tourist Board and an industrial marketing analyst for Jamaica Investment Promotions in New York City, both highly successful marketing operations. Mr. Hyton holds the AB, MBA, and JD degrees from Harvard University.

Joseph S. Iandiorio is a partner in a law firm in Waltham, Massachusetts. The firm specializes in patents, trademarks, copyrights, trade secrets, licensing and litigation of intellectual property matters, employee and consultant contracts, confidential disclosure agreements, and other, related areas of intellectual property. Mr. Iandiorio has over 30 years of experience, including a period as an examiner in the U.S. Patent and Trademark Office. He is actively involved in fostering the creation and growth of small businesses and high-technology companies. He was chosen as the SBA's Lawyer Small Business Advocate of the Year. He is Director and Treasurer of the Massachusetts Technology Development Corporation, a venture capital fund; Chairman and Director of the Smaller Business Association of New England; and a member of the Massachusetts Small Business Advisory Council and the Science and Technology Advisory Board.

Bruce A. Kirchhoff is Professor of Entrepreneurship at New Jersey Institute of Technology. His prior credentials include service as Chief Economist for the U.S. Small Business Administration and as Assistant Director of the Minority Business Development Agency in the U.S. Department of Commerce. He was Director of the Center for Entrepreneurship and Public Policy at Fairleigh Dickinson University and Director of Research in Babson College's Entrepreneurship Center, and he served as Director of the Babson Entrepreneurship Research Conference in 1987 and 1988. Dr. Kirchhoff has published over 100 articles and papers on entrepreneurship, economic development, and business strategy. His book *Entrepreneurship and Dynamic Capitalism* describes how small firms contribute to economic growth. Dr. Kirchhoff earned his Ph.D. in Business Administration and an MBA from the University of Utah. He has extensive consulting experience, having supervised and conducted consultations with over 200 small businesses in the United States and Latin America. He has received six awards for excellence in small business consulting from the U.S. Small Business Administration. Drawing together his business experience and his academic interests, Dr. Kirchhoff joined with two others to found SCT, Inc. in 1984 to manufacture computer-based theft deterrence systems for retail stores. In 1979 he cofounded Pathfinder Systems, Inc., a manufacturer of guidance systems for farm tractors.

Richard P. Mandel is Associate Professor of Law at Babson College, where he teaches a variety of courses in business law and taxation. He is also a partner in the law firm Bowditch and Dewey, of Worcester and Framingham, Massachusetts, where he specializes in the representation of small businesses and their executives. Mr. Mandel has written a number of articles regarding the representation of small businesses. He holds an AB from Cornell University and a JD from Harvard Law School.

J. William Petty, Professor of Finance and the W. W. Caruth Chairholder in Entrepreneurship, teaches in the Department of Finance at Baylor University. One of his primary responsibilities is teaching entrepreneurial finance, at both the undergraduate and graduate levels. He has also taught the course Financing the Small Firm at the University of Texas at Austin. He is coauthor of a leading corporate finance textbook, *Basic Financial Management,* and coauthor of *Financial Management of the Small Firm.* In 1992 he served as the Program Chair for the annual meetings of the Academy of Small Business Finance, and he is a member of the founding board of the academy. Petty has published research in numerous academic and practitioner journals, including *Financial Management, Accounting Review, Journal of Financial and Quantitative Analysis, Journal of Managerial Finance,* and the *Journal of Small Business Finance.* He served as a coeditor for the *Journal of Financial Research,* and he currently serves as an associate editor for *Entrepreneurship: Theory and Practice* and for the *Journal of Small Business Finance.* He has served as a consultant to several small and middle-market companies, primarily in consumer products and energy-related businesses. Petty received his undergraduate degree in marketing from Abilene Christian University, and both his MBA and Ph.D. in finance and accounting from the University of Texas at Austin. He is a CPA in the state of Texas.

Dr. Robert Ronstadt is Professor of Entrepreneurship at Pepperdine University and the author of numerous books, articles, and cases about entrepreneurs. He is the founder or cofounder of several businesses and the originator of *Ronstadt's Financials,* a powerful software program equipped with the financial and accounting expertise to empower people to produce integrated financial projections that are timely and technically correct. He received his undergraduate degree from the University of California at Berkeley, his master's degree from the University of Oregon, and his doctorate in business administration from Harvard Business School.

Joel Shulman is the Robert Weissman professor of finance at Babson College, where he teaches Financial Strategies, Working Captial Management, Investments, and Financial Management. He has previously taught Portfolio Management, Taxation, Securities Analysis, Managerial Finance, Cost Accounting, and Special Topics in Finance at Harvard University, Michigan State University, and Wayne State University. He has a Ph.D. in finance and is also a Chartered Financial Analyst (CFA), Certified Management Accountant (CMA), and Certified Cash Manager (CCM). His publications include a number of scholarly articles in his field as well as seven coauthored books published by American Management Association: *Leasing For Profit, Alternatives to Conventional Financing, Planning Cash Flow, How to Effectively Manage Corporate Cash, A Manager's Guide to Financial Analysis, The Job of the Corporate Controller,* and *How to Manage and Evaluate Capital Expenditures.* He has consulted for many small, entrepreneurial firms as well as Coldwell Banker, First Albany, Ford

Motor, Freddie Mac, K mart, Loomis Sayles, Merrill Lynch, Raytheon, Rockwell International, Salomon Brothers, Sears, and UNISYS.

Stephen Spinelli, Jr. was a founding shareholder of Jiffy Lube International and the founder, chairman, and CEO of American Oil Change Corporation, where he had chief executive responsibility for 47 Jiffy Lube service centers in Massachusetts, Connecticut, and New York. He is a lecturer in entrepreneurship at Babson College, and he has given seminars on franchising to MBA students at INSEAD and the University of London's Management School and to undergraduate students at the American College in London. He has also conducted a conference on entrepreneurship at Ernst & Young. He has an MBA from Babson College and a BA in economics from Western Maryland College; he is currently pursuing his doctoral degree in economics from the University of London's Imperial College Management School.

Jeffry A. Timmons is internationally recognized for his work in entrepreneurship. He is the first to hold a joint appointment at the Harvard Business School, as the first MBA Class of 1954 Professor of New Ventures, and at Babson College, where he was first to hold the Frederic C. Hamilton Professorship and heads the Price-Babson College Fellows Program. He has authored or coauthored several books, including *New Venture Creation,* 3rd ed., 1990 (Richard D. Irwin) and *Venture Capital at the Crossroads,* 1992 (HBS Press). He is cofounder, investor, or director of several companies, and is an advisor to a $285 million growth capital fund and Ernst & Young's National Entrepreneurial Services Group. A special advisor to the Ewing Marion Kauffman Foundation of Kansas City, he also serves on the board of the foundation's Center for Entrepreneurial Leadership and as a Trustee of Colgate University, his alma mater. He received his MBA and doctorate from the Harvard Business School.

Karl H. Vesper, BSME, MSME, earned a Ph.D. from Stanford and an MBA from Harvard. He is a Professor of Business Administration, Mechanical Engineering, and Marine Studies. His latest book is *New Venture Experience.* Others include *New Venture Mechanics, The Washington Entrepreneur's Guide, New Venture Strategies, Frontiers on Entrepreneurship Research* (with others), *Encyclopedia of Entrepreneurship* (with Kent and Sexton), and *Entrepreneurship and National Policy.* From 1982 to 1985 he served as Chairman of the Management and Organization Department at the University of Washington, where he has been on the faculty since 1969. He has held visiting appointments as the Schoen Professor of Entrepreneurship at Baylor University in 1980 and the Babson Professor of Entrepreneurship at Babson College in 1981. During the 1986–87 academic year he was on leave at the University of Calgary, where he held the first endowed professorship in the Faculty of Management. He was a Fulbright Distinguished Lecturer at Trinity College in Dublin in 1989.

William E. Wetzel, Jr. is the Forbes Professor of Management at the Whittemore School of Business and Economics and Director of the Center for Venture Research, University of New Hampshire. His professional and research interests include the role of the entrepreneur in economic development, the financial management of high-growth private companies and the informal venture capital markets. Professor Wetzel is a founding member of the New Hampshire High Technology Council and a past president of the Council. He founded Venture Capital Network, Inc. in 1984. He is a member of the Smaller Business Association of New England (SBANE) and served on its board of directors from 1983 through 1986. Professor Wetzel also serves on the boards of directors of Yankee Equipment Systems, Inc.; C.I.M. Industries, Inc.; M.I.T. Technology Capital Network, Inc.; New Hampshire Business Development Corp.; and RVA Associates, Inc.; and on the advisory board of Kearsarge Ventures, L.P.

INDEX

The Portable MBA
Executive Service

An Exclusive Benefit for *Portable MBA* Readers

The Portable MBA Executive Service is a quarterly newsletter in the spirit of *The Portable MBA Series*, providing readers with a continuing business education. Each issue will feature articles on current and emerging trends in business today, and helpful, practical tips on a broad range of topics.

FREE
1-year
subscription

$39.95 value

Best of all, a 1 year membership in this exclusive service is available to readers of ***The Portable MBA Series*** *through a FREE introductory offer.*

Send your name and address to:
The Portable MBA Executive Service
P.O. Box 2575
Secaucus, NJ 07096-2575 *

* In Canada, send to:
The Portable MBA Executive Service, Professional Reference & Trade Division,
John Wiley & Sons Canada Limited, 22 Worcester Road, Rexdale, Ontario, M9W1L1

...and "Get BusinessWise" with
The Portable MBA Executive Service

WILEY

...Because Your Business Education Doesn't Stop with a Diploma